The 1995 Baseball Encyclopedia® Update

Complete Career Records
for All Players Who Played
in the 1994 Season

MACMILLAN • USA

MACMILLAN
A Prentice Hall Macmillan Company
15 Columbus Circle
New York, NY 10023

ISBN 0-02-860089-4

10 9 8 7 6 5 4 3 2 1

Printed in the United States of America

Contents

Acknowledgments

Macmillan gratefully acknowledges the efforts of the following people, without whose help *The Baseball Encyclopedia®* *Update* could not have been produced. From Stats, Inc: John Dewan, Art Ashley, and Bob Mecca. From Black Dot Graphics: Al Arduino, Martin Parrish, Sherry Pickrum, Paul Thomson, Darlene White, and Randall Zubow. And from Macmillan: Ken Samelson, Jeanine Bucek, David Frost, Eric Wechter, and publisher Natalie Chapman.

The Teams and
Their Players

The Teams and Their Players lists, for the 1994 season, each team, along with its manager and record, the regulars at each position, as well as the pitchers and the leading substitutes. The teams are presented in the order of the standings of the division. Substitutes are listed if they had at least 112 at bats or 20 runs batted in; pitchers are listed if they pitched 112 innings or had 7 or more decisions (including saves).

Fielding statistics listed for regulars are for the indicated position only. The position listed for substitutes may vary. If a substitute played 70% of his games at one position, that is the only position listed for him. If he did not play 70% of his games at one position, but played 90% of his games at two positions, he is listed with a combination position, such as "S2" for shortstop and second base, or "CO" for catcher and outfield. In such cases, the fielding statistics listed are combined for both positions. All outfield positions are considered one position for these purposes. If a player failed to meet either the 70% or 90% requirement listed above, he is listed as a utility player ("UT").

Any statistic that appears in boldfaced print is a league-leading total for that category. An asterisk (*) next to a particular statistic would indicate that the player led the league, but since he was traded during the season, the figure listed there is not necessarily his league-leading final total or average. For batting averages, a batter must have 3.1 plate appearances for each of his team's games to qualify for the title. Pitchers must have one inning pitched for every game played by his team to qualify in any pitching category. Fielders must have appeared in 75 games at the position to qualify. Catchers must appear in half the games played by their club.

NATIONAL LEAGUE 1994

		POS	Player	AB	BA	HR	RBI	PO	A	E	DP	TC/G	FA	Pitcher	G	IP	W	L	SV	ERA
East	Montreal	1B	C. Floyd	334	.281	4	41	527	40	5	43	7.4	.991	K. Hill	23	155	**16**	5	0	3.32
		2B	M. Lansing	394	.266	5	35	144	206	6	46	4.3	.983	P. Martinez	24	145	11	5	1	3.42
	W-74 L-40	SS	W. Cordero	415	.294	15	63	124	316	22	55	4.2	.952	J. Fassero	21	139	8	6	0	2.99
		3B	S. Berry	320	.278	11	41	66	147	14	8	2.3	.938	B. Henry	24	107	8	3	1	2.43
	Felipe Alou	RF	L. Walker	395	.322	19	86	140	5	4	1	2.2	.973	K. Rueter	20	92	7	3	0	5.17
		CF	M. Grissom	475	.288	11	45	**321**	7	5	0	**3.1**	.985	M. Rojas	58	84	3	2	16	3.32
		LF	M. Alou	422	.339	22	78	201	4	3	0	2.0	.986	G. Heredia	39	75	6	3	0	3.46
		C	D. Fletcher	285	.260	10	57	479	20	2	2	6.2	.996	J. Shaw	46	67	5	2	1	3.88
		C	L. Webster	143	.273	5	23	237	19	1	0	5.6	.996	J. Wetteland	52	64	4	6	25	2.83
		OF	L. Frazier	140	.271	0	14	55	2	0	1	1.6	1.000	T. Scott	40	53	5	2	1	2.70
	Atlanta	1B	F. McGriff	424	.318	34	94	**1004**	66	7	73	9.6	.994	G. Maddux	25	**202**	**16**	6	0	**1.56**
		2B	M. Lemke	350	.294	3	31	208	300	3	54	5.0	**.994**	T. Glavine	25	165	13	9	0	3.97
	W-68 L-46	SS	J. Blauser	380	.258	6	45	126	289	13	44	4.5	.970	S. Avery	24	152	8	3	0	4.04
		3B	T. Pendleton	309	.252	7	30	60	147	11	12	2.8	.950	J. Smoltz	21	135	6	10	0	4.14
	Bobby Cox	RF	D. Justice	352	.313	19	59	193	6	**11**	0	2.1	.948	K. Mercker	20	112	9	4	0	3.45
		CF	R. Kelly	255	.286	6	24	128	3	2	0	2.1	.985	G. McMichael	51	59	4	6	21	3.84
		LF	R. Klesko	245	.278	17	47	67	3	6	0	1.0	.921	M. Wohlers	51	51	7	2	1	4.59
		C	J. Lopez	277	.245	13	35	560	35	3	0	**8.0**	.995	M. Stanton	49	46	3	1	3	3.55
		OF	D. Sanders	191	.288	4	21	99	0	2	0	2.2	.980							
		OF	D. Gallagher	152	.224	2	14	87	1	1	0	1.2	.989							
		C	C. O'Brien	152	.243	8	28	308	26	3	1	7.0	.991							
		OF	T. Tarasco	132	.273	5	19	42	1	0	0	.9	1.000							
		S2	R. Belliard	120	.242	0	9	45	86	1	16		.992							
		3B	B. Pecota	112	.214	2	16	16	59	2	4	2.5	.974							
	New York	1B	D. Segui	336	.241	10	43	665	51	3	65	9.2	**.996**	B. Saberhagen	24	177	14	4	0	2.74
		2B	J. Kent	415	.292	14	68	221	338	**14**	76	5.4	.976	B. Jones	24	160	12	7	0	3.15
	W-55 L-58	SS	J. Vizcaino	410	.256	3	33	137	291	13	55	4.3	.971	P. Smith	21	131	4	10	0	5.55
		3B	B. Bonilla	403	.290	20	67	77	217	**18**	**24**	2.9	.942	M. Gozzo	23	69	3	5	0	4.83
	Dallas Green	RF	J. Orsulak	292	.260	8	42	129	9	3	2	1.6	.979	J. Jacome	8	54	4	3	0	2.67
		CF	R. Thompson	334	.225	18	59	274	5	3	1	2.9	.989	R. Mason	41	51	2	4	1	3.51
		LF	K. McReynolds	180	.256	4	21	91	1	0	1	2.0	1.000	D. Linton	32	50	6	2	0	4.47
		C	T. Hundley	291	.237	16	42	448	28	5	0	5.9	.990	J. Franco	47	50	1	4	**30**	2.70
		C	K. Stinnett	150	.253	2	14	211	20	5	2	5.4	.979	J. Manzanillo	37	47	3	2	2	2.66
		OF	J. Burnitz	143	.238	3	15	63	1	2	0	1.6	.970	D. Gooden	7	41	3	4	0	6.31
		OF	J. Lindeman	137	.270	7	20	54	1	3	0	1.8	.948							
		1B	R. Brogna	131	.351	7	20	308	28	1	29	9.6	.997							
		UT	F. Vina	124	.250	0	6	46	59	4	5		.963							
	Philadelphia	1B	J. Kruk	255	.302	5	38	540	46	3	45	8.5	.995	D. Jackson	25	179	14	6	0	3.26
		2B	M. Morandini	274	.292	2	26	167	216	6	38	4.9	.985	B. Munoz	21	104	7	5	1	2.67
	W-54 L-61	SS	K. Stocker	271	.273	2	28	118	253	16	46	4.7	.959	D. West	31	99	4	10	0	3.55
		3B	D. Hollins	162	.222	4	26	37	47	11	1	2.2	.884	S. Boskie	18	84	4	6	0	5.23
	Jim Fregosi	RF	J. Eisenreich	290	.300	4	43	178	4	2	2	2.0	.989	C. Schilling	13	82	2	8	0	4.48
		CF	L. Dykstra	315	.273	5	24	235	4	4	0	2.9	.984	D. Jones	47	54	2	4	27	2.17
		LF	M. Thompson	220	.273	3	30	119	1	0	1	1.5	1.000*	B. Rivera	9	38	3	4	0	6.87
		C	D. Daulton	257	.300	15	56	435	41	3	2	7.0	.994							
		UT	M. Duncan	347	.268	8	48	148	188	12	38		.966							
		OF	P. Incaviglia	244	.230	13	32	90	2	2	0	1.5	.979							
		1B	R. Jordan	220	.282	8	37	430	14	3	41	9.1	.993							
		3B	K. Batiste	209	.234	1	13	31	71	9	3	2.6	.919							
		OF	T. Longmire	139	.237	0	17	45	3	3	1	1.6	.941							
		OF	B. Hatcher	134	.246	2	13	68	4	0	0	1.8	1.000							
	Florida	1B	G. Colbrunn	155	.303	6	31	303	26	4	28	8.1	.988	D. Weathers	24	135	8	12	0	5.27
		2B	B. Barberie	372	.301	5	31	223	320	**14**	61	5.3	.975	P. Rapp	24	133	7	8	0	3.85
	W-51 L-64	SS	K. Abbott	345	.249	9	33	165	258	13	57	4.4	.966	C. Hough	21	114	5	9	0	5.15
		3B	J. Browne	329	.295	3	30	44	87	10	8	2.3	.929	M. Gardner	20	92	4	4	0	4.87
	Rene Lachemann	RF	G. Sheffield	322	.276	27	78	153	7	5	2	1.9	.970	C. Hammond	13	73	4	4	0	3.07
		CF	C. Carr	433	.263	2	30	297	4	6	0	3.0	.980	R. Nen	44	58	5	5	15	2.95
		LF	J. Conine	451	.319	18	82	182	4	5	0	2.0	.974	J. Hernandez	21	23	3	3	9	2.70
		C	B. Santiago	337	.273	11	41	511	**64**	5	3	6.0	.991							
		3B	D. Magadan	211	.275	1	17	21	71	4	5	2.0	.958							
		OF	M. Carrillo	136	.250	0	9	49	5	1	1	1.1	.982							
		1B	O. Destrade	130	.208	5	15	273	19	5	29	8.0	.983							
		S3	A. Arias	113	.239	0	15	37	52	2	9		.978							
Central	Cincinnati	1B	H. Morris	436	.335	10	78	899	77	6	76	8.8	.994	J. Rijo	26	172	9	6	0	3.08
		2B	B. Boone	381	.320	12	68	191	267	12	57	4.4	.974	J. Smiley	24	159	11	10	0	3.86
	W-66 L-48	SS	B. Larkin	427	.279	9	52	**178**	312	10	56	4.5	.980	E. Hanson	22	123	5	5	0	4.11
		3B	T. Fernandez	366	.279	8	50	54	165	2	10	2.4	**.991**	J. Roper	16	92	6	2	0	4.50
	Davey Johnson	RF	R. Sanders	400	.263	17	62	217	12	6	2	2.3	.974	P. Schourek	22	81	7	2	0	4.09
		CF	D. Sanders	184	.277	0	7	110	2	0	0	2.5	1.000	J. Ruffin	51	70	7	2	1	3.09
		LF	K. Mitchell	310	.326	30	77	132	9	4	0	1.6	.972	J. Brantley	50	65	6	6	15	2.48
		C	B. Dorsett	216	.245	5	26	412	34	4	2	6.2	.991	C. McElroy	52	58	1	2	5	2.34
		OF	R. Kelly	179	.302	3	21	119	2	1	0	2.6	.992	H. Carrasco	45	56	5	6	6	2.24
		OF	T. Howard	178	.264	5	24	80	2	3	1	1.5	.965							
		C	E. Taubensee	177	.294	8	21	361	17	4	1	6.3	.990							
		OF	J. Brumfield	122	.311	4	11	74	1	1	0	1.8	.987							

NATIONAL LEAGUE 1994, *cont.*

Houston
W-66 L-49 — Terry Collins

POS	Player	AB	BA	HR	RBI	PO	A	E	DP	TC/G	FA
1B	J. Bagwell	400	.368	39	116	923	117	9	93	9.6	.991
2B	C. Biggio	437	.318	6	56	225	339	7	63	5.1	.988
SS	A. Cedeno	342	.263	9	49	130	280	23	69	4.6	.947
3B	K. Caminiti	406	.283	18	75	79	201	9	17	2.7	.969
RF	J. Mouton	310	.245	2	16	163	5	3	2	1.8	.982
CF	S. Finley	373	.276	11	33	214	9	4	0	2.5	.982
LF	L. Gonzalez	392	.273	8	67	228	5	2	1	2.1	.991
C	S. Servais	251	.195	9	41	481	29	2	1	6.6	.996
OF	K. Bass	203	.310	6	35	82	3	2	1	1.5	.977
C	T. Eusebio	159	.296	5	30	263	24	2	1	5.6	.993
OF	M. Felder	117	.239	0	13	36	2	1	0	1.2	.974

Pitcher	G	IP	W	L	SV	ERA
D. Drabek	23	165	12	6	0	2.84
G. Swindell	24	148	8	9	0	4.37
D. Kile	24	148	9	6	0	4.57
S. Reynolds	33	124	8	5	0	3.05
P. Harnisch	17	95	8	5	0	5.40
B. Williams	20	78	6	5	0	5.74
T. Jones	48	73	5	2	5	2.72
D. Veres	32	41	3	3	1	2.41
J. Hudek	42	39	0	2	16	2.97
M. Williams	25	20	1	4	6	7.65

Pittsburgh
W-53 L-61 — Jim Leyland

POS	Player	AB	BA	HR	RBI	PO	A	E	DP	TC/G	FA
1B	B. Hunter	233	.227	11	47	488	38	5	48	9.0	.991
2B	C. Garcia	412	.277	6	28	226	316	12	78	5.7	.978
SS	J. Bell	424	.276	9	45	152	380	15	67	5.0	.973
3B	J. King	339	.263	5	42	59	193	12	24	2.9	.955
RF	O. Merced	386	.272	9	51	100	3	2	1	1.5	.981
CF	A. Van Slyke	374	.246	6	30	238	9	2	1	2.5	.992
LF	A. Martin	276	.286	9	33	129	8	3	1	1.8	.979
C	D. Slaught	240	.288	2	21	425	36	3	4	6.3	.994
OF	D. Clark	223	.296	10	46	107	5	3	1	2.0	.974
C	L. Parrish	126	.270	3	16	225	15	3	1	6.4	.988
UT	T. Foley	123	.236	3	15	51	94	3	25		.980
13	K. Young	122	.205	1	11	177	45	3	21		.987

Pitcher	G	IP	W	L	SV	ERA
Z. Smith	25	157	10	8	0	3.27
D. Neagle	24	137	9	10	0	5.12
S. Cooke	25	134	4	11	0	5.02
P. Wagner	29	120	7	8	0	4.59
J. Lieber	17	109	6	7	0	3.73
R. White	43	75	4	5	6	3.82
R. Manzanillo	46	50	4	2	1	4.14
A. Pena	22	29	3	2	7	5.02

St. Louis
W-53 L-61 — Joe Torre

POS	Player	AB	BA	HR	RBI	PO	A	E	DP	TC/G	FA
1B	G. Jefferies	397	.325	12	55	890	52	7	91	9.3	.993
2B	G. Pena	213	.254	11	34	119	170	3	42	4.9	.990
SS	O. Smith	381	.262	3	30	136	292	6	65	4.5	.982
3B	T. Zeile	415	.267	19	75	66	224	12	24	2.7	.960
RF	M. Whiten	334	.293	14	53	234	9	9	0	2.8	.964
CF	R. Lankford	416	.267	19	57	259	5	6	1	2.6	.978
LF	B. Gilkey	380	.253	6	45	168	9	3	3	1.8	.983
C	T. Pagnozzi	243	.272	7	40	369	41	1	3	5.9	.998
2B	L. Alicea	205	.278	5	29	124	148	4	38	5.2	.986
OF	B. Jordan	178	.258	5	15	105	5	1	1	2.4	.991
S2	J. Oquendo	129	.264	0	9	53	98	4	22		.974
C	T. McGriff	114	.219	0	13	207	23	2	0	5.9	.991

Pitcher	G	IP	W	L	SV	ERA
B. Tewksbury	24	156	12	10	0	5.32
V. Palacios	31	118	3	8	1	4.44
A. Watson	22	116	6	5	0	5.52
R. Arocha	45	83	4	4	11	4.01
T. Urbani	20	80	3	7	0	5.15
O. Olivares	14	74	3	4	1	5.74
R. Sutcliffe	16	68	6	4	0	6.52
R. Rodriguez	56	60	3	5	0	4.03
R. Murphy	50	40	4	3	2	3.79
M. Perez	36	31	2	3	12	8.71

Chicago
W-49 L-64 — Tom Trebelhorn

POS	Player	AB	BA	HR	RBI	PO	A	E	DP	TC/G	FA
1B	M. Grace	403	.298	6	44	925	76	7	90	9.8	.993
2B	R. Sandberg	223	.238	5	24	96	202	4	35	5.3	.987
SS	S. Dunston	331	.278	11	35	121	219	12	47	4.2	.966
3B	S. Buechele	339	.242	14	52	55	136	5	12	2.0	.974
RF	S. Sosa	426	.300	25	70	248	5	7	0	2.5	.973
CF	K. Rhodes	269	.234	8	19	142	4	5	1	2.0	.967
LF	D. May	345	.284	8	51	154	4	1	0	1.7	.994
C	R. Wilkins	313	.227	7	39	546	51	4	1	6.3	.993
UT	R. Sanchez	291	.285	0	24	152	275	9	52		.979
OF	G. Hill	269	.297	10	38	150	0	2	0	1.9	.987
UT	J. Hernandez	132	.242	1	9	46	85	4	15		.970
O1	E. Zambrano	116	.259	6	18	84	5	2	6		.978

Pitcher	G	IP	W	L	SV	ERA
S. Trachsel	22	146	9	7	0	3.21
W. Banks	23	138	8	12	0	5.40
A. Young	20	115	4	6	0	3.92
J. Bullinger	33	100	6	2	2	3.60
K. Foster	13	81	3	4	0	2.89
M. Morgan	15	81	2	10	0	6.69
J. Bautista	58	69	4	5	1	3.89
C. Crim	49	64	5	4	2	4.48
R. Myers	38	40	1	5	21	3.79

West

Los Angeles
W-58 L-56 — Tom Lasorda

POS	Player	AB	BA	HR	RBI	PO	A	E	DP	TC/G	FA
1B	E. Karros	406	.266	14	46	896	116	9	79	9.4	.991
2B	D. DeShields	320	.250	2	33	155	277	6	47	5.0	.986
SS	J. Offerman	243	.210	1	25	123	194	11	45	4.6	.966
3B	T. Wallach	414	.280	23	78	81	174	11	9	2.4	.959
RF	R. Mondesi	434	.306	16	56	206	16	8	1	2.1	.965
CF	B. Butler	417	.314	8	33	260	8	2	1	2.4	.993
LF	H. Rodriguez	306	.268	8	49	141	4	2	0	1.7	.986
C	M. Piazza	405	.319	24	92	640	38	10	3	6.6	.985
UT	C. Snyder	153	.235	6	18	92	23	7	9		.943
SS	R. Bournigal	116	.224	0	11	56	97	3	19	3.9	.981

Pitcher	G	IP	W	L	SV	ERA
R. Martinez	24	170	12	7	0	3.97
K. Gross	25	157	9	7	1	3.60
T. Candiotti	23	153	7	7	0	4.12
P. Astacio	23	149	6	8	0	4.29
O. Hershiser	21	135	6	6	0	3.79
T. Worrell	38	42	6	5	11	4.29
J. Gott	37	36	5	3	2	5.94
D. Dreifort	27	29	0	5	6	6.21

San Francisco
W-55 L-60 — Dusty Baker

POS	Player	AB	BA	HR	RBI	PO	A	E	DP	TC/G	FA
1B	T. Benzinger	328	.265	9	31	781	55	5	69	8.5	.994
2B	J. Patterson	240	.238	3	32	120	163	6	32	4.6	.979
SS	R. Clayton	385	.236	3	30	178	331	14	62	4.8	.973
3B	M. Williams	445	.267	43	96	79	234	12	21	3.0	.963
RF	D. Martinez	235	.247	4	27	86	3	0	1	1.5	1.000
CF	D. Lewis	451	.257	4	29	281	5	2	1	2.5	.993
LF	B. Bonds	391	.312	37	81	198	10	3	0	1.9	.986
C	K. Manwaring	316	.250	1	29	540	53	4	4	6.2	.993
OF	W. McGee	156	.282	5	23	79	2	1	0	2.0	.988
2B	R. Thompson	129	.209	2	7	67	121	2	24	5.4	.989
OF	M. Carreon	100	.270	3	20	44	0	1	0	1.4	.978

Pitcher	G	IP	W	L	SV	ERA
J. Burkett	25	159	6	8	0	3.62
M. Portugal	21	137	10	8	0	3.93
B. Swift	17	109	8	7	0	3.38
B. Hickerson	28	98	4	8	1	5.40
S. Torres	16	84	2	8	0	5.44
W. VanLandingham	16	84	8	2	0	3.54
D. Burba	57	74	3	6	0	4.38
R. Beck	48	49	2	4	28	2.77
R. Monteleone	39	45	4	3	0	3.18
M. Jackson	36	42	3	2	4	1.49

NATIONAL LEAGUE 1994, cont.

	POS	Player	AB	BA	HR	RBI	PO	A	E	DP	TC/G	FA	Pitcher	G	IP	W	L	SV	ERA
Colorado	1B	A. Galarraga	417	.319	31	85	954	64	8	89	10.0	.992	G. Harris	29	130	3	12	1	6.65
	2B	N. Liriano	255	.255	3	31	144	222	10	42	4.8	.973	D. Nied	22	122	9	7	0	4.80
W-53 L-64	SS	W. Weiss	423	.251	1	32	157	318	13	68	4.4	.973	M. Freeman	19	113	10	2	0	2.80
	3B	C. Hayes	423	.288	10	50	72	216	17	19	2.8	.944	M. Harkey	24	92	1	6	0	5.79
Don Baylor	RF	D. Bichette	**484**	.304	27	95	210	10	2	**3**	1.9	.991	W. Blair	47	78	0	5	3	5.79
	CF	M. Kingery	301	.349	4	41	185	5	4	0	2.0	.979	L. Painter	15	74	4	6	0	6.11
	LF	H. Johnson	227	.211	10	40	90	2	2	0	1.5	.979	K. Ritz	15	74	5	6	0	5.62
	C	J. Girardi	330	.276	4	34	548	55	5	**5**	6.5	.992	S. Reed	**61**	64	3	2	3	3.94
	OF	E. Young	228	.272	7	30	97	4	2	0	1.7	.981	B. Ruffin	56	56	4	5	16	4.04
	OF	E. Burks	149	.322	13	24	79	2	3	0	2.2	.964	A. Reynoso	9	52	3	4	0	4.82
	UT	V. Castilla	130	.331	3	18	67	78	2	23		.986	M. Munoz	57	46	4	2	1	3.74
	2B	R. Mejia	116	.241	4	14	70	93	7	19	5.0	.959							
San Diego	1B	E. Williams	175	.331	11	42	382	29	5	28	9.0	.988	A. Benes	25	172	6	**14**	0	3.86
	2B	B. Roberts	403	.320	2	31	147	221	9	41	4.2	.976	A. Ashby	24	164	6	11	0	3.40
W-47 L-70	SS	R. Gutierrez	275	.240	1	28	85	186	22	33	3.8	.925	S. Sanders	23	111	4	8	1	4.78
	3B	C. Shipley	240	.333	4	30	25	63	6	3	1.8	.936	J. Hamilton	16	109	9	6	0	2.98
Jim Riggleman	RF	T. Gwynn	419	**.394**	12	64	191	6	3	1	1.9	.985	P. Martinez	48	68	3	2	3	2.90
	CF	D. Bell	434	.311	14	54	247	3	10	0	2.4	.962	W. Whitehurst	13	64	4	7	0	4.92
	LF	P. Plantier	341	.220	18	41	159	5	2	0	1.8	.988	T. Hoffman	47	56	4	4	20	2.57
	C	B. Ausmus	327	.251	7	24	**684**	59	7	2	7.6	.991	T. Mauser	35	49	2	4	2	3.49
	S2	L. Lopez	235	.277	2	20	97	169	14	23		.950							
	3B	S. Livingstone	180	.272	2	10	20	78	6	6	2.1	.942							
	UT	P. Clark	149	.215	5	20	148	14	4	14		.976							
	31	A. Cianfrocco	146	.219	4	13	58	65	7	7		.946							
	OF	B. Bean	135	.215	0	14	46	0	0	1	1.2	1.000							
	1B	T. Hyers	118	.254	0	7	258	23	4	19	7.0	.986							

BATTING AND BASE RUNNING LEADERS

Batting Average
T. Gwynn, SD .394
J. Bagwell, HOU .368
M. Alou, MON .339
H. Morris, CIN .335
K. Mitchell, CIN .326

Slugging Average
J. Bagwell, HOU .750
K. Mitchell, CIN .681
B. Bonds, SF .647
F. McGriff, ATL .623
M. Williams, SF .607

Home Runs
M. Williams, SF 43
J. Bagwell, HOU 39
B. Bonds, SF 37
F. McGriff, ATL 34
A. Galarraga, CLR 31

Total Bases
J. Bagwell, HOU 300
M. Williams, SF 270
D. Bichette, CLR 265
F. McGriff, ATL 264
B. Bonds, SF 253

Runs Batted In
J. Bagwell, HOU 116
M. Williams, SF 96
D. Bichette, CLR 95
F. McGriff, ATL 94
M. Piazza, LA 92

Stolen Bases
C. Biggio, HOU 39
D. Sanders, ATL, CIN 38
M. Grissom, MON 36
C. Carr, FLA 32
D. Lewis, SF 30

Hits
T. Gwynn, SD 165
J. Bagwell, HOU 147
D. Bichette, CLR 147
H. Morris, CIN 146

Base on Balls
B. Bonds, SF 74
D. Justice, ATL 69
L. Dykstra, PHI 68
B. Butler, LA 68

Home Run Percentage
J. Bagwell, HOU 9.8
K. Mitchell, CIN 9.7
M. Williams, SF 9.7
B. Bonds, SF 9.5

Runs Scored
J. Bagwell, HOU 104
M. Grissom, MON 96
B. Bonds, SF 89
R. Lankford, STL 89

Doubles
L. Walker, MON 44
C. Biggio, HOU 44
T. Gwynn, SD 35
J. Bell, PIT 35

Triples
B. Butler, LA 9
D. Lewis, SF 9
M. Kingery, CLR 8
R. Sanders, CIN 8
R. Mondesi, LA 8

PITCHING LEADERS

Winning Percentage
B. Saberhagen, NY .778
K. Hill, MON .762
G. Maddux, ATL .727
D. Jackson, PHI .700
P. Martinez, MON .688

Earned Run Average
G. Maddux, ATL 1.56
B. Saberhagen, NY 2.74
D. Drabek, HOU 2.84
J. Fassero, MON 2.99
S. Reynolds, HOU 3.05

Wins
K. Hill, MON 16
G. Maddux, ATL 16
B. Saberhagen, NY 14
D. Jackson, PHI 14
T. Glavine, ATL 13

Saves
J. Franco, NY 30
R. Beck, SF 28
D. Jones, PHI 27
J. Wetteland, MON 25
R. Myers, CHI 21
G. McMichael, ATL 21

Strikeouts
A. Benes, SD 189
J. Rijo, CIN 171
G. Maddux, ATL 156
B. Saberhagen, NY 143
P. Martinez, MON 142

Complete Games
G. Maddux, ATL 10
D. Drabek, HOU 6
T. Candiotti, LA 5

Fewest Hits/9 Innings
G. Maddux, ATL 6.68
P. Martinez, MON 7.15
D. Drabek, HOU 7.21
S. Avery, ATL 7.54

Shutouts
R. Martinez, LA 3
G. Maddux, ATL 3
D. Drabek, HOU 2
A. Benes, SD 2

Fewest Walks/9 Innings
B. Saberhagen, NY 0.66
B. Tewksbury, STL 1.27
G. Maddux, ATL 1.38
S. Reynolds, HOU 1.52

Most Strikeouts/9 Inn.
A. Benes, SD 9.87
J. Rijo, CIN 8.93
P. Martinez, MON 8.83
D. Neagle, PIT 8.01

Innings
G. Maddux, ATL 202
D. Jackson, PHI 179
B. Saberhagen, NY 177
J. Rijo, CIN 172
A. Benes, SD 172

Games Pitched
S. Reed, CLR 61
M. Rojas, MON 58
J. Bautista, CHI 58
D. Burba, SF 57
M. Munoz, CLR 57

		W	L	PCT	GB	R	OR	2B	3B	HR	BA	SA	SB	E	DP	FA	CG	BB	SO	ShO	SV	ERA
East	Montreal	74	40	.649		585	454	246	30	108	.278	.435	**137**	94	86	.979	4	**288**	805	**8**	**46**	**3.56**
	Atlanta	68	46	.596	6	542	**448**	198	18	**137**	.267	.434	48	81	79	.982	16	378	**865**	**8**	26	3.57
	New York	55	58	.487	18.5	506	526	164	21	117	.250	.394	25	89	111	.980	7	332	640	3	35	4.13
	Philadelphia	54	61	.470	20.5	521	497	208	28	80	.262	.390	67	94	93	.978	7	377	699	6	30	3.85
	Florida	51	64	.443	23.5	468	576	180	24	94	.266	.396	65	95	101	.978	5	428	649	7	30	4.50
Central	Cincinnati	66	48	.579		**609**	490	211	36	124	**.286**	**.449**	119	73	84	.983	6	339	799	6	27	3.78
	Houston	66	49	.574	.5	602	503	**252**	25	120	.278	.445	124	76	108	.983	9	367	739	6	29	3.97
	Pittsburgh	53	61	.465	13	466	580	198	23	80	.259	.384	53	91	**124**	.980	8	370	650	2	24	4.64
	St. Louis	53	61	.465	13	535	621	213	27	108	.263	.414	76	80	112	.982	7	355	632	7	29	5.14
	Chicago	49	64	.434	16.5	500	549	189	26	109	.259	.404	69	81	105	.982	5	392	717	5	27	4.47
West	Los Angeles	58	56	.509		532	509	160	29	115	.270	.414	74	88	92	.980	14	354	732	5	20	4.17
	San Francisco	55	60	.478	3.5	504	500	159	32	123	.249	.402	114	**68**	105	**.985**	2	372	655	4	33	3.99
	Colorado	53	64	.453	6.5	573	638	206	**39**	125	.274	.439	91	84	112	.981	4	448	703	5	28	5.15
	San Diego	47	70	.402	12.5	479	531	200	19	92	.275	.401	79	111	81	.975	8	393	862	6	27	4.08
						7422	7422	2784	377	1532	.267	.415	1141	1205	1393	.980	102	5193	10147	78	411	4.21

THE TEAMS AND THEIR PLAYERS

AMERICAN LEAGUE 1994

East — New York
W-70 L-43 — Buck Showalter

POS	Player	AB	BA	HR	RBI	PO	A	E	DP	TC/G	FA	Pitcher	G	IP	W	L	SV	ERA
1B	D. Mattingly	372	.304	6	51	916	66	2	95	10.1	.998	J. Key	25	168	17	4	0	3.27
2B	P. Kelly	286	.280	3	41	182	257	10	69	4.8	.978	J. Abbott	24	160	9	8	0	4.55
SS	M. Gallego	306	.239	6	41	106	245	11	53	5.0	.970	M. Perez	22	151	9	4	0	4.10
3B	W. Boggs	366	.342	11	55	40	213	10	19	2.8	.962	T. Mulholland	24	121	6	7	0	6.49
RF	P. O'Neill	368	.359	21	83	203	7	1	0	2.1	.995	S. Kamieniecki	22	117	8	6	0	3.76
CF	B. Williams	408	.289	12	57	277	7	3	1	2.7	.990	B. Wickman	53	70	5	4	6	3.09
LF	L. Polonia	350	.311	1	36	154	9	4	2	2.0	.976	S. Hitchcock	23	49	4	1	2	4.20
C	M. Stanley	290	.300	17	57	391	30	3	1	5.9	.993	X. Hernandez	31	40	4	4	6	5.85
DH	D. Tartabull	399	.256	19	67							S. Howe	40	40	3	0	15	1.80
UT	R. Velarde	280	.279	9	34	94	188	19	37		.937							
UT	J. Leyritz	249	.265	17	58	282	15	0	6		1.000							

Baltimore
W-63 L-49 — Johnny Oates

POS	Player	AB	BA	HR	RBI	PO	A	E	DP	TC/G	FA	Pitcher	G	IP	W	L	SV	ERA
1B	R. Palmeiro	436	.319	23	76	958	67	4	86	9.3	.996	M. Mussina	24	176	16	5	0	3.06
2B	M. McLemore	343	.257	3	29	202	270	9	53	5.0	.981	B. McDonald	24	157	14	7	0	4.06
SS	C. Ripken	444	.315	13	75	130	321	7	70	4.1	.985	J. Moyer	23	149	5	7	0	4.77
3B	L. Gomez	285	.274	15	56	54	139	5	12	2.5	.975	S. Fernandez	19	115	6	6	0	5.15
RF	J. Hammonds	250	.296	8	31	147	5	6	0	2.4	.962	M. Eichhorn	43	71	6	5	1	2.15
CF	M. Devereaux	301	.203	9	33	203	3	1	1	2.5	.995	A. Rhodes	10	53	3	5	0	5.81
LF	B. Anderson	453	.263	12	48	247	4	1	0	2.3	.996	A. Mills	47	45	3	3	2	5.16
C	C. Hoiles	332	.247	19	53	615	36	7	2	6.7	.989	L. Smith	41	38	1	4	33	3.29
DH	H. Baines	326	.294	16	54													
UT	C. Sabo	258	.256	11	42	52	49	4	5		.962							
OF	J. Voigt	141	.241	3	20	88	2	1	0	1.7	.989							

Toronto
W-55 L-60 — Cito Gaston

POS	Player	AB	BA	HR	RBI	PO	A	E	DP	TC/G	FA	Pitcher	G	IP	W	L	SV	ERA
1B	J. Olerud	384	.297	12	67	823	68	6	82	8.6	.993	P. Hentgen	24	175	13	8	0	3.40
2B	R. Alomar	392	.306	8	38	176	275	4	69	4.3	.991	J. Guzman	25	147	12	11	0	5.68
SS	D. Schofield	325	.255	4	32	150	235	11	58	4.2	.972	T. Stottlemyre	26	141	7	7	1	4.22
3B	E. Sprague	405	.240	11	44	99	147	14	18	2.4	.946	D. Stewart	22	133	7	8	0	5.87
RF	J. Carter	435	.271	27	103	205	4	2	1	1.9	.991	A. Leiter	20	112	6	7	0	5.08
CF	D. White	403	.270	13	49	267	3	6	1	2.8	.978	T. Castillo	41	68	5	2	1	2.51
LF	M. Huff	207	.304	3	25	126	4	1	1	1.7	.992	D. Hall	30	32	2	3	17	3.41
C	P. Borders	295	.247	3	26	583	59	8	2	7.6	.988							
DH	P. Molitor	454	.341	14	75													
UT	D. Coles	143	.210	4	15	103	9	4	7		.966							
OF	C. Delgado	130	.215	9	24	55	2	2	0	1.4	.966							
C	R. Knorr	124	.242	7	19	247	21	2	1	6.8	.993							

Boston
W-54 L-61 — Butch Hobson

POS	Player	AB	BA	HR	RBI	PO	A	E	DP	TC/G	FA	Pitcher	G	IP	W	L	SV	ERA
1B	M. Vaughn	394	.310	26	82	879	57	10	103	8.8	.989	R. Clemens	24	171	9	7	0	2.85
2B	S. Fletcher	185	.227	3	11	118	163	1	40	5.2	.996	A. Sele	22	143	8	7	0	3.83
SS	J. Valentin	301	.316	9	49	134	239	8	54	4.6	.979	J. Hesketh	25	114	8	5	0	4.26
3B	S. Cooper	369	.282	13	53	51	219	16	20	2.8	.944	D. Darwin	13	76	7	5	0	6.30
RF	B. Hatcher	164	.244	1	18	87	3	3	1	2.2	.968	K. Ryan	42	48	2	3	13	2.44
CF	O. Nixon	398	.274	0	25	254	4	3	1	2.5	.989	G. Harris	35	46	3	4	2	8.28
LF	M. Greenwell	327	.269	11	44	141	10	1	1	1.8	.993	C. Nabholz	8	42	3	4	0	6.64
C	D. Berryhill	255	.263	6	34	409	29	2	2	6.6	.995	J. Russell	29	28	0	5	12	5.14
DH	A. Dawson	292	.240	16	48													
UT	T. Naehring	297	.276	7	42	190	182	6	45		.984							
OF	T. Brunansky	177	.237	10	34	84	1	1	1	2.0	.988							
S2	C. Rodriguez	174	.287	1	13	86	129	5	36		.977							
OF	W. Chamberlain	164	.256	4	20	69	5	0	0	2.2	1.000							
OF	L. Tinsley	144	.222	2	14	114	1	1	1	1.9	.991							
C	R. Rowland	118	.229	9	20	195	12	6	0	5.5	.972							

Detroit
W-53 L-62 — Sparky Anderson

POS	Player	AB	BA	HR	RBI	PO	A	E	DP	TC/G	FA	Pitcher	G	IP	W	L	SV	ERA
1B	C. Fielder	425	.259	28	90	887	108	7	72	9.8	.993	T. Belcher	25	162	7	15	0	5.89
2B	L. Whitaker	322	.301	12	43	135	246	12	43	4.7	.969	M. Moore	25	154	11	10	0	5.42
SS	A. Trammell	292	.267	8	28	117	180	10	43	4.9	.967	B. Gullickson	21	115	4	5	0	5.93
3B	T. Fryman	464	.263	18	85	78	222	14	12	2.8	.955	D. Wells	16	111	5	7	0	3.96
RF	J. Felix	301	.306	13	49	188	4	4	0	2.4	.980	J. Doherty	18	101	6	7	0	6.48
CF	E. Davis	120	.183	3	13	85	1	1	1	2.5	.989	J. Boever	46	81	9	2	3	3.98
LF	T. Phillips	438	.281	19	61	236	6	5	1	2.4	.980	M. Gardiner	38	59	2	2	5	4.14
C	C. Kreuter	170	.224	1	19	278	22	4	1	4.8	.987	M. Henneman	30	35	1	3	8	5.19
DH	K. Gibson	330	.276	22	72													
UT	M. Tettleton	339	.248	17	51	367	30	5	7		.988							
S2	C. Gomez	296	.257	8	53	141	210	8	39		.978							
UT	J. Samuel	136	.309	5	21	82	28	1	4		.991							
OF	M. Cuyler	116	.241	1	11	78	1	2	0	1.8	.975							

Central — Chicago
W-67 L-46 — Gene Lamont

POS	Player	AB	BA	HR	RBI	PO	A	E	DP	TC/G	FA	Pitcher	G	IP	W	L	SV	ERA
1B	F. Thomas	399	.353	38	101	735	45	7	74	7.9	.991	J. McDowell	25	181	10	9	0	3.73
2B	J. Cora	312	.276	2	30	161	195	8	47	4.3	.978	A. Fernandez	24	170	11	7	0	3.86
SS	O. Guillen	365	.288	1	39	141	235	16	44	4.0	.959	W. Alvarez	24	162	12	8	0	3.45
3B	R. Ventura	401	.282	18	78	80	176	18	21	2.5	.934	J. Bere	24	142	12	2	0	3.81
RF	D. Jackson	369	.312	10	51	225	2	1	1	2.2	.996	S. Sanderson	18	92	8	4	0	5.09
CF	L. Johnson	412	.277	3	54	317	1	0	0	3.1	1.000	D. DeLeon	42	67	3	2	2	3.36
LF	T. Raines	384	.266	10	52	203	3	4	1	2.0	.981	K. McCaskill	40	53	1	4	3	3.42
C	R. Karkovice	207	.213	11	29	417	19	3	1	5.8	.993	R. Hernandez	45	48	4	4	14	4.91
DH	J. Franco	433	.319	20	98													
C	M. LaValliere	139	.281	1	24	305	21	3	1	5.7	.991							
UT	N. Martin	131	.275	1	16	58	77	2	11		.985							

AMERICAN LEAGUE 1994, *cont.*

	POS	Player	AB	BA	HR	RBI	PO	A	E	DP	TC/G	FA	Pitcher	G	IP	W	L	SV	ERA
Cleveland	1B	P. Sorrento	322	.280	14	62	798	58	4	79	10.0	.995	D. Martinez	24	177	11	6	0	3.52
	2B	C. Baerga	442	.314	19	80	205	334	**15**	70	5.4	.973	C. Nagy	23	169	10	8	0	3.45
W-66 L-47	SS	O. Vizquel	286	.273	1	33	114	204	6	53	4.7	.981	J. Morris	23	141	10	6	0	5.60
	3B	J. Thome	321	.268	20	52	62	173	15	12	2.7	.940	M. Clark	20	127	11	3	0	3.82
Mike Hargrove	RF	M. Ramirez	290	.269	17	60	150	7	1	2	1.9	.994	J. Grimsley	14	83	5	2	0	4.57
	CF	K. Lofton	459	.349	12	57	276	**13**	2	**3**	2.6	.993	J. Mesa	51	73	7	5	2	3.82
	LF	A. Belle	412	.357	36	101	205	8	6	0	2.1	.973	E. Plunk	41	71	7	2	3	2.54
	C	S. Alomar	292	.288	14	43	453	40	2	0	6.3	.996	J. Russell	13	13	1	1	5	4.97
	DH	E. Murray	433	.254	17	76													
	UT	A. Espinoza	231	.238	1	19	93	209	10	42		.968							
	OF	W. Kirby	191	.293	5	23	92	2	4	1	1.4	.959							
	C	T. Pena	112	.295	2	10	209	17	1	0	5.7	.996							
Kansas City	1B	W. Joyner	363	.311	8	57	779	64	8	67	9.9	.991	D. Cone	23	172	16	5	0	2.94
	2B	J. Lind	290	.269	1	31	149	252	5	44	4.8	.988	T. Gordon	24	155	11	7	0	4.35
W-64 L-51	SS	G. Gagne	375	.259	7	51	**189**	323	12	63	4.9	.977	K. Appier	23	155	7	6	0	3.83
	3B	G. Gaetti	327	.287	12	57	61	162	4	15	2.7	**.982**	M. Gubicza	22	130	7	9	0	4.50
Hal McRae	RF	F. Jose	366	.303	11	55	193	7	4	1	2.1	.980	H. Pichardo	45	68	5	3	3	4.92
	CF	B. McRae	436	.273	4	40	252	2	3	0	2.3	.988	R. Meacham	36	51	3	3	4	3.73
	LF	V. Coleman	438	.240	2	33	163	11	7	1	1.8	.961	J. Montgomery	42	45	2	3	27	4.03
	C	M. Macfarlane	314	.255	14	47	498	39	4	**2**	6.7	.993	B. Brewer	50	39	4	1	3	2.56
	DH	B. Hamelin	312	.282	24	65													
	OF	D. Henderson	198	.247	5	31	72	4	3	0	2.0	.962							
	23	T. Shumpert	183	.240	8	24	68	127	8	15		.961							
	C	B. Mayne	144	.257	2	20	246	13	1	1	6.2	.996							
Minnesota	1B	K. Hrbek	274	.270	10	53	567	41	2	51	8.5	.997	K. Tapani	24	156	11	7	0	4.62
	2B	C. Knoblauch	445	.312	5	51	190	284	3	60	4.4	.994	S. Erickson	23	144	8	11	0	5.44
W-53 L-60	SS	P. Meares	229	.266	2	24	134	209	13	45	4.5	.963	J. Deshaies	25	130	6	12	0	7.39
	3B	S. Leius	350	.246	14	49	63	184	8	13	2.7	.969	P. Mahomes	21	120	9	5	0	4.73
Tom Kelly	RF	K. Puckett	439	.317	20	**112**	204	**13**	3	1	2.3	.986	C. Pulido	19	84	3	7	0	5.98
	CF	A. Cole	345	.296	4	23	245	4	8	0	2.6	.969	C. Willis	49	59	2	4	3	5.92
	LF	S. Mack	303	.333	15	61	201	2	2	0	2.7	.990	M. Guthrie	50	51	4	2	1	6.14
	C	M. Walbeck	338	.204	5	35	496	45	4	0	5.7	.993	D. Stevens	24	45	5	2	0	6.80
	DH	D. Winfield	294	.252	10	43							R. Aguilera	44	45	1	4	23	3.63
	OF	P. Munoz	244	.295	11	36	110	1	4	0	2.0	.965							
	UT	J. Reboulet	189	.259	3	23	150	131	7	29		.976							
	1O	D. McCarty	131	.260	1	12	244	27	5	19		.982							
	UT	C. Hale	118	.263	1	11	45	51	3	7		.970							
Milwaukee	1B	J. Jaha	291	.241	12	39	660	47	8	60	9.8	.989	C. Eldred	25	179	11	11	0	4.68
	2B	J. Reed	399	.271	2	37	**231**	351	3	**72**	5.5	.995	R. Bones	24	171	10	9	0	3.43
W-53 L-62	SS	J. Valentin	285	.239	11	46	129	285	**20**	60	**5.2**	.954	B. Wegman	19	116	8	4	0	4.51
	3B	K. Seitzer	309	.314	5	49	25	72	8	6	2.4	.924	B. Scanlan	30	103	2	6	2	4.11
Phil Garner	RF	M. Mieske	259	.259	10	38	155	7	4	1	2.1	.976	J. Navarro	29	90	4	9	0	6.62
	CF	A. Diaz	187	.251	1	17	137	5	1	0	2.0	.993	G. Lloyd	43	47	2	3	3	5.17
	LF	G. Vaughn	370	.254	19	55	162	5	3	0	2.1	.982	A. Miranda	8	46	2	5	0	5.28
	C	D. Nilsson	397	.275	12	69	295	15	2	0	5.2	.994	M. Fetters	42	46	1	4	17	2.54
	DH	B. Harper	251	.291	4	32													
	OF	T. Ward	367	.232	9	45	260	8	4	1	2.7	.985							
	S3	B. Spiers	214	.252	0	17	70	128	8	26		.961							
	OF	D. Hamilton	141	.262	1	13	60	2	0	1	1.9	1.000							
	UT	B. Surhoff	134	.261	5	22	121	29	4	12		.974							
	3B	J. Cirillo	126	.238	3	12	23	59	3	7	2.3	.965							
West Texas	1B	W. Clark	389	.329	13	80	**968**	73	**10**	85	9.8	.990	K. Brown	26	170	7	9	0	4.82
	2B	J. Frye	205	.327	0	18	89	135	4	28	4.2	.982	K. Rogers	24	167	11	8	0	4.46
W-52 L-62	SS	M. Lee	335	.278	2	38	132	255	13	49	4.7	.968	H. Fajardo	18	83	5	7	0	6.91
	3B	D. Palmer	342	.246	19	59	50	181	**22**	7	2.8	.913	C. Carpenter	47	59	2	5	5	5.03
Kevin Kennedy	RF	R. Greer	277	.314	10	46	159	2	4	2	2.3	.976	R. Pavlik	11	50	2	5	0	7.69
	CF	D. Hulse	310	.255	1	19	179	0	4	0	2.4	.978	J. Howell	40	43	4	1	2	5.44
	LF	J. Gonzalez	422	.275	19	85	223	9	2	1	2.2	.991	T. Henke	37	38	3	6	15	3.79
	C	I. Rodriguez	363	.298	16	57	600	44	5	2	6.6	.992							
	DH	J. Canseco	429	.282	31	90													
	2B	D. Strange	226	.212	5	26	78	146	7	36	4.4	.970							
	OF	O. McDowell	183	.262	1	13	113	2	2	0	2.2	.983							
	OF	C. James	133	.256	7	19	63	2	0	0	1.4	1.000							
	SS	E. Beltre	131	.282	0	12	53	121	7	21	4.4	.961							
Oakland	1B	T. Neel	278	.266	15	48	295	23	2	34	7.1	.994	R. Darling	25	160	10	11	0	4.50
	2B	B. Gates	233	.283	2	24	105	160	7	28	4.3	.974	B. Witt	24	136	8	10	0	5.04
W-51 L-63	SS	M. Bordick	391	.253	2	37	182	308	13	64	4.5	.974	T. Van Poppel	23	117	7	10	0	6.09
	3B	S. Brosius	324	.238	14	49	69	154	13	18	2.5	.945	S. Ontiveros	27	115	6	4	0	**2.65**
Tony LaRussa	RF	R. Sierra	426	.268	23	92	155	8	**9**	2	1.8	.948	B. Welch	25	69	3	6	0	7.08
	CF	S. Javier	419	.272	10	44	270	3	4	0	2.6	.986	J. Briscoe	37	49	4	2	1	4.01
	LF	R. Henderson	296	.260	6	20	166	4	4	0	2.5	.977	D. Eckersley	45	44	5	4	19	4.26
	C	T. Steinbach	369	.285	11	57	568	**59**	1	**2**	6.8	**.998**							
	DH	G. Berroa	340	.306	13	65													
	UT	S. Hemond	198	.222	3	20	245	93	6	17		.983							
	O1	M. Aldrete	179	.242	4	18	207	14	1	15		.995							
	1B	M. McGwire	135	.252	9	25	311	17	4	25	8.3	.988							

AMERICAN LEAGUE 1994, *cont.*

	POS	Player	AB	BA	HR	RBI	PO	A	E	DP	TC/G	FA	Pitcher	G	IP	W	L	SV	ERA
Seattle	1B	T. Martinez	329	.261	20	61	705	45	2	62	9.2	.997	R. Johnson	23	172	13	6	0	3.19
	2B	R. Amaral	228	.263	4	18	81	102	11	19	4.6	.943	C. Bosio	19	125	4	10	0	4.32
W-49 L-63	SS	F. Fermin	379	.317	1	35	115	180	8	40	3.9	.974	D. Fleming	23	117	7	11	0	6.46
	3B	E. Martinez	326	.285	13	51	44	127	9	8	2.8	.950	R. Salkeld	13	59	2	5	0	7.17
Lou Piniella	RF	J. Buhner	358	.279	21	68	179	11	2	2	2.0	.990	B. Ayala	46	57	4	3	18	2.86
	CF	K. Griffey	433	.323	40	90	225	12	4	1	2.3	.983	B. Risley	37	52	9	6	0	3.44
	LF	E. Anthony	262	.237	10	30	126	4	2	0	1.9	.985							
	C	D. Wilson	282	.216	3	27	602	41	9	2	7.2	.986							
	DH	R. Jefferson	162	.327	8	32													
	UT	M. Blowers	270	.289	9	49	141	108	9	15		.965							
	2S	L. Sojo	213	.277	6	22	97	185	7	36		.976							
	OF	K. Mitchell	128	.227	5	15	49	0	1	0	1.3	.980							
	OF	B. Turang	112	.188	1	8	44	1	1	0	1.5	.978							
California	1B	J. Snow	223	.220	8	30	489	37	2	56	8.7	.996	C. Finley	25	183	10	10	0	4.32
	2B	H. Reynolds	207	.232	0	11	116	130	1	24	3.8	.996	M. Langston	18	119	7	8	0	4.68
W-47 L-68	SS	G. DiSarcina	389	.260	3	33	160	359	9	66	4.8	.983	P. Leftwich	20	114	5	10	0	5.68
	3B	S. Owen	268	.310	3	37	42	128	8	13	2.5	.955	B. Anderson	18	102	7	5	0	5.22
Buck Rodgers	RF	T. Salmon	373	.287	23	70	219	9	8	1	2.4	.966	M. Leiter	40	95	4	7	2	4.72
W-16 L-23	CF	C. Curtis	453	.256	11	50	331	9	4	0	3.0	.988	J. Magrane	20	74	2	6	0	7.30
	LF	J. Edmonds	289	.273	5	37	145	9	3	0	2.0	.981	J. Grahe	40	43	2	5	13	6.65
Bobby Knoop	C	C. Turner	149	.242	1	12	268	29	1	0	5.2	.997							
W-1 L-1	DH	C. Davis	392	.311	26	84													
Marcel Lachemann	32	D. Easley	316	.215	6	30	122	178	7	34		.977							
W-30 L-44	OF	B. Jackson	201	.279	13	43	77	3	3	0	1.8	.964							
	1B	E. Perez	129	.209	5	16	305	15	1	29	8.4	.997							
	C	J. Fabregas	127	.283	0	16	217	16	3	1	5.8	.987							
	C	G. Myers	126	.246	2	8	194	28	2	0	5.5	.991							
	UT	R. Hudler	124	.298	8	20	71	61	5	20		.964							
	OF	D. Smith	122	.262	5	18	50	2	5	1	1.8	.912							

BATTING AND BASE RUNNING LEADERS

Batting Average
P. O'Neill, NY	.359
A. Belle, CLE	.357
F. Thomas, CHI	.353
K. Lofton, CLE	.349
W. Boggs, NY	.342

Slugging Average
F. Thomas, CHI	.729
A. Belle, CLE	.714
K. Griffey, SEA	.674
P. O'Neill, NY	.603
B. Hamelin, KC	.599

Home Runs
K. Griffey, SEA	40
F. Thomas, CHI	38
A. Belle, CLE	36
J. Canseco, TEX	31
C. Fielder, DET	28

Total Bases
A. Belle, CLE	294
K. Griffey, SEA	292
F. Thomas, CHI	291
K. Lofton, CLE	246
R. Palmeiro, BAL	240

Runs Batted In
K. Puckett, MIN	112
J. Carter, TOR	103
F. Thomas, CHI	101
A. Belle, CLE	101
J. Franco, CHI	98

Stolen Bases
K. Lofton, CLE	60
V. Coleman, KC	50
O. Nixon, BOS	42
C. Knoblauch, MIN	35
B. Anderson, BAL	31

Hits
K. Lofton, CLE	160
P. Molitor, TOR	155
A. Belle, CLE	147
F. Thomas, CHI	141

Base on Balls
F. Thomas, CHI	109
M. Tettleton, DET	97
T. Phillips, DET	95
R. Henderson, OAK	72
P. O'Neill, NY	72

Home Run Percentage
F. Thomas, CHI	9.5
K. Griffey, SEA	9.2
A. Belle, CLE	8.7
B. Hamelin, KC	7.7

Runs Scored
F. Thomas, CHI	106
K. Lofton, CLE	105
K. Griffey, SEA	94
T. Phillips, DET	91

Doubles
C. Knoblauch, MIN	45
A. Belle, CLE	35
F. Thomas, CHI	34
T. Fryman, DET	34

Triples
L. Johnson, CHI	14
V. Coleman, KC	12
K. Lofton, CLE	9
A. Diaz, MIL	7

PITCHING LEADERS

Winning Percentage
J. Key, NY	.810
M. Mussina, BAL	.762
D. Cone, KC	.762
R. Johnson, SEA	.684
B. McDonald, BAL	.667

Earned Run Average
S. Ontiveros, OAK	2.65
R. Clemens, BOS	2.85
D. Cone, KC	2.94
M. Mussina, BAL	3.06
R. Johnson, SEA	3.19

Wins
J. Key, NY	17
D. Cone, KC	16
M. Mussina, BAL	16
B. McDonald, BAL	14
R. Johnson, SEA	13
P. Hentgen, TOR	13

Saves
L. Smith, BAL	33
J. Montgomery, KC	27
R. Aguilera, MIN	23
D. Eckersley, OAK	19
B. Ayala, SEA	18

Strikeouts
R. Johnson, SEA	204
R. Clemens, BOS	168
C. Finley, CAL	148
P. Hentgen, TOR	147
K. Appier, KC	145

Complete Games
R. Johnson, SEA	9
D. Martinez, CLE	7
C. Finley, CAL	7

Fewest Hits/9 Innings
R. Clemens, BOS	6.54
D. Cone, KC	6.82
R. Johnson, SEA	6.91
S. Ontiveros, OAK	7.26

Shutouts
| R. Johnson, SEA | 4 |

Fewest Walks/9 Innings
M. Gubicza, KC	1.80
B. Gullickson, DET	1.95
B. Wegman, MIL	2.02
S. Ontiveros, OAK	2.03

Most Strikeouts/9 Inn.
R. Johnson, SEA	10.67
R. Clemens, BOS	8.86
K. Appier, KC	8.42
M. Langston, CAL	8.22

Innings
C. Finley, CAL	183
J. McDowell, CHI	181
C. Eldred, MIL	179
D. Martinez, CLE	177

Games Pitched
B. Wickman, NY	53
J. Mesa, CLE	51
M. Guthrie, MIN	50
B. Brewer, KC	50

		W	L	PCT	GB	R	OR	2B	3B	HR	BA	SA	SB	E	DP	FA	CG	BB	SO	ShO	SV	ERA
East	New York	70	43	.619		670	534	238	16	139	.290	.462	55	80	119	.982	8	398	656	2	31	4.34
	Baltimore	63	49	.563	6.5	589	497	185	20	139	.272	.438	69	57	96	.986	13	351	666	4	37	4.31
	Toronto	55	60	.478	16	566	579	210	30	115	.269	.424	79	81	100	.981	13	482	832	4	26	4.70
	Boston	54	61	.470	17	552	621	222	19	120	.263	.421	81	81	121	.981	6	450	729	3	30	4.93
	Detroit	53	62	.461	18	652	671	216	25	161	.265	.454	46	82	88	.981	15	449	560	1	20	5.38
Central	Chicago	67	46	.593		633	498	175	39	121	.287	.444	77	79	87	.981	13	377	754	9	20	3.96
	Cleveland	66	47	.584	1	679	562	240	20	167	.290	.484	131	90	113	.980	17	404	666	5	21	4.36
	Kansas City	64	51	.557	4	574	532	211	38	100	.269	.419	140	80	94	.982	5	392	717	6	38	4.23
	Minnesota	53	60	.469	14	594	688	239	23	100	.276	.427	94	75	93	.982	6	388	602	4	29	5.68
	Milwaukee	53	62	.461	15	547	586	238	21	99	.263	.408	59	85	128	.981	11	421	577	3	20	4.62
West	Texas	52	62	.456		613	697	198	27	124	.280	.436	82	106	102	.976	10	394	683	4	26	5.45
	Oakland	51	63	.447	1	549	589	178	13	113	.260	.399	91	88	100	.979	12	510	732	9	23	4.80
	Seattle	49	63	.438	2	569	616	211	18	153	.269	.451	48	95	93	.977	13	486	763	7	21	4.99
	California	47	68	.409	5.5	543	660	178	16	120	.264	.409	65	76	99	.983	11	436	682	4	21	5.42
						8330	8330	2939	325	1774	.273	.434	1117	1155	1433	.981	153	5938	9619	65	366	4.80

Player Register

The Player Register is an alphabetical listing of the career batting and fielding records of every man who appeared in a game in the 1994 season, with the exception of players who are primarily pitchers. Pitchers who have appeared in a minimum of 25 non-pitching games (pinch-hitting, pinch-running, or playing other positions) are listed in this section; all others have abbreviated batting records listed in the Pitcher Register.

Any statistics that appear in boldfaced type indicate that the player led his league in that category that year. Where there is a tie for the league lead, all tied leaders are listed with boldfaced figures. If a superscript "1" appears next to a statistic, as with Rickey Henderson's stolen base total in 1982, it indicates that he is the all-time single season leader in the category. Figures appearing in bold beneath a player's career totals means that the player ranks in the top ten in baseball history in that category. (Rickey Henderson, naturally, has "1st" beneath his career stolen base total.) Career leaders are also highlighted underneath the World Series totals.

Kurt Abbott

ABBOTT, KURT THOMAS
B. June 2, 1969, Zanesville, Ohio

BR TR 5'11" 180 lbs.

Year	Team	Games	BA	SA	AB	H	2B	3B	HR	HR%	R	RBI	BB	SO	SB	Pinch Hit AB	Pinch Hit H	PO	A	E	DP	TC/G	FA	G by Pos
1993	OAK A	20	.246	.410	61	15	1	0	3	4.9	11	9	3	20	2	2	1	36	13	2	2	2.6	.961	OF-13, SS-6, 2B-2
1994	FLA N	101	.249	.394	345	86	17	3	9	2.6	41	33	16	98	3	3	2	165	258	15	57	4.3	.966	SS-99
2 yrs.		121	.249	.397	406	101	18	3	12	3.0	52	42	19	118	5	5	3	201	271	17	59	4.0	.965	SS-105, OF-13, 2B-2

Mike Aldrete

ALDRETE, MICHAEL PETER
B. Jan. 29, 1961, Carmel, Calif.

BL TL 5'11" 180 lbs.

Year	Team	Games	BA	SA	AB	H	2B	3B	HR	HR%	R	RBI	BB	SO	SB	Pinch Hit AB	Pinch Hit H	PO	A	E	DP	TC/G	FA	G by Pos
1986	SF N	84	.250	.389	216	54	18	3	2	0.9	27	25	33	34	1	16	4	317	36	1	34	4.2	.997	1B-37, OF-31
1987		126	.325	.462	357	116	18	2	9	2.5	50	51	43	50	6	25	6	328	18	3	21	2.8	.991	OF-79, 1B-33
1988		139	.267	.329	389	104	15	0	3	0.8	44	50	56	65	6	29	11	272	8	4	3	2.0	.986	OF-115, 1B-10
1989	MON N	76	.221	.316	136	30	8	1	1	0.7	12	12	19	30	1	26	8	109	9	1	8	1.6	.992	OF-37, 1B-10
1990		96	.242	.317	161	39	7	1	1	0.6	22	18	37	31	1	36	9	160	12	1	16	1.8	.994	OF-38, 1B-18
1991	2 teams	SD N (12G – .000)			CLE A (85G – .262)																			
"	total	97	.242	.298	198	48	6	1	1	0.5	24	20	39	41	1	20	2	341	24	2	31	3.8	.995	1B-47, OF-21, DH-7
1993	OAK A	95	.267	.443	255	68	13	1	10	3.9	40	33	34	45	1	17	7	407	28	2	39	4.6	.995	1B-59, OF-20, DH-6
1994		76	.242	.337	178	43	5	0	4	2.2	23	18	20	35	2	25	3	207	14	1	15	2.9	.995	OF-35, 1B-27, DH-1
8 yrs.		789	.266	.372	1890	502	90	9	31	1.6	242	227	281	331	19	194	50	2141	149	15	167	2.9	.993	OF-376, 1B-241, DH-14

LEAGUE CHAMPIONSHIP SERIES

Year	Team	Games	BA	SA	AB	H	2B	3B	HR	HR%	R	RBI	BB	SO	SB	Pinch Hit AB	Pinch Hit H	PO	A	E	DP	TC/G	FA	G by Pos
1987	SF N	5	.100	.100	10	1	0	0	0	0.0	0	1	1	0	2	0	2	5	0	0	0	1.0	1.000	OF-3

Luis Alicea

ALICEA, LUIS RENE
Born Luis Rene Alicea (DeJesus).
B. July 29, 1965, Santurce, Puerto Rico.

BB TR 5'9" 165 lbs.

Year	Team	Games	BA	SA	AB	H	2B	3B	HR	HR%	R	RBI	BB	SO	SB	Pinch Hit AB	Pinch Hit H	PO	A	E	DP	TC/G	FA	G by Pos
1988	STL N	93	.212	.283	297	63	10	4	1	0.3	20	24	25	32	1	5	1	206	240	14	52	4.9	.970	2B-91
1991		56	.191	.235	68	13	3	0	0	0.0	5	0	8	19	0	39	8	19	23	0	4	0.8	1.000	2B-11, 3B-2, SS-1
1992		85	.245	.385	265	65	9	11	2	0.8	26	32	27	40	2	6	0	136	233	7	38	4.4	.981	2B-75, SS-4
1993		115	.279	.373	362	101	19	3	3	0.8	50	46	47	54	11	17	6	210	281	11	61	4.4	.978	2B-96, OF-4, 3B-1
1994		88	.278	.459	205	57	12	5	5	2.4	32	29	30	38	4	34	8	126	148	4	38	3.2	.986	2B-53, OF-2
5 yrs.		437	.250	.360	1197	299	53	23	11	0.9	133	131	137	183	18	101	23	697	925	36	193	3.8	.978	2B-326, OF-6, SS-5, 3B-3

Roberto Alomar

ALOMAR, ROBERTO
Born Roberto Alomar (Velazquez).
Son of Sandy Alomar. Brother of Sandy Alomar.
B. Feb. 5, 1968, Ponce, Puerto Rico.

BB TR 6' 184 lbs.

Year	Team	Games	BA	SA	AB	H	2B	3B	HR	HR%	R	RBI	BB	SO	SB	Pinch Hit AB	Pinch Hit H	PO	A	E	DP	TC/G	FA	G by Pos
1988	SD N	143	.266	.382	545	145	24	6	9	1.7	84	41	47	83	24	0	0	319	459	16	88	5.6	.980	2B-143
1989		158	.295	.376	623	184	27	1	7	1.1	82	56	53	76	42	1	0	341	472	28	91	5.3	.967	2B-157
1990		147	.287	.381	586	168	27	5	6	1.0	80	60	48	72	24	3	0	316	404	19	77	5.0	.974	2B-137, SS-5
1991	TOR A	161	.295	.436	637	188	41	11	9	1.4	88	69	57	86	53	1	0	333	447	15	79	4.9	.981	2B-160
1992		152	.310	.427	571	177	27	8	8	1.4	105	76	87	52	49	0	0	287	377	5	66	4.4	.993	2B-150, DH-1
1993		153	.326	.492	589	192	35	6	17	2.9	109	93	80	67	55	2	1	254	439	14	92	4.6	.980	2B-151
1994		107	.306	.452	392	120	25	4	8	2.0	78	38	51	41	19	4	0	176	275	4	69	4.3	.991	2B-106
7 yrs.		1021	.298	.419	3943	1174	206	41	64	1.6	626	433	423	477	266	11	1	2026	2873	101	562	4.9	.980	2B-1004, SS-5, DH-1

LEAGUE CHAMPIONSHIP SERIES

Year	Team	Games	BA	SA	AB	H	2B	3B	HR	HR%	R	RBI	BB	SO	SB	Pinch Hit AB	Pinch Hit H	PO	A	E	DP	TC/G	FA	G by Pos
1991	TOR A	5	.474	.474	19	9	0	0	0	0.0	3	4	2	3	2	0	0	14	9	0	4	4.6	1.000	2B-5
1992		6	.423	.692	26	11	1	0	2	7.7	4	4	2	1	5	0	0	16	15	0	5	5.2	1.000	2B-6
1993		6	.292	.333	24	7	1	0	0	0.0	3	4	4	3	4	0	0	14	19	0	5	5.5	1.000	2B-6
3 yrs.		17	.391	.507	69	27	2	0	2	2.9	10	12	8	7	11	0	0	44	43	0	12	5.1	1.000	2B-17

WORLD SERIES

Year	Team	Games	BA	SA	AB	H	2B	3B	HR	HR%	R	RBI	BB	SO	SB	Pinch Hit AB	Pinch Hit H	PO	A	E	DP	TC/G	FA	G by Pos
1992	TOR A	6	.208	.250	24	5	1	0	0	0.0	3	0	3	3	3	0	0	5	12	0	0	2.8	1.000	2B-6
1993		6	.480	.640	25	12	2	1	0	0.0	5	6	2	3	4	0	0	9	21	2	2	5.3	.938	2B-6
2 yrs.		12	.347	.449	49	17	3	1	0	0.0	8	6	5	6	7	0	0	14	33	2	2	4.1	.959	2B-12

9th

Sandy Alomar

ALOMAR, SANTOS, JR.
Born Santos Alomar (Velazquez).
Son of Sandy Alomar. Brother of Roberto Alomar.
B. June 18, 1966, Salinas, Puerto Rico.

BR TR 6'5" 200 lbs.

Year	Team	Games	BA	SA	AB	H	2B	3B	HR	HR%	R	RBI	BB	SO	SB	Pinch Hit AB	Pinch Hit H	PO	A	E	DP	TC/G	FA	G by Pos
1988	SD N	1	.000	.000	1	0	0	0	0	0.0	0	0	0	1	0	1	0	0	0	0	0	0.0	–	C-6
1989		7	.211	.421	19	4	1	0	1	5.3	1	6	3	3	0	1	0	33	1	0	1	4.9	1.000	C-6
1990	CLE A	132	.290	.418	445	129	26	2	9	2.0	60	66	25	46	4	9	2	686	46	14	6	5.7	.981	C-129
1991		51	.217	.266	184	40	9	0	0	0.0	10	7	8	24	0	1	0	280	19	4	4	5.9	.987	C-46, DH-4
1992		89	.251	.324	299	75	16	0	2	0.7	22	26	13	32	3	1	0	477	39	2	6	5.8	.996	C-88, DH-1
1993		64	.270	.395	215	58	7	1	6	2.8	24	32	11	28	3	1	1	342	25	6	4	5.8	.984	C-64
1994		80	.288	.490	292	84	15	1	14	4.8	44	43	25	31	8	2	0	453	40	2	0	6.2	.996	C-78
7 yrs.		424	.268	.390	1455	390	74	4	32	2.2	161	180	85	165	18	17	3	2271	170	28	21	5.8	.989	C-411, DH-5

Moises Alou

ALOU, MOISES ROJAS
Son of Felipe Alou.
B. July 3, 1966, Atlanta, Ga.

BR TR 6'3" 185 lbs.

Year	Team	Games	BA	SA	AB	H	2B	3B	HR	HR%	R	RBI	BB	SO	SB	Pinch Hit AB	Pinch Hit H	PO	A	E	DP	TC/G	FA	G by Pos
1990	2 teams	PIT N (2G – .200)			MON N (14G – .200)																			
"	total	16	.200	.300	20	4	0	1	0	0.0	4	0	0	3	0	5	1	9	1	0	0	0.6	1.000	OF-7
1992	MON N	115	.282	.455	341	96	28	2	9	2.6	53	56	25	46	16	15	7	170	6	4	1	1.6	.978	OF-100
1993		136	.286	.483	482	138	29	6	18	3.7	70	85	38	53	17	3	1	254	11	4	2	2.0	.985	OF-136
1994		107	.339	.592	422	143	31	5	22	5.2	81	78	42	63	7	1	0	201	4	3	0	1.9	.986	OF-106
4 yrs.		374	.301	.509	1265	381	88	14	49	3.9	208	219	105	165	40	24	9	634	22	11	3	1.8	.984	OF-349

Year Team	Games	BA	SA	AB	H	2B	3B	HR	HR%	R	RBI	BB	SO	SB	Pinch Hit AB	Pinch Hit H	PO	A	E	DP	TC/G	FA	G by Pos

Rich Amaral

AMARAL, RICHARD LOUIS
B. Apr. 1, 1962, Visalia, Calif.
BR TR 6'   175 lbs.

Year Team	Games	BA	SA	AB	H	2B	3B	HR	HR%	R	RBI	BB	SO	SB	PH AB	PH H	PO	A	E	DP	TC/G	FA	G by Pos
1991 SEA A	14	.063	.063	16	1	0	0	0	0.0	2	0	1	5	0	2	0	13	16	2	6	2.2	.935	2B-5, 3B-2, DH-2, SS-2, 1B-1
1992	35	.240	.300	100	24	3	0	1	1.0	9	7	5	16	4	2	0	33	68	3	10	3.0	.971	3B-17, SS-17, OF-3, 1B-2, 2B-1
1993	110	.290	.367	373	108	24	1	1	0.3	53	44	33	54	19	5	3	180	270	10	71	4.2	.978	2B-77, 3B-19, SS-14, DH-9, 1B-3
1994	77	.263	.377	228	60	10	2	4	1.8	37	18	24	28	5	6	2	108	117	15	24	3.1	.938	2B-42, OF-16, SS-7, DH-5, 1B-2
4 yrs.	236	.269	.354	717	193	37	3	6	0.8	101	69	63	103	28	15	5	334	471	30	111	3.5	.964	2B-125, SS-40, 3B-38, OF-19, DH-16, 1B-8

Ruben Amaro

AMARO, RUBEN, JR.
Son of Ruben Amaro.
B. Feb. 12, 1965, Philadelphia, Pa.
BB TR 5'10"   170 lbs.

Year Team	Games	BA	SA	AB	H	2B	3B	HR	HR%	R	RBI	BB	SO	SB	PH AB	PH H	PO	A	E	DP	TC/G	FA	G by Pos
1991 CAL A	10	.217	.261	23	5	1	0	0	0.0	0	2	3	3	0	2	0	9	6	1	1	1.6	.938	OF-5, 2B-4, DH-1
1992 PHI N	126	.219	.348	374	82	15	6	7	1.9	43	34	37	54	11	14	2	232	5	2	1	1.9	.992	OF-113
1993	25	.333	.521	48	16	2	2	1	2.1	7	6	6	5	0	8	0	25	1	1	1	1.1	.963	OF-16
1994 CLE A	26	.217	.522	23	5	1	0	2	8.7	5	5	2	3	2	11	1	10	0	1	0	0.4	.909	OF-12, DH-3
4 yrs.	187	.231	.370	468	108	19	8	10	2.1	55	47	48	65	13	35	3	276	12	5	3	1.6	.983	OF-146, 2B-4, DH-4

Brady Anderson

ANDERSON, BRADY KEVIN
B. Jan. 18, 1964, Silver Spring, Md.
BL TL 6'1"   170 lbs.

Year Team	Games	BA	SA	AB	H	2B	3B	HR	HR%	R	RBI	BB	SO	SB	PH AB	PH H	PO	A	E	DP	TC/G	FA	G by Pos
1988 2 teams	BOS A (41G – .230)			BAL A (53G – .198)																			
" total	94	.212	.286	325	69	13	4	1	0.3	31	21	23	75	10	7	0	243	4	4	1	2.7	.984	OF-90
1989 BAL A	94	.207	.312	266	55	12	2	4	1.5	44	16	43	45	16	6	1	191	3	3	0	2.1	.985	OF-79, DH-8
1990	89	.231	.308	234	54	5	2	3	1.3	24	24	31	46	15	18	6	149	3	2	1	1.7	.987	OF-63, DH-11
1991	113	.230	.324	256	59	12	3	2	0.8	40	27	38	44	12	14	4	150	3	3	0	1.4	.981	OF-101, DH-3
1992	159	.271	.449	623	169	28	10	21	3.4	100	80	98	98	53	1	0	382	10	8	6	2.5	.980	OF-158
1993	142	.263	.425	560	147	36	8	13	2.3	87	66	82	99	24	1	0	296	7	2	0	2.1	.993	OF-140, DH-2
1994	111	.263	.419	453	119	25	5	12	2.6	78	48	57	75	31	1	0	247	4	1	0	2.3	.996	OF-109
7 yrs.	802	.247	.382	2717	672	131	34	56	2.1	404	282	372	482	161	48	11	1658	34	23	8	2.1	.987	OF-740, DH-24

Garret Anderson

ANDERSON, GARRET JOSEPH
B. June 30, 1972, Los Angeles, Calif.
BL TL 6'3"   190 lbs.

Year Team	Games	BA	SA	AB	H	2B	3B	HR	HR%	R	RBI	BB	SO	SB	PH AB	PH H	PO	A	E	DP	TC/G	FA	G by Pos
1994 CAL A	5	.385	.385	13	5	0	0	0	0.0	0	1	0	2	0	1	1	10	0	0	0	2.0	1.000	OF-4

Eric Anthony

ANTHONY, ERIC TODD
B. Nov. 8, 1967, San Diego, Calif.
BL TL 6'2"   195 lbs.

Year Team	Games	BA	SA	AB	H	2B	3B	HR	HR%	R	RBI	BB	SO	SB	PH AB	PH H	PO	A	E	DP	TC/G	FA	G by Pos
1989 HOU N	25	.180	.410	61	11	2	0	4	6.6	7	7	9	16	0	5	2	34	1	0	0	1.4	1.000	OF-21
1990	84	.192	.351	239	46	8	0	10	4.2	26	29	29	78	5	11	1	124	5	4	0	1.6	.970	OF-71
1991	39	.153	.229	118	18	6	0	1	0.8	11	7	12	41	1	2	0	64	5	1	1	1.8	.986	OF-37
1992	137	.239	.407	440	105	15	1	19	4.3	45	80	38	98	5	22	5	173	6	5	0	1.3	.973	OF-115
1993	145	.249	.397	486	121	19	4	15	3.1	70	66	49	88	3	16	2	233	6	3	0	1.7	.988	OF-131
1994 SEA A	79	.237	.412	262	62	14	1	10	3.8	31	30	23	66	6	9	1	126	4	2	0	1.7	.985	OF-71, DH-4
6 yrs.	509	.226	.384	1606	363	64	6	59	3.7	190	219	160	387	20	65	11	754	27	15	1	1.6	.981	OF-446, DH-4

Alex Arias

ARIAS, ALEJANDRO
B. Nov. 20, 1967, New York, N. Y.
BR TR 6'3"   185 lbs.

Year Team	Games	BA	SA	AB	H	2B	3B	HR	HR%	R	RBI	BB	SO	SB	PH AB	PH H	PO	A	E	DP	TC/G	FA	G by Pos
1992 CHI N	32	.293	.354	99	29	6	0	0	0.0	14	7	11	13	0	0	0	43	74	4	8	3.8	.967	SS-30
1993 FLA N	96	.269	.321	249	67	5	1	2	0.8	27	20	27	18	1	25	4	94	144	6	25	2.5	.975	2B-30, 3B-22, SS-18
1994	59	.239	.283	113	27	5	0	0	0.0	4	15	9	19	0	27	9	37	52	2	9	1.5	.978	SS-20, 3B-15
3 yrs.	187	.267	.319	461	123	16	1	2	0.4	45	42	47	50	1	52	13	174	270	12	42	2.4	.974	SS-68, 3B-37, 2B-30

Billy Ashley

ASHLEY, BILLY MANUAL
B. July 11, 1970, Trenton, Mich.
BR TR 6'7"   220 lbs.

Year Team	Games	BA	SA	AB	H	2B	3B	HR	HR%	R	RBI	BB	SO	SB	PH AB	PH H	PO	A	E	DP	TC/G	FA	G by Pos
1992 LA N	29	.221	.337	95	21	5	0	2	2.1	6	6	5	34	0	4	2	34	2	6	0	1.4	.857	OF-27
1993	14	.243	.243	37	9	0	0	0	0.0	0	0	2	11	0	3	1	11	3	0	0	1.0	1.000	OF-11
1994	2	.333	.500	6	2	1	0	0	0.0	0	0	0	2	0	0	0	3	0	0	0	1.5	1.000	OF-2
3 yrs.	45	.232	.319	138	32	6	0	2	1.4	6	6	7	47	0	7	3	48	5	6	0	1.3	.898	OF-40

Brad Ausmus

AUSMUS, BRADLEY DAVID
B. Apr. 14, 1969, New Haven, Conn.
BR TR 5'11"   190 lbs.

Year Team	Games	BA	SA	AB	H	2B	3B	HR	HR%	R	RBI	BB	SO	SB	PH AB	PH H	PO	A	E	DP	TC/G	FA	G by Pos
1993 SD N	49	.256	.413	160	41	8	1	5	3.1	18	12	6	28	2	0	0	272	34	8	5	6.4	.975	C-49
1994	101	.251	.358	327	82	12	1	7	2.1	45	24	30	63	5	0	0	687	59	7	2	7.5	.991	C-99, 1B-1
2 yrs.	150	.253	.376	487	123	20	2	12	2.5	63	36	36	91	7	0	0	959	93	15	7	7.1	.986	C-148, 1B-1

Carlos Baerga

BAERGA, CARLOS OBED
Born Carlos Obed Baerga (Ortiz).
B. Nov. 4, 1968, Santurce, Puerto Rico
BB TR 5'11"   165 lbs.

Year Team	Games	BA	SA	AB	H	2B	3B	HR	HR%	R	RBI	BB	SO	SB	PH AB	PH H	PO	A	E	DP	TC/G	FA	G by Pos
1990 CLE A	108	.260	.394	312	81	17	2	7	2.2	46	47	16	57	0	31	11	79	164	17	27	2.4	.935	3B-50, SS-48, 2B-8
1991	158	.288	.398	593	171	28	2	11	1.9	80	69	48	74	3	4	1	217	421	27	73	4.2	.959	3B-89, 2B-75, SS-2
1992	161	.312	.455	657	205	32	1	20	3.0	92	105	35	76	10	0	0	399	475	19	138	5.5	.979	2B-160, DH-1
1993	154	.321	.486	624	200	28	6	21	3.4	105	114	34	68	15	1	0	347	445	17	108	5.3	.979	2B-150, DH-4
1994	103	.314	.525	442	139	32	2	19	4.3	81	80	10	45	8	0	0	205	334	15	70	5.4	.973	2B-102, DH-1
5 yrs.	684	.303	.454	2628	796	137	13	78	3.0	404	415	143	320	36	36	12	1247	1839	95	416	4.7	.970	2B-495, 3B-139, SS-50, DH-6

Year	Team	Games	BA	SA	AB	H	2B	3B	HR	HR%	R	RBI	BB	SO	SB	Pinch Hit AB	Pinch Hit H	PO	A	E	DP	TC/G	FA	G by Pos

Jeff Bagwell

BAGWELL, JEFFREY ROBERT
B. May 27, 1968, Boston, Mass.

BR TR 6′ 195 lbs.

Year	Team	Games	BA	SA	AB	H	2B	3B	HR	HR%	R	RBI	BB	SO	SB	AB	H	PO	A	E	DP	TC/G	FA	G by Pos
1991	HOU N	156	.294	.437	554	163	26	4	15	2.7	79	82	75	116	7	4	2	1270	106	12	97	8.9	.991	1B-155
1992		162	.273	.444	586	160	34	6	18	3.1	87	96	84	97	10	4	2	1334	133	7	110	9.1	.995	1B-159
1993		142	.320	.516	535	171	37	4	20	3.7	76	88	62	73	13	2	1	1200	113	9	106	9.3	.993	1B-141
1994		110	.368	**.750**	400	147	32	2	39	**9.8**	104	116	65	65	15	1	0	924	118	9	93	9.6	.991	1B-109, OF-1
4 yrs.		570	.309	.520	2075	641	129	16	92	4.4	346	382	286	351	45	11	5	4728	470	37	406	9.2	.993	1B-564, OF-1

Harold Baines

BAINES, HAROLD DOUGLAS
B. Mar. 15, 1959, Easton, Md.

BL TL 6′2″ 175 lbs.

Year	Team	Games	BA	SA	AB	H	2B	3B	HR	HR%	R	RBI	BB	SO	SB	AB	H	PO	A	E	DP	TC/G	FA	G by Pos
1980	CHI A	141	.255	.405	491	125	23	6	13	2.6	55	49	19	65	2	9	1	229	6	9	1	1.7	.963	OF-137, DH-1
1981		82	.286	.482	280	80	11	7	10	3.6	42	41	12	41	6	5	1	120	10	2	1	1.6	.985	OF-80, DH-1
1982		161	.271	.469	608	165	29	8	25	4.1	89	105	49	95	10	1	0	326	10	7	4	2.1	.980	OF-161
1983		156	.280	.443	596	167	33	2	20	3.4	76	99	49	85	7	1	1	312	10	9	3	2.1	.973	OF-155
1984		147	.304	**.541**	569	173	28	10	29	5.1	72	94	54	75	1	1	0	307	8	6	1	2.2	.981	OF-147
1985		160	.309	.467	640	198	29	3	22	3.4	86	113	42	89	1	1	0	318	8	2	2	2.1	.994	OF-159, DH-1
1986		145	.296	.465	570	169	29	2	21	3.7	72	88	38	89	2	1	0	295	15	5	5	2.2	.984	OF-141, DH-3
1987		132	.293	.479	505	148	26	4	20	4.0	59	93	46	82	0	9	3	13	0	0	0	0.1	1.000	DH-117, OF-8
1988		158	.277	.411	599	166	39	1	13	2.2	55	81	67	109	0	4	2	14	1	2	0	0.1	.882	DH-147, OF-9
1989	2 teams	CHI A	(96G – .321)		TEX A	(50G – .285)																		
"	total	146	.309	.465	505	156	29	1	16	3.2	73	72	73	79	0	8	1	54	0	2	0	0.4	.964	DH-116, OF-26
1990	2 teams	TEX A	(103G – .290)		OAK A	(32G – .266)																		
"	total	135	.284	.441	415	118	15	1	16	3.9	52	65	67	80	0	13	4	5	0	1	0	0.0	.833	DH-125, OF-2
1991	OAK A	141	.295	.473	488	144	25	1	20	4.1	76	90	72	67	0	11	5	11	1	1	0	0.1	.923	DH-125, OF-12
1992		140	.253	.391	478	121	18	0	16	3.3	58	76	59	61	1	9	3	27	0	1	0	0.2	.964	DH-116, OF-23
1993	BAL A	118	.313	.510	416	130	22	0	20	4.8	64	78	57	52	0	6	2	0	0	0	0	0.0	–	DH-116
1994		94	.294	.485	326	96	12	1	16	4.9	44	54	30	49	0	10	4	0	0	0	0	0.0	–	DH-91
15 yrs.		2056	.288	.461	7486	2156	368	47	277	3.7	973	1198	734	1118	30	89	27	2031	69	47	17	1.0	.978	OF-1060, DH-959

LEAGUE CHAMPIONSHIP SERIES

Year	Team	Games	BA	SA	AB	H	2B	3B	HR	HR%	R	RBI	BB	SO	SB	AB	H	PO	A	E	DP	TC/G	FA	G by Pos
1983	CHI A	4	.125	.125	16	2	0	0	0	0.0	0	0	1	3	0	0	0	6	1	0	0	1.8	1.000	OF-4
1990	OAK A	4	.357	.429	14	5	1	0	0	0.0	2	3	2	1	1	0	0	0	0	0	0	0.0	–	DH-4
1992		6	.440	.640	25	11	2	0	1	4.0	6	4	0	3	0	0	0	0	0	0	0	0.0	–	DH-6
3 yrs.		14	.327	.436	55	18	3	0	1	1.8	8	7	3	7	1	0	0	6	1	0	0	0.5	1.000	DH-10, OF-4

WORLD SERIES

Year	Team	Games	BA	SA	AB	H	2B	3B	HR	HR%	R	RBI	BB	SO	SB	AB	H	PO	A	E	DP	TC/G	FA	G by Pos
1990	OAK A	3	.143	.571	7	1	0	0	1	14.3	1	1	2	1	1	0	1	0	0	0	0	0.0	–	DH-2

Bret Barberie

BARBERIE, BRET EDWARD
B. Aug. 16, 1967, Long Beach, Calif.

BB TR 5′11″ 185 lbs.

Year	Team	Games	BA	SA	AB	H	2B	3B	HR	HR%	R	RBI	BB	SO	SB	AB	H	PO	A	E	DP	TC/G	FA	G by Pos
1991	MON N	57	.353	.515	136	48	12	2	2	1.5	16	18	20	22	0	16	1	53	90	5	15	2.6	.966	SS-19, 2B-10, 3B-10, 1B-1
1992		111	.232	.281	285	66	11	0	1	0.4	26	24	47	62	9	22	8	66	188	13	18	2.4	.951	3B-63, 2B-26, SS-1
1993	FLA N	99	.277	.371	375	104	16	2	5	1.3	45	33	33	58	2	2	0	201	303	9	62	5.2	.982	2B-97
1994		107	.301	.406	372	112	20	2	5	1.3	40	31	23	65	2	5	2	223	320	14	61	5.2	.975	2B-106
4 yrs.		374	.283	.377	1168	330	59	6	13	1.1	127	106	123	207	13	45	11	543	901	41	156	4.0	.972	2B-239, 3B-73, SS-20, 1B-1

Skeeter Barnes

BARNES, WILLIAM HENRY
B. Mar. 3, 1957, Cincinnati, Ohio.

BR TR 5′11″ 170 lbs.

Year	Team	Games	BA	SA	AB	H	2B	3B	HR	HR%	R	RBI	BB	SO	SB	AB	H	PO	A	E	DP	TC/G	FA	G by Pos
1983	CIN N	15	.206	.294	34	7	0	0	1	2.9	5	5	7	3	2	2	0	45	11	1	7	3.8	.982	1B-7, 3B-7
1984		32	.119	.190	42	5	0	0	1	2.4	5	3	4	6	0	16	1	7	15	0	0	0.7	1.000	3B-11, OF-3
1985	MON N	19	.154	.192	26	4	1	0	0	0.0	0	0	0	2	0	10	1	13	6	0	1	1.0	1.000	3B-4, OF-3, 1B-1
1987	STL N	4	.250	1.000	4	1	0	0	1	25.0	1	3	0	0	0	3	0	0	0	0	0	0.0	–	3B-1
1989	CIN N	5	.000	.000	3	0	0	0	0	0.0	1	0	0	0	0	0	0	0	0	0	0	0.0	–	
1991	DET A	75	.289	.491	159	46	13	2	5	3.1	28	17	9	24	10	11	0	92	38	2	4	1.8	.985	OF-33, 3B-17, 1B-9, 2B-7, DH-3
1992		95	.273	.388	165	45	8	1	3	1.8	27	25	10	18	3	16	3	127	78	11	16	2.3	.949	3B-39, 1B-17, OF-15, 2B-7, DH-6
1993		84	.281	.381	160	45	4	1	2	1.3	24	27	11	19	5	17	6	158	37	4	7	2.4	.980	1B-27, OF-18, 3B-13, DH-13, 2B-10, SS-2
1994		24	.286	.429	21	6	0	0	1	4.8	4	4	0	2	0	5	1	20	2	1	2	1.0	.957	1B-15, OF-4, DH-1
9 yrs.		353	.259	.389	614	159	30	4	14	2.3	95	83	41	74	20	83	12	462	187	19	37	1.9	.972	3B-92, 1B-76, OF-76, 2B-24, DH-23, SS-2

Kevin Bass

BASS, KEVIN CHARLES
B. May 12, 1959, Redwood City, Calif.

BB TR 6′ 183 lbs.

Year	Team	Games	BA	SA	AB	H	2B	3B	HR	HR%	R	RBI	BB	SO	SB	AB	H	PO	A	E	DP	TC/G	FA	G by Pos
1982	2 teams	MIL A	(18G – .000)		HOU N	(12G – .042)																		
"	total	30	.030	.030	33	1	0	0	0	0.0	6	1	1	9	0	1	0	18	0	1	0	0.6	.947	OF-21, DH-2
1983	HOU N	88	.236	.333	195	46	7	3	2	1.0	25	18	6	27	2	43	11	68	1	4	1	0.8	.945	OF-52
1984		121	.260	.360	331	86	17	5	2	0.6	33	29	6	57	5	44	13	149	4	4	2	1.3	.975	OF-81
1985		150	.269	.427	539	145	27	5	16	3.0	72	68	31	63	19	12	4	328	10	1	1	2.3	.997	OF-141
1986		157	.311	.486	591	184	33	5	20	3.4	83	79	38	72	22	2	2	303	12	5	4	2.0	.984	OF-155
1987		157	.284	.449	592	168	31	5	19	3.2	83	85	53	77	21	2	1	287	11	4	2	1.9	.987	OF-155
1988		157	.255	.390	541	138	27	2	14	2.6	57	72	42	65	31	16	6	267	7	6	2	1.8	.979	OF-147
1989	SF N	87	.300	.435	313	94	19	4	5	1.6	42	44	29	44	11	2	1	186	6	3	0	2.2	.985	OF-84
1990		61	.252	.402	214	54	9	1	7	3.3	25	32	14	26	2	5	1	88	2	3	0	1.5	.968	OF-55
1991		124	.233	.366	361	84	10	4	10	2.8	43	40	36	56	7	24	3	159	9	4	2	1.4	.977	OF-101
1992	2 teams	SF N	(89G – .268)		NY N	(46G – .270)																		
"	total	135	.269	.418	402	108	23	5	9	2.2	40	39	23	70	14	29	7	191	2	3	0	1.5	.985	OF-111
1993	HOU N	111	.284	.402	229	65	18	0	3	1.3	31	27	27	52	10	52	9	83	3	1	0	0.8	.989	OF-64
1994		82	.310	.483	203	63	15	1	6	3.0	37	35	28	24	2	26	9	82	3	2	1	1.1	.977	OF-57
13 yrs.		1460	.272	.416	4544	1236	236	40	113	2.5	577	579	333	621	143	258	72	2209	70	41	15	1.6	.982	OF-1224, DH-2

LEAGUE CHAMPIONSHIP SERIES

Year	Team	Games	BA	SA	AB	H	2B	3B	HR	HR%	R	RBI	BB	SO	SB	AB	H	PO	A	E	DP	TC/G	FA	G by Pos
1986	HOU N	6	.292	.375	24	7	2	0	0	0.0	0	4	4	1	2	0	0	16	0	1	0	2.0	.941	OF-6

Year Team	Games	BA	SA	AB	H	2B	3B	HR	HR%	R	RBI	BB	SO	SB	Pinch Hit AB	H	PO	A	E	DP	TC/G	FA	G by Pos

Kim Batiste

BATISTE, KIMOTHY EMIL
B. Mar. 15, 1968, New Orleans, La.

BR TR 6' 175 lbs.

Year Team	Games	BA	SA	AB	H	2B	3B	HR	HR%	R	RBI	BB	SO	SB	PH AB	PH H	PO	A	E	DP	TC/G	FA	G by Pos
1991 PHI N	10	.222	.222	27	6	0	0	0	0.0	2	1	1	8	0	2	0	10	22	1	4	3.3	.970	SS-7
1992	44	.206	.257	136	28	4	0	1	0.7	9	10	4	18	0	2	0	69	85	13	17	3.8	.922	SS-41
1993	79	.282	.436	156	44	7	1	5	3.2	14	29	3	29	0	0	0	72	108	10	15	2.4	.947	3B-58, SS-24
1994	64	.234	.278	209	49	6	0	1	0.5	17	13	1	32	1	7	2	52	116	12	13	2.8	.933	3B-42, SS-17
4 yrs.	197	.241	.316	528	127	17	1	7	1.3	42	53	9	87	1	11	2	203	331	36	49	2.9	.937	3B-100, SS-89
LEAGUE CHAMPIONSHIP SERIES
1993 PHI N	4	1.000	1.000	1	1	0	0	0	0.0	0	1	0	0	0	0	0	2	0	2	0	1.0	.500	3B-4
WORLD SERIES
1993 PHI N	3	—	—	0	0	0	0	0	—	0	0	0	0	0	0	0	0	1	0	0	0.3	1.000	3B-3

Danny Bautista

BAUTISTA, DANIEL
Born Daniel Bautista (Alcantara).
B. May 24, 1972, Santo Domingo, Dominican Republic

BR TR 5'11" 170 lbs.

Year Team	Games	BA	SA	AB	H	2B	3B	HR	HR%	R	RBI	BB	SO	SB	PH AB	PH H	PO	A	E	DP	TC/G	FA	G by Pos
1993 DET A	17	.311	.410	61	19	3	0	1	1.6	6	9	1	10	3	0	0	38	2	0	0	2.4	1.000	OF-16, DH-1
1994	31	.232	.414	99	23	4	1	4	4.0	12	15	3	18	1	3	1	66	0	0	0	2.1	1.000	OF-30, DH-1
2 yrs.	48	.263	.413	160	42	7	1	5	3.1	18	24	4	28	4	3	1	104	2	0	0	2.2	1.000	OF-46, DH-2

Billy Bean

BEAN, WILLIAM DARO
B. May 11, 1964, Santa Ana, Calif.

BL TL 6' 185 lbs.

Year Team	Games	BA	SA	AB	H	2B	3B	HR	HR%	R	RBI	BB	SO	SB	PH AB	PH H	PO	A	E	DP	TC/G	FA	G by Pos
1987 DET A	26	.258	.288	66	17	2	0	0	0.0	6	4	5	11	1	5	0	54	1	0	0	2.1	1.000	OF-24
1988	10	.182	.364	11	2	0	1	0	0.0	2	0	0	2	0	4	2	8	1	0	0	0.9	1.000	OF-4, 1B-2, DH-1
1989 2 teams	DET A (9G – .000)				LA N	(51G – .197)																	
" total	60	.171	.220	82	14	4	0	0	0.0	7	3	6	13	0	7	1	61	0	2	1	1.1	.968	OF-50, 1B-2
1993 SD N	88	.260	.395	177	46	9	0	5	2.8	19	32	2	27	6	122	9	1	5	1.5	.992	OF-54, 1B-12	
1994	84	.215	.267	135	29	5	1	0	0.0	7	14	7	25	0	33	12	96	5	0	4	1.2	1.000	OF-39, 1B-16
5 yrs.	268	.229	.312	471	108	20	2	5	1.1	41	53	24	80	3	76	21	341	16	3	12	1.3	.992	OF-171, 1B-32, DH-1

Rich Becker

BECKER, RICHARD GODHARD
B. Feb. 1, 1972, Aurora, Ill.

BB TL 5'10" 180 lbs.

Year Team	Games	BA	SA	AB	H	2B	3B	HR	HR%	R	RBI	BB	SO	SB	PH AB	PH H	PO	A	E	DP	TC/G	FA	G by Pos
1993 MIN A	3	.286	.571	7	2	2	0	0	0.0	5	4	1	0	1	0	7	0	1	0	2.7	.875	OF-3	
1994	28	.265	.327	98	26	3	0	1	1.0	12	8	13	25	6	2	1	87	2	1	1	3.2	.989	OF-26, DH-1
2 yrs.	31	.267	.343	105	28	5	0	1	1.0	15	8	18	29	7	2	1	94	2	2	1	3.2	.980	OF-29, DH-1

Derek Bell

BELL, DEREK NATHANIEL
B. Dec. 11, 1968, Tampa, Fla.

BR TR 6'2" 200 lbs.

Year Team	Games	BA	SA	AB	H	2B	3B	HR	HR%	R	RBI	BB	SO	SB	PH AB	PH H	PO	A	E	DP	TC/G	FA	G by Pos
1991 TOR A	18	.143	.143	28	4	0	0	0	0.0	5	1	6	5	3	0	0	16	0	2	0	1.0	.889	OF-13
1992	61	.242	.354	161	39	6	3	2	1.2	23	15	15	34	7	2	0	105	4	0	1	1.8	1.000	OF-56, DH-1
1993 SD N	150	.262	.417	542	142	19	1	21	3.9	73	72	23	122	26	8	0	334	37	17	7	2.6	.956	OF-125, 3B-19
1994	108	.311	.454	434	135	20	0	14	3.2	54	54	29	88	24	1	0	247	3	10	0	2.4	.962	OF-108
4 yrs.	337	.275	.415	1165	320	45	4	37	3.2	155	142	73	249	60	11	0	702	44	29	8	2.3	.963	OF-302, 3B-19, DH-1
LEAGUE CHAMPIONSHIP SERIES
1992 TOR A	2	—	—	0	0	0	0	0	—	1	0	1	0	1	0	0	1	0	0	0	0.5	1.000	OF-2
WORLD SERIES
1992 TOR A	2	.000	.000	1	0	0	0	0	0.0	1	0	1	0	1	0	0	0	0	0	0	0.0	—	

Jay Bell

BELL, JAY STUART
B. Dec. 11, 1965, Eglin Air Force Base, Fla.

BR TR 6'1" 180 lbs.

Year Team	Games	BA	SA	AB	H	2B	3B	HR	HR%	R	RBI	BB	SO	SB	PH AB	PH H	PO	A	E	DP	TC/G	FA	G by Pos
1986 CLE A	5	.357	.714	14	5	2	0	1	7.1	3	4	2	3	0	1	0	1	6	2	1	1.8	.778	2B-2, DH-2
1987	38	.216	.352	125	27	9	1	2	1.6	14	13	8	31	2	0	0	67	93	9	22	4.4	.947	SS-38
1988	73	.218	.280	211	46	5	1	2	0.9	23	21	21	53	4	0	0	103	170	10	37	3.9	.965	SS-72
1989 PIT N	78	.258	.351	271	70	13	3	2	0.7	33	27	19	47	5	3	1	109	197	10	41	4.1	.968	SS-78
1990	159	.254	.362	583	148	28	7	7	1.2	93	52	65	109	10	2	1	260	459	22	85	4.7	.970	SS-159
1991	157	.270	.428	608	164	32	8	16	2.6	96	67	52	99	10	2	0	239	491	24	78	4.8	.968	SS-156
1992	159	.264	.383	632	167	36	6	9	1.4	87	55	55	103	7	0	0	268	526	22	94	5.1	.973	SS-159
1993	154	.310	.437	604	187	32	9	9	1.5	102	51	77	122	16	0	0	256	527	11	100	5.2	.986	SS-154
1994	110	.276	.441	424	117	35	4	9	2.1	68	45	49	82	2	1	0	152	380	15	67	5.0	.973	SS-110
9 yrs.	933	.268	.395	3472	931	192	39	57	1.6	519	335	348	649	56	9	2	1455	2849	125	525	4.7	.972	SS-926, 2B-2, DH-2
LEAGUE CHAMPIONSHIP SERIES
1990 PIT N	6	.250	.450	20	5	1	0	1	5.0	3	1	4	3	0	0	0	4	22	1	2	4.5	.963	SS-6
1991	7	.414	.586	29	12	2	0	1	3.4	2	1	0	10	0	0	0	13	19	1	2	4.7	.970	SS-7
1992	7	.172	.345	29	5	2	0	1	3.4	3	4	3	4	0	0	0	6	8	1	0	2.1	.933	SS-7
3 yrs.	20	.282	.462	78	22	5	0	3	3.8	8	6	7	17	0	0	0	23	49	3	4	3.8	.960	SS-20

Juan Bell

BELL, JUAN
Born Juan Bell (Mathey).
Brother of George Bell.
B. Mar. 29, 1968, San Pedro de Macoris, Dominican Republic.

BR TR 5'11" 172 lbs.

Year Team	Games	BA	SA	AB	H	2B	3B	HR	HR%	R	RBI	BB	SO	SB	PH AB	PH H	PO	A	E	DP	TC/G	FA	G by Pos
1989 BAL A	8	.000	.000	4	0	0	0	0	0.0	2	0	1	1	1	0	0	2	6	0	1	1.0	1.000	DH-4, 2B-2, SS-2
1990	5	.000	.000	2	0	0	0	0	0.0	2	0	0	1	0	0	0	1	1	0	0	0.4	1.000	DH-1, SS-1
1991	100	.172	.249	209	36	9	2	1	0.5	26	15	8	51	0	5	0	107	199	9	40	3.2	.971	2B-77, SS-15, DH-4, OF-1
1992 PHI N	46	.204	.259	147	30	3	1	1	0.7	12	8	18	29	5	1	0	82	129	6	22	4.7	.972	SS-46
1993 2 teams	PHI N (24G – .200)				MIL A	(91G – .234)																	
" total	115	.228	.322	351	80	12	3	5	1.4	47	36	41	76	6	2	0	218	281	21	64	4.5	.960	SS-62, 2B-47, OF-3, DH-2
1994 MON N	38	.278	.381	97	27	4	0	2	2.1	12	10	15	21	4	9	2	43	72	2	15	3.1	.983	2B-25, 3B-3, SS-1
6 yrs.	312	.214	.296	810	173	28	6	9	1.1	100	69	82	179	16	17	2	453	688	38	142	3.8	.968	2B-151, SS-127, DH-11, OF-4, 3B-3

Year	Team	Games	BA	SA	AB	H	2B	3B	HR	HR%	R	RBI	BB	SO	SB	Pinch Hit AB	Pinch Hit H	PO	A	E	DP	TC/G	FA	G by Pos

Albert Belle

BELLE, ALBERT JOJUAN
B. Aug. 25, 1966, Shreveport, La.
BR TR 6'1" 190 lbs.

Year	Team	Games	BA	SA	AB	H	2B	3B	HR	HR%	R	RBI	BB	SO	SB	PH AB	PH H	PO	A	E	DP	TC/G	FA	G by Pos
1989	CLE A	62	.225	.394	218	49	8	4	7	3.2	22	37	12	55	2	2	1	92	3	2	1	1.6	.979	OF-44, DH-17
1990		9	.174	.304	23	4	0	0	1	4.3	1	3	1	6	0	2	0	0	0	0	0	0.0	–	DH-6, OF-1
1991		123	.282	.540	461	130	31	2	28	6.1	60	95	25	99	3	4	1	170	8	9	1	1.5	.952	OF-89, DH-32
1992		153	.260	.477	585	152	23	1	34	5.8	81	112	52	128	8	1	0	94	1	3	0	0.6	.969	DH-100, OF-52
1993		159	.290	.552	594	172	36	3	38	6.4	93	**129**	76	96	23	1	0	338	16	5	7	2.3	.986	OF-150, DH-9
1994		106	.357	.714	412	147	35	2	36	8.7	90	101	58	71	9	0	0	205	8	6	0	2.1	.973	OF-104, DH-2
6 yrs.		612	.285	.542	2293	654	133	12	144	6.3	347	477	224	455	45	10	2	899	36	25	9	1.6	.974	OF-440, DH-166

Rafael Belliard

BELLIARD, RAFAEL LEONIDAS
Born Rafael Leonidas Belliard (Matias).
B. Oct. 24, 1961, Puerto Nuevo Mao, Dominican Republic.
BR TR 5'6" 160 lbs.
BB 1982

Year	Team	Games	BA	SA	AB	H	2B	3B	HR	HR%	R	RBI	BB	SO	SB	PH AB	PH H	PO	A	E	DP	TC/G	FA	G by Pos
1982	PIT N	9	.500	.500	2	1	0	0	0	0.0	3	0	0	0	1	1	1	2	2	0	0	0.4	1.000	SS-4
1983		4	.000	.000	1	0	0	0	0	0.0	1	0	0	1	0	0	0	1	3	0	1	1.0	1.000	SS-3
1984		20	.227	.227	22	5	0	0	0	0.0	3	0	0	1	4	0	0	12	13	3	4	1.4	.893	SS-12, 2B-1
1985		17	.200	.200	20	4	0	0	0	0.0	1	1	0	5	0	2	0	13	23	2	3	2.2	.947	SS-12
1986		117	.233	.262	309	72	5	2	0	0.0	33	31	26	54	12	4	0	147	317	12	50	4.1	.975	SS-96, 2B-23
1987		81	.207	.271	203	42	4	3	1	0.5	26	15	20	25	5	1	0	113	191	6	31	3.8	.981	SS-71, 2B-7
1988		122	.213	.241	286	61	0	4	0	0.0	28	11	26	47	7	1	0	134	261	9	51	3.3	.978	SS-117, 2B-3
1989		67	.214	.240	154	33	4	0	0	0.0	10	8	8	22	5	1	0	71	138	3	20	3.2	.986	SS-40, 2B-20, 3B-6
1990		47	.204	.259	54	11	3	0	0	0.0	10	6	5	13	1	10	2	37	36	2	8	1.6	.973	2B-21, SS-10, 3B-5
1991	ATL N	149	.249	.286	353	88	9	2	0	0.0	36	27	22	63	3	3	0	168	361	18	53	3.7	.967	SS-145
1992		144	.211	.239	285	60	6	1	0	0.0	20	14	14	43	0	1	0	152	291	14	48	3.2	.969	SS-139, 2B-1
1993		91	.228	.291	79	18	5	0	0	0.0	6	6	4	13	0	4	0	53	99	1	18	1.7	.993	SS-58, 2B-24
1994		46	.242	.317	120	29	7	1	0	0.0	9	9	2	29	0	3	0	45	86	1	16	2.9	.992	SS-26, 2B-18
13 yrs.		914	.225	.263	1888	424	43	13	1	0.1	186	128	127	316	38	31	5	948	1821	71	303	3.1	.975	SS-733, 2B-118, 3B-11

LEAGUE CHAMPIONSHIP SERIES

Year	Team	Games	BA	SA	AB	H	2B	3B	HR	HR%	R	RBI	BB	SO	SB	PH AB	PH H	PO	A	E	DP	TC/G	FA	G by Pos
1991	ATL N	7	.211	.211	19	4	0	0	0	0.0	0	1	3	3	0	0	0	9	15	1	4	3.6	.960	SS-7
1992		4	.000	.000	2	0	0	0	0	0.0	1	0	1	0	0	0	0	2	3	0	0	1.3	1.000	SS-3, 2B-1
1993		2	.000	.000	1	0	0	0	0	0.0	1	0	0	1	0	0	0	0	0	0	0	0.0	–	2B-1, SS-1
3 yrs.		13	.182	.182	22	4	0	0	0	0.0	2	1	4	4	0	0	0	11	18	1	4	2.3	.967	SS-11, 2B-2

WORLD SERIES

Year	Team	Games	BA	SA	AB	H	2B	3B	HR	HR%	R	RBI	BB	SO	SB	PH AB	PH H	PO	A	E	DP	TC/G	FA	G by Pos
1991	ATL N	7	.375	.438	16	6	1	0	0	0.0	0	4	1	2	0	0	0	8	21	0	4	4.1	1.000	SS-7
1992		4	–	–	0	0	0	0	0	–	0	0	0	0	0	0	0	2	2	0	1	1.0	1.000	SS-3, 2B-1
2 yrs.		11	.375	.438	16	6	1	0	0	0.0	0	4	1	2	0	0	0	10	23	0	5	3.0	1.000	SS-10, 2B-1

Esteban Beltre

BELTRE, ESTEBAN
Born Esteban Beltre (Valera).
B. Dec. 26, 1967, Ingenio Quesqueya, Dominican Republic.
BR TR 5'10" 155 lbs.

Year	Team	Games	BA	SA	AB	H	2B	3B	HR	HR%	R	RBI	BB	SO	SB	PH AB	PH H	PO	A	E	DP	TC/G	FA	G by Pos
1991	CHI A	8	.167	.167	6	1	0	0	0	0.0	0	0	1	1	1	0	0	1	5	0	1	0.8	1.000	SS-8
1992		49	.191	.236	110	21	2	0	1	0.9	21	10	3	18	1	0	0	53	92	12	12	3.2	.924	SS-43, DH-4
1994	TEX A	48	.282	.321	131	37	5	0	0	0.0	12	12	16	25	2	1	0	59	132	9	23	4.2	.955	SS-41, 3B-5, 2B-1
3 yrs.		105	.239	.279	247	59	7	0	1	0.4	33	22	20	44	4	1	0	113	229	21	36	3.5	.942	SS-92, 3B-5, DH-4, 2B-1

Freddie Benavides

BENAVIDES, ALFREDO
B. Apr. 7, 1966, Laredo, Tex.
BR TR 6'2" 180 lbs.

Year	Team	Games	BA	SA	AB	H	2B	3B	HR	HR%	R	RBI	BB	SO	SB	PH AB	PH H	PO	A	E	DP	TC/G	FA	G by Pos
1991	CIN N	24	.286	.302	63	18	1	0	0	0.0	11	3	1	15	1	2	0	33	53	2	6	3.7	.977	SS-20, 2B-3
1992		74	.231	.318	173	40	10	1	1	0.6	14	17	10	34	0	11	3	80	129	6	26	2.9	.972	2B-37, SS-34, 3B-1
1993	CLR N	74	.286	.404	213	61	10	3	3	1.4	20	26	6	27	3	5	1	98	158	13	27	3.6	.952	SS-48, 2B-19, 3B-5, 1B-1
1994	MON N	47	.188	.271	85	16	5	1	0	0.0	8	6	3	15	0	8	3	52	47	2	12	2.1	.980	2B-36, 3B-5, 1B-3, SS-3
4 yrs.		219	.253	.343	534	135	26	5	4	0.7	53	52	20	91	4	26	7	263	387	23	71	3.1	.966	SS-105, 2B-95, 3B-11, 1B-4

Mike Benjamin

BENJAMIN, MICHAEL PAUL
B. Nov. 22, 1965, Euclid, Ohio.
BR TR 6'3" 195 lbs.

Year	Team	Games	BA	SA	AB	H	2B	3B	HR	HR%	R	RBI	BB	SO	SB	PH AB	PH H	PO	A	E	DP	TC/G	FA	G by Pos
1989	SF N	14	.167	.167	6	1	0	0	0	0.0	6	0	0	1	0	1	1	4	4	0	0	0.6	1.000	SS-8
1990		22	.214	.411	56	12	3	1	2	3.6	7	3	3	10	1	2	0	29	53	1	10	3.8	.988	SS-21
1991		54	.123	.208	106	13	3	0	2	1.9	12	8	7	26	3	2	1	64	123	3	23	3.5	.984	SS-51, 3B-1
1992		40	.173	.267	75	13	2	1	1	1.3	4	3	4	15	1	2	0	34	71	1	13	2.7	.991	SS-33, 3B-2
1993		63	.199	.329	146	29	7	0	4	2.7	22	16	9	23	0	0	0	74	133	5	33	3.4	.976	2B-23, SS-23, 3B-16
1994		38	.258	.419	62	16	5	1	1	1.6	9	9	5	16	5	0	0	33	69	3	14	2.8	.971	SS-18, 2B-10, 3B-5
6 yrs.		231	.186	.310	451	84	20	3	10	2.2	60	39	28	91	10	7	2	238	453	13	93	3.0	.982	SS-154, 2B-33, 3B-24

Todd Benzinger

BENZINGER, TODD ERIC
B. Feb. 11, 1963, Dayton, Ky.
BB TR 6'1" 185 lbs.

Year	Team	Games	BA	SA	AB	H	2B	3B	HR	HR%	R	RBI	BB	SO	SB	PH AB	PH H	PO	A	E	DP	TC/G	FA	G by Pos
1987	BOS A	73	.278	.444	223	62	11	1	8	3.6	36	43	22	41	5	8	2	155	7	2	2	2.2	.988	OF-61, 1B-2
1988		120	.254	.425	405	103	28	1	13	3.2	47	70	22	80	2	7	3	602	38	6	47	5.4	.991	1B-85, OF-48, DH-1
1989	CIN N	161	.245	.381	**628**	154	28	3	17	2.7	79	76	44	120	3	3	1	1417	73	7	96	9.3	.995	1B-158
1990		118	.253	.340	376	95	14	2	5	1.3	35	46	19	69	3	15	0	733	52	6	58	6.7	.992	1B-95, OF-10
1991	2 teams		CIN N (51G – .187)				KC A (78G – .294)																	
"	total	129	.262	.351	416	109	14	0	3	0.7	36	51	27	66	4	22	3	797	51	5	64	6.6	.994	1B-96, OF-15, DH-1
1992	LA N	121	.239	.348	293	70	16	2	4	1.4	24	31	15	54	2	48	13	263	18	1	17	2.3	.996	OF-51, 1B-42
1993	SF N	86	.288	.452	177	51	7	2	6	3.4	25	26	13	35	0	41	8	299	15	0	27	3.7	1.000	1B-40, OF-7, 3B-1
1994		107	.265	.399	328	87	13	2	9	2.7	32	31	17	84	2	14	5	781	55	5	69	7.9	.994	1B-99
8 yrs.		915	.257	.385	2846	731	135	18	65	2.3	314	374	179	549	21	158	35	5047	309	32	380	5.9	.994	1B-617, OF-192, DH-2, 3B-1

LEAGUE CHAMPIONSHIP SERIES

Year	Team	Games	BA	SA	AB	H	2B	3B	HR	HR%	R	RBI	BB	SO	SB	PH AB	PH H	PO	A	E	DP	TC/G	FA	G by Pos
1988	BOS A	4	.091	.091	11	1	0	0	0	0.0	0	0	1	3	0	1	0	21	1	0	2	5.5	1.000	1B-3
1990	CIN N	5	.333	.333	9	3	0	0	0	0.0	0	0	2	0	0	2	2	17	0	0	0	3.4	1.000	1B-2
2 yrs.		9	.200	.200	20	4	0	0	0	0.0	0	0	3	3	0	3	2	38	1	0	2	4.3	1.000	1B-5

Year	Team	Games	BA	SA	AB	H	2B	3B	HR	HR%	R	RBI	BB	SO	SB	Pinch Hit AB	Pinch Hit H	PO	A	E	DP	TC/G	FA	G by Pos

Todd Benzinger *continued*

WORLD SERIES
| | | | | | | | | | | | | | | | | | | | | | | | | |
|1990|CIN N|4|.182|.182|11|2|0|0|0|0.0|1|0|0|0|0|0|1|0|24|0|0|1|6.0|1.000|1B-3|

Geronimo Berroa

BERROA, GERONIMO EMILIANO
Born Geronimo Emiliano Letta (Berroa).
B. Mar. 18, 1965, Santo Domingo, Dominican Republic.
BR TR 6' 165 lbs.

|1989|ATL N|81|.265|.338|136|36|4|0|2|1.5|7|9|7|32|0|47|11|67|1|2|0|0.9|.971|OF-34|
|1990| |7|.000|.000|4|0|0|0|0|0.0|0|0|1|1|0|3|0|1|0|0|0|0.1|1.000|OF-3|
1992	CIN N	13	.267	.333	15	4	1	0	0	0.0	2	1	2	1	0	9	1	2	1	0	0	0.2	1.000	OF-3
1993	FLA N	14	.118	.147	34	4	1	0	0	0.0	3	0	2	7	0	5	0	9	1	2	0	0.9	.833	OF-9
1994	OAK A	96	.306	.485	340	104	18	2	13	3.8	55	65	41	62	7	8	1	131	5	1	6	1.4	.993	DH-44, OF-42, 1B-9
5 yrs.		211	.280	.418	529	148	24	2	15	2.8	67	74	53	103	7	72	13	210	8	5	6	1.1	.978	OF-91, DH-44, 1B-9

Sean Berry

BERRY, SEAN ROBERT
B. Mar. 22, 1966, Santa Monica, Calif.
BR TR 5'11" 200 lbs.

|1990|KC A|8|.217|.348|23|5|1|1|0|0.0|2|4|2|5|0|0|0|7|10|1|2|2.3|.944|3B-8|
|1991| |31|.133|.183|60|8|3|0|0|0.0|5|1|5|23|0|1|0|13|52|2|3|2.2|.970|3B-30|
|1992|MON N|24|.333|.404|57|19|1|0|1|1.8|5|4|1|11|2|5|3|10|19|4|1|1.4|.879|3B-20|
|1993| |122|.261|.465|299|78|15|2|14|4.7|50|49|41|70|12|30|7|66|153|15|13|1.9|.936|3B-96|
|1994| |103|.278|.453|320|89|19|2|11|3.4|43|41|32|50|14|3|0|66|147|14|8|2.2|.938|3B-100|
|5 yrs.| |288|.262|.430|759|199|39|5|26|3.4|105|99|81|159|28|39|10|162|381|36|27|2.0|.938|3B-254|

Damon Berryhill

BERRYHILL, DAMON SCOTT
B. Dec. 3, 1963, South Laguna, Calif.
BB TR 6' 205 lbs.

|1987|CHI N|12|.179|.214|28|5|1|0|0|0.0|2|1|3|5|0|1|0|37|3|4|0|3.7|.909|C-11|
|1988| |95|.259|.395|309|80|19|1|7|2.3|19|38|17|56|1|6|1|448|54|9|5|5.4|.982|C-90|
|1989| |91|.257|.341|334|86|13|0|5|1.5|37|41|16|54|1|6|2|473|41|4|4|5.7|.992|C-89|
|1990| |17|.189|.321|53|10|4|0|1|1.9|6|9|5|14|0|1|0|87|3|2|0|5.4|.978|C-15|
1991	2 teams	CHI N (62G – .189)			ATL N (1G – .000)																			
"	total	63	.188	.325	160	30	7	0	5	3.1	13	14	11	42	1	17	2	214	24	8	2	3.9	.967	C-49
1992	ATL N	101	.228	.384	307	70	16	1	10	3.3	21	43	17	67	0	16	4	426	31	1	5	4.5	.998	C-84
1993		115	.245	.382	335	82	18	2	8	2.4	24	43	21	64	0	12	2	570	52	6	2	5.5	.990	C-105
1994	BOS A	82	.263	.416	255	67	17	2	6	2.4	30	34	19	59	0	13	4	409	29	2	2	5.4	.995	C-67, DH-6
8 yrs.		576	.241	.372	1781	430	95	6	42	2.4	152	223	109	361	3	72	15	2664	237	36	20	5.1	.988	C-510, DH-6

LEAGUE CHAMPIONSHIP SERIES
|1992|ATL N|7|.167|.208|24|4|1|0|0|0.0|1|1|3|2|0|0|0|43|5|0|0|6.9|1.000|C-7|
|1993| |6|.211|.368|19|4|0|0|1|5.3|2|3|1|5|0|0|0|42|0|0|0|7.0|1.000|C-6|
|2 yrs.| |13|.186|.279|43|8|1|0|1|2.3|3|4|4|7|0|0|0|85|5|0|0|6.9|1.000|C-13|

WORLD SERIES
|1992|ATL N|6|.091|.227|22|2|0|0|1|4.5|1|3|1|11|0|0|0|33|2|0|0|5.8|1.000|C-6|

Dante Bichette

BICHETTE, ALPHONSE DANTE
B. Nov. 18, 1963, West Palm Beach, Fla.
BR TR 6'3" 215 lbs.

|1988|CAL A|21|.261|.304|46|12|0|0|0|0.0|1|8|0|7|0|0|0|44|2|1|0|2.2|.979|OF-21|
|1989| |48|.210|.326|138|29|7|0|3|2.2|13|15|6|24|3|9|0|95|6|1|2|2.1|.990|OF-40, DH-1|
|1990| |109|.255|.433|349|89|15|1|15|4.3|40|53|16|79|5|8|2|183|12|7|5|1.9|.965|OF-105|
|1991|MIL A|134|.238|.393|445|106|18|3|15|3.4|53|59|22|107|14|10|4|270|14|7|7|2.2|.976|OF-127, 3B-1|
|1992| |112|.287|.406|387|111|27|2|5|1.3|37|41|16|74|18|10|1|188|6|2|2|1.8|.990|OF-101, DH-4|
|1993|CLR N|141|.310|.526|538|167|43|5|21|3.9|93|89|28|99|14|4|0|308|14|9|3|2.3|.973|OF-137|
|1994| |116|.304|.548|484|147|33|2|27|5.6|74|95|19|70|21|2|1|210|10|2|3|1.9|.991|OF-116|
|7 yrs.| |681|.277|.457|2387|661|145|13|86|3.6|311|360|107|460|75|43|8|1298|64|29|22|2.0|.979|OF-647, DH-5, 3B-1|

Craig Biggio

BIGGIO, CRAIG ALAN
B. Dec. 14, 1965, Smithtown, N.Y.
BR TR 5'11" 185 lbs.

|1988|HOU N|50|.211|.350|123|26|6|1|3|2.4|14|5|7|29|6|0|0|292|28|3|0|6.5|.991|C-50|
|1989| |134|.257|.402|443|114|21|2|13|2.9|64|60|49|64|21|4|3|742|56|9|6|6.0|.989|C-125, OF-5|
|1990| |150|.276|.348|555|153|24|2|4|0.7|53|42|53|79|25|3|2|657|60|13|4|4.9|.982|C-113, OF-50|
|1991| |149|.295|.374|546|161|23|4|4|0.7|79|46|53|71|19|9|3|894|73|11|11|6.6|.989|C-139, 2B-3, OF-2|
|1992| |162|.277|.369|613|170|32|3|6|1.0|96|39|94|95|38|1|0|344|413|12|81|4.7|.984|2B-161|
|1993| |155|.287|.474|610|175|41|5|21|3.4|98|64|77|93|15|0|0|306|447|14|90|4.9|.982|2B-155|
|1994| |114|.318|.483|437|139|44|5|6|1.4|88|56|62|58|39|2|0|225|339|7|63|5.0|.988|2B-113|
|7 yrs.| |914|.282|.404|3327|938|191|22|57|1.7|492|312|395|489|163|19|8|3460|1416|69|255|5.4|.986|2B-432, C-427, OF-57|

Jeff Blauser

BLAUSER, JEFFREY MICHAEL
B. Nov. 8, 1965, Los Gatos, Calif.
BR TR 6' 170 lbs.

|1987|ATL N|51|.242|.352|165|40|6|3|2|1.2|11|15|18|34|7|1|0|65|166|9|28|4.7|.963|SS-50|
|1988| |18|.239|.403|67|16|3|1|2|3.0|7|7|2|11|0|1|0|35|59|4|8|5.4|.959|2B-9, SS-8|
|1989| |142|.270|.410|456|123|24|2|12|2.6|63|46|38|101|5|9|4|137|254|21|28|2.9|.949|3B-78, 2B-39, SS-30, OF-2|
|1990| |115|.269|.409|386|104|24|3|8|2.1|46|39|35|70|3|4|2|169|288|16|54|4.1|.966|SS-93, 2B-14, 3B-9, OF-1|
|1991| |129|.259|.409|352|91|14|3|11|3.1|49|54|54|59|5|26|6|136|219|17|37|2.9|.954|SS-85, 2B-32, 3B-18|
|1992| |123|.262|.458|343|90|19|3|14|4.1|61|46|46|82|5|16|2|119|225|14|34|2.9|.961|SS-106, 2B-21, 3B-1|
|1993| |161|.305|.436|597|182|29|2|15|2.5|110|73|85|109|16|2|0|189|426|19|86|3.9|.970|SS-161|
|1994| |96|.258|.382|380|98|21|4|6|1.6|56|45|38|64|1|0|0|126|289|13|44|4.5|.970|SS-96|
|8 yrs.| |835|.271|.414|2746|744|140|21|70|2.5|403|325|316|530|42|59|14|976|1926|113|319|3.6|.963|SS-629, 2B-115, 3B-106, OF-3|

LEAGUE CHAMPIONSHIP SERIES
|1991|ATL N|2|.000|.000|2|0|0|0|0|0.0|0|0|0|0|0|1|0|0|1|1|0|1.0|.500|SS-2|
|1992| |7|.208|.417|24|5|0|1|1|4.2|3|4|3|2|0|0|0|7|15|2|1|3.4|.917|SS-7|
|1993| |6|.280|.560|25|7|1|0|2|8.0|5|4|4|7|0|0|0|6|14|0|0|3.3|1.000|SS-6|
|3 yrs.| |15|.235|.471|51|12|1|1|3|5.9|8|8|7|9|0|1|0|13|30|3|1|3.1|.935|SS-15|

Year Team	Games	BA	SA	AB	H	2B	3B	HR	HR%	R	RBI	BB	SO	SB	Pinch Hit AB	Pinch Hit H	PO	A	E	DP	TC/G	FA	G by Pos

Jeff Blauser *continued*

WORLD SERIES

1991 ATL N	5	.167	.167	6	1	0	0	0	0.0	0	0	1	1	0	4	0	3	3	0	1	1.2	1.000	SS-5
1992	6	.250	.250	24	6	0	0	0	0.0	2	0	1	9	2	0	0	7	22	0	5	4.8	1.000	SS-6
2 yrs.	11	.233	.233	30	7	0	0	0	0.0	2	0	2	10	2	4	0	10	25	0	6	3.2	1.000	SS-11

Greg Blosser

BLOSSER, GREGORY BRENT
B. June 26, 1971, Manatee, Fla.
BL TL 6'3" 200 lbs.

1993 BOS A	17	.071	.107	28	2	1	0	0	0.0	1	1	2	7	1	7	0	11	1	0	0	0.7	1.000	OF-9, DH-1
1994	5	.091	.091	11	1	0	0	0	0.0	2	1	4	4	0	1	0	8	0	3	0	2.2	.727	OF-3, DH-1
2 yrs.	22	.077	.103	39	3	1	0	0	0.0	3	2	6	11	1	8	0	19	1	3	0	1.0	.870	OF-12, DH-2

Mike Blowers

BLOWERS, MICHAEL ROY
B. Apr. 24, 1965, Wurzburg, West Germany.
BR TR 6'2" 190 lbs.

1989 NY A	13	.263	.263	38	10	0	0	0	0.0	2	3	3	13	0	1	0	9	14	4	3	2.1	.852	3B-13
1990	48	.188	.319	144	27	4	0	5	3.5	16	21	12	50	1	3	0	26	63	10	4	2.1	.899	3B-45, DH-2
1991	15	.200	.286	35	7	0	0	1	2.9	3	1	4	3	0	1	0	4	16	3	1	1.5	.870	3B-14
1992 SEA A	31	.192	.274	73	14	3	0	1	1.4	7	2	6	20	0	1	0	28	44	1	8	2.4	.986	3B-29, 1B-3
1993	127	.280	.475	379	106	23	3	15	4.0	55	57	44	98	1	6	2	70	225	15	14	2.4	.952	3B-117, DH-2, OF-2, 1B-1, C-1
1994	85	.289	.437	270	78	13	0	9	3.3	37	49	25	60	2	14	4	141	108	9	15	3.0	.965	3B-48, 1B-20, DH-9, OF-9
6 yrs.	319	.258	.409	939	242	43	3	31	3.3	120	133	94	244	4	26	6	278	470	42	45	2.5	.947	3B-266, 1B-24, DH-13, OF-11, C-1

Tim Bogar

BOGAR, TIMOTHY PAUL
B. Oct. 28, 1966, Indianapolis, Ind.
BR TR 6'2" 198 lbs.

1993 NY N	78	.244	.351	205	50	13	0	3	1.5	19	25	14	29	0	4	0	105	217	9	42	4.2	.973	SS-66, 3B-7, 2B-6
1994	50	.154	.269	52	8	0	0	2	3.8	5	5	4	11	1	5	1	77	37	1	16	2.3	.991	3B-22, 1B-14, SS-7, 2B-1, OF-1
2 yrs.	128	.226	.335	257	58	13	0	5	1.9	24	30	18	40	1	9	1	182	254	10	58	3.5	.978	SS-73, 3B-29, 1B-14, 2B-7, OF-1

Wade Boggs

BOGGS, WADE ANTHONY
B. June 15, 1958, Omaha, Neb.
BL TR 6'2" 190 lbs.

1982 BOS A	104	.349	.441	338	118	14	1	5	1.5	51	44	35	21	1	13	4	489	168	8	51	6.4	.988	1B-49, 3B-44, DH-3, OF-1
1983	153	.361	.486	582	210	44	7	5	0.9	100	74	92	36	3	0	0	118	368	27	40	3.4	.947	3B-153
1984	158	.325	.416	625	203	31	4	6	1.0	109	55	89	44	3	1	0	141	330	20	30	3.1	.959	3B-155, DH-2
1985	161	.368	.478	653	240	42	3	8	1.2	107	78	96	61	2	0	0	134	335	17	30	3.0	.965	3B-161
1986	149	.357	.486	580	207	47	2	8	1.4	107	71	105	44	0	0	0	121	267	19	30	2.7	.953	3B-149
1987	147	.363	.588	551	200	40	6	24	4.4	108	89	105	48	1	1	0	112	277	14	37	2.7	.965	3B-145, 1B-1, DH-1
1988	155	.366	.490	584	214	45	6	5	0.9	128	58	125	34	2	1	1	122	250	11	17	2.5	.971	3B-151, DH-3
1989	156	.330	.449	621	205	51	7	3	0.5	113	54	107	51	2	1	0	123	264	17	29	2.6	.958	3B-152, DH-3
1990	155	.302	.418	619	187	44	5	6	1.0	89	63	87	68	0	0	0	108	241	20	18	2.4	.946	3B-152, DH-3
1991	144	.332	.460	546	181	42	2	8	1.5	93	51	89	32	1	3	2	89	276	12	34	2.6	.968	3B-140
1992	143	.259	.358	514	133	22	4	7	1.4	62	50	74	31	1	4	0	70	229	15	23	2.2	.952	3B-117, DH-21
1993 NY A	143	.302	.363	560	169	26	1	2	0.4	83	59	74	49	0	6	1	75	311	12	29	2.8	.970	3B-134, DH-8
1994	97	.342	.489	366	125	19	1	11	3.0	61	55	61	29	2	5	1	66	217	10	21	3.0	.966	3B-93, 1B-4
13 yrs.	1865	.335	.455	7139	2392	467	49	98	1.4	1211	801	1139	548	18	35	9	1768	3533	202	389	3.0	.963	3B-1746, 1B-54, DH-44, OF-1

LEAGUE CHAMPIONSHIP SERIES

1986 BOS A	7	.233	.333	30	7	1	1	0	0.0	3	2	4	1	0	0	0	7	14	2	1	3.3	.913	3B-7
1988	4	.385	.385	13	5	0	0	0	0.0	2	3	3	4	0	0	0	6	6	0	1	3.0	1.000	3B-4
1990	4	.438	.688	16	7	1	0	1	6.3	1	1	0	3	0	0	0	6	10	0	2	4.0	1.000	3B-4
3 yrs.	15	.322	.441	59	19	2	1	1	1.7	6	6	7	8	0	0	0	19	30	2	4	3.4	.961	3B-15

WORLD SERIES

| 1986 BOS A | 7 | .290 | .387 | 31 | 9 | 3 | 0 | 0 | 0.0 | 3 | 3 | 3 | 2 | 0 | 0 | 0 | 4 | 15 | 0 | 1 | 2.7 | 1.000 | 3B-7 |

Barry Bonds

BONDS, BARRY LAMAR
Son of Bobby Bonds.
B. July 24, 1964, Riverside, Calif.
BL TL 6'1" 185 lbs.

1986 PIT N	113	.223	.416	413	92	26	3	16	3.9	72	48	65	102	36	3	1	280	9	5	2	2.6	.983	OF-110
1987	150	.261	.492	551	144	34	9	25	4.5	99	59	54	88	32	7	1	330	15	5	3	2.3	.986	OF-145
1988	144	.283	.491	538	152	30	5	24	4.5	97	58	72	82	17	11	2	292	5	6	0	2.1	.980	OF-136
1989	159	.248	.426	580	144	34	6	19	3.3	96	58	93	93	32	8	3	365	14	6	1	2.4	.984	OF-156
1990	151	.301	.565	519	156	32	3	33	6.4	104	114	93	83	52	2	0	338	14	6	1	2.4	.983	OF-150
1991	153	.292	.514	510	149	28	5	25	4.9	95	116	107	73	43	3	1	321	13	3	1	2.2	.991	OF-150
1992	140	.311	.624	473	147	36	5	34	7.2	109	103	127	69	39	2	0	310	4	3	0	2.3	.991	OF-139
1993 SF N	159	.336	.677	539	181	38	4	46	8.5	129	123	126	79	29	3	0	310	7	5	0	2.0	.984	OF-157
1994	112	.312	.647	391	122	18	1	37	9.5	89	81	74	43	29	0	0	198	10	3	0	1.9	.986	OF-112
9 yrs.	1281	.285	.537	4514	1287	276	41	259	5.7	890	760	811	712	309	39	8	2744	91	42	9	2.2	.985	OF-1255

LEAGUE CHAMPIONSHIP SERIES

1990 PIT N	6	.167	.167	18	3	0	0	0	0.0	4	1	6	5	2	0	0	13	0	0	0	2.2	1.000	OF-6
1991	7	.148	.185	27	4	1	0	0	0.0	1	0	2	4	3	0	0	14	1	1	0	2.3	.938	OF-7
1992	7	.261	.435	23	6	1	0	1	4.3	5	2	6	4	1	0	0	17	0	0	0	2.4	1.000	OF-7
3 yrs.	20	.191	.265	68	13	2	0	1	1.5	10	3	14	13	6	0	0	44	1	1	0	2.3	.978	OF-20

Bobby Bonilla

BONILLA, ROBERTO MARTIN ANTONIO
B. Feb. 23, 1963, Bronx, N. Y.
BB TR 6'3" 210 lbs.

| 1986 2 teams | CHI A (75G – .269) | | | PIT N (63G – .240) | | | | | | | | | | | | | | | | | | | |
| " total | 138 | .256 | .333 | 426 | 109 | 16 | 4 | 3 | 0.7 | 55 | 43 | 62 | 88 | 8 | 19 | 2 | 451 | 38 | 5 | 29 | 3.6 | .990 | OF-94, 1B-34, 3B-4 |

17

Year Team	Games	BA	SA	AB	H	2B	3B	HR	HR%	R	RBI	BB	SO	SB	Pinch Hit AB	Pinch Hit H	PO	A	E	DP	TC/G	FA	G by Pos

Bobby Bonilla *continued*

Year Team	Games	BA	SA	AB	H	2B	3B	HR	HR%	R	RBI	BB	SO	SB	AB	H	PO	A	E	DP	TC/G	FA	G by Pos
1987 PIT N	141	.300	.481	466	140	33	3	15	3.2	58	77	39	64	3	17	6	142	139	16	13	2.1	.946	3B-89, OF-46, 1B-6
1988	159	.274	.476	584	160	32	7	24	4.1	87	100	85	82	3	0	0	121	336	32	17	3.1	.935	3B-159
1989	163	.281	.490	616	173	37	10	24	3.9	96	86	76	93	8	1	0	190	334	35	37	3.4	.937	3B-156, 1B-8, OF-1
1990	160	.280	.518	625	175	39	7	32	5.1	112	120	45	103	4	1	0	315	35	15	2	2.3	.959	OF-149, 3B-14, 1B-3
1991	157	.302	.492	577	174	**44**	6	18	3.1	102	100	90	67	2	2	0	247	144	15	19	2.6	.963	OF-104, 3B-67, 1B-4
1992 NY N	128	.249	.432	438	109	23	0	19	4.3	62	70	66	73	4	5	2	277	9	4	3	2.3	.986	OF-121, 1B-6
1993	139	.265	.522	502	133	21	3	34	6.8	81	87	72	96	3	0	0	238	112	17	11	2.6	.954	OF-85, 3B-52, 1B-6
1994	108	.290	.504	403	117	24	1	20	5.0	60	67	55	101	1	0	0	77	217	18	24	2.9	.942	3B-107
9 yrs.	1293	.278	.476	4637	1290	269	41	189	4.1	713	750	590	767	36	45	10	2058	1364	157	155	2.8	.956	3B-648, OF-600, 1B-67

LEAGUE CHAMPIONSHIP SERIES

Year Team	Games	BA	SA	AB	H	2B	3B	HR	HR%	R	RBI	BB	SO	SB	AB	H	PO	A	E	DP	TC/G	FA	G by Pos
1990 PIT N	6	.190	.238	21	4	1	0	0	0.0	0	1	3	1	0	0	0	4	5	1	1	1.7	.900	OF-5, 3B-3
1991	7	.304	.391	23	7	2	0	0	0.0	2	1	6	2	0	0	0	12	1	0	0	1.9	1.000	OF-7
2 yrs.	13	.250	.318	44	11	3	0	0	0.0	2	2	9	3	0	0	0	16	6	1	1	1.8	.957	OF-12, 3B-3

Bret Boone

BOONE, BRET ROBERT
Son of Bob Boone.
B. Apr. 6, 1969, El Cajon, Calif.

BR TR 5'10" 180 lbs.

Year Team	Games	BA	SA	AB	H	2B	3B	HR	HR%	R	RBI	BB	SO	SB	AB	H	PO	A	E	DP	TC/G	FA	G by Pos
1992 SEA A	33	.194	.318	129	25	4	0	4	3.1	15	15	4	34	1	1	0	72	96	6	22	5.3	.966	2B-32, 3B-6
1993	76	.251	.443	271	68	12	2	12	4.4	31	38	17	52	2	0	0	140	177	3	55	4.2	.991	2B-74, DH-1
1994 CIN N	108	.320	.491	381	122	25	2	12	3.1	59	68	24	74	3	2	1	192	269	12	57	4.4	.975	2B-106, 3B-2
3 yrs.	217	.275	.446	781	215	41	4	28	3.6	105	121	45	160	6	3	1	404	542	21	134	4.5	.978	2B-212, 3B-8, DH-1

Pat Borders

BORDERS, PATRICK LANCE
B. May 14, 1963, Columbus, Ohio.

BR TR 6'2" 190 lbs.

Year Team	Games	BA	SA	AB	H	2B	3B	HR	HR%	R	RBI	BB	SO	SB	AB	H	PO	A	E	DP	TC/G	FA	G by Pos
1988 TOR A	56	.273	.448	154	42	6	3	5	3.2	15	21	3	24	0	15	5	205	19	7	0	4.1	.970	C-43, 2B-1, 3B-1
1989	94	.257	.349	241	62	11	1	3	1.2	22	29	11	45	2	20	5	261	27	6	1	3.1	.980	C-68, DH-18
1990	125	.286	.497	346	99	24	2	15	4.3	36	49	18	57	0	25	5	515	46	4	6	4.5	.993	C-115, DH-1
1991	105	.244	.354	291	71	17	0	5	1.7	22	36	11	45	0	18	5	505	48	4	4	5.3	.993	C-102
1992	138	.242	.385	480	116	26	2	13	2.7	47	53	33	75	1	3	3	784	88	8	7	6.4	.991	C-137
1993	138	.254	.371	488	124	30	0	9	1.8	38	55	20	66	2	0	0	869	80	13	12	7.0	.986	C-138
1994	85	.247	.329	295	73	13	1	3	1.0	24	26	15	50	1	0	0	583	59	8	2	7.6	.988	C-85
7 yrs.	741	.256	.388	2295	587	127	9	53	2.3	204	269	111	362	6	81	23	3722	367	50	32	5.6	.988	C-688, DH-19, 2B-1, 3B-1

LEAGUE CHAMPIONSHIP SERIES

Year Team	Games	BA	SA	AB	H	2B	3B	HR	HR%	R	RBI	BB	SO	SB	AB	H	PO	A	E	DP	TC/G	FA	G by Pos
1989 TOR A	1	1.000	1.000	1	1	0	0	0	0.0	0	1	0	0	0	1	1	1	0	0	0	1.0	1.000	C-1
1991	5	.263	.316	19	5	1	0	0	0.0	0	0	0	0	0	0	0	38	3	2	0	8.6	.953	C-5
1992	6	.318	.455	22	7	0	0	1	4.5	3	3	1	0	0	0	0	38	3	1	1	7.0	.976	C-6
1993	6	.250	.292	24	6	1	0	0	0.0	1	3	0	7	1	0	0	41	4	0	1	7.5	1.000	C-6
4 yrs.	18	.288	.364	66	19	2	0	1	1.5	4	9	1	7	1	1	1	118	10	3	2	7.3	.977	C-18

WORLD SERIES

Year Team	Games	BA	SA	AB	H	2B	3B	HR	HR%	R	RBI	BB	SO	SB	AB	H	PO	A	E	DP	TC/G	FA	G by Pos
1992 TOR A	6	.450	.750	20	9	3	0	1	5.0	2	3	2	1	0	0	0	48	5	1	0	9.0	.981	C-6
1993	6	.304	.304	23	7	0	0	0	0.0	2	1	2	1	0	0	0	50	2	1	0	8.8	.981	C-6
2 yrs.	12	.372	.512	43	16	3	0	1	2.3	4	4	4	2	0	0	0	98	7	2	2	8.9	.981	C-12

Mike Bordick

BORDICK, MICHAEL TODD
B. July 21, 1965, Marquette, Mich.

BR TR 5'11" 170 lbs.

Year Team	Games	BA	SA	AB	H	2B	3B	HR	HR%	R	RBI	BB	SO	SB	AB	H	PO	A	E	DP	TC/G	FA	G by Pos
1990 OAK A	25	.071	.071	14	1	0	0	0	0.0	0	0	1	4	0	4	1	9	8	0	0	0.7	1.000	3B-10, SS-9, 2B-7
1991	90	.238	.268	235	56	5	1	0	0.0	21	21	14	37	3	2	0	146	213	11	46	4.1	.970	SS-84, 2B-5, 3B-1
1992	154	.300	.371	504	151	19	4	3	0.6	62	48	40	59	12	1	0	311	449	16	107	5.0	.979	2B-95, SS-70
1993	159	.249	.311	546	136	21	2	3	0.5	60	48	60	58	10	2	0	285	420	13	110	4.5	.982	SS-159, 2B-1
1994	114	.253	.335	391	99	18	4	2	0.5	38	37	38	44	7	0	0	190	320	14	67	4.6	.973	SS-112, 2B-4
5 yrs.	542	.262	.327	1690	443	63	11	8	0.5	181	154	153	202	32	9	1	941	1410	54	330	4.4	.978	SS-434, 2B-112, 3B-11

LEAGUE CHAMPIONSHIP SERIES

Year Team	Games	BA	SA	AB	H	2B	3B	HR	HR%	R	RBI	BB	SO	SB	AB	H	PO	A	E	DP	TC/G	FA	G by Pos
1992 OAK A	6	.053	.053	19	1	0	0	0	0.0	1	1	0	1	2	1	0	15	14	0	4	4.8	1.000	SS-4, 2B-2

WORLD SERIES

Year Team	Games	BA	SA	AB	H	2B	3B	HR	HR%	R	RBI	BB	SO	SB	AB	H	PO	A	E	DP	TC/G	FA	G by Pos
1990 OAK A	3	–	–	0	0	0	0	0	–	0	0	0	0	0	0	0	0	2	0	0	0.7	1.000	SS-3

Daryl Boston

BOSTON, DARYL LAMONT
B. Jan. 4, 1963, Cincinnati, Ohio.

BL TL 6'3" 185 lbs.

Year Team	Games	BA	SA	AB	H	2B	3B	HR	HR%	R	RBI	BB	SO	SB	AB	H	PO	A	E	DP	TC/G	FA	G by Pos
1984 CHI A	35	.169	.229	83	14	3	1	0	0.0	8	3	4	20	6	2	1	59	2	6	1	1.9	.910	OF-34, DH-1
1985	95	.228	.332	232	53	13	1	3	1.3	20	15	14	44	8	5	1	179	7	2	1	2.0	.989	OF-93, DH-2
1986	56	.266	.427	199	53	11	3	5	2.5	29	22	21	33	9	1	0	152	3	5	1	2.9	.969	OF-53, DH-1
1987	103	.258	.421	337	87	21	2	10	3.0	51	29	25	68	12	10	2	207	7	2	3	2.1	.991	OF-92, DH-5
1988	105	.217	.434	281	61	12	2	15	5.3	37	31	21	44	9	13	3	190	4	10	2	1.9	.951	OF-85, DH-5
1989	101	.252	.372	218	55	3	4	5	2.3	34	23	24	31	7	16	4	134	2	4	0	1.4	.971	OF-75, DH-9
1990 2 teams		CHI A (5G – .000)						NY N (115G – .273)															
" total	120	.272	.439	367	100	24	2	12	3.3	65	45	28	50	19	18	3	203	3	3	1	1.7	.986	OF-110, DH-3
1991 NY N	137	.275	.416	255	70	16	4	4	1.6	40	21	30	42	15	27	6	156	2	3	1	1.2	.981	OF-115
1992	130	.249	.426	289	72	14	2	11	3.8	37	35	38	60	12	40	7	133	5	1	1	1.1	.993	OF-95
1993 CLR N	124	.261	.464	291	76	15	1	14	4.8	46	40	26	57	1	37	9	124	5	2	1	1.1	.985	OF-79
1994 NY A	52	.182	.364	77	14	2	0	4	5.2	11	14	6	20	1	25	5	15	1	0	0	0.3	1.000	OF-16, DH-8
11 yrs.	1058	.249	.410	2629	655	131	22	83	3.2	378	278	237	469	98	194	41	1552	37	38	12	1.5	.977	OF-847, DH-34

Rafael Bournigal

BOURNIGAL, RAFAEL ANTONIO
Born Rafael Antonio Bournigal (Pelletier).
B. May 12, 1966, Azua, Dominican Republic.

BR TR 5'11" 160 lbs.

Year Team	Games	BA	SA	AB	H	2B	3B	HR	HR%	R	RBI	BB	SO	SB	AB	H	PO	A	E	DP	TC/G	FA	G by Pos
1992 LA N	10	.150	.200	20	3	1	0	0	0.0	1	0	1	2	0	1	0	12	17	1	6	3.0	.967	SS-9
1993	8	.500	.556	18	9	1	0	0	0.0	0	3	0	2	0	2	1	5	14	0	3	2.4	1.000	2B-4, SS-4
1994	40	.224	.267	116	26	3	1	0	0.0	2	11	9	5	0	0	0	56	97	3	19	3.9	.981	SS-40
3 yrs.	58	.247	.292	154	38	5	1	0	0.0	3	14	10	9	0	3	1	73	128	4	28	3.5	.980	SS-53, 2B-4

Year Team	Games	BA	SA	AB	H	2B	3B	HR	HR%	R	RBI	BB	SO	SB	Pinch Hit AB	Pinch Hit H	PO	A	E	DP	TC/G	FA	G by Pos

Jim Bowie
BOWIE, JAMES R.
B. Feb. 17, 1965, Tokyo, Japan.   BL TL 6'   205 lbs.

Year Team	Games	BA	SA	AB	H	2B	3B	HR	HR%	R	RBI	BB	SO	SB	PH AB	PH H	PO	A	E	DP	TC/G	FA	G by Pos
1994 OAK A	6	.214	.214	14	3	0	0	0	0.0	0	0	0	2	0	1	0	44	2	0	5	7.7	1.000	1B-6

Darren Bragg
BRAGG, DARREN WILLIAM
B. Sept. 7, 1969, Waterbury, Conn.   BL TR 5'9"   180 lbs.

Year Team	Games	BA	SA	AB	H	2B	3B	HR	HR%	R	RBI	BB	SO	SB	PH AB	PH H	PO	A	E	DP	TC/G	FA	G by Pos
1994 SEA A	8	.158	.211	19	3	1	0	0	0.0	4	2	2	5	0	1	0	1	0	0	0	0.1	1.000	DH-3, OF-3

Jeff Branson
BRANSON, JEFFERY GLENN
B. Jan. 26, 1967, Waynesboro, Miss.   BL TR 6'   180 lbs.

Year Team	Games	BA	SA	AB	H	2B	3B	HR	HR%	R	RBI	BB	SO	SB	PH AB	PH H	PO	A	E	DP	TC/G	FA	G by Pos
1992 CIN N	72	.296	.374	115	34	7	1	0	0.0	12	15	5	16	0	34	13	46	63	7	19	1.6	.940	2B-33, 3B-8, SS-1
1993	125	.241	.310	381	92	15	1	3	0.8	40	22	19	73	4	17	6	185	260	11	56	3.6	.976	SS-59, 2B-45, 3B-14, 1B-1
1994	58	.284	.505	109	31	4	1	6	5.5	18	16	5	16	0	19	5	39	52	1	6	1.6	.989	2B-19, 3B-18, SS-8, 1B-2
3 yrs.	255	.260	.357	605	157	26	3	9	1.5	70	53	29	105	4	70	24	270	375	19	81	2.6	.971	2B-97, SS-68, 3B-40, 1B-3

Sid Bream
BREAM, SIDNEY EUGENE
B. Aug. 3, 1960, Carlisle, Pa.   BL TL 6'4"   215 lbs.

Year Team	Games	BA	SA	AB	H	2B	3B	HR	HR%	R	RBI	BB	SO	SB	PH AB	PH H	PO	A	E	DP	TC/G	FA	G by Pos
1983 LA N	15	.182	.182	11	2	0	0	0	0.0	0	2	2	2	0	10	2	8	0	0	1	0.5	1.000	1B-4
1984	27	.184	.245	49	9	3	0	0	0.0	2	6	6	9	1	11	1	95	11	0	9	3.9	1.000	1B-14
1985 2 teams	LA N (24G – .132)		PIT N (26G – .284)																				
" total	50	.230	.399	148	34	7	0	6	4.1	18	21	18	24	0	10	2	367	35	3	29	8.1	.993	1B-41
1986 PIT N	154	.268	.450	522	140	37	5	16	3.1	73	77	60	73	13	5	1	1320	166	17	107	9.8	.989	1B-153, OF-2
1987	149	.275	.411	516	142	25	3	13	2.5	64	65	49	69	9	7	2	1236	127	17	109	9.3	.988	1B-144
1988	148	.264	.409	462	122	37	0	10	2.2	50	65	47	64	9	16	6	1118	140	6	88	8.5	.995	1B-138
1989	19	.222	.306	36	8	3	0	0	0.0	3	4	12	10	0	2	0	111	7	1	5	6.3	.992	1B-13
1990	147	.270	.455	389	105	23	2	15	3.9	39	67	48	65	8	14	2	971	104	8	80	7.4	.993	1B-142
1991 ATL N	91	.253	.423	265	67	12	0	11	4.2	32	45	25	31	0	9	5	668	50	3	53	7.9	.996	1B-85
1992	125	.261	.414	372	97	25	1	10	2.7	30	61	46	51	6	12	4	856	73	10	69	7.5	.989	1B-120
1993	117	.260	.415	277	72	14	1	9	3.2	33	35	31	43	4	29	10	627	62	3	62	5.9	.996	1B-90
1994 HOU N	46	.344	.426	61	21	5	0	0	0.0	7	7	9	9	0	32	13	60	11	1	8	1.6	.986	1B-10
12 yrs.	1088	.264	.420	3108	819	191	12	90	2.9	351	455	353	450	50	157	48	7437	786	69	620	7.6	.992	1B-954, OF-2
LEAGUE CHAMPIONSHIP SERIES																							
1990 PIT N	4	.500	1.000	8	4	1	0	1	12.5	1	3	2	3	0	1	0	26	3	0	3	7.3	1.000	1B-4
1991 ATL N	4	.300	.600	10	3	0	0	1	10.0	1	3	0	1	0	1	0	19	3	0	2	5.5	1.000	1B-4
1992	7	.273	.545	22	6	3	0	1	4.5	5	2	3	0	0	0	0	53	3	0	3	8.0	1.000	1B-7
1993	1	1.000	1.000	1	1	0	0	0	0.0	1	0	0	0	0	0	0	1	0	0	0	1.0	1.000	1B-1
4 yrs.	16	.341	.659	41	14	4	0	3	7.3	8	8	5	4	0	2	0	99	9	0	8	6.8	1.000	1B-16
WORLD SERIES																							
1991 ATL N	7	.125	.208	24	3	2	0	0	0.0	0	0	3	4	0	0	0	69	7	0	6	10.9	1.000	1B-7
1992	5	.200	.200	15	3	0	0	0	0.0	1	0	4	0	0	0	0	41	1	1	4	8.6	.977	1B-5
2 yrs.	12	.154	.205	39	6	2	0	0	0.0	1	0	7	4	0	0	0	110	8	1	10	9.9	.992	1B-12

Rico Brogna
BROGNA, RICO JOSEPH
B. Apr. 18, 1970, Turner Falls, Mass.   BL TL 6'2"   190 lbs.

Year Team	Games	BA	SA	AB	H	2B	3B	HR	HR%	R	RBI	BB	SO	SB	PH AB	PH H	PO	A	E	DP	TC/G	FA	G by Pos
1992 DET A	9	.192	.346	26	5	1	0	1	3.8	3	3	3	5	0	0	0	48	6	1	9	6.1	.982	1B-8, DH-2
1994 NY N	39	.351	.626	131	46	11	2	7	5.3	16	20	6	29	1	4	1	308	28	1	29	8.6	.997	1B-35
2 yrs.	48	.325	.580	157	51	12	2	8	5.1	19	23	9	34	1	4	1	356	34	2	38	8.2	.995	1B-43, DH-2

Hubie Brooks
BROOKS, HUBERT, JR.
B. Sept. 24, 1956, Los Angeles, Calif.   BR TR 6'   178 lbs.

Year Team	Games	BA	SA	AB	H	2B	3B	HR	HR%	R	RBI	BB	SO	SB	PH AB	PH H	PO	A	E	DP	TC/G	FA	G by Pos
1980 NY N	24	.309	.395	81	25	2	1	1	1.2	8	10	5	9	1	1	0	16	40	2	2	2.4	.966	3B-23
1981	98	.307	.411	358	110	21	2	4	1.1	34	38	23	65	9	2	0	67	193	21	14	2.9	.925	3B-93, OF-3, SS-1
1982	126	.249	.317	457	114	21	2	2	0.4	40	40	28	76	6	1	0	89	237	24	21	2.8	.931	3B-126
1983	150	.251	.321	586	147	18	4	5	0.9	53	58	24	96	6	2	1	116	303	21	28	2.9	.952	3B-145, 2B-7
1984	153	.283	.417	561	159	23	2	16	2.9	61	73	48	79	6	0	0	112	284	29	41	2.8	.932	3B-129, SS-26
1985 MON N	156	.269	.413	605	163	34	7	13	2.1	67	100	34	79	6	2	1	203	441	28	81	4.3	.958	SS-155
1986	80	.340	.569	306	104	18	5	14	4.6	50	58	25	60	4	0	0	116	222	15	37	4.4	.958	SS-80
1987	112	.263	.426	430	113	22	3	14	3.3	57	72	24	72	4	3	2	131	271	20	53	3.8	.953	SS-109
1988	151	.279	.447	588	164	35	2	20	3.4	61	90	35	108	7	2	1	261	8	9	1	1.8	.968	OF-149
1989	148	.268	.404	542	145	30	1	14	2.6	56	70	39	108	6	8	0	234	6	9	2	1.7	.964	OF-140
1990 LA N	153	.266	.424	568	151	28	1	20	3.5	74	91	33	108	2	1	0	255	9	10	2	1.8	.964	OF-150
1991 NY N	103	.238	.409	357	85	11	1	16	4.5	48	50	44	62	3	4	0	166	6	5	0	1.7	.972	OF-100
1992 CAL A	82	.216	.337	306	66	13	0	8	2.6	28	36	12	46	3	8	2	64	4	1	4	0.8	.986	DH-70, 1B-6
1993 KC A	75	.286	.375	168	48	12	0	1	0.6	14	24	11	27	0	33	10	72	6	2	2	1.1	.975	OF-40, DH-9, 1B-3
1994	34	.230	.311	61	14	2	0	1	1.6	5	14	2	10	1	20	5	33	1	0	3	1.0	1.000	DH-19, 1B-4
15 yrs.	1645	.269	.403	5974	1608	290	31	149	2.5	656	824	387	1005	64	87	22	1935	2031	196	287	2.5	.953	OF-582, 3B-516, SS-371, DH-98, 1B-13, 2B-7

Scott Brosius
BROSIUS, SCOTT DAVID
B. Aug. 15, 1966, Hillsboro, Ore.   BR TR 6'1"   185 lbs.

Year Team	Games	BA	SA	AB	H	2B	3B	HR	HR%	R	RBI	BB	SO	SB	PH AB	PH H	PO	A	E	DP	TC/G	FA	G by Pos
1991 OAK A	36	.235	.397	68	16	5	0	2	2.9	9	4	3	11	3	4	2	31	16	0	3	1.3	1.000	2B-18, OF-13, 3B-7, DH-1
1992	38	.218	.379	87	19	2	0	4	4.6	13	13	3	13	3	2	0	68	15	1	2	2.2	.988	OF-20, 3B-12, 1B-3, DH-1, SS-1
1993	70	.249	.390	213	53	10	1	6	2.8	26	25	14	37	6	6	2	173	29	2	10	2.9	.990	OF-46, 1B-11, 3B-10, SS-6, DH-2
1994	96	.238	.417	324	77	14	1	14	4.3	31	49	24	57	2	0	0	81	154	13	19	2.6	.948	3B-93, OF-7, 1B-1
4 yrs.	240	.238	.402	692	165	31	2	26	3.8	79	91	44	118	14	12	4	353	214	16	34	2.4	.973	3B-122, OF-86, 2B-18, 1B-15, SS-7, DH-4

Year	Team	Games	BA	SA	AB	H	2B	3B	HR	HR%	R	RBI	BB	SO	SB	Pinch Hit AB	Pinch Hit H	PO	A	E	DP	TC/G	FA	G by Pos

Jarvis Brown

BROWN, JARVIS ARDEL
B. Mar. 26, 1967, Waukegan, Ill.

BR TR 5'7" 165 lbs.

Year	Team	Games	BA	SA	AB	H	2B	3B	HR	HR%	R	RBI	BB	SO	SB	PH AB	PH H	PO	A	E	DP	TC/G	FA	G by Pos
1991	MIN A	38	.216	.216	37	8	0	0	0	0.0	10	0	2	8	7	2	0	21	0	1	0	0.6	.955	OF-32, DH-4
1992		35	.067	.067	15	1	0	0	0	0.0	8	0	2	4	2	0	0	20	0	1	0	0.6	.952	OF-31, DH-1
1993	SD N	47	.233	.331	133	31	9	2	0	0.0	21	8	15	26	3	5	1	109	2	2	0	2.4	.982	OF-43
1994	ATL N	17	.133	.400	15	2	1	0	1	6.7	3	1	0	2	0	4	1	10	0	0	0	0.6	1.000	OF-9
4 yrs.		137	.210	.295	200	42	10	2	1	0.5	42	9	19	40	12	11	2	160	2	4	0	1.2	.976	OF-115, DH-5

LEAGUE CHAMPIONSHIP SERIES

Year	Team	Games	BA	SA	AB	H	2B	3B	HR	HR%	R	RBI	BB	SO	SB	PH AB	PH H	PO	A	E	DP	TC/G	FA	G by Pos
1991	MIN A	1	–	–	0	0	0	0	0	–	1	0	0	0	0	0	0	0	0	0	0	0.0	–	DH-1

WORLD SERIES

Year	Team	Games	BA	SA	AB	H	2B	3B	HR	HR%	R	RBI	BB	SO	SB	PH AB	PH H	PO	A	E	DP	TC/G	FA	G by Pos
1991	MIN A	3	.000	.000	2	0	0	0	0	0.0	0	0	0	1	0	1	0	0	0	0	0	0.0	–	OF-2, DH-1

Jerry Browne

BROWNE, JEROME AUSTIN
B. Feb. 13, 1966, Christiansted, Virgin Islands.

BB TR 5'10" 140 lbs.

Year	Team	Games	BA	SA	AB	H	2B	3B	HR	HR%	R	RBI	BB	SO	SB	PH AB	PH H	PO	A	E	DP	TC/G	FA	G by Pos
1986	TEX A	11	.417	.500	24	10	2	0	0	0.0	6	3	1	4	0	1	0	9	15	2	4	2.4	.923	2B-8
1987		132	.271	.339	454	123	16	6	1	0.2	63	38	61	50	27	5	0	258	338	12	66	4.6	.980	2B-130, DH-1
1988		73	.229	.304	214	49	9	2	1	0.5	26	17	25	32	7	3	0	112	139	11	27	3.6	.958	2B-70, DH-1
1989	CLE A	153	.299	.390	598	179	31	4	5	0.8	83	45	68	64	14	2	0	305	380	15	67	4.6	.979	2B-151, DH-2
1990		140	.267	.372	513	137	26	5	6	1.2	92	50	72	46	12	3	1	286	382	10	69	4.8	.985	2B-139
1991		107	.228	.269	290	66	5	2	1	0.3	28	29	27	29	2	34	11	113	141	14	21	2.5	.948	2B-47, OF-17, 3B-15, DH-7
1992	OAK A	111	.287	.364	324	93	12	2	3	0.9	43	40	40	40	3	15	7	149	88	5	11	2.2	.979	3B-58, OF-43, 2B-19, DH-1, SS-1
1993		76	.250	.323	260	65	13	4	2	0.8	27	19	22	17	4	10	1	149	28	6	6	2.4	.967	OF-56, 3B-13, 2B-3, 1B-2
1994	FLA N	101	.295	.398	329	97	17	4	3	0.9	42	30	52	23	3	8	2	117	125	15	12	2.5	.942	3B-62, OF-30, 2B-15
9 yrs.		904	.272	.355	3006	819	131	25	22	0.7	410	271	368	305	72	81	22	1498	1636	90	283	3.6	.972	2B-582, 3B-148, OF-146, DH-12, 1B-2, SS-1

LEAGUE CHAMPIONSHIP SERIES

Year	Team	Games	BA	SA	AB	H	2B	3B	HR	HR%	R	RBI	BB	SO	SB	PH AB	PH H	PO	A	E	DP	TC/G	FA	G by Pos
1992	OAK A	4	.400	.400	10	4	0	0	0	0.0	3	2	2	0	0	0	0	6	0	0	0	1.5	1.000	3B-2, OF-1

Jacob Brumfield

BRUMFIELD, JACOB DONNELL
B. May 27, 1965, Bogalusa, La.

BR TR 6' 170 lbs.

Year	Team	Games	BA	SA	AB	H	2B	3B	HR	HR%	R	RBI	BB	SO	SB	PH AB	PH H	PO	A	E	DP	TC/G	FA	G by Pos
1992	CIN N	24	.133	.133	30	4	0	0	0	0.0	6	2	2	4	6	5	1	20	1	0	0	0.9	1.000	OF-16
1993		103	.268	.419	272	73	17	3	6	2.2	40	23	21	47	20	5	0	178	16	7	4	2.0	.965	OF-96, 2B-4
1994		68	.311	.525	122	38	10	2	4	3.3	36	11	15	18	6	19	2	74	1	1	0	1.1	.987	OF-43
3 yrs.		195	.271	.429	424	115	27	5	10	2.4	82	36	38	69	32	29	3	272	18	8	4	1.5	.973	OF-155, 2B-4

Mike Brumley

BRUMLEY, ANTHONY MICHAEL
Son of Mike Brumley.
B. Apr. 9, 1963, Oklahoma City, Okla.

BB TR 5'10" 165 lbs.

Year	Team	Games	BA	SA	AB	H	2B	3B	HR	HR%	R	RBI	BB	SO	SB	PH AB	PH H	PO	A	E	DP	TC/G	FA	G by Pos
1987	CHI N	39	.202	.288	104	21	2	2	1	1.0	8	9	10	30	7	3	0	43	93	5	24	3.6	.965	SS-34, 2B-1
1989	DET A	92	.198	.255	212	42	5	2	1	0.5	33	11	14	45	8	3	0	80	160	12	24	2.7	.952	SS-42, 2B-24, 3B-11, DH-8, OF-4
1990	SEA A	62	.224	.313	147	33	5	4	0	0.0	19	7	10	22	2	7	2	63	123	5	26	3.1	.974	SS-47, 2B-6, 3B-3, OF-2, DH-1
1991	BOS A	63	.212	.254	118	25	5	0	0	0.0	16	5	10	22	2	4	0	46	116	7	20	2.7	.959	SS-31, 3B-17, 2B-7, OF-4, DH-2
1992		2	.000	.000	1	0	0	0	0	0.0	0	0	0	0	0	1	0	0	0	0	0	0.0	–	
1993	HOU N	8	.300	.300	10	3	0	0	0	0.0	1	2	1	3	0	7	2	1	1	0	0	0.3	1.000	3B-1, OF-1, SS-1
1994	OAK A	11	.240	.240	25	6	0	0	0	0.0	0	2	1	8	0	1	0	10	9	2	2	1.9	.905	2B-4, 3B-4, OF-3, SS-1
7 yrs.		277	.211	.274	617	130	17	8	2	0.3	77	36	46	130	19	27	4	243	502	31	96	2.8	.960	SS-156, 2B-42, 3B-36, OF-14, DH-11

Tom Brunansky

BRUNANSKY, THOMAS ANDREW (Bruno)
B. Aug. 20, 1960, Covina, Calif.

BR TR 6'4" 205 lbs.

Year	Team	Games	BA	SA	AB	H	2B	3B	HR	HR%	R	RBI	BB	SO	SB	PH AB	PH H	PO	A	E	DP	TC/G	FA	G by Pos
1981	CAL A	11	.152	.424	33	5	0	0	3	9.1	7	6	8	10	1	0	0	27	3	2	1	2.9	.938	OF-11
1982	MIN A	127	.272	.471	463	126	30	1	20	4.3	77	46	71	101	1	0	0	343	8	5	0	2.8	.986	OF-127
1983		151	.227	.445	542	123	24	5	28	5.2	70	82	61	95	2	2	0	375	16	6	8	2.6	.985	OF-146, DH-4
1984		155	.252	.459	567	143	21	0	32	5.6	75	85	57	94	4	2	0	304	13	5	6	2.1	.984	OF-153, DH-1
1985		157	.242	.448	567	137	28	4	27	4.8	71	90	71	86	5	3	1	300	14	5	2	2.0	.984	OF-155
1986		157	.256	.423	593	152	28	1	23	3.9	69	75	53	98	12	5	1	315	10	6	1	2.1	.982	OF-152, DH-2
1987		155	.259	.489	532	138	22	2	32	6.0	83	85	74	104	11	1	1	273	10	3	1	1.8	.990	OF-138, DH-17
1988	2 teams		MIN A (14G – .184)				STL N (143G – .245)																	
"	total	157	.240	.414	572	137	23	4	23	4.0	74	85	86	93	17	0	0	286	9	5	1	1.9	.987	OF-156, DH-1
1989	STL N	158	.239	.410	556	133	29	3	20	3.6	67	85	59	107	5	6	0	291	9	7	2	1.9	.977	OF-155, 1B-1
1990	2 teams		STL N (19G – .158)				BOS A (129G – .267)																	
"	total	148	.255	.419	518	132	27	5	16	3.1	66	73	66	115	5	6	2	304	8	7	2	2.2	.978	OF-138, DH-7
1991	BOS A	142	.229	.390	459	105	24	1	16	3.5	54	70	49	72	1	5	2	265	5	3	2	1.9	.989	OF-137, DH-1
1992		138	.266	.445	458	122	31	3	15	3.3	47	74	66	96	2	7	2	373	16	6	22	2.9	.985	OF-92, 1B-28, DH-17
1993	MIL A	80	.183	.321	224	41	7	3	6	2.7	20	29	25	59	3	8	0	146	4	2	0	1.9	.987	OF-71, DH-6
1994	2 teams		MIL A (16G – .214)				BOS A (48G – .237)																	
"	total	64	.234	.449	205	48	12	1	10	4.9	24	34	24	57	0	7	1	142	2	1	8	2.3	.993	OF-49, 1B-7, DH-5
14 yrs.		1800	.245	.434	6289	1542	306	33	271	4.3	804	919	770	1187	69	52	10	3744	128	62	55	2.2	.984	OF-1680, DH-61, 1B-36

LEAGUE CHAMPIONSHIP SERIES

Year	Team	Games	BA	SA	AB	H	2B	3B	HR	HR%	R	RBI	BB	SO	SB	PH AB	PH H	PO	A	E	DP	TC/G	FA	G by Pos
1987	MIN A	5	.412	1.000	17	7	4	0	2	11.8	5	9	4	3	0	0	0	10	0	0	0	2.0	1.000	OF-5
1990	BOS A	4	.083	.083	12	1	0	0	0	0.0	0	0	1	3	0	0	0	13	0	0	0	3.3	1.000	OF-4
2 yrs.		9	.276	.621	29	8	4	0	2	6.9	5	9	5	6	0	0	0	23	0	0	0	2.6	1.000	OF-9

WORLD SERIES

Year	Team	Games	BA	SA	AB	H	2B	3B	HR	HR%	R	RBI	BB	SO	SB	PH AB	PH H	PO	A	E	DP	TC/G	FA	G by Pos
1987	MIN A	7	.200	.200	25	5	0	0	0	0.0	5	2	4	4	1	1	0	14	0	0	0	2.0	1.000	OF-7

Year	Team	Games	BA	SA	AB	H	2B	3B	HR	HR%	R	RBI	BB	SO	SB	Pinch Hit AB	Pinch Hit H	PO	A	E	DP	TC/G	FA	G by Pos

Steve Buechele

BUECHELE, STEVEN BERNARD
B. Sept. 26, 1961, Lancaster, Calif.

BR TR 6'2" 190 lbs.

Year	Team	Games	BA	SA	AB	H	2B	3B	HR	HR%	R	RBI	BB	SO	SB	Pinch Hit AB	Pinch Hit H	PO	A	E	DP	TC/G	FA	G by Pos
1985	TEX A	69	.219	.356	219	48	6	3	6	2.7	22	21	14	38	3	0	0	52	138	6	17	2.8	.969	3B-69, 2B-1
1986		153	.243	.410	461	112	19	2	18	3.9	54	54	35	98	5	2	1	174	292	12	42	3.1	.975	3B-137, 2B-33, OF-2
1987		136	.237	.399	363	86	20	0	13	3.6	45	50	28	66	2	2	1	89	211	9	20	2.3	.971	3B-123, 2B-18, OF-2
1988		155	.250	.404	503	126	21	4	16	3.2	68	58	65	79	2	1	0	114	300	16	25	2.8	.963	3B-153, 2B-2
1989		155	.235	.387	486	114	22	2	16	3.3	60	59	36	107	1	1	0	128	288	12	29	2.8	.972	3B-145, 2B-18, DH-1, SS-1
1990		91	.215	.339	251	54	10	0	7	2.8	30	30	27	63	1	2	0	72	160	8	7	2.6	.967	3B-88, 2B-4
1991	2 teams					TEX A (121G – .267)				PIT N (31G – .246)														
"	total	152	.262	.440	530	139	22	3	22	4.2	74	85	49	97	0	5	2	121	339	7	28	3.1	.985	3B-142, 2B-13, SS-4
1992	2 teams					PIT N (80G – .249)				CHI N (65G – .276)														
"	total	145	.261	.372	524	137	23	4	9	1.7	52	64	52	105	1	1	1	103	289	17	16	2.8	.958	3B-143, 2B-2
1993	CHI N	133	.272	.437	460	125	27	2	15	3.3	53	65	48	87	1	3	0	97	232	8	25	2.5	.976	3B-129, 1B-6
1994		104	.242	.404	339	82	11	1	14	4.1	33	52	39	80	1	2	0	101	144	5	13	2.4	.980	3B-99, 1B-6, 2B-1
10 yrs.		1293	.247	.400	4136	1023	181	21	136	3.3	491	538	393	820	17	20	5	1051	2393	100	222	2.7	.972	3B-1228, 2B-92, 1B-12, SS-5, OF-4, DH-1

LEAGUE CHAMPIONSHIP SERIES

Year	Team	Games	BA	SA	AB	H	2B	3B	HR	HR%	R	RBI	BB	SO	SB	Pinch Hit AB	Pinch Hit H	PO	A	E	DP	TC/G	FA	G by Pos
1991	PIT N	7	.304	.391	23	7	2	0	0	0.0	2	0	4	6	0	0	0	8	14	0	1	3.1	1.000	3B-7

Damon Buford

BUFORD, DAMON JACKSON
Son of Don Buford.
B. June 12, 1970, Baltimore, Md.

BR TR 5'10" 170 lbs.

Year	Team	Games	BA	SA	AB	H	2B	3B	HR	HR%	R	RBI	BB	SO	SB	Pinch Hit AB	Pinch Hit H	PO	A	E	DP	TC/G	FA	G by Pos
1993	BAL A	53	.228	.367	79	18	5	0	2	2.5	18	9	9	19	2	3	1	61	2	1	2	1.2	.984	OF-30, DH-16
1994		4	.500	.500	2	1	0	0	0	0.0	2	0	0	1	0	0	0	0	0	0	0	0.0	–	DH-1, OF-1
2 yrs.		57	.235	.370	81	19	5	0	2	2.5	20	9	9	20	2	3	1	61	2	1	2	1.1	.984	OF-31, DH-17

Jay Buhner

BUHNER, JAY CAMPBELL
B. Aug. 13, 1964, Louisville, Ky.

BR TR 6'3" 205 lbs.

Year	Team	Games	BA	SA	AB	H	2B	3B	HR	HR%	R	RBI	BB	SO	SB	Pinch Hit AB	Pinch Hit H	PO	A	E	DP	TC/G	FA	G by Pos
1987	NY A	7	.227	.318	22	5	2	0	0	0.0	0	1	1	6	0	0	0	11	1	0	1	1.7	1.000	OF-7
1988	2 teams					NY A (25G – .188)				SEA A (60G – .224)														
"	total	85	.215	.421	261	56	13	1	13	5.0	36	38	28	93	1	4	1	186	9	3	3	2.3	.985	OF-81
1989	SEA A	58	.275	.490	204	56	15	1	9	4.4	27	33	19	55	1	0	0	106	6	4	3	2.0	.966	OF-57
1990		51	.276	.479	163	45	12	0	7	4.3	16	33	17	50	2	3	0	55	1	2	0	1.1	.966	OF-40, DH-10
1991		137	.244	.498	406	99	14	4	27	6.7	64	77	53	117	0	10	1	244	15	5	4	1.9	.981	OF-131
1992		152	.243	.422	543	132	16	3	25	4.6	69	79	71	146	0	3	1	314	14	2	4	2.2	.994	OF-150
1993		158	.272	.476	563	153	28	3	27	4.8	91	98	100	144	2	2	1	263	8	6	2	1.8	.978	OF-148, DH-10
1994		101	.279	.542	358	100	23	4	21	5.9	74	68	66	63	0	3	1	179	11	2	1	1.9	.990	OF-96, DH-4
8 yrs.		749	.256	.471	2520	646	123	16	129	5.1	377	427	355	674	6	25	5	1358	65	24	19	1.9	.983	OF-710, DH-24

Ellis Burks

BURKS, ELLIS RENA
B. Sept. 11, 1964, Vicksburg, Miss.

BR TR 6'2" 175 lbs.

Year	Team	Games	BA	SA	AB	H	2B	3B	HR	HR%	R	RBI	BB	SO	SB	Pinch Hit AB	Pinch Hit H	PO	A	E	DP	TC/G	FA	G by Pos
1987	BOS A	133	.272	.441	558	152	30	2	20	3.6	94	59	41	98	27	0	0	320	15	4	2	2.5	.988	OF-132
1988		144	.294	.481	540	159	37	5	18	3.3	93	92	62	89	25	0	0	370	9	9	0	2.7	.977	OF-142, DH-2
1989		97	.303	.471	399	121	19	6	12	3.0	73	61	36	52	21	0	0	245	7	6	3	2.7	.977	OF-95, DH-1
1990		152	.296	.486	588	174	33	8	21	3.6	89	89	48	82	9	3	1	324	7	2	0	2.2	.994	OF-143, DH-6
1991		130	.251	.422	474	119	33	3	14	3.0	56	56	39	81	6	2	0	283	2	2	1	2.2	.993	OF-126, DH-2
1992		66	.255	.417	235	60	8	3	8	3.4	35	30	25	48	5	3	0	120	3	2	0	1.9	.984	OF-63, DH-1
1993	CHI A	146	.275	.441	499	137	24	4	17	3.4	75	74	60	97	6	5	2	313	6	6	1	2.2	.982	OF-146
1994	CLR N	42	.322	.678	149	48	8	3	13	8.7	33	24	16	39	3	3	0	79	2	3	0	2.0	.964	OF-39
8 yrs.		910	.282	.465	3442	970	192	34	123	3.6	548	485	327	586	102	16	3	2054	51	34	7	2.4	.984	OF-886, DH-12

LEAGUE CHAMPIONSHIP SERIES

Year	Team	Games	BA	SA	AB	H	2B	3B	HR	HR%	R	RBI	BB	SO	SB	Pinch Hit AB	Pinch Hit H	PO	A	E	DP	TC/G	FA	G by Pos
1988	BOS A	4	.235	.294	17	4	1	0	0	0.0	2	1	0	3	0	0	0	10	0	0	0	2.5	1.000	OF-4
1990		4	.267	.400	15	4	2	0	0	0.0	1	0	1	1	1	0	0	9	1	0	0	2.5	1.000	OF-4
1993	CHI A	6	.304	.478	23	7	1	0	1	4.3	4	3	3	5	0	0	0	15	0	0	0	2.5	1.000	OF-6
3 yrs.		14	.273	.400	55	15	4	0	1	1.8	7	4	4	9	1	0	0	34	1	0	0	2.5	1.000	OF-14

Jeromy Burnitz

BURNITZ, JEROMY NEAL
B. Apr. 15, 1969, Westminster, Calif.

BL TR 6' 190 lbs.

Year	Team	Games	BA	SA	AB	H	2B	3B	HR	HR%	R	RBI	BB	SO	SB	Pinch Hit AB	Pinch Hit H	PO	A	E	DP	TC/G	FA	G by Pos
1993	NY N	86	.243	.475	263	64	10	6	13	4.9	49	38	38	66	3	10	3	165	6	4	2	2.0	.977	OF-79
1994		45	.238	.329	143	34	4	0	3	2.1	26	15	23	45	1	3	1	63	1	2	0	1.5	.970	OF-42
2 yrs.		131	.241	.424	406	98	14	6	16	3.9	75	53	61	111	4	13	4	228	7	6	2	1.8	.975	OF-121

Brett Butler

BUTLER, BRETT MORGAN
B. June 15, 1957, Los Angeles, Calif.

BL TL 5'10" 160 lbs.

Year	Team	Games	BA	SA	AB	H	2B	3B	HR	HR%	R	RBI	BB	SO	SB	Pinch Hit AB	Pinch Hit H	PO	A	E	DP	TC/G	FA	G by Pos
1981	ATL N	40	.254	.317	126	32	2	3	0	0.0	17	4	19	17	9	2	1	76	2	1	0	2.0	.987	OF-37
1982		89	.217	.225	240	52	2	0	0	0.0	35	7	25	35	21	6	1	129	2	0	0	1.5	1.000	OF-77
1983		151	.281	.393	549	154	21	13	5	0.9	84	37	54	56	39	6	1	284	13	4	4	2.0	.987	OF-143
1984	CLE A	159	.269	.355	602	162	25	9	3	0.5	108	49	86	62	52	3	0	448	13	4	3	2.9	.991	OF-156
1985		152	.311	.431	591	184	28	14	5	0.8	106	50	63	42	47	1	0	437	19	1	5	3.0	.998	OF-150, DH-1
1986		161	.278	.375	587	163	17	**14**	4	0.7	92	51	70	65	32	1	0	434	9	3	3	2.8	.993	OF-159
1987	SF N	137	.295	.425	522	154	25	8	9	1.7	91	41	91	55	33	0	0	393	4	4	2	2.9	.990	OF-136
1988		157	.287	.398	568	163	27	9	6	1.1	**109**	43	97	64	43	2	0	395	3	5	1	2.6	.988	OF-155
1989		154	.283	.354	594	168	22	4	4	0.7	100	36	59	69	31	0	0	407	11	6	3	2.8	.986	OF-152
1990		160	.309	.384	622	**192**	20	9	3	0.5	108	44	90	62	51	1	0	420	4	6	0	2.7	.986	OF-159
1991	LA N	161	.296	.343	615	182	13	5	2	0.3	**112**	38	**108**	79	38	1	0	372	8	0	3	2.4	1.000	OF-161
1992		157	.309	.391	553	171	14	11	3	0.5	86	39	95	67	41	3	1	353	9	2	3	2.3	.995	OF-155
1993		156	.298	.371	607	181	21	10	1	0.2	80	42	86	69	39	1	0	369	6	0	0	2.4	1.000	OF-155
1994		111	.314	.446	417	131	13	**9**	8	1.9	79	33	68	52	27	0	0	260	8	2	1	2.4	.993	OF-111
14 yrs.		1945	.290	.380	7193	2089	250	118	53	0.7	1207	514	1011	794	503	27	4	4777	111	38	28	2.5	.992	OF-1906, DH-1

Year Team	Games	BA	SA	AB	H	2B	3B	HR	HR%	R	RBI	BB	SO	SB	Pinch Hit AB	Pinch Hit H	PO	A	E	DP	TC/G	FA	G by Pos

Brett Butler *continued*

LEAGUE CHAMPIONSHIP SERIES

Year Team	Games	BA	SA	AB	H	2B	3B	HR	HR%	R	RBI	BB	SO	SB	PH AB	PH H	PO	A	E	DP	TC/G	FA	G by Pos
1982 ATL N	2	.000	.000	1	0	0	0	0	0.0	0	0	0	0	0	1	0	0	0	0	0	0.0	–	OF-1
1989 SF N	5	.211	.211	19	4	0	0	0	0.0	6	0	3	3	0	0	0	9	0	0	0	1.8	1.000	OF-5
2 yrs.	7	.200	.200	20	4	0	0	0	0.0	6	0	3	3	0	1	0	9	0	0	0	1.3	1.000	OF-6

WORLD SERIES

Year Team	Games	BA	SA	AB	H	2B	3B	HR	HR%	R	RBI	BB	SO	SB	PH AB	PH H	PO	A	E	DP	TC/G	FA	G by Pos
1989 SF N	4	.286	.357	14	4	1	0	0	0.0	1	1	2	1	2	0	0	9	0	0	0	2.3	1.000	OF-4

Rob Butler

BUTLER, ROBERT FRANK JOHN
B. Apr. 10, 1970, East York, Ont., Canada

BL TL 5'11" 185 lbs.

Year Team	Games	BA	SA	AB	H	2B	3B	HR	HR%	R	RBI	BB	SO	SB	PH AB	PH H	PO	A	E	DP	TC/G	FA	G by Pos
1993 TOR A	17	.271	.354	48	13	4	0	0	0.0	8	2	7	12	2	1	0	32	0	1	0	1.9	.970	OF-16
1994	41	.176	.203	74	13	0	1	0	0.0	13	5	7	8	0	4	0	43	0	1	0	1.1	.977	OF-31, DH-1
2 yrs.	58	.213	.262	122	26	4	1	0	0.0	21	7	14	20	2	5	0	75	0	2	0	1.3	.974	OF-47, DH-1

WORLD SERIES

Year Team	Games	BA	SA	AB	H	2B	3B	HR	HR%	R	RBI	BB	SO	SB	PH AB	PH H	PO	A	E	DP	TC/G	FA	G by Pos
1993 TOR A	2	.500	.500	2	1	0	0	0	0.0	1	0	0	0	0	2	1	0	0	0	0	0.0	–	

Ken Caminiti

CAMINITI, KENNETH GENE
B. Apr. 21, 1963, Hanford, Calif.

BB TR 6' 200 lbs.

Year Team	Games	BA	SA	AB	H	2B	3B	HR	HR%	R	RBI	BB	SO	SB	PH AB	PH H	PO	A	E	DP	TC/G	FA	G by Pos
1987 HOU N	63	.246	.335	203	50	7	1	3	1.5	10	23	12	44	0	9	2	50	98	8	11	2.5	.949	3B-61
1988	30	.181	.241	83	15	2	0	1	1.2	5	7	5	18	0	5	0	12	43	3	2	1.9	.948	3B-28
1989	161	.255	.369	585	149	31	3	10	1.7	71	72	51	93	4	2	0	126	335	22	27	3.0	.954	3B-160
1990	153	.242	.309	541	131	20	2	4	0.7	52	51	48	97	9	10	1	118	243	21	20	2.5	.945	3B-149
1991	152	.253	.383	574	145	30	3	13	2.3	65	80	46	85	4	2	0	129	293	23	29	2.9	.948	3B-152
1992	135	.294	.441	506	149	31	2	13	2.6	68	62	44	68	10	6	1	102	210	11	19	2.4	.966	3B-129
1993	143	.262	.390	543	142	31	0	13	2.4	75	75	49	88	8	1	0	123	264	24	23	2.9	.942	3B-143
1994	111	.283	.495	406	115	28	2	18	4.4	63	75	43	71	4	6	0	79	201	9	17	2.6	.969	3B-108
8 yrs.	948	.260	.386	3441	896	180	13	75	2.2	409	445	298	564	39	41	4	739	1687	121	150	2.7	.952	3B-930

John Cangelosi

CANGELOSI, JOHN ANTHONY
B. Mar. 10, 1963, Brooklyn, N. Y.

BB TL 5'8" 150 lbs.

Year Team	Games	BA	SA	AB	H	2B	3B	HR	HR%	R	RBI	BB	SO	SB	PH AB	PH H	PO	A	E	DP	TC/G	FA	G by Pos
1985 CHI A	5	.000	.000	2	0	0	0	0	0.0	2	0	0	1	0	0	0	1	0	0	0	0.2	1.000	OF-3, DH-2
1986	137	.235	.299	438	103	16	3	2	0.5	65	32	71	61	50	1	0	276	7	9	1	2.1	.969	OF-129, DH-3
1987 PIT N	104	.275	.418	182	50	8	3	4	2.2	44	18	46	33	21	50	10	74	3	3	0	0.8	.963	OF-47
1988	75	.254	.305	118	30	4	1	0	0.0	18	8	17	16	9	42	12	52	0	2	0	0.7	.963	OF-24, P-1
1989	112	.219	.269	160	35	4	2	0	0.0	18	9	35	20	11	68	12	71	1	2	0	0.7	.973	OF-46
1990	58	.197	.224	76	15	2	0	0	0.0	13	1	11	12	7	36	8	24	0	0	0	0.4	1.000	OF-12
1992 TEX A	73	.188	.247	85	16	2	0	1	1.2	12	6	18	16	6	5	2	76	4	3	1	1.1	.964	OF-65, DH-6
1994 NY N	62	.252	.288	111	28	4	0	0	0.0	14	4	19	20	5	19	5	64	5	0	1	1.1	1.000	OF-50
8 yrs.	626	.236	.304	1172	277	40	9	7	0.6	186	78	217	179	109	221	49	638	20	19	3	1.1	.972	OF-376, DH-11, P-1

Jose Canseco

CANSECO, JOSE
Born Jose Canseco (Capas).
Brother of Ozzie Canseco.
B. July 2, 1964, Havana, Cuba.

BR TR 6'3" 185 lbs.

Year Team	Games	BA	SA	AB	H	2B	3B	HR	HR%	R	RBI	BB	SO	SB	PH AB	PH H	PO	A	E	DP	TC/G	FA	G by Pos
1985 OAK A	29	.302	.490	96	29	3	0	5	5.2	16	13	4	31	1	4	1	56	2	3	1	2.1	.951	OF-26
1986	157	.240	.457	600	144	29	1	33	5.5	85	117	65	175	15	1	1	319	4	14	1	2.1	.958	OF-155, DH-1
1987	159	.257	.470	630	162	35	3	31	4.9	81	113	50	157	15	1	0	263	12	7	3	1.8	.975	OF-130, DH-30
1988	158	.307	**.569**	610	187	34	0	**42**	**6.9**	120	124	78	128	40	1	0	304	11	7	3	2.0	.978	OF-144, DH-13
1989	65	.269	.542	227	61	9	1	17	7.5	40	57	23	69	6	3	1	119	5	3	2	2.0	.976	OF-56, DH-5
1990	131	.274	.543	481	132	14	2	37	7.7	83	101	72	158	19	2	1	182	7	1	2	1.5	.995	OF-88, DH-43
1991	154	.266	.556	572	152	32	1	**44**	**7.7**	115	122	78	152	26	6	2	245	5	9	0	1.7	.965	OF-131, DH-24
1992 2 teams	OAK A (97G – .246)			TEX A	(22G – .233)																		
" total	119	.244	.456	439	107	15	0	26	5.9	74	87	63	128	6	3	0	195	5	3	3	1.7	.985	OF-90, DH-28
1993 TEX A	60	.255	.455	231	59	14	1	10	4.3	30	46	16	62	6	3	0	94	4	3	2	1.7	.970	OF-49, DH-9, P-1
1994	111	.282	.552	429	121	19	2	31	7.2	88	90	69	114	15	0	0	0	0	0	0	0.0	–	DH-111
10 yrs.	1143	.267	.512	4315	1154	204	11	276	6.4 **9th**	732	870	518	1174	149	24	6	1777	55	50	17	1.6	.973	OF-869, DH-264, P-1

LEAGUE CHAMPIONSHIP SERIES

Year Team	Games	BA	SA	AB	H	2B	3B	HR	HR%	R	RBI	BB	SO	SB	PH AB	PH H	PO	A	E	DP	TC/G	FA	G by Pos
1988 OAK A	4	.313	.938	16	5	1	0	3	18.8	4	4	1	2	1	0	0	6	0	0	0	1.5	1.000	OF-4
1989	5	.294	.471	17	5	0	0	1	5.9	1	3	3	7	0	1	0	6	1	1	0	1.6	.875	OF-5
1990	4	.182	.182	11	2	0	0	0	0.0	3	1	5	5	2	0	0	14	0	0	0	3.5	1.000	OF-4
3 yrs.	13	.273	.568	44	12	1	0	4	9.1	8	8	9	14	3	1	0	26	1	1	0	2.2	.964	OF-13

WORLD SERIES

Year Team	Games	BA	SA	AB	H	2B	3B	HR	HR%	R	RBI	BB	SO	SB	PH AB	PH H	PO	A	E	DP	TC/G	FA	G by Pos
1988 OAK A	5	.053	.211	19	1	0	1	1	5.3	1	5	2	5	1	0	0	8	0	0	0	1.6	1.000	OF-5
1989	4	.357	.571	14	5	0	0	1	7.1	5	3	4	3	1	0	0	6	0	0	0	1.5	1.000	OF-4
1990	4	.083	.333	12	1	0	0	1	8.3	1	2	2	3	0	0	0	4	0	0	0	1.0	1.000	OF-3
3 yrs.	13	.156	.356	45	7	0	0	3	6.7	7	10	8	11	2	0	0	18	0	0	0	1.4	1.000	OF-12

Chuck Carr

CARR, CHARLES LEE GLENN
B. Aug. 10, 1968, San Bernardino, Calif.

BB TR 5'10" 155 lbs.

Year Team	Games	BA	SA	AB	H	2B	3B	HR	HR%	R	RBI	BB	SO	SB	PH AB	PH H	PO	A	E	DP	TC/G	FA	G by Pos
1990 NY N	4	.000	.000	2	0	0	0	0	0.0	1	0	0	2	1	2	0	0	0	0	0	0.0	–	OF-1
1991	12	.182	.182	11	2	0	0	0	0.0	1	1	0	2	1	3	0	9	0	0	0	0.8	1.000	OF-9
1992 STL N	22	.219	.266	64	14	3	0	0	0.0	8	3	9	6	10	1	0	39	1	0	0	1.8	1.000	OF-19
1993 FLA N	142	.267	.330	551	147	19	2	4	0.7	75	41	49	74	58	1	0	393	7	6	2	2.9	.985	OF-139
1994	106	.263	.330	433	114	19	2	2	0.5	61	30	22	71	32	3	1	297	4	6	0	2.9	.980	OF-104
5 yrs.	286	.261	.324	1061	277	41	4	6	0.6	145	75	80	155	102	9	1	738	12	12	2	2.7	.984	OF-272

Mark Carreon

CARREON, MARK STEVEN
Son of Camilo Carreon.
B. July 19, 1963, Chicago, Ill.

BR TL 6' 170 lbs.

Year Team	Games	BA	SA	AB	H	2B	3B	HR	HR%	R	RBI	BB	SO	SB	PH AB	PH H	PO	A	E	DP	TC/G	FA	G by Pos
1987 NY N	9	.250	.250	12	3	0	0	0	0.0	1	1	1	1	0	5	1	4	0	1	0	0.6	.800	OF-5
1988	7	.556	1.111	9	5	2	0	1	11.1	5	1	2	1	0	2	0	1	0	0	0	0.1	1.000	OF-4

Year	Team	Games	BA	SA	AB	H	2B	3B	HR	HR%	R	RBI	BB	SO	SB	Pinch Hit AB	Pinch Hit H	PO	A	E	DP	TC/G	FA	G by Pos

Mark Carreon *continued*

1989		68	.308	.489	133	41	6	0	6	4.5	20	16	12	17	2	27	10	57	0	1	0	0.9	.983	OF-39
1990		82	.250	.473	188	47	12	0	10	5.3	30	26	15	29	1	24	4	87	1	0	0	1.1	1.000	OF-60
1991		106	.260	.331	254	66	6	0	4	1.6	18	21	12	26	2	35	12	96	4	3	1	1.0	.971	OF-77
1992	DET A	101	.232	.360	336	78	11	1	10	3.0	34	41	22	57	3	8	2	178	5	4	2	1.9	.979	OF-83, DH-13
1993	SF N	78	.327	.540	150	49	9	1	7	4.7	22	33	13	16	1	35	10	54	4	3	1	0.8	.951	OF-41, 1B-3
1994		51	.270	.400	100	27	4	0	3	3.0	8	20	7	20	0	21	6	44	0	1	0	0.9	.978	OF-33
8 yrs.		502	.267	.417	1182	316	50	2	41	3.5	137	159	84	167	9	157	45	521	14	13	4	1.1	.976	OF-342, DH-13, 1B-3

Matias Carrillo

CARRILLO, MATIAS
Born Matias Carrillo (Garcia).
B. Feb. 24, 1963, Los Mochis, Mexico.

BL TL 5'11" 190 lbs.

1991	MIL A	3	–	–	0	0	0	0	0	–	0	0	0	0	0	0	0	0	0	0	0	0.0	–	OF-3
1993	FLA N	24	.255	.364	55	14	6	0	0	0.0	4	3	1	7	0	9	0	21	0	0	0	0.9	1.000	OF-16
1994		80	.250	.301	136	34	7	0	0	0.0	13	9	9	31	3	27	6	49	5	1	1	0.7	.982	OF-49
3 yrs.		107	.251	.319	191	48	13	0	0	0.0	17	12	10	38	3	36	6	70	5	1	1	0.7	.987	OF-68

Joe Carter

CARTER, JOSEPH CHRIS
B. Mar. 7, 1960, Oklahoma City, Okla.

BR TR 6'3" 210 lbs.

1983	CHI N	23	.176	.235	51	9	1	1	0	0.0	6	1	0	21	1	5	1	26	0	0	0	1.1	1.000	OF-16
1984	CLE A	66	.275	.467	244	67	6	1	13	5.3	32	41	11	48	2	7	5	169	11	6	4	2.8	.968	OF-59, 1B-7
1985		143	.262	.409	489	128	27	0	15	3.1	64	59	25	74	24	4	0	311	17	6	4	2.3	.982	OF-135, 1B-11, DH-7, 2B-1, 3B-1
1986		162	.302	.514	663	200	36	9	29	4.4	108	**121**	32	95	29	1	1	800	55	10	52	5.3	.988	OF-104, 1B-70
1987		149	.264	.480	588	155	27	2	32	5.4	83	106	27	105	31	2	0	782	46	17	61	5.7	.980	1B-84, OF-62, DH-5
1988		157	.271	.478	621	168	36	6	27	4.3	85	98	35	82	27	1	0	444	8	7	3	2.9	.985	OF-156
1989		162	.243	.465	**651**	158	32	4	35	5.4	84	105	39	112	13	0	0	443	20	9	7	2.9	.981	OF-146, 1B-11, DH-8
1990	SD N	162	.232	.391	**634**	147	27	1	24	3.8	79	115	48	93	22	1	0	492	16	11	19	3.2	.979	OF-150, 1B-14
1991	TOR A	162	.273	.503	638	174	42	3	33	5.2	89	108	49	112	20	0	0	283	13	8	2	1.9	.974	OF-151, DH-11
1992		158	.264	.498	622	164	30	7	34	5.5	97	119	36	109	12	1	0	284	13	9	3	1.9	.971	OF-129, DH-24, 1B-4
1993		155	.254	.489	603	153	33	5	33	5.5	92	121	47	113	8	1	0	289	7	8	0	2.0	.974	OF-151, DH-3
1994		111	.271	.524	435	118	25	2	27	6.2	70	103	33	64	11	1	0	205	4	2	1	1.9	.991	OF-110, DH-1
12 yrs.		1610	.263	.473	6239	1641	322	41	302	4.8	889	1097	382	1028	200	23	7	4528	210	93	156	3.0	.981	OF-1369, 1B-201, DH-59, 2B-1, 3B-1

LEAGUE CHAMPIONSHIP SERIES

1991	TOR A	5	.263	.526	19	5	2	0	1	5.3	3	4	1	5	0	0	0	4	1	0	0	1.0	1.000	OF-3, DH-2
1992		6	.192	.308	26	5	0	0	1	3.8	2	3	2	4	2	0	0	16	1	1	1	3.0	.944	OF-6, 1B-2
1993		6	.259	.259	27	7	0	0	0	0.0	2	2	1	5	0	0	0	12	1	0	0	2.2	1.000	OF-6
3 yrs.		17	.236	.347	72	17	2	0	2	2.8	7	9	4	14	2	0	0	32	3	1	1	2.1	.972	OF-15, DH-2, 1B-2

WORLD SERIES

1992	TOR A	6	.273	.636	22	6	2	0	2	9.1	2	3	3	2	0	0	0	27	1	0	0	4.7	1.000	OF-4, 1B-2
1993		6	.280	.560	25	7	1	0	2	8.0	6	8	0	4	0	0	0	13	0	2	0	2.5	.867	OF-6
2 yrs.		12	.277	.596	47	13	3	0	4	8.5	8	11	3	6	0	0	0	40	1	2	0	3.6	.953	OF-10, 1B-2

Vinny Castilla

CASTILLA, VINICIO
Born Vinicio Castilla (Soria).
B. July 4, 1967, Oaxaca, Mexico.

BR TR 6'1" 175 lbs.

1991	ATL N	12	.200	.200	5	1	0	0	0	0.0	1	0	0	2	0	0	0	6	6	0	0	1.0	1.000	SS-12
1992		9	.250	.313	16	4	1	0	0	0.0	1	1	0	4	0	0	0	2	12	1	1	1.7	.933	3B-4, SS-4
1993	CLR N	105	.255	.404	337	86	9	7	9	2.7	36	30	13	45	2	2	0	141	282	11	67	4.1	.975	SS-104
1994		52	.331	.500	130	43	11	1	3	2.3	16	18	7	23	2	10	3	67	78	2	23	2.8	.986	SS-18, 2B-14, 3B-9, 1B-2
4 yrs.		178	.275	.424	488	134	21	8	12	2.5	54	49	21	74	4	12	3	216	378	14	91	3.4	.977	SS-138, 2B-14, 3B-13, 1B-2

Andujar Cedeno

CEDENO, ANDUJAR
Born Andujar Cedeno (Donastorg).
Brother of Domingo Cedeno.
B. Aug. 21, 1969, La Romana, Dominican Republic.

BR TR 6'1" 170 lbs.

1990	HOU N	7	.000	.000	8	0	0	0	0	0.0	0	0	0	5	0	2	0	3	2	1	0	0.9	.833	SS-3
1991		67	.243	.418	251	61	13	2	9	3.6	27	36	9	74	4	1	0	88	151	18	36	3.8	.930	SS-66
1992		71	.173	.277	220	38	13	2	2	0.9	15	13	14	71	2	1	0	82	175	11	27	3.8	.959	SS-70
1993		149	.283	.412	505	143	24	4	11	2.2	69	56	48	97	9	1	1	155	376	25	78	3.7	.955	SS-149, 3B-1
1994		98	.263	.418	342	90	26	0	9	2.6	38	49	29	79	1	3	1	130	280	23	69	4.4	.947	SS-95
5 yrs.		392	.250	.390	1326	332	76	8	31	2.3	149	154	100	326	16	8	2	458	984	78	210	3.9	.949	SS-383, 3B-1

Domingo Cedeno

CEDENO, DOMINGO ANTONIO
Born Domingo Antonio Cedeno (Donastorg).
Brother of Andujar Cedeno.
B. Nov. 4, 1968, La Romana, Dominican Republic

BB TR 6'1" 170 lbs.

1993	TOR A	15	.174	.174	46	8	0	0	0	0.0	5	7	1	10	1	1	0	10	39	1	5	3.3	.980	SS-10, 2B-5
1994		47	.196	.278	97	19	2	3	0	0.0	14	10	10	31	1	3	0	40	64	8	11	2.4	.929	2B-28, SS-8, 3B-6, OF-1
2 yrs.		62	.189	.245	143	27	2	3	0	0.0	19	17	11	41	2	4	0	50	103	9	16	2.6	.944	2B-33, SS-18, 3B-6, OF-1

Wes Chamberlain

CHAMBERLAIN, WESLEY POLK
B. Apr. 13, 1966, Chicago, Ill.

BR TR 6'2" 210 lbs.

1990	PHI N	18	.283	.478	46	13	3	0	2	4.3	9	4	1	9	4	8	0	23	0	1	0	1.3	.958	OF-10
1991		101	.240	.399	383	92	16	3	13	3.4	51	50	31	73	9	3	0	199	4	3	0	2.0	.985	OF-98
1992		76	.258	.422	275	71	18	0	9	3.3	26	41	10	55	4	4	1	132	3	4	1	1.8	.971	OF-73
1993		96	.282	.493	284	80	20	2	12	4.2	34	45	17	51	2	20	4	131	10	1	3	1.5	.993	OF-76
1994	2 teams		PHI N	(24G – .275)		BOS A	(51G – .256)																	
"	total	75	.262	.408	233	61	14	1	6	2.6	20	26	15	50	1	0	15	96	8	0	1	1.4	1.000	OF-52, DH-12
5 yrs.		366	.260	.431	1221	317	71	6	42	3.4	140	166	74	238	19	50	6	581	25	9	5	1.7	.985	OF-309, DH-12

Wes Chamberlain *continued*

LEAGUE CHAMPIONSHIP SERIES

Year Team	Games	BA	SA	AB	H	2B	3B	HR	HR%	R	RBI	BB	SO	SB	Pinch Hit AB	Pinch Hit H	PO	A	E	DP	TC/G	FA	G by Pos
1993 PHI N	4	.364	.636	11	4	3	0	0	0.0	1	1	1	3	0	1	0	2	2	0	0	1.0	1.000	OF-3

WORLD SERIES

Year Team	Games	BA	SA	AB	H	2B	3B	HR	HR%	R	RBI	BB	SO	SB	Pinch Hit AB	Pinch Hit H	PO	A	E	DP	TC/G	FA	G by Pos
1993 PHI N	2	.000	.000	2	0	0	0	0	0.0	0	0	0	1	0	1	0	2	0	0	0	0.0	—	

Archi Cianfrocco

CIANFROCCO, ANGELO DOMINIC — B. Oct. 6, 1966, Rome, N. Y. — BR TR 6'5" 200 lbs.

Year Team	Games	BA	SA	AB	H	2B	3B	HR	HR%	R	RBI	BB	SO	SB	Pinch Hit AB	Pinch Hit H	PO	A	E	DP	TC/G	FA	G by Pos
1992 MON N	86	.241	.358	232	56	5	2	6	2.6	25	30	11	66	3	10	2	387	66	8	26	5.4	.983	1B-56, 3B-19, OF-5
1993 2 teams	MON N (12G – .235)		SD N (84G – .244)																				
" total	96	.243	.416	296	72	11	2	12	4.1	30	48	17	69	2	2	2	243	97	10	29	3.6	.971	3B-64, 1B-42
1994 SD N	59	.219	.356	146	32	8	0	4	2.7	9	13	3	39	2	12	2	58	67	7	7	2.2	.947	3B-37, 1B-16, SS-1
3 yrs.	241	.237	.383	674	160	24	4	22	3.3	64	91	31	174	7	24	6	688	230	25	62	3.9	.973	3B-120, 1B-114, OF-5, SS-1

Jeff Cirillo

CIRILLO, JEFFREY HOWARD — B. Sept. 23, 1969, Pasadena, Calif. — BR TR 6'2" 190 lbs.

Year Team	Games	BA	SA	AB	H	2B	3B	HR	HR%	R	RBI	BB	SO	SB	Pinch Hit AB	Pinch Hit H	PO	A	E	DP	TC/G	FA	G by Pos
1994 MIL A	39	.238	.381	126	30	9	0	3	2.4	17	12	11	16	0	3	1	23	60	3	7	2.2	.965	3B-37, 2B-1

Dave Clark

CLARK, DAVID EARL — B. Sept. 3, 1962, Tupelo, Miss. — BL TR 6'2" 200 lbs.

Year Team	Games	BA	SA	AB	H	2B	3B	HR	HR%	R	RBI	BB	SO	SB	Pinch Hit AB	Pinch Hit H	PO	A	E	DP	TC/G	FA	G by Pos
1986 CLE A	18	.276	.448	58	16	1	0	3	5.2	10	9	7	11	1	0	0	26	0	0	0	1.4	1.000	OF-10, DH-7
1987	29	.207	.368	87	18	5	0	3	3.4	11	12	2	24	1	6	0	24	1	0	0	0.9	1.000	OF-13, DH-12
1988	63	.263	.359	156	41	4	1	3	1.9	11	18	17	28	0	19	4	36	0	2	0	0.6	.947	DH-27, OF-23
1989	102	.237	.379	253	60	12	0	8	3.2	21	29	30	63	0	29	7	27	0	1	0	0.3	.964	DH-55, OF-21
1990 CHI N	84	.275	.409	171	47	4	2	5	2.9	22	20	8	40	7	42	11	60	2	0	0	0.7	1.000	OF-39
1991 KC A	11	.200	.200	10	2	0	0	0	0.0	0	1	1	1	0	10	2	0	0	0	0	0.0	—	DH-1, OF-1
1992 PIT N	23	.212	.394	33	7	0	0	2	6.1	3	7	6	8	0	11	2	10	0	0	0	0.4	1.000	OF-8
1993	110	.271	.444	277	75	11	2	11	4.0	43	46	38	58	1	23	3	132	3	6	1	1.3	.957	OF-91
1994	86	.296	.489	223	66	11	1	10	4.5	37	46	22	48	2	24	8	107	5	3	1	1.3	.974	OF-57
9 yrs.	526	.262	.416	1268	332	48	6	45	3.5	159	188	131	281	12	163	37	422	11	12	2	0.8	.973	OF-263, DH-102

Phil Clark

CLARK, PHILLIP BENJAMIN — Brother of Jerald Clark. B. May 6, 1968, Crockett, Tex. — BR TR 6' 180 lbs.

Year Team	Games	BA	SA	AB	H	2B	3B	HR	HR%	R	RBI	BB	SO	SB	Pinch Hit AB	Pinch Hit H	PO	A	E	DP	TC/G	FA	G by Pos
1992 DET A	23	.407	.537	54	22	4	0	1	1.9	3	5	6	9	1	6	3	27	0	2	0	1.3	.931	OF-13, DH-7
1993 SD N	102	.313	.496	240	75	17	0	9	3.8	33	33	8	31	2	37	13	243	35	8	14	2.8	.972	OF-36, 1B-24, C-11, 3B-5
1994	61	.215	.356	149	32	6	0	5	3.4	14	20	5	17	1	20	4	148	14	4	14	2.7	.976	1B-24, OF-17, C-5, 3B-1
3 yrs.	186	.291	.454	443	129	27	0	15	3.4	50	58	19	57	4	63	20	418	49	14	28	2.6	.971	OF-66, 1B-48, C-16, DH-7, 3B-6

Will Clark

CLARK, WILLIAM NUSCHLER (The Thrill) — B. Mar. 13, 1964, New Orleans, La. — BL TL 6'2" 190 lbs.

Year Team	Games	BA	SA	AB	H	2B	3B	HR	HR%	R	RBI	BB	SO	SB	Pinch Hit AB	Pinch Hit H	PO	A	E	DP	TC/G	FA	G by Pos
1986 SF N	111	.287	.444	408	117	27	2	11	2.7	66	41	34	76	4	9	6	942	72	11	76	9.2	.989	1B-102
1987	150	.308	.580	529	163	29	5	35	6.6	89	91	49	98	5	11	3	1253	103	13	130	9.1	.991	1B-139
1988	162	.282	.508	575	162	31	6	29	5.0	102	**109**	100	129	9	5	0	1492	104	12	126	9.9	.993	1B-158
1989	159	.333	.546	588	196	38	9	23	3.9	**104**	111	74	103	8	1	0	1445	111	10	117	9.8	.994	1B-158
1990	154	.295	.448	600	177	25	5	19	3.2	91	95	62	97	8	1	0	1456	119	12	118	10.3	.992	1B-153
1991	148	.301	**.536**	565	170	32	7	29	5.1	84	116	51	91	4	3	1	1273	110	4	115	9.4	.997	1B-144
1992	144	.300	.476	513	154	40	1	16	3.1	69	73	73	68	12	2	1	1275	105	10	130	9.7	.993	1B-141
1993	132	.283	.432	491	139	27	2	14	2.9	82	73	63	68	2	2	0	1078	88	14	113	8.9	.988	1B-129
1994 TEX A	110	.329	.501	389	128	24	2	13	3.3	73	80	71	59	5	2	0	968	73	10	85	9.6	.990	1B-107, DH-1
9 yrs.	1270	.302	.499	4658	1406	273	39	189	4.1	760	789	577	803	57	36	11	11182	885	96	1010	9.6	.992	1B-1231, DH-1

LEAGUE CHAMPIONSHIP SERIES

Year Team	Games	BA	SA	AB	H	2B	3B	HR	HR%	R	RBI	BB	SO	SB	Pinch Hit AB	Pinch Hit H	PO	A	E	DP	TC/G	FA	G by Pos
1987 SF N	7	.360	.560	25	9	2	1	1	4.0	3	3	3	6	1	0	0	63	7	1	10	10.1	.986	1B-7
1989	5	.650	1.200	20	13	3	1	2	10.0	8	8	2	2	0	0	0	43	6	0	6	9.8	1.000	1B-5
2 yrs.	12	.489	.844	45	22	5	1	3	6.7	11	11	5	8	1	0	0	106	13	1	16	10.0	.992	1B-12

WORLD SERIES

Year Team	Games	BA	SA	AB	H	2B	3B	HR	HR%	R	RBI	BB	SO	SB	Pinch Hit AB	Pinch Hit H	PO	A	E	DP	TC/G	FA	G by Pos
1989 SF N	4	.250	.313	16	4	1	0	0	0.0	2	0	1	3	0	0	0	40	2	0	2	10.5	1.000	1B-4

Royce Clayton

CLAYTON, ROYCE SPENCER — B. Jan. 2, 1970, Burbank, Calif. — BR TR 6' 175 lbs.

Year Team	Games	BA	SA	AB	H	2B	3B	HR	HR%	R	RBI	BB	SO	SB	Pinch Hit AB	Pinch Hit H	PO	A	E	DP	TC/G	FA	G by Pos
1991 SF N	9	.115	.154	26	3	1	0	0	0.0	0	2	1	6	0	0	0	16	6	3	1	2.8	.880	SS-8
1992	98	.224	.308	321	72	7	4	4	1.2	31	24	26	63	8	1	0	142	257	11	51	4.2	.973	SS-94, 3B-1
1993	153	.282	.372	549	155	21	5	6	1.1	54	70	38	91	11	1	0	251	449	27	103	4.8	.963	SS-153
1994	108	.236	.327	385	91	14	6	3	0.8	38	30	30	74	23	1	0	178	331	14	62	4.8	.973	SS-108
4 yrs.	368	.251	.338	1281	321	43	15	13	1.0	123	126	95	234	42	3	0	587	1043	55	217	4.6	.967	SS-363, 3B-1

Greg Colbrunn

COLBRUNN, GREGORY JOSEPH — B. July 26, 1969, Fontana, Calif. — BR TR 6' 190 lbs.

Year Team	Games	BA	SA	AB	H	2B	3B	HR	HR%	R	RBI	BB	SO	SB	Pinch Hit AB	Pinch Hit H	PO	A	E	DP	TC/G	FA	G by Pos
1992 MON N	52	.268	.351	168	45	8	0	2	1.2	12	18	6	34	3	5	0	363	29	3	24	7.6	.992	1B-47
1993	70	.255	.392	153	39	9	0	4	2.6	15	23	6	33	4	10	4	372	27	2	31	5.7	.995	1B-61
1994 FLA N	47	.303	.484	155	47	10	0	6	3.9	17	31	9	27	1	5	2	303	26	4	28	7.1	.988	1B-41
3 yrs.	169	.275	.408	476	131	27	0	12	2.5	44	72	21	94	8	20	6	1038	82	9	83	6.7	.992	1B-149

Year	Team	Games	BA	SA	AB	H	2B	3B	HR	HR%	R	RBI	BB	SO	SB	Pinch Hit AB	Pinch Hit H	PO	A	E	DP	TC/G	FA	G by Pos

Alex Cole

COLE, ALEXANDER, JR.
B. Aug. 17, 1965, Fayetteville, N. C.   BL TL 6'2" 170 lbs.

Year	Team	Games	BA	SA	AB	H	2B	3B	HR	HR%	R	RBI	BB	SO	SB	PH AB	PH H	PO	A	E	DP	TC/G	FA	G by Pos
1990	CLE A	63	.300	.357	227	68	5	4	0	0.0	43	13	28	38	40	1	0	145	3	6	1	2.4	.961	OF-59, DH-1
1991		122	.295	.354	387	114	17	3	0	0.0	58	21	58	47	27	7	1	256	6	8	1	2.2	.970	OF-107, DH-6
1992	2 teams	CLE A (41G – .206)		PIT N (64G – .278)																				
"	total	105	.255	.315	302	77	4	7	0	0.0	44	15	28	67	16	30	4	118	6	2	1	1.2	.984	OF-77, DH-3
1993	CLR N	126	.256	.305	348	89	9	4	0	0.0	50	24	43	58	30	28	6	219	5	4	1	1.8	.982	OF-93
1994	MIN A	105	.296	.403	345	102	15	5	4	1.2	68	23	44	60	29	9	2	245	4	8	0	2.4	.969	OF-100, DH-1
5 yrs.		521	.280	.347	1609	450	50	23	4	0.2	263	96	201	270	142	74	13	983	24	28	4	2.0	.973	OF-436, DH-11

LEAGUE CHAMPIONSHIP SERIES

Year	Team	Games	BA	SA	AB	H	2B	3B	HR	HR%	R	RBI	BB	SO	SB	PH AB	PH H	PO	A	E	DP	TC/G	FA	G by Pos
1992	PIT N	4	.200	.200	10	2	0	0	0	0.0	2	1	3	2	1	0	0	7	1	0	1	2.0	1.000	OF-4

Vince Coleman

COLEMAN, VINCENT MAURICE
B. Sept. 22, 1961, Jacksonville, Fla.   BB TR 6' 170 lbs.

Year	Team	Games	BA	SA	AB	H	2B	3B	HR	HR%	R	RBI	BB	SO	SB	PH AB	PH H	PO	A	E	DP	TC/G	FA	G by Pos
1985	STL N	151	.267	.335	636	170	20	10	1	0.2	107	40	50	115	110	1	0	305	16	7	1	2.2	.979	OF-150
1986		154	.232	.280	600	139	13	8	0	0.0	94	29	60	98	107	2	1	300	12	9	2	2.1	.972	OF-149
1987		151	.289	.358	623	180	14	10	3	0.5	121	43	70	126	109	1	0	274	16	9	3	2.0	.970	OF-150
1988		153	.260	.339	616	160	20	10	3	0.5	77	38	49	111	81	2	0	290	14	9	1	2.0	.971	OF-150
1989		145	.254	.334	563	143	21	9	2	0.4	94	28	50	90	65	5	2	247	5	10	1	1.8	.962	OF-142
1990		124	.292	.400	497	145	18	9	6	1.2	73	39	35	88	77	5	0	244	12	5	2	2.1	.981	OF-120
1991	NY N	72	.255	.327	278	71	7	5	1	0.4	45	17	39	47	37	2	0	132	5	3	0	1.9	.979	OF-70
1992		71	.275	.358	229	63	11	1	2	0.9	37	21	27	41	24	8	3	112	2	1	2	1.6	.991	OF-61
1993		92	.279	.375	373	104	14	8	2	0.5	64	25	21	58	38	3	1	162	5	3	0	1.8	.982	OF-90
1994	KC A	104	.240	.340	438	105	14	12	2	0.5	61	33	29	72	50	0	0	163	11	7	1	1.7	.961	OF-99, DH-4
10 yrs.		1217	.264	.342	4853	1280	152	82	22	0.5	773	313	430	846	698 8th	29	7	2229	98	63	13	2.0	.974	OF-1181, DH-4

LEAGUE CHAMPIONSHIP SERIES

Year	Team	Games	BA	SA	AB	H	2B	3B	HR	HR%	R	RBI	BB	SO	SB	PH AB	PH H	PO	A	E	DP	TC/G	FA	G by Pos
1985	STL N	3	.286	.286	14	4	0	0	0	0.0	2	1	0	2	1	0	0	8	0	0	0	2.7	1.000	OF-3
1987		7	.269	.308	26	7	1	0	0	0.0	3	4	4	6	1	0	0	9	1	0	0	1.4	1.000	OF-7
2 yrs.		10	.275	.300	40	11	1	0	0	0.0	5	5	4	8	2	0	0	17	1	0	0	1.8	1.000	OF-10

WORLD SERIES

Year	Team	Games	BA	SA	AB	H	2B	3B	HR	HR%	R	RBI	BB	SO	SB	PH AB	PH H	PO	A	E	DP	TC/G	FA	G by Pos
1987	STL N	7	.143	.214	28	4	2	0	0	0.0	5	2	1	10	6	0	0	10	2	0	0	1.7	1.000	OF-7

Darnell Coles

COLES, DARNELL
B. June 2, 1962, San Bernardino, Calif.   BR TR 6'1" 185 lbs.

Year	Team	Games	BA	SA	AB	H	2B	3B	HR	HR%	R	RBI	BB	SO	SB	PH AB	PH H	PO	A	E	DP	TC/G	FA	G by Pos
1983	SEA A	27	.283	.391	92	26	7	1	1	1.1	9	6	7	12	0	1	0	17	47	4	8	2.5	.941	3B-26
1984		48	.161	.196	143	23	3	1	0	0.0	15	6	17	26	2	0	0	31	63	8	10	2.1	.922	3B-42, DH-3, OF-3
1985		27	.237	.356	59	14	4	0	1	1.7	8	5	9	17	0	3	0	25	44	6	10	2.8	.920	SS-15, 3B-7, DH-2, OF-2
1986	DET A	142	.273	.453	521	142	30	2	20	3.8	67	86	45	84	6	1	0	111	242	23	23	2.6	.939	3B-133, DH-7, OF-2, SS-2
1987	2 teams	DET A (53G – .181)		PIT N (40G – .227)																				
"	total	93	.201	.369	268	54	13	1	10	3.7	34	39	34	43	1	9	2	123	87	20	6	2.5	.913	3B-46, OF-34, 1B-10, DH-3, SS-1
1988	2 teams	PIT N (68G – .232)		SEA A (55G – .292)																				
"	total	123	.261	.438	406	106	23	2	15	3.7	52	70	37	67	4	11	0	166	3	3	0	1.4	.983	OF-102, DH-7, 1B-2, 3B-1
1989	SEA A	146	.252	.359	535	135	21	3	10	1.9	54	59	27	61	5	8	1	317	76	12	20	2.8	.970	OF-89, 3B-26, 1B-18, DH-12
1990	2 teams	SEA A (37G – .215)		DET A (52G – .204)																				
"	total	89	.209	.293	215	45	7	1	3	1.4	22	20	16	38	0	27	8	69	42	9	3	1.3	.925	DH-31, OF-31, 3B-14, 1B-4
1991	SF N	11	.214	.214	14	3	0	0	0	0.0	1	0	0	2	0	7	1	4	0	0	0	0.4	1.000	OF-3, 1B-1
1992	CIN N	55	.312	.482	141	44	11	2	3	2.1	16	18	3	15	1	10	3	161	42	0	8	3.7	1.000	3B-23, 1B-20, OF-5
1993	TOR A	64	.253	.371	194	49	9	1	4	2.1	26	26	16	29	1	4	1	77	20	7	0	1.6	.933	OF-44, 3B-16, 1B-1, DH-1
1994		48	.210	.350	143	30	6	1	4	2.8	15	15	10	25	0	4	2	103	5	4	7	2.4	.966	OF-29, 1B-8, 3B-7, DH-1
12 yrs.		873	.246	.383	2731	671	134	14	71	2.6	319	350	221	419	20	85	17	1204	675	96	95	2.3	.951	OF-344, 3B-341, DH-67, 1B-66, SS-18

Jeff Conine

CONINE, JEFFREY GUY
B. June 27, 1966, Tacoma, Wash.   BR TR 6'1" 205 lbs.

Year	Team	Games	BA	SA	AB	H	2B	3B	HR	HR%	R	RBI	BB	SO	SB	PH AB	PH H	PO	A	E	DP	TC/G	FA	G by Pos
1990	KC A	9	.250	.350	20	5	2	0	0	0.0	3	2	2	5	0	0	0	39	4	1	7	4.9	.977	1B-9
1992		28	.253	.352	91	23	5	2	0	0.0	10	9	8	23	0	0	0	75	3	0	1	2.8	1.000	OF-23, 1B-4, DH-1
1993	FLA N	162	.292	.403	595	174	24	3	12	2.0	75	79	52	135	2	4	1	403	25	2	11	2.7	.995	OF-147, 1B-43
1994		115	.319	.525	451	144	27	6	18	4.0	60	82	40	92	1	1	0	409	24	6	19	3.8	.986	OF-97, 1B-46
4 yrs.		314	.299	.446	1157	346	58	11	30	2.6	148	172	102	255	3	5	1	926	56	9	38	3.2	.991	OF-267, 1B-102, DH-1

Scott Coolbaugh

COOLBAUGH, SCOTT ROBERT
B. June 13, 1966, Binghamton, N. Y.   BR TR 5'10" 185 lbs.

Year	Team	Games	BA	SA	AB	H	2B	3B	HR	HR%	R	RBI	BB	SO	SB	PH AB	PH H	PO	A	E	DP	TC/G	FA	G by Pos
1989	TEX A	25	.275	.412	51	14	1	0	2	3.9	7	7	4	12	0	0	0	7	39	2	3	1.9	.958	3B-23, DH-2
1990		67	.200	.267	180	36	6	0	2	1.1	21	13	15	47	1	2	1	42	118	10	12	2.5	.941	3B-66
1991	SD N	60	.217	.306	180	39	8	1	2	1.1	12	15	19	45	0	6	0	32	108	7	8	2.5	.952	3B-54
1994	STL N	15	.190	.476	21	4	0	0	2	9.5	4	6	1	4	0	7	2	24	6	0	3	2.0	1.000	1B-4, 3B-4
4 yrs.		167	.215	.310	432	93	15	1	8	1.9	44	41	39	108	1	15	3	105	271	19	26	2.4	.952	3B-147, 1B-4, DH-2

Scott Cooper

COOPER, SCOTT KENDRICK
B. Oct. 13, 1967, St. Louis, Mo.   BL TR 6'3" 200 lbs.

Year	Team	Games	BA	SA	AB	H	2B	3B	HR	HR%	R	RBI	BB	SO	SB	PH AB	PH H	PO	A	E	DP	TC/G	FA	G by Pos
1990	BOS A	2	.000	.000	1	0	0	0	0	0.0	0	0	0	1	0	1	0	0	0	0	0	0.0	–	
1991		14	.457	.686	35	16	4	2	0	0.0	6	7	2	2	0	2	1	6	22	2	1	2.1	.933	3B-13
1992		123	.276	.383	337	93	21	0	5	1.5	34	33	37	33	1	15	5	472	137	9	49	5.0	.985	1B-62, 3B-47, DH-2, 2B-1, SS-1
1993		156	.279	.397	526	147	29	3	9	1.7	67	63	58	81	5	4	2	112	244	24	23	2.4	.937	3B-154, 1B-2, SS-1
1994		104	.282	.453	369	104	16	4	13	3.5	49	53	30	65	0	2	0	51	219	16	20	2.8	.944	3B-104
5 yrs.		399	.284	.417	1268	360	70	9	27	2.1	156	156	127	182	6	24	8	641	622	51	93	3.3	.961	3B-318, 1B-64, DH-2, SS-2, 2B-1

Joey Cora

CORA, JOSE MANUEL
Born Jose Manuel Cora (Amaro).
B. May 14, 1965, Caguas, Puerto Rico.
BB TR 5'7" 150 lbs.

Year Team	Games	BA	SA	AB	H	2B	3B	HR	HR%	R	RBI	BB	SO	SB	Pinch Hit AB	Pinch Hit H	PO	A	E	DP	TC/G	FA	G by Pos
1987 SD N	77	.237	.282	241	57	7	2	0	0.0	23	13	28	26	15	8	2	123	200	10	32	4.3	.970	2B-66, SS-6
1989	12	.316	.368	19	6	1	0	0	0.0	5	1	1	0	1	0	0	11	15	2	3	2.3	.929	SS-7, 3B-2, 2B-1
1990	51	.270	.300	100	27	3	0	0	0.0	12	2	6	9	8	8	0	59	49	11	15	2.3	.908	SS-21, 2B-15, C-1
1991 CHI A	100	.241	.276	228	55	2	3	0	0.0	37	18	20	21	11	7	1	107	192	10	36	3.1	.968	2B-80, SS-5, DH-2
1992	68	.246	.320	122	30	7	1	0	0.0	27	9	22	13	10	9	2	60	84	3	22	2.2	.980	2B-28, DH-16, SS-6, 3B-5
1993	153	.268	.349	579	155	15	13	2	0.3	95	51	67	63	20	3	0	296	413	19	85	4.8	.974	2B-151, 3B-3
1994	90	.276	.362	312	86	13	4	2	0.6	55	30	38	32	8	6	2	161	195	8	47	4.0	.978	2B-84
7 yrs.	551	.260	.326	1601	416	48	23	4	0.2	254	124	182	164	73	41	7	817	1148	63	240	3.7	.969	2B-425, SS-45, DH-18, 3B-10, C-1

LEAGUE CHAMPIONSHIP SERIES

Year Team	Games	BA	SA	AB	H	2B	3B	HR	HR%	R	RBI	BB	SO	SB	Pinch Hit AB	Pinch Hit H	PO	A	E	DP	TC/G	FA	G by Pos
1993 CHI A	6	.136	.136	22	3	0	0	0	0.0	1	1	3	6	0	0	0	18	20	3	2	6.8	.927	2B-6

Wil Cordero

CORDERO, WILFREDO
Born Wilfredo Cordero (Nieva).
B. Oct. 3, 1971, Mayaguez, Puerto Rico.
BR TR 6'2" 185 lbs.

Year Team	Games	BA	SA	AB	H	2B	3B	HR	HR%	R	RBI	BB	SO	SB	Pinch Hit AB	Pinch Hit H	PO	A	E	DP	TC/G	FA	G by Pos
1992 MON N	45	.302	.397	126	38	4	1	2	1.6	17	8	9	31	0	2	2	51	92	8	12	3.4	.947	SS-35, 2B-9
1993	138	.248	.387	475	118	32	2	10	2.1	56	58	34	60	12	4	1	183	373	36	61	4.1	.937	SS-134, 3B-2
1994	110	.294	.489	415	122	30	3	15	3.6	65	63	41	62	16	1	1	124	316	22	55	4.2	.952	SS-109
3 yrs.	293	.274	.430	1016	278	66	6	27	2.7	138	129	84	153	28	7	4	338	781	66	128	4.0	.944	SS-278, 2B-9, 3B-2

Rod Correia

CORREIA, RONALD DOUGLAS
B. Sept. 13, 1967, Providence, R. I.
BR TR 5'11" 185 lbs.

Year Team	Games	BA	SA	AB	H	2B	3B	HR	HR%	R	RBI	BB	SO	SB	Pinch Hit AB	Pinch Hit H	PO	A	E	DP	TC/G	FA	G by Pos
1993 CAL A	64	.266	.305	128	34	5	0	0	0.0	12	9	6	20	2	0	0	87	121	3	22	3.3	.986	SS-40, 2B-11, 3B-3, DH-3
1994	6	.235	.294	17	4	1	0	0	0.0	4	0	0	0	0	0	0	12	9	0	3	3.5	1.000	2B-5, SS-1
2 yrs.	70	.262	.303	145	38	6	0	0	0.0	16	9	6	20	2	0	0	99	130	3	25	3.3	.987	SS-41, 2B-16, 3B-3, DH-3

Tripp Cromer

CROMER, ROY BUNYON III
B. Nov. 21, 1967, Lake City, S. C.
BR TR 6'2" 165 lbs.

Year Team	Games	BA	SA	AB	H	2B	3B	HR	HR%	R	RBI	BB	SO	SB	Pinch Hit AB	Pinch Hit H	PO	A	E	DP	TC/G	FA	G by Pos
1993 STL N	10	.087	.087	23	2	0	0	0	0.0	1	0	1	6	0	1	0	13	18	3	3	3.4	.912	SS-9
1994	2	-	-	0	0	0	0	0	-	1	0	0	0	0	0	0	0	0	1	0	0.5	.000	SS-2
2 yrs.	12	.087	.087	23	2	0	0	0	0.0	2	0	1	6	0	1	0	13	18	4	3	2.9	.886	SS-11

Fausto Cruz

CRUZ, FAUSTO SANTIAGO
B. May 1, 1972, Monte Cristi, Dominican Republic.
BR TR 5'10" 165 lbs.

Year Team	Games	BA	SA	AB	H	2B	3B	HR	HR%	R	RBI	BB	SO	SB	Pinch Hit AB	Pinch Hit H	PO	A	E	DP	TC/G	FA	G by Pos
1994 OAK A	17	.107	.107	28	3	0	0	0	0.0	2	0	4	6	0	4	0	17	23	2	3	2.5	.952	SS-10, 3B-4, 2B-1

Midre Cummings

CUMMINGS, MIDRE ALMERIC
B. Oct. 14, 1971, St. Croix, Virgin Islands
BB TR 6'1" 190 lbs.

Year Team	Games	BA	SA	AB	H	2B	3B	HR	HR%	R	RBI	BB	SO	SB	Pinch Hit AB	Pinch Hit H	PO	A	E	DP	TC/G	FA	G by Pos
1993 PIT N	13	.111	.139	36	4	1	0	0	0.0	5	3	4	9	0	2	0	21	0	0	0	1.6	1.000	OF-11
1994	24	.244	.326	86	21	4	0	1	1.2	11	12	4	18	0	0	0	48	1	2	1	2.1	.961	OF-24
2 yrs.	37	.205	.270	122	25	5	0	1	0.8	16	15	8	27	0	2	0	69	1	2	1	1.9	.972	OF-35

Chad Curtis

CURTIS, CHAD DAVID
B. Nov. 6, 1968, Marion, Ind.
BR TR 5'10" 175 lbs.

Year Team	Games	BA	SA	AB	H	2B	3B	HR	HR%	R	RBI	BB	SO	SB	Pinch Hit AB	Pinch Hit H	PO	A	E	DP	TC/G	FA	G by Pos
1992 CAL A	139	.259	.372	441	114	16	2	10	2.3	59	46	51	71	43	5	0	250	16	6	3	2.0	.978	OF-135, DH-1
1993	152	.285	.369	583	166	25	3	6	1.0	94	59	70	89	48	2	1	428	14	9	6	3.0	.980	OF-151, 2B-3
1994	114	.256	.397	453	116	23	4	11	2.4	67	50	37	69	25	0	0	331	9	4	0	3.0	.988	OF-114
3 yrs.	405	.268	.378	1477	396	64	9	27	1.8	220	155	158	229	116	7	1	1009	39	19	9	2.6	.982	OF-400, 2B-3, DH-1

Milt Cuyler

CUYLER, MILTON
B. Oct. 7, 1968, Macon, Ga.
BB TR 5'10" 175 lbs.

Year Team	Games	BA	SA	AB	H	2B	3B	HR	HR%	R	RBI	BB	SO	SB	Pinch Hit AB	Pinch Hit H	PO	A	E	DP	TC/G	FA	G by Pos
1990 DET A	19	.255	.353	51	13	3	1	0	0.0	8	8	5	10	1	0	0	38	2	1	0	2.2	.976	OF-17
1991	154	.257	.337	475	122	15	7	3	0.6	77	33	52	92	41	1	0	411	7	6	3	2.8	.986	OF-151
1992	89	.241	.316	291	70	11	1	3	1.0	39	28	10	62	8	0	0	232	4	4	1	2.7	.983	OF-89
1993	82	.213	.313	249	53	11	7	0	0.0	46	19	19	53	13	2	0	211	2	7	1	2.7	.968	OF-80
1994	48	.241	.310	116	28	3	1	1	0.9	20	11	13	21	5	0	0	78	1	2	0	1.7	.975	OF-46
5 yrs.	392	.242	.325	1182	286	43	17	7	0.6	190	99	99	238	68	3	0	970	16	20	5	2.6	.980	OF-383

Mark Dalesandro

DALESANDRO, MARK ANTHONY
B. May 14, 1968, Chicago, Ill.
BR TR 6' 185 lbs.

Year Team	Games	BA	SA	AB	H	2B	3B	HR	HR%	R	RBI	BB	SO	SB	Pinch Hit AB	Pinch Hit H	PO	A	E	DP	TC/G	FA	G by Pos
1994 CAL A	19	.200	.360	25	5	1	0	1	4.0	5	2	2	4	0	5	1	19	5	1	1	1.3	.960	C-11, 3B-5, OF-2

Darren Daulton

DAULTON, DARREN ARTHUR
B. Jan. 3, 1962, Arkansas City, Kans.
BL TR 6'2" 195 lbs.

Year Team	Games	BA	SA	AB	H	2B	3B	HR	HR%	R	RBI	BB	SO	SB	Pinch Hit AB	Pinch Hit H	PO	A	E	DP	TC/G	FA	G by Pos
1983 PHI N	2	.333	.333	3	1	0	0	0	0.0	1	0	1	1	0	0	0	8	0	0	0	4.0	1.000	C-2
1985	36	.204	.369	103	21	3	1	4	3.9	14	11	16	37	3	5	0	160	15	1	1	4.9	.994	C-28
1986	49	.225	.428	138	31	4	0	8	5.8	18	21	38	41	2	1	0	244	21	4	6	5.5	.985	C-48
1987	53	.194	.310	129	25	6	0	3	2.3	10	13	16	37	0	12	3	210	13	2	6	4.2	.991	C-40, 1B-1
1988	58	.208	.271	144	30	6	0	1	0.7	13	12	17	26	2	15	4	205	15	6	1	3.9	.973	C-44, 1B-1
1989	131	.201	.310	368	74	12	2	8	2.2	29	44	52	58	2	11	2	627	56	11	8	5.3	.984	C-126
1990	143	.268	.416	459	123	30	1	12	2.6	62	57	72	72	7	10	2	683	70	8	10	5.3	.989	C-139
1991	89	.196	.365	285	56	12	0	12	4.2	36	42	41	66	5	4	1	493	33	8	5	6.0	.985	C-88
1992	145	.270	.524	485	131	32	5	27	5.6	80	**109**	88	103	11	5	1	760	69	11	8	5.8	.987	C-141
1993	147	.257	.482	510	131	35	4	24	4.7	90	105	117	111	5	2	1	981	67	9	19	7.2	.991	C-147
1994	69	.300	.549	257	77	17	1	15	5.8	43	56	33	43	4	1	0	435	41	3	2	6.9	.994	C-68
11 yrs.	922	.243	.426	2881	700	157	14	114	4.0	396	470	491	595	41	66	14	4806	400	63	66	5.7	.988	C-871, 1B-2

LEAGUE CHAMPIONSHIP SERIES

Year Team	Games	BA	SA	AB	H	2B	3B	HR	HR%	R	RBI	BB	SO	SB	Pinch Hit AB	Pinch Hit H	PO	A	E	DP	TC/G	FA	G by Pos
1993 PHI N	6	.263	.474	19	5	1	0	1	5.3	2	3	6	3	0	0	0	54	3	0	0	9.5	1.000	C-6

Darren Daulton *continued*

WORLD SERIES

Year Team	Games	BA	SA	AB	H	2B	3B	HR	HR%	R	RBI	BB	SO	SB	Pinch Hit AB	Pinch Hit H	PO	A	E	DP	TC/G	FA	G by Pos
1993 PHI N	6	.217	.435	23	5	2	0	1	4.3	4	4	4	5	0	0	0	31	4	0	1	5.8	1.000	C-6

Butch Davis

DAVIS, WALLACE McARTHUR
B. June 19, 1958, Williamston, N. C.

BR TR 6′ 185 lbs.

Year Team	Games	BA	SA	AB	H	2B	3B	HR	HR%	R	RBI	BB	SO	SB	Pinch Hit AB	Pinch Hit H	PO	A	E	DP	TC/G	FA	G by Pos
1983 KC A	33	.344	.508	122	42	2	6	2	1.6	13	18	4	19	4	0	0	83	1	2	0	2.6	.977	OF-33
1984	41	.147	.224	116	17	3	0	2	1.7	11	12	10	19	4	4	0	69	2	3	1	1.8	.959	OF-35, DH-2
1987 PIT N	7	.143	.286	7	1	1	0	0	0.0	3	0	1	3	0	5	0	3	0	0	0	0.4	1.000	OF-1
1988 BAL A	13	.240	.280	25	6	1	0	0	0.0	2	0	0	8	1	1	0	16	1	0	1	1.3	1.000	OF-10, DH-1
1989	5	.167	.333	6	1	1	0	0	0.0	1	0	0	3	0	1	0	3	0	0	0	0.6	1.000	OF-3, DH-1
1991 LA N	1	.000	.000	1	0	0	0	0	0.0	0	0	0	0	0	1	0	0	0	0	0	0.0	–	
1993 TEX A	62	.245	.415	159	39	10	4	3	1.9	24	20	5	28	3	9	3	94	2	4	1	1.6	.960	OF-44, DH-11
1994	4	.235	.412	17	4	3	0	0	0.0	2	0	0	3	1	0	0	6	1	0	0	1.8	1.000	OF-4
8 yrs.	166	.243	.380	453	110	21	10	7	1.5	56	50	20	83	13	21	3	274	7	9	3	1.7	.969	OF-130, DH-15

Chili Davis

DAVIS, CHARLES THEODORE
B. Jan. 17, 1960, Kingston, Jamaica.

BB TR 6′3″ 195 lbs.

Year Team	Games	BA	SA	AB	H	2B	3B	HR	HR%	R	RBI	BB	SO	SB	Pinch Hit AB	Pinch Hit H	PO	A	E	DP	TC/G	FA	G by Pos
1981 SF N	8	.133	.133	15	2	0	0	0	0.0	1	0	1	2	2	3	1	7	0	0	0	0.9	1.000	OF-6
1982	154	.261	.410	641	167	27	6	19	3.0	86	76	45	115	24	1	1	404	16	12	4	2.8	.972	OF-153
1983	137	.233	.352	486	113	21	2	11	2.3	54	59	55	108	10	4	1	357	7	9	1	2.7	.976	OF-133
1984	137	.315	.507	499	157	21	6	21	4.2	87	81	42	74	12	15	6	292	9	9	2	2.3	.971	OF-123
1985	136	.270	.412	481	130	25	2	13	2.7	53	56	62	74	15	9	2	279	10	6	2	2.2	.980	OF-126
1986	153	.278	.416	526	146	28	3	13	2.5	71	70	84	96	16	7	1	303	9	9	2	2.1	.972	OF-148
1987	149	.250	.442	500	125	22	1	24	4.8	80	76	72	109	16	20	3	265	6	7	2	1.9	.975	OF-135
1988 CAL A	158	.268	.432	600	161	29	3	21	3.5	81	93	56	118	9	1	0	299	10	19	1	2.1	.942	OF-153, DH-3
1989	154	.271	.436	560	152	24	1	22	3.9	81	90	61	109	3	2	0	270	5	6	0	1.8	.979	OF-147, DH-6
1990	113	.265	.398	412	109	17	1	12	2.9	58	58	61	89	1	2	0	77	5	3	1	0.8	.965	DH-60, OF-52
1991 MIN A	153	.277	.507	534	148	34	1	29	5.4	84	93	95	117	5	2	0	2	0	0	0	0.0	1.000	DH-150, OF-2
1992	138	.288	.439	444	128	27	2	12	2.7	63	66	73	76	4	16	5	6	0	0	0	0.0	1.000	DH-125, OF-4, 1B-1
1993 CAL A	152	.243	.440	573	139	32	0	27	4.7	74	112	71	135	4	1	0	0	0	0	0	0.0	–	DH-150, P-1
1994	108	.311	.561	392	122	18	1	26	6.6	72	84	69	84	3	0	0	5	0	0	0	0.0	1.000	DH-106, OF-2
14 yrs.	1850	.270	.440	6663	1799	325	29	250	3.8	945	1014	847	1306	124	83	20	2566	77	80	15	1.5	.971	OF-1184, DH-600, 1B-1, P-1

LEAGUE CHAMPIONSHIP SERIES

Year Team	Games	BA	SA	AB	H	2B	3B	HR	HR%	R	RBI	BB	SO	SB	Pinch Hit AB	Pinch Hit H	PO	A	E	DP	TC/G	FA	G by Pos
1987 SF N	6	.150	.200	20	3	1	0	0	0.0	2	0	1	4	0	0	0	11	1	1	1	2.2	.923	OF-6
1991 MIN A	5	.294	.412	17	5	2	0	0	0.0	3	2	5	8	1	0	0	0	0	0	0	0.0	–	DH-5
2 yrs.	11	.216	.297	37	8	3	0	0	0.0	5	2	6	12	1	0	0	11	1	1	1	1.2	.923	OF-6, DH-5

WORLD SERIES

Year Team	Games	BA	SA	AB	H	2B	3B	HR	HR%	R	RBI	BB	SO	SB	Pinch Hit AB	Pinch Hit H	PO	A	E	DP	TC/G	FA	G by Pos
1991 MIN A	6	.222	.556	18	4	0	0	2	11.1	4	4	2	3	0	1	1	1	0	0	0	0.2	1.000	DH-4, OF-1

Eric Davis

DAVIS, ERIC KEITH
B. May 29, 1962, Los Angeles, Calif.

BR TR 6′3″ 175 lbs.

Year Team	Games	BA	SA	AB	H	2B	3B	HR	HR%	R	RBI	BB	SO	SB	Pinch Hit AB	Pinch Hit H	PO	A	E	DP	TC/G	FA	G by Pos
1984 CIN N	57	.224	.466	174	39	10	1	10	5.7	33	30	24	48	10	6	1	125	4	1	2	2.3	.992	OF-51
1985	56	.246	.516	122	30	3	3	8	6.6	26	18	7	39	16	8	1	75	3	1	1	1.4	.987	OF-47
1986	132	.277	.523	415	115	15	3	27	6.5	97	71	68	100	80	4	0	274	2	7	0	2.1	.975	OF-121
1987	129	.293	.593	474	139	23	4	37	7.8	120	100	84	134	50	1	0	380	10	4	4	3.1	.990	OF-128
1988	135	.273	.489	472	129	18	3	26	5.5	81	93	65	124	35	3	1	300	2	6	0	2.3	.981	OF-130
1989	131	.281	.541	462	130	14	2	34	7.4	74	101	68	116	21	3	1	298	2	5	1	2.3	.984	OF-125
1990	127	.260	.486	453	118	26	2	24	5.3	84	86	60	100	21	6	1	257	11	2	1	2.1	.993	OF-122
1991	89	.235	.386	285	67	10	0	11	3.9	39	33	48	92	14	8	2	190	5	3	2	2.2	.985	OF-82
1992 LA N	76	.228	.322	267	61	8	1	5	1.9	21	32	36	71	19	0	0	123	0	5	0	1.7	.961	OF-74
1993 2 teams	LA N (108G – .234)			DET A (23G – .253)																			
" total	131	.237	.415	451	107	18	1	20	4.4	71	68	55	106	35	4	0	273	7	3	2	2.2	.989	OF-121, DH-5
1994 DET A	37	.183	.292	120	22	4	0	3	2.5	19	13	18	45	5	2	0	85	1	1	1	2.4	.989	OF-35
11 yrs.	1100	.259	.477	3695	957	149	20	205	5.5	665	645	533	975	306	45	7	2380	47	38	14	2.2	.985	OF-1036, DH-5

LEAGUE CHAMPIONSHIP SERIES

Year Team	Games	BA	SA	AB	H	2B	3B	HR	HR%	R	RBI	BB	SO	SB	Pinch Hit AB	Pinch Hit H	PO	A	E	DP	TC/G	FA	G by Pos
1990 CIN N	6	.174	.217	23	4	1	0	0	0.0	2	2	1	9	0	0	0	12	1	0	0	2.2	1.000	OF-6

WORLD SERIES

Year Team	Games	BA	SA	AB	H	2B	3B	HR	HR%	R	RBI	BB	SO	SB	Pinch Hit AB	Pinch Hit H	PO	A	E	DP	TC/G	FA	G by Pos
1990 CIN N	4	.286	.500	14	4	0	0	1	7.1	3	5	0	0	0	0	0	4	0	0	0	1.0	1.000	OF-4

Russ Davis

DAVIS, RUSSELL STUART
B. Sept. 13, 1969, Birmingham, Ala.

BR TR 6′ 170 lbs.

Year Team	Games	BA	SA	AB	H	2B	3B	HR	HR%	R	RBI	BB	SO	SB	Pinch Hit AB	Pinch Hit H	PO	A	E	DP	TC/G	FA	G by Pos
1994 NY A	4	.143	.143	14	2	0	0	0	0.0	0	1	0	4	0	0	0	2	6	0	0	2.0	1.000	3B-4

Andre Dawson

DAWSON, ANDRE FERNANDO (The Hawk)
B. July 10, 1954, Miami, Fla.

BR TR 6′3″ 180 lbs.

Year Team	Games	BA	SA	AB	H	2B	3B	HR	HR%	R	RBI	BB	SO	SB	Pinch Hit AB	Pinch Hit H	PO	A	E	DP	TC/G	FA	G by Pos
1976 MON N	24	.235	.306	85	20	4	1	0	0.0	9	7	5	13	1	0	0	61	1	2	1	2.7	.969	OF-24
1977	139	.282	.474	525	148	26	9	19	3.6	64	65	34	93	21	5	0	352	9	4	1	2.6	.989	OF-136
1978	157	.253	.442	609	154	24	8	25	4.1	84	72	30	128	28	5	2	411	17	5	2	2.8	.988	OF-153
1979	155	.275	.468	639	176	24	12	25	3.9	90	92	27	115	35	0	0	394	7	5	1	2.6	.988	OF-153
1980	151	.308	.492	577	178	41	7	17	2.9	96	87	44	69	34	3	1	410	14	6	3	2.8	.986	OF-147
1981	103	.302	.553	394	119	21	3	24	6.1	71	64	35	50	26	0	0	327	10	7	1	3.3	.980	OF-103
1982	148	.301	.498	608	183	37	7	23	3.8	107	83	34	96	39	0	0	419	8	8	2	2.9	.982	OF-147
1983	159	.299	.539	633	**189**	36	10	32	5.1	104	113	38	81	25	1	1	435	6	9	2	2.8	.980	OF-157
1984	138	.248	.409	533	132	23	6	17	3.2	73	86	41	80	13	4	0	297	11	8	2	2.3	.975	OF-134
1985	139	.255	.444	529	135	27	2	23	4.3	65	91	29	92	13	9	3	248	9	7	1	1.9	.973	OF-131
1986	130	.284	.478	496	141	32	2	20	4.0	65	78	37	79	18	3	1	200	11	3	2	1.6	.986	OF-127
1987 CHI N	153	.287	.568	621	178	24	2	**49**	7.9	90	**137**	32	103	11	2	1	271	12	4	0	1.9	.986	OF-152
1988	157	.303	.504	591	179	31	8	24	4.1	78	79	37	73	12	8	2	267	7	3	1	1.8	.989	OF-147
1989	118	.252	.476	416	105	18	6	21	5.0	62	77	35	62	8	5	2	227	4	3	0	2.0	.987	OF-112
1990	147	.310	.535	529	164	28	5	27	5.1	72	100	42	65	16	7	2	250	10	5	4	1.8	.981	OF-139

Andre Dawson *continued*

Year Team	Games	BA	SA	AB	H	2B	3B	HR	HR%	R	RBI	BB	SO	SB	Pinch Hit AB	Pinch Hit H	PO	A	E	DP	TC/G	FA	G by Pos
1991	149	.272	.488	563	153	21	4	31	5.5	69	104	22	80	4	12	2	243	7	3	2	1.7	.988	OF-137
1992	143	.277	.456	542	150	27	2	22	4.1	60	90	30	70	6	6	1	225	11	2	3	1.7	.992	OF-139
1993 BOS A	121	.273	.425	461	126	29	1	13	2.8	44	67	17	49	2	4	2	42	0	0	0	0.3	1.000	DH-97, OF-20
1994	75	.240	.466	292	70	18	0	16	5.5	34	48	9	53	2	2	1	0	0	0	0	0.0	–	DH-74
19 yrs.	2506	.280	.484	9643	2700	491	95	428	4.4	1337	1540	578	1451	314	76	21	5079	154	84	28	2.1	.984	OF-2258, DH-171
DIVISIONAL PLAYOFF SERIES																							
1981 MON N	5	.300	.400	20	6	0	1	0	0.0	1	0	1	6	2	1	0	12	1	1	0	2.8	.929	OF-5
LEAGUE CHAMPIONSHIP SERIES																							
1981 MON N	5	.150	.150	20	3	0	0	0	0.0	2	0	0	4	0	0	0	12	0	0	0	2.4	1.000	OF-5
1989 CHI N	5	.105	.158	19	2	1	0	0	0.0	0	3	2	6	0	0	0	4	0	0	0	0.8	1.000	OF-5
2 yrs.	10	.128	.154	39	5	1	0	0	0.0	2	3	2	10	0	0	0	16	0	0	0	1.6	1.000	OF-10

Carlos Delgado

DELGADO, CARLOS JUAN
Born Carlos Juan Delgado (Hernandez).
B. June 25, 1972, Mayaguez, Puerto Rico   BL TR 6'3" 215 lbs.

Year Team	Games	BA	SA	AB	H	2B	3B	HR	HR%	R	RBI	BB	SO	SB	Pinch Hit AB	Pinch Hit H	PO	A	E	DP	TC/G	FA	G by Pos
1993 TOR A	2	.000	.000	1	0	0	0	0	0.0	0	0	1	0	0	1	0	2	0	0	0	1.0	1.000	C-1, DH-1
1994	43	.215	.438	130	28	2	0	9	6.9	17	24	25	46	1	3	0	56	2	2	0	1.4	.967	OF-41, C-1
2 yrs.	45	.214	.435	131	28	2	0	9	6.9	17	24	26	46	1	4	0	58	2	2	0	1.4	.968	OF-41, C-2, DH-1

Delino DeShields

DeSHIELDS, DELINO LAMONT
B. Jan. 15, 1969, Seaford, Del.   BL TR 6'1" 170 lbs.

Year Team	Games	BA	SA	AB	H	2B	3B	HR	HR%	R	RBI	BB	SO	SB	Pinch Hit AB	Pinch Hit H	PO	A	E	DP	TC/G	FA	G by Pos
1990 MON N	129	.289	.393	499	144	28	6	4	0.8	69	45	66	96	42	4	0	236	371	12	65	4.8	.981	2B-128
1991	151	.238	.332	563	134	15	4	10	1.8	83	51	95	151	56	5	0	285	405	27	72	4.7	.962	2B-148
1992	135	.292	.398	530	155	19	8	7	1.3	82	56	54	108	46	0	0	251	360	15	71	4.6	.976	2B-134
1993	123	.295	.372	481	142	17	7	2	0.4	75	29	72	64	43	0	0	243	381	11	74	5.2	.983	2B-123
1994 LA N	89	.250	.322	320	80	11	3	2	0.6	51	33	54	53	27	2	1	156	282	7	48	5.0	.984	2B-88, SS-10
5 yrs.	627	.274	.366	2393	655	90	28	25	1.0	360	214	341	472	214	11	1	1171	1799	72	330	4.9	.976	2B-621, SS-10

Orestes Destrade

DESTRADE, ORESTES
Born Orestes Destrade (Cucuas).
B. May 8, 1962, Santiago, Cuba.   BB TR 6'4" 210 lbs.

Year Team	Games	BA	SA	AB	H	2B	3B	HR	HR%	R	RBI	BB	SO	SB	Pinch Hit AB	Pinch Hit H	PO	A	E	DP	TC/G	FA	G by Pos
1987 NY A	9	.263	.263	19	5	0	0	0	0.0	5	1	5	5	0	4	0	20	1	0	2	2.3	1.000	1B-3, DH-2
1988 PIT N	36	.149	.234	47	7	1	0	1	2.1	2	3	5	17	0	24	4	61	2	0	3	1.8	1.000	1B-8
1993 FLA N	153	.255	.406	569	145	20	3	20	3.5	61	87	58	130	0	1	0	1313	90	19	109	9.3	.987	1B-152
1994	39	.208	.354	130	27	4	0	5	3.8	12	15	19	32	1	1	1	273	19	5	29	7.6	.983	1B-37
4 yrs.	237	.241	.383	765	184	25	3	26	3.4	80	106	87	184	1	30	5	1667	112	24	143	7.6	.987	1B-200, DH-2

Mike Devereaux

DEVEREAUX, MICHAEL
B. Apr. 10, 1963, Casper, Wyo.   BR TR 6' 195 lbs.

Year Team	Games	BA	SA	AB	H	2B	3B	HR	HR%	R	RBI	BB	SO	SB	Pinch Hit AB	Pinch Hit H	PO	A	E	DP	TC/G	FA	G by Pos
1987 LA N	19	.222	.278	54	12	3	0	0	0.0	7	4	3	10	3	5	0	21	1	0	0	1.2	1.000	OF-18
1988	30	.116	.140	43	5	1	0	0	0.0	4	2	2	10	0	7	1	29	0	0	0	1.0	1.000	OF-26
1989 BAL A	122	.266	.379	391	104	14	3	8	2.0	55	46	36	60	22	14	0	288	1	5	0	2.4	.983	OF-112, DH-3
1990	108	.240	.392	367	88	18	1	12	3.3	48	49	28	48	13	6	3	281	4	5	1	2.7	.983	OF-104, DH-3
1991	149	.260	.431	608	158	27	10	19	3.1	82	59	47	115	16	8	2	399	10	3	1	2.8	.993	OF-149
1992	156	.276	.464	653	180	29	11	24	3.7	76	107	44	94	10	1	1	431	5	5	3	2.8	.989	OF-155
1993	131	.250	.400	527	132	31	3	14	2.7	72	75	43	99	3	0	0	311	8	4	3	2.5	.988	OF-130
1994	85	.203	.332	301	61	8	2	9	3.0	35	33	22	72	1	2	1	203	3	1	1	2.4	.995	OF-84, DH-1
8 yrs.	800	.251	.404	2944	740	131	30	86	2.9	379	375	225	508	68	43	8	1963	32	23	9	2.5	.989	OF-778, DH-9

Alex Diaz

DIAZ, ALEXIS
B. Oct. 5, 1968, Brooklyn, N.Y.   BB TR 5'11" 175 lbs.

Year Team	Games	BA	SA	AB	H	2B	3B	HR	HR%	R	RBI	BB	SO	SB	Pinch Hit AB	Pinch Hit H	PO	A	E	DP	TC/G	FA	G by Pos
1992 MIL A	22	.111	.111	9	1	0	0	0	0.0	5	1	0	3	3	0	0	10	0	0	0	0.5	1.000	OF-11, DH-2
1993	32	.319	.348	69	22	2	0	0	0.0	9	1	0	12	5	4	1	46	1	1	0	1.5	.979	OF-28, DH-1
1994	79	.251	.369	187	47	5	7	1	0.5	17	17	10	19	5	1	1	138	11	2	0	1.9	.987	OF-73, 2B-2, DH-1
3 yrs.	133	.264	.355	265	70	7	7	1	0.4	31	19	10	31	13	5	2	194	12	3	0	1.6	.986	OF-112, DH-4, 2B-2

Mario Diaz

DIAZ, MARIO RAFAEL
Born Mario Rafael Diaz (Torres).
B. Jan. 10, 1962, Humacao, Puerto Rico.   BR TR 5'10" 145 lbs.

Year Team	Games	BA	SA	AB	H	2B	3B	HR	HR%	R	RBI	BB	SO	SB	Pinch Hit AB	Pinch Hit H	PO	A	E	DP	TC/G	FA	G by Pos
1987 SEA A	11	.304	.391	23	7	0	1	0	0.0	4	3	0	4	0	1	0	10	25	1	6	3.3	.972	SS-10
1988	28	.306	.375	72	22	5	0	0	0.0	6	9	3	5	0	3	1	31	47	1	11	2.8	.987	SS-21, 2B-4, 1B-1, 3B-1
1989	52	.135	.176	74	10	0	0	1	1.4	9	7	7	7	0	3	1	35	54	5	10	1.8	.947	SS-37, 2B-14, 3B-3
1990 NY N	16	.136	.182	22	3	1	0	0	0.0	0	1	0	3	0	7	2	5	18	1	1	1.5	.958	SS-10, 2B-1
1991 TEX A	96	.264	.319	182	48	7	0	1	0.5	24	22	15	18	0	14	3	93	143	7	32	2.5	.971	SS-65, 2B-20, 3B-8, DH-1
1992	19	.226	.258	31	7	1	0	0	0.0	2	1	1	2	0	1	0	16	26	1	2	2.5	.977	SS-16, 2B-3, 3B-1
1993	71	.273	.361	205	56	10	1	2	1.0	24	24	8	13	1	3	1	90	153	3	29	3.5	.988	SS-57, 3B-12, 1B-1
1994 FLA N	32	.325	.429	77	25	4	2	0	0.0	10	11	6	6	0	13	5	19	40	1	11	1.9	.983	3B-11, 2B-7, SS-7
8 yrs.	325	.259	.329	686	178	28	4	4	0.6	79	78	40	58	1	45	13	299	506	20	102	2.5	.976	SS-223, 2B-49, 3B-36, 1B-2, DH-1

Gary DiSarcina

DiSARCINA, GARY THOMAS
B. Nov. 19, 1967, Malden, Mass.   BR TR 6'1" 170 lbs.

Year Team	Games	BA	SA	AB	H	2B	3B	HR	HR%	R	RBI	BB	SO	SB	Pinch Hit AB	Pinch Hit H	PO	A	E	DP	TC/G	FA	G by Pos
1989 CAL A	2	–	–	0	0	0	0	0	–	0	0	0	0	0	0	0	0	0	0	0	0.0	–	SS-1
1990	18	.140	.193	57	8	1	1	0	0.0	8	0	3	10	1	1	0	17	57	4	9	4.3	.949	SS-14, 2B-3
1991	18	.211	.246	57	12	2	0	0	0.0	5	3	3	4	0	1	0	29	45	4	5	4.3	.949	SS-10, 2B-7, 3B-2
1992	157	.247	.301	518	128	19	0	3	0.6	48	42	20	50	9	1	0	250	486	25	109	4.8	.967	SS-157
1993	126	.238	.313	416	99	20	1	3	0.7	44	45	15	38	5	1	0	193	362	14	77	4.5	.975	SS-126
1994	112	.260	.329	389	101	14	2	3	0.8	53	33	18	28	3	2	1	160	359	9	66	4.7	.983	SS-110
6 yrs.	433	.242	.305	1437	348	56	4	9	0.6	158	123	59	130	18	5	1	649	1309	56	266	4.7	.972	SS-418, 2B-10, 3B-2

Year	Team	Games	BA	SA	AB	H	2B	3B	HR	HR%	R	RBI	BB	SO	SB	Pinch Hit AB	Pinch Hit H	PO	A	E	DP	TC/G	FA	G by Pos

Chris Donnels

DONNELS, CHRIS BARTON
B. Apr. 21, 1966, Los Angeles, Calif.   BL TR 6'   185 lbs.

1991	NY N	37	.225	.247	89	20	2	0	0	0.0	7	5	14	19	1	13	1	131	34	2	13	4.5	.988	1B-15, 3B-11
1992		45	.174	.207	121	21	4	0	0	0.0	8	6	17	25	1	4	0	34	77	5	6	2.6	.957	3B-29, 2B-12
1993	HOU N	88	.257	.391	179	46	14	2	2	1.1	18	24	19	33	2	34	7	169	54	8	21	2.6	.965	3B-31, 1B-23, 2B-1
1994		54	.267	.430	86	23	5	0	3	3.5	12	5	13	18	1	30	8	42	27	0	5	1.3	1.000	3B-14, 1B-4, 2B-4
4 yrs.		224	.232	.324	475	110	25	2	5	1.1	45	40	63	95	5	81	16	376	192	15	45	2.6	.974	3B-85, 1B-42, 2B-17

Brian Dorsett

DORSETT, BRIAN RICHARD
B. Apr. 9, 1961, Terre Haute, Ind.   BR TR 6'3"   215 lbs.

1987	CLE A	5	.273	.545	11	3	0	0	1	9.1	2	3	0	3	0	2	1	12	0	0	0	2.4	1.000	C-4
1988	CAL A	7	.091	.091	11	1	0	0	0	0.0	0	2	1	5	0	0	0	19	3	0	1	3.1	1.000	C-7
1989	NY A	8	.364	.409	22	8	1	0	0	0.0	3	4	1	3	0	0	0	29	3	0	1	4.0	1.000	C-8
1990		14	.143	.200	35	5	2	0	0	0.0	2	0	2	4	0	2	0	31	0	0	1	2.2	1.000	C-9, DH-5
1991	SD N	11	.083	.083	12	1	0	0	0	0.0	0	1	0	3	0	10	1	4	1	0	0	0.5	1.000	1B-2
1993	CIN N	25	.254	.413	63	16	4	0	2	3.2	7	12	3	14	0	8	2	119	5	0	0	5.0	1.000	C-18, 1B-3
1994		76	.245	.352	216	53	8	0	5	2.3	21	26	21	33	0	8	3	413	34	4	2	5.9	.991	C-73, 1B-1
7 yrs.		146	.235	.341	370	87	15	0	8	2.2	35	48	28	65	0	30	7	627	46	4	5	4.6	.994	C-119, 1B-6, DH-5

Rob Ducey

DUCEY, ROBERT THOMAS
B. May 24, 1965, Toronto, Ont., Canada.   BL TR 6'2"   175 lbs.

1987	TOR A	34	.188	.271	48	9	1	0	1	2.1	12	6	8	10	2	3	1	31	0	0	0	0.9	1.000	OF-28
1988		27	.315	.426	54	17	4	1	0	0.0	15	6	5	7	1	0	0	35	1	0	0	1.3	1.000	OF-26
1989		41	.211	.263	76	16	4	0	0	0.0	5	7	9	25	2	6	0	56	3	0	2	1.4	1.000	OF-35, DH-1
1990		19	.302	.396	53	16	5	0	0	0.0	7	7	7	15	1	0	0	37	0	0	0	1.9	1.000	OF-19
1991		39	.235	.368	68	16	2	2	1	1.5	8	4	6	26	2	14	3	32	1	4	0	0.9	.892	OF-24, DH-2
1992	2 teams		TOR A	(23G – .048)		CAL A		(31G – .237)																
"	total	54	.188	.238	80	15	4	0	0	0.0	7	2	5	22	2	10	3	43	2	0	0	0.9	.957	OF-33, DH-5
1993	TEX A	27	.282	.494	85	24	6	3	2	2.4	15	9	10	17	2	1	1	51	1	0	0	1.9	1.000	OF-26
1994		11	.172	.207	29	5	1	0	0	0.0	1	1	2	1	0	1	0	15	0	2	0	1.5	.882	OF-10
8 yrs.		252	.239	.343	493	118	27	6	4	0.8	70	42	52	123	12	35	8	300	8	8	2	1.3	.975	OF-201, DH-8

LEAGUE CHAMPIONSHIP SERIES

| 1991 | TOR A | 1 | 1.000 | .000 | 1 | 0 | 0 | 0 | 0 | 0.0 | 0 | 0 | 0 | 0 | 0 | 0 | 0 | 0 | 0 | 0 | 0 | 0.0 | – | OF-1 |

Mariano Duncan

DUNCAN, MARIANO
Born Mariano Duncan (Nolasco).
B. Mar. 13, 1963, San Pedro de Macoris, Dominican Republic.   BR TR 6'   165 lbs.
                                                                           BB 1985-87

1985	LA N	142	.244	.340	562	137	24	6	6	1.1	74	39	38	113	38	2	1	224	430	30	64	4.8	.956	SS-123, 2B-19
1986		109	.229	.305	407	93	7	0	8	2.0	47	30	30	78	48	2	0	172	317	25	46	4.7	.951	SS-106
1987		76	.215	.322	261	56	8	1	6	2.3	31	18	17	62	·11	1	0	101	213	21	40	4.4	.937	SS-67, 2B-7, OF-2
1989	2 teams		LA N	(49G – .250)		CIN N		(45G – .247)																
"	total	94	.248	.357	258	64	15	2	3	1.2	32	21	8	51	9	18	7	101	155	14	30	2.9	.948	SS-60, 2B-13, OF-7
1990	CIN N	125	.306	.476	435	133	22	11	10	2.3	67	55	24	67	13	5	0	265	303	18	55	4.7	.969	2B-115, SS-12, OF-1
1991		100	.258	.411	333	86	7	4	12	3.6	46	40	12	57	5	8	2	169	212	9	41	3.9	.977	2B-62, SS-32, OF-7
1992	PHI N	142	.267	.389	574	153	40	3	8	1.4	71	50	17	108	23	3	1	256	210	16	43	3.4	.967	OF-85, 2B-52, SS-42, 3B-4
1993		124	.282	.417	496	140	26	4	11	2.2	68	73	12	88	6	10	4	180	304	21	50	4.1	.958	2B-65, SS-59
1994		88	.268	.406	347	93	22	1	8	2.3	49	48	17	72	10	3	2	148	188	12	38	4.0	.966	2B-37, 3B-28, SS-19, 1B-6
9 yrs.		1000	.260	.383	3673	955	171	32	72	2.0	485	374	175	696	163	52	17	1616	2332	166	407	4.1	.960	SS-520, 2B-370, OF-82, 3B-32, 1B-6

LEAGUE CHAMPIONSHIP SERIES

1985	LA N	5	.222	.444	18	4	2	1	0	0.0	2	1	1	3	1	0	0	7	16	1	3	4.8	.958	SS-5
1990	CIN N	6	.300	.450	20	6	0	0	1	5.0	1	4	0	8	0	0	0	6	11	1	0	3.0	.944	2B-6
1993	PHI N	3	.267	.533	15	4	0	2	0	0.0	3	0	0	5	0	0	0	5	6	1	0	4.0	.917	2B-3
3 yrs.		14	.264	.472	53	14	2	3	1	1.9	6	5	1	16	1	0	0	18	33	3	3	3.9	.944	2B-9, SS-5

WORLD SERIES

1990	CIN N	4	.143	.143	14	2	0	0	0	0.0	1	1	2	2	1	0	0	9	9	0	2	4.5	1.000	2B-4
1993	PHI N	6	.345	.414	29	10	0	1	0	0.0	5	2	1	7	3	0	0	11	17	1	5	4.8	.966	2B-5, DH-1
2 yrs.		10	.279	.326	43	12	0	1	0	0.0	6	3	3	9	4	0	0	20	26	1	7	4.7	.979	2B-9, DH-1

Steve Dunn

DUNN, STEVEN ROBERT
B. Apr. 18, 1970, Champaign, Ill.   BL TL 6'4"   225 lbs.

| 1994 | MIN A | 14 | .229 | .371 | 35 | 8 | 5 | 0 | 0 | 0.0 | 2 | 4 | 1 | 12 | 0 | 2 | 1 | 91 | 8 | 1 | 11 | 7.1 | .990 | 1B-12 |

Shawon Dunston

DUNSTON, SHAWON DONNELL
B. Mar. 21, 1963, Brooklyn, N.Y.   BR TR 6'1"   175 lbs.

1985	CHI N	74	.260	.388	250	65	12	4	4	1.6	40	18	19	42	11	0	0	144	248	17	39	5.5	.958	SS-73
1986		150	.250	.410	581	145	36	3	17	2.9	66	68	21	114	13	2	1	320	465	32	96	5.4	.961	SS-149
1987		95	.246	.358	346	85	18	3	5	1.4	40	22	10	68	12	1	0	160	271	14	54	4.7	.969	SS-94
1988		155	.249	.357	575	143	23	6	9	1.6	69	56	16	108	30	3	0	257	455	20	76	4.7	.973	SS-151
1989		138	.278	.403	471	131	20	6	9	1.9	52	60	30	86	19	1	0	213	379	17	76	4.4	.972	SS-138
1990		146	.262	.426	545	143	22	8	17	3.1	73	66	15	87	25	0	0	255	392	20	77	4.6	.970	SS-144
1991		142	.260	.407	492	128	22	7	12	2.4	59	50	23	64	21	2	1	261	383	21	69	4.7	.968	SS-142
1992		18	.315	.384	73	23	3	1	0	0.0	8	2	3	13	2	0	0	28	42	1	9	3.9	.986	SS-18
1993		7	.400	.600	10	4	2	0	0	0.0	3	2	0	1	0	5	2	5	0	0	0	0.7	1.000	SS-2
1994		88	.278	.435	331	92	19	0	11	3.3	38	35	16	48	3	3	2	121	219	12	47	4.0	.966	SS-84
10 yrs.		1013	.261	.398	3674	959	177	38	84	2.3	448	379	153	631	136	17	6	1764	2854	154	543	4.7	.968	SS-995

LEAGUE CHAMPIONSHIP SERIES

| 1989 | CHI N | 5 | .316 | .316 | 19 | 6 | 0 | 0 | 0 | 0.0 | 1 | 2 | 0 | 1 | 1 | 1 | 0 | 10 | 14 | 1 | 1 | 5.0 | .960 | SS-5 |

Len Dykstra

DYKSTRA, LEONARD KYLE (Nails)
B. Feb. 10, 1963, Santa Ana, Calif.

BL TL 5'10" 160 lbs.

Year	Team	Games	BA	SA	AB	H	2B	3B	HR	HR%	R	RBI	BB	SO	SB	Pinch Hit AB	H	PO	A	E	DP	TC/G	FA	G by Pos
1985	NY N	83	.254	.331	236	60	9	3	1	0.4	40	19	30	24	15	9	3	165	6	1	2	2.1	.994	OF-74
1986		147	.295	.445	431	127	27	7	8	1.9	77	45	58	55	31	14	4	283	8	3	2	2.0	.990	OF-139
1987		132	.285	.455	431	123	37	3	10	2.3	86	43	40	67	27	18	5	239	4	3	1	1.9	.988	OF-118
1988		126	.270	.385	429	116	19	3	8	1.9	57	33	30	43	30	12	5	270	3	1	0	2.2	.996	OF-112
1989 2 teams	NY N	(56G – .270)			PHI N	(90G – .222)																		
" total		146	.237	.356	511	121	32	4	7	1.4	66	32	60	53	30	9	3	332	10	4	0	2.4	.988	OF-139
1990	PHI N	149	.325	.441	590	192	35	3	9	1.5	106	60	89	48	33	1	0	439	7	6	5	3.0	.987	OF-149
1991		63	.297	.427	246	73	13	5	3	1.2	48	12	37	20	24	1	1	167	3	4	2	2.8	.977	OF-63
1992		85	.301	.406	345	104	18	0	6	1.7	53	39	40	32	30	0	0	253	6	3	4	3.1	.989	OF-85
1993		161	.305	.482	637	194	44	6	19	3.0	143	66	129	64	37	1	0	469	2	10	0	3.0	.979	OF-160
1994		84	.273	.435	315	86	26	5	5	1.6	68	24	68	44	15	1	1	235	4	4	0	2.9	.984	OF-83
10 yrs.		1176	.287	.422	4171	1196	260	39	76	1.8	744	373	581	450	272	66	22	2852	53	39	16	2.5	.987	OF-1122

LEAGUE CHAMPIONSHIP SERIES

Year	Team	Games	BA	SA	AB	H	2B	3B	HR	HR%	R	RBI	BB	SO	SB	Pinch Hit AB	H	PO	A	E	DP	TC/G	FA	G by Pos
1986	NY N	6	.304	.565	23	7	1	1	1	4.3	3	3	2	4	1	2	1	10	0	0	0	1.7	1.000	OF-6
1988		7	.429	.857	14	6	3	0	1	7.1	6	3	4	0	0	0	0	9	0	0	0	1.3	1.000	OF-7
1993	PHI N	6	.280	.560	25	7	1	0	2	8.0	5	2	5	8	0	0	0	13	0	0	0	2.2	1.000	OF-6
3 yrs.		19	.323	.629	62	20	5	1	4	6.5	14	8	11	12	1	2	1	32	0	0	0	1.7	1.000	OF-19

WORLD SERIES

Year	Team	Games	BA	SA	AB	H	2B	3B	HR	HR%	R	RBI	BB	SO	SB	Pinch Hit AB	H	PO	A	E	DP	TC/G	FA	G by Pos
1986	NY N	7	.296	.519	27	8	0	0	2	7.4	4	3	2	7	0	1	1	14	0	0	0	2.0	1.000	OF-7
1993	PHI N	6	.348	.913	23	8	1	0	4	17.4	9	8	7	4	4	0	0	18	1	0	0	3.2	1.000	OF-6
2 yrs.		13	.320	.700	50	16	1	0	6	12.0	13	11	9	11	4	1	1	32	1	0	0	2.5	1.000	OF-13
				4th						1st														

Damion Easley

EASLEY, JACINTO DAMION
B. Nov. 11, 1969, New York, N. Y.

BR TR 5'11" 155 lbs.

Year	Team	Games	BA	SA	AB	H	2B	3B	HR	HR%	R	RBI	BB	SO	SB	Pinch Hit AB	H	PO	A	E	DP	TC/G	FA	G by Pos
1992	CAL A	47	.258	.311	151	39	5	0	1	0.7	14	12	8	26	9	4	1	30	102	5	13	2.9	.964	3B-45, SS-3
1993		73	.313	.413	230	72	13	2	2	0.9	33	22	28	35	6	3	1	111	157	6	29	3.8	.978	2B-54, 3B-14, DH-1
1994		88	.215	.329	316	68	16	1	6	1.9	41	30	29	48	4	3	1	122	178	7	34	3.5	.977	3B-47, 2B-40
3 yrs.		208	.257	.353	697	179	34	3	9	1.3	88	64	65	109	19	10	3	263	437	18	76	3.5	.975	3B-106, 2B-94, SS-3, DH-1

Jim Edmonds

EDMONDS, JAMES PATRICK
B. June 27, 1970, Fullerton, Calif.

BL TL 6'1" 190 lbs.

Year	Team	Games	BA	SA	AB	H	2B	3B	HR	HR%	R	RBI	BB	SO	SB	Pinch Hit AB	H	PO	A	E	DP	TC/G	FA	G by Pos
1993	CAL A	18	.246	.344	61	15	4	1	0	0.0	5	4	2	16	0	1	1	47	4	1	2	2.9	.981	OF-17
1994		94	.273	.377	289	79	13	1	5	1.7	35	37	30	72	4	4	0	301	20	3	10	3.4	.991	OF-77, 1B-22
2 yrs.		112	.269	.371	350	94	17	2	5	1.4	40	41	32	88	4	5	1	348	24	4	12	3.4	.989	OF-94, 1B-22

Robert Eenhoorn

EENHOORN, ROBERT
B. Feb. 9, 1968, Rotterdam, Netherlands

BR TR 6'3" 170 lbs.

Year	Team	Games	BA	SA	AB	H	2B	3B	HR	HR%	R	RBI	BB	SO	SB	Pinch Hit AB	H	PO	A	E	DP	TC/G	FA	G by Pos
1994	NY A	3	.500	.750	4	2	1	0	0	0.0	1	0	0	0	0	0	2	0	0	1	0	1	0.3	1.000	SS-3

Jim Eisenreich

EISENREICH, JAMES MICHAEL
B. Apr. 18, 1959, St. Cloud, Minn.

BL TL 5'11" 175 lbs.

Year	Team	Games	BA	SA	AB	H	2B	3B	HR	HR%	R	RBI	BB	SO	SB	Pinch Hit AB	H	PO	A	E	DP	TC/G	FA	G by Pos
1982	MIN A	34	.303	.424	99	30	6	0	2	2.0	10	9	11	13	0	3	1	72	0	2	0	2.2	.973	OF-30
1983		2	.286	.429	7	2	1	0	0	0.0	1	0	1	1	0	0	0	6	1	0	0	3.5	1.000	OF-2
1984		12	.219	.250	32	7	1	0	0	0.0	1	3	2	4	2	3	1	5	0	0	0	0.4	1.000	DH-6, OF-3
1987	KC A	44	.238	.467	105	25	8	2	4	3.8	10	21	7	13	1	15	5	0	0	0	0	0.0	–	DH-26
1988		82	.218	.282	202	44	8	1	1	0.5	26	19	6	31	9	9	1	109	0	4	0	1.4	.965	OF-64, DH-13
1989		134	.293	.448	475	139	33	7	9	1.9	64	59	37	44	27	6	2	273	4	3	0	2.1	.989	OF-123, DH-10
1990		142	.280	.397	496	139	29	7	5	1.0	61	51	42	51	12	8	4	261	6	1	3	1.9	.996	OF-138, DH-2
1991		135	.301	.392	375	113	22	3	2	0.5	47	47	20	35	5	32	7	243	12	5	12	1.9	.981	OF-105, 1B-15, DH-1
1992		113	.269	.340	353	95	13	3	2	0.6	31	28	24	36	11	27	10	180	1	1	0	1.6	.995	OF-88, DH-8
1993	PHI N	153	.318	.445	362	115	17	4	7	1.9	51	54	26	36	5	21	3	223	6	1	0	1.5	.996	OF-137, 1B-1
1994		104	.300	.421	290	87	15	4	4	1.4	42	43	33	31	6	17	4	178	4	2	2	1.8	.989	OF-93
11 yrs.		955	.285	.400	2796	796	153	31	36	1.3	344	334	209	295	78	141	38	1550	34	19	17	1.7	.988	OF-783, DH-66, 1B-16

LEAGUE CHAMPIONSHIP SERIES

Year	Team	Games	BA	SA	AB	H	2B	3B	HR	HR%	R	RBI	BB	SO	SB	Pinch Hit AB	H	PO	A	E	DP	TC/G	FA	G by Pos
1993	PHI N	6	.133	.200	15	2	1	0	0	0.0	0	1	0	2	0	1	1	6	0	0	0	1.0	1.000	OF-5

WORLD SERIES

Year	Team	Games	BA	SA	AB	H	2B	3B	HR	HR%	R	RBI	BB	SO	SB	Pinch Hit AB	H	PO	A	E	DP	TC/G	FA	G by Pos
1993	PHI N	6	.231	.346	26	6	0	0	1	3.8	3	7	2	4	0	0	0	18	0	0	0	3.0	1.000	OF-6

Kevin Elster

ELSTER, KEVIN DANIEL
B. Aug. 3, 1964, San Pedro, Calif.

BR TR 6'2" 180 lbs.

Year	Team	Games	BA	SA	AB	H	2B	3B	HR	HR%	R	RBI	BB	SO	SB	Pinch Hit AB	H	PO	A	E	DP	TC/G	FA	G by Pos
1986	NY N	19	.167	.200	30	5	1	0	0	0.0	3	0	3	8	0	0	0	16	35	2	6	2.8	.962	SS-19
1987		5	.400	.600	10	4	0	0	0	0.0	1	1	0	1	0	2	2	4	6	1	0	2.2	.909	SS-3
1988		149	.214	.313	406	87	11	1	9	2.2	41	37	35	47	2	1	0	196	345	13	61	3.7	.977	SS-148
1989		151	.231	.360	458	106	25	2	10	2.2	52	55	34	77	4	0	0	235	374	15	63	4.1	.976	SS-150
1990		92	.207	.363	314	65	20	1	9	2.9	36	45	30	54	2	0	0	159	251	17	42	4.6	.960	SS-92
1991		115	.241	.351	348	84	16	2	6	1.7	33	36	40	53	2	9	2	149	299	14	39	4.0	.970	SS-107
1992		6	.222	.222	18	4	0	0	0	0.0	0	0	0	2	0	1	0	8	10	0	3	3.0	1.000	SS-5
1994	NY A	7	.000	.000	20	0	0	0	0	0.0	0	0	1	6	0	0	0	5	27	0	7	4.6	1.000	SS-7
8 yrs.		544	.221	.339	1604	355	75	6	34	2.1	166	174	143	248	10	13	4	772	1347	62	221	4.0	.972	SS-531

LEAGUE CHAMPIONSHIP SERIES

Year	Team	Games	BA	SA	AB	H	2B	3B	HR	HR%	R	RBI	BB	SO	SB	Pinch Hit AB	H	PO	A	E	DP	TC/G	FA	G by Pos
1986	NY N	4	.000	.000	3	0	0	0	0	0.0	0	0	0	1	0	0	0	2	3	0	1	1.3	1.000	SS-4
1988		5	.250	.375	8	2	1	0	0	0.0	1	1	3	0	0	0	0	7	7	2	2	3.2	.875	SS-5
2 yrs.		9	.182	.273	11	2	1	0	0	0.0	1	1	3	1	0	0	0	9	10	2	2	2.3	.905	SS-9

WORLD SERIES

Year	Team	Games	BA	SA	AB	H	2B	3B	HR	HR%	R	RBI	BB	SO	SB	Pinch Hit AB	H	PO	A	E	DP	TC/G	FA	G by Pos
1986	NY N	1	.000	.000	1	0	0	0	0	0.0	0	0	0	0	0	0	0	3	3	1	1	7.0	.857	SS-1

Year Team	Games	BA	SA	AB	H	2B	3B	HR	HR%	R	RBI	BB	SO	SB	Pinch Hit AB	Pinch Hit H	PO	A	E	DP	TC/G	FA	G by Pos

Alvaro Espinoza

ESPINOZA, ALVARO ALBERTO
Born Alvaro Alberto Espinoza (Ramirez).
B. Feb. 19, 1962, Valencia, Venezuela.
BR TR 6' 160 lbs.

Year Team	Games	BA	SA	AB	H	2B	3B	HR	HR%	R	RBI	BB	SO	SB	PH AB	PH H	PO	A	E	DP	TC/G	FA	G by Pos
1984 MIN A	1	–	–	0	0	0	0	0	–	0	0	0	0	0	0	0	0	0	0	0	0.0	–	SS-1
1985	32	.263	.298	57	15	2	0	0	0.0	5	9	1	9	0	0	0	25	69	5	15	3.1	.949	SS-31
1986	37	.214	.238	42	9	1	0	0	0.0	4	1	1	10	0	1	0	23	52	4	11	2.1	.949	2B-19, SS-18
1988 NY A	3	.000	.000	3	0	0	0	0	0.0	0	0	0	0	0	0	0	5	2	0	1	2.3	1.000	2B-2, SS-1
1989	146	.282	.332	503	142	23	1	0	0.0	51	41	14	60	3	0	0	237	471	22	114	5.0	.970	SS-146
1990	150	.224	.274	438	98	12	2	2	0.5	31	20	16	54	1	0	0	268	447	17	100	4.9	.977	SS-150
1991	148	.256	.344	480	123	23	2	5	1.0	51	33	16	57	4	1	0	225	441	21	113	4.6	.969	SS-147, 3B-2, P-1
1993 CLE A	129	.278	.380	263	73	15	0	4	1.5	34	27	8	36	2	9	3	66	157	12	24	1.8	.949	3B-99, SS-35, 2B-2
1994	90	.238	.307	231	55	13	0	1	0.4	27	19	6	33	1	1	0	93	209	10	42	3.5	.968	3B-37, SS-36, 2B-20, 1B-3
9 yrs.	736	.255	.322	2017	515	89	5	12	0.6	203	150	62	259	11	12	3	942	1848	91	420	3.9	.968	SS-565, 3B-138, 2B-43, 1B-3, P-1

Tony Eusebio

EUSEBIO, RAUL ANTONIO
Born Raul Antonio Bare (Eusebio).
B. Apr. 27, 1967, San Jose de Los Llamos, Dominican Republic.
BR TR 6'2" 180 lbs.

Year Team	Games	BA	SA	AB	H	2B	3B	HR	HR%	R	RBI	BB	SO	SB	PH AB	PH H	PO	A	E	DP	TC/G	FA	G by Pos
1991 HOU N	10	.105	.158	19	2	1	0	0	0.0	4	0	6	8	0	1	0	49	4	1	0	5.4	.981	C-9
1994	55	.296	.459	159	47	9	1	5	3.1	18	30	8	33	0	3	1	263	24	2	1	5.3	.993	C-52
2 yrs.	65	.275	.427	178	49	10	1	5	2.8	22	30	14	41	0	4	1	312	28	3	1	5.3	.991	C-61

Carl Everett

EVERETT, CARL EDWARD
B. June 3, 1970, Tampa, Fla.
BB TR 6' 180 lbs.

Year Team	Games	BA	SA	AB	H	2B	3B	HR	HR%	R	RBI	BB	SO	SB	PH AB	PH H	PO	A	E	DP	TC/G	FA	G by Pos
1993 FLA N	11	.105	.105	19	2	0	0	0	0.0	0	1	1	9	1	3	0	6	0	1	0	0.6	.857	OF-8
1994	16	.216	.353	51	11	1	0	2	3.9	7	6	3	15	4	1	0	28	2	0	0	1.9	1.000	OF-16
2 yrs.	27	.186	.286	70	13	1	0	2	2.9	7	6	4	24	5	4	0	34	2	1	0	1.4	.973	OF-24

Jorge Fabregas

FABREGAS, JORGE
B. Mar. 13, 1970, Miami, Fla.
BL TR 6'3" 205 lbs.

Year Team	Games	BA	SA	AB	H	2B	3B	HR	HR%	R	RBI	BB	SO	SB	PH AB	PH H	PO	A	E	DP	TC/G	FA	G by Pos
1994 CAL A	43	.283	.307	127	36	3	0	0	0.0	12	16	7	18	2	7	3	217	16	3	1	5.5	.987	C-41

Rikkert Faneyte

FANEYTE, RIKKERT
B. May 31, 1969, Amsterdam, Netherlands
BR TR 6' 170 lbs.

Year Team	Games	BA	SA	AB	H	2B	3B	HR	HR%	R	RBI	BB	SO	SB	PH AB	PH H	PO	A	E	DP	TC/G	FA	G by Pos
1993 SF N	7	.133	.133	15	2	0	0	0	0.0	2	0	2	4	0	1	0	10	0	0	0	1.4	1.000	OF-6
1994	19	.115	.231	26	3	3	0	0	0.0	2	4	3	11	0	12	1	9	0	1	0	0.5	.900	OF-6
2 yrs.	26	.122	.195	41	5	3	0	0	0.0	4	4	5	15	0	13	1	19	0	1	0	0.8	.950	OF-12

Mike Felder

FELDER, MICHAEL OTIS
B. Nov. 18, 1961, Vallejo, Calif.
BB TR 5'8" 160 lbs.

Year Team	Games	BA	SA	AB	H	2B	3B	HR	HR%	R	RBI	BB	SO	SB	PH AB	PH H	PO	A	E	DP	TC/G	FA	G by Pos
1985 MIL A	15	.196	.214	56	11	1	0	0	0.0	8	0	5	6	4	1	1	32	1	0	0	2.2	1.000	OF-14
1986	44	.239	.323	155	37	2	4	1	0.6	24	13	13	16	16	0	0	98	0	0	0	2.2	1.000	OF-42, DH-1
1987	108	.266	.353	289	77	5	7	2	0.7	48	31	28	23	34	7	1	190	10	5	3	1.9	.976	OF-99, DH-3, 2B-1
1988	50	.173	.185	81	14	1	0	0	0.0	14	5	0	11	8	2	0	40	1	1	0	0.8	.976	OF-28, DH-16, 2B-1
1989	117	.241	.324	315	76	11	3	3	1.0	50	23	23	38	26	7	3	203	24	4	7	2.0	.983	OF-93, DH-11, 2B-10
1990	121	.274	.359	237	65	7	2	3	1.3	38	27	22	17	20	8	1	167	9	5	6	1.5	.972	OF-107, 2B-1, 3B-1, DH-1
1991 SF N	132	.264	.328	348	92	10	6	0	0.0	51	18	30	31	21	36	10	193	10	4	3	1.6	.981	OF-109, 3B-3, 2B-1
1992	145	.286	.382	322	92	13	3	4	1.2	44	23	21	29	14	49	11	159	3	1	0	1.1	.994	OF-105, 2B-3
1993 SEA A	109	.211	.269	342	72	7	5	1	0.3	31	20	22	34	15	23	3	143	12	2	1	1.4	.987	OF-95, DH-6, 3B-2
1994 HOU N	58	.239	.291	117	28	2	2	0	0.0	10	13	4	12	3	27	5	36	2	1	0	0.7	.974	OF-32
10 yrs.	899	.249	.322	2262	564	59	32	14	0.6	318	173	168	217	161	160	35	1261	72	23	20	1.5	.983	OF-724, DH-38, 2B-17, 3B-6

Junior Felix

FELIX, JUNIOR FRANCISCO
Born Junior Francisco Felix (Sanchez).
B. Oct. 3, 1967, Laguna Salada, Dominican Republic.
BB TR 6' 170 lbs.

Year Team	Games	BA	SA	AB	H	2B	3B	HR	HR%	R	RBI	BB	SO	SB	PH AB	PH H	PO	A	E	DP	TC/G	FA	G by Pos
1989 TOR A	110	.258	.395	415	107	14	8	9	2.2	62	46	33	101	18	2	0	243	9	9	0	2.4	.966	OF-107, DH-2
1990	127	.263	.441	463	122	23	7	15	3.2	73	65	45	99	13	2	0	244	11	9	3	2.1	.966	OF-125, DH-1
1991 CAL A	66	.283	.370	230	65	10	2	2	0.9	32	26	11	55	7	1	0	126	1	3	0	2.0	.977	OF-65
1992	139	.246	.361	509	125	22	5	9	1.8	63	72	33	128	8	7	1	340	9	6	3	2.6	.983	OF-128, DH-8
1993 FLA N	57	.238	.397	214	51	11	1	7	3.3	25	22	10	50	2	5	1	91	3	6	0	1.8	.940	OF-52
1994 DET A	86	.306	.525	301	92	25	1	13	4.3	54	49	26	76	1	4	0	188	4	4	0	2.3	.980	OF-81, DH-2
6 yrs.	585	.264	.413	2132	562	105	24	55	2.6	309	280	158	509	49	21	2	1232	37	37	6	2.2	.972	OF-558, DH-13
LEAGUE CHAMPIONSHIP SERIES																							
1989 TOR A	3	.273	.364	11	3	1	0	0	0.0	0	3	0	2	0	0	0	8	0	0	0	2.7	1.000	OF-3

Felix Fermin

FERMIN, FELIX JOSE
Born Felix Jose Fermin (Minaya).
B. Oct. 9, 1963, Mao Valverde, Dominican Republic.
BR TR 5'11" 160 lbs.

Year Team	Games	BA	SA	AB	H	2B	3B	HR	HR%	R	RBI	BB	SO	SB	PH AB	PH H	PO	A	E	DP	TC/G	FA	G by Pos
1987 PIT N	23	.250	.250	68	17	0	0	0	0.0	6	4	4	9	0	0	0	36	62	2	13	4.3	.980	SS-23
1988	43	.276	.322	87	24	0	2	0	0.0	9	2	8	10	3	1	0	51	76	6	14	3.1	.955	SS-43
1989 CLE A	156	.238	.260	484	115	9	1	0	0.0	50	21	41	27	6	0	0	253	517	26	84	5.1	.967	SS-153, 2B-2
1990	148	.256	.304	414	106	13	2	1	0.2	47	40	26	22	3	0	0	214	423	16	81	4.4	.975	SS-147, 2B-1
1991	129	.262	.302	424	111	13	2	0	0.0	30	31	26	27	5	0	0	214	372	12	74	4.6	.980	SS-129
1992	79	.270	.321	215	58	7	2	0	0.0	27	13	18	10	0	2	1	78	168	8	42	3.2	.969	SS-55, 3B-17, 2B-7, 1B-2
1993	140	.263	.317	480	126	16	2	2	0.4	48	45	24	14	4	0	0	211	346	23	87	4.1	.960	SS-140
1994 SEA A	101	.317	.380	379	120	21	0	1	0.3	52	35	11	22	4	0	0	168	251	10	57	4.2	.977	SS-77, 2B-25
8 yrs.	819	.265	.310	2551	677	79	11	4	0.2	269	191	158	141	25	3	1	1225	2215	103	452	4.3	.971	SS-767, 2B-35, 3B-17, 1B-2

Year Team	Games	BA	SA	AB	H	2B	3B	HR	HR%	R	RBI	BB	SO	SB	Pinch Hit AB	Pinch Hit H	PO	A	E	DP	TC/G	FA	G by Pos

Tony Fernandez

FERNANDEZ, OCTAVIO ANTONIO
Born Octavio Antonio Fernando (Castro).
B. June 30, 1962, San Pedro de Macoris, Dominican Republic.

BB TR 6'1" 160 lbs.

Year Team	Games	BA	SA	AB	H	2B	3B	HR	HR%	R	RBI	BB	SO	SB	AB	H	PO	A	E	DP	TC/G	FA	G by Pos
1983 TOR A	15	.265	.353	34	9	1	1	0	0.0	5	2	2	2	0	2	1	16	17	0	6	2.2	1.000	SS-13, DH-1
1984	88	.270	.356	233	63	5	3	3	1.3	29	19	17	15	5	6	1	119	195	9	41	3.7	.972	SS-73, 3B-10, DH-1
1985	161	.289	.390	564	163	31	10	2	0.4	71	51	43	41	13	3	1	283	478	30	109	4.9	.962	SS-160
1986	163	.310	.428	687	213	33	9	10	1.5	91	65	27	52	25	1	1	294	445	13	103	4.6	.983	SS-163
1987	146	.322	.426	578	186	29	8	5	0.9	90	67	51	48	32	1	0	270	396	14	88	4.7	.979	SS-146
1988	154	.287	.386	648	186	41	4	5	0.8	76	70	45	65	15	0	0	247	470	14	106	4.7	.981	SS-154
1989	140	.257	.389	573	147	25	9	11	1.9	64	64	29	51	22	0	0	260	475	6	93	5.3	.992	SS-140
1990	161	.276	.391	635	175	27	17	4	0.6	84	66	71	70	26	0	0	297	480	9	93	4.9	.989	SS-161
1991 SD N	145	.272	.360	558	152	27	5	4	0.7	81	38	55	74	23	2	0	247	440	20	78	4.9	.972	SS-145
1992	155	.275	.359	622	171	32	4	4	0.6	84	37	56	62	20	0	0	240	406	11	65	4.2	.983	SS-154
1993 2 teams		NY N	(48G – .225)		TOR A	(94G – .306)																	
" total	142	.279	.394	526	147	23	11	5	1.0	65	64	56	45	21	0	0	279	410	13	90	4.9	.981	SS-142
1994 CIN N	104	.279	.426	366	102	18	6	8	2.2	50	50	44	40	12	5	1	67	194	4	13	2.5	.985	3B-93, SS-9, 2B-5
12 yrs.	1574	.285	.392	6024	1714	292	87	61	1.0	790	593	496	565	214	20	5	2619	4406	143	885	4.6	.980	SS-1460, 3B-103, 2B-5, DH-2

LEAGUE CHAMPIONSHIP SERIES

Year Team	Games	BA	SA	AB	H	2B	3B	HR	HR%	R	RBI	BB	SO	SB	AB	H	PO	A	E	DP	TC/G	FA	G by Pos
1985 TOR A	7	.333	.417	24	8	2	0	0	0.0	2	2	1	2	0	0	0	11	14	2	2	3.9	.926	SS-7
1989	5	.350	.500	20	7	3	0	0	0.0	6	1	1	2	5	0	0	9	15	0	3	4.8	1.000	SS-5
1993	6	.318	.318	22	7	0	0	0	0.0	1	1	2	4	0	0	0	12	8	0	5	3.3	1.000	SS-6
3 yrs.	18	.333	.409	66	22	5	0	0	0.0	9	4	4	8	5	0	0	32	37	2	10	3.9	.972	SS-18

WORLD SERIES

Year Team	Games	BA	SA	AB	H	2B	3B	HR	HR%	R	RBI	BB	SO	SB	AB	H	PO	A	E	DP	TC/G	FA	G by Pos
1993 TOR A	6	.333	.381	21	7	1	0	0	0.0	2	9	3	3	0	0	0	11	8	0	4	3.2	1.000	SS-6

Cecil Fielder

FIELDER, CECIL GRANT
B. Sept. 21, 1963, Los Angeles, Calif.

BR TR 6'3" 230 lbs.

Year Team	Games	BA	SA	AB	H	2B	3B	HR	HR%	R	RBI	BB	SO	SB	AB	H	PO	A	E	DP	TC/G	FA	G by Pos
1985 TOR A	30	.311	.527	74	23	4	0	4	5.4	6	16	6	16	0	4	1	171	17	4	21	6.4	.979	1B-25
1986	34	.157	.325	83	13	2	0	4	4.8	7	13	6	27	0	9	1	37	4	1	3	1.2	.976	DH-22, 1B-7, 3B-2, OF-1
1987	82	.269	.560	175	47	7	1	14	8.0	30	32	20	48	0	19	4	98	6	0	12	1.3	1.000	DH-55, 1B-16, 3B-2
1988	74	.230	.431	174	40	6	1	9	5.2	24	23	14	53	0	21	5	101	12	1	10	1.5	.991	DH-50, 1B-17, 3B-3, 2B-2
1990 DET A	159	.277	.592	573	159	25	1	51	8.9	104	132	90	182	0	3	0	1190	111	14	137	8.3	.989	1B-143, DH-15
1991	162	.261	.513	624	163	25	0	44	7.1	102	133	78	151	0	0	0	1055	83	8	110	7.1	.993	1B-122, DH-42
1992	155	.244	.458	594	145	22	0	35	5.9	80	124	73	151	0	0	0	957	92	10	98	6.8	.991	1B-114, DH-43
1993	154	.267	.464	573	153	23	0	30	5.2	80	117	90	125	0	1	0	971	78	10	84	6.9	.991	1B-119, DH-36
1994	109	.259	.504	425	110	16	2	28	6.6	67	90	50	110	0	0	0	887	108	7	72	9.2	.993	1B-102, DH-7
9 yrs.	959	.259	.501	3295	853	130	5	219	6.6	500	680	427	863	0	57	11	5467	511	55	547	6.3	.991	1B-665, DH-270, 3B-7, 2B-2, OF-1

LEAGUE CHAMPIONSHIP SERIES

Year Team	Games	BA	SA	AB	H	2B	3B	HR	HR%	R	RBI	BB	SO	SB	AB	H	PO	A	E	DP	TC/G	FA	G by Pos
1985 TOR A	3	.333	.667	3	1	1	0	0	0.0	0	0	0	1	0	3	1	0	0	0	0	0.0	–	

Steve Finley

FINLEY, STEVEN ALLEN
B. May 12, 1965, Paducah, Tenn.

BL TL 6'2" 175 lbs.

Year Team	Games	BA	SA	AB	H	2B	3B	HR	HR%	R	RBI	BB	SO	SB	AB	H	PO	A	E	DP	TC/G	FA	G by Pos
1989 BAL A	81	.249	.318	217	54	5	2	2	0.9	35	25	15	30	17	5	1	144	1	2	0	1.8	.986	OF-76, DH-3
1990	142	.256	.328	464	119	16	4	3	0.6	46	37	32	53	22	12	0	298	4	7	1	2.2	.977	OF-133, DH-2
1991 HOU N	159	.285	.406	596	170	28	10	8	1.3	84	54	42	65	34	9	2	323	13	5	2	2.1	.985	OF-153
1992	162	.292	.407	607	177	29	13	5	0.8	84	55	58	63	44	2	0	418	8	3	3	2.6	.993	OF-160
1993	142	.266	.385	545	145	15	13	8	1.5	69	44	28	65	19	3	2	329	12	4	4	2.4	.988	OF-140
1994	94	.276	.434	373	103	16	13	11	2.9	64	33	28	52	13	2	0	214	9	4	0	2.4	.982	OF-92
6 yrs.	780	.274	.386	2802	768	109	47	37	1.3	382	248	203	328	149	33	5	1726	47	25	10	2.3	.986	OF-754, DH-5

John Flaherty

FLAHERTY, JOHN TIMOTHY
B. Oct. 21, 1967, New York, N. Y.

BR TR 6'1" 195 lbs.

Year Team	Games	BA	SA	AB	H	2B	3B	HR	HR%	R	RBI	BB	SO	SB	AB	H	PO	A	E	DP	TC/G	FA	G by Pos
1992 BOS A	35	.197	.227	66	13	2	0	0	0.0	3	2	3	7	0	1	0	102	7	2	3	3.2	.982	C-34
1993	13	.120	.200	25	3	2	0	0	0.0	3	2	2	6	0	0	0	35	9	0	0	3.4	1.000	C-13
1994 DET A	34	.150	.175	40	6	1	0	0	0.0	2	4	1	11	0	1	0	78	9	0	0	2.6	1.000	C-33, DH-1
3 yrs.	82	.168	.206	131	22	5	0	0	0.0	8	8	6	24	0	2	0	215	25	2	2	3.0	.992	C-80, DH-1

Darrin Fletcher

FLETCHER, DARRIN GLEN
Son of Tom Fletcher.
B. Oct. 3, 1966, Elmhurst, Ill.

BL TR 6'2" 195 lbs.

Year Team	Games	BA	SA	AB	H	2B	3B	HR	HR%	R	RBI	BB	SO	SB	AB	H	PO	A	E	DP	TC/G	FA	G by Pos
1989 LA N	5	.500	.875	8	4	0	0	1	12.5	1	2	1	0	0	2	1	16	1	0	0	3.4	1.000	C-5
1990 2 teams		LA N	(2G – .000)		PHI N	(9G – .136)																	
" total	11	.130	.174	23	3	1	0	0	0.0	3	1	1	6	0	4	0	30	1	0	0	3.0	1.000	C-7
1991 PHI N	46	.228	.309	136	31	8	0	1	0.7	5	12	5	15	0	1	0	242	22	2	1	5.8	.992	C-45
1992 MON N	83	.243	.333	222	54	10	2	2	0.9	13	26	14	28	0	16	4	360	33	2	3	4.8	.995	C-69
1993	133	.255	.379	396	101	20	1	9	2.3	33	60	34	40	0	16	7	620	41	8	3	5.0	.988	C-127
1994	94	.260	.435	285	74	18	1	10	3.5	28	57	25	23	0	12	2	479	20	2	2	5.3	.996	C-81
6 yrs.	372	.250	.375	1070	267	57	4	23	2.1	83	158	80	112	0	51	14	1747	120	14	9	5.1	.993	C-334

Scott Fletcher

FLETCHER, SCOTT BRIAN
B. July 30, 1958, Fort Walton Beach, Fla.

BR TR 5'11" 168 lbs.

Year Team	Games	BA	SA	AB	H	2B	3B	HR	HR%	R	RBI	BB	SO	SB	AB	H	PO	A	E	DP	TC/G	FA	G by Pos
1981 CHI N	19	.217	.304	46	10	4	0	0	0.0	6	1	2	4	0	0	0	34	44	3	10	4.3	.963	2B-13, SS-4, 3B-1
1982	11	.167	.167	24	4	0	0	0	0.0	4	1	4	5	1	0	0	11	23	0	3	3.1	1.000	SS-11
1983 CHI A	114	.237	.370	262	62	16	5	3	1.1	42	31	29	22	5	0	0	126	308	16	64	3.9	.964	SS-100, 2B-12, 3B-7, DH-1
1984	149	.250	.311	456	114	13	3	3	0.7	46	35	46	46	10	0	0	234	439	19	89	4.6	.973	SS-134, 2B-28, 3B-3
1985	119	.256	.309	301	77	8	1	2	0.7	38	31	35	47	5	12	3	123	208	8	36	2.8	.976	3B-55, SS-44, 2B-37, DH-2

Year Team	Games	BA	SA	AB	H	2B	3B	HR	HR%	R	RBI	BB	SO	SB	Pinch Hit AB	Pinch Hit H	PO	A	E	DP	TC/G	FA	G by Pos

Scott Fletcher *continued*

Year Team	Games	BA	SA	AB	H	2B	3B	HR	HR%	R	RBI	BB	SO	SB	AB	H	PO	A	E	DP	TC/G	FA	G by Pos
1986 TEX A	147	.300	.400	530	159	34	5	3	0.6	82	50	47	59	12	0	0	216	388	16	93	4.2	.974	SS-136, 3B-12, 2B-11, DH-1
1987	156	.287	.374	588	169	28	4	5	0.9	82	63	61	66	13	3	1	249	413	23	98	4.4	.966	SS-155
1988	140	.276	.328	515	142	19	4	0	0.0	59	47	62	34	8	2	0	215	414	11	90	4.6	.983	SS-139
1989 2 teams		TEX A	(83G – .239)		CHI A	(59G – .272)																	
" total	142	.253	.311	546	138	25	2	1	0.2	77	43	64	60	2	1	0	241	362	15	88	4.4	.976	SS-89, 2B-53, DH-1
1990 CHI A	151	.242	.312	509	123	18	3	4	0.8	54	56	45	63	1	0	0	305	436	9	115	5.0	.988	2B-151
1991	90	.206	.266	248	51	10	1	1	0.4	14	28	17	26	0	6	2	178	192	3	49	4.1	.992	2B-86, 3B-4
1992 MIL A	123	.275	.360	386	106	18	3	3	0.8	53	51	30	33	17	4	0	236	382	9	84	5.1	.986	2B-106, SS-22, 3B-1
1993 BOS A	121	.285	.402	480	137	31	5	5	1.0	81	45	37	35	16	4	0	217	371	11	68	5.0	.982	2B-116, SS-2, 3B-1, DH-1
1994	63	.227	.335	185	42	9	1	3	1.6	31	16	16	14	8	2	0	118	163	1	40	4.5	.996	2B-54, DH-4
14 yrs.	1545	.263	.343	5076	1334	233	37	33	0.7	669	493	495	514	98	34	6	2503	4143	144	927	4.4	.979	SS-836, 2B-667, 3B-84, DH-10

LEAGUE CHAMPIONSHIP SERIES

Year Team	Games	BA	SA	AB	H	2B	3B	HR	HR%	R	RBI	BB	SO	SB	AB	H	PO	A	E	DP	TC/G	FA	G by Pos
1983 CHI A	3	1.000	.000	7	0	0	0	0	0.0	0	1	0	0	0	0	0	3	8	0	1	3.7	1.000	SS-3

Cliff Floyd

FLOYD, CORNELIUS CLIFFORD
B. Dec. 5, 1972, Chicago, Ill.

BL TL 6'5" 220 lbs.

Year Team	Games	BA	SA	AB	H	2B	3B	HR	HR%	R	RBI	BB	SO	SB	AB	H	PO	A	E	DP	TC/G	FA	G by Pos
1993 MON N	10	.226	.323	31	7	0	1	1	3.2	3	2	0	9	0	2	0	79	4	0	5	8.3	1.000	1B-10
1994	100	.281	.398	334	94	19	4	4	1.2	43	41	24	63	10	6	3	565	41	6	43	6.1	.990	1B-77, OF-26
2 yrs.	110	.277	.392	365	101	19	4	5	1.4	46	43	24	72	10	8	3	644	45	6	48	6.3	.991	1B-87, OF-26

Tom Foley

FOLEY, THOMAS MICHAEL
B. Sept. 9, 1959, Fort Benning, Ga.

BL TR 6'1" 160 lbs.

Year Team	Games	BA	SA	AB	H	2B	3B	HR	HR%	R	RBI	BB	SO	SB	AB	H	PO	A	E	DP	TC/G	FA	G by Pos
1983 CIN N	68	.204	.265	98	20	4	1	0	0.0	7	9	13	17	1	20	4	54	76	2	16	1.9	.985	SS-37, 2B-5
1984	106	.253	.357	277	70	8	3	5	1.8	26	27	24	36	3	13	5	119	228	11	36	3.4	.969	SS-83, 2B-10, 3B-1
1985 2 teams		CIN N	(43G – .196)		PHI N	(46G – .266)																	
" total	89	.240	.336	250	60	13	1	3	1.2	24	23	19	34	2	12	4	127	202	7	47	3.8	.979	SS-60, 2B-18, 3B-1
1986 2 teams		PHI N	(39G – .295)		MON N	(64G – .257)																	
" total	103	.266	.357	263	70	15	3	1	0.4	26	23	30	37	10	22	5	117	190	6	29	3.0	.981	SS-53, 2B-26, 3B-16
1987 MON N	106	.293	.432	280	82	18	3	5	1.8	35	28	11	40	6	24	5	134	190	9	43	3.1	.973	SS-49, 2B-39, 3B-9
1988	127	.265	.377	377	100	21	3	5	1.3	33	43	30	49	2	14	1	204	324	15	61	4.3	.972	2B-89, SS-32, 3B-9
1989	122	.229	.347	375	86	19	3	7	1.9	34	39	45	53	2	12	2	203	317	8	58	4.3	.985	2B-108, 3B-16, SS-14, P-1
1990	73	.213	.238	164	35	2	1	0	0.0	11	12	12	22	0	10	1	80	123	5	26	2.8	.976	SS-45, 2B-20, 3B-7, 1B-1
1991	86	.208	.286	168	35	11	1	0	0.0	12	15	14	30	2	14	3	200	93	6	23	3.5	.980	SS-43, 1B-31, 3B-6, 2B-2
1992	72	.174	.217	115	20	3	1	0	0.0	7	5	8	21	3	11	3	74	97	5	20	2.4	.972	SS-33, 2B-13, 1B-12, 3B-4, OF-1
1993 PIT N	86	.253	.366	194	49	11	1	3	1.5	18	22	11	26	0	32	9	116	105	5	29	2.6	.978	2B-35, 1B-12, 3B-7, SS-6
1994	59	.236	.366	123	29	7	0	3	2.4	13	15	13	18	0	17	2	51	94	3	25	2.5	.980	2B-17, 3B-14, SS-8, 1B-3
12 yrs.	1097	.244	.344	2684	656	132	20	32	1.2	246	261	230	383	31	201	41	1479	2039	82	413	3.3	.977	SS-463, 2B-382, 3B-90, 1B-59, P-1, OF-1

Eric Fox

FOX, ERIC HOLLIS
B. Aug. 15, 1963, Lemoore, Calif.

BB TL 5'10" 180 lbs.

Year Team	Games	BA	SA	AB	H	2B	3B	HR	HR%	R	RBI	BB	SO	SB	AB	H	PO	A	E	DP	TC/G	FA	G by Pos
1992 OAK A	51	.238	.364	143	34	5	2	3	2.1	24	13	13	29	3	4	0	92	3	1	1	1.9	.990	OF-43, DH-3
1993	29	.143	.214	56	8	1	0	1	1.8	5	5	2	7	0	3	0	47	0	0	1	1.6	1.000	OF-26, DH-1
1994	26	.205	.318	44	9	2	0	1	2.3	7	1	3	8	2	4	1	32	1	0	0	1.3	1.000	OF-24
3 yrs.	106	.210	.321	243	51	8	2	5	2.1	36	19	18	44	5	11	1	171	4	1	2	1.7	.994	OF-93, DH-4

LEAGUE CHAMPIONSHIP SERIES

Year Team	Games	BA	SA	AB	H	2B	3B	HR	HR%	R	RBI	BB	SO	SB	AB	H	PO	A	E	DP	TC/G	FA	G by Pos
1992 OAK A	4	1.000	.000	1	0	0	0	0	0.0	0	0	1	0	2	0	0	1	0	0	0	0.3	1.000	DH-1, OF-1

Julio Franco

FRANCO, JULIO CESAR
Born Julio Cesar Robles (Franco).
B. Aug. 23, 1958, Hato Mayor, Dominican Republic.

BR TR 6' 160 lbs.

Year Team	Games	BA	SA	AB	H	2B	3B	HR	HR%	R	RBI	BB	SO	SB	AB	H	PO	A	E	DP	TC/G	FA	G by Pos
1982 PHI N	16	.276	.310	29	8	1	0	0	0.0	3	3	2	4	0	0	0	8	25	0	2	2.1	1.000	SS-11, 3B-2
1983 CLE A	149	.273	.388	560	153	24	8	8	1.4	68	80	27	50	32	0	0	247	438	28	92	4.8	.961	SS-149
1984	160	.286	.348	658	188	22	5	3	0.5	82	79	43	68	19	0	0	280	481	36	116	5.0	.955	SS-159, DH-1
1985	160	.288	.381	636	183	33	4	6	0.9	97	90	54	74	13	2	0	252	437	36	99	4.5	.950	SS-151, 2B-8, DH-1
1986	149	.306	.422	599	183	30	5	10	1.7	80	74	32	66	10	1	0	248	413	19	90	4.6	.972	SS-134, 2B-13, DH-3
1987	128	.319	.428	495	158	24	3	8	1.6	86	52	57	56	32	1	1	175	313	18	56	4.0	.964	SS-111, 2B-9, DH-8
1988	152	.303	.409	613	186	23	6	10	1.6	88	54	56	72	25	0	0	310	434	14	87	5.0	.982	2B-151, DH-1
1989 TEX A	150	.316	.462	548	173	31	5	13	2.4	80	92	66	69	21	1	1	256	386	13	70	4.4	.980	2B-140, DH-10
1990	157	.296	.402	582	172	27	1	11	1.9	96	69	82	83	31	1	1	310	444	19	101	4.9	.975	2B-152, DH-3
1991	146	.341	.474	589	201	27	3	15	2.5	108	78	65	78	36	2	1	294	372	14	80	4.7	.979	2B-146
1992	35	.234	.355	107	25	7	2	2	1.9	19	8	15	17	1	7	3	21	17	3	2	1.2	.927	DH-15, 2B-9, OF-4
1993	144	.289	.438	532	154	31	3	14	2.6	85	84	62	95	9	3	1	0	0	0	0	0.0	–	DH-140
1994 CHI A	112	.319	.510	433	138	19	2	20	4.6	72	98	62	75	8	0	0	88	7	3	9	0.9	.969	DH-99, 1B-14
13 yrs.	1658	.301	.419	6381	1922	299	45	120	1.9	964	861	623	807	237	18	8	2489	3767	203	804	3.9	.969	SS-715, 2B-628, DH-281, 1B-14, OF-4, 3B-2

Lou Frazier

FRAZIER, ARTHUR LOUIS
B. Jan. 26, 1965, St. Louis, Mo.

BB TR 6'2" 175 lbs.

Year Team	Games	BA	SA	AB	H	2B	3B	HR	HR%	R	RBI	BB	SO	SB	AB	H	PO	A	E	DP	TC/G	FA	G by Pos
1993 MON N	112	.286	.349	189	54	7	1	1	0.5	27	16	16	24	17	48	12	98	9	2	1	1.0	.982	OF-60, 1B-8, 2B-1
1994	76	.271	.307	140	38	3	1	0	0.0	25	14	18	23	20	24	5	61	4	1	1	0.9	.985	OF-36, 2B-6, 1B-1
2 yrs.	188	.280	.331	329	92	10	2	1	0.3	52	30	34	47	37	72	17	159	13	3	2	0.9	.983	OF-96, 1B-9, 2B-7

Jeff Frye

FRYE, JEFFREY DUSTIN
B. Aug. 31, 1966, Oakland, Calif.

BR TR 5'9" 180 lbs.

Year Team	Games	BA	SA	AB	H	2B	3B	HR	HR%	R	RBI	BB	SO	SB	AB	H	PO	A	E	DP	TC/G	FA	G by Pos
1992 TEX A	67	.256	.327	199	51	9	1	1	0.5	24	12	16	27	1	0	0	120	196	3	43	4.8	.978	2B-67
1994	57	.327	.454	205	67	20	3	0	0.0	37	18	29	23	6	2	1	89	135	4	28	4.0	.982	2B-54, 3B-1, DH-1
2 yrs.	124	.292	.391	404	118	29	4	1	0.2	61	30	45	50	7	2	1	209	331	11	71	4.4	.980	2B-121, 3B-1, DH-1

Travis Fryman

FRYMAN, DAVID TRAVIS
B. Mar. 25, 1969, Lexington, Ky.

BR TR 6′1″ 180 lbs.

Year Team	Games	BA	SA	AB	H	2B	3B	HR	HR%	R	RBI	BB	SO	SB	Pinch Hit AB	Pinch Hit H	PO	A	E	DP	TC/G	FA	G by Pos
1990 **DET A**	66	.297	.470	232	69	11	1	9	3.9	32	27	17	51	3	1	0	47	145	14	21	3.1	.932	3B-48, SS-17, DH-1
1991	149	.259	.447	557	144	36	3	21	3.8	65	91	40	149	12	1	1	153	354	23	61	3.6	.957	3B-86, SS-71
1992	161	.266	.416	**659**	175	31	4	20	3.0	87	96	45	144	8	0	0	219	489	22	95	4.5	.970	SS-137, 3B-26
1993	151	.300	.486	607	182	37	5	22	3.6	98	97	77	128	9	0	0	169	382	23	70	3.8	.960	SS-81, 3B-69, DH-1
1994	114	.263	.474	**464**	122	34	5	18	3.9	66	85	45	**128**	2	0	0	78	222	14	12	2.8	.955	3B-114
5 yrs.	641	.275	.455	2519	692	149	18	90	3.6	348	396	224	600	34	2	1	666	1592	96	259	3.7	.959	3B-343, SS-306, DH-2

Gary Gaetti

GAETTI, GARY JOSEPH
B. Aug. 19, 1958, Centralia, Ill.

BR TR 6′ 180 lbs.

Year Team	Games	BA	SA	AB	H	2B	3B	HR	HR%	R	RBI	BB	SO	SB	Pinch Hit AB	Pinch Hit H	PO	A	E	DP	TC/G	FA	G by Pos
1981 **MIN A**	9	.192	.423	26	5	0	0	2	7.7	4	3	0	6	0	0	0	5	17	0	1	2.4	1.000	3B-8, DH-1
1982	145	.230	.443	508	117	25	4	25	4.9	59	84	37	107	0	1	0	106	291	17	36	2.9	.959	3B-142, SS-2
1983	157	.245	.414	584	143	30	3	21	3.6	81	78	54	121	7	2	1	131	361	17	46	3.2	.967	3B-154, SS-3, DH-1
1984	162	.262	.350	588	154	29	4	5	0.9	55	65	44	81	11	0	0	163	335	21	27	3.2	.960	3B-154, OF-8, SS-2
1985	160	.246	.409	560	138	31	0	20	3.6	71	63	37	89	13	1	0	162	316	18	31	3.1	.964	3B-156, OF-4, 1B-1, DH-1
1986	157	.287	.518	596	171	34	1	34	5.7	91	108	52	108	14	1	0	120	335	21	36	3.0	.956	3B-156, SS-2, 2B-1, OF-1
1987	154	.257	.485	584	150	36	2	31	5.3	95	109	37	92	10	3	2	134	261	11	28	2.6	.973	3B-150, DH-2
1988	133	.301	.551	468	141	29	2	28	6.0	66	88	36	85	7	14	4	105	191	7	24	2.3	.977	3B-115, DH-5, SS-2
1989	130	.251	.404	498	125	11	4	19	3.8	63	75	25	87	6	3	1	115	253	10	24	2.9	.974	3B-125, DH-3, 1B-2
1990	154	.229	.376	577	132	27	5	16	2.8	61	85	36	101	6	2	0	125	319	18	36	3.0	.961	3B-151, 1B-2, SS-2
1991 **CAL A**	152	.246	.379	586	144	22	1	18	3.1	58	66	33	104	5	1	1	111	353	17	39	3.2	.965	3B-152
1992	130	.226	.342	456	103	13	2	12	2.6	41	48	21	79	3	7	2	423	196	22	53	4.9	.966	3B-67, 1B-44, DH-17
1993 **2 teams**	**CAL A** (20G – .180)			**KC A** (82G – .256)																			
" **total**	102	.245	.438	331	81	20	1	14	4.2	40	50	21	87	1	8	1	185	153	7	29	3.4	.980	3B-79, 1B-24, DH-6
1994 **KC A**	90	.287	.462	327	94	15	3	12	3.7	53	57	19	63	0	2	1	99	166	4	20	3.0	.985	3B-85, 1B-9
14 yrs.	1835	.254	.427	6689	1698	322	32	257	3.8	838	979	452	1210	83	45	13	1984	3547	190	430	3.1	.967	3B-1694, 1B-82, DH-36, OF-13, SS-13, 2B-1
LEAGUE CHAMPIONSHIP SERIES																							
1987 **MIN A**	5	.300	.650	20	6	1	0	2	10.0	5	5	1	3	0	0	0	8	7	0	1	3.0	1.000	3B-5
WORLD SERIES																							
1987 **MIN A**	7	.259	.519	27	7	2	1	1	3.7	4	4	2	5	2	0	0	6	15	0	2	3.0	1.000	3B-7

Greg Gagne

GAGNE, GREGORY CHRISTOPHER
B. Nov. 12, 1961, Fall River, Mass.

BR TR 5′11″ 175 lbs.

Year Team	Games	BA	SA	AB	H	2B	3B	HR	HR%	R	RBI	BB	SO	SB	Pinch Hit AB	Pinch Hit H	PO	A	E	DP	TC/G	FA	G by Pos
1983 **MIN A**	10	.111	.148	27	3	1	0	0	0.0	2	3	0	6	0	0	0	10	14	2	2	2.6	.923	SS-10
1984	2	.000	.000	1	0	0	0	0	0.0	0	0	0	0	0	1	0	0	0	0	0	0.0	–	
1985	114	.225	.317	293	66	15	3	2	0.7	37	23	20	57	10	4	1	149	269	14	48	3.8	.968	SS-106, DH-5
1986	156	.250	.398	472	118	22	6	12	2.5	63	54	30	108	12	0	0	228	381	26	96	4.1	.959	SS-155, 2B-4
1987	137	.265	.430	437	116	28	7	10	2.3	68	40	25	84	6	0	0	196	391	18	75	4.4	.970	SS-136, OF-4, 2B-1
1988	149	.236	.397	461	109	20	6	14	3.0	70	48	27	110	15	1	0	202	373	18	79	4.0	.970	SS-146, OF-2, 2B-1, 3B-1
1989	149	.272	.424	460	125	29	7	9	2.0	69	48	17	80	11	5	0	218	389	18	66	4.2	.971	SS-146, OF-1
1990	138	.235	.361	388	91	22	3	7	1.8	38	38	24	76	8	2	0	184	377	14	62	4.2	.976	SS-135, DH-2, OF-1
1991	139	.265	.395	408	108	23	3	8	2.0	52	42	26	72	11	2	1	181	377	9	69	4.1	.984	SS-137, DH-1
1992	146	.246	.346	439	108	23	0	7	1.6	53	39	19	83	6	1	0	208	438	18	83	4.5	.973	SS-141
1993 **KC A**	159	.280	.406	540	151	32	3	10	1.9	66	57	33	93	10	1	0	266	451	10	93	4.6	.986	SS-159
1994	107	.259	.392	375	97	23	3	7	1.9	39	51	27	79	10	0	0	189	323	12	63	4.9	.977	SS-106
12 yrs.	1406	.254	.388	4301	1092	238	41	86	2.0	557	443	248	848	99	17	2	2031	3783	159	736	4.2	.973	SS-1377, OF-8, DH-8, 2B-6, 3B-1
LEAGUE CHAMPIONSHIP SERIES																							
1987 **MIN A**	5	.278	.778	18	5	3	0	2	11.1	5	3	3	4	0	0	0	9	13	2	2	4.8	.917	SS-5
1991	5	.235	.235	17	4	0	0	0	0.0	1	1	1	5	0	0	0	9	9	2	1	4.0	.900	SS-5
2 yrs.	10	.257	.514	35	9	3	0	2	5.7	6	4	4	9	0	0	0	18	22	4	3	4.4	.909	SS-10
WORLD SERIES																							
1987 **MIN A**	7	.200	.333	30	6	1	0	1	3.3	5	3	1	6	0	0	0	6	20	2	2	4.0	.929	SS-7
1991	7	.167	.333	24	4	1	0	1	4.2	1	3	0	7	0	0	0	13	24	0	5	5.3	1.000	SS-7
2 yrs.	14	.185	.333	54	10	2	0	2	3.7	6	6	1	13	0	0	0	19	44	2	7	4.6	.969	SS-14

Andres Galarraga

GALARRAGA, ANDRES JOSE (Big Cat)
Born Andres Jose Padovani (Galarraga).
B. June 18, 1961, Caracas, Venezuela.

BR TR 6′3″ 235 lbs.

Year Team	Games	BA	SA	AB	H	2B	3B	HR	HR%	R	RBI	BB	SO	SB	Pinch Hit AB	Pinch Hit H	PO	A	E	DP	TC/G	FA	G by Pos
1985 **MON N**	24	.187	.280	75	14	1	0	2	2.7	9	4	3	18	1	2	1	173	22	1	14	8.2	.995	1B-23
1986	105	.271	.405	321	87	13	0	10	3.1	39	42	30	79	6	7	1	805	40	4	59	8.1	.995	1B-102
1987	147	.305	.459	551	168	40	3	13	2.4	72	90	41	127	7	1	0	1300	103	10	96	9.6	.993	1B-146
1988	157	.302	.540	609	**184**	**42**	8	29	4.8	99	92	39	**153**	13	2	1	1464	103	15	124	10.1	.991	1B-156
1989	152	.257	.434	572	147	30	1	23	4.0	76	85	48	**158**	12	6	1	1335	91	11	97	9.5	.992	1B-147
1990	155	.256	.409	579	148	29	0	20	3.5	65	87	40	**169**	10	7	0	1300	94	10	93	9.1	.993	1B-154
1991	107	.219	.336	375	82	13	2	9	2.4	34	33	23	86	5	2	0	887	80	9	68	9.1	.991	1B-105
1992 **STL N**	95	.243	.391	325	79	14	2	10	3.1	38	39	11	69	5	6	0	777	62	8	71	8.9	.991	1B-90
1993 **CLR N**	120	**.370**	.602	470	174	35	4	22	4.7	71	98	24	73	2	1	0	1018	103	11	88	9.4	.990	1B-119
1994	103	.319	.592	417	133	21	0	31	7.4	77	85	19	93	8	0	0	954	64	8	89	10.0	.992	1B-103
10 yrs.	1165	.283	.466	4294	1216	238	20	169	3.9	580	655	278	1025	69	34	4	10013	762	87	799	9.3	.992	1B-1145

Dave Gallagher

GALLAGHER, DAVID THOMAS
B. Sept. 20, 1960, Trenton, N. J.

BR TR 6′ 180 lbs.

Year Team	Games	BA	SA	AB	H	2B	3B	HR	HR%	R	RBI	BB	SO	SB	Pinch Hit AB	Pinch Hit H	PO	A	E	DP	TC/G	FA	G by Pos
1987 **CLE A**	15	.111	.194	36	4	1	1	0	0.0	2	1	2	5	2	0	0	34	1	1	1	2.4	.972	OF-14
1988 **CHI A**	101	.303	.406	347	105	15	3	5	1.4	59	31	29	40	5	11	2	228	5	0	2	2.3	1.000	OF-95, DH-2
1989	161	.266	.314	601	160	22	2	1	0.2	74	46	46	79	5	2	0	390	8	3	4	2.5	.993	OF-160, DH-1
1990 **2 teams**	**CHI A** (45G – .280)			**BAL A** (23G – .216)																			
" **total**	68	.254	.302	126	32	4	1	0	0.0	12	7	7	12	1	10	2	96	3	2	2	1.5	.980	OF-57, DH-6
1991 **CAL A**	90	.293	.367	270	79	17	0	1	0.4	32	30	24	43	2	11	4	180	8	0	1	2.1	1.000	OF-87, DH-2
1992 **NY N**	98	.240	.331	175	42	11	1	1	0.6	20	21	19	16	4	30	5	105	4	2	3	1.1	.982	OF-76

Year Team	Games	BA	SA	AB	H	2B	3B	HR	HR%	R	RBI	BB	SO	SB	Pinch Hit AB	Pinch Hit H	PO	A	E	DP	TC/G	FA	G by Pos

Dave Gallagher *continued*

Year Team	Games	BA	SA	AB	H	2B	3B	HR	HR%	R	RBI	BB	SO	SB	AB	H	PO	A	E	DP	TC/G	FA	G by Pos
1993	99	.274	.443	201	55	12	2	6	3.0	34	28	20	18	1	27	10	139	7	0	1	1.5	1.000	OF-72, 1B-9
1994 ATL N	89	.224	.296	152	34	5	0	2	1.3	27	14	22	17	0	21	4	93	4	1	1	1.1	.990	OF-77, 1B-1
8 yrs.	721	.268	.349	1908	511	87	10	16	0.8	260	178	169	230	20	112	27	1265	40	9	15	1.8	.993	OF-638, DH-11, 1B-10

Mike Gallego

GALLEGO, MICHAEL ANTHONY
B. Oct. 31, 1960, Whittier, Calif.

BR TR 5'8" 160 lbs.

Year Team	Games	BA	SA	AB	H	2B	3B	HR	HR%	R	RBI	BB	SO	SB	AB	H	PO	A	E	DP	TC/G	FA	G by Pos
1985 OAK A	76	.208	.338	77	16	5	1	1	1.3	13	9	12	14	1	2	0	57	94	1	25	2.0	.993	2B-42, SS-21, 3B-12
1986	20	.270	.324	37	10	2	0	0	0.0	2	4	1	6	0	0	0	24	51	1	6	3.8	.987	2B-19, 3B-2, SS-1
1987	72	.250	.347	124	31	6	0	2	1.6	18	14	12	21	0	4	1	75	122	8	29	2.8	.961	2B-31, 3B-24, SS-17
1988	129	.209	.260	277	58	8	0	2	0.7	38	20	34	53	2	3	0	155	254	8	49	3.2	.981	2B-83, SS-42, 3B-16
1989	133	.252	.328	357	90	14	2	3	0.8	45	30	35	43	7	2	0	211	363	19	84	4.5	.968	SS-94, 2B-41, 3B-3, DH-1
1990	140	.206	.272	389	80	13	2	3	0.8	36	34	35	50	5	2	1	207	379	13	78	4.3	.978	2B-83, SS-38, 3B-27, DH-1, OF-1
1991	159	.247	.369	482	119	15	4	12	2.5	67	49	67	84	6	0	0	283	446	12	90	4.7	.984	2B-135, SS-55
1992 NY A	53	.254	.358	173	44	7	1	3	1.7	24	14	20	22	0	0	0	112	153	6	41	5.1	.978	2B-40, SS-14
1993	119	.283	.412	403	114	20	1	10	2.5	63	54	50	65	3	1	0	169	368	13	76	4.6	.976	SS-55, 2B-52, 3B-27, DH-1
1994	89	.239	.359	306	73	17	2	6	2.0	39	41	38	46	0	0	0	141	311	11	69	5.2	.976	SS-72, 2B-26
10 yrs.	990	.242	.340	2625	635	107	12	42	1.6	345	269	304	404	24	14	2	1434	2541	92	549	4.1	.977	2B-552, SS-409, 3B-111, DH-3, OF-1
LEAGUE CHAMPIONSHIP SERIES																							
1988 OAK A	4	.083	.083	12	1	0	0	0	0.0	1	0	0	3	0	0	0	7	6	0	4	3.3	1.000	2B-4
1989	4	.273	.364	11	3	1	0	0	0.0	3	1	0	2	0	0	0	6	14	0	2	5.0	1.000	2B-2, SS-2
1990	4	.400	.500	10	4	1	0	0	0.0	1	2	1	1	0	0	0	8	9	0	2	4.3	1.000	SS-3, 2B-2
3 yrs.	12	.242	.303	33	8	2	0	0	0.0	5	3	1	6	0	0	0	21	29	0	8	4.2	1.000	2B-8, SS-5
WORLD SERIES																							
1988 OAK A	1	–	–	0	0	0	0	0	–	0	0	0	0	0	0	0	0	0	0	0	0.0	–	2B-1
1989	2	.000	.000	1	0	0	0	0	0.0	0	0	0	0	0	1	0	0	0	0	0	0.0	–	2B-1, 3B-1
1990	4	.091	.091	11	1	0	0	0	0.0	0	1	1	3	1	0	0	7	10	1	3	4.5	.944	SS-4
3 yrs.	7	.083	.083	12	1	0	0	0	0.0	0	1	1	3	1	1	0	7	10	1	3	2.6	.944	SS-4, 2B-2, 3B-1

Carlos Garcia

GARCIA, CARLOS JESUS
Born Carlos Jesus Garcia (Guerrero).
B. Oct. 15, 1967, Tachira, Venezuela.

BR TR 6'1" 185 lbs.

Year Team	Games	BA	SA	AB	H	2B	3B	HR	HR%	R	RBI	BB	SO	SB	AB	H	PO	A	E	DP	TC/G	FA	G by Pos
1990 PIT N	4	.500	.500	4	2	0	0	0	0.0	1	0	0	2	0	1	1	0	4	0	1	1.0	1.000	SS-3
1991	12	.250	.417	24	6	0	2	0	0.0	2	1	1	8	0	1	0	11	18	1	3	2.5	.967	SS-9, 3B-2, 2B-1
1992	22	.205	.231	39	8	1	0	0	0.0	4	4	0	9	0	3	1	25	35	2	11	2.8	.968	2B-14, SS-8
1993	141	.269	.399	546	147	25	5	12	2.2	77	47	31	67	18	2	1	299	347	11	87	4.7	.983	2B-140, SS-3
1994	98	.277	.367	412	114	15	2	6	1.5	49	28	16	67	18	0	0	226	316	12	78	5.7	.978	2B-98
5 yrs.	277	.270	.380	1025	277	41	9	18	1.8	133	80	48	153	36	7	3	561	720	26	180	4.7	.980	2B-253, SS-23, 3B-2
LEAGUE CHAMPIONSHIP SERIES																							
1992 PIT N	1	.000	.000	1	0	0	0	0	0.0	0	0	0	0	0	0	0	0	0	0	0	0.0	–	2B-1

Jeff Gardner

GARDNER, JEFFREY SCOTT
B. Feb. 4, 1964, Newport Beach, Calif.

BL TR 5'11" 165 lbs.

Year Team	Games	BA	SA	AB	H	2B	3B	HR	HR%	R	RBI	BB	SO	SB	AB	H	PO	A	E	DP	TC/G	FA	G by Pos
1991 NY N	13	.162	.162	37	6	0	0	0	0.0	3	1	4	6	0	2	1	11	29	6	2	3.5	.870	SS-8, 2B-3
1992 SD N	15	.105	.105	19	2	0	0	0	0.0	0	0	1	8	0	4	0	10	18	0	3	1.9	1.000	2B-10
1993	140	.262	.356	404	106	21	7	1	0.2	53	24	45	69	2	17	2	213	295	10	48	3.7	.981	2B-133, 3B-1, SS-1
1994 MON N	18	.219	.281	32	7	0	1	0	0.0	4	1	3	5	0	8	2	6	4	2	1	0.7	.833	3B-9, 2B-4
4 yrs.	186	.246	.327	492	121	21	8	1	0.2	60	26	53	88	2	31	5	240	346	18	54	3.2	.970	2B-150, 3B-10, SS-9

Brent Gates

GATES, BRENT ROBERT
B. Mar. 14, 1970, Grand Rapids, Mich.

BB TR 6'1" 180 lbs.

Year Team	Games	BA	SA	AB	H	2B	3B	HR	HR%	R	RBI	BB	SO	SB	AB	H	PO	A	E	DP	TC/G	FA	G by Pos
1993 OAK A	139	.290	.391	535	155	29	2	7	1.3	64	69	56	75	7	3	1	281	431	14	88	5.2	.981	2B-139
1994	64	.283	.365	233	66	11	1	2	0.9	29	24	21	32	3	2	1	112	160	8	28	4.4	.971	2B-63, 1B-1
2 yrs.	203	.288	.383	768	221	40	3	9	1.2	93	93	77	107	10	5	2	393	591	22	116	5.0	.978	2B-202, 1B-1

Kirk Gibson

GIBSON, KIRK HAROLD
B. May 28, 1957, Pontiac, Mich.

BL TL 6'3" 215 lbs.

Year Team	Games	BA	SA	AB	H	2B	3B	HR	HR%	R	RBI	BB	SO	SB	AB	H	PO	A	E	DP	TC/G	FA	G by Pos
1979 DET A	12	.237	.395	38	9	3	0	1	2.6	3	4	1	3	3	2	0	15	0	0	0	1.3	1.000	OF-10
1980	51	.263	.440	175	46	2	1	9	5.1	23	16	10	45	4	5	1	122	1	1	0	2.4	.992	OF-49, DH-1
1981	83	.328	.479	290	95	11	3	9	3.1	41	40	18	64	17	8	1	142	1	4	0	1.8	.973	OF-67, DH-9
1982	69	.278	.444	266	74	16	2	8	3.0	34	35	25	41	9	1	0	167	4	1	3	2.5	.994	OF-64, DH-4
1983	128	.227	.414	401	91	12	9	15	3.7	60	51	53	96	14	20	5	116	2	3	0	0.9	.975	DH-66, OF-54
1984	149	.282	.516	531	150	23	10	27	5.1	92	91	63	103	29	11	1	245	4	12	2	1.8	.954	OF-139, DH-6
1985	154	.287	.518	581	167	37	5	29	5.0	96	97	71	137	30	3	2	286	1	11	0	1.9	.963	OF-144, DH-8
1986	119	.268	.492	441	118	11	2	28	6.3	84	86	68	107	34	2	1	190	2	2	1	1.6	.990	OF-114, DH-4
1987	128	.277	.489	487	135	25	3	24	4.9	95	79	71	117	26	3	0	253	6	7	0	2.1	.974	OF-121, DH-4
1988 LA N	150	.290	.483	542	157	28	1	25	4.6	106	76	73	120	31	3	0	311	6	12	3	2.2	.964	OF-148
1989	71	.213	.368	253	54	8	2	9	3.6	35	28	35	55	12	2	1	146	3	3	2	2.1	.980	OF-70
1990	89	.260	.400	315	82	20	0	8	2.5	59	38	39	65	26	6	1	191	4	1	1	2.2	.995	OF-81
1991 KC A	132	.236	.403	462	109	17	6	16	3.5	81	55	69	103	18	9	2	162	3	4	1	1.3	.976	OF-94, DH-30
1992 PIT N	16	.196	.304	56	11	0	0	2	3.6	6	5	3	12	3	3	0	25	1	0	1	1.6	1.000	OF-13
1993 DET A	116	.261	.432	403	105	18	4	13	3.2	62	62	44	87	15	11	2	76	0	1	0	0.7	.987	DH-76, OF-32
1994	98	.276	.548	330	91	17	2	23	7.0	71	72	42	69	4	8	2	76	3	1	0	0.8	.988	DH-56, OF-38
16 yrs.	1565	.268	.464	5571	1494	248	52	246	4.4	948	835	685	1224	275	97	19	2523	41	63	12	1.7	.976	OF-1238, DH-264
LEAGUE CHAMPIONSHIP SERIES																							
1984 DET A	3	.417	.750	12	5	1	0	1	8.3	2	2	2	2	1	0	0	7	0	0	0	2.3	1.000	OF-3
1987	5	.286	.476	21	6	1	0	1	4.8	4	4	3	8	3	0	0	10	1	0	0	2.2	1.000	OF-5
1988 LA N	7	.154	.385	26	4	0	0	2	7.7	2	6	3	6	2	0	0	17	1	1	0	2.7	.947	OF-7
3 yrs.	15	.254	.492	59	15	2	0	4	6.8	8	12	8	15	6	0	0	34	2	1	0	2.5	.973	OF-15

Year Team	Games	BA	SA	AB	H	2B	3B	HR	HR%	R	RBI	BB	SO	SB	Pinch Hit AB	H	PO	A	E	DP	TC/G	FA	G by Pos

Kirk Gibson *continued*

WORLD SERIES

Year Team	Games	BA	SA	AB	H	2B	3B	HR	HR%	R	RBI	BB	SO	SB	AB	H	PO	A	E	DP	TC/G	FA	G by Pos
1984 DET A	5	.333	.667	18	6	0	0	2	11.1	4	7	4	4	3	0	0	5	1	2	0	1.6	.750	OF-5
1988 LA N	1	1.000	4.000	1	1	0	0	1	100.0	1	2	0	0	0	1	1	0	0	0	0	0.0	–	
2 yrs.	6	.368	.842	19	7	0	0	3	15.8	5	9	4	4	3	1	1	5	1	2	0	1.3	.750	

Bernard Gilkey

GILKEY, OTIS BERNARD
B. Sept. 24, 1966, St. Louis, Mo.

BR TR 6′ 170 lbs.

Year Team	Games	BA	SA	AB	H	2B	3B	HR	HR%	R	RBI	BB	SO	SB	AB	H	PO	A	E	DP	TC/G	FA	G by Pos
1990 STL N	18	.297	.484	64	19	5	2	1	1.6	11	3	8	5	6	0	0	47	2	2	0	2.8	.961	OF-18
1991	81	.216	.313	268	58	7	2	5	1.9	28	20	39	33	14	7	1	164	6	1	1	2.1	.994	OF-74
1992	131	.302	.427	384	116	19	4	7	1.8	56	43	39	52	18	20	4	217	9	5	3	1.8	.978	OF-111
1993	137	.305	.481	557	170	40	5	16	2.9	99	70	56	66	15	1	1	251	20	8	4	2.0	.971	OF-134, 1B-3
1994	105	.253	.363	380	96	22	1	6	1.6	52	45	39	65	15	4	2	168	9	3	3	1.8	.983	OF-102
5 yrs.	472	.278	.414	1653	459	93	14	35	2.1	246	181	181	221	68	32	8	847	46	19	11	1.9	.979	OF-439, 1B-3

Joe Girardi

GIRARDI, JOSEPH ELLIOTT
B. Oct. 14, 1964, Peoria, Ill.

BR TR 5′11″ 195 lbs.

Year Team	Games	BA	SA	AB	H	2B	3B	HR	HR%	R	RBI	BB	SO	SB	AB	H	PO	A	E	DP	TC/G	FA	G by Pos
1989 CHI N	59	.248	.331	157	39	10	0	1	0.6	15	14	11	26	2	0	0	332	28	7	1	6.2	.981	C-59
1990	133	.270	.344	419	113	24	2	1	0.2	36	38	17	50	8	0	0	653	61	11	5	5.5	.985	C-133
1991	21	.191	.234	47	9	2	0	0	0.0	3	6	6	6	0	1	1	95	11	3	1	5.2	.972	C-21
1992	91	.270	.300	270	73	3	1	1	0.4	19	12	19	38	0	10	5	369	51	4	6	4.7	.991	C-86
1993 CLR N	86	.290	.397	310	90	14	5	3	1.0	35	31	24	41	6	2	0	479	45	6	7	6.2	.989	C-84
1994	93	.276	.364	330	91	9	4	4	1.2	47	34	21	48	3	0	0	548	55	5	5	6.5	.992	C-93
6 yrs.	483	.271	.346	1533	415	62	12	10	0.7	155	135	98	209	19	13	6	2476	251	36	25	5.7	.987	C-476

LEAGUE CHAMPIONSHIP SERIES

Year Team	Games	BA	SA	AB	H	2B	3B	HR	HR%	R	RBI	BB	SO	SB	AB	H	PO	A	E	DP	TC/G	FA	G by Pos
1989 CHI N	4	.100	.100	10	1	0	0	0	0.0	1	1	0	2	0	0	0	20	0	0	0	5.0	1.000	C-4

Jerry Goff

GOFF, JERRY LEROY
B. Apr. 12, 1964, San Rafael, Calif.

BL TR 6′3″ 205 lbs.

Year Team	Games	BA	SA	AB	H	2B	3B	HR	HR%	R	RBI	BB	SO	SB	AB	H	PO	A	E	DP	TC/G	FA	G by Pos
1990 MON N	52	.227	.311	119	27	1	0	3	2.5	14	7	21	36	0	6	3	216	17	9	3	4.7	.963	C-38, 1B-3, 3B-3
1992	3	.000	.000	3	0	0	0	0	0.0	0	0	0	3	0	3	0	0	0	0	0	0.0	–	
1993 PIT N	14	.297	.514	37	11	2	0	2	5.4	5	6	8	9	0	2	1	54	7	1	0	4.4	.984	C-14
1994	8	.080	.080	25	2	0	0	0	0.0	0	1	0	11	0	1	0	34	4	2	0	5.0	.950	C-7
4 yrs.	77	.217	.315	184	40	3	0	5	2.7	19	14	29	59	0	12	4	304	28	12	3	4.5	.965	C-59, 1B-3, 3B-3

Chris Gomez

GOMEZ, CHRISTOPHER CORY
B. June 16, 1971, Los Angeles, Calif.

BR TR 6′1″ 183 lbs.

Year Team	Games	BA	SA	AB	H	2B	3B	HR	HR%	R	RBI	BB	SO	SB	AB	H	PO	A	E	DP	TC/G	FA	G by Pos
1993 DET A	46	.250	.320	128	32	7	1	0	0.0	11	11	9	17	2	0	0	68	119	5	23	4.2	.974	SS-29, 2B-17, DH-1
1994	84	.257	.402	296	76	19	0	8	2.7	32	53	33	64	5	0	0	141	210	8	39	4.3	.978	SS-57, 2B-30
2 yrs.	130	.255	.377	424	108	26	1	8	1.9	43	64	42	81	7	0	0	209	329	13	62	4.2	.976	SS-86, 2B-47, DH-1

Leo Gomez

GOMEZ, LEONARDO
Born Leonardo Gomez (Velez).
B. Mar. 2, 1966, Canovanas, Puerto Rico.

BR TR 6′ 180 lbs.

Year Team	Games	BA	SA	AB	H	2B	3B	HR	HR%	R	RBI	BB	SO	SB	AB	H	PO	A	E	DP	TC/G	FA	G by Pos
1990 BAL A	12	.231	.231	39	9	0	0	0	0.0	3	1	8	7	0	0	0	11	20	4	2	2.9	.886	3B-12
1991	118	.233	.409	391	91	17	2	16	4.1	40	45	40	82	1	5	0	78	184	7	20	2.3	.974	3B-105, DH-10, 1B-3
1992	137	.265	.425	468	124	24	0	17	3.6	62	64	63	78	2	0	0	106	246	18	19	2.7	.951	3B-137
1993	71	.197	.348	244	48	7	0	10	4.1	30	25	32	60	0	0	0	48	145	10	16	2.9	.951	3B-70, DH-1
1994	84	.274	.502	285	78	20	0	15	5.3	46	56	41	55	0	2	0	56	141	5	12	2.4	.975	3B-78, DH-5, 1B-1
5 yrs.	422	.245	.418	1427	350	68	2	58	4.1	181	191	184	282	3	7	0	299	736	44	69	2.6	.959	3B-402, DH-16, 1B-4

Rene Gonzales

GONZALES, RENE ADRIAN
B. Sept. 23, 1960, Austin, Tex.

BR TR 6′3″ 180 lbs.

Year Team	Games	BA	SA	AB	H	2B	3B	HR	HR%	R	RBI	BB	SO	SB	AB	H	PO	A	E	DP	TC/G	FA	G by Pos
1984 MON N	29	.233	.267	30	7	1	0	0	0.0	5	2	2	5	0	0	0	17	28	2	5	1.6	.957	SS-27
1986	11	.115	.115	26	3	0	0	0	0.0	1	0	2	7	0	0	0	7	19	0	3	2.4	1.000	SS-6, 3B-5
1987 BAL A	37	.267	.383	60	16	2	1	1	1.7	14	7	3	11	1	0	0	22	43	2	5	1.8	.970	3B-29, 2B-6, SS-1
1988	92	.215	.266	237	51	6	0	2	0.8	13	15	13	32	2	0	0	66	185	8	26	2.8	.969	3B-80, 2B-14, SS-2, 1B-1, OF-1
1989	71	.217	.259	166	36	4	0	1	0.6	16	11	12	30	5	2	0	103	146	7	37	3.6	.973	2B-54, 3B-17, SS-1
1990	67	.214	.291	103	22	3	1	1	1.0	13	12	12	14	1	0	0	68	114	2	23	2.7	.989	2B-43, 3B-16, SS-9, OF-1
1991 TOR A	71	.195	.246	118	23	3	0	1	0.8	16	6	12	22	0	2	1	61	118	7	17	2.6	.962	SS-36, 3B-26, 2B-11, 1B-2
1992 CAL A	104	.277	.398	329	91	17	1	7	2.1	47	38	41	46	7	2	1	191	229	9	49	4.1	.979	3B-53, 2B-42, 1B-13, SS-8
1993	117	.251	.319	335	84	17	0	2	0.6	34	31	49	45	5	2	2	234	170	12	46	3.6	.971	3B-79, 1B-31, SS-5, 2B-4, P-1
1994 CLE A	22	.348	.609	23	8	1	1	1	4.3	6	5	5	3	2	3	1	17	21	1	2	1.8	.974	3B-13, 1B-4, SS-4, 2B-1
10 yrs.	621	.239	.316	1427	341	54	4	16	1.1	165	127	151	215	23	14	5	786	1073	50	213	3.1	.974	3B-318, 2B-175, SS-99, 1B-51, OF-2, P-1

LEAGUE CHAMPIONSHIP SERIES

Year Team	Games	BA	SA	AB	H	2B	3B	HR	HR%	R	RBI	BB	SO	SB	AB	H	PO	A	E	DP	TC/G	FA	G by Pos
1991 TOR A	2	–	–	0	0	0	0	0	–	0	0	0	0	0	0	0	2	0	0	0	1.0	1.000	1B-1, SS-1

Alex Gonzalez

GONZALEZ, ALEXANDER SCOTT
B. Apr. 8, 1973, Miami, Fla.

BR TR 6′ 180 lbs.

Year Team	Games	BA	SA	AB	H	2B	3B	HR	HR%	R	RBI	BB	SO	SB	AB	H	PO	A	E	DP	TC/G	FA	G by Pos
1994 TOR A	15	.151	.245	53	8	3	1	0	0.0	7	1	4	17	3	0	0	18	49	6	5	4.9	.918	SS-15

Juan Gonzalez

GONZALEZ, JUAN ALBERTO
Born Juan Alberto Gonzalez (Vasquez).
B. Oct. 16, 1969, Vega Baja, Puerto Rico.

BR TR 6′3″ 175 lbs.

Year Team	Games	BA	SA	AB	H	2B	3B	HR	HR%	R	RBI	BB	SO	SB	AB	H	PO	A	E	DP	TC/G	FA	G by Pos
1989 TEX A	24	.150	.250	60	9	3	0	1	1.7	6	7	6	17	0	1	0	53	0	2	0	2.3	.964	OF-24
1990	25	.289	.522	90	26	7	1	4	4.4	11	12	2	18	0	3	1	33	0	0	0	1.3	1.000	OF-16, DH-9

Year Team	Games	BA	SA	AB	H	2B	3B	HR	HR%	R	RBI	BB	SO	SB	Pinch Hit AB	Pinch Hit H	PO	A	E	DP	TC/G	FA	G by Pos

Juan Gonzalez *continued*

Year Team	Games	BA	SA	AB	H	2B	3B	HR	HR%	R	RBI	BB	SO	SB	AB	H	PO	A	E	DP	TC/G	FA	G by Pos
1991	142	.264	.479	545	144	34	1	27	5.0	78	102	42	118	4	3	0	310	6	6	1	2.3	.981	OF-136, DH-4
1992	155	.260	.529	584	152	24	2	43	7.4	77	109	35	143	0	6	1	379	9	10	2	2.6	.975	OF-148, DH-4
1993	140	.310	**.632**	536	166	33	1	46	8.6	105	118	37	99	4	1	1	265	5	4	0	2.0	.985	OF-129, DH-10
1994	107	.275	.472	422	116	18	4	19	4.5	57	85	30	66	6	0	0	223	9	2	1	2.2	.991	OF-107
6 yrs.	593	.274	.523	2237	613	119	9	140	6.3	334	433	152	461	14	14	3	1263	29	24	4	2.2	.982	OF-560, DH-27

Luis Gonzalez

GONZALEZ, LUIS EMILIO
B. Sept. 3, 1967, Tampa, Fla.   BL TR 6'   180 lbs.

Year Team	Games	BA	SA	AB	H	2B	3B	HR	HR%	R	RBI	BB	SO	SB	AB	H	PO	A	E	DP	TC/G	FA	G by Pos
1990 HOU N	12	.190	.286	21	4	2	0	0	0.0	1	0	2	5	0	5	1	22	10	0	1	2.7	1.000	3B-4, 1B-2
1991	137	.254	.433	473	120	28	9	13	2.7	51	69	40	101	10	5	1	294	6	5	1	2.2	.984	OF-133
1992	122	.243	.385	387	94	19	3	10	2.6	40	55	24	52	7	17	5	261	5	2	1	2.2	.993	OF-111
1993	154	.300	.457	540	162	34	3	15	2.8	82	72	47	83	20	6	3	347	10	8	2	2.4	.978	OF-149
1994	112	.273	.429	392	107	29	4	8	2.0	57	67	49	57	15	2	1	228	5	2	1	2.1	.991	OF-111
5 yrs.	537	.269	.427	1813	487	112	19	46	2.5	231	263	162	298	52	35	11	1152	36	17	6	2.2	.986	OF-504, 3B-4, 1B-2

Tom Goodwin

GOODWIN, THOMAS JONES
B. July 27, 1968, Fresno, Calif.   BL TR 6'1"   165 lbs.

Year Team	Games	BA	SA	AB	H	2B	3B	HR	HR%	R	RBI	BB	SO	SB	AB	H	PO	A	E	DP	TC/G	FA	G by Pos
1991 LA N	16	.143	.143	7	1	0	0	0	0.0	3	0	0	0	1	1	0	8	0	0	0	0.5	1.000	OF-5
1992	57	.233	.274	73	17	1	1	0	0.0	15	3	6	10	7	5	2	43	0	0	0	0.8	1.000	OF-45
1993	30	.294	.353	17	5	1	0	0	0.0	6	1	1	4	1	5	1	8	0	0	0	0.3	1.000	OF-12
1994 KC A	2	.000	.000	2	0	0	0	0	0.0	0	0	0	1	0	0	0	1	0	0	0	0.5	1.000	DH-1, OF-1
4 yrs.	105	.232	.273	99	23	2	1	0	0.0	24	4	7	15	9	11	3	60	0	0	0	0.6	1.000	OF-63, DH-1

Mark Grace

GRACE, MARK EUGENE
B. June 28, 1964, Winston-Salem, N. C.   BL TL 6'2"   190 lbs.

Year Team	Games	BA	SA	AB	H	2B	3B	HR	HR%	R	RBI	BB	SO	SB	AB	H	PO	A	E	DP	TC/G	FA	G by Pos
1988 CHI N	134	.296	.403	486	144	23	4	7	1.4	65	57	60	43	3	7	3	1182	87	17	91	9.6	.987	1B-133
1989	142	.314	.457	510	160	28	3	13	2.5	74	79	80	42	14	1	1	1230	126	6	93	9.6	.996	1B-142
1990	157	.309	.413	589	182	32	1	9	1.5	72	82	59	54	15	7	2	1324	180	12	116	9.7	.992	1B-153
1991	160	.273	.373	**619**	169	28	5	8	1.3	87	58	70	53	3	4	0	1520	167	8	106	10.6	.995	1B-160
1992	158	.307	.430	603	185	37	5	9	1.5	72	79	72	36	6	1	0	1580	141	4	119	10.9	.998	1B-157
1993	155	.325	.475	594	193	39	4	14	2.4	86	98	71	32	8	1	0	1455	109	5	136	10.1	.997	1B-154
1994	106	.298	.414	403	120	23	3	6	1.5	55	44	48	41	0	5	2	925	76	7	90	9.5	.993	1B-103
7 yrs.	1012	.303	.424	3804	1153	210	25	66	1.7	511	497	460	301	49	26	8	9216	886	59	751	10.0	.994	1B-1002

LEAGUE CHAMPIONSHIP SERIES

Year Team	Games	BA	SA	AB	H	2B	3B	HR	HR%	R	RBI	BB	SO	SB	AB	H	PO	A	E	DP	TC/G	FA	G by Pos
1989 CHI N	5	.647	1.118	17	11	3	1	1	5.9	3	8	4	1	1	0	0	44	3	0	1	9.4	1.000	1B-5

Craig Grebeck

GREBECK, CRAIG ALLEN
B. Dec. 29, 1964, Johnstown, Pa.   BR TR 5'8"   160 lbs.

Year Team	Games	BA	SA	AB	H	2B	3B	HR	HR%	R	RBI	BB	SO	SB	AB	H	PO	A	E	DP	TC/G	FA	G by Pos
1990 CHI A	59	.168	.235	119	20	3	1	1	0.8	7	9	8	24	0	4	1	36	98	3	10	2.3	.978	3B-35, SS-16, 2B-6, DH-1
1991	107	.281	.460	224	63	16	3	6	2.7	37	31	38	40	1	14	3	104	183	10	34	2.8	.966	3B-49, 2B-36, SS-26
1992	88	.268	.387	287	77	21	2	3	1.0	24	35	30	34	0	0	0	112	283	8	47	4.6	.980	SS-85, 3B-7, OF-2
1993	72	.226	.268	190	43	5	0	1	0.5	25	12	26	26	1	3	0	91	185	5	39	3.9	.982	SS-46, 2B-16, 3B-14
1994	35	.309	.361	97	30	5	0	0	0.0	17	5	12	5	0	1	0	44	65	2	13	3.2	.982	2B-14, SS-14, 3B-7
5 yrs.	361	.254	.358	917	233	50	6	11	1.2	110	92	114	129	2	22	4	387	814	28	143	3.4	.977	SS-187, 3B-112, 2B-72, OF-2, DH-1

LEAGUE CHAMPIONSHIP SERIES

Year Team	Games	BA	SA	AB	H	2B	3B	HR	HR%	R	RBI	BB	SO	SB	AB	H	PO	A	E	DP	TC/G	FA	G by Pos
1993 CHI A	1	1.000	1.000	1	1	0	0	0	0.0	0	0	0	0	0	1	1	0	0	0	0	0.0	–	3B-1

Shawn Green

GREEN, SHAWN DAVID
B. Nov. 10, 1972, Des Plaines, Ill.   BL TL 6'4"   190 lbs.

Year Team	Games	BA	SA	AB	H	2B	3B	HR	HR%	R	RBI	BB	SO	SB	AB	H	PO	A	E	DP	TC/G	FA	G by Pos
1993 TOR A	3	.000	.000	6	0	0	0	0	0.0	0	0	0	1	0	0	0	1	0	0	0	0.3	1.000	OF-2, DH-1
1994	14	.091	.121	33	3	1	0	0	0.0	1	1	1	8	1	0	0	12	2	0	0	1.0	1.000	OF-14
2 yrs.	17	.077	.103	39	3	1	0	0	0.0	1	1	1	9	1	0	0	13	2	0	0	0.9	1.000	OF-16, DH-1

Willie Greene

GREENE, WILLIE LOUIS
B. Sept. 23, 1971, Milledgeville, Ga.   BL TR 5'11"   180 lbs.

Year Team	Games	BA	SA	AB	H	2B	3B	HR	HR%	R	RBI	BB	SO	SB	AB	H	PO	A	E	DP	TC/G	FA	G by Pos
1992 CIN N	29	.269	.430	93	25	5	2	2	2.2	10	13	10	23	0	4	0	16	40	3	6	2.0	.949	3B-25
1993	15	.160	.340	50	8	1	1	2	4.0	7	5	2	19	0	1	0	19	37	1	8	3.8	.982	SS-10, 3B-5
1994	16	.216	.270	37	8	2	0	0	0.0	5	3	6	14	0	4	1	2	21	1	1	1.5	.958	3B-13, OF-1
3 yrs.	60	.228	.372	180	41	8	3	4	2.2	22	21	18	56	0	9	1	37	98	5	15	2.3	.964	3B-43, SS-10, OF-1

Mike Greenwell

GREENWELL, MICHAEL LEWIS
B. July 18, 1963, Louisville, Ky.   BL TR 6'   170 lbs.

Year Team	Games	BA	SA	AB	H	2B	3B	HR	HR%	R	RBI	BB	SO	SB	AB	H	PO	A	E	DP	TC/G	FA	G by Pos
1985 BOS A	17	.323	.742	31	10	1	0	4	12.9	7	8	3	4	1	1	0	14	0	0	0	0.8	1.000	OF-17
1986	31	.314	.371	35	11	2	0	0	0.0	4	4	5	7	0	12	2	18	1	0	1	0.6	1.000	OF-15, DH-3
1987	125	.328	.570	412	135	31	6	19	4.6	71	89	35	40	5	17	5	165	8	6	0	1.4	.966	OF-91, DH-15, C-1
1988	158	.325	.531	590	192	39	8	22	3.7	86	119	87	38	16	0	0	302	6	6	2	2.0	.981	OF-147, DH-11
1989	145	.308	.443	578	178	36	0	14	2.4	87	95	56	44	13	1	1	220	11	8	1	1.6	.967	OF-139, DH-5
1990	159	.297	.434	610	181	30	6	14	2.3	71	73	65	43	8	1	0	287	13	7	1	1.9	.977	OF-159
1991	147	.300	.419	544	163	26	6	9	1.7	76	83	43	35	15	4	1	263	9	3	3	1.9	.989	OF-143, DH-1
1992	49	.233	.278	180	42	2	0	2	1.1	16	18	18	19	2	2	2	85	1	0	0	1.8	1.000	OF-41, DH-6
1993	146	.315	.480	540	170	38	6	13	2.4	77	72	54	46	5	3	0	261	6	2	1	1.8	.993	OF-134, DH-10
1994	95	.269	.453	327	88	25	1	11	3.4	60	45	38	26	2	7	2	141	10	1	1	1.6	.993	OF-84, DH-6
10 yrs.	1072	.304	.465	3847	1170	230	33	108	2.8	555	606	404	302	67	48	13	1756	65	33	10	1.7	.982	OF-970, DH-57, C-1

LEAGUE CHAMPIONSHIP SERIES

Year Team	Games	BA	SA	AB	H	2B	3B	HR	HR%	R	RBI	BB	SO	SB	AB	H	PO	A	E	DP	TC/G	FA	G by Pos
1986 BOS A	2	.500	.500	2	1	0	0	0	0.0	0	0	0	0	0	1	1	0	0	0	0	0.0	–	
1988	4	.214	.500	14	3	1	0	1	7.1	2	3	3	0	0	0	0	4	0	0	0	1.0	1.000	OF-4
1990	4	.000	.000	14	0	0	0	0	0.0	1	0	2	2	0	0	0	3	0	1	0	1.0	.750	OF-4
3 yrs.	10	.133	.267	30	4	1	0	1	3.3	3	3	5	2	0	1	1	7	0	1	0	0.8	.875	OF-8

Year	Team	Games	BA	SA	AB	H	2B	3B	HR	HR%	R	RBI	BB	SO	SB	Pinch Hit AB	Pinch Hit H	PO	A	E	DP	TC/G	FA	G by Pos

Mike Greenwell *continued*

WORLD SERIES

| 1986 | BOS A | 4 | 1.000 | .000 | 3 | 0 | 0 | 0 | 0 | 0.0 | 0 | 0 | 1 | 2 | 0 | 3 | 0 | 0 | 0 | 0 | 0 | 0.0 | – | |

Rusty Greer

GREER, THURMAN CLYDE III
B. Jan. 21, 1969, Fort Rucker, Ala.
BL TL 6' 190 lbs.

| 1994 | TEX A | 80 | .314 | .487 | 277 | 87 | 16 | 1 | 10 | 3.6 | 36 | 46 | 46 | 46 | 0 | 2 | 0 | 216 | 4 | 6 | 10 | 2.8 | .973 | OF-73, 1B-9 |

Ken Griffey

GRIFFEY, GEORGE KENNETH, JR.
Son of Ken Griffey.
B. Nov. 21, 1969, Donora, Pa.
BL TL 6'3" 195 lbs.

1989	SEA A	127	.264	.420	455	120	23	0	16	3.5	61	61	44	83	16	3	1	302	12	10	6	2.6	.969	OF-127
1990		155	.300	.481	597	179	28	7	22	3.7	91	80	63	81	16	3	1	330	8	7	1	2.2	.980	OF-151, DH-2
1991		154	.327	.527	548	179	42	1	22	4.0	76	100	71	82	18	4	1	360	15	4	4	2.5	.989	OF-152, DH-1
1992		142	.308	.535	565	174	39	4	27	4.8	83	103	44	67	10	3	1	359	8	1	4	2.6	.997	OF-137, DH-3
1993		156	.309	.617	582	180	38	3	45	7.7	113	109	96	91	17	0	0	317	8	3	3	2.1	.991	OF-139, DH-19, 1B-1
1994		111	.323	.674	433	140	24	4	**40**	9.2	94	90	56	73	11	0	0	225	12	4	1	2.2	.983	OF-103, DH-9
6 yrs.		845	.306	.541	3180	972	194	19	172	5.4	518	543	374	477	88	13	4	1893	63	29	19	2.3	.985	OF-809, DH-34, 1B-1

Marquis Grissom

GRISSOM, MARQUIS DEON
B. Apr. 17, 1967, Atlanta, Ga.
BR TR 5'11" 190 lbs.

1989	MON N	26	.257	.324	74	19	2	0	1	1.4	16	2	12	21	1	3	0	32	1	2	0	1.3	.943	OF-23
1990		98	.257	.351	288	74	14	2	3	1.0	42	29	27	40	22	21	6	165	5	2	0	1.8	.988	OF-87
1991		148	.267	.373	558	149	23	9	6	1.1	73	39	34	89	**76**	8	1	350	15	6	2	2.5	.984	OF-138
1992		159	.276	.418	**653**	180	39	6	14	2.1	99	66	42	81	**78**	1	0	401	7	7	2	2.6	.983	OF-157
1993		157	.298	.438	630	188	27	2	19	3.0	104	95	52	76	53	1	0	416	8	7	3	2.7	.984	OF-157
1994		110	.288	.427	475	137	25	4	11	2.3	96	45	41	66	36	1	1	321	7	5	0	3.0	.985	OF-109
6 yrs.		698	.279	.405	2678	747	130	23	54	2.0	430	276	208	373	266	35	8	1685	43	29	7	2.5	.983	OF-671

Ozzie Guillen

GUILLEN, OSWALDO JOSE
Born Oswaldo Jose Guillen (Barrios).
B. Jan. 20, 1964, Oculare del Tuy, Venezuela.
BL TR 5'11" 160 lbs.

1985	CHI A	150	.273	.358	491	134	21	9	1	0.2	71	33	12	36	7	13	1	220	382	12	80	4.1	.980	SS-150
1986		159	.250	.311	547	137	19	4	2	0.4	58	47	12	52	8	2	0	261	459	22	93	4.7	.970	SS-157, DH-1
1987		149	.279	.354	560	156	22	7	2	0.4	64	51	22	52	25	2	1	266	475	19	105	5.1	.975	SS-149
1988		156	.261	.314	566	148	16	7	0	0.0	58	39	25	40	25	0	0	273	570	20	115	5.5	.977	SS-156
1989		155	.253	.318	597	151	20	8	1	0.2	63	54	15	48	36	0	0	272	512	22	106	5.2	.973	SS-155
1990		160	.279	.341	516	144	21	4	1	0.2	61	58	26	37	13	2	0	252	474	17	100	4.6	.977	SS-159
1991		154	.273	.340	524	143	20	3	3	0.6	52	49	11	38	21	6	1	249	439	21	88	4.6	.970	SS-149
1992		12	.200	.300	40	8	4	0	0	0.0	5	7	1	5	1	0	0	20	39	0	7	4.9	1.000	SS-12
1993		134	.280	.374	457	128	23	4	4	0.9	44	50	10	41	5	3	1	189	361	16	82	4.2	.972	SS-133
1994		100	.288	.348	365	105	9	5	1	0.3	46	39	14	35	5	2	0	141	235	16	44	3.9	.959	SS-99
10 yrs.		1329	.269	.338	4663	1254	175	51	15	0.3	522	427	148	384	146	30	4	2143	3946	165	820	4.7	.974	SS-1319, DH-1

LEAGUE CHAMPIONSHIP SERIES

| 1993 | CHI A | 6 | .273 | .318 | 22 | 6 | 1 | 0 | 0 | 0.0 | 4 | 2 | 1 | 0 | 2 | 1 | 0 | 12 | 14 | 0 | 4 | 4.3 | 1.000 | SS-6 |

Ricky Gutierrez

GUTIERREZ, RICARDO
B. May 23, 1970, Miami, Fla.
BR TR 6'1" 175 lbs.

1993	SD N	133	.251	.331	438	110	10	5	5	1.1	76	26	50	97	4	8	2	194	305	14	55	3.9	.973	SS-117, 2B-6, OF-5, 3B-4
1994		90	.240	.305	275	66	11	2	1	0.4	27	28	32	54	2	6	1	93	202	22	34	3.5	.931	SS-78, 2B-7
2 yrs.		223	.247	.321	713	176	21	7	6	0.8	103	54	82	151	6	14	3	287	507	36	89	3.7	.957	SS-195, 2B-13, OF-5, 3B-4

Chris Gwynn

GWYNN, CHRISTOPHER KARLTON
Brother of Tony Gwynn.
B. Oct. 13, 1964, Los Angeles, Calif.
BL TL 6' 200 lbs.

1987	LA N	17	.219	.250	32	7	1	0	0	0.0	2	2	1	7	0	6	0	12	0	0	0	0.7	1.000	OF-10
1988		12	.182	.182	11	2	0	0	0	0.0	1	0	1	2	0	9	2	0	0	0	0	0.0	–	OF-4
1989		32	.235	.324	68	16	4	1	0	0.0	8	7	2	9	1	14	3	26	1	0	0	0.8	1.000	OF-19
1990		101	.284	.418	141	40	2	1	5	3.5	19	22	7	28	0	**56**	13	39	1	0	0	0.4	1.000	OF-44
1991		94	.252	.410	139	35	5	1	5	3.6	18	22	10	23	1	**56**	13	37	2	0	0	0.4	1.000	OF-41
1992	KC A	34	.286	.405	84	24	3	2	1	1.2	10	7	3	10	0	10	2	33	0	0	0	1.0	1.000	OF-19, DH-2
1993		103	.300	.387	287	86	14	4	1	0.3	36	25	24	34	0	16	6	161	7	1	1	1.6	.994	OF-83, DH-5, 1B-1
1994	LA N	58	.268	.394	71	19	0	0	3	4.2	9	13	7	7	0	35	11	14	0	0	0	0.2	1.000	OF-20
8 yrs.		451	.275	.385	833	229	29	9	15	1.8	103	98	55	120	2	202	50	322	11	1	2	0.7	.997	OF-240, DH-7, 1B-1

Tony Gwynn

GWYNN, ANTHONY KEITH
Brother of Chris Gwynn.
B. May 9, 1960, Los Angeles, Calif.
BL TL 5'11" 185 lbs.

1982	SD N	54	.289	.389	190	55	12	2	1	0.5	33	17	14	16	8	4	1	110	1	1	0	2.1	.991	OF-52
1983		86	.309	.372	304	94	12	2	1	0.3	34	37	23	21	7	6	1	163	9	1	1	2.0	.994	OF-81
1984		158	**.351**	.444	606	**213**	21	10	5	0.8	88	71	59	23	33	2	1	345	11	4	4	2.3	.989	OF-156
1985		154	.317	.408	622	197	29	5	6	1.0	90	46	45	33	14	2	0	337	14	4	2	2.3	.989	OF-152
1986		160	.329	.467	642	211	33	7	14	2.2	**107**	59	52	35	37	1	0	337	19	4	3	2.3	.989	OF-160
1987		157	**.370**	.511	589	218	36	13	7	1.2	119	54	82	35	56	2	1	298	13	6	1	2.0	.981	OF-156
1988		133	**.313**	.415	521	163	22	5	7	1.3	64	70	51	40	26	0	0	264	8	5	1	2.1	.982	OF-133
1989		158	**.336**	.424	604	**203**	27	7	4	0.7	82	62	56	30	40	0	0	353	13	6	1	2.4	.984	OF-157
1990		141	.309	.415	573	177	29	10	4	0.7	79	72	44	23	17	0	0	327	11	5	2	2.4	.985	OF-141
1991		134	.317	.432	530	168	27	11	4	0.8	69	62	34	19	8	1	0	291	8	3	2	2.3	.990	OF-134
1992		128	.317	.415	520	165	27	3	6	1.2	77	41	46	16	3	1	0	270	9	5	2	2.2	.982	OF-127
1993		122	.358	.497	489	175	41	3	7	1.4	70	59	36	19	14	2	0	244	8	5	2	2.1	.981	OF-121

Year	Team	Games	BA	SA	AB	H	2B	3B	HR	HR%	R	RBI	BB	SO	SB	Pinch Hit AB	Pinch Hit H	PO	A	E	DP	TC/G	FA	G by Pos

Tony Gwynn *continued*

Year	Team	Games	BA	SA	AB	H	2B	3B	HR	HR%	R	RBI	BB	SO	SB	PH AB	PH H	PO	A	E	DP	TC/G	FA	G by Pos
1994		110	.394	.568	419	165	35	1	12	2.9	79	64	48	19	5	5	1	191	6	3	1	1.8	.985	OF-106
13 yrs.		1695	.333	.446	6609	2204	351	79	78	1.2	991	714	590	329	268	26	5	3530	130	52	22	2.2	.986	OF-1676

LEAGUE CHAMPIONSHIP SERIES

Year	Team	Games	BA	SA	AB	H	2B	3B	HR	HR%	R	RBI	BB	SO	SB	PH AB	PH H	PO	A	E	DP	TC/G	FA	G by Pos
1984	SD N	5	.368	.526	19	7	3	0	0	0.0	6	3	1	2	1	0	0	9	0	0	0	1.8	1.000	OF-5

WORLD SERIES

Year	Team	Games	BA	SA	AB	H	2B	3B	HR	HR%	R	RBI	BB	SO	SB	PH AB	PH H	PO	A	E	DP	TC/G	FA	G by Pos
1984	SD N	5	.263	.263	19	5	0	0	0	0.0	1	0	3	2	1	0	0	12	1	1	1	2.8	.929	OF-5

Chip Hale

HALE, WALTER WILLIAM
B. Dec. 2, 1964, Santa Clara, Calif. — BL TR 5'11" 180 lbs.

Year	Team	Games	BA	SA	AB	H	2B	3B	HR	HR%	R	RBI	BB	SO	SB	PH AB	PH H	PO	A	E	DP	TC/G	FA	G by Pos
1989	MIN A	28	.209	.254	67	14	3	0	0	0.0	6	4	1	6	0	8	0	15	40	1	8	2.0	.982	2B-16, 3B-9, DH-2
1990		1	.000	.000	2	0	0	0	0	0.0	0	2	0	1	0	0	0	2	6	0	2	8.0	1.000	2B-1
1993		69	.333	.425	186	62	6	1	3	1.6	25	27	18	17	2	17	7	38	64	4	11	1.5	.962	2B-21, 3B-19, DH-19, 1B-1, SS-1
1994		67	.263	.364	118	31	9	0	1	0.8	13	11	16	14	0	31	11	45	51	3	7	1.5	.970	3B-21, DH-10, 1B-7, 2B-5, OF-1
4 yrs.		165	.287	.373	373	107	18	1	4	1.1	44	44	35	38	2	56	18	100	161	8	28	1.6	.970	3B-49, 2B-43, DH-31, 1B-8, SS-1, OF-1

Joe Hall

HALL, JOSEPH GEROY
B. Mar. 6, 1966, Paducah, Ky. — BR TR 6' 180 lbs.

Year	Team	Games	BA	SA	AB	H	2B	3B	HR	HR%	R	RBI	BB	SO	SB	PH AB	PH H	PO	A	E	DP	TC/G	FA	G by Pos
1994	CHI A	17	.393	.607	28	11	3	0	1	3.6	6	5	2	4	0	8	3	11	0	1	0	0.7	.917	OF-9, DH-2

Bob Hamelin

HAMELIN, ROBERT JAMES III (The Hammer)
B. Nov. 29, 1967, Elizabeth, N. J. — BL TL 6'1" 240 lbs.

Year	Team	Games	BA	SA	AB	H	2B	3B	HR	HR%	R	RBI	BB	SO	SB	PH AB	PH H	PO	A	E	DP	TC/G	FA	G by Pos
1993	KC A	16	.224	.408	49	11	3	0	2	4.1	2	5	6	15	0	1	0	129	9	2	11	8.8	.986	1B-15
1994		101	.282	.599	312	88	25	1	24	7.7	64	65	56	62	4	6	2	234	18	2	11	2.5	.992	DH-70, 1B-24
2 yrs.		117	.274	.573	361	99	28	1	26	7.2	66	70	62	77	4	7	2	363	27	4	22	3.4	.990	DH-70, 1B-39

Darryl Hamilton

HAMILTON, DARRYL QUINN
B. Dec. 3, 1963, Baton Rouge, La. — BL TR 6'1" 180 lbs.

Year	Team	Games	BA	SA	AB	H	2B	3B	HR	HR%	R	RBI	BB	SO	SB	PH AB	PH H	PO	A	E	DP	TC/G	FA	G by Pos
1988	MIL A	44	.184	.252	103	19	4	0	1	1.0	14	11	12	9	7	3	1	75	0	0	0	1.7	1.000	OF-37, DH-3
1990		89	.295	.346	156	46	5	0	1	0.6	27	18	9	12	10	5	1	120	1	1	0	1.4	.992	OF-72, DH-9
1991		122	.311	.385	405	126	15	6	1	0.2	64	57	33	38	16	3	3	234	3	1	0	2.0	.996	OF-117
1992		128	.298	.400	470	140	19	7	5	1.1	67	62	45	42	41	3	1	279	10	0	0	2.3	1.000	OF-124
1993		135	.310	.406	520	161	21	1	9	1.7	74	48	45	62	21	5	0	340	10	3	1	2.6	.992	OF-129
1994		36	.262	.369	141	37	10	1	1	0.7	23	13	15	17	3	0	0	60	2	0	1	1.7	1.000	OF-32, DH-3
6 yrs.		554	.295	.383	1795	529	74	15	18	1.0	269	209	159	180	98	19	6	1108	27	5	2	2.1	.996	OF-511, DH-15

Jeffrey Hammonds

HAMMONDS, JEFFREY BRYAN
B. Mar. 5, 1971, Plainfield, N. J. — BR TR 6' 195 lbs.

Year	Team	Games	BA	SA	AB	H	2B	3B	HR	HR%	R	RBI	BB	SO	SB	PH AB	PH H	PO	A	E	DP	TC/G	FA	G by Pos
1993	BAL A	33	.305	.467	105	32	8	0	3	2.9	10	19	2	16	4	2	2	47	2	2	0	1.5	.961	OF-23, DH-7
1994		68	.296	.480	250	74	18	2	8	3.2	45	31	17	39	5	0	0	147	5	6	0	2.3	.962	OF-67
2 yrs.		101	.299	.476	355	106	26	2	11	3.1	55	50	19	55	9	2	2	194	7	8	0	2.1	.962	OF-90, DH-7

Todd Haney

HANEY, TODD MICHAEL
B. July 30, 1965, Galveston, Tex. — BR TR 5'9" 165 lbs.

Year	Team	Games	BA	SA	AB	H	2B	3B	HR	HR%	R	RBI	BB	SO	SB	PH AB	PH H	PO	A	E	DP	TC/G	FA	G by Pos
1992	MON N	7	.300	.400	10	3	1	0	0	0.0	0	1	0	0	0	1	0	2	6	0	1	1.1	1.000	2B-5
1994	CHI N	17	.162	.243	37	6	0	0	1	2.7	6	2	3	3	2	1	0	20	28	1	8	2.9	.980	2B-11, 3B-3
2 yrs.		24	.191	.277	47	9	1	0	1	2.1	6	3	3	3	2	2	0	22	34	1	9	2.4	.982	2B-16, 3B-3

Dave Hansen

HANSEN, DAVID ANDREW
B. Nov. 24, 1968, Long Beach, Calif. — BL TR 6' 180 lbs.

Year	Team	Games	BA	SA	AB	H	2B	3B	HR	HR%	R	RBI	BB	SO	SB	PH AB	PH H	PO	A	E	DP	TC/G	FA	G by Pos
1990	LA N	5	.143	.143	7	1	0	0	0	0.0	0	0	1	0	3	0	3	0	0	1	1	0	0.4	.500	3B-2
1991		53	.268	.393	56	15	4	0	1	1.8	3	5	2	12	1	32	10	5	19	0	2	0.5	1.000	3B-21, SS-1
1992		132	.214	.299	341	73	11	0	6	1.8	30	22	34	49	0	25	5	61	183	8	13	1.9	.968	3B-108
1993		84	.362	.505	105	38	7	0	4	3.8	13	30	21	13	0	55	18	11	27	3	1	0.5	.927	3B-18
1994		40	.341	.409	44	15	3	0	0	0.0	3	5	5	5	0	31	8	0	6	1	0	0.2	.857	3B-7
5 yrs.		314	.257	.354	553	142	21	0	11	2.0	49	63	62	82	1	146	41	77	236	13	16	1.0	.960	3B-156, SS-1

Shawn Hare

HARE, SHAWN ROBERT
B. Mar. 26, 1967, St. Louis, Mo. — BL TL 6'2" 190 lbs.

Year	Team	Games	BA	SA	AB	H	2B	3B	HR	HR%	R	RBI	BB	SO	SB	PH AB	PH H	PO	A	E	DP	TC/G	FA	G by Pos
1991	DET A	9	.053	.105	19	1	1	0	0	0.0	0	0	2	1	0	2	0	9	1	0	0	1.1	1.000	OF-6, DH-2
1992		15	.115	.154	26	3	1	0	0	0.0	0	5	2	4	0	4	3	33	2	0	2	2.3	1.000	OF-9, 1B-4
1994	NY N	22	.225	.300	40	9	1	1	0	0.0	7	2	4	11	0	7	1	23	0	0	0	1.0	1.000	OF-14
3 yrs.		46	.153	.212	85	13	3	1	0	0.0	7	7	8	16	0	13	4	65	3	0	2	1.5	1.000	OF-29, 1B-4, DH-2

Brian Harper

HARPER, BRIAN DAVID
B. Oct. 16, 1959, Los Angeles, Calif. — BR TR 6'2" 195 lbs.

Year	Team	Games	BA	SA	AB	H	2B	3B	HR	HR%	R	RBI	BB	SO	SB	PH AB	PH H	PO	A	E	DP	TC/G	FA	G by Pos
1979	CAL A	1	.000	.000	2	0	0	0	0	0.0	0	0	0	1	0	1	0	0	0	0	0	0.0	—	DH-1
1981		4	.273	.273	11	3	0	0	0	0.0	1	1	0	0	1	1	0	5	0	0	0	1.5	.833	OF-2, DH-1
1982	PIT N	20	.276	.517	29	8	1	0	2	6.9	4	4	1	4	0	12	5	10	0	0	0	0.5	1.000	OF-8
1983		61	.221	.427	131	29	4	1	7	5.3	16	20	2	15	0	27	6	40	0	0	0	0.7	1.000	OF-35, 1B-1
1984		48	.259	.348	112	29	4	0	2	1.8	4	11	5	11	0	11	2	57	3	1	0	1.3	.984	OF-37, C-2
1985	STL N	43	.250	.327	52	13	4	0	0	0.0	5	8	2	3	0	26	7	15	5	0	0	0.5	1.000	OF-13, 3B-6, C-2, 1B-1
1986	DET A	19	.139	.167	36	5	1	0	0	0.0	2	3	3	3	0	4	2	25	2	1	2	1.5	.964	OF-11, DH-6, 1B-2, C-2
1987	OAK A	11	.235	.294	17	4	1	0	0	0.0	1	3	0	4	0	4	1	0	0	0	0	0.0	—	DH-7, OF-1
1988	MIN A	60	.295	.428	166	49	11	1	3	1.8	15	20	10	12	0	7	1	208	15	2	0	3.8	.991	C-48, DH-5, 3B-2
1989		126	.325	.449	385	125	24	0	8	2.1	40	57	10	16	2	7	1	462	36	11	7	4.0	.978	C-101, DH-19, OF-3, 1B-2, 3B-2

Brian Harper *continued*

Year Team	Games	BA	SA	AB	H	2B	3B	HR	HR%	R	RBI	BB	SO	SB	Pinch Hit AB	Pinch Hit H	PO	A	E	DP	TC/G	FA	G by Pos
1990	134	.294	.432	479	141	42	3	6	1.3	61	54	19	27	3	1	0	686	58	11	5	5.6	.985	C-120, DH-11, 3B-3, 1B-2
1991	123	.311	.447	441	137	28	1	10	2.3	54	69	14	22	1	2	0	643	33	8	7	5.6	.988	C-119, DH-2, 1B-1, OF-1
1992	140	.307	.410	502	154	25	0	9	1.8	58	73	26	22	0	8	1	744	58	13	8	5.8	.984	C-133, DH-2
1993	147	.304	.425	530	161	26	1	12	2.3	52	73	29	29	1	8	5	736	64	10	6	5.5	.988	C-134, DH-7
1994 MIL A	64	.291	.398	251	73	15	0	4	1.6	23	32	9	18	0	1	0	143	13	3	2	2.5	.981	DH-36, C-25, OF-3
15 yrs.	1001	.296	.420	3144	931	186	7	63	2.0	339	428	133	187	8	120	31	3774	287	61	37	4.1	.985	C-686, OF-114, DH-97, 3B-13, 1B-9

LEAGUE CHAMPIONSHIP SERIES

Year Team	Games	BA	SA	AB	H	2B	3B	HR	HR%	R	RBI	BB	SO	SB	Pinch Hit AB	Pinch Hit H	PO	A	E	DP	TC/G	FA	G by Pos
1985 STL N	1	.000	.000	1	0	0	0	0	0.0	0	0	0	0	0	1	0	0	0	0	0	0.0	–	
1991 MIN A	5	.278	.389	18	5	2	0	0	0.0	1	1	0	2	0	0	0	23	1	1	0	5.0	.960	C-5
2 yrs.	6	.263	.368	19	5	2	0	0	0.0	1	1	0	2	0	1	0	23	1	1	0	4.2	.960	

WORLD SERIES

Year Team	Games	BA	SA	AB	H	2B	3B	HR	HR%	R	RBI	BB	SO	SB	Pinch Hit AB	Pinch Hit H	PO	A	E	DP	TC/G	FA	G by Pos
1985 STL N	4	.250	.250	4	1	0	0	0	0.0	0	1	0	1	0	4	1	0	0	0	0	0.0	–	
1991 MIN A	7	.381	.476	21	8	2	0	0	0.0	2	1	2	2	0	2	0	33	5	1	1	5.6	.974	C-7
2 yrs.	11	.360	.440	25	9	2	0	0	0.0	2	2	2	3	0	6	1	33	5	1	1	3.5	.974	

Lenny Harris

HARRIS, LEONARD ANTHONY
B. Oct. 28, 1964, Miami, Fla.

BL TR 5'10" 195 lbs.

Year Team	Games	BA	SA	AB	H	2B	3B	HR	HR%	R	RBI	BB	SO	SB	Pinch Hit AB	Pinch Hit H	PO	A	E	DP	TC/G	FA	G by Pos
1988 CIN N	16	.372	.395	43	16	1	0	1	0.0	7	8	5	4	4	0	0	14	33	1	2	3.0	.979	3B-10, 2B-6
1989 2 teams				CIN N (61G – .223)						LA N (54G – .252)													
" total	115	.236	.299	335	79	10	1	3	0.9	36	26	20	33	14	20	8	147	168	15	32	2.9	.955	2B-46, 3B-24, OF-21, SS-18
1990 LA N	137	.304	.374	431	131	16	4	2	0.5	61	29	29	31	15	23	3	140	205	11	24	2.6	.969	3B-94, 2B-44, OF-2, SS-1
1991	145	.287	.350	429	123	16	1	3	0.7	59	38	37	32	12	24	3	125	250	20	35	2.7	.949	3B-113, 2B-27, SS-20, OF-1
1992	135	.271	.303	347	94	11	0	0	0.0	28	30	24	24	19	29	6	199	248	27	48	3.5	.943	2B-81, 3B-33, OF-15, SS-10
1993	107	.238	.325	160	38	6	1	2	1.3	20	11	15	15	3	45	8	61	99	3	11	1.5	.982	2B-35, 3B-17, SS-3, OF-2
1994 CIN N	66	.310	.360	100	31	3	1	0	0.0	13	14	5	13	7	45	12	27	29	6	2	0.9	.903	3B-15, 1B-4, OF-3, 2B-2
7 yrs.	721	.278	.337	1845	512	63	8	10	0.5	224	156	135	152	74	186	40	713	1032	83	154	2.5	.955	3B-306, 2B-241, SS-52, OF-44, 1B-4

Bill Haselman

HASELMAN, WILLIAM JOSEPH
B. May 25, 1966, Long Branch, N. J.

BR TR 6'3" 205 lbs.

Year Team	Games	BA	SA	AB	H	2B	3B	HR	HR%	R	RBI	BB	SO	SB	Pinch Hit AB	Pinch Hit H	PO	A	E	DP	TC/G	FA	G by Pos
1990 TEX A	7	.154	.154	13	2	0	0	0	0.0	0	3	1	5	0	3	1	8	0	0	0	1.1	1.000	DH-3, C-1
1992 SEA A	8	.263	.263	19	5	0	0	0	0.0	1	0	0	7	0	1	1	19	2	0	0	2.6	1.000	C-5, OF-2
1993	58	.255	.423	137	35	8	0	5	3.6	21	16	12	19	2	6	1	236	17	2	2	4.4	.992	C-49, DH-4, OF-2
1994	38	.193	.337	83	16	7	1	1	1.2	11	8	3	11	1	3	1	157	5	3	0	4.3	.982	C-33, DH-2, OF-2
4 yrs.	111	.230	.369	252	58	15	1	6	2.4	33	27	16	42	3	13	4	420	24	5	2	4.0	.989	C-88, DH-9, OF-6

Billy Hatcher

HATCHER, WILLIAM AUGUSTUS
B. Oct. 4, 1960, Williams, Ariz.

BR TR 5'9" 175 lbs.

Year Team	Games	BA	SA	AB	H	2B	3B	HR	HR%	R	RBI	BB	SO	SB	Pinch Hit AB	Pinch Hit H	PO	A	E	DP	TC/G	FA	G by Pos
1984 CHI N	8	.111	.111	9	1	0	0	0	0.0	1	0	1	0	2	3	0	2	1	0	0	0.4	1.000	OF-4
1985	53	.245	.368	163	40	12	1	2	1.2	24	10	8	12	2	9	1	77	2	1	0	1.5	.988	OF-44
1986 HOU N	127	.258	.356	419	108	15	4	6	1.4	55	36	22	52	38	4	0	226	7	4	0	1.9	.983	OF-121
1987	141	.296	.415	564	167	28	3	11	2.0	96	63	42	70	53	1	1	276	16	4	6	2.1	.986	OF-140
1988	145	.268	.370	530	142	25	4	7	1.3	79	52	37	56	32	5	1	280	7	5	2	2.0	.983	OF-142
1989 2 teams				HOU N (108G – .228)						PIT N (27G – .244)													
" total	135	.231	.308	481	111	19	3	4	0.8	59	51	30	62	24	15	5	250	1	1	1	1.9	.992	OF-124
1990 CIN N	139	.276	.381	504	139	28	5	5	1.0	68	25	33	42	30	13	3	308	10	1	2	2.3	.997	OF-131
1991	138	.262	.360	442	116	25	3	4	0.9	45	41	26	55	11	19	3	248	4	5	0	1.9	.981	OF-121
1992 2 teams				CIN N (43G – .287)						BOS N (75G – .238)													
" total	118	.249	.328	409	102	19	2	3	0.7	47	33	22	52	4	21	5	174	5	6	0	1.6	.968	OF-98
1993 BOS A	136	.287	.400	508	146	24	3	9	1.8	71	57	28	46	14	4	1	284	6	2	1	2.1	.993	OF-130, 2B-2
1994 2 teams				BOS A (44G – .244)						PHI N (43G – .246)													
" total	87	.245	.336	298	73	14	2	3	1.0	39	31	17	28	8	5	3	155	7	3	1	1.9	.982	OF-83, DH-1
11 yrs.	1227	.265	.364	4327	1145	209	30	54	1.2	584	399	266	475	218	99	23	2280	66	33	13	1.9	.986	OF-1138, 2B-2, DH-1

LEAGUE CHAMPIONSHIP SERIES

Year Team	Games	BA	SA	AB	H	2B	3B	HR	HR%	R	RBI	BB	SO	SB	Pinch Hit AB	Pinch Hit H	PO	A	E	DP	TC/G	FA	G by Pos
1986 HOU N	6	.280	.400	25	7	0	0	1	4.0	4	2	3	2	1	0	0	11	0	1	0	2.0	.917	OF-6
1990 CIN N	4	.333	.600	15	5	1	0	1	6.7	2	2	0	2	2	0	0	5	1	0	0	1.5	1.000	OF-4
2 yrs.	10	.300	.475	40	12	1	0	2	5.0	6	4	3	4	3	0	0	16	1	1	0	1.8	.944	OF-10

WORLD SERIES

Year Team	Games	BA	SA	AB	H	2B	3B	HR	HR%	R	RBI	BB	SO	SB	Pinch Hit AB	Pinch Hit H	PO	A	E	DP	TC/G	FA	G by Pos
1990 CIN N	4	.750	1.250	12	9	4	1	1	0.0	6	2	2	0	0	0	0	11	0	0	0	2.8	1.000	OF-4

Charlie Hayes

HAYES, CHARLES DEWAYNE
B. May 29, 1965, Hattiesburg, Miss.

BR TR 6' 224 lbs.

Year Team	Games	BA	SA	AB	H	2B	3B	HR	HR%	R	RBI	BB	SO	SB	Pinch Hit AB	Pinch Hit H	PO	A	E	DP	TC/G	FA	G by Pos
1988 SF N	7	.091	.091	11	1	0	0	0	0.0	0	1	0	0	0	3	0	1	2	0	1	0.7	1.000	OF-4, 3B-3
1989 2 teams				SF N (3G – .200)						PHI N (84G – .258)													
" total	87	.257	.391	304	78	15	1	8	2.6	26	43	11	50	3	5	2	51	174	22	15	2.8	.911	3B-85
1990 PHI N	152	.258	.348	561	145	20	0	10	1.8	56	57	28	91	4	6	2	151	329	20	31	3.3	.960	3B-146, 1B-4, 2B-1
1991	142	.230	.363	460	106	23	1	12	2.6	34	53	16	75	3	8	4	88	240	15	25	2.4	.956	3B-138, SS-2
1992 NY A	142	.257	.409	509	131	19	2	18	3.5	52	66	28	100	3	1	0	125	249	13	32	2.7	.966	3B-139, 1B-4
1993 CLR N	157	.305	.522	573	175	45	2	25	4.4	89	98	43	82	11	6	1	123	292	20	22	2.8	.954	3B-154, SS-1
1994	113	.288	.433	423	122	23	4	10	2.4	46	50	36	71	3	3	1	72	216	17	19	2.7	.944	3B-110
7 yrs.	800	.267	.413	2841	758	145	10	83	2.9	303	367	162	472	27	31	10	615	1500	107	144	2.8	.952	3B-775, 1B-8, OF-4, SS-3, 2B-1

Year	Team	Games	BA	SA	AB	H	2B	3B	HR	HR%	R	RBI	BB	SO	SB	Pinch Hit AB	Pinch Hit H	PO	A	E	DP	TC/G	FA	G by Pos

Eric Helfand

HELFAND, ERIC JAMES
B. Mar. 25, 1969, Erie, Pa.

BL TR 6' 195 lbs.

Year	Team	Games	BA	SA	AB	H	2B	3B	HR	HR%	R	RBI	BB	SO	SB	PH AB	PH H	PO	A	E	DP	TC/G	FA	G by Pos
1993	OAK A	8	.231	.231	13	3	0	0	0	0.0	1	1	0	1	0	3	1	25	5	0	1	3.8	1.000	C-5
1994		7	.167	.167	6	1	0	0	0	0.0	1	1	0	1	0	3	0	12	2	0	0	2.0	1.000	C-6
2 yrs.		15	.211	.211	19	4	0	0	0	0.0	2	2	0	2	0	6	1	37	7	0	1	2.9	1.000	C-11

Scott Hemond

HEMOND, SCOTT MATHEW
B. Nov. 18, 1965, Taunton, Mass.

BR TR 6' 205 lbs.

Year	Team	Games	BA	SA	AB	H	2B	3B	HR	HR%	R	RBI	BB	SO	SB	PH AB	PH H	PO	A	E	DP	TC/G	FA	G by Pos
1989	OAK A	4	–	–	0	0	0	0	0		2	0	0	0	0	0	0	0	0	0	0	0.0	–	
1990		7	.154	.154	13	2	0	0	0	0.0	0	1	0	5	0	0	0	2	5	0	0	1.0	1.000	3B-7, 2B-1
1991		23	.217	.217	23	5	0	0	0	0.0	4	0	1	7	1	0	0	27	14	1	3	1.8	.976	C-8, 2B-7, DH-4, 3B-2, SS-1
1992 2 teams	OAK A (17G – .222)				CHI A (8G – .231)																			
" total		25	.225	.275	40	9	2	0	0	0.0	8	2	4	13	1	3	1	34	6	1	0	1.6	.976	C-9, DH-5, OF-4, 3B-3, SS-3
1993	OAK A	91	.256	.414	215	55	16	0	6	2.8	31	26	32	55	14	3	1	404	39	4	6	4.9	.991	C-75, OF-6, DH-3, 1B-1, 2B-1
1994		91	.222	.323	198	44	11	0	3	1.5	23	20	16	51	7	4	0	245	93	6	17	3.8	.983	C-39, 2B-25, 3B-12, 1B-7, DH-2, OF-2
6 yrs.		241	.235	.350	489	115	29	0	9	1.8	68	49	53	131	23	10	2	712	157	12	26	3.7	.986	C-131, 2B-34, 3B-24, DH-14, OF-12, 1B-8, SS-4

Dave Henderson

HENDERSON, DAVID LEE (Hendu)
B. July 21, 1958, Merced, Calif.

BR TR 6'2" 210 lbs.

Year	Team	Games	BA	SA	AB	H	2B	3B	HR	HR%	R	RBI	BB	SO	SB	PH AB	PH H	PO	A	E	DP	TC/G	FA	G by Pos
1981	SEA A	59	.167	.333	126	21	3	0	6	4.8	17	13	16	24	2	6	1	105	4	0	1	1.8	1.000	OF-58
1982		104	.253	.441	324	82	17	1	14	4.3	47	48	36	67	2	4	0	249	11	4	4	2.5	.985	OF-101
1983		137	.269	.444	484	130	24	5	17	3.5	50	55	28	93	9	4	1	304	17	6	4	2.4	.982	OF-133, DH-3
1984		112	.280	.466	350	98	23	0	14	4.0	42	43	19	56	5	5	1	242	11	3	5	2.3	.988	OF-97, DH-10
1985		139	.241	.388	502	121	28	2	14	2.8	70	68	48	104	6	2	1	335	8	5	3	2.5	.986	OF-138
1986 2 teams	SEA A (103G – .276)				BOS A (36G – .196)																			
" total		139	.265	.459	388	103	22	4	15	3.9	59	47	39	110	2	8	2	234	11	5	1	1.8	.980	OF-112, DH-22
1987 2 teams	BOS A (75G – .234)				SF N (15G – .238)																			
" total		90	.234	.410	205	48	12	0	8	3.9	32	26	30	53	3	15	3	124	1	5	0	1.4	.962	OF-73
1988	OAK A	146	.304	.525	507	154	38	1	24	4.7	100	94	47	92	2	6	3	382	5	7	2	2.7	.982	OF-143
1989		152	.250	.380	579	145	24	3	15	2.6	77	80	54	131	8	4	0	385	5	9	1	2.6	.977	OF-149, DH-2
1990		127	.271	.467	450	122	28	0	20	4.4	65	63	40	105	3	7	1	319	5	4	1	2.6	.988	OF-116, DH-6
1991		150	.276	.465	572	158	33	0	25	4.4	86	85	58	113	6	7	0	362	10	1	2	2.5	.997	OF-140, DH-7, 2B-1
1992		20	.143	.159	63	9	1	0	0	0.0	1	2	2	16	0	6	0	19	0	1	0	1.0	.950	OF-12, DH-4
1993		107	.220	.427	382	84	19	0	20	5.2	37	53	32	113	0	8	1	205	7	2	4	2.0	.991	OF-76, DH-28
1994	KC A	56	.247	.404	198	49	14	1	5	2.5	27	31	16	28	2	3	1	72	4	3	0	1.4	.962	OF-40, DH-16
14 yrs.		1538	.258	.436	5130	1324	286	17	197	3.8	710	708	465	1105	50	85	15	3334	99	55	28	2.3	.984	OF-1388, DH-98, 2B-1
LEAGUE CHAMPIONSHIP SERIES																								
1986	BOS A	5	.111	.444	9	1	0	0	1	11.1	3	4	2	2	0	0	0	11	0	0	0	2.2	1.000	OF-5
1988	OAK A	4	.375	.625	16	6	1	0	1	6.3	2	4	1	7	0	0	0	11	0	2	0	3.3	.846	OF-4
1989		5	.263	.579	19	5	3	0	1	5.3	4	1	2	5	0	0	0	22	0	0	0	4.4	1.000	OF-5
1990		2	.167	.167	6	1	0	0	0	0.0	0	1	0	2	1	0	0	7	0	0	0	3.5	1.000	OF-2
4 yrs.		16	.260	.520	50	13	4	0	3	6.0	9	10	5	16	1	0	0	51	0	2	0	3.3	.962	OF-16
WORLD SERIES																								
1986	BOS A	7	.400	.760	25	10	1	1	2	8.0	6	5	2	6	0	0	0	22	0	0	0	3.1	1.000	OF-7
1988	OAK A	5	.300	.400	20	6	2	0	0	0.0	1	1	2	7	0	0	0	12	0	0	0	2.4	1.000	OF-5
1989		4	.308	.923	13	4	2	0	2	15.4	6	4	4	3	0	0	0	13	0	0	0	3.3	1.000	OF-4
1990		4	.231	.308	13	3	1	0	0	0.0	2	0	1	3	0	0	0	7	0	0	0	1.8	1.000	OF-3
4 yrs.		20	.324	.606	71	23	6	1	4	5.6	15	10	9	19	0	0	0	54	0	0	0	2.7	1.000	OF-19

Rickey Henderson

HENDERSON, RICKEY HENLEY
B. Dec. 25, 1957, Chicago, Ill.

BR TL 5'10" 180 lbs.

Year	Team	Games	BA	SA	AB	H	2B	3B	HR	HR%	R	RBI	BB	SO	SB	PH AB	PH H	PO	A	E	DP	TC/G	FA	G by Pos
1979	OAK A	89	.274	.336	351	96	13	3	1	0.3	49	26	34	39	33	0	0	215	5	6	0	2.5	.973	OF-88
1980		158	.303	.399	591	179	22	4	9	1.5	111	53	117	54	100	0	0	407	15	7	1	2.7	.984	OF-157, DH-1
1981		108	.319	.437	423	135	18	7	6	1.4	89	35	64	68	56	1	0	327	7	7	0	3.2	.979	OF-107
1982		149	.267	.382	536	143	24	4	10	1.9	119	51	116	94	130¹	1	0	379	2	9	0	2.6	.977	OF-144, DH-4
1983		145	.292	.421	513	150	25	7	9	1.8	105	48	103	80	108	6	1	349	9	3	1	2.5	.992	OF-142, DH-1
1984		142	.293	.458	502	147	27	4	16	3.2	113	58	86	81	66	2	0	341	7	11	1	2.5	.969	OF-140
1985	NY A	143	.314	.516	547	172	28	5	24	4.4	146	72	99	65	80	1	0	439	7	9	3	3.2	.980	OF-141, DH-1
1986		153	.263	.469	608	160	31	5	28	4.6	130	74	89	81	87	3	0	426	4	6	0	2.8	.986	OF-146, DH-5
1987		95	.291	.497	358	104	17	3	17	4.7	78	37	80	52	41	2	0	189	3	4	1	2.1	.980	OF-69, DH-24
1988		140	.305	.399	554	169	30	2	6	1.1	118	50	82	54	93	0	0	320	7	12	5	2.4	.965	OF-136, DH-3
1989 2 teams	NY A (65G – .247)				OAK A (85G – .294)																			
" total		150	.274	.399	541	148	26	3	12	2.2	113	57	126	68	77	2	2	335	6	4	1	2.3	.988	OF-147, DH-3
1990	OAK A	136	.325	.577	489	159	33	3	28	5.7	119	61	97	60	65	1	0	289	5	5	0	2.2	.983	OF-118, DH-15
1991		134	.268	.423	470	126	17	1	18	3.8	105	57	98	73	58	6	1	249	10	8	1	2.0	.970	OF-119, DH-10
1992		117	.283	.457	396	112	18	3	15	3.8	77	46	95	56	48	2	1	231	9	4	2	2.1	.984	OF-108, DH-6
1993 2 teams	OAK A (90G – .327)				TOR A (44G – .215)																			
" total		134	.289	.474	481	139	22	2	21	4.4	114	59	120	65	53	2	0	258	6	7	1	2.0	.974	OF-118, DH-16
1994	OAK A	87	.260	.365	296	77	13	0	6	2.0	66	20	72	45	22	3	0	166	4	4	0	2.0	.977	OF-71, DH-13
16 yrs.		2080	.289	.440	7656	2216	364	56	226	3.0	1652	804	1478	1035	1117 1st	32	5	4920	106	106	17	2.5	.979	OF-1951, DH-102
DIVISIONAL PLAYOFF SERIES																								
1981	OAK A	3	.182	.182	11	2	0	0	0	0.0	3	0	2	0	2	0	0	8	0	0	0	2.7	1.000	OF-3
LEAGUE CHAMPIONSHIP SERIES																								
1981	OAK A	3	.364	.727	11	4	2	1	0	0.0	0	1	1	2	1	0	0	6	0	1	0	2.3	.857	OF-3
1989		5	.400	1.000	15	6	1	1	2	13.3	8	5	7	8	8	0	0	13	0	1	0	2.8	.929	OF-5
1990		4	.294	.294	17	5	0	0	0	0.0	1	3	1	2	2	0	0	10	0	0	0	2.5	1.000	OF-4
1992		6	.261	.261	23	6	0	0	0	0.0	5	1	4	4	2	0	0	15	0	3	0	3.0	.833	OF-6
1993	TOR A	6	.120	.200	25	3	2	0	0	0.0	4	0	4	5	2	0	0	9	0	1	0	1.7	.900	OF-6
5 yrs.		24	.264	.429	91	24	5	2	2	2.2	18	10	17	13	16	0	0	53	0	6	0	2.5	.898	OF-24

Year Team	Games	BA	SA	AB	H	2B	3B	HR	HR%	R	RBI	BB	SO	SB	Pinch Hit AB	H	PO	A	E	DP	TC/G	FA	G by Pos

Rickey Henderson *continued*

WORLD SERIES

Year Team	Games	BA	SA	AB	H	2B	3B	HR	HR%	R	RBI	BB	SO	SB	AB	H	PO	A	E	DP	TC/G	FA	G by Pos
1989 **OAK A**	4	.474	.895	19	9	1	2	1	5.3	4	3	2	2	3	0	0	9	0	0	0	2.3	1.000	OF-4
1990	4	.333	.667	15	5	2	0	1	6.7	2	1	3	4	1	0	0	12	1	0	0	3.3	1.000	OF-4
1993 **TOR A**	6	.227	.318	22	5	2	0	0	0.0	6	2	5	2	1	0	0	8	0	0	0	1.3	1.000	OF-6
3 yrs.	14	.339	.607	56	19	5	2	2	3.6	12	6	10	8	7	0	0	29	1	0	0	2.1	1.000	OF-14
														9th									

Carlos Hernandez

HERNANDEZ, CARLOS ALBERTO
Born Carlos Alberto Hernandez (Almeida).
B. May 24, 1967, San Felix, Venezuela.

BR TR 5'11" 185 lbs.

Year Team	Games	BA	SA	AB	H	2B	3B	HR	HR%	R	RBI	BB	SO	SB	AB	H	PO	A	E	DP	TC/G	FA	G by Pos
1990 **LA N**	10	.200	.250	20	4	1	0	0	0.0	2	1	0	2	0	0	0	37	2	0	0	3.9	1.000	C-10
1991	15	.214	.286	14	3	1	0	0	0.0	1	1	0	5	1	2	0	24	4	1	0	1.9	.966	C-13, 3B-1
1992	69	.260	.335	173	45	4	0	3	1.7	11	17	11	21	1	10	0	295	37	7	4	4.9	.979	C-63
1993	50	.253	.364	99	25	5	0	2	2.0	6	7	2	11	0	11	2	181	15	7	0	4.1	.966	C-43
1994	32	.219	.344	64	14	2	0	2	3.1	6	6	1	14	0	6	0	104	12	0	0	3.6	1.000	C-27
5 yrs.	176	.246	.338	370	91	13	0	7	1.9	26	32	14	53	1	29	2	641	70	15	4	4.1	.979	C-156, 3B-1

Jose Hernandez

HERNANDEZ, JOSE ANTONIO
Born Jose Antonio Hernandez (Figueroa).
B. July 14, 1969, Rio Piedras, Puerto Rico.

BR TR 6'1" 180 lbs.

Year Team	Games	BA	SA	AB	H	2B	3B	HR	HR%	R	RBI	BB	SO	SB	AB	H	PO	A	E	DP	TC/G	FA	G by Pos
1991 **TEX A**	45	.184	.224	98	18	2	1	0	0.0	8	4	3	31	0	0	0	49	111	4	18	3.6	.976	SS-44, 3B-1
1992 **CLE A**	3	.000	.000	4	0	0	0	0	0.0	0	0	0	2	0	0	0	3	3	1	0	2.3	.857	SS-3
1994 **CHI N**	56	.242	.326	132	32	2	3	1	0.8	18	9	8	29	2	8	2	46	85	4	15	2.4	.970	3B-28, SS-21, 2B-8, OF-1
3 yrs.	104	.214	.278	234	50	4	4	1	0.4	26	13	11	62	2	8	2	98	199	9	33	2.9	.971	SS-68, 3B-29, 2B-8, OF-1

Glenallen Hill

HILL, GLENALLEN
B. Mar. 22, 1965, Santa Cruz, Calif.

BR TR 6'3" 210 lbs.

Year Team	Games	BA	SA	AB	H	2B	3B	HR	HR%	R	RBI	BB	SO	SB	AB	H	PO	A	E	DP	TC/G	FA	G by Pos
1989 **TOR A**	19	.288	.346	52	15	0	0	1	1.9	4	7	3	12	2	0	0	27	0	1	0	1.5	.964	OF-16, DH-3
1990	84	.231	.435	260	60	11	3	12	4.6	47	32	18	62	8	7	2	115	4	2	0	1.4	.983	OF-60, DH-20
1991 **2 teams**		**TOR A** (35G – .253)					**CLE A** (37G – .262)																
" total	72	.258	.421	221	57	8	2	8	3.6	29	25	23	54	6	2	0	118	0	3	0	1.7	.975	OF-46, DH-17
1992 **CLE A**	102	.241	.436	369	89	16	1	18	4.9	38	49	20	73	9	9	1	126	5	6	1	1.3	.956	OF-59, DH-34
1993 **2 teams**		**CLE A** (66G – .224)					**CHI N** (31G – .345)																
" total	97	.264	.506	261	69	14	2	15	5.7	33	47	17	71	8	19	6	104	3	6	1	1.2	.947	OF-60, DH-18
1994 **CHI N**	89	.297	.461	269	80	12	1	10	3.7	48	38	29	57	19	20	5	150	0	2	0	1.7	.987	OF-78
6 yrs.	463	.258	.448	1432	370	61	9	64	4.5	199	198	110	329	52	57	14	640	12	20	2	1.5	.970	OF-319, DH-92

Denny Hocking

HOCKING, DENNIS LEE
B. Apr. 2, 1970, Torrance, Calif.

BB TR 5'10" 180 lbs.

Year Team	Games	BA	SA	AB	H	2B	3B	HR	HR%	R	RBI	BB	SO	SB	AB	H	PO	A	E	DP	TC/G	FA	G by Pos
1993 **MIN A**	15	.139	.167	36	5	1	0	0	0.0	7	0	6	8	1	1	0	19	23	1	11	2.9	.977	SS-12, 2B-1
1994	11	.323	.419	31	10	3	0	0	0.0	3	2	0	4	2	1	1	11	27	0	5	3.5	1.000	SS-10
2 yrs.	26	.224	.284	67	15	4	0	0	0.0	10	2	6	12	3	6	1	30	50	1	16	3.1	.988	SS-22, 2B-1

Chris Hoiles

HOILES, CHRISTOPHER ALLEN
B. Mar. 20, 1965, Bowling Green, Ohio.

BR TR 6' 195 lbs.

Year Team	Games	BA	SA	AB	H	2B	3B	HR	HR%	R	RBI	BB	SO	SB	AB	H	PO	A	E	DP	TC/G	FA	G by Pos
1989 **BAL A**	6	.111	.222	9	1	1	0	0	0.0	0	1	1	3	0	2	0	11	0	0	0	1.8	1.000	C-3, DH-3
1990	23	.190	.286	63	12	3	0	1	1.6	7	6	5	12	0	3	0	62	6	0	6	3.0	1.000	C-7, DH-7, 1B-6
1991	107	.243	.384	341	83	15	0	11	3.2	36	31	29	61	0	6	1	443	44	1	6	4.6	.998	C-89, DH-13, 1B-2
1992	96	.274	.506	310	85	10	1	20	6.5	49	40	55	60	0	0	0	500	31	3	6	5.6	.994	C-95, DH-1
1993	126	.310	.585	419	130	28	0	29	6.9	80	82	69	94	1	3	0	696	64	5	11	6.1	.993	C-124, DH-2
1994	99	.247	.449	332	82	10	0	19	5.7	45	53	63	73	2	3	0	615	36	7	2	6.6	.989	C-98
6 yrs.	457	.267	.476	1474	393	67	1	80	5.4	217	213	222	303	3	17	1	2327	181	16	31	5.5	.994	C-416, DH-26, 1B-8

Ray Holbert

HOLBERT, RAY ARTHUR III
B. Sept. 25, 1970, Torrance, Calif.

BR TR 6' 170 lbs.

Year Team	Games	BA	SA	AB	H	2B	3B	HR	HR%	R	RBI	BB	SO	SB	AB	H	PO	A	E	DP	TC/G	FA	G by Pos
1994 **SD N**	5	.200	.200	5	1	0	0	0	0.0	1	0	1	0	4	0	1	4	1	1	0	0	0	0.0	–	SS-1

Dave Hollins

HOLLINS, DAVID MICHAEL
B. May 25, 1966, Buffalo, N. Y.

BB TR 6'1" 195 lbs.

Year Team	Games	BA	SA	AB	H	2B	3B	HR	HR%	R	RBI	BB	SO	SB	AB	H	PO	A	E	DP	TC/G	FA	G by Pos
1990 **PHI N**	72	.184	.316	114	21	0	0	5	4.4	14	15	10	28	0	37	8	27	37	4	0	0.9	.941	3B-30, 1B-1
1991	56	.298	.510	151	45	10	2	6	4.0	18	21	17	26	1	14	3	67	62	8	6	2.4	.942	3B-36, 1B-6
1992	156	.270	.469	586	158	28	4	27	4.6	104	93	76	110	9	0	0	120	253	18	22	2.5	.954	3B-156, 1B-1
1993	143	.273	.442	543	148	30	4	18	3.3	104	93	85	109	2	0	0	73	215	27	9	2.2	.914	3B-143
1994	44	.222	.352	162	36	7	1	4	2.5	28	26	23	32	1	0	0	38	47	11	1	2.2	.885	3B-43, OF-1
5 yrs.	471	.262	.440	1556	408	75	11	60	3.9	268	248	211	305	13	51	11	325	614	68	38	2.1	.932	3B-408, 1B-8, OF-1

LEAGUE CHAMPIONSHIP SERIES

Year Team	Games	BA	SA	AB	H	2B	3B	HR	HR%	R	RBI	BB	SO	SB	AB	H	PO	A	E	DP	TC/G	FA	G by Pos
1993 **PHI N**	6	.200	.550	20	4	1	0	2	10.0	2	4	5	4	1	1	0	5	4	0	0	1.5	1.000	3B-6

WORLD SERIES

Year Team	Games	BA	SA	AB	H	2B	3B	HR	HR%	R	RBI	BB	SO	SB	AB	H	PO	A	E	DP	TC/G	FA	G by Pos
1993 **PHI N**	6	.261	.304	23	6	1	0	0	0.0	5	2	6	5	0	0	0	9	9	0	0	3.0	1.000	3B-6

Chris Howard

HOWARD, CHRISTOPHER HUGH
B. Feb. 27, 1966, San Diego, Calif.

BR TR 6'2" 200 lbs.

Year Team	Games	BA	SA	AB	H	2B	3B	HR	HR%	R	RBI	BB	SO	SB	AB	H	PO	A	E	DP	TC/G	FA	G by Pos
1991 **SEA A**	9	.167	.333	6	1	1	0	0	0.0	1	0	1	2	0	0	0	13	2	0	1	1.7	1.000	C-9
1993	4	.000	.000	1	0	0	0	0	0.0	0	0	0	0	0	0	0	5	0	0	0	1.3	1.000	C-4
1994	9	.200	.240	25	5	1	0	0	0.0	2	2	1	6	0	0	0	44	3	0	0	5.2	1.000	C-9
3 yrs.	22	.188	.250	32	6	2	0	0	0.0	3	2	2	8	0	0	0	62	5	0	1	3.0	1.000	C-22

Year Team	Games	BA	SA	AB	H	2B	3B	HR	HR%	R	RBI	BB	SO	SB	Pinch Hit AB	Pinch Hit H	PO	A	E	DP	TC/G	FA	G by Pos

Dave Howard

HOWARD, DAVID WAYNE
Son of Bruce Howard.
B. Feb. 26, 1967, Sarasota, Fla.
BB TR 6' 165 lbs.

Year Team	Games	BA	SA	AB	H	2B	3B	HR	HR%	R	RBI	BB	SO	SB	AB	H	PO	A	E	DP	TC/G	FA	G by Pos
1991 KC A	94	.216	.258	236	51	7	0	1	0.4	20	17	16	45	3	1	0	129	248	12	40	4.1	.969	SS-63, 2B-26, 3B-1, DH-1, OF-1
1992	74	.224	.283	219	49	6	2	1	0.5	19	18	15	43	3	0	0	124	204	8	52	4.5	.976	SS-74, OF-2
1993	15	.333	.417	24	8	0	1	0	0.0	5	2	2	5	1	0	0	17	28	3	2	3.2	.938	2B-7, SS-3, 3B-2, OF-1
1994	46	.229	.313	83	19	4	0	1	1.2	9	13	11	23	3	0	0	27	79	1	7	2.3	.991	3B-25, SS-15, 2B-3, DH-2, OF-1, P-1
4 yrs.	229	.226	.283	562	127	17	3	3	0.5	53	50	44	116	10	1	0	297	559	24	101	3.8	.973	SS-155, 2B-36, 3B-28, OF-5, DH-3, P-1

Thomas Howard

HOWARD, THOMAS SYLVESTER
B. Dec. 11, 1964, Middletown, Ohio.
BB TR 6'2" 200 lbs.

Year Team	Games	BA	SA	AB	H	2B	3B	HR	HR%	R	RBI	BB	SO	SB	AB	H	PO	A	E	DP	TC/G	FA	G by Pos
1990 SD N	20	.273	.318	44	12	2	0	0	0.0	4	0	0	11	0	8	1	19	0	1	0	1.0	.950	OF-13
1991	106	.249	.356	281	70	12	3	4	1.4	30	22	24	57	10	26	3	182	4	1	1	1.8	.995	OF-86
1992 2 teams	SD N	(5G – .333)		CLE A	(117G – .277)																		
" total	122	.277	.346	361	100	15	2	2	0.6	37	32	17	60	15	22	7	187	5	2	0	1.6	.990	OF-97, DH-2
1993 2 teams	CLE A	(74G – .236)		CIN N	(38G – .277)																		
" total	112	.254	.386	319	81	15	3	7	2.2	48	36	24	63	10	29	6	154	7	3	2	1.5	.982	OF-84, DH-7
1994 CIN N	83	.264	.410	178	47	11	0	5	2.8	24	24	10	30	4	32	9	80	2	3	1	1.0	.965	OF-57
5 yrs.	443	.262	.368	1183	310	55	8	18	1.5	143	114	75	221	39	117	26	622	18	10	4	1.5	.985	OF-337, DH-9

Dann Howitt

HOWITT, DANN PAUL JOHN
B. Feb. 13, 1964, Battle Creek, Mich.
BL TR 6'5" 205 lbs.

Year Team	Games	BA	SA	AB	H	2B	3B	HR	HR%	R	RBI	BB	SO	SB	AB	H	PO	A	E	DP	TC/G	FA	G by Pos
1989 OAK A	3	.000	.000	3	0	0	0	0	0.0	0	0	0	2	0	1	0	2	0	0	0	0.7	1.000	1B-1, OF-1
1990	14	.136	.227	22	3	0	1	0	0.0	3	1	3	12	0	2	0	34	1	0	3	2.5	1.000	OF-11, 1B-5, 3B-1
1991	21	.167	.262	42	7	1	0	1	2.4	5	3	1	12	0	6	1	36	0	0	0	1.7	1.000	OF-20, 1B-1
1992 2 teams	OAK A	(22G – .125)		SEA A	(13G – .270)																		
" total	35	.188	.329	85	16	4	1	2	2.4	7	10	8	9	1	2	0	63	5	2	3	2.0	.971	OF-30, 1B-4, DH-1
1993 SEA A	32	.211	.355	76	16	3	1	2	2.6	6	8	4	18	0	4	0	42	1	0	1	1.3	1.000	OF-29, DH-2
1994 CHI A	10	.357	.571	14	5	3	0	0	0.0	4	0	1	7	0	2	1	15	1	0	1	1.6	1.000	OF-7, 1B-4
6 yrs.	115	.194	.326	242	47	11	3	5	2.1	25	22	17	60	1	17	2	192	8	2	7	1.8	.990	OF-98, 1B-15, DH-3, 3B-1

Kent Hrbek

HRBEK, KENT ALLEN (Herbie)
B. May 21, 1960, Minneapolis, Minn.
BL TR 6'4" 240 lbs.

Year Team	Games	BA	SA	AB	H	2B	3B	HR	HR%	R	RBI	BB	SO	SB	AB	H	PO	A	E	DP	TC/G	FA	G by Pos
1981 MIN A	24	.239	.358	67	16	5	0	1	1.5	5	7	5	9	0	5	2	124	6	0	14	5.3	1.000	1B-13, DH-8
1982	140	.301	.485	532	160	21	4	23	4.3	82	92	54	80	3	1	0	1174	88	9	125	9.1	.993	1B-138, DH-2
1983	141	.297	.489	515	153	41	5	16	3.1	75	84	57	71	4	3	0	1151	89	13	125	8.9	.990	1B-137, DH-2
1984	149	.311	.522	559	174	31	3	27	4.8	80	107	65	87	1	1	1	1320	99	14	113	9.6	.990	1B-148, DH-1
1985	158	.278	.444	593	165	31	2	21	3.5	78	93	67	87	1	5	2	1339	114	8	114	9.2	.995	1B-156, DH-2
1986	149	.267	.478	550	147	27	1	29	5.3	85	91	71	81	2	3	0	1218	104	10	137	8.9	.992	1B-147, DH-1
1987	143	.285	.545	477	136	20	1	34	7.1	85	90	84	60	5	5	1	1179	68	5	112	8.8	.996	1B-137, DH-1
1988	143	.312	.520	510	159	31	0	25	4.9	75	76	67	54	0	2	1	842	57	3	92	6.3	.997	1B-105, DH-37
1989	109	.272	.517	375	102	17	0	25	6.7	59	84	53	35	3	4	1	723	60	4	66	7.2	.995	1B-89, DH-18
1990	143	.287	.474	492	141	26	0	22	4.5	61	79	69	45	5	4	2	1057	83	3	100	8.0	.997	1B-120, DH-20, 3B-1
1991	132	.284	.461	462	131	20	1	20	4.3	72	89	67	48	4	4	3	1138	95	8	110	9.4	.994	1B-128
1992	112	.244	.409	394	96	20	1	15	3.8	52	58	71	56	5	2	1	954	68	3	75	9.2	.997	1B-104, DH-8
1993	123	.242	.467	392	95	11	1	25	6.4	60	83	71	57	4	8	1	941	80	5	98	8.3	.995	1B-115, DH-2
1994	81	.270	.420	274	74	11	0	10	3.6	34	53	37	28	0	8	5	567	41	2	51	7.5	.997	1B-72, DH-4
14 yrs.	1747	.282	.481	6192	1749	312	18	293	4.7	903	1086	838	798	37	55	20	13727	1050	87	1332	8.5	.994	1B-1609, DH-106, 3B-1

LEAGUE CHAMPIONSHIP SERIES

Year Team	Games	BA	SA	AB	H	2B	3B	HR	HR%	R	RBI	BB	SO	SB	AB	H	PO	A	E	DP	TC/G	FA	G by Pos
1987 MIN A	5	.150	.300	20	3	0	0	1	5.0	4	1	3	0	0	0	0	40	3	0	3	8.6	1.000	1B-5
1991	5	.143	.143	21	3	0	0	0	0.0	0	3	1	3	0	0	0	40	7	0	3	9.4	1.000	1B-5
2 yrs.	10	.146	.220	41	6	0	0	1	2.4	4	4	4	3	0	0	0	80	10	0	6	9.0	1.000	1B-10

WORLD SERIES

Year Team	Games	BA	SA	AB	H	2B	3B	HR	HR%	R	RBI	BB	SO	SB	AB	H	PO	A	E	DP	TC/G	FA	G by Pos
1987 MIN A	7	.208	.333	24	5	0	0	1	4.2	4	6	5	3	0	0	0	68	2	0	3	10.0	1.000	1B-7
1991	7	.115	.269	26	3	1	0	1	3.8	2	2	2	6	0	0	0	65	8	0	4	10.4	1.000	1B-7
2 yrs.	14	.160	.300	50	8	1	0	2	4.0	6	8	7	9	0	0	0	133	10	0	7	10.2	1.000	1B-14

Trenidad Hubbard

HUBBARD, TRENIDAD AVIEL (Trent)
B. May 11, 1964, Chicago, Ill.
BR TR 5'8" 180 lbs.

Year Team	Games	BA	SA	AB	H	2B	3B	HR	HR%	R	RBI	BB	SO	SB	AB	H	PO	A	E	DP	TC/G	FA	G by Pos
1994 CLR N	18	.280	.520	25	7	1	1	1	4.0	3	3	3	4	0	12	5	4	0	0	0	0.2	1.000	OF-5

Rex Hudler

HUDLER, REX ALLEN
B. Sept. 2, 1960, Tempe, Ariz.
BR TR 6'1" 180 lbs.

Year Team	Games	BA	SA	AB	H	2B	3B	HR	HR%	R	RBI	BB	SO	SB	AB	H	PO	A	E	DP	TC/G	FA	G by Pos
1984 NY A	9	.143	.286	7	1	1	0	0	0.0	2	0	1	5	0	0	0	4	7	0	1	1.2	1.000	2B-9
1985	20	.157	.196	51	8	0	1	0	0.0	4	1	1	9	0	0	0	42	51	2	14	4.8	.979	2B-16, 1B-1, SS-1
1986 BAL A	14	.000	.000	1	0	0	0	0	0.0	1	0	0	0	1	0	0	2	3	1	0	0.4	.833	2B-13, 3B-1
1988 MON N	77	.273	.412	216	59	14	2	4	1.9	38	14	10	34	29	3	0	116	168	10	30	3.8	.966	2B-41, OF-27, OF-4
1989	92	.245	.406	155	38	7	0	6	3.9	21	13	6	23	15	27	4	59	59	7	13	1.4	.944	2B-38, OF-23, SS-18
1990 2 teams	MON N	(4G – .333)		STL N	(89G – .281)																		
" total	93	.282	.445	220	62	11	2	7	3.2	31	22	12	32	18	21	4	158	42	5	9	2.2	.976	OF-45, 2B-10, 1B-6, 3B-6, SS-1
1991 STL N	101	.227	.309	207	47	10	2	1	0.5	21	15	10	29	12	27	4	130	6	2	6	1.4	.986	OF-58, 1B-12, 2B-5
1992	61	.245	.378	98	24	4	0	3	3.1	17	5	2	23	2	29	7	44	39	3	6	1.4	.965	2B-26, OF-18, 3B-4
1994 CAL A	56	.298	.556	124	37	8	0	8	6.5	17	20	6	28	2	10	0	71	61	5	20	2.4	.964	2B-22, OF-18, 3B-4, DH-4, 1B-1
9 yrs.	523	.256	.400	1079	276	55	7	29	2.7	152	90	48	183	79	117	19	626	436	35	99	2.1	.968	2B-170, OF-160, SS-47, 1B-28, 3B-11, DH-4

Mike Huff

HUFF, MICHAEL KALE
B. Aug. 11, 1963, Honolulu, Hawaii.

BR TR 6'1" 180 lbs.

Year	Team		Games	BA	SA	AB	H	2B	3B	HR	HR%	R	RBI	BB	SO	SB	Pinch Hit AB	H	PO	A	E	DP	TC/G	FA	G by Pos
1989	LA	N	12	.200	.360	25	5	1	0	1	4.0	4	2	3	6	0	3	1	18	0	0	0	1.5	1.000	OF-9
1991	2 teams		CLE A (51G – .240)			CHI A (51G – .268)																			
"	total		102	.251	.346	243	61	10	2	3	1.2	42	25	37	48	14	12	0	168	7	2	1	1.7	.989	OF-96, 2B-4, DH-2
1992	CHI	A	60	.209	.252	115	24	5	0	0	0.0	13	8	10	24	1	16	5	68	2	0	0	1.2	1.000	OF-56, DH-1
1993			43	.182	.295	44	8	2	0	1	2.3	4	6	9	15	1	2	0	40	0	0	0	0.9	1.000	OF-43
1994	TOR	A	80	.304	.449	207	63	15	3	3	1.4	31	25	27	27	2	9	3	126	4	1	1	1.6	.992	OF-76
5 yrs.			297	.254	.360	634	161	33	5	8	1.3	94	66	86	120	18	42	9	420	13	3	2	1.5	.993	OF-280, 2B-4, DH-3

Tim Hulett

HULETT, TIMOTHY CRAIG
B. Jan. 20, 1960, Springfield, Ill.

BR TR 6' 185 lbs.

Year	Team		Games	BA	SA	AB	H	2B	3B	HR	HR%	R	RBI	BB	SO	SB	Pinch Hit AB	H	PO	A	E	DP	TC/G	FA	G by Pos
1983	CHI	A	6	.200	.200	5	1	0	0	0	0.0	0	0	0	0	1	0	0	8	6	2	1	2.7	.875	2B-6
1984			8	.000	.000	7	0	0	0	0	0.0	1	0	1	4	1	1	0	4	15	0	2	2.4	1.000	3B-4, 2B-3
1985			141	.268	.375	395	106	19	4	5	1.3	52	36	30	81	6	2	1	117	256	24	41	2.8	.940	3B-115, 2B-28, OF-1
1986			150	.231	.379	520	120	16	5	17	3.3	53	44	21	91	4	5	1	179	331	15	54	3.5	.971	3B-89, 2B-66
1987			68	.217	.346	240	52	10	0	7	2.9	20	28	10	41	0	0	0	55	142	9	19	3.0	.956	3B-61, 2B-8
1989	BAL	A	33	.278	.423	97	27	5	0	3	3.1	12	18	10	17	0	1	0	70	71	4	13	4.4	.972	2B-23, 3B-11
1990			53	.255	.373	153	39	7	1	3	2.0	16	16	15	41	1	9	1	44	101	4	15	2.8	.973	3B-24, 2B-16, DH-8
1991			79	.204	.350	206	42	9	0	7	3.4	29	18	13	49	1	10	2	47	96	4	13	1.9	.973	3B-39, 2B-26, DH-15, SS-1
1992			57	.289	.408	142	41	7	2	2	1.4	11	21	10	31	0	9	2	25	92	7	11	2.2	.944	3B-27, DH-13, 2B-10, SS-5
1993			85	.300	.381	260	78	15	0	2	0.8	40	23	23	56	1	6	1	58	176	8	26	2.8	.967	3B-75, SS-8, 2B-4, DH-2
1994			36	.228	.337	92	21	2	1	2	2.2	11	15	12	24	0	2	0	61	93	4	24	4.4	.981	2B-23, 3B-9, SS-6
11 yrs.			716	.249	.372	2117	527	90	13	48	2.3	245	219	145	435	14	45	8	668	1379	80	219	3.0	.962	3B-454, 2B-213, DH-38, SS-20, OF-1

David Hulse

HULSE, DAVID LINDSEY
B. Feb. 25, 1968, San Angelo, Texas.

BL TL 5'11" 170 lbs.

Year	Team		Games	BA	SA	AB	H	2B	3B	HR	HR%	R	RBI	BB	SO	SB	Pinch Hit AB	H	PO	A	E	DP	TC/G	FA	G by Pos
1992	TEX	A	32	.304	.348	92	28	4	0	0	0.0	14	2	3	18	3	0	0	61	0	1	0	1.9	.984	OF-31, DH-1
1993			114	.290	.369	407	118	9	10	1	0.2	71	29	26	57	29	6	5	244	3	3	0	2.2	.988	OF-112, DH-2
1994			77	.255	.316	310	79	8	4	1	0.3	58	19	21	53	18	0	0	179	0	4	0	2.4	.978	OF-76
3 yrs.			223	.278	.346	809	225	21	14	2	0.2	143	50	50	128	50	6	5	484	3	8	0	2.2	.984	OF-219, DH-3

Todd Hundley

HUNDLEY, TODD RANDOLPH
Son of Randy Hundley.
B. May 27, 1969, Martinsville, Va.

BB TR 5'11" 170 lbs.

Year	Team		Games	BA	SA	AB	H	2B	3B	HR	HR%	R	RBI	BB	SO	SB	Pinch Hit AB	H	PO	A	E	DP	TC/G	FA	G by Pos
1990	NY	N	36	.209	.299	67	14	6	0	0	0.0	8	2	6	18	0	3	0	162	8	2	2	4.8	.988	C-36
1991			21	.133	.217	60	8	0	1	1	1.7	5	7	6	14	0	3	1	85	11	0	1	4.6	1.000	C-20
1992			123	.209	.316	358	75	17	0	7	2.0	32	32	19	76	3	7	1	700	48	3	2	6.1	.996	C-121
1993			130	.228	.357	417	95	17	2	11	2.6	40	53	23	62	1	15	3	592	63	8	6	5.1	.988	C-123
1994			91	.237	.443	291	69	10	1	16	5.5	45	42	25	73	2	15	4	448	28	5	0	5.3	.990	C-82
5 yrs.			401	.219	.355	1193	261	50	4	35	2.9	130	136	79	243	6	43	9	1987	158	18	11	5.4	.992	C-382

Brian Hunter

HUNTER, BRIAN LEE
B. Mar. 5, 1971, Portland, Ore.

BR TR 6'4" 180 lbs.

Year	Team		Games	BA	SA	AB	H	2B	3B	HR	HR%	R	RBI	BB	SO	SB	Pinch Hit AB	H	PO	A	E	DP	TC/G	FA	G by Pos
1994	HOU	N	6	.250	.292	24	6	1	0	0	0.0	2	0	1	6	2	0	0	13	1	1	1	2.5	.933	OF-6

Brian Hunter

HUNTER, BRIAN RAYNOLD
B. Mar. 4, 1968, Torrance, Calif.

BR TL 6' 195 lbs.

Year	Team		Games	BA	SA	AB	H	2B	3B	HR	HR%	R	RBI	BB	SO	SB	Pinch Hit AB	H	PO	A	E	DP	TC/G	FA	G by Pos
1991	ATL	N	97	.251	.450	271	68	16	1	12	4.4	32	50	17	48	0	18	3	624	46	8	42	7.0	.988	1B-85, OF-6
1992			102	.239	.487	238	57	13	2	14	5.9	34	41	21	50	1	21	5	542	50	4	35	5.8	.993	1B-92, OF-6
1993			37	.138	.200	80	11	3	1	0	0.0	4	8	2	15	0	11	1	168	13	1	19	4.9	.995	1B-29, OF-2
1994	2 teams		PIT N (76G – .227)			CIN N (9G – .304)																			
"	total		85	.234	.480	256	60	16	1	15	5.9	34	57	17	56	0	17	5	515	39	5	48	6.6	.991	1B-60, OF-10
4 yrs.			321	.232	.446	845	196	48	5	41	4.9	104	156	57	169	1	67	14	1849	148	18	144	6.3	.991	1B-266, OF-24

LEAGUE CHAMPIONSHIP SERIES

1991	ATL	N	5	.333	.611	18	6	2	0	1	5.6	2	4	0	4	0	0	0	30	4	0	3	6.8	1.000	1B-5
1992			3	.200	.200	5	1	0	0	0	0.0	0	0	1	0	0	2	0	7	0	0	0	2.3	1.000	1B-2
2 yrs.			8	.304	.522	23	7	2	0	1	4.3	2	4	1	4	0	2	0	37	4	0	3	5.1	1.000	1B-7

WORLD SERIES

1991	ATL	N	7	.190	.381	21	4	1	0	1	4.8	2	3	0	2	0	3	1	6	1	1	1	1.1	.875	1B-4, OF-4
1992			4	.200	.200	5	1	0	0	0	0.0	0	2	0	1	0	0	0	14	1	0	2	3.8	1.000	1B-3
2 yrs.			11	.192	.346	26	5	1	0	1	3.8	2	5	0	3	0	4	1	20	2	1	3	2.1	.957	1B-7, OF-4

Tim Hyers

HYERS, TIMOTHY JAMES
B. Oct. 3, 1971, Atlanta, Ga.

BL TL 6'1" 185 lbs.

Year	Team		Games	BA	SA	AB	H	2B	3B	HR	HR%	R	RBI	BB	SO	SB	Pinch Hit AB	H	PO	A	E	DP	TC/G	FA	G by Pos
1994	SD	N	52	.254	.280	118	30	3	0	0	0.0	9	7	9	15	3	9	3	258	23	4	19	5.5	.986	1B-41, OF-2

Pete Incaviglia

INCAVIGLIA, PETER JOSEPH (Inky)
B. Apr. 2, 1964, Pebble Beach, Calif.

BR TR 6'1" 225 lbs.

Year	Team		Games	BA	SA	AB	H	2B	3B	HR	HR%	R	RBI	BB	SO	SB	Pinch Hit AB	H	PO	A	E	DP	TC/G	FA	G by Pos
1986	TEX	A	153	.250	.463	540	135	21	2	30	5.6	82	88	55	185	3	4	0	157	6	14	1	1.2	.921	OF-114, DH-36
1987			139	.271	.497	509	138	26	4	27	5.3	85	80	48	168	9	3	0	216	8	13	0	1.7	.945	OF-132, DH-6
1988			116	.249	.467	418	104	19	3	22	5.3	59	54	39	153	6	0	0	172	12	2	1	1.6	.989	OF-93, DH-21
1989			133	.236	.453	453	107	27	4	21	4.6	48	81	32	136	5	5	2	213	7	6	2	1.7	.973	OF-125, DH-5
1990			153	.233	.420	529	123	27	0	24	4.5	59	85	45	146	3	13	2	290	12	8	2	2.0	.974	OF-145, DH-2
1991	DET	A	97	.214	.353	337	72	12	1	11	3.3	38	38	36	92	1	3	0	106	4	3	2	1.2	.973	OF-54, DH-41
1992	HOU	N	113	.266	.430	349	93	22	1	11	3.2	31	44	25	99	2	18	4	188	8	6	1	1.8	.970	OF-98
1993	PHI	N	116	.274	.530	368	101	16	3	24	6.5	60	89	21	82	1	24	6	164	4	5	1	1.5	.971	OF-97
1994			80	.230	.439	244	56	10	1	13	5.3	28	32	16	71	1	20	7	90	2	2	0	1.2	.979	OF-63
9 yrs.			1100	.248	.453	3747	929	180	19	183	4.9	490	591	317	1132	31	90	21	1596	63	59	10	1.6	.966	OF-921, DH-111

Year Team	Games	BA	SA	AB	H	2B	3B	HR	HR%	R	RBI	BB	SO	SB	Pinch Hit AB	H	PO	A	E	DP	TC/G	FA	G by Pos

Pete Incaviglia *continued*

LEAGUE CHAMPIONSHIP SERIES
| 1993 PHI N | 3 | .167 | .417 | 12 | 2 | 0 | 0 | 1 | 8.3 | 2 | 1 | 0 | 3 | 0 | 0 | 0 | 8 | 0 | 0 | 0 | 2.7 | 1.000 | OF-3 |

WORLD SERIES
| 1993 PHI N | 4 | .125 | .125 | 8 | 1 | 0 | 0 | 0 | 0.0 | 0 | 1 | 0 | 4 | 0 | 1 | 1 | 7 | 0 | 0 | 0 | 1.8 | 1.000 | OF-4 |

Garey Ingram

INGRAM, GAREY LAMAR
B. July 25, 1970, Columbus, Ga.   BR TR 5'11" 180 lbs.
| 1994 LA N | 26 | .282 | .410 | 78 | 22 | 1 | 0 | 3 | 3.8 | 10 | 8 | 7 | 22 | 0 | 2 | 1 | 44 | 68 | 2 | 14 | 4.4 | .982 | 2B-23 |

Riccardo Ingram

INGRAM, RICCARDO BENAY
B. Sept. 10, 1966, Douglas, Ga.   BR TR 6' 205 lbs.
| 1994 DET A | 12 | .217 | .217 | 23 | 5 | 0 | 0 | 0 | 0.0 | 3 | 2 | 1 | 2 | 0 | 1 | 0 | 13 | 1 | 0 | 0 | 1.2 | 1.000 | OF-8, DH-1 |

Bo Jackson

JACKSON, VINCENT EDWARD
B. Nov. 30, 1962, Bessemer, Ala.   BR TR 6'1" 222 lbs.
1986 KC A	25	.207	.329	82	17	2	1	2	2.4	9	9	7	34	3	0	0	29	2	4	0	1.4	.886	OF-23, DH-1
1987	116	.235	.455	396	93	17	2	22	5.6	46	53	30	158	10	2	0	180	9	9	1	1.7	.955	OF-113, DH-1
1988	124	.246	.472	439	108	16	4	25	5.7	63	68	25	146	27	1	0	246	11	7	2	2.1	.973	OF-121, DH-2
1989	135	.256	.495	515	132	15	6	32	6.2	86	105	39	172	26	1	0	224	11	8	2	1.8	.967	OF-110, DH-24
1990	111	.272	.523	405	110	16	1	28	6.9	74	78	44	128	15	4	1	230	8	12	2	2.3	.952	OF-97, DH-10
1991 CHI A	23	.225	.408	71	16	4	0	3	4.2	8	14	12	25	0	2	1	0	0	0	0	0.0	—	DH-21
1993	85	.232	.433	284	66	9	0	16	5.6	32	45	23	106	0	8	3	89	5	1	1	1.1	.989	OF-47, DH-36
1994 CAL A	75	.279	.507	201	56	7	0	13	6.5	23	43	20	72	1	15	4	77	3	3	0	1.1	.964	OF-46, DH-9
8 yrs.	694	.250	.474	2393	598	86	14	141	5.9	341	415	200	841	82	33	9	1075	49	44	8	1.7	.962	OF-557, DH-104

LEAGUE CHAMPIONSHIP SERIES
| 1993 CHI A | 3 | .000 | .000 | 10 | 0 | 0 | 0 | 0 | 0.0 | 1 | 0 | 3 | 6 | 0 | 0 | 0 | 0 | 0 | 0 | 0 | 0.0 | — | DH-3 |

Chuck Jackson

JACKSON, CHARLES LEO
B. Mar. 19, 1963, Seattle, Wash.   BR TR 6' 185 lbs.
1987 HOU N	35	.211	.296	71	15	3	0	1	1.4	3	6	7	19	1	5	1	12	39	2	4	1.5	.962	3B-16, OF-13, SS-1
1988	46	.229	.349	83	19	5	1	1	1.2	7	8	7	16	1	9	2	12	51	7	6	1.5	.900	3B-32, OF-3, SS-3
1994 TEX A	1	.000	.000	2	0	0	0	0	0.0	0	0	0	0	0	0	0	0	0	0	0	0.0	—	3B-1
3 yrs.	82	.218	.321	156	34	8	1	2	1.3	10	14	14	35	2	14	3	24	90	9	10	1.5	.927	3B-49, OF-16, SS-4

Darrin Jackson

JACKSON, DARRIN JAY
B. Aug. 22, 1963, Los Angeles, Calif.   BR TR 6' 185 lbs.
1985 CHI N	5	.091	.091	11	1	0	0	0	0.0	0	0	0	3	0	0	0	7	0	0	0	1.4	1.000	OF-4
1987	7	.800	1.000	5	4	1	0	0	0.0	2	0	0	0	0	4	3	1	0	0	0	0.1	1.000	OF-5
1988	100	.266	.452	188	50	11	3	6	3.2	29	20	5	28	4	21	5	116	1	2	0	1.2	.983	OF-74
1989 2 teams	CHI N (45G – .229)			SD N (25G – .207)
" total	70	.218	.329	170	37	7	0	4	2.4	17	20	13	34	1	14	1	121	5	5	4	1.9	.962	OF-63
1990 SD N	58	.257	.363	113	29	3	0	3	2.7	10	9	5	24	3	18	4	63	1	1	1	1.1	.985	OF-39
1991	122	.262	.476	359	94	12	1	21	5.8	51	49	27	66	5	23	3	243	2	2	2	2.0	.992	OF-98, P-1
1992	155	.249	.392	587	146	23	5	17	2.9	72	70	26	106	14	2	0	435	18	2	9	2.9	.996	OF-153
1993 2 teams	TOR A (46G – .216)			NY N (31G – .195)
" total	77	.209	.312	263	55	9	0	6	2.3	19	26	10	75	0	8	2	137	6	1	2	1.9	.993	OF-72
1994 CHI A	104	.312	.455	369	115	17	3	10	2.7	43	51	27	56	7	8	3	225	2	1	1	2.2	.996	OF-102
9 yrs.	698	.257	.406	2065	531	83	12	67	3.2	243	245	113	392	34	99	21	1348	35	14	19	2.0	.990	OF-610, P-1

John Jaha

JAHA, JOHN EMIL
B. May 27, 1966, Portland, Ore.   BR TR 6'1" 195 lbs.
1992 MIL A	47	.226	.308	133	30	3	1	2	1.5	17	10	12	30	10	3	2	286	22	0	22	6.6	1.000	1B-38, DH-8, OF-1
1993	153	.264	.416	515	136	21	0	19	3.7	78	70	51	109	13	4	0	1187	128	10	116	8.7	.992	1B-150, 2B-1, 3B-1
1994	84	.241	.412	291	70	14	0	12	4.1	45	39	32	75	3	1	0	660	47	8	60	8.5	.989	1B-73, DH-11
3 yrs.	284	.251	.399	939	236	38	1	33	3.5	140	119	95	214	26	8	2	2133	197	18	198	8.3	.992	1B-261, DH-19, OF-1, 2B-1, 3B-1

Chris James

JAMES, DONALD CHRIS
B. Oct. 4, 1962, Rusk, Tex.   BR TR 6'1" 190 lbs.
1986 PHI N	16	.283	.413	46	13	3	0	1	2.2	5	5	1	13	0	6	1	19	0	0	0	1.2	1.000	OF-11
1987	115	.293	.525	358	105	20	6	17	4.7	48	54	27	67	3	9	5	198	5	2	1	1.8	.990	OF-108
1988	150	.242	.389	566	137	24	1	19	3.4	57	66	31	73	7	4	1	282	51	9	6	2.3	.974	OF-116, 3B-31
1989 2 teams	PHI N (45G – .207)			SD N (87G – .264)
" total	132	.243	.367	482	117	17	2	13	2.7	55	65	26	68	5	8	2	215	27	7	4	1.9	.972	OF-116, 3B-17
1990 CLE A	140	.299	.443	528	158	32	4	12	2.3	62	70	31	71	4	6	2	25	1	0	0	0.2	1.000	DH-124, OF-14
1991	115	.238	.318	437	104	16	2	5	1.1	31	41	18	61	3	7	2	173	10	0	8	1.6	1.000	DH-60, OF-39, 1B-15
1992 SF N	111	.242	.375	248	60	10	4	5	2.0	25	32	14	45	2	44	9	112	2	3	2	1.1	.974	OF-62
1993 2 teams	HOU N (65G – .256)			TEX A (8G – .355)
" total	73	.275	.525	160	44	11	1	9	5.6	24	26	18	40	2	28	7	79	4	3	1	1.2	.965	OF-41
1994 TEX A	52	.256	.534	133	34	8	4	7	5.3	28	19	20	38	0	12	3	63	2	0	0	1.3	1.000	OF-48
9 yrs.	904	.261	.414	2958	772	141	24	88	3.0	335	378	186	476	26	124	33	1166	102	24	22	1.4	.981	OF-555, DH-184, 3B-48, 1B-15

Stan Javier

JAVIER, STANLEY JULIAN
Born Stanley Julian Javier (DeJavier).
Son of Julian Javier.
B. Jan. 9, 1964, San Francisco De Macoris, Dominican Republic.   BB TR 6' 180 lbs.
| 1984 NY A | 7 | .143 | .143 | 7 | 1 | 0 | 0 | 0 | 0.0 | 1 | 0 | 0 | 1 | 0 | 0 | 0 | 3 | 0 | 0 | 0 | 0.4 | 1.000 | OF-5 |
| 1986 OAK A | 59 | .202 | .272 | 114 | 23 | 8 | 0 | 0 | 0.0 | 13 | 8 | 16 | 27 | 8 | 0 | 0 | 118 | 1 | 0 | 1 | 2.0 | 1.000 | OF-51, DH-2 |

Stan Javier *continued*

Year Team	Games	BA	SA	AB	H	2B	3B	HR	HR%	R	RBI	BB	SO	SB	Pinch Hit AB	Pinch Hit H	PO	A	E	DP	TC/G	FA	G by Pos
1987	81	.185	.258	151	28	3	1	2	1.3	22	9	19	33	3	7	0	149	5	3	4	1.9	.981	OF-71, 1B-6, DH-1
1988	125	.257	.320	397	102	13	3	2	0.5	49	35	32	63	20	9	2	274	7	5	5	2.3	.983	OF-115, 1B-4, DH-2
1989	112	.248	.316	310	77	12	3	1	0.3	42	28	31	45	12	7	0	221	8	2	2	2.1	.991	OF-107, 1B-1, 2B-1
1990 **2 teams**		**OAK A** (19G – .242)		**LA N** (104G – .304)																			
" total	123	.298	.395	309	92	9	6	3	1.0	60	27	40	50	15	31	8	223	2	0	1	1.8	1.000	OF-100, DH-2
1991 LA N	121	.205	.284	176	36	5	3	1	0.6	21	11	16	36	7	52	5	90	4	3	1	0.8	.969	OF-69, 1B-2
1992 **2 teams**		**LA N** (56G – .190)		**PHI N** (74G – .261)																			
" total	130	.249	.314	334	83	17	1	1	0.3	42	29	37	54	18	30	7	229	7	3	1	1.8	.987	OF-101
1993 CAL A	92	.291	.405	237	69	10	4	3	1.3	33	28	27	33	12	27	7	167	4	4	2	1.9	.977	OF-64, 1B-12, 2B-2, DH-1
1994 OAK A	109	.272	.399	419	114	23	0	10	2.4	75	44	49	76	24	1	0	274	4	4	0	2.6	.986	OF-108, 1B-1, 3B-1
10 yrs.	959	.255	.341	2454	625	100	21	23	0.9	358	219	267	418	119	164	29	1748	42	24	17	1.9	.987	OF-791, 1B-26, DH-8, 2B-3, 3B-1

LEAGUE CHAMPIONSHIP SERIES

Year Team	Games	BA	SA	AB	H	2B	3B	HR	HR%	R	RBI	BB	SO	SB	Pinch Hit AB	Pinch Hit H	PO	A	E	DP	TC/G	FA	G by Pos
1988 OAK A	2	.500	.500	4	2	0	0	0	0.0	0	1	1	0	0	0	0	5	0	0	0	2.5	1.000	OF-2
1989	1	.000	.000	2	0	0	0	0	0.0	0	0	0	0	0	0	0	1	0	0	0	1.0	1.000	OF-1
2 yrs.	3	.333	.333	6	2	0	0	0	0.0	0	1	1	0	0	0	0	6	0	0	0	2.0	1.000	OF-3

WORLD SERIES

Year Team	Games	BA	SA	AB	H	2B	3B	HR	HR%	R	RBI	BB	SO	SB	Pinch Hit AB	Pinch Hit H	PO	A	E	DP	TC/G	FA	G by Pos
1988 OAK A	3	.500	.500	4	2	0	0	0	0.0	0	2	0	0	0	0	0	1	0	0	0	0.3	1.000	OF-2
1989	1	–	–	0	0	0	0	0	–	0	0	0	0	0	0	0	0	0	0	0	0.0	–	OF-1
2 yrs.	4	.500	.500	4	2	0	0	0	0.0	0	2	0	0	0	0	0	1	0	0	0	0.3	1.000	OF-3

Gregg Jefferies

JEFFERIES, GREGORY SCOTT
B. Aug. 1, 1967, Burlingame, Calif.   BB TR 5'11" 175 lbs.

Year Team	Games	BA	SA	AB	H	2B	3B	HR	HR%	R	RBI	BB	SO	SB	Pinch Hit AB	Pinch Hit H	PO	A	E	DP	TC/G	FA	G by Pos
1987 NY N	6	.500	.667	6	3	0	0	0	0.0	2	0	0	0	0	6	3	0	0	0	0	0.0	–	SS-0
1988	29	.321	.596	109	35	8	2	6	5.5	19	17	8	10	5	1	0	33	46	2	9	2.8	.975	3B-20, 2B-10
1989	141	.258	.392	508	131	28	2	12	2.4	72	56	39	46	21	7	1	242	280	14	44	3.8	.974	2B-123, 3B-20
1990	153	.283	.434	604	171	**40**	3	15	2.5	96	68	46	40	11	4	1	242	341	16	54	3.9	.973	2B-118, 3B-34
1991	136	.272	.374	486	132	19	2	9	1.9	59	62	47	38	26	9	2	170	271	17	21	3.4	.963	2B-77, 3B-51
1992 KC A	152	.285	.404	604	172	36	3	10	1.7	66	75	43	29	19	3	0	96	304	26	22	2.8	.939	3B-146, 2B-1, DH-1
1993 STL N	142	.342	.485	544	186	24	3	16	2.9	89	83	62	32	46	1	1	1281	77	9	115	9.6	.993	1B-140, 2B-1
1994	103	.325	.489	397	129	27	1	12	3.0	52	55	45	26	12	3	2	890	52	7	91	9.2	.993	1B-102
8 yrs.	862	.294	.434	3258	959	183	16	80	2.5	453	418	290	221	140	34	10	2954	1371	91	356	5.1	.979	2B-330, 3B-271, 1B-242, DH-1, SS-0

LEAGUE CHAMPIONSHIP SERIES

Year Team	Games	BA	SA	AB	H	2B	3B	HR	HR%	R	RBI	BB	SO	SB	Pinch Hit AB	Pinch Hit H	PO	A	E	DP	TC/G	FA	G by Pos
1988 NY N	7	.333	.407	27	9	2	0	0	0.0	2	1	4	0	1	0	0	5	8	1	0	2.0	.929	3B-7

Reggie Jefferson

JEFFERSON, REGINALD JIROD
B. Sept. 25, 1968, Tallahassee, Fla.   BB TL 6'4" 210 lbs.

Year Team	Games	BA	SA	AB	H	2B	3B	HR	HR%	R	RBI	BB	SO	SB	Pinch Hit AB	Pinch Hit H	PO	A	E	DP	TC/G	FA	G by Pos
1991 **2 teams**		**CIN N** (5G – .143)		**CLE A** (26G – .198)																			
" total	31	.194	.306	108	21	3	0	3	2.8	11	13	4	24	0	2	0	266	25	2	31	9.5	.993	1B-28
1992 CLE A	24	.337	.483	89	30	6	2	1	1.1	8	6	1	17	0	2	1	129	12	1	9	5.9	.993	1B-15, DH-7
1993	113	.249	.372	366	91	11	2	10	2.7	35	34	28	78	1	17	3	112	10	3	10	1.1	.976	DH-88, 1B-15
1994 SEA A	63	.327	.543	162	53	11	0	8	4.9	24	32	17	32	0	16	7	95	10	2	14	1.7	.981	DH-32, 1B-13, OF-2
4 yrs.	231	.269	.414	725	195	31	4	22	3.0	78	85	50	151	1	37	11	602	57	8	64	2.9	.988	DH-127, 1B-71, OF-2

Brian Johnson

JOHNSON, BRIAN DAVID
B. Jan. 8, 1968, Oakland, Calif.   BR TR 6'2" 210 lbs.

Year Team	Games	BA	SA	AB	H	2B	3B	HR	HR%	R	RBI	BB	SO	SB	Pinch Hit AB	Pinch Hit H	PO	A	E	DP	TC/G	FA	G by Pos
1994 SD N	36	.247	.409	93	23	4	1	3	3.2	7	16	5	21	0	10	4	185	15	0	1	5.6	1.000	C-24, 1B-5

Charles Johnson

JOHNSON, CHARLES EDWARD, JR.
B. July 20, 1971, Fort Pierce, Fla.   BR TR 6'2" 215 lbs.

Year Team	Games	BA	SA	AB	H	2B	3B	HR	HR%	R	RBI	BB	SO	SB	Pinch Hit AB	Pinch Hit H	PO	A	E	DP	TC/G	FA	G by Pos
1994 FLA N	4	.455	.818	11	5	1	0	1	9.1	5	4	1	4	0	0	0	18	2	0	0	5.0	1.000	C-4

Erik Johnson

JOHNSON, ERIK ANTHONY
B. Oct. 11, 1965, Oakland, Calif.   BR TR 5'11" 175 lbs.

Year Team	Games	BA	SA	AB	H	2B	3B	HR	HR%	R	RBI	BB	SO	SB	Pinch Hit AB	Pinch Hit H	PO	A	E	DP	TC/G	FA	G by Pos
1993 SF N	4	.400	.800	5	2	0	0	0	0.0	1	0	0	1	0	1	0	1	1	0	0	0.5	1.000	2B-2, 3B-1, SS-1
1994	5	.154	.154	13	2	0	0	0	0.0	0	0	0	4	0	2	0	8	7	0	3	3.0	1.000	2B-2, SS-1
2 yrs.	9	.222	.333	18	4	0	0	0	0.0	1	0	0	5	0	3	0	9	8	0	3	1.9	1.000	2B-4, SS-2, 3B-1

Howard Johnson

JOHNSON, HOWARD MICHAEL (Hojo)
B. Nov. 29, 1960, Clearwater, Fla.   BB TR 5'11" 175 lbs.

Year Team	Games	BA	SA	AB	H	2B	3B	HR	HR%	R	RBI	BB	SO	SB	Pinch Hit AB	Pinch Hit H	PO	A	E	DP	TC/G	FA	G by Pos
1982 DET A	54	.316	.426	155	49	5	0	4	2.6	23	14	16	30	7	7	1	36	40	7	6	1.5	.916	3B-33, DH-10, OF-9
1983	27	.212	.348	66	14	0	0	3	4.5	11	5	7	10	0	6	2	10	30	7	2	1.7	.851	3B-21, DH-2
1984	116	.248	.394	355	88	14	1	12	3.4	43	50	40	67	10	7	2	63	150	14	21	2.0	.938	3B-108, SS-9, DH-4, 1B-1, OF-1
1985 NY N	126	.242	.393	389	94	18	4	11	2.8	38	46	34	78	6	12	4	78	190	18	27	2.3	.937	3B-113, SS-7, OF-1
1986	88	.245	.445	220	54	14	0	10	4.5	30	39	31	64	8	17	2	52	136	20	24	2.4	.904	3B-45, SS-34, OF-1
1987	157	.265	.504	554	147	22	1	36	6.5	93	99	83	113	32	2	1	118	305	26	27	2.9	.942	3B-140, SS-38, OF-2
1988	148	.230	.422	495	114	21	1	24	4.8	85	68	86	104	23	3	1	110	274	18	37	2.7	.955	3B-131, SS-52
1989	153	.287	.559	571	164	41	3	36	6.3	**104**	101	77	126	41	0	0	97	217	24	22	2.2	.929	3B-143, SS-31
1990	154	.244	.434	590	144	37	3	23	3.9	89	90	69	100	34	1	0	150	335	28	39	3.3	.945	3B-92, SS-28
1991	156	.259	.535	564	146	34	4	**38**	6.7	108	**117**	78	120	30	1	0	161	264	31	26	2.9	.932	3B-104, OF-30, SS-28
1992	100	.223	.337	350	78	19	0	7	2.0	48	43	55	79	22	3	0	206	3	4	0	2.1	.981	OF-98
1993	72	.238	.379	235	56	8	2	7	3.0	32	26	43	43	6	3	1	52	135	11	11	2.8	.944	3B-68
1994 CLR N	93	.211	.405	227	48	10	2	10	4.4	30	40	39	73	11	33	10	98	2	0	0	1.1	.980	OF-62, 1B-1
13 yrs.	1444	.251	.449	4771	1196	243	21	221	4.6	734	738	658	1007	230	95	23	1231	2081	210	242	2.4	.940	3B-998, SS-272, OF-204, DH-16, 1B-2

Year	Team	Games	BA	SA	AB	H	2B	3B	HR	HR%	R	RBI	BB	SO	SB	Pinch Hit AB	Pinch Hit H	PO	A	E	DP	TC/G	FA	G by Pos

Howard Johnson *continued*

LEAGUE CHAMPIONSHIP SERIES

Year	Team	Games	BA	SA	AB	H	2B	3B	HR	HR%	R	RBI	BB	SO	SB	PH AB	PH H	PO	A	E	DP	TC/G	FA	G by Pos
1986	NY N	2	.000	.000	2	0	0	0	0	0.0	0	0	0	0	0	2	0	0	0	0	0	0.0	–	
1988		6	.056	.056	18	1	0	0	0	0.0	3	0	1	6	1	2	0	6	9	1	0	2.7	.938	SS-5, 3B-1
2 yrs.		8	.050	.050	20	1	0	0	0	0.0	3	0	1	6	1	4	0	6	9	1	0	2.0	.938	

WORLD SERIES

Year	Team	Games	BA	SA	AB	H	2B	3B	HR	HR%	R	RBI	BB	SO	SB	PH AB	PH H	PO	A	E	DP	TC/G	FA	G by Pos
1984	DET A	1	.000	.000	1	0	0	0	0	0.0	0	0	0	0	0	1	0	0	0	0	0	0.0	–	
1986	NY N	2	.000	.000	5	0	0	0	0	0.0	0	0	0	2	0	1	0	1	0	0	0	0.5	1.000	3B-1, SS-1
2 yrs.		3	.000	.000	6	0	0	0	0	0.0	0	0	0	2	0	2	0	1	0	0	0	0.3	1.000	

Lance Johnson

JOHNSON, KENNETH LANCE
B. July 6, 1963, Cincinnati, Ohio.   BL TL 5'10" 160 lbs.

Year	Team	Games	BA	SA	AB	H	2B	3B	HR	HR%	R	RBI	BB	SO	SB	PH AB	PH H	PO	A	E	DP	TC/G	FA	G by Pos
1987	STL N	33	.220	.288	59	13	2	1	0	0.0	4	7	4	6	6	8	2	27	0	2	0	0.9	.931	OF-25
1988	CHI A	33	.185	.234	124	23	4	1	0	0.0	11	6	6	11	6	3	2	63	1	2	0	2.0	.970	OF-31, DH-1
1989		50	.300	.367	180	54	8	2	0	0.0	28	16	17	24	16	3	1	113	0	2	0	2.3	.983	OF-45, DH-1
1990		151	.285	.357	541	154	18	9	1	0.2	76	51	33	45	36	17	4	353	5	10	3	2.4	.973	OF-148, DH-1
1991		160	.274	.342	588	161	14	**13**	0	0.0	72	49	26	58	26	4	2	425	11	2	3	2.7	.995	OF-158
1992		157	.279	.363	567	158	15	**12**	0	0.5	67	47	34	33	41	3	1	433	11	6	3	2.9	.987	OF-157
1993		147	.311	.396	540	168	18	**14**	0	0.0	75	47	36	33	35	2	0	427	7	9	1	3.0	.980	OF-146
1994		106	.277	.393	412	114	11	**14**	3	0.7	56	54	26	23	26	3	0	317	1	0	0	3.0	1.000	OF-103, DH-1
8 yrs.		837	.281	.361	3011	845	90	66	7	0.2	389	277	182	233	192	43	10	2158	36	33	10	2.7	.985	OF-813, DH-4

LEAGUE CHAMPIONSHIP SERIES

Year	Team	Games	BA	SA	AB	H	2B	3B	HR	HR%	R	RBI	BB	SO	SB	PH AB	PH H	PO	A	E	DP	TC/G	FA	G by Pos
1987	STL N	1	–	–	0	0	0	0	0	–	1	0	0	0	1	0	0	0	0	0	0	0.0	–	OF-0
1993	CHI A	6	.217	.478	23	5	1	1	1	4.3	2	6	2	1	1	0	0	15	0	0	0	2.5	1.000	OF-6
2 yrs.		7	.217	.478	23	5	1	1	1	4.3	3	6	2	1	2	0	0	15	0	0	0	2.1	1.000	OF-6

WORLD SERIES

Year	Team	Games	BA	SA	AB	H	2B	3B	HR	HR%	R	RBI	BB	SO	SB	PH AB	PH H	PO	A	E	DP	TC/G	FA	G by Pos
1987	STL N	1	–	–	0	0	0	0	0	–	0	0	0	0	1	1	0	0	0	0	0	0.0	–	OF-0

Chris Jones

JONES, CHRISTOPHER CARLOS
B. Dec. 16, 1965, Utica, N. Y.   BR TR 6'2" 200 lbs.

Year	Team	Games	BA	SA	AB	H	2B	3B	HR	HR%	R	RBI	BB	SO	SB	PH AB	PH H	PO	A	E	DP	TC/G	FA	G by Pos
1991	CIN N	52	.292	.416	89	26	1	2	2	2.2	14	6	2	31	2	26	8	27	1	0	0	0.5	1.000	OF-26
1992	HOU N	54	.190	.302	63	12	2	1	1	1.6	7	4	7	21	3	14	1	26	0	2	0	0.5	.929	OF-43
1993	CLR N	86	.273	.450	209	57	11	4	6	2.9	29	31	10	48	9	22	8	114	2	2	0	1.4	.983	OF-70
1994		21	.300	.400	40	12	2	1	0	0.0	6	2	2	14	0	9	1	16	0	1	0	0.8	.941	OF-14
4 yrs.		213	.267	.414	401	107	16	8	9	2.2	56	43	21	114	14	71	18	183	3	5	0	0.9	.974	OF-153

Brian Jordan

JORDAN, BRIAN O'NEAL
B. Mar. 29, 1967, Baltimore, Md.   BR TR 6'1" 205 lbs.

Year	Team	Games	BA	SA	AB	H	2B	3B	HR	HR%	R	RBI	BB	SO	SB	PH AB	PH H	PO	A	E	DP	TC/G	FA	G by Pos
1992	STL N	55	.207	.373	193	40	9	4	5	2.6	17	22	10	48	7	5	1	101	4	1	0	1.9	.991	OF-53
1993		67	.309	.543	223	69	10	6	10	4.5	33	44	12	35	6	2	0	140	4	4	0	2.2	.973	OF-65
1994		53	.258	.410	178	46	8	2	5	2.8	14	15	16	40	4	5	3	105	6	1	1	2.1	.991	OF-46, 1B-1
3 yrs.		175	.261	.448	594	155	27	12	20	3.4	64	81	38	123	17	12	4	346	14	6	1	2.1	.984	OF-164, 1B-1

Ricky Jordan

JORDAN, PAUL SCOTT
B. May 26, 1965, Richmond, Calif.   BR TR 6'5" 210 lbs.

Year	Team	Games	BA	SA	AB	H	2B	3B	HR	HR%	R	RBI	BB	SO	SB	PH AB	PH H	PO	A	E	DP	TC/G	FA	G by Pos
1988	PHI N	69	.308	.491	273	84	15	1	11	4.0	41	43	7	39	1	0	0	579	35	5	41	9.0	.992	1B-69
1989		144	.285	.407	523	149	22	3	12	2.3	63	75	23	62	4	10	4	1271	61	9	99	9.3	.993	1B-140
1990		92	.241	.352	324	78	21	0	5	1.5	32	44	13	39	2	8	2	743	37	4	65	8.5	.995	1B-84
1991		101	.272	.452	301	82	21	3	9	3.0	38	49	14	49	0	28	9	626	37	9	37	6.7	.987	1B-72
1992		94	.304	.417	276	84	19	0	4	1.4	33	34	5	44	3	28	8	427	27	2	34	4.9	.996	1B-54, OF-11
1993		90	.289	.421	159	46	4	1	5	3.1	21	18	8	32	0	53	16	201	4	2	20	2.3	.990	1B-33
1994		72	.282	.473	220	62	14	2	8	3.6	29	37	6	32	0	23	4	430	14	3	41	6.2	.993	1B-49
7 yrs.		662	.282	.425	2076	585	116	10	54	2.6	257	300	76	297	10	150	43	4277	215	34	337	6.8	.992	1B-501, OF-11

LEAGUE CHAMPIONSHIP SERIES

Year	Team	Games	BA	SA	AB	H	2B	3B	HR	HR%	R	RBI	BB	SO	SB	PH AB	PH H	PO	A	E	DP	TC/G	FA	G by Pos
1993	PHI N	2	1.000	.000	1	0	0	0	0	0.0	0	0	1	0	1	0	1	0	0	0	0.0	–	

WORLD SERIES

Year	Team	Games	BA	SA	AB	H	2B	3B	HR	HR%	R	RBI	BB	SO	SB	PH AB	PH H	PO	A	E	DP	TC/G	FA	G by Pos
1993	PHI N	3	.200	.200	10	2	0	0	0	0.0	0	0	0	2	0	0	1	0	0	0	0	0.0	–	DH-2

Felix Jose

JOSE, DOMINGO FELIX
Born Domingo Felix Andujar (Felix).
B. May 8, 1965, Santo Domingo, Dominican Republic.   BB TR 6'1" 190 lbs.

Year	Team	Games	BA	SA	AB	H	2B	3B	HR	HR%	R	RBI	BB	SO	SB	PH AB	PH H	PO	A	E	DP	TC/G	FA	G by Pos
1988	OAK A	8	.333	.500	6	2	1	0	0	0.0	2	1	0	1	1	2	0	8	0	0	0	1.0	1.000	OF-6
1989		20	.193	.228	57	11	2	0	0	0.0	3	5	4	13	0	3	1	35	2	1	0	1.9	.974	OF-19
1990	2 teams		OAK A	(101G – .264)	STL N	(25G – .271)																		
"	total	126	.265	.385	426	113	16	1	11	2.6	54	52	24	81	12	13	2	254	5	5	1	2.1	.981	OF-115, DH-7
1991	STL N	154	.305	.438	568	173	40	6	8	1.4	69	77	50	113	20	1	1	268	15	3	2	1.9	.990	OF-153
1992		131	.295	.432	509	150	22	3	14	2.8	62	75	40	100	28	5	2	273	11	6	1	2.2	.979	OF-127
1993	KC A	149	.253	.349	499	126	24	3	6	1.2	64	43	36	95	31	9	2	237	6	7	3	1.7	.972	OF-144, DH-1
1994		99	.303	.475	366	111	28	1	11	3.0	56	55	35	75	10	2	1	193	7	4	1	2.1	.980	OF-98
7 yrs.		687	.282	.410	2431	686	133	14	50	2.1	310	308	189	478	102	35	9	1268	46	26	8	2.0	.981	OF-662, DH-8

Wally Joyner

JOYNER, WALLACE KEITH (Wally World)
B. June 16, 1962, Atlanta, Ga.   BL TL 6'2" 185 lbs.

Year	Team	Games	BA	SA	AB	H	2B	3B	HR	HR%	R	RBI	BB	SO	SB	PH AB	PH H	PO	A	E	DP	TC/G	FA	G by Pos
1986	CAL A	154	.290	.457	593	172	27	3	22	3.7	82	100	57	58	5	4	1	1222	139	15	128	8.9	.989	1B-152
1987		149	.285	.528	564	161	33	1	34	6.0	100	117	72	64	8	2	0	1276	92	10	133	9.2	.993	1B-149
1988		158	.295	.419	597	176	31	2	13	2.2	81	85	55	51	8	2	0	1369	143	8	148	9.6	.995	1B-156
1989		159	.282	.420	593	167	30	2	16	2.7	78	79	46	58	3	2	1	1487	99	4	146	10.0	.997	1B-159
1990		83	.268	.394	310	83	15	0	8	2.6	35	41	41	34	2	1	0	727	62	4	78	9.6	.995	1B-83
1991		143	.301	.488	551	166	34	3	21	3.8	79	96	52	66	2	2	0	1335	98	8	124	10.1	.994	1B-141
1992	KC A	149	.269	.386	572	154	36	2	9	1.6	66	66	55	50	11	1	0	1236	137	10	138	9.3	.993	1B-145, DH-4

Year Team	Games	BA	SA	AB	H	2B	3B	HR	HR%	R	RBI	BB	SO	SB	Pinch Hit AB	H	PO	A	E	DP	TC/G	FA	G by Pos

Wally Joyner *continued*

Year Team	Games	BA	SA	AB	H	2B	3B	HR	HR%	R	RBI	BB	SO	SB	AB	H	PO	A	E	DP	TC/G	FA	G by Pos
1993	141	.292	.467	497	145	36	3	15	3.0	83	65	66	67	5	1	0	1116	145	7	116	9.0	.994	1B-140
1994	97	.311	.449	363	113	20	3	8	2.2	52	57	47	43	3	0	0	779	64	8	67	8.8	.991	1B-86, DH-11
9 yrs.	1233	.288	.447	4640	1337	262	19	146	3.1	656	706	491	491	47	17	4	10547	979	74	1078	9.4	.994	1B-1211, DH-15

LEAGUE CHAMPIONSHIP SERIES

Year Team	Games	BA	SA	AB	H	2B	3B	HR	HR%	R	RBI	BB	SO	SB	AB	H	PO	A	E	DP	TC/G	FA	G by Pos
1986 CAL A	3	.455	.909	11	5	2	0	1	9.1	3	2	2	2	0	0	0	26	1	0	2	9.0	1.000	1B-3

David Justice

JUSTICE, DAVID CHRISTOPHER
B. Apr. 14, 1966, Cincinnati, Ohio. BL TL 6'3" 195 lbs.

Year Team	Games	BA	SA	AB	H	2B	3B	HR	HR%	R	RBI	BB	SO	SB	AB	H	PO	A	E	DP	TC/G	FA	G by Pos
1989 ATL N	16	.235	.353	51	12	3	0	1	2.0	7	3	3	9	2	0	0	24	0	0	0	1.5	1.000	OF-16
1990	127	.282	.535	439	124	23	2	28	6.4	76	78	64	92	11	5	2	604	42	14	44	5.2	.979	1B-69, OF-61
1991	109	.275	.503	396	109	25	1	21	5.3	67	87	65	81	8	3	0	204	9	7	0	2.0	.968	OF-106
1992	144	.256	.446	484	124	19	5	21	4.3	78	72	79	85	2	3	0	313	8	8	2	2.3	.976	OF-140
1993	157	.270	.515	585	158	15	4	40	6.8	90	120	78	90	3	0	0	323	9	5	2	2.1	.985	OF-157
1994	104	.313	.531	352	110	16	2	19	5.4	61	59	69	45	2	2	1	193	6	11	0	2.0	.948	OF-102
6 yrs.	657	.276	.501	2307	637	101	14	130	5.6	379	419	358	402	28	13	3	1661	74	45	48	2.7	.975	OF-582, 1B-69

LEAGUE CHAMPIONSHIP SERIES

Year Team	Games	BA	SA	AB	H	2B	3B	HR	HR%	R	RBI	BB	SO	SB	AB	H	PO	A	E	DP	TC/G	FA	G by Pos
1991 ATL N	7	.200	.360	25	5	1	0	1	4.0	4	2	3	7	0	0	0	17	0	1	0	2.6	.944	OF-7
1992	7	.280	.560	25	7	1	0	2	8.0	5	6	6	2	0	0	0	19	3	0	0	3.1	1.000	OF-7
1993	6	.143	.190	21	3	1	0	0	0.0	2	4	3	3	0	0	0	14	0	1	0	2.5	.933	OF-6
3 yrs.	20	.211	.380	71	15	3	0	3	4.2	11	12	12	12	0	0	0	50	3	2	0	2.8	.964	OF-20

WORLD SERIES

Year Team	Games	BA	SA	AB	H	2B	3B	HR	HR%	R	RBI	BB	SO	SB	AB	H	PO	A	E	DP	TC/G	FA	G by Pos
1991 ATL N	7	.259	.481	27	7	0	0	2	7.4	5	6	5	5	2	0	0	21	1	1	0	3.3	.957	OF-7
1992	6	.158	.316	19	3	0	0	1	5.3	4	3	6	5	1	0	0	15	0	1	0	2.7	.938	OF-6
2 yrs.	13	.217	.413	46	10	0	0	3	6.5	9	9	11	10	3	0	0	36	1	2	0	3.0	.949	OF-13

Ron Karkovice

KARKOVICE, RONALD JOSEPH
B. Aug. 8, 1963, Union, N. J. BR TR 6'1" 210 lbs.

Year Team	Games	BA	SA	AB	H	2B	3B	HR	HR%	R	RBI	BB	SO	SB	AB	H	PO	A	E	DP	TC/G	FA	G by Pos
1986 CHI A	37	.247	.443	97	24	7	0	4	4.1	13	13	9	37	1	0	0	227	19	1	4	6.7	.996	C-37
1987	39	.071	.141	85	6	0	0	2	2.4	7	7	7	40	3	0	0	147	20	3	3	4.4	.982	C-37
1988	46	.174	.287	115	20	4	0	3	2.6	10	9	7	30	4	0	0	190	24	1	4	4.7	.995	C-46
1989	71	.264	.385	182	48	9	2	3	1.6	21	24	10	56	0	0	0	299	47	5	6	4.9	.986	C-68, DH-2
1990	68	.246	.399	183	45	10	0	6	3.3	30	20	16	52	2	4	2	296	31	2	4	4.8	.994	C-64, DH-1
1991	75	.246	.413	167	41	13	0	5	3.0	25	22	15	42	0	4	0	309	28	4	6	4.5	.988	C-69, OF-1
1992	123	.237	.392	342	81	12	1	13	3.8	39	50	30	89	10	4	0	536	53	6	8	4.8	.990	C-119, OF-1
1993	128	.228	.424	403	92	17	1	20	5.0	60	54	29	126	2	2	0	769	63	5	4	6.5	.994	C-127
1994	77	.213	.425	207	44	9	1	11	5.3	33	29	36	68	0	6	0	417	19	3	1	5.7	.993	C-76
9 yrs.	664	.225	.389	1781	401	81	5	67	3.8	238	228	159	540	22	20	2	3190	304	30	40	5.3	.991	C-643, DH-3, OF-2

LEAGUE CHAMPIONSHIP SERIES

Year Team	Games	BA	SA	AB	H	2B	3B	HR	HR%	R	RBI	BB	SO	SB	AB	H	PO	A	E	DP	TC/G	FA	G by Pos
1993 CHI A	6	.000	.000	15	0	0	0	0	0.0	0	0	1	7	0	0	0	30	2	0	0	5.3	1.000	C-6

Eric Karros

KARROS, ERIC PETER
B. Nov. 4, 1967, Hackensack, N. J. BR TR 6'4" 205 lbs.

Year Team	Games	BA	SA	AB	H	2B	3B	HR	HR%	R	RBI	BB	SO	SB	AB	H	PO	A	E	DP	TC/G	FA	G by Pos
1991 LA N	14	.071	.143	14	1	0	0	0	0.0	0	1	0	6	0	4	1	33	2	0	5	2.5	1.000	1B-10
1992	149	.257	.426	545	140	30	1	20	3.7	63	88	37	103	2	7	4	1211	125	9	98	9.0	.993	1B-143
1993	158	.247	.409	619	153	27	2	23	3.7	74	80	34	82	0	1	0	1335	147	12	118	9.5	.992	1B-157
1994	111	.266	.426	406	108	21	1	14	3.4	51	46	29	53	2	2	0	896	116	9	79	9.2	.991	1B-109
4 yrs.	432	.254	.417	1584	402	79	4	57	3.6	188	215	101	244	4	14	5	3475	390	30	300	9.0	.992	1B-419

Mike Kelly

KELLY, MICHAEL RAYMOND
B. June 2, 1970, Los Angeles, Calif. BR TR 6'4" 195 lbs.

Year Team	Games	BA	SA	AB	H	2B	3B	HR	HR%	R	RBI	BB	SO	SB	AB	H	PO	A	E	DP	TC/G	FA	G by Pos
1994 ATL N	30	.273	.506	77	21	10	1	2	2.6	14	9	2	17	1	6	0	25	0	1	0	0.9	.962	OF-25

Pat Kelly

KELLY, PATRICK FRANKLIN
B. Oct. 14, 1967, Philadelphia, Pa. BR TR 6' 180 lbs.

Year Team	Games	BA	SA	AB	H	2B	3B	HR	HR%	R	RBI	BB	SO	SB	AB	H	PO	A	E	DP	TC/G	FA	G by Pos
1991 NY A	96	.242	.339	298	72	12	4	3	1.0	35	23	15	52	12	0	0	78	204	18	29	3.1	.940	3B-80, 2B-19
1992	106	.226	.374	318	72	22	2	7	2.2	38	27	25	72	8	0	0	203	296	11	64	4.8	.978	2B-101, DH-1
1993	127	.273	.389	406	111	24	1	7	1.7	49	51	24	68	14	1	0	245	369	14	84	4.9	.978	2B-125
1994	93	.280	.399	286	80	21	2	3	1.0	35	41	19	51	6	1	0	182	257	10	69	4.8	.978	2B-93
4 yrs.	422	.256	.376	1308	335	79	9	20	1.5	157	142	83	243	40	3	0	708	1126	53	246	4.5	.972	2B-338, 3B-80, DH-1

Roberto Kelly

KELLY, ROBERTO CONRADO
Born Roberto Conrado Kelly (Gray).
B. Oct. 1, 1964, Panama City, Panama. BR TR 6'2" 180 lbs.

Year Team	Games	BA	SA	AB	H	2B	3B	HR	HR%	R	RBI	BB	SO	SB	AB	H	PO	A	E	DP	TC/G	FA	G by Pos
1987 NY A	23	.269	.385	52	14	3	0	1	1.9	12	7	5	15	9	0	0	42	0	2	0	1.9	.955	OF-17
1988	38	.247	.364	77	19	4	1	1	1.3	9	7	3	15	5	1	1	70	1	1	0	1.9	.986	OF-30
1989	137	.302	.417	441	133	18	3	9	2.0	65	48	41	89	35	3	2	353	9	6	2	2.7	.984	OF-137
1990	162	.285	.418	641	183	32	4	15	2.3	85	61	33	148	42	4	1	420	5	5	0	2.7	.988	OF-160, DH-1
1991	126	.267	.444	486	130	22	2	20	4.1	68	69	45	77	32	2	1	268	8	4	1	2.2	.986	OF-125
1992	152	.272	.384	580	158	31	2	10	1.7	81	66	41	96	28	5	0	389	8	7	3	2.7	.983	OF-146
1993 CIN N	78	.319	.475	320	102	17	3	9	2.8	44	35	17	43	21	0	0	198	3	1	1	2.6	.995	OF-78
1994 2 teams		CIN N (47G – .302)		ATL N (63G – .286)																			
" total	110	.293	.422	434	127	23	3	9	2.1	73	45	35	71	19	0	0	247	5	3	0	2.3	.988	OF-110
8 yrs.	826	.286	.420	3031	866	150	18	74	2.4	437	338	220	554	191	14	5	1987	39	29	7	2.5	.986	OF-803, DH-1

Jeff Kent

KENT, JEFFREY FRANKLIN
B. Mar. 7, 1968, Bellflower, Calif. BR TR 6'1" 185 lbs.

Year Team	Games	BA	SA	AB	H	2B	3B	HR	HR%	R	RBI	BB	SO	SB	AB	H	PO	A	E	DP	TC/G	FA	G by Pos
1992 2 teams		TOR A (65G – .240)		NY N (37G – .239)																			
" total	102	.239	.430	305	73	14	2	11	3.6	52	50	27	76	2	3	1	124	205	14	23	3.4	.959	2B-51, 3B-50, 1B-3, SS-1

Year	Team	Games	BA	SA	AB	H	2B	3B	HR	HR%	R	RBI	BB	SO	SB	Pinch Hit AB	Pinch Hit H	PO	A	E	DP	TC/G	FA	G by Pos

Jeff Kent *continued*

1993	NY N	140	.270	.446	496	134	24	0	21	4.2	65	80	30	88	4	1	0	261	341	22	73	4.5	.965	2B-127, 3B-12, SS-2
1994		107	.292	.475	415	121	24	5	14	3.4	53	68	23	84	1	0	0	221	338	14	76	5.4	.976	2B-107
3 yrs.		349	.270	.451	1216	328	69	7	46	3.8	170	198	80	248	7	4	1	606	884	50	172	4.4	.968	2B-285, 3B-62, 1B-3, SS-3

Jeff King

KING, JEFFREY WAYNE
B. Dec. 26, 1964, Marion, Ind.

BR TR 6'1" 175 lbs.

1989	PIT N	75	.195	.353	215	42	13	3	5	2.3	31	19	20	34	4	15	3	403	59	4	36	6.2	.991	1B-46, 3B-13, 2B-7, SS-1
1990		127	.245	.410	371	91	17	1	14	3.8	46	53	21	50	3	19	5	61	215	18	15	2.3	.939	3B-115, 1B-1
1991		33	.239	.376	109	26	1	1	4	3.7	16	18	14	15	3	0	0	15	62	2	0	2.4	.975	3B-33
1992		130	.231	.371	480	111	21	2	14	2.9	56	65	27	56	4	7	1	368	234	12	58	4.7	.980	3B-73, 1B-32, 2B-32, SS-6, OF-1
1993		158	.295	.406	611	180	35	3	9	1.5	82	98	59	54	8	1	0	108	362	18	30	3.1	.963	3B-156, 2B-2, SS-2
1994		94	.263	.375	339	89	23	0	5	1.5	36	42	30	38	3	1	0	61	198	13	26	2.9	.952	3B-91, 1B-1
6 yrs.		617	.254	.387	2125	539	110	10	51	2.4	267	295	171	247	25	43	9	1016	1130	67	165	3.6	.970	3B-481, 1B-79, 2B-42, SS-9, OF-1

LEAGUE CHAMPIONSHIP SERIES

1990	PIT N	5	.100	.100	10	1	0	0	0	0.0	1	0	1	5	0	2	0	1	4	0	0	1.0	1.000	3B-4
1992		7	.241	.379	29	7	4	0	0	0.0	4	2	0	1	0	0	0	11	19	1	5	4.4	.968	3B-7
2 yrs.		12	.205	.308	39	8	4	0	0	0.0	4	2	1	6	0	2	0	12	23	1	5	3.0	.972	3B-11

Mike Kingery

KINGERY, MICHAEL SCOTT
B. Mar. 29, 1961, St. James, Minn.

BL TL 6' 180 lbs.

1986	KC A	62	.258	.388	209	54	8	5	3	1.4	25	14	12	30	7	5	2	102	6	3	2	1.8	.973	OF-59
1987	SEA A	120	.280	.449	354	99	25	4	9	2.5	38	52	27	43	7	9	3	226	15	2	3	2.0	.992	OF-114, DH-4
1988		57	.203	.276	123	25	6	0	1	0.8	21	9	19	23	3	5	0	102	6	2	1	1.9	.982	OF-44, 1B-10
1989		31	.224	.342	76	17	3	0	2	2.6	14	6	7	14	1	6	0	70	0	0	0	2.3	1.000	OF-23
1990	SF N	105	.295	.338	207	61	7	1	0	0.0	24	24	12	19	6	17	7	126	7	3	2	1.3	.978	OF-95
1991		91	.182	.236	110	20	2	2	0	0.0	13	8	15	21	1	44	11	60	2	1	2	0.7	.984	OF-38, 1B-6
1992	OAK A	12	.107	.107	28	3	0	0	0	0.0	3	1	1	3	0	3	0	14	0	0	0	1.2	1.000	OF-10
1994	CLR N	105	.349	.532	301	105	27	8	4	1.3	56	41	30	26	5	12	3	187	5	4	1	1.9	.980	OF-98, 1B-1
8 yrs.		583	.273	.397	1408	384	78	20	19	1.3	194	155	123	179	30	101	26	887	41	15	11	1.6	.984	OF-481, 1B-17, DH-4

Wayne Kirby

KIRBY, WAYNE LEONARD
B. Jan. 22, 1964, Williamsburg, Va.

BL TR 5'11" 185 lbs.

1991	CLE A	21	.209	.256	43	9	2	0	0	0.0	4	5	2	6	1	1	0	40	1	0	0	2.0	1.000	OF-21
1992		21	.167	.389	18	3	1	0	1	5.6	9	1	3	2	0	9	2	3	0	0	0	0.1	1.000	DH-4, OF-2
1993		131	.269	.371	458	123	19	5	6	1.3	71	60	37	58	17	10	0	273	19	5	5	2.3	.983	OF-123, DH-5
1994		78	.293	.403	191	56	6	0	5	2.6	33	23	13	30	11	15	5	92	2	4	1	1.3	.959	OF-68, DH-2
4 yrs.		251	.269	.373	710	191	28	5	12	1.7	117	89	55	96	29	35	7	408	22	9	6	1.7	.979	OF-214, DH-11

Ryan Klesko

KLESKO, RYAN ANTHONY
B. June 12, 1971, Westminster, Calif.

BL TL 6'3" 220 lbs.

1992	ATL N	13	.000	.000	14	0	0	0	0	0.0	0	1	0	5	0	7	0	25	0	0	2	1.9	1.000	1B-5
1993		22	.353	.765	17	6	1	0	2	11.8	3	5	3	4	0	15	6	8	0	0	0	0.4	1.000	1B-3, OF-2
1994		92	.278	.563	245	68	13	3	17	6.9	42	47	26	48	1	14	3	89	3	7	1	1.1	.929	OF-74, 1B-6
3 yrs.		127	.268	.547	276	74	14	3	19	6.9	45	53	29	57	1	36	9	122	3	7	3	1.0	.947	OF-76, 1B-14

Chuck Knoblauch

KNOBLAUCH, EDWARD CHARLES
B. July 7, 1968, Houston, Tex.

BR TR 5'9" 175 lbs.

1991	MIN A	151	.281	.350	565	159	24	6	1	0.2	78	50	59	40	25	3	2	249	460	18	94	4.8	.975	2B-148, SS-2
1992		155	.297	.358	600	178	19	6	2	0.3	104	56	88	60	34	1	0	306	416	6	104	4.7	.992	2B-154, DH-1, SS-1
1993		153	.277	.346	602	167	27	4	2	0.3	82	41	65	44	29	4	0	302	431	9	100	4.8	.988	2B-148, SS-6, OF-1
1994		109	.312	.461	445	139	**45**	3	5	1.1	85	51	41	56	35	0	0	190	285	3	60	4.4	.994	2B-109, SS-1
4 yrs.		568	.291	.373	2212	643	115	19	10	0.5	349	198	253	200	123	8	2	1047	1592	36	358	4.7	.987	2B-559, SS-10, DH-1, OF-1

LEAGUE CHAMPIONSHIP SERIES

| 1991 | MIN A | 5 | .350 | .450 | 20 | 7 | 2 | 0 | 0 | 0.0 | 5 | 3 | 3 | 3 | 2 | 0 | 0 | 8 | 14 | 0 | 3 | 4.4 | 1.000 | 2B-5 |

WORLD SERIES

| 1991 | MIN A | 7 | .308 | .346 | 26 | 8 | 1 | 0 | 0 | 0.0 | 3 | 2 | 4 | 2 | 4 | 0 | 0 | 15 | 14 | 1 | 1 | 4.3 | .967 | 2B-7 |

Randy Knorr

KNORR, RANDY DUANE
B. Nov. 12, 1968, San Gabriel, Calif.

BR TR 6'2" 205 lbs.

1991	TOR A	3	.000	.000	1	0	0	0	0	0.0	0	0	0	1	0	0	0	6	1	0	0	2.3	1.000	C-3
1992		8	.263	.421	19	5	0	0	1	5.3	1	2	1	5	0	0	0	33	3	0	0	4.5	1.000	C-8, DH-1
1993		39	.248	.436	101	25	3	2	4	4.0	11	20	9	29	0	1	0	168	20	0	4	4.8	1.000	C-39
1994		40	.242	.427	124	30	2	0	7	5.6	20	19	10	35	0	1	0	247	21	2	1	6.8	.993	C-40
4 yrs.		90	.245	.429	245	60	5	2	12	4.9	32	41	21	70	0	2	0	454	45	2	5	5.6	.996	C-90, DH-1

WORLD SERIES

| 1993 | TOR A | 1 | — | — | 0 | 0 | 0 | 0 | 0 | — | 0 | 0 | 0 | 0 | 0 | 0 | 0 | 3 | 0 | 0 | 0 | 3.0 | 1.000 | C-1 |

Kevin Koslofski

KOSLOFSKI, KEVIN CRAIG
B. Sept. 24, 1966, Decatur, Ill.

BL TR 5'8" 165 lbs.

1992	KC A	55	.248	.346	133	33	0	2	3	2.3	20	13	12	23	2	5	2	107	5	0	0	2.1	.991	OF-52
1993		15	.269	.385	26	7	0	0	1	3.8	4	2	4	5	0	1	0	20	2	0	2	1.5	1.000	OF-13, DH-1
1994		2	.250	.250	4	1	0	0	0	0.0	2	0	2	1	0	1	1	2	1	2	0	2.0	.750	OF-2
3 yrs.		72	.252	.350	163	41	0	2	4	2.5	26	15	18	29	2	7	3	129	8	2	2	1.9	.986	OF-67, DH-1

Year Team	Games	BA	SA	AB	H	2B	3B	HR	HR%	R	RBI	BB	SO	SB	Pinch Hit AB	Pinch Hit H	PO	A	E	DP	TC/G	FA	G by Pos

Chad Kreuter

KREUTER, CHADDEN MICHAEL
B. Aug. 26, 1964, Greenbrae, Calif.

BB TR 6'2" 190 lbs.

Year Team	Games	BA	SA	AB	H	2B	3B	HR	HR%	R	RBI	BB	SO	SB	PH AB	PH H	PO	A	E	DP	TC/G	FA	G by Pos
1988 TEX A	16	.275	.412	51	14	2	1	1	2.0	3	5	7	13	0	0	0	93	8	1	0	6.4	.990	C-16
1989	87	.152	.266	158	24	3	0	5	3.2	16	9	27	40	0	1	0	453	26	4	4	5.6	.992	C-85
1990	22	.045	.091	22	1	1	0	0	0.0	2	2	8	9	0	0	0	39	4	1	0	2.0	.977	C-20, DH-1
1991	3	.000	.000	4	0	0	0	0	0.0	0	0	0	1	0	1	0	5	0	0	0	1.7	1.000	C-1
1992 DET A	67	.253	.332	190	48	9	0	2	1.1	22	16	20	38	0	3	2	271	22	5	6	4.4	.983	C-62, DH-1
1993	119	.286	.484	374	107	23	3	15	4.0	59	51	49	92	2	8	4	522	70	7	10	5.0	.988	C-112, DH-2, 1B-1
1994	65	.224	.288	170	38	8	0	1	0.6	17	19	28	36	0	1	1	280	22	4	1	4.7	.987	C-64, 1B-1, OF-1
7 yrs.	379	.239	.369	969	232	46	4	24	2.5	119	102	139	229	2	14	7	1663	152	22	21	4.8	.988	C-360, DH-4, 1B-2, OF-1

John Kruk

KRUK, JOHN MARTIN
B. Feb. 9, 1961, Charleston, W. Va.

BL TL 5'10" 220 lbs.

Year Team	Games	BA	SA	AB	H	2B	3B	HR	HR%	R	RBI	BB	SO	SB	PH AB	PH H	PO	A	E	DP	TC/G	FA	G by Pos
1986 SD N	122	.309	.424	278	86	16	2	4	1.4	33	38	45	58	2	32	8	139	6	3	3	1.2	.980	OF-74, 1B-9
1987	138	.313	.488	447	140	14	2	20	4.5	72	91	73	93	18	12	6	911	78	5	74	7.2	.995	1B-101, OF-29
1988	120	.241	.362	378	91	17	1	9	2.4	54	44	80	68	5	7	2	634	37	3	45	5.6	.996	1B-63, OF-55
1989 2 teams					SD N	(31G – .184)			PHI N	(81G – .331)													
" total	112	.300	.437	357	107	13	6	8	2.2	53	44	44	53	3	8	1	212	9	4	4	2.0	.982	OF-99, 1B-7
1990 PHI N	142	.291	.431	443	129	25	8	7	1.6	52	67	69	70	10	13	5	543	45	4	34	4.2	.993	OF-87, 1B-61
1991	152	.294	.483	538	158	27	6	21	3.9	84	92	67	100	7	9	2	848	53	3	55	5.9	.997	1B-102, OF-52
1992	144	.323	.458	507	164	30	4	10	2.0	86	70	92	88	3	1	0	1037	58	8	76	7.7	.993	1B-121, OF-35
1993	150	.316	.475	535	169	33	5	14	2.6	100	85	111	87	6	7	1	1149	69	8	79	8.2	.993	1B-144
1994	75	.302	.427	255	77	17	0	5	2.0	35	38	42	51	4	4	3	540	46	3	45	7.9	.995	1B-69
9 yrs.	1155	.300	.448	3738	1121	192	34	98	2.6	569	569	623	668	58	93	28	6013	401	41	415	5.6	.994	1B-677, OF-431

LEAGUE CHAMPIONSHIP SERIES

Year Team	Games	BA	SA	AB	H	2B	3B	HR	HR%	R	RBI	BB	SO	SB	PH AB	PH H	PO	A	E	DP	TC/G	FA	G by Pos
1993 PHI N	6	.250	.542	24	6	2	1	1	4.2	4	5	4	5	0	0	0	44	2	0	2	7.7	1.000	1B-6

WORLD SERIES

Year Team	Games	BA	SA	AB	H	2B	3B	HR	HR%	R	RBI	BB	SO	SB	PH AB	PH H	PO	A	E	DP	TC/G	FA	G by Pos
1993 PHI N	6	.348	.391	23	8	1	0	0	0.0	4	4	7	7	0	0	0	42	3	0	4	7.5	1.000	1B-6

Ray Lankford

LANKFORD, RAYMOND LEWIS
B. June 5, 1967, Los Angeles, Calif.

BL TL 5'11" 180 lbs.

Year Team	Games	BA	SA	AB	H	2B	3B	HR	HR%	R	RBI	BB	SO	SB	PH AB	PH H	PO	A	E	DP	TC/G	FA	G by Pos
1990 STL N	39	.286	.452	126	36	10	1	3	2.4	12	12	13	27	8	7	3	92	1	1	0	2.4	.989	OF-35
1991	151	.251	.392	566	142	23	15	9	1.6	83	69	41	114	44	5	1	367	7	6	2	2.5	.984	OF-149
1992	153	.293	.480	598	175	40	6	20	3.3	87	86	72	147	42	1	0	438	5	2	0	2.9	.996	OF-153
1993	127	.238	.346	407	97	17	3	7	1.7	64	45	81	111	14	8	1	312	6	7	0	2.6	.978	OF-121
1994	109	.267	.488	416	111	25	5	19	4.6	89	57	58	113	11	5	0	259	5	6	1	2.5	.978	OF-104
5 yrs.	579	.265	.431	2113	561	115	30	58	2.7	335	269	265	512	119	26	5	1468	24	22	3	2.6	.985	OF-562

Mike Lansing

LANSING, MICHAEL THOMAS (The Laser)
B. Apr. 3, 1968, Rawlins, Wyo.

BR TR 6' 175 lbs.

Year Team	Games	BA	SA	AB	H	2B	3B	HR	HR%	R	RBI	BB	SO	SB	PH AB	PH H	PO	A	E	DP	TC/G	FA	G by Pos
1993 MON N	141	.287	.369	491	141	29	1	3	0.6	64	45	46	56	23	4	1	136	336	24	53	3.5	.952	3B-81, SS-51, 2B-25
1994	106	.266	.368	394	105	21	2	5	1.3	44	35	30	37	12	0	0	164	283	10	54	4.3	.978	2B-82, 3B-28, SS-12
2 yrs.	247	.278	.368	885	246	50	3	8	0.9	108	80	76	93	35	4	1	300	619	34	107	3.9	.964	3B-109, 2B-107, SS-63

Barry Larkin

LARKIN, BARRY LOUIS
B. Apr. 28, 1964, Cincinnati, Ohio.

BR TR 6' 185 lbs.

Year Team	Games	BA	SA	AB	H	2B	3B	HR	HR%	R	RBI	BB	SO	SB	PH AB	PH H	PO	A	E	DP	TC/G	FA	G by Pos
1986 CIN N	41	.283	.403	159	45	4	3	3	1.9	27	19	9	21	8	4	0	51	125	4	22	4.4	.978	SS-36, 2B-3
1987	125	.244	.371	439	107	16	2	12	2.7	64	43	36	52	21	4	1	168	358	19	72	4.4	.965	SS-119
1988	151	.296	.429	588	174	32	5	12	2.0	91	56	41	24	40	2	0	231	470	29	67	4.8	.960	SS-148
1989	97	.342	.446	325	111	14	4	4	1.2	47	36	20	23	10	10	4	142	267	10	31	4.3	.976	SS-82
1990	158	.301	.396	614	185	25	6	7	1.1	85	67	49	49	30	3	1	254	469	17	86	4.7	.977	SS-156
1991	123	.302	.506	464	140	27	4	20	4.3	88	69	55	64	24	2	0	226	372	15	65	5.0	.976	SS-119
1992	140	.304	.454	533	162	32	6	12	2.3	76	78	63	58	15	0	0	233	408	11	67	4.7	.983	SS-140
1993	100	.315	.445	384	121	20	3	8	2.1	57	51	51	33	14	0	0	159	281	16	56	4.6	.965	SS-99
1994	110	.279	.419	439	119	23	5	9	2.1	78	52	64	58	26	0	0	178	312	10	56	4.5	.980	SS-110
9 yrs.	1045	.296	.431	3933	1164	193	38	87	2.2	613	471	388	382	188	25	6	1642	3062	131	522	4.6	.973	SS-1009, 2B-3

LEAGUE CHAMPIONSHIP SERIES

Year Team	Games	BA	SA	AB	H	2B	3B	HR	HR%	R	RBI	BB	SO	SB	PH AB	PH H	PO	A	E	DP	TC/G	FA	G by Pos
1990 CIN N	6	.261	.348	23	6	2	0	0	0.0	5	1	3	1	3	0	0	21	15	1	2	6.2	.973	SS-6

WORLD SERIES

Year Team	Games	BA	SA	AB	H	2B	3B	HR	HR%	R	RBI	BB	SO	SB	PH AB	PH H	PO	A	E	DP	TC/G	FA	G by Pos
1990 CIN N	4	.353	.529	17	6	1	1	0	0.0	3	1	2	0	0	0	0	1	14	0	2	3.8	1.000	SS-4

Mike LaValliere

LaVALLIERE, MICHAEL EUGENE (Spanky)
B. Aug. 18, 1960, Charlotte, N. C.

BL TR 5'10" 180 lbs.

Year Team	Games	BA	SA	AB	H	2B	3B	HR	HR%	R	RBI	BB	SO	SB	PH AB	PH H	PO	A	E	DP	TC/G	FA	G by Pos
1984 PHI N	6	.000	.000	7	0	0	0	0	0.0	0	0	2	2	0	0	0	20	2	0	0	3.7	1.000	C-6
1985 STL N	12	.147	.176	34	5	1	0	0	0.0	2	6	7	3	0	0	0	48	5	0	3	4.4	1.000	C-12
1986	110	.234	.310	303	71	10	2	3	1.0	18	30	36	37	0	4	0	468	47	6	8	4.7	.988	C-108
1987 PIT N	121	.300	.365	340	102	19	0	1	0.3	33	36	43	32	0	14	5	584	70	5	11	5.4	.992	C-112
1988	120	.261	.330	352	92	18	0	2	0.6	24	47	50	34	3	10	1	565	55	8	6	5.2	.987	C-114
1989	68	.316	.400	190	60	10	0	2	1.1	15	23	29	24	0	3	3	306	24	3	3	4.9	.991	C-65
1990	96	.258	.344	279	72	15	0	3	1.1	27	31	44	20	0	2	1	478	36	5	6	5.4	.990	C-95
1991	108	.289	.360	336	97	11	2	3	0.9	25	41	33	27	2	3	0	565	46	1	4	5.7	.998	C-105
1992	95	.256	.328	293	75	13	1	2	0.7	22	29	44	21	0	1	0	421	63	3	6	5.1	.994	C-92, 3B-1
1993 2 teams					PIT N	(1G – .200)			CHI A	(37G – .258)													
" total	38	.255	.275	102	26	2	0	0	0.0	6	8	14	10	0	0	0	176	28	0	2	5.4	1.000	C-38
1994 CHI A	59	.281	.331	139	39	4	0	1	0.7	6	24	20	15	0	2	0	305	21	3	1	5.6	.991	C-58
11 yrs.	833	.269	.338	2375	639	103	5	17	0.7	178	275	312	229	5	39	7	3936	397	34	50	5.2	.992	C-805, 3B-1

LEAGUE CHAMPIONSHIP SERIES

Year Team	Games	BA	SA	AB	H	2B	3B	HR	HR%	R	RBI	BB	SO	SB	PH AB	PH H	PO	A	E	DP	TC/G	FA	G by Pos
1990 PIT N	3	.000	.000	6	0	0	0	0	0.0	1	0	1	0	0	0	0	17	2	0	0	6.3	1.000	C-3
1991	3	.333	.333	6	2	0	0	0	0.0	0	1	2	0	0	1	1	14	3	0	0	5.7	1.000	C-3
1992	3	.200	.200	10	2	0	0	0	0.0	1	0	3	0	0	0	0	14	0	0	0	4.7	1.000	C-3
1993 CHI A	2	.333	.333	3	1	0	0	0	0.0	0	0	0	0	0	0	0	8	0	0	0	4.0	1.000	C-2
4 yrs.	11	.200	.200	25	5	0	0	0	0.0	2	1	6	0	0	1	1	53	5	0	0	5.3	1.000	C-11

Year Team	Games	BA	SA	AB	H	2B	3B	HR	HR%	R	RBI	BB	SO	SB	Pinch Hit AB	Pinch Hit H	PO	A	E	DP	TC/G	FA	G by Pos

Manny Lee

LEE, MANUEL
Born Manuel Lora (Lee).
B. June 17, 1965, San Pedro de Macoris, Dominican Republic.
BB TR 5'9" 150 lbs.

Year Team	Games	BA	SA	AB	H	2B	3B	HR	HR%	R	RBI	BB	SO	SB	PH AB	PH H	PO	A	E	DP	TC/G	FA	G by Pos
1985 **TOR A**	64	.200	.200	40	8	0	0	0	0.0	9	0	2	9	1	3	1	34	56	3	11	1.5	.968	2B-38, DH-8, SS-8, 3B-5
1986	35	.205	.269	78	16	0	1	1	1.3	8	7	4	10	0	0	0	36	76	2	11	3.3	.982	2B-29, SS-5, 3B-2
1987	56	.256	.347	121	31	2	3	1	0.8	14	11	6	13	2	3	2	77	110	5	26	3.4	.974	2B-27, SS-26
1988	116	.291	.365	381	111	16	3	2	0.5	38	38	26	64	3	2	0	250	308	12	71	4.9	.979	2B-98, SS-23, 3B-8
1989	99	.260	.333	300	78	9	2	3	1.0	27	34	20	60	4	13	1	152	201	11	51	3.7	.970	2B-40, SS-28, 3B-17, DH-13, OF-1
1990	117	.243	.340	391	95	12	4	6	1.5	45	41	26	90	3	3	0	265	301	4	66	4.9	.993	2B-112, SS-9
1991	138	.234	.288	445	104	18	3	0	0.0	41	29	24	107	7	0	0	194	360	19	52	4.2	.967	SS-138
1992	128	.263	.316	396	104	10	1	3	0.8	49	39	50	73	6	0	0	187	332	7	67	4.1	.987	SS-128
1993 **TEX A**	73	.220	.259	205	45	3	1	1	0.5	31	12	22	39	2	0	0	96	205	10	35	4.3	.968	SS-72
1994	95	.278	.361	335	93	18	2	2	0.6	41	38	21	66	3	0	0	152	281	13	53	4.7	.971	SS-85, 2B-13
10 yrs.	921	.254	.323	2692	685	88	20	19	0.7	303	249	201	531	31	24	4	1443	2230	86	443	4.1	.977	SS-522, 2B-357, 3B-32, DH-21, OF-1

LEAGUE CHAMPIONSHIP SERIES

Year Team	Games	BA	SA	AB	H	2B	3B	HR	HR%	R	RBI	BB	SO	SB	PH AB	PH H	PO	A	E	DP	TC/G	FA	G by Pos
1985 **TOR A**	1	–	–	0	0	0	0	0	–	0	0	0	0	0	0	0	0	0	0	0	0.0	–	2B-1
1989	2	.250	.250	8	2	0	0	0	0.0	0	0	0	1	0	0	0	4	1	0	1	2.5	1.000	2B-2
1991	5	.125	.125	16	2	0	0	0	0.0	3	0	1	5	0	0	0	8	16	1	3	5.0	.960	SS-5
1992	6	.278	.444	18	5	1	1	0	0.0	2	3	1	2	0	0	0	12	15	3	5	5.0	.900	SS-6
4 yrs.	14	.214	.286	42	9	1	1	0	0.0	7	3	2	8	0	0	0	24	32	4	9	4.3	.933	SS-11, 2B-3

WORLD SERIES

Year Team	Games	BA	SA	AB	H	2B	3B	HR	HR%	R	RBI	BB	SO	SB	PH AB	PH H	PO	A	E	DP	TC/G	FA	G by Pos
1992 **TOR A**	6	.105	.105	19	2	0	0	0	0.0	1	0	1	2	0	0	0	14	10	1	4	4.2	.960	SS-6

Scott Leius

LEIUS, SCOTT THOMAS
B. Sept. 24, 1965, Yonkers, N. Y.
BR TR 6'3" 180 lbs.

Year Team	Games	BA	SA	AB	H	2B	3B	HR	HR%	R	RBI	BB	SO	SB	PH AB	PH H	PO	A	E	DP	TC/G	FA	G by Pos
1990 **MIN A**	14	.240	.400	25	6	1	0	1	4.0	4	4	2	2	0	0	0	20	25	0	10	3.2	1.000	SS-12, 3B-1
1991	109	.286	.417	199	57	7	2	5	2.5	35	20	30	35	5	25	11	56	129	7	15	1.8	.964	3B-79, SS-19, OF-2
1992	129	.249	.318	409	102	18	2	2	0.5	50	35	34	61	6	3	2	63	261	15	13	2.6	.956	3B-125, SS-10
1993	10	.167	.167	18	3	0	0	0	0.0	4	2	2	4	0	0	0	10	26	2	7	3.8	.947	SS-9
1994	97	.246	.417	350	86	16	1	14	4.0	57	49	37	58	2	5	1	63	184	8	13	2.6	.969	3B-95, SS-2
5 yrs.	359	.254	.372	1001	254	42	5	22	2.2	150	110	105	160	13	33	14	212	625	32	58	2.4	.963	3B-300, SS-52, OF-2

LEAGUE CHAMPIONSHIP SERIES

Year Team	Games	BA	SA	AB	H	2B	3B	HR	HR%	R	RBI	BB	SO	SB	PH AB	PH H	PO	A	E	DP	TC/G	FA	G by Pos
1991 **MIN A**	3	.000	.000	4	0	0	0	0	0.0	0	0	1	1	0	0	0	1	4	0	1	1.7	1.000	3B-3

WORLD SERIES

Year Team	Games	BA	SA	AB	H	2B	3B	HR	HR%	R	RBI	BB	SO	SB	PH AB	PH H	PO	A	E	DP	TC/G	FA	G by Pos
1991 **MIN A**	7	.357	.571	14	5	0	0	1	7.1	2	2	1	2	1	0	0	5	8	1	0	2.0	.929	3B-6, SS-1

Mark Lemke

LEMKE, MARK ALAN
B. Aug. 13, 1965, Utica, N. Y.
BB TR 5'10" 167 lbs.

Year Team	Games	BA	SA	AB	H	2B	3B	HR	HR%	R	RBI	BB	SO	SB	PH AB	PH H	PO	A	E	DP	TC/G	FA	G by Pos
1988 **ATL N**	16	.224	.293	58	13	4	0	0	0.0	8	2	4	5	0	0	0	47	51	3	11	6.3	.970	2B-16
1989	14	.182	.364	55	10	2	1	2	3.6	4	10	5	7	0	1	1	25	40	0	7	4.6	1.000	2B-14
1990	102	.226	.280	239	54	13	0	0	0.0	22	21	21	22	0	15	2	90	193	4	29	2.8	.986	3B-45, 2B-44, SS-1
1991	136	.234	.312	269	63	11	2	2	0.7	36	23	29	27	1	27	9	162	215	10	40	2.8	.974	2B-110, 3B-15
1992	155	.227	.304	427	97	7	4	6	1.4	38	26	50	39	0	10	0	236	335	9	56	3.7	.984	2B-145, 3B-13
1993	151	.252	.341	493	124	19	2	7	1.4	52	49	65	50	1	1	0	329	442	14	100	5.2	.982	2B-150
1994	104	.294	.363	350	103	15	0	3	0.9	40	31	38	37	0	2	0	208	300	3	54	4.9	.994	2B-103
7 yrs.	678	.245	.324	1891	464	71	9	20	1.1	200	162	212	187	2	56	12	1097	1576	43	297	4.0	.984	2B-582, 3B-73, SS-1

LEAGUE CHAMPIONSHIP SERIES

Year Team	Games	BA	SA	AB	H	2B	3B	HR	HR%	R	RBI	BB	SO	SB	PH AB	PH H	PO	A	E	DP	TC/G	FA	G by Pos
1991 **ATL N**	7	.200	.250	20	4	1	0	0	0.0	1	1	4	0	0	0	0	12	10	1	2	3.3	.957	2B-7
1992	7	.333	.381	21	7	1	0	0	0.0	2	2	5	3	0	0	0	11	16	0	3	3.9	1.000	2B-7, 3B-1
1993	6	.208	.292	24	5	2	0	0	0.0	2	4	1	6	0	0	0	6	19	2	1	4.5	.926	2B-6
3 yrs.	20	.246	.308	65	16	4	0	0	0.0	5	7	10	9	0	0	0	29	45	3	6	3.9	.961	2B-20, 3B-1

WORLD SERIES

Year Team	Games	BA	SA	AB	H	2B	3B	HR	HR%	R	RBI	BB	SO	SB	PH AB	PH H	PO	A	E	DP	TC/G	FA	G by Pos
1991 **ATL N**	6	.417	.708	24	10	1	3	0	0.0	4	4	2	4	0	0	0	14	19	1	4	5.7	.971	2B-6
1992	6	.211	.211	19	4	0	0	0	0.0	0	2	1	3	0	0	0	19	12	0	5	5.2	1.000	2B-6
2 yrs.	12	.326	.488	43	14	1	3 (4th)	0	0.0	4	6	3	7	0	0	0	33	31	1	9	5.4	.985	2B-12

Mark Leonard

LEONARD, MARK DAVID
B. Aug. 14, 1964, Mountain View, Calif.
BL TR 6'1" 195 lbs.

Year Team	Games	BA	SA	AB	H	2B	3B	HR	HR%	R	RBI	BB	SO	SB	PH AB	PH H	PO	A	E	DP	TC/G	FA	G by Pos
1990 **SF N**	11	.176	.412	17	3	1	0	1	5.9	3	2	3	8	0	4	0	10	0	0	0	0.9	1.000	OF-7
1991	64	.240	.357	129	31	7	1	2	1.6	14	14	12	25	0	26	7	41	0	0	0	0.6	1.000	OF-34
1992	55	.234	.383	128	30	7	0	4	3.1	13	16	16	31	0	14	3	61	2	1	2	1.2	.984	OF-37
1993 **BAL A**	10	.067	.133	15	1	1	0	0	0.0	1	3	3	7	0	2	0	5	0	1	0	0.6	.833	OF-4, DH-3
1994 **SF N**	14	.364	.636	11	4	1	1	0	0.0	2	2	3	2	0	10	4	1	0	0	0	0.1	1.000	OF-2
5 yrs.	154	.230	.370	300	69	17	2	7	2.3	33	37	37	73	0	56	14	118	2	2	2	0.8	.984	OF-84, DH-3

Jesse Levis

LEVIS, JESSE
B. Apr. 14, 1968, Philadelphia, Pa.
BL TR 5'9" 180 lbs.

Year Team	Games	BA	SA	AB	H	2B	3B	HR	HR%	R	RBI	BB	SO	SB	PH AB	PH H	PO	A	E	DP	TC/G	FA	G by Pos
1992 **CLE A**	28	.279	.442	43	12	4	0	1	2.3	2	3	0	5	0	12	1	59	5	1	0	2.3	.985	C-21, DH-1
1993	31	.175	.206	63	11	2	0	0	0.0	7	4	2	10	0	8	1	108	8	1	4	3.8	.991	C-29
1994	1	1.000	1.000	1	1	0	0	0	0.0	0	0	0	0	0	1	1	0	0	0	0	–		
3 yrs.	60	.224	.308	107	24	6	0	1	0.9	9	7	2	15	0	21	3	167	13	2	4	3.0	.989	C-50, DH-1

Darren Lewis

LEWIS, DARREN JOEL
B. Aug. 28, 1967, Berkeley, Calif.
BR TR 6' 180 lbs.

Year Team	Games	BA	SA	AB	H	2B	3B	HR	HR%	R	RBI	BB	SO	SB	PH AB	PH H	PO	A	E	DP	TC/G	FA	G by Pos
1990 **OAK A**	25	.229	.229	35	8	0	0	0	0.0	4	1	7	4	2	4	0	33	0	0	0	1.3	1.000	OF-23, DH-2
1991 **SF N**	72	.248	.311	222	55	5	3	1	0.5	41	15	36	30	13	4	1	159	2	0	0	2.2	1.000	OF-68
1992	100	.231	.272	320	74	8	1	1	0.3	38	18	29	46	28	6	1	225	3	0	2	2.3	1.000	OF-94
1993	136	.253	.324	522	132	17	7	2	0.4	84	48	30	40	46	9	2	344	4	0	3	2.6	1.000	OF-131
1994	114	.257	.357	451	116	15	9	4	0.9	70	29	53	50	30	1	0	281	5	2	1	2.5	.993	OF-113
5 yrs.	447	.240	.319	1550	383	43	20	8	0.5	237	111	155	170	119	24	4	1042	14	2	6	2.4	.998	OF-429, DH-2

Year	Team	Games	BA	SA	AB	H	2B	3B	HR	HR%	R	RBI	BB	SO	SB	Pinch Hit AB	H	PO	A	E	DP	TC/G	FA	G by Pos

Mark Lewis

LEWIS, MARK DAVID
B. Nov. 30, 1969, Hamilton, Ohio.
BR TR 6'1" 190 lbs.

1991	CLE A	84	.264	.318	314	83	15	1	0	0.0	29	30	15	45	2	2	2	129	231	9	47	4.4	.976	2B-50, SS-36
1992		122	.264	.351	413	109	21	0	5	1.2	44	30	25	69	4	0	0	184	336	26	71	4.5	.952	SS-121, 3B-1
1993		14	.250	.346	52	13	2	0	1	1.9	6	5	0	7	3	0	0	22	31	2	10	3.9	.964	SS-13
1994		20	.205	.315	73	15	5	0	1	1.4	6	8	2	13	1	0	0	17	40	6	4	3.2	.905	SS-13, 3B-6, 2B-1
4 yrs.		240	.258	.336	852	220	43	1	7	0.8	85	73	42	134	10	2	2	352	638	43	132	4.3	.958	SS-183, 2B-51, 3B-7

Jim Leyritz

LEYRITZ, JAMES JOSEPH
B. Dec. 27, 1963, Lakewood, Ohio.
BR TR 6' 190 lbs.

1990	NY A	92	.257	.356	303	78	13	1	5	1.7	28	25	27	51	2	4	2	117	107	13	5	2.6	.945	3B-69, OF-14, C-11
1991		32	.182	.221	77	14	3	0	0	0.0	8	4	13	15	0	9	2	38	21	3	3	1.9	.952	3B-18, C-5, 1B-3, DH-1
1992		63	.257	.444	144	37	6	0	7	4.9	17	26	14	22	0	10	1	96	15	1	2	1.8	.991	DH-31, C-18, 1B-2, 3B-2, 2B-1
1993		95	.309	.525	259	80	14	0	14	5.4	43	53	37	59	0	13	4	333	15	2	22	3.7	.994	1B-29, OF-28, DH-21, C-12
1994		75	.265	.518	249	66	12	0	17	6.8	47	58	35	61	0	7	1	282	15	0	6	4.0	1.000	C-37, DH-25, 1B-10
5 yrs.		357	.266	.440	1032	275	48	1	43	4.2	143	166	126	208	2	43	10	866	173	19	38	3.0	.982	3B-89, C-83, DH-78, OF-44, 1B-44, 2B-1

Mike Lieberthal

LIEBERTHAL, MICHAEL SCOTT
B. Jan. 18, 1972, Glendale, Calif.
BR TR 6' 170 lbs.

| 1994 | PHI N | 24 | .266 | .367 | 79 | 21 | 3 | 1 | 1 | 1.3 | 6 | 5 | 3 | 5 | 0 | 2 | 0 | 122 | 5 | 4 | 0 | 5.5 | .969 | C-22 |

Jose Lind

LIND, JOSE
Born Jose Lind (Salgado).
B. May 1, 1964, Toabaja, Puerto Rico.
BR TR 5'11" 155 lbs.

1987	PIT N	35	.322	.434	143	46	8	4	0	0.0	21	11	8	12	2	0	0	53	139	1	12	5.5	.995	2B-35
1988		154	.262	.324	611	160	24	4	2	0.3	82	49	42	75	15	4	2	333	473	11	73	5.3	.987	2B-153
1989		153	.232	.289	578	134	21	3	2	0.3	52	48	39	64	15	5	2	309	438	18	81	5.0	.976	2B-151
1990		152	.261	.340	514	134	28	5	1	0.2	46	48	35	52	8	0	0	330	449	7	74	5.2	.991	2B-152
1991		150	.265	.339	502	133	16	6	3	0.6	53	54	30	56	7	1	0	349	438	9	79	5.3	.989	2B-149
1992		135	.235	.269	468	110	14	1	0	0.0	38	39	26	29	3	1	0	311	428	6	78	5.5	.992	2B-134
1993	KC A	136	.248	.288	431	107	13	2	0	0.0	33	37	13	36	3	1	1	269	362	4	75	4.7	.994	2B-136
1994		85	.269	.348	290	78	16	2	1	0.3	34	31	16	34	9	1	0	149	252	5	44	4.8	.988	2B-84, DH-1
8 yrs.		1000	.255	.318	3537	902	140	27	9	0.3	359	317	209	358	62	13	5	2103	2979	61	516	5.1	.988	2B-994, DH-1

LEAGUE CHAMPIONSHIP SERIES

1990	PIT N	6	.238	.524	21	5	1	1	1	4.8	1	2	1	4	0	0	0	19	19	0	4	6.3	1.000	2B-6
1991		7	.160	.160	25	4	0	0	0	0.0	0	3	0	6	0	0	0	12	24	1	1	5.3	.973	2B-7
1992		7	.222	.481	27	6	2	1	1	3.7	5	5	1	4	0	0	0	16	23	2	3	5.9	.951	2B-7
3 yrs.		20	.205	.384	73	15	3	2	2	2.7	6	10	2	14	0	0	0	47	66	3	8	5.8	.974	2B-20

Jim Lindeman

LINDEMAN, JAMES WILLIAM
B. Jan. 10, 1962, Evanston, Ill.
BR TR 6'1" 200 lbs.

1986	STL N	19	.255	.327	55	14	1	0	1	1.8	7	6	2	10	1	2	1	118	10	1	8	6.8	.992	1B-17, 3B-1, OF-1
1987		75	.208	.386	207	43	13	0	8	3.9	20	28	11	56	3	13	2	196	14	3	13	2.8	.986	OF-49, 1B-20
1988		17	.209	.372	43	9	1	0	2	4.7	3	7	2	9	0	4	2	36	2	1	2	2.3	.974	OF-12, 1B-3
1989		73	.111	.133	45	5	1	0	0	0.0	8	2	3	18	0	26	2	93	6	1	7	1.4	.990	1B-42, OF-5
1990	DET A	12	.219	.438	32	7	1	0	2	6.3	5	8	2	13	0	5	0	5	0	0	0	0.4	1.000	DH-10, 1B-1, OF-1
1991	PHI N	65	.337	.389	95	32	5	0	0	0.0	13	12	13	14	1	36	13	35	1	0	1	0.6	1.000	OF-30, 1B-1
1992		29	.256	.359	39	10	1	0	1	2.6	6	6	3	11	0	21	8	6	0	0	0	0.2	1.000	OF-9
1993	HOU N	9	.348	.478	23	8	3	0	0	0.0	2	0	1	7	0	4	0	40	5	0	6	5.0	1.000	1B-9
1994	NY N	52	.270	.496	137	37	8	1	7	5.1	18	20	6	35	0	15	4	74	2	4	4	1.5	.950	OF-33, 1B-4
9 yrs.		351	.244	.391	676	165	34	1	21	3.1	82	89	42	173	4	126	32	603	40	10	41	1.9	.985	OF-140, 1B-97, DH-10, 3B-1

LEAGUE CHAMPIONSHIP SERIES

| 1987 | STL N | 5 | .308 | .538 | 13 | 4 | 0 | 0 | 1 | 7.7 | 1 | 3 | 0 | 3 | 0 | 1 | 0 | 33 | 2 | 0 | 3 | 7.0 | 1.000 | 1B-5 |

WORLD SERIES

| 1987 | STL N | 6 | .333 | .400 | 15 | 5 | 0 | 0 | 0 | 0.0 | 3 | 2 | 0 | 3 | 0 | 1 | 0 | 28 | 2 | 3 | 2 | 5.5 | .909 | 1B-6, OF-1 |

Nelson Liriano

LIRIANO, NELSON ARTURO
Born Nelson Arturo Liriano (Bonilla).
B. June 3, 1964, Santo Domingo, Dominican Republic.
BB TR 5'10" 165 lbs.

1987	TOR A	37	.241	.342	158	38	6	2	2	1.3	29	10	16	22	13	1	1	83	107	1	28	5.2	.995	2B-37
1988		99	.264	.333	276	73	6	2	3	1.1	36	23	11	40	12	16	4	121	177	12	48	3.1	.961	2B-80, DH-11, 3B-1
1989		132	.263	.376	418	110	26	3	5	1.2	51	53	43	51	16	7	4	267	330	12	76	4.6	.980	2B-122, DH-5
1990	2 teams		TOR A	(50G - .212)		MIN A		(53G - .254)																
"	total	103	.234	.327	355	83	12	9	1	0.3	46	28	38	44	8	5	2	176	260	11	53	4.3	.975	2B-99, DH-2, SS-1
1991	KC A	10	.409	.409	22	9	0	0	0	0.0	5	1	0	2	0	0	0	11	23	0	3	3.4	1.000	2B-10
1993	CLR N	48	.305	.424	151	46	6	3	2	1.3	28	15	18	22	6	3	2	65	103	6	20	3.6	.966	SS-35, 2B-16, 3B-1
1994		87	.255	.396	255	65	17	5	3	1.2	39	31	42	44	0	3	1	146	225	10	42	4.4	.974	2B-79, SS-3, 3B-2
7 yrs.		516	.259	.363	1635	424	73	24	16	1.0	234	161	168	225	55	35	14	869	1225	52	270	4.2	.976	2B-443, SS-39, DH-18, 3B-4

LEAGUE CHAMPIONSHIP SERIES

| 1989 | TOR A | 3 | .429 | .429 | 7 | 3 | 0 | 0 | 0 | 0.0 | 1 | 1 | 2 | 0 | 3 | 0 | 0 | 4 | 3 | 1 | 1 | 2.7 | .875 | 2B-3 |

Pat Listach

LISTACH, PATRICK ALAN
B. Sept. 12, 1967, Natchitoches, La.
BR TR 5'9" 170 lbs.

1992	MIL A	149	.290	.349	579	168	19	6	1	0.2	93	47	55	124	54	1	0	238	449	24	89	4.8	.966	SS-148, 2B-1, OF-1
1993		98	.244	.317	356	87	15	1	3	0.8	50	30	37	70	18	2	1	135	267	10	53	4.2	.976	2B-80, OF-6
1994		16	.296	.352	54	16	3	0	0	0.0	8	2	3	8	2	1	0	19	51	3	10	4.6	.959	SS-16
3 yrs.		263	.274	.338	989	271	37	7	4	0.4	151	79	95	202	74	4	1	392	767	37	152	4.5	.969	SS-259, OF-7, 2B-1

Year Team	Games	BA	SA	AB	H	2B	3B	HR	HR%	R	RBI	BB	SO	SB	Pinch Hit AB	Pinch Hit H	PO	A	E	DP	TC/G	FA	G by Pos

Greg Litton
LITTON, JON GREGORY
B. July 13, 1964, New Orleans, La. BR TR 6' 175 lbs.

Year Team	Games	BA	SA	AB	H	2B	3B	HR	HR%	R	RBI	BB	SO	SB	PH AB	PH H	PO	A	E	DP	TC/G	FA	G by Pos
1989 SF N	71	.252	.413	143	36	5	3	4	2.8	12	17	7	29	0	27	9	44	66	3	5	1.6	.973	3B-34, 2B-15, SS-9, OF-6, C-2
1990	93	.245	.314	204	50	9	1	1	0.5	17	24	11	45	1	35	5	90	43	1	10	1.4	.993	OF-56, 2B-18, SS-7, 3B-5
1991	59	.181	.276	127	23	7	1	1	0.8	13	15	11	25	0	13	3	121	65	2	21	3.2	.989	1B-15, 2B-15, 3B-11, SS-9, OF-6, C-1, P-1
1992	68	.229	.350	140	32	5	0	4	2.9	9	15	11	33	0	16	4	82	85	4	26	2.5	.977	2B-31, 3B-10, 1B-8, SS-3, OF-1
1993 SEA A	72	.299	.448	174	52	17	0	3	1.7	25	25	18	30	0	15	6	135	52	0	28	2.6	1.000	OF-22, 2B-17, 1B-13, DH-12, 3B-7, SS-5
1994 BOS A	11	.095	.095	21	2	0	0	0	0.0	2	1	0	5	0	1	1	14	12	0	1	2.4	1.000	2B-4, 1B-3, 3B-3, DH-1
6 yrs.	374	.241	.355	809	195	43	5	13	1.6	78	97	58	167	1	107	28	486	323	10	91	2.2	.988	2B-100, OF-91, 3B-70, 1B-39, SS-33, DH-13, C-3, P-1

LEAGUE CHAMPIONSHIP SERIES

Year Team	Games	BA	SA	AB	H	2B	3B	HR	HR%	R	RBI	BB	SO	SB	PH AB	PH H	PO	A	E	DP	TC/G	FA	G by Pos
1989 SF N	1	1.000	1.000	1	1	0	0	0	0.0	0	0	0	0	0	0	0	1	1	0	0	0.0	-	1

WORLD SERIES

Year Team	Games	BA	SA	AB	H	2B	3B	HR	HR%	R	RBI	BB	SO	SB	PH AB	PH H	PO	A	E	DP	TC/G	FA	G by Pos
1989 SF N	2	.500	1.167	6	3	1	0	1	16.7	1	3	0	0	0	0	1	2	3	0	0	2.5	1.000	2B-2, 3B-1

Scott Livingstone
LIVINGSTONE, SCOTT LOUIS
B. July 15, 1965, Dallas, Tex. BL TR 6' 190 lbs.

Year Team	Games	BA	SA	AB	H	2B	3B	HR	HR%	R	RBI	BB	SO	SB	PH AB	PH H	PO	A	E	DP	TC/G	FA	G by Pos
1991 DET A	44	.291	.378	127	37	5	0	2	1.6	19	11	10	25	2	2	1	32	67	2	6	2.3	.980	3B-43
1992	117	.282	.376	354	100	21	0	4	1.1	43	46	21	36	1	13	3	67	189	10	15	2.3	.962	3B-112
1993	98	.293	.359	304	89	10	2	2	0.7	39	39	19	32	1	9	3	33	94	6	6	1.4	.955	3B-62, DH-32
1994 2 teams	DET A (15G – .217)			SD N (57G – .272)																			
" total	72	.266	.369	203	54	13	1	2	1.0	11	11	7	26	2	9	3	26	81	6	7	1.6	.947	3B-51, 1B-6, DH-5
4 yrs.	331	.283	.369	988	280	49	3	10	1.0	112	107	57	119	6	33	10	158	431	24	34	1.9	.961	3B-268, DH-37, 1B-6

Keith Lockhart
LOCKHART, KEITH VIRGIL
B. Nov. 10, 1964, Whittier, Calif. BL TR 5'10" 170 lbs.

Year Team	Games	BA	SA	AB	H	2B	3B	HR	HR%	R	RBI	BB	SO	SB	PH AB	PH H	PO	A	E	DP	TC/G	FA	G by Pos
1994 SD N	27	.209	.349	43	9	0	0	2	4.7	4	6	4	10	1	13	3	10	21	1	3	1.2	.969	3B-13, 2B-5, OF-1, SS-1

Kenny Lofton
LOFTON, KENNETH
B. May 31, 1967, East Chicago, Ind. BL TL 6' 180 lbs.

Year Team	Games	BA	SA	AB	H	2B	3B	HR	HR%	R	RBI	BB	SO	SB	PH AB	PH H	PO	A	E	DP	TC/G	FA	G by Pos
1991 HOU N	20	.203	.216	74	15	1	0	0	0.0	9	0	5	19	2	1	0	41	1	1	0	2.2	.977	OF-20
1992 CLE A	148	.285	.365	576	164	15	8	5	0.9	96	42	68	54	66	2	0	420	14	8	3	3.0	.982	OF-143
1993	148	.325	.408	569	185	28	8	1	0.2	116	42	81	83	70	2	0	402	11	9	3	2.9	.979	OF-147
1994	112	.349	.536	459	160	32	9	12	2.6	105	57	52	56	60	0	0	276	13	2	3	2.6	.993	OF-112
4 yrs.	428	.312	.420	1678	524	76	25	18	1.1	326	141	206	212	198	5	0	1139	39	20	9	2.8	.983	OF-422

Tony Longmire
LONGMIRE, ANTHONY EUGENE
B. Aug. 12, 1968, Vallejo, Calif. BL TR 6'1" 197 lbs.

Year Team	Games	BA	SA	AB	H	2B	3B	HR	HR%	R	RBI	BB	SO	SB	PH AB	PH H	PO	A	E	DP	TC/G	FA	G by Pos
1993 PHI N	11	.231	.231	13	3	0	0	0	0.0	1	1	0	1	0	8	3	4	0	0	0	0.4	1.000	OF-2
1994	69	.237	.317	139	33	11	0	0	0.0	10	17	10	27	2	31	8	45	3	3	1	0.7	.941	OF-32
2 yrs.	80	.237	.309	152	36	11	0	0	0.0	11	18	10	28	2	39	11	49	3	3	1	0.7	.945	OF-34

LEAGUE CHAMPIONSHIP SERIES

Year Team	Games	BA	SA	AB	H	2B	3B	HR	HR%	R	RBI	BB	SO	SB	PH AB	PH H	PO	A	E	DP	TC/G	FA	G by Pos
1993 PHI N	1	.000	.000	1	0	0	0	0	0.0	0	0	0	0	0	1	0	0	0	0	0	0.0	-	1

Javier Lopez
LOPEZ, JAVIER
Born Javier Lopez (Torres).
B. Nov. 5, 1970, Ponce, Puerto Rico. BR TR 6'3" 185 lbs.

Year Team	Games	BA	SA	AB	H	2B	3B	HR	HR%	R	RBI	BB	SO	SB	PH AB	PH H	PO	A	E	DP	TC/G	FA	G by Pos
1992 ATL N	9	.375	.500	16	6	2	0	0	0.0	3	2	0	1	0	2	1	28	2	0	0	3.3	1.000	C-9
1993	8	.375	.750	16	6	1	1	1	6.3	1	2	0	2	0	2	0	37	2	1	0	5.0	.975	C-7
1994	80	.245	.419	277	68	9	0	13	4.7	27	35	17	61	0	6	1	560	35	3	0	7.5	.995	C-75
3 yrs.	97	.259	.440	309	80	12	1	14	4.5	31	39	17	64	0	10	2	625	39	4	0	6.9	.994	C-91

LEAGUE CHAMPIONSHIP SERIES

Year Team	Games	BA	SA	AB	H	2B	3B	HR	HR%	R	RBI	BB	SO	SB	PH AB	PH H	PO	A	E	DP	TC/G	FA	G by Pos
1992 ATL N	1	.000	.000	1	0	0	0	0	0.0	0	0	0	0	0	0	0	2	0	0	0	2.0	1.000	C-1

Luis Lopez
LOPEZ, LUIS MANUEL
Born Luis Manuel Lopez (Santos).
B. Sept. 4, 1970, Cidra, Puerto Rico BB TR 5'11" 175 lbs.

Year Team	Games	BA	SA	AB	H	2B	3B	HR	HR%	R	RBI	BB	SO	SB	PH AB	PH H	PO	A	E	DP	TC/G	FA	G by Pos
1993 SD N	17	.116	.140	43	5	1	0	0	0.0	1	1	0	8	0	1	1	23	34	1	5	3.4	.983	2B-15
1994	77	.277	.379	235	65	16	1	2	0.9	29	20	15	39	3	8	1	101	174	14	23	3.8	.952	SS-43, 2B-29, 3B-5
2 yrs.	94	.252	.342	278	70	17	1	2	0.7	30	21	15	47	3	9	2	124	208	15	28	3.7	.957	2B-44, SS-43, 3B-5

Torey Lovullo
LOVULLO, SALVATORE ANTHONY
B. July 25, 1965, Santa Monica, Calif. BB TR 6' 185 lbs.

Year Team	Games	BA	SA	AB	H	2B	3B	HR	HR%	R	RBI	BB	SO	SB	PH AB	PH H	PO	A	E	DP	TC/G	FA	G by Pos
1988 DET A	12	.381	.667	21	8	1	1	1	4.8	2	2	1	2	0	0	0	12	19	0	2	2.6	1.000	2B-9, 3B-3
1989	29	.115	.172	87	10	2	0	1	1.1	8	4	14	20	0	4	0	134	24	1	15	5.5	.994	1B-18, 3B-11
1991 NY A	22	.176	.216	51	9	2	0	0	0.0	0	2	5	7	0	0	0	14	33	3	1	2.3	.940	3B-22
1993 CAL A	116	.251	.354	367	92	20	0	6	1.6	42	30	36	49	7	12	5	209	249	11	70	4.0	.977	2B-91, 3B-14, SS-9, OF-2, 1B-1
1994 SEA A	36	.222	.375	72	16	5	0	2	2.8	9	7	9	13	0	8	2	19	49	1	8	1.9	.986	2B-20, 3B-5, DH-1
5 yrs.	215	.226	.329	598	135	30	1	10	1.7	61	45	65	91	8	24	7	388	374	16	96	3.6	.979	2B-120, 3B-55, 1B-19, SS-9, OF-2, DH-1

John Mabry
MABRY, JOHN STEVEN
B. Oct. 17, 1970, Wilmington, Del. BL TR 6'4" 195 lbs.

Year Team	Games	BA	SA	AB	H	2B	3B	HR	HR%	R	RBI	BB	SO	SB	PH AB	PH H	PO	A	E	DP	TC/G	FA	G by Pos
1994 STL N	6	.304	.435	23	7	3	0	0	0.0	2	3	2	4	0	0	0	16	0	0	0	2.7	1.000	OF-6

Mike Macfarlane

MACFARLANE, MICHAEL ANDREW (Mac)
B. Apr. 12, 1964, Stockton, Calif.
BR TR 6'1" 200 lbs.

Year Team	Games	BA	SA	AB	H	2B	3B	HR	HR%	R	RBI	BB	SO	SB	Pinch Hit AB	Pinch Hit H	PO	A	E	DP	TC/G	FA	G by Pos
1987 KC A	8	.211	.263	19	4	1	0	0	0.0	0	3	2	1	0	0	0	29	2	0	0	3.9	1.000	C-8
1988	70	.265	.393	211	56	15	0	4	1.9	25	26	21	37	0	4	0	309	18	2	3	4.7	.994	C-68
1989	69	.223	.299	157	35	6	0	2	1.3	13	19	7	27	0	12	2	249	17	1	4	3.9	.996	C-59, DH-4
1990	124	.255	.380	400	102	24	4	6	1.5	37	58	25	69	1	13	3	660	23	6	9	5.6	.991	C-112, DH-5
1991	84	.277	.506	267	74	18	2	13	4.9	34	41	17	52	1	13	4	391	28	3	4	5.0	.993	C-69, DH-4
1992	129	.234	.445	402	94	28	3	17	4.2	51	48	30	89	1	16	4	527	43	4	7	4.4	.993	C-104, DH-13
1993	117	.273	.497	388	106	27	0	20	5.2	55	67	40	83	2	12	5	647	68	11	11	6.2	.985	C-114
1994	92	.255	.462	314	80	17	3	14	4.5	53	47	35	71	1	6	1	498	39	4	2	5.9	.993	C-81, DH-8
8 yrs.	693	.255	.435	2158	551	136	12	76	3.5	268	309	177	430	6	76	19	3310	238	31	40	5.2	.991	C-615, DH-34

Quinn Mack

MACK, QUINN DAVID
Brother of Shane Mack.
B. Sept. 11, 1965, Los Angeles, Calif.
BL TL 5'10" 185 lbs.

Year Team	Games	BA	SA	AB	H	2B	3B	HR	HR%	R	RBI	BB	SO	SB	Pinch Hit AB	Pinch Hit H	PO	A	E	DP	TC/G	FA	G by Pos
1994 SEA A	5	.238	.381	21	5	3	0	0	0.0	1	2	1	3	2	0	0	6	0	0	0	1.2	1.000	OF-4, DH-1

Shane Mack

MACK, SHANE LEE
Brother of Quinn Mack.
B. Dec. 7, 1963, Los Angeles, Calif.
BR TR 6' 185 lbs.

Year Team	Games	BA	SA	AB	H	2B	3B	HR	HR%	R	RBI	BB	SO	SB	Pinch Hit AB	Pinch Hit H	PO	A	E	DP	TC/G	FA	G by Pos
1987 SD N	105	.239	.361	238	57	11	3	4	1.7	28	25	18	47	4	20	3	159	1	3	0	1.6	.982	OF-91
1988	56	.244	.269	119	29	3	0	0	0.0	13	12	14	21	5	5	0	110	4	2	1	2.1	.983	OF-55
1990 MIN A	125	.326	.460	313	102	10	4	8	2.6	50	44	29	69	13	16	7	230	8	3	1	1.9	.988	OF-109, DH-4
1991	143	.310	.529	442	137	27	8	18	4.1	79	74	34	79	13	8	3	290	6	7	2	2.1	.977	OF-140, DH-1
1992	156	.315	.467	600	189	31	6	16	2.7	101	75	64	106	26	2	1	322	9	4	2	2.1	.988	OF-155
1993	128	.276	.412	503	139	30	4	10	2.0	66	61	41	76	15	1	0	347	8	5	1	2.8	.986	OF-128
1994	81	.333	.564	303	101	21	2	15	5.0	55	61	32	51	4	2	1	201	2	2	0	2.5	.990	OF-75, DH-4
7 yrs.	794	.299	.458	2518	754	133	27	71	2.8	392	352	232	449	80	49	15	1659	38	26	7	2.2	.985	OF-753, DH-9

LEAGUE CHAMPIONSHIP SERIES

Year Team	Games	BA	SA	AB	H	2B	3B	HR	HR%	R	RBI	BB	SO	SB	Pinch Hit AB	Pinch Hit H	PO	A	E	DP	TC/G	FA	G by Pos
1991 MIN A	5	.333	.500	18	6	1	1	0	0.0	4	3	2	4	2	0	0	3	0	1	0	0.8	.750	OF-5

WORLD SERIES

Year Team	Games	BA	SA	AB	H	2B	3B	HR	HR%	R	RBI	BB	SO	SB	Pinch Hit AB	Pinch Hit H	PO	A	E	DP	TC/G	FA	G by Pos
1991 MIN A	6	.130	.174	23	3	1	0	0	0.0	0	1	0	7	0	0	0	11	0	0	0	1.8	1.000	OF-6

Dave Magadan

MAGADAN, DAVID JOSEPH
B. Sept. 30, 1962, Tampa, Fla.
BL TR 6'3" 190 lbs.

Year Team	Games	BA	SA	AB	H	2B	3B	HR	HR%	R	RBI	BB	SO	SB	Pinch Hit AB	Pinch Hit H	PO	A	E	DP	TC/G	FA	G by Pos
1986 NY N	10	.444	.444	18	8	0	0	0	0.0	3	3	3	1	0	1	1	48	5	0	5	5.3	1.000	1B-9
1987	85	.318	.443	192	61	13	1	3	1.6	21	24	22	22	0	30	6	88	92	4	9	2.2	.978	3B-50, 1B-13
1988	112	.277	.334	314	87	15	0	1	0.3	39	35	60	39	0	12	1	459	99	10	42	5.1	.982	1B-71, 3B-48
1989	127	.286	.393	374	107	22	3	4	1.1	47	41	49	37	1	23	5	587	89	7	54	5.4	.990	1B-87, 3B-28
1990	144	.328	.457	451	148	28	6	6	1.3	74	72	74	55	2	22	9	837	99	3	53	6.5	.997	1B-113, 3B-19
1991	124	.258	.342	418	108	23	0	4	1.0	58	51	83	50	1	4	3	1035	90	5	73	9.1	.996	1B-122
1992	99	.283	.346	321	91	9	1	3	0.9	33	28	56	44	1	5	0	54	136	11	11	2.0	.945	3B-93, 1B-2
1993 2 teams	FLA N (66G – .286)			SEA A (71G – .259)																			
" total	137	.273	.356	455	124	23	0	5	1.1	49	50	80	63	2	10	3	381	192	12	50	4.3	.979	3B-90, 1B-43, DH-2
1994 FLA N	74	.275	.322	211	58	7	0	1	0.5	30	17	39	25	0	14	6	127	78	4	12	2.8	.981	3B-48, 1B-16
9 yrs.	912	.288	.376	2754	792	140	11	27	1.0	354	321	466	336	7	121	34	3616	880	56	309	5.0	.988	1B-476, 3B-376, DH-2

LEAGUE CHAMPIONSHIP SERIES

Year Team	Games	BA	SA	AB	H	2B	3B	HR	HR%	R	RBI	BB	SO	SB	Pinch Hit AB	Pinch Hit H	PO	A	E	DP	TC/G	FA	G by Pos
1988 NY N	3	1.000	.000	3	0	0	0	0	0.0	0	0	0	2	0	3	0	0	0	0	0	0.0	–	

Mike Maksudian

MAKSUDIAN, MICHAEL BRYANT
B. May 28, 1966, Belleville, Ill.
BL TR 5'11" 220 lbs.

Year Team	Games	BA	SA	AB	H	2B	3B	HR	HR%	R	RBI	BB	SO	SB	Pinch Hit AB	Pinch Hit H	PO	A	E	DP	TC/G	FA	G by Pos
1992 TOR A	3	.000	.000	3	0	0	0	0	0.0	0	0	0	0	0	3	0	0	0	0	0	0.0	–	1B-1
1993 MIN A	5	.167	.250	12	2	1	0	0	0.0	2	2	4	2	0	1	0	28	6	0	3	6.8	1.000	1B-4, 3B-1
1994 CHI N	26	.269	.346	26	7	2	0	0	0.0	6	4	10	4	0	13	4	18	5	0	3	0.9	1.000	1B-3, 3B-2, C-2
3 yrs.	34	.220	.293	41	9	3	0	0	0.0	8	6	14	6	0	17	4	46	11	0	6	1.7	1.000	1B-8, 3B-3, C-2

Candy Maldonado

MALDONADO, CANDIDO
Born Candido Maldonado (Guadarrama).
B. Sept. 5, 1960, Humacao, Puerto Rico.
BR TR 6' 185 lbs.

Year Team	Games	BA	SA	AB	H	2B	3B	HR	HR%	R	RBI	BB	SO	SB	Pinch Hit AB	Pinch Hit H	PO	A	E	DP	TC/G	FA	G by Pos
1981 LA N	11	.083	.083	12	1	0	0	0	0.0	0	0	0	5	0	4	0	8	0	0	0	0.7	1.000	OF-9
1982	6	.000	.000	4	0	0	0	0	0.0	0	0	0	1	0	2	0	5	0	0	0	0.8	1.000	OF-3
1983	42	.194	.290	62	12	1	1	1	1.6	5	6	5	14	0	9	2	26	0	0	0	0.6	1.000	OF-33
1984	116	.268	.382	254	68	14	0	5	2.0	25	28	19	29	0	31	9	124	5	8	0	1.2	.942	OF-102, 3B-4
1985	121	.225	.338	213	48	7	1	5	2.3	20	19	19	40	1	31	7	121	6	2	0	1.1	.984	OF-113
1986 SF N	133	.252	.477	405	102	31	3	18	4.4	49	85	20	77	4	40	17	161	11	3	0	1.3	.983	OF-101, 3B-1
1987	118	.292	.509	442	129	28	4	20	4.5	69	85	34	78	8	4	1	176	7	5	0	1.6	.973	OF-116
1988	142	.255	.377	499	127	23	1	12	2.4	53	68	37	88	6	5	0	251	5	10	1	1.9	.962	OF-139
1989	129	.217	.362	345	75	23	0	9	2.6	39	41	37	69	4	30	7	181	6	5	1	1.5	.974	OF-116
1990 CLE A	155	.273	.446	590	161	32	2	22	3.7	76	95	49	134	3	1	0	293	9	2	1	2.0	.993	OF-134, DH-20
1991 2 teams	MIL A (34G – .207)			TOR A (52G – .277)																			
" total	86	.250	.427	288	72	15	0	12	4.2	37	48	36	76	4	1	0	139	2	2	0	1.7	.986	OF-76, DH-9
1992 TOR A	137	.272	.462	489	133	25	4	20	4.1	64	66	59	112	2	2	0	260	12	6	1	2.0	.978	OF-132, DH-4
1993 2 teams	CHI N (70G – .186)			CLE A (28G – .247)																			
" total	98	.208	.348	221	46	7	0	8	3.6	19	35	24	58	0	36	6	88	4	6	2	1.0	.939	OF-68, DH-2
1994 CLE A	42	.196	.435	92	18	5	1	5	5.4	14	12	19	31	1	12	2	6	0	0	0	0.1	1.000	DH-25, OF-5
14 yrs.	1336	.253	.421	3916	992	211	17	137	3.5	470	588	359	814	33	210	53	1839	67	49	6	1.5	.975	OF-1147, DH-60, 3B-5

LEAGUE CHAMPIONSHIP SERIES

Year Team	Games	BA	SA	AB	H	2B	3B	HR	HR%	R	RBI	BB	SO	SB	Pinch Hit AB	Pinch Hit H	PO	A	E	DP	TC/G	FA	G by Pos
1983 LA N	2	.000	.000	2	0	0	0	0	0.0	0	0	0	1	0	2	0	0	0	0	0	0.0	–	
1985	4	.143	.143	7	1	0	0	0	0.0	0	1	0	3	0	1	0	4	0	1	0	1.3	.800	OF-3

Year	Team		Games	BA	SA	AB	H	2B	3B	HR	HR%	R	RBI	BB	SO	SB	Pinch Hit AB	Pinch Hit H	PO	A	E	DP	TC/G	FA	G by Pos

Candy Maldonado *continued*

Year	Team		Games	BA	SA	AB	H	2B	3B	HR	HR%	R	RBI	BB	SO	SB	AB	H	PO	A	E	DP	TC/G	FA	G by Pos
1987	SF	N	5	.211	.263	19	4	1	0	0	0.0	2	2	0	3	0	0	0	7	0	0	0	1.4	1.000	OF-5
1989			3	.000	.000	3	0	0	0	0	0.0	1	1	2	0	0	1	0	2	0	0	0	0.7	1.000	OF-3
1991	TOR	A	5	.100	.150	20	2	1	0	0	0.0	1	1	1	6	0	0	0	4	0	0	0	0.8	1.000	OF-3
1992			6	.273	.545	22	6	0	0	2	9.1	3	6	3	4	0	0	0	9	1	0	1	1.7	1.000	OF-6
6 yrs.			25	.178	.288	73	13	2	0	2	2.7	7	11	6	17	0	4	0	26	1	1	1	1.1	.964	OF-20
WORLD SERIES																									
1989	SF	N	4	.091	.273	11	1	0	1	0	0.0	1	0	0	4	0	1	1	5	0	0	0	1.3	1.000	OF-3
1992	TOR	A	6	.158	.316	19	3	0	0	1	5.3	1	2	2	5	0	1	0	8	2	0	1	1.7	1.000	OF-5
2 yrs.			10	.133	.300	30	4	0	1	1	3.3	2	2	2	9	0	2	1	13	2	0	1	1.5	1.000	OF-8

Kirt Manwaring

MANWARING, KIRT DEAN
B. July 15, 1965, Elmira, N. Y. — BR TR 5′11″ 185 lbs.

Year	Team		Games	BA	SA	AB	H	2B	3B	HR	HR%	R	RBI	BB	SO	SB	AB	H	PO	A	E	DP	TC/G	FA	G by Pos
1987	SF	N	6	.143	.143	7	1	0	0	0	0.0	0	0	0	1	0	0	0	9	1	1	0	1.8	.909	C-6
1988			40	.250	.336	116	29	7	0	1	0.9	12	15	2	21	0	0	0	162	24	4	2	4.8	.979	C-40
1989			85	.210	.250	200	42	4	2	0	0.0	14	18	11	28	2	9	2	289	32	6	3	3.8	.982	C-81
1990			8	.154	.308	13	2	0	1	0	0.0	0	1	0	3	0	0	0	22	3	0	1	3.1	1.000	C-8
1991			67	.225	.275	178	40	9	0	0	0.0	16	19	9	22	1	1	1	315	28	4	7	5.2	.988	C-67
1992			109	.244	.335	349	85	10	5	4	1.1	24	26	29	42	2	2	1	564	68	4	12	5.8	.994	C-108
1993			130	.275	.350	432	119	15	1	5	1.2	48	49	41	76	1	0	0	739	70	2	12	6.2	.998	C-130
1994			97	.250	.320	316	79	17	1	1	0.3	30	29	25	50	1	0	0	540	53	4	4	6.2	.993	C-97
8 yrs.			542	.246	.318	1611	397	62	10	11	0.7	144	157	117	243	7	12	4	2640	279	25	41	5.4	.992	C-537
LEAGUE CHAMPIONSHIP SERIES																									
1989	SF	N	3	.000	.000	2	0	0	0	0	0.0	0	0	0	0	0	0	0	5	0	0	0	1.7	1.000	C-3
WORLD SERIES																									
1989	SF	N	1	1.000	2.000	1	1	0	0	0	0.0	1	0	0	0	0	0	0	0	0	0	0	0.0	—	C-1

Tom Marsh

MARSH, THOMAS OWEN
B. Dec. 27, 1965, Toledo, Ohio. — BR TR 6′2″ 180 lbs.

Year	Team		Games	BA	SA	AB	H	2B	3B	HR	HR%	R	RBI	BB	SO	SB	AB	H	PO	A	E	DP	TC/G	FA	G by Pos
1992	PHI	N	42	.200	.304	125	25	3	2	2	1.6	7	16	2	23	0	8	2	66	0	2	0	1.6	.971	OF-35
1994			8	.278	.444	18	5	1	1	0	0.0	3	3	1	1	0	3	1	8	0	1	0	1.1	.889	OF-7
2 yrs.			50	.210	.322	143	30	4	3	2	1.4	10	19	3	24	0	11	3	74	0	3	0	1.5	.961	OF-42

Al Martin

MARTIN, ALBERT LEE
B. Nov. 24, 1967, West Covina, Calif. — BL TL 6′2″ 220 lbs.

Year	Team		Games	BA	SA	AB	H	2B	3B	HR	HR%	R	RBI	BB	SO	SB	AB	H	PO	A	E	DP	TC/G	FA	G by Pos
1992	PIT	N	12	.167	.333	12	2	0	1	0	0.0	1	2	0	5	0	6	1	6	0	0	0	0.5	1.000	OF-7
1993			143	.281	.481	480	135	26	8	18	3.8	85	64	42	122	16	14	5	268	6	7	0	2.0	.975	OF-136
1994			82	.286	.457	276	79	12	4	9	3.3	48	33	34	56	15	3	0	129	8	3	1	1.7	.979	OF-77
3 yrs.			237	.281	.470	768	216	38	13	27	3.5	134	99	76	183	31	23	6	403	14	10	1	1.8	.977	OF-220

Norberto Martin

MARTIN, NORBERTO ENRIQUE (Paco)
Born Norberto Enrique Martin (McDonald).
B. Dec. 10, 1966, San Pedro de Macoris, Dominican Republic — BR TR 5′10″ 175 lbs.

Year	Team		Games	BA	SA	AB	H	2B	3B	HR	HR%	R	RBI	BB	SO	SB	AB	H	PO	A	E	DP	TC/G	FA	G by Pos
1993	CHI	A	8	.357	.357	14	5	0	0	0	0.0	3	2	1	1	0	1	0	13	9	1	4	2.9	.957	2B-5, DH-1
1994			45	.275	.366	131	36	7	1	1	0.8	19	16	9	16	4	5	1	58	77	2	11	3.0	.985	2B-28, SS-6, 3B-5, OF-2, DH-1
2 yrs.			53	.283	.366	145	41	7	1	1	0.7	22	18	10	17	4	6	1	71	86	3	15	3.0	.981	2B-33, SS-6, 3B-5, DH-2, OF-2

Dave Martinez

MARTINEZ, DAVID
B. Sept. 26, 1964, New York, N. Y. — BL TL 5′10″ 150 lbs.

Year	Team		Games	BA	SA	AB	H	2B	3B	HR	HR%	R	RBI	BB	SO	SB	AB	H	PO	A	E	DP	TC/G	FA	G by Pos
1986	CHI	N	53	.139	.194	108	15	1	1	1	0.9	13	7	6	22	4	5	1	77	2	1	1	1.5	.988	OF-46
1987			142	.292	.418	459	134	18	8	8	1.7	70	36	57	96	16	11	3	283	10	6	1	2.1	.980	OF-139
1988	2 teams		CHI N	(75G – .254)		MON N	(63G – .257)																		
"	total		138	.255	.351	447	114	13	6	6	1.3	51	46	38	94	23	11	1	281	4	6	1	2.1	.979	OF-132
1989	MON	N	126	.274	.382	361	99	16	7	3	0.8	41	27	27	57	23	11	3	199	7	7	1	1.7	.967	OF-118
1990			118	.279	.422	391	109	13	5	11	2.8	60	39	24	48	13	14	3	257	6	3	1	2.3	.989	OF-108, P-1
1991			124	.295	.419	396	117	18	5	7	1.8	47	42	20	54	16	11	4	213	10	4	0	1.8	.982	OF-112
1992	CIN	N	135	.254	.354	393	100	20	5	3	0.8	47	31	42	54	12	12	0	382	18	6	23	3.0	.985	OF-111, 1B-21
1993	SF	N	91	.241	.361	241	58	12	1	5	2.1	28	27	27	39	6	20	3	131	6	1	2	1.5	.993	OF-73
1994			97	.247	.362	235	58	9	3	4	1.7	23	27	21	22	3	25	8	255	18	3	17	2.8	.989	OF-58, 1B-25
9 yrs.			1024	.265	.379	3031	804	120	41	48	1.6	380	282	262	486	116	120	26	2078	81	37	47	2.1	.983	OF-897, 1B-46, P-1

Edgar Martinez

MARTINEZ, EDGAR
B. Jan. 2, 1963, New York, N. Y. — BR TR 6′ 175 lbs.

Year	Team		Games	BA	SA	AB	H	2B	3B	HR	HR%	R	RBI	BB	SO	SB	AB	H	PO	A	E	DP	TC/G	FA	G by Pos
1987	SEA	A	13	.372	.581	43	16	5	2	0	0.0	6	5	2	5	0	1	0	13	19	0	1	2.5	1.000	3B-12, DH-1
1988			14	.281	.406	32	9	4	0	0	0.0	0	5	4	7	0	1	1	5	8	1	1	1.0	.929	3B-13
1989			65	.240	.304	171	41	5	0	2	1.2	20	20	17	26	2	8	1	40	72	6	9	1.8	.949	3B-61
1990			144	.302	.433	487	147	27	2	11	2.3	71	49	74	62	1	1	0	89	259	27	16	2.6	.928	3B-143, DH-2
1991			150	.307	.452	544	167	35	1	14	2.6	98	52	84	72	0	1	0	84	299	15	25	2.7	.962	3B-144, DH-2
1992			135	**.343**	.544	528	181	**46**	3	18	3.4	100	73	54	61	14	3	0	88	211	17	25	2.3	.946	3B-103, DH-28, 1B-2
1993			42	.237	.378	135	32	7	0	4	3.0	20	13	28	19	0	2	1	5	11	2	1	0.4	.889	DH-24, 3B-16
1994			89	.285	.482	326	93	23	1	13	4.0	47	51	53	42	6	0	0	44	127	9	8	2.0	.950	3B-65, DH-23
8 yrs.			652	.303	.460	2266	686	152	9	62	2.7	362	268	316	294	23	19	4	368	1006	77	86	2.2	.947	3B-557, DH-80, 1B-2

Tino Martinez

MARTINEZ, CONSTANTINO
B. Dec. 7, 1967, Tampa, Fla. — BL TR 6′2″ 205 lbs.

Year	Team		Games	BA	SA	AB	H	2B	3B	HR	HR%	R	RBI	BB	SO	SB	AB	H	PO	A	E	DP	TC/G	FA	G by Pos
1990	SEA	A	24	.221	.279	68	15	4	0	0	0.0	5	9	9	9	0	2	0	155	12	0	25	7.0	1.000	1B-23
1991			36	.205	.330	112	23	2	0	4	3.6	11	9	11	24	0	5	2	249	22	2	24	7.6	.992	1B-29, DH-5

Year Team	Games	BA	SA	AB	H	2B	3B	HR	HR%	R	RBI	BB	SO	SB	Pinch Hit AB	Pinch Hit H	PO	A	E	DP	TC/G	FA	G by Pos

Tino Martinez *continued*

Year Team	Games	BA	SA	AB	H	2B	3B	HR	HR%	R	RBI	BB	SO	SB	PH AB	PH H	PO	A	E	DP	TC/G	FA	G by Pos
1992	136	.257	.411	460	118	19	2	16	3.5	53	66	42	77	2	11	1	678	58	4	62	5.4	.995	1B-78, DH-47
1993	109	.265	.456	408	108	25	1	17	4.2	48	60	45	56	0	0	0	933	60	3	89	9.1	.997	1B-103, DH-6
1994	97	.261	.508	329	86	21	0	20	6.1	42	61	29	52	1	5	1	705	45	2	62	7.8	.997	1B-82, DH-8
5 yrs.	402	.254	.434	1377	350	71	3	57	4.1	158	201	136	218	3	23	4	2720	197	11	262	7.3	.996	1B-315, DH-66

Mike Matheny

MATHENY, MICHAEL SCOTT
B. Sept. 22, 1970, Columbus, Ohio
BR TR 6'3" 205 lbs.

Year Team	Games	BA	SA	AB	H	2B	3B	HR	HR%	R	RBI	BB	SO	SB	PH AB	PH H	PO	A	E	DP	TC/G	FA	G by Pos
1994 MIL A	28	.226	.340	53	12	3	0	1	1.9	3	2	3	13	0	2	0	81	8	1	1	3.2	.989	C-27

Francisco Matos

MATOS, FRANCISCO AGUIRRE
Born Francisco Aguirre Matos (Mancebo).
B. July 23, 1969, Santo Domingo, Dominican Republic
BR TR 6'1" 160 lbs.

Year Team	Games	BA	SA	AB	H	2B	3B	HR	HR%	R	RBI	BB	SO	SB	PH AB	PH H	PO	A	E	DP	TC/G	FA	G by Pos
1994 OAK A	14	.250	.286	28	7	1	0	0	0.0	1	2	1	2	1	2	0	13	24	3	4	2.9	.925	2B-12, DH-2

Don Mattingly

MATTINGLY, DONALD ARTHUR
B. Apr. 20, 1961, Evansville, Ind.
BL TL 6' 185 lbs.

Year Team	Games	BA	SA	AB	H	2B	3B	HR	HR%	R	RBI	BB	SO	SB	PH AB	PH H	PO	A	E	DP	TC/G	FA	G by Pos
1982 NY A	7	.167	.167	12	2	0	0	0	0.0	0	1	0	1	0	1	0	15	1	0	0	2.3	1.000	OF-6, 1B-1
1983	91	.283	.409	279	79	15	4	4	1.4	34	32	21	31	0	8	1	350	15	3	31	4.0	.992	OF-48, 1B-42, 2B-1
1984	153	**.343**	.537	603	**207**	**44**	2	23	3.8	91	110	41	33	1	3	1	1143	126	6	136	8.3	.995	1B-133, OF-19
1985	159	.324	.567	652	211	**48**	3	35	5.4	107	**145**	56	41	2	0	0	1318	87	7	154	8.9	.995	1B-159
1986	162	.352	**.573**	677	**238**	**53**	2	31	4.6	117	113	53	35	0	0	0	1378	111	7	134	9.2	.995	1B-160, 3B-3, DH-1
1987	141	.327	.559	569	186	38	2	30	5.3	93	115	51	38	1	1	0	1239	91	5	122	9.5	.996	1B-140, DH-1
1988	144	.311	.462	599	186	37	0	18	3.0	94	88	41	29	1	1	0	1250	99	9	131	9.4	.993	1B-143, DH-1, OF-1
1989	158	.303	.477	631	191	37	2	23	3.6	79	113	51	30	3	0	0	1276	87	7	143	8.7	.995	1B-145, DH-17, OF-1
1990	102	.256	.335	394	101	16	0	5	1.3	40	42	28	20	1	4	2	800	78	3	81	8.6	.997	1B-89, DH-13, OF-1
1991	152	.288	.394	587	169	35	0	9	1.5	64	68	46	42	2	4	1	1119	77	5	135	7.9	.996	1B-127, DH-22
1992	157	.288	.416	640	184	40	0	14	2.2	89	86	39	43	3	2	0	1211	115	4	129	8.5	.997	1B-143, DH-15
1993	134	.291	.445	530	154	27	2	17	3.2	78	86	61	42	0	2	1	1258	84	3	123	10.0	.998	1B-130, DH-5
1994	97	.304	.411	372	113	20	1	6	1.6	62	51	60	24	0	0	0	916	66	2	95	10.1	.998	1B-97
13 yrs.	1657	.309	.475	6545	2021	410	18	215	3.3	948	1050	548	409	14	28	7	13273	1037	61	1414	8.7	.996	1B-1509, OF-76, DH-75, 3B-3, 2B-1

Derrick May

MAY, DERRICK BRANT
Son of Dave May.
B. July 14, 1968, Rochester, N. Y.
BL TR 6'4" 210 lbs.

Year Team	Games	BA	SA	AB	H	2B	3B	HR	HR%	R	RBI	BB	SO	SB	PH AB	PH H	PO	A	E	DP	TC/G	FA	G by Pos
1990 CHI N	17	.246	.344	61	15	3	0	1	1.6	8	11	2	7	1	0	0	34	1	1	0	2.1	.972	OF-17
1991	15	.227	.455	22	5	2	0	1	4.5	4	3	2	7	1	7	1	11	1	0	0	0.8	1.000	OF-7
1992	124	.274	.373	351	96	11	0	8	2.3	33	45	14	40	5	21	6	153	3	5	0	1.3	.969	OF-108
1993	128	.295	.422	465	137	25	2	10	2.2	62	77	31	41	10	10	1	220	8	7	1	1.8	.970	OF-122
1994	100	.284	.420	345	98	19	2	8	2.3	43	51	30	34	3	11	1	154	4	1	0	1.6	.994	OF-92
5 yrs.	384	.282	.404	1244	351	60	4	28	2.3	150	187	79	123	19	49	9	572	17	14	1	1.6	.977	OF-346

Brent Mayne

MAYNE, BRENT DANEM
B. Apr. 19, 1968, Loma Linda, Calif.
BL TR 6'1" 195 lbs.

Year Team	Games	BA	SA	AB	H	2B	3B	HR	HR%	R	RBI	BB	SO	SB	PH AB	PH H	PO	A	E	DP	TC/G	FA	G by Pos
1990 KC A	5	.231	.231	13	3	0	0	0	0.0	2	1	3	3	0	1	0	29	3	1	0	6.6	.970	C-5
1991	85	.251	.325	231	58	8	0	3	1.3	22	31	23	42	2	8	2	425	38	6	4	5.5	.987	C-80, DH-1
1992	82	.225	.272	213	48	10	0	0	0.0	16	18	11	26	0	14	4	281	33	3	2	3.9	.991	C-62, 3B-8, DH-1
1993	71	.254	.337	205	52	9	1	2	1.0	22	22	18	31	3	4	1	356	27	2	1	5.4	.995	C-68, DH-1
1994	46	.257	.347	144	37	5	1	2	1.4	19	20	14	27	1	4	0	246	13	1	1	5.7	.996	C-42, DH-3
5 yrs.	289	.246	.316	806	198	32	2	7	0.9	81	92	69	129	6	31	7	1337	114	13	8	5.1	.991	C-257, 3B-8, DH-6

David McCarty

McCARTY, DAVID ANDREW
B. Nov. 23, 1969, Houston, Tex.
BR TL 6'5" 210 lbs.

Year Team	Games	BA	SA	AB	H	2B	3B	HR	HR%	R	RBI	BB	SO	SB	PH AB	PH H	PO	A	E	DP	TC/G	FA	G by Pos
1993 MIN A	98	.214	.286	350	75	15	2	2	0.6	36	21	19	80	2	5	1	412	38	8	25	4.7	.983	OF-67, 1B-36, DH-2
1994	44	.260	.374	131	34	8	2	1	0.8	21	12	7	32	2	3	0	244	27	5	19	6.3	.982	1B-32, OF-14
2 yrs.	142	.227	.310	481	109	23	4	3	0.6	57	33	26	112	4	8	1	656	65	13	44	5.2	.982	OF-81, 1B-68, DH-2

Lloyd McClendon

McCLENDON, LLOYD GLENN
B. Jan. 11, 1959, Gary, Ind.
BR TR 5'10" 190 lbs.

Year Team	Games	BA	SA	AB	H	2B	3B	HR	HR%	R	RBI	BB	SO	SB	PH AB	PH H	PO	A	E	DP	TC/G	FA	G by Pos
1987 CIN N	45	.208	.361	72	15	5	0	2	2.8	8	13	4	15	1	24	6	80	5	2	3	1.9	.977	C-12, 1B-5, 3B-1, OF-1
1988	72	.219	.314	137	30	4	0	3	2.2	9	14	15	22	4	24	6	197	13	4	11	3.0	.981	C-23, OF-17, 1B-12, 3B-2
1989 CHI N	92	.286	.479	259	74	12	1	12	4.6	47	40	37	31	6	16	5	310	18	6	21	3.6	.982	OF-45, 1B-28, 3B-6, C-5
1990 2 teams		CHI N (49G – .159)		PIT N (4G – .333)																			
" total	53	.164	.245	110	18	2	1	2	1.8	6	12	14	22	1	16	2	120	9	1	5	2.5	.992	OF-24, 1B-8, C-8
1991 PIT N	85	.288	.460	163	47	7	0	7	4.3	24	24	18	23	2	33	9	163	12	3	13	2.1	.983	OF-32, 1B-22, C-2
1992	84	.253	.353	190	48	8	1	3	1.6	26	20	28	24	1	16	5	136	9	3	3	1.8	.980	OF-60, 1B-18
1993	88	.221	.326	181	40	11	1	2	1.1	21	19	23	17	0	32	6	98	5	3	2	1.2	.972	OF-61, 1B-6
1994	51	.239	.413	92	22	4	0	4	4.3	9	12	4	11	0	29	8	46	2	1	5	1.0	.980	OF-20, 1B-2
8 yrs.	570	.244	.381	1204	294	54	3	35	2.9	150	154	143	165	15	190	47	1150	73	23	63	2.2	.982	OF-260, 1B-101, C-50, 3B-9

LEAGUE CHAMPIONSHIP SERIES

Year Team	Games	BA	SA	AB	H	2B	3B	HR	HR%	R	RBI	BB	SO	SB	PH AB	PH H	PO	A	E	DP	TC/G	FA	G by Pos
1989 CHI N	3	.667	.667	3	2	0	0	0	0.0	0	0	1	0	0	2	1	3	0	0	0	1.0	1.000	C-2, OF-1
1991 PIT N	3	.000	.000	2	0	0	0	0	0.0	0	0	0	1	0	2	0	0	0	0	0	0.0	–	1B-1
1992	5	.727	1.182	11	8	2	0	1	9.1	4	4	4	1	0	0	0	10	0	0	0	2.0	1.000	OF-5
3 yrs.	11	.625	.938	16	10	2	0	1	6.3	4	4	5	2	0	4	1	13	0	0	0	1.2	1.000	OF-6, C-2, 1B-1

Ray McDavid

McDAVID, RAY DARNELL
B. July 20, 1971, San Diego, Calif.
BL TR 6'3" 190 lbs.

Year Team	Games	BA	SA	AB	H	2B	3B	HR	HR%	R	RBI	BB	SO	SB	PH AB	PH H	PO	A	E	DP	TC/G	FA	G by Pos
1994 SD N	9	.250	.286	28	7	1	0	0	0.0	2	2	1	8	1	2	1	11	0	0	0	1.2	1.000	OF-7

Year Team	Games	BA	SA	AB	H	2B	3B	HR	HR%	R	RBI	BB	SO	SB	Pinch Hit AB	Pinch Hit H	PO	A	E	DP	TC/G	FA	G by Pos

Oddibe McDowell

McDOWELL, ODDIBE, JR.
B. Aug. 25, 1962, Hollywood, Fla.

BL TL 5'9" 165 lbs.

Year Team	Games	BA	SA	AB	H	2B	3B	HR	HR%	R	RBI	BB	SO	SB	AB	H	PO	A	E	DP	TC/G	FA	G by Pos
1985 **TEX A**	111	.239	.431	406	97	14	5	18	4.4	63	42	36	85	25	8	2	282	9	2	2	2.6	.993	OF-103, DH-4
1986	154	.266	.427	572	152	24	7	18	3.1	105	49	65	112	33	8	2	325	13	3	3	2.2	.991	OF-148, DH-1
1987	128	.241	.428	407	98	26	4	14	3.4	65	52	51	99	24	11	1	263	5	3	1	2.1	.989	OF-125
1988	120	.247	.355	437	108	19	5	6	1.4	55	37	41	89	33	9	2	267	2	3	1	2.3	.989	OF-113, DH-3
1989 **2 teams**		**CLE A**	(69G – .222)		**ATL N**	(76G – .304)																	
" total	145	.266	.391	519	138	23	6	10	1.9	89	46	52	73	27	9	3	303	7	5	1	2.2	.984	OF-132, DH-2
1990 **ATL N**	113	.243	.357	305	74	14	0	7	2.3	47	25	21	53	13	34	7	134	2	4	0	1.2	.971	OF-72
1994 **TEX A**	59	.262	.317	183	48	5	1	1	0.5	34	15	28	39	14	5	0	113	2	2	0	2.0	.983	OF-53, DH-2
7 yrs.	830	.253	.395	2829	715	125	28	74	2.6	458	266	294	550	169	84	17	1687	40	22	8	2.1	.987	OF-746, DH-12

Willie McGee

McGEE, WILLIE DEAN
B. Nov. 2, 1958, San Francisco, Calif.

BB TR 6'1" 176 lbs.

Year Team	Games	BA	SA	AB	H	2B	3B	HR	HR%	R	RBI	BB	SO	SB	AB	H	PO	A	E	DP	TC/G	FA	G by Pos
1982 **STL N**	123	.296	.391	422	125	12	8	4	0.9	43	56	12	58	24	15	6	245	3	11	0	2.1	.958	OF-117
1983	147	.286	.374	601	172	22	8	5	0.8	75	75	26	98	39	3	2	385	7	5	1	2.7	.987	OF-145
1984	145	.291	.394	571	166	19	11	6	1.1	82	50	29	80	43	5	0	374	10	6	4	2.7	.985	OF-141
1985	152	**.353**	.503	612	**216**	26	**18**	10	1.6	114	82	34	86	56	4	2	382	11	9	2	2.6	.978	OF-149
1986	124	.256	.370	497	127	22	7	7	1.4	65	48	37	82	19	2	0	325	9	3	0	2.7	.991	OF-121
1987	153	.285	.434	620	177	37	11	11	1.8	76	105	24	90	16	2	1	354	10	7	1	2.4	.981	OF-152, SS-1
1988	137	.292	.372	562	164	24	6	3	0.5	73	50	32	84	41	2	1	348	9	9	0	2.7	.975	OF-135
1989	58	.236	.352	199	47	10	2	3	1.5	23	17	10	34	8	10	2	118	2	3	0	2.1	.976	OF-47
1990 **2 teams**		**STL N**	(125G – **.335**)		**OAK A**	(29G – .274)																	
" total	154	.324	.419	614	199	35	7	3	0.5	99	77	48	104	31	2	0	413	14	17	5	2.9	.962	OF-152, DH-1
1991 **SF N**	131	.312	.408	497	155	30	3	4	0.8	67	43	34	74	17	4	2	259	6	6	3	2.1	.978	OF-128
1992	138	.297	.354	474	141	20	2	1	0.2	56	36	29	88	13	21	11	231	11	6	2	1.8	.976	OF-119
1993	130	.301	.389	475	143	28	1	4	0.8	53	46	38	67	10	7	1	224	9	5	1	1.8	.979	OF-126
1994	45	.282	.397	156	44	3	0	5	3.2	19	23	15	24	3	4	0	79	2	1	0	1.8	.988	OF-42
13 yrs.	1637	.298	.402	6300	1876	288	84	66	1.0	845	708	368	969	320	81	28	3737	103	88	19	2.4	.978	OF-1574, SS-1, DH-1
LEAGUE CHAMPIONSHIP SERIES																							
1982 **STL N**	3	.308	.846	13	4	0	2	1	7.7	4	5	0	5	0	0	0	12	0	1	0	4.3	.923	OF-3
1985	6	.269	.308	26	7	1	0	0	0.0	6	3	3	6	2	0	0	17	0	0	0	2.8	1.000	OF-6
1987	7	.308	.423	26	8	1	1	0	0.0	2	5	0	5	0	0	0	16	0	0	0	2.3	1.000	OF-7
1990 **OAK A**	3	.222	.333	9	2	1	0	0	0.0	3	0	1	2	2	0	0	2	0	0	0	0.7	1.000	OF-2
4 yrs.	19	.284	.446	74	21	3	3	1	1.4	15	10	4	18	4	0	0	47	0	1	0	2.5	.979	OF-18
WORLD SERIES																							
1982 **STL N**	6	.240	.480	25	6	0	0	2	8.0	6	5	1	3	2	0	0	24	0	0	0	4.0	1.000	OF-6
1985	7	.259	.444	27	7	2	0	1	3.7	2	2	1	3	1	0	0	15	0	0	0	2.1	1.000	OF-7
1987	7	.370	.444	27	10	2	0	0	0.0	0	4	0	9	0	0	0	21	1	1	0	3.3	.957	OF-7
1990 **OAK A**	4	.200	.300	10	2	1	0	0	0.0	1	0	0	2	1	1	0	5	0	0	0	1.3	1.000	OF-3
4 yrs.	24	.281	.438	89	25	5	0	3	3.4	11	11	2	17	4	1	0	65	1	1	0	2.8	.985	OF-23

Fred McGriff

McGRIFF, FREDERICK STANLEY
B. Oct. 31, 1963, Tampa, Fla.

BL TL 6'3" 200 lbs.

Year Team	Games	BA	SA	AB	H	2B	3B	HR	HR%	R	RBI	BB	SO	SB	AB	H	PO	A	E	DP	TC/G	FA	G by Pos
1986 **TOR A**	3	.200	.200	5	1	0	0	0	0.0	1	0	2	2	0	0	0	3	0	0	0	1.0	1.000	DH-2, 1B-1
1987	107	.247	.505	295	73	16	0	20	6.8	58	43	60	104	3	14	1	108	7	2	5	1.1	.983	DH-90, 1B-14
1988	154	.282	.552	536	151	35	4	34	6.3	100	82	79	149	6	5	2	1344	93	5	143	9.4	.997	1B-153
1989	161	.269	.525	551	148	27	3	**36**	6.5	98	92	119	132	7	1	0	1460	115	17	148	9.9	.989	1B-159, DH-2
1990	153	.300	.530	557	167	21	1	35	6.3	91	88	94	108	5	0	0	1246	126	6	119	9.0	.996	1B-147, DH-6
1991 **SD N**	153	.278	.494	528	147	19	1	31	5.9	84	106	105	135	4	0	0	1370	87	14	111	9.6	.990	1B-153
1992	152	.286	.556	531	152	30	4	**35**	6.6	79	104	96	108	8	1	0	1219	108	12	95	8.8	.991	1B-151
1993 **2 teams**		**SD N**	(83G – .275)		**ATL N**	(68G – .310)																	
" total	151	.291	.549	557	162	29	2	37	6.6	111	101	76	106	5	2	1	1203	92	17	102	8.7	.987	1B-149
1994 **ATL N**	113	.318	.623	424	135	25	1	34	8.0	81	94	50	76	7	1	0	1004	66	7	73	9.5	.994	1B-112
9 yrs.	1147	.285	.541	3984	1136	202	16	262	6.6	703	710	679	920	45	24	4	8957	694	80	796	8.5	.992	1B-1039, DH-100
LEAGUE CHAMPIONSHIP SERIES																							
1989 **TOR A**	5	.143	.143	21	3	0	0	0	0.0	1	3	0	4	0	0	0	35	2	1	3	7.6	.974	1B-5
1993 **ATL N**	6	.435	.652	23	10	2	0	1	4.3	6	4	4	7	0	0	0	50	3	0	1	8.8	1.000	1B-6
2 yrs.	11	.295	.409	44	13	2	0	1	2.3	7	7	4	11	0	0	0	85	5	1	4	8.3	.989	1B-11

Terry McGriff

McGRIFF, TERENCE ROY
B. Sept. 23, 1963, Fort Pierce, Fla.

BR TR 6'2" 190 lbs.

Year Team	Games	BA	SA	AB	H	2B	3B	HR	HR%	R	RBI	BB	SO	SB	AB	H	PO	A	E	DP	TC/G	FA	G by Pos
1987 **CIN N**	34	.225	.326	89	20	3	0	2	2.2	6	11	8	17	0	0	0	160	14	3	1	5.2	.983	C-33
1988	35	.198	.260	96	19	3	0	1	1.0	9	4	12	31	1	1	0	177	14	2	1	5.5	.990	C-32
1989	6	.273	.273	11	3	0	0	0	0.0	1	2	2	3	0	0	0	23	3	2	0	4.7	.929	C-6
1990 **2 teams**		**CIN N**	(2G – .000)		**HOU N**	(4G – .000)																	
" total	6	.000	.000	9	0	0	0	0	0.0	0	0	0	1	0	1	0	13	2	1	1	2.7	.938	C-5
1993 **FLA N**	3	.000	.000	7	0	0	0	0	0.0	0	0	1	2	0	1	0	12	0	0	0	4.0	1.000	C-3
1994 **STL N**	42	.219	.272	114	25	6	0	0	0.0	10	13	13	11	0	2	1	207	23	2	0	5.5	.991	C-39
6 yrs.	126	.206	.270	326	67	12	0	3	0.9	26	30	36	65	1	5	1	592	56	10	3	5.2	.985	C-118

Mark McGwire

McGWIRE, MARK DAVID
B. Oct. 1, 1963, Pomona, Calif.

BR TR 6'5" 215 lbs.

Year Team	Games	BA	SA	AB	H	2B	3B	HR	HR%	R	RBI	BB	SO	SB	AB	H	PO	A	E	DP	TC/G	FA	G by Pos
1986 **OAK A**	18	.189	.377	53	10	1	0	3	5.7	10	9	4	18	0	3	1	10	20	6	1	2.0	.833	3B-16
1987	151	.289	**.618**	557	161	28	4	**49**	8.8	97	118	71	131	1	2	1	1176	101	13	91	8.5	.990	1B-145, 3B-8, OF-3
1988	155	.260	.478	550	143	22	1	32	5.8	87	99	76	117	0	4	2	1228	88	9	118	8.5	.993	1B-154, OF-1
1989	143	.231	.467	490	113	17	0	33	6.7	74	95	83	94	1	1	0	1170	114	6	122	9.0	.995	1B-141, DH-2
1990	156	.235	.489	523	123	16	0	39	7.5	87	108	**110**	116	2	1	0	1329	95	5	126	9.2	.997	1B-154, DH-2
1991	154	.201	.383	483	97	22	0	22	4.6	62	75	93	116	2	4	1	1191	101	4	120	8.4	.997	1B-152
1992	139	.268	**.585**	467	125	22	0	42	**9.0**	87	104	90	105	0	1	0	1110	71	6	118	8.6	.995	1B-139, DH-1

Year	Team	Games	BA	SA	AB	H	2B	3B	HR	HR%	R	RBI	BB	SO	SB	Pinch Hit AB	Pinch Hit H	PO	A	E	DP	TC/G	FA	G by Pos

Mark McGwire *continued*

Year	Team	Games	BA	SA	AB	H	2B	3B	HR	HR%	R	RBI	BB	SO	SB	PH AB	PH H	PO	A	E	DP	TC/G	FA	G by Pos
1993		27	.333	.726	84	28	6	0	9	10.7	16	24	21	19	0	1	0	197	14	0	20	7.8	1.000	1B-25
1994		47	.252	.474	135	34	3	0	9	6.7	26	25	37	40	0	2	0	311	17	4	25	7.1	.988	1B-40, DH-5
9 yrs.		990	.250	.507	3342	834	137	5	238	7.1	546	657	585	756	6	19	5	7730	621	53	741	8.5	.994	1B-950, 3B-24, DH-10, OF-4

LEAGUE CHAMPIONSHIP SERIES

Year	Team	Games	BA	SA	AB	H	2B	3B	HR	HR%	R	RBI	BB	SO	SB	PH AB	PH H	PO	A	E	DP	TC/G	FA	G by Pos
1988	OAK A	4	.333	.533	15	5	0	0	1	6.7	4	3	1	5	0	0	0	24	2	0	4	6.5	1.000	1B-4
1989		5	.389	.611	18	7	1	0	1	5.6	3	3	1	4	0	0	0	46	1	1	4	9.6	.979	1B-5
1990		4	.154	.154	13	2	0	0	0	0.0	2	2	3	3	0	0	0	40	0	0	3	10.0	1.000	1B-4
1992		6	.150	.300	20	3	0	0	1	5.0	1	3	5	4	0	0	0	46	2	1	3	8.2	.980	1B-6
4 yrs.		19	.258	.409	66	17	1	0	3	4.5	10	11	10	16	0	0	0	156	5	2	14	8.6	.988	1B-19

WORLD SERIES

Year	Team	Games	BA	SA	AB	H	2B	3B	HR	HR%	R	RBI	BB	SO	SB	PH AB	PH H	PO	A	E	DP	TC/G	FA	G by Pos
1988	OAK A	5	.059	.235	17	1	0	0	1	5.9	1	1	3	4	0	0	0	40	3	0	2	8.6	1.000	1B-5
1989		4	.294	.353	17	5	1	0	0	0.0	0	1	1	3	0	0	0	28	2	0	1	7.5	1.000	1B-4
1990		4	.214	.214	14	3	0	0	0	0.0	1	0	2	4	0	0	0	42	1	2	5	11.3	.956	1B-4
3 yrs.		13	.188	.271	48	9	1	0	1	2.1	2	2	6	11	0	0	0	110	6	2	8	9.1	.983	1B-13

Jeff McKnight

McKNIGHT, JEFFERSON ALAN
Son of Jim McKnight.
B. Feb. 18, 1963, Conway, Ark.

BB TR 6′ 170 lbs.

Year	Team	Games	BA	SA	AB	H	2B	3B	HR	HR%	R	RBI	BB	SO	SB	PH AB	PH H	PO	A	E	DP	TC/G	FA	G by Pos
1989	NY N	6	.250	.250	12	3	0	0	0	0.0	2	0	2	1	0	3	1	4	5	1	1	1.7	.900	2B-4, 1B-1, 3B-1, SS-1
1990	BAL A	29	.200	.267	75	15	2	0	1	1.3	11	4	5	17	0	2	0	106	20	0	11	4.3	1.000	1B-15, OF-8, 2B-5, DH-1, SS-1
1991		16	.171	.195	41	7	1	0	0	0.0	2	2	2	7	1	4	1	22	2	0	1	1.5	1.000	OF-7, DH-4, 1B-2
1992	NY N	31	.271	.400	85	23	3	1	2	2.4	10	13	2	8	0	13	3	82	40	3	8	4.0	.976	2B-14, 1B-9, 3B-3, SS-3, OF-1
1993		105	.256	.323	164	42	3	1	2	1.2	19	13	13	31	0	59	19	86	88	10	19	1.8	.946	SS-29, 2B-15, 1B-10, 3B-9, C-1
1994		31	.148	.185	27	4	0	0	0	0.0	1	2	4	12	0	26	4	8	0	0	0	0.3	1.000	1B-2
6 yrs.		218	.233	.304	404	94	10	2	5	1.2	45	34	28	76	1	107	28	308	155	14	40	2.2	.971	1B-39, 2B-38, SS-34, OF-16, 3B-13, DH-5, C-1

Mark McLemore

McLEMORE, MARK TREMELL
B. Oct. 4, 1964, San Diego, Calif.

BB TR 5′11″ 175 lbs.

Year	Team	Games	BA	SA	AB	H	2B	3B	HR	HR%	R	RBI	BB	SO	SB	PH AB	PH H	PO	A	E	DP	TC/G	FA	G by Pos
1986	CAL A	5	.000	.000	4	0	0	0	0	0.0	0	0	1	2	0	0	0	3	10	0	1	2.6	1.000	2B-2
1987		138	.236	.300	433	102	13	3	3	0.7	61	41	48	72	25	1	0	293	363	17	98	4.9	.975	2B-132, SS-6, DH-3
1988		77	.240	.330	233	56	11	2	2	0.9	38	16	25	28	13	9	3	108	178	6	53	3.8	.979	2B-63, 3B-5, DH-1
1989		32	.243	.291	103	25	3	1	0	0.0	12	14	7	19	6	1	0	55	88	5	24	4.6	.966	2B-27, DH-1
1990	2 teams	28	.150	.183	60	9	2	0	0	0.0	6	2	4	15	1	2	0	37	39	4	10	2.9	.950	2B-11, SS-8, 3B-4, DH-2
"	total	CAL A (20G – .146)			CLE A (8G – .167)																			
1991	HOU N	21	.148	.164	61	9	1	0	0	0.0	6	2	6	13	0	2	0	25	54	2	8	3.9	.975	2B-19
1992	BAL A	101	.246	.294	228	56	7	2	0	0.0	40	27	21	26	11	11	4	126	186	7	47	3.2	.978	2B-70, DH-16
1993		148	.284	.368	581	165	27	5	4	0.7	81	72	64	92	21	0	0	335	80	6	23	2.8	.986	OF-124, 2B-25, 3B-4, DH-1
1994		104	.257	.321	343	88	11	1	3	0.9	44	29	51	50	20	4	0	220	270	9	53	4.8	.982	2B-96, OF-7, DH-1
9 yrs.		654	.249	.317	2046	510	75	14	12	0.6	288	203	227	317	97	30	7	1202	1268	56	317	3.9	.978	2B-445, OF-131, DH-25, SS-14, 3B-13

Brian McRae

McRAE, BRIAN WESLEY
Son of Hal McRae.
B. Aug. 27, 1967, Bradenton, Fla.

BB TR 6′ 175 lbs.

Year	Team	Games	BA	SA	AB	H	2B	3B	HR	HR%	R	RBI	BB	SO	SB	PH AB	PH H	PO	A	E	DP	TC/G	FA	G by Pos
1990	KC A	46	.286	.405	168	48	8	3	2	1.2	21	23	9	29	4	1	1	120	1	0	0	2.6	1.000	OF-45
1991		152	.261	.372	629	164	28	9	8	1.3	86	64	24	99	20	2	1	405	2	3	0	2.7	.993	OF-150
1992		149	.223	.308	533	119	23	5	4	0.8	63	52	42	88	18	5	2	419	8	3	2	2.9	.993	OF-148, DH-1
1993		153	.282	.413	627	177	28	9	12	1.9	78	69	37	105	23	3	0	394	4	7	3	2.6	.983	OF-153
1994		114	.273	.378	436	119	22	6	4	0.9	71	40	54	67	28	1	0	252	2	3	0	2.3	.988	OF-110, DH-4
5 yrs.		614	.262	.372	2393	627	109	32	30	1.3	319	248	166	388	93	12	4	1590	17	16	5	2.6	.990	OF-606, DH-5

Kevin McReynolds

McREYNOLDS, WALTER KEVIN (Big Mac)
B. Oct. 16, 1959, Little Rock, Ark.

BR TR 6′1″ 205 lbs.

Year	Team	Games	BA	SA	AB	H	2B	3B	HR	HR%	R	RBI	BB	SO	SB	PH AB	PH H	PO	A	E	DP	TC/G	FA	G by Pos
1983	SD N	39	.221	.343	140	31	3	1	4	2.9	15	14	12	29	2	2	1	87	4	1	1	2.4	.989	OF-38
1984		147	.278	.465	525	146	26	6	20	3.8	68	75	34	69	3	5	1	422	10	4	1	3.0	.991	OF-143
1985		152	.234	.371	564	132	24	4	15	2.7	61	75	43	81	4	2	0	430	12	3	3	2.9	.993	OF-150
1986		158	.288	.504	560	161	31	6	26	4.6	89	96	66	83	8	4	1	332	9	8	4	2.2	.977	OF-154
1987	NY N	151	.276	.495	590	163	32	5	29	4.9	86	95	39	70	14	3	2	286	8	4	0	2.0	.987	OF-150
1988		147	.288	.496	552	159	30	2	27	4.9	82	99	38	56	21	3	1	252	18	4	5	1.85	.985	OF-147
1989		148	.272	.450	545	148	25	3	22	4.0	74	85	46	74	15	3	1	307	10	10	3	2.2	.969	OF-145
1990		147	.269	.455	521	140	23	1	24	4.6	75	82	71	61	9	2	1	237	14	3	2	1.7	.988	OF-144
1991		143	.259	.416	522	135	32	1	16	3.1	65	74	49	46	6	4	2	281	9	2	1	2.0	.993	OF-141
1992	KC A	109	.247	.418	373	92	25	0	13	3.5	45	49	67	48	7	4	0	204	4	3	0	1.9	.986	OF-106, DH-1
1993		110	.245	.425	351	86	22	0	11	3.1	44	42	37	56	2	16	2	191	5	2	0	1.8	.990	OF-104, DH-1
1994	NY N	51	.256	.406	180	46	11	0	4	2.2	23	21	20	34	2	4	0	91	1	0	1	1.8	1.000	OF-47
12 yrs.		1502	.265	.447	5423	1439	284	35	211	3.9	727	807	522	707	93	52	12	3120	104	44	21	2.2	.987	OF-1469, DH-2

LEAGUE CHAMPIONSHIP SERIES

Year	Team	Games	BA	SA	AB	H	2B	3B	HR	HR%	R	RBI	BB	SO	SB	PH AB	PH H	PO	A	E	DP	TC/G	FA	G by Pos
1984	SD N	4	.300	.600	10	3	0	0	1	10.0	2	4	3	1	0	0	0	10	0	0	0	2.5	1.000	OF-4
1988	NY N	7	.250	.536	28	7	2	0	2	7.1	4	4	3	5	2	0	0	19	0	0	0	2.7	1.000	OF-7
2 yrs.		11	.263	.553	38	10	2	0	3	7.9	6	8	6	6	2	0	0	29	0	0	0	2.6	1.000	OF-11

Year Team	Games	BA	SA	AB	H	2B	3B	HR	HR%	R	RBI	BB	SO	SB	Pinch Hit AB	Pinch Hit H	PO	A	E	DP	TC/G	FA	G by Pos

Pat Meares — MEARES, PATRICK JAMES — B. Sept. 6, 1968, Salina, Kans. — BR TR 6' 185 lbs.

Year Team	Games	BA	SA	AB	H	2B	3B	HR	HR%	R	RBI	BB	SO	SB	PH AB	PH H	PO	A	E	DP	TC/G	FA	G by Pos
1993 MIN A	111	.251	.309	346	87	14	3	0	0.0	33	33	7	52	4	1	0	165	304	19	71	4.4	.961	SS-111
1994	80	.266	.354	229	61	12	1	2	0.9	29	24	14	50	5	1	0	134	209	13	45	4.5	.963	SS-79
2 yrs.	191	.257	.327	575	148	26	4	2	0.3	62	57	21	102	9	2	0	299	513	32	116	4.4	.962	SS-190

Roberto Mejia — MEJIA, ROBERTO ANTONIO — Born Roberto Antonio (Diaz). — B. Apr. 14, 1972, Hato Mayor, Dominican Republic — BR TR 5'11" 160 lbs.

Year Team	Games	BA	SA	AB	H	2B	3B	HR	HR%	R	RBI	BB	SO	SB	PH AB	PH H	PO	A	E	DP	TC/G	FA	G by Pos
1993 CLR N	65	.231	.402	229	53	14	5	5	2.2	31	20	13	63	4	0	0	126	184	12	38	5.0	.963	2B-65
1994	38	.241	.431	116	28	8	1	4	3.4	11	14	15	33	3	3	0	70	93	7	19	4.5	.959	2B-34
2 yrs.	103	.235	.412	345	81	22	6	9	2.6	42	34	28	96	7	3	0	196	277	19	57	4.8	.961	2B-99

Bob Melvin — MELVIN, ROBERT PAUL — B. Oct. 28, 1961, Palo Alto, Calif. — BR TR 6'4" 205 lbs.

Year Team	Games	BA	SA	AB	H	2B	3B	HR	HR%	R	RBI	BB	SO	SB	PH AB	PH H	PO	A	E	DP	TC/G	FA	G by Pos
1985 DET A	41	.220	.293	82	18	4	1	0	0.0	10	4	3	21	0	0	0	175	13	2	1	4.6	.989	C-41
1986 SF N	89	.224	.347	268	60	14	2	5	1.9	24	25	15	69	3	6	1	443	60	6	7	5.7	.988	C-84, 3B-1
1987	84	.199	.366	246	49	8	0	11	4.5	31	31	17	44	0	8	1	414	44	1	8	5.5	.998	C-78, 1B-1
1988	92	.234	.377	273	64	13	1	8	2.9	23	27	13	46	0	4	1	406	31	7	4	4.8	.984	C-89, 1B-1
1989 BAL A	85	.241	.295	278	67	10	1	1	0.4	22	32	15	53	1	5	0	303	20	3	1	3.8	.991	C-75, DH-9
1990	93	.243	.346	301	73	14	1	5	1.7	30	37	11	53	0	11	2	365	26	1	2	4.2	.997	C-76, DH-10, 1B-1
1991	79	.250	.307	228	57	10	0	1	0.4	11	23	11	46	0	5	2	383	31	1	8	5.3	.998	C-72, DH-4
1992 KC A	32	.314	.386	70	22	5	0	0	0.0	5	6	5	13	0	8	1	99	9	1	5	3.4	.991	C-21, 1B-3
1993 BOS A	77	.222	.313	176	39	7	0	3	1.7	13	23	7	44	0	3	1	309	19	2	5	4.3	.994	C-76, 1B-1
1994 2 teams	NY A (9G – .286)			CHI A	(11G – .158)																		
" total	20	.212	.303	33	7	0	0	1	3.0	5	4	1	7	0	1	0	64	0	0	2	3.2	1.000	C-15, 1B-4, DH-1
10 yrs.	692	.233	.337	1955	456	85	6	35	1.8	174	212	98	396	4	51	10	2961	253	24	43	4.7	.993	C-627, DH-24, 1B-11, 3B-1

LEAGUE CHAMPIONSHIP SERIES

Year Team	Games	BA	SA	AB	H	2B	3B	HR	HR%	R	RBI	BB	SO	SB	PH AB	PH H	PO	A	E	DP	TC/G	FA	G by Pos
1987 SF N	3	.429	.429	7	3	0	0	0	0.0	0	0	1	1	0	0	0	14	1	0	0	5.0	1.000	C-2

Orlando Merced — MERCED, ORLANDO LUIS — Born Orlando Luis Merced (Villanueva). — B. Nov. 2, 1966, Hato Rey, Puerto Rico. — BB TR 6' 180 lbs.

Year Team	Games	BA	SA	AB	H	2B	3B	HR	HR%	R	RBI	BB	SO	SB	PH AB	PH H	PO	A	E	DP	TC/G	FA	G by Pos
1990 PIT N	25	.208	.250	24	5	1	0	0	0.0	3	0	1	9	0	24	5	0	0	0	0	0.0	–	C-1, OF-1
1991	120	.275	.399	411	113	17	2	10	2.4	83	50	64	81	8	17	6	916	60	12	64	8.2	.988	1B-105, OF-7
1992	134	.247	.385	405	100	28	5	6	1.5	50	60	52	63	5	25	10	905	76	5	74	7.4	.995	1B-114, OF-17
1993	137	.313	.443	447	140	26	4	8	1.8	68	70	77	64	3	15	9	485	31	10	28	3.8	.981	OF-109, 1B-42
1994	108	.272	.412	386	105	21	3	9	2.3	48	51	42	58	4	2	0	509	29	5	46	5.0	.991	OF-68, 1B-55
5 yrs.	524	.277	.408	1673	463	93	14	33	2.0	252	231	236	275	20	83	30	2815	196	32	212	5.8	.989	1B-316, OF-202, C-1

LEAGUE CHAMPIONSHIP SERIES

Year Team	Games	BA	SA	AB	H	2B	3B	HR	HR%	R	RBI	BB	SO	SB	PH AB	PH H	PO	A	E	DP	TC/G	FA	G by Pos
1991 PIT N	3	.222	.556	9	2	0	0	1	11.1	1	1	0	1	0	0	0	13	0	1	0	4.7	.929	1B-2
1992	4	.100	.200	10	1	1	0	0	0.0	0	2	2	4	0	1	0	27	2	1	3	7.5	.967	1B-4
2 yrs.	7	.158	.368	19	3	1	0	1	5.3	1	3	2	5	0	1	0	40	2	2	3	6.3	.955	1B-6

Matt Merullo — MERULLO, MATTHEW BATES — B. Aug. 4, 1965, Winchester, Mass. — BL TR 6'2" 200 lbs.

Year Team	Games	BA	SA	AB	H	2B	3B	HR	HR%	R	RBI	BB	SO	SB	PH AB	PH H	PO	A	E	DP	TC/G	FA	G by Pos
1989 CHI A	31	.222	.272	81	18	1	0	1	1.2	5	8	6	14	0	7	3	100	10	3	0	3.6	.973	C-27, DH-1
1991	80	.229	.343	140	32	1	0	5	3.6	8	21	9	18	0	41	7	159	14	2	11	2.2	.989	C-27, 1B-16, DH-6
1992	24	.180	.240	50	9	1	1	0	0.0	3	3	1	8	0	7	0	64	3	2	0	2.9	.971	C-16, DH-1
1993	8	.050	.050	20	1	0	0	0	0.0	1	0	1	1	0	3	0	0	0	0	0	0.0	–	DH-6
1994 CLE A	4	.100	.100	10	1	0	0	0	0.0	1	0	1	1	0	0	0	22	0	1	0	5.8	.957	C-4
5 yrs.	147	.203	.279	301	61	3	1	6	2.0	18	32	18	42	0	58	10	345	27	8	11	2.6	.979	C-74, 1B-16, DH-14

Matt Mieske — MIESKE, MATTHEW TODD — B. Feb. 13, 1968, Midland, Mich. — BR TR 6' 185 lbs.

Year Team	Games	BA	SA	AB	H	2B	3B	HR	HR%	R	RBI	BB	SO	SB	PH AB	PH H	PO	A	E	DP	TC/G	FA	G by Pos
1993 MIL A	23	.241	.397	58	14	0	0	3	5.2	9	7	4	14	0	0	0	43	1	3	0	2.0	.936	OF-22
1994	84	.259	.432	259	67	13	1	10	3.9	39	38	21	62	3	0	0	155	7	4	1	2.0	.976	OF-80, DH-1
2 yrs.	107	.256	.426	317	81	13	1	13	4.1	48	45	25	76	3	0	0	198	8	7	1	2.0	.967	OF-102, DH-1

Keith Miller — MILLER, KEITH ALAN — B. June 12, 1963, Midland, Mich. — BR TR 5'11" 175 lbs.

Year Team	Games	BA	SA	AB	H	2B	3B	HR	HR%	R	RBI	BB	SO	SB	PH AB	PH H	PO	A	E	DP	TC/G	FA	G by Pos
1987 NY N	25	.373	.490	51	19	2	2	0	0.0	14	1	2	6	8	0	0	21	38	2	6	2.4	.967	2B-16
1988	40	.214	.300	70	15	1	1	1	1.4	9	5	6	10	0	9	2	34	24	5	3	1.6	.921	2B-16, 1B-6, OF-1
1989	57	.231	.301	143	33	7	0	1	0.7	15	7	5	27	6	7	2	90	52	5	8	2.6	.966	2B-23, OF-14, SS-8, 3B-2
1990	88	.258	.305	233	60	8	0	1	0.4	42	12	23	46	16	16	4	168	21	4	8	2.2	.979	OF-61, 2B-11, SS-4
1991	98	.280	.411	275	77	22	1	4	1.5	41	23	23	44	14	11	2	165	154	10	30	3.4	.970	2B-60, OF-28, 3B-2, SS-2
1992 KC A	106	.284	.389	416	118	24	4	4	1.0	57	38	31	46	16	2	0	230	250	15	60	4.7	.970	2B-93, OF-16, DH-1
1993	37	.167	.194	108	18	3	0	0	0.0	9	9	8	19	3	5	0	18	35	6	3	1.6	.898	3B-21, DH-6, OF-4, 2B-3
1994	5	.133	.133	15	2	0	0	0	0.0	1	0	0	3	0	0	0	7	2	0	0	1.8	1.000	OF-4, 3B-2
8 yrs.	456	.261	.349	1311	342	67	8	11	0.8	188	89	98	201	63	50	10	733	576	47	118	3.0	.965	2B-222, OF-128, 3B-33, SS-22, DH-7

Orlando Miller — MILLER, ORLANDO SALMON — Born Orlando Salmon Miller (Dixon). — B. Jan. 13, 1969, Changuinola, Panama — BR TR 6'1" 180 lbs.

Year Team	Games	BA	SA	AB	H	2B	3B	HR	HR%	R	RBI	BB	SO	SB	PH AB	PH H	PO	A	E	DP	TC/G	FA	G by Pos
1994 HOU N	16	.325	.525	40	13	0	1	2	5.0	3	9	2	12	1	3	0	12	30	0	4	2.6	1.000	SS-11, 2B-3

Randy Milligan

MILLIGAN, RANDY ANDRE (Moose)
B. Nov. 27, 1961, San Diego, Calif.
BR TR 6'2" 200 lbs.

Year Team	Games	BA	SA	AB	H	2B	3B	HR	HR%	R	RBI	BB	SO	SB	Pinch Hit AB	Pinch Hit H	PO	A	E	DP	TC/G	FA	G by Pos
1987 NY N	3	.000	.000	1	0	0	0	0	0.0	0	0	1	1	0	1	0	0	0	0	0	0.0	–	1B-0
1988 PIT N	40	.220	.390	82	18	5	0	3	3.7	10	8	20	24	1	13	3	213	15	3	19	5.8	.987	1B-25, OF-1
1989 BAL A	124	.268	.458	365	98	23	5	12	3.3	56	45	74	75	9	11	2	914	83	5	92	8.1	.995	1B-117, DH-1
1990	109	.265	.492	362	96	20	1	20	5.5	64	60	88	68	6	0	0	846	87	9	94	8.6	.990	1B-98, DH-9
1991	141	.263	.406	483	127	17	2	16	3.3	57	70	84	108	0	6	1	948	81	11	92	7.4	.989	1B-106, DH-25, OF-9
1992	137	.240	.361	462	111	21	1	11	2.4	71	53	106	81	0	3	0	1009	76	7	110	8.0	.994	1B-129, DH-6
1993 2 teams	CIN N (83G – .274)			CLE A (19G – .426)																			
" total	102	.299	.434	281	84	18	1	6	2.1	37	36	60	53	0	18	7	578	64	5	63	6.3	.992	1B-79, OF-9, DH-1
1994 MON N	47	.232	.329	82	19	2	0	2	2.4	10	12	14	21	0	12	2	157	19	4	16	3.8	.978	1B-33
8 yrs.	703	.261	.420	2118	553	106	10	70	3.3	305	284	447	431	16	64	15	4665	425	44	486	7.3	.991	1B-587, DH-42, OF-19

Keith Mitchell

MITCHELL, KEITH ALEXANDER
B. Aug. 6, 1969, San Diego, Calif.
BR TR 5'10" 180 lbs.

Year Team	Games	BA	SA	AB	H	2B	3B	HR	HR%	R	RBI	BB	SO	SB	Pinch Hit AB	Pinch Hit H	PO	A	E	DP	TC/G	FA	G by Pos
1991 ATL N	48	.318	.409	66	21	0	0	2	3.0	11	5	8	12	3	10	2	31	1	1	0	0.7	.970	OF-34
1994 SEA A	46	.227	.359	128	29	2	0	5	3.9	21	15	18	22	0	6	1	49	0	1	0	1.1	.980	OF-39, DH-6
2 yrs.	94	.258	.376	194	50	2	0	7	3.6	32	20	26	34	3	16	3	80	1	2	0	0.9	.976	OF-73, DH-6
LEAGUE CHAMPIONSHIP SERIES																							
1991 ATL N	5	.000	.000	4	0	0	0	0	0.0	0	0	0	1	0	1	0	2	0	0	0	0.4	1.000	OF-5
WORLD SERIES																							
1991 ATL N	3	.000	.000	2	0	0	0	0	0.0	0	0	0	1	0	0	0	0	0	0	0	0.0	–	OF-3

Kevin Mitchell

MITCHELL, KEVIN DARNELL (Mitch, World)
B. Jan. 13, 1962, San Diego, Calif.
BR TR 5'10" 210 lbs.

Year Team	Games	BA	SA	AB	H	2B	3B	HR	HR%	R	RBI	BB	SO	SB	Pinch Hit AB	Pinch Hit H	PO	A	E	DP	TC/G	FA	G by Pos
1984 NY N	7	.214	.214	14	3	0	0	0	0.0	0	1	0	3	0	4	1	1	4	1	2	0.9	.833	3B-5
1986	108	.277	.466	328	91	22	2	12	3.7	51	43	33	61	3	20	3	158	69	10	10	2.2	.958	OF-68, SS-24, 3B-7, 1B-2
1987 2 teams	SD N (62G – .245)			SF N (69G – .306)																			
" total	131	.280	.474	464	130	20	2	22	4.7	68	70	48	88	9	9	2	76	240	15	19	2.5	.955	3B-119, OF-6, SS-1
1988 SF N	148	.251	.442	505	127	25	7	19	3.8	60	80	48	85	5	10	2	118	205	22	18	2.3	.936	3B-102, OF-40
1989	154	.291	**.635**	543	158	34	6	**47**	**8.7**	100	**125**	87	115	3	3	1	305	10	7	0	2.1	.978	OF-147, 3B-2
1990	140	.290	.544	524	152	24	2	35	6.7	90	93	58	87	4	2	1	295	9	9	3	2.2	.971	OF-138
1991	113	.256	.515	371	95	13	1	27	7.3	52	69	43	57	2	13	0	188	6	6	1	1.8	.970	OF-100, 1B-1
1992 SEA A	99	.286	.428	360	103	24	0	9	2.5	48	67	35	46	0	5	3	130	4	0	0	1.4	1.000	OF-69, DH-26
1993 CIN N	93	.341	.601	323	110	21	3	19	5.9	56	64	25	48	1	3	0	149	7	7	2	1.8	.957	OF-88
1994	95	.326	.681	310	101	18	1	30	9.7	57	77	59	62	2	4	1	139	10	4	2	1.6	.974	OF-89, 1B-1
10 yrs.	1088	.286	.529	3742	1070	201	24	220	5.9	582	689	436	652	29	73	14	1559	564	81	57	2.0	.963	OF-745, 3B-235, DH-26, SS-25, 1B-4
LEAGUE CHAMPIONSHIP SERIES																							
1986 NY N	2	.250	.250	8	2	0	0	0	0.0	1	0	0	1	0	0	0	3	0	0	0	1.5	1.000	OF-2
1987 SF N	7	.267	.400	30	8	1	0	1	3.3	2	2	0	3	1	0	0	4	10	1	1	2.1	.933	3B-7
1989	5	.353	.706	17	6	0	0	2	11.8	5	7	3	3	0	0	0	15	1	1	1	3.4	.941	OF-5
3 yrs.	14	.291	.473	55	16	1	0	3	5.5	8	9	3	7	1	0	0	22	11	2	2	2.5	.943	3B-7, OF-7
WORLD SERIES																							
1986 NY N	5	.250	.250	8	2	0	0	0	0.0	1	0	0	3	0	2	1	0	2	0	0	0.4	1.000	OF-2, DH-1
1989 SF N	4	.294	.471	17	5	0	0	1	5.9	2	2	0	3	0	0	0	10	0	1	0	2.8	.909	OF-4
2 yrs.	9	.280	.400	25	7	0	0	1	4.0	3	2	0	6	0	2	1	10	2	1	0	1.4	.923	OF-6, DH-1

Paul Molitor

MOLITOR, PAUL LEO
B. Aug. 22, 1956, St. Paul, Minn.
BR TR 6' 185 lbs.

Year Team	Games	BA	SA	AB	H	2B	3B	HR	HR%	R	RBI	BB	SO	SB	Pinch Hit AB	Pinch Hit H	PO	A	E	DP	TC/G	FA	G by Pos
1978 MIL A	125	.273	.372	521	142	26	4	6	1.2	73	45	19	54	30	3	0	253	401	22	74	5.4	.967	2B-91, SS-31, DH-2, 3B-1
1979	140	.322	.469	584	188	27	16	9	1.5	88	62	48	48	33	2	0	309	440	16	84	5.5	.979	2B-122, SS-10, DH-8
1980	111	.304	.438	450	137	29	2	9	2.0	81	37	48	48	34	2	1	260	336	20	90	5.5	.968	2B-91, SS-12, DH-7, 3B-1
1981	64	.267	.335	251	67	11	0	2	0.8	45	19	25	29	10	1	0	119	4	3	1	2.0	.976	OF-46, DH-16
1982	160	.302	.450	**666**	201	26	8	19	2.9	**136**	71	69	93	41	0	0	134	350	32	48	3.2	.938	3B-150, DH-6, SS-4
1983	152	.270	.410	608	164	28	6	15	2.5	95	47	59	74	41	2	0	105	343	16	37	3.1	.966	3B-146, DH-2
1984	13	.217	.239	46	10	1	0	0	0.0	3	6	2	8	1	2	0	7	21	2	3	2.3	.933	3B-7, DH-4
1985	140	.297	.408	576	171	28	3	10	1.7	93	48	54	80	21	1	0	126	263	19	30	2.9	.953	3B-135, DH-4
1986	105	.281	.426	437	123	24	6	9	2.1	62	55	40	81	20	0	0	86	171	15	25	2.6	.945	3B-91, DH-10, OF-4
1987	118	.353	.566	465	164	**41**	5	16	3.4	**114**	75	69	67	45	1	0	60	113	5	24	1.5	.972	DH-58, 3B-41, 2B-19
1988	154	.312	.452	609	190	34	6	13	2.1	115	60	71	54	41	0	0	87	188	17	15	1.9	.942	3B-105, DH-49, 2B-1
1989	155	.315	.439	615	194	35	4	11	1.8	84	56	64	67	27	0	0	106	287	18	27	2.7	.956	3B-112, DH-28, 2B-16
1990	103	.285	.464	418	119	27	6	12	2.9	64	45	37	51	18	1	0	463	222	10	65	6.7	.986	2B-60, 1B-37, DH-4, 3B-2
1991	158	.325	.489	**665**	**216**	32	**13**	17	2.6	**133**	75	77	62	19	0	0	389	32	6	52	2.7	.986	DH-112, 1B-46
1992	158	.320	.461	609	195	36	7	12	2.0	89	89	73	66	31	2	0	461	26	2	44	3.1	.996	DH-108, 1B-48
1993 TOR A	160	.332	.509	636	**211**	37	5	22	3.5	121	111	77	71	22	0	0	178	14	3	16	1.2	.985	DH-137, 1B-23
1994	115	.341	.518	454	155	30	4	14	3.1	86	75	55	48	20	0	0	47	3	0	6	0.4	1.000	DH-110, 1B-5
17 yrs.	2131	.307	.453	8610	2647	472	95	196	2.3	1482	976	887	1001	454	17	1	3190	3214	206	641	3.1	.969	3B-791, DH-665, 2B-400, 1B-159, SS-57, OF-50
DIVISIONAL PLAYOFF SERIES																							
1981 MIL A	5	.250	.400	20	5	0	0	1	5.0	2	1	2	5	0	0	0	12	0	0	0	2.4	1.000	OF-5
LEAGUE CHAMPIONSHIP SERIES																							
1982 MIL A	5	.316	.684	19	6	1	0	2	10.5	4	5	2	3	1	0	0	4	11	2	2	3.4	.882	3B-5
1993 TOR A	6	.391	.696	23	9	2	1	1	4.3	7	5	3	3	0	0	0	0	0	0	0	0.0	–	DH-6
2 yrs.	11	.357	.690	42	15	3	1	3	7.1	11	10	5	6	1	0	0	4	11	2	2	1.5	.882	DH-6, 3B-5
WORLD SERIES																							
1982 MIL A	7	.355	.355	31	11	0	0	0	0.0	5	2	2	4	1	0	0	4	9	0	1	1.9	1.000	3B-7
1993 TOR A	6	.500	1.000	24	12	2	2	2	8.3	10	8	3	0	1	0	0	7	3	0	2	1.7	1.000	DH-3, 3B-2, 1B-1
2 yrs.	13	.418 1st	.636 7th	55	23	2	2	2	3.6	15	10	5	4	2	0	0	11	12	0	3	1.8	1.000	3B-9, DH-3, 1B-1

Year	Team	Games	BA	SA	AB	H	2B	3B	HR	HR%	R	RBI	BB	SO	SB	Pinch Hit AB	H	PO	A	E	DP	TC/G	FA	G by Pos

Raul Mondesi

MONDESI, RAUL RAMON
Born Raul Ramon Mondesi. (Avilino).
B. Mar. 12, 1971, San Cristobal, Dominican Republic
BR TR 5'11" 202 lbs.

Year	Team	Games	BA	SA	AB	H	2B	3B	HR	HR%	R	RBI	BB	SO	SB	AB	H	PO	A	E	DP	TC/G	FA	G by Pos
1993	LA N	42	.291	.488	86	25	3	1	4	4.7	13	10	4	16	4	7	3	55	3	3	1	1.5	.951	OF-40
1994		112	.306	.516	434	133	27	8	16	3.7	63	56	16	78	11	0	0	206	16	8	1	2.1	.965	OF-112
2 yrs.		154	.304	.512	520	158	30	9	20	3.8	76	66	20	94	15	7	3	261	19	11	2	1.9	.962	OF-152

Mickey Morandini

MORANDINI, MICHAEL ROBERT
B. Apr. 22, 1966, Kittanning, Pa.
BL TR 5'11" 170 lbs.

Year	Team	Games	BA	SA	AB	H	2B	3B	HR	HR%	R	RBI	BB	SO	SB	AB	H	PO	A	E	DP	TC/G	FA	G by Pos
1990	PHI N	25	.241	.329	79	19	4	0	1	1.3	9	3	6	19	3	1	0	37	61	1	10	4.0	.990	2B-25
1991		98	.249	.317	325	81	11	4	1	0.3	38	20	29	45	13	0	0	183	254	6	45	4.5	.986	2B-97
1992		127	.265	.344	422	112	8	8	3	0.7	47	30	25	64	8	6	3	239	336	6	65	4.6	.990	2B-124, SS-3
1993		120	.247	.355	425	105	19	9	3	0.7	57	33	34	73	13	11	3	208	288	5	48	4.2	.990	2B-111
1994		87	.292	.409	274	80	16	5	2	0.7	40	26	34	33	10	8	3	167	216	6	38	4.5	.985	2B-79
5 yrs.		457	.260	.352	1525	397	58	26	10	0.7	191	112	128	234	47	26	9	834	1155	24	206	4.4	.988	2B-436, SS-3

LEAGUE CHAMPIONSHIP SERIES

| 1993 | PHI N | 4 | .250 | .375 | 16 | 4 | 0 | 1 | 0 | 0.0 | 1 | 2 | 0 | 3 | 1 | 1 | 1 | 8 | 9 | 1 | 2 | 4.5 | .944 | 2B-4 |

WORLD SERIES

| 1993 | PHI N | 3 | .200 | .200 | 5 | 1 | 0 | 0 | 0 | 0.0 | 1 | 0 | 1 | 2 | 0 | 1 | 0 | 2 | 0 | 0 | 0 | 0.7 | 1.000 | 2B-1 |

Mike Mordecai

MORDECAI, MICHAEL HOWARD
B. Dec. 13, 1967, Birmingham, Ala.
BB TR 5'11" 175 lbs.

| 1994 | ATL N | 4 | .250 | 1.000 | 4 | 1 | 0 | 0 | 1 | 25.0 | 1 | 3 | 1 | 0 | 0 | 0 | 0 | 1 | 4 | 0 | 0 | 1.3 | 1.000 | SS-4 |

Russ Morman

MORMAN, RUSSELL LEE
B. Apr. 28, 1962, Independence, Mo.
BR TR 6'4" 215 lbs.

Year	Team	Games	BA	SA	AB	H	2B	3B	HR	HR%	R	RBI	BB	SO	SB	AB	H	PO	A	E	DP	TC/G	FA	G by Pos
1986	CHI A	49	.252	.358	159	40	5	0	4	2.5	18	17	16	36	1	1	0	342	26	4	31	7.6	.989	1B-47
1988		40	.240	.267	75	18	2	0	0	0.0	8	3	3	17	0	5	2	114	5	2	8	3.0	.983	1B-22, OF-10, DH-3
1989		37	.224	.259	58	13	2	0	0	0.0	5	8	6	16	1	2	2	157	13	2	21	4.6	.988	1B-35, DH-1
1990	KC A	12	.270	.568	37	10	4	2	1	2.7	5	3	3	3	0	1	0	27	4	0	1	2.6	1.000	OF-8, 1B-3, DH-1
1991		12	.261	.261	23	6	0	0	0	0.0	1	1	1	5	0	4	0	47	3	0	2	4.2	1.000	1B-8, OF-2, DH-1
1994	FLA N	13	.212	.364	33	7	0	1	1	3.0	2	2	2	9	0	4	0	66	9	1	9	5.8	.987	1B-8
6 yrs.		163	.244	.340	385	94	13	3	6	1.6	39	34	31	86	2	17	4	753	60	9	72	5.0	.989	1B-123, OF-20, DH-6

Hal Morris

MORRIS, WILLIAM HAROLD
B. Apr. 9, 1965, Fort Rucker, Ala.
BL TL 6'3" 200 lbs.

Year	Team	Games	BA	SA	AB	H	2B	3B	HR	HR%	R	RBI	BB	SO	SB	AB	H	PO	A	E	DP	TC/G	FA	G by Pos
1988	NY A	15	.100	.100	20	2	0	0	0	0.0	1	0	1	9	0	10	2	7	0	0	0	0.5	1.000	OF-4, DH-1
1989		15	.278	.278	18	5	0	0	0	0.0	2	4	1	4	0	9	1	12	0	0	2	0.8	1.000	OF-5, 1B-2, DH-1
1990	CIN N	107	.340	.498	309	105	22	3	7	2.3	50	36	21	32	9	21	7	595	53	4	50	6.1	.994	1B-80, OF-6
1991		136	.318	.479	478	152	33	1	14	2.9	72	59	46	61	10	9	3	979	100	9	87	8.0	.992	1B-128, OF-1
1992		115	.271	.385	395	107	21	3	6	1.5	41	53	45	53	6	8	2	841	86	1	65	8.1	.999	1B-109
1993		101	.317	.420	379	120	18	0	7	1.8	48	49	34	51	2	4	0	745	76	5	61	8.2	.994	1B-98
1994		112	.335	.491	436	146	30	4	10	2.3	60	78	34	62	6	1	0	899	77	6	76	8.8	.994	1B-112
7 yrs.		601	.313	.450	2035	637	124	11	44	2.2	274	279	181	272	33	62	15	4078	392	25	341	7.5	.994	1B-529, OF-16, DH-2

LEAGUE CHAMPIONSHIP SERIES

| 1990 | CIN N | 5 | .417 | .500 | 12 | 5 | 1 | 0 | 0 | 0.0 | 3 | 1 | 1 | 0 | 0 | 1 | 1 | 20 | 2 | 0 | 2 | 4.4 | 1.000 | 1B-4 |

WORLD SERIES

| 1990 | CIN N | 4 | .071 | .071 | 14 | 1 | 0 | 0 | 0 | 0.0 | 0 | 2 | 1 | 1 | 1 | 0 | 0 | 18 | 1 | 0 | 1 | 4.8 | 1.000 | 1B-2, DH-2 |

James Mouton

MOUTON, JAMES RALEIGH
B. Dec. 29, 1968, Denver, Colo.
BR TR 5'9" 175 lbs.

| 1994 | HOU N | 99 | .245 | .300 | 310 | 76 | 11 | 0 | 2 | 0.6 | 43 | 16 | 27 | 69 | 24 | 3 | 2 | 163 | 5 | 3 | 2 | 1.7 | .982 | OF-96 |

Pedro Munoz

MUNOZ, PEDRO JAVIER
Born Pedro Javier Munoz (Gonzalez).
B. Sept. 19, 1968, Ponce, Puerto Rico.
BR TR 5'11" 170 lbs.

Year	Team	Games	BA	SA	AB	H	2B	3B	HR	HR%	R	RBI	BB	SO	SB	AB	H	PO	A	E	DP	TC/G	FA	G by Pos
1990	MIN A	22	.271	.341	85	23	4	1	0	0.0	13	5	2	16	3	0	0	34	1	1	1	1.6	.972	OF-21, DH-1
1991		51	.283	.500	138	39	7	1	7	5.1	15	26	9	31	3	6	1	89	3	1	2	1.8	.989	OF-44, DH-2
1992		127	.270	.409	418	113	16	3	12	2.9	44	71	17	90	4	6	1	220	8	3	4	1.8	.987	OF-122, DH-3
1993		104	.233	.393	326	76	11	1	13	4.0	34	38	25	97	1	3	0	172	5	3	2	1.7	.983	OF-102
1994		75	.295	.508	244	72	15	2	11	4.5	35	36	19	67	0	7	1	110	1	4	0	1.5	.965	OF-58, DH-12
5 yrs.		379	.267	.430	1211	323	53	8	43	3.6	141	176	72	301	11	22	3	625	18	12	9	1.7	.982	OF-347, DH-18

Eddie Murray

MURRAY, EDDIE CLARENCE
Brother of Rich Murray.
B. Feb. 24, 1956, Los Angeles, Calif.
BB TR 6'2" 190 lbs.

Year	Team	Games	BA	SA	AB	H	2B	3B	HR	HR%	R	RBI	BB	SO	SB	AB	H	PO	A	E	DP	TC/G	FA	G by Pos
1977	BAL A	160	.283	.470	611	173	29	2	27	4.4	81	88	48	104	0	4	0	375	17	3	34	2.5	.992	DH-111, 1B-42, OF-3
1978		161	.285	.480	610	174	32	3	27	4.4	85	95	70	97	6	0	0	1507	112	6	144	10.1	.996	1B-157, 3B-3, DH-1
1979		159	.295	.475	606	179	30	2	25	4.1	90	99	72	78	10	0	0	1456	107	10	135	9.9	.994	1B-157, DH-2
1980		158	.300	.519	621	186	36	2	32	5.2	100	116	54	71	7	3	1	1369	77	9	158	9.2	.994	1B-154, DH-1
1981		99	.294	.534	378	111	21	2	22	5.8	57	78	40	43	2	0	0	899	91	1	98	10.0	.999	1B-99
1982		151	.316	.549	550	174	30	1	32	5.8	87	110	70	82	7	0	0	1269	97	4	106	9.1	.997	1B-149, DH-2
1983		156	.306	.538	582	178	30	3	33	5.7	115	111	86	90	5	2	0	1393	114	10	136	9.7	.993	1B-153, DH-2
1984		162	.306	.509	588	180	26	3	29	4.9	97	110	107	87	10	0	0	1538	143	13	152	10.5	.992	1B-159, DH-3
1985		156	.297	.523	583	173	37	1	31	5.3	111	124	84	68	5	0	0	1338	152	19	154	9.7	.987	1B-154, DH-2
1986		137	.305	.463	495	151	25	1	17	3.4	61	84	78	49	3	2	0	1045	88	13	100	8.4	.989	1B-119, DH-16
1987		160	.277	.477	618	171	28	3	30	4.9	89	91	73	80	1	0	0	1371	145	10	146	9.5	.993	1B-156, DH-4
1988		161	.284	.474	603	171	27	2	28	4.6	75	84	75	78	5	0	0	867	106	11	101	6.1	.989	1B-103, DH-58
1989	LA N	160	.247	.401	594	147	29	1	20	3.4	66	88	87	85	7	1	1	1316	137	6	122	9.1	.996	1B-159, 3B-2
1990		155	.330	.520	558	184	22	3	26	4.7	96	95	82	64	8	4	0	1180	113	10	88	8.4	.992	1B-150
1991		153	.260	.403	576	150	23	1	19	3.3	69	96	55	74	10	3	2	1327	128	7	96	9.6	.995	1B-149, 3B-1

Year	Team	Games	BA	SA	AB	H	2B	3B	HR	HR%	R	RBI	BB	SO	SB	Pinch Hit AB	H	PO	A	E	DP	TC/G	FA	G by Pos

Eddie Murray *continued*

Year	Team	Games	BA	SA	AB	H	2B	3B	HR	HR%	R	RBI	BB	SO	SB	AB	H	PO	A	E	DP	TC/G	FA	G by Pos
1992	NY N	156	.261	.423	551	144	37	2	16	2.9	64	93	66	74	4	3	1	1283	96	12	109	8.9	.991	1B-154
1993		154	.285	.467	610	174	28	1	27	4.4	77	100	40	61	2	0	0	1319	109	18	118	9.4	.988	1B-154
1994	CLE A	108	.254	.425	433	110	21	1	17	3.9	57	76	31	53	8	0	0	241	14	3	25	2.4	.988	DH-82, 1B-26
18 yrs.		2706	.288	.480	10167	2930	511	34	458	4.5	1477	1738	1218	1338	100	22	5	21093	1846	165	2022	8.5	.993	1B-2394, DH-284, 3B-6, OF-3

LEAGUE CHAMPIONSHIP SERIES

Year	Team	Games	BA	SA	AB	H	2B	3B	HR	HR%	R	RBI	BB	SO	SB	AB	H	PO	A	E	DP	TC/G	FA	G by Pos
1979	BAL A	4	.417	.667	12	5	0	0	1	8.3	3	5	5	2	0	0	0	44	3	2	4	12.3	.959	1B-4
1983		4	.267	.467	15	4	0	0	1	6.7	5	3	3	3	1	0	0	36	2	1	2	9.8	.974	1B-4
2 yrs.		8	.333	.556	27	9	0	0	2	7.4	8	8	8	5	1	0	0	80	5	3	6	11.0	.966	1B-8

WORLD SERIES

Year	Team	Games	BA	SA	AB	H	2B	3B	HR	HR%	R	RBI	BB	SO	SB	AB	H	PO	A	E	DP	TC/G	FA	G by Pos
1979	BAL A	7	.154	.308	26	4	1	0	1	3.8	3	2	4	4	1	0	0	60	7	0	5	9.6	1.000	1B-7
1983		5	.250	.550	20	5	0	0	2	10.0	2	3	1	4	0	0	0	46	1	1	5	9.6	.979	1B-5
2 yrs.		12	.196	.413	46	9	1	0	3	6.5	5	5	5	8	1	0	0	106	8	1	10	9.6	.991	1B-12

Greg Myers

MYERS, GREGORY RICHARD
B. Apr. 14, 1966, Riverside, Calif.

BL TR 6'1" 200 lbs.

Year	Team	Games	BA	SA	AB	H	2B	3B	HR	HR%	R	RBI	BB	SO	SB	AB	H	PO	A	E	DP	TC/G	FA	G by Pos
1987	TOR A	7	.111	.111	9	1	0	0	0	0.0	1	0	0	3	0	0	0	24	1	0	0	3.6	1.000	C-7
1989		17	.114	.159	44	5	2	0	0	0.0	0	1	2	9	0	1	0	46	6	0	1	3.1	1.000	C-11, DH-6
1990		87	.236	.332	250	59	7	1	5	2.0	33	22	22	33	0	7	2	411	30	3	4	5.1	.993	C-87
1991		107	.262	.411	309	81	22	0	8	2.6	25	36	21	45	0	10	2	484	37	11	5	5.0	.979	C-104
1992	2 teams		TOR A	(22G – .230)		CAL A	(8G – .235)																	
"	total	30	.231	.359	78	18	7	0	1	1.3	4	13	5	11	0	4	1	125	16	1	1	4.7	.993	C-26, DH-1
1993	CAL A	108	.255	.362	290	74	10	0	7	2.4	27	40	17	47	0	25	8	369	44	6	5	3.9	.986	C-97, DH-2
1994		45	.246	.341	126	31	6	0	2	1.6	10	8	10	27	0	6	0	194	28	2	0	5.0	.991	C-41, DH-1
7 yrs.		401	.243	.356	1106	269	54	1	23	2.1	100	120	77	175	3	53	13	1653	162	23	16	4.6	.987	C-373, DH-10

Tim Naehring

NAEHRING, TIMOTHY JAMES
B. Feb. 1, 1967, Cincinnati, Ohio.

BR TR 6'2" 190 lbs.

Year	Team	Games	BA	SA	AB	H	2B	3B	HR	HR%	R	RBI	BB	SO	SB	AB	H	PO	A	E	DP	TC/G	FA	G by Pos
1990	BOS A	24	.271	.412	85	23	6	0	2	2.4	10	12	8	15	0	0	0	36	66	9	13	4.6	.919	SS-19, 3B-5, 2B-1
1991		20	.109	.127	55	6	1	0	0	0.0	1	3	6	15	0	1	0	17	53	3	9	3.7	.959	SS-17, 3B-2, 2B-1
1992		72	.231	.323	186	43	8	0	3	1.6	12	14	18	31	0	8	0	95	170	3	31	3.7	.989	SS-30, 2B-23, 3B-10, DH-4, OF-1
1993		39	.331	.433	127	42	10	0	1	0.8	14	17	10	26	1	6	2	46	43	2	14	2.3	.978	2B-15, DH-10, 3B-9, SS-4
1994		80	.276	.414	297	82	18	1	7	2.4	41	42	30	56	1	2	1	190	182	6	45	4.7	.984	2B-49, 3B-11, SS-9, 1B-8, DH-7
5 yrs.		235	.261	.373	750	196	43	1	13	1.7	78	88	72	143	2	17	3	384	514	23	112	3.9	.975	2B-89, SS-79, 3B-37, DH-21, 1B-8, OF-1

Bob Natal

NATAL, ROBERT MARCEL
B. Nov. 13, 1965, Long Beach, Calif.

BR TR 5'11" 190 lbs.

Year	Team	Games	BA	SA	AB	H	2B	3B	HR	HR%	R	RBI	BB	SO	SB	AB	H	PO	A	E	DP	TC/G	FA	G by Pos
1992	MON N	5	.000	.000	6	0	0	0	0	0.0	0	0	1	1	0	1	0	10	0	1	0	2.2	.909	C-4
1993	FLA N	41	.214	.291	117	25	4	1	1	0.9	3	6	6	22	1	2	0	196	18	0	2	5.2	1.000	C-38
1994		10	.276	.345	29	8	2	0	0	0.0	2	2	5	5	1	2	0	50	9	1	0	6.0	.983	C-8
3 yrs.		56	.217	.289	152	33	6	1	1	0.7	5	8	12	28	2	5	0	256	27	2	2	5.1	.993	C-50

Troy Neel

NEEL, TROY LEE
B. Sept. 14, 1965, Freeport, Tex.

BL TR 6'4" 210 lbs.

Year	Team	Games	BA	SA	AB	H	2B	3B	HR	HR%	R	RBI	BB	SO	SB	AB	H	PO	A	E	DP	TC/G	FA	G by Pos
1992	OAK A	24	.264	.491	53	14	3	0	3	5.7	8	9	5	15	0	7	3	16	1	3	0	0.8	.850	DH-9, OF-9, 1B-2
1993		123	.290	.473	427	124	21	0	19	4.4	59	63	49	101	3	7	1	236	22	5	25	2.1	.981	DH-85, 1B-34
1994		83	.266	.475	278	74	13	0	15	5.4	43	48	38	61	2	6	2	295	23	2	34	3.9	.994	1B-45, DH-35
3 yrs.		230	.280	.475	758	212	37	0	37	4.9	110	120	92	177	5	20	6	547	46	10	59	2.6	.983	DH-129, 1B-81, OF-9

Marc Newfield

NEWFIELD, MARC ALEXANDER
B. Oct. 19, 1972, Sacramento, Calif.

BR TR 6'4" 205 lbs.

Year	Team	Games	BA	SA	AB	H	2B	3B	HR	HR%	R	RBI	BB	SO	SB	AB	H	PO	A	E	DP	TC/G	FA	G by Pos
1993	SEA A	22	.227	.318	66	15	3	0	1	1.5	5	7	2	8	0	3	0	0	0	0	0	0.0	–	DH-15, OF-5
1994		12	.184	.289	38	7	1	0	1	2.6	3	4	2	4	0	2	0	2	0	0	0	0.2	1.000	DH-9, OF-3
2 yrs.		34	.212	.308	104	22	4	0	2	1.9	8	11	4	12	0	5	0	2	0	0	0	0.1	1.000	DH-24, OF-8

Warren Newson

NEWSON, WARREN DALE
B. July 3, 1964, Newnan, Ga.

BL TL 5'7" 190 lbs.

Year	Team	Games	BA	SA	AB	H	2B	3B	HR	HR%	R	RBI	BB	SO	SB	AB	H	PO	A	E	DP	TC/G	FA	G by Pos
1991	CHI A	71	.295	.424	132	39	5	0	4	3.0	20	25	28	34	2	22	8	48	3	2	0	0.7	.962	OF-50, DH-3
1992		63	.221	.265	136	30	3	0	1	0.7	19	11	37	38	3	15	3	67	5	0	3	1.1	1.000	OF-50, DH-4
1993		26	.300	.450	40	12	0	0	2	5.0	9	6	9	12	0	11	5	5	0	0	0	0.2	1.000	DH-10, OF-5
1994		63	.255	.363	102	26	5	0	2	2.0	16	7	14	23	1	25	7	45	1	1	1	0.7	.979	OF-34, DH-3
4 yrs.		223	.261	.359	410	107	13	0	9	2.2	64	49	88	107	6	73	23	165	9	3	4	0.8	.983	OF-139, DH-20

LEAGUE CHAMPIONSHIP SERIES

Year	Team	Games	BA	SA	AB	H	2B	3B	HR	HR%	R	RBI	BB	SO	SB	AB	H	PO	A	E	DP	TC/G	FA	G by Pos
1993	CHI A	2	.200	.800	5	1	0	0	1	20.0	1	1	1	0	0	1	0	0	0	0	0	0.0	–	DH-1

Melvin Nieves

NIEVES, MELVIN
Born Melvin Nieves (Ramos).
B. Dec. 28, 1971, San Juan, Puerto Rico.

BB TR 6'2" 185 lbs.

Year	Team	Games	BA	SA	AB	H	2B	3B	HR	HR%	R	RBI	BB	SO	SB	AB	H	PO	A	E	DP	TC/G	FA	G by Pos
1992	ATL N	12	.211	.263	19	4	0	0	0	0.0	0	2	7	7	0	6	1	8	0	3	0	0.9	.727	OF-6
1993	SD N	19	.191	.319	47	9	0	0	2	4.3	4	3	3	21	0	6	0	27	0	2	0	1.5	.931	OF-15
1994		10	.263	.474	19	5	1	0	1	5.3	2	4	3	10	0	4	1	11	1	0	0	1.2	1.000	OF-6
3 yrs.		41	.212	.341	85	18	2	0	3	3.5	6	8	8	38	0	16	2	46	1	5	0	1.3	.904	OF-27

Dave Nilsson

NILSSON, DAVID WAYNE
B. Dec. 14, 1969, Brisbane, Australia.

BL TR 6'3" 185 lbs.

Year	Team	Games	BA	SA	AB	H	2B	3B	HR	HR%	R	RBI	BB	SO	SB	AB	H	PO	A	E	DP	TC/G	FA	G by Pos
1992	MIL A	51	.232	.354	164	38	8	0	4	2.4	15	25	17	18	2	1	0	231	16	2	2	4.9	.992	C-46, 1B-3, DH-2
1993		100	.257	.375	296	76	10	2	7	2.4	35	40	37	36	3	4	1	457	33	9	6	5.0	.982	C-91, 1B-4, DH-4

Year Team	Games	BA	SA	AB	H	2B	3B	HR	HR%	R	RBI	BB	SO	SB	Pinch Hit AB	Pinch Hit H	PO	A	E	DP	TC/G	FA	G by Pos

Dave Nilsson *continued*

Year Team	Games	BA	SA	AB	H	2B	3B	HR	HR%	R	RBI	BB	SO	SB	AB	H	PO	A	E	DP	TC/G	FA	G by Pos
1994	109	.275	.451	397	109	28	3	12	3.0	51	69	34	61	1	5	1	315	15	2	4	3.0	.994	C-60, DH-43, 1B-5
3 yrs.	260	.260	.406	857	223	46	5	23	2.7	101	134	88	115	6	10	2	1003	64	13	12	4.2	.988	C-197, DH-49, 1B-12

Otis Nixon

NIXON, OTIS JUNIOR
Brother of Donell Nixon.
B. Jan. 9, 1959, Evergreen, N. C.

BB TR 6'2" 175 lbs.

Year Team	Games	BA	SA	AB	H	2B	3B	HR	HR%	R	RBI	BB	SO	SB	AB	H	PO	A	E	DP	TC/G	FA	G by Pos
1983 NY A	13	.143	.143	14	2	0	0	0	0.0	2	0	1	5	2	0	0	14	1	1	0	1.2	.938	OF-9
1984 CLE A	49	.154	.154	91	14	0	0	0	0.0	16	1	8	11	12	0	0	81	3	0	0	1.7	1.000	OF-46
1985	104	.235	.315	162	38	4	0	3	1.9	34	9	8	27	20	2	0	129	5	4	1	1.3	.971	OF-80, DH-11
1986	105	.263	.326	95	25	4	1	0	0.0	33	8	13	12	23	3	1	90	3	3	0	0.9	.969	OF-95, DH-5
1987	19	.059	.059	17	1	0	0	0	0.0	2	1	3	4	2	0	0	21	0	0	0	1.1	1.000	OF-17
1988 MON N	90	.244	.288	271	66	8	2	0	0.0	47	15	28	42	46	11	6	176	2	1	1	2.0	.994	OF-82
1989	126	.217	.260	258	56	7	2	0	0.0	41	21	33	36	37	21	2	160	2	2	0	1.3	.988	OF-98
1990	119	.251	.307	231	58	6	2	1	0.4	46	20	28	33	50	28	6	149	6	1	1	1.3	.994	OF-88, SS-1
1991 ATL N	124	.297	.327	401	119	10	1	0	0.0	81	26	47	40	72	8	3	218	6	3	1	1.8	.987	OF-115
1992	120	.294	.346	456	134	14	2	2	0.4	79	22	39	54	41	9	4	333	6	3	1	2.9	.991	OF-111
1993	134	.269	.315	461	124	12	3	1	0.2	77	24	61	63	47	13	2	308	4	3	1	2.4	.990	OF-116
1994 BOS A	103	.274	.317	398	109	15	1	0	0.0	60	25	55	65	42	0	0	254	4	3	1	2.5	.989	OF-103
12 yrs.	1106	.261	.306	2855	746	80	14	7	0.2	518	172	324	392	394	95	24	1933	42	24	7	1.8	.988	OF-960, DH-16, SS-1

LEAGUE CHAMPIONSHIP SERIES

Year Team	Games	BA	SA	AB	H	2B	3B	HR	HR%	R	RBI	BB	SO	SB	AB	H	PO	A	E	DP	TC/G	FA	G by Pos
1992 ATL N	7	.286	.357	28	8	2	0	0	0.0	5	2	4	4	3	0	0	16	0	0	0	2.3	1.000	OF-7
1993	6	.348	.435	23	8	2	0	0	0.0	3	4	5	6	0	0	0	13	0	0	0	2.2	1.000	OF-6
2 yrs.	13	.314	.392	51	16	4	0	0	0.0	8	6	9	10	3	0	0	29	0	0	0	2.2	1.000	OF-13

WORLD SERIES

Year Team	Games	BA	SA	AB	H	2B	3B	HR	HR%	R	RBI	BB	SO	SB	AB	H	PO	A	E	DP	TC/G	FA	G by Pos
1992 ATL N	6	.296	.333	27	8	1	0	0	0.0	3	1	1	3	5	0	0	18	0	0	0	3.0	1.000	OF-6

Junior Noboa

NOBOA, MILCIADES ARTURO
Born Milciades Arturo Noboa (Diaz).
B. Nov. 10, 1964, Azua, Dominican Republic.

BR TR 5'10" 155 lbs.

Year Team	Games	BA	SA	AB	H	2B	3B	HR	HR%	R	RBI	BB	SO	SB	AB	H	PO	A	E	DP	TC/G	FA	G by Pos
1984 CLE A	23	.364	.364	11	4	0	0	0	0.0	3	0	0	2	1	0	0	7	13	0	4	0.9	1.000	2B-19, DH-1
1987	39	.225	.275	80	18	2	1	0	0.0	7	7	3	6	1	2	0	28	66	3	8	2.5	.969	2B-21, SS-8, 3B-5
1988 CAL A	21	.063	.063	16	1	0	0	0	0.0	4	0	0	1	0	0	0	8	24	1	7	1.6	.970	2B-9, SS-3, 3B-2
1989 MON N	21	.227	.227	44	10	0	0	0	0.0	3	1	1	3	0	5	3	17	45	0	7	3.0	1.000	2B-13, SS-4, 3B-1
1990	81	.266	.335	158	42	7	2	0	0.0	15	14	7	14	4	35	10	47	52	2	10	1.2	.980	2B-31, OF-9, 3B-8, SS-7, P-1
1991	67	.242	.305	95	23	3	0	1	1.1	5	2	1	8	2	46	**14**	20	19	1	4	0.6	.975	OF-7, 2B-6, 3B-2, SS-2, 1B-1
1992 NY N	46	.149	.149	47	7	0	0	0	0.0	7	3	3	8	0	20	2	19	30	3	6	1.1	.942	2B-16, 3B-3, SS-2
1994 2 teams	OAK A	(17G – .325)		PIT N	(2G – .000)																		
" total	19	.310	.381	42	13	1	0	0	0.0	3	6	2	5	1	3	0	19	33	3	7	2.9	.945	2B-14, SS-2
8 yrs.	317	.239	.288	493	118	13	4	1	0.2	47	33	17	47	9	111	29	165	282	13	53	1.5	.972	2B-129, SS-28, 3B-21, OF-16, DH-1, P-1, 1B-1

Matt Nokes

NOKES, MATTHEW DODGE
B. Oct. 31, 1963, San Diego, Calif.

BL TR 6'1" 180 lbs.

Year Team	Games	BA	SA	AB	H	2B	3B	HR	HR%	R	RBI	BB	SO	SB	AB	H	PO	A	E	DP	TC/G	FA	G by Pos
1985 SF N	19	.208	.358	53	11	2	0	2	3.8	3	5	1	9	0	5	0	84	2	2	0	4.6	.977	C-14
1986 DET A	7	.333	.500	24	8	1	0	1	4.2	2	2	1	1	0	0	0	43	2	0	2	6.4	1.000	C-7
1987	135	.289	.536	461	133	14	2	32	6.9	69	87	35	70	2	19	4	600	32	5	2	4.7	.992	C-109, OF-3, 3B-2
1988	122	.251	.424	382	96	18	0	16	4.2	53	53	34	58	0	16	3	574	45	7	8	5.1	.989	C-110, DH-4
1989	87	.250	.388	268	67	10	0	9	3.4	15	39	17	37	1	11	1	235	26	6	3	3.1	.978	C-51, DH-33
1990 2 teams	DET A	(44G – .270)		NY A	(92G – .238)																		
" total	136	.248	.373	351	87	9	1	11	3.1	33	40	24	47	2	34	8	237	34	2	6	2.0	.993	C-65, DH-54, OF-2
1991 NY A	135	.268	.469	456	122	20	0	24	5.3	52	77	25	49	3	17	4	690	48	6	7	5.5	.992	C-130, DH-3
1992	121	.224	.424	384	86	9	1	22	5.7	42	59	37	62	0	13	4	551	48	4	6	5.0	.993	C-111
1993	76	.249	.424	217	54	8	0	10	4.6	25	35	16	31	0	9	5	245	19	2	6	3.5	.992	C-56, DH-11
1994	28	.291	.595	79	23	3	0	7	8.9	11	19	5	16	0	6	0	106	6	3	7	4.1	.974	C-17, DH-5, 1B-4
10 yrs.	866	.257	.445	2675	687	94	4	134	5.0	305	416	195	380	8	130	29	3365	262	37	41	4.2	.990	C-670, DH-110, OF-5, 1B-4, 3B-2

LEAGUE CHAMPIONSHIP SERIES

Year Team	Games	BA	SA	AB	H	2B	3B	HR	HR%	R	RBI	BB	SO	SB	AB	H	PO	A	E	DP	TC/G	FA	G by Pos
1987 DET A	5	.143	.357	14	2	0	0	1	7.1	2	1	2	4	0	2	0	11	2	0	0	2.6	1.000	C-3, DH-2

Charlie O'Brien

O'BRIEN, CHARLES HUGH
B. May 1, 1960, Tulsa, Okla.

BR TR 6'2" 195 lbs.

Year Team	Games	BA	SA	AB	H	2B	3B	HR	HR%	R	RBI	BB	SO	SB	AB	H	PO	A	E	DP	TC/G	FA	G by Pos
1985 OAK A	16	.273	.364	11	3	1	0	0	0.0	3	1	3	3	0	0	0	23	0	1	0	1.5	.958	C-16
1987 MIL A	10	.200	.343	35	7	3	1	0	0.0	2	0	4	4	0	0	0	78	11	0	1	8.9	1.000	C-10
1988	40	.220	.322	118	26	6	0	2	1.7	12	9	5	16	0	0	0	210	20	2	4	5.8	.991	C-40
1989	62	.234	.383	188	44	10	0	6	3.2	22	35	21	11	0	0	0	314	36	5	5	5.7	.986	C-62
1990 2 teams	MIL A	(46G – .186)		NY N	(28G – .162)																		
" total	74	.178	.244	213	38	10	2	0	0.0	17	20	21	34	0	0	0	408	45	5	6	6.2	.989	C-74
1991 NY N	69	.185	.256	168	31	6	0	2	1.2	16	14	17	25	0	2	0	396	37	4	7	6.3	.991	C-67
1992	68	.212	.327	156	33	12	0	2	1.3	15	13	16	18	0	4	0	287	44	7	4	5.0	.979	C-64
1993	67	.255	.378	188	48	11	0	4	2.1	15	23	14	14	1	3	1	325	39	5	5	5.5	.986	C-65
1994 ATL N	51	.243	.474	152	37	11	0	8	5.3	24	28	15	24	0	3	1	308	26	3	1	6.6	.991	C-48
9 yrs.	457	.217	.338	1229	267	70	3	24	2.0	126	143	116	149	1	12	2	2349	258	32	32	5.8	.988	C-446

Jose Offerman

OFFERMAN, JOSE ANTONIO
Born Jose Antonio Oferman (Dono).
B. Nov. 8, 1968, San Pedro de Macoris, Dominican Republic.

BB TR 6' 150 lbs.

Year Team	Games	BA	SA	AB	H	2B	3B	HR	HR%	R	RBI	BB	SO	SB	AB	H	PO	A	E	DP	TC/G	FA	G by Pos
1990 LA N	29	.155	.207	58	9	0	0	1	1.7	7	7	4	14	1	1	0	30	40	4	5	2.6	.946	SS-27
1991	52	.195	.212	113	22	0	0	0	0.0	10	3	25	32	3	2	0	50	121	10	17	3.5	.945	SS-50

Year Team	Games	BA	SA	AB	H	2B	3B	HR	HR%	R	RBI	BB	SO	SB	Pinch Hit AB	Pinch Hit H	PO	A	E	DP	TC/G	FA	G by Pos

Jose Offerman *continued*

Year Team	Games	BA	SA	AB	H	2B	3B	HR	HR%	R	RBI	BB	SO	SB	AB	H	PO	A	E	DP	TC/G	FA	G by Pos
1992	149	.260	.333	534	139	20	8	1	0.2	67	30	57	98	23	1	0	208	398	42	74	4.3	.935	SS-149
1993	158	.269	.331	590	159	21	6	1	0.2	77	62	71	75	30	1	0	250	454	37	95	4.7	.950	SS-158
1994	72	.210	.288	243	51	8	4	1	0.4	27	25	38	38	2	0	0	123	194	11	45	4.6	.966	SS-72
5 yrs.	460	.247	.311	1538	380	51	18	4	0.3	188	127	195	257	59	5	0	661	1207	104	236	4.3	.947	SS-456

Greg O'Halloran

O'HALLORAN, GREGORY JOSEPH
B. May 21, 1968, Toronto, Ont., Canada

BL TR 6'2" 205 lbs.

Year Team	Games	BA	SA	AB	H	2B	3B	HR	HR%	R	RBI	BB	SO	SB	AB	H	PO	A	E	DP	TC/G	FA	G by Pos
1994 FLA N	12	.182	.182	11	2	0	0	0	0.0	1	1	1	0	1	11	2	2	0	0	0	0.2	1.000	C-1

Troy O'Leary

O'LEARY, TROY FRANKLIN
B. Aug. 4, 1969, Compton, Calif.

BL TL 6' 175 lbs.

Year Team	Games	BA	SA	AB	H	2B	3B	HR	HR%	R	RBI	BB	SO	SB	AB	H	PO	A	E	DP	TC/G	FA	G by Pos
1993 MIL A	19	.293	.366	41	12	3	0	0	0.0	3	3	5	9	0	2	1	32	1	0	0	1.7	1.000	OF-19
1994	27	.273	.409	66	18	1	1	2	3.0	9	7	5	12	1	4	1	37	2	0	1	1.4	1.000	OF-21, DH-1
2 yrs.	46	.280	.393	107	30	4	1	2	1.9	12	10	10	21	1	6	2	69	3	0	1	1.6	1.000	OF-40, DH-1

John Olerud

OLERUD, JOHN GARRETT
B. Aug. 5, 1968, Seattle, Wash.

BL TL 6'5" 205 lbs.

Year Team	Games	BA	SA	AB	H	2B	3B	HR	HR%	R	RBI	BB	SO	SB	AB	H	PO	A	E	DP	TC/G	FA	G by Pos
1989 TOR A	6	.375	.375	8	3	0	0	0	0.0	2	0	0	1	0	1	0	19	2	0	0	3.5	1.000	1B-5, DH-1
1990	111	.265	.430	358	95	15	1	14	3.9	43	48	57	75	0	7	1	133	10	2	10	1.3	.986	DH-90, 1B-18
1991	139	.256	.438	454	116	30	1	17	3.7	64	68	68	84	0	9	1	1120	78	5	77	8.7	.996	1B-135, DH-1
1992	138	.284	.450	458	130	28	0	16	3.5	68	66	70	61	1	10	4	1057	81	7	72	8.3	.994	1B-133, DH-1
1993	158	**.363**	.599	551	200	**54**	2	24	4.4	109	107	114	65	0	1	0	1160	97	10	107	8.0	.992	1B-137, DH-20
1994	108	.297	.477	384	114	29	2	12	3.1	47	67	61	53	1	3	0	823	68	6	82	8.3	.993	1B-104, DH-3
6 yrs.	660	.297	.486	2213	658	156	6	83	3.8	333	356	370	339	2	31	6	4312	336	30	348	7.1	.994	1B-532, DH-116

LEAGUE CHAMPIONSHIP SERIES

Year Team	Games	BA	SA	AB	H	2B	3B	HR	HR%	R	RBI	BB	SO	SB	AB	H	PO	A	E	DP	TC/G	FA	G by Pos
1991 TOR A	5	.158	.158	19	3	0	0	0	0.0	1	3	3	1	0	0	0	40	3	0	5	8.6	1.000	1B-5
1992	6	.348	.565	23	8	2	0	1	4.3	4	4	2	5	0	0	0	51	1	0	6	8.7	1.000	1B-6
1993	6	.348	.391	23	8	1	0	0	0.0	5	3	4	1	0	0	0	48	9	1	5	9.7	.983	1B-6
3 yrs.	17	.292	.385	65	19	3	0	1	1.5	10	10	9	7	0	0	0	139	13	1	16	9.0	.993	1B-17

WORLD SERIES

Year Team	Games	BA	SA	AB	H	2B	3B	HR	HR%	R	RBI	BB	SO	SB	AB	H	PO	A	E	DP	TC/G	FA	G by Pos
1992 TOR A	4	.308	.308	13	4	0	0	0	0.0	2	0	0	4	0	0	0	25	3	0	2	7.0	1.000	1B-4
1993	5	.235	.471	17	4	1	0	1	5.9	5	2	4	1	0	0	0	36	0	0	3	7.2	1.000	1B-5
2 yrs.	9	.267	.400	30	8	1	0	1	3.3	7	2	4	5	0	0	0	61	3	0	5	7.1	1.000	1B-9

Jose Oliva

OLIVA, JOSE
Born Jose Oliva (Galvez).
B. Mar. 3, 1971, San Pedro de Macoris, Dominican Republic

BR TR 6'3" 215 lbs.

Year Team	Games	BA	SA	AB	H	2B	3B	HR	HR%	R	RBI	BB	SO	SB	AB	H	PO	A	E	DP	TC/G	FA	G by Pos
1994 ATL N	19	.288	.678	59	17	5	0	6	10.2	9	11	7	10	0	3	1	9	32	3	2	2.3	.932	3B-16

Joe Oliver

OLIVER, JOSEPH MELTON
B. July 24, 1965, Memphis, Tenn.

BR TR 6'3" 215 lbs.

Year Team	Games	BA	SA	AB	H	2B	3B	HR	HR%	R	RBI	BB	SO	SB	AB	H	PO	A	E	DP	TC/G	FA	G by Pos
1989 CIN N	49	.272	.384	151	41	8	0	3	2.0	13	23	6	28	0	7	2	260	21	4	1	5.8	.986	C-47
1990	121	.231	.360	364	84	23	0	8	2.2	34	52	37	75	1	8	4	686	59	6	8	6.2	.992	C-118
1991	94	.216	.379	269	58	11	0	11	4.1	21	41	18	53	0	7	0	496	40	11	6	5.8	.980	C-90
1992	143	.270	.388	485	131	25	1	10	2.1	42	57	35	75	2	2	1	925	64	8	8	7.0	.992	C-141, 1B-1
1993	139	.239	.384	482	115	28	0	14	2.9	40	75	27	91	0	3	1	825	70	7	13	6.9	.992	C-133, 1B-12, OF-1
1994	6	.211	.368	19	4	0	0	1	5.3	1	5	2	3	0	0	0	48	2	1	0	8.5	.980	C-6
6 yrs.	552	.245	.379	1770	433	95	1	47	2.7	151	253	125	325	3	27	8	3240	256	37	36	6.4	.990	C-535, 1B-13, OF-1

LEAGUE CHAMPIONSHIP SERIES

Year Team	Games	BA	SA	AB	H	2B	3B	HR	HR%	R	RBI	BB	SO	SB	AB	H	PO	A	E	DP	TC/G	FA	G by Pos
1990 CIN N	5	.143	.143	14	2	0	0	0	0.0	1	0	1	0	0	0	0	27	1	0	0	5.6	1.000	C-5

WORLD SERIES

Year Team	Games	BA	SA	AB	H	2B	3B	HR	HR%	R	RBI	BB	SO	SB	AB	H	PO	A	E	DP	TC/G	FA	G by Pos
1990 CIN N	4	.333	.500	18	6	3	0	0	0.0	2	2	1	0	1	0	0	27	1	3	0	7.8	.903	C-4

Paul O'Neill

O'NEILL, PAUL ANDREW
B. Feb. 25, 1963, Columbus, Ohio.

BL TL 6'4" 200 lbs.

Year Team	Games	BA	SA	AB	H	2B	3B	HR	HR%	R	RBI	BB	SO	SB	AB	H	PO	A	E	DP	TC/G	FA	G by Pos
1985 CIN N	5	.333	.417	12	4	1	0	0	0.0	1	1	0	2	0	3	1	3	1	0	0	0.8	1.000	OF-2
1986	3	.000	.000	2	0	0	0	0	0.0	0	0	1	1	0	2	0	0	0	0	0	0.0	—	
1987	84	.256	.488	160	41	14	1	7	4.4	24	28	18	29	2	37	11	90	2	4	2	1.1	.958	OF-42, 1B-2, P-1
1988	145	.252	.414	485	122	25	3	16	3.3	58	73	38	65	8	11	0	410	13	6	14	3.0	.986	OF-118, 1B-21
1989	117	.276	.446	428	118	24	2	15	3.5	49	74	46	64	20	3	3	223	7	4	1	2.0	.983	OF-115
1990	145	.270	.421	503	136	28	0	16	3.2	59	78	53	103	13	8	2	271	12	2	0	2.0	.993	OF-141
1991	152	.256	.481	532	136	36	0	28	5.3	71	91	73	107	12	4	1	301	13	2	2	2.1	.994	OF-150
1992	148	.246	.373	496	122	19	1	14	2.8	59	66	77	85	6	9	3	291	12	1	2	2.1	.997	OF-143
1993 NY A	141	.311	.504	498	155	34	1	20	4.0	71	75	44	69	2	12	1	230	7	2	0	1.7	.992	OF-138, DH-2
1994	103	**.359**	.603	368	132	25	1	21	5.7	68	83	72	56	5	9	4	203	7	1	0	2.0	.995	OF-99, DH-4
10 yrs.	1043	.277	.460	3484	966	206	9	137	3.9	460	569	422	581	68	98	26	2022	74	22	21	2.0	.990	OF-948, 1B-23, DH-6, P-1

LEAGUE CHAMPIONSHIP SERIES

Year Team	Games	BA	SA	AB	H	2B	3B	HR	HR%	R	RBI	BB	SO	SB	AB	H	PO	A	E	DP	TC/G	FA	G by Pos
1990 CIN N	5	.471	.824	17	8	3	0	1	5.9	1	4	1	1	1	0	0	9	2	0	1	2.2	1.000	OF-5

WORLD SERIES

Year Team	Games	BA	SA	AB	H	2B	3B	HR	HR%	R	RBI	BB	SO	SB	AB	H	PO	A	E	DP	TC/G	FA	G by Pos
1990 CIN N	4	.083	.083	12	1	0	0	0	0.0	2	1	5	2	1	0	0	11	0	0	0	2.8	1.000	OF-4

Jose Oquendo

OQUENDO, JOSE MANUEL
Born Jose Manuel Oquendo (Contreras).
B. July 4, 1963, Rio Piedras, Puerto Rico.

BB TR 5'10" 160 lbs.
BR 1984

Year Team	Games	BA	SA	AB	H	2B	3B	HR	HR%	R	RBI	BB	SO	SB	AB	H	PO	A	E	DP	TC/G	FA	G by Pos
1983 NY N	120	.213	.244	328	70	7	0	1	0.3	29	17	19	60	8	1	0	182	326	21	65	4.4	.960	SS-116
1984	81	.222	.249	189	42	5	0	0	0.0	23	10	15	26	10	3	2	95	152	7	33	3.1	.972	SS-67

Year	Team	Games	BA	SA	AB	H	2B	3B	HR	HR%	R	RBI	BB	SO	SB	Pinch Hit AB	Pinch Hit H	PO	A	E	DP	TC/G	FA	G by Pos

Jose Oquendo *continued*

Year	Team	Games	BA	SA	AB	H	2B	3B	HR	HR%	R	RBI	BB	SO	SB	PH AB	PH H	PO	A	E	DP	TC/G	FA	G by Pos
1986	STL N	76	.297	.341	138	41	4	1	0	0.0	20	13	15	20	2	27	6	52	94	8	23	2.0	.948	SS-29, 2B-21, 3B-1, OF-1
1987		116	.286	.335	248	71	9	0	1	0.4	43	24	54	29	4	26	10	149	133	4	31	2.5	.986	OF-46, 2B-32, SS-23, 3B-8, 1B-3, P-1
1988		148	.277	.350	451	125	10	1	7	1.6	36	46	52	40	4	10	2	268	315	11	61	4.0	.981	2B-69, 3B-47, SS-17, 1B-16, OF-15, C-1, P-1
1989		163	.291	.372	556	162	28	7	1	0.2	59	48	79	59	3	1	1	356	523	6	108	5.4	.993	2B-156, SS-7, 1B-1
1990		156	.252	.316	469	118	17	5	1	0.2	38	37	74	46	1	3	0	294	403	4	67	4.5	.994	2B-150, SS-4
1991		127	.240	.301	366	88	11	4	1	0.3	37	26	67	48	1	0	0	271	368	9	65	5.1	.986	2B-118, SS-22, 1B-3, P-1
1992		14	.257	.400	35	9	3	1	0	0.0	3	3	5	3	0	2	0	18	30	1	7	3.5	.980	2B-9, SS-5
1993		46	.205	.205	73	15	0	0	0	0.0	7	4	12	8	0	6	1	52	82	1	15	2.9	.993	SS-22, 2B-16
1994		55	.264	.310	129	34	2	1	0	0.0	13	9	21	16	1	12	4	53	98	4	22	2.8	.974	SS-28, 2B-16
11 yrs.		1102	.260	.318	2982	775	96	21	12	0.4	308	237	413	355	34	91	26	1790	2524	76	497	4.0	.983	2B-587, SS-340, OF-62, 3B-56, 1B-23, P-3, C-1

LEAGUE CHAMPIONSHIP SERIES

| 1987 | STL N | 5 | .167 | .417 | 12 | 2 | 0 | 0 | 1 | 8.3 | 3 | 4 | 3 | 2 | 0 | 1 | 0 | 7 | 0 | 0 | 0 | 1.4 | 1.000 | OF-5, 3B-1 |

WORLD SERIES

| 1987 | STL N | 7 | .250 | .250 | 24 | 6 | 0 | 0 | 0 | 0.0 | 2 | 2 | 1 | 4 | 0 | 0 | 0 | 8 | 10 | 0 | 0 | 2.6 | 1.000 | 3B-4, OF-3 |

Joe Orsulak

ORSULAK, JOSEPH MICHAEL
B. May 31, 1962, Glen Ridge, N. J.   BL TL 6'1" 185 lbs.

Year	Team	Games	BA	SA	AB	H	2B	3B	HR	HR%	R	RBI	BB	SO	SB	PH AB	PH H	PO	A	E	DP	TC/G	FA	G by Pos
1983	PIT N	7	.182	.182	11	2	0	0	0	0.0	0	1	0	2	0	3	0	2	2	0	0	0.6	1.000	OF-4
1984		32	.254	.328	67	17	1	2	0	0.0	12	3	1	7	3	6	1	41	1	0	0	1.3	1.000	OF-25
1985		121	.300	.365	397	119	14	6	0	0.0	54	21	26	27	24	8	4	229	10	6	1	2.0	.976	OF-115
1986		138	.249	.342	401	100	19	6	2	0.5	60	19	28	38	24	22	4	193	11	4	2	1.5	.981	OF-120
1988	BAL A	125	.288	.422	379	109	21	3	8	2.1	48	27	23	30	9	17	4	228	6	5	2	1.9	.979	OF-117
1989		123	.285	.421	390	111	22	5	7	1.8	59	55	41	35	5	15	6	250	10	4	2	2.1	.985	OF-109, DH-5
1990		124	.269	.397	413	111	14	3	11	2.7	49	57	46	48	6	14	3	267	5	3	2	2.2	.989	OF-109, DH-5
1991		143	.278	.358	486	135	22	1	5	1.0	57	43	28	45	6	14	3	273	22	1	4	2.1	.997	OF-132, DH-2
1992		117	.289	.381	391	113	18	3	4	1.0	45	39	28	34	5	8	1	228	9	4	1	2.1	.983	OF-110, DH-1
1993	NY N	134	.284	.399	409	116	15	4	8	2.0	59	35	28	25	5	31	10	231	10	5	1	1.8	.980	OF-114, 1B-4
1994		96	.260	.353	292	76	3	0	8	2.7	39	42	16	21	4	13	2	148	9	3	3	1.7	.981	OF-90, 1B-6
11 yrs.		1160	.278	.380	3636	1009	149	33	53	1.5	482	342	265	312	91	151	38	2090	95	35	18	1.9	.984	OF-1045, DH-13, 1B-10

Junior Ortiz

ORTIZ, ADALBERTO
Born Adalberto Ortiz (Colon).
B. Oct. 24, 1959, Humacao, Puerto Rico.   BR TR 5'11" 174 lbs.

Year	Team	Games	BA	SA	AB	H	2B	3B	HR	HR%	R	RBI	BB	SO	SB	PH AB	PH H	PO	A	E	DP	TC/G	FA	G by Pos
1982	PIT N	7	.200	.267	15	3	1	0	0	0.0	1	0	1	3	0	1	0	27	3	0	0	4.3	1.000	C-7
1983 2 teams	PIT N (5G – .125)				NY N	(68G – .254)																		
" total		73	.249	.275	193	48	5	0	0	0.0	11	12	4	14	1	5	2	293	31	11	2	4.6	.967	C-71
1984	NY N	40	.198	.231	91	18	3	0	0	0.0	6	11	5	15	1	10	1	136	13	3	3	3.8	.980	C-32
1985	PIT N	23	.292	.361	72	21	2	0	1	1.4	4	5	3	17	1	1	0	115	14	2	3	5.7	.985	C-23
1986		49	.336	.391	110	37	6	0	0	0.0	11	14	9	13	0	11	3	165	13	2	2	3.7	.983	C-36
1987		75	.271	.339	192	52	8	1	1	0.5	16	22	15	23	0	8	2	313	39	9	2	4.8	.975	C-72
1988		49	.280	.381	118	33	6	0	2	1.7	8	18	9	9	1	12	3	152	23	3	2	3.6	.983	C-40
1989		91	.217	.265	230	50	6	1	1	0.4	16	22	20	20	2	13	1	334	32	2	2	4.0	.995	C-84
1990	MIN A	71	.335	.388	170	57	7	1	0	0.0	18	18	12	16	0	3	1	247	25	0	6	3.8	1.000	C-68, DH-3
1991		61	.209	.261	134	28	5	1	0	0.0	9	11	15	12	0	1	0	203	17	1	2	3.6	.995	C-60
1992	CLE A	86	.250	.279	244	61	7	0	0	0.0	20	24	12	23	1	3	2	402	38	5	2	5.2	.989	C-86
1993		95	.221	.273	249	55	13	0	0	0.0	19	20	11	26	1	2	0	441	58	5	13	5.3	.990	C-95
1994	TEX A	28	.276	.303	76	21	2	0	0	0.0	3	9	5	11	0	2	0	106	18	1	1	4.3	.992	C-28
13 yrs.		749	.256	.305	1894	484	71	4	5	0.3	142	186	121	222	8	71	15	2934	324	45	40	4.4	.986	C-702, DH-3

LEAGUE CHAMPIONSHIP SERIES

| 1991 | MIN A | 3 | .000 | .000 | 3 | 0 | 0 | 0 | 0 | 0.0 | 0 | 0 | 0 | 0 | 0 | 0 | 0 | 10 | 0 | 0 | 0 | 3.3 | 1.000 | C-3 |

WORLD SERIES

| 1991 | MIN A | 3 | .200 | .200 | 5 | 1 | 0 | 0 | 0 | 0.0 | 1 | 0 | 1 | 0 | 0 | 0 | 0 | 9 | 0 | 0 | 0 | 3.0 | 1.000 | C-3 |

Luis Ortiz

ORTIZ, LUIS ALBERTO
Born Luis Alberto Ortiz (Galarza).
B. May 25, 1970, Santo Domingo, Dominican Republic   BR TR 6' 190 lbs.

Year	Team	Games	BA	SA	AB	H	2B	3B	HR	HR%	R	RBI	BB	SO	SB	PH AB	PH H	PO	A	E	DP	TC/G	FA	G by Pos
1993	BOS A	9	.250	.250	12	3	0	0	0	0.0	0	1	0	2	0	5	1	2	2	0	1	0.4	1.000	3B-5, DH-2
1994		7	.167	.278	18	3	2	0	0	0.0	3	6	1	5	0	1	0	0	0	0	0	0.0	–	DH-6
2 yrs.		16	.200	.267	30	6	2	0	0	0.0	3	7	1	7	0	6	1	2	2	0	1	0.3	1.000	DH-8, 3B-5

Spike Owen

OWEN, SPIKE DEE
Brother of Dave Owen.
B. Apr. 19, 1961, Cleburne, Tex.   BB TR 5'9" 160 lbs.

Year	Team	Games	BA	SA	AB	H	2B	3B	HR	HR%	R	RBI	BB	SO	SB	PH AB	PH H	PO	A	E	DP	TC/G	FA	G by Pos
1983	SEA A	80	.196	.271	306	60	11	3	2	0.7	36	21	24	44	10	1	0	122	233	11	45	4.6	.970	SS-80
1984		152	.245	.326	530	130	18	8	3	0.6	67	43	46	63	16	1	1	245	463	17	86	4.8	.977	SS-151
1985		118	.259	.372	352	91	10	6	6	1.7	41	37	34	27	11	0	0	196	361	14	76	4.8	.975	SS-117
1986 2 teams	SEA A (112G – .246)				BOS A	(42G – .183)																		
" total		154	.231	.309	528	122	24	7	1	0.2	67	45	51	51	4	0	0	279	467	21	133	5.0	.973	SS-154
1987	BOS A	132	.259	.343	437	113	17	7	2	0.5	50	48	53	43	11	1	0	176	336	13	69	4.0	.975	SS-130
1988		89	.249	.370	257	64	14	1	5	1.9	40	18	27	27	0	6	1	102	192	10	34	3.4	.967	SS-76, DH-7
1989	MON N	142	.233	.332	437	102	17	4	6	1.4	52	41	74	44	3	1	0	232	388	13	65	4.5	.979	SS-142
1990		149	.234	.342	453	106	24	5	5	1.1	55	35	70	60	8	5	0	216	340	6	52	3.8	.989	SS-148
1991		139	.255	.366	424	108	22	8	3	0.7	39	26	42	61	2	6	2	189	376	8	64	4.1	.986	SS-133
1992	NY A	122	.269	.381	386	104	16	3	7	1.8	52	40	50	30	9	5	1	187	300	9	44	4.1	.982	SS-116
1993	NY A	103	.234	.311	334	78	16	2	2	0.6	41	20	29	30	3	4	0	116	312	14	44	4.3	.968	SS-96, DH-1

Year Team	Games	BA	SA	AB	H	2B	3B	HR	HR%	R	RBI	BB	SO	SB	Pinch Hit AB	H	PO	A	E	DP	TC/G	FA	G by Pos

Spike Owen *continued*

Year Team	Games	BA	SA	AB	H	2B	3B	HR	HR%	R	RBI	BB	SO	SB	AB	H	PO	A	E	DP	TC/G	FA	G by Pos
1994 **CAL** A	82	.310	.422	268	83	17	2	3	1.1	30	37	49	17	2	1	1	64	137	8	18	2.5	.962	3B-70, SS-5, 1B-4, DH-2, 2B-1
12 yrs.	1462	.246	.343	4712	1161	206	56	45	1.0	570	411	551	497	79	31	6	2124	3905	144	730	4.2	.977	SS-1348, 3B-70, DH-10, 1B-4, 2B-1

LEAGUE CHAMPIONSHIP SERIES

Year Team	Games	BA	SA	AB	H	2B	3B	HR	HR%	R	RBI	BB	SO	SB	AB	H	PO	A	E	DP	TC/G	FA	G by Pos
1986 **BOS** A	7	.429	.524	21	9	0	1	0	0.0	5	3	2	2	1	0	0	12	21	5	2	5.4	.868	SS-7
1988	1	–	–	0	0	0	0	0	–	0	0	1	0	0	0	0	0	0	0	0	0.0	–	
2 yrs.	8	.429	.524	21	9	0	1	0	0.0	5	3	3	2	1	0	0	12	21	5	2	4.8	.868	

WORLD SERIES

Year Team	Games	BA	SA	AB	H	2B	3B	HR	HR%	R	RBI	BB	SO	SB	AB	H	PO	A	E	DP	TC/G	FA	G by Pos
1986 **BOS** A	7	.300	.300	20	6	0	0	0	0.0	2	2	5	6	0	0	0	10	13	0	3	3.3	1.000	SS-7

Jayhawk Owens

OWENS, CLAUDE JAYHAWK
B. Feb. 10, 1969, Cincinnati, Ohio

BR TR 6'1" 213 lbs.

Year Team	Games	BA	SA	AB	H	2B	3B	HR	HR%	R	RBI	BB	SO	SB	AB	H	PO	A	E	DP	TC/G	FA	G by Pos
1993 **CLR** N	33	.209	.372	86	18	5	0	3	3.5	12	6	6	30	1	2	0	138	19	7	3	5.0	.957	C-32
1994	6	.250	.417	12	3	0	1	0	0.0	4	1	3	3	0	0	0	25	3	0	0	4.7	1.000	C-6
2 yrs.	39	.214	.378	98	21	5	1	3	3.1	16	7	9	33	1	2	0	163	22	7	3	4.9	.964	C-38

Tom Pagnozzi

PAGNOZZI, THOMAS ALAN
B. July 30, 1962, Tucson, Ariz.

BR TR 6' 190 lbs.

Year Team	Games	BA	SA	AB	H	2B	3B	HR	HR%	R	RBI	BB	SO	SB	AB	H	PO	A	E	DP	TC/G	FA	G by Pos
1987 **STL** N	27	.188	.333	48	9	1	0	2	4.2	8	9	4	13	1	7	2	61	5	0	2	2.4	1.000	C-25, 1B-1
1988	81	.282	.328	195	55	9	0	0	0.0	17	15	11	32	0	26	4	340	30	4	11	4.6	.989	1B-28, C-28, 3B-5
1989	52	.150	.175	80	12	2	0	0	0.0	3	3	6	19	0	15	2	100	9	2	1	2.1	.982	C-38, 1B-2, 3B-1
1990	69	.277	.373	220	61	15	0	2	0.9	20	23	14	37	1	4	2	345	39	4	4	5.6	.990	C-63, 1B-2
1991	140	.264	.351	459	121	24	5	2	0.4	38	57	36	63	9	0	0	682	81	7	9	5.5	.991	C-139, 1B-3
1992	139	.249	.359	485	121	26	3	7	1.4	33	44	28	64	2	3	0	688	53	1	10	5.3	.999	C-138
1993	92	.258	.373	330	85	15	1	7	2.1	31	41	19	30	1	1	0	421	44	4	4	5.1	.991	C-92
1994	70	.272	.416	243	66	12	1	7	2.9	21	40	21	39	0	0	0	370	41	1	3	5.9	.998	C-70, 1B-1
8 yrs.	670	.257	.357	2060	530	104	10	27	1.3	171	232	139	297	14	56	10	3007	302	23	44	5.0	.993	C-593, 1B-37, 3B-6

LEAGUE CHAMPIONSHIP SERIES

Year Team	Games	BA	SA	AB	H	2B	3B	HR	HR%	R	RBI	BB	SO	SB	AB	H	PO	A	E	DP	TC/G	FA	G by Pos
1987 **STL** N	1	.000	.000	1	0	0	0	0	0.0	0	0	0	0	0	1	0	0	0	0	0	0.0	–	C-0

WORLD SERIES

Year Team	Games	BA	SA	AB	H	2B	3B	HR	HR%	R	RBI	BB	SO	SB	AB	H	PO	A	E	DP	TC/G	FA	G by Pos
1987 **STL** N	2	.250	.250	4	1	0	0	0	0.0	0	0	0	1	0	1	0	0	0	0	0	0.0	–	DH-1

Rafael Palmeiro

PALMEIRO, RAFAEL
Born Rafael Palmeiro (Corrales).
B. Sept. 24, 1964, Havana, Cuba.

BL TL 6' 180 lbs.

Year Team	Games	BA	SA	AB	H	2B	3B	HR	HR%	R	RBI	BB	SO	SB	AB	H	PO	A	E	DP	TC/G	FA	G by Pos
1986 **CHI** N	22	.247	.425	73	18	4	0	3	4.1	9	12	4	6	1	2	0	34	2	4	1	1.8	.900	OF-20
1987	84	.276	.543	221	61	15	1	14	6.3	32	30	20	26	2	27	5	176	9	1	16	2.2	.995	OF-45, 1B-18
1988	152	.307	.436	580	178	41	5	8	1.4	75	53	38	34	12	5	0	322	11	5	2	2.2	.985	OF-147, 1B-5
1989 **TEX** A	156	.275	.374	559	154	23	4	8	1.4	76	64	63	48	4	3	1	1167	119	12	106	8.3	.991	1B-147, DH-6
1990	154	.319	.468	598	191	35	6	14	2.3	72	89	40	59	3	4	0	1215	91	7	123	8.5	.995	1B-146, DH-6
1991	159	.322	.532	631	203	49	3	26	4.1	115	88	68	72	4	3	2	1305	96	12	119	8.9	.992	1B-157, DH-2
1992	159	.268	.434	608	163	27	4	22	3.6	84	85	72	83	2	3	0	1251	143	7	131	8.8	.995	1B-156, DH-2
1993	160	.295	.554	597	176	40	2	37	6.2	124	105	73	85	22	1	0	1388	147	5	133	9.6	.997	1B-160
1994 **BAL** A	111	.319	.550	436	139	32	0	23	5.3	82	76	54	63	7	0	0	958	67	4	86	9.3	.996	1B-111
9 yrs.	1157	.298	.480	4303	1283	266	25	155	3.6	669	602	432	476	57	48	8	7816	685	57	717	7.4	.993	1B-900, OF-212, DH-16

Dean Palmer

PALMER, DEAN WILLIAM
B. Dec. 27, 1968, Tallahassee, Fla.

BR TR 6'1" 175 lbs.

Year Team	Games	BA	SA	AB	H	2B	3B	HR	HR%	R	RBI	BB	SO	SB	AB	H	PO	A	E	DP	TC/G	FA	G by Pos
1989 **TEX** A	16	.105	.211	19	2	2	0	0	0.0	0	1	0	12	0	6	0	3	4	2	0	0.6	.778	3B-6, DH-6, OF-1, SS-1
1991	81	.187	.403	268	50	9	2	15	5.6	38	37	32	98	0	5	2	69	75	9	6	1.9	.941	3B-50, OF-29, DH-5
1992	152	.229	.420	541	124	25	0	26	4.8	74	72	62	154	10	4	2	124	254	22	24	2.6	.945	3B-150
1993	148	.245	.503	519	127	31	4	33	6.4	88	96	53	154	11	0	0	86	258	29	21	2.5	.922	3B-148, SS-1
1994	93	.246	.465	342	84	14	2	19	5.6	50	59	26	89	3	3	1	50	181	22	7	2.7	.913	3B-91
5 yrs.	490	.229	.449	1689	387	81	6	93	5.5	250	265	173	507	24	18	5	332	772	84	58	2.4	.929	3B-445, OF-30, DH-11, SS-2

Erik Pappas

PAPPAS, ERIK DANIEL
B. Apr. 25, 1966, Chicago, Ill.

BR TR 6' 190 lbs.

Year Team	Games	BA	SA	AB	H	2B	3B	HR	HR%	R	RBI	BB	SO	SB	AB	H	PO	A	E	DP	TC/G	FA	G by Pos
1991 **CHI** N	7	.176	.176	17	3	0	0	0	0.0	1	2	1	5	0	1	1	35	1	0	0	5.1	1.000	C-6, DH-1
1993 **STL** N	82	.276	.342	228	63	12	0	1	0.4	25	28	35	35	1	3	0	337	32	6	6	4.6	.984	C-63, OF-16, 1B-2
1994	15	.091	.114	44	4	1	0	0	0.0	8	5	10	13	0	0	0	80	4	4	1	5.9	.955	C-15
3 yrs.	104	.242	.298	289	70	13	0	1	0.3	34	35	46	53	1	4	1	452	37	10	7	4.8	.980	C-84, OF-16, 1B-2, DH-1

Craig Paquette

PAQUETTE, CRAIG HAROLD
B. Mar. 28, 1969, Long Beach, Calif.

BR TR 6' 190 lbs.

Year Team	Games	BA	SA	AB	H	2B	3B	HR	HR%	R	RBI	BB	SO	SB	AB	H	PO	A	E	DP	TC/G	FA	G by Pos
1993 **OAK** A	105	.219	.382	393	86	20	4	12	3.1	35	46	14	108	4	4	1	82	165	13	17	2.5	.950	3B-104, DH-1, OF-1
1994	14	.143	.184	49	7	2	0	0	0.0	0	0	0	14	1	1	0	14	22	0	3	2.6	1.000	3B-14
2 yrs.	119	.210	.360	442	93	22	4	12	2.7	35	46	14	122	5	5	1	96	187	13	20	2.5	.956	3B-118, DH-1, OF-1

Mark Parent

PARENT, MARK ALAN
B. Sept. 16, 1961, Ashland, Ore.

BR TR 6'5" 215 lbs.

Year Team	Games	BA	SA	AB	H	2B	3B	HR	HR%	R	RBI	BB	SO	SB	AB	H	PO	A	E	DP	TC/G	FA	G by Pos
1986 **SD** N	8	.143	.143	14	2	0	0	0	0.0	1	0	1	3	0	4	0	16	0	2	0	2.3	.889	C-3
1987	12	.080	.080	25	2	0	0	0	0.0	0	2	0	9	0	2	0	36	3	0	0	3.3	1.000	C-10
1988	41	.195	.373	118	23	3	0	6	5.1	9	15	6	23	0	3	1	203	15	3	3	5.4	.986	C-36
1989	52	.191	.369	141	27	4	0	7	5.0	12	21	8	34	1	9	2	246	17	0	2	5.1	1.000	C-41, 1B-1
1990	65	.222	.328	189	42	11	0	3	1.6	13	16	16	29	1	5	1	324	31	3	6	5.5	.992	C-60
1991 **TEX** A	3	.000	.000	1	0	0	0	0	0.0	0	0	0	1	0	0	0	5	0	0	0	1.7	1.000	C-3
1992 **BAL** A	17	.235	.441	34	8	1	0	2	5.9	4	4	3	7	0	1	0	73	7	1	1	4.8	.988	C-16

Year	Team	Games	BA	SA	AB	H	2B	3B	HR	HR%	R	RBI	BB	SO	SB	Pinch Hit AB	Pinch Hit H	PO	A	E	DP	TC/G	FA	G by Pos

Mark Parent *continued*

1993		22	.259	.519	54	14	2	0	4	7.4	7	12	3	14	0	2	1	83	5	1	0	4.0	.989	C-21, DH-1
1994	CHI N	44	.263	.394	99	26	4	0	3	3.0	8	16	13	24	0	4	2	184	21	5	1	4.8	.976	C-37
9 yrs.		264	.213	.361	675	144	25	0	25	3.7	54	86	50	144	2	30	7	1170	99	15	13	4.9	.988	C-227, 1B-1, DH-1

Rick Parker

PARKER, RICHARD ALAN
B. Mar. 20, 1963, Kansas City, Mo.
BR TR 6'   185 lbs.

1990	SF N	54	.243	.346	107	26	5	0	2	1.9	19	14	10	15	6	19	4	45	3	2	0	0.9	.960	OF-35, 2B-2, 3B-1, SS-1
1991		13	.071	.071	14	1	0	0	0	0.0	0	1	0	5	0	8	0	5	0	0	0	0.4	1.000	OF-4
1993	HOU N	45	.333	.400	45	15	3	0	0	0.0	11	4	3	8	1	18	5	18	0	0	0	0.4	1.000	OF-16, 2B-1, SS-1
1994	NY N	8	.063	.063	16	1	0	0	0	0.0	1	0	1	2	0	1	0	14	1	0	0	1.9	1.000	OF-6
4 yrs.		120	.236	.313	182	43	8	0	2	1.1	31	19	14	30	7	46	9	82	4	2	0	0.7	.977	OF-61, 2B-3, SS-2, 3B-1

Derek Parks

PARKS, DEREK GAVIN
B. Sept. 29, 1968, Covina, Calif.
BR TR 6'   205 lbs.

1992	MIN A	7	.333	.333	6	2	0	0	0	0.0	1	1	0	1	0	0	0	18	1	0	0	2.7	1.000	C-7
1993		7	.200	.200	20	4	0	0	0	0.0	3	1	1	2	0	0	0	28	4	1	1	4.7	.970	C-7
1994		31	.191	.292	89	17	6	0	1	1.1	6	9	4	20	0	3	3	119	16	1	0	4.4	.993	C-31
3 yrs.		45	.200	.278	115	23	6	0	1	0.9	10	10	6	23	0	3	3	165	21	2	1	4.2	.989	C-45

Lance Parrish

PARRISH, LANCE MICHAEL
B. June 15, 1956, Clairton, Pa.
BR TR 6'3"   210 lbs.

1977	DET A	12	.196	.435	46	9	2	0	3	6.5	10	7	5	12	0	0	0	76	6	0	0	6.8	1.000	C-12
1978		85	.219	.424	288	63	11	3	14	4.9	37	41	11	71	0	6	1	353	39	5	5	4.7	.987	C-79
1979		143	.276	.456	493	136	26	3	19	3.9	65	65	49	105	6	3	1	707	79	9	10	5.6	.989	C-142
1980		144	.286	.499	553	158	34	6	24	4.3	79	82	31	109	6	4	1	607	67	7	15	4.7	.990	C-121, DH-16, 1B-5, OF-5
1981		96	.244	.394	348	85	18	2	10	2.9	39	46	34	52	2	0	0	407	40	3	6	4.7	.993	C-90, DH-5
1982		133	.284	.529	486	138	19	2	32	6.6	75	87	40	99	3	2	1	627	76	8	8	5.3	.989	C-132, DH-1
1983		155	.269	.483	605	163	42	3	27	4.5	80	114	44	106	1	2	0	695	73	4	8	5.0	.995	C-131, DH-27
1984		147	.237	.443	578	137	16	2	33	5.7	75	98	41	120	2	3	1	720	67	7	11	5.4	.991	C-127, DH-22
1985		140	.273	.479	549	150	27	1	28	5.1	64	98	41	90	2	1	1	695	53	5	9	5.4	.993	C-120, DH-22
1986		91	.257	.483	327	84	6	1	22	6.7	53	62	38	83	0	4	0	483	48	6	5	5.9	.989	C-85, DH-6
1987	PHI N	130	.245	.399	466	114	21	0	17	3.6	42	67	47	104	0	4	0	724	66	9	1	6.1	.989	C-127
1988		123	.215	.370	424	91	17	2	15	3.5	44	60	47	93	0	3	2	640	73	9	12	5.9	.988	C-117, 1B-1
1989	CAL A	124	.238	.388	433	103	12	1	17	3.9	48	50	42	104	1	2	0	638	63	5	7	5.7	.993	C-122, DH-2
1990		133	.268	.451	470	126	14	0	24	5.1	54	70	46	107	2	1	0	794	90	6	21	6.7	.993	C-131, 1B-4, DH-1
1991		119	.216	.388	402	87	12	0	19	4.7	38	51	35	117	0	5	2	670	57	2	11	6.1	.997	C-111, DH-5, 1B-3
1992	2 teams	CAL A	(24G – .229)				SEA A		(69G – .234)															
"	total	93	.233	.418	275	64	13	1	12	4.4	26	32	24	70	1	11	0	383	23	6	15	4.4	.985	C-56, 1B-16, DH-16
1993	CLE A	10	.200	.400	20	4	1	0	1	5.0	2	2	4	5	1	1	0	47	10	3	1	6.0	.950	C-10
1994	PIT N	40	.270	.381	126	34	5	0	3	2.4	10	16	18	28	1	2	0	228	15	4	1	6.2	.984	C-38, 1B-1
18 yrs.		1918	.253	.444	6889	1746	296	27	320	4.6	841	1048	597	1475	28	54	10	9494	945	98	146	5.5	.991	C-1751, DH-122, 1B-30, OF-6

LEAGUE CHAMPIONSHIP SERIES

| 1984 | DET A | 3 | .250 | .583 | 12 | 3 | 1 | 0 | 1 | 8.3 | 1 | 3 | 0 | 3 | 0 | 0 | 0 | 21 | 2 | 0 | 0 | 7.7 | 1.000 | C-3 |

WORLD SERIES

| 1984 | DET A | 5 | .278 | .500 | 18 | 5 | 1 | 0 | 1 | 5.6 | 3 | 2 | 3 | 2 | 1 | 0 | 0 | 30 | 3 | 1 | 1 | 6.8 | .971 | C-5 |

Dan Pasqua

PASQUA, DANIEL ANTHONY
B. Oct. 17, 1961, Yonkers, N.Y.
BL TL 6'   205 lbs.

1985	NY A	60	.209	.426	148	31	3	1	9	6.1	17	25	16	38	0	15	2	72	2	0	0	1.2	1.000	OF-37, DH-14
1986		102	.293	.525	280	82	17	0	16	5.7	44	45	47	78	2	22	7	172	4	2	6	1.7	.989	OF-81, 1B-5, DH-3
1987		113	.233	.421	318	74	7	1	17	5.3	42	42	40	99	0	22	3	214	10	2	2	2.0	.991	OF-74, DH-20, 1B-12
1988	CHI A	129	.227	.417	422	96	16	2	20	4.7	48	50	46	100	1	15	1	316	14	2	13	2.6	.994	OF-112, DH-2, 1B-2
1989		73	.248	.427	246	61	9	1	11	4.5	26	47	25	58	1	3	2	149	3	1	2	2.1	.993	OF-66, DH-5
1990		112	.274	.495	325	89	27	3	13	4.0	43	58	37	66	1	18	4	71	5	3	1	0.7	.962	DH-57, OF-43
1991		134	.259	.465	417	108	22	5	18	4.3	71	66	62	86	0	13	3	587	46	6	47	4.8	.991	1B-83, OF-59, DH-8
1992		93	.211	.347	265	56	16	1	6	2.3	26	33	36	57	0	8	2	185	7	6	4	2.1	.970	OF-81, 1B-5, DH-1
1993		78	.205	.358	176	36	10	1	5	2.8	22	20	26	51	2	7	1	204	12	3	15	2.8	.986	OF-37, 1B-32, DH-6
1994		11	.217	.565	23	5	2	0	2	8.7	2	4	0	9	0	3	0	15	0	4	1	1.7	.789	OF-5, 1B-3
10 yrs.		905	.244	.438	2620	638	129	15	117	4.5	341	390	335	642	7	126	25	1985	103	29	91	2.3	.986	OF-595, 1B-147, DH-116

LEAGUE CHAMPIONSHIP SERIES

| 1993 | CHI A | 2 | .000 | .000 | 6 | 0 | 0 | 0 | 0 | 0.0 | 1 | 0 | 1 | 2 | 0 | 0 | 0 | 13 | 2 | 1 | 2 | 8.0 | .938 | 1B-2 |

John Patterson

PATTERSON, JOHN ALLEN
B. Feb. 11, 1967, Key West, Fla.
BB TR 5'9"   160 lbs.

1992	SF N	32	.184	.214	103	19	1	1	0	0.0	10	4	5	24	5	6	1	66	54	4	16	3.9	.968	2B-22, OF-5
1993		16	.188	.375	16	3	0	0	1	6.3	1	2	0	5	0	16	3	0	0	0	0	0.0	–	
1994		85	.238	.325	240	57	10	1	3	1.3	36	32	16	43	13	23	3	120	163	6	32	3.4	.979	2B-63
3 yrs.		133	.220	.295	359	79	11	2	4	1.1	47	38	21	72	18	45	7	186	217	10	48	3.1	.976	2B-85, OF-5

Bill Pecota

PECOTA, WILLIAM JOSEPH
B. Feb. 16, 1960, Redwood City, Calif.
BR TR 6'2"   195 lbs.

1986	KC A	12	.207	.276	29	6	2	0	0	0.0	3	2	3	3	0	0	0	7	31	1	1	3.3	.974	3B-12, SS-2
1987		66	.276	.378	156	43	5	1	3	1.9	22	14	15	25	5	7	0	67	135	6	28	3.2	.971	SS-36, 3B-17, 2B-15
1988		90	.208	.275	178	37	3	3	1	0.6	25	15	18	34	7	1	1	98	145	6	25	2.8	.976	SS-41, 3B-21, 1B-11, OF-9, DH-4, 2B-3, C-1
1989		65	.205	.410	83	17	4	2	3	3.6	21	5	7	9	5	0	0	50	79	2	14	2.0	.985	SS-29, OF-15, 2B-12, 3B-7, 1B-4, DH-1
1990		87	.242	.383	240	58	15	2	5	2.1	43	20	33	39	8	2	0	160	195	5	44	4.1	.986	2B-50, SS-21, 3B-11, OF-6, 1B-4, DH-2

Bill Pecota *continued*

Year Team	Games	BA	SA	AB	H	2B	3B	HR	HR%	R	RBI	BB	SO	SB	Pinch Hit AB	Pinch Hit H	PO	A	E	DP	TC/G	FA	G by Pos
1991	125	.286	.399	398	114	23	2	6	1.5	53	45	41	45	16	6	2	163	206	4	28	3.0	.989	3B-102, 2B-34, SS-9, 1B-8, DH-2, OF-1, P-1
1992 NY N	117	.227	.297	269	61	13	0	2	0.7	28	26	25	40	9	20	6	92	218	12	33	2.8	.963	3B-48, SS-39, 2B-38, 1B-1, P-1
1993 ATL N	72	.323	.387	62	20	2	1	0	0.0	17	5	2	5	1	30	8	9	13	0	1	0.3	1.000	3B-23, 2B-4, OF-1
1994	64	.214	.313	112	24	5	0	2	1.8	11	16	16	16	1	29	9	16	61	2	4	1.2	.975	3B-31, 2B-1, OF-1
9 yrs.	698	.249	.354	1527	380	72	11	22	1.4	223	148	160	216	52	95	26	662	1083	38	178	2.6	.979	3B-272, SS-177, 2B-157, OF-33, 1B-28, DH-9, P-2, C-1

LEAGUE CHAMPIONSHIP SERIES

Year Team	Games	BA	SA	AB	H	2B	3B	HR	HR%	R	RBI	BB	SO	SB	Pinch Hit AB	Pinch Hit H	PO	A	E	DP	TC/G	FA	G by Pos
1993 ATL N	4	.333	.333	3	1	0	0	0	0.0	1	0	1	1	0	3	1	0	0	0	0	0.0	-	

Steve Pegues

PEGUES, STEVEN ANTONE
B. May 21, 1968, Pontotoc, Miss.
BR TR 6'2" 190 lbs.

Year Team	Games	BA	SA	AB	H	2B	3B	HR	HR%	R	RBI	BB	SO	SB	Pinch Hit AB	Pinch Hit H	PO	A	E	DP	TC/G	FA	G by Pos
1994 2 teams	CIN N (11G – .300)			PIT N (7G – .385)																			
" total	18	.361	.417	36	13	2	0	0	0.0	2	2	2	5	1	6	2	13	0	1	0	0.8	.929	OF-11

Geronimo Pena

PENA, GERONIMO
Born Geronimo Pena (Martinez).
B. Mar. 29, 1967, Distrito Nacional, Dominican Republic.
BB TR 6'1" 170 lbs.

Year Team	Games	BA	SA	AB	H	2B	3B	HR	HR%	R	RBI	BB	SO	SB	Pinch Hit AB	Pinch Hit H	PO	A	E	DP	TC/G	FA	G by Pos
1990 STL N	18	.244	.289	45	11	2	0	0	0.0	5	2	4	14	1	6	3	24	30	1	7	3.1	.982	2B-11
1991	104	.243	.400	185	45	8	3	5	2.7	38	17	18	45	15	11	3	101	146	6	28	2.4	.976	2B-83, OF-4
1992	62	.305	.478	203	62	12	1	7	3.4	31	31	24	37	13	3	2	125	184	5	40	5.1	.984	2B-57
1993	74	.256	.406	254	65	19	2	5	2.0	34	30	25	71	13	8	0	140	200	12	47	4.8	.966	2B-64
1994	83	.254	.479	213	54	13	1	11	5.2	33	34	24	54	9	17	2	119	170	3	42	3.5	.990	2B-59, 3B-1
5 yrs.	341	.263	.432	900	237	54	7	28	3.1	141	114	95	221	51	45	10	509	730	27	164	3.7	.979	2B-274, OF-4, 3B-1

Tony Pena

PENA, ANTONIO FRANCESCO
Born Antonio Francesco Pena (Padilla).
Brother of Ramon Pena.
B. June 4, 1957, Monte Cristi, Dominican Republic.
BR TR 6' 175 lbs.

Year Team	Games	BA	SA	AB	H	2B	3B	HR	HR%	R	RBI	BB	SO	SB	Pinch Hit AB	Pinch Hit H	PO	A	E	DP	TC/G	FA	G by Pos
1980 PIT N	8	.429	.571	21	9	1	1	0	0.0	1	1	0	4	0	2	1	38	2	2	0	5.3	.952	C-6
1981	66	.300	.381	210	63	9	1	2	1.0	16	17	8	23	1	2	1	286	41	5	10	5.0	.985	C-64
1982	138	.296	.435	497	147	28	4	11	2.2	53	63	17	57	2	0	0	763	89	16	6	6.3	.982	C-137
1983	151	.301	.435	542	163	22	3	15	2.8	51	70	31	73	6	2	1	976	90	9	9	7.1	.992	C-149
1984	147	.286	.425	546	156	27	2	15	2.7	77	78	36	79	12	1	1	895	95	9	15	6.8	.991	C-146
1985	147	.249	.361	546	136	27	2	10	1.8	53	59	29	67	12	0	0	925	102	12	9	7.1	.988	C-146, 1B-1
1986	144	.288	.406	510	147	26	2	10	2.0	56	52	53	69	9	7	1	824	99	18	13	6.5	.981	C-139, 1B-4
1987 STL N	116	.214	.307	384	82	13	4	5	1.3	40	44	36	54	6	4	1	624	51	8	8	5.9	.988	C-112, 1B-4, OF-2
1988	149	.263	.372	505	133	23	1	10	2.0	55	51	33	60	6	8	1	796	72	6	9	5.9	.993	C-142, 1B-3
1989	141	.259	.337	424	110	17	2	4	0.9	36	37	35	33	5	7	1	675	70	2	13	5.3	.997	C-134, OF-1
1990 BOS A	143	.263	.348	491	129	19	1	7	1.4	62	56	43	71	8	5	2	866	74	5	13	6.6	.995	C-142, 1B-1
1991	141	.231	.321	464	107	23	2	5	1.1	45	48	37	53	8	1	0	864	60	5	15	6.6	.995	C-140
1992	133	.241	.305	410	99	21	1	1	0.2	39	38	24	61	3	1	1	786	57	6	12	6.4	.993	C-132
1993	126	.181	.257	304	55	11	0	4	1.3	20	19	25	46	1	0	0	698	53	4	6	6.0	.995	C-125
1994 CLE A	40	.295	.438	112	33	8	1	2	1.8	18	10	9	11	0	0	0	209	17	1	0	5.7	.996	C-40
15 yrs.	1790	.263	.369	5966	1569	275	27	101	1.7	622	643	416	761	79	40	11	10225	972	108	138	6.3	.990	C-1754, 1B-13, OF-3

LEAGUE CHAMPIONSHIP SERIES

Year Team	Games	BA	SA	AB	H	2B	3B	HR	HR%	R	RBI	BB	SO	SB	Pinch Hit AB	Pinch Hit H	PO	A	E	DP	TC/G	FA	G by Pos
1987 STL N	7	.381	.476	21	8	0	1	0	0.0	5	0	3	4	1	0	0	55	5	0	0	8.6	1.000	C-7
1990 BOS A	4	.214	.214	14	3	0	0	0	0.0	0	0	0	0	0	0	0	22	4	1	1	6.8	.963	C-4
2 yrs.	11	.314	.371	35	11	0	1	0	0.0	5	0	3	4	1	0	0	77	9	1	1	7.9	.989	C-11

WORLD SERIES

Year Team	Games	BA	SA	AB	H	2B	3B	HR	HR%	R	RBI	BB	SO	SB	Pinch Hit AB	Pinch Hit H	PO	A	E	DP	TC/G	FA	G by Pos
1987 STL N	7	.409	.455	22	9	1	0	0	0.0	2	4	3	2	1	0	0	32	1	1	0	4.9	.971	C-6, DH-1

Terry Pendleton

PENDLETON, TERRY LEE
B. July 16, 1960, Los Angeles, Calif.
BB TR 5'9" 180 lbs.

Year Team	Games	BA	SA	AB	H	2B	3B	HR	HR%	R	RBI	BB	SO	SB	Pinch Hit AB	Pinch Hit H	PO	A	E	DP	TC/G	FA	G by Pos
1984 STL N	67	.324	.420	262	85	16	3	1	0.4	37	33	16	32	20	1	0	59	155	13	10	3.4	.943	3B-66
1985	149	.240	.306	559	134	16	3	5	0.9	56	69	37	75	17	2	1	129	361	18	26	3.4	.965	3B-149
1986	159	.239	.306	578	138	26	5	1	0.2	56	59	34	59	24	3	0	133	371	20	36	3.3	.962	3B-156, OF-1
1987	159	.286	.412	583	167	29	4	12	2.1	82	96	70	74	19	1	1	117	369	26	27	3.2	.949	3B-158
1988	110	.253	.361	391	99	20	2	6	1.5	44	53	21	51	3	11	4	75	239	12	13	3.0	.963	3B-101
1989	162	.264	.390	613	162	28	5	13	2.1	83	74	44	81	9	3	0	113	392	15	25	3.2	.971	3B-161
1990	121	.230	.324	447	103	20	2	6	1.3	46	58	30	58	7	5	3	91	248	19	18	3.0	.947	3B-117
1991 ATL N	153	.319	.517	586	187	34	8	22	3.8	94	86	43	70	10	4	1	108	349	24	31	3.1	.950	3B-148
1992	160	.311	.473	640	199	39	1	21	3.3	98	105	37	67	5	2	0	133	325	19	27	3.0	.960	3B-158
1993	161	.272	.408	633	172	33	1	17	2.7	81	84	36	97	5	2	0	129	318	19	32	2.9	.959	3B-161
1994	77	.252	.398	309	78	18	3	7	2.3	25	30	12	57	2	0	0	60	147	11	12	2.8	.950	3B-77
11 yrs.	1478	.272	.395	5601	1524	279	37	111	2.0	702	747	380	721	121	34	10	1147	3274	196	257	3.1	.958	3B-1452, OF-1

LEAGUE CHAMPIONSHIP SERIES

Year Team	Games	BA	SA	AB	H	2B	3B	HR	HR%	R	RBI	BB	SO	SB	Pinch Hit AB	Pinch Hit H	PO	A	E	DP	TC/G	FA	G by Pos
1985 STL N	6	.208	.250	24	5	1	0	0	0.0	2	4	1	2	0	0	0	6	18	1	2	4.2	.960	3B-6
1987	6	.211	.316	19	4	0	1	0	0.0	3	1	0	6	0	0	0	3	11	0	1	2.3	1.000	3B-6
1991 ATL N	7	.167	.267	30	5	1	1	0	0.0	1	1	1	3	0	0	0	5	11	0	1	2.3	1.000	3B-7
1992	7	.233	.300	30	7	2	0	0	0.0	2	3	0	2	0	0	0	4	18	0	1	3.1	1.000	3B-7
1993	6	.346	.500	26	9	1	0	1	3.8	4	1	1	2	0	0	0	7	5	0	1	2.0	1.000	3B-6
5 yrs.	32	.233	.326	129	30	5	2	1	0.8	12	14	2	15	0	0	0	25	63	1	7	2.8	.989	3B-32

WORLD SERIES

Year Team	Games	BA	SA	AB	H	2B	3B	HR	HR%	R	RBI	BB	SO	SB	Pinch Hit AB	Pinch Hit H	PO	A	E	DP	TC/G	FA	G by Pos
1985 STL N	7	.261	.391	23	6	1	0	1	4.3	3	3	2	4	0	0	0	6	14	1	3	3.0	.952	3B-7
1987	3	.429	.429	7	3	0	0	0	0.0	1	1	1	2	0	0	0	0	0	0	0	0.0	-	DH-2
1991 ATL N	7	.367	.667	30	11	3	0	2	6.7	6	3	3	1	0	0	0	3	20	2	2	3.6	.920	3B-7
1992	6	.240	.320	25	6	2	0	0	0.0	2	2	1	5	0	0	0	4	19	0	1	3.8	1.000	3B-6
4 yrs.	23	.306	.471	85	26	6	1	2	2.4	13	9	8	9	2	0	0	13	53	3	6	3.0	.957	3B-20, DH-2

Year Team	Games	BA	SA	AB	H	2B	3B	HR	HR%	R	RBI	BB	SO	SB	Pinch Hit AB	Pinch Hit H	PO	A	E	DP	TC/G	FA	G by Pos

William Pennyfeather

PENNYFEATHER, WILLIAM NATHANIEL
B. May 25, 1968, Perth Amboy, N. J.

BR TR 6'2" 195 lbs.

Year Team	Games	BA	SA	AB	H	2B	3B	HR	HR%	R	RBI	BB	SO	SB	AB	H	PO	A	E	DP	TC/G	FA	G by Pos
1992 PIT N	15	.222	.222	9	2	0	0	0	0.0	2	0	0	0	0	1	0	8	0	0	0	0.5	1.000	OF-10
1993	21	.206	.235	34	7	1	0	0	0.0	4	2	0	6	0	5	0	21	0	0	0	1.0	1.000	OF-17
1994	4	.000	.000	3	0	0	0	0	0.0	0	0	0	0	0	3	0	0	0	0	0	0.0	–	OF-1
3 yrs.	40	.196	.217	46	9	1	0	0	0.0	6	2	0	6	0	9	0	29	0	0	0	0.7	1.000	OF-28

Eduardo Perez

PEREZ, EDUARDO ATANACIO
Son of Tony Perez.
B. Sept. 11, 1969, Cincinnati, Ohio

BR TR 6'4" 215 lbs.

Year Team	Games	BA	SA	AB	H	2B	3B	HR	HR%	R	RBI	BB	SO	SB	AB	H	PO	A	E	DP	TC/G	FA	G by Pos
1993 CAL A	52	.250	.372	180	45	6	2	4	2.2	16	30	9	39	5	4	0	24	101	5	7	2.5	.962	3B-45, DH-3
1994	38	.209	.380	129	27	7	0	5	3.9	10	16	12	29	3	1	0	305	15	1	29	8.4	.997	1B-38
2 yrs.	90	.233	.375	309	72	13	2	9	2.9	26	46	21	68	8	5	0	329	116	6	36	5.0	.987	3B-45, 1B-38, DH-3

Robert Perez

PEREZ, ROBERT ALEXANDER
Born Robert Alexander Perez (Jimenez).
B. June 4, 1969, Bolivar, Venezuela.

BR TR 6'3" 205 lbs.

Year Team	Games	BA	SA	AB	H	2B	3B	HR	HR%	R	RBI	BB	SO	SB	AB	H	PO	A	E	DP	TC/G	FA	G by Pos
1994 TOR A	4	.125	.125	8	1	0	0	0	0.0	0	0	0	1	0	0	0	3	1	0	0	1.0	1.000	OF-4

Gerald Perry

PERRY, GERALD JUNE
B. Oct. 30, 1960, Savannah, Ga.

BL TR 5'11" 172 lbs.

Year Team	Games	BA	SA	AB	H	2B	3B	HR	HR%	R	RBI	BB	SO	SB	AB	H	PO	A	E	DP	TC/G	FA	G by Pos
1983 ATL N	27	.359	.487	39	14	2	0	1	2.6	5	6	5	4	0	16	7	55	0	1	5	2.1	.982	1B-7, OF-1
1984	122	.265	.372	347	92	12	2	7	2.0	52	47	61	38	15	16	8	550	28	12	41	4.8	.980	1B-64, OF-53
1985	110	.214	.273	238	51	5	0	3	1.3	22	13	23	28	9	44	6	541	37	9	48	5.3	.985	1B-55, OF-5
1986	29	.271	.386	70	19	2	0	2	2.9	6	11	8	4	0	11	3	24	1	2	2	0.9	.926	OF-21, 1B-1
1987	142	.270	.411	533	144	35	2	12	2.3	77	74	48	63	42	5	1	1297	72	14	118	9.7	.990	1B-136, OF-7
1988	141	.300	.400	547	164	29	1	8	1.5	61	74	36	49	29	0	0	1282	106	17	102	10.0	.988	1B-141
1989	72	.252	.338	266	67	11	0	4	1.5	24	21	32	28	10	0	0	618	51	9	49	9.4	.987	1B-72
1990 KC A	133	.254	.361	465	118	22	2	8	1.7	57	57	39	56	17	12	0	394	40	6	41	3.3	.986	DH-68, 1B-51
1991 STL N	109	.240	.380	242	58	8	4	6	2.5	29	36	22	34	15	41	11	413	29	5	30	4.1	.989	1B-61, OF-5
1992	87	.238	.315	143	34	8	0	1	0.7	13	18	15	23	3	54	12	221	11	3	23	2.7	.987	1B-29
1993	96	.337	.510	98	33	5	0	4	4.1	21	16	18	23	1	**70**	**24**	79	3	2	5	0.9	.976	1B-15, OF-1
1994	60	.325	.532	77	25	7	0	3	3.9	12	18	15	12	1	40	12	96	4	1	9	1.7	.990	1B-13
12 yrs.	1128	.267	.380	3065	819	146	11	59	1.9	379	391	322	362	142	309	84	5570	382	81	473	5.3	.987	1B-645, OF-89, DH-68

Herbert Perry

PERRY, HERBERT EDWARD, JR.
B. Sept. 15, 1969, Live Oak, Fla.

BR TR 6'2" 210 lbs.

Year Team	Games	BA	SA	AB	H	2B	3B	HR	HR%	R	RBI	BB	SO	SB	AB	H	PO	A	E	DP	TC/G	FA	G by Pos
1994 CLE A	4	.111	.111	9	1	0	0	0	0.0	1	1	3	1	0	0	0	25	5	1	1	7.8	.968	1B-2, 3B-2

Roberto Petagine

PETAGINE, ROBERTO ANTONIO
Born Roberto Antonio Petagine (Guerra).
B. June 7, 1971, Nueva Esparita, Venezuela

BL TL 6'1" 172 lbs.

Year Team	Games	BA	SA	AB	H	2B	3B	HR	HR%	R	RBI	BB	SO	SB	AB	H	PO	A	E	DP	TC/G	FA	G by Pos
1994 HOU N	8	.000	.000	7	0	0	0	0	0.0	0	0	1	3	0	6	0	3	0	0	0	0.4	1.000	1B-2

J. R. Phillips

PHILLIPS, CHARLES GENE
B. Apr. 29, 1970, West Covina, Calif.

BL TL 6'2" 205 lbs.

Year Team	Games	BA	SA	AB	H	2B	3B	HR	HR%	R	RBI	BB	SO	SB	AB	H	PO	A	E	DP	TC/G	FA	G by Pos
1993 SF N	11	.313	.688	16	5	1	1	1	6.3	1	4	0	5	0	6	1	32	2	1	1	3.2	.971	1B-5
1994	15	.132	.211	38	5	0	0	1	2.6	1	3	1	13	1	5	0	79	10	1	7	6.0	.989	1B-10
2 yrs.	26	.185	.352	54	10	1	1	2	3.7	2	7	1	18	1	11	1	111	12	2	8	4.8	.984	1B-15

Tony Phillips

PHILLIPS, KEITH ANTHONY
B. Apr. 25, 1959, Atlanta, Ga.

BB TR 5'9" 155 lbs.

Year Team	Games	BA	SA	AB	H	2B	3B	HR	HR%	R	RBI	BB	SO	SB	AB	H	PO	A	E	DP	TC/G	FA	G by Pos
1982 OAK A	40	.210	.284	81	17	2	2	0	0.0	11	8	12	26	2	0	0	46	95	7	17	3.7	.953	SS-39
1983	148	.248	.320	412	102	12	3	4	1.0	54	35	48	70	16	1	1	218	383	30	85	4.3	.952	SS-101, 2B-63, 3B-4, DH-1
1984	154	.266	.359	451	120	24	3	4	0.9	62	37	42	86	10	2	0	255	391	28	90	4.4	.958	SS-91, 2B-90, OF-1
1985	42	.280	.453	161	45	12	2	4	2.5	23	17	13	34	3	1	0	54	103	3	13	3.8	.981	3B-31, 2B-24
1986	118	.256	.345	441	113	14	5	5	1.1	76	52	76	82	15	0	0	191	326	13	43	4.5	.975	2B-88, 3B-30, OF-4, DH-2, SS-1
1987	111	.240	.372	379	91	20	0	10	2.6	48	46	57	76	7	6	1	179	299	14	47	4.4	.972	2B-87, 3B-11, SS-9, OF-2
1988	79	.203	.307	212	43	8	4	2	0.9	32	17	36	50	0	5	1	84	80	10	18	2.2	.943	3B-32, OF-31, 2B-27, SS-10, 1B-3
1989	143	.262	.348	451	118	15	6	4	0.9	48	47	58	66	3	10	3	184	321	15	54	3.6	.971	2B-84, SS-49, SS-17, OF-16, 1B-1
1990 DET A	152	.251	.351	573	144	23	5	8	1.4	97	55	99	85	19	1	0	180	368	23	62	3.8	.960	3B-104, 2B-47, SS-11, OF-8, DH-4
1991	146	.284	.438	564	160	28	4	17	3.0	87	72	79	95	10	6	2	269	237	8	51	3.5	.984	OF-56, 3B-46, 2B-36, DH-18, SS-13
1992	159	.276	.388	606	167	32	3	10	1.7	**114**	64	114	93	12	1	0	301	195	11	45	3.2	.978	OF-69, 2B-57, DH-34, 3B-20, SS-1
1993	151	.313	.398	566	177	27	0	7	1.2	113	57	**132**	102	16	3	2	321	165	13	34	3.3	.974	OF-108, 2B-51, DH-4, 3B-1
1994	114	.281	.468	438	123	19	3	19	4.3	91	61	95	105	13	1	1	254	42	6	7	2.6	.980	OF-104, 2B-12, DH-6
13 yrs.	1557	.266	.378	5335	1420	236	40	94	1.8	856	568	861	970	126	37	11	2536	3005	181	566	3.7	.968	2B-666, OF-399, 3B-328, SS-293, DH-69, 1B-4
LEAGUE CHAMPIONSHIP SERIES
1988 OAK A	2	.286	.429	7	2	1	0	0	0.0	0	0	1	3	0	0	0	10	0	0	1	5.0	1.000	OF-2, 2B-1
1989	5	.167	.222	18	3	1	0	0	0.0	1	1	2	4	2	0	0	4	14	0	2	3.6	1.000	2B-3, 3B-3
2 yrs.	7	.200	.280	25	5	2	0	0	0.0	1	1	3	7	2	0	0	14	14	0	3	4.0	1.000	2B-4, 3B-3, OF-2

Year Team	Games	BA	SA	AB	H	2B	3B	HR	HR%	R	RBI	BB	SO	SB	Pinch Hit AB	Pinch Hit H	PO	A	E	DP	TC/G	FA	G by Pos

Tony Phillips *continued*

WORLD SERIES
1988 **OAK A**	2	.250	.250	4	1	0	0	0	0.0	1	0	1	2	0	0	0	3	5	0	1	4.0	1.000	2B-1, OF-1
1989	4	.235	.471	17	4	1	0	1	5.9	2	3	0	3	0	0	0	8	15	0	1	5.8	1.000	2B-4, 3B-2, OF-1
2 yrs.	6	.238	.429	21	5	1	0	1	4.8	3	3	1	5	0	0	0	11	20	0	2	5.2	1.000	2B-5, 3B-2, OF-2

Mike Piazza

PIAZZA, MICHAEL JOSEPH
B. Sept. 4, 1968, Norristown, Pa.

BR TR 6'3" 200 lbs.

1992 **LA N**	21	.232	.319	69	16	3	0	1	1.4	5	7	4	12	0	5	2	94	7	1	1	4.9	.990	C-16
1993	149	.318	.561	547	174	24	2	35	6.4	81	112	46	86	3	5	0	900	99	11	11	6.8	.989	C-146, 1B-1
1994	107	.319	.541	405	129	18	0	24	5.9	64	92	33	65	1	8	3	640	38	10	3	6.4	.985	C-104
3 yrs.	277	.312	.537	1021	319	45	2	60	5.9	150	211	83	163	4	18	5	1634	144	22	15	6.5	.988	C-266, 1B-1

Greg Pirkl

PIRKL, GREGORY DANIEL
B. Aug. 7, 1970, Long Beach, Calif.

BR TR 6'5" 225 lbs.

1993 **SEA A**	7	.174	.304	23	4	0	0	1	4.3	1	4	0	4	0	0	0	42	5	0	8	6.7	1.000	1B-5, DH-2
1994	19	.264	.660	53	14	3	0	6	11.3	7	11	1	12	0	4	3	56	1	1	3	3.1	.983	DH-10, 1B-7
2 yrs.	26	.237	.553	76	18	3	0	7	9.2	8	15	1	16	0	4	3	98	6	1	11	4.0	.990	1B-12, DH-12

Phil Plantier

PLANTIER, PHILLIP ALAN
B. Jan. 27, 1969, Manchester, N. H.

BL TR 6' 175 lbs.

1990 **BOS A**	14	.133	.200	15	2	1	0	0	0.0	1	3	4	6	0	6	1	0	0	0	0	0.0	–	DH-4, OF-1
1991	53	.331	.615	148	49	7	1	11	7.4	27	35	23	38	1	8	3	80	1	2	0	1.6	.976	OF-40, DH-5
1992	108	.246	.361	349	86	19	0	7	2.0	46	30	44	83	2	12	4	148	6	4	0	1.5	.975	OF-76, DH-23
1993 **SD N**	138	.240	.509	462	111	20	1	34	7.4	67	100	61	124	4	5	0	271	14	3	3	2.1	.990	OF-134
1994	96	.220	.440	341	75	21	0	18	5.3	44	44	36	91	3	6	0	159	5	2	0	1.7	.988	OF-91
5 yrs.	409	.246	.460	1315	323	68	2	70	5.3	185	209	168	342	10	37	8	658	26	11	3	1.7	.984	OF-342, DH-32

Luis Polonia

POLONIA, LUIS ANDREW
Born Luis Andrew Polonia (Almonte).
B. Oct. 12, 1964, Santiago City, Dominican Republic.

BL TL 5'8" 155 lbs.
BB 1987

1987 **OAK A**	125	.287	.398	435	125	16	10	4	0.9	78	49	32	64	29	8	3	235	2	5	1	1.9	.979	OF-104, DH-18
1988	84	.292	.378	288	84	11	4	2	0.7	51	27	21	40	24	9	2	155	3	2	1	1.9	.988	OF-76, DH-2
1989 **2 teams**				**OAK A** (59G – .286)						**NY A** (66G – .313)													
" total	125	.300	.388	433	130	17	6	3	0.7	70	46	25	44	22	14	6	231	9	4	2	2.0	.984	OF-108, DH-9
1990 **2 teams**				**NY A** (11G – .318)						**CAL A** (109G – .336)													
" total	120	.335	.412	403	135	7	9	2	0.5	52	35	25	43	21	19	6	142	3	3	2	1.2	.980	OF-85, DH-15
1991 **CAL A**	150	.296	.379	604	179	28	8	2	0.3	92	50	52	74	48	5	1	246	9	5	1	1.7	.981	OF-143, DH-4
1992	149	.286	.329	577	165	17	4	0	0.0	83	35	45	64	51	4	1	192	8	4	1	1.4	.980	OF-99, DH-47
1993	152	.271	.326	576	156	17	6	1	0.2	75	32	48	53	55	8	2	286	12	5	3	2.0	.983	OF-141, DH-3
1994 **NY A**	95	.311	.414	350	109	21	6	1	0.3	62	36	37	36	20	10	4	154	9	4	2	1.8	.976	OF-84, DH-2
8 yrs.	1000	.295	.373	3666	1083	134	53	15	0.4	563	310	285	418	270	77	25	1641	55	32	13	1.7	.981	OF-840, DH-100

LEAGUE CHAMPIONSHIP SERIES
| 1988 **OAK A** | 3 | .400 | .400 | 5 | 2 | 0 | 0 | 0 | 0.0 | 0 | 0 | 1 | 2 | 0 | 0 | 0 | 2 | 0 | 0 | 0 | 0.7 | 1.000 | OF-1 |

WORLD SERIES
| 1988 **OAK A** | 3 | .111 | .111 | 9 | 1 | 0 | 0 | 0 | 0.0 | 1 | 0 | 2 | 2 | 0 | 2 | 0 | 2 | 0 | 0 | 0 | 0.7 | 1.000 | OF-2 |

Todd Pratt

PRATT, TODD ALAN
B. Feb. 9, 1967, Bellevue, Neb.

BR TR 6'3" 195 lbs.

1992 **PHI N**	16	.283	.435	46	13	1	0	2	4.3	6	10	4	12	0	4	0	65	4	2	1	4.4	.972	C-11
1993	33	.287	.529	87	25	6	0	5	5.7	8	13	5	19	0	6	1	169	7	2	3	5.4	.989	C-26
1994	28	.196	.333	102	20	6	1	2	2.0	10	9	12	29	0	0	0	172	9	0	1	6.5	1.000	C-28
3 yrs.	77	.247	.426	235	58	13	1	9	3.8	24	32	21	60	0	10	1	406	20	4	5	5.6	.991	C-65

LEAGUE CHAMPIONSHIP SERIES
| 1993 **PHI N** | 1 | 1.000 | .000 | 1 | 0 | 0 | 0 | 0 | 0.0 | 0 | 0 | 0 | 1 | 0 | 0 | 0 | 1 | 0 | 0 | 0 | 1.0 | 1.000 | C-1 |

Tom Prince

PRINCE, THOMAS ALBERT
B. Aug. 13, 1964, Kankakee, Ill.

BR TR 5'11" 185 lbs.

1987 **PIT N**	4	.222	.667	9	2	1	0	1	11.1	1	2	0	2	0	0	0	14	3	0	0	4.3	1.000	C-4
1988	29	.176	.203	74	13	2	0	0	0.0	3	6	4	15	0	2	0	108	8	2	1	4.1	.983	C-28
1989	21	.135	.212	52	7	4	0	0	0.0	1	5	6	12	1	0	0	85	11	4	1	4.8	.960	C-21
1990	4	.100	.100	10	1	0	0	0	0.0	1	0	1	2	0	1	0	16	1	0	0	4.3	1.000	C-3
1991	26	.265	.441	34	9	3	0	1	2.9	4	2	7	3	0	5	0	53	9	1	0	2.4	.984	C-19, 1B-1
1992	27	.091	.136	44	4	2	0	0	0.0	1	5	4	6	1	6	0	76	8	2	0	3.2	.977	C-19, 3B-1
1993	66	.196	.307	179	35	14	0	2	1.1	14	24	13	38	1	8	3	270	32	5	6	4.7	.984	C-59
1994 **LA N**	3	.333	.333	6	2	0	0	0	0.0	2	1	1	3	0	0	0	11	1	0	0	4.0	1.000	C-3
8 yrs.	180	.179	.272	408	73	26	0	4	1.0	27	45	38	84	3	22	3	633	73	14	8	4.0	.981	C-156, 1B-1, 3B-1

Kirby Puckett

PUCKETT, KIRBY
B. Mar. 14, 1961, Chicago, Ill.

BR TR 5'8" 215 lbs.

1984 **MIN A**	128	.296	.336	557	165	12	5	0	0.0	63	31	16	69	14	0	0	438	16	3	4	3.6	.993	OF-128
1985	161	.288	.385	691	199	29	13	4	0.6	80	74	41	87	21	1	0	465	19	8	5	3.1	.984	OF-161
1986	161	.328	.537	680	223	37	6	31	4.6	119	96	34	99	20	4	1	429	8	6	3	2.8	.986	OF-160
1987	157	.332	.534	624	207	32	5	28	4.5	96	99	32	91	12	2	0	341	8	5	2	2.3	.986	OF-147, DH-8
1988	158	.356	.545	657	234	42	5	24	3.7	109	121	23	83	6	1	0	450	12	3	4	2.9	.994	OF-158
1989	159	.339	.465	635	215	45	4	9	1.4	75	85	41	59	11	2	1	438	13	4	3	2.9	.991	OF-157, DH-2
1990	146	.298	.446	551	164	40	3	12	2.2	82	80	57	73	5	1	1	354	9	4	3	2.5	.989	OF-141, DH-4, 2B-1, 3B-1, SS-1

Year	Team	Games	BA	SA	AB	H	2B	3B	HR	HR%	R	RBI	BB	SO	SB	Pinch Hit AB	Pinch Hit H	PO	A	E	DP	TC/G	FA	G by Pos

Kirby Puckett *continued*

Year	Team	Games	BA	SA	AB	H	2B	3B	HR	HR%	R	RBI	BB	SO	SB	AB	H	PO	A	E	DP	TC/G	FA	G by Pos
1991		152	.319	.460	611	195	29	6	15	2.5	92	89	31	78	11	0	0	373	13	6	5	2.6	.985	OF-152
1992		160	.329	.490	639	210	38	4	19	3.0	104	110	44	97	17	2	1	394	9	3	3	2.5	.993	OF-149, DH-9, 2B-2, 3B-2, SS-1
1993		156	.296	.474	622	184	39	3	22	3.5	89	89	47	93	8	0	0	312	13	2	2	2.1	.994	OF-139, DH-17
1994		108	.317	.540	439	139	32	3	20	4.6	79	112	28	47	6	0	0	204	13	3	1	2.0	.986	OF-95, DH-13
11 yrs.		1646	.318	.474	6706	2135	375	57	184	2.7	988	986	394	876	131	13	4	4198	133	47	35	2.7	.989	OF-1587, DH-53, 2B-3, 3B-3, SS-2

LEAGUE CHAMPIONSHIP SERIES

Year	Team	Games	BA	SA	AB	H	2B	3B	HR	HR%	R	RBI	BB	SO	SB	AB	H	PO	A	E	DP	TC/G	FA	G by Pos
1987	MIN A	5	.208	.375	24	5	1	0	1	4.2	3	3	0	5	1	0	0	7	0	0	0	1.4	1.000	OF-5
1991		5	.429	.762	21	9	1	0	2	9.5	4	6	1	4	0	0	0	13	1	0	0	2.8	1.000	OF-5
2 yrs.		10	.311	.556	45	14	2	0	3	6.7	7	9	1	9	1	0	0	20	1	0	0	2.1	1.000	OF-10

WORLD SERIES

Year	Team	Games	BA	SA	AB	H	2B	3B	HR	HR%	R	RBI	BB	SO	SB	AB	H	PO	A	E	DP	TC/G	FA	G by Pos
1987	MIN A	7	.357	.464	28	10	1	1	0	0.0	5	3	2	1	1	0	0	15	1	1	0	2.4	.941	OF-7
1991		7	.250	.583	24	6	0	1	2	8.3	4	4	5	7	1	0	0	16	1	0	0	2.4	1.000	OF-7
2 yrs.		14	.308	.519	52	16	1	2	2	3.8	9	7	7	8	2	0	0	31	2	1	0	2.4	.971	OF-14

Eddie Pye

PYE, ROBERT EDWARD
B. Feb. 13, 1967, Columbia, Tenn.

BR TR 5'10" 175 lbs.

Year	Team	Games	BA	SA	AB	H	2B	3B	HR	HR%	R	RBI	BB	SO	SB	AB	H	PO	A	E	DP	TC/G	FA	G by Pos
1994	LA N	7	.100	.100	10	1	0	0	0	0.0	2	0	1	4	0	2	1	4	13	0	4	2.4	1.000	2B-3, SS-3

Tom Quinlan

QUINLAN, THOMAS RAYMOND
B. Mar. 27, 1968, St. Paul, Minn.

BR TR 6'3" 200 lbs.

Year	Team	Games	BA	SA	AB	H	2B	3B	HR	HR%	R	RBI	BB	SO	SB	AB	H	PO	A	E	DP	TC/G	FA	G by Pos
1990	TOR A	1	.500	.500	2	1	0	0	0	0.0	0	0	0	1	0	0	0	0	1	0	0	1.0	1.000	3B-1
1992		13	.067	.133	15	1	1	0	0	0.0	2	2	2	9	0	1	0	4	6	1	0	0.8	.909	3B-13
1994	PHI N	24	.200	.343	35	7	2	0	1	2.9	6	3	3	13	0	4	0	9	19	1	1	1.2	.966	3B-20
3 yrs.		38	.173	.288	52	9	3	0	1	1.9	8	5	5	23	0	5	0	13	26	2	1	1.1	.951	3B-34

Tim Raines

RAINES, TIMOTHY (Rock)
B. Sept. 16, 1959, Sanford, Fla.

BB TR 5'8" 160 lbs.

Year	Team	Games	BA	SA	AB	H	2B	3B	HR	HR%	R	RBI	BB	SO	SB	AB	H	PO	A	E	DP	TC/G	FA	G by Pos
1979	MON N	6	–	–	0	0	0	0	0	–	3	0	0	0	2	0	0	0	0	0	0	0.0	–	
1980		15	.050	.050	20	1	0	0	0	0.0	5	0	6	3	5	0	0	15	16	0	2	2.1	1.000	2B-7, OF-1
1981		88	.304	.438	313	95	13	7	5	1.6	61	37	45	31	71	0	0	162	8	4	0	2.0	.977	OF-81, 2B-1
1982		156	.277	.369	647	179	32	8	4	0.6	90	43	75	83	78	0	0	293	126	8	12	2.7	.981	OF-120, 2B-36
1983		156	.298	.429	615	183	32	8	11	1.8	133	71	97	70	90	1	1	314	23	4	3	2.2	.988	OF-154, 2B-7
1984		160	.309	.437	622	192	38	9	8	1.3	106	60	87	69	75	0	0	420	8	6	1	2.7	.986	OF-160, 2B-2
1985		150	.320	.475	575	184	30	13	11	1.9	115	41	81	60	70	7	0	284	8	2	4	2.0	.993	OF-145
1986		151	.334	.476	580	194	35	10	9	1.6	91	62	78	60	70	4	1	270	13	6	1	1.9	.979	OF-147
1987		139	.330	.526	530	175	34	8	18	3.4	123	68	90	52	50	0	0	297	9	4	1	2.2	.987	OF-139
1988		109	.270	.431	429	116	19	7	12	2.8	66	48	53	44	33	1	0	235	5	3	1	2.2	.988	OF-108
1989		145	.286	.418	517	148	29	6	9	1.7	76	60	93	48	41	4	3	253	7	1	0	1.8	.996	OF-139
1990		130	.287	.392	457	131	11	5	9	2.0	65	62	70	43	49	8	2	239	3	6	1	1.9	.976	OF-123
1991	CHI A	155	.268	.345	609	163	20	6	5	0.8	102	50	83	68	51	5	0	273	12	3	3	1.9	.990	OF-133, DH-19
1992		144	.294	.405	551	162	22	9	7	1.3	102	54	81	48	45	4	3	312	12	2	0	2.3	.994	OF-129, DH-14
1993		115	.306	.480	415	127	16	4	16	3.9	75	54	64	35	21	4	1	200	5	0	2	1.8	1.000	OF-112
1994		101	.266	.409	384	102	15	5	10	2.6	80	52	61	43	13	6	0	203	3	4	1	2.1	.981	OF-97
16 yrs.		1920	.296	.428	7264	2152	346	105	134	1.8	1293	762	1064	757	764 **4th**	44	11	3770	258	53	32	2.1	.987	OF-1788, 2B-53, DH-33

LEAGUE CHAMPIONSHIP SERIES

Year	Team	Games	BA	SA	AB	H	2B	3B	HR	HR%	R	RBI	BB	SO	SB	AB	H	PO	A	E	DP	TC/G	FA	G by Pos
1981	MON N	5	.238	.333	21	5	2	0	0	0.0	1	1	0	3	0	0	0	9	0	0	0	1.8	1.000	OF-5
1993	CHI A	6	.444	.519	27	12	2	0	0	0.0	5	1	2	2	1	0	0	12	2	0	0	2.3	1.000	OF-6
2 yrs.		11	.354	.438	48	17	4	0	0	0.0	6	2	2	5	1	0	0	21	2	0	0	2.1	1.000	OF-11

Manny Ramirez

RAMIREZ, MANUEL ARISTIDES
Born Manuel Aristides Ramirez (Onelcida).
B. May 30, 1972, Santo Domingo, Dominican Republic

BR TR 6' 190 lbs.

Year	Team	Games	BA	SA	AB	H	2B	3B	HR	HR%	R	RBI	BB	SO	SB	AB	H	PO	A	E	DP	TC/G	FA	G by Pos
1993	CLE A	22	.170	.302	53	9	1	0	2	3.8	5	5	2	8	0	4	1	3	0	0	0	0.1	1.000	DH-20, OF-1
1994		91	.269	.521	290	78	22	0	17	5.9	51	60	42	72	4	5	0	150	7	1	2	1.7	.994	OF-84, DH-5
2 yrs.		113	.254	.487	343	87	23	0	19	5.5	56	65	44	80	4	9	1	153	7	1	2	1.4	.994	OF-85, DH-25

Randy Ready

READY, RANDY MAX
B. Jan. 8, 1960, San Mateo, Calif.

BR TR 5'11" 175 lbs.

Year	Team	Games	BA	SA	AB	H	2B	3B	HR	HR%	R	RBI	BB	SO	SB	AB	H	PO	A	E	DP	TC/G	FA	G by Pos
1983	MIL A	12	.405	.676	37	15	3	2	1	2.7	8	6	6	3	0	1	0	5	8	0	1	1.1	1.000	DH-6, 3B-4
1984		37	.187	.325	123	23	6	1	3	2.4	13	13	14	18	0	1	0	29	76	6	4	3.0	.946	3B-36
1985		48	.265	.387	181	48	9	5	1	0.6	29	21	14	23	0	2	0	93	14	1	1	2.3	.991	OF-37, 3B-7, 2B-3, DH-2
1986	2 teams		MIL A (23G – .190)		SD N (1G – .000)																			
"	total	24	.183	.268	82	15	4	0	1	1.2	8	4	9	10	2	2	0	35	23	4	4	2.6	.935	OF-11, 2B-7, 3B-4, DH-1
1987	SD N	124	.309	.520	350	108	26	6	12	3.4	69	54	67	44	7	25	6	124	220	15	35	2.9	.958	3B-52, 2B-51, OF-16
1988		114	.266	.390	331	88	16	2	7	2.1	43	39	39	38	6	24	5	112	153	11	22	2.4	.960	3B-57, 2B-26, OF-16
1989	2 teams		SD N (28G – .254)		PHI N (72G – .267)																			
"	total	100	.264	.425	254	67	13	2	8	3.1	37	26	42	37	4	28	6	80	72	9	13	1.6	.944	OF-37, 3B-32, 2B-9
1990	PHI N	101	.244	.309	217	53	9	1	1	0.5	26	26	29	35	3	45	12	78	86	2	18	1.6	.988	OF-30, 2B-28
1991		76	.249	.322	205	51	10	1	1	0.5	32	20	47	25	2	12	2	127	145	3	22	3.6	.989	2B-66
1992	OAK A	61	.200	.288	125	25	2	0	3	2.4	17	17	25	23	1	16	6	53	19	5	5	1.3	.935	DH-24, OF-24, 3B-7, 1B-4, 2B-4
1993	MON N	40	.254	.351	134	34	8	1	1	0.7	22	10	23	8	2	1	0	135	92	8	22	5.9	.966	2B-28, 1B-13, 3B-3
1994	PHI N	17	.381	.476	42	16	1	0	1	2.4	5	3	8	3	0	1	1	18	27	0	3	2.6	1.000	2B-11, 3B-1
12 yrs.		754	.261	.390	2081	543	107	21	40	1.9	309	239	323	270	27	160	38	889	935	64	150	2.5	.966	2B-233, 3B-203, OF-171, DH-33, 1B-17

LEAGUE CHAMPIONSHIP SERIES

Year	Team	Games	BA	SA	AB	H	2B	3B	HR	HR%	R	RBI	BB	SO	SB	AB	H	PO	A	E	DP	TC/G	FA	G by Pos
1992	OAK A	1	.000	.000	1	0	0	0	0	0.0	1	0	0	1	0	1	0	0	0	0	0	0.0	–	

Year	Team	Games	BA	SA	AB	H	2B	3B	HR	HR%	R	RBI	BB	SO	SB	Pinch Hit AB	Pinch Hit H	PO	A	E	DP	TC/G	FA	G by Pos

Jeff Reboulet

REBOULET, JEFFREY ALLEN
B. Apr. 30, 1967, Dayton, Ohio. BR TR 6' 167 lbs.

Year	Team	Games	BA	SA	AB	H	2B	3B	HR	HR%	R	RBI	BB	SO	SB	PH AB	PH H	PO	A	E	DP	TC/G	FA	G by Pos
1992	MIN A	73	.190	.277	137	26	7	1	1	0.7	15	16	23	26	3	2	0	71	162	5	31	3.3	.979	SS-36, 3B-22, 2B-13, OF-7, DH-1
1993		109	.258	.304	240	62	8	0	1	0.4	33	15	35	37	5	5	1	122	215	6	40	3.1	.983	SS-62, 3B-35, 2B-11, OF-3, DH-1
1994		74	.259	.376	189	49	11	1	3	1.6	28	23	18	23	0	3	2	150	131	7	29	3.9	.976	SS-42, 2B-14, 1B-10, 3B-6, OF-4, DH-1
3 yrs.		256	.242	.322	566	137	26	2	5	0.9	76	54	76	86	8	10	3	343	508	18	100	3.4	.979	SS-140, 3B-63, 2B-38, OF-14, 1B-10, DH-3

Gary Redus

REDUS, GARY EUGENE
B. Nov. 1, 1956, Tanner, Ala. BR TR 6'1" 180 lbs.

Year	Team	Games	BA	SA	AB	H	2B	3B	HR	HR%	R	RBI	BB	SO	SB	PH AB	PH H	PO	A	E	DP	TC/G	FA	G by Pos
1982	CIN N	20	.217	.337	83	18	3	2	1	1.2	12	7	5	21	11	0	0	29	3	1	0	1.7	.970	OF-20
1983		125	.247	.444	453	112	20	9	17	3.8	90	51	71	111	39	4	2	235	11	7	0	2.0	.972	OF-120
1984		123	.254	.376	394	100	21	3	7	1.8	69	22	52	71	48	10	3	200	6	7	3	1.7	.967	OF-114
1985		101	.252	.415	246	62	14	4	6	2.4	51	28	44	52	48	17	6	140	3	2	0	1.4	.986	OF-85
1986	PHI N	90	.247	.432	340	84	22	4	11	3.2	62	33	47	78	25	2	0	185	8	4	2	2.2	.980	OF-89
1987	CHI A	130	.236	.392	475	112	26	6	12	2.5	78	48	69	90	52	0	0	262	13	6	4	2.2	.979	OF-123, DH-4
1988	2 teams				CHI A (77G – .263)				PIT N	(30G – .197)														
"	total	107	.249	.381	333	83	12	4	8	2.4	54	38	48	71	31	16	4	182	9	4	1	1.8	.979	OF-87, DH-2
1989	PIT N	98	.283	.462	279	79	18	7	6	2.2	42	33	40	51	25	12	3	583	55	9	43	6.6	.986	1B-72, OF-16
1990		96	.247	.419	227	56	15	3	6	2.6	32	23	33	38	11	19	3	461	36	8	29	5.3	.984	1B-72, OF-7
1991		98	.246	.393	252	62	12	4	7	2.8	45	24	28	39	17	31	9	403	26	6	35	4.4	.986	1B-47, OF-33
1992		76	.256	.381	176	45	7	3	3	1.7	26	12	17	25	11	16	3	301	16	1	14	4.2	.997	1B-36, OF-15
1993	TEX A	77	.288	.459	222	64	12	4	6	2.7	28	31	23	35	4	21	5	124	4	3	5	1.7	.977	OF-61, 1B-5, 2B-1, DH-1
1994		18	.273	.303	33	9	1	0	0	0.0	2	2	4	6	0	9	0	41	2	0	3	2.4	1.000	OF-7, 1B-5
13 yrs.		1159	.252	.410	3513	886	183	51	90	2.6	591	352	481	688	322	157	40	3146	192	58	139	2.9	.983	OF-777, 1B-237, DH-7, 2B-1

LEAGUE CHAMPIONSHIP SERIES

Year	Team	Games	BA	SA	AB	H	2B	3B	HR	HR%	R	RBI	BB	SO	SB	PH AB	PH H	PO	A	E	DP	TC/G	FA	G by Pos
1990	PIT N	5	.250	.250	8	2	0	0	0	0.0	1	0	1	3	1	3	1	16	0	0	0	3.2	1.000	1B-2
1991		5	.158	.158	19	3	0	0	0	0.0	1	0	1	4	2	0	0	51	0	2	2	10.6	.962	1B-5
1992		5	.438	.813	16	7	4	1	0	0.0	4	3	2	3	0	1	0	31	4	0	1	7.0	1.000	1B-5
3 yrs.		15	.279	.419	43	12	4	1	0	0.0	6	3	4	10	3	4	1	98	4	2	3	6.9	.981	1B-12

Jeff Reed

REED, JEFFREY SCOTT
B. Nov. 12, 1962, Joliet, Ill. BL TR 6'2" 190 lbs.

Year	Team	Games	BA	SA	AB	H	2B	3B	HR	HR%	R	RBI	BB	SO	SB	PH AB	PH H	PO	A	E	DP	TC/G	FA	G by Pos
1984	MIN A	18	.143	.286	21	3	3	0	0	0.0	1	2	6	0	0	0	0	41	2	1	1	2.4	.977	C-18
1985		7	.200	.200	10	2	0	0	0	0.0	2	0	0	3	0	1	0	9	3	0	0	1.7	1.000	C-7
1986		68	.236	.321	165	39	6	1	2	1.2	13	9	16	19	1	7	3	332	19	2	5	5.2	.994	C-64
1987	MON N	75	.213	.280	207	44	11	0	1	0.5	15	21	12	20	0	5	1	357	36	12	6	5.4	.970	C-74
1988	2 teams				MON N (43G – .220)				CIN N	(49G – .232)														
"	total	92	.226	.287	265	60	9	2	1	0.4	20	16	28	41	1	6	1	468	38	3	3	5.5	.994	C-88
1989	CIN N	102	.223	.293	287	64	11	0	3	1.0	16	23	34	46	0	5	0	504	50	7	2	5.5	.988	C-99
1990		72	.251	.360	175	44	8	1	3	1.7	12	16	24	26	0	3	0	358	26	5	1	5.4	.987	C-70
1991		91	.267	.370	270	72	15	2	3	1.1	20	31	23	38	0	4	1	527	29	5	7	6.2	.991	C-89
1992		15	.160	.160	25	4	0	0	0	0.0	2	1	4	9	0	2	0	29	2	0	0	2.1	1.000	C-6
1993	SF N	66	.261	.437	119	31	3	0	6	5.0	10	12	16	22	0	33	6	180	14	0	4	2.9	1.000	C-37
1994		50	.175	.233	103	18	3	0	1	1.0	11	7	11	21	0	19	4	138	9	1	1	3.0	.993	C-33
11 yrs.		656	.231	.317	1647	381	69	6	20	1.2	124	138	167	246	2	92	16	2943	228	36	30	4.9	.989	C-585

LEAGUE CHAMPIONSHIP SERIES

Year	Team	Games	BA	SA	AB	H	2B	3B	HR	HR%	R	RBI	BB	SO	SB	PH AB	PH H	PO	A	E	DP	TC/G	FA	G by Pos
1990	CIN N	4	1.000	.000	7	0	0	0	0	0.0	0	0	0	2	0	0	0	24	1	0	0	6.3	1.000	C-4

Jody Reed

REED, JODY ERIC
B. July 26, 1962, Tampa, Fla. BR TR 5'9" 170 lbs.

Year	Team	Games	BA	SA	AB	H	2B	3B	HR	HR%	R	RBI	BB	SO	SB	PH AB	PH H	PO	A	E	DP	TC/G	FA	G by Pos
1987	BOS A	9	.300	.400	30	9	1	1	0	0.0	4	8	4	4	1	0	0	11	26	0	9	4.1	1.000	SS-6, 2B-2, 3B-1
1988		109	.293	.376	338	99	23	1	1	0.3	60	28	45	21	1	0	0	147	282	11	57	4.0	.975	SS-94, 2B-11, 3B-4
1989		146	.288	.393	524	151	42	2	3	0.6	76	40	73	44	4	3	1	255	423	19	88	4.8	.973	SS-77, 2B-70, 3B-4, DH-1, OF-1
1990		155	.289	.390	598	173	45	0	5	0.8	70	51	75	65	4	1	0	278	478	16	103	5.0	.979	2B-119, SS-50, DH-1
1991		153	.283	.382	618	175	42	2	5	0.8	87	60	60	53	6	0	0	314	449	14	110	5.1	.982	2B-152, SS-6
1992		143	.247	.316	550	136	27	1	3	0.5	64	40	62	44	7	0	0	304	472	14	113	5.5	.982	2B-142, DH-1
1993	LA N	132	.276	.346	445	123	21	2	2	0.4	48	31	38	40	1	1	1	280	413	6	76	5.3	.993	2B-132
1994	MIL A	108	.271	.341	399	108	22	0	2	0.5	48	37	57	34	5	2	0	231	351	3	72	5.4	.995	2B-106
8 yrs.		955	.278	.365	3502	974	223	9	21	0.6	457	295	414	301	29	7	2	1820	2894	82	628	5.0	.983	2B-734, SS-233, 3B-9, DH-3, OF-1

LEAGUE CHAMPIONSHIP SERIES

Year	Team	Games	BA	SA	AB	H	2B	3B	HR	HR%	R	RBI	BB	SO	SB	PH AB	PH H	PO	A	E	DP	TC/G	FA	G by Pos
1988	BOS A	4	.273	.364	11	3	1	0	0	0.0	0	0	2	1	0	0	0	3	10	0	2	3.3	1.000	SS-4
1990		4	.133	.133	15	2	0	0	0	0.0	0	1	0	2	0	0	0	11	11	0	4	5.5	1.000	2B-4, SS-3
2 yrs.		8	.192	.231	26	5	1	0	0	0.0	0	1	2	3	0	0	0	14	21	0	6	4.4	1.000	SS-7, 2B-4

Rick Renteria

RENTERIA, RICHARD AVINA
B. Dec. 25, 1961, Harbor City, Calif. BR TR 5'9" 172 lbs.

Year	Team	Games	BA	SA	AB	H	2B	3B	HR	HR%	R	RBI	BB	SO	SB	PH AB	PH H	PO	A	E	DP	TC/G	FA	G by Pos
1986	PIT N	10	.250	.333	12	3	1	0	0	0.0	2	1	0	4	0	9	2	1	2	2	0	0.5	.600	3B-1
1987	SEA A	12	.100	.200	10	1	1	0	0	0.0	0	2	2	3	0	1	0	3	4	1	1	0.7	.875	2B-4, DH-4, SS-1
1988		31	.205	.307	88	18	9	0	0	0.0	6	6	2	8	1	1	1	33	44	3	10	2.6	.963	SS-11, 3B-5, 2B-4
1993	FLA N	103	.255	.327	263	67	9	2	2	0.8	27	30	21	31	0	31	5	84	151	2	20	2.3	.992	2B-45, 3B-25, OF-1
1994		28	.224	.347	49	11	0	0	2	4.1	5	4	1	4	0	11	1	10	22	1	7	1.2	.970	3B-14, 2B-6, OF-2
5 yrs.		184	.237	.322	422	100	20	2	4	0.9	42	41	25	49	2	61	9	131	223	9	38	2.0	.975	2B-59, 3B-45, SS-12, DH-4, OF-3

Year	Team	Games	BA	SA	AB	H	2B	3B	HR	HR%	R	RBI	BB	SO	SB	Pinch Hit AB	Pinch Hit H	PO	A	E	DP	TC/G	FA	G by Pos

Harold Reynolds

REYNOLDS, HAROLD CRAIG
Brother of Don Reynolds.
B. Nov. 26, 1960, Eugene, Ore.

BB TR 5'11" 165 lbs.

Year	Team	Games	BA	SA	AB	H	2B	3B	HR	HR%	R	RBI	BB	SO	SB	PH AB	PH H	PO	A	E	DP	TC/G	FA	G by Pos
1983	SEA A	20	.203	.305	59	12	4	1	0	0.0	8	1	2	9	0	0	0	30	48	2	14	4.0	.975	2B-18
1984		10	.300	.300	10	3	0	0	0	0.0	3	0	0	1	1	0	0	8	12	0	3	2.0	1.000	2B-6
1985		66	.144	.192	104	15	3	1	0	0.0	15	6	17	14	3	2	0	69	123	8	22	3.0	.960	2B-61
1986		126	.222	.290	445	99	19	4	1	0.2	46	24	29	42	30	0	0	278	415	16	111	5.6	.977	2B-126
1987		160	.275	.370	530	146	31	8	1	0.2	73	35	39	34	**60**	0	0	347	507	20	111	5.5	.977	2B-160
1988		158	.283	.383	598	169	26	**11**	4	0.7	61	41	51	51	35	0	0	303	471	18	111	5.0	.977	2B-158
1989		153	.300	.369	613	184	24	9	0	0.0	87	43	55	45	25	2	0	311	506	17	109	5.5	.980	2B-151, DH-1
1990		160	.252	.347	**642**	162	36	5	5	0.8	100	55	81	52	31	0	0	330	499	19	110	5.3	.978	2B-160
1991		161	.254	.341	631	160	34	6	3	0.5	95	57	72	63	28	2	0	348	463	18	133	5.1	.978	2B-159, DH-1
1992		140	.247	.330	458	113	23	3	3	0.7	55	33	45	41	15	11	2	303	362	12	88	4.8	.982	2B-134, DH-1, OF-1
1993	BAL A	145	.252	.334	485	122	20	4	4	0.8	64	47	66	47	12	3	1	306	396	10	110	4.9	.986	2B-141, DH-1
1994	CAL A	74	.232	.290	207	48	10	1	0	0.0	33	11	23	18	10	12	5	116	130	1	24	3.3	.996	2B-65, DH-1
12 yrs.		1373	.258	.341	4782	1233	230	53	21	0.4	640	353	480	417	250	32	8	2749	3932	141	946	5.0	.979	2B-1339, DH-5, OF-1

Karl Rhodes

RHODES, KARL DERRICK (Tuffy)
B. Aug. 21, 1968, Cincinnati, Ohio.

BL TL 6' 175 lbs.

Year	Team	Games	BA	SA	AB	H	2B	3B	HR	HR%	R	RBI	BB	SO	SB	PH AB	PH H	PO	A	E	DP	TC/G	FA	G by Pos
1990	HOU N	38	.244	.372	86	21	6	1	1	1.2	12	3	13	12	4	6	3	61	2	3	0	1.7	.955	OF-30
1991		44	.213	.272	136	29	3	1	1	0.7	7	12	14	26	2	3	0	87	4	4	1	2.2	.958	OF-44
1992		5	.000	.000	4	0	0	0	0	0.0	0	0	0	2	0	4	0	0	0	0	0	0.0	–	OF-1
1993	2 teams		HOU N	(5G – .000)		CHI N	(15G – .288)																	
"	total	20	.278	.519	54	15	2	1	3	5.6	12	7	11	9	2	3	0	33	1	1	0	1.8	.971	OF-18
1994	CHI N	95	.234	.387	269	63	17	0	8	3.0	39	19	33	64	6	21	7	142	4	5	1	1.6	.967	OF-76
5 yrs.		202	.233	.366	549	128	28	3	13	2.4	70	41	71	113	14	37	10	323	11	13	2	1.7	.963	OF-169

Billy Ripken

RIPKEN, WILLIAM OLIVER
Son of Cal Ripken. Brother of Cal Ripken.
B. Dec. 16, 1964, Havre de Grace, Md.

BR TR 6'1" 180 lbs.

Year	Team	Games	BA	SA	AB	H	2B	3B	HR	HR%	R	RBI	BB	SO	SB	PH AB	PH H	PO	A	E	DP	TC/G	FA	G by Pos
1987	BAL A	58	.308	.372	234	72	9	0	2	0.9	27	20	21	23	4	0	0	133	162	3	53	5.1	.990	2B-58
1988		150	.207	.258	512	106	18	1	2	0.4	52	34	33	63	8	0	0	310	440	12	110	5.1	.984	2B-149, 3B-2
1989		115	.239	.305	318	76	11	2	2	0.6	31	26	22	53	1	0	0	255	335	9	81	5.2	.985	2B-114, DH-1
1990		129	.291	.387	406	118	28	1	3	0.7	48	38	28	43	5	1	1	250	366	8	84	4.8	.987	2B-127
1991		104	.216	.261	287	62	11	1	0	0.0	24	14	15	31	0	0	0	201	284	7	75	4.7	.986	2B-103
1992		111	.230	.312	330	76	15	2	4	1.2	35	36	18	26	2	0	0	217	317	4	66	4.8	.993	2B-108, DH-2
1993	TEX A	50	.189	.220	132	25	4	0	0	0.0	12	11	11	19	0	0	0	80	123	2	28	4.1	.990	2B-34, SS-18, 3B-1
1994		32	.309	.370	81	25	5	0	0	0.0	9	6	9	11	2	4	1	29	50	2	10	2.5	.975	3B-18, 2B-3, SS-2, 1B-1
8 yrs.		749	.243	.309	2300	560	101	5	13	0.6	238	185	151	269	22	5	2	1475	2077	47	507	4.8	.987	2B-705, 3B-21, SS-20, DH-3, 1B-1

Cal Ripken

RIPKEN, CALVIN EDWIN, JR.
Son of Cal Ripken. Brother of Billy Ripken.
B. Aug. 24, 1960, Havre de Grace, Md.

BR TR 6'4" 200 lbs.

Year	Team	Games	BA	SA	AB	H	2B	3B	HR	HR%	R	RBI	BB	SO	SB	PH AB	PH H	PO	A	E	DP	TC/G	FA	G by Pos
1981	BAL A	23	.128	.128	39	5	0	0	0	0.0	1	0	1	8	0	4	0	13	30	3	6	2.0	.935	SS-12, 3B-6
1982		160	.264	.475	598	158	32	5	28	4.7	90	93	46	95	3	0	0	221	440	19	64	4.3	.972	SS-94, 3B-71
1983		162	.318	.517	663	211	47	2	27	4.1	**121**	102	58	97	0	0	0	272	534	25	113	5.1	.970	SS-162
1984		162	.304	.510	641	195	37	7	27	4.2	103	86	71	89	2	0	0	297	583	26	122	5.6	.971	SS-162
1985		161	.282	.469	642	181	32	5	26	4.0	116	110	67	68	2	0	0	286	474	26	123	4.9	.967	SS-161
1986		162	.282	.461	627	177	35	1	25	4.0	98	81	70	60	4	0	0	240	482	13	105	4.6	.982	SS-162
1987		162	.252	.436	624	157	28	3	27	4.3	97	98	81	77	3	0	0	240	480	20	103	4.6	.973	SS-162
1988		161	.264	.431	575	152	25	1	23	4.0	87	81	102	69	2	0	0	284	480	21	119	4.9	.973	SS-161
1989		162	.257	.401	646	166	30	0	21	3.3	80	93	57	72	3	0	0	276	531	8	119	5.0	.990	SS-162
1990		161	.250	.415	600	150	28	4	21	3.5	78	84	82	66	3	0	0	242	435	3	94	4.2	.996	SS-161
1991		162	.323	.566	650	210	46	5	34	5.2	99	114	53	46	6	0	0	267	528	11	114	5.0	.986	SS-162
1992		162	.251	.366	637	160	29	1	14	2.2	73	72	64	50	4	0	0	288	445	12	119	4.6	.984	SS-162
1993		162	.257	.420	641	165	26	3	24	3.7	87	90	65	58	1	0	0	227	494	17	101	4.6	.977	SS-162
1994		112	.315	.459	444	140	19	3	13	2.9	71	75	32	41	1	0	0	130	321	7	70	4.1	.985	SS-112
14 yrs.		2074	.277	.455	8027	2227	414	40	310	3.9	1201	1179	849	896	34	4	0	3283	6257	211	1372	4.7	.978	SS-1997, 3B-77

LEAGUE CHAMPIONSHIP SERIES

Year	Team	Games	BA	SA	AB	H	2B	3B	HR	HR%	R	RBI	BB	SO	SB	PH AB	PH H	PO	A	E	DP	TC/G	FA	G by Pos
1983	BAL A	4	.400	.533	15	6	2	0	0	0.0	5	1	2	3	0	0	0	7	11	0	2	4.5	1.000	SS-4

WORLD SERIES

Year	Team	Games	BA	SA	AB	H	2B	3B	HR	HR%	R	RBI	BB	SO	SB	PH AB	PH H	PO	A	E	DP	TC/G	FA	G by Pos
1983	BAL A	5	.167	.167	18	3	0	0	0	0.0	2	1	3	4	0	0	0	6	14	0	3	4.0	1.000	SS-5

Luis Rivera

RIVERA, LUIS ANTONIO
Born Luis Antonio Rivera (Pedraza).
B. Jan. 3, 1964, Cidra, Puerto Rico.

BR TR 5'9" 170 lbs.

Year	Team	Games	BA	SA	AB	H	2B	3B	HR	HR%	R	RBI	BB	SO	SB	PH AB	PH H	PO	A	E	DP	TC/G	FA	G by Pos
1986	MON N	55	.205	.283	166	34	11	1	0	0.0	20	13	17	33	1	2	0	64	119	9	24	3.5	.953	SS-55
1987		18	.156	.219	32	5	2	0	0	0.0	0	1	1	8	0	3	1	9	27	3	4	2.2	.923	SS-15
1988		123	.224	.318	371	83	17	3	4	1.1	35	30	24	69	3	8	2	160	301	18	69	3.9	.962	SS-116
1989	BOS A	93	.257	.362	323	83	17	1	5	1.5	35	29	20	60	2	1	0	127	240	16	59	4.1	.958	SS-90, 2B-1, DH-1
1990		118	.225	.344	346	78	20	0	7	2.0	38	45	25	58	4	2	1	187	310	18	69	4.4	.965	SS-112, 2B-3, 3B-1
1991		129	.258	.384	414	107	22	3	8	1.9	64	40	35	86	4	0	0	180	386	24	87	4.6	.959	SS-129
1992		102	.215	.260	288	62	11	1	0	0.0	17	29	26	56	4	6	0	120	287	14	57	4.1	.967	SS-93, 2B-1, 3B-1, DH-1, OF-1
1993		62	.208	.308	130	27	8	1	1	0.8	13	7	11	36	1	4	1	65	111	6	28	2.9	.967	2B-27, SS-27, DH-5, 3B-2
1994	NY N	32	.279	.581	43	12	2	1	3	7.0	11	5	4	14	0	17	6	19	29	2	9	1.6	.960	SS-11, 2B-5
9 yrs.		732	.232	.335	2113	491	110	11	28	1.3	233	199	163	420	19	43	11	931	1810	110	406	3.9	.961	SS-648, 2B-37, DH-7, 3B-4, OF-1

LEAGUE CHAMPIONSHIP SERIES

Year	Team	Games	BA	SA	AB	H	2B	3B	HR	HR%	R	RBI	BB	SO	SB	PH AB	PH H	PO	A	E	DP	TC/G	FA	G by Pos
1990	BOS A	4	.222	.333	9	2	1	0	0	0.0	1	0	0	2	0	0	0	6	16	1	3	5.8	.957	SS-4

Year Team	Games	BA	SA	AB	H	2B	3B	HR	HR%	R	RBI	BB	SO	SB	Pinch Hit AB	Pinch Hit H	PO	A	E	DP	TC/G	FA	G by Pos

Kevin Roberson
ROBERSON, KEVIN LYNN
B. Jan. 29, 1968, Decatur, Ill.
BB TR 6'4" 210 lbs.

Year Team	Games	BA	SA	AB	H	2B	3B	HR	HR%	R	RBI	BB	SO	SB	PH AB	PH H	PO	A	E	DP	TC/G	FA	G by Pos
1993 CHI N	62	.189	.372	180	34	4	1	9	5.0	23	27	12	48	0	14	5	77	3	3	0	1.3	.963	OF-51
1994	44	.218	.509	55	12	4	0	4	7.3	8	9	2	14	0	35	9	7	1	2	0	0.2	.800	OF-9
2 yrs.	106	.196	.404	235	46	8	1	13	5.5	31	36	14	62	0	49	11	84	3	5	0	0.9	.946	OF-60

Bip Roberts
ROBERTS, LEON JOSEPH
B. Oct. 27, 1963, Berkeley, Calif.
BB TR 5'7" 150 lbs.

Year Team	Games	BA	SA	AB	H	2B	3B	HR	HR%	R	RBI	BB	SO	SB	PH AB	PH H	PO	A	E	DP	TC/G	FA	G by Pos
1986 SD N	101	.253	.303	241	61	5	2	1	0.4	34	12	14	29	14	3	1	166	172	10	33	3.4	.971	2B-87
1988	5	.333	.333	9	3	0	0	0	0.0	1	0	1	2	0	2	0	2	3	1	1	1.2	.833	3B-2, 2B-1
1989	117	.301	.422	329	99	15	8	3	0.9	81	25	49	45	21	17	6	134	113	9	17	2.2	.965	OF-54, 3B-37, SS-14, 2B-9
1990	149	.309	.433	556	172	36	3	9	1.6	104	44	55	65	46	5	0	227	160	13	22	2.7	.968	OF-75, 3B-56, SS-18, 2B-8
1991	117	.281	.347	424	119	13	3	3	0.7	66	32	37	71	26	7	1	239	185	10	35	3.7	.977	2B-68, OF-46
1992 CIN N	147	.323	.432	532	172	34	6	4	0.8	92	45	62	54	44	12	4	209	152	7	13	2.5	.981	OF-79, 2B-42, 3B-36
1993	83	.240	.295	292	70	13	0	1	0.3	46	18	38	46	26	3	0	152	176	6	31	4.0	.982	2B-65, OF-12, 3B-3, SS-1
1994 SD N	105	.320	.397	403	129	15	5	2	0.5	52	31	39	57	21	2	2	177	221	9	41	3.9	.978	2B-90, OF-20
8 yrs.	824	.296	.387	2786	825	131	27	23	0.8	476	207	295	369	198	51	14	1306	1182	65	193	3.1	.975	2B-370, OF-286, 3B-134, SS-33

Alex Rodriguez
RODRIGUEZ, ALEXANDER EMMANUEL
B. July 27, 1975, New York, N.Y.
BR TR 6'3" 190 lbs.

Year Team	Games	BA	SA	AB	H	2B	3B	HR	HR%	R	RBI	BB	SO	SB	PH AB	PH H	PO	A	E	DP	TC/G	FA	G by Pos
1994 SEA A	17	.204	.204	54	11	0	0	0	0.0	4	2	3	20	3	0	0	20	45	6	9	4.2	.915	SS-17

Carlos Rodriguez
RODRIGUEZ, CARLOS
Born Carlos Rodriguez (Marquez).
B. Nov. 1, 1967, Mexico City, Mexico.
BB TR 5'9" 160 lbs.

Year Team	Games	BA	SA	AB	H	2B	3B	HR	HR%	R	RBI	BB	SO	SB	PH AB	PH H	PO	A	E	DP	TC/G	FA	G by Pos
1991 NY A	15	.189	.189	37	7	0	0	0	0.0	1	2	1	2	0	2	0	11	34	2	9	3.1	.957	SS-11, 2B-3
1994 BOS A	57	.287	.397	174	50	14	1	1	0.6	15	13	11	13	1	3	2	87	132	6	36	3.9	.973	SS-32, 2B-20, 3B-4
2 yrs.	72	.270	.360	211	57	14	1	1	0.5	16	15	12	15	1	5	2	98	166	8	45	3.8	.971	SS-43, 2B-23, 3B-4

Henry Rodriguez
RODRIGUEZ, HENRY ANDERSON
Born Henry Anderson Rodriguez (Lorenzo).
B. Nov. 8, 1967, Santo Domingo, Dominican Republic.
BL TL 6'1" 180 lbs.

Year Team	Games	BA	SA	AB	H	2B	3B	HR	HR%	R	RBI	BB	SO	SB	PH AB	PH H	PO	A	E	DP	TC/G	FA	G by Pos
1992 LA N	53	.219	.329	146	32	7	0	3	2.1	11	14	8	30	0	15	4	68	8	3	2	1.5	.962	OF-48, 1B-1
1993	76	.222	.415	176	39	10	0	8	4.5	20	23	11	39	1	15	4	128	8	1	2	1.8	.993	OF-48, 1B-13
1994	104	.268	.405	306	82	14	2	8	2.6	33	49	17	58	0	15	4	198	9	2	3	2.0	.990	OF-86, 1B-17
3 yrs.	233	.244	.390	628	153	31	2	19	3.0	64	86	36	127	1	35	8	394	25	6	7	1.8	.986	OF-182, 1B-31

Ivan Rodriguez
RODRIGUEZ, IVAN (Pudge)
Born Ivan Rodriguez (Torres).
B. Nov. 27, 1971, Manati, Puerto Rico.
BR TR 5'9" 165 lbs.

Year Team	Games	BA	SA	AB	H	2B	3B	HR	HR%	R	RBI	BB	SO	SB	PH AB	PH H	PO	A	E	DP	TC/G	FA	G by Pos
1991 TEX A	88	.264	.354	280	74	16	0	3	1.1	24	27	5	42	0	2	0	517	62	10	6	6.7	.983	C-88
1992	123	.260	.360	420	109	16	1	8	1.9	39	37	24	73	0	9	1	763	85	15	10	7.0	.983	C-116, DH-2
1993	137	.273	.412	473	129	28	4	10	2.1	56	66	29	70	8	5	3	801	76	8	6	6.5	.991	C-134, DH-1
1994	99	.298	.488	363	108	19	1	16	4.4	56	57	31	42	6	1	0	600	44	5	2	6.6	.992	C-99
4 yrs.	447	.273	.405	1536	420	79	6	37	2.4	175	187	89	227	14	17	4	2681	267	38	24	6.7	.987	C-437, DH-3

Rich Rowland
ROWLAND, RICHARD GARNET
B. Feb. 25, 1964, Cloverdale, Calif.
BR TR 6'1" 210 lbs.

Year Team	Games	BA	SA	AB	H	2B	3B	HR	HR%	R	RBI	BB	SO	SB	PH AB	PH H	PO	A	E	DP	TC/G	FA	G by Pos
1990 DET A	7	.158	.211	19	3	1	0	0	0.0	3	0	2	4	0	1	0	29	0	1	0	4.3	.967	C-5, DH-2
1991	4	.250	.250	4	1	0	0	0	0.0	0	1	1	2	0	1	0	2	1	0	0	0.8	1.000	C-2, DH-1
1992	6	.214	.214	14	3	0	0	0	0.0	2	0	3	3	0	0	0	12	1	0	1	2.2	1.000	C-3, DH-2, 1B-1, 3B-1
1993	21	.217	.283	46	10	3	0	0	0.0	2	4	5	16	0	3	2	75	7	1	1	4.0	.988	C-17, DH-3
1994 BOS A	46	.229	.483	118	27	3	0	9	7.6	14	20	11	35	0	5	0	196	12	6	0	4.7	.972	C-39, DH-4, 1B-1
5 yrs.	84	.219	.388	201	44	7	0	9	4.5	21	25	22	60	0	10	2	314	21	8	2	4.1	.977	C-66, DH-12, 1B-2, 3B-1

Stan Royer
ROYER, STANLEY DEAN
B. Aug. 31, 1967, Olney, Ill.
BR TR 6'3" 195 lbs.

Year Team	Games	BA	SA	AB	H	2B	3B	HR	HR%	R	RBI	BB	SO	SB	PH AB	PH H	PO	A	E	DP	TC/G	FA	G by Pos
1991 STL N	9	.286	.333	21	6	1	0	0	0.0	1	1	1	2	0	3	1	5	4	0	0	1.0	1.000	3B-5
1992	13	.323	.581	31	10	2	0	2	6.5	6	9	1	4	0	3	1	34	11	3	9	3.7	.938	3B-5, 1B-4
1993	46	.304	.413	46	14	2	0	1	2.2	4	8	2	14	0	12	4	22	16	3	1	1.7	.927	3B-10, 1B-2
1994 2 teams	STL N (39G – .175)			BOS A	(4G – .111)																		
" total	43	.167	.288	66	11	5	0	1	1.5	3	3	0	21	0	27	3	41	14	3	2	1.3	.948	1B-12, 3B-8
4 yrs.	89	.250	.384	164	41	10	0	4	2.4	14	21	4	41	0	45	9	102	45	9	12	1.8	.942	3B-28, 1B-18

Chris Sabo
SABO, CHRISTOPHER ANDREW (Spuds)
B. Jan. 19, 1962, Detroit, Mich.
BR TR 5'11" 185 lbs.

Year Team	Games	BA	SA	AB	H	2B	3B	HR	HR%	R	RBI	BB	SO	SB	PH AB	PH H	PO	A	E	DP	TC/G	FA	G by Pos
1988 CIN N	137	.271	.414	538	146	40	2	11	2.0	74	44	29	52	46	2	0	75	318	14	31	3.0	.966	3B-135, SS-2
1989	82	.260	.395	304	79	21	1	6	2.0	40	29	25	33	14	5	0	36	145	11	12	2.3	.943	3B-76
1990	148	.270	.476	567	153	38	2	25	4.4	95	71	61	58	25	1	0	70	273	12	17	2.4	.966	3B-146
1991	153	.301	.505	582	175	35	3	26	4.5	91	88	44	79	19	1	1	86	255	12	24	2.3	.966	3B-151
1992	96	.244	.422	344	84	19	3	12	3.5	42	43	30	54	4	2	0	60	159	9	13	2.4	.961	3B-93
1993	148	.259	.440	552	143	33	2	21	3.8	86	82	43	105	6	0	0	79	242	11	16	2.2	.967	3B-148
1994 BAL A	68	.256	.465	258	66	15	3	11	4.3	41	42	20	38	1	2	0	52	49	4	5	1.5	.962	3B-37, OF-22, DH-10
7 yrs.	832	.269	.450	3145	846	201	16	112	3.6	469	399	252	419	115	14	1	458	1441	73	118	2.4	.963	3B-786, OF-22, DH-10, SS-2

LEAGUE CHAMPIONSHIP SERIES

Year Team	Games	BA	SA	AB	H	2B	3B	HR	HR%	R	RBI	BB	SO	SB	PH AB	PH H	PO	A	E	DP	TC/G	FA	G by Pos
1990 CIN N	6	.227	.364	22	5	0	0	1	4.5	1	3	1	4	0	0	0	7	7	0	1	2.3	1.000	3B-6

WORLD SERIES

Year Team	Games	BA	SA	AB	H	2B	3B	HR	HR%	R	RBI	BB	SO	SB	PH AB	PH H	PO	A	E	DP	TC/G	FA	G by Pos
1990 CIN N	4	.563	1.000	16	9	1	0	2	12.5	2	5	2	2	0	0	0	3	14	0	0	4.3	1.000	3B-4

Year Team	Games	BA	SA	AB	H	2B	3B	HR	HR%	R	RBI	BB	SO	SB	Pinch Hit AB	Pinch Hit H	PO	A	E	DP	TC/G	FA	G by Pos

Olmedo Saenz

SAENZ, OLMEDO BR TR 6'2" 185 lbs.
Born Olmedo Saenz (Sanchez).
B. Oct. 8, 1970, Chitre Herrera, Panama

Year Team	Games	BA	SA	AB	H	2B	3B	HR	HR%	R	RBI	BB	SO	SB	Pinch Hit AB	Pinch Hit H	PO	A	E	DP	TC/G	FA	G by Pos
1994 **CHI A**	5	.143	.286	14	2	0	1	0	0.0	2	0	0	5	0	0	0	3	6	0	0	1.8	1.000	3B-5

Tim Salmon

SALMON, TIMOTHY JAMES BR TR 6'3" 200 lbs.
B. Aug. 24, 1968, Long Beach, Calif.

Year Team	Games	BA	SA	AB	H	2B	3B	HR	HR%	R	RBI	BB	SO	SB	Pinch Hit AB	Pinch Hit H	PO	A	E	DP	TC/G	FA	G by Pos
1992 **CAL A**	23	.177	.266	79	14	1	0	2	2.5	8	6	11	23	1	0	0	40	1	2	1	1.9	.953	OF-21
1993	142	.283	.536	515	146	35	1	31	6.0	93	95	82	135	5	0	0	335	12	7	2	2.5	.980	OF-141, DH-1
1994	100	.287	.531	373	107	18	2	23	6.2	67	70	54	102	1	1	1	219	9	8	1	2.4	.966	OF-99
3 yrs.	265	.276	.512	967	267	54	3	56	5.8	168	171	147	260	7	1	1	594	22	17	4	2.4	.973	OF-261, DH-1

Juan Samuel

SAMUEL, JUAN MILTON (Sammy) BR TR 5'11" 170 lbs.
Born Juan Milton Romero (Samuel).
B. Dec. 9, 1960, San Pedro de Macoris, Dominican Republic.

Year Team	Games	BA	SA	AB	H	2B	3B	HR	HR%	R	RBI	BB	SO	SB	Pinch Hit AB	Pinch Hit H	PO	A	E	DP	TC/G	FA	G by Pos
1983 **PHI N**	18	.277	.446	65	18	1	2	2	3.1	14	5	4	16	3	0	0	44	54	9	9	5.9	.916	2B-18
1984	160	.272	.442	**701**	191	36	**19**	15	2.1	105	69	28	**168**	72	2	1	388	438	33	77	5.4	.962	2B-160
1985	161	.264	.436	**663**	175	31	13	19	2.9	101	74	33	**141**	53	1	0	389	463	15	88	5.4	.983	2B-159
1986	145	.266	.448	591	157	36	12	16	2.7	90	78	26	**142**	42	2	2	290	440	25	83	5.2	.967	2B-143
1987	160	.272	.502	**655**	178	37	**15**	28	4.3	113	100	60	**162**	35	0	0	374	434	18	99	5.2	.978	2B-160
1988	157	.243	.380	629	153	32	9	12	1.9	68	67	39	151	33	1	1	351	387	16	92	4.8	.979	2B-152, OF-3, 3B-1
1989 **2 teams**	**PHI N** (51G – .246)			**NY N** (86G – .228)																			
" **total**	137	.235	.335	532	125	16	2	11	2.1	69	48	42	120	42	2	1	339	6	4	3	2.5	.989	OF-134
1990 **LA N**	143	.242	.382	492	119	24	3	13	2.6	62	52	51	126	38	6	1	273	262	16	47	3.9	.971	2B-108, OF-31
1991	153	.271	.389	594	161	22	6	12	2.0	74	58	49	133	23	2	1	300	442	17	73	5.0	.978	2B-152
1992 **2 teams**	**LA N** (47G – .262)			**KC A** (29G – .284)																			
" **total**	76	.272	.344	224	61	8	4	0	0.0	22	23	14	49	8	15	4	121	106	11	22	3.1	.954	2B-48, OF-19
1993 **CIN N**	103	.230	.345	261	60	10	4	4	1.5	31	26	23	53	9	18	3	151	172	10	33	3.2	.970	2B-70, 1B-6, 3B-4, OF-3
1994 **DET A**	59	.309	.559	136	42	9	5	5	3.7	32	21	10	26	5	5	2	82	28	1	4	1.9	.991	OF-27, DH-10, 2B-8, 1B-2
12 yrs.	1472	.260	.415	5543	1440	262	94	137	2.5	781	621	379	1287	363	54	16	3102	3232	175	630	4.4	.973	2B-1178, OF-217, DH-10, 1B-8, 3B-5
LEAGUE CHAMPIONSHIP SERIES																							
1983 **PHI N**	1	–	–	0	0	0	0	0	–	0	0	0	0	0	0	0	0	0	0	0	0.0	–	
WORLD SERIES																							
1983 **PHI N**	3	.000	.000	1	0	0	0	0	0.0	0	0	0	0	0	1	0	0	0	0	0	0.0	–	

Rey Sanchez

SANCHEZ, REY FRANCISCO BR TR 5'10" 180 lbs.
Born Rey Francisco Sanchez (Guadalupe).
B. Oct. 5, 1967, Rio Piedras, Puerto Rico.

Year Team	Games	BA	SA	AB	H	2B	3B	HR	HR%	R	RBI	BB	SO	SB	Pinch Hit AB	Pinch Hit H	PO	A	E	DP	TC/G	FA	G by Pos
1991 **CHI N**	13	.261	.261	23	6	0	0	0	0.0	1	2	4	3	0	0	0	11	25	0	1	2.8	1.000	SS-10, 2B-2
1992	74	.251	.341	255	64	14	3	1	0.4	24	19	10	17	2	3	1	148	202	9	52	4.9	.975	SS-68, 2B-4
1993	105	.282	.326	344	97	11	2	0	0.0	35	28	15	22	1	10	4	158	317	15	62	4.7	.969	SS-98
1994	96	.285	.337	291	83	13	1	0	0.0	26	24	20	29	2	7	1	152	275	9	52	4.5	.979	2B-50, SS-30, 3B-17
4 yrs.	288	.274	.332	913	250	38	6	1	0.1	86	73	49	71	5	20	6	469	819	33	167	4.6	.975	SS-206, 2B-56, 3B-17

Ryne Sandberg

SANDBERG, RYNE DEE (Ryno) BR TR 6'1" 175 lbs.
B. Sept. 18, 1959, Spokane, Wash.

Year Team	Games	BA	SA	AB	H	2B	3B	HR	HR%	R	RBI	BB	SO	SB	Pinch Hit AB	Pinch Hit H	PO	A	E	DP	TC/G	FA	G by Pos
1981 **PHI N**	13	.167	.167	6	1	0	0	0	0.0	2	0	0	1	0	0	0	7	7	0	1	1.1	1.000	SS-5, 2B-1
1982 **CHI N**	156	.271	.372	635	172	33	5	7	1.1	103	54	36	90	32	1	0	136	373	12	28	3.3	.977	3B-133, 2B-24
1983	158	.261	.351	633	165	25	4	8	1.3	94	48	51	79	37	4	2	330	571	13	126	5.8	.986	2B-157, SS-1
1984	156	.314	.520	636	200	36	**19**	19	3.0	**114**	84	52	101	32	0	0	314	550	6	102	5.6	.993	2B-156
1985	153	.305	.504	609	186	31	6	26	4.3	113	83	57	97	54	1	0	353	501	12	99	5.7	.986	2B-153, SS-1
1986	154	.284	.411	627	178	28	5	14	2.2	68	76	46	79	34	1	1	309	492	5	86	5.2	.994	2B-153
1987	132	.294	.442	523	154	25	2	16	3.1	81	59	59	79	21	2	1	294	375	10	84	5.1	.985	2B-131
1988	155	.264	.419	618	163	23	8	19	3.1	77	69	54	91	25	2	0	291	522	11	79	5.3	.987	2B-153
1989	157	.290	.497	606	176	25	5	30	5.0	**104**	76	59	85	15	2	0	294	466	6	80	4.9	.992	2B-155
1990	155	.306	.559	615	188	30	3	**40**	6.5	**116**	100	50	84	25	2	0	278	469	8	81	4.9	.989	2B-154
1991	158	.291	.485	585	170	32	2	26	4.4	104	100	87	89	22	3	1	267	515	4	66	5.0	.995	2B-157
1992	158	.304	.510	612	186	32	8	26	4.2	100	87	68	73	17	1	0	283	539	8	94	5.3	.990	2B-157
1993	117	.309	.412	456	141	20	0	9	2.0	67	45	37	62	9	3	1	209	347	7	77	4.8	.988	2B-115
1994	57	.238	.390	223	53	9	5	5	2.2	36	24	23	40	2	0	0	96	202	4	35	5.3	.987	2B-57
14 yrs.	1879	.289	.455	7384	2133	349	72	245	3.3	1179	905	679	1050	325	22	6	3461	5929	106	1038	5.1	.989	2B-1723, 3B-133, SS-7
LEAGUE CHAMPIONSHIP SERIES																							
1984 **CHI N**	5	.368	.474	19	7	2	0	0	0.0	3	2	3	2	3	0	0	12	18	1	6	6.2	.968	2B-5
1989	5	.400	.800	20	8	3	1	1	5.0	6	4	3	4	0	0	0	7	11	0	1	3.6	1.000	2B-5
2 yrs.	10	.385	.641	39	15	5	1	1	2.6	9	6	6	6	3	0	0	19	29	1	7	4.9	.980	2B-10

Deion Sanders

SANDERS, DEION LUWYNN (Neon, Prime Time) BL TL 6'1" 195 lbs.
B. Aug. 9, 1967, Fort Myers, Fla.

Year Team	Games	BA	SA	AB	H	2B	3B	HR	HR%	R	RBI	BB	SO	SB	Pinch Hit AB	Pinch Hit H	PO	A	E	DP	TC/G	FA	G by Pos
1989 **NY A**	14	.234	.404	47	11	2	0	2	4.3	7	7	3	8	1	1	0	30	1	1	0	2.3	.969	OF-14
1990	57	.158	.271	133	21	2	2	3	2.3	24	9	13	27	8	4	0	69	2	2	1	1.3	.973	OF-42, DH-4
1991 **ATL N**	54	.191	.345	110	21	1	2	4	3.6	16	13	12	23	11	4	0	57	3	3	0	1.2	.952	OF-44
1992	97	.304	.495	303	92	6	**14**	8	2.6	54	28	18	52	26	14	5	174	4	3	0	1.9	.983	OF-75
1993	95	.276	.452	272	75	18	6	6	2.2	42	28	16	42	19	29	12	137	1	2	1	1.5	.986	OF-60
1994 **2 teams**	**ATL N** (46G – .288)			**CIN N** (46G – .277)																			
" **total**	92	.283	.381	375	106	17	4	4	1.1	58	28	32	63	38	3	1	209	2	2	0	2.3	.991	OF-91
6 yrs.	409	.263	.410	1240	326	46	28	27	2.2	201	113	94	215	103	55	18	676	13	13	2	1.7	.981	OF-326, DH-4
LEAGUE CHAMPIONSHIP SERIES																							
1992 **ATL N**	4	.000	.000	5	0	0	0	0	0.0	0	0	0	3	0	3	0	1	0	0	0	0.3	1.000	OF-3
1993	5	.000	.000	3	0	0	0	0	0.0	0	0	0	1	0	3	0	0	0	0	0	0.0	–	OF-1
2 yrs.	9	.000	.000	8	0	0	0	0	0.0	0	0	0	4	0	6	0	1	0	0	0	0.1	1.000	OF-4

Year Team	Games	BA	SA	AB	H	2B	3B	HR	HR%	R	RBI	BB	SO	SB	Pinch Hit AB	Pinch Hit H	PO	A	E	DP	TC/G	FA	G by Pos

Deion Sanders *continued*

WORLD SERIES

Year Team	Games	BA	SA	AB	H	2B	3B	HR	HR%	R	RBI	BB	SO	SB	PH AB	PH H	PO	A	E	DP	TC/G	FA	G by Pos
1992 ATL N	4	.533	.667	15	8	2	0	0	0.0	4	1	2	1	5	0	0	5	1	0	0	1.5	1.000	OF-4

Reggie Sanders

SANDERS, REGINALD LAVERNE
B. Dec. 1, 1967, Florence, S. C.

BR TR 6' 180 lbs.

Year Team	Games	BA	SA	AB	H	2B	3B	HR	HR%	R	RBI	BB	SO	SB	PH AB	PH H	PO	A	E	DP	TC/G	FA	G by Pos
1991 CIN N	9	.200	.275	40	8	0	0	1	2.5	6	3	0	9	1	0	0	22	0	0	0	2.4	1.000	OF-9
1992	116	.270	.462	385	104	26	6	12	3.1	62	36	48	98	16	11	3	262	11	6	4	2.4	.978	OF-110
1993	138	.274	.444	496	136	16	4	20	4.0	90	83	51	118	27	1	0	312	3	8	0	2.3	.975	OF-137
1994	107	.263	.480	400	105	20	8	17	4.3	66	62	41	**114**	21	3	0	217	12	6	2	2.2	.974	OF-104
4 yrs.	370	.267	.455	1321	353	62	18	50	3.8	224	184	140	339	65	15	3	813	26	20	6	2.3	.977	OF-360

Benito Santiago

SANTIAGO, BENITO
Born Benito Santiago (Rivera).
B. Mar. 9, 1965, Ponce, Puerto Rico.

BR TR 6'1" 180 lbs.

Year Team	Games	BA	SA	AB	H	2B	3B	HR	HR%	R	RBI	BB	SO	SB	PH AB	PH H	PO	A	E	DP	TC/G	FA	G by Pos
1986 SD N	17	.290	.468	62	18	2	0	3	4.8	10	6	2	12	0	0	0	80	7	5	2	5.4	.946	C-17
1987	146	.300	.467	546	164	33	2	18	3.3	64	79	16	112	21	0	0	817	80	22	12	6.3	.976	C-146
1988	139	.248	.362	492	122	22	2	10	2.0	49	46	24	82	15	7	2	725	75	12	11	5.8	.985	C-136
1989	129	.236	.387	462	109	16	3	16	3.5	50	62	26	89	11	2	0	685	81	20	10	6.1	.975	C-127
1990	100	.270	.419	344	93	8	5	11	3.2	42	53	27	55	5	4	1	538	51	12	6	6.0	.980	C-98
1991	152	.267	.403	580	155	22	3	17	2.9	60	87	23	114	8	2	2	830	100	14	14	6.2	.985	C-151, OF-1
1992	106	.251	.383	386	97	21	0	10	2.6	37	42	21	52	2	4	1	584	53	12	6	6.1	.982	C-103
1993 FLA N	139	.230	.380	469	108	19	6	13	2.8	49	50	37	88	10	5	1	741	63	11	4	5.9	.987	C-136, OF-1
1994	101	.273	.424	337	92	14	2	11	3.3	35	41	25	57	1	8	2	511	64	5	3	5.7	.991	C-97
9 yrs.	1029	.260	.405	3678	958	157	23	109	3.0	396	466	201	661	73	32	9	5511	574	113	68	6.0	.982	C-1011, OF-2

Mackey Sasser

SASSER, MACK DANIEL
B. Aug. 3, 1962, Fort Gaines, Ga.

BL TR 6'1" 190 lbs.

Year Team	Games	BA	SA	AB	H	2B	3B	HR	HR%	R	RBI	BB	SO	SB	PH AB	PH H	PO	A	E	DP	TC/G	FA	G by Pos
1987 2 teams	SF N (2G – .000)			PIT N (12G – .217)																			
" total	14	.185	.185	27	5	0	0	0	0.0	2	2	0	2	0	9	4	29	0	0	0	2.1	1.000	C-6
1988 NY N	60	.285	.407	123	35	10	1	1	0.8	9	17	6	9	0	19	3	235	17	6	2	4.3	.977	C-42, 3B-1, OF-1
1989	72	.291	.407	182	53	14	2	1	0.5	17	22	7	15	0	17	5	335	19	3	3	5.0	.992	C-62, 3B-1
1990	100	.307	.426	270	83	14	0	6	2.2	31	41	15	19	0	25	6	501	43	14	4	5.6	.975	C-87, 1B-1
1991	96	.272	.417	228	62	14	2	5	2.2	18	35	9	19	0	38	10	271	21	3	6	3.1	.990	C-43, OF-21, 1B-10
1992	92	.241	.326	141	34	6	0	2	1.4	7	18	3	10	0	55	8	131	5	1	4	1.5	.993	C-27, 1B-12, OF-9
1993 SEA A	83	.218	.309	188	41	10	2	1	0.5	18	21	15	30	1	23	6	60	4	3	0	0.8	.955	OF-37, DH-19, C-4, 1B-1
1994	3	.000	.000	4	0	0	0	0	0.0	0	0	0	0	0	2	0	0	0	0	0	–	–	C-1, OF-1
8 yrs.	520	.269	.381	1163	313	68	7	16	1.4	102	156	55	104	1	188	42	1562	109	30	19	3.3	.982	C-272, OF-69, 1B-24, DH-19, 3B-2

LEAGUE CHAMPIONSHIP SERIES

Year Team	Games	BA	SA	AB	H	2B	3B	HR	HR%	R	RBI	BB	SO	SB	PH AB	PH H	PO	A	E	DP	TC/G	FA	G by Pos
1988 NY N	4	.200	.200	5	1	0	0	0	0.0	0	0	0	1	0	2	0	2	0	0	0	0.5	1.000	C-2

Steve Sax

SAX, STEPHEN LOUIS
Brother of Dave Sax.
B. Jan. 29, 1960, Sacramento, Calif.

BR TR 5'11" 185 lbs.

Year Team	Games	BA	SA	AB	H	2B	3B	HR	HR%	R	RBI	BB	SO	SB	PH AB	PH H	PO	A	E	DP	TC/G	FA	G by Pos
1981 LA N	31	.277	.345	119	33	2	0	2	1.7	15	9	7	14	5	2	1	64	93	4	22	5.2	.975	2B-29
1982	150	.282	.359	638	180	23	7	4	0.6	88	47	49	53	49	1	1	347	452	19	83	5.5	.977	2B-149
1983	155	.281	.350	623	175	18	5	5	0.8	94	41	58	73	56	4	1	331	399	30	74	4.9	.961	2B-152
1984	145	.243	.304	569	138	24	4	1	0.2	70	35	47	53	34	3	0	318	450	21	99	5.4	.973	2B-141
1985	136	.279	.318	488	136	8	4	1	0.2	62	42	54	43	27	1	0	330	358	22	84	5.2	.969	2B-135, 3B-1
1986	157	.332	.441	633	210	43	4	6	0.9	91	56	59	58	40	3	1	367	432	16	71	5.2	.980	2B-154
1987	157	.280	.369	610	171	22	7	6	1.0	84	46	44	61	37	5	0	343	420	14	92	4.9	.982	2B-152, 3B-1, OF-1
1988	160	.277	.343	632	175	19	4	5	0.8	70	57	45	51	42	2	2	276	429	14	69	4.5	.981	2B-158
1989 NY A	158	.315	.387	651	205	26	3	5	0.8	88	63	52	44	43	0	0	312	460	10	117	4.9	.987	2B-158
1990	155	.260	.325	615	160	24	2	4	0.7	70	42	49	46	43	0	0	292	457	10	102	4.9	.987	2B-154
1991	158	.304	.414	652	198	38	2	10	1.5	85	56	41	38	31	0	0	277	454	10	107	4.7	.987	2B-149, 3B-5, DH-4
1992 CHI A	143	.236	.317	567	134	26	4	4	0.7	74	47	43	42	30	1	0	305	390	20	75	5.0	.972	2B-141, DH-1
1993	57	.235	.303	119	28	5	0	1	0.8	20	8	8	6	7	0	0	39	3	0	0	0.7	1.000	OF-32, DH-20, 2B-1
1994 OAK A	7	.250	.333	24	6	0	1	0	0.0	2	1	0	2	0	1	1	16	20	0	3	5.1	1.000	2B-6
14 yrs.	1769	.281	.358	6940	1949	278	47	54	0.8	913	550	556	584	444	31	7	3617	4817	190	998	4.9	.978	2B-1679, OF-33, DH-25, 3B-7

DIVISIONAL PLAYOFF SERIES

Year Team	Games	BA	SA	AB	H	2B	3B	HR	HR%	R	RBI	BB	SO	SB	PH AB	PH H	PO	A	E	DP	TC/G	FA	G by Pos
1981 LA N	1	–	–	0	0	0	0	0	–	0	0	0	0	0	0	0	0	0	0	0	0.0	–	2B-1

LEAGUE CHAMPIONSHIP SERIES

Year Team	Games	BA	SA	AB	H	2B	3B	HR	HR%	R	RBI	BB	SO	SB	PH AB	PH H	PO	A	E	DP	TC/G	FA	G by Pos
1981 LA N	1	–	–	0	0	0	0	0	–	0	0	0	0	0	0	0	0	1	0	0	1.0	1.000	2B-1
1983	4	.250	.250	16	4	0	0	0	0.0	0	0	1	0	1	0	0	11	12	0	3	5.8	1.000	2B-4
1985	6	.300	.450	20	6	3	0	0	0.0	1	1	1	0	0	0	0	12	20	0	6	5.3	1.000	2B-6
1988	7	.267	.267	30	8	0	0	0	0.0	7	3	3	3	5	0	0	12	22	0	6	4.9	1.000	2B-7
4 yrs.	18	.273	.318	66	18	3	0	0	0.0	8	4	5	3	6	0	0	35	55	0	9	5.0	1.000	2B-18

WORLD SERIES

Year Team	Games	BA	SA	AB	H	2B	3B	HR	HR%	R	RBI	BB	SO	SB	PH AB	PH H	PO	A	E	DP	TC/G	FA	G by Pos
1981 LA N	2	.000	.000	1	0	0	0	0	0.0	0	0	0	1	0	1	0	0	0	0	0	0.0	–	2B-1
1988	5	.300	.300	20	6	0	0	0	0.0	3	0	1	1	1	0	0	11	11	0	2	4.4	1.000	2B-5
2 yrs.	7	.286	.286	21	6	0	0	0	0.0	3	0	1	1	1	1	0	11	11	0	2	3.1	1.000	2B-6

Steve Scarsone

SCARSONE, STEVEN WAYNE
B. Apr. 11, 1966, Anaheim, Calif.

BR TR 6'2" 170 lbs.

Year Team	Games	BA	SA	AB	H	2B	3B	HR	HR%	R	RBI	BB	SO	SB	PH AB	PH H	PO	A	E	DP	TC/G	FA	G by Pos
1992 2 teams	PHI N (7G – .154)			BAL A (11G – .176)																			
" total	18	.167	.167	30	5	0	0	0	0.0	3	0	2	12	0	5	1	8	11	2	5	1.2	.905	2B-8, 3B-2, SS-1
1993 SF N	44	.252	.398	103	26	9	0	2	1.9	16	15	4	32	0	10	3	53	44	1	11	2.2	.990	2B-20, 3B-8, 1B-6
1994	52	.272	.408	103	28	8	0	2	1.9	21	13	10	20	0	15	4	66	80	2	23	2.8	.986	2B-22, 3B-8, 1B-6, SS-1
3 yrs.	114	.250	.373	236	59	17	0	4	1.7	40	28	16	64	0	30	8	127	135	5	39	2.3	.981	2B-50, 3B-18, 1B-12, SS-2

Year Team	Games	BA	SA	AB	H	2B	3B	HR	HR%	R	RBI	BB	SO	SB	Pinch Hit AB	Pinch Hit H	PO	A	E	DP	TC/G	FA	G by Pos

Jeff Schaefer

SCHAEFER, JEFFREY SCOTT
B. May 31, 1960, Patchogue, N. Y.

BR TR 5'10" 170 lbs.

Year Team	Games	BA	SA	AB	H	2B	3B	HR	HR%	R	RBI	BB	SO	SB	PH AB	PH H	PO	A	E	DP	TC/G	FA	G by Pos
1989 CHI A	15	.100	.100	10	1	0	0	0	0.0	2	0	0	2	1	0	0	5	7	2	4	0.9	.857	SS-5, 2B-4, 3B-4, DH-1
1990 SEA A	55	.206	.234	107	22	3	0	0	0.0	11	6	3	11	4	2	1	52	87	5	20	2.6	.965	3B-26, SS-24, 2B-3
1991	84	.250	.323	164	41	7	1	1	0.6	19	11	5	25	3	3	0	79	120	6	31	2.4	.971	SS-46, 3B-30, 2B-11, DH-1
1992	65	.114	.186	70	8	2	0	1	1.4	5	3	2	10	0	0	0	36	91	9	10	2.1	.934	SS-33, 3B-21, 2B-7, DH-1
1994 OAK A	6	.125	.125	8	1	0	0	0	0.0	0	0	0	1	0	1	0	4	2	1	0	1.2	.857	3B-3, SS-2, 1B-1
5 yrs.	225	.203	.259	359	73	12	1	2	0.6	37	20	10	49	8	6	1	176	307	23	65	2.2	.955	SS-110, 3B-84, 2B-25, DH-3, 1B-1

Dick Schofield

SCHOFIELD, RICHARD CRAIG
Son of Dick Schofield.
B. Nov. 21, 1962, Springfield, Ill.

BR TR 5'10" 175 lbs.

Year Team	Games	BA	SA	AB	H	2B	3B	HR	HR%	R	RBI	BB	SO	SB	PH AB	PH H	PO	A	E	DP	TC/G	FA	G by Pos
1983 CAL A	21	.204	.407	54	11	2	0	3	5.6	4	4	6	8	0	0	0	24	67	7	10	4.7	.929	SS-21
1984	140	.193	.263	400	77	10	3	4	1.0	39	21	33	79	4	0	0	218	420	12	95	4.6	.982	SS-140
1985	147	.219	.331	438	96	19	3	8	1.8	50	41	35	70	11	1	0	261	397	25	108	4.6	.963	SS-147
1986	139	.249	.397	458	114	17	6	13	2.8	67	57	48	55	23	0	0	246	389	18	103	4.7	.972	SS-137
1987	134	.251	.355	479	120	17	3	9	1.9	52	46	37	63	19	0	0	205	351	9	76	4.2	.984	SS-131, 2B-2, DH-1
1988	155	.239	.317	527	126	11	6	6	1.1	61	34	40	57	20	0	0	278	492	13	125	5.1	.983	SS-155
1989	91	.228	.318	302	69	11	2	4	1.3	42	26	28	47	9	1	1	118	276	7	56	4.4	.983	SS-90
1990	99	.255	.297	310	79	8	1	1	0.3	41	18	52	61	3	0	0	170	318	17	77	5.1	.966	SS-99
1991	134	.225	.260	427	96	9	3	0	0.0	44	31	50	69	8	3	0	186	398	15	83	4.5	.975	SS-133
1992 2 teams		CAL A	(1G – .333)	NY N	(142G – .205)																		
" total	143	.206	.286	423	87	18	2	4	0.9	52	36	61	82	11	0	0	208	392	7	78	4.2	.988	SS-142
1993 TOR A	36	.191	.236	110	21	1	2	0	0.0	11	5	16	25	3	0	0	61	106	4	23	4.8	.977	SS-36
1994	95	.255	.342	325	83	14	1	4	1.2	38	32	34	62	7	0	0	150	235	11	58	4.2	.972	SS-95
12 yrs.	1334	.230	.317	4253	979	137	32	56	1.3	501	351	440	678	118	5	1	2125	3841	145	892	4.6	.976	SS-1326, 2B-2, DH-1

LEAGUE CHAMPIONSHIP SERIES

Year Team	Games	BA	SA	AB	H	2B	3B	HR	HR%	R	RBI	BB	SO	SB	PH AB	PH H	PO	A	E	DP	TC/G	FA	G by Pos
1986 CAL A	7	.300	.433	30	9	1	0	1	3.3	4	2	1	5	1	1	0	12	23	2	3	5.3	.946	SS-7

David Segui

SEGUI, DAVID VINCENT
Son of Diego Segui.
B. June 19, 1966, Kansas City, Kans.

BB TL 6'1" 170 lbs.

Year Team	Games	BA	SA	AB	H	2B	3B	HR	HR%	R	RBI	BB	SO	SB	PH AB	PH H	PO	A	E	DP	TC/G	FA	G by Pos
1990 BAL A	40	.244	.350	123	30	7	0	2	1.6	14	15	11	15	0	0	0	283	26	3	24	7.8	.990	1B-36, DH-4
1991	86	.278	.340	212	59	7	0	2	0.9	15	22	12	19	1	24	6	264	23	3	22	3.4	.990	1B-42, OF-33, DH-4
1992	115	.233	.296	189	44	9	0	1	0.5	21	17	20	23	1	11	4	406	35	1	42	3.8	.998	1B-95, OF-18
1993	146	.273	.400	450	123	27	0	10	2.2	54	60	58	53	2	2	0	1152	98	5	122	8.6	.996	1B-144, DH-1
1994 NY N	92	.241	.387	336	81	17	1	10	3.0	46	43	33	43	0	1	0	696	52	5	65	8.2	.993	1B-78, OF-21
5 yrs.	479	.257	.367	1310	337	67	1	25	1.9	150	157	134	153	4	38	10	2801	234	17	275	6.4	.994	1B-395, OF-72, DH-9

Kevin Seitzer

SEITZER, KEVIN LEE
B. Mar. 26, 1962, Springfield, Ill.

BR TR 5'11" 180 lbs.

Year Team	Games	BA	SA	AB	H	2B	3B	HR	HR%	R	RBI	BB	SO	SB	PH AB	PH H	PO	A	E	DP	TC/G	FA	G by Pos
1986 KC A	28	.323	.448	96	31	4	1	2	2.1	16	11	19	14	0	1	1	224	19	3	17	8.8	.988	1B-22, OF-5, 3B-3
1987	161	.323	.470	641	**207**	33	8	15	2.3	105	83	80	85	12	0	0	290	315	24	51	3.9	.962	3B-141, 1B-25, OF-3
1988	149	.304	.406	559	170	32	5	5	0.9	90	60	72	64	10	1	0	93	297	26	33	2.8	.938	3B-147, 1B-1, OF-1
1989	160	.281	.337	597	168	17	2	4	0.7	78	48	102	76	17	0	0	118	277	20	30	2.6	.952	3B-159, SS-6, OF-3, 1B-2
1990	158	.275	.370	622	171	31	5	6	1.0	91	38	67	66	7	5	3	118	281	19	36	2.6	.955	3B-152, 2B-10
1991	85	.265	.350	234	62	11	3	1	0.4	28	25	29	21	4	20	11	45	127	11	8	2.2	.940	3B-68, DH-3
1992 MIL A	148	.270	.367	540	146	35	1	5	0.9	74	71	57	44	13	0	0	102	277	12	18	2.6	.969	3B-146, 2B-2, 1B-1
1993 2 teams		OAK A	(73G – .255)	MIL A	(47G – .290)																		
" total	120	.269	.396	417	112	16	2	11	2.6	45	57	44	48	7	13	2	275	152	12	43	3.7	.973	3B-79, 1B-31, DH-6, OF-4, 2B-3, P-1, SS-1
1994 MIL A	80	.314	.453	309	97	24	2	5	1.6	44	49	30	38	2	1	1	329	104	11	51	5.6	.975	1B-43, 1B-35, DH-4
9 yrs.	1089	.290	.395	4015	1164	203	29	54	1.3	571	442	500	456	72	41	18	1594	1849	138	287	3.3	.961	3B-938, 1B-116, OF-16, 2B-15, DH-14, SS-7, P-1

Scott Servais

SERVAIS, SCOTT DANIEL
B. June 14, 1967, LaCrosse, Wis.

BR TR 6'2" 195 lbs.

Year Team	Games	BA	SA	AB	H	2B	3B	HR	HR%	R	RBI	BB	SO	SB	PH AB	PH H	PO	A	E	DP	TC/G	FA	G by Pos
1991 HOU N	16	.162	.243	37	6	3	0	0	0.0	0	6	4	8	0	2	0	77	4	1	0	5.1	.988	C-14
1992	77	.239	.283	205	49	9	0	0	0.0	12	15	11	25	0	7	1	386	27	2	5	5.4	.995	C-73
1993	85	.244	.415	258	63	11	0	11	4.3	24	32	22	45	0	5	0	493	40	2	9	6.3	.996	C-82
1994	78	.195	.371	251	49	15	1	9	3.6	27	41	10	44	0	0	0	481	29	2	1	6.6	.996	C-78
4 yrs.	256	.222	.356	751	167	38	1	20	2.7	63	94	47	122	0	14	1	1437	100	7	15	6.0	.995	C-247

Danny Sheaffer

SHEAFFER, DANNY TODD
B. Aug. 2, 1961, Jacksonville, Fla.

BR TR 6' 185 lbs.

Year Team	Games	BA	SA	AB	H	2B	3B	HR	HR%	R	RBI	BB	SO	SB	PH AB	PH H	PO	A	E	DP	TC/G	FA	G by Pos
1987 BOS A	25	.121	.182	66	8	1	0	1	1.5	5	5	0	14	0	1	1	121	5	3	1	5.2	.977	C-25
1989 CLE A	7	.063	.063	16	1	0	0	0	0.0	1	0	2	2	0	1	0	4	0	0	0	0.6	1.000	DH-3, 3B-2, OF-1
1993 CLR N	82	.278	.384	216	60	9	1	4	1.9	26	32	8	15	2	7	2	337	32	2	6	4.5	.995	C-65, 1B-7, OF-2, 3B-1
1994	44	.218	.282	110	24	4	0	1	0.9	11	12	10	11	0	11	3	181	17	1	3	4.5	.995	C-30, 1B-2, OF-1
4 yrs.	158	.228	.311	408	93	14	1	6	1.5	43	49	20	42	2	20	6	643	54	6	10	4.4	.991	C-120, 1B-9, OF-4, DH-3, 3B-3

Gary Sheffield

SHEFFIELD, GARY ANTONIAN
B. Nov. 18, 1968, Tampa, Fla.

BR TR 5'11" 190 lbs.

Year Team	Games	BA	SA	AB	H	2B	3B	HR	HR%	R	RBI	BB	SO	SB	PH AB	PH H	PO	A	E	DP	TC/G	FA	G by Pos
1988 MIL A	24	.238	.400	80	19	1	0	4	5.0	12	12	7	7	3	0	0	39	48	3	9	3.8	.967	SS-24
1989	95	.247	.337	368	91	18	0	5	1.4	34	32	27	33	10	0	0	100	238	16	44	3.7	.955	SS-70, 3B-21, DH-4
1990	125	.294	.421	487	143	30	1	10	2.1	67	67	44	41	25	0	0	98	254	25	16	3.0	.934	3B-125
1991	50	.194	.320	175	34	12	2	2	1.1	25	22	19	15	5	0	0	29	65	8	7	2.0	.922	3B-43, DH-5
1992 SD N	146	**.330**	.580	557	184	34	3	33	5.9	87	100	48	40	5	2	1	99	299	16	25	2.8	.961	3B-144
1993 2 teams		SD N	(68G – .295)	FLA N	(72G – .292)																		
" total	140	.294	.476	494	145	20	5	20	4.0	67	73	47	64	17	1	1	79	225	34	15	2.4	.899	3B-133

Year Team	Games	BA	SA	AB	H	2B	3B	HR	HR%	R	RBI	BB	SO	SB	Pinch Hit AB	Pinch Hit H	PO	A	E	DP	TC/G	FA	G by Pos

Gary Sheffield *continued*

Year Team	Games	BA	SA	AB	H	2B	3B	HR	HR%	R	RBI	BB	SO	SB	AB	H	PO	A	E	DP	TC/G	FA	G by Pos
1994 FLA N	87	.276	.584	322	89	16	1	27	8.4	61	78	51	50	12	1	1	153	7	5	2	1.9	.970	OF-87
7 yrs.	667	.284	.468	2483	705	131	12	101	4.1	353	384	243	250	77	7	3	597	1136	107	118	2.8	.942	3B-466, SS-94, OF-87, DH-9

Craig Shipley

SHIPLEY, CRAIG BARRY
B. Jan. 7, 1963, Parramatta, Australia.

BR TR 6'1" 175 lbs.

Year Team	Games	BA	SA	AB	H	2B	3B	HR	HR%	R	RBI	BB	SO	SB	AB	H	PO	A	E	DP	TC/G	FA	G by Pos
1986 LA N	12	.111	.148	27	3	1	0	0	0.0	3	4	2	5	0	0	0	16	18	3	4	3.1	.919	SS-10, 2B-1, 3B-1
1987	26	.257	.286	35	9	1	0	0	0.0	3	2	0	6	0	2	0	15	28	3	2	1.8	.935	SS-18, 3B-6
1989 NY N	4	.143	.143	7	1	0	0	0	0.0	3	0	0	1	0	0	0	0	4	0	0	1.0	1.000	SS-3, 3B-2
1991 SD N	37	.275	.341	91	25	3	0	1	1.1	6	6	2	14	0	4	0	39	70	7	14	3.1	.940	SS-19, 2B-14
1992	52	.248	.305	105	26	6	0	0	0.0	7	7	2	21	1	14	6	52	74	1	18	2.4	.992	SS-23, 2B-11, 3B-8
1993	105	.235	.326	230	54	9	0	4	1.7	25	22	10	31	12	28	6	84	121	7	15	2.0	.967	SS-38, 3B-37, 2B-12, OF-5
1994	81	.333	.475	240	80	14	4	4	1.7	32	30	9	28	6	13	6	65	108	9	12	2.2	.951	3B-53, SS-14, 2B-13, OF-2, 1B-1
7 yrs.	317	.269	.363	735	198	34	4	9	1.2	79	71	25	106	19	61	18	271	423	30	65	2.3	.959	SS-125, 3B-107, 2B-51, OF-7, 1B-1

Terry Shumpert

SHUMPERT, TERRANCE DARNELL
B. Aug. 16, 1966, Paducah, Ky.

BR TR 5'11" 190 lbs.

Year Team	Games	BA	SA	AB	H	2B	3B	HR	HR%	R	RBI	BB	SO	SB	AB	H	PO	A	E	DP	TC/G	FA	G by Pos
1990 KC A	32	.275	.363	91	25	6	1	0	0.0	7	8	2	17	3	0	0	56	74	3	15	4.2	.977	2B-27, DH-3
1991	144	.217	.322	369	80	16	4	5	1.4	45	34	30	75	17	0	0	249	368	16	81	4.4	.975	2B-144
1992	36	.149	.255	94	14	5	1	1	1.1	6	11	3	17	2	0	0	50	77	4	17	3.6	.969	2B-33, DH-1, SS-1
1993	8	.100	.100	10	1	0	0	0	0.0	0	0	2	2	1	0	0	11	11	0	3	2.8	1.000	2B-8
1994	64	.240	.426	183	44	6	2	8	4.4	28	24	13	39	18	1	0	69	129	8	16	3.2	.961	2B-38, 3B-24, DH-2, SS-1
5 yrs.	284	.220	.341	747	164	33	8	14	1.9	86	77	50	150	41	1	0	435	659	31	132	4.0	.972	2B-250, 3B-24, DH-6, SS-2

Ruben Sierra

SIERRA, RUBEN ANGEL
Born Ruben Angel Sierra (Garcia).
B. Oct. 6, 1965, Rio Piedras, Puerto Rico.

BB TR 6'1" 175 lbs.

Year Team	Games	BA	SA	AB	H	2B	3B	HR	HR%	R	RBI	BB	SO	SB	AB	H	PO	A	E	DP	TC/G	FA	G by Pos
1986 TEX A	113	.264	.476	382	101	13	10	16	4.2	50	55	22	65	7	6	1	200	7	6	1	1.9	.972	OF-107, DH-3
1987	158	.263	.470	643	169	35	4	30	4.7	97	109	39	114	16	2	0	272	17	11	6	1.9	.963	OF-157
1988	156	.254	.424	615	156	32	2	23	3.7	77	91	44	91	18	3	1	310	11	7	3	2.1	.979	OF-153, DH-1
1989	162	.306	.543	634	194	35	14	29	4.6	101	119	43	82	8	0	0	313	13	9	2	2.1	.973	OF-162
1990	159	.280	.426	608	170	37	2	16	2.6	70	96	49	86	9	2	1	283	7	10	1	1.9	.967	OF-151, DH-7
1991	161	.307	.502	661	203	44	5	25	3.8	110	116	56	91	16	1	1	305	15	7	3	2.0	.979	OF-161
1992 2 teams	TEX A (124G – .278)						OAK A	(27G – .277)															
" total	151	.278	.443	601	167	34	7	17	2.8	83	87	45	68	14	1	0	283	6	7	0	2.0	.976	OF-144, DH-6
1993 OAK A	158	.233	.390	630	147	23	5	22	3.5	77	101	52	97	25	2	0	291	9	7	3	1.9	.977	OF-133, DH-25
1994	110	.268	.484	426	114	21	1	23	5.4	71	92	23	64	8	3	2	155	8	9	2	1.6	.948	OF-98, DH-10
9 yrs.	1328	.273	.461	5200	1421	274	50	201	3.9	736	866	373	758	121	22	7	2412	93	73	21	1.9	.972	OF-1266, DH-52

LEAGUE CHAMPIONSHIP SERIES

Year Team	Games	BA	SA	AB	H	2B	3B	HR	HR%	R	RBI	BB	SO	SB	AB	H	PO	A	E	DP	TC/G	FA	G by Pos
1992 OAK A	6	.333	.625	24	8	2	1	1	4.2	4	7	2	1	1	0	0	12	0	0	0	2.0	1.000	OF-6

Dave Silvestri

SILVESTRI, DAVID JOSEPH
B. Sept. 29, 1967, St. Louis, Mo.

BR TR 6' 180 lbs.

Year Team	Games	BA	SA	AB	H	2B	3B	HR	HR%	R	RBI	BB	SO	SB	AB	H	PO	A	E	DP	TC/G	FA	G by Pos
1992 NY A	7	.308	.615	13	4	0	2	0	0.0	3	1	0	3	0	1	0	3	12	2	3	2.4	.882	SS-6
1993	7	.286	.476	21	6	1	0	1	4.8	4	4	5	3	0	0	0	9	20	3	4	4.6	.906	SS-4, 3B-3
1994	12	.111	.389	18	2	0	1	1	5.6	3	2	4	9	0	1	0	14	16	1	3	2.6	.968	2B-9, 3B-2, SS-1
3 yrs.	26	.231	.481	52	12	1	3	2	3.8	10	7	9	15	0	2	0	26	48	6	10	3.1	.925	SS-11, 2B-9, 3B-5

Mike Simms

SIMMS, MICHAEL HOWARD
B. Jan. 12, 1967, Orange, Calif.

BR TR 6'4" 185 lbs.

Year Team	Games	BA	SA	AB	H	2B	3B	HR	HR%	R	RBI	BB	SO	SB	AB	H	PO	A	E	DP	TC/G	FA	G by Pos
1990 HOU N	12	.308	.615	13	4	1	0	1	7.7	3	2	0	4	0	5	0	20	1	0	2	1.8	1.000	1B-6
1991	49	.203	.317	123	25	5	0	3	2.4	18	16	18	38	1	8	1	44	4	6	0	1.1	.889	OF-41
1992	15	.250	.417	24	6	1	0	1	4.2	1	3	2	9	0	6	1	10	2	1	0	0.8	.990	OF-9, 1B-1
1994	6	.083	.167	12	1	1	0	0	0.0	1	0	0	5	1	2	0	6	0	1	0	1.2	.857	OF-3
4 yrs.	82	.209	.343	172	36	8	0	5	2.9	23	21	20	56	2	21	2	80	7	7	2	1.1	.926	OF-53, 1B-7

Duane Singleton

SINGLETON, DUANE EARL
B. Aug. 6, 1972, Staten Island, N. Y.

BL TR 6'1" 170 lbs.

Year Team	Games	BA	SA	AB	H	2B	3B	HR	HR%	R	RBI	BB	SO	SB	AB	H	PO	A	E	DP	TC/G	FA	G by Pos
1994 MIL A	2	–	–	0	0	0	0	0	–	0	0	0	0	0	0	0	1	0	0	0	0.5	1.000	OF-2

Don Slaught

SLAUGHT, DONALD MARTIN (Sluggo)
B. Sept. 11, 1958, Long Beach, Calif.

BR TR 6'1" 190 lbs.

Year Team	Games	BA	SA	AB	H	2B	3B	HR	HR%	R	RBI	BB	SO	SB	AB	H	PO	A	E	DP	TC/G	FA	G by Pos
1982 KC A	43	.278	.409	115	32	6	0	3	2.6	14	8	9	12	0	0	0	156	7	1	1	3.8	.994	C-43
1983	83	.312	.388	276	86	13	4	0	0.0	21	28	11	27	3	5	2	299	18	12	7	4.0	.964	C-79, DH-1
1984	124	.264	.379	409	108	27	4	4	1.0	48	42	20	55	0	5	2	547	44	11	8	4.9	.982	C-123, DH-1
1985 TEX A	102	.280	.423	343	96	17	4	8	2.3	34	35	20	41	5	1	0	550	33	6	4	5.8	.990	C-102
1986	95	.264	.449	314	83	17	1	13	4.1	39	46	16	59	3	3	3	533	40	4	1	6.1	.993	C-91, DH-2
1987	95	.224	.405	237	53	15	2	8	3.4	25	16	24	51	0	22	6	429	39	7	5	5.0	.985	C-85, DH-5
1988 NY A	97	.283	.450	322	91	25	1	9	2.8	33	43	24	54	1	6	2	496	24	11	4	5.5	.979	C-94, DH-1
1989	117	.251	.371	350	88	21	3	5	1.4	34	38	30	57	1	12	3	493	44	5	8	4.6	.991	C-105, DH-3
1990 PIT N	84	.300	.457	230	69	18	3	4	1.7	27	29	27	27	0	16	5	345	36	8	4	4.6	.979	C-78
1991	77	.295	.395	220	65	17	1	1	0.5	19	29	21	32	1	13	2	338	31	5	4	4.9	.987	C-69, 3B-1
1992	87	.345	.482	255	88	17	3	4	1.6	26	37	17	23	2	14	4	365	35	5	4	4.7	.988	C-79
1993	116	.300	.440	377	113	19	2	10	2.7	34	55	29	56	2	13	6	540	50	4	10	5.1	.993	C-105
1994	76	.288	.342	240	69	7	0	2	0.8	21	21	34	31	0	2	0	425	36	3	4	6.1	.994	C-74
13 yrs.	1196	.282	.415	3688	1041	219	28	71	1.9	375	427	282	525	18	112	34	5516	437	82	64	5.0	.986	C-1127, DH-13, 3B-1

Year Team	Games	BA	SA	AB	H	2B	3B	HR	HR%	R	RBI	BB	SO	SB	Pinch Hit AB	Pinch Hit H	PO	A	E	DP	TC/G	FA	G by Pos

Don Slaught *continued*

LEAGUE CHAMPIONSHIP SERIES

Year Team	Games	BA	SA	AB	H	2B	3B	HR	HR%	R	RBI	BB	SO	SB	AB	H	PO	A	E	DP	TC/G	FA	G by Pos
1984 KC A	3	.364	.364	11	4	0	0	0	0.0	0	0	0	0	0	0	0	17	0	3	0	6.7	.850	C-3
1990 PIT N	4	.091	.182	11	1	1	0	0	0.0	0	1	2	3	0	0	0	22	1	1	0	6.0	.958	C-4
1991	6	.235	.235	17	4	0	0	0	0.0	0	1	1	4	0	1	1	30	5	0	1	5.8	1.000	C-6
1992	5	.333	.667	12	4	1	0	1	8.3	5	5	6	3	0	1	0	17	1	0	0	3.6	1.000	C-5
4 yrs.	18	.255	.353	51	13	2	0	1	2.0	5	7	9	10	0	2	1	86	7	4	1	5.4	.959	C-18

Dwight Smith

SMITH, JOHN DWIGHT
B. Nov. 8, 1963, Tallahassee, Fla.

BL TR 5'11" 175 lbs.

Year Team	Games	BA	SA	AB	H	2B	3B	HR	HR%	R	RBI	BB	SO	SB	AB	H	PO	A	E	DP	TC/G	FA	G by Pos
1989 CHI N	109	.324	.493	343	111	19	6	9	2.6	52	52	31	51	9	15	8	188	7	5	3	1.8	.975	OF-102
1990	117	.262	.376	290	76	15	0	6	2.1	34	27	28	46	11	34	8	139	4	2	2	1.2	.986	OF-81
1991	90	.228	.347	167	38	7	2	3	1.8	16	21	11	32	2	45	11	73	3	3	1	0.9	.962	OF-42
1992	109	.276	.392	217	60	10	3	3	1.4	28	24	13	40	9	49	14	92	2	2	0	0.9	.979	OF-63
1993	111	.300	.494	310	93	17	5	11	3.5	51	35	25	51	8	24	9	163	5	8	1	1.6	.955	OF-89
1994 2 teams	CAL A	(45G – .262)		BAL A	(28G – .311)																		
" total	73	.281	.459	196	55	7	2	8	4.1	31	30	12	37	2	19	5	81	2	7	1	1.2	.922	OF-53, DH-5
6 yrs.	609	.284	.436	1523	433	75	18	40	2.6	212	189	120	257	41	186	55	736	23	27	8	1.3	.966	OF-430, DH-5

LEAGUE CHAMPIONSHIP SERIES

Year Team	Games	BA	SA	AB	H	2B	3B	HR	HR%	R	RBI	BB	SO	SB	AB	H	PO	A	E	DP	TC/G	FA	G by Pos
1989 CHI N	4	.200	.267	15	3	1	0	0	0.0	0	2	0	2	1	0	0	10	0	0	0	2.5	1.000	OF-4

Lonnie Smith

SMITH, LONNIE
B. Dec. 22, 1955, Chicago, Ill.

BR TR 5'9" 170 lbs.

Year Team	Games	BA	SA	AB	H	2B	3B	HR	HR%	R	RBI	BB	SO	SB	AB	H	PO	A	E	DP	TC/G	FA	G by Pos
1978 PHI N	17	.000	.000	4	0	0	0	0	0.0	6	0	4	3	4	1	0	5	1	0	0	0.4	1.000	OF-11
1979	17	.167	.233	30	5	2	0	0	0.0	4	3	1	7	2	4	0	19	1	0	0	1.2	1.000	OF-11
1980	100	.339	.443	298	101	14	4	3	1.0	69	20	26	48	33	8	2	121	2	4	0	1.3	.969	OF-82
1981	62	.324	.472	176	57	14	3	2	1.1	40	11	18	14	21	5	3	89	10	3	2	1.6	.971	OF-51
1982 STL N	156	.307	.434	592	182	35	8	8	1.4	120	69	64	74	68	9	1	303	16	10	3	2.1	.970	OF-149
1983	130	.321	.453	492	158	31	5	8	1.6	83	45	41	55	43	5	1	225	14	15	4	2.0	.941	OF-126
1984	145	.250	.341	504	126	20	4	6	1.2	77	49	70	90	50	3	1	184	18	11	0	1.5	.948	OF-140
1985 2 teams	STL N	(28G – .260)		KC A	(120G – .257)																		
" total	148	.257	.358	544	140	25	6	6	1.1	92	48	56	89	52	2	0	238	11	9	4	1.7	.965	OF-147
1986 KC A	134	.287	.411	508	146	25	7	8	1.6	80	44	46	78	26	4	2	245	5	9	1	1.9	.965	OF-118, DH-10
1987	48	.251	.359	167	42	7	1	3	1.8	26	8	24	31	9	1	0	52	2	5	0	1.2	.915	OF-32, DH-15
1988 ATL N	43	.237	.342	114	27	3	0	3	2.6	14	9	10	25	4	14	3	59	2	2	0	1.5	.968	OF-35
1989	134	.315	.533	482	152	34	4	21	4.4	89	79	76	95	25	3	0	289	3	2	0	2.2	.993	OF-132
1990	135	.305	.459	466	142	27	9	9	1.9	72	42	58	69	10	19	5	254	6	12	2	2.0	.956	OF-122
1991	122	.275	.394	353	97	19	1	7	2.0	58	44	50	64	9	22	4	134	5	5	2	1.2	.965	OF-99
1992	84	.247	.437	158	39	8	2	6	3.8	23	33	17	37	4	43	8	60	2	3	0	0.8	.954	OF-35
1993 2 teams	PIT N	(94G – .286)		BAL A	(9G – .208)																		
" total	103	.278	.448	223	62	6	4	8	3.6	43	27	51	52	9	31	8	109	2	2	0	1.1	.982	OF-64, DH-5
1994 BAL A	35	.203	.254	59	12	3	0	0	0.0	13	2	11	18	1	6	0	2	1	0	0	0.1	1.000	DH-30, OF-2
17 yrs.	1613	.288	.420	5170	1488	273	58	98	1.9	909	533	623	849	370	180	39	2388	101	92	18	1.6	.964	OF-1356, DH-60

DIVISIONAL PLAYOFF SERIES

Year Team	Games	BA	SA	AB	H	2B	3B	HR	HR%	R	RBI	BB	SO	SB	AB	H	PO	A	E	DP	TC/G	FA	G by Pos
1981 PHI N	5	.263	.316	19	5	1	0	0	0.0	1	0	0	4	1	0	0	6	1	0	0	1.4	1.000	OF-5

LEAGUE CHAMPIONSHIP SERIES

Year Team	Games	BA	SA	AB	H	2B	3B	HR	HR%	R	RBI	BB	SO	SB	AB	H	PO	A	E	DP	TC/G	FA	G by Pos
1980 PHI N	3	.600	.600	5	3	0	0	0	0.0	2	0	0	0	1	0	0	2	1	0	1	1.0	1.000	OF-2
1982 STL N	3	.273	.273	11	3	0	0	0	0.0	1	1	0	1	1	0	0	2	0	0	0	0.7	1.000	OF-3
1985 KC A	7	.250	.321	28	7	2	0	0	0.0	2	1	3	6	1	0	0	8	3	1	0	1.7	.917	OF-7
1991 ATL N	7	.250	.375	24	6	3	0	0	0.0	3	0	4	5	1	0	0	10	2	0	1	1.7	1.000	OF-7
1992	6	.333	.667	6	2	0	1	0	0.0	1	1	0	0	0	6	2	0	0	0	0	0.0	–	
5 yrs.	26	.284	.378	74	21	5	1	0	0.0	9	3	7	12	3	6	2	22	6	1	2	1.1	.966	OF-19

WORLD SERIES

Year Team	Games	BA	SA	AB	H	2B	3B	HR	HR%	R	RBI	BB	SO	SB	AB	H	PO	A	E	DP	TC/G	FA	G by Pos
1980 PHI N	6	.263	.316	19	5	1	0	0	0.0	2	1	1	1	0	0	0	4	1	0	0	0.8	1.000	OF-4, DH-1
1982 STL N	7	.321	.536	28	9	4	1	0	0.0	6	1	1	5	2	0	0	11	0	0	0	1.6	1.000	OF-6, DH-1
1985 KC A	7	.333	.444	27	9	3	0	0	0.0	4	4	3	8	2	0	0	7	2	0	0	1.3	1.000	OF-7
1991 ATL N	7	.231	.577	26	6	0	0	3	11.5	5	3	3	4	1	0	0	2	0	0	0	0.3	1.000	DH-4, OF-3
1992	5	.167	.417	12	2	0	1	1	8.3	1	5	1	4	0	0	0	0	0	0	0	0.0	–	DH-3
5 yrs.	32	.277	.473	112	31	8	1	4	3.6	18	14	9	22	5	0	0	24	3	0	0	0.8	1.000	OF-20, DH-9
							6th																	

Mark Smith

SMITH, MARK EDWARD
B. May 7, 1970, Pasadena, Calif.

BR TR 6'3" 205 lbs.

Year Team	Games	BA	SA	AB	H	2B	3B	HR	HR%	R	RBI	BB	SO	SB	AB	H	PO	A	E	DP	TC/G	FA	G by Pos
1994 BAL A	3	.143	.143	7	1	0	0	0	0.0	0	2	0	2	0	0	0	8	0	0	0	2.7	1.000	OF-3

Ozzie Smith

SMITH, OSBORNE EARL (The Wizard)
B. Dec. 26, 1954, Mobile, Ala.

BB TR 5'11" 150 lbs.

Year Team	Games	BA	SA	AB	H	2B	3B	HR	HR%	R	RBI	BB	SO	SB	AB	H	PO	A	E	DP	TC/G	FA	G by Pos
1978 SD N	159	.258	.312	590	152	17	6	1	0.2	69	46	47	43	40	1	0	264	548	25	98	5.3	.970	SS-159
1979	156	.211	.262	587	124	18	6	0	0.0	77	27	37	37	28	0	0	256	555	20	86	5.3	.976	SS-155
1980	158	.230	.276	609	140	18	5	0	0.0	67	35	71	49	57	0	0	288	621	24	113	5.9	.974	SS-158
1981	110	.222	.256	450	100	11	2	0	0.0	53	21	41	37	22	0	0	220	422	16	72	6.0	.976	SS-110
1982 STL N	140	.248	.314	488	121	24	1	2	0.4	58	43	68	32	25	1	0	279	535	13	101	5.9	.984	SS-139
1983	159	.243	.335	552	134	30	6	3	0.5	69	50	64	36	34	2	0	304	519	21	100	5.3	.975	SS-158
1984	124	.257	.337	412	106	20	5	1	0.2	53	44	56	17	35	0	0	233	437	12	94	5.5	.982	SS-124
1985	158	.276	.361	537	148	22	3	6	1.1	70	54	65	27	31	2	0	264	549	14	111	5.2	.983	SS-158
1986	153	.280	.333	514	144	19	4	0	0.0	67	54	79	27	31	8	2	229	453	15	96	4.6	.978	SS-144
1987	158	.303	.383	600	182	40	4	0	0.0	104	75	89	36	43	2	1	245	516	10	111	4.9	.987	SS-158
1988	153	.270	.336	575	155	27	1	3	0.5	80	51	74	43	57	2	0	234	519	22	79	5.1	.972	SS-150
1989	155	.273	.361	593	162	30	8	2	0.3	82	50	55	37	29	2	1	209	483	17	73	4.6	.976	SS-153
1990	143	.254	.305	512	130	21	1	1	0.2	61	50	61	33	32	2	0	212	378	12	66	4.2	.980	SS-140
1991	150	.285	.367	550	157	30	3	3	0.5	96	50	83	36	35	0	0	244	387	8	79	4.3	.987	SS-150
1992	132	.295	.342	518	153	20	2	0	0.0	73	31	59	34	43	0	0	232	420	10	82	5.0	.985	SS-132

Year Team	Games	BA	SA	AB	H	2B	3B	HR	HR%	R	RBI	BB	SO	SB	Pinch Hit AB	Pinch Hit H	PO	A	E	DP	TC/G	FA	G by Pos

Ozzie Smith *continued*

Year Team	Games	BA	SA	AB	H	2B	3B	HR	HR%	R	RBI	BB	SO	SB	AB	H	PO	A	E	DP	TC/G	FA	G by Pos
1993	141	.288	.356	545	157	22	6	1	0.2	75	53	43	18	21	5	0	251	451	19	98	5.1	.974	SS-134
1994	98	.262	.349	381	100	18	3	3	0.8	51	30	38	26	6	2	0	136	292	8	65	4.4	.982	SS-96
17 yrs.	2447	.262	.329	9013	2365	387	66	26	0.3	1205	764	1030	568	569	27	4	4100	8085	266	1524	5.1	.979	SS-2418

LEAGUE CHAMPIONSHIP SERIES

Year Team	Games	BA	SA	AB	H	2B	3B	HR	HR%	R	RBI	BB	SO	SB	AB	H	PO	A	E	DP	TC/G	FA	G by Pos
1982 STL N	3	.556	.556	9	5	0	0	0	0.0	0	3	3	0	1	0	0	4	11	0	1	5.0	1.000	SS-3
1985	6	.435	.696	23	10	1	1	1	4.3	4	3	3	1	1	0	0	6	16	0	2	3.7	1.000	SS-6
1987	7	.200	.280	25	5	0	1	0	0.0	2	1	3	4	0	0	0	10	19	1	4	4.3	.967	SS-7
3 yrs.	16	.351	.491	57	20	1	2	1	1.8	6	7	9	5	2	0	0	20	46	1	7	4.2	.985	SS-16

WORLD SERIES

Year Team	Games	BA	SA	AB	H	2B	3B	HR	HR%	R	RBI	BB	SO	SB	AB	H	PO	A	E	DP	TC/G	FA	G by Pos
1982 STL N	7	.208	.208	24	5	0	0	0	0.0	3	1	3	0	1	0	0	22	17	0	5	5.6	1.000	SS-7
1985	7	.087	.087	23	2	0	0	0	0.0	1	0	4	0	1	0	0	10	16	1	5	3.9	.963	SS-7
1987	7	.214	.214	28	6	0	0	0	0.0	3	2	2	3	2	0	0	7	19	0	1	3.7	1.000	SS-7
3 yrs.	21	.173	.173	75	13	0	0	0	0.0	7	3	9	3	4	0	0	39	52	1	11	4.4	.989	SS-21

J. T. Snow

SNOW, JACK THOMAS
B. Feb. 26, 1968, Long Beach, Calif.

BB TL 6'2" 200 lbs.

Year Team	Games	BA	SA	AB	H	2B	3B	HR	HR%	R	RBI	BB	SO	SB	AB	H	PO	A	E	DP	TC/G	FA	G by Pos
1992 NY A	7	.143	.214	14	2	1	0	0	0.0	1	2	5	5	0	0	0	43	2	0	7	6.4	1.000	1B-6, DH-1
1993 CAL A	129	.241	.408	419	101	18	2	16	3.8	60	57	55	88	3	2	0	1010	81	6	103	8.5	.995	1B-129
1994	61	.220	.345	223	49	4	0	8	3.6	22	30	19	48	0	0	0	489	37	2	56	8.7	.996	1B-61
3 yrs.	197	.232	.383	656	152	23	2	24	3.7	83	89	79	141	3	2	0	1542	120	8	166	8.5	.995	1B-196, DH-1

Cory Snyder

SNYDER, JAMES CORY
B. Nov. 11, 1962, Inglewood, Calif.

BR TR 6'4" 175 lbs.

Year Team	Games	BA	SA	AB	H	2B	3B	HR	HR%	R	RBI	BB	SO	SB	AB	H	PO	A	E	DP	TC/G	FA	G by Pos
1986 CLE A	103	.272	.500	416	113	21	1	24	5.8	58	69	16	123	2	0	0	213	84	10	22	3.0	.967	OF-74, SS-34, 3B-11, DH-1
1987	157	.236	.456	577	136	24	1	33	5.7	74	82	31	166	5	7	2	313	53	15	9	2.4	.961	OF-139, SS-18
1988	142	.272	.483	511	139	24	3	26	5.1	71	75	42	101	5	1	0	314	16	5	0	2.4	.985	OF-141
1989	132	.215	.360	489	105	17	0	18	3.7	49	59	23	134	6	4	0	297	32	1	7	2.5	.997	OF-125, SS-7, DH-2
1990	123	.233	.404	438	102	27	3	14	3.2	46	55	21	118	1	4	1	229	18	7	4	2.1	.972	OF-120, SS-5
1991 2 teams		CHI A	(50G – .188)		TOR A	(21G – .143)																	
" total	71	.175	.265	166	29	4	1	3	1.8	14	17	9	60	0	15	2	195	17	3	10	3.0	.986	OF-43, 1B-22, 3B-3, DH-3
1992 SF N	124	.269	.444	390	105	22	2	14	3.6	48	57	23	96	4	15	2	301	53	6	18	2.9	.983	OF-70, 1B-27, 3B-14, 2B-4, SS-3
1993 LA N	143	.266	.397	516	137	33	1	11	2.1	61	56	47	**147**	4	5	1	210	46	9	8	1.9	.966	OF-115, 3B-23, 1B-12, SS-2
1994	73	.235	.392	153	36	6	0	6	3.9	18	18	14	47	1	20	4	92	23	7	9	1.7	.943	OF-50, 1B-9, 3B-6, SS-4, 2B-3
9 yrs.	1068	.247	.425	3656	902	178	13	149	4.1	439	488	226	992	28	75	12	2164	342	63	87	2.4	.975	OF-877, SS-73, 1B-70, 3B-57, 2B-7, DH-6

Luis Sojo

SOJO, LUIS BELTRAN
Born Luis Beltran Sojo (Sojo).
B. Jan. 3, 1966, Caracas, Venezuela.

BR TR 5'11" 172 lbs.

Year Team	Games	BA	SA	AB	H	2B	3B	HR	HR%	R	RBI	BB	SO	SB	AB	H	PO	A	E	DP	TC/G	FA	G by Pos
1990 TOR A	33	.225	.300	80	18	3	0	1	1.3	14	9	5	5	1	4	0	34	31	5	7	2.1	.929	2B-15, OF-5, SS-5, 3B-4, DH-3
1991 CAL A	113	.258	.327	364	94	14	1	3	0.8	38	20	14	26	4	0	0	233	335	11	78	5.1	.981	2B-107, SS-2, 3B-1, DH-1, OF-1
1992	106	.272	.378	368	100	12	3	7	1.9	37	43	14	24	7	4	1	196	292	9	73	4.7	.982	2B-96, 3B-9, SS-5
1993 TOR A	19	.170	.213	47	8	2	0	0	0.0	5	6	4	2	0	1	0	24	35	2	8	3.2	.967	2B-8, SS-8, 3B-3
1994 SEA A	63	.277	.423	213	59	9	2	6	2.8	32	22	8	25	2	1	1	97	186	7	36	4.6	.976	2B-40, SS-24, DH-2, 3B-1
5 yrs.	334	.260	.356	1072	279	40	6	17	1.6	126	100	45	82	14	11	2	584	879	34	202	4.5	.977	2B-266, SS-44, 3B-18, OF-6, DH-6

Paul Sorrento

SORRENTO, PAUL ANTHONY
B. Nov. 17, 1965, Somerville, Mass.

BL TR 6'2" 195 lbs.

Year Team	Games	BA	SA	AB	H	2B	3B	HR	HR%	R	RBI	BB	SO	SB	AB	H	PO	A	E	DP	TC/G	FA	G by Pos
1989 MIN A	14	.238	.238	21	5	0	0	0	0.0	2	1	5	4	0	3	0	13	0	0	1	0.9	1.000	1B-5, DH-5
1990	41	.207	.380	121	25	4	1	5	4.1	11	13	12	31	1	6	2	118	7	1	14	3.1	.992	DH-23, 1B-15
1991	26	.255	.553	47	12	2	0	4	8.5	6	13	4	11	0	12	3	70	7	0	7	3.0	1.000	1B-13, DH-2
1992 CLE A	140	.269	.443	458	123	24	1	18	3.9	52	60	51	89	0	14	2	996	78	8	108	7.7	.993	1B-121, DH-11
1993	148	.257	.434	463	119	26	1	18	3.9	75	65	58	121	3	13	3	1015	86	6	107	7.5	.995	1B-144, OF-3, DH-1
1994	95	.280	.453	322	90	14	0	14	4.3	43	62	34	68	0	8	2	798	58	4	79	9.1	.995	1B-86, DH-8
6 yrs.	464	.261	.438	1432	374	70	3	59	4.1	189	214	164	324	4	56	12	3010	236	19	316	7.0	.994	1B-384, DH-50, OF-3

LEAGUE CHAMPIONSHIP SERIES

Year Team	Games	BA	SA	AB	H	2B	3B	HR	HR%	R	RBI	BB	SO	SB	AB	H	PO	A	E	DP	TC/G	FA	G by Pos
1991 MIN A	1	.000	.000	1	0	0	0	0	0.0	0	0	0	1	0	1	0	0	0	0	0	0.0	–	

WORLD SERIES

Year Team	Games	BA	SA	AB	H	2B	3B	HR	HR%	R	RBI	BB	SO	SB	AB	H	PO	A	E	DP	TC/G	FA	G by Pos
1991 MIN A	3	.000	.000	2	0	0	0	0	0.0	0	0	1	2	0	2	0	1	1	0	1	0.7	1.000	1B-1

Sammy Sosa

SOSA, SAMUEL
Born Samuel Sosa (Peralta).
B. Nov. 10, 1968, San Pedro de Macoris, Dominican Republic.

BR TR 6' 165 lbs.

Year Team	Games	BA	SA	AB	H	2B	3B	HR	HR%	R	RBI	BB	SO	SB	AB	H	PO	A	E	DP	TC/G	FA	G by Pos
1989 2 teams		TEX A	(25G – .238)		CHI A	(33G – .273)																	
" total	58	.257	.366	183	47	8	0	4	2.2	27	13	11	47	7	4	0	94	2	4	0	1.7	.960	OF-52, DH-6
1990 CHI A	153	.233	.404	532	124	26	10	15	2.8	72	70	33	150	32	0	0	315	14	13	1	2.2	.962	OF-152
1991	116	.203	.335	316	64	10	1	10	3.2	39	33	14	98	13	7	2	214	6	6	0	1.9	.973	OF-111, DH-2
1992 CHI N	67	.260	.393	262	68	7	2	8	3.1	41	25	19	63	15	0	0	145	4	6	1	2.3	.961	OF-67
1993	159	.261	.485	598	156	25	5	33	5.5	92	93	38	135	36	2	1	344	17	9	4	2.3	.976	OF-158
1994	105	.300	.545	426	128	17	6	25	5.9	59	70	25	92	22	0	0	248	5	7	0	2.5	.973	OF-105
6 yrs.	658	.253	.437	2317	587	93	24	95	4.1	330	304	140	585	125	13	3	1360	48	45	6	2.2	.969	OF-645, DH-8

Year Team	Games	BA	SA	AB	H	2B	3B	HR	HR%	R	RBI	BB	SO	SB	Pinch Hit AB	Pinch Hit H	PO	A	E	DP	TC/G	FA	G by Pos

Tim Spehr

SPEHR, TIMOTHY JOSEPH
B. July 2, 1966, Excelsior Springs, Mo.
BR TR 6'2" 205 lbs.

Year Team	Games	BA	SA	AB	H	2B	3B	HR	HR%	R	RBI	BB	SO	SB	AB	H	PO	A	E	DP	TC/G	FA	G by Pos
1991 KC A	37	.189	.378	74	14	5	0	3	4.1	7	14	9	18	1	1	0	190	19	3	3	5.7	.986	C-37
1993 MON N	53	.230	.368	87	20	6	0	2	2.3	14	10	6	20	2	3	0	166	22	9	3	3.7	.954	C-49
1994	52	.250	.389	36	9	3	1	0	0.0	8	5	4	11	2	2	1	104	6	0	1	2.1	1.000	C-46, OF-2
3 yrs.	142	.218	.376	197	43	14	1	5	2.5	29	29	19	49	5	6	1	460	47	12	7	3.7	.977	C-132, OF-2

Bill Spiers

SPIERS, WILLIAM JAMES
B. June 5, 1966, Orangeburg, S. C.
BL TR 6'2" 190 lbs.

Year Team	Games	BA	SA	AB	H	2B	3B	HR	HR%	R	RBI	BB	SO	SB	AB	H	PO	A	E	DP	TC/G	FA	G by Pos
1989 MIL A	114	.255	.333	345	88	9	3	4	1.2	44	33	21	63	10	4	3	164	295	21	62	4.2	.956	SS-89, 3B-12, 2B-4, DH-4, 1B-2
1990	112	.242	.317	363	88	15	3	2	0.6	44	36	16	45	11	2	1	159	326	12	72	4.4	.976	SS-111
1991	133	.283	.401	414	117	13	6	8	1.9	71	54	34	55	14	1	0	201	345	17	93	4.2	.970	SS-128, DH-2, OF-1
1992	12	.313	.438	16	5	2	0	0	0.0	2	2	1	4	1	1	0	6	6	0	0	1.0	1.000	SS-5, 2B-4, 3B-1, DH-1
1993	113	.238	.303	340	81	8	4	2	0.6	43	36	29	51	9	3	1	213	231	13	55	4.0	.972	2B-104, OF-7, SS-4, DH-1
1994	73	.252	.308	214	54	10	1	0	0.0	27	17	19	42	7	10	0	70	128	8	26	2.8	.961	3B-35, SS-35, DH-3, OF-2, 1B-1
6 yrs.	557	.256	.338	1692	433	57	17	16	0.9	231	178	120	260	52	21	5	813	1331	71	308	4.0	.968	SS-372, 2B-112, 3B-48, DH-11, OF-10, 1B-3

Ed Sprague

SPRAGUE, EDWARD NELSON, JR.
Son of Ed Sprague.
B. July 25, 1967, Castro Valley, Calif.
BR TR 6'2" 215 lbs.

Year Team	Games	BA	SA	AB	H	2B	3B	HR	HR%	R	RBI	BB	SO	SB	AB	H	PO	A	E	DP	TC/G	FA	G by Pos
1991 TOR A	61	.275	.394	160	44	7	0	4	2.5	17	20	19	43	0	11	4	167	72	14	14	4.1	.945	3B-35, 1B-22, C-2, DH-2
1992	22	.234	.340	47	11	2	0	1	2.1	6	7	3	7	0	3	2	82	5	1	1	4.0	.989	C-15, 1B-4, DH-2, 3B-1
1993	150	.260	.386	546	142	31	1	12	2.2	50	73	32	85	1	0	0	128	231	17	21	2.5	.955	3B-150
1994	109	.240	.373	405	97	19	1	11	2.7	38	44	23	95	1	0	0	118	147	14	20	2.6	.950	3B-107, 1B-3
4 yrs.	342	.254	.381	1158	294	59	2	28	2.4	111	144	77	230	2	4	3	495	455	46	56	2.9	.954	3B-293, 1B-29, C-17, DH-4

LEAGUE CHAMPIONSHIP SERIES

Year Team	Games	BA	SA	AB	H	2B	3B	HR	HR%	R	RBI	BB	SO	SB	AB	H	PO	A	E	DP	TC/G	FA	G by Pos
1992 TOR A	2	.500	.500	2	1	0	0	0	0.0	0	0	0	1	0	2	1	0	0	0	0	0.0	–	
1993	6	.286	.381	21	6	0	1	0	0.0	0	4	2	4	0	0	0	5	9	0	1	2.3	1.000	3B-6
2 yrs.	8	.304	.391	23	7	0	1	0	0.0	0	4	2	5	0	2	1	5	9	0	1	1.8	1.000	

WORLD SERIES

Year Team	Games	BA	SA	AB	H	2B	3B	HR	HR%	R	RBI	BB	SO	SB	AB	H	PO	A	E	DP	TC/G	FA	G by Pos
1992 TOR A	3	.500	2.000	2	1	0	0	1	50.0	1	2	1	0	0	2	1	0	0	0	0	0.0	–	1B-1
1993	5	.067	.067	15	1	0	0	0	0.0	0	2	1	6	0	1	0	4	9	2	1	3.0	.867	3B-4, 1B-1
2 yrs.	8	.118	.294	17	2	0	0	1	5.9	1	4	2	6	0	3	1	4	9	2	1	1.9	.867	3B-4, 1B-2

Andy Stankiewicz

STANKIEWICZ, ANDREW NEAL
B. Aug. 10, 1964, Inglewood, Calif.
BR TR 5'9" 165 lbs.

Year Team	Games	BA	SA	AB	H	2B	3B	HR	HR%	R	RBI	BB	SO	SB	AB	H	PO	A	E	DP	TC/G	FA	G by Pos
1992 NY A	116	.268	.348	400	107	22	2	2	0.5	52	25	38	42	9	3	0	185	346	12	74	4.7	.978	SS-81, 2B-34, DH-1
1993	16	.000	.000	9	0	0	0	0	0.0	0	0	5	1	0	0	0	7	15	0	4	1.4	1.000	2B-6, 3B-4, DH-1, SS-1
1994 HOU N	37	.259	.370	54	14	3	0	1	1.9	10	5	12	12	1	8	3	12	45	0	7	1.5	1.000	SS-17, 2B-6, 3B-1
3 yrs.	169	.261	.343	463	121	25	2	3	0.6	67	30	51	55	10	11	3	204	406	12	85	3.7	.981	SS-99, 2B-46, 3B-5, DH-2

Mike Stanley

STANLEY, ROBERT MICHAEL
B. June 25, 1963, Fort Lauderdale, Fla.
BR TR 6'1" 185 lbs.

Year Team	Games	BA	SA	AB	H	2B	3B	HR	HR%	R	RBI	BB	SO	SB	AB	H	PO	A	E	DP	TC/G	FA	G by Pos
1986 TEX A	15	.333	.533	30	10	3	0	1	3.3	4	1	3	7	1	5	2	14	8	1	2	1.5	.957	3B-7, C-4, DH-3, OF-1
1987	78	.273	.403	216	59	8	1	6	2.8	34	37	31	48	3	6	4	389	26	7	7	5.4	.983	C-61, 1B-12, OF-1
1988	94	.229	.297	249	57	8	0	3	1.2	21	27	37	62	0	15	3	342	17	4	4	3.9	.989	C-64, 1B-7, 3B-2
1989	67	.246	.311	122	30	3	1	1	0.8	9	11	12	29	1	23	6	117	8	3	3	1.9	.977	C-25, DH-21, 1B-7, 3B-3
1990	103	.249	.333	189	47	8	1	2	1.1	21	19	30	25	1	27	7	261	25	4	2	2.8	.986	C-63, DH-8, 1B-8, 3B-6
1991	95	.249	.381	181	45	13	1	3	1.7	25	25	34	44	0	27	6	288	20	6	2	3.3	.981	C-58, 1B-12, 3B-6, OF-1
1992 NY A	68	.249	.428	173	43	7	0	8	4.6	24	27	33	45	0	5	1	287	30	6	5	4.8	.981	C-55, DH-4, 1B-4
1993	130	.305	.534	423	129	17	1	26	6.1	70	84	57	85	1	11	3	652	46	3	5	5.4	.996	C-122, DH-2
1994	82	.300	.545	290	87	20	0	17	5.9	54	57	39	56	0	1	0	444	33	5	3	5.9	.990	C-72, 1B-7, DH-4
9 yrs.	732	.271	.430	1873	507	87	5	67	3.6	262	288	276	401	7	120	32	2794	213	39	33	4.2	.987	C-524, DH-56, 1B-55, 3B-26, OF-3

Dave Staton

STATON, DAVID ALAN
B. Apr. 12, 1968, Seattle, Wash.
BR TR 6'5" 215 lbs.

Year Team	Games	BA	SA	AB	H	2B	3B	HR	HR%	R	RBI	BB	SO	SB	AB	H	PO	A	E	DP	TC/G	FA	G by Pos
1993 SD N	17	.262	.690	42	11	3	0	5	11.9	7	9	3	12	0	6	3	68	12	0	10	4.7	1.000	1B-12
1994	29	.182	.394	66	12	2	0	4	6.1	6	6	10	18	0	7	0	152	20	0	9	5.9	1.000	1B-20
2 yrs.	46	.213	.509	108	23	5	0	9	8.3	13	15	13	30	0	13	3	220	32	0	19	5.5	1.000	1B-32

Terry Steinbach

STEINBACH, TERRY LEE
B. Mar. 2, 1962, New Ulm, Minn.
BR TR 6'1" 195 lbs.

Year Team	Games	BA	SA	AB	H	2B	3B	HR	HR%	R	RBI	BB	SO	SB	AB	H	PO	A	E	DP	TC/G	FA	G by Pos
1986 OAK A	6	.333	.733	15	5	0	0	2	13.3	3	4	1	0	0	2	1	21	4	1	1	4.3	.962	C-5
1987	122	.284	.463	391	111	16	3	16	4.1	66	56	32	66	1	7	4	642	44	10	6	5.7	.986	C-107, 3B-10, 1B-1
1988	104	.265	.402	351	93	19	1	9	2.6	42	51	33	47	3	4	2	536	58	9	10	5.8	.985	C-84, 3B-9, 1B-8, DH-7, OF-1
1989	130	.273	.352	454	124	13	1	7	1.5	37	42	30	66	1	8	2	612	47	11	14	5.2	.984	C-103, OF-14, 1B-10, DH-4, 3B-3
1990	114	.251	.372	379	95	15	2	9	2.4	32	57	19	66	0	14	4	401	31	5	1	3.8	.989	C-83, DH-25, 1B-3
1991	129	.274	.386	456	125	31	1	6	1.3	50	67	22	70	2	7	4	639	53	15	11	5.5	.979	C-117, 1B-9, DH-2
1992	128	.279	.411	438	122	20	1	12	2.7	48	53	45	58	2	5	0	598	72	10	10	5.3	.985	C-124, 1B-5, DH-2
1993	104	.285	.416	389	111	19	1	10	2.6	47	43	25	65	3	4	1	524	47	7	18	5.6	.988	C-86, 1B-15, DH-6
1994	103	.285	.442	369	105	21	2	11	3.0	51	57	26	62	2	0	0	592	60	1	7	6.3	.998	C-93, DH-6, 1B-5
9 yrs.	940	.275	.406	3242	891	154	12	82	2.5	376	430	233	500	14	51	18	4565	416	69	78	5.4	.986	C-802, 1B-56, DH-52, 3B-22, OF-15

Year Team	Games	BA	SA	AB	H	2B	3B	HR	HR%	R	RBI	BB	SO	SB	Pinch Hit AB	Pinch Hit H	PO	A	E	DP	TC/G	FA	G by Pos

Terry Steinbach *continued*

LEAGUE CHAMPIONSHIP SERIES

Year Team	Games	BA	SA	AB	H	2B	3B	HR	HR%	R	RBI	BB	SO	SB	AB	H	PO	A	E	DP	TC/G	FA	G by Pos
1988 **OAK A**	2	.250	.250	4	1	0	0	0	0.0	0	0	2	0	0	0	0	12	0	0	0	6.0	1.000	C-2
1989	4	.200	.200	15	3	0	0	0	0.0	0	1	1	5	0	0	0	17	0	0	0	4.3	1.000	C-3, DH-1
1990	3	.455	.455	11	5	0	0	0	0.0	2	1	1	2	0	0	0	11	0	0	0	3.7	1.000	C-3
1992	6	.292	.417	24	7	0	0	1	4.2	1	5	2	7	0	0	0	30	7	0	0	6.2	1.000	C-6
4 yrs.	15	.296	.352	54	16	0	0	1	1.9	3	7	6	14	0	0	0	70	7	0	0	5.1	1.000	C-14, DH-1

WORLD SERIES

Year Team	Games	BA	SA	AB	H	2B	3B	HR	HR%	R	RBI	BB	SO	SB	AB	H	PO	A	E	DP	TC/G	FA	G by Pos
1988 **OAK A**	3	.364	.455	11	4	1	0	0	0.0	0	0	0	2	0	0	0	11	3	0	0	4.7	1.000	C-2, DH-1
1989	4	.250	.563	16	4	0	1	1	6.3	3	7	2	1	0	0	0	27	2	0	0	7.3	1.000	C-4
1990	3	.125	.125	8	1	0	0	0	0.0	0	0	0	1	0	0	0	8	1	0	0	3.0	1.000	C-3
3 yrs.	10	.257	.429	35	9	1	1	1	2.9	3	7	2	4	0	0	0	46	6	0	0	5.2	1.000	C-9, DH-1

Kelly Stinnett

STINNETT, KELLY LEE
B. Feb. 14, 1970, Lawton, Okla.

BR TR 5'11" 195 lbs.

Year Team	Games	BA	SA	AB	H	2B	3B	HR	HR%	R	RBI	BB	SO	SB	AB	H	PO	A	E	DP	TC/G	FA	G by Pos
1994 **NY N**	47	.253	.360	150	38	6	2	2	1.3	20	14	11	28	2	4	0	211	20	5	2	5.0	.979	C-44

Kevin Stocker

STOCKER, KEVIN DOUGLAS
B. Feb. 13, 1970, Spokane, Wash.

BB TR 6'1" 175 lbs.

Year Team	Games	BA	SA	AB	H	2B	3B	HR	HR%	R	RBI	BB	SO	SB	AB	H	PO	A	E	DP	TC/G	FA	G by Pos
1993 **PHI N**	70	.324	.417	259	84	12	3	2	0.8	46	31	30	43	5	0	0	118	202	14	44	4.8	.958	SS-70
1994	82	.273	.351	271	74	11	2	2	0.7	38	28	44	41	2	0	0	118	253	16	46	4.7	.959	SS-82
2 yrs.	152	.298	.383	530	158	23	5	4	0.8	84	59	74	84	7	0	0	236	455	30	90	4.7	.958	SS-152

LEAGUE CHAMPIONSHIP SERIES

Year Team	Games	BA	SA	AB	H	2B	3B	HR	HR%	R	RBI	BB	SO	SB	AB	H	PO	A	E	DP	TC/G	FA	G by Pos
1993 **PHI N**	6	.182	.227	22	4	1	0	0	0.0	0	1	2	5	0	0	0	9	14	1	1	4.0	.958	SS-6

WORLD SERIES

Year Team	Games	BA	SA	AB	H	2B	3B	HR	HR%	R	RBI	BB	SO	SB	AB	H	PO	A	E	DP	TC/G	FA	G by Pos
1993 **PHI N**	6	.211	.263	19	4	1	0	0	0.0	1	1	5	5	0	0	0	8	13	0	4	3.5	1.000	SS-6

Doug Strange

STRANGE, JOSEPH DOUGLAS
B. Apr. 13, 1964, Greenville, S. C.

BB TR 6'2" 170 lbs.

Year Team	Games	BA	SA	AB	H	2B	3B	HR	HR%	R	RBI	BB	SO	SB	AB	H	PO	A	E	DP	TC/G	FA	G by Pos
1989 **DET A**	64	.214	.260	196	42	4	1	1	0.5	16	14	17	36	3	3	0	53	118	19	17	3.0	.900	3B-54, 2B-9, SS-9, DH-1
1991 **CHI N**	3	.444	.556	9	4	1	0	0	0.0	0	1	0	1	1	0	0	1	3	1	0	1.7	.800	3B-3
1992	52	.160	.202	94	15	1	0	1	1.1	7	5	10	15	1	10	1	24	51	6	4	1.6	.926	3B-33, 2B-12
1993 **TEX A**	145	.256	.360	484	124	29	0	7	1.4	58	60	43	69	6	12	4	276	374	13	83	4.6	.980	2B-135, 3B-9, SS-1
1994	73	.212	.341	226	48	12	1	5	2.2	26	26	15	38	1	6	1	88	174	11	39	3.7	.960	2B-53, 3B-13, OF-3
5 yrs.	337	.231	.323	1009	233	47	2	14	1.4	107	106	85	159	12	31	6	442	720	50	143	3.6	.959	2B-209, 3B-112, SS-10, OF-3, DH-1

Darryl Strawberry

STRAWBERRY, DARRYL EUGENE (The Straw Man)
B. Mar. 12, 1962, Los Angeles, Calif.

BL TL 6'6" 190 lbs.

Year Team	Games	BA	SA	AB	H	2B	3B	HR	HR%	R	RBI	BB	SO	SB	AB	H	PO	A	E	DP	TC/G	FA	G by Pos
1983 **NY N**	122	.257	.512	420	108	15	7	26	6.2	63	74	47	128	19	4	0	232	8	4	0	2.0	.984	OF-117
1984	147	.251	.467	522	131	27	4	26	5.0	75	97	75	131	27	4	2	276	11	6	3	2.0	.980	OF-146
1985	111	.277	.557	393	109	15	4	29	7.4	78	79	73	96	26	2	0	211	5	2	2	2.0	.991	OF-110
1986	136	.259	.507	475	123	27	5	27	5.7	76	93	72	141	28	8	0	226	10	6	3	1.8	.975	OF-131
1987	154	.284	.583	532	151	32	5	39	7.3	108	104	97	122	36	3	1	272	6	8	3	1.9	.972	OF-151
1988	153	.269	**.545**	543	146	27	3	**39**	7.2	101	101	85	127	29	2	0	297	4	9	3	2.0	.971	OF-150
1989	134	.225	.466	476	107	26	1	29	6.1	69	77	61	105	11	6	1	272	4	8	2	2.1	.972	OF-131
1990	152	.277	.518	542	150	18	1	37	6.8	92	108	70	110	15	5	0	268	10	3	4	1.8	.989	OF-149
1991 **LA N**	139	.265	.491	505	134	22	4	28	5.5	86	99	75	125	10	3	1	209	11	5	2	1.6	.978	OF-136
1992	43	.237	.385	156	37	8	0	5	3.2	20	25	19	34	3	2	1	67	2	1	0	1.6	.986	OF-42
1993	32	.140	.310	100	14	2	0	5	5.0	12	12	16	19	1	3	1	37	1	4	0	1.3	.905	OF-29
1994 **SF N**	29	.239	.424	92	22	3	1	4	4.3	13	17	19	22	0	0	0	61	1	2	1	2.2	.969	OF-27
12 yrs.	1352	.259	.506	4756	1232	222	35	294	6.2	793	886	709	1160	205	42	7	2428	73	58	23	1.9	.977	OF-1319

LEAGUE CHAMPIONSHIP SERIES

Year Team	Games	BA	SA	AB	H	2B	3B	HR	HR%	R	RBI	BB	SO	SB	AB	H	PO	A	E	DP	TC/G	FA	G by Pos
1986 **NY N**	6	.227	.545	22	5	1	0	2	9.1	4	5	3	12	1	0	0	9	0	0	0	1.5	1.000	OF-6
1988	7	.300	.467	30	9	2	0	1	3.3	5	6	2	5	0	0	0	11	0	0	0	1.6	1.000	OF-7
2 yrs.	13	.269	.500	52	14	3	0	3	5.8	9	11	5	17	1	0	0	20	0	0	0	1.5	1.000	OF-13

WORLD SERIES

Year Team	Games	BA	SA	AB	H	2B	3B	HR	HR%	R	RBI	BB	SO	SB	AB	H	PO	A	E	DP	TC/G	FA	G by Pos
1986 **NY N**	7	.208	.375	24	5	1	0	1	4.2	4	1	4	6	3	0	0	19	0	0	0	2.7	1.000	OF-7

B. J. Surhoff

SURHOFF, WILLIAM JAMES
Brother of Rich Surhoff.
B. Aug. 4, 1964, Bronx, N. Y.

BL TR 6'1" 185 lbs.

Year Team	Games	BA	SA	AB	H	2B	3B	HR	HR%	R	RBI	BB	SO	SB	AB	H	PO	A	E	DP	TC/G	FA	G by Pos
1987 **MIL A**	115	.299	.423	395	118	22	3	7	1.8	50	68	36	30	11	10	3	648	56	11	12	6.2	.985	C-98, 3B-10, 1B-1
1988	139	.245	.318	493	121	21	0	5	1.0	47	38	31	49	21	9	2	550	94	8	3	4.7	.988	C-106, 3B-31, 1B-2, OF-1, SS-1
1989	126	.248	.339	436	108	17	4	5	1.1	42	55	25	29	14	5	0	530	58	10	7	4.7	.983	C-106, DH-12, 3B-6
1990	135	.276	.376	474	131	21	4	6	1.3	55	59	41	37	18	8	2	619	62	12	11	5.1	.983	C-125, 3B-11
1991	143	.289	.372	505	146	19	4	5	1.0	57	68	26	33	5	10	2	665	71	4	11	5.2	.995	C-127, DH-6, 3B-5, OF-2, 2B-1
1992	139	.252	.321	480	121	19	1	4	0.8	63	62	46	41	14	4	1	699	74	6	25	5.6	.992	C-109, 1B-17, DH-9, OF-7, 3B-3
1993	148	.274	.391	552	151	38	3	7	1.3	66	79	36	47	12	5	2	175	220	18	21	2.8	.956	3B-121, OF-24, 1B-8, C-3, DH-1
1994	40	.261	.485	134	35	11	2	5	3.7	20	22	16	14	0	1	0	121	29	4	12	3.9	.974	3B-18, C-12, 1B-8, OF-3, DH-1
8 yrs.	985	.268	.367	3469	931	168	21	44	1.3	400	451	257	280	95	52	12	4007	664	73	102	4.8	.985	C-686, 3B-205, OF-37, 1B-36, DH-29, SS-1, 2B-1

Year Team	Games	BA	SA	AB	H	2B	3B	HR	HR%	R	RBI	BB	SO	SB	Pinch Hit AB	Pinch Hit H	PO	A	E	DP	TC/G	FA	G by Pos

Dale Sveum

SVEUM, DALE CURTIS
B. Nov. 23, 1963, Richmond, Calif.

BB TR 6'2" 185 lbs.

Year Team	Games	BA	SA	AB	H	2B	3B	HR	HR%	R	RBI	BB	SO	SB	PH AB	PH H	PO	A	E	DP	TC/G	FA	G by Pos
1986 MIL A	91	.246	.366	317	78	13	2	7	2.2	35	35	32	63	4	2	0	92	179	30	19	3.3	.900	3B-65, 2B-13, SS-13
1987	153	.252	.454	535	135	27	3	25	4.7	86	95	40	133	2	1	1	242	396	23	89	4.3	.965	SS-142, 2B-13
1988	129	.242	.347	467	113	14	4	9	1.9	41	51	21	122	1	0	0	209	375	27	94	4.7	.956	SS-127, 2B-1, DH-1
1990	48	.197	.282	117	23	7	0	1	0.9	15	12	12	30	0	6	0	59	63	6	10	2.7	.953	3B-22, 2B-16, 1B-5, SS-5
1991	90	.241	.365	266	64	19	1	4	1.5	33	43	32	78	2	6	0	85	189	10	33	3.2	.965	SS-51, 3B-38, DH-3, 2B-2
1992 2 teams		PHI	N	(54G – .178)							CHI	A	(40G – .219)										
" total	94	.197	.297	249	49	13	0	4	1.6	28	28	28	68	1	19	1	121	198	16	38	3.6	.952	SS-71, 3B-7, 1B-6
1993 OAK A	30	.177	.304	79	14	2	1	2	2.5	12	6	16	21	0	7	3	128	17	3	13	4.9	.980	1B-14, 3B-7, 2B-4, DH-2, OF-1, SS-1
1994 SEA A	10	.185	.296	27	5	0	0	1	3.7	3	2	2	10	0	4	0	2	8	1	0	1.1	.909	DH-4, 3B-3
8 yrs.	645	.234	.368	2057	481	95	11	53	2.6	253	272	183	525	10	45	5	938	1425	116	296	3.8	.953	SS-410, 3B-142, 2B-49, 1B-25, DH-10, OF-1

Jeff Tackett

TACKETT, JEFFREY WILSON
B. Dec. 1, 1965, Fresno, Calif.

BR TR 6'2" 200 lbs.

Year Team	Games	BA	SA	AB	H	2B	3B	HR	HR%	R	RBI	BB	SO	SB	PH AB	PH H	PO	A	E	DP	TC/G	FA	G by Pos
1991 BAL A	6	.125	.125	8	1	0	0	0	0.0	1	0	2	2	0	0	0	22	0	0	0	3.7	1.000	C-6
1992	65	.240	.380	179	43	8	1	5	2.8	21	24	17	28	0	1	0	311	32	1	5	5.3	.997	C-64, 3B-1
1993	38	.172	.207	87	15	3	0	0	0.0	8	9	13	28	0	0	0	167	16	2	1	4.9	.989	C-38, P-1
1994	26	.226	.434	53	12	3	1	2	3.8	5	9	5	13	0	0	0	86	11	2	0	3.8	.980	C-26
4 yrs.	135	.217	.336	327	71	14	2	7	2.1	35	42	37	71	0	1	0	586	59	5	6	4.8	.992	C-134, 3B-1, P-1

Tony Tarasco

TARASCO, ANTONIO GIACINTO
B. Dec. 9, 1970, New York, N. Y.

BL TR 6' 185 lbs.

Year Team	Games	BA	SA	AB	H	2B	3B	HR	HR%	R	RBI	BB	SO	SB	PH AB	PH H	PO	A	E	DP	TC/G	FA	G by Pos
1993 ATL N	24	.229	.286	35	8	2	0	0	0.0	6	2	0	5	0	13	4	11	0	0	0	0.5	1.000	OF-12
1994	87	.273	.432	132	36	6	0	5	3.8	16	19	9	17	5	46	10	42	1	0	0	0.5	1.000	OF-46
2 yrs.	111	.263	.401	167	44	8	0	5	3.0	22	21	9	22	5	59	14	53	1	0	0	0.5	1.000	OF-58

LEAGUE CHAMPIONSHIP SERIES

Year Team	Games	BA	SA	AB	H	2B	3B	HR	HR%	R	RBI	BB	SO	SB	PH AB	PH H	PO	A	E	DP	TC/G	FA	G by Pos
1993 ATL N	2	1.000	.000	1	0	0	0	0	0.0	0	0	0	1	0	0	0	0	0	0	0	0.0	–	OF-2

Danny Tartabull

TARTABULL, DANILO
Born Danilo Tartabull (Mora).
Son of Jose Tartabull.
B. Oct. 30, 1962, San Juan, Puerto Rico.

BR TR 6'1" 185 lbs.

Year Team	Games	BA	SA	AB	H	2B	3B	HR	HR%	R	RBI	BB	SO	SB	PH AB	PH H	PO	A	E	DP	TC/G	FA	G by Pos
1984 SEA A	10	.300	.650	20	6	1	0	2	10.0	3	7	2	3	0	1	0	8	21	2	5	3.1	.935	SS-8, 2B-1
1985	19	.328	.525	61	20	7	1	1	1.6	8	7	8	14	1	3	1	28	43	4	11	3.9	.947	SS-16, 3B-4
1986	137	.270	.489	511	138	25	6	25	4.9	76	96	61	157	4	2	1	233	111	18	28	2.6	.950	OF-101, 2B-31, DH-3, 3B-1
1987 KC A	158	.309	.541	582	180	27	3	34	5.8	95	101	79	136	9	3	0	228	11	6	1	1.6	.976	OF-149, DH-6
1988	146	.274	.515	507	139	38	3	26	5.1	80	102	76	119	8	4	1	227	8	9	1	1.7	.963	OF-130, DH-13
1989	133	.268	.440	441	118	22	0	18	4.1	54	62	69	123	4	4	1	108	3	2	0	0.8	.982	OF-71, DH-55
1990	88	.268	.473	313	84	19	0	15	4.8	41	60	36	93	1	4	1	81	1	3	0	1.0	.965	OF-52, DH-32
1991	132	.316	.593	484	153	35	3	31	6.4	78	100	65	121	6	1	0	190	4	7	0	1.5	.965	OF-124, DH-5
1992 NY A	123	.266	.489	421	112	19	0	25	5.9	72	85	103	115	2	3	0	142	3	3	1	1.2	.980	OF-69, DH-53
1993	138	.250	.503	513	128	33	2	31	6.0	87	102	92	156	0	0	0	88	3	2	2	0.7	.978	DH-88, OF-50
1994	104	.256	.464	399	102	24	1	19	4.8	68	67	66	111	1	3	1	43	1	0	0	0.4	1.000	DH-78, OF-26
11 yrs.	1188	.278	.505	4252	1180	250	19	227	5.3	662	789	657	1148	36	28	6	1376	209	56	49	1.4	.966	OF-772, DH-334, 2B-32, SS-24, 3B-5

Eddie Taubensee

TAUBENSEE, EDWARD KENNETH
B. Oct. 31, 1968, Beeville, Tex.

BL TR 6'4" 205 lbs.

Year Team	Games	BA	SA	AB	H	2B	3B	HR	HR%	R	RBI	BB	SO	SB	PH AB	PH H	PO	A	E	DP	TC/G	FA	G by Pos
1991 CLE A	26	.242	.303	66	16	2	1	0	0.0	5	8	5	16	0	2	0	89	6	2	1	3.7	.979	C-25
1992 HOU N	104	.222	.323	297	66	15	0	5	1.7	23	28	31	78	2	4	0	557	66	5	6	6.0	.992	C-103
1993	94	.250	.389	288	72	11	1	9	3.1	26	42	21	44	1	7	2	552	40	5	5	6.4	.992	C-90
1994 2 teams		HOU	N	(5G – .100)							CIN	N	(61G – .294)										
" total	66	.283	.476	187	53	8	2	8	4.3	29	21	15	31	2	4	0	380	19	4	1	6.1	.990	C-66
4 yrs.	290	.247	.378	838	207	36	4	22	2.6	83	99	72	169	5	17	2	1578	131	16	13	5.9	.991	C-284

Jesus Tavarez

TAVAREZ, JESUS RAFAEL
B. Mar. 26, 1971, Santo Domingo, Dominican Republic

BB TR 6' 170 lbs.

Year Team	Games	BA	SA	AB	H	2B	3B	HR	HR%	R	RBI	BB	SO	SB	PH AB	PH H	PO	A	E	DP	TC/G	FA	G by Pos
1994 FLA N	17	.179	.179	39	7	0	0	0	0.0	4	4	1	5	1	6	2	28	1	0	0	1.7	1.000	OF-11

Mickey Tettleton

TETTLETON, MICKEY LEE
B. Sept. 16, 1960, Oklahoma City, Okla.

BB TR 6'2" 190 lbs.

Year Team	Games	BA	SA	AB	H	2B	3B	HR	HR%	R	RBI	BB	SO	SB	PH AB	PH H	PO	A	E	DP	TC/G	FA	G by Pos
1984 OAK A	33	.263	.355	76	20	2	1	1	1.3	10	5	11	21	0	3	0	112	10	1	1	3.7	.992	C-32
1985	78	.251	.351	211	53	12	0	3	1.4	23	15	28	59	2	3	1	344	24	4	9	4.8	.989	C-76, DH-1
1986	90	.204	.389	211	43	9	0	10	4.7	26	35	39	51	7	2	0	463	32	8	6	5.6	.984	C-89
1987	82	.194	.322	211	41	3	0	8	3.8	19	26	30	65	1	2	0	435	29	6	1	5.7	.987	C-80, 1B-1, DH-1
1988 BAL A	86	.261	.424	283	74	11	1	11	3.9	31	37	28	70	0	9	0	361	31	3	1	4.6	.992	C-80
1989	117	.258	.509	411	106	21	2	26	6.3	72	65	73	117	3	3	1	297	42	2	1	2.9	.994	C-75, DH-43
1990	135	.223	.381	444	99	21	2	15	3.4	68	51	106	160	2	2	1	458	39	5	4	3.7	.990	C-90, DH-40, 1B-5, OF-1
1991 DET A	154	.263	.491	501	132	17	2	31	6.2	85	89	101	131	3	13	4	562	55	6	2	4.0	.990	C-125, DH-24, OF-3, 1B-1
1992	157	.238	.469	525	125	25	0	32	6.1	82	83	**122**	137	0	4	1	481	47	2	11	3.4	.996	C-113, DH-40, 1B-3, OF-2
1993	152	.245	.492	522	128	25	4	32	6.1	79	110	109	139	3	4	1	723	48	6	43	5.1	.992	1B-59, C-56, OF-55, DH-4
1994	107	.248	.463	339	84	18	0	17	5.0	57	51	97	98	1	3	1	367	30	5	7	3.8	.988	C-53, 1B-24, DH-22, OF-18
11 yrs.	1191	.242	.443	3734	905	164	14	186	5.0	552	567	744	1048	21	47	10	4603	387	48	86	4.2	.990	C-869, DH-175, 1B-93, OF-79

Year Team	Games	BA	SA	AB	H	2B	3B	HR	HR%	R	RBI	BB	SO	SB	Pinch Hit AB	Pinch Hit H	PO	A	E	DP	TC/G	FA	G by Pos

Frank Thomas

THOMAS, FRANK EDWARD (The Big Hurt)
B. May 27, 1968, Columbus, Ga.　　　　　　　　　　　　　BR TR 6'5"　240 lbs.

Year Team	Games	BA	SA	AB	H	2B	3B	HR	HR%	R	RBI	BB	SO	SB	AB	H	PO	A	E	DP	TC/G	FA	G by Pos
1990 CHI A	60	.330	.529	191	63	11	3	7	3.7	39	31	44	54	0	1	1	428	26	5	53	7.7	.989	1B-51, DH-8
1991	158	.318	.553	559	178	31	2	32	5.7	104	109	138	112	1	1	1	459	27	2	43	3.1	.996	DH-101, 1B-56
1992	160	.323	.536	573	185	46	2	24	4.2	108	115	122	88	6	1	0	1428	92	13	112	9.6	.992	1B-158, DH-2
1993	153	.317	.607	549	174	36	0	41	7.5	106	128	112	54	4	0	0	1222	83	15	128	8.6	.989	1B-150, DH-4
1994	113	.353	.729	399	141	34	1	38	9.5	106	101	109	61	2	1	0	735	45	7	74	7.0	.991	1B-99, DH-13
5 yrs.	644	.326	.590	2271	741	158	8	142	6.3	463	484	525	369	13	4	2	4272	273	42	410	7.1	.991	1B-514, DH-128
LEAGUE CHAMPIONSHIP SERIES																							
1993 CHI A	6	.353	.529	17	6	0	0	1	5.9	2	3	10	5	0	0	0	24	3	0	3	4.5	1.000	1B-4, DH-2

Jim Thome

THOME, JAMES HOWARD
B. Aug. 27, 1970, Peoria, Ill.　　　　　　　　　　　　　BL TR 6'3"　190 lbs.

Year Team	Games	BA	SA	AB	H	2B	3B	HR	HR%	R	RBI	BB	SO	SB	AB	H	PO	A	E	DP	TC/G	FA	G by Pos
1991 CLE A	27	.255	.367	98	25	4	2	1	1.0	7	9	5	16	1	0	0	12	60	8	6	3.0	.900	3B-27
1992	40	.205	.299	117	24	3	1	2	1.7	8	12	10	34	2	1	0	21	61	11	3	2.3	.882	3B-40
1993	47	.266	.474	154	41	11	0	7	4.5	28	22	29	36	2	2	0	29	86	6	10	2.6	.950	3B-47
1994	98	.268	.523	321	86	20	1	20	6.2	58	52	46	84	3	7	2	62	173	15	12	2.6	.940	3B-94
4 yrs.	212	.255	.452	690	176	38	4	30	4.3	101	95	90	170	8	10	2	124	380	40	31	2.6	.926	3B-208

Milt Thompson

THOMPSON, MILTON BERNARD
B. Jan. 5, 1959, Washington, D. C.　　　　　　　　　　　BL TR 5'11"　170 lbs.

Year Team	Games	BA	SA	AB	H	2B	3B	HR	HR%	R	RBI	BB	SO	SB	AB	H	PO	A	E	DP	TC/G	FA	G by Pos
1984 ATL N	25	.303	.374	99	30	1	0	2	2.0	16	4	11	11	14	2	2	37	6	2	1	1.8	.956	OF-25
1985 PHI N	73	.302	.363	182	55	7	2	0	0.0	17	6	7	36	9	30	13	78	2	3	0	1.1	.964	OF-49
1986 PHI N	96	.251	.341	299	75	7	1	6	2.0	38	23	26	62	19	10	1	212	1	2	1	2.2	.991	OF-89
1987	150	.302	.425	527	159	26	9	7	1.3	86	43	42	87	46	15	5	354	4	4	1	2.4	.989	OF-146
1988	122	.288	.357	378	109	16	2	2	0.5	53	33	39	59	17	16	4	278	5	5	1	2.4	.983	OF-112
1989 STL N	155	.290	.393	545	158	28	8	4	0.7	60	68	39	91	27	10	1	348	5	8	1	2.3	.978	OF-147
1990	135	.218	.328	418	91	14	7	6	1.4	42	30	39	60	25	21	4	232	4	7	0	1.8	.971	OF-116
1991	115	.307	.442	326	100	16	5	6	1.8	55	34	32	53	16	28	10	207	8	2	1	1.9	.991	OF-91
1992	109	.293	.404	208	61	9	1	4	1.9	31	17	16	39	18	58	16	74	1	2	1	0.7	.974	OF-45
1993 PHI N	129	.262	.350	340	89	14	2	4	1.2	42	44	40	57	9	25	4	162	6	1	1	1.3	.994	OF-106
1994 2 teams		PHI N	(87G – .273)			HOU	N	(9G – .286)															
" total	96	.274	.353	241	66	7	0	4	1.7	34	33	24	30	9	13	2	126	2	0	1	1.3	1.000	OF-85
11 yrs.	1205	.279	.378	3563	993	145	37	45	1.3	474	335	315	585	209	228	66	2108	44	36	9	1.8	.984	OF-1011
LEAGUE CHAMPIONSHIP SERIES																							
1993 PHI N	6	.231	.308	13	3	1	0	0	0.0	2	0	1	2	0	1	0	8	0	1	0	1.5	.889	OF-5
WORLD SERIES																							
1993 PHI N	6	.313	.688	16	5	1	1	1	6.3	3	6	1	2	0	0	0	10	0	1	0	1.8	.909	OF-6

Robby Thompson

THOMPSON, ROBERT RANDALL
B. May 10, 1962, West Palm Beach, Fla.　　　　　　　　BR TR 5'11"　165 lbs.

Year Team	Games	BA	SA	AB	H	2B	3B	HR	HR%	R	RBI	BB	SO	SB	AB	H	PO	A	E	DP	TC/G	FA	G by Pos
1986 SF N	149	.271	.370	549	149	27	3	7	1.3	73	47	42	112	12	1	0	255	451	17	97	4.9	.976	2B-149, SS-1
1987	132	.262	.419	420	110	26	5	10	2.4	62	44	40	91	16	4	2	246	341	17	99	4.6	.972	2B-126
1988	138	.264	.384	477	126	24	6	7	1.5	66	48	40	111	14	5	1	255	365	14	88	4.6	.978	2B-134
1989	148	.241	.400	547	132	26	11	13	2.4	91	50	51	133	12	0	0	307	425	8	88	5.0	.989	2B-148
1990	144	.245	.392	498	122	22	3	15	3.0	67	56	34	96	14	3	1	287	441	8	94	5.1	.989	2B-142
1991	144	.262	.447	492	129	24	5	19	3.9	74	48	63	95	14	0	0	320	402	11	98	5.1	.985	2B-144
1992	128	.260	.415	443	115	25	1	14	3.2	54	49	43	75	5	8	1	296	382	15	101	5.4	.978	2B-120
1993	128	.312	.496	494	154	30	2	19	3.8	85	65	45	97	10	2	1	273	384	8	95	5.2	.988	2B-128
1994	35	.209	.349	129	27	8	2	2	1.6	13	7	15	32	3	0	0	67	121	2	24	5.4	.989	2B-35
9 yrs.	1146	.263	.412	4049	1064	212	38	106	2.6	585	414	373	842	100	23	6	2306	3312	100	784	5.0	.983	2B-1126, SS-1
LEAGUE CHAMPIONSHIP SERIES																							
1987 SF N	7	.100	.350	20	2	0	1	1	5.0	4	2	5	7	2	1	0	11	19	1	6	4.4	.968	2B-6
1989	5	.278	.611	18	5	0	0	2	11.1	5	3	3	2	0	0	0	10	13	0	4	4.6	1.000	2B-5
2 yrs.	12	.184	.474	38	7	0	1	3	7.9	9	5	8	9	2	1	0	21	32	1	10	4.5	.981	2B-11
WORLD SERIES																							
1989 SF N	4	.091	.091	11	1	0	0	0	0.0	0	2	0	4	0	1	1	4	10	0	2	3.5	1.000	2B-4

Ryan Thompson

THOMPSON, RYAN ORLANDO
B. Nov. 4, 1967, Chestertown, Md.　　　　　　　　　　　BR TR 6'3"　200 lbs.

Year Team	Games	BA	SA	AB	H	2B	3B	HR	HR%	R	RBI	BB	SO	SB	AB	H	PO	A	E	DP	TC/G	FA	G by Pos
1992 NY N	30	.222	.389	108	24	7	1	3	2.8	15	10	8	24	2	1	0	77	2	1	0	2.7	.988	OF-29
1993	80	.250	.444	288	72	19	2	11	3.8	34	26	19	81	2	1	1	228	4	3	0	2.9	.987	OF-76
1994	98	.225	.434	334	75	14	1	18	5.4	39	59	28	94	1	0	0	274	5	3	1	2.9	.989	OF-98
3 yrs.	208	.234	.432	730	171	40	4	32	4.4	88	95	55	199	5	2	1	579	11	7	1	2.9	.988	OF-203

Ron Tingley

TINGLEY, RONALD IRVIN
B. May 27, 1959, Presque Isle, Me.　　　　　　　　　　BR TR 6'2"　160 lbs.

Year Team	Games	BA	SA	AB	H	2B	3B	HR	HR%	R	RBI	BB	SO	SB	AB	H	PO	A	E	DP	TC/G	FA	G by Pos
1982 SD N	8	.100	.100	20	2	0	0	0	0.0	0	0	0	7	0	0	0	40	4	2	1	5.8	.957	C-8
1988 CLE A	9	.167	.292	24	4	0	0	1	4.2	1	2	2	8	0	0	1	48	6	0	1	6.0	1.000	C-9
1989 CAL A	4	.333	.333	3	1	0	0	0	0.0	0	0	1	0	0	0	0	7	1	1	0	2.3	.889	C-4
1990	5	.000	.000	3	0	0	0	0	0.0	0	0	1	1	0	0	0	12	0	0	0	2.4	1.000	C-5
1991	45	.200	.287	115	23	7	0	1	0.9	11	13	8	34	1	0	0	222	32	3	2	5.7	.988	C-45
1992	71	.197	.299	127	25	2	1	3	2.4	15	8	13	35	0	3	0	270	35	4	2	4.4	.987	C-69
1993	58	.200	.278	90	18	7	0	0	0.0	7	12	9	22	1	0	0	200	20	1	3	3.8	.995	C-58
1994 2 teams		FLA	N	(19G – .173)			CHI	A	(5G – .000)													
" total	24	.158	.298	57	9	3	1	1	1.8	4	2	5	20	0	2	1	107	10	1	1	4.9	.992	C-23
8 yrs.	224	.187	.280	439	82	19	2	6	1.4	38	37	39	127	2	6	2	906	108	12	10	4.6	.988	C-221

84

Year Team	Games	BA	SA	AB	H	2B	3B	HR	HR%	R	RBI	BB	SO	SB	Pinch Hit AB	H	PO	A	E	DP	TC/G	FA	G by Pos

Lee Tinsley
TINSLEY, LEE OWEN
B. Mar. 4, 1969, Shelbyville, Ky.
BB TR 5'11" 190 lbs.

Year Team	Games	BA	SA	AB	H	2B	3B	HR	HR%	R	RBI	BB	SO	SB	PH AB	PH H	PO	A	E	DP	TC/G	FA	G by Pos
1993 SEA A	11	.158	.368	19	3	1	0	1	5.3	2	2	2	9	0	5	1	9	0	1	0	0.9	.900	OF-6, DH-2
1994 BOS A	78	.222	.292	144	32	4	0	2	1.4	27	14	19	36	13	4	0	114	1	1	1	1.5	.991	OF-60, DH-9
2 yrs.	89	.215	.301	163	35	5	0	3	1.8	29	16	21	45	13	9	1	123	1	2	1	1.4	.984	OF-66, DH-11

Andy Tomberlin
TOMBERLIN, ANDY LEE
B. Nov. 7, 1966, Monroe, N. C.
BL TL 5'11" 160 lbs.

Year Team	Games	BA	SA	AB	H	2B	3B	HR	HR%	R	RBI	BB	SO	SB	PH AB	PH H	PO	A	E	DP	TC/G	FA	G by Pos
1993 PIT N	27	.286	.405	42	12	0	1	1	2.4	4	5	2	14	0	18	4	9	1	0	0	0.4	1.000	OF-7
1994 BOS A	17	.194	.333	36	7	0	1	1	2.8	1	1	6	12	1	4	1	12	2	0	1	0.8	1.000	OF-11, DH-5, P-1
2 yrs.	44	.244	.372	78	19	0	2	2	2.6	5	6	8	26	1	22	5	21	3	0	1	0.5	1.000	OF-18, DH-5, P-1

Alan Trammell
TRAMMELL, ALAN STUART
B. Feb. 21, 1958, Garden Grove, Calif.
BR TR 6' 165 lbs.

Year Team	Games	BA	SA	AB	H	2B	3B	HR	HR%	R	RBI	BB	SO	SB	PH AB	PH H	PO	A	E	DP	TC/G	FA	G by Pos
1977 DET A	19	.186	.186	43	8	0	0	0	0.0	6	0	4	12	0	0	0	15	34	2	5	2.7	.961	SS-19
1978	139	.268	.339	448	120	14	6	2	0.4	49	34	45	56	3	0	0	239	421	14	95	4.8	.979	SS-139
1979	142	.276	.357	460	127	11	4	6	1.3	68	50	43	55	17	0	0	245	388	26	99	4.6	.961	SS-142
1980	146	.300	.404	560	168	21	5	9	1.6	107	65	69	63	12	2	0	225	412	13	89	4.5	.980	SS-144
1981	105	.258	.327	392	101	15	3	2	0.5	52	31	49	31	10	1	1	181	347	9	65	5.1	.983	SS-105
1982	157	.258	.395	489	126	34	3	9	1.8	66	57	52	47	19	0	0	259	459	16	97	4.7	.978	SS-157
1983	142	.319	.471	505	161	31	2	14	2.8	83	66	57	64	30	0	0	236	367	13	71	4.3	.979	SS-140
1984	139	.314	.468	555	174	34	5	14	2.5	85	69	60	63	19	3	1	180	314	10	71	3.6	.980	SS-114, DH-22
1985	149	.258	.380	605	156	21	7	13	2.1	79	57	50	71	14	0	0	225	400	15	89	4.3	.977	SS-149
1986	151	.277	.469	574	159	33	7	21	3.7	107	75	59	57	25	1	0	238	445	22	99	4.7	.969	SS-149, DH-2
1987	151	.343	.551	597	205	34	3	28	4.7	109	105	60	47	21	3	0	222	421	19	94	4.4	.971	SS-149
1988	128	.311	.464	466	145	24	1	15	3.2	73	69	46	46	7	2	2	195	355	11	67	4.4	.980	SS-125
1989	121	.243	.334	449	109	20	3	5	1.1	54	43	45	45	10	2	1	188	396	9	71	4.9	.985	SS-117, DH-2
1990	146	.304	.449	559	170	37	1	14	2.5	71	89	68	55	12	2	0	232	409	14	102	4.5	.979	SS-142, DH-3
1991	101	.248	.373	375	93	20	0	9	2.4	57	55	37	39	11	4	1	131	296	9	60	4.3	.979	SS-92, DH-6
1992	29	.275	.392	102	28	7	1	1	1.0	11	11	15	4	2	0	0	46	80	3	16	4.4	.977	SS-27
1993	112	.329	.496	401	132	25	3	12	3.0	72	60	38	38	12	11	2	113	238	9	31	3.2	.975	SS-63, 3B-35, OF-8, DH-6
1994	76	.267	.414	292	78	17	1	8	2.7	38	28	16	35	3	6	1	117	180	10	43	4.0	.967	SS-63, DH-11
18 yrs.	2153	.287	.421	7872	2260	398	55	182	2.3	1187	964	813	828	227	37	9	3287	5962	224	1264	4.4	.976	SS-2036, DH-52, 3B-35, OF-8

LEAGUE CHAMPIONSHIP SERIES

Year Team	Games	BA	SA	AB	H	2B	3B	HR	HR%	R	RBI	BB	SO	SB	PH AB	PH H	PO	A	E	DP	TC/G	FA	G by Pos
1984 DET A	3	.364	.818	11	4	0	1	1	9.1	2	3	3	1	0	0	0	1	8	0	0	3.0	1.000	SS-3
1987	5	.200	.250	20	4	1	0	0	0.0	3	2	1	2	0	0	0	6	9	1	1	3.2	.938	SS-5
2 yrs.	8	.258	.452	31	8	1	1	1	3.2	5	5	4	3	0	0	0	7	17	1	1	3.1	.960	SS-8

WORLD SERIES

Year Team	Games	BA	SA	AB	H	2B	3B	HR	HR%	R	RBI	BB	SO	SB	PH AB	PH H	PO	A	E	DP	TC/G	FA	G by Pos
1984 DET A	5	.450	.800	20	9	1	0	2	10.0	5	6	2	2	1	0	0	8	9	1	0	3.6	.944	SS-5

Jeff Treadway
TREADWAY, HUGH JEFFERY
B. Jan. 22, 1963, Columbus, Ga.
BL TR 5'10" 170 lbs.

Year Team	Games	BA	SA	AB	H	2B	3B	HR	HR%	R	RBI	BB	SO	SB	PH AB	PH H	PO	A	E	DP	TC/G	FA	G by Pos
1987 CIN N	23	.333	.452	84	28	4	0	2	2.4	9	4	2	6	1	2	1	44	48	3	14	4.2	.958	2B-21
1988	103	.252	.362	301	76	19	4	2	0.7	30	23	27	30	2	7	4	189	253	8	50	4.4	.982	2B-97, 3B-2
1989 ATL N	134	.277	.378	473	131	18	3	8	1.7	58	40	30	38	3	11	3	273	341	12	80	4.7	.981	2B-123, 3B-6
1990	128	.283	.403	474	134	20	2	11	2.3	56	59	25	42	3	6	2	241	360	15	72	4.8	.976	2B-122
1991	106	.320	.418	306	98	17	2	3	1.0	41	32	23	19	2	14	4	155	206	15	33	3.5	.960	2B-93
1992	61	.222	.286	126	28	6	1	0	0.0	5	5	9	16	1	17	3	53	85	1	25	2.3	.993	2B-45, 3B-1
1993 CLE A	97	.303	.403	221	67	14	1	2	0.9	25	27	14	21	1	36	9	46	111	10	13	1.7	.940	3B-42, 2B-19, DH-4
1994 LA N	52	.299	.343	67	20	3	0	0	0.0	14	5	5	8	1	27	13	21	37	3	7	1.2	.951	2B-24, 3B-3
8 yrs.	704	.284	.386	2052	582	101	13	28	1.4	238	195	135	180	14	120	39	1022	1441	68	294	3.6	.973	2B-544, 3B-54, DH-4

LEAGUE CHAMPIONSHIP SERIES

Year Team	Games	BA	SA	AB	H	2B	3B	HR	HR%	R	RBI	BB	SO	SB	PH AB	PH H	PO	A	E	DP	TC/G	FA	G by Pos
1991 ATL N	1	.333	.333	3	1	0	0	0	0.0	0	0	0	0	0	0	0	2	2	0	1	4.0	1.000	2B-1
1992	3	.667	.667	3	2	0	0	0	0.0	1	0	0	0	0	0	0	0	1	0	0	0.3	1.000	2B-1
2 yrs.	4	.500	.500	6	3	0	0	0	0.0	1	0	0	0	0	0	0	2	3	0	1	1.3	1.000	2B-2

WORLD SERIES

Year Team	Games	BA	SA	AB	H	2B	3B	HR	HR%	R	RBI	BB	SO	SB	PH AB	PH H	PO	A	E	DP	TC/G	FA	G by Pos
1991 ATL N	3	.250	.250	4	1	0	0	0	0.0	1	0	1	2	0	1	0	1	3	1	1	1.7	.800	2B-1
1992	1	.000	.000	1	0	0	0	0	0.0	0	0	0	0	0	1	0	0	0	0	0	0.0	—	
2 yrs.	4	.200	.200	5	1	0	0	0	0.0	1	0	1	2	0	2	0	1	3	1	1	1.3	.800	2B-1

Brian Turang
TURANG, BRIAN CRAIG
B. June 14, 1967, Long Beach, Calif.
BR TR 5'10" 170 lbs.

Year Team	Games	BA	SA	AB	H	2B	3B	HR	HR%	R	RBI	BB	SO	SB	PH AB	PH H	PO	A	E	DP	TC/G	FA	G by Pos
1993 SEA A	40	.250	.343	140	35	11	1	0	0.0	22	7	17	20	6	2	1	72	2	1	0	1.9	.987	OF-38, 3B-2, 2B-1, DH-1
1994	38	.188	.277	112	21	5	1	1	0.9	9	8	7	25	3	1	0	52	10	2	3	1.7	.969	OF-30, 2B-5, DH-4
2 yrs.	78	.222	.313	252	56	16	2	1	0.4	31	15	24	45	9	3	1	124	12	3	3	1.8	.978	OF-68, 2B-6, DH-5, 3B-2

Chris Turner
TURNER, CHRISTOPHER WAN
B. Mar. 23, 1969, Bowling Green, Ky.
BR TR 6'2" 190 lbs.

Year Team	Games	BA	SA	AB	H	2B	3B	HR	HR%	R	RBI	BB	SO	SB	PH AB	PH H	PO	A	E	DP	TC/G	FA	G by Pos
1993 CAL A	25	.280	.387	75	21	5	0	1	1.3	9	13	9	16	1	0	0	116	14	1	0	5.2	.992	C-25
1994	58	.242	.322	149	36	7	1	1	0.7	23	12	10	29	3	2	0	268	29	1	0	5.1	.997	C-57
2 yrs.	83	.254	.344	224	57	12	1	2	0.9	32	25	19	45	4	2	0	384	43	2	0	5.2	.995	C-82

John Valentin
VALENTIN, JOHN WILLIAM
B. Feb. 18, 1967, Mineola, N. Y.
BR TR 6' 170 lbs.

Year Team	Games	BA	SA	AB	H	2B	3B	HR	HR%	R	RBI	BB	SO	SB	PH AB	PH H	PO	A	E	DP	TC/G	FA	G by Pos
1992 BOS A	58	.276	.427	185	51	13	0	5	2.7	21	25	20	17	1	0	0	79	181	10	45	4.7	.963	SS-58
1993	144	.278	.447	468	130	40	3	11	2.4	50	66	49	77	3	1	0	238	432	20	96	4.8	.971	SS-144
1994	84	.316	.505	301	95	26	2	9	3.0	53	49	42	38	3	1	0	134	239	8	54	4.5	.979	SS-83, DH-1
3 yrs.	286	.289	.461	954	276	79	5	25	2.6	124	140	111	132	7	2	0	451	852	38	195	4.7	.972	SS-285, DH-1

Year Team	Games	BA	SA	AB	H	2B	3B	HR	HR%	R	RBI	BB	SO	SB	Pinch Hit AB	Pinch Hit H	PO	A	E	DP	TC/G	FA	G by Pos

Jose Valentin

VALENTIN, JOSE ANTONIO
Born Jose Antonio Valentin (Rosario).
B. Oct. 12, 1969, Manati, Puerto Rico.

BB TR 5'10" 175 lbs.

Year Team	Games	BA	SA	AB	H	2B	3B	HR	HR%	R	RBI	BB	SO	SB	PH AB	PH H	PO	A	E	DP	TC/G	FA	G by Pos
1992 MIL A	4	.000	.000	3	0	0	0	0	0.0	1	1	0	0	0	0	0	1	1	1	0	0.8	.667	2B-1, SS-1
1993	19	.245	.396	53	13	1	2	1	1.9	10	7	7	16	1	0	0	20	51	6	9	4.1	.922	SS-19
1994	97	.239	.421	285	68	19	0	11	3.9	47	46	38	75	12	0	0	150	336	20	71	5.2	.960	SS-83, 2B-18, 3B-1, DH-1
3 yrs.	120	.238	.413	341	81	20	2	12	3.5	58	54	45	91	13	0	0	171	388	27	80	4.9	.954	SS-103, 2B-19, 3B-1, DH-1

Dave Valle

VALLE, DAVID
B. Oct. 30, 1960, Bayside, N.Y.

BR TR 6'2" 200 lbs.

Year Team	Games	BA	SA	AB	H	2B	3B	HR	HR%	R	RBI	BB	SO	SB	PH AB	PH H	PO	A	E	DP	TC/G	FA	G by Pos
1984 SEA A	13	.296	.444	27	8	1	0	1	3.7	4	4	1	5	0	0	0	56	5	0	0	4.7	1.000	C-13
1985	31	.157	.171	70	11	1	0	0	0.0	2	4	1	17	0	0	0	117	7	3	0	4.1	.976	C-31
1986	22	.340	.679	53	18	3	0	5	9.4	10	15	7	7	0	8	2	90	3	2	3	4.3	.979	C-12, 1B-4
1987	95	.256	.435	324	83	16	3	12	3.7	40	53	15	46	2	10	1	422	34	5	2	4.9	.989	C-75, 1B-2, OF-1
1988	93	.231	.400	290	67	15	2	10	3.4	29	50	18	38	0	10	5	490	47	6	8	5.8	.989	C-84, DH-3, 1B-1
1989	94	.237	.354	316	75	10	3	7	2.2	32	34	29	32	0	3	2	496	52	4	3	5.9	.993	C-93
1990	107	.214	.331	308	66	15	0	7	2.3	37	33	45	48	1	3	0	633	44	2	9	6.3	.997	C-104, 1B-1
1991	132	.194	.299	324	63	8	1	8	2.5	38	32	34	49	0	3	0	676	52	6	9	5.6	.992	C-129, 1B-2
1992	124	.240	.362	367	88	16	1	9	2.5	39	30	27	58	0	3	2	606	62	7	10	5.4	.990	C-122
1993	135	.258	.395	423	109	19	0	13	3.1	48	63	48	56	1	3	0	881	71	5	13	7.1	.995	C-135
1994 2 teams	BOS A	(30G – .158)		MIL A	(16G – .389)																		
" total	46	.232	.375	112	26	8	1	2	1.8	14	10	18	22	0	2	0	204	7	3	1	4.7	.986	C-40, 1B-2, DH-2
11 yrs.	892	.235	.371	2614	614	112	11	74	2.8	293	328	243	378	4	42	12	4671	384	43	58	5.7	.992	C-838, 1B-12, DH-5, OF-1

Ty Van Burkleo

VAN BURKLEO, TYLER LEE
B. Oct. 7, 1963, Oakland, Calif.

BL TL 6'5" 230 lbs.

Year Team	Games	BA	SA	AB	H	2B	3B	HR	HR%	R	RBI	BB	SO	SB	PH AB	PH H	PO	A	E	DP	TC/G	FA	G by Pos
1993 CAL A	12	.152	.333	33	5	3	0	1	3.0	2	1	6	9	1	1	0	99	3	0	8	8.5	1.000	1B-12
1994 CLR N	2	.000	.000	5	0	0	0	0	0.0	0	0	0	1	0	1	0	15	1	0	1	8.0	1.000	1B-2
2 yrs.	14	.132	.289	38	5	3	0	1	2.6	2	1	6	10	1	2	0	114	4	0	9	8.4	1.000	1B-14

John Vander Wal

VANDER WAL, JOHN HENRY
B. Apr. 29, 1966, Grand Rapids, Mich.

BL TL 6'1" 180 lbs.

Year Team	Games	BA	SA	AB	H	2B	3B	HR	HR%	R	RBI	BB	SO	SB	PH AB	PH H	PO	A	E	DP	TC/G	FA	G by Pos
1991 MON N	21	.213	.361	61	13	4	1	1	1.6	4	8	1	18	0	4	1	29	0	0	0	1.4	1.000	OF-17
1992	105	.239	.352	213	51	8	2	4	1.9	21	20	24	36	3	35	6	122	6	2	3	1.2	.985	OF-57, 1B-7
1993	106	.233	.372	215	50	7	4	5	2.3	34	30	27	30	6	30	7	271	14	4	17	2.7	.986	1B-42, OF-38
1994 CLR N	91	.245	.427	110	27	3	1	5	4.5	12	15	16	31	2	58	14	106	3	0	11	1.2	1.000	1B-14, OF-7
4 yrs.	323	.235	.374	599	141	22	8	15	2.5	71	73	68	115	11	127	28	528	23	6	31	1.7	.989	OF-119, 1B-63

Andy Van Slyke

VAN SLYKE, ANDREW JAMES (Slick)
B. Dec. 21, 1960, Utica, N.Y.

BL TR 6'1" 190 lbs.

Year Team	Games	BA	SA	AB	H	2B	3B	HR	HR%	R	RBI	BB	SO	SB	PH AB	PH H	PO	A	E	DP	TC/G	FA	G by Pos
1983 STL N	101	.262	.421	309	81	15	5	8	2.6	51	38	46	64	21	5	1	203	59	6	16	2.7	.978	OF-69, 3B-30, 1B-9
1984	137	.244	.368	361	88	16	4	7	1.9	45	50	63	71	28	11	4	357	82	8	40	3.3	.982	OF-81, 3B-32, 1B-30
1985	146	.259	.439	424	110	25	6	13	3.1	61	55	47	54	34	19	4	237	13	1	6	1.7	.996	OF-142, 1B-1
1986	137	.270	.452	418	113	23	7	13	3.1	48	61	47	85	21	10	2	415	34	8	25	3.3	.982	OF-110, 1B-38
1987 PIT N	157	.293	.507	564	165	36	11	21	3.7	93	82	56	122	34	7	1	338	10	4	9	2.2	.989	OF-150, 1B-1
1988	154	.288	.506	587	169	23	15	25	4.3	101	100	57	126	30	5	0	406	12	4	2	2.7	.991	OF-152
1989	130	.237	.370	476	113	18	9	9	1.9	64	53	47	100	16	10	1	344	9	4	6	2.7	.989	OF-123, 1B-2
1990	136	.284	.465	493	140	26	6	17	3.4	67	77	66	89	14	4	0	326	6	8	0	2.5	.976	OF-133
1991	138	.265	.446	491	130	24	7	17	3.5	87	83	71	85	10	4	0	273	8	1	1	2.0	.996	OF-135
1992	154	.324	.505	614	199	45	12	14	2.3	103	89	58	99	12	0	0	421	11	5	3	2.8	.989	OF-154
1993	83	.310	.449	323	100	13	4	8	2.5	42	50	24	40	11	6	0	205	2	1	1	2.5	.995	OF-78
1994	105	.246	.358	374	92	18	3	6	1.6	41	30	52	72	7	7	1	238	9	2	1	2.4	.992	OF-99
12 yrs.	1578	.276	.448	5434	1500	282	89	158	2.9	803	768	634	1007	238	88	14	3763	255	52	110	2.6	.987	OF-1426, 1B-82, 3B-62

LEAGUE CHAMPIONSHIP SERIES

Year Team	Games	BA	SA	AB	H	2B	3B	HR	HR%	R	RBI	BB	SO	SB	PH AB	PH H	PO	A	E	DP	TC/G	FA	G by Pos
1985 STL N	5	.091	.091	11	1	0	0	0	0.0	1	1	2	1	0	0	0	7	0	0	0	1.4	1.000	OF-5
1990 PIT N	6	.208	.333	24	5	1	1	0	0.0	3	3	1	7	1	0	0	13	1	0	0	2.3	1.000	OF-6
1991	7	.160	.360	25	4	2	0	1	4.0	3	2	5	5	1	0	0	18	1	0	0	2.7	1.000	OF-7
1992	7	.276	.448	29	8	3	1	0	0.0	1	4	1	5	0	0	0	20	0	0	0	2.9	1.000	OF-7
4 yrs.	25	.202	.348	89	18	6	2	1	1.1	8	10	9	18	2	0	0	58	2	0	0	2.4	1.000	OF-25

WORLD SERIES

Year Team	Games	BA	SA	AB	H	2B	3B	HR	HR%	R	RBI	BB	SO	SB	PH AB	PH H	PO	A	E	DP	TC/G	FA	G by Pos
1985 STL N	6	.091	.091	11	1	0	0	0	0.0	0	0	0	5	0	0	0	8	0	0	0	1.3	1.000	OF-6

Gary Varsho

VARSHO, GARY ANDREW
B. June 20, 1961, Marshfield, Wis.

BL TR 5'11" 190 lbs.

Year Team	Games	BA	SA	AB	H	2B	3B	HR	HR%	R	RBI	BB	SO	SB	PH AB	PH H	PO	A	E	DP	TC/G	FA	G by Pos
1988 CHI N	46	.274	.315	73	20	3	0	0	0.0	6	5	1	6	5	28	11	29	0	3	0	0.7	.906	OF-18
1989	61	.184	.276	87	16	4	0	0	0.0	10	6	4	13	3	36	5	25	1	2	0	0.5	.929	OF-21
1990	46	.250	.333	48	12	4	0	0	0.0	10	1	1	6	2	43	11	2	0	0	0	0.0	1.000	OF-3
1991 PIT N	99	.273	.417	187	51	11	2	4	2.1	23	23	19	34	9	41	9	95	2	1	1	1.0	.990	OF-54, 1B-3
1992	103	.222	.370	162	36	6	3	4	2.5	22	22	10	32	5	55	13	62	1	1	0	0.6	.984	OF-44
1993 CIN N	77	.232	.358	95	22	6	0	2	2.1	8	11	9	19	1	44	9	27	1	0	1	0.4	1.000	OF-22
1994 PIT N	67	.256	.402	82	21	6	3	0	0.0	15	5	4	19	0	28	8	25	0	2	0	0.4	.926	OF-36, 1B-1
7 yrs.	499	.243	.365	734	178	40	10	10	1.4	94	73	48	129	25	275	66	265	5	9	2	0.6	.968	OF-198, 1B-4

LEAGUE CHAMPIONSHIP SERIES

Year Team	Games	BA	SA	AB	H	2B	3B	HR	HR%	R	RBI	BB	SO	SB	PH AB	PH H	PO	A	E	DP	TC/G	FA	G by Pos
1991 PIT N	2	.500	.500	2	1	0	0	0	0.0	0	0	0	1	0	2	1	0	0	0	0	0.0	—	
1992	2	.500	.500	2	1	0	0	0	0.0	0	0	0	0	0	2	1	0	0	0	0	0.0	—	OF-1
2 yrs.	4	.500	.500	4	2	0	0	0	0.0	0	0	0	1	0	4	2	0	0	0	0	0.0	—	

Greg Vaughn

VAUGHN, GREGORY LAMONT
B. July 3, 1965, Sacramento, Calif.

BR TR 6' 195 lbs.

Year Team	Games	BA	SA	AB	H	2B	3B	HR	HR%	R	RBI	BB	SO	SB	PH AB	PH H	PO	A	E	DP	TC/G	FA	G by Pos
1989 MIL A	38	.265	.425	113	30	3	0	5	4.4	18	23	13	23	4	1	0	32	1	2	0	0.9	.943	OF-24, DH-13
1990	120	.220	.432	382	84	26	2	17	4.5	51	61	33	91	7	5	0	195	8	7	1	1.8	.967	OF-106, DH-8

Year Team	Games	BA	SA	AB	H	2B	3B	HR	HR%	R	RBI	BB	SO	SB	Pinch Hit AB	Pinch Hit H	PO	A	E	DP	TC/G	FA	G by Pos

Greg Vaughn *continued*

Year Team	Games	BA	SA	AB	H	2B	3B	HR	HR%	R	RBI	BB	SO	SB	AB	H	PO	A	E	DP	TC/G	FA	G by Pos
1991	145	.244	.456	542	132	24	5	27	5.0	81	98	62	125	2	2	0	315	5	2	1	2.2	.994	OF-135, DH-10
1992	141	.228	.409	501	114	18	2	23	4.6	77	78	60	123	15	4	0	288	6	3	0	2.1	.990	OF-131, DH-7
1993	154	.267	.482	569	152	28	2	30	5.3	97	97	89	118	10	2	0	214	1	3	1	1.4	.986	OF-94, DH-58
1994	95	.254	.478	370	94	24	1	19	5.1	59	55	51	93	9	0	0	162	5	3	0	1.8	.982	OF-81, DH-14
6 yrs.	693	.245	.451	2477	606	123	12	121	4.9	383	412	308	573	47	14	0	1206	26	20	3	1.8	.984	OF-571, DH-110

Mo Vaughn

VAUGHN, MAURICE SAMUEL
B. Dec. 15, 1967, Norwalk, Conn.
BL TR 6'1" 225 lbs.

Year Team	Games	BA	SA	AB	H	2B	3B	HR	HR%	R	RBI	BB	SO	SB	AB	H	PO	A	E	DP	TC/G	FA	G by Pos
1991 BOS A	74	.260	.370	219	57	12	0	4	1.8	21	32	26	43	2	9	3	378	26	6	43	5.5	.985	1B-49, DH-16
1992	113	.234	.400	355	83	16	2	13	3.7	42	57	47	67	3	13	4	741	57	15	76	7.2	.982	1B-85, DH-20
1993	152	.297	.525	539	160	34	1	29	5.4	86	101	79	130	4	2	0	1110	70	16	104	7.9	.987	1B-131, DH-19
1994	111	.310	.576	394	122	25	1	26	6.6	65	82	57	112	4	3	0	879	57	10	103	8.5	.989	1B-107, DH-1
4 yrs.	450	.280	.486	1507	422	87	4	72	4.8	214	272	209	352	13	27	7	3108	210	47	326	7.5	.986	1B-372, DH-56

Randy Velarde

VELARDE, RANDY LEE
B. Nov. 24, 1962, Midland, Tex.
BR TR 6' 185 lbs.

Year Team	Games	BA	SA	AB	H	2B	3B	HR	HR%	R	RBI	BB	SO	SB	AB	H	PO	A	E	DP	TC/G	FA	G by Pos
1987 NY A	8	.182	.182	22	4	0	0	0	0.0	1	1	0	6	0	0	0	8	20	2	3	3.8	.933	SS-8
1988	48	.174	.357	115	20	6	0	5	4.3	18	12	8	24	1	0	0	72	98	8	26	3.7	.955	2B-24, SS-14, 3B-11
1989	33	.340	.480	100	34	4	2	2	2.0	12	11	7	14	0	2	1	26	61	4	16	2.8	.956	3B-27, SS-9
1990	95	.210	.319	229	48	6	2	5	2.2	21	19	20	53	0	7	1	70	159	12	18	2.5	.950	3B-74, SS-15, OF-5, 2B-3, DH-3
1991	80	.245	.332	184	45	11	1	1	0.5	19	15	18	43	3	7	4	64	148	15	24	2.8	.934	3B-50, SS-31, OF-2
1992	121	.272	.386	412	112	24	1	7	1.7	57	46	38	78	7	3	2	179	257	15	50	3.7	.967	SS-75, 3B-26, OF-23, 2B-3
1993	85	.301	.469	226	68	13	2	7	3.1	28	24	18	39	2	13	4	102	92	9	20	2.4	.956	OF-50, SS-26, 3B-16, DH-1
1994	77	.279	.439	280	78	16	1	9	3.2	47	34	22	61	4	0	0	94	188	19	37	3.9	.937	SS-49, 3B-27, OF-7, 2B-5
8 yrs.	547	.261	.392	1568	409	80	9	36	2.3	203	162	131	318	17	32	12	615	1023	84	194	3.1	.951	3B-231, SS-227, OF-87, 2B-35, DH-4

Robin Ventura

VENTURA, ROBIN MARK
B. July 14, 1967, Santa Maria, Calif.
BL TR 6'1" 185 lbs.

Year Team	Games	BA	SA	AB	H	2B	3B	HR	HR%	R	RBI	BB	SO	SB	AB	H	PO	A	E	DP	TC/G	FA	G by Pos
1989 CHI A	16	.178	.244	45	8	3	0	0	0.0	5	7	8	6	0	1	0	17	33	2	2	3.3	.962	3B-16
1990	150	.249	.318	493	123	17	1	5	1.0	48	54	55	53	1	7	2	116	268	25	32	2.7	.939	3B-147, 1B-1
1991	157	.284	.442	606	172	25	1	23	3.8	92	100	80	67	2	3	0	225	291	18	37	3.4	.966	3B-151, 1B-31
1992	157	.282	.431	592	167	38	1	16	2.7	85	93	93	71	2	0	0	141	375	23	29	3.4	.957	3B-157, 1B-2
1993	157	.262	.433	554	145	27	1	22	4.0	85	94	105	82	1	2	0	119	278	14	27	2.6	.966	3B-155, 1B-4
1994	109	.282	.459	401	113	15	1	18	4.5	57	78	61	69	3	1	0	88	180	20	22	2.6	.931	3B-108, 1B-3, SS-1
6 yrs.	746	.271	.414	2691	728	125	5	84	3.1	372	426	402	348	9	14	2	706	1425	102	149	3.0	.954	3B-734, 1B-41, SS-1

LEAGUE CHAMPIONSHIP SERIES

Year Team	Games	BA	SA	AB	H	2B	3B	HR	HR%	R	RBI	BB	SO	SB	AB	H	PO	A	E	DP	TC/G	FA	G by Pos
1993 CHI A	6	.200	.350	20	4	0	0	1	5.0	2	5	6	6	0	0	0	9	6	1	0	2.7	.938	3B-6, 1B-1

Fernando Vina

VINA, FERNANDO
B. Apr. 16, 1969, Sacramento, Calif.
BL TR 5'9" 170 lbs.

Year Team	Games	BA	SA	AB	H	2B	3B	HR	HR%	R	RBI	BB	SO	SB	AB	H	PO	A	E	DP	TC/G	FA	G by Pos
1993 SEA A	24	.222	.267	45	10	2	0	0	0.0	5	2	4	3	6	1	0	28	40	0	12	2.8	1.000	2B-16, SS-4, DH-2
1994 NY N	79	.250	.298	124	31	6	0	0	0.0	20	6	12	11	3	34	6	46	59	4	5	1.4	.963	2B-13, 3B-12, SS-9, OF-6
2 yrs.	103	.243	.290	169	41	8	0	0	0.0	25	8	16	14	9	35	6	74	99	4	17	1.7	.977	2B-29, SS-13, 3B-12, OF-6, DH-2

Jose Vizcaino

VIZCAINO, JOSE LUIS
Born Jose Luis Vizcaino (Pimental).
B. Mar. 26, 1968, San Cristobal, Dominican Republic.
BB TR 6'1" 150 lbs.

Year Team	Games	BA	SA	AB	H	2B	3B	HR	HR%	R	RBI	BB	SO	SB	AB	H	PO	A	E	DP	TC/G	FA	G by Pos
1989 LA N	7	.200	.200	10	2	0	0	0	0.0	2	0	0	1	0	1	1	6	9	2	2	2.4	.882	SS-5
1990	37	.275	.333	51	14	1	1	0	0.0	3	2	4	8	1	15	2	23	27	2	6	1.4	.962	SS-11, 2B-6
1991 CHI N	93	.262	.297	145	38	5	0	0	0.0	7	10	5	18	2	6	1	49	118	7	19	1.9	.960	3B-57, SS-33, 2B-9
1992	86	.225	.298	285	64	10	4	1	0.4	25	17	14	35	3	6	1	93	195	9	34	3.5	.970	SS-50, 3B-29, 2B-5
1993	151	.287	.358	551	158	19	4	4	0.7	74	54	46	71	12	8	2	218	407	17	73	4.3	.974	SS-81, 3B-44, 2B-34
1994 NY N	103	.256	.324	410	105	13	3	3	0.7	47	33	33	62	1	2	1	137	291	13	55	4.3	.971	SS-102
6 yrs.	477	.262	.329	1452	381	48	12	8	0.6	158	116	102	195	19	38	8	526	1047	50	189	3.4	.969	SS-282, 3B-130, 2B-54

Omar Vizquel

VIZQUEL, OMAR ENRIQUE
Born Omar Enrique Vizquel (Gonzalez).
B. May 15, 1967, Caracas, Venezuela.
BB TR 5'9" 155 lbs.

Year Team	Games	BA	SA	AB	H	2B	3B	HR	HR%	R	RBI	BB	SO	SB	AB	H	PO	A	E	DP	TC/G	FA	G by Pos
1989 SEA A	143	.220	.261	387	85	7	3	1	0.3	45	20	28	40	1	2	0	208	388	18	102	4.3	.971	SS-143
1990	81	.247	.298	255	63	3	2	2	0.8	19	18	18	22	4	0	0	103	239	7	48	4.3	.980	SS-81
1991	142	.230	.293	426	98	16	4	1	0.2	42	41	45	37	7	8	0	224	422	13	105	4.6	.980	SS-138, 2B-1
1992	136	.294	.352	483	142	20	4	0	0.0	49	21	32	38	15	5	0	223	403	7	92	4.7	.989	SS-136
1993	158	.255	.298	560	143	14	2	2	0.4	68	31	50	71	12	1	1	245	475	15	108	4.7	.980	SS-155, DH-2
1994 CLE A	69	.273	.325	286	78	10	1	1	0.3	39	33	23	23	13	1	1	114	204	6	53	4.7	.981	SS-69
6 yrs.	729	.254	.305	2397	609	70	16	7	0.3	262	164	196	231	52	17	2	1117	2131	66	508	4.5	.980	SS-722, DH-2, 2B-1

Jack Voigt

VOIGT, JOHN DAVID
B. May 17, 1966, Sarasota, Fla.
BR TR 6'1" 170 lbs.

Year Team	Games	BA	SA	AB	H	2B	3B	HR	HR%	R	RBI	BB	SO	SB	AB	H	PO	A	E	DP	TC/G	FA	G by Pos
1992 BAL A	1	–	–	0	0	0	0	0	0	0	0	0	0	0	0	0	0	0	0	0	0.0	–	
1993	64	.296	.500	152	45	11	1	6	3.9	32	23	25	33	1	10	2	101	6	1	3	1.7	.991	OF-43, DH-8, 1B-5, 3B-3
1994	59	.241	.340	141	34	5	0	3	2.1	15	20	18	25	0	3	1	114	5	2	2	2.1	.983	OF-54, 1B-6, DH-2
3 yrs.	124	.270	.423	293	79	16	1	9	3.1	47	43	43	58	1	13	3	215	11	3	5	1.8	.987	OF-97, 1B-11, DH-10, 3B-3

Year Team	Games	BA	SA	AB	H	2B	3B	HR	HR%	R	RBI	BB	SO	SB	Pinch Hit AB	Pinch Hit H	PO	A	E	DP	TC/G	FA	G by Pos

Matt Walbeck
WALBECK, MATTHEW LOVICK
B. Oct. 2, 1969, Sacramento, Calif.   BB TR 5'11" 195 lbs.

Year Team	Games	BA	SA	AB	H	2B	3B	HR	HR%	R	RBI	BB	SO	SB	AB	H	PO	A	E	DP	TC/G	FA	G by Pos
1993 CHI N	11	.200	.367	30	6	2	0	1	3.3	2	6	1	6	0	3	1	49	2	0	0	4.6	1.000	C-11
1994 MIN A	97	.204	.284	338	69	12	0	5	1.5	31	35	17	37	1	3	0	496	45	4	0	5.6	.993	C-95, DH-1
2 yrs.	108	.204	.291	368	75	14	0	6	1.6	33	41	18	43	1	6	1	545	47	4	0	5.5	.993	C-106, DH-1

Larry Walker
WALKER, LARRY KENNETH ROBERT
B. Dec. 1, 1966, Maple Ridge, B. C., Canada.   BL TR 6'2" 185 lbs.

Year Team	Games	BA	SA	AB	H	2B	3B	HR	HR%	R	RBI	BB	SO	SB	AB	H	PO	A	E	DP	TC/G	FA	G by Pos
1989 MON N	20	.170	.170	47	8	0	0	0	0.0	4	4	5	13	1	7	0	19	2	0	1	1.1	1.000	OF-15
1990	133	.241	.434	419	101	18	3	19	4.5	59	51	49	112	21	11	1	249	12	4	5	2.0	.985	OF-124
1991	137	.290	.458	487	141	30	2	16	3.3	59	64	42	102	14	2	1	536	36	6	30	4.2	.990	OF-102, 1B-39
1992	143	.301	.506	528	159	31	4	23	4.4	85	93	41	97	18	3	1	269	16	2	2	2.0	.993	OF-139
1993	138	.265	.469	490	130	24	5	22	4.5	85	86	80	76	29	2	0	316	16	6	4	2.4	.982	OF-132, 1B-4
1994	103	.322	.587	395	127	44	2	19	4.8	76	86	47	74	15	1	0	423	29	9	21	4.5	.980	OF-68, 1B-35
6 yrs.	674	.281	.483	2366	666	147	16	99	4.2	368	384	264	474	98	26	3	1812	111	27	63	2.9	.986	OF-580, 1B-78

Tim Wallach
WALLACH, TIMOTHY CHARLES
B. Sept. 14, 1957, Huntington Park, Calif.   BR TR 6'3" 220 lbs.

Year Team	Games	BA	SA	AB	H	2B	3B	HR	HR%	R	RBI	BB	SO	SB	AB	H	PO	A	E	DP	TC/G	FA	G by Pos
1980 MON N	5	.182	.455	11	2	0	1	1	9.1	1	2	1	5	0	2	0	12	0	0	0	2.4	1.000	OF-3, 1B-1
1981	71	.236	.344	212	50	9	1	4	1.9	19	13	15	37	0	6	1	207	31	1	9	3.4	.996	OF-35, 1B-16, 3B-15
1982	158	.268	.471	596	160	31	3	28	4.7	89	97	36	81	6	3	1	132	287	23	23	2.8	.948	3B-156, OF-2, 1B-1
1983	156	.269	.434	581	156	33	3	19	3.3	54	70	55	97	0	0	0	151	265	19	26	2.8	.956	3B-156
1984	160	.246	.395	582	143	25	4	18	3.1	55	72	50	101	3	0	0	162	332	21	29	3.2	.959	3B-160, SS-1
1985	155	.260	.450	569	148	36	3	22	3.9	70	81	38	79	9	2	0	148	383	18	34	3.5	.967	3B-154
1986	134	.233	.396	480	112	22	1	18	3.8	50	71	44	72	8	1	0	94	270	16	26	2.8	.958	3B-132
1987	153	.298	.514	593	177	42	4	26	4.4	89	123	37	98	9	3	0	128	292	21	21	2.9	.952	3B-150, P-1
1988	159	.257	.389	592	152	32	5	12	2.0	52	69	38	88	2	8	2	124	329	18	32	3.0	.962	3B-153, 2B-1
1989	154	.277	.419	573	159	42	0	13	2.3	76	77	58	81	3	1	1	113	302	18	20	2.8	.958	3B-153, P-1
1990	161	.296	.471	626	185	37	5	21	3.4	69	98	42	80	6	0	0	128	309	21	23	2.8	.954	3B-161
1991	151	.225	.334	577	130	22	1	13	2.3	60	73	50	100	2	0	0	107	310	14	27	2.9	.968	3B-149
1992	150	.223	.331	537	120	29	1	9	1.7	53	59	50	90	2	3	0	690	244	15	59	6.3	.984	3B-85, 1B-71
1993 LA N	133	.222	.342	477	106	19	1	12	2.5	42	62	32	70	0	5	0	121	229	15	15	2.7	.959	3B-130, 1B-1
1994	113	.280	.502	414	116	21	1	23	5.6	68	78	46	80	0	1	0	81	174	11	9	2.4	.959	3B-113
15 yrs.	2013	.258	.418	7420	1916	400	33	239	3.2	847	1045	592	1159	50	35	5	2398	3757	231	352	3.2	.964	3B-1867, 1B-90, OF-40, P-2, SS-1, 2B-1

DIVISIONAL PLAYOFF SERIES
Year Team	Games	BA	SA	AB	H	2B	3B	HR	HR%	R	RBI	BB	SO	SB	AB	H	PO	A	E	DP	TC/G	FA	G by Pos
1981 MON N	4	.250	.500	4	1	1	0	0	0.0	1	0	4	0	0	0	0	4	0	0	0	1.0	1.000	OF-3

LEAGUE CHAMPIONSHIP SERIES
Year Team	Games	BA	SA	AB	H	2B	3B	HR	HR%	R	RBI	BB	SO	SB	AB	H	PO	A	E	DP	TC/G	FA	G by Pos
1981 MON N	1	.000	.000	1	0	0	0	0	0.0	0	0	0	0	0	1	0	0	0	0	0	0.0	—

Jerome Walton
WALTON, JEROME O'TERRELL
B. July 8, 1965, Newnan, Ga.   BR TR 6'1" 175 lbs.

Year Team	Games	BA	SA	AB	H	2B	3B	HR	HR%	R	RBI	BB	SO	SB	AB	H	PO	A	E	DP	TC/G	FA	G by Pos
1989 CHI N	116	.293	.385	475	139	23	3	5	1.1	64	46	27	77	24	0	0	289	2	3	1	2.5	.990	OF-115
1990	101	.263	.329	392	103	16	2	2	0.5	63	21	50	70	14	0	0	247	3	6	0	2.5	.977	OF-98
1991	123	.219	.330	270	59	13	1	5	1.9	42	17	19	55	7	25	5	170	2	3	1	1.4	.983	OF-101
1992	30	.127	.164	55	7	0	1	0	0.0	7	1	9	13	1	5	0	34	0	2	0	1.2	.944	OF-24
1993 CAL A	5	.000	.000	2	0	0	0	0	0.0	2	0	1	2	1	0	0	2	0	0	0	0.4	1.000	DH-3, OF-1
1994 CIN N	46	.309	.412	68	21	4	0	1	1.5	10	9	4	12	1	15	2	58	1	1	2	1.3	.983	OF-26, 1B-7
6 yrs.	421	.261	.347	1262	329	56	7	13	1.0	188	94	110	229	48	45	7	800	8	15	4	2.0	.982	OF-365, 1B-7, DH-3

LEAGUE CHAMPIONSHIP SERIES
Year Team	Games	BA	SA	AB	H	2B	3B	HR	HR%	R	RBI	BB	SO	SB	AB	H	PO	A	E	DP	TC/G	FA	G by Pos
1989 CHI N	5	.364	.364	22	8	0	0	0	0.0	4	2	2	2	1	0	0	11	0	0	0	2.2	1.000	OF-5

Turner Ward
WARD, TURNER MAX
B. Apr. 11, 1965, Orlando, Fla.   BB TR 6'2" 200 lbs.

Year Team	Games	BA	SA	AB	H	2B	3B	HR	HR%	R	RBI	BB	SO	SB	AB	H	PO	A	E	DP	TC/G	FA	G by Pos
1990 CLE A	14	.348	.500	46	16	2	1	1	2.2	10	10	3	8	3	0	0	20	2	1	0	1.6	.957	OF-13, DH-1
1991 2 teams		CLE A	(40G – .230)		TOR A	(8G – .308)																	
" total	48	.239	.301	113	27	7	0	0	0.0	12	7	11	18	0	3	1	70	1	0	0	1.5	1.000	OF-44
1992 TOR A	18	.345	.552	29	10	3	0	1	3.4	7	3	4	4	0	4	0	18	1	0	0	1.1	1.000	OF-12
1993	72	.192	.311	167	32	4	2	4	2.4	20	28	23	26	3	7	2	97	2	1	0	1.4	.990	OF-65, 1B-1
1994 MIL A	102	.232	.357	367	85	15	2	9	2.5	55	45	52	68	6	1	0	260	9	4	1	2.7	.985	OF-99, 3B-1
5 yrs.	254	.235	.355	722	170	31	5	15	2.1	104	93	93	124	12	15	3	465	15	6	1	1.9	.988	OF-233, DH-1, 1B-1, 3B-1

Lenny Webster
WEBSTER, LEONARD IRELL
B. Feb. 10, 1965, New Orleans, La.   BR TR 5'9" 185 lbs.

Year Team	Games	BA	SA	AB	H	2B	3B	HR	HR%	R	RBI	BB	SO	SB	AB	H	PO	A	E	DP	TC/G	FA	G by Pos
1989 MIN A	14	.300	.400	20	6	2	0	0	0.0	3	1	3	2	0	1	1	32	0	0	0	2.3	1.000	C-14
1990	2	.333	.500	6	2	1	0	0	0.0	1	0	1	1	0	0	0	9	0	0	0	4.5	1.000	C-2
1991	18	.294	.588	34	10	1	0	3	8.8	7	8	6	10	0	2	0	61	10	1	1	4.0	.986	C-17
1992	53	.280	.407	118	33	10	1	1	0.8	10	13	9	11	0	6	5	190	11	1	3	3.8	.995	C-49, DH-1
1993	49	.198	.245	106	21	2	0	1	0.9	14	8	11	8	1	3	0	177	13	0	1	3.9	1.000	C-45, DH-1
1994 MON N	57	.273	.448	143	39	10	0	5	3.5	13	23	16	24	0	13	1	237	19	1	0	4.5	.996	C-46
6 yrs.	193	.260	.396	427	111	26	1	10	2.3	48	53	46	56	1	25	7	706	53	3	5	3.9	.996	C-173, DH-2

Mitch Webster
WEBSTER, MITCHELL DEAN
B. May 16, 1959, Larned, Kans.   BB TL 6'1½" 170 lbs.

Year Team	Games	BA	SA	AB	H	2B	3B	HR	HR%	R	RBI	BB	SO	SB	AB	H	PO	A	E	DP	TC/G	FA	G by Pos
1983 TOR A	11	.182	.182	11	2	0	0	0	0.0	2	0	1	1	0	1	0	5	0	0	0	0.5	1.000	OF-7, DH-2
1984	26	.227	.409	22	5	2	1	0	0.0	9	4	1	7	0	7	1	16	0	2	1	0.7	.889	OF-10, DH-9, 1B-1
1985 2 teams		TOR A	(4G – .000)		MON N	(74G – .274)																	
" total	78	.272	.484	213	58	6	11	5.2	32	30	20	33	15	5	0	133	3	1	0	1.8	.993	OF-66, DH-2
1986 MON N	151	.290	.431	576	167	31	13	8	1.4	89	49	57	78	36	4	1	325	12	8	3	2.3	.977	OF-146

Year Team	Games	BA	SA	AB	H	2B	3B	HR	HR%	R	RBI	BB	SO	SB	Pinch Hit AB	Pinch Hit H	PO	A	E	DP	TC/G	FA	G by Pos

Mitch Webster *continued*

Year Team	Games	BA	SA	AB	H	2B	3B	HR	HR%	R	RBI	BB	SO	SB	AB	H	PO	A	E	DP	TC/G	FA	G by Pos
1987	156	.281	.435	588	165	30	8	15	2.6	101	63	70	95	33	7	4	266	8	5	0	1.8	.982	OF-153
1988 2 teams	MON N (81G – .255)			CHI N (70G – .265)																			
" total	151	.260	.356	523	136	16	8	6	1.1	69	39	55	87	22	17	3	322	3	6	0	2.2	.982	OF-136
1989 CHI N	98	.257	.364	272	70	12	4	3	1.1	40	19	30	55	14	30	4	161	3	6	0	1.7	.965	OF-74
1990 CLE A	128	.252	.407	437	110	20	6	12	2.7	58	55	20	61	22	12	4	345	3	5	2	2.8	.986	OF-118, 1B-3, DH-3
1991 3 teams	CLE A (13G – .125)			PIT N (36G – .175)				LA N (58G – .284)															
" total	107	.207	.325	203	42	8	5	2	1.0	23	19	21	61	2	35	7	111	2	2	1	1.1	.983	OF-75, 1B-1
1992 LA N	135	.267	.420	262	70	12	5	6	2.3	33	35	27	49	11	47	17	130	0	3	0	1.0	.977	OF-90
1993	88	.244	.337	172	42	6	2	2	1.2	26	14	11	24	4	35	6	75	1	4	0	0.9	.950	OF-56
1994	82	.274	.464	84	23	4	0	4	4.8	16	12	8	13	1	31	9	29	0	0	0	0.4	1.000	OF-48
12 yrs.	1211	.265	.403	3363	890	149	54	69	2.1	498	339	321	564	160	235	57	1918	35	42	7	1.6	.979	OF-979, DH-16, 1B-5

LEAGUE CHAMPIONSHIP SERIES

| 1989 CHI N | 3 | .333 | .333 | 3 | 1 | 0 | 0 | 0 | 0.0 | 0 | 0 | 0 | 0 | 0 | 1 | 1 | 0 | 0 | 0 | 0 | 0.0 | – | OF-2 |

Eric Wedge

WEDGE, ERIC MICHAEL
B. Jan. 27, 1968, Fort Wayne, Ind.

BR TR 6'3" 215 lbs.

Year Team	Games	BA	SA	AB	H	2B	3B	HR	HR%	R	RBI	BB	SO	SB	AB	H	PO	A	E	DP	TC/G	FA	G by Pos
1991 BOS A	1	1.000	1.000	1	1	0	0	0	0.0	0	0	0	0	0	1	1	0	0	0	0	0.0	–	DH-1
1992	27	.250	.500	68	17	2	0	5	7.4	11	11	13	18	0	5	2	19	2	0	1	0.8	1.000	DH-20, C-5
1993 CLR N	9	.182	.182	11	2	0	0	0	0.0	2	1	0	4	0	8	2	6	1	0	0	0.8	1.000	C-1
1994 BOS A	2	.000	.000	6	0	0	0	0	0.0	0	0	1	3	0	0	0	0	0	0	0	0.0	–	DH-2
4 yrs.	39	.233	.430	86	20	2	0	5	5.8	13	12	14	25	0	14	5	25	3	0	1	0.7	1.000	DH-23, C-6

John Wehner

WEHNER, JOHN PAUL
B. June 29, 1967, Pittsburgh, Pa.

BR TR 6'3" 205 lbs.

Year Team	Games	BA	SA	AB	H	2B	3B	HR	HR%	R	RBI	BB	SO	SB	AB	H	PO	A	E	DP	TC/G	FA	G by Pos
1991 PIT N	37	.340	.406	106	36	7	0	0	0.0	15	7	7	17	3	3	2	23	65	6	9	2.5	.936	3B-36
1992	55	.179	.228	123	22	6	0	0	0.0	11	4	12	22	3	12	5	96	63	4	17	3.0	.975	3B-34, 1B-13, 2B-5
1993	29	.143	.143	35	5	0	0	0	0.0	3	0	6	10	0	9	0	17	8	0	3	0.9	1.000	OF-13, 2B-3, 3B-3
1994	2	.250	.500	4	1	1	0	0	0.0	1	3	0	1	0	1	1	0	2	0	0	1.0	1.000	3B-1
4 yrs.	123	.239	.291	268	64	14	0	0	0.0	30	14	25	50	6	25	8	136	138	10	29	2.3	.965	3B-74, 1B-13, OF-13, 2B-8

LEAGUE CHAMPIONSHIP SERIES

| 1992 PIT N | 2 | .000 | .000 | 2 | 0 | 0 | 0 | 0 | 0.0 | 0 | 0 | 0 | 2 | 0 | 2 | 0 | 0 | 0 | 0 | 0 | 0.0 | – | |

Walt Weiss

WEISS, WALTER WILLIAM
B. Nov. 28, 1963, Tuxedo, N. Y.

BB TR 6' 175 lbs.

Year Team	Games	BA	SA	AB	H	2B	3B	HR	HR%	R	RBI	BB	SO	SB	AB	H	PO	A	E	DP	TC/G	FA	G by Pos
1987 OAK A	16	.462	.615	26	12	4	0	0	0.0	3	1	2	2	1	1	0	8	30	1	4	2.4	.974	SS-11
1988	147	.250	.321	452	113	17	3	3	0.7	44	39	35	56	4	1	0	254	431	15	83	4.8	.979	SS-147
1989	84	.233	.318	236	55	11	0	3	1.3	30	21	21	39	6	0	0	106	195	15	44	3.8	.953	SS-84
1990	138	.265	.321	445	118	17	1	2	0.4	50	35	46	53	9	3	1	194	373	12	77	4.2	.979	SS-137
1991	40	.226	.286	133	30	6	1	0	0.0	15	13	12	14	6	1	1	64	99	5	21	4.2	.970	SS-40
1992	103	.212	.241	316	67	5	2	0	0.0	36	21	43	39	6	1	0	144	270	19	57	4.2	.956	SS-103
1993 FLA N	158	.266	.308	500	133	14	2	1	0.2	50	39	79	73	7	6	0	229	406	15	80	4.1	.977	SS-153
1994 CLR N	110	.251	.303	423	106	11	4	1	0.2	58	32	56	58	12	2	0	157	318	13	68	4.4	.973	SS-110
8 yrs.	796	.250	.306	2531	634	85	13	10	0.4	286	201	294	334	51	15	2	1156	2122	95	434	4.2	.972	SS-785

LEAGUE CHAMPIONSHIP SERIES

1988 OAK A	4	.333	.467	15	5	2	0	0	0.0	0	2	0	4	0	0	0	7	10	0	3	4.3	1.000	SS-4
1989	4	.111	.222	9	1	1	0	0	0.0	2	0	1	1	1	0	0	5	9	0	2	3.5	1.000	SS-4
1990	2	.000	.000	7	0	0	0	0	0.0	2	0	2	2	0	0	0	2	7	1	1	5.0	.900	SS-2
1992	3	.167	.167	6	1	0	0	0	0.0	1	0	2	1	2	0	0	5	6	0	1	3.7	1.000	SS-3
4 yrs.	13	.189	.270	37	7	3	0	0	0.0	7	2	5	8	3	0	0	19	32	1	7	4.0	.981	SS-13

WORLD SERIES

1988 OAK A	5	.063	.063	16	1	0	0	0	0.0	1	0	0	2	1	0	0	5	11	1	1	3.4	.941	SS-5
1989	4	.133	.333	15	2	0	0	1	6.7	3	1	2	2	0	0	0	7	8	0	1	3.8	1.000	SS-4
2 yrs.	9	.097	.194	31	3	0	0	1	3.2	4	1	2	4	1	0	0	12	19	1	2	3.6	.969	SS-9

Lou Whitaker

WHITAKER, LOUIS RODMAN (Sweet Lou)
B. May 12, 1957, Brooklyn, N. Y.

BL TR 5'11" 160 lbs.

Year Team	Games	BA	SA	AB	H	2B	3B	HR	HR%	R	RBI	BB	SO	SB	AB	H	PO	A	E	DP	TC/G	FA	G by Pos
1977 DET A	11	.250	.281	32	8	1	0	0	0.0	5	2	4	6	2	0	0	17	18	0	2	3.2	1.000	2B-9
1978	139	.285	.357	484	138	12	7	3	0.6	71	58	61	65	7	6	3	301	458	17	95	5.6	.978	2B-136, DH-2
1979	127	.286	.378	423	121	14	8	3	0.7	75	42	78	66	20	5	0	280	369	9	103	5.2	.986	2B-126
1980	145	.233	.283	477	111	19	1	1	0.2	68	45	73	79	8	8	2	340	428	12	93	5.4	.985	2B-143
1981	109	.263	.373	335	88	14	4	5	1.5	48	36	40	42	5	2	1	227	354	9	77	5.4	.985	2B-108
1982	152	.286	.434	560	160	22	8	15	2.7	76	65	48	58	11	4	1	331	470	10	120	5.3	.988	2B-149, DH-1
1983	161	.320	.457	643	206	40	6	12	1.9	94	72	67	70	17	7	3	299	447	13	92	4.7	.983	2B-160
1984	143	.289	.407	558	161	25	1	13	2.3	90	56	62	63	6	6	1	290	405	15	83	5.0	.979	2B-142
1985	152	.280	.457	608	170	29	8	21	3.5	102	73	80	56	6	4	0	314	414	11	101	4.9	.985	2B-150
1986	144	.269	.437	584	157	26	6	20	3.4	95	73	63	70	13	6	4	276	421	11	98	4.9	.984	2B-141
1987	149	.265	.427	604	160	38	6	16	2.6	110	59	71	108	13	3	1	275	416	17	99	4.8	.976	2B-148
1988	115	.275	.419	403	111	18	2	12	3.0	54	55	66	61	2	9	3	218	284	8	53	4.4	.984	2B-110
1989	148	.251	.462	509	128	21	1	28	5.5	77	85	89	59	6	6	0	327	393	11	99	4.9	.985	2B-146, DH-2
1990	132	.237	.407	472	112	22	2	18	3.8	75	60	74	71	8	11	1	286	372	6	98	5.0	.991	2B-130, DH-1
1991	138	.279	.489	470	131	26	2	23	4.9	94	78	90	45	4	13	4	255	361	4	91	4.5	.994	2B-135, DH-3
1992	130	.278	.461	453	126	26	0	19	4.2	77	71	81	46	6	8	0	257	313	9	73	4.5	.984	2B-119, DH-10
1993	119	.290	.449	383	111	32	1	9	2.3	72	67	78	46	3	16	5	236	322	11	75	4.8	.981	2B-110
1994	92	.301	.491	322	97	21	2	12	3.7	67	43	41	42	2	12	2	135	246	12	43	4.3	.969	2B-83, DH-5
18 yrs.	2306	.276	.423	8320	2296	406	65	230	2.8	1350	1040	1166	1058	139	126	31	4664	6491	185	1495	4.9	.984	2B-2245, DH-24

LEAGUE CHAMPIONSHIP SERIES

1984 DET A	3	.143	.143	14	2	0	0	0	0.0	3	0	0	3	0	0	0	5	6	0	0	3.7	1.000	2B-3
1987	5	.176	.353	17	3	0	0	1	5.9	4	1	7	3	1	0	0	11	14	0	1	5.0	1.000	2B-5
2 yrs.	8	.161	.258	31	5	0	0	1	3.2	7	1	7	6	1	0	0	16	20	0	1	4.5	1.000	2B-8

Year Team	Games	BA	SA	AB	H	2B	3B	HR	HR%	R	RBI	BB	SO	SB	Pinch Hit AB	Pinch Hit H	PO	A	E	DP	TC/G	FA	G by Pos

Lou Whitaker *continued*

WORLD SERIES

Year Team	Games	BA	SA	AB	H	2B	3B	HR	HR%	R	RBI	BB	SO	SB	AB	H	PO	A	E	DP	TC/G	FA	G by Pos
1984 DET A	5	.278	.389	18	5	2	0	0	0.0	6	0	4	4	0	0	0	15	18	0	2	6.6	1.000	2B-5

Devon White

WHITE, DEVON MARKES B. Dec. 29, 1962, Kingston, Jamaica. BB TR 6'1" 170 lbs.

Year Team	Games	BA	SA	AB	H	2B	3B	HR	HR%	R	RBI	BB	SO	SB	AB	H	PO	A	E	DP	TC/G	FA	G by Pos
1985 CAL A	21	.143	.143	7	1	0	0	0	0.0	7	0	1	3	3	0	0	10	1	0	0	0.5	1.000	OF-16
1986	28	.235	.353	51	12	1	1	1	2.0	8	3	6	8	6	0	0	49	0	2	0	1.8	.961	OF-28
1987	159	.263	.443	639	168	33	5	24	3.8	103	87	39	135	32	0	0	424	16	9	3	2.8	.980	OF-159
1988	122	.259	.389	455	118	22	2	11	2.4	76	51	23	84	17	5	2	364	7	9	2	3.1	.976	OF-116
1989	156	.245	.371	636	156	18	13	12	1.9	86	56	31	129	44	1	0	430	10	5	3	2.9	.989	OF-154, DH-1
1990	125	.217	.343	443	96	17	3	11	2.5	57	44	44	116	21	3	0	302	11	9	4	2.6	.972	OF-122
1991 TOR A	156	.282	.455	642	181	40	10	17	2.6	110	60	55	135	33	0	0	439	8	1	2	2.9	.998	OF-156
1992	153	.248	.390	641	159	26	7	17	2.7	98	60	47	133	37	0	0	443	8	7	2	3.0	.985	OF-152, DH-1
1993	146	.273	.438	598	163	42	6	15	2.5	116	52	57	127	34	0	0	399	6	3	2	2.8	.993	OF-145
1994	100	.270	.457	403	109	24	6	13	3.2	67	49	21	80	11	1	1	267	3	6	1	2.8	.978	OF-98
10 yrs.	1166	.258	.411	4515	1163	223	53	121	2.7	728	462	324	950	238	10	3	3127	70	51	19	2.8	.984	OF-1146, DH-2

LEAGUE CHAMPIONSHIP SERIES

Year Team	Games	BA	SA	AB	H	2B	3B	HR	HR%	R	RBI	BB	SO	SB	AB	H	PO	A	E	DP	TC/G	FA	G by Pos
1986 CAL A	3	.500	.500	2	1	0	0	0	0.0	2	0	0	1	0	0	0	2	0	0	0	0.7	1.000	OF-3
1991 TOR A	5	.364	.409	22	8	1	0	0	0.0	5	0	2	3	3	0	0	16	0	0	0	3.2	1.000	OF-5
1992	6	.348	.435	23	8	2	0	0	0.0	2	2	5	6	0	0	0	16	0	1	0	2.8	.941	OF-6
1993	6	.444	.667	27	12	1	1	1	3.7	3	2	1	5	0	0	0	15	0	0	0	2.5	1.000	OF-6
4 yrs.	20	.392	.514	74	29	4	1	1	1.4	12	4	8	15	3	0	0	49	0	1	0	2.5	.980	OF-20

WORLD SERIES

Year Team	Games	BA	SA	AB	H	2B	3B	HR	HR%	R	RBI	BB	SO	SB	AB	H	PO	A	E	DP	TC/G	FA	G by Pos
1992 TOR A	6	.231	.269	26	6	1	0	0	0.0	2	2	0	6	1	0	0	22	1	0	1	3.8	1.000	OF-6
1993	6	.292	.708	24	7	3	2	1	4.2	8	7	4	7	1	0	0	16	0	0	0	2.7	1.000	OF-6
2 yrs.	12	.260	.480	50	13	4	2	1	2.0	10	9	4	13	2	0	0	38	1	0	1	3.3	1.000	OF-12

Rondell White

WHITE, RONDELL BERNARD B. Feb. 23, 1972, Milledgeville, Ga. BR TR 6'1" 193 lbs.

Year Team	Games	BA	SA	AB	H	2B	3B	HR	HR%	R	RBI	BB	SO	SB	AB	H	PO	A	E	DP	TC/G	FA	G by Pos
1993 MON N	23	.260	.411	73	19	3	1	2	2.7	9	15	7	16	1	1	0	33	0	0	0	1.4	1.000	OF-21
1994	40	.278	.464	97	27	10	1	2	2.1	16	13	9	18	1	10	0	34	1	2	0	0.9	.946	OF-29
2 yrs.	63	.271	.441	170	46	13	2	4	2.4	25	28	16	34	2	11	0	67	1	2	0	1.1	.971	OF-50

Mark Whiten

WHITEN, MARK ANTHONY B. Nov. 25, 1966, Pensacola, Fla. BB TR 6'3" 210 lbs.

Year Team	Games	BA	SA	AB	H	2B	3B	HR	HR%	R	RBI	BB	SO	SB	AB	H	PO	A	E	DP	TC/G	FA	G by Pos
1990 TOR A	33	.273	.375	88	24	1	1	2	2.3	12	7	7	14	2	3	0	60	3	0	0	1.9	1.000	OF-30, DH-2
1991 2 teams	TOR A (46G – .221)			CLE A (70G – .256)																			
" total	116	.243	.388	407	99	18	7	9	2.2	46	45	30	85	4	5	0	256	13	7	2	2.4	.975	OF-109, DH-3
1992 CLE A	148	.254	.360	508	129	19	4	9	1.8	73	43	72	102	16	1	1	321	14	7	1	2.3	.980	OF-144, DH-2
1993 STL N	152	.253	.423	562	142	13	4	25	4.4	81	99	58	110	15	6	2	329	9	10	1	2.3	.971	OF-148
1994	92	.293	.485	334	98	18	2	14	4.2	57	53	37	75	10	2	1	234	9	9	0	2.7	.964	OF-90
5 yrs.	541	.259	.408	1899	492	69	18	59	3.1	269	247	204	386	47	17	4	1200	48	33	4	2.4	.974	OF-521, DH-7

Darrell Whitmore

WHITMORE, DARRELL LAMONT B. Nov. 18, 1968, Front Royal, Va. BL TR 6'1" 210 lbs.

Year Team	Games	BA	SA	AB	H	2B	3B	HR	HR%	R	RBI	BB	SO	SB	AB	H	PO	A	E	DP	TC/G	FA	G by Pos
1993 FLA N	76	.204	.300	250	51	8	2	4	1.6	24	19	10	72	4	6	0	140	3	3	1	1.9	.979	OF-69
1994	9	.227	.273	22	5	1	0	0	0.0	1	0	3	5	0	2	0	14	0	0	0	1.6	1.000	OF-6
2 yrs.	85	.206	.298	272	56	9	2	4	1.5	25	19	13	77	4	8	0	154	3	3	1	1.9	.981	OF-75

Rick Wilkins

WILKINS, RICHARD DAVID B. June 4, 1967, Jacksonville, Fla. BL TR 6'2" 210 lbs.

Year Team	Games	BA	SA	AB	H	2B	3B	HR	HR%	R	RBI	BB	SO	SB	AB	H	PO	A	E	DP	TC/G	FA	G by Pos
1991 CHI N	86	.222	.355	203	45	9	0	6	3.0	21	22	19	56	2	5	2	373	42	3	6	4.9	.993	C-82
1992	83	.270	.414	244	66	9	1	8	3.3	20	22	28	53	0	15	5	408	47	3	5	5.5	.993	C-73
1993	136	.303	.561	446	135	23	1	30	6.7	78	73	50	99	2	9	4	717	89	3	8	5.9	.996	C-133
1994	100	.227	.387	313	71	25	2	7	2.2	44	39	40	86	4	9	0	550	51	4	1	6.1	.993	C-95, 1B-2
4 yrs.	405	.263	.451	1206	317	66	4	51	4.2	163	156	137	294	9	38	11	2048	229	13	20	5.7	.994	C-383, 1B-2

Jerry Willard

WILLARD, GERALD DUANE, JR. B. Mar. 14, 1960, Oxnard, Calif. BL TR 6'2" 200 lbs.

Year Team	Games	BA	SA	AB	H	2B	3B	HR	HR%	R	RBI	BB	SO	SB	AB	H	PO	A	E	DP	TC/G	FA	G by Pos
1984 CLE A	87	.224	.386	246	55	8	1	10	4.1	21	37	26	55	1	12	1	335	35	7	7	4.3	.981	C-76, DH-1
1985	104	.270	.383	300	81	13	0	7	2.3	39	36	28	59	0	10	2	427	52	5	11	4.7	.990	C-96, DH-1
1986 OAK A	75	.267	.385	161	43	7	0	4	2.5	17	26	22	28	0	7	4	300	12	2	1	4.2	.994	C-71, DH-7
1987	7	.167	.167	6	1	0	0	0	0.0	0	0	1	0	0	1	0	1	0	0	1	0.1	1.000	DH-3, 1B-1, 3B-1
1990 CHI A	3	.000	.000	3	0	0	0	0	0.0	0	0	0	0	0	2	0	0	0	0	0	0.0	–	C-1
1991 ATL N	17	.214	.429	14	3	0	0	1	7.1	1	4	2	5	0	12	2	3	0	0	0	0.2	1.000	C-1
1992 2 teams	ATL N (26G – .348)			MON N (21G – .120)																			
" total	47	.229	.375	48	11	1	0	2	4.2	2	8	2	10	0	39	9	19	3	1	0	0.5	.957	1B-5, C-1
1994 SEA A	6	.200	.800	5	1	0	0	1	20.0	1	3	1	1	0	4	1	0	0	0	0	0.0	–	C-1, DH-1
8 yrs.	346	.249	.384	783	195	29	1	25	3.2	82	114	83	161	1	87	19	1085	102	15	20	3.5	.988	C-247, DH-13, 1B-6, 3B-1

LEAGUE CHAMPIONSHIP SERIES

Year Team	Games	BA	SA	AB	H	2B	3B	HR	HR%	R	RBI	BB	SO	SB	AB	H	PO	A	E	DP	TC/G	FA	G by Pos
1991 ATL N	2	1.000	.000	2	0	0	0	0	0.0	0	1	0	0	0	2	0	0	0	0	0	0.0	–	

WORLD SERIES

Year Team	Games	BA	SA	AB	H	2B	3B	HR	HR%	R	RBI	BB	SO	SB	AB	H	PO	A	E	DP	TC/G	FA	G by Pos
1991 ATL N	1	–	–	0	0	0	0	0	–	0	1	1	0	0	0	0	0	0	0	0	0.0	–	

Bernie Williams

WILLIAMS, BERNABE Born Bernabe Williams (Figueroa). B. Sept. 13, 1968, San Juan, Puerto Rico. BB TR 6'2" 180 lbs.

Year Team	Games	BA	SA	AB	H	2B	3B	HR	HR%	R	RBI	BB	SO	SB	AB	H	PO	A	E	DP	TC/G	FA	G by Pos
1991 NY A	85	.238	.350	320	76	19	4	3	0.9	43	34	48	57	10	0	0	230	3	5	0	2.8	.979	OF-85
1992	62	.280	.406	261	73	14	2	5	1.9	39	26	29	36	7	0	0	187	5	1	2	3.1	.995	OF-62

Year Team	Games	BA	SA	AB	H	2B	3B	HR	HR%	R	RBI	BB	SO	SB	Pinch Hit AB	Pinch Hit H	PO	A	E	DP	TC/G	FA	G by Pos

Bernie Williams *continued*

Year Team	Games	BA	SA	AB	H	2B	3B	HR	HR%	R	RBI	BB	SO	SB	AB	H	PO	A	E	DP	TC/G	FA	G by Pos
1993	139	.268	.400	567	152	31	4	12	2.1	67	68	53	106	9	0	0	366	5	4	1	2.7	.989	OF-139
1994	108	.289	.453	408	118	29	1	12	2.9	80	57	61	54	16	3	1	277	7	3	1	2.7	.990	OF-107
4 yrs.	394	.269	.405	1556	419	93	11	32	2.1	229	185	191	253	42	3	1	1060	20	13	4	2.8	.988	OF-393

Eddie Williams

WILLIAMS, EDWARD LAQUAN
B. Nov. 1, 1964, Shreveport, La.   BR TR 6'   175 lbs.

Year Team	Games	BA	SA	AB	H	2B	3B	HR	HR%	R	RBI	BB	SO	SB	AB	H	PO	A	E	DP	TC/G	FA	G by Pos
1986 CLE A	5	.143	.143	7	1	0	0	0	0.0	2	1	0	3	0	2	0	0	0	0	0	0.0	–	OF-4
1987	22	.172	.281	64	11	4	0	1	1.6	9	4	9	19	0	0	0	17	37	1	6	2.5	.982	3B-22
1988	10	.190	.190	21	4	0	0	0	0.0	3	1	0	3	0	0	0	3	18	0	0	2.1	1.000	3B-10
1989 CHI A	66	.274	.358	201	55	8	0	3	1.5	25	10	18	31	1	1	0	37	123	16	21	2.7	.909	3B-65
1990 SD N	14	.286	.571	42	12	3	0	3	7.1	5	4	5	6	0	2	0	5	21	3	2	2.1	.897	3B-13
1994	49	.331	.594	175	58	11	1	11	6.3	32	42	15	26	0	2	0	382	29	5	28	8.5	.988	1B-46, 3B-1
6 yrs.	166	.276	.437	510	141	26	1	18	3.5	76	62	47	88	1	7	0	444	228	25	57	4.2	.964	3B-111, 1B-46, OF-4

Gerald Williams

WILLIAMS, GERALD FLOYD
B. Aug. 10, 1966, New Orleans, La.   BR TR 6'2"   190 lbs.

Year Team	Games	BA	SA	AB	H	2B	3B	HR	HR%	R	RBI	BB	SO	SB	AB	H	PO	A	E	DP	TC/G	FA	G by Pos
1992 NY A	15	.296	.704	27	8	2	0	3	11.1	7	6	0	3	2	0	0	20	1	2	0	1.5	.913	OF-12
1993	42	.149	.269	67	10	2	3	0	0.0	11	6	1	14	2	4	1	41	2	2	0	1.1	.956	OF-37
1994	57	.291	.523	86	25	8	0	4	4.7	19	13	4	17	1	6	1	43	2	2	0	0.8	.957	OF-43, DH-2
3 yrs.	114	.239	.456	180	43	12	3	7	3.9	37	25	5	34	5	10	2	104	5	6	0	1.0	.948	OF-92, DH-2

Matt Williams

WILLIAMS, MATTHEW DERRICK
B. Nov. 28, 1965, Bishop, Calif.   BR TR 6'2"   205 lbs.

Year Team	Games	BA	SA	AB	H	2B	3B	HR	HR%	R	RBI	BB	SO	SB	AB	H	PO	A	E	DP	TC/G	FA	G by Pos
1987 SF N	84	.188	.339	245	46	9	2	8	3.3	28	21	16	68	4	3	2	110	234	9	52	4.2	.975	SS-70, 3B-17
1988	52	.205	.410	156	32	6	1	8	5.1	17	19	8	41	0	2	0	48	108	7	9	3.1	.957	3B-43, SS-14
1989	84	.202	.455	292	59	18	1	18	6.2	31	50	14	72	1	3	0	90	168	10	15	3.2	.963	3B-73, SS-30
1990	159	.277	.488	617	171	27	2	33	5.3	87	122	33	138	7	1	1	140	306	19	33	2.9	.959	3B-159
1991	157	.268	.499	589	158	24	5	34	5.8	72	98	33	128	5	3	0	134	295	16	32	2.8	.964	3B-155, SS-4
1992	146	.227	.384	529	120	13	5	20	3.8	58	66	39	109	7	5	1	105	289	23	33	2.9	.945	3B-144
1993	145	.294	.561	579	170	33	4	38	6.6	105	110	27	80	1	1	0	117	266	12	34	2.7	.970	3B-144
1994	112	.267	.607	445	119	16	3	**43**	9.7	74	96	33	87	1	2	0	79	234	12	21	2.9	.963	3B-110
8 yrs.	939	.253	.485	3452	875	146	23	202	5.9	472	582	203	723	26	20	4	823	1900	108	229	3.0	.962	3B-845, SS-118

LEAGUE CHAMPIONSHIP SERIES

Year Team	Games	BA	SA	AB	H	2B	3B	HR	HR%	R	RBI	BB	SO	SB	AB	H	PO	A	E	DP	TC/G	FA	G by Pos
1989 SF N	5	.300	.650	20	6	1	0	2	10.0	2	9	0	2	0	0	0	5	12	0	2	3.4	1.000	3B-5, SS-1

WORLD SERIES

Year Team	Games	BA	SA	AB	H	2B	3B	HR	HR%	R	RBI	BB	SO	SB	AB	H	PO	A	E	DP	TC/G	FA	G by Pos
1989 SF N	4	.125	.313	16	2	0	0	1	6.3	1	1	0	6	0	0	0	4	12	0	2	4.0	1.000	SS-4, 3B-3

Dan Wilson

WILSON, DANIEL ALLEN
B. Mar. 25, 1969, Arlington Heights, Ill.   BR TR 6'3"   190 lbs.

Year Team	Games	BA	SA	AB	H	2B	3B	HR	HR%	R	RBI	BB	SO	SB	AB	H	PO	A	E	DP	TC/G	FA	G by Pos
1992 CIN N	12	.360	.400	25	9	1	0	0	0.0	2	3	3	8	0	4	2	42	4	0	0	3.8	1.000	C-9
1993	36	.224	.263	76	17	3	0	0	0.0	6	8	9	16	0	3	1	146	9	1	2	4.3	.994	C-35
1994 SEA A	91	.216	.312	282	61	14	2	3	1.1	24	27	10	57	1	0	0	602	41	9	2	7.2	.986	C-91
3 yrs.	139	.227	.308	383	87	18	2	3	0.8	32	38	22	81	1	7	3	790	54	10	4	6.1	.988	C-135

Willie Wilson

WILSON, WILLIE JAMES
B. July 9, 1955, Montgomery, Ala.   BB TR 6'3"   190 lbs.

Year Team	Games	BA	SA	AB	H	2B	3B	HR	HR%	R	RBI	BB	SO	SB	AB	H	PO	A	E	DP	TC/G	FA	G by Pos
1976 KC A	12	.167	.167	6	1	0	0	0	0.0	0	0	0	2	2	0	0	6	1	1	0	0.7	.875	OF-6
1977	13	.324	.382	34	11	2	0	0	0.0	10	1	1	8	6	0	0	24	0	1	0	1.9	.960	OF-9, DH-2
1978	127	.217	.278	198	43	8	2	0	0.0	43	16	16	33	46	0	0	171	6	4	2	1.4	.978	OF-112, DH-6
1979	154	.315	.420	588	185	18	13	6	1.0	113	49	28	92	**83**	0	0	384	13	6	0	2.6	.985	OF-152, DH-2
1980	161	.326	.421	705¹	230	28	15	3	0.4	**133**	49	28	81	79	3	0	482	9	6	1	3.1	.988	OF-159
1981	102	.303	.364	439	133	10	7	1	0.2	54	32	18	42	34	0	0	299	14	4	3	3.1	.987	OF-101
1982	136	**.332**	.431	585	194	19	15	3	0.5	87	46	26	81	37	1	0	376	4	5	0	2.8	.987	OF-135
1983	137	.276	.352	576	159	22	8	2	0.3	90	33	33	75	59	3	1	354	3	9	0	2.7	.975	OF-136
1984	128	.301	.390	541	163	24	9	2	0.4	81	44	39	56	47	0	0	383	6	4	2	3.1	.990	OF-128
1985	141	.278	.408	605	168	25	21	4	0.7	87	43	29	94	43	0	0	378	4	1	1	2.7	.995	OF-140
1986	156	.269	.366	631	170	20	7	9	1.4	77	44	31	97	34	6	0	408	4	3	2	2.7	.993	OF-155
1987	146	.279	.377	610	170	18	15	4	0.7	97	30	32	88	59	1	0	342	3	1	1	2.4	.997	OF-143, DH-2
1988	147	.262	.333	591	155	17	11	1	0.2	81	37	22	106	35	4	1	365	1	4	0	2.5	.989	OF-142
1989	112	.253	.358	383	97	17	7	3	0.8	58	43	27	78	24	2	2	252	2	6	0	2.3	.977	OF-108, DH-1
1990	115	.290	.371	307	89	13	3	2	0.7	49	42	30	57	24	9	0	187	2	0	1	1.6	1.000	OF-106, DH-1
1991 OAK A	113	.238	.313	294	70	14	4	0	0.0	38	28	18	43	20	21	6	176	2	3	0	1.6	.983	OF-87, DH-9
1992	132	.270	.333	396	107	15	5	0	0.0	38	37	35	65	28	10	3	355	2	7	2	2.8	.981	OF-120, DH-5
1993 CHI N	105	.258	.348	221	57	11	3	1	0.5	29	11	11	40	7	37	9	109	1	1	0	1.1	.991	OF-82
1994	17	.238	.429	21	5	0	2	0	0.0	4	0	1	6	1	6	2	9	0	0	0	0.5	1.000	OF-10
19 yrs.	2154	.285	.376	7731	2207	281	147	41	0.5	1169	585	425	1144	668 10th	103	24	5060	77	67	15	2.4	.987	OF-2031, DH-28

DIVISIONAL PLAYOFF SERIES

Year Team	Games	BA	SA	AB	H	2B	3B	HR	HR%	R	RBI	BB	SO	SB	AB	H	PO	A	E	DP	TC/G	FA	G by Pos
1981 KC A	3	.308	.308	13	4	0	0	0	0.0	1	1	0	0	0	0	0	6	0	0	0	2.0	1.000	OF-3

LEAGUE CHAMPIONSHIP SERIES

Year Team	Games	BA	SA	AB	H	2B	3B	HR	HR%	R	RBI	BB	SO	SB	AB	H	PO	A	E	DP	TC/G	FA	G by Pos
1978 KC A	3	.250	.250	4	1	0	0	0	0.0	0	0	0	2	0	0	0	2	0	0	0	0.7	1.000	OF-3
1980	3	.308	.615	13	4	2	1	0	0.0	4	1	2	0	0	0	0	6	1	0	0	2.3	1.000	OF-3
1984	3	.154	.154	13	2	0	0	0	0.0	0	0	1	2	0	0	0	10	0	0	0	3.3	1.000	OF-3
1985	7	.310	.414	29	9	0	0	1	3.4	5	2	1	5	1	0	0	12	0	0	0	1.7	1.000	OF-7
1992 OAK A	6	.227	.273	22	5	1	0	0	0.0	0	1	5	7	0	0	0	16	0	0	0	2.7	1.000	OF-6, DH-1
5 yrs.	22	.259	.358	81	21	3	1	1	1.2	7	6	4	16	1	0	0	46	1	0	0	2.1	1.000	OF-22, DH-1

WORLD SERIES

Year Team	Games	BA	SA	AB	H	2B	3B	HR	HR%	R	RBI	BB	SO	SB	AB	H	PO	A	E	DP	TC/G	FA	G by Pos
1980 KC A	6	.154	.192	26	4	1	0	0	0.0	3	0	4	12	2	0	0	15	1	0	0	2.7	1.000	OF-6
1985	7	.367	.433	30	11	0	1	0	0.0	2	3	1	4	3	0	0	19	1	0	0	2.9	1.000	OF-7
2 yrs.	13	.268	.321	56	15	1	1	0	0.0	5	3	5	16	5	0	0	34	2	0	0	2.8	1.000	OF-13

Year	Team	Games	BA	SA	AB	H	2B	3B	HR	HR%	R	RBI	BB	SO	SB	Pinch Hit AB	H	PO	A	E	DP	TC/G	FA	G by Pos

Dave Winfield

WINFIELD, DAVID MARK
B. Oct. 3, 1951, St. Paul, Minn.   BR TR 6'6" 220 lbs.

Year	Team	Games	BA	SA	AB	H	2B	3B	HR	HR%	R	RBI	BB	SO	SB	PH AB	PH H	PO	A	E	DP	TC/G	FA	G by Pos
1973	SD N	56	.277	.383	141	39	4	1	3	2.1	9	12	12	19	0	17	8	65	1	3	0	1.2	.957	OF-36, 1B-1
1974		145	.265	.438	498	132	18	4	20	4.0	57	75	40	96	9	15	4	276	11	12	2	2.1	.960	OF-131
1975		143	.267	.403	509	136	20	2	15	2.9	74	76	69	82	23	2	0	302	9	9	1	2.2	.972	OF-138
1976		137	.283	.431	492	139	26	4	13	2.6	81	69	65	78	26	2	1	304	15	6	4	2.4	.982	OF-134
1977		157	.275	.467	615	169	29	7	25	4.1	104	92	58	75	16	2	1	368	15	11	3	2.5	.972	OF-156
1978		158	.308	.499	587	181	30	5	24	4.1	88	97	55	81	21	5	1	328	8	7	1	2.2	.980	OF-154, 1B-2
1979		159	.308	.558	597	184	27	10	34	5.7	97	118	85	71	15	2	0	344	14	5	3	2.3	.986	OF-157
1980		162	.276	.450	558	154	25	6	20	3.6	89	87	79	83	23	9	3	273	20	4.	4	1.8	.987	OF-159
1981	NY A	105	.294	.464	388	114	25	1	13	3.4	52	68	43	41	11	4	3	196	1	3	0	1.9	.985	OF-102, DH-1
1982		140	.280	.560	539	151	24	8	37	6.9	84	106	45	64	5	1	0	279	17	8	2	2.2	.974	OF-135, DH-4
1983		152	.283	.513	598	169	26	8	32	5.4	99	116	58	77	15	3	2	313	5	7	2	2.1	.978	OF-151
1984		141	.340	.515	567	193	34	4	19	3.4	106	100	53	71	6	0	0	306	3	2	1	2.2	.994	OF-140
1985		155	.275	.471	633	174	34	6	26	4.1	105	114	52	96	19	1	1	316	13	3	3	2.1	.991	OF-152, DH-2
1986		154	.262	.462	565	148	31	5	24	4.2	90	104	77	106	6	7	1	292	9	5	5	2.0	.984	OF-145, DH-6, 3B-2
1987		156	.275	.457	575	158	22	1	27	4.7	83	97	76	96	5	4	2	253	6	3	1	1.7	.989	OF-145, DH-8
1988		149	.322	.530	559	180	37	2	25	4.5	96	107	69	88	9	4	0	276	3	3	1	1.9	.989	OF-141, DH-4
1990	2 teams	NY A (20G – .213)			CAL A (112G – .275)																			
"	total	132	.267	.453	475	127	21	2	21	4.4	70	78	52	81	0	7	1	177	7	2	1	1.4	.989	OF-120, DH-10
1991	CAL A	150	.262	.472	568	149	27	4	28	4.9	75	86	56	109	7	1	0	198	7	2	1	1.4	.990	OF-115, DH-34
1992	TOR A	156	.290	.491	583	169	33	3	26	4.5	92	108	82	89	2	0	0	52	1	0	0	0.3	1.000	DH-130, OF-26
1993	MIN A	143	.271	.442	547	148	27	2	21	3.8	72	76	45	106	2	2	5	91	3	0	3	0.7	1.000	DH-105, OF-31, 1B-5
1994		77	.252	.425	294	74	15	3	10	3.4	35	43	31	51	2	0	0	3	0	0	0	0.0	1.000	DH-76, OF-1
21 yrs.		2927	.284	.476	10888	3088	535	88	463	4.3	1658	1829	1202	1660	222	91	30	5012	168	95	38	1.8	.982	OF-2469, DH-380, 1B-8, 3B-2
			8th			7th																		

DIVISIONAL PLAYOFF SERIES

Year	Team	Games	BA	SA	AB	H	2B	3B	HR	HR%	R	RBI	BB	SO	SB	PH AB	PH H	PO	A	E	DP	TC/G	FA	G by Pos
1981	NY A	5	.350	.500	20	7	3	0	0	0.0	2	0	1	5	0	0	0	10	1	0	0	2.2	1.000	OF-5

LEAGUE CHAMPIONSHIP SERIES

Year	Team	Games	BA	SA	AB	H	2B	3B	HR	HR%	R	RBI	BB	SO	SB	PH AB	PH H	PO	A	E	DP	TC/G	FA	G by Pos
1981	NY A	3	.154	.231	13	2	1	0	0	0.0	2	2	2	2	1	0	0	6	0	0	0	2.0	1.000	OF-3
1992	TOR A	6	.250	.542	24	6	1	0	2	8.3	7	3	4	2	0	0	0	0	0	0	0	0.0	–	DH-6
2 yrs.		9	.216	.432	37	8	2	0	2	5.4	9	5	6	4	1	0	0	6	0	0	0	0.7	1.000	DH-6, OF-3

WORLD SERIES

Year	Team	Games	BA	SA	AB	H	2B	3B	HR	HR%	R	RBI	BB	SO	SB	PH AB	PH H	PO	A	E	DP	TC/G	FA	G by Pos
1981	NY A	6	.045	.045	22	1	0	0	0	0.0	0	1	5	4	1	0	0	13	1	0	0	2.3	1.000	OF-6
1992	TOR A	6	.227	.273	22	5	1	0	0	0.0	0	3	2	3	0	0	0	7	0	0	0	1.2	1.000	DH-3, OF-3
2 yrs.		12	.136	.159	44	6	1	0	0	0.0	0	4	7	7	1	0	0	20	1	0	0	1.8	1.000	OF-9, DH-3

Tony Womack

WOMACK, ANTHONY DARRELL
B. Sept. 25, 1969, Danville, Va.   BL TR 5'9" 160 lbs.

Year	Team	Games	BA	SA	AB	H	2B	3B	HR	HR%	R	RBI	BB	SO	SB	PH AB	PH H	PO	A	E	DP	TC/G	FA	G by Pos
1993	PIT N	15	.083	.083	24	2	0	0	0	0.0	5	0	3	3	2	3	0	11	22	1	6	2.3	.971	SS-6
1994		5	.333	.333	12	4	0	0	0	0.0	4	1	2	3	0	0	0	3	6	2	2	2.2	.818	2B-3, SS-2
2 yrs.		20	.167	.167	36	6	0	0	0	0.0	9	1	5	6	2	3	0	14	28	3	8	2.3	.933	SS-8, 2B-3

Rick Wrona

WRONA, RICHARD JAMES
B. Dec. 10, 1963, Tulsa, Okla.   BR TR 6'1" 185 lbs.

Year	Team	Games	BA	SA	AB	H	2B	3B	HR	HR%	R	RBI	BB	SO	SB	PH AB	PH H	PO	A	E	DP	TC/G	FA	G by Pos
1988	CHI N	4	.000	.000	6	0	0	0	0	0.0	0	0	0	1	0	1	0	11	1	0	0	3.0	1.000	C-2
1989		38	.283	.391	92	26	2	1	2	2.2	11	14	2	21	0	3	2	158	15	3	1	4.6	.983	C-37
1990		16	.172	.172	29	5	0	0	0	0.0	3	0	2	11	1	0	0	55	9	2	2	4.1	.970	C-16
1992	CIN N	11	.174	.174	23	4	0	0	0	0.0	0	0	0	3	0	0	0	52	5	2	0	5.4	.966	C-10, 1B-1
1993	CHI A	4	.125	.125	8	1	0	0	0	0.0	0	1	0	4	0	0	0	12	0	0	0	3.0	1.000	C-4
1994	MIL A	6	.500	1.200	10	5	4	0	1	10.0	2	3	1	1	0	2	1	10	2	1	0	2.2	.923	C-5, 1B-1
6 yrs.		79	.244	.345	168	41	6	1	3	1.8	16	18	5	41	1	6	3	298	32	8	3	4.3	.976	C-74, 1B-2

LEAGUE CHAMPIONSHIP SERIES

Year	Team	Games	BA	SA	AB	H	2B	3B	HR	HR%	R	RBI	BB	SO	SB	PH AB	PH H	PO	A	E	DP	TC/G	FA	G by Pos
1989	CHI N	2	1.000	.000	5	0	0	0	0	0.0	0	0	0	3	0	0	0	9	1	0	0	5.0	1.000	C-2

Eric Young

YOUNG, ERIC ORLANDO
B. Nov. 26, 1966, Jacksonville, Fla.   BR TR 5'9" 180 lbs.

Year	Team	Games	BA	SA	AB	H	2B	3B	HR	HR%	R	RBI	BB	SO	SB	PH AB	PH H	PO	A	E	DP	TC/G	FA	G by Pos
1992	LA N	49	.258	.288	132	34	1	0	1	0.8	9	11	8	9	6	0	0	85	115	9	20	4.3	.957	2B-43
1993	CLR N	144	.269	.353	490	132	16	8	3	0.6	82	42	63	41	42	14	5	255	229	18	44	3.5	.964	2B-79, OF-52
1994		90	.272	.430	228	62	13	1	7	3.1	37	30	38	17	18	21	3	97	4	2	0	1.1	.981	OF-60, 2B-1
3 yrs.		283	.268	.364	850	228	30	9	11	1.3	128	83	109	67	66	35	8	437	348	29	64	2.9	.964	2B-123, OF-112

Ernie Young

YOUNG, ERNEST WESLEY
B. July 8, 1969, Chicago, Ill.   BR TR 6'1" 190 lbs.

Year	Team	Games	BA	SA	AB	H	2B	3B	HR	HR%	R	RBI	BB	SO	SB	PH AB	PH H	PO	A	E	DP	TC/G	FA	G by Pos
1994	OAK A	11	.067	.100	30	2	1	0	0	0.0	2	3	1	8	0	2	0	22	1	1	0	2.2	.958	OF-10, DH-1

Gerald Young

YOUNG, GERALD ANTHONY
B. Oct. 22, 1964, Tele, Honduras.   BB TR 6'2" 185 lbs.

Year	Team	Games	BA	SA	AB	H	2B	3B	HR	HR%	R	RBI	BB	SO	SB	PH AB	PH H	PO	A	E	DP	TC/G	FA	G by Pos
1987	HOU N	71	.321	.380	274	88	9	2	1	0.4	44	15	26	27	26	2	1	143	5	3	1	2.1	.980	OF-67
1988		149	.257	.325	576	148	21	9	0	0.0	79	37	66	65	65	5	2	357	10	3	1	2.5	.992	OF-145
1989		146	.233	.276	533	124	17	3	0	0.0	71	38	74	60	34	2	1	412	15	1	5	2.9	.998	OF-143
1990		57	.175	.234	154	27	4	1	1	0.6	15	4	20	23	6	5	0	99	4	1	1	1.8	.990	OF-50
1991		108	.218	.275	142	31	3	1	1	0.7	26	11	24	17	16	23	3	96	4	0	1	0.9	1.000	OF-84
1992		74	.184	.224	76	14	1	1	0	0.0	14	4	10	11	6	20	1	53	0	2	0	0.7	.964	OF-57
1993	CLR N	19	.053	.053	19	1	0	0	0	0.0	5	1	4	1	0	5	0	15	0	2	0	0.9	.882	OF-11
1994	STL N	16	.317	.488	41	13	3	2	0	0.0	9	3	3	8	2	4	1	19	0	0	0	1.2	1.000	OF-11
8 yrs.		640	.246	.304	1815	446	58	19	3	0.2	259	113	227	213	155	66	9	1194	38	12	9	1.9	.990	OF-568

Year	Team	Games	BA	SA	AB	H	2B	3B	HR	HR%	R	RBI	BB	SO	SB	Pinch Hit AB	Pinch Hit H	PO	A	E	DP	TC/G	FA	G by Pos

Kevin Young

YOUNG, KEVIN STACEY
B. June 16, 1969, Alpena, Mich.

BR TR 6'3" 210 lbs.

Year	Team	Games	BA	SA	AB	H	2B	3B	HR	HR%	R	RBI	BB	SO	SB	PH AB	PH H	PO	A	E	DP	TC/G	FA	G by Pos
1992	PIT N	10	.571	.571	7	4	0	0	0	0.0	2	4	2	0	1	1	0	3	1	1	0	0.5	.800	3B-7, 1B-1
1993		141	.236	.343	449	106	24	3	6	1.3	38	47	36	82	2	6	2	1122	112	3	108	8.8	.998	1B-135, 3B-6
1994		59	.205	.320	122	25	7	2	1	0.8	15	11	8	34	0	10	0	178	45	3	21	3.8	.987	1B-37, 3B-17, OF-1
3 yrs.		210	.234	.341	578	135	31	5	7	1.2	55	62	46	116	3	17	2	1303	158	7	129	7.0	.995	1B-173, 3B-30, OF-1

Eddie Zambrano

ZAMBRANO, EDUARDO JOSE
Born Eduardo Jose Zambrano (Guerra).
B. Feb. 1, 1966, Maracaibo, Venezuela

BR TR 6'2" 175 lbs.

Year	Team	Games	BA	SA	AB	H	2B	3B	HR	HR%	R	RBI	BB	SO	SB	PH AB	PH H	PO	A	E	DP	TC/G	FA	G by Pos
1993	CHI N	8	.294	.294	17	5	0	0	0	0.0	1	2	1	3	0	3	2	14	0	1	1	1.9	.933	OF-4, 1B-2
1994		67	.259	.474	116	30	7	0	6	5.2	17	18	16	29	2	26	7	84	5	2	6	1.4	.978	OF-27, 1B-9, 3B-4
2 yrs.		75	.263	.451	133	35	7	0	6	4.5	18	20	17	32	2	29	9	98	5	3	7	1.4	.972	OF-31, 1B-11, 3B-4

Todd Zeile

ZEILE, TODD EDWARD
B. Sept. 9, 1965, Van Nuys, Calif.

BR TR 6'1" 190 lbs.

Year	Team	Games	BA	SA	AB	H	2B	3B	HR	HR%	R	RBI	BB	SO	SB	PH AB	PH H	PO	A	E	DP	TC/G	FA	G by Pos
1989	STL N	28	.256	.354	82	21	3	1	1	1.2	7	8	9	14	0	5	0	125	10	4	1	5.0	.971	C-23
1990		144	.244	.398	495	121	25	3	15	3.0	62	57	67	77	2	3	0	648	106	15	12	5.3	.980	C-105, 3B-24, 1B-11, OF-1
1991		155	.280	.412	565	158	36	3	11	1.9	76	81	62	94	17	0	0	124	290	25	18	2.8	.943	3B-154
1992		126	.257	.364	439	113	18	4	7	1.6	51	48	68	70	7	3	0	80	235	13	19	2.6	.960	3B-124
1993		157	.277	.433	571	158	36	1	17	3.0	82	103	70	76	5	3	1	83	310	33	26	2.7	.923	3B-153
1994		113	.267	.470	415	111	25	1	19	4.6	62	75	52	56	1	2	0	66	224	12	24	2.7	.960	3B-112
6 yrs.		723	.266	.413	2567	682	143	13	70	2.7	340	372	328	387	32	16	1	1126	1175	102	100	3.3	.958	3B-567, C-128, 1B-11, OF-1

Bob Zupcic

ZUPCIC, ROBERT
B. Aug. 18, 1966, Pittsburgh, Pa.

BR TR 6'4" 220 lbs.

Year	Team	Games	BA	SA	AB	H	2B	3B	HR	HR%	R	RBI	BB	SO	SB	PH AB	PH H	PO	A	E	DP	TC/G	FA	G by Pos
1991	BOS A	18	.160	.280	25	4	0	0	1	4.0	3	3	1	6	0	1	0	14	0	2	0	0.9	.875	OF-16
1992		124	.276	.352	392	108	19	1	3	0.8	46	43	25	60	2	10	2	241	11	6	3	2.1	.977	OF-114, DH-5
1993		141	.241	.360	286	69	24	2	2	0.7	40	26	27	54	5	9	2	179	7	4	2	1.3	.979	OF-122, DH-5
1994 2 teams	BOS A (4G – .000)		CHI A	(32G – .205)																				
" total		36	.196	.293	92	18	4	1	1	1.1	10	8	4	17	0	3	2	49	4	0	0	1.5	1.000	OF-30, 3B-2, 1B-1, DH-1
4 yrs.		319	.250	.346	795	199	47	4	7	0.9	99	80	57	137	7	23	6	483	22	12	5	1.6	.977	OF-282, DH-11, 3B-2, 1B-1

Pitcher Register

The Pitcher Register is an alphabetical listing of every man who pitched in the major leagues in 1994. Also included are those players who played in 1994 and had pitched (however briefly) in previous seasons.

As in the Batter Register, boldfaced print indicates a league leader for the season. A superscript "1" means that the figure is the all-time single season record (since 1893, when the mound was fixed at a distance of 60 feet 6 inches), and figures underneath a player's career and World Series career totals provide his rank in the top ten all-time.

Partial innings pitched are indicated by adding ".1" or ".2" to the figure in the IP column; "55.2" would mean that he had pitched fifty-five and two-third innings. Meaningless averages are indicated with a dash; these would include the winning percentage of a pitcher with an 0-0 record, or the batting average of a pitcher with no at bats. Any time the infinity symbol "∞" is shown for a pitcher's earned run average, it means that he allowed at least one run in that season without retiring a batter.

An asterisk (*) shown in the lifetime batting totals means that that pitcher's complete batting record is included in the Player Register.

Year	Team	W	L	PCT	ERA	G	GS	CG	IP	H	BB	SO	ShO	W	L	SV	AB	H	HR	BA	PO	A	E	DP	TC/G	FA
														Relief Pitching			**Batting**									

Jim Abbott

ABBOTT, JAMES ANTHONY
B. Sept. 19, 1967, Flint, Mich.
BL TL 6'3" 200 lbs.

Year	Team	W	L	PCT	ERA	G	GS	CG	IP	H	BB	SO	ShO	W	L	SV	AB	H	HR	BA	PO	A	E	DP	TC/G	FA
1989	CAL A	12	12	.500	3.92	29	29	4	181.1	190	74	115	2	0	0	0	0	0	0	–	6	26	3	1	1.2	.914
1990		10	14	.417	4.51	33	33	4	211.2	**246**	72	105	1	0	0	0	0	0	0	–	8	36	1	4	1.4	.978
1991		18	11	.621	2.89	34	34	5	243	222	73	158	1	0	0	0	0	0	0	–	19	46	2	3	2.0	.970
1992		7	15	.318	2.77	29	29	7	211	208	68	130	0	0	0	0	0	0	0	–	11	35	0	1	1.6	1.000
1993	NY A	11	14	.440	4.37	32	32	4	214	221	73	95	1	0	0	0	0	0	0	–	4	42	1	3	1.5	.979
1994		9	8	.529	4.55	24	24	2	160.1	167	64	90	0	0	0	0	0	0	0	–	8	23	1	1	1.3	.969
6 yrs.		67	74	.475	3.78	181	181	26	1221.1	1254	424	693	5	0	0	0	0	0	0	–	56	208	8	13	1.5	.971

Mark Acre

ACRE, MARK ROBERT
B. Sept. 16, 1968, Concord, Calif.
BR TR 6'8" 235 lbs.

Year	Team	W	L	PCT	ERA	G	GS	CG	IP	H	BB	SO	ShO	W	L	SV	AB	H	HR	BA	PO	A	E	DP	TC/G	FA
1994	OAK A	5	1	.833	3.41	34	0	0	34.1	24	23	21	0	5	1	0	0	0	0	–	0	3	1	0	0.1	.750

Rick Aguilera

AGUILERA, RICHARD WARREN (Aggie)
B. Dec. 31, 1961, San Gabriel, Calif.
BR TR 6'4" 195 lbs.

Year	Team	W	L	PCT	ERA	G	GS	CG	IP	H	BB	SO	ShO	W	L	SV	AB	H	HR	BA	PO	A	E	DP	TC/G	FA
1985	NY N	10	7	.588	3.24	21	19	2	122.1	118	37	74	0	1	0	0	36	10	0	.278	8	16	0	1	1.1	1.000
1986		10	7	.588	3.88	28	20	2	141.2	145	36	104	0	1	1	0	51	8	2	.157	13	26	0	1	1.4	1.000
1987		11	3	.786	3.60	18	17	1	115	124	33	77	0	0	0	0	40	9	1	.225	7	29	2	1	2.1	.947
1988		0	4	.000	6.93	11	3	0	24.2	29	10	16	0	0	2	0	4	1	0	.250	3	5	0	0	0.7	1.000
1989	2 teams				NY N	(36G 6–6)		MIN A	(11G 3–5)																	
"	total	9	11	.450	2.79	47	11	3	145	130	38	137	0	6	6	7	7	0	0	.000	6	21	1	2	0.6	.964
1990	MIN A	5	3	.625	2.76	56	0	0	65.1	55	19	61	0	5	3	32	0	0	0	–	2	4	0	0	0.1	1.000
1991		4	5	.444	2.35	63	0	0	69	44	30	61	0	4	5	42	0	0	0	–	7	5	0	0	0.2	1.000
1992		2	6	.250	2.84	64	0	0	66.2	60	17	52	0	2	6	41	0	0	0	–	2	5	0	0	0.1	1.000
1993		4	3	.571	3.11	65	0	0	72.1	60	14	59	0	4	3	34	0	0	0	–	12	8	0	0	0.3	1.000
1994		1	4	.200	3.63	44	0	0	44.2	57	10	46	0	1	4	23	0	0	0	–	4	9	0	0	0.3	1.000
10 yrs.		56	53	.514	3.29	417	70	8	866.2	822	244	687	0	24	30	179	138	28	3	.203	64	128	3	5	0.5	.985

LEAGUE CHAMPIONSHIP SERIES

Year	Team	W	L	PCT	ERA	G	GS	CG	IP	H	BB	SO	ShO	W	L	SV	AB	H	HR	BA	PO	A	E	DP	TC/G	FA
1986	NY N	0	0	–	0.00	2	0	0	5	2	2	2	0	0	0	0	0	0	0	–	1	1	0	0	1.0	1.000
1988		0	0	–	1.29	3	0	0	7	3	2	4	0	0	0	0	1	0	0	.000	0	1	0	0	0.3	1.000
1991	MIN A	0	0	–	0.00	3	0	0	3.1	1	0	3	0	0	0	3	0	0	0	–	0	0	0	0	0.0	–
3 yrs.		0	0	–	0.59	8	0	0	15.1	6	4	9	0	0	0	3	1	0	0	.000	1	2	0	0	0.4	1.000

WORLD SERIES

Year	Team	W	L	PCT	ERA	G	GS	CG	IP	H	BB	SO	ShO	W	L	SV	AB	H	HR	BA	PO	A	E	DP	TC/G	FA
1986	NY N	1	0	1.000	12.00	2	0	0	3	8	1	4	0	1	0	0	0	0	0	–	0	0	0	0	0.0	–
1991	MIN A	1	1	.500	1.80	4	0	0	5	6	1	3	0	1	1	2	1	0	0	.000	0	0	0	0	0.0	–
2 yrs.		2	1	.667	5.63	6	0	0	8	14	2	7	0	2	1	2	1	0	0	.000	0	0	0	0	0.0	–

Wilson Alvarez

ALVAREZ, WILSON EDUARDO
Born Wilson Eduardo Alvarez (Funemayor).
B. Mar. 24, 1970, Maracaibo, Venezuela.
BL TL 6'1" 175 lbs.

Year	Team	W	L	PCT	ERA	G	GS	CG	IP	H	BB	SO	ShO	W	L	SV	AB	H	HR	BA	PO	A	E	DP	TC/G	FA
1989	TEX A	0	1	.000	∞	1	1	0		3	2	0	0	0	0	0	0	0	0	–	0	0	0	0	0.0	–
1991	CHI A	3	2	.600	3.51	10	9	2	56.1	47	29	32	1	0	0	0	0	0	0	–	1	7	0	1	0.8	1.000
1992		5	3	.625	5.20	34	9	0	100.1	103	65	66	0	2	2	1	0	0	0	–	4	14	2	1	0.6	.900
1993		15	8	.652	2.95	31	31	1	207.2	168	**122**	155	1	0	0	0	0	0	0	–	5	28	1	2	1.1	.971
1994		12	8	.600	3.45	24	24	2	161.2	147	62	108	1	0	0	0	0	0	0	–	6	13	0	1	0.8	1.000
5 yrs.		35	22	.614	3.64	100	74	5	526	468	280	361	3	2	2	1	0	0	0	–	16	62	3	5	0.8	.963

LEAGUE CHAMPIONSHIP SERIES

Year	Team	W	L	PCT	ERA	G	GS	CG	IP	H	BB	SO	ShO	W	L	SV	AB	H	HR	BA	PO	A	E	DP	TC/G	FA
1993	CHI A	1	0	1.000	1.00	1	1	1	9	7	2	6	0	0	0	0	0	0	0	–	0	2	0	1	2.0	1.000

Larry Andersen

ANDERSEN, LARRY EUGENE
B. May 6, 1953, Portland, Ore.
BR TR 6'3" 200 lbs.

Year	Team	W	L	PCT	ERA	G	GS	CG	IP	H	BB	SO	ShO	W	L	SV	AB	H	HR	BA	PO	A	E	DP	TC/G	FA
1975	CLE A	0	0	–	4.76	3	0	0	5.2	4	2	4	0	0	0	0	0	0	0	–	1	1	0	0	0.7	1.000
1977		0	1	.000	3.21	11	0	0	14	10	9	8	0	0	1	0	0	0	0	–	3	6	2	4	1.0	.818
1979		0	0	–	7.41	8	0	0	17	25	4	7	0	0	0	0	0	0	0	–	0	4	0	1	0.5	1.000
1981	SEA A	3	3	.500	2.65	41	0	0	68	57	18	40	0	3	3	5	0	0	0	–	5	9	0	1	0.3	1.000
1982		0	0	–	5.99	40	1	0	79.2	100	23	32	0	0	0	1	0	0	0	–	8	14	0	2	0.6	1.000
1983	PHI N	1	0	1.000	2.39	17	0	0	26.1	19	9	14	0	1	0	0	2	0	0	.000	2	6	0	0	0.5	1.000
1984		3	7	.300	2.38	64	0	5	90.2	85	25	54	0	3	7	4	4	0	0	.000	5	16	4	1	0.4	.840
1985		3	3	.500	4.32	57	0	0	73	78	26	50	0	3	3	3	4	0	0	.000	5	21	2	2	0.5	.929
1986	2 teams				PHI N	(10G 0–0)		HOU N	(38G 2–1)																	
"	total	2	1	.667	3.03	48	0	0	77.1	83	26	42	0	2	1	1	4	0	0	.000	10	11	2	3	0.5	.913
1987	HOU N	9	5	.643	3.45	67	0	0	101.2	95	41	94	0	9	5	5	6	1	0	.167	12	10	3	0	0.4	.880
1988		2	4	.333	2.94	53	0	0	82.2	82	20	66	0	2	4	5	6	2	0	.333	9	9	2	1	0.4	.900
1989		4	4	.500	1.54	60	0	0	87.2	63	24	85	0	4	4	3	3	1	0	.333	10	13	4	0	0.5	.852
1990	2 teams				HOU N	(50G 5–2)		BOS A	(15G 0–0)																	
"	total	5	2	.714	1.79	65	0	0	95.2	79	27	93	0	5	2	7	3	0	0	.000	13	12	2	1	0.4	.926
1991	SD N	3	4	.429	2.30	38	0	0	47	39	13	40	0	3	4	13	2	0	0	.000	5	7	1	0	0.3	.923
1992		1	1	.500	3.34	34	0	0	35	26	8	35	0	1	1	2	1	0	0	.000	4	5	1	0	0.3	.900
1993	PHI N	3	2	.600	2.92	64	0	0	61.2	54	21	67	0	3	2	0	1	1	0	1.000	3	4	1	1	0.1	.875
1994		1	2	.333	4.41	29	0	0	32.2	33	15	27	0	1	2	0	0	0	0	–	2	3	1	0	0.2	.833
17 yrs.		40	39	.506	3.15	699	1	0	995.2	932	311	758	0	40	39	49	38	5	0	.132	97	151	25	17	0.4	.908

LEAGUE CHAMPIONSHIP SERIES

Year	Team	W	L	PCT	ERA	G	GS	CG	IP	H	BB	SO	ShO	W	L	SV	AB	H	HR	BA	PO	A	E	DP	TC/G	FA
1986	HOU N	0	0	–	0.00	2	0	0	5	1	2	3	0	0	0	0	0	0	0	–	0	0	0	0	0.0	–
1990	BOS A	0	1	.000	6.00	3	0	0	3	3	3	3	0	0	1	0	0	0	0	–	1	0	0	0	0.3	1.000
1993	PHI N	0	0	–	15.43	3	0	0	2.1	4	1	3	0	0	0	0	0	0	0	–	0	0	0	0	0.0	–
3 yrs.		0	1	.000	5.23	8	0	0	10.1	8	6	9	0	0	1	0	0	0	0	–	1	0	0	0	0.3	1.000

WORLD SERIES

Year	Team	W	L	PCT	ERA	G	GS	CG	IP	H	BB	SO	ShO	W	L	SV	AB	H	HR	BA	PO	A	E	DP	TC/G	FA
1983	PHI N	0	0	–	2.25	2	0	0	4	4	0	1	0	0	0	0	0	0	0	–	1	0	0	1	1.0	1.000
1993		0	0	–	12.27	4	0	0	3.2	5	3	3	0	0	0	0	0	0	0	–	0	0	0	0	0.0	–
2 yrs.		0	0	–	7.04	6	0	0	7.2	9	3	4	0	0	0	0	0	0	0	–	1	0	0	1	0.3	1.000

Year	Team		W	L	PCT	ERA	G	GS	CG	IP	H	BB	SO	ShO	Relief Pitching W	L	SV	Batting AB	H	HR	BA	PO	A	E	DP	TC/G	FA

Brian Anderson — ANDERSON, BRIAN JAMES
B. Apr. 26, 1972, Portsmouth, Va. — BL TL 6'1" 190 lbs.

Year	Team		W	L	PCT	ERA	G	GS	CG	IP	H	BB	SO	ShO	W	L	SV	AB	H	HR	BA	PO	A	E	DP	TC/G	FA
1993	CAL	A	0	0	–	3.97	4	1	0	11.1	11	2	4	0	0	0	0	0	0	0	–	0	1	0	0	0.3	1.000
1994			7	5	.583	5.22	18	18	0	101.2	120	27	47	0	0	0	0	0	0	0	–	6	10	1	0	0.9	.941
2 yrs.			7	5	.583	5.10	22	19	0	113	131	29	51	0	0	0	0	0	0	0	–	6	11	1	0	0.8	.944

Kevin Appier — APPIER, ROBERT KEVIN
B. Dec. 6, 1967, Lancaster, Calif. — BR TR 6'2" 180 lbs.

Year	Team		W	L	PCT	ERA	G	GS	CG	IP	H	BB	SO	ShO	W	L	SV	AB	H	HR	BA	PO	A	E	DP	TC/G	FA
1989	KC	A	1	4	.200	9.14	6	5	0	21.2	34	12	10	0	0	0	0	0	0	0	–	1	0	0	0	0.2	1.000
1990			12	8	.600	2.76	32	24	3	185.2	179	54	127	3	0	0	0	0	0	0	–	15	21	3	3	1.2	.923
1991			13	10	.565	3.42	34	31	6	207.2	205	61	158	3	0	1	0	0	0	0	–	20	26	2	0	1.4	.958
1992			15	8	.652	2.46	30	30	3	208.1	167	68	150	0	0	0	0	0	0	0	–	19	21	1	4	1.4	.976
1993			18	8	.692	**2.56**	34	34	5	238.2	183	81	186	1	0	0	0	0	0	0	–	26	14	1	4	1.2	.976
1994			7	6	.538	3.83	23	23	1	155	137	63	145	0	0	0	0	0	0	0	–	7	13	0	1	0.9	1.000
6 yrs.			66	44	.600	3.09	159	147	18	1017	905	339	776	7	0	1	0	0	0	0	–	88	95	7	12	1.2	.963

Luis Aquino — AQUINO, LUIS ANTONIO
Born Luis Antonio Aquino (Colon).
B. May 19, 1964, Santurce, Puerto Rico. — BR TR 6' 155 lbs.

Year	Team		W	L	PCT	ERA	G	GS	CG	IP	H	BB	SO	ShO	W	L	SV	AB	H	HR	BA	PO	A	E	DP	TC/G	FA
1986	TOR	A	1	1	.500	6.35	7	0	0	11.1	14	3	5	0	1	1	0	0	0	0	–	1	1	0	0	0.3	1.000
1988	KC	A	1	0	1.000	2.79	7	5	1	29	33	17	11	1	0	0	0	0	0	0	–	2	2	1	1	0.7	.800
1989			6	8	.429	3.50	34	16	2	141.1	148	35	68	1	2	0	0	0	0	0	–	11	23	0	3	1.0	1.000
1990			4	1	.800	3.16	20	3	0	68.1	59	27	28	0	2	0	0	0	0	0	–	4	10	0	2	0.7	1.000
1991			8	4	.667	3.44	38	18	1	157	152	47	80	1	2	0	3	0	0	0	–	14	21	3	3	1.0	.921
1992			3	6	.333	4.52	15	13	0	67.2	81	20	11	0	0	1	0	0	0	0	–	4	16	0	1	1.3	1.000
1993	FLA	N	6	8	.429	3.42	38	13	0	110.2	115	40	67	0	2	2	0	25	2	0	.080	10	30	1	5	1.1	.976
1994			2	1	.667	3.73	29	1	0	50.2	39	22	22	0	2	1	0	6	1	0	.167	5	10	0	2	0.5	1.000
8 yrs.			31	29	.517	3.58	188	69	5	636	641	211	292	3	11	5	3	31	3	0	.097	51	113	5	17	0.9	.970

Jack Armstrong — ARMSTRONG, JACK WILLIAM
B. Mar. 7, 1965, Englewood, N. J. — BR TR 6'5" 220 lbs.

Year	Team		W	L	PCT	ERA	G	GS	CG	IP	H	BB	SO	ShO	W	L	SV	AB	H	HR	BA	PO	A	E	DP	TC/G	FA
1988	CIN	N	4	7	.364	5.79	14	13	0	65.1	63	38	45	0	0	0	0	21	2	0	.095	3	13	0	0	1.1	1.000
1989			2	3	.400	4.64	9	8	0	42.2	40	21	23	0	0	0	0	8	0	0	.000	1	9	0	0	1.1	1.000
1990			12	9	.571	3.42	29	27	2	166	151	59	110	1	0	0	0	47	5	0	.106	15	20	0	2	1.2	1.000
1991			7	13	.350	5.48	27	24	1	139.2	158	54	93	0	0	0	0	43	4	0	.093	16	16	2	0	1.3	.941
1992	CLE	A	6	15	.286	4.64	35	23	1	166.2	176	67	114	0	3	0	0	0	0	0	–	13	25	4	2	1.2	.905
1993	FLA	N	9	17	.346	4.49	36	33	0	196.1	210	78	118	0	1	0	0	66	10	0	.152	13	28	2	1	1.2	.953
1994	TEX	A	0	1	.000	3.60	2	2	0	10	9	2	7	0	0	0	0	0	0	0	–	1	0	0	0	0.5	1.000
7 yrs.			40	65	.381	4.58	152	130	4	786.2	807	319	510	1	4	0	0	185	21	0	.114	62	111	8	5	1.2	.956

WORLD SERIES

| 1990 | CIN | N | 0 | 0 | – | 0.00 | 1 | 0 | 0 | 3 | 1 | 1 | 3 | 0 | 0 | 0 | 0 | 0 | 0 | 0 | – | 0 | 0 | 0 | 0 | 0.0 | – |

Rene Arocha — AROCHA, RENE
Born Rene Arocha (Magaly).
B. Feb. 24, 1966, Havana, Cuba — BR TR 6' 180 lbs.

Year	Team		W	L	PCT	ERA	G	GS	CG	IP	H	BB	SO	ShO	W	L	SV	AB	H	HR	BA	PO	A	E	DP	TC/G	FA
1993	STL	N	11	8	.579	3.78	32	29	1	188	197	31	96	0	0	1	0	58	6	0	.103	9	28	4	3	1.3	.902
1994			4	4	.500	4.01	45	7	1	83	94	21	62	1	3	1	11	9	1	0	.111	3	11	0	0	0.3	1.000
2 yrs.			15	12	.556	3.85	77	36	2	271	291	52	158	1	3	2	11	67	7	0	.104	12	39	4	3	0.7	.927

Andy Ashby — ASHBY, ANDREW JASON
B. July 11, 1967, Kansas City, Mo. — BR TR 6'5" 180 lbs.

Year	Team		W	L	PCT	ERA	G	GS	CG	IP	H	BB	SO	ShO	W	L	SV	AB	H	HR	BA	PO	A	E	DP	TC/G	FA
1991	PHI	N	1	5	.167	6.00	8	8	0	42	41	19	26	0	0	0	0	12	1	0	.083	7	4	0	1	1.4	1.000
1992			1	3	.250	7.54	10	8	0	37	42	21	24	0	0	0	0	11	1	0	.091	1	6	0	0	0.7	1.000
1993	2 teams	CLR N (20G 0–4)								SD N (12G 3–6)																	
"	total		3	10	.231	6.80	32	21	0	123	168	56	77	0	0	0	1	36	5	0	.139	14	20	0	1	1.1	1.000
1994	SD	N	6	11	.353	3.40	24	24	4	164.1	145	43	121	0	0	0	0	49	8	0	.163	14	22	0	0	1.5	1.000
4 yrs.			11	29	.275	5.26	74	61	4	366.1	396	139	248	0	0	0	1	108	15	0	.139	36	52	0	2	1.2	1.000

Paul Assenmacher — ASSENMACHER, PAUL ANDRE
B. Dec. 10, 1960, Detroit, Mich. — BL TL 6'3" 195 lbs.

Year	Team		W	L	PCT	ERA	G	GS	CG	IP	H	BB	SO	ShO	W	L	SV	AB	H	HR	BA	PO	A	E	DP	TC/G	FA
1986	ATL	N	7	3	.700	2.50	61	0	0	68.1	61	26	56	0	7	3	7	6	0	0	.000	5	15	0	1	0.3	1.000
1987			1	1	.500	5.10	52	0	0	54.2	58	24	39	0	1	1	2	4	0	0	.000	2	3	0	0	0.1	1.000
1988			8	7	.533	3.06	64	0	0	79.1	72	32	71	0	8	7	5	3	1	0	.333	6	11	0	2	0.3	1.000
1989	2 teams	ATL N (49G 1–3)								CHI N (14G 2–1)																	
"	total		3	4	.429	3.99	63	0	0	76.2	74	28	79	0	3	4	0	5	0	0	.000	3	13	0	0	0.3	1.000
1990	CHI	N	7	2	.778	2.80	74	1	0	103	90	36	95	0	7	2	10	8	0	0	.000	1	18	0	0	0.3	1.000
1991			7	8	.467	3.24	75	0	0	102.2	85	31	117	0	7	8	15	4	1	0	.250	4	10	1	0	0.2	.933
1992			4	4	.500	4.10	70	0	0	68	72	26	67	0	4	4	8	4	0	0	.000	3	6	0	1	0.1	1.000
1993	2 teams	CHI N (46G 2–1)								NY A (26G 2–2)																	
"	total		4	3	.571	3.38	72	0	0	56	54	22	45	0	4	3	0	2	1	0	.500	1	4	1	2	0.1	.833
1994	CHI	A	1	2	.333	3.55	44	0	0	33	26	13	29	0	1	2	1	0	0	0	–	2	5	0	2	0.2	1.000
9 yrs.			42	34	.553	3.44	575	1	0	641.2	592	238	598	0	42	34	48	36	3	0	.083	27	85	2	8	0.2	.982

LEAGUE CHAMPIONSHIP SERIES

| 1989 | CHI | N | 0 | 0 | – | 13.50 | 2 | 0 | 0 | 0.2 | 3 | 0 | 0 | 0 | 0 | 0 | 0 | 0 | 0 | 0 | – | 0 | 0 | 0 | 0 | 0.0 | – |

Pedro Astacio — ASTACIO, PEDRO JULIO
Born Pedro Julio Astacio (Pura).
B. Nov. 28, 1969, Hato Mayor, Dominican Republic. — BR TR 6'2" 174 lbs.

Year	Team		W	L	PCT	ERA	G	GS	CG	IP	H	BB	SO	ShO	W	L	SV	AB	H	HR	BA	PO	A	E	DP	TC/G	FA
1992	LA	N	5	5	.500	1.98	11	11	4	82	80	20	43	4	0	0	0	24	3	0	.125	4	13	2	1	1.7	.895
1993			14	9	.609	3.57	31	31	3	186.1	165	68	122	2	0	0	0	62	10	0	.161	23	17	2	1	1.4	.952

Year	Team	W	L	PCT	ERA	G	GS	CG	IP	H	BB	SO	ShO	W	L	SV	AB	H	HR	BA	PO	A	E	DP	TC/G	FA
														Relief Pitching			**Batting**									

Pedro Astacio *continued*

Year	Team	W	L	PCT	ERA	G	GS	CG	IP	H	BB	SO	ShO	W	L	SV	AB	H	HR	BA	PO	A	E	DP	TC/G	FA
1994		6	8	.429	4.29	23	23	3	149	142	47	108	1	0	0	0	47	3	0	.064	19	13	0	0	1.4	1.000
3 yrs.		25	22	.532	3.52	65	65	10	417.1	387	135	273	7	0	0	0	133	16	0	.120	46	43	4	2	1.4	.957

Joe Ausanio

AUSANIO, JOSEPH JOHN, JR.
B. Dec. 9, 1965, Kingston, N. Y.

BR TR 6'1" 205 lbs.

Year	Team	W	L	PCT	ERA	G	GS	CG	IP	H	BB	SO	ShO	W	L	SV	AB	H	HR	BA	PO	A	E	DP	TC/G	FA
1994	NY A	2	1	.667	5.17	13	0	0	15.2	16	6	15	0	2	1	0	0	0	0	—	1	2	0	0	0.2	1.000

Steve Avery

AVERY, STEVEN THOMAS
B. Apr. 14, 1970, Trenton, Mich.

BL TL 6'4" 180 lbs.

Year	Team	W	L	PCT	ERA	G	GS	CG	IP	H	BB	SO	ShO	W	L	SV	AB	H	HR	BA	PO	A	E	DP	TC/G	FA
1990	ATL N	3	11	.214	5.64	21	20	1	99	121	45	75	1	0	1	0	30	4	0	.133	4	22	2	0	1.3	.929
1991		18	8	.692	3.38	35	35	3	210.1	189	65	137	1	0	0	0	79	17	0	.215	9	31	1	2	1.2	.976
1992		11	11	.500	3.20	35	**35**	2	233.2	216	71	129	2	0	0	0	76	13	0	.171	16	36	3	1	1.6	.945
1993		18	6	.750	2.94	35	35	3	223.1	216	43	125	1	0	0	0	75	12	0	.160	4	47	0	2	1.5	1.000
1994		8	3	.727	4.04	24	24	1	151.2	127	55	122	0	0	0	0	49	5	0	.102	4	26	1	0	1.3	.968
5 yrs.		58	39	.598	3.58	150	149	10	918	869	279	588	5	0	1	0	309	51	0	.165	37	162	7	5	1.4	.966

LEAGUE CHAMPIONSHIP SERIES

Year	Team	W	L	PCT	ERA	G	GS	CG	IP	H	BB	SO	ShO	W	L	SV	AB	H	HR	BA	PO	A	E	DP	TC/G	FA
1991	ATL N	2	0	1.000	0.00	2	2	0	16.1	9	4	17	0	0	0	0	7	1	0	.143	1	2	0	0	1.5	1.000
1992		1	1	.500	9.00	3	2	0	8	13	2	3	0	0	0	0	2	0	0	.000	0	0	0	0	0.0	—
1993		0	0	—	2.77	2	2	0	13	9	6	10	0	0	0	0	4	2	0	.500	0	2	0	0	1.0	1.000
3 yrs.		3	1	.750	2.89	7	6	0	37.1	31	12	30	0	0	0	0	13	3	0	.231	1	4	0	0	0.7	1.000

WORLD SERIES

Year	Team	W	L	PCT	ERA	G	GS	CG	IP	H	BB	SO	ShO	W	L	SV	AB	H	HR	BA	PO	A	E	DP	TC/G	FA
1991	ATL N	0	0	—	3.46	2	2	0	13	10	1	8	0	0	0	0	3	0	0	.000	1	0	0	0	0.5	1.000
1992		0	1	.000	3.75	2	2	0	12	11	3	11	0	0	0	0	1	0	0	.000	0	2	0	0	1.0	1.000
2 yrs.		0	1	.000	3.60	4	4	0	25	21	4	19	0	0	0	0	4	0	0	.000	1	2	0	0	0.8	1.000

Bobby Ayala

AYALA, ROBERT JOSEPH
B. July 8, 1969, Ventura, Calif.

BR TR 6'2" 190 lbs.

Year	Team	W	L	PCT	ERA	G	GS	CG	IP	H	BB	SO	ShO	W	L	SV	AB	H	HR	BA	PO	A	E	DP	TC/G	FA
1992	CIN N	2	1	.667	4.34	5	5	0	29	33	13	23	0	0	0	0	9	0	0	.000	3	8	0	1	2.2	1.000
1993		7	10	.412	5.60	43	9	0	98	106	45	65	0	5	4	3	21	2	0	.095	12	10	6	1	0.7	.786
1994	SEA A	4	3	.571	2.86	46	0	0	56.2	42	26	76	0	4	3	18	0	0	0	—	2	5	2	0	0.2	.778
3 yrs.		13	14	.481	4.56	94	14	0	183.2	181	84	164	0	9	7	21	30	2	0	.067	17	23	8	2	0.5	.833

Cory Bailey

BAILEY, PHILLIP CORY
B. Jan. 24, 1971, Herrin, Ill.

BR TR 6' 195 lbs.

Year	Team	W	L	PCT	ERA	G	GS	CG	IP	H	BB	SO	ShO	W	L	SV	AB	H	HR	BA	PO	A	E	DP	TC/G	FA
1993	BOS A	0	1	.000	3.45	11	0	0	15.2	12	12	11	0	0	1	0	0	0	0	—	0	5	0	0	0.5	1.000
1994		0	1	.000	12.46	5	0	0	4.1	10	3	4	0	0	1	0	0	0	0	—	0	0	0	0	0.0	—
2 yrs.		0	2	.000	5.40	16	0	0	20	22	15	15	0	0	2	0	0	0	0	—	0	5	0	0	0.3	1.000

Jeff Ballard

BALLARD, JEFFREY SCOTT
B. Aug. 13, 1963, Billings, Mont.

BL TL 6'3" 210 lbs.

Year	Team	W	L	PCT	ERA	G	GS	CG	IP	H	BB	SO	ShO	W	L	SV	AB	H	HR	BA	PO	A	E	DP	TC/G	FA
1987	BAL A	2	8	.200	6.59	14	14	0	69.2	100	35	27	0	0	0	0	0	0	0	—	5	10	0	1	1.1	1.000
1988		8	12	.400	4.40	25	25	6	153.1	167	42	41	1	0	0	0	0	0	0	—	9	13	0	3	0.9	1.000
1989		18	8	.692	3.43	35	35	4	215.1	240	57	62	1	0	0	0	0	0	0	—	13	55	2	6	2.0	.971
1990		2	11	.154	4.93	44	17	0	133.1	152	42	50	0	1	1	0	0	0	0	—	11	20	1	0	0.7	.969
1991		6	12	.333	5.60	26	22	0	123.2	153	28	37	0	0	0	0	0	0	0	—	4	15	1	3	0.8	.950
1993	PIT N	4	1	.800	4.86	25	5	0	53.2	70	15	16	0	3	0	0	11	4	0	.364	7	21	1	3	0.7	.941
1994		1	1	.500	6.66	28	0	0	24.1	32	10	11	0	1	1	2	2	1	0	.500	1	3	0	0	0.1	1.000
7 yrs.		41	53	.436	4.71	197	118	10	773.1	914	229	244	2	5	2	2	13	5	0	.385	47	128	5	16	0.9	.972

Scott Bankhead

BANKHEAD, MICHAEL SCOTT
B. July 31, 1963, Raleigh, N. C.

BR TR 5'10" 175 lbs.

Year	Team	W	L	PCT	ERA	G	GS	CG	IP	H	BB	SO	ShO	W	L	SV	AB	H	HR	BA	PO	A	E	DP	TC/G	FA
1986	KC A	8	9	.471	4.61	24	17	0	121	121	37	94	0	2	1	0	0	0	0	—	11	12	1	0	1.0	.958
1987	SEA A	9	8	.529	5.42	27	25	2	149.1	168	37	95	0	0	0	0	0	0	0	—	9	9	0	1	0.7	1.000
1988		7	9	.438	3.07	21	21	0	135	115	38	102	1	0	0	0	0	0	0	—	7	11	0	0	0.9	1.000
1989		14	6	.700	3.34	33	33	3	210.1	187	63	140	2	0	0	0	0	0	0	—	14	19	0	2	1.0	1.000
1990		0	2	.000	11.08	4	4	0	13	18	7	10	0	0	0	0	0	0	0	—	0	0	0	0	0.0	—
1991		3	6	.333	4.90	17	9	0	60.2	73	21	28	0	1	1	0	0	0	0	—	5	7	0	1	0.7	1.000
1992	CIN N	10	4	.714	2.93	54	0	0	70.2	57	29	53	0	10	4	1	9	2	0	.222	5	2	2	0	0.2	.778
1993	BOS A	2	1	.667	3.50	40	0	0	64.1	59	29	47	0	2	1	0	0	0	0	—	1	4	1	0	0.2	.833
1994		3	2	.600	4.54	27	0	0	37.2	34	12	25	0	3	2	0	0	0	0	—	1	0	0	0	0.0	1.000
9 yrs.		56	47	.544	4.09	247	109	7	862	832	273	594	3	18	9	1	9	2	0	.222	53	64	4	4	0.5	.967

Willie Banks

BANKS, WILLIE ANTHONY
B. Feb. 27, 1969, Jersey City, N. J.

BR TR 6'1" 190 lbs.

Year	Team	W	L	PCT	ERA	G	GS	CG	IP	H	BB	SO	ShO	W	L	SV	AB	H	HR	BA	PO	A	E	DP	TC/G	FA
1991	MIN A	1	1	.500	5.71	5	3	0	17.1	21	12	16	0	0	0	0	0	0	0	—	0	0	0	0	0.0	—
1992		4	4	.500	5.70	16	12	0	71	80	37	37	0	0	0	0	0	0	0	—	9	5	0	0	0.9	1.000
1993		11	12	.478	4.04	31	30	0	171.1	186	78	138	0	0	0	0	0	0	0	—	13	15	6	1	1.1	.824
1994	CHI N	8	12	.400	5.40	23	23	1	138.1	139	56	91	1	0	0	0	41	5	0	.122	9	13	1	0	1.0	.957
4 yrs.		24	29	.453	4.88	75	68	1	398	426	183	282	1	0	0	0	41	5	0	.122	31	33	7	1	0.9	.901

Brian Barnes

BARNES, BRIAN KEITH
B. Mar. 25, 1967, Roanoke Rapids, N. C.

BL TL 5'9" 170 lbs.

Year	Team	W	L	PCT	ERA	G	GS	CG	IP	H	BB	SO	ShO	W	L	SV	AB	H	HR	BA	PO	A	E	DP	TC/G	FA
1990	MON N	1	1	.500	2.89	4	4	1	28	25	7	23	0	0	0	0	9	0	0	.000	4	3	1	0	2.0	.875
1991		5	8	.385	4.22	28	27	1	160	135	84	117	0	0	0	0	49	4	0	.082	7	31	2	1	1.4	.950
1992		6	6	.500	2.97	21	17	0	100	77	46	65	0	0	0	0	29	8	0	.276	5	18	0	1	1.1	1.000
1993		2	6	.250	4.41	52	8	0	100	105	48	60	0	1	3	3	20	3	0	.150	3	15	0	1	0.3	1.000
1994	2 teams	CLE A (6G 0–1)				LA N (5G 0–0)																				
"	total	0	1	.000	5.89	11	0	0	18.1	22	19	10	0	0	1	0	0	0	0	—	1	2	1	0	0.4	.750
5 yrs.		14	22	.389	3.94	116	56	2	406.1	364	204	275	0	1	4	3	107	15	0	.140	20	69	4	2	0.8	.957

Year	Team	W	L	PCT	ERA	G	GS	CG	IP	H	BB	SO	ShO	Relief Pitching W	L	SV	Batting AB	H	HR	BA	PO	A	E	DP	TC/G	FA

Jose Bautista

BAUTISTA, JOSE JOAQUIN
Born Jose Joaquin Bautista (Arias).
B. July 25, 1964, Bani, Dominican Republic.　　　　BR TR 6'1" 177 lbs.

Year	Team	W	L	PCT	ERA	G	GS	CG	IP	H	BB	SO	ShO	W	L	SV	AB	H	HR	BA	PO	A	E	DP	TC/G	FA
1988	BAL A	6	15	.286	4.30	33	25	3	171.2	171	45	76	0	0	1	0	0	0	0	–	27	11	1	3	1.2	.974
1989		3	4	.429	5.31	15	10	0	78	84	15	30	0	0	0	0	0	0	0	–	3	10	1	0	0.9	.929
1990		1	0	1.000	4.05	22	0	0	26.2	28	7	15	0	1	0	0	0	0	0	–	1	2	0	0	0.1	1.000
1991		0	1	.000	16.88	5	0	0	5.1	13	5	3	0	0	1	0	0	0	0	–	0	1	0	0	0.2	1.000
1993	CHI N	10	3	.769	2.82	58	7	1	111.2	105	27	63	0	6	1	2	21	4	0	.190	14	18	2	2	0.6	.941
1994		4	5	.444	3.89	58	0	0	69.1	75	17	45	0	4	5	1	2	0	0	.000	5	9	0	0	0.2	1.000
6 yrs.		24	28	.462	4.18	191	42	4	462.2	476	116	232	0	11	8	3	23	4	0	.174	50	51	4	5	0.5	.962

Rod Beck

BECK, RODNEY ROY
B. Aug. 3, 1968, Burbank, Calif.　　　　BR TR 6'1" 215 lbs.

Year	Team	W	L	PCT	ERA	G	GS	CG	IP	H	BB	SO	ShO	W	L	SV	AB	H	HR	BA	PO	A	E	DP	TC/G	FA
1991	SF N	1	1	.500	3.78	31	0	0	52.1	53	13	38	0	1	1	1	2	1	0	.500	1	10	0	0	0.4	1.000
1992		3	3	.500	1.76	65	0	0	92	62	15	87	0	3	3	17	2	1	0	.500	2	13	1	0	0.2	.938
1993		3	1	.750	2.16	76	0	0	79.1	57	13	86	0	3	1	48	4	0	0	.000	0	8	1	0	0.1	.889
1994		2	4	.333	2.77	48	0	0	48.2	49	13	39	0	2	4	28	3	0	0	.000	4	4	0	0	0.2	1.000
4 yrs.		9	9	.500	2.45	220	0	0	272.1	221	54	250	0	9	9	94	11	2	0	.182	7	35	2	1	0.2	.955

Steve Bedrosian

BEDROSIAN, STEPHEN WAYNE (Bedrock)
B. Dec. 6, 1957, Methuen, Mass.　　　　BR TR 6'3" 200 lbs.

Year	Team	W	L	PCT	ERA	G	GS	CG	IP	H	BB	SO	ShO	W	L	SV	AB	H	HR	BA	PO	A	E	DP	TC/G	FA
1981	ATL N	1	2	.333	4.50	15	1	0	24	15	15	9	0	1	1	0	2	0	0	.000	1	2	0	1	0.2	1.000
1982		8	6	.571	2.42	64	3	0	137.2	102	57	123	0	7	4	11	26	1	0	.038	12	14	1	2	0.4	.963
1983		9	10	.474	3.60	70	1	0	120	100	51	114	0	9	10	19	19	2	0	.105	4	16	0	2	0.3	1.000
1984		9	6	.600	2.37	40	4	0	83.2	65	33	81	0	6	5	11	17	2	0	.118	1	8	1	0	0.3	.900
1985		7	15	.318	3.83	37	37	0	206.2	198	111	134	0	0	0	0	64	5	0	.078	13	23	4	3	1.1	.900
1986	PHI N	8	6	.571	3.39	68	0	0	90.1	79	34	82	0	8	6	29	5	1	0	.200	2	10	0	1	0.2	1.000
1987		5	3	.625	2.83	65	0	0	89	79	28	74	0	5	3	40	4	0	0	.000	3	7	0	0	0.2	1.000
1988		6	6	.500	3.75	57	0	0	74.1	75	27	61	0	6	6	28	2	0	0	.000	5	9	0	0	0.2	1.000
1989	2 teams	PHI N	(28G 2–3)		SF N	(40G 1–4)																				
"	total	3	7	.300	2.87	68	0	0	84.2	56	39	58	0	3	7	23	6	1	0	.167	2	5	1	1	0.1	.875
1990	SF N	9	9	.500	4.20	68	0	0	79.1	72	44	43	0	9	9	17	4	2	0	.500	9	11	1	1	0.3	.952
1991	MIN A	5	3	.625	4.42	56	0	0	77.1	70	35	44	0	5	3	6	0	0	0	–	6	5	0	0	0.2	1.000
1993	ATL N	5	2	.714	1.63	49	0	0	49.2	34	14	33	0	5	2	0	2	0	0	.000	3	5	0	0	0.2	1.000
1994		0	2	.000	3.33	46	0	0	46	41	18	43	0	0	2	0	2	1	0	.500	3	4	1	0	0.2	.875
13 yrs.		75	77	.493	3.31	703	46	0	1162.2	986	506	899	0	64	58	184	153	15	0	.098	64	119	9	11	0.3	.953

LEAGUE CHAMPIONSHIP SERIES

Year	Team	W	L	PCT	ERA	G	GS	CG	IP	H	BB	SO	ShO	W	L	SV	AB	H	HR	BA	PO	A	E	DP	TC/G	FA
1982	ATL N	0	0	–	18.00	2	0	0	1	3	1	2	0	0	0	0	0	0	0	–	0	0	0	0	0.0	–
1989	SF N	0	0	–	2.70	4	0	0	3.1	4	2	2	0	0	0	3	0	0	0	–	0	0	0	0	0.0	–
1991	MIN A	0	0	–	0.00	2	0	0	1.1	3	2	2	0	0	0	0	0	0	0	–	0	0	0	0	0.0	–
3 yrs.		0	0	–	4.76	8	0	0	5.2	10	5	6	0	0	0	3	0	0	0	–	0	0	0	0	0.0	–

WORLD SERIES

Year	Team	W	L	PCT	ERA	G	GS	CG	IP	H	BB	SO	ShO	W	L	SV	AB	H	HR	BA	PO	A	E	DP	TC/G	FA
1989	SF N	0	0	–	0.00	2	0	0	2.2	0	2	2	0	0	0	0	0	0	0	–	0	0	0	0	0.0	–
1991	MIN A	0	0	–	5.40	3	0	0	3.1	3	0	2	0	0	0	0	0	0	0	–	0	1	0	0	0.3	1.000
2 yrs.		0	0	–	3.00	5	0	0	6	3	2	4	0	0	0	0	0	0	0	–	0	1	0	0	0.2	1.000

Tim Belcher

BELCHER, TIMOTHY WAYNE
B. Oct. 19, 1961, Mount Gilead, Ohio.　　　　BR TR 6'3" 210 lbs.

Year	Team	W	L	PCT	ERA	G	GS	CG	IP	H	BB	SO	ShO	W	L	SV	AB	H	HR	BA	PO	A	E	DP	TC/G	FA
1987	LA N	4	2	.667	2.38	6	5	0	34	30	7	23	0	1	0	0	10	2	0	.200	1	5	0	0	1.0	1.000
1988		12	6	.667	2.91	36	27	4	179.2	143	51	152	1	1	0	4	56	4	1	.071	14	19	0	2	0.9	1.000
1989		15	12	.556	2.82	39	30	10	230	182	80	200	8	1	1	0	70	7	0	.100	21	18	3	3	1.1	.929
1990		9	9	.500	4.00	24	24	5	153	136	48	102	2	0	0	0	43	7	0	.163	11	11	0	1	0.9	1.000
1991		10	9	.526	2.62	33	33	2	209.1	189	75	156	1	0	0	0	67	8	0	.119	11	20	2	2	1.0	.939
1992	CIN N	15	14	.517	3.91	35	34	2	227.2	201	80	149	1	0	1	0	76	8	1	.105	23	27	1	2	1.5	.980
1993	2 teams	CIN N	(22G 9–6)		CHI A	(12G 3–5)																				
"	total	12	11	.522	4.44	34	33	5	208.2	198	74	135	3	0	0	0	50	10	0	.200	19	17	2	2	1.1	.947
1994	DET A	7	15	.318	5.89	25	25	0	162	192	78	76	0	0	0	0	0	0	0	–	19	25	4	4	1.9	.917
8 yrs.		84	78	.519	3.69	232	211	31	1404.1	1271	493	993	16	3	3	5	372	46	2	.124	119	142	12	16	1.2	.956

LEAGUE CHAMPIONSHIP SERIES

Year	Team	W	L	PCT	ERA	G	GS	CG	IP	H	BB	SO	ShO	W	L	SV	AB	H	HR	BA	PO	A	E	DP	TC/G	FA
1988	LA N	2	0	1.000	4.11	2	2	0	15.1	12	4	16	0	0	0	0	8	1	0	.125	1	0	0	0	0.5	1.000
1993	CHI A	1	0	1.000	2.45	1	0	0	3.2	3	3	1	0	1	0	0	0	0	0	–	1	1	0	0	2.0	1.000
2 yrs.		3	0	1.000	3.79	3	2	0	19	15	7	17	0	1	0	0	8	1	0	.125	2	1	0	0	1.0	1.000

WORLD SERIES

Year	Team	W	L	PCT	ERA	G	GS	CG	IP	H	BB	SO	ShO	W	L	SV	AB	H	HR	BA	PO	A	E	DP	TC/G	FA
1988	LA N	1	0	1.000	6.23	2	2	0	8.2	10	6	10	0	0	0	0	0	0	0	–	0	0	0	0	0.0	–

Stan Belinda

BELINDA, STANLEY PETER
B. Aug. 6, 1966, Huntingdon, Pa.　　　　BR TR 6'3" 185 lbs.

Year	Team	W	L	PCT	ERA	G	GS	CG	IP	H	BB	SO	ShO	W	L	SV	AB	H	HR	BA	PO	A	E	DP	TC/G	FA
1989	PIT N	0	1	.000	6.10	8	0	0	10.1	13	2	10	0	0	1	0	0	0	0	–	0	0	0	0	0.0	–
1990		3	4	.429	3.55	55	0	0	58.1	48	29	55	0	3	4	8	5	0	0	.000	2	4	0	0	0.1	1.000
1991		7	5	.583	3.45	60	0	0	78.1	50	35	71	0	7	5	16	7	0	0	.000	5	5	0	1	0.2	1.000
1992		6	4	.600	3.15	59	0	0	71.1	58	29	57	0	6	4	18	3	2	0	.667	4	4	0	1	0.1	1.000
1993	2 teams	PIT N	(40G 3–1)		KC A	(23G 1–1)																				
"	total	4	2	.667	3.88	63	0	0	69.2	65	17	55	0	4	2	19	1	0	0	.000	4	5	0	1	0.1	1.000
1994	KC A	2	2	.500	5.14	37	0	0	49	47	24	37	0	2	2	1	0	0	0	–	0	2	0	0	0.1	1.000
6 yrs.		22	18	.550	3.82	282	0	0	337	281	136	285	0	22	18	62	16	2	0	.125	15	22	0	3	0.1	1.000

LEAGUE CHAMPIONSHIP SERIES

Year	Team	W	L	PCT	ERA	G	GS	CG	IP	H	BB	SO	ShO	W	L	SV	AB	H	HR	BA	PO	A	E	DP	TC/G	FA
1990	PIT N	0	0	–	2.45	3	0	0	3.2	3	0	4	0	0	0	0	0	0	0	–	0	0	0	0	0.0	–
1991		1	0	1.000	0.00	3	0	0	5	0	3	4	0	1	0	0	0	0	0	–	0	2	0	1	0.7	1.000
1992		0	0	–	0.00	2	0	0	1.2	2	1	2	0	0	0	0	0	0	0	–	0	0	0	0	0.0	–
3 yrs.		1	0	1.000	0.87	8	0	0	10.1	5	4	10	0	1	0	0	0	0	0	–	0	2	0	1	0.3	1.000

Year	Team	W	L	PCT	ERA	G	GS	CG	IP	H	BB	SO	ShO	Relief Pitching W	L	SV	Batting AB	H	HR	BA	PO	A	E	DP	TC/G	FA

Andy Benes

BENES, ANDREW CHARLES
B. Aug. 20, 1967, Evansville, Ind. — BR TR 6'6" 235 lbs.

Year	Team	W	L	PCT	ERA	G	GS	CG	IP	H	BB	SO	ShO	W	L	SV	AB	H	HR	BA	PO	A	E	DP	TC/G	FA
1989	SD N	6	3	.667	3.51	10	10	0	66.2	51	31	66	0	0	0	0	24	6	1	.250	4	8	0	1	1.2	1.000
1990		10	11	.476	3.60	32	31	2	192.1	177	69	140	0	0	0	0	60	6	0	.100	15	9	1	1	0.8	.960
1991		15	11	.577	3.03	33	33	4	223	194	59	167	1	0	0	0	62	2	1	.032	8	29	0	3	1.1	1.000
1992		13	14	.481	3.35	34	34	2	231.1	**230**	61	169	2	0	0	0	67	10	1	.149	14	34	1	1	1.4	.980
1993		15	15	.500	3.78	34	34	4	230.2	200	86	179	2	0	0	0	72	9	1	.125	16	15	1	2	0.9	.969
1994		6	**14**	.300	3.86	25	25	2	172.1	155	**51**	**189**	2	0	0	0	49	8	0	.163	21	19	0	2	1.6	1.000
6 yrs.		65	68	.489	3.51	168	167	14	1116.1	1007	357	910	7	0	0	0	334	41	4	.123	78	114	3	10	1.2	.985

Armando Benitez

BENITEZ, ARMANDO GERMAN
B. Nov. 3, 1972, Ramon Santana, Dominican Republic. — BR TR 6'4" 180 lbs.

Year	Team	W	L	PCT	ERA	G	GS	CG	IP	H	BB	SO	ShO	W	L	SV	AB	H	HR	BA	PO	A	E	DP	TC/G	FA
1994	BAL A	0	0	—	0.90	3	0	0	10	8	4	14	0	0	0	0	0	0	0	—	0	1	0	0	0.3	1.000

Jason Bere

BERE, JASON PHILLIP
B. May 26, 1971, Cambridge, Mass. — BR TR 6'3" 185 lbs.

Year	Team	W	L	PCT	ERA	G	GS	CG	IP	H	BB	SO	ShO	W	L	SV	AB	H	HR	BA	PO	A	E	DP	TC/G	FA
1993	CHI A	12	5	.706	3.47	24	24	1	142.2	109	81	129	0	0	0	0	0	0	0	—	11	14	2	1	1.1	.926
1994		12	2	.857	3.81	24	24	0	141.2	119	80	127	0	0	0	0	0	0	0	—	9	12	2	1	1.0	.913
2 yrs.		24	7	.774	3.64	48	48	1	284.1	228	161	256	0	0	0	0	0	0	0	—	20	26	4	2	1.0	.920

LEAGUE CHAMPIONSHIP SERIES

Year	Team	W	L	PCT	ERA	G	GS	CG	IP	H	BB	SO	ShO	W	L	SV	AB	H	HR	BA	PO	A	E	DP	TC/G	FA
1993	CHI A	0	0	—	11.57	1	1	0	2.1	5	2	3	0	0	0	0	0	0	0	—	0	0	0	0	0.0	—

Sean Bergman

BERGMAN, SEAN FREDERICK
B. Apr. 11, 1970, Joliet, Ill. — BR TR 6'4" 205 lbs.

Year	Team	W	L	PCT	ERA	G	GS	CG	IP	H	BB	SO	ShO	W	L	SV	AB	H	HR	BA	PO	A	E	DP	TC/G	FA
1993	DET A	1	4	.200	5.67	9	6	1	39.2	47	23	19	0	1	0	0	0	0	0	—	3	6	0	1	1.0	1.000
1994		2	1	.667	5.60	3	3	0	17.2	22	7	12	0	0	0	0	0	0	0	—	2	1	0	0	1.0	1.000
2 yrs.		3	5	.375	5.65	12	9	1	57.1	69	30	31	0	1	0	0	0	0	0	—	5	7	0	1	1.0	1.000

Mike Bielecki

BIELECKI, MICHAEL JOSEPH
B. July 31, 1959, Baltimore, Md. — BR TR 6'3" 195 lbs.

Year	Team	W	L	PCT	ERA	G	GS	CG	IP	H	BB	SO	ShO	W	L	SV	AB	H	HR	BA	PO	A	E	DP	TC/G	FA
1984	PIT N	0	0	—	0.00	4	0	0	4.1	4	0	1	0	0	0	0	0	0	0	—	0	1	0	0	0.3	1.000
1985		2	3	.400	4.53	12	7	0	45.2	45	31	22	0	0	0	0	10	0	0	.000	5	11	0	0	1.3	1.000
1986		6	11	.353	4.66	31	27	0	148.2	149	83	83	0	0	0	0	48	3	0	.063	17	16	1	1	1.1	.971
1987		2	3	.400	4.73	8	8	2	45.2	43	12	25	0	0	0	0	16	1	0	.063	6	5	1	0	1.5	.917
1988	CHI N	2	2	.500	3.35	19	5	0	48.1	55	16	33	0	1	0	0	10	1	0	.100	4	5	0	0	0.5	1.000
1989		18	7	**.720**	3.14	33	33	4	212.1	187	81	147	3	0	0	0	70	3	0	.043	18	21	1	0	1.2	.975
1990		8	11	.421	4.93	36	29	0	168	188	70	103	0	0	0	1	43	7	0	.163	17	33	3	2	1.5	.943
1991	2 teams	CHI N	(39G 13–11)		ATL N	(2G 0–0)																				
"	total	13	11	.542	4.46	41	25	0	173.2	171	56	75	0	3	3	0	46	3	0	.065	22	24	0	3	1.1	1.000
1992	ATL N	2	4	.333	2.57	19	14	1	80.2	77	27	62	1	0	0	0	24	3	0	.125	5	14	0	0	1.0	1.000
1993	CLE A	4	5	.444	5.90	13	13	0	68.2	90	23	38	0	0	0	0	0	0	0	—	5	11	0	1	1.2	1.000
1994	ATL N	2	0	1.000	4.00	19	1	0	27	28	12	18	0	2	0	0	3	0	0	.000	3	4	0	1	0.4	1.000
11 yrs.		59	57	.509	4.17	235	162	7	1023	1037	411	607	4	7	3	1	270	21	0	.078	102	145	6	8	1.1	.976

LEAGUE CHAMPIONSHIP SERIES

Year	Team	W	L	PCT	ERA	G	GS	CG	IP	H	BB	SO	ShO	W	L	SV	AB	H	HR	BA	PO	A	E	DP	TC/G	FA
1989	CHI N	0	1	.000	3.65	2	2	0	12.1	7	6	11	0	0	0	0	5	1	0	.200	1	2	0	0	1.5	1.000

Bud Black

BLACK, HARRY RALSTON
B. June 30, 1957, San Mateo, Calif. — BL TL 6'2" 180 lbs.

Year	Team	W	L	PCT	ERA	G	GS	CG	IP	H	BB	SO	ShO	W	L	SV	AB	H	HR	BA	PO	A	E	DP	TC/G	FA
1981	SEA A	0	0	—	0.00	2	0	0	1	2	3	0	0	0	0	0	0	0	0	—	0	1	0	0	0.5	1.000
1982	KC A	4	6	.400	4.58	22	14	0	88.1	92	34	40	0	0	0	0	0	0	0	—	6	12	1	1	0.9	.947
1983		10	7	.588	3.79	24	24	3	161.1	159	43	58	0	0	0	0	0	0	0	—	7	32	1	5	1.7	.975
1984		17	12	.586	3.12	35	35	8	257	226	64	140	1	0	0	0	0	0	0	—	13	51	2	2	1.9	.970
1985		10	15	.400	4.33	33	33	5	205.2	216	59	122	2	0	0	0	0	0	0	—	6	30	4	0	1.2	.900
1986		5	10	.333	3.20	56	4	0	121	100	43	68	0	4	7	9	0	0	0	—	3	21	0	1	0.4	1.000
1987		8	6	.571	3.60	29	18	0	122.1	126	35	61	0	1	1	1	0	0	0	—	4	19	0	0	0.8	1.000
1988	2 teams	KC A	(17G 2–1)		CLE A	(16G 2–3)																				
"	total	4	4	.500	5.00	33	7	0	81	82	34	63	0	3	2	1	0	0	0	—	5	12	0	0	0.5	1.000
1989	CLE A	12	11	.522	3.36	33	32	6	222.1	213	52	88	3	0	0	0	0	0	0	—	13	33	2	3	1.5	.958
1990	2 teams	CLE A	(29G 11–10)		TOR A	(3G 2–1)																				
"	total	13	11	.542	3.57	32	31	5	206.2	181	61	106	2	0	0	0	0	0	0	—	7	33	1	2	1.3	.976
1991	SF N	12	**16**	.429	3.99	34	34	3	214.1	201	71	104	3	0	0	0	71	13	0	.183	14	38	0	4	1.5	1.000
1992		10	12	.455	3.97	28	28	2	177	178	59	82	1	0	0	0	54	3	0	.056	5	37	0	4	1.5	1.000
1993		8	2	.800	3.56	16	16	0	93.2	89	33	45	0	0	0	0	37	9	0	.243	3	22	2	2	1.7	.926
1994		4	2	.667	4.47	10	10	0	54.1	50	16	28	0	0	0	0	17	1	0	.059	3	7	0	1	1.0	1.000
14 yrs.		117	114	.506	3.77	387	286	32	2006	1915	607	1005	12	10	10	11	179	26	0	.145	89	348	13	25	1.2	.971

LEAGUE CHAMPIONSHIP SERIES

Year	Team	W	L	PCT	ERA	G	GS	CG	IP	H	BB	SO	ShO	W	L	SV	AB	H	HR	BA	PO	A	E	DP	TC/G	FA
1984	KC A	0	1	.000	7.20	1	1	0	5	7	1	3	0	0	0	0	0	0	0	—	1	1	0	0	2.0	1.000
1985		0	0	—	1.69	3	1	0	10.2	11	4	8	0	0	0	0	0	0	0	—	1	2	0	1	1.0	1.000
2 yrs.		0	1	.000	3.45	4	2	0	15.2	18	5	11	0	0	0	0	0	0	0	—	2	3	0	1	1.3	1.000

WORLD SERIES

Year	Team	W	L	PCT	ERA	G	GS	CG	IP	H	BB	SO	ShO	W	L	SV	AB	H	HR	BA	PO	A	E	DP	TC/G	FA
1985	KC A	0	1	.000	5.06	2	1	0	5.1	4	5	4	0	0	0	0	1	0	0	.000	1	2	1	1	2.0	.750

Willie Blair

BLAIR, WILLIAM ALLEN
B. Dec. 18, 1965, Paintsville, Ky. — BR TR 6'1" 185 lbs.

Year	Team	W	L	PCT	ERA	G	GS	CG	IP	H	BB	SO	ShO	W	L	SV	AB	H	HR	BA	PO	A	E	DP	TC/G	FA
1990	TOR A	3	5	.375	4.06	27	6	0	68.2	66	28	43	0	3	2	0	0	0	0	—	3	6	0	0	0.3	1.000
1991	CLE A	2	3	.400	6.75	11	5	0	36	58	10	13	0	0	1	0	0	0	0	—	2	5	0	1	0.6	1.000
1992	HOU N	5	7	.417	4.00	29	8	0	78.2	74	25	48	0	4	2	0	17	1	0	.059	4	7	2	0	0.4	.846
1993	CLR N	6	10	.375	4.75	46	18	1	146	184	42	84	0	2	0	0	36	4	0	.111	9	16	0	0	0.5	1.000
1994		0	5	.000	5.79	47	1	0	77.2	98	39	68	0	0	4	3	6	0	0	.000	3	7	1	0	0.2	.909
5 yrs.		16	30	.348	4.86	160	38	1	407	480	144	256	0	9	9	3	59	5	0	.085	21	41	3	1	0.4	.954

Year	Team		W	L	PCT	ERA	G	GS	CG	IP	H	BB	SO	ShO	Relief Pitching			Batting			BA	PO	A	E	DP	TC/G	FA
															W	L	SV	AB	H	HR							

Joe Boever

BOEVER, JOSEPH MARTIN
B. Oct. 4, 1960, Kirkwood, Mo.
BR TR 6'1" 200 lbs.

Year	Team		W	L	PCT	ERA	G	GS	CG	IP	H	BB	SO	ShO	W	L	SV	AB	H	HR	BA	PO	A	E	DP	TC/G	FA
1985	STL	N	0	0	–	4.41	13	0	0	16.1	17	4	20	0	0	0	0	0	0	0	–	0	0	0	0	0.0	–
1986			0	1	.000	1.66	11	0	0	21.2	19	11	8	0	0	1	0	2	1	0	.500	1	2	0	0	0.3	1.000
1987	ATL	N	1	0	1.000	7.36	14	0	0	18.1	29	12	18	0	1	0	0	0	0	0	–	0	2	0	0	0.1	1.000
1988			0	2	.000	1.77	16	0	0	20.1	12	1	7	0	0	2	1	0	0	0	–	2	3	0	1	0.3	1.000
1989			4	11	.267	3.94	66	0	0	82.1	78	34	68	0	4	11	21	1	0	0	.000	7	15	0	0	0.3	1.000
1990	2 teams		ATL	N	(33G 1–3)		PHI	N	(34G 2–3)																		
"	total		3	6	.333	3.36	67	0	0	88.1	77	51	75	0	3	6	14	3	0	0	.000	6	7	2	1	0.2	.867
1991	PHI	N	3	5	.375	3.84	68	0	0	98.1	90	54	89	0	3	5	0	3	1	0	.333	1	10	0	0	0.2	1.000
1992	HOU	N	3	6	.333	2.51	81	0	0	111.1	103	45	67	0	3	6	2	7	0	0	.000	4	19	2	2	0.3	.920
1993	2 teams		OAK	A	(42G 4–2)		DET	A	(19G 2–1)																		
"	total		6	3	.667	3.61	61	0	0	102.1	101	44	63	0	6	3	3	0	0	–		9	12	1	1	0.4	.955
1994	DET	A	9	2	.818	3.98	46	0	0	81.1	80	37	49	0	9	2	3	0	0	0	–	10	13	1	1	0.5	.958
10 yrs.			29	36	.446	3.51	443	0	0	640.2	606	293	464	0	29	36	44	16	2	0	.125	40	83	6	6	0.3	.953

Brian Bohanon

BOHANON, BRIAN EDWARD
B. Aug. 1, 1968, Denton, Tex.
BL TL 6'2" 210 lbs.

Year	Team		W	L	PCT	ERA	G	GS	CG	IP	H	BB	SO	ShO	W	L	SV	AB	H	HR	BA	PO	A	E	DP	TC/G	FA
1990	TEX	A	0	3	.000	6.62	11	6	0	34	40	18	15	0	0	0	0	0	0	0	–	1	10	0	2	1.0	1.000
1991			4	3	.571	4.84	11	11	1	61.1	66	23	34	0	0	0	0	0	0	0	–	3	6	0	1	0.8	1.000
1992			1	1	.500	6.31	18	7	0	45.2	57	25	29	0	0	0	0	0	0	0	–	5	3	1	0	0.5	.889
1993			4	4	.500	4.76	36	8	0	92.2	107	46	45	0	3	1	0	0	0	0	–	5	18	0	4	0.6	1.000
1994			2	2	.500	7.23	11	5	0	37.1	51	8	26	0	0	0	0	0	0	0	–	3	6	0	0	0.8	1.000
5 yrs.			11	13	.458	5.61	87	37	1	271	321	120	149	0	3	1	0	0	0	0	–	17	43	1	7	0.7	.984

Tom Bolton

BOLTON, THOMAS EDWARD
B. May 6, 1962, Nashville, Tenn.
BL TL 6'2" 172 lbs.

Year	Team		W	L	PCT	ERA	G	GS	CG	IP	H	BB	SO	ShO	W	L	SV	AB	H	HR	BA	PO	A	E	DP	TC/G	FA
1987	BOS	A	1	0	1.000	4.38	29	0	0	61.2	83	27	49	0	1	0	0	0	0	0	–	3	9	0	1	0.4	1.000
1988			1	3	.250	4.75	28	0	0	30.1	35	14	21	0	1	3	1	0	0	0	–	1	10	0	0	0.4	1.000
1989			0	4	.000	8.31	4	4	0	17.1	21	10	9	0	0	0	0	0	0	0	–	1	2	0	0	0.8	1.000
1990			10	5	.667	3.38	21	16	3	119.2	111	47	65	0	2	0	0	0	0	0	–	4	21	1	1	1.2	.962
1991			8	9	.471	5.24	25	19	0	110	136	51	64	0	1	0	0	0	0	0	–	1	15	2	3	0.7	.889
1992	2 teams		BOS	A	(21G 1–2)		CIN	N	(16G 3–3)																		
"	total		4	5	.444	4.54	37	9	0	75.1	86	37	50	0	2	1	0	14	0	0	.000	3	14	1	1	0.5	.944
1993	DET	A	6	6	.500	4.47	43	8	0	102.2	113	45	66	0	1	4	0	0	0	0	–	6	15	2	2	0.5	.913
1994	BAL	A	1	2	.333	5.40	22	0	0	23.1	29	13	12	0	1	2	0	0	0	0	–	3	3	0	1	0.3	1.000
8 yrs.			31	34	.477	4.56	209	56	3	540.1	614	244	336	0	9	10	1	14	0	0	.000	22	89	6	9	0.6	.949

LEAGUE CHAMPIONSHIP SERIES

Year	Team		W	L	PCT	ERA	G	GS	CG	IP	H	BB	SO	ShO	W	L	SV	AB	H	HR	BA	PO	A	E	DP	TC/G	FA
1990	BOS	A	0	0	–	0.00	2	0	0	3	2	2	3	0	0	0	0	0	0	0	–	0	0	0	0	0.0	–

Ricky Bones

BONES, RICARDO
B. Apr. 7, 1969, Salinas, Puerto Rico.
BR TR 5'10" 175 lbs.

Year	Team		W	L	PCT	ERA	G	GS	CG	IP	H	BB	SO	ShO	W	L	SV	AB	H	HR	BA	PO	A	E	DP	TC/G	FA
1991	SD	N	4	6	.400	4.83	11	11	0	54	57	18	31	0	0	0	0	13	1	0	.077	1	2	0	0	0.3	1.000
1992	MIL	A	9	10	.474	4.57	31	28	0	163.1	169	48	65	0	0	0	0	0	0	0	–	17	13	2	1	1.0	.938
1993			11	11	.500	4.86	32	31	3	203.2	222	63	63	0	0	0	0	0	0	0	–	26	22	1	2	1.5	.980
1994			10	9	.526	3.43	24	24	4	170.2	166	45	57	0	0	0	0	0	0	0	–	8	14	1	2	1.0	.957
4 yrs.			34	36	.486	4.37	98	94	7	591.2	614	174	216	1	0	0	0	13	1	0	.077	52	51	4	5	1.1	.963

Toby Borland

BORLAND, TOBY SHAWN
B. May 29, 1969, Quitman, La.
BR TR 6'6" 186 lbs.

Year	Team		W	L	PCT	ERA	G	GS	CG	IP	H	BB	SO	ShO	W	L	SV	AB	H	HR	BA	PO	A	E	DP	TC/G	FA
1994	PHI	N	1	0	1.000	2.36	24	0	0	34.1	31	14	26	0	1	0	1	3	0	0	.000	5	1	0	0	0.3	1.000

Chris Bosio

BOSIO, CHRISTOPHER LOUIS
B. Apr. 3, 1963, Carmichael, Calif.
BR TR 6'3" 220 lbs.

Year	Team		W	L	PCT	ERA	G	GS	CG	IP	H	BB	SO	ShO	W	L	SV	AB	H	HR	BA	PO	A	E	DP	TC/G	FA
1986	MIL	A	0	4	.000	7.01	10	4	0	34.2	41	13	29	0	0	1	0	0	0	0	–	4	5	1	1	1.0	.900
1987			11	8	.579	5.24	46	19	2	170	187	50	150	1	3	1	2	0	0	0	–	14	24	4	5	0.9	.905
1988			7	15	.318	3.36	38	22	9	182	190	38	84	1	1	3	6	0	0	0	–	22	33	3	7	1.5	.948
1989			15	10	.600	2.95	33	33	8	234.2	225	48	173	2	0	0	0	0	0	0	–	16	35	2	2	1.6	.962
1990			4	9	.308	4.00	20	20	4	132.2	131	38	76	1	0	0	0	0	0	0	–	12	24	1	2	1.9	.973
1991			14	10	.583	3.25	32	32	5	204.2	187	58	117	1	0	0	0	0	0	0	–	20	21	2	4	1.3	.953
1992			16	6	.727	3.62	33	33	4	231.1	223	44	120	2	0	0	0	0	0	0	–	20	26	0	5	1.4	1.000
1993	SEA	A	9	9	.500	3.45	29	24	3	164.1	138	59	119	1	1	0	1	0	0	0	–	13	21	1	1	1.2	.971
1994			4	10	.286	4.32	19	19	4	125	137	40	67	0	0	0	0	0	0	0	–	11	24	0	3	1.8	1.000
9 yrs.			80	81	.497	3.77	260	206	39	1479.1	1459	388	935	9	5	5	9	0	0	0	–	132	213	14	30	1.4	.961

Shawn Boskie

BOSKIE, SHAWN KEALOHA
B. May 28, 1967, Hawthorne, Nev.
BR TR 6'3" 205 lbs.

Year	Team		W	L	PCT	ERA	G	GS	CG	IP	H	BB	SO	ShO	W	L	SV	AB	H	HR	BA	PO	A	E	DP	TC/G	FA
1990	CHI	N	5	6	.455	3.69	15	15	1	97.2	99	31	49	0	0	0	0	36	8	0	.222	12	12	0	2	1.6	1.000
1991			4	9	.308	5.23	28	20	0	129	150	52	62	0	1	0	0	41	7	1	.171	14	21	2	0	1.3	.946
1992			5	11	.313	5.01	23	18	0	91.2	96	36	39	0	2	1	0	27	5	0	.185	8	21	1	2	1.3	.967
1993			5	3	.625	3.43	39	2	0	65.2	63	21	39	0	4	2	0	11	3	0	.273	3	5	1	0	0.2	.889
1994	3 teams		CHI	N	(2G 0–0)		PHI	N	(18G 4–6)		SEA	A	(2G 0–1)														
"	total		4	7	.364	5.06	22	15	1	90.2	92	30	61	0	0	0	0	26	3	0	.115	8	13	1	2	1.0	.955
5 yrs.			23	36	.390	4.59	127	70	2	474.2	500	170	250	0	7	3	0	141	26	1	.184	45	72	5	6	1.0	.959

Ricky Bottalico

BOTTALICO, RICHARD PAUL
B. Aug. 26, 1969, New Britain, Conn.
BL TR 6'1" 200 lbs.

Year	Team		W	L	PCT	ERA	G	GS	CG	IP	H	BB	SO	ShO	W	L	SV	AB	H	HR	BA	PO	A	E	DP	TC/G	FA
1994	PHI	N	0	0	–	0.00	3	0	0	3	3	1	3	0	0	0	0	0	0	0	–	0	0	0	0	0.0	–

Year	Team	W	L	PCT	ERA	G	GS	CG	IP	H	BB	SO	ShO	Relief Pitching W	L	SV	Batting AB	H	HR	BA	PO	A	E	DP	TC/G	FA

Kent Bottenfield

BOTTENFIELD, KENT DENNIS
B. Nov. 14, 1968, Portland, Ore.   BB TR 6'3"   225 lbs.

Year	Team	W	L	PCT	ERA	G	GS	CG	IP	H	BB	SO	ShO	W	L	SV	AB	H	HR	BA	PO	A	E	DP	TC/G	FA
1992	MON N	1	2	.333	2.23	10	4	0	32.1	26	11	14	0	0	1	1	8	3	0	.375	2	2	0	0	0.4	1.000
1993	2 teams												MON N (23G 2–5)		CLR N (14G 3–5)											
"	total	5	10	.333	5.07	37	25	1	159.2	179	71	63	0	0	1	0	50	11	0	.220	9	32	2	6	1.2	.953
1994	2 teams												CLR N (15G 3–1)		SF N (1G 0–0)											
"	total	3	1	.750	6.15	16	1	0	26.1	33	10	15	0	3	0	1	1	0	0	.000	1	2	1	0	0.3	.750
	3 yrs.	9	13	.409	4.78	63	30	1	218.1	238	92	92	0	3	2	2	59	14	0	.237	12	36	3	6	0.8	.941

Denis Boucher

BOUCHER, DENIS
B. Mar. 7, 1968, Montreal, Que., Canada.   BR TL 6'1"   195 lbs.

Year	Team	W	L	PCT	ERA	G	GS	CG	IP	H	BB	SO	ShO	W	L	SV	AB	H	HR	BA	PO	A	E	DP	TC/G	FA
1991	2 teams												TOR A (7G 0–3)		CLE A (5G 1–4)											
"	total	1	7	.125	6.05	12	12	0	58	74	24	29	0	0	0	0	0	0	0	–	2	13	2	2	1.4	.882
1992	CLE A	2	2	.500	6.37	8	7	0	41	48	20	17	0	0	0	0	0	0	0	–	3	3	0	0	0.8	1.000
1993	MON N	3	1	.750	1.91	5	5	0	28.1	24	3	14	0	0	0	0	6	1	0	.167	1	4	0	0	1.0	1.000
1994		0	1	.000	6.75	10	2	0	18.2	24	7	17	0	0	0	0	3	1	0	.333	1	3	0	0	0.4	1.000
	4 yrs.	6	11	.353	5.42	35	26	0	146	170	54	77	0	0	0	0	9	2	0	.222	7	23	2	2	0.9	.938

Ryan Bowen

BOWEN, RYAN EUGENE
B. Feb. 10, 1968, Hanford, Calif.   BR TR 6'   185 lbs.

Year	Team	W	L	PCT	ERA	G	GS	CG	IP	H	BB	SO	ShO	W	L	SV	AB	H	HR	BA	PO	A	E	DP	TC/G	FA
1991	HOU N	6	4	.600	5.15	14	13	0	71.2	73	36	49	0	1	0	0	22	4	0	.182	4	3	2	0	0.6	.778
1992		0	7	.000	10.96	11	9	0	33.2	48	30	22	0	0	0	0	9	1	0	.111	0	3	0	0	0.3	1.000
1993	FLA N	8	12	.400	4.42	27	27	2	156.2	156	87	98	1	0	0	0	51	6	0	.118	7	24	2	0	1.2	.939
1994		1	5	.167	4.94	8	8	1	47.1	50	19	32	0	0	0	0	14	5	0	.357	0	3	1	0	0.5	.750
	4 yrs.	15	28	.349	5.38	60	57	3	309.1	327	172	201	1	1	0	0	96	16	0	.167	11	33	5	0	0.8	.898

Jeff Brantley

BRANTLEY, JEFFREY HOKE
B. Sept. 5, 1963, Florence, Ala.   BR TR 5'11"   180 lbs.

Year	Team	W	L	PCT	ERA	G	GS	CG	IP	H	BB	SO	ShO	W	L	SV	AB	H	HR	BA	PO	A	E	DP	TC/G	FA
1988	SF N	0	1	.000	5.66	9	1	0	20.2	22	6	11	0	0	0	1	2	1	0	.500	0	7	0	0	0.8	1.000
1989		7	1	.875	4.07	59	1	0	97.1	101	37	69	0	7	0	0	12	1	0	.083	3	16	0	0	0.3	1.000
1990		5	3	.625	1.56	55	0	0	86.2	77	33	61	0	5	3	19	7	2	0	.286	6	11	1	1	0.3	.944
1991		5	2	.714	2.45	67	0	0	95.1	78	52	81	0	5	2	15	3	0	0	.000	4	9	0	1	0.2	1.000
1992		7	7	.500	2.95	56	4	0	91.2	67	45	86	0	4	7	7	9	1	0	.111	4	9	0	0	0.2	1.000
1993		5	6	.455	4.28	53	12	0	113.2	112	46	76	0	2	1	0	28	3	0	.107	6	9	2	0	0.3	.882
1994	CIN N	6	6	.500	2.48	50	0	0	65.1	46	28	63	0	6	6	15	3	0	0	.000	2	10	0	1	0.2	1.000
	7 yrs.	35	26	.574	3.15	349	18	0	570.2	503	247	447	0	29	19	57	64	8	0	.125	25	71	3	3	0.3	.970

LEAGUE CHAMPIONSHIP SERIES

| 1989 | SF N | 0 | 0 | – | 0.00 | 3 | 0 | 0 | 5 | 1 | 2 | 3 | 0 | 0 | 0 | 0 | 0 | 0 | 0 | – | 0 | 0 | 0 | 0 | 0.0 | – |

WORLD SERIES

| 1989 | SF N | 0 | 0 | – | 4.15 | 3 | 0 | 0 | 4.1 | 5 | 3 | 1 | 0 | 0 | 0 | 0 | 0 | 0 | 0 | – | 1 | 0 | 0 | 0 | 0.3 | 1.000 |

Billy Brewer

BREWER, WILLIAM ROBERT
B. Apr. 15, 1968, Fort Worth, Tex.   BL TL 6'1"   175 lbs.

Year	Team	W	L	PCT	ERA	G	GS	CG	IP	H	BB	SO	ShO	W	L	SV	AB	H	HR	BA	PO	A	E	DP	TC/G	FA
1993	KC A	2	2	.500	3.46	46	0	0	39	31	20	28	0	2	2	0	0	0	0	–	1	4	2	0	0.2	.714
1994		4	1	.800	2.56	50	0	0	38.2	28	16	25	0	4	1	3	0	0	0	–	2	6	1	0	0.2	.889
	2 yrs.	6	3	.667	3.01	96	0	0	77.2	59	36	53	0	6	3	3	0	0	0	–	3	10	3	0	0.2	.813

Brad Brink

BRINK, BRADFORD ALBERT
B. Jan. 20, 1965, Roseville, Calif.   BR TR 6'2"   195 lbs.

Year	Team	W	L	PCT	ERA	G	GS	CG	IP	H	BB	SO	ShO	W	L	SV	AB	H	HR	BA	PO	A	E	DP	TC/G	FA
1992	PHI N	0	4	.000	4.14	8	7	0	41.1	53	13	16	0	0	0	0	12	1	0	.083	0	2	1	0	0.4	.667
1993		0	0	–	3.00	2	0	0	6	3	3	8	0	0	0	0	1	0	0	.000	0	0	0	0	0.5	.000
1994	SF N	0	0	–	1.08	4	0	0	8.1	4	4	3	0	0	0	0	1	0	0	.000	1	1	0	0	0.5	1.000
	3 yrs.	0	4	.000	3.56	14	7	0	55.2	60	20	27	0	0	0	0	14	1	0	.071	1	3	2	0	0.4	.667

John Briscoe

BRISCOE, JOHN ERIC
B. Sept. 22, 1967, La Grange, Ill.   BR TR 6'3"   185 lbs.

Year	Team	W	L	PCT	ERA	G	GS	CG	IP	H	BB	SO	ShO	W	L	SV	AB	H	HR	BA	PO	A	E	DP	TC/G	FA
1991	OAK A	0	0	–	7.07	11	0	0	14	12	10	9	0	0	0	0	0	0	0	–	0	1	0	0	0.1	1.000
1992		0	1	.000	6.43	2	2	0	7	12	9	4	0	0	0	0	0	0	0	–	0	1	1	0	1.0	.500
1993		1	0	1.000	8.03	17	0	0	24.2	26	26	24	0	1	0	0	0	0	0	–	1	4	0	0	0.3	1.000
1994		4	2	.667	4.01	37	0	0	49.1	31	39	45	0	4	2	1	0	0	0	–	2	2	0	1	0.1	1.000
	4 yrs.	5	3	.625	5.68	67	2	0	95	81	84	82	0	5	2	1	0	0	0	–	3	8	1	1	0.2	.917

Doug Brocail

BROCAIL, DOUGLAS KEITH
B. May 16, 1967, Clearfield, Pa.   BL TR 6'5"   220 lbs.

Year	Team	W	L	PCT	ERA	G	GS	CG	IP	H	BB	SO	ShO	W	L	SV	AB	H	HR	BA	PO	A	E	DP	TC/G	FA
1992	SD N	0	0	–	6.43	3	3	0	14	17	5	15	0	0	0	0	5	1	0	.200	2	3	1	0	2.0	.833
1993		4	13	.235	4.56	24	24	0	128.1	143	42	70	0	0	0	0	33	6	0	.182	8	20	2	1	1.3	.933
1994		0	0	–	5.82	12	0	0	17	21	5	11	0	0	0	0	2	0	0	.000	1	2	1	0	0.3	.750
	3 yrs.	4	13	.235	4.86	39	27	0	159.1	181	52	96	0	0	0	0	40	7	0	.175	11	25	4	1	1.0	.900

Jeff Bronkey

BRONKEY, JACOB JEFFREY
B. Sept. 18, 1965, Kabul, Afghanistan   BR TR 6'3"   215 lbs.

Year	Team	W	L	PCT	ERA	G	GS	CG	IP	H	BB	SO	ShO	W	L	SV	AB	H	HR	BA	PO	A	E	DP	TC/G	FA
1993	TEX A	1	1	.500	4.00	21	0	0	36	39	11	18	0	1	1	1	1	0	0	.000	3	10	0	1	0.6	1.000
1994	MIL A	1	1	.500	4.35	16	0	0	20.2	20	12	13	0	1	1	1	0	0	0	–	1	4	0	0	0.3	1.000
	2 yrs.	2	2	.500	4.13	37	0	0	56.2	59	23	31	0	2	2	2	1	0	0	.000	4	14	0	1	0.5	1.000

Scott Brow

BROW, SCOTT JOHN
B. Mar. 17, 1969, Butte, Mont.   BR TR 6'3"   200 lbs.

Year	Team	W	L	PCT	ERA	G	GS	CG	IP	H	BB	SO	ShO	W	L	SV	AB	H	HR	BA	PO	A	E	DP	TC/G	FA
1993	TOR A	1	1	.500	6.00	6	3	0	18	19	10	7	0	0	0	0	0	0	0	–	3	8	0	1	1.8	1.000
1994		0	3	.000	5.90	18	0	0	29	34	19	15	0	0	3	2	0	0	0	–	1	4	0	1	0.3	1.000
	2 yrs.	1	4	.200	5.94	24	3	0	47	53	29	22	0	0	3	2	0	0	0	–	4	12	0	2	0.7	1.000

Year	Team		W	L	PCT	ERA	G	GS	CG	IP	H	BB	SO	ShO	Relief Pitching W	L	SV	Batting AB	H	HR	BA	PO	A	E	DP	TC/G	FA

Kevin Brown

BROWN, JAMES KEVIN
B. Mar. 14, 1965, Milledgeville, Ga.   BR TR 6'4"   195 lbs.

Year	Team		W	L	PCT	ERA	G	GS	CG	IP	H	BB	SO	ShO	W	L	SV	AB	H	HR	BA	PO	A	E	DP	TC/G	FA
1986	TEX	A	1	0	1.000	3.60	1	1	0	5	6	0	4	0	0	0	0	0	0	0	–	0	1	0	0	1.0	1.000
1988			1	1	.500	4.24	4	4	1	23.1	33	8	12	0	0	0	0	0	0	0	–	1	2	0	0	0.8	1.000
1989			12	9	.571	3.35	28	28	7	191	167	70	104	0	0	0	0	0	0	0	–	15	41	2	6	2.1	.966
1990			12	10	.545	3.60	26	26	6	180	175	60	88	2	0	0	0	1	0	0	.000	15	24	3	0	1.6	.929
1991			9	12	.429	4.40	33	33	0	210.2	233	90	96	0	0	0	0	0	0	0	–	18	32	2	3	1.6	.962
1992			**21**	11	.656	3.32	35	35	11	**265.2**	**262**	76	173	1	0	0	0	0	0	0	–	37	36	8	4	2.3	.901
1993			15	12	.556	3.59	34	34	12	233	228	74	142	3	0	0	0	0	0	0	–	29	42	3	2	2.2	.959
1994			7	9	.438	4.82	26	**25**	3	170	**218**	50	123	0	0	1	0	0	0	0	–	20	29	4	2	2.0	.925
8 yrs.			78	64	.549	3.81	187	186	40	1278.2	1322	428	742	6	0	1	0	1	0	0	.000	135	207	22	17	1.9	.940

Tom Browning

BROWNING, THOMAS LEO
B. Apr. 28, 1960, Casper, Wyo.   BL TL 6'1"   190 lbs.

Year	Team		W	L	PCT	ERA	G	GS	CG	IP	H	BB	SO	ShO	W	L	SV	AB	H	HR	BA	PO	A	E	DP	TC/G	FA
1984	CIN	N	1	0	1.000	1.54	3	3	0	23.1	27	5	14	0	0	0	0	7	1	0	.143	1	3	0	0	1.3	1.000
1985			20	9	.690	3.55	38	38	6	261.1	242	73	155	4	0	0	0	88	17	0	.193	12	34	2	1	1.3	.958
1986			14	13	.519	3.81	39	**39**	4	243.1	225	70	147	2	0	0	0	86	14	0	.163	11	26	3	5	1.0	.925
1987			10	13	.435	5.02	32	31	2	183	201	61	117	0	0	0	0	52	8	0	.154	5	23	3	1	1.0	.903
1988			18	5	.783	3.41	36	**36**	5	250.2	205	64	124	0	0	0	0	83	12	0	.145	8	30	3	3	1.1	.927
1989			15	12	.556	3.39	37	**37**	9	249.2	241	64	118	2	0	0	0	78	7	0	.090	8	35	0	3	1.2	1.000
1990			15	9	.625	3.80	35	**35**	2	227.2	235	52	99	1	0	0	0	75	7	0	.093	8	27	3	1	1.1	.921
1991			14	14	.500	4.18	36	36	1	230.1	241	56	115	0	0	0	0	70	12	1	.171	8	24	5	2	1.0	.865
1992			6	5	.545	5.07	16	16	0	87	108	28	33	0	0	0	0	31	7	0	.226	6	14	1	3	1.3	.952
1993			7	7	.500	4.74	21	20	0	114	159	20	53	0	0	0	0	37	8	1	.216	10	21	0	2	1.5	1.000
1994			3	1	.750	4.20	7	7	2	40.2	34	13	22	1	0	0	0	14	2	0	.143	1	6	0	0	1.0	1.000
11 yrs.			123	88	.583	3.92	300	298	31	1911	1918	506	997	12	0	0	0	621	95	2	.153	78	243	20	21	1.1	.941

LEAGUE CHAMPIONSHIP SERIES

1990	CIN	N	1	1	.500	3.27	2	2	0	11	9	6	5	0	0	0	0	3	0	0	.000	1	1	0	0	1.0	1.000

WORLD SERIES

1990	CIN	N	1	0	1.000	4.50	1	1	0	6	6	2	2	0	0	0	0	0	0	0	–	0	0	0	0	0.0	–

Duff Brumley

BRUMLEY, DUFF LECHAUN
B. Aug. 25, 1970, Cleveland, Tenn.   BR TR 6'4"   195 lbs.

1994	TEX	A	0	0	–	16.20	2	0	0	3.1	6	5	4	0	0	0	0	0	0	0	–	0	0	0	0	0.0	–

Gary Buckels

BUCKELS, GARY SCOTT
B. July 22, 1965, La Mirada, Calif.   BR TR 6'   185 lbs.

1994	STL	N	0	1	.000	2.25	10	0	0	12	8	7	9	0	0	1	0	1	0	0	.000	2	2	0	0	0.4	1.000

Jim Bullinger

BULLINGER, JAMES ERIC
B. Aug. 21, 1965, New Orleans, La.   BR TR 6'2"   185 lbs.

1992	CHI	N	2	8	.200	4.66	39	9	1	85	72	54	36	0	1	2	7	20	5	1	.250	17	17	0	2	0.9	1.000
1993			1	0	1.000	4.32	15	0	0	16.2	18	9	10	0	1	0	1	1	0	0	.000	1	1	0	0	0.1	1.000
1994			6	2	.750	3.60	33	10	1	100	87	34	72	0	2	0	2	22	3	0	.136	6	11	0	0	0.5	1.000
3 yrs.			9	10	.474	4.11	87	19	2	201.2	177	97	118	0	4	2	10	43	8	1	.186	24	29	0	2	0.6	1.000

Dave Burba

BURBA, DAVID ALLEN
B. July 7, 1966, Dayton, Ohio.   BR TR 6'4"   220 lbs.

1990	SEA	A	0	0	–	4.50	6	0	0	8	8	2	4	0	0	0	0	0	0	0	–	1	2	1	0	0.7	.750
1991			2	2	.500	3.68	22	2	0	36.2	34	14	16	0	1	1	1	0	0	0	–	2	4	0	0	0.3	1.000
1992	SF	N	2	7	.222	4.97	23	11	0	70.2	80	31	47	0	1	1	0	15	1	0	.067	3	8	0	0	0.5	1.000
1993			10	3	.769	4.25	54	5	0	95.1	95	37	88	0	7	2	0	17	5	0	.294	7	12	1	0	0.4	.950
1994			3	6	.333	4.38	57	0	0	74	59	45	84	0	3	**6**	0	3	0	0	.000	3	5	0	1	0.1	1.000
5 yrs.			17	18	.486	4.39	162	18	0	284.2	276	129	239	0	12	10	1	35	6	0	.171	16	31	2	1	0.3	.959

John Burkett

BURKETT, JOHN DAVID
B. Nov. 28, 1964, New Brighton, Pa.   BR TR 6'2"   175 lbs.

1987	SF	N	0	0	–	4.50	3	0	0	6	7	3	5	0	0	0	0	1	0	0	.000	0	1	0	1	0.3	1.000
1990			14	7	.667	3.79	33	32	2	204	201	61	118	0	0	0	1	63	3	0	.048	11	25	1	4	1.1	.973
1991			12	11	.522	4.18	36	34	3	206.2	223	60	131	1	0	0	0	55	5	0	.091	13	25	1	2	1.1	.974
1992			13	9	.591	3.84	32	32	3	189.2	194	45	107	1	0	0	0	55	1	0	.018	11	18	1	0	0.9	.967
1993			**22**	7	.759	3.65	34	34	2	231.2	224	40	145	1	0	0	0	76	9	0	.118	21	36	0	2	1.7	1.000
1994			6	8	.429	3.62	25	25	0	159.1	176	36	85	0	0	0	0	51	3	0	.059	14	23	0	1	1.5	1.000
6 yrs.			67	42	.615	3.83	163	157	10	997.1	1025	245	591	3	0	0	1	301	21	0	.070	70	128	3	10	1.2	.985

Terry Burrows

BURROWS, TERRY DALE
B. Nov. 28, 1968, Lake Charles, La.   BL TL 6'1"   185 lbs.

1994	TEX	A	0	0	–	9.00	1	0	0	1	1	1	1	0	0	0	0	0	0	0	–	0	0	0	0	0.0	–

Mike Butcher

BUTCHER, MICHAEL DANA
B. May 10, 1965, Davenport, Iowa.   BR TR 6'1"   200 lbs.

1992	CAL	A	2	2	.500	3.25	19	0	0	27.2	29	13	24	0	2	2	0	0	0	0	–	0	3	0	0	0.2	1.000
1993			1	0	1.000	2.86	23	0	0	28.1	21	15	24	0	1	0	8	0	0	0	–	1	0	0	0	0.1	1.000
1994			2	1	.667	6.67	33	0	0	29.2	31	23	19	0	2	1	1	0	0	0	–	2	9	0	3	0.3	1.000
3 yrs.			5	3	.625	4.31	75	0	0	85.2	81	51	67	0	5	3	9	0	0	0	–	3	13	0	3	0.2	1.000

Year	Team	W	L	PCT	ERA	G	GS	CG	IP	H	BB	SO	ShO	W	L	SV	AB	H	HR	BA	PO	A	E	DP	TC/G	FA
														Relief Pitching			Batting									

Greg Cadaret

CADARET, GREGORY JAMES
B. Feb. 27, 1962, Detroit, Mich. BL TL 6'3" 200 lbs.

Year	Team	W	L	PCT	ERA	G	GS	CG	IP	H	BB	SO	ShO	W	L	SV	AB	H	HR	BA	PO	A	E	DP	TC/G	FA
1987	OAK A	6	2	.750	4.54	29	0	0	39.2	37	24	30	0	6	2	0	0	0	0	–	6	6	0	1	0.4	1.000
1988		5	2	.714	2.89	58	0	0	71.2	60	36	64	0	5	2	3	0	0	0	–	3	9	0	1	0.2	1.000
1989	2 teams	OAK A	(26G 0–0)		NY A	(20G 5–5)																				
"	total	5	5	.500	4.05	46	13	3	120	130	57	80	1	1	0	0	0	0	0	–	9	21	2	2	0.7	.938
1990	NY A	5	4	.556	4.15	54	6	0	121.1	120	64	80	0	4	1	3	0	0	0	–	7	27	1	1	0.6	.971
1991		8	6	.571	3.62	68	5	0	121.2	110	59	105	0	5	5	3	0	0	0	–	5	17	1	5	0.3	.957
1992		4	8	.333	4.25	46	11	1	103.2	104	74	73	1	1	3	1	0	0	0	–	5	18	0	2	0.5	1.000
1993	2 teams	CIN N	(34G 2–1)		KC A	(13G 1–1)																				
"	total	3	2	.600	4.31	47	0	0	48	54	30	25	0	3	2	1	2	0	0	.000	4	6	0	0	0.2	1.000
1994	2 teams	TOR A	(21G 0–1)		DET A	(17G 1–0)																				
"	total	1	1	.500	4.73	38	0	0	40	41	33	29	0	1	1	2	0	0	0	–	2	7	0	1	0.2	1.000
8 yrs.		37	30	.552	3.99	386	35	4	666	656	377	486	2	26	16	13	2	0	0	.000	41	111	4	13	0.4	.974

LEAGUE CHAMPIONSHIP SERIES

| 1988 | OAK A | 0 | 0 | – | 27.00 | 1 | 0 | 0 | 0.1 | 1 | 1 | 0 | 0 | 0 | 0 | 0 | 0 | 0 | 0 | – | 0 | 0 | 0 | 0 | 0.0 | – |

WORLD SERIES

| 1988 | OAK A | 0 | 0 | – | 0.00 | 3 | 0 | 0 | 2 | 2 | 0 | 3 | 0 | 0 | 0 | 0 | 0 | 0 | 0 | – | 0 | 0 | 0 | 0 | 0.0 | – |

Kevin Campbell

CAMPBELL, KEVIN WADE
B. Dec. 6, 1964, Marianna, Ark. BR TR 6'2" 225 lbs.

Year	Team	W	L	PCT	ERA	G	GS	CG	IP	H	BB	SO	ShO	W	L	SV	AB	H	HR	BA	PO	A	E	DP	TC/G	FA
1991	OAK A	1	0	1.000	2.74	14	0	0	23	13	14	16	0	1	0	0	0	0	0	–	3	2	0	0	0.4	1.000
1992		2	3	.400	5.12	32	5	0	65	66	45	38	0	1	2	1	0	0	0	–	1	6	0	0	0.2	1.000
1993		0	0	–	7.31	11	0	0	16	20	11	9	0	0	0	0	0	0	0	–	0	1	0	0	0.1	1.000
1994	MIN A	1	0	1.000	2.92	14	0	0	24.2	20	5	15	0	1	0	0	0	0	0	–	0	7	0	0	0.5	1.000
4 yrs.		4	3	.571	4.55	71	5	0	128.2	119	75	78	0	3	2	1	0	0	0	–	4	16	0	0	0.3	1.000

Mike Campbell

CAMPBELL, MICHAEL THOMAS
B. Feb. 17, 1964, Seattle, Wash. BR TR 6'3" 210 lbs.

Year	Team	W	L	PCT	ERA	G	GS	CG	IP	H	BB	SO	ShO	W	L	SV	AB	H	HR	BA	PO	A	E	DP	TC/G	FA
1987	SEA A	1	4	.200	4.74	9	9	1	49.1	41	25	35	0	0	0	0	0	0	0	–	6	5	0	0	1.2	1.000
1988		6	10	.375	5.89	20	20	2	114.2	128	43	63	0	0	0	0	0	0	0	–	7	13	3	1	1.2	.870
1989		1	2	.333	7.29	5	5	0	21	28	10	6	0	0	0	0	0	0	0	–	2	1	0	0	0.6	1.000
1992	TEX A	0	1	.000	9.82	1	0	0	3.2	3	2	2	0	0	1	0	0	0	0	–	0	0	0	0	0.0	–
1994	SD N	1	1	.500	12.96	3	2	0	8.1	13	5	10	0	1	0	0	3	1	0	.333	0	0	0	0	0.0	–
5 yrs.		9	18	.333	6.12	38	36	3	197	213	85	116	0	1	1	0	3	1	0	.333	15	19	3	1	1.0	.919

Tom Candiotti

CANDIOTTI, THOMAS CAESAR
B. Aug. 31, 1957, Walnut Creek, Calif. BR TR 6'3" 205 lbs.

Year	Team	W	L	PCT	ERA	G	GS	CG	IP	H	BB	SO	ShO	W	L	SV	AB	H	HR	BA	PO	A	E	DP	TC/G	FA
1983	MIL A	4	4	.500	3.23	10	8	2	55.2	62	16	21	1	0	0	0	0	0	0	–	4	5	0	1	0.9	1.000
1984		2	2	.500	5.29	8	6	0	32.1	38	10	23	0	0	0	0	0	0	0	–	3	1	0	0	0.5	1.000
1986	CLE A	16	12	.571	3.57	36	34	17	252.1	234	106	167	3	0	0	0	0	0	0	–	27	41	3	7	2.0	.958
1987		7	18	.280	4.78	32	32	7	201.2	193	93	111	2	0	0	0	0	0	0	–	17	29	1	1	1.5	.979
1988		14	8	.636	3.28	31	31	11	216.2	225	53	137	1	0	0	0	0	0	0	–	17	36	1	2	1.7	.981
1989		13	10	.565	3.10	31	31	4	206	188	55	124	0	0	0	0	0	0	0	–	28	41	1	1	2.3	.986
1990		15	11	.577	3.65	31	29	3	202	207	55	128	1	0	0	0	0	0	0	–	22	37	2	1	2.0	.967
1991	2 teams	CLE A	(15G 7–6)		TOR A	(19G 6–7)																				
"	total	13	13	.500	2.65	34	34	6	238	202	73	167	0	0	0	0	0	0	0	–	19	28	1	1	1.4	.979
1992	LA N	11	15	.423	3.00	32	30	6	203.2	177	63	152	2	1	0	0	56	6	0	.107	16	32	1	3	1.5	.980
1993		8	10	.444	3.12	33	32	2	213.2	192	71	155	0	0	0	0	60	8	0	.133	10	30	3	3	1.3	.930
1994		7	7	.500	4.12	23	22	5	153	149	54	102	0	0	0	0	50	7	0	.140	14	22	0	1	1.6	1.000
11 yrs.		110	110	.500	3.46	301	289	63	1975	1867	649	1287	10	1	0	0	166	21	0	.127	177	302	13	21	1.6	.974

LEAGUE CHAMPIONSHIP SERIES

| 1991 | TOR A | 0 | 1 | .000 | 8.22 | 2 | 2 | 0 | 7.2 | 17 | 2 | 5 | 0 | 0 | 0 | 0 | 0 | 0 | 0 | – | 2 | 0 | 1 | 1.0 | 1.000 |

John Cangelosi

CANGELOSI, JOHN ANTHONY
B. Mar. 10, 1963, Brooklyn, N.Y. BB TL 5'8" 150 lbs.

Year	Team	W	L	PCT	ERA	G	GS	CG	IP	H	BB	SO	ShO	W	L	SV	AB	H	HR	BA	PO	A	E	DP	TC/G	FA
1988	PIT N	0	0	–	0.00	1	0	0	2	1	1	0	0	0	0	0	*				0	0	0	0	0.0	–

Jose Canseco

CANSECO, JOSE
Born Jose Canseco (Capas).
Brother of Ozzie Canseco.
B. July 2, 1964, Havana, Cuba. BR TR 6'3" 185 lbs.

Year	Team	W	L	PCT	ERA	G	GS	CG	IP	H	BB	SO	ShO	W	L	SV	AB	H	HR	BA	PO	A	E	DP	TC/G	FA
1993	TEX A	0	0	–	27.00	1	0	0	1	2	3	0	0	0	0	0	*				0	0	0	0	0.0	–

Cris Carpenter

CARPENTER, CRIS HOWELL
B. Apr. 5, 1965, St. Augustine, Fla. BR TR 6'1" 195 lbs.

Year	Team	W	L	PCT	ERA	G	GS	CG	IP	H	BB	SO	ShO	W	L	SV	AB	H	HR	BA	PO	A	E	DP	TC/G	FA
1988	STL N	2	3	.400	4.72	8	8	1	47.2	56	9	24	0	0	0	0	14	2	0	.143	6	4	0	1	1.3	1.000
1989		4	4	.500	3.18	36	5	0	68	70	26	35	0	3	2	0	9	4	0	.444	3	10	0	1	0.4	1.000
1990		0	0	–	4.50	4	0	0	8	5	2	6	0	0	0	0	1	0	0	.000	0	0	1	0	0.3	.000
1991		10	4	.714	4.23	59	0	0	66	53	20	47	0	10	4	0	3	1	0	.333	4	8	0	0	0.2	1.000
1992		5	4	.556	2.97	73	0	0	88	69	27	46	0	5	4	1	3	1	0	.333	7	10	0	1	0.2	1.000
1993	2 teams	FLA N	(29G 0–1)		TEX A	(27G 4–1)																				
"	total	4	2	.667	3.50	56	0	0	69.1	64	25	53	0	4	2	1	0	0	0	–	3	12	0	1	0.3	1.000
1994	TEX A	2	5	.286	5.03	47	0	0	59	69	20	39	0	2	5	5	0	0	0	–	2	8	1	1	0.2	.909
7 yrs.		27	22	.551	3.83	283	13	1	406	386	129	250	0	24	17	7	30	8	0	.267	25	52	2	5	0.3	.975

Hector Carrasco

CARRASCO, HECTOR
Born Hector Carrasco (Pacheco).
B. Oct. 22, 1969, San Pedro de Macoris, Dominican Republic BR TR 6'2" 175 lbs.

Year	Team	W	L	PCT	ERA	G	GS	CG	IP	H	BB	SO	ShO	W	L	SV	AB	H	HR	BA	PO	A	E	DP	TC/G	FA
1994	CIN N	5	6	.455	2.24	45	0	0	56.1	42	30	41	0	5	6	6	6	0	0	.000	3	7	1	0	0.2	.909

Year	Team	W	L	PCT	ERA	G	GS	CG	IP	H	BB	SO	ShO	W	L	SV	AB	H	HR	BA	PO	A	E	DP	TC/G	FA
														Relief Pitching			**Batting**									

Andy Carter
CARTER, ANDREW GODFREY
B. Nov. 9, 1968, Philadelphia, Pa.　　　　BL TL 6'5" 200 lbs.

Year	Team	W	L	PCT	ERA	G	GS	CG	IP	H	BB	SO	ShO	W	L	SV	AB	H	HR	BA	PO	A	E	DP	TC/G	FA
1994	PHI N	0	2	.000	4.46	20	0	0	34.1	34	12	18	0	0	2	0	6	0	0	.000	1	2	0	0	0.2	1.000

Larry Casian
CASIAN, LAWRENCE PAUL
B. Oct. 28, 1965, Lynwood, Calif.　　　　BR TL 6'1" 170 lbs.

Year	Team	W	L	PCT	ERA	G	GS	CG	IP	H	BB	SO	ShO	W	L	SV	AB	H	HR	BA	PO	A	E	DP	TC/G	FA
1990	MIN A	2	1	.667	3.22	5	3	0	22.1	26	4	11	0	1	0	0	0	0	0	—	0	3	0	1	0.6	1.000
1991		0	0	—	7.36	15	0	0	18.1	28	7	6	0	0	0	0	0	0	0	—	3	4	0	0	0.5	1.000
1992		1	0	1.000	2.70	6	0	0	6.2	7	1	2	0	1	0	0	0	0	0	—	1	1	0	1	0.3	1.000
1993		5	3	.625	3.02	54	0	0	56.2	59	14	31	0	5	3	1	0	0	0	—	4	4	0	0	0.1	1.000
1994	2 teams	MIN A (33G 1-3)					CLE A (7G 0-2)																			
"	total	1	5	.167	7.35	40	0	0	49	73	16	20	0	1	5	1	0	0	0	—	2	14	0	0	0.4	1.000
5 yrs.		9	9	.500	4.94	120	3	0	153	193	42	70	0	8	8	2	0	0	0	—	10	26	0	2	0.3	1.000

Frank Castillo
CASTILLO, FRANK ANTHONY
B. Apr. 1, 1969, El Paso, Tex.　　　　BR TR 6'1" 180 lbs.

Year	Team	W	L	PCT	ERA	G	GS	CG	IP	H	BB	SO	ShO	W	L	SV	AB	H	HR	BA	PO	A	E	DP	TC/G	FA
1991	CHI N	6	7	.462	4.35	18	18	4	111.2	107	33	73	0	0	0	0	35	5	0	.143	6	16	0	0	1.2	1.000
1992		10	11	.476	3.46	33	33	0	205.1	179	63	135	0	0	0	0	65	6	0	.092	10	28	1	2	1.2	.974
1993		5	8	.385	4.84	29	25	2	141.1	162	39	84	0	0	0	0	43	7	0	.163	7	34	1	2	1.4	.976
1994		2	1	.667	4.30	4	4	1	23	25	5	19	0	0	0	0	9	0	0	.000	1	3	2	0	1.5	.667
4 yrs.		23	27	.460	4.11	84	80	7	481.1	473	140	311	0	0	0	0	152	18	0	.118	24	81	4	4	1.3	.963

Juan Castillo
CASTILLO, JUAN FRANCISCO
B. June 23, 1970, Caracas, Venezuela.　　　　BR TR 6'5" 205 lbs.

Year	Team	W	L	PCT	ERA	G	GS	CG	IP	H	BB	SO	ShO	W	L	SV	AB	H	HR	BA	PO	A	E	DP	TC/G	FA
1994	NY N	0	0	—	6.94	2	2	0	11.2	17	5	1	0	0	0	0	5	1	0	.200	3	6	0	1	4.5	1.000

Tony Castillo
CASTILLO, ANTONIO JOSE
Born Antonio Jose Castillo (Jimenez).
B. Mar. 1, 1963, Quibor, Venezuela.　　　　BL TL 5'10" 177 lbs.

Year	Team	W	L	PCT	ERA	G	GS	CG	IP	H	BB	SO	ShO	W	L	SV	AB	H	HR	BA	PO	A	E	DP	TC/G	FA
1988	TOR A	1	0	1.000	3.00	14	0	0	15	10	2	14	0	1	0	0	0	0	0	—	0	3	0	0	0.2	1.000
1989	2 teams	TOR A (17G 1-1)					ATL N (12G 0-1)																			
"	total	1	2	.333	5.67	29	0	0	27	31	14	15	0	1	2	1	1	0	0	.000	2	3	0	0	0.2	1.000
1990	ATL N	5	1	.833	4.23	52	3	0	76.2	93	20	64	0	3	1	1	7	1	0	.143	5	13	0	1	0.3	1.000
1991	2 teams	ATL N (7G 1-1)					NY N (10G 1-0)																			
"	total	2	1	.667	3.34	17	3	0	32.1	40	11	18	0	1	1	0	4	0	0	.000	3	6	0	0	0.5	1.000
1993	TOR A	3	2	.600	3.38	51	0	0	50.2	44	22	28	0	3	2	0	0	0	0	—	3	9	1	1	0.3	.923
1994		5	2	.714	2.51	41	0	0	68	66	28	43	0	5	2	1	0	0	0	—	4	16	1	0	0.5	.952
6 yrs.		17	8	.680	3.60	204	6	0	269.2	284	97	182	0	14	8	3	12	1	0	.083	17	50	2	2	0.3	.971

LEAGUE CHAMPIONSHIP SERIES

Year	Team	W	L	PCT	ERA	G	GS	CG	IP	H	BB	SO	ShO	W	L	SV	AB	H	HR	BA	PO	A	E	DP	TC/G	FA
1993	TOR A	0	0	—	0.00	2	0	0	2	0	1	1	0	0	0	0	0	0	0	—	0	1	0	0	0.5	1.000

WORLD SERIES

Year	Team	W	L	PCT	ERA	G	GS	CG	IP	H	BB	SO	ShO	W	L	SV	AB	H	HR	BA	PO	A	E	DP	TC/G	FA
1993	TOR A	1	0	1.000	8.10	2	0	0	3.1	6	3	1	0	1	0	0	1	0	0	.000	0	0	0	0	0.0	—

Frank Cimorelli
CIMORELLI, FRANK THOMAS
B. Aug. 2, 1968, Poughkeepsie, N. Y.　　　　BR TR 6' 175 lbs.

Year	Team	W	L	PCT	ERA	G	GS	CG	IP	H	BB	SO	ShO	W	L	SV	AB	H	HR	BA	PO	A	E	DP	TC/G	FA
1994	STL N	0	0	—	8.78	11	0	0	13.1	20	10	1	0	0	0	1	2	0	0	.000	1	1	2	0	0.4	.500

Mark Clark
CLARK, MARK WILLARD
B. May 12, 1968, Bath, Ill.　　　　BR TR 6'5" 225 lbs.

Year	Team	W	L	PCT	ERA	G	GS	CG	IP	H	BB	SO	ShO	W	L	SV	AB	H	HR	BA	PO	A	E	DP	TC/G	FA
1991	STL N	1	1	.500	4.03	7	2	0	22.1	17	11	13	0	1	1	0	7	0	0	.000	2	1	0	0	0.4	1.000
1992		3	10	.231	4.45	20	20	1	113.1	117	36	44	1	0	0	0	36	5	0	.139	2	13	1	0	0.8	.938
1993	CLE A	7	5	.583	4.28	26	15	1	109.1	119	25	57	0	0	0	0	0	0	0	—	4	10	2	0	0.6	.875
1994		11	3	.786	3.82	20	20	4	127.1	133	40	60	1	0	0	0	0	0	0	—	5	23	0	3	1.4	1.000
4 yrs.		22	19	.537	4.16	73	57	6	372.1	386	112	174	2	1	1	0	43	5	0	.116	13	47	3	3	0.9	.952

Roger Clemens
CLEMENS, WILLIAM ROGER (Rocket Man)
B. Aug. 4, 1962, Dayton, Ohio.　　　　BR TR 6'4" 205 lbs.

Year	Team	W	L	PCT	ERA	G	GS	CG	IP	H	BB	SO	ShO	W	L	SV	AB	H	HR	BA	PO	A	E	DP	TC/G	FA
1984	BOS A	9	4	.692	4.32	21	20	5	133.1	146	29	126	1	0	0	0	0	0	0	—	11	14	0	0	1.2	1.000
1985		7	5	.583	3.29	15	15	3	98.1	83	37	74	1	0	0	0	0	0	0	—	12	9	0	1	1.4	1.000
1986		24	4	.857	2.48	33	33	10	254	179	67	238	1	0	0	0	0	0	0	—	27	21	4	0	1.6	.923
1987		20	9	.690	2.97	36	36	18	281.2	248	83	256	7	0	0	0	0	0	0	—	15	25	0	1	1.1	1.000
1988		18	12	.600	2.93	35	35	14	264	217	62	291	8	0	0	0	0	0	0	—	17	17	1	1	1.0	.971
1989		17	11	.607	3.13	35	35	8	253.1	215	93	230	3	0	0	0	0	0	0	—	17	27	0	1	1.3	1.000
1990		21	6	.778	1.93	31	31	7	228.1	193	54	209	4	0	0	0	0	0	0	—	23	26	2	1	1.6	.961
1991		18	10	.643	2.62	35	35	13	271.1	219	65	241	4	0	0	0	0	0	0	—	31	30	1	0	1.8	.984
1992		18	11	.621	2.41	32	32	11	246.2	203	62	208	5	0	0	0	0	0	0	—	19	25	1	0	1.4	.978
1993		11	14	.440	4.46	29	29	2	191.2	175	67	160	1	0	0	0	0	0	0	—	11	20	1	1	1.1	.969
1994		9	7	.563	2.85	24	24	3	170.2	124	71	168	1	0	0	0	0	0	0	—	8	19	2	2	1.2	.931
11 yrs.		172	93	.649	2.93	326	325	94	2393.1	2002	690	2201	36	0	0	0	0	0	0	—	191	233	12	9	1.3	.972

LEAGUE CHAMPIONSHIP SERIES

Year	Team	W	L	PCT	ERA	G	GS	CG	IP	H	BB	SO	ShO	W	L	SV	AB	H	HR	BA	PO	A	E	DP	TC/G	FA
1986	BOS A	1	1	.500	4.37	3	3	0	22.2	22	7	17	0	0	0	0	0	0	0	—	1	2	0	0	1.0	1.000
1988		0	0	—	3.86	1	1	0	7	6	0	8	0	0	0	0	0	0	0	—	0	0	1	0	1.0	.000
1990		0	1	.000	3.52	2	2	0	7.2	7	5	4	0	0	0	0	0	0	0	—	0	1	0	0	0.5	1.000
3 yrs.		1	2	.333	4.10	6	6	0	37.1	35	12	29	0	0	0	0	0	0	0	—	1	3	1	0	0.8	.800

WORLD SERIES

Year	Team	W	L	PCT	ERA	G	GS	CG	IP	H	BB	SO	ShO	W	L	SV	AB	H	HR	BA	PO	A	E	DP	TC/G	FA
1986	BOS A	0	0	—	3.18	2	2	0	11.1	9	6	11	0	0	0	0	4	0	0	.000	1	2	0	0	1.5	1.000

David Cone
CONE, DAVID BRIAN
B. Jan. 2, 1963, Kansas City, Mo.　　　　BL TR 6'1" 180 lbs.

Year	Team	W	L	PCT	ERA	G	GS	CG	IP	H	BB	SO	ShO	W	L	SV	AB	H	HR	BA	PO	A	E	DP	TC/G	FA
1986	KC A	0	0	—	5.56	11	0	0	22.2	29	13	21	0	0	0	0	0	0	0	—	4	0	0	0	0.4	1.000
1987	NY N	5	6	.455	3.71	21	13	1	99.1	87	44	68	0	1	1	1	31	2	0	.065	12	10	1	0	1.1	.957

Year	Team	W	L	PCT	ERA	G	GS	CG	IP	H	BB	SO	ShO	W	L	SV	AB	H	HR	BA	PO	A	E	DP	TC/G	FA

David Cone *continued*

Year	Team	W	L	PCT	ERA	G	GS	CG	IP	H	BB	SO	ShO	W	L	SV	AB	H	HR	BA	PO	A	E	DP	TC/G	FA
1988		20	3	.870	2.22	35	28	8	231.1	178	80	213	4	2	0	0	80	12	0	.150	17	23	1	0	1.2	.976
1989		14	8	.636	3.52	34	33	7	219.2	183	74	190	2	0	0	0	77	18	0	.234	21	14	1	0	1.1	.972
1990		14	10	.583	3.23	31	30	6	211.2	177	65	**233**	2	0	0	0	70	14	0	.200	17	20	3	1	1.3	.925
1991		14	14	.500	3.29	34	34	5	232.2	204	73	**241**	2	0	0	0	72	9	0	.125	18	26	4	2	1.4	.917
1992	2 teams	NY N	(27G 13–7)		TOR A	(8G 4–3)																				
"	total	17	10	.630	2.81	35	34	7	249.2	201	111	261	5	0	0	0	65	6	0	.092	18	22	2	1	1.2	.952
1993	KC A	11	14	.440	3.33	34	34	6	254	205	114	191	1	0	0	0	0	0	0	–	24	24	1	4	1.4	.980
1994		16	5	.762	2.94	23	23	4	171.2	130	54	132	3	0	0	0	0	0	0	–	20	18	3	3	1.8	.927
9 yrs.		111	70	.613	3.12	258	229	44	1692.2	1394	628	1550	19	3	1	1	395	61	0	.154	151	157	16	11	1.3	.951

LEAGUE CHAMPIONSHIP SERIES

Year	Team	W	L	PCT	ERA	G	GS	CG	IP	H	BB	SO	ShO	W	L	SV	AB	H	HR	BA	PO	A	E	DP	TC/G	FA
1988	NY N	1	1	.500	4.50	3	2	1	12	10	5	9	0	0	0	0	4	0	0	.000	1	0	0	0	0.3	1.000
1992	TOR A	1	1	.500	3.00	2	2	0	12	11	5	9	0	0	0	0	0	0	0	–	0	1	1	0	1.0	.500
2 yrs.		2	2	.500	3.75	5	4	1	24	21	10	18	0	0	0	0	4	0	0	.000	1	1	1	0	0.6	.667

WORLD SERIES

Year	Team	W	L	PCT	ERA	G	GS	CG	IP	H	BB	SO	ShO	W	L	SV	AB	H	HR	BA	PO	A	E	DP	TC/G	FA
1992	TOR A	0	0	–	3.48	2	2	0	10.1	9	8	8	0	0	0	0	4	2	0	.500	0	0	0	0	0.0	–

Jim Converse

CONVERSE, JAMES DANIEL
B. Aug. 17, 1971, San Francisco, Calif.

BL TR 5'9" 180 lbs.

Year	Team	W	L	PCT	ERA	G	GS	CG	IP	H	BB	SO	ShO	W	L	SV	AB	H	HR	BA	PO	A	E	DP	TC/G	FA
1993	SEA A	1	3	.250	5.31	4	4	0	20.1	23	14	10	0	0	0	0	0	0	0	–	2	6	0	0	2.0	1.000
1994		0	5	.000	8.69	13	8	0	48.2	73	40	39	0	0	0	0	0	0	0	–	3	6	1	0	0.8	.900
2 yrs.		1	8	.111	7.70	17	12	0	69	96	54	49	0	0	0	0	0	0	0	–	5	12	1	0	1.1	.944

Dennis Cook

COOK, DENNIS BRYAN
B. Oct. 4, 1962, LaMarque, Tex.

BL TL 6'3" 185 lbs.

Year	Team	W	L	PCT	ERA	G	GS	CG	IP	H	BB	SO	ShO	W	L	SV	AB	H	HR	BA	PO	A	E	DP	TC/G	FA
1988	SF N	2	1	.667	2.86	4	4	1	22	9	11	13	1	1	0	0	4	0	0	.000	1	0	0	0	0.3	1.000
1989	2 teams	SF N	(2G 1–0)		PHI N	(21G 6–8)																				
"	total	7	8	.467	3.72	23	18	2	121	110	38	67	1	0	1	0	42	9	0	.214	4	16	3	0	1.0	.870
1990	2 teams	PHI N	(42G 8–3)		LA N	(5G 1–1)																				
"	total	9	4	.692	3.92	47	16	2	156	155	56	64	0	3	1	1	49	15	1	.306	10	22	0	1	0.7	1.000
1991	LA N	1	0	1.000	0.51	20	1	0	17.2	12	7	8	0	1	0	0	1	0	0	.000	0	4	0	0	0.2	1.000
1992	CLE A	5	7	.417	3.82	32	25	1	158	156	50	96	0	0	1	0	0	0	0	–	3	15	1	2	0.6	.947
1993		5	5	.500	5.67	25	6	0	54	62	16	34	0	4	2	0	0	0	0	–	2	6	2	1	0.4	.800
1994	CHI A	3	1	.750	3.55	38	0	0	33	29	14	26	0	3	1	0	0	0	0	–	2	2	0	0	0.1	1.000
7 yrs.		32	26	.552	3.85	189	70	6	561.2	533	192	308	3	11	5	1	96	24	1	.250	21	66	6	4	0.5	.935

Steve Cooke

COOKE, STEVEN MONTAGUE
B. Jan. 14, 1970, Lihue, Hawaii.

BR TL 6'6" 220 lbs.

Year	Team	W	L	PCT	ERA	G	GS	CG	IP	H	BB	SO	ShO	W	L	SV	AB	H	HR	BA	PO	A	E	DP	TC/G	FA
1992	PIT N	2	0	1.000	3.52	11	0	0	23	22	4	10	0	2	0	0	3	1	0	.333	0	3	0	0	0.3	1.000
1993		10	10	.500	3.89	32	32	3	210.2	207	59	132	1	0	0	0	71	11	0	.155	7	23	3	1	1.0	.909
1994		4	11	.267	5.02	25	23	2	134.1	157	46	74	0	1	0	0	42	8	0	.190	3	16	1	1	0.8	.950
3 yrs.		16	21	.432	4.28	68	55	5	368	386	109	216	1	3	0	0	116	20	0	.172	10	42	4	2	0.8	.929

Rheal Cormier

CORMIER, RHEAL PAUL
B. Apr. 23, 1967, Moncton, N. B., Canada.

BL TL 5'10" 185 lbs.

Year	Team	W	L	PCT	ERA	G	GS	CG	IP	H	BB	SO	ShO	W	L	SV	AB	H	HR	BA	PO	A	E	DP	TC/G	FA
1991	STL N	4	5	.444	4.12	11	10	2	67.2	74	8	38	0	0	0	0	21	5	0	.238	3	8	0	1	1.0	1.000
1992		10	10	.500	3.68	31	30	3	186	194	33	117	0	0	0	0	59	6	0	.102	9	34	0	2	1.4	1.000
1993		7	6	.538	4.33	38	21	1	145.1	163	27	75	0	1	1	0	47	11	0	.234	8	27	3	2	1.0	.921
1994		3	2	.600	5.45	7	7	0	39.2	40	7	26	0	0	0	0	14	4	0	.286	1	3	1	0	0.7	.800
4 yrs.		24	23	.511	4.12	87	68	6	438.2	471	75	256	0	1	1	0	141	26	0	.184	21	72	4	4	1.1	.959

Brad Cornett

CORNETT, BRAD BYRON
B. Feb. 4, 1969, LaMesa, Tex.

BR TR 6'3" 190 lbs.

Year	Team	W	L	PCT	ERA	G	GS	CG	IP	H	BB	SO	ShO	W	L	SV	AB	H	HR	BA	PO	A	E	DP	TC/G	FA
1994	TOR A	1	3	.250	6.68	9	4	0	31	40	11	22	0	0	0	0	0	0	0	–	0	5	0	0	0.6	1.000

Danny Cox

COX, DANNY BRADFORD
B. Sept. 21, 1959, Northampton, England.

BR TR 6'4" 220 lbs.

Year	Team	W	L	PCT	ERA	G	GS	CG	IP	H	BB	SO	ShO	W	L	SV	AB	H	HR	BA	PO	A	E	DP	TC/G	FA
1983	STL N	3	6	.333	3.25	12	12	0	83	92	23	36	0	0	0	0	27	2	0	.074	9	16	2	1	2.3	.926
1984		9	11	.450	4.03	29	27	1	156.1	171	54	70	1	1	0	0	53	7	0	.132	11	27	1	4	1.3	.974
1985		18	9	.667	2.88	35	35	10	241	226	64	131	4	0	0	0	79	12	0	.152	22	31	2	1	1.6	.964
1986		12	13	.480	2.90	32	32	8	220	189	60	108	2	0	0	0	65	5	0	.077	22	10	5	0	1.2	.865
1987		11	9	.550	3.88	31	31	2	199.1	224	71	101	0	0	0	0	69	8	0	.116	23	24	1	1	1.5	.979
1988		3	8	.273	3.98	13	13	0	86	89	25	47	0	0	0	0	23	1	0	.043	10	12	0	2	1.7	1.000
1991	PHI N	4	6	.400	4.57	23	17	0	102.1	98	39	46	0	0	0	0	29	3	0	.103	10	11	0	1	0.9	1.000
1992	2 teams	PHI N	(9G 2–2)		PIT N	(16G 3–1)																				
"	total	5	3	.625	4.60	25	7	0	62.2	66	27	48	0	3	1	3	14	1	0	.071	8	9	2	1	0.8	.895
1993	TOR A	7	6	.538	3.12	44	0	0	83.2	73	29	84	0	7	6	2	0	0	0	–	4	4	1	0	0.2	.889
1994		1	1	.500	1.45	10	0	0	18.2	7	7	14	0	1	1	3	0	0	0	–	2	1	0	0	0.3	1.000
10 yrs.		73	72	.503	3.51	254	174	21	1253	1235	399	685	5	12	8	8	359	39	0	.109	121	145	14	11	1.1	.950

LEAGUE CHAMPIONSHIP SERIES

Year	Team	W	L	PCT	ERA	G	GS	CG	IP	H	BB	SO	ShO	W	L	SV	AB	H	HR	BA	PO	A	E	DP	TC/G	FA
1985	STL N	1	0	1.000	3.00	1	1	0	6	4	5	4	0	0	0	0	2	0	0	.000	0	3	0	0	3.0	1.000
1987		1	1	.500	2.12	2	2	2	17	17	3	11	1	0	0	0	6	2	0	.333	4	5	0	2	4.5	1.000
1992	PIT N	0	0	–	0.00	2	0	0	1.1	1	1	1	0	0	0	0	0	0	0	–	0	0	0	0	0.0	–
1993	TOR A	0	0	–	0.00	2	0	0	5	3	2	5	0	0	0	0	0	0	0	–	0	1	0	0	0.5	1.000
4 yrs.		2	1	.667	1.84	7	3	2	29.1	25	11	21	1	0	0	0	8	2	0	.250	4	9	0	2	1.9	1.000

WORLD SERIES

Year	Team	W	L	PCT	ERA	G	GS	CG	IP	H	BB	SO	ShO	W	L	SV	AB	H	HR	BA	PO	A	E	DP	TC/G	FA
1985	STL N	0	0	–	1.29	2	2	0	14	14	4	13	0	0	0	0	4	0	0	.000	1	2	0	1	1.5	1.000
1987		0	2	.333	7.71	3	2	0	11.2	16	8	9	0	0	1	0	3	0	0	.000	1	1	0	1	0.7	1.000
1993	TOR A	0	0	–	8.10	3	0	0	3.1	3	5	6	0	0	0	0	0	0	0	–	1	0	0	0	0.3	1.000
3 yrs.		1	2	.333	4.66	8	4	0	29	33	17	28	0	0	1	0	7	0	0	.000	3	3	0	2	0.8	1.000

Year	Team	W	L	PCT	ERA	G	GS	CG	IP	H	BB	SO	ShO	W	L	SV	AB	H	HR	BA	PO	A	E	DP	TC/G	FA
														Relief Pitching			**Batting**									

Chuck Crim

CRIM, CHARLES ROBERT
B. July 23, 1961, Van Nuys, Calif.
BR TR 6' 175 lbs.

Year	Team	W	L	PCT	ERA	G	GS	CG	IP	H	BB	SO	ShO	W	L	SV	AB	H	HR	BA	PO	A	E	DP	TC/G	FA
1987	MIL A	6	8	.429	3.67	53	5	0	130	133	39	56	0	5	4	12	0	0	0	–	14	17	4	3	0.7	.886
1988		7	6	.538	2.91	70	0	0	105	95	28	58	0	7	6	9	0	0	0	–	12	13	3	1	0.4	.893
1989		9	7	.563	2.83	76	0	0	117.2	114	36	59	0	9	7	7	0	0	0	–	5	13	1	2	0.3	.947
1990		3	5	.375	3.47	67	0	0	85.2	88	23	39	0	3	5	11	0	0	0	–	10	12	1	1	0.3	.957
1991		8	5	.615	4.63	66	0	0	91.1	115	25	39	0	8	5	3	0	0	0	–	8	14	1	0	0.3	.957
1992	CAL A	7	6	.538	5.17	57	0	0	87	100	29	30	0	7	6	1	0	0	0	–	7	12	1	0	0.4	.950
1993		2	2	.500	5.87	11	0	0	15.1	17	5	10	0	2	2	0	0	0	0	–	0	5	0	0	0.5	1.000
1994	CHI N	5	4	.556	4.48	49	1	0	64.1	69	24	43	0	4	4	2	2	0	0	.000	6	8	0	1	0.3	1.000
8 yrs.		47	43	.522	3.83	449	6	0	696.1	731	209	334	0	45	39	45	2	0	0	.000	62	94	11	8	0.4	.934

John Cummings

CUMMINGS, JOHN RUSSELL
B. May 10, 1969, Torrance, Calif.
BL TL 6'3" 200 lbs.

Year	Team	W	L	PCT	ERA	G	GS	CG	IP	H	BB	SO	ShO	W	L	SV	AB	H	HR	BA	PO	A	E	DP	TC/G	FA
1993	SEA A	0	6	.000	6.02	10	8	1	46.1	59	16	19	0	0	0	0	0	0	0	–	3	6	2	0	1.1	.818
1994		2	4	.333	5.63	17	8	0	64	66	37	33	0	1	0	0	0	0	0	–	2	5	0	0	0.4	1.000
2 yrs.		2	10	.167	5.79	27	16	1	110.1	125	53	52	0	1	0	0	0	0	0	–	5	11	2	0	0.7	.889

Jim Czajkowski

CZAJKOWSKI, JAMES MARK
B. Dec. 18, 1963, Parma, Ohio.
BB TR 6'4" 215 lbs.

Year	Team	W	L	PCT	ERA	G	GS	CG	IP	H	BB	SO	ShO	W	L	SV	AB	H	HR	BA	PO	A	E	DP	TC/G	FA
1994	CLR N	0	0	–	4.15	5	0	0	8.2	9	6	2	0	0	0	0	0	0	0	–	1	3	0	0	0.8	1.000

Omar Daal

DAAL, OMAR JESUS
Born Omar Jesus Daal (Cordero).
B. Mar. 1, 1972, Maracaibo, Venezuela.
BL TL 6'3" 160 lbs.

Year	Team	W	L	PCT	ERA	G	GS	CG	IP	H	BB	SO	ShO	W	L	SV	AB	H	HR	BA	PO	A	E	DP	TC/G	FA
1993	LA N	2	3	.400	5.09	47	0	0	35.1	36	21	19	0	2	3	0	0	0	0	–	5	6	0	0	0.2	1.000
1994		0	0	–	3.29	24	0	0	13.2	12	5	9	0	0	0	0	0	0	0	–	1	2	1	0	0.2	.750
2 yrs.		2	3	.400	4.59	71	0	0	49	48	26	28	0	2	3	0	0	0	0	–	6	8	1	0	0.2	.933

Ron Darling

DARLING, RONALD MAURICE, JR.
B. Aug. 19, 1960, Honolulu, Hawaii.
BR TR 6'3" 205 lbs.

Year	Team	W	L	PCT	ERA	G	GS	CG	IP	H	BB	SO	ShO	W	L	SV	AB	H	HR	BA	PO	A	E	DP	TC/G	FA
1983	NY N	1	3	.250	2.80	5	5	1	35.1	31	17	23	0	0	0	0	10	1	0	.100	2	6	0	1	1.6	1.000
1984		12	9	.571	3.81	33	33	2	205.2	179	104	136	2	0	0	0	67	10	0	.149	17	38	3	3	1.8	.948
1985		16	6	.727	2.90	36	35	4	248	214	114	167	2	0	0	0	76	13	0	.171	24	47	2	5	2.0	.973
1986		15	6	.714	2.81	34	34	4	237	203	81	184	2	0	0	0	81	8	0	.099	24	47	7	7	2.3	.910
1987		12	8	.600	4.29	32	32	2	207.2	183	96	167	0	0	0	0	65	8	0	.123	17	43	3	5	2.0	.952
1988		17	9	.654	3.25	34	34	7	240.2	218	60	161	4	0	0	0	82	18	0	.220	17	35	3	4	1.6	.945
1989		14	14	.500	3.52	33	33	4	217.1	214	70	153	0	0	0	0	73	9	2	.123	15	37	4	5	1.7	.929
1990		7	9	.438	4.50	33	18	1	126	135	44	99	0	1	2	0	31	4	0	.129	7	22	2	0	0.9	.935
1991	3 teams					NY N	(17G 5–6)	MON N	(3G 0–2)	OAK A	(12G 3–7)															
"	total	8	15	.348	4.26	32	32	0	194.1	185	71	129	0	0	0	0	40	5	0	.125	18	27	6	2	1.6	.882
1992	OAK A	15	10	.600	3.66	33	33	4	206.1	198	72	99	3	0	0	0	0	0	0	–	11	26	4	2	1.2	.902
1993		5	9	.357	5.16	31	29	3	178	198	72	95	0	0	0	0	0	0	0	–	12	17	1	0	1.0	.967
1994		10	11	.476	4.50	25	25	4	160	162	59	108	0	0	0	0	1	0	0	.000	3	27	2	1	1.3	.938
12 yrs.		132	109	.548	3.77	361	343	36	2256.1	2120	860	1521	13	1	2	0	526	76	2	.144	167	372	37	35	1.6	.936

LEAGUE CHAMPIONSHIP SERIES

Year	Team	W	L	PCT	ERA	G	GS	CG	IP	H	BB	SO	ShO	W	L	SV	AB	H	HR	BA	PO	A	E	DP	TC/G	FA
1986	NY N	0	0	–	7.20	1	1	0	5	6	2	5	0	0	0	0	1	0	0	.000	1	2	0	0	3.0	1.000
1988		0	1	.000	7.71	2	2	0	7	11	4	7	0	0	0	0	3	0	0	.000	1	3	0	0	2.0	1.000
1992	OAK A	0	1	.000	3.00	1	1	0	6	4	2	3	0	0	0	0	0	0	0	–	1	0	0	0	1.0	1.000
3 yrs.		0	2	.000	6.00	4	4	0	18	21	8	15	0	0	0	0	4	0	0	.000	3	5	0	0	2.0	1.000

WORLD SERIES

Year	Team	W	L	PCT	ERA	G	GS	CG	IP	H	BB	SO	ShO	W	L	SV	AB	H	HR	BA	PO	A	E	DP	TC/G	FA
1986	NY N	1	1	.500	1.53	3	3	0	17.2	13	10	12	1	0	0	0	3	0	0	.000	0	4	0	0	1.3	1.000

Danny Darwin

DARWIN, DANIEL WAYNE
Brother of Jeff Darwin.
B. Oct. 25, 1955, Bonham, Tex.
BR TR 6'3" 185 lbs.

Year	Team	W	L	PCT	ERA	G	GS	CG	IP	H	BB	SO	ShO	W	L	SV	AB	H	HR	BA	PO	A	E	DP	TC/G	FA
1978	TEX A	1	0	1.000	4.15	3	1	0	8.2	11	1	8	0	0	0	0	0	0	0	–	0	0	0	0	0.0	–
1979		4	4	.500	4.04	20	6	1	78	50	30	58	0	1	3	0	0	0	0	–	2	6	0	0	0.4	1.000
1980		13	4	.765	2.62	53	2	0	110	98	50	104	0	12	3	8	0	0	0	–	7	11	0	1	0.3	1.000
1981		9	9	.500	3.64	22	22	6	146	115	57	98	2	0	0	0	0	0	0	–	8	16	2	3	1.2	.923
1982		10	8	.556	3.44	56	1	0	89	95	37	61	0	10	7	7	0	0	0	–	5	19	0	0	0.4	1.000
1983		8	13	.381	3.49	28	26	9	183	175	62	92	2	0	0	0	0	0	0	–	20	18	3	1	1.5	.927
1984		8	12	.400	3.94	35	32	5	223.2	249	54	123	1	0	0	0	0	0	0	–	13	21	3	2	1.1	.919
1985	MIL A	8	18	.308	3.80	39	29	11	217.2	212	65	125	1	1	2	0	0	0	0	–	15	16	2	1	0.8	.939
1986	2 teams					MIL A	(27G 6–8)	HOU N	(12G 5–2)																		
"	total	11	10	.524	3.17	39	22	6	184.2	170	44	120	1	3	1	0	16	1	0	.063	10	27	3	2	1.0	.925
1987	HOU N	9	10	.474	3.59	33	30	3	195.2	184	69	134	1	0	0	0	66	12	0	.182	10	22	2	0	1.0	.941
1988		8	13	.381	3.84	44	20	3	192	189	48	129	0	4	3	3	56	4	1	.071	14	37	1	2	1.2	.981
1989		11	4	.733	2.36	68	0	0	122	92	33	104	0	11	4	7	17	2	0	.118	2	12	2	2	0.2	.875
1990		11	4	.733	2.21	48	17	3	162.2	136	31	109	2	2	1	2	38	5	0	.132	11	15	1	1	0.6	.963
1991	BOS A	3	6	.333	5.16	12	12	0	68	71	15	42	0	0	0	0	0	0	0	–	6	9	0	0	1.3	1.000
1992		9	9	.500	3.96	51	15	2	161.1	159	53	124	1	5	4	3	0	0	0	–	9	13	1	2	0.5	.957
1993		15	11	.577	3.26	34	34	2	229.1	196	49	130	1	0	0	0	0	0	0	–	14	31	2	2	1.4	.957
1994		7	5	.583	6.30	13	13	0	75.2	101	24	54	0	0	0	0	0	0	0	–	5	8	0	0	1.0	1.000
17 yrs.		145	140	.509	3.56	598	282	51	2447.1	2303	722	1615	9	49	28	32	193	24	1	.124	151	281	22	19	0.8	.952

Jeff Darwin

DARWIN, JEFFREY SCOTT
Brother of Danny Darwin.
B. July 6, 1969, Sherman, Tex.
BR TR 6'3" 180 lbs.

Year	Team	W	L	PCT	ERA	G	GS	CG	IP	H	BB	SO	ShO	W	L	SV	AB	H	HR	BA	PO	A	E	DP	TC/G	FA
1994	SEA A	0	0	–	13.50	2	0	0	4	7	3	1	0	0	0	0	0	0	0	–	0	0	0	0	0.0	–

Year	Team	W	L	PCT	ERA	G	GS	CG	IP	H	BB	SO	ShO	Relief Pitching W	L	SV	Batting AB	H	HR	BA	PO	A	E	DP	TC/G	FA

Chili Davis

DAVIS, CHARLES THEODORE
B. Jan. 17, 1960, Kingston, Jamaica.   BB TR 6'3"   195 lbs.

| 1993 | CAL A | 0 | 0 | – | 0.00 | 1 | 0 | 0 | 2 | 0 | 0 | 0 | 0 | 0 | 0 | 0 | * | | 1 | | 0 | 0 | 0 | 0 | 0.0 | – |

Mark Davis

DAVIS, MARK WILLIAM
B. Oct. 19, 1960, Livermore, Calif.   BL TL 6'3"   180 lbs.

1980	PHI N	0	0	–	2.57	2	1	0	7	4	5	5	0	0	0	0	2	1	0	.500	0	0	0	0	0.0	–
1981		1	4	.200	7.74	9	9	0	43	49	24	29	0	0	0	0	11	1	0	.091	0	6	0	0	0.7	1.000
1983	SF N	6	4	.600	3.49	20	20	2	111	93	50	83	2	0	0	0	30	4	0	.133	4	13	0	0	0.9	1.000
1984		5	17	.227	5.36	46	27	1	174.2	201	54	124	0	3	4	0	46	6	0	.130	1	22	3	1	0.6	.885
1985		5	12	.294	3.54	77	1	0	114.1	89	41	131	0	5	11	7	12	3	0	.250	2	12	0	0	0.2	1.000
1986		5	7	.417	2.99	67	2	0	84.1	63	34	90	0	5	6	4	8	1	0	.125	3	11	3	1	0.3	.824
1987	2 teams	SF N	(20G 4–5)	SD N	(43G 5–3)																					
"	total	9	8	.529	3.99	63	11	1	133	123	59	98	0	5	3	2	30	7	0	.233	4	20	2	3	0.4	.923
1988	SD N	5	10	.333	2.01	62	0	0	98.1	70	42	102	0	5	10	28	10	2	1	.200	4	21	1	2	0.4	.962
1989		4	3	.571	1.85	70	0	0	92.2	66	31	92	0	4	3	44	13	0	0	.000	1	11	3	0	0.2	.800
1990	KC A	2	7	.222	5.11	53	3	0	68.2	71	52	73	0	2	5	6	0	0	0	–	1	6	1	0	0.2	.875
1991		6	3	.667	4.45	29	5	0	62.2	55	39	47	0	3	2	1	0	0	0	–	1	7	0	1	0.3	1.000
1992	2 teams	KC A	(13G 1–3)	ATL N	(14G 1–0)																					
"	total	2	3	.400	7.13	27	6	0	53	64	41	34	0	1	0	0	1	0	0	.000	3	6	1	0	0.4	.900
1993	2 teams	PHI N	(25G 1–2)	SD N	(35G 0–3)																					
"	total	1	5	.167	4.26	60	0	0	69.2	79	44	70	0	1	5	4	4	1	0	.250	3	8	2	1	0.2	.846
1994	SD N	0	1	.000	8.82	20	0	0	16.1	20	13	15	0	0	1	0	0	0	0	–	0	3	0	0	0.2	1.000
14 yrs.		51	84	.378	4.15	605	85	4	1128.2	1047	529	993	2	34	50	96	167	26	1	.156	27	146	16	9	0.3	.915

Storm Davis

DAVIS, GEORGE EARL
B. Dec. 26, 1961, Dallas, Tex.   BR TR 6'4"   210 lbs.

1982	BAL A	8	4	.667	3.49	29	8	1	100.2	96	28	67	0	3	2	0	0	0	0	–	6	12	1	0	0.7	.947
1983		13	7	.650	3.59	34	29	6	200.1	180	64	125	1	0	0	0	0	0	0	–	14	19	3	1	1.1	.917
1984		14	9	.609	3.12	35	31	10	225	205	71	105	2	0	1	1	0	0	0	–	15	18	2	1	1.0	.943
1985		10	8	.556	4.53	31	28	8	175	172	70	93	1	0	0	0	0	0	0	–	15	20	0	0	1.1	1.000
1986		9	12	.429	3.62	25	25	2	154	166	49	96	0	0	0	0	0	0	0	–	22	21	1	3	1.8	.977
1987	2 teams	SD N	(21G 2–7)	OAK A	(5G 1–1)																					
"	total	3	8	.273	5.23	26	15	0	93	98	47	65	0	0	1	0	16	1	0	.063	8	9	1	0	0.7	.944
1988	OAK A	16	7	.696	3.70	33	33	1	201.2	211	91	127	0	0	0	0	0	0	0	–	6	21	1	2	0.8	.964
1989		19	7	.731	4.36	31	31	1	169.1	187	68	91	0	0	0	0	0	0	0	–	12	17	2	0	1.0	.935
1990	KC A	7	10	.412	4.74	21	20	0	112	129	35	62	0	0	0	0	0	0	0	–	4	10	1	3	0.7	.933
1991		3	9	.250	4.96	51	9	1	114.1	140	46	53	1	1	4	2	0	0	0	–	5	12	0	0	0.3	1.000
1992	BAL A	7	3	.700	3.43	48	2	0	89.1	79	36	53	0	7	3	4	0	0	0	–	3	14	0	3	0.4	1.000
1993	2 teams	OAK A	(19G 2–6)	DET A	(24G 0–2)																					
"	total	2	8	.200	5.05	43	8	0	98	93	48	73	0	0	0	0	0	0	0	–	5	14	1	1	0.5	.950
1994	DET A	2	4	.333	3.56	35	0	0	48	36	34	38	0	2	4	0	0	0	0	–	6	9	0	1	0.4	1.000
13 yrs.		113	96	.541	4.02	442	239	30	1780.2	1792	687	1048	5	14	19	11	16	1	0	.063	121	196	13	15	0.7	.961

LEAGUE CHAMPIONSHIP SERIES

1983	BAL A	0	0	–	0.00	1	1	0	6	5	2	2	0	0	0	0	0	0	0	–	0	0	0	0	0.0	–
1988	OAK A	0	0	–	0.00	1	1	0	6.1	2	5	4	0	0	0	0	0	0	0	–	0	2	0	0	2.0	1.000
1989		0	1	.000	7.11	1	1	0	6.1	5	2	3	0	0	0	0	0	0	0	–	0	0	0	0	0.0	–
3 yrs.		0	1	.000	2.41	3	3	0	18.2	12	9	9	0	0	0	0	0	0	0	–	0	2	0	0	0.7	1.000

WORLD SERIES

1983	BAL A	1	0	1.000	5.40	1	1	0	5	6	1	3	0	0	0	0	2	0	0	.000	0	1	0	0	1.0	1.000
1988	OAK A	0	2	.000	11.25	2	2	0	8	14	1	7	0	0	0	0	1	0	0	.000	2	1	0	0	1.5	1.000
2 yrs.		1	2	.333	9.00	3	3	0	13	20	2	10	0	0	0	0	3	0	0	.000	2	2	0	0	1.3	1.000

Tim Davis

DAVIS, TIMOTHY HOWARD
B. July 14, 1970, Marianna, Fla.   BL TL 5'11"   165 lbs.

| 1994 | SEA A | 2 | 2 | .500 | 4.01 | 42 | 1 | 0 | 49.1 | 57 | 25 | 28 | 0 | 1 | 2 | 2 | 0 | 0 | 0 | – | 2 | 8 | 0 | 0 | 0.2 | 1.000 |

Jose DeJesus

DeJESUS, JOSE LUIS
B. Jan. 6, 1965, Brooklyn, N. Y.   BR TR 6'5"   175 lbs.

1988	KC A	0	1	.000	27.00	2	1	0	2.2	6	5	2	0	0	0	0	0	0	0	–	0	0	0	0	0.0	–
1989		0	0	–	4.50	3	1	0	8	7	8	2	0	0	0	0	0	0	0	–	0	1	0	0	0.3	1.000
1990	PHI N	7	8	.467	3.74	22	22	3	130	97	73	87	1	0	0	0	38	3	0	.079	9	14	2	1	1.1	.920
1991		10	9	.526	3.42	31	29	3	181.2	147	128	118	0	0	0	1	62	8	0	.129	4	18	1	0	0.7	.957
1994	KC A	3	1	.750	4.73	5	4	0	26.2	27	13	12	0	0	0	0	0	0	0	–	2	1	0	0	0.6	1.000
5 yrs.		20	19	.513	3.84	63	57	6	349	284	227	221	1	0	0	1	100	11	0	.110	15	34	3	1	0.8	.942

Jose DeLeon

DeLEON, JOSE
Born Jose DeLeon (Chestaro).
B. Dec. 20, 1960, La Vega, Dominican Republic.   BR TR 6'3"   195 lbs.

1983	PIT N	7	3	.700	2.83	15	15	3	108	75	47	118	2	0	0	0	34	2	0	.059	6	9	1	0	1.1	.938
1984		7	13	.350	3.74	30	28	5	192.1	147	92	153	1	1	0	0	59	5	0	.085	6	16	2	1	0.8	.917
1985		2	19	.095	4.70	31	25	1	162.2	138	89	149	0	0	1	3	36	2	0	.056	9	16	1	1	0.8	.962
1986	2 teams	PIT N	(9G 1–3)	CHI A	(13G 4–5)																					
"	total	5	8	.385	3.87	22	14	1	95.1	66	59	79	0	1	2	1	1	0	0	.000	6	14	1	2	1.0	.952
1987	CHI A	11	12	.478	4.02	33	31	2	206	177	97	153	0	0	0	0	0	0	0	–	10	14	3	0	0.8	.889
1988	STL N	13	10	.565	3.67	34	34	3	225.1	198	86	208	1	0	0	0	72	10	0	.139	10	21	0	0	0.9	1.000

Year	Team	W	L	PCT	ERA	G	GS	CG	IP	H	BB	SO	ShO	Relief Pitching W	L	SV	Batting AB	H	HR	BA	PO	A	E	DP	TC/G	FA

Jose DeLeon *continued*

Year	Team	W	L	PCT	ERA	G	GS	CG	IP	H	BB	SO	ShO	W	L	SV	AB	H	HR	BA	PO	A	E	DP	TC/G	FA
1989		16	12	.571	3.05	36	36	5	244.2	173	80	**201**	3	0	0	0	83	8	0	.096	9	16	5	0	0.8	.833
1990		7	**19**	.269	4.43	32	32	0	182.2	168	86	164	0	0	0	0	56	6	0	.107	8	15	2	0	0.8	.920
1991		5	9	.357	2.71	28	28	1	162.2	144	61	118	0	0	0	0	46	2	0	.043	5	17	0	0	0.8	1.000
1992	**2 teams**	**STL N**	(29G 2–7)		**PHI**	**N**	(3G 0–1)																			
"	total	2	8	.200	4.37	32	18	0	117.1	111	48	79	0	0	0	0	26	3	0	.115	7	10	0	0	0.5	1.000
1993	**2 teams**	**PHI N**	(24G 3–0)		**CHI**	**A**	(11G 0–0)																			
"	total	3	0	1.000	2.98	35	3	0	57.1	44	30	40	0	3	0	0	6	0	0	.000	2	3	0	0	0.1	1.000
1994	CHI A	3	2	.600	3.36	42	0	0	67	48	31	67	0	3	2	2	0	0	0	–	1	6	0	0	0.2	1.000
12 yrs.		81	115	.413	3.69	370	264	21	1821.1	1489	806	1529	7	8	5	6	419	38	0	.091	79	157	15	4	0.7	.940

LEAGUE CHAMPIONSHIP SERIES

| 1993 | CHI A | 0 | 0 | – | 1.93 | 2 | 0 | 0 | 4.2 | 7 | 1 | 6 | 0 | 0 | 0 | 0 | 0 | 0 | 0 | – | 0 | 0 | 0 | 0 | 0.0 | – |

Rich DeLucia

DeLUCIA, RICHARD ANTHONY
B. Oct. 7, 1964, Reading, Pa.

BR TR 6' .185 lbs.

Year	Team	W	L	PCT	ERA	G	GS	CG	IP	H	BB	SO	ShO	W	L	SV	AB	H	HR	BA	PO	A	E	DP	TC/G	FA
1990	SEA A	1	2	.333	2.00	5	5	1	36	30	9	20	0	0	0	0	0	0	0	–	3	2	1	0	1.2	.833
1991		12	13	.480	5.09	32	31	0	182	176	78	98	0	1	0	0	0	0	0	–	8	19	0	1	0.8	1.000
1992		3	6	.333	5.49	30	11	0	83.2	100	35	66	0	0	0	1	0	0	0	–	8	6	1	0	0.5	.933
1993		3	6	.333	4.64	30	1	0	42.2	46	23	48	0	3	5	0	0	0	0	–	2	7	0	0	0.3	1.000
1994	CIN N	0	0	–	4.22	8	0	0	10.2	9	5	15	0	0	0	0	0	0	0	–	1	0	0	0	0.1	1.000
5 yrs.		19	27	.413	4.79	105	48	1	355	361	150	247	0	4	5	1	0	0	0	–	22	34	2	1	0.6	.966

Jim Deshaies

DESHAIES, JAMES JOSEPH
B. June 23, 1960, Massena, N. Y.

BL TL 6'4" 222 lbs.

Year	Team	W	L	PCT	ERA	G	GS	CG	IP	H	BB	SO	ShO	W	L	SV	AB	H	HR	BA	PO	A	E	DP	TC/G	FA
1984	NY A	0	1	.000	11.57	2	2	0	7	14	7	5	0	0	0	0	0	0	0	–	0	1	0	0	0.5	1.000
1985	HOU N	0	0	–	0.00	2	0	0	3	1	0	2	0	0	0	0	0	0	0	–	0	0	0	0	0.0	–
1986		12	5	.706	3.25	26	26	1	144	124	59	128	1	0	0	0	43	2	0	.047	9	13	2	0	0.9	.917
1987		11	6	.647	4.62	26	25	1	152	149	57	104	0	0	0	0	53	5	0	.094	5	22	1	0	1.1	.964
1988		11	14	.440	3.00	31	31	3	207	164	72	127	2	0	0	0	63	3	0	.048	7	25	2	1	1.1	.941
1989		15	10	.600	2.91	34	34	6	225.2	180	79	153	3	0	0	0	75	9	0	.120	8	31	3	2	1.2	.929
1990		7	12	.368	3.78	34	34	2	209.1	186	84	119	0	0	0	0	63	4	0	.063	3	32	2	1	1.1	.946
1991		5	12	.294	4.98	28	28	1	161	156	72	98	0	0	0	0	41	4	0	.098	4	18	3	1	0.9	.880
1992	SD N	4	7	.364	3.28	15	15	0	96	92	33	46	0	0	0	0	29	6	0	.207	2	22	0	1	1.6	1.000
1993	**2 teams**	**MIN A**	(27G 11–13)		**SF**	**N**	(5G 2–2)																			
"	total	13	15	.464	4.39	32	31	1	184.1	183	57	85	0	0	0	0	5	0	0	.000	4	25	0	0	0.9	1.000
1994	MIN A	6	12	.333	7.39	25	**25**	0	130.1	170	54	78	0	0	0	0	0	0	0	–	3	15	1	1	0.8	.947
11 yrs.		84	94	.472	4.09	255	251	15	1519.2	1419	574	945	6	0	0	0	372	33	0	.089	45	204	14	7	1.0	.947

John Dettmer

DETTMER, JOHN FRANKLIN
B. Mar. 4, 1970, Centerville, Ill.

BR TR 6' 185 lbs.

Year	Team	W	L	PCT	ERA	G	GS	CG	IP	H	BB	SO	ShO	W	L	SV	AB	H	HR	BA	PO	A	E	DP	TC/G	FA
1994	TEX A	0	6	.000	4.33	11	9	0	54	63	20	27	0	0	0	0	0	0	0	–	5	6	0	0	1.0	1.000

Mark Dewey

DEWEY, MARK ALAN
B. Jan. 3, 1965, Grand Rapids, Mich.

BR TR 6' 185 lbs.

Year	Team	W	L	PCT	ERA	G	GS	CG	IP	H	BB	SO	ShO	W	L	SV	AB	H	HR	BA	PO	A	E	DP	TC/G	FA
1990	SF N	1	1	.500	2.78	14	0	0	22.2	22	5	11	0	1	1	0	1	0	0	.000	2	2	0	1	0.3	1.000
1992	NY N	1	0	1.000	4.32	20	0	0	33.1	37	10	24	0	1	0	0	1	0	0	.000	3	5	0	0	0.4	1.000
1993	PIT N	1	2	.333	2.36	21	0	0	26.2	14	10	14	0	1	2	7	0	0	0	–	2	6	0	0	0.4	1.000
1994		2	1	.667	3.68	45	0	0	51.1	61	19	30	0	2	1	1	1	1	0	1.000	4	4	1	1	0.2	.889
4 yrs.		5	4	.556	3.43	100	0	0	134	134	44	79	0	5	4	8	3	1	0	.333	11	17	1	2	0.3	.966

Jerry DiPoto

DiPOTO, GERALD PETER III
B. May 24, 1968, Jersey City, N. J.

BR TR 6'2" 203 lbs.

Year	Team	W	L	PCT	ERA	G	GS	CG	IP	H	BB	SO	ShO	W	L	SV	AB	H	HR	BA	PO	A	E	DP	TC/G	FA
1993	CLE A	4	4	.500	2.40	46	0	0	56.1	57	30	41	0	4	4	11	0	0	0	–	4	10	2	1	0.3	.875
1994		0	0	–	8.04	7	0	0	15.2	26	10	9	0	0	0	0	0	0	0	–	0	1	0	0	0.1	1.000
2 yrs.		4	4	.500	3.63	53	0	0	72	83	40	50	0	4	4	11	0	0	0	–	4	11	2	1	0.3	.882

Steve Dixon

DIXON, STEVEN ROSS
B. Aug. 3, 1969, Cincinnati, Ohio

BL TL 6' 190 lbs.

Year	Team	W	L	PCT	ERA	G	GS	CG	IP	H	BB	SO	ShO	W	L	SV	AB	H	HR	BA	PO	A	E	DP	TC/G	FA
1993	STL N	0	0	–	33.75	4	0	0	2.2	7	5	2	0	0	0	0	0	0	0	–	0	1	0	0	0.3	1.000
1994		0	0	–	23.14	2	0	0	2.1	3	8	1	0	0	0	0	0	0	0	–	0	0	0	0	0.0	–
2 yrs.		0	0	–	28.80	6	0	0	5	10	13	3	0	0	0	0	0	0	0	–	0	1	0	0	0.2	1.000

John Doherty

DOHERTY, JOHN HAROLD
B. June 11, 1967, Bronx, N. Y.

BR TR 6'4" 190 lbs.

Year	Team	W	L	PCT	ERA	G	GS	CG	IP	H	BB	SO	ShO	W	L	SV	AB	H	HR	BA	PO	A	E	DP	TC/G	FA
1992	DET A	7	4	.636	3.88	47	11	0	116	131	25	37	0	2	2	3	0	0	0	–	10	19	1	4	0.6	.967
1993		14	11	.560	4.44	32	31	3	184.2	205	48	63	2	0	0	0	0	0	0	–	14	20	5	1	1.2	.872
1994		6	7	.462	6.48	18	17	2	101.1	139	26	28	0	0	0	0	0	0	0	–	6	25	0	4	1.7	1.000
3 yrs.		27	22	.551	4.79	97	59	5	402	475	99	128	2	2	2	3	0	0	0	–	30	64	6	9	1.0	.940

John Dopson

DOPSON, JOHN ROBERT, JR.
B. July 14, 1963, Baltimore, Md.

BL TR 6'4" 205 lbs.

Year	Team	W	L	PCT	ERA	G	GS	CG	IP	H	BB	SO	ShO	W	L	SV	AB	H	HR	BA	PO	A	E	DP	TC/G	FA
1985	MON N	0	2	.000	11.08	4	3	0	13	25	4	4	0	0	0	0	4	0	0	.000	0	2	0	0	0.5	1.000
1988		3	11	.214	3.04	26	26	1	168.2	150	58	101	0	0	0	0	51	3	0	.059	10	15	2	1	1.0	.926
1989	BOS A	12	8	.600	3.99	29	28	2	169.1	166	69	95	0	1	0	0	0	0	0	–	20	34	1	1	1.9	.982
1990		0	0	–	2.04	4	4	0	17.2	13	9	9	0	0	0	0	0	0	0	–	1	5	0	0	1.5	1.000
1991		0	0	–	18.00	1	0	0	1	2	1	0	0	0	0	0	0	0	0	–	0	1	0	0	1.0	1.000
1992		7	11	.389	4.08	25	25	0	141.1	159	38	55	0	0	0	0	0	0	0	–	19	18	1	1	1.5	.974
1993		7	11	.389	4.97	34	28	0	155.2	170	59	89	1	0	2	0	0	0	0	–	17	22	0	0	1.1	1.000
1994	CAL A	1	4	.200	6.14	21	5	0	58.2	67	26	33	0	0	1	1	0	0	0	–	3	10	0	0	0.6	1.000
8 yrs.		30	47	.390	4.27	144	119	4	725.1	752	264	386	1	1	3	1	55	3	0	.055	70	107	4	3	1.3	.978

Year	Team	W	L	PCT	ERA	G	GS	CG	IP	H	BB	SO	ShO	Relief Pitching W	L	SV	Batting AB	H	HR	BA	PO	A	E	DP	TC/G	FA

Doug Drabek

DRABEK, DOUGLAS DEAN
B. July 25, 1962, Victoria, Tex.

BR TR 6'1" 185 lbs.

Year	Team		W	L	PCT	ERA	G	GS	CG	IP	H	BB	SO	ShO	W	L	SV	AB	H	HR	BA	PO	A	E	DP	TC/G	FA
1986	NY	A	7	8	.467	4.10	27	21	0	131.2	126	50	76	1	0	0	0	0	0	0	–	5	13	0	0	0.7	1.000
1987	PIT	N	11	12	.478	3.88	29	28	1	176.1	165	46	120	1	0	0	0	59	7	0	.119	24	23	2	0	1.7	.959
1988			15	7	.682	3.08	33	32	3	219.1	194	50	127	1	0	0	0	76	13	0	.171	29	21	6	6	1.7	.893
1989			14	12	.538	2.80	35	34	8	244.1	215	69	123	5	1	0	0	77	8	0	.104	24	34	2	0	1.7	.967
1990			**22**	6	**.786**	2.76	33	33	9	231.1	190	56	131	3	0	0	0	84	18	1	.214	25	36	1	1	1.9	.984
1991			15	14	.517	3.07	35	35	5	234.2	245	62	142	2	0	0	0	84	15	0	.179	27	41	5	1	2.1	.932
1992			15	11	.577	2.77	34	34	10	256.2	218	54	177	4	0	0	0	89	14	0	.157	29	36	3	4	2.0	.956
1993	HOU	N	9	18	.333	3.79	34	34	7	237.2	242	60	157	2	0	0	0	71	6	1	.085	19	32	0	2	1.5	1.000
1994			12	6	.667	2.84	23	23	6	164.2	132	45	121	2	0	0	0	58	14	0	.241	21	28	3	2	2.3	.942
9 yrs.			120	94	.561	3.17	283	274	49	1896.2	1727	492	1174	20	1	0	0	598	95	2	.159	203	264	22	16	1.7	.955

LEAGUE CHAMPIONSHIP SERIES

Year	Team		W	L	PCT	ERA	G	GS	CG	IP	H	BB	SO	ShO	W	L	SV	AB	H	HR	BA	PO	A	E	DP	TC/G	FA
1990	PIT	N	1	1	.500	1.65	2	2	1	16.1	12	3	13	0	0	0	0	6	1	0	.167	1	6	1	0	4.0	.875
1991			1	1	.500	0.60	2	2	1	15	10	5	10	0	0	0	0	5	1	0	.200	3	0	0	0	1.5	1.000
1992			0	3	.000	3.71	3	3	0	17	18	6	10	0	0	0	0	6	0	0	.000	0	0	0	0	0.0	–
3 yrs.			2	5	.286	2.05	7	7	2	48.1	40	14	33	0	0	0	0	17	2	0	.118	4	6	1	0	1.6	.909

Brian Drahman

DRAHMAN, BRIAN STACY
B. Nov. 7, 1966, Kenton, Ky.

BR TR 6'3" 205 lbs.

Year	Team		W	L	PCT	ERA	G	GS	CG	IP	H	BB	SO	ShO	W	L	SV	AB	H	HR	BA	PO	A	E	DP	TC/G	FA
1991	CHI	A	3	2	.600	3.23	28	0	0	30.2	21	13	18	0	3	2	0	0	0	0	–	1	5	1	0	0.3	.857
1992			0	0	–	2.57	5	0	0	7	6	2	1	0	0	0	0	0	0	0	–	1	0	1	0	0.4	.500
1993			0	0	–	0.00	5	0	0	5.1	7	2	3	0	0	0	1	0	0	0	–	0	1	0	0	0.2	1.000
1994	FLA	N	0	0	–	6.23	9	0	0	13	15	6	7	0	0	0	0	0	0	0	–	1	2	0	1	0.3	1.000
4 yrs.			3	2	.600	3.54	47	0	0	56	49	23	29	0	3	2	1	0	0	0	–	3	8	2	1	0.3	.846

Darren Dreifort

DREIFORT, DARREN JAMES
B. May 18, 1972, Wichita, Kans.

BR TR 6'2" 205 lbs.

Year	Team		W	L	PCT	ERA	G	GS	CG	IP	H	BB	SO	ShO	W	L	SV	AB	H	HR	BA	PO	A	E	DP	TC/G	FA
1994	LA	N	0	5	.000	6.21	27	0	0	29	45	15	22	0	0	5	6	1	1	0	1.000	2	8	2	0	0.4	.833

Steve Dreyer

DREYER, STEVEN WILLIAM
B. Nov. 19, 1969, Ames, Iowa

BR TR 6'3" 185 lbs.

Year	Team		W	L	PCT	ERA	G	GS	CG	IP	H	BB	SO	ShO	W	L	SV	AB	H	HR	BA	PO	A	E	DP	TC/G	FA
1993	TEX	A	3	3	.500	5.71	10	6	0	41	48	20	23	0	0	0	0	0	0	0	–	2	4	0	0	0.6	1.000
1994			1	1	.500	5.71	5	3	0	17.1	19	8	11	0	0	0	0	0	0	0	–	2	0	0	0	0.4	1.000
2 yrs.			4	4	.500	5.71	15	9	0	58.1	67	28	34	0	0	0	0	0	0	0	–	4	4	0	0	0.5	1.000

Mike Dyer

DYER, MICHAEL LAWRENCE
B. Sept. 8, 1966, Upland, Calif.

BR TR 6'3" 195 lbs.

Year	Team		W	L	PCT	ERA	G	GS	CG	IP	H	BB	SO	ShO	W	L	SV	AB	H	HR	BA	PO	A	E	DP	TC/G	FA
1989	MIN	A	4	7	.364	4.82	16	12	1	71	74	37	37	0	0	1	0	0	0	0	–	6	3	0	1	0.6	1.000
1994	PIT	N	1	1	.500	5.87	14	0	0	15.1	15	12	13	0	1	1	4	1	0	0	.000	0	1	0	0	0.1	1.000
2 yrs.			5	8	.385	5.00	30	12	1	86.1	89	49	50	0	1	2	4	1	0	0	.000	6	4	0	1	0.3	1.000

Dennis Eckersley

ECKERSLEY, DENNIS LEE (The Eck)
B. Oct. 3, 1954, Oakland, Calif.

BR TR 6'2" 190 lbs.

Year	Team		W	L	PCT	ERA	G	GS	CG	IP	H	BB	SO	ShO	W	L	SV	AB	H	HR	BA	PO	A	E	DP	TC/G	FA
1975	CLE	A	13	7	.650	2.60	34	24	6	186.2	147	90	152	2	1	0	2	0	0	0	–	7	12	1	0	0.6	.950
1976			13	12	.520	3.44	36	30	9	199	155	78	200	3	1	0	1	0	0	0	–	9	20	1	1	0.8	.967
1977			14	13	.519	3.53	33	33	12	247	214	54	191	3	0	0	0	0	0	0	–	6	22	2	1	0.9	.933
1978	BOS	A	20	8	.714	2.99	35	35	16	268.1	258	71	162	3	0	0	0	0	0	0	–	19	29	0	1	1.4	1.000
1979			17	10	.630	2.99	33	33	17	247	234	59	150	2	0	0	0	0	0	0	–	12	42	6	3	1.8	.900
1980			12	14	.462	4.27	30	30	8	198	188	44	121	0	0	0	0	0	0	0	–	10	24	3	0	1.2	.919
1981			9	8	.529	4.27	23	23	8	154	160	35	79	2	0	0	0	0	0	0	–	12	19	1	1	1.4	.969
1982			13	13	.500	3.73	33	33	11	224.1	228	43	127	3	0	0	0	0	0	0	–	21	21	1	2	1.3	.977
1983			9	13	.409	5.61	28	28	2	176.1	223	39	77	0	0	0	0	0	0	0	–	19	18	1	0	1.4	.974
1984	2 teams	BOS A (9G 4–4)				CHI N (24G 10–8)																					
"	total		14	12	.538	3.60	33	33	4	225	223	49	114	0	0	0	0	55	6	0	.109	27	38	5	3	2.1	.929
1985	CHI	N	11	7	.611	3.08	25	25	6	169.1	145	19	117	2	0	0	0	56	7	1	.125	10	26	3	1	1.6	.923
1986			6	11	.353	4.57	33	32	1	201	226	43	137	0	0	0	0	69	11	2	.159	16	28	3	3	1.4	.936
1987	OAK	A	6	8	.429	3.03	54	2	0	115.2	99	17	113	0	6	6	16	0	0	0	–	4	13	1	0	0.3	.944
1988			4	2	.667	2.35	60	0	0	72.2	52	11	70	0	4	2	**45**	0	0	0	–	7	3	0	0	0.2	1.000
1989			4	0	1.000	1.56	51	0	0	57.2	32	3	55	0	4	0	33	0	0	0	–	4	4	0	1	0.2	1.000
1990			4	2	.667	0.61	63	0	0	73.1	41	4	73	0	4	2	48	0	0	0	–	3	1	0	0	0.1	1.000
1991			5	4	.556	2.96	67	0	0	76	60	9	87	0	5	4	43	0	0	0	–	6	9	0	0	0.2	1.000
1992			7	1	.875	1.91	69	0	0	80	62	11	93	0	7	1	**51**	0	0	0	–	3	10	0	0	0.2	1.000
1993			2	4	.333	4.16	64	0	0	67	67	13	80	0	2	4	36	0	0	0	–	2	1	0	0	0.1	1.000
1994			5	4	.556	4.26	45	0	0	44.1	49	13	47	0	5	4	19	0	0	0	–	2	1	0	0	0.1	1.000
20 yrs.			188	153	.551	3.46	849	361	100	3082.2	2863	705	2245	20	39	23	294 6th	180	24	3	.133	197	345	28	18	0.7	.951

LEAGUE CHAMPIONSHIP SERIES

Year	Team		W	L	PCT	ERA	G	GS	CG	IP	H	BB	SO	ShO	W	L	SV	AB	H	HR	BA	PO	A	E	DP	TC/G	FA
1984	CHI	N	0	1	.000	8.44	1	1	0	5.1	9	0	0	0	0	0	0	2	0	0	.000	0	0	0	0	0.0	–
1988	OAK	A	0	0	–	0.00	4	0	0	6	1	2	5	0	0	0	4	0	0	0	–	2	0	0	0	0.5	1.000
1989			0	0	–	1.59	4	0	0	5.2	4	0	2	0	0	0	3	0	0	0	–	0	1	0	0	0.3	1.000
1990			0	0	–	0.00	3	0	0	3.1	2	0	3	0	0	0	1	0	0	0	–	0	0	0	0	0.0	–
1992			0	0	–	6.00	3	0	0	3	8	0	2	0	0	0	1	0	0	0	–	0	0	0	0	0.0	–
5 yrs.			0	1	.000	3.09	15	1	0	23.1	24	2	12	0	0	0	10	2	0	0	.000	2	1	0	0	0.2	1.000

WORLD SERIES

Year	Team		W	L	PCT	ERA	G	GS	CG	IP	H	BB	SO	ShO	W	L	SV	AB	H	HR	BA	PO	A	E	DP	TC/G	FA
1988	OAK	A	0	1	.000	10.80	2	0	0	1.2	2	1	2	0	0	1	0	0	0	0	–	0	0	0	0	0.0	–
1989			0	0	–	0.00	2	0	0	1.2	0	0	0	0	0	0	1	0	0	0	–	1	0	0	0	0.5	1.000
1990			0	1	.000	6.75	2	0	0	1.1	3	0	1	0	0	1	0	0	0	0	–	0	0	0	0	0.0	–
3 yrs.			0	2	.000	5.79	6	0	0	4.2	5	1	3	0	0	2	1	0	0	0	–	1	0	0	0	0.2	1.000

Year	Team	W	L	PCT	ERA	G	GS	CG	IP	H	BB	SO	ShO	W	L	SV	AB	H	HR	BA	PO	A	E	DP	TC/G	FA

Tom Edens — EDENS, THOMAS PATRICK. B. June 9, 1961, Ontario, Ore. — BR TR 6'3" 185 lbs.

Year	Team	W	L	PCT	ERA	G	GS	CG	IP	H	BB	SO	ShO	W	L	SV	AB	H	HR	BA	PO	A	E	DP	TC/G	FA
1987	NY N	0	0	—	6.75	2	2	0	8	15	4	4	0	0	0	0	3	0	0	.000	0	4	1	0	2.5	.800
1990	MIL A	4	5	.444	4.45	35	6	0	89	89	33	40	0	2	3	2	0	0	0	—	7	10	3	0	0.6	.850
1991	MIN A	2	2	.500	4.09	8	6	0	33	34	10	19	0	0	0	0	0	0	0	—	5	5	0	0	1.3	1.000
1992		6	3	.667	2.83	52	0	0	76.1	65	36	57	0	6	3	3	0	0	0	—	8	4	0	0	0.2	1.000
1993	HOU N	1	1	.500	3.12	38	0	0	49	47	19	21	0	1	1	0	1	0	0	.000	3	10	1	0	0.4	.929
1994	2 teams	HOU N	(39G 4–1)		PHI N	(3G 1–0)																				
"	total	5	1	.833	4.33	42	0	0	54	59	18	39	0	5	1	1	2	0	0	.000	6	13	0	1	0.5	1.000
6 yrs.		18	12	.600	3.84	177	14	0	309.1	309	120	180	0	14	8	6	6	0	0	.000	29	46	5	1	0.5	.938

Mark Eichhorn — EICHHORN, MARK ANTHONY. B. Nov. 21, 1960, San Jose, Calif. — BR TR 6'4" 200 lbs.

Year	Team	W	L	PCT	ERA	G	GS	CG	IP	H	BB	SO	ShO	W	L	SV	AB	H	HR	BA	PO	A	E	DP	TC/G	FA
1982	TOR A	0	3	.000	5.45	7	7	0	38	40	14	16	0	0	0	0	0	0	0	—	1	3	0	0	0.6	1.000
1986		14	6	.700	1.72	69	0	0	157	105	45	166	0	14	6	10	0	0	0	—	16	21	0	1	0.5	1.000
1987		10	6	.625	3.17	89	0	0	127.2	110	52	96	0	10	6	4	0	0	0	—	2	30	1	2	0.4	.970
1988		0	3	.000	4.19	37	0	0	66.2	79	27	28	0	0	3	1	0	0	0	—	5	13	0	1	0.5	1.000
1989	ATL N	5	5	.500	4.35	45	0	0	68.1	70	19	49	0	5	5	0	2	0	0	.000	9	17	0	1	0.6	1.000
1990	CAL A	2	5	.286	3.08	60	0	0	84.2	98	23	69	0	2	5	13	0	0	0	—	7	16	0	0	0.4	1.000
1991		3	3	.500	1.98	70	0	0	81.2	63	13	49	0	3	3	1	0	0	0	—	4	18	0	2	0.3	1.000
1992	2 teams	CAL A	(42G 2–4)		TOR A	(23G 2–0)																				
"	total	4	4	.500	3.08	65	0	0	87.2	86	25	61	0	4	4	2	0	0	0	—	5	19	1	0	0.4	.960
1993	TOR A	3	1	.750	2.72	54	0	0	72.2	76	22	47	0	3	1	0	0	0	0	—	7	18	0	1	0.5	1.000
1994	BAL A	6	5	.545	2.15	43	0	0	71	62	19	35	0	6	5	1	0	0	0	—	3	19	0	1	0.5	1.000
10 yrs.		47	41	.534	2.93	539	7	0	855.1	789	259	616	0	47	38	32	2	0	0	.000	59	174	2	9	0.4	.991

LEAGUE CHAMPIONSHIP SERIES

Year	Team	W	L	PCT	ERA	G	GS	CG	IP	H	BB	SO	ShO	W	L	SV	AB	H	HR	BA	PO	A	E	DP	TC/G	FA
1992	TOR A	0	0	—	0.00	1	0	0	1	0	0	0	0	0	0	0	0	0	0	—	0	0	0	0	0.0	—
1993		0	0	—	0.00	1	0	0	2	1	1	1	0	0	0	0	0	0	0	—	0	0	0	0	0.0	—
2 yrs.		0	0	—	0.00	2	0	0	3	1	1	1	0	0	0	0	0	0	0	—	0	0	0	0	0.0	—

WORLD SERIES

Year	Team	W	L	PCT	ERA	G	GS	CG	IP	H	BB	SO	ShO	W	L	SV	AB	H	HR	BA	PO	A	E	DP	TC/G	FA
1992	TOR A	0	0	—	0.00	1	0	0	1	0	0	1	0	0	0	0	0	0	0	—	0	0	0	0	0.0	—
1993		0	0	—	0.00	1	0	0	0.1	1	1	0	0	0	0	0	0	0	0	—	0	0	0	0	0.0	—
2 yrs.		0	0	—	0.00	2	0	0	1.1	1	1	1	0	0	0	0	0	0	0	—	0	0	0	0	0.0	—

Joey Eischen — EISCHEN, JOSEPH RAYMOND. B. May 25, 1970, West Covina, Calif. — BL TL 6'1" 190 lbs.

Year	Team	W	L	PCT	ERA	G	GS	CG	IP	H	BB	SO	ShO	W	L	SV	AB	H	HR	BA	PO	A	E	DP	TC/G	FA
1994	MON N	0	0	—	54.00	1	0	0	0.2	4	0	1	0	0	0	0	0	0	0	—	0	0	0	0	0.0	—

Cal Eldred — ELDRED, CALVIN JOHN. B. Nov. 24, 1967, Cedar Rapids, Iowa. — BR TR 6'4" 215 lbs.

Year	Team	W	L	PCT	ERA	G	GS	CG	IP	H	BB	SO	ShO	W	L	SV	AB	H	HR	BA	PO	A	E	DP	TC/G	FA
1991	MIL A	2	0	1.000	4.50	3	3	0	16	20	6	10	0	0	0	0	0	0	0	—	2	1	0	0	1.0	1.000
1992		11	2	.846	1.79	14	14	2	100.1	76	23	62	1	0	0	0	0	0	0	—	4	12	1	0	1.2	.941
1993		16	16	.500	4.01	36	36	8	258	232	91	180	1	0	0	0	0	0	0	—	26	27	2	4	1.5	.964
1994		11	11	.500	4.68	25	25	6	179	158	84	98	0	0	0	0	0	0	0	—	20	23	0	2	1.7	1.000
4 yrs.		40	29	.580	3.84	78	78	16	553.1	486	204	350	2	0	0	0	0	0	0	—	52	63	3	6	1.5	.975

Donnie Elliott — ELLIOTT, DONALD GLENN. B. Sept. 20, 1968, Pasadena, Tex. — BR TR 6'4" 190 lbs.

Year	Team	W	L	PCT	ERA	G	GS	CG	IP	H	BB	SO	ShO	W	L	SV	AB	H	HR	BA	PO	A	E	DP	TC/G	FA
1994	SD N	0	1	.000	3.27	30	1	0	33	31	21	24	0	0	1	0	1	0	0	.000	4	2	0	1	0.2	1.000

Scott Erickson — ERICKSON, SCOTT GAVIN. B. Feb. 2, 1968, Long Beach, Calif. — BR TR 6'4" 220 lbs.

Year	Team	W	L	PCT	ERA	G	GS	CG	IP	H	BB	SO	ShO	W	L	SV	AB	H	HR	BA	PO	A	E	DP	TC/G	FA
1990	MIN A	8	4	.667	2.87	19	17	1	113	108	51	53	0	0	0	0	0	0	0	—	10	13	0	0	1.2	1.000
1991		20	8	.714	3.18	32	32	5	204	189	71	108	3	0	0	0	0	0	0	—	19	31	1	3	1.6	.980
1992		13	12	.520	3.40	32	32	5	212	197	83	101	3	0	0	0	0	0	0	—	18	34	1	3	1.7	.981
1993		8	19	.296	5.19	34	34	1	218.2	266	71	116	0	0	0	0	0	0	0	—	18	34	3	3	1.6	.945
1994		8	11	.421	5.44	23	23	2	144	173	59	104	1	0	0	0	0	0	0	—	9	23	4	4	1.6	.889
5 yrs.		57	54	.514	4.05	140	138	14	891.2	933	335	482	7	0	0	0	0	0	0	—	74	135	9	13	1.6	.959

LEAGUE CHAMPIONSHIP SERIES

Year	Team	W	L	PCT	ERA	G	GS	CG	IP	H	BB	SO	ShO	W	L	SV	AB	H	HR	BA	PO	A	E	DP	TC/G	FA
1991	MIN A	0	0	—	4.50	1	1	0	4	3	5	2	0	0	0	0	0	0	0	—	1	1	0	0	2.0	1.000

WORLD SERIES

Year	Team	W	L	PCT	ERA	G	GS	CG	IP	H	BB	SO	ShO	W	L	SV	AB	H	HR	BA	PO	A	E	DP	TC/G	FA
1991	MIN A	0	0	—	5.06	2	2	0	10.2	10	4	5	0	0	0	0	1	0	0	.000	1	0	0	0	0.5	1.000

Alvaro Espinoza — ESPINOZA, ALVARO ALBERTO. Born Alvaro Alberto Espinoza (Ramirez). B. Feb. 19, 1962, Valencia, Venezuela. — BR TR 6' 160 lbs.

Year	Team	W	L	PCT	ERA	G	GS	CG	IP	H	BB	SO	ShO	W	L	SV	AB	H	HR	BA	PO	A	E	DP	TC/G	FA
1991	NY A	0	0	—	0.00	1	0	0	0.2	0	0	0	0	0	0	0	*				0	0	0	0	0.0	—

Bryan Eversgerd — EVERSGERD, BRYAN DAVID. B. Feb. 11, 1969, Centralia, Ill. — BR TL 6'1" 190 lbs.

Year	Team	W	L	PCT	ERA	G	GS	CG	IP	H	BB	SO	ShO	W	L	SV	AB	H	HR	BA	PO	A	E	DP	TC/G	FA
1994	STL N	2	3	.400	4.52	40	1	0	67.2	75	20	47	0	1	3	0	6	0	0	.000	5	13	0	2	0.5	1.000

Hector Fajardo — FAJARDO, HECTOR. Born Hector Fajardo (Nabaratte). B. Nov. 16, 1970, Sahuayo, Mexico. — BR TR 6'4" 185 lbs.

Year	Team	W	L	PCT	ERA	G	GS	CG	IP	H	BB	SO	ShO	W	L	SV	AB	H	HR	BA	PO	A	E	DP	TC/G	FA
1991	2 teams	PIT N	(2G 0–0)		TEX A	(4G 0–2)																				
"	total	0	2	.000	6.75	6	5	0	25.1	35	11	23	0	0	0	0	3	0	0	.000	1	1	0	0	0.3	1.000
1993	TEX A	0	0	—	0.00	1	0	0	0.2	0	0	1	0	0	0	0	0	0	0	—	0	0	0	0	0.0	—
1994		5	7	.417	6.91	18	12	0	83.1	95	26	45	0	0	0	0	0	0	0	—	3	11	0	0	0.8	1.000
3 yrs.		5	9	.357	6.83	25	17	0	109.1	130	37	69	0	0	0	0	3	0	0	.000	4	12	0	0	0.6	1.000

Year	Team	W	L	PCT	ERA	G	GS	CG	IP	H	BB	SO	ShO	W	L	SV	AB	H	HR	BA	PO	A	E	DP	TC/G	FA
														Relief	**Pitching**		**Batting**									

Steve Farr

FARR, STEVEN MICHAEL
B. Dec. 12, 1956, Cheverly, Md.
BR TR 5'10" 190 lbs.

Year	Team		W	L	PCT	ERA	G	GS	CG	IP	H	BB	SO	ShO	W	L	SV	AB	H	HR	BA	PO	A	E	DP	TC/G	FA
1984	CLE	A	3	11	.214	4.58	31	16	0	116	106	46	83	0	1	2	1	0	0	0	–	7	18	2	1	0.9	.926
1985	KC	A	2	1	.667	3.11	16	3	0	37.2	34	20	36	0	1	0	1	0	0	0	–	3	6	0	0	0.6	1.000
1986			8	4	.667	3.13	56	0	0	109.1	90	39	83	0	8	4	8	0	0	0	–	8	16	0	1	0.4	1.000
1987			4	3	.571	4.15	47	0	0	91	97	44	88	0	4	3	1	0	0	0	–	3	6	2	0	0.2	.818
1988			5	4	.556	2.50	62	1	0	82.2	74	30	72	0	4	4	20	0	0	0	–	3	7	0	0	0.2	1.000
1989			2	5	.286	4.12	51	2	0	63.1	75	22	56	0	1	5	18	0	0	0	–	7	4	0	0	0.2	1.000
1990			13	7	.650	1.98	57	6	1	127	99	48	94	1	8	6	1	0	0	0	–	7	18	2	1	0.5	.926
1991	NY	A	5	5	.500	2.19	60	0	0	70	57	20	60	0	5	5	23	0	0	0	–	7	11	0	1	0.3	1.000
1992			2	2	.500	1.56	50	0	0	52	34	19	37	0	2	2	30	0	0	0	–	2	4	2	0	0.2	.750
1993			2	2	.500	4.21	49	0	0	47	44	28	39	0	2	2	25	0	0	0	–	6	10	0	0	0.3	1.000
1994	2 teams	CLE A (19G 1–1)		BOS A (11G 1–0)																							
"	total		2	1	.667	5.72	30	0	0	28.1	41	18	20	0	2	1	4	0	0	0	–	2	2	1	0	0.2	.800
	11 yrs.		48	45	.516	3.25	509	28	1	824.1	751	334	668	1	38	34	132	0	0	0	–	55	102	9	4	0.3	.946
LEAGUE CHAMPIONSHIP SERIES																											
1985	KC	A	1	0	1.000	1.42	2	0	0	6.1	4	1	3	0	1	0	0	0	0	0	–	0	1	0	1	0.5	1.000

John Farrell

FARRELL, JOHN EDWARD
B. Aug. 4, 1962, Monmouth Beach, N. J.
BR TR 6'4" 210 lbs.

Year	Team		W	L	PCT	ERA	G	GS	CG	IP	H	BB	SO	ShO	W	L	SV	AB	H	HR	BA	PO	A	E	DP	TC/G	FA
1987	CLE	A	5	1	.833	3.39	10	9	1	69	68	22	28	0	1	0	0	0	0	0	–	8	7	2	1	1.7	.882
1988			14	10	.583	4.24	31	30	4	210.1	216	67	92	0	0	0	0	0	0	0	–	21	23	0	2	1.4	1.000
1989			9	14	.391	3.63	31	31	7	208	196	71	132	2	0	0	0	0	0	0	–	18	20	2	1	1.3	.950
1990			4	5	.444	4.28	17	17	1	96.2	108	33	44	0	0	0	0	0	0	0	–	8	12	2	1	1.3	.909
1993	CAL	A	3	12	.200	7.35	21	17	0	90.2	110	44	45	0	0	1	0	0	0	0	–	5	11	0	0	0.8	1.000
1994			1	2	.333	9.00	3	3	0	13	16	8	10	0	0	0	0	0	0	0	–	1	6	1	1	2.7	.875
	6 yrs.		36	44	.450	4.48	113	107	13	687.2	714	245	351	2	1	1	0	0	0	0	–	61	79	7	6	1.3	.952

Jeff Fassero

FASSERO, JEFFREY JOSEPH
B. Jan. 15, 1963, Springfield, Ill.
BL TL 6'1" 180 lbs.

Year	Team		W	L	PCT	ERA	G	GS	CG	IP	H	BB	SO	ShO	W	L	SV	AB	H	HR	BA	PO	A	E	DP	TC/G	FA
1991	MON	N	2	5	.286	2.44	51	0	0	55.1	39	17	42	0	2	5	8	3	0	0	.000	3	11	1	1	0.3	.933
1992			8	7	.533	2.84	70	0	0	85.2	81	34	63	0	8	7	1	7	1	0	.143	1	15	0	0	0.2	1.000
1993			12	5	.706	2.29	56	15	1	149.2	119	54	140	0	5	1	1	32	2	0	.063	5	22	3	0	0.5	.900
1994			8	6	.571	2.99	21	21	1	138.2	119	40	119	0	0	0	0	44	3	0	.068	9	33	0	1	2.0	1.000
	4 yrs.		30	23	.566	2.64	198	36	2	429.1	358	145	364	0	15	13	10	86	6	0	.070	18	81	4	2	0.5	.961

Alex Fernandez

FERNANDEZ, ALEXANDER
B. Aug. 13, 1969, Miami, Fla.
BR TR 6'2" 200 lbs.

Year	Team		W	L	PCT	ERA	G	GS	CG	IP	H	BB	SO	ShO	W	L	SV	AB	H	HR	BA	PO	A	E	DP	TC/G	FA
1990	CHI	A	5	5	.500	3.80	13	13	3	87.2	89	34	61	0	0	0	0	0	0	0	–	3	12	2	0	1.3	.882
1991			9	13	.409	4.51	34	32	2	191.2	186	88	145	0	0	0	0	0	0	0	–	7	31	3	2	1.2	.927
1992			8	11	.421	4.27	29	29	4	187.2	199	50	95	2	0	0	0	0	0	0	–	10	33	2	5	1.6	.956
1993			18	9	.667	3.13	34	34	3	247.1	221	67	169	1	0	0	0	0	0	0	–	18	38	0	1	1.6	1.000
1994			11	7	.611	3.86	24	24	4	170.1	163	50	122	3	0	0	0	0	0	0	–	16	39	1	4	2.3	.982
	5 yrs.		51	45	.531	3.88	134	132	16	884.2	858	289	592	6	0	0	0	0	0	0	–	54	153	8	13	1.6	.963
LEAGUE CHAMPIONSHIP SERIES																											
1993	CHI	A	0	2	.000	1.80	2	2	0	15	15	6	10	0	0	0	0	0	0	0	–	2	1	0	1	1.5	1.000

Sid Fernandez

FERNANDEZ, CHARLES SIDNEY (El Sid)
B. Oct. 12, 1962, Honolulu, Hawaii.
BL TL 6'1" 220 lbs.

Year	Team		W	L	PCT	ERA	G	GS	CG	IP	H	BB	SO	ShO	W	L	SV	AB	H	HR	BA	PO	A	E	DP	TC/G	FA
1983	LA	N	0	1	.000	6.00	2	1	0	6	7	7	9	0	0	0	0	1	1	0	1.000	1	1	0	0	1.0	1.000
1984	NY	N	6	6	.500	3.50	15	15	0	90	74	34	62	0	0	0	0	28	5	0	.179	0	6	0	0	0.4	1.000
1985			9	9	.500	2.80	26	26	3	170.1	108	80	180	0	0	0	0	52	11	0	.212	1	23	0	0	0.9	1.000
1986			16	6	.727	3.52	32	31	2	204.1	161	91	200	1	0	0	1	68	11	0	.162	3	18	1	1	0.7	.955
1987			12	8	.600	3.81	28	27	3	156	130	67	134	1	0	0	0	43	7	0	.163	4	12	1	0	0.6	.941
1988			12	10	.545	3.03	31	31	1	187	127	70	189	1	0	0	0	56	14	0	.250	2	13	0	0	0.5	1.000
1989			14	5	.737	2.83	35	32	6	219.1	157	75	198	2	0	0	0	71	15	1	.211	4	13	0	2	0.5	1.000
1990			9	14	.391	3.46	30	30	2	179.1	130	67	181	1	0	0	0	58	11	0	.190	1	16	2	0	0.6	.895
1991			1	3	.250	2.86	8	8	0	44	36	9	31	0	0	0	0	13	2	0	.154	1	11	0	0	1.5	1.000
1992			14	11	.560	2.73	32	32	5	214.2	162	67	193	2	0	0	0	74	15	0	.203	4	21	1	1	0.8	.962
1993			5	6	.455	2.93	18	18	1	119.2	82	36	81	1	0	0	0	32	3	0	.094	2	10	0	1	0.7	1.000
1994	BAL	A	6	6	.500	5.15	19	19	2	115.1	109	46	95	0	0	0	0	0	0	0	–	1	9	0	0	0.5	1.000
	12 yrs.		104	85	.550	3.29	276	270	25	1706	1283	649	1553	9	0	0	1	496	95	1	.192	24	153	5	5	0.7	.973
LEAGUE CHAMPIONSHIP SERIES																											
1986	NY	N	0	1	.000	4.50	1	1	0	6	3	1	5	0	0	0	0	1	0	0	.000	0	0	0	0	0.0	–
1988			0	1	.000	13.50	1	1	0	4	7	1	5	0	0	0	0	1	0	0	.000	0	0	0	0	0.0	–
	2 yrs.		0	2	.000	8.10	2	2	0	10	10	2	10	0	0	0	0	2	0	0	.000	0	0	0	0	0.0	–
WORLD SERIES																											
1986	NY	N	0	0	–	1.35	3	0	0	6.2	6	1	10	0	0	0	0	0	0	0	–	0	0	0	0	0.0	–

Mike Fetters

FETTERS, MICHAEL LEE
B. Dec. 19, 1964, Van Nuys, Calif.
BR TR 6'4" 200 lbs.

Year	Team		W	L	PCT	ERA	G	GS	CG	IP	H	BB	SO	ShO	W	L	SV	AB	H	HR	BA	PO	A	E	DP	TC/G	FA
1989	CAL	A	0	0	–	8.10	1	1	0	3.1	5	1	4	0	0	0	0	0	0	0	–	0	1	0	0	1.0	1.000
1990			1	1	.500	4.12	26	2	0	67.2	77	20	35	0	1	1	1	0	0	0	–	9	11	1	0	0.8	.952
1991			2	5	.286	4.84	19	4	0	44.2	53	28	24	0	2	1	0	0	0	0	–	2	4	1	0	0.4	.857
1992	MIL	A	5	1	.833	1.87	50	0	0	62.2	38	24	43	0	5	1	2	0	0	0	–	3	11	0	1	0.3	1.000
1993			3	3	.500	3.34	45	0	0	59.1	59	22	23	0	3	3	0	0	0	0	–	5	7	1	4	0.3	.923
1994			1	4	.200	2.54	42	0	0	46	41	27	31	0	1	4	17	0	0	0	–	3	5	1	1	0.2	.889
	6 yrs.		12	14	.462	3.36	183	6	0	283.2	273	122	160	0	12	10	20	0	0	0	–	22	39	4	6	0.4	.938

Year	Team	W	L	PCT	ERA	G	GS	CG	IP	H	BB	SO	ShO	W	L	SV	AB	H	HR	BA	PO	A	E	DP	TC/G	FA
														Relief Pitching			Batting									

Chuck Finley

FINLEY, CHARLES EDWARD
B. Nov. 26, 1962, Monroe, La. BL TL 6'6" 220 lbs.

Year	Team	W	L	PCT	ERA	G	GS	CG	IP	H	BB	SO	ShO	W	L	SV	AB	H	HR	BA	PO	A	E	DP	TC/G	FA
1986	CAL A	3	1	.750	3.30			0	46.1	40	23	37	0	3	1	0	0	0	0	–	8	8	0	1	0.6	1.000
1987		2	7	.222	4.67	35	3	0	90.2	102	43	63	0	2	6	0	0	0	0	–	6	11	1	1	0.5	.944
1988		9	15	.375	4.17	31	31	2	194.1	191	82	111	0	0	0	0	0	0	0	–	5	24	1	1	1.0	.967
1989		16	9	.640	2.57	29	29	9	199.2	171	82	156	1	0	0	0	0	0	0	–	4	16	2	0	0.8	.909
1990		18	9	.667	2.40	32	32	7	236	210	81	177	2	0	0	0	0	0	0	–	14	21	5	2	1.3	.875
1991		18	9	.667	3.80	34	34	4	227.1	205	101	171	2	0	0	0	0	0	0	–	11	16	2	3	0.9	.931
1992		7	12	.368	3.96	31	31	4	204.1	212	98	124	1	0	0	0	0	0	0	–	3	17	3	1	0.7	.870
1993		16	14	.533	3.15	35	35	13	251.1	243	82	187	2	0	0	0	0	0	0	–	10	26	5	0	1.2	.878
1994		10	10	.500	4.32	25	25	7	183.1	178	71	148	2	0	0	0	0	0	0	–	9	17	4	1	1.2	.867
9 yrs.		99	86	.535	3.50	277	220	46	1633.1	1552	663	1174	10	5	7	0	0	0	0	–	70	156	23	10	0.9	.908

LEAGUE CHAMPIONSHIP SERIES

Year	Team	W	L	PCT	ERA	G	GS	CG	IP	H	BB	SO	ShO	W	L	SV	AB	H	HR	BA	PO	A	E	DP	TC/G	FA
1986	CAL A	0	0	–	0.00	3	0	0	2	1	0	1	0	0	0	0	0	0	0	–	0	0	0	0	0.0	–

Gar Finnvold

FINNVOLD, ANDERS GAR
B. Mar. 11, 1968, Boynton Beach, Fla. BR TR 6'5" 195 lbs.

Year	Team	W	L	PCT	ERA	G	GS	CG	IP	H	BB	SO	ShO	W	L	SV	AB	H	HR	BA	PO	A	E	DP	TC/G	FA
1994	BOS A	0	4	.000	5.94	8	8	0	36.1	45	15	17	0	0	0	0	0	0	0	–	3	2	1	0	0.8	.833

Dave Fleming

FLEMING, DAVID ANTHONY
B. Nov. 7, 1969, Jackson Heights, N. Y. BL TL 6'3" 200 lbs.

Year	Team	W	L	PCT	ERA	G	GS	CG	IP	H	BB	SO	ShO	W	L	SV	AB	H	HR	BA	PO	A	E	DP	TC/G	FA
1991	SEA A	1	0	1.000	6.62	9	3	0	17.2	19	3	11	0	0	0	0	0	0	0	–	3	6	0	2	1.0	1.000
1992		17	10	.630	3.39	33	33	7	228.1	225	60	112	4	0	0	0	0	0	0	–	4	33	1	4	1.2	.974
1993		12	5	.706	4.36	26	26	1	167.1	189	67	75	1	0	0	0	0	0	0	–	9	28	0	1	1.4	1.000
1994		7	11	.389	6.46	23	23	0	117	152	65	65	0	0	0	0	0	0	0	–	8	15	1	1	1.0	.958
4 yrs.		37	26	.587	4.48	91	85	8	530.1	585	195	263	5	0	0	0	0	0	0	–	24	82	2	8	1.2	.981

Bryce Florie

FLORIE, BRYCE BETTENCOURT
B. May 21, 1970, Charleston, S. C. BR TR 6' 185 lbs.

Year	Team	W	L	PCT	ERA	G	GS	CG	IP	H	BB	SO	ShO	W	L	SV	AB	H	HR	BA	PO	A	E	DP	TC/G	FA
1994	SD N	0	0	–	0.96	9	0	0	9.1	8	3	8	0	0	0	0	0	0	0	–	2	3	0	0	0.6	1.000

Tom Foley

FOLEY, THOMAS MICHAEL
B. Sept. 9, 1959, Fort Benning, Ga. BL TR 6'1" 160 lbs.

Year	Team	W	L	PCT	ERA	G	GS	CG	IP	H	BB	SO	ShO	W	L	SV	AB	H	HR	BA	PO	A	E	DP	TC/G	FA
1989	MON N	0	0	–	27.00	1	0	0	0.1	1	1	0	0	0	0	0	*				0	0	0	0	0.0	–

Tim Fortugno

FORTUGNO, TIMOTHY SHAWN
B. Apr. 11, 1962, Clinton, Mass. BL TL 6'1" 195 lbs.

Year	Team	W	L	PCT	ERA	G	GS	CG	IP	H	BB	SO	ShO	W	L	SV	AB	H	HR	BA	PO	A	E	DP	TC/G	FA
1992	CAL A	1	1	.500	5.18	14	5	1	41.2	37	19	31	1	0	0	0	0	0	0	–	0	4	0	0	0.3	1.000
1994	CIN N	1	0	1.000	4.20	25	0	0	30	32	14	29	0	1	0	0	3	1	0	.333	2	6	0	1	0.3	1.000
2 yrs.		2	1	.667	4.77	39	5	1	71.2	69	33	60	1	1	0	1	3	1	0	.333	2	10	0	1	0.3	1.000

Tony Fossas

FOSSAS, EMILIO ANTONIO
Born Emilio Antonio Fossas (Morejon).
B. Sept. 23, 1957, Havana, Cuba. BL TL 6' 195 lbs.

Year	Team	W	L	PCT	ERA	G	GS	CG	IP	H	BB	SO	ShO	W	L	SV	AB	H	HR	BA	PO	A	E	DP	TC/G	FA
1988	TEX A	0	0	–	4.76	5	0	0	5.2	11	2	0	0	0	0	0	0	0	0	–	1	1	0	1	0.4	1.000
1989	MIL A	2	2	.500	3.54	51	0	0	61	57	22	42	0	2	2	1	0	0	0	–	1	12	2	0	0.3	.867
1990		2	3	.400	6.44	32	0	0	29.1	44	10	24	0	2	3	0	0	0	0	–	1	4	3	0	0.3	.625
1991	BOS A	3	2	.600	3.47	64	0	0	57	49	28	29	0	3	2	1	0	0	0	–	6	12	2	2	0.3	.900
1992		1	2	.333	2.43	60	0	0	29.2	31	14	19	0	1	2	2	0	0	0	–	2	6	0	0	0.1	1.000
1993		1	1	.500	5.18	71	0	0	40	38	15	39	0	1	1	0	0	0	0	–	1	6	1	0	0.1	.875
1994		2	0	1.000	4.76	44	0	0	34	35	15	31	0	2	0	1	0	0	0	–	0	5	2	0	0.2	.714
7 yrs.		11	10	.524	4.17	327	0	0	256.2	265	106	184	0	11	10	5	0	0	0	–	12	46	10	3	0.2	.853

Kevin Foster

FOSTER, KEVIN CHRISTOPHER
B. Jan. 13, 1969, Evanston, Ill. BR TR 6'1" 160 lbs.

Year	Team	W	L	PCT	ERA	G	GS	CG	IP	H	BB	SO	ShO	W	L	SV	AB	H	HR	BA	PO	A	E	DP	TC/G	FA
1993	PHI N	0	1	.000	14.85	2	1	0	6.2	13	7	6	0	0	0	0	2	0	0	.000	1	0	0	0	0.5	1.000
1994	CHI N	3	4	.429	2.89	13	13	0	81	70	35	75	0	0	0	0	27	2	0	.074	4	5	0	0	0.7	1.000
2 yrs.		3	5	.375	3.80	15	14	0	87.2	83	42	81	0	0	0	0	29	2	0	.069	5	5	0	0	0.7	1.000

John Franco

FRANCO, JOHN ANTHONY
B. Sept. 17, 1960, Brooklyn, N. Y. BL TL 5'10" 175 lbs.

Year	Team	W	L	PCT	ERA	G	GS	CG	IP	H	BB	SO	ShO	W	L	SV	AB	H	HR	BA	PO	A	E	DP	TC/G	FA
1984	CIN N	6	2	.750	2.61	54	0	0	79.1	74	36	55	0	6	2	4	3	0	0	.000	5	15	0	1	0.4	1.000
1985		12	3	.800	2.18	67	0	0	99	83	40	61	0	12	3	12	6	2	0	.333	9	21	1	1	0.5	.968
1986		6	6	.500	2.94	74	0	0	101	90	44	84	0	6	6	29	4	0	0	.000	6	22	4	2	0.4	.875
1987		8	5	.615	2.52	68	0	0	82	76	27	61	0	8	5	32	4	0	0	.000	4	7	0	0	0.2	1.000
1988		6	6	.500	1.57	70	0	0	86	60	27	46	0	6	6	39	1	0	0	.000	3	18	1	1	0.3	.955
1989		4	8	.333	3.12	60	0	0	80.2	77	36	60	0	4	8	32	3	1	0	.333	2	19	1	1	0.4	.955
1990	NY N	5	3	.625	2.53	55	0	0	67.2	66	21	56	0	5	3	33	5	0	0	.000	3	13	1	0	0.3	.944
1991		5	9	.357	2.93	52	0	0	55.1	61	18	45	0	5	9	30	1	0	0	.000	3	10	1	1	0.3	.929
1992		6	2	.750	1.64	31	0	0	33	24	11	20	0	6	2	15	1	0	0	.000	2	12	0	2	0.5	1.000
1993		4	3	.571	5.20	35	0	0	36.1	46	19	29	0	4	3	10	1	0	0	.000	4	7	0	1	0.3	1.000
1994		1	4	.200	2.70	47	0	0	50	47	19	42	0	1	4	30	3	0	0	.000	4	7	0	1	0.2	1.000
11 yrs.		63	51	.553	2.63	613	0	0	770.1	704	298	559	0	63	51	266	30	3	0	.100	45	153	9	9	0.3	.957
																8th										

John Frascatore

FRASCATORE, JOHN VINCENT
B. Feb. 4, 1970, Ozone Park, N. Y. BR TR 6'1" 200 lbs.

Year	Team	W	L	PCT	ERA	G	GS	CG	IP	H	BB	SO	ShO	W	L	SV	AB	H	HR	BA	PO	A	E	DP	TC/G	FA
1994	STL N	0	1	.000	16.20	1	1	0	3.1	7	2	2	0	0	0	0	1	0	0	.000	0	1	0	0	1.0	1.000

Year	Team	W	L	PCT	ERA	G	GS	CG	IP	H	BB	SO	ShO	W	L	SV	AB	H	HR	BA	PO	A	E	DP	TC/G	FA

Willie Fraser   FRASER, WILLIAM PATRICK   B. May 26, 1964, New York, N. Y.   BR TR 6'1"   200 lbs.

Year	Team	W	L	PCT	ERA	G	GS	CG	IP	H	BB	SO	ShO	RW	RL	SV	AB	H	HR	BA	PO	A	E	DP	TC/G	FA
1986	CAL A	0	0	–	8.31	1	1	0	4.1	6	1	2	0	0	0	0	0	0	0	–	0	0	0	0	0.0	–
1987		10	10	.500	3.92	36	23	5	176.2	160	63	106	1	3	1	1	0	0	0	–	6	15	1	0	0.6	.955
1988		12	13	.480	5.41	34	32	2	194.2	203	80	86	0	1	0	0	0	0	0	–	21	20	3	3	1.3	.932
1989		4	7	.364	3.24	44	0	0	91.2	80	23	46	0	4	7	2	0	0	0	–	6	14	0	1	0.5	1.000
1990		5	4	.556	3.08	45	0	0	76	69	24	32	0	5	4	2	0	0	0	–	2	6	0	0	0.2	1.000
1991	2 teams	TOR A	(13G 0–2)	STL N	(35G 3–3)																					
"	total	3	5	.375	5.35	48	1	0	75.2	77	32	37	0	3	4	0	2	0	0	.000	3	6	0	0	0.2	1.000
1994	FLA N	2	0	1.000	5.84	9	0	0	12.1	20	6	7	0	2	0	0	0	0	0	–	0	1	0	0	0.1	1.000
7 yrs.		36	39	.480	4.42	217	57	7	631.1	615	229	316	1	18	16	5	2	0	0	.000	38	62	4	4	0.5	.962

Marvin Freeman   FREEMAN, MARVIN (Starvin' Marvin)   B. Apr. 10, 1963, Chicago, Ill.   BR TR 6'7"   200 lbs.

Year	Team	W	L	PCT	ERA	G	GS	CG	IP	H	BB	SO	ShO	RW	RL	SV	AB	H	HR	BA	PO	A	E	DP	TC/G	FA
1986	PHI N	2	0	1.000	2.25	3	3	0	16	6	10	8	0	0	0	0	6	0	0	.000	0	1	0	0	0.3	1.000
1988		2	3	.400	6.10	11	11	0	51.2	55	43	37	0	0	0	0	14	3	0	.214	2	9	0	0	1.0	1.000
1989		0	0	–	6.00	1	1	0	3	2	5	0	0	0	0	0	2	0	0	.000	0	0	0	0	0.0	–
1990	2 teams	PHI N	(16G 0–2)	ATL N	(9G 1–0)																					
"	total	1	2	.333	4.31	25	3	0	48	41	17	38	0	1	1	1	7	0	0	.000	1	6	1	1	0.3	.875
1991	ATL N	1	0	1.000	3.00	34	0	0	48	37	13	34	0	1	0	0	7	0	0	.000	3	4	0	0	0.2	1.000
1992		7	5	.583	3.22	58	0	0	64.1	61	29	41	0	7	5	3	4	2	0	.500	4	5	2	0	0.2	.818
1993		2	0	1.000	6.08	21	0	0	23.2	24	10	25	0	2	0	0	0	0	0	–	1	0	0	0	0.0	1.000
1994	CLR N	10	2	.833	2.80	19	18	0	112.2	113	23	67	0	1	0	0	36	4	1	.111	8	20	0	0	1.5	1.000
8 yrs.		25	12	.676	3.77	172	36	0	367.1	339	150	250	0	12	6	5	76	9	1	.118	19	45	3	1	0.4	.955

LEAGUE CHAMPIONSHIP SERIES

Year	Team	W	L	PCT	ERA	G	GS	CG	IP	H	BB	SO	ShO	RW	RL	SV	AB	H	HR	BA	PO	A	E	DP	TC/G	FA
1992	ATL N	0	0	–	14.73	3	0	0	3.2	8	2	1	0	0	0	0	0	0	0	–	0	2	0	0	0.7	1.000

Steve Frey   FREY, STEVEN FRANCIS   B. July 29, 1963, Meadowbrook, Pa.   BR TL 5'9"   170 lbs.

Year	Team	W	L	PCT	ERA	G	GS	CG	IP	H	BB	SO	ShO	RW	RL	SV	AB	H	HR	BA	PO	A	E	DP	TC/G	FA
1989	MON N	3	2	.600	5.48	20	0	0	21.1	29	11	15	0	3	2	0	0	0	0	–	1	2	0	0	0.2	1.000
1990		8	2	.800	2.10	51	0	0	55.2	44	29	29	0	8	2	9	1	0	0	.000	4	7	1	0	0.2	.917
1991		0	1	.000	4.99	31	0	0	39.2	43	23	21	0	0	1	1	2	0	0	.000	1	4	0	0	0.2	1.000
1992	CAL A	4	2	.667	3.57	51	0	0	45.1	39	22	24	0	4	2	4	0	0	0	–	4	5	0	1	0.2	1.000
1993		2	3	.400	2.98	55	0	0	48.1	41	26	22	0	2	3	13	0	0	0	–	2	6	0	0	0.1	1.000
1994	SF N	1	0	1.000	4.94	44	0	0	31	37	15	20	0	1	0	0	0	0	0	–	2	4	0	0	0.1	1.000
6 yrs.		18	10	.643	3.69	252	0	0	241.1	233	126	131	0	18	10	27	3	0	0	.000	14	28	1	1	0.2	.977

Todd Frohwirth   FROHWIRTH, TODD GERARD   B. Sept. 28, 1962, Milwaukee, Wis.   BR TR 6'4"   190 lbs.

Year	Team	W	L	PCT	ERA	G	GS	CG	IP	H	BB	SO	ShO	RW	RL	SV	AB	H	HR	BA	PO	A	E	DP	TC/G	FA
1987	PHI N	1	0	1.000	0.00	10	0	0	11	12	2	9	0	1	0	0	1	0	0	.000	1	1	0	1	0.2	1.000
1988		1	2	.333	8.25	12	0	0	12	16	11	11	0	1	2	0	0	0	0	–	0	5	0	0	0.4	1.000
1989		1	0	1.000	3.59	45	0	0	62.2	56	18	39	0	1	0	0	1	0	0	.000	5	8	0	0	0.3	1.000
1990		0	1	.000	18.00	5	0	0	3	6	6	1	0	0	1	0	0	0	0	–	0	1	1	0	0.4	.500
1991	BAL A	7	3	.700	1.87	51	0	0	96.1	64	29	77	0	7	3	3	0	0	0	–	14	24	3	3	0.8	.927
1992		4	3	.571	2.46	65	0	0	106	97	41	58	0	4	3	4	0	0	0	–	8	24	1	4	0.5	.970
1993		6	7	.462	3.83	70	0	0	96.1	91	44	50	0	6	7	3	0	0	0	–	8	21	1	3	0.4	.967
1994	BOS A	0	3	.000	10.80	22	0	0	26.2	40	17	13	0	0	3	1	0	0	0	–	1	8	1	0	0.5	.900
8 yrs.		20	19	.513	3.50	280	0	0	412	379	168	258	0	20	19	11	2	0	0	.000	37	92	7	11	0.5	.949

Keith Garagozzo   GARAGOZZO, KEITH JOHN   B. Oct. 25, 1969, Camden, N. J.   BL TL 6'   170 lbs.

Year	Team	W	L	PCT	ERA	G	GS	CG	IP	H	BB	SO	ShO	RW	RL	SV	AB	H	HR	BA	PO	A	E	DP	TC/G	FA
1994	MIN A	0	0	–	9.64	7	0	0	9.1	9	13	3	0	0	0	0	0	0	0	–	0	2	0	0	0.3	1.000

Mike Gardiner   GARDINER, MICHAEL JAMES   B. Oct. 19, 1965, Sarina, Ont., Canada.   BB TR 6'   185 lbs.

Year	Team	W	L	PCT	ERA	G	GS	CG	IP	H	BB	SO	ShO	RW	RL	SV	AB	H	HR	BA	PO	A	E	DP	TC/G	FA
1990	SEA A	0	2	.000	10.66	5	3	0	12.2	22	5	6	0	0	0	0	0	0	0	–	1	2	0	0	0.6	1.000
1991	BOS A	9	10	.474	4.85	22	22	0	130	140	47	91	0	0	0	0	0	0	0	–	12	13	1	2	1.2	.962
1992		4	10	.286	4.75	28	18	0	130.2	126	58	79	0	2	2	0	0	0	0	–	13	15	1	2	1.0	.966
1993	2 teams	MON N	(24G 2–3)	DET A	(10G 0–0)																					
"	total	2	3	.400	4.93	34	2	0	49.1	52	26	25	0	1	2	0	4	0	0	.000	1	7	0	0	0.2	1.000
1994	DET A	2	2	.500	4.14	38	1	0	58.2	53	23	31	0	2	2	5	0	0	0	–	6	2	0	0	0.2	1.000
5 yrs.		17	27	.386	4.91	127	46	0	381.1	393	159	232	0	5	6	5	4	0	0	.000	33	39	2	4	0.6	.973

Mark Gardner   GARDNER, MARK ALLAN   B. Mar. 1, 1962, Los Angeles, Calif.   BR TR 6'1"   190 lbs.

Year	Team	W	L	PCT	ERA	G	GS	CG	IP	H	BB	SO	ShO	RW	RL	SV	AB	H	HR	BA	PO	A	E	DP	TC/G	FA
1989	MON N	0	3	.000	5.13	7	4	0	26.1	26	11	21	0	0	0	0	6	1	0	.167	1	3	0	0	0.6	1.000
1990		7	9	.438	3.42	27	26	3	152.2	129	61	135	3	0	1	0	44	5	0	.114	9	25	0	4	1.3	1.000
1991		9	11	.450	3.85	27	27	0	168.1	139	75	107	0	0	0	0	55	5	0	.091	12	15	1	1	1.0	.964
1992		12	10	.545	4.36	33	30	0	179.2	179	60	132	0	1	0	0	50	7	0	.140	14	22	2	0	1.2	.947
1993	KC A	4	6	.400	6.19	17	16	0	91.2	92	36	54	0	0	0	0	0	0	0	–	6	5	1	1	0.7	.917
1994	FLA N	4	4	.500	4.87	20	14	0	92.1	97	30	57	0	0	0	0	25	1	0	.040	8	8	0	0	0.8	1.000
6 yrs.		36	43	.456	4.37	131	117	3	711	662	273	506	3	1	1	0	180	19	0	.106	50	78	4	6	1.0	.970

Paul Gibson   GIBSON, PAUL MARSHALL   B. Jan. 4, 1960, Southampton, N. Y.   BR TL 6'   165 lbs.

Year	Team	W	L	PCT	ERA	G	GS	CG	IP	H	BB	SO	ShO	RW	RL	SV	AB	H	HR	BA	PO	A	E	DP	TC/G	FA
1988	DET A	4	2	.667	2.93	40	1	0	92	83	34	50	0	3	2	0	0	0	0	–	7	11	0	2	0.5	1.000
1989		4	8	.333	4.64	45	13	0	132	129	57	77	0	3	3	0	0	0	0	–	6	20	2	0	0.6	.929
1990		5	4	.556	3.05	61	0	0	97.1	99	44	56	0	5	4	3	0	0	0	–	9	11	0	1	0.3	1.000
1991		5	7	.417	4.59	68	0	0	96	112	48	52	0	5	7	8	0	0	0	–	6	13	0	0	0.3	1.000
1992	NY N	0	1	.000	5.23	43	1	0	62	70	25	49	0	0	1	0	6	0	0	.000	2	6	0	0	0.2	1.000
1993	2 teams	NY N	(8G 1–1)	NY A	(20G 2–0)																					
"	total	3	1	.750	3.48	28	0	0	44	45	11	37	0	3	1	0	0	0	0	–	3	5	0	1	0.3	1.000

Year	Team	W	L	PCT	ERA	G	GS	CG	IP	H	BB	SO	ShO	Relief Pitching W	L	SV	Batting AB	H	HR	BA	PO	A	E	DP	TC/G	FA

Paul Gibson *continued*

Year	Team	W	L	PCT	ERA	G	GS	CG	IP	H	BB	SO	ShO	W	L	SV	AB	H	HR	BA	PO	A	E	DP	TC/G	FA
1994	NY A	1	1	.500	4.97	30	0	0	29	26	17	21	0	1	1	0	0	0	0	–	2	4	0	0	0.2	1.000
7 yrs.		22	24	.478	4.06	315	15	0	552.1	564	236	342	0	20	19	11	6	0	0	.000	35	70	2	4	0.3	.981

Tom Glavine

GLAVINE, THOMAS MICHAEL
B. Mar. 25, 1966, Concord, Mass.   BL TL 6'   175 lbs.

Year	Team	W	L	PCT	ERA	G	GS	CG	IP	H	BB	SO	ShO	W	L	SV	AB	H	HR	BA	PO	A	E	DP	TC/G	FA
1987	ATL N	2	4	.333	5.54	9	9	0	50.1	55	33	20	0	0	0	0	16	2	0	.125	1	13	1	0	1.7	.933
1988		7	17	.292	4.56	34	34	1	195.1	201	63	84	0	0	0	0	60	11	0	.183	12	41	4	3	1.7	.930
1989		14	8	.636	3.68	29	29	6	186	172	40	90	4	0	0	0	67	10	0	.149	7	37	4	4	1.7	.917
1990		10	12	.455	4.28	33	33	1	214.1	232	78	129	0	0	0	0	62	7	0	.113	19	33	1	1	1.6	.981
1991		20	11	.645	2.55	34	34	9	246.2	201	69	192	1	0	0	0	74	17	0	.230	16	45	0	4	1.8	1.000
1992		20	8	.714	2.76	33	33	7	225	197	70	129	5	0	0	0	77	19	0	.247	18	31	0	2	1.5	1.000
1993		22	6	.786	3.20	36	36	4	239.1	236	90	120	2	0	0	0	81	14	0	.173	17	36	2	4	1.5	.964
1994		13	9	.591	3.97	25	25	2	165.1	173	70	140	0	0	0	0	56	10	0	.179	11	33	1	1	1.8	.978
8 yrs.		108	75	.590	3.58	233	233	30	1522.1	1467	513	904	12	0	0	0	493	90	0	.183	101	269	13	19	1.6	.966

LEAGUE CHAMPIONSHIP SERIES

Year	Team	W	L	PCT	ERA	G	GS	CG	IP	H	BB	SO	ShO	W	L	SV	AB	H	HR	BA	PO	A	E	DP	TC/G	FA
1991	ATL N	0	2	.000	3.21	2	2	0	14	12	6	11	0	0	0	0	4	1	0	.250	1	3	0	0	2.0	1.000
1992		0	2	.000	12.27	2	2	0	7.1	13	3	2	0	0	0	0	2	0	0	.000	1	2	0	0	1.5	1.000
1993		1	0	1.000	2.57	1	1	0	7	6	0	5	0	0	0	0	3	0	0	.000	0	3	0	0	3.0	1.000
3 yrs.		1	4	.200	5.40	5	5	0	28.1	31	9	18	0	0	0	0	9	1	0	.111	2	8	0	0	2.0	1.000

WORLD SERIES

Year	Team	W	L	PCT	ERA	G	GS	CG	IP	H	BB	SO	ShO	W	L	SV	AB	H	HR	BA	PO	A	E	DP	TC/G	FA
1991	ATL N	1	1	.500	2.70	2	2	1	13.1	8	7	8	0	0	0	0	2	0	0	.000	0	3	0	1	1.5	1.000
1992		1	1	.500	1.59	2	2	2	17	10	4	8	0	0	0	0	2	0	0	.000	0	2	0	0	1.0	1.000
2 yrs.		2	2	.500	2.08	4	4	3	30.1	18	11	16	0	0	0	0	4	0	0	.000	0	5	0	1	1.3	1.000

George Glinatsis

GLINATSIS, GEORGE, JR.
B. June 29, 1969, Youngstown, Ohio.   BR TR 6'4"   195 lbs.

Year	Team	W	L	PCT	ERA	G	GS	CG	IP	H	BB	SO	ShO	W	L	SV	AB	H	HR	BA	PO	A	E	DP	TC/G	FA
1994	SEA A	0	1	.000	13.50	2	2	0	5.1	9	6	1	0	0	0	0	0	0	0	–	0	0	0	0	0.0	–

Greg Gohr

GOHR, GREGORY JAMES
B. Oct. 29, 1967, Santa Clara, Calif.   BR TR 6'3"   205 lbs.

Year	Team	W	L	PCT	ERA	G	GS	CG	IP	H	BB	SO	ShO	W	L	SV	AB	H	HR	BA	PO	A	E	DP	TC/G	FA
1993	DET A	0	0	–	5.96	16	0	0	22.2	26	14	23	0	0	0	0	0	0	0	–	1	1	0	1	0.1	1.000
1994		2	2	.500	4.50	8	6	0	34	36	21	21	0	1	0	0	0	0	0	–	2	1	0	0	0.4	1.000
2 yrs.		2	2	.500	5.08	24	6	0	56.2	62	35	44	0	1	0	0	0	0	0	–	3	2	0	1	0.2	1.000

Pat Gomez

GOMEZ, PATRICK ALEXANDER
B. Mar. 17, 1968, Roseville, Calif.   BL TL 6'   190 lbs.

Year	Team	W	L	PCT	ERA	G	GS	CG	IP	H	BB	SO	ShO	W	L	SV	AB	H	HR	BA	PO	A	E	DP	TC/G	FA
1993	SD N	1	2	.333	5.12	27	1	0	31.2	35	19	26	0	1	1	0	5	0	0	.000	0	3	1	0	0.1	.750
1994	SF N	0	1	.000	3.78	26	0	0	33.1	23	20	14	0	0	1	0	2	0	0	.000	3	2	1	0	0.2	.833
2 yrs.		1	3	.250	4.43	53	1	0	65	58	39	40	0	1	2	0	7	0	0	.000	3	5	2	0	0.2	.800

Rene Gonzales

GONZALES, RENE ADRIAN
B. Sept. 23, 1960, Austin, Tex.   BR TR 6'3"   180 lbs.

Year	Team	W	L	PCT	ERA	G	GS	CG	IP	H	BB	SO	ShO	W	L	SV	AB	H	HR	BA	PO	A	E	DP	TC/G	FA
1993	CAL A	0	0	–	0.00	1	0	0	1	0	0	0	0	0	0	0	*				1	1	0	0	1.0	1.000

Dwight Gooden

GOODEN, DWIGHT EUGENE (Doc)
B. Nov. 16, 1964, Tampa, Fla.   BR TR 6'2"   190 lbs.

Year	Team	W	L	PCT	ERA	G	GS	CG	IP	H	BB	SO	ShO	W	L	SV	AB	H	HR	BA	PO	A	E	DP	TC/G	FA
1984	NY N	17	9	.654	2.60	31	31	7	218	161	73	276	3	0	0	0	70	14	0	.200	21	22	2	0	1.5	.956
1985		24	4	.857	1.53	35	35	16	276.2	198	69	268	8	0	0	0	93	21	1	.226	25	38	2	6	1.9	.969
1986		17	6	.739	2.84	33	33	12	250	197	80	200	2	0	0	0	81	7	0	.086	36	36	2	5	2.2	.973
1987		15	7	.682	3.21	25	25	7	179.2	162	53	148	3	0	0	0	64	14	0	.219	15	22	3	3	1.6	.925
1988		18	9	.667	3.19	34	34	10	248.1	242	57	175	3	0	0	0	90	16	1	.178	27	56	5	3	2.6	.943
1989		9	4	.692	2.89	19	17	0	118.1	93	47	101	0	0	0	1	40	8	0	.200	8	16	3	0	1.4	.889
1990		19	7	.731	3.83	34	34	2	232.2	229	70	223	1	0	0	0	75	14	1	.187	15	35	4	5	1.6	.926
1991		13	7	.650	3.60	27	27	3	190	185	56	150	1	0	0	0	63	15	1	.238	15	28	2	3	1.7	.956
1992		10	13	.435	3.67	31	31	3	206	197	70	145	0	0	0	0	72	19	1	.264	9	40	6	1	1.8	.891
1993		12	15	.444	3.45	29	29	7	208.2	188	61	149	2	0	0	0	70	14	2	.200	19	24	2	1	1.6	.956
1994		3	4	.429	6.31	7	7	0	41.1	46	15	40	0	0	0	0	12	2	0	.167	1	11	1	1	1.9	.923
11 yrs.		157	85	.649	3.10	305	303	67	2169.2	1898	651	1875	23	0	0	1	730	144	7	.197	191	328	32	28	1.8	.942

LEAGUE CHAMPIONSHIP SERIES

Year	Team	W	L	PCT	ERA	G	GS	CG	IP	H	BB	SO	ShO	W	L	SV	AB	H	HR	BA	PO	A	E	DP	TC/G	FA
1986	NY N	0	1	.000	1.06	2	2	0	17	16	5	9	0	0	0	0	5	0	0	.000	3	2	0	0	2.5	1.000
1988		0	0	–	2.95	3	2	0	18.1	10	8	20	0	0	0	0	5	1	0	.200	1	3	0	0	1.3	1.000
2 yrs.		0	1	.000	2.04	5	4	0	35.1	26	13	29	0	0	0	0	10	1	0	.100	4	5	0	0	1.8	1.000

WORLD SERIES

Year	Team	W	L	PCT	ERA	G	GS	CG	IP	H	BB	SO	ShO	W	L	SV	AB	H	HR	BA	PO	A	E	DP	TC/G	FA
1986	NY N	0	2	.000	8.00	2	2	0	9	17	4	9	0	0	0	0	2	1	0	.500	1	2	0	0	1.5	1.000

Tom Gordon

GORDON, THOMAS (Flash)
B. Nov. 18, 1967, Sebring, Fla.   BR TR 5'9"   160 lbs.

Year	Team	W	L	PCT	ERA	G	GS	CG	IP	H	BB	SO	ShO	W	L	SV	AB	H	HR	BA	PO	A	E	DP	TC/G	FA
1988	KC A	0	2	.000	5.17	5	2	0	15.2	16	7	18	0	0	0	0	0	0	0	–	2	2	0	0	0.8	1.000
1989		17	9	.654	3.64	49	16	1	163	122	86	153	1	10	2	1	0	0	0	–	15	26	0	7	0.8	1.000
1990		12	11	.522	3.73	32	32	6	195.1	192	99	175	1	0	0	0	0	0	0	–	17	24	1	1	1.3	.976
1991		9	14	.391	3.87	45	14	1	158	129	87	167	0	4	7	1	0	0	0	–	12	17	2	1	0.7	.935
1992		6	10	.375	4.59	40	11	0	117.2	116	55	98	0	6	5	0	0	0	0	–	11	14	1	1	0.7	.962
1993		12	6	.667	3.58	48	14	2	155.2	125	77	143	0	4	2	1	0	0	0	–	18	21	2	0	0.9	.951
1994		11	7	.611	4.35	24	24	0	155.1	136	87	126	0	0	0	0	0	0	0	–	12	25	2	3	1.6	.949
7 yrs.		67	59	.532	3.94	243	113	10	960.2	836	498	880	2	24	16	3	0	0	0	–	87	129	8	13	0.9	.964

Year	Team	W	L	PCT	ERA	G	GS	CG	IP	H	BB	SO	ShO	Relief Pitching W	L	SV	Batting AB	H	HR	BA	PO	A	E	DP	TC/G	FA

Goose Gossage

GOSSAGE, RICHARD MICHAEL
B. July 5, 1951, Colorado Springs, Colo.
BR TR 6'3" 180 lbs.

Year	Team	W	L	PCT	ERA	G	GS	CG	IP	H	BB	SO	ShO	W	L	SV	AB	H	HR	BA	PO	A	E	DP	TC/G	FA
1972	CHI A	7	1	.875	4.28	36	1	0	80	72	44	57	0	7	0	2	16	0	0	.000	3	10	1	1	0.4	.929
1973		0	4	.000	7.43	20	4	1	49.2	57	37	33	0	0	0	0	0	0	0	–	5	5	1	0	0.6	.909
1974		4	6	.400	4.15	39	3	0	89	92	47	64	0	4	5	1	0	0	0	–	3	14	2	1	0.5	.895
1975		9	8	.529	1.84	62	0	0	141.2	99	70	130	0	9	8	26	0	0	0	–	3	25	3	3	0.5	.903
1976		9	17	.346	3.94	31	29	15	224	214	90	135	0	0	1	1	0	0	0	–	18	27	3	1	1.5	.938
1977	PIT N	11	9	.550	1.62	72	0	0	133	78	49	151	0	**11**	9	26	23	5	0	.217	4	10	1	0	0.2	.933
1978	NY A	10	11	.476	2.01	63	0	0	134.1	87	59	122	0	10	11	**27**	0	0	0	–	6	12	3	0	0.3	.857
1979		5	3	.625	2.64	36	0	0	58	48	19	41	0	5	3	18	0	0	0	–	1	4	0	0	0.1	1.000
1980		6	2	.750	2.27	64	0	0	99	74	37	103	0	6	2	**33**	0	0	0	–	1	10	2	0	0.2	.846
1981		3	2	.600	0.77	32	0	0	47	22	14	48	0	3	2	20	0	0	0	–	2	7	1	1	0.3	.900
1982		4	5	.444	2.23	56	0	0	93	63	28	102	0	4	5	30	0	0	0	–	2	6	0	1	0.1	1.000
1983		13	5	.722	2.27	57	0	0	87.1	82	25	90	0	13	5	22	0	0	0	–	2	3	1	0	0.1	.833
1984	SD N	10	6	.625	2.90	62	0	0	102.1	75	36	84	0	10	6	25	22	4	0	.182	5	8	0	0	0.2	1.000
1985		5	3	.625	1.82	50	0	0	79	64	17	52	0	5	3	26	11	0	0	.000	5	7	0	1	0.2	1.000
1986		5	7	.417	4.45	45	0	0	64.2	69	20	63	0	5	7	21	7	0	0	.000	2	5	0	0	0.2	1.000
1987		5	4	.556	3.12	40	0	0	52	47	19	44	0	5	4	11	4	0	0	.000	2	5	0	0	0.2	1.000
1988	CHI N	4	4	.500	4.33	46	0	0	43.2	50	15	30	0	4	4	13	1	0	0	.000	1	7	0	0	0.2	1.000
1989	2 teams	SF N	(31G 2–1)		NY A	(11G 1–0)																				
"	total	3	1	.750	2.95	42	0	0	58	46	30	30	0	3	1	5	0	0	0	.000	7	4	1	1	0.3	.917
1991	TEX A	4	2	.667	3.57	44	0	0	40.1	33	16	28	0	4	2	1	0	0	0	–	2	2	1	0	0.1	.800
1992	OAK A	0	2	.000	2.84	30	0	0	38	32	19	26	0	0	2	0	0	0	0	–	2	4	0	0	0.2	1.000
1993		4	5	.444	4.53	39	0	0	47.2	49	26	40	0	4	5	1	0	0	0	–	5	3	1	0	0.2	.889
1994	SEA A	3	0	1.000	4.18	36	0	0	47.1	44	15	29	0	3	0	1	0	0	0	–	2	2	0	1	0.1	1.000
22 yrs.		124	107	.537	3.01 **3rd**	1002	37	16	1809	1497	732	1502	0	115 **3rd**	85	310 **4th**	85	9	0	.106	78	180	21	11	0.3	.925

DIVISIONAL PLAYOFF SERIES

Year	Team	W	L	PCT	ERA	G	GS	CG	IP	H	BB	SO	ShO	W	L	SV	AB	H	HR	BA	PO	A	E	DP	TC/G	FA
1981	NY A	0	0	–	0.00	3	0	0	6.2	3	2	8	0	0	0	3	0	0	0	–	0	0	0	0	0.0	–

LEAGUE CHAMPIONSHIP SERIES

Year	Team	W	L	PCT	ERA	G	GS	CG	IP	H	BB	SO	ShO	W	L	SV	AB	H	HR	BA	PO	A	E	DP	TC/G	FA
1978	NY A	1	0	1.000	4.50	2	0	0	4	3	0	3	0	1	0	1	0	0	0	–	0	1	0	0	0.5	1.000
1980		0	1	.000	54.00	1	0	0	0.1	3	0	0	0	0	1	0	0	0	0	–	0	0	0	0	0.0	–
1981		0	0	–	0.00	2	0	0	2.2	1	0	2	0	0	0	1	0	0	0	–	0	0	0	0	0.0	–
1984	SD N	0	0	–	4.50	3	0	0	4	5	1	5	0	0	0	1	0	0	0	–	0	0	0	0	0.0	–
4 yrs.		1	1	.500	4.91	8	0	0	11	12	1	10	0	1	1	3	0	0	0	–	0	1	0	0	0.1	1.000

WORLD SERIES

Year	Team	W	L	PCT	ERA	G	GS	CG	IP	H	BB	SO	ShO	W	L	SV	AB	H	HR	BA	PO	A	E	DP	TC/G	FA
1978	NY A	1	0	1.000	0.00	3	0	0	6	1	1	4	0	1	0	1	0	0	0	–	0	0	0	0	0.0	–
1981		0	0	–	0.00	3	0	0	5	2	2	5	0	0	0	2	1	0	0	.000	0	0	0	0	0.0	–
1984	SD N	0	0	–	13.50	2	0	0	2.2	3	1	2	0	0	0	0	0	0	0	–	0	1	0	0	0.5	1.000
3 yrs.		1	0	1.000	2.63	8	0	0	13.2	6	4	11	0	1	0	2	1	0	0	.000	0	1	0	0	0.1	1.000

Jim Gott

GOTT, JAMES WILLIAM
B. Aug. 3, 1959, Hollywood, Calif.
BR TR 6'4" 200 lbs.

Year	Team	W	L	PCT	ERA	G	GS	CG	IP	H	BB	SO	ShO	W	L	SV	AB	H	HR	BA	PO	A	E	DP	TC/G	FA
1982	TOR A	5	10	.333	4.43	30	23	1	136	134	66	82	1	0	0	0	0	0	0	–	6	18	1	2	0.8	.960
1983		9	14	.391	4.74	34	30	6	176.2	195	68	121	1	0	1	0	0	0	0	–	9	20	1	2	0.9	.967
1984		7	6	.538	4.02	35	12	1	109.2	93	49	73	1	2	1	2	0	0	0	–	6	9	1	0	0.5	.938
1985	SF N	7	10	.412	3.88	26	26	2	148.1	144	51	78	0	0	0	0	51	10	3	.196	9	28	0	1	1.4	1.000
1986		0	0	–	7.62	9	2	0	13	16	13	9	0	0	0	1	3	0	0	.000	0	2	0	0	0.2	1.000
1987	2 teams	SF N	(30G 1–0)		PIT N	(25G 0–2)																				
"	total	1	2	.333	3.41	55	3	0	87	81	40	90	0	1	2	13	11	1	1	.091	5	10	1	0	0.3	.938
1988	PIT N	6	6	.500	3.49	67	0	0	77.1	68	22	76	0	6	6	34	1	0	0	.000	4	8	0	0	0.2	1.000
1989		0	0	–	0.00	1	0	0	0.2	1	1	1	0	0	0	0	0	0	0	–	0	0	0	0	0.0	–
1990	LA N	3	5	.375	2.90	50	0	0	62	59	34	44	0	3	5	3	1	0	0	.000	6	5	0	0	0.2	1.000
1991		4	3	.571	2.96	55	0	0	76	63	32	73	0	4	3	2	2	1	0	.500	10	9	0	1	0.3	1.000
1992		3	3	.500	2.45	68	0	0	88	72	41	75	0	3	3	6	2	1	0	.500	11	15	0	0	0.4	1.000
1993		4	8	.333	2.32	62	0	0	77.2	71	17	67	0	4	8	25	1	0	0	.000	8	8	0	1	0.3	1.000
1994		5	3	.625	5.94	37	0	0	36.1	46	20	29	0	5	3	2	0	0	0	–	3	6	2	1	0.3	.818
13 yrs.		54	70	.435	3.80	529	96	10	1088.2	1043	454	818	3	28	32	88	72	13	4	.181	77	138	6	7	0.4	.973

Mauro Gozzo

GOZZO, MAURO PAUL (Goose)
B. Mar. 7, 1966, New Britain, Conn.
BR TR 6'2" 210 lbs.

Year	Team	W	L	PCT	ERA	G	GS	CG	IP	H	BB	SO	ShO	W	L	SV	AB	H	HR	BA	PO	A	E	DP	TC/G	FA
1989	TOR A	4	1	.800	4.83	9	3	0	31.2	35	9	10	0	1	1	0	0	0	0	–	3	3	0	0	0.7	1.000
1990	CLE A	0	0	–	0.00	2	0	0	3	2	2	2	0	0	0	0	0	0	0	–	0	0	0	0	0.0	–
1991		0	0	–	19.29	2	2	0	4.2	9	7	3	0	0	0	0	0	0	0	–	0	0	0	0	0.0	–
1992	MIN A	0	0	–	27.00	2	0	0	1.2	7	0	1	0	0	0	0	0	0	0	–	0	0	0	0	0.0	–
1993	NY N	0	1	.000	2.57	10	0	0	14	11	5	6	0	0	1	1	0	0	0	–	0	0	0	0	0.0	–
1994		3	5	.375	4.83	23	8	0	69	86	28	33	0	1	2	0	16	4	0	.250	3	9	0	0	0.5	1.000
6 yrs.		7	7	.500	5.30	48	13	0	124	150	51	55	0	2	4	1	16	4	0	.250	6	12	0	0	0.4	1.000

Joe Grahe

GRAHE, JOSEPH MILTON
B. Aug. 14, 1967, West Palm Beach, Fla.
BR TR 6'1" 196 lbs.

Year	Team	W	L	PCT	ERA	G	GS	CG	IP	H	BB	SO	ShO	W	L	SV	AB	H	HR	BA	PO	A	E	DP	TC/G	FA
1990	CAL A	3	4	.429	4.98	8	8	0	43.1	51	23	25	0	0	0	0	0	0	0	–	2	11	0	2	1.6	1.000
1991		3	7	.300	4.81	18	10	1	73	84	33	40	0	1	0	0	0	0	0	–	4	11	1	0	0.9	.938
1992		5	6	.455	3.52	46	7	0	94.2	85	39	39	0	3	3	21	0	0	0	–	12	13	3	1	0.6	.893
1993		4	1	.800	2.86	45	0	0	56.2	54	25	31	0	4	1	11	0	0	0	–	3	13	0	1	0.4	1.000
1994		2	5	.286	6.65	40	0	0	43.1	68	18	26	0	2	5	13	0	0	0	–	3	8	0	0	0.3	1.000
5 yrs.		17	23	.425	4.34	157	25	1	311	342	138	161	0	10	9	45	0	0	0	–	24	56	4	4	0.5	.952

Jeff Granger

GRANGER, JEFFREY ADAM
B. Dec. 16, 1971, San Pedro, Calif.
BR TL 6'4" 200 lbs.

Year	Team	W	L	PCT	ERA	G	GS	CG	IP	H	BB	SO	ShO	W	L	SV	AB	H	HR	BA	PO	A	E	DP	TC/G	FA
1993	KC A	0	0	–	27.00	1	0	0	1	3	2	1	0	0	0	0	0	0	0	–	0	0	0	0	0.0	–
1994		0	1	.000	6.75	2	2	0	9.1	13	6	3	0	0	0	0	0	0	0	–	2	0	0	0	1.0	1.000
2 yrs.		0	1	.000	8.71	3	2	0	10.1	16	8	4	0	0	0	0	0	0	0	–	2	0	0	0	0.7	1.000

Year	Team	W	L	PCT	ERA	G	GS	CG	IP	H	BB	SO	ShO	Relief Pitching W	L	SV	Batting AB	H	HR	BA	PO	A	E	DP	TC/G	FA

Tommy Greene
GREENE, IRA THOMAS
B. Apr. 6, 1967, Lumberton, N. C. BR TR 6'5" 225 lbs.

Year	Team	W	L	PCT	ERA	G	GS	CG	IP	H	BB	SO	ShO	W	L	SV	AB	H	HR	BA	PO	A	E	DP	TC/G	FA
1989	ATL N	1	2	.333	4.10	4	4	1	26.1	22	6	17	1	0	0	0	10	1	0	.100	2	2	0	0	1.0	1.000
1990	2 teams	ATL N	(5G 1–0)		PHI N	(10G 2–3)																				
"	total	3	3	.500	5.08	15	9	0	51.1	50	26	21	0	0	0	0	12	2	0	.167	3	6	1	0	0.7	.900
1991	PHI N	13	7	.650	3.38	36	27	3	207.2	177	66	154	2	1	0	0	71	19	2	.268	14	16	1	0	0.9	.968
1992		3	3	.500	5.32	13	12	0	64.1	75	34	39	0	0	0	0	24	3	0	.125	3	7	3	0	1.0	.769
1993		16	4	.800	3.42	31	30	7	200	175	62	167	2	0	0	0	72	16	2	.222	5	23	1	3	0.9	.966
1994		2	0	1.000	4.54	7	7	0	35.2	37	22	28	0	0	0	0	13	5	0	.385	1	4	0	2	0.7	1.000
6 yrs.		38	19	.667	3.86	106	89	11	585.1	536	216	426	5	1	0	0	202	46	4	.228	28	58	6	5	0.9	.935

LEAGUE CHAMPIONSHIP SERIES

| 1993 | PHI N | 1 | 1 | .500 | 9.64 | 2 | 2 | 0 | 9.1 | 12 | 7 | 7 | 0 | 0 | 0 | 0 | 0 | 0 | 0 | – | 0 | 3 | 0 | 0 | 1.5 | 1.000 |

WORLD SERIES

| 1993 | PHI N | 0 | 0 | – | 27.00 | 1 | 1 | 0 | 2.1 | 7 | 4 | 1 | 0 | 0 | 0 | 0 | 1 | 1 | 0 | 1.000 | 0 | 0 | 0 | 0 | 0.0 | – |

Jason Grimsley
GRIMSLEY, JASON ALAN
B. Aug. 7, 1967, Cleveland, Tex. BR TR 6'3" 180 lbs.

Year	Team	W	L	PCT	ERA	G	GS	CG	IP	H	BB	SO	ShO	W	L	SV	AB	H	HR	BA	PO	A	E	DP	TC/G	FA
1989	PHI N	1	3	.250	5.89	4	4	0	18.1	19	19	7	0	0	0	0	5	0	0	.000	1	4	1	1	1.5	.833
1990		3	2	.600	3.30	11	11	0	57.1	47	43	41	0	0	0	0	16	3	0	.188	13	8	1	2	2.0	.955
1991		1	7	.125	4.87	12	12	0	61	54	41	42	0	0	0	0	17	1	0	.059	2	14	1	3	1.4	.941
1993	CLE A	3	4	.429	5.31	10	6	0	42.1	52	20	27	0	1	2	0	0	0	0	–	4	4	0	0	0.8	1.000
1994		5	2	.714	4.57	14	13	1	82.2	91	34	59	0	0	0	0	0	0	0	–	6	9	0	1	1.1	1.000
5 yrs.		13	18	.419	4.57	51	46	1	261.2	263	157	176	0	1	2	0	38	4	0	.105	26	39	3	7	1.3	.956

Buddy Groom
GROOM, WEDSEL GARY
B. July 10, 1965, Dallas, Tex. BL TL 6'2" 200 lbs.

Year	Team	W	L	PCT	ERA	G	GS	CG	IP	H	BB	SO	ShO	W	L	SV	AB	H	HR	BA	PO	A	E	DP	TC/G	FA
1992	DET A	0	5	.000	5.82	12	7	0	38.2	48	22	15	0	0	0	1	0	0	0	–	0	6	0	0	0.5	1.000
1993		0	2	.000	6.14	19	3	0	36.2	48	13	15	0	0	1	0	0	0	0	–	1	7	1	0	0.5	.889
1994		0	1	.000	3.94	40	0	0	32	31	13	27	0	0	1	1	0	0	0	–	0	0	0	0	0.0	–
3 yrs.		0	8	.000	5.37	71	10	0	107.1	127	48	57	0	0	2	2	0	0	0	–	1	13	1	0	0.2	.933

Kevin Gross
GROSS, KEVIN FRANK
B. June 8, 1961, Downey, Calif. BR TR 6'5" 200 lbs.

Year	Team	W	L	PCT	ERA	G	GS	CG	IP	H	BB	SO	ShO	W	L	SV	AB	H	HR	BA	PO	A	E	DP	TC/G	FA
1983	PHI N	4	6	.400	3.56	17	17	1	96	100	35	66	1	0	0	0	33	3	0	.091	11	13	0	0	1.4	1.000
1984		8	5	.615	4.12	44	14	1	129	140	44	84	0	4	0	1	30	2	0	.067	9	22	2	3	0.8	.939
1985		15	13	.536	3.41	38	31	6	205.2	194	81	151	2	1	2	0	65	9	1	.138	18	34	3	0	1.4	.945
1986		12	12	.500	4.02	37	36	7	241.2	240	94	154	2	0	0	0	80	15	2	.188	25	28	2	2	1.5	.964
1987		9	16	.360	4.35	34	33	3	200.2	205	87	110	1	1	0	0	63	12	1	.190	13	23	3	1	1.1	.923
1988		12	14	.462	3.69	33	33	5	231.2	209	89	162	1	0	0	0	75	13	0	.173	13	34	2	2	1.5	.959
1989	MON N	11	12	.478	4.38	31	31	4	201.1	188	88	158	3	0	0	0	64	9	0	.141	15	25	2	1	1.4	.952
1990		9	12	.429	4.57	31	26	2	163.1	171	65	111	1	0	0	0	50	10	1	.200	6	13	1	0	0.6	.950
1991	LA N	10	11	.476	3.58	46	10	0	115.2	123	50	95	0	6	6	3	25	7	0	.280	9	14	1	0	0.5	.958
1992		8	13	.381	3.17	34	30	4	204.2	182	77	158	3	0	0	0	63	6	0	.095	11	25	1	2	1.1	.973
1993		13	13	.500	4.14	33	32	3	202.1	224	74	150	0	0	0	0	64	13	1	.203	11	40	0	1	1.5	1.000
1994		9	7	.563	3.60	25	23	1	157.1	162	43	124	0	0	0	1	47	7	1	.149	14	29	1	1	1.8	.977
12 yrs.		120	134	.472	3.89	403	316	37	2149.1	2138	827	1523	14	13	9	5	659	106	6	.161	155	300	18	13	1.2	.962

Eddie Guardado
GUARDADO, EDWARD ADRIAN
B. Oct. 2, 1970, Stockton, Calif. BR TL 6' 195 lbs.

Year	Team	W	L	PCT	ERA	G	GS	CG	IP	H	BB	SO	ShO	W	L	SV	AB	H	HR	BA	PO	A	E	DP	TC/G	FA
1993	MIN A	3	8	.273	6.18	19	16	0	94.2	123	36	46	0	0	0	0	0	0	0	–	6	9	0	1	0.8	1.000
1994		0	2	.000	8.47	4	4	0	17	26	4	8	0	0	0	0	0	0	0	–	0	0	0	0	0.0	–
2 yrs.		3	10	.231	6.53	23	20	0	111.2	149	40	54	0	0	0	0	0	0	0	–	6	9	0	1	0.7	1.000

Mark Gubicza
GUBICZA, MARK STEVEN
B. Aug. 14, 1962, Philadelphia, Pa. BR TR 6'6" 215 lbs.

Year	Team	W	L	PCT	ERA	G	GS	CG	IP	H	BB	SO	ShO	W	L	SV	AB	H	HR	BA	PO	A	E	DP	TC/G	FA
1984	KC A	10	14	.417	4.05	29	29	4	189	172	75	111	2	0	0	0	0	0	0	–	19	31	2	1	1.8	.962
1985		14	10	.583	4.06	29	28	0	177.1	160	77	99	0	1	0	0	0	0	0	–	23	26	0	4	1.7	1.000
1986		12	6	.667	3.64	35	24	3	180.2	155	84	118	0	1	1	0	0	0	0	–	17	32	0	3	1.4	1.000
1987		13	18	.419	3.98	35	35	10	241.2	231	120	166	2	0	0	0	0	0	0	–	32	40	2	7	2.1	.973
1988		20	8	.714	2.70	35	35	8	269.2	237	83	183	4	0	0	0	0	0	0	–	29	44	1	3	2.1	.986
1989		15	11	.577	3.04	36	36	8	255	252	63	173	2	0	0	0	0	0	0	–	18	49	5	0	2.0	.931
1990		4	7	.364	4.50	16	16	2	94	101	38	71	0	0	0	0	0	0	0	–	9	10	1	3	1.3	.950
1991		9	12	.429	5.68	26	26	0	133	168	42	89	0	0	0	0	0	0	0	–	8	29	3	5	1.5	.925
1992		7	6	.538	3.72	18	18	2	111.1	110	36	81	1	0	0	0	0	0	0	–	10	12	0	2	1.2	1.000
1993		5	8	.385	4.66	49	6	0	104.1	128	43	80	0	5	4	2	0	0	0	–	11	7	1	0	0.4	.947
1994		7	9	.438	4.50	22	22	0	130	158	26	59	0	0	0	0	0	0	0	–	17	20	3	1	1.8	.925
11 yrs.		116	109	.516	3.86	330	275	37	1886	1872	687	1230	13	7	5	2	0	0	0	–	193	300	18	29	1.5	.965

LEAGUE CHAMPIONSHIP SERIES

| 1985 | KC A | 1 | 0 | 1.000 | 3.24 | 2 | 1 | 0 | 8.1 | 4 | 4 | 4 | 0 | 0 | 0 | 0 | 0 | 0 | 0 | – | 0 | 1 | 0 | 1 | 0.5 | 1.000 |

Bill Gullickson
GULLICKSON, WILLIAM LEE
B. Feb. 20, 1959, Marshall, Minn. BR TR 6'3" 200 lbs.

Year	Team	W	L	PCT	ERA	G	GS	CG	IP	H	BB	SO	ShO	W	L	SV	AB	H	HR	BA	PO	A	E	DP	TC/G	FA
1979	MON N	0	0	–	0.00	1	0	0	1	2	0	0	0	0	0	0	0	0	0	–	0	0	0	0	0.0	–
1980		10	5	.667	3.00	24	19	5	141	127	50	120	2	0	1	0	40	7	0	.175	4	21	1	2	1.1	.962
1981		7	9	.438	2.81	22	22	3	157	142	34	115	2	0	0	0	46	7	0	.152	12	16	1	2	1.3	.966
1982		12	14	.462	3.57	34	34	6	236.2	231	61	155	0	0	0	0	82	10	0	.122	16	18	3	1	1.1	.919
1983		17	12	.586	3.75	34	34	10	242.1	230	59	120	1	0	0	0	82	11	1	.134	27	25	1	3	1.6	.981
1984		12	9	.571	3.61	32	32	3	226.2	230	37	100	0	0	0	0	73	8	0	.110	14	19	4	2	1.2	.892
1985		14	12	.538	3.52	29	29	4	181.1	187	47	68	1	0	0	0	64	12	0	.188	10	26	1	0	1.3	.973

Year	Team	W	L	PCT	ERA	G	GS	CG	IP	H	BB	SO	ShO	W	L	SV	AB	H	HR	BA	PO	A	E	DP	TC/G	FA

Bill Gullickson *continued*

Year	Team	W	L	PCT	ERA	G	GS	CG	IP	H	BB	SO	ShO	W	L	SV	AB	H	HR	BA	PO	A	E	DP	TC/G	FA
1986	CIN N	15	12	.556	3.38	37	37	6	244.2	245	60	121	2	0	0	0	79	6	0	.076	14	32	3	3	1.3	.939
1987	2 teams	CIN N	(27G 10–11)		NY A	(8G 4–2)																				
"	total	14	13	.519	4.86	35	35	4	213	218	50	117	1	0	0	0	53	11	1	.208	16	21	0	0	1.1	1.000
1990	HOU N	10	14	.417	3.82	32	32	2	193.1	221	61	73	1	0	0	0	57	9	1	.158	11	13	0	1	0.8	1.000
1991	DET A	20	9	.690	3.90	35	35	2	226.1	256	44	91	0	0	0	0	0	0	0	–	14	21	0	0	1.0	1.000
1992		14	13	.519	4.34	34	34	4	221.2	228	50	64	1	0	0	0	0	0	0	–	21	26	1	3	1.4	.979
1993		13	9	.591	5.37	28	28	2	159.1	186	44	70	0	0	0	0	0	0	0	–	11	24	0	1	1.3	1.000
1994		4	5	.444	5.93	21	19	1	115.1	156	25	65	0	0	0	0	0	0	0	–	15	14	1	0	1.4	.967
14 yrs.		162	136	.544	3.93	398	390	54	2559.2	2659	622	1279	11	0	1	0	576	81	3	.141	185	276	16	18	1.2	.966

DIVISIONAL PLAYOFF SERIES

Year	Team	W	L	PCT	ERA	G	GS	CG	IP	H	BB	SO	ShO	W	L	SV	AB	H	HR	BA	PO	A	E	DP	TC/G	FA
1981	MON N	1	0	1.000	1.17	1	1	0	7.2	6	1	3	0	0	0	0	3	0	0	.000	0	0	0	0	0.0	–

LEAGUE CHAMPIONSHIP SERIES

Year	Team	W	L	PCT	ERA	G	GS	CG	IP	H	BB	SO	ShO	W	L	SV	AB	H	HR	BA	PO	A	E	DP	TC/G	FA
1981	MON N	0	2	.000	2.51	2	2	0	14.1	12	6	12	0	0	0	0	3	0	0	.000	0	2	0	0	1.0	1.000

Eric Gunderson

GUNDERSON, ERIC ANDREW
B. Mar. 29, 1966, Portland, Ore.

BR TL 6'   175 lbs.

Year	Team	W	L	PCT	ERA	G	GS	CG	IP	H	BB	SO	ShO	W	L	SV	AB	H	HR	BA	PO	A	E	DP	TC/G	FA
1990	SF N	1	2	.333	5.49	7	4	0	19.2	14	11	14	0	0	0	0	6	0	0	.000	0	4	0	0	0.6	1.000
1991		0	0	–	5.40	2	0	0	3.1	6	1	2	0	0	0	1	0	0	0	–	0	1	0	0	0.5	1.000
1992	SEA A	2	1	.667	8.68	9	0	0	9.1	12	5	2	0	2	1	0	0	0	0	–	1	2	0	0	0.3	1.000
1994	NY N	0	0	–	0.00	14	0	0	9	5	4	4	0	0	0	0	0	0	0	–	0	1	0	0	0.1	1.000
4 yrs.		3	3	.500	5.01	32	4	0	41.1	47	21	22	0	2	1	1	6	0	0	.000	1	8	0	0	0.3	1.000

Mark Guthrie

GUTHRIE, MARK ANDREW
B. Sept. 22, 1965, Buffalo, N. Y.

BB TR 6'4"   192 lbs.

Year	Team	W	L	PCT	ERA	G	GS	CG	IP	H	BB	SO	ShO	W	L	SV	AB	H	HR	BA	PO	A	E	DP	TC/G	FA
1989	MIN A	2	4	.333	4.55	13	8	0	57.1	66	21	38	0	0	0	0	0	0	0	–	2	8	0	0	0.8	1.000
1990		7	9	.438	3.79	24	21	3	144.2	154	39	101	1	1	0	0	0	0	0	–	5	23	1	0	1.2	.966
1991		7	5	.583	4.32	41	12	0	98	116	41	72	0	2	1	2	0	0	0	–	5	10	1	0	0.4	.938
1992		2	3	.400	2.88	54	0	0	75	59	23	76	0	2	3	5	0	0	0	–	4	6	1	0	0.2	.909
1993		2	1	.667	4.71	22	0	0	21	20	16	15	0	2	1	0	0	0	0	–	0	5	0	0	0.2	1.000
1994		4	2	.667	6.14	50	2	0	51.1	65	18	38	0	4	1	1	0	0	0	–	3	8	0	0	0.2	1.000
6 yrs.		24	24	.500	4.16	204	43	3	447.1	480	158	340	1	11	6	8	0	0	0	–	19	60	3	0	0.4	.963

LEAGUE CHAMPIONSHIP SERIES

Year	Team	W	L	PCT	ERA	G	GS	CG	IP	H	BB	SO	ShO	W	L	SV	AB	H	HR	BA	PO	A	E	DP	TC/G	FA
1991	MIN A	1	0	1.000	0.00	2	0	0	2.2	0	1	0	0	1	0	0	0	0	0	–	0	1	0	0	0.5	1.000

WORLD SERIES

Year	Team	W	L	PCT	ERA	G	GS	CG	IP	H	BB	SO	ShO	W	L	SV	AB	H	HR	BA	PO	A	E	DP	TC/G	FA
1991	MIN A	0	1	.000	2.25	4	0	0	4	3	4	3	0	0	1	0	0	0	0	–	0	1	0	0	0.3	1.000

Jose Guzman

GUZMAN, JOSE ALBERTO
Born Jose Alberto Guzman (Mirabel).
B. Apr. 9, 1963, Santa Isabel, Puerto Rico.

BR TR 6'2"   172 lbs.

Year	Team	W	L	PCT	ERA	G	GS	CG	IP	H	BB	SO	ShO	W	L	SV	AB	H	HR	BA	PO	A	E	DP	TC/G	FA
1985	TEX A	3	2	.600	2.76	5	5	0	32.2	27	14	24	0	0	0	0	0	0	0	–	0	5	0	0	1.0	1.000
1986		9	15	.375	4.54	29	29	2	172.1	199	60	87	0	0	0	0	0	0	0	–	13	24	0	0	1.3	1.000
1987		14	14	.500	4.67	37	37	6	208.1	196	82	143	0	3	0	0	0	0	0	–	14	34	2	3	1.4	.960
1988		11	13	.458	3.70	30	30	6	206.2	180	82	157	2	0	0	0	0	0	0	–	15	24	3	1	1.4	.929
1991		13	7	.650	3.08	25	25	5	169.2	152	84	125	1	0	0	0	0	0	0	–	12	32	1	2	1.8	.978
1992		16	11	.593	3.66	33	33	5	224	229	73	179	0	0	0	0	0	0	0	–	16	22	1	3	1.2	.974
1993	CHI N	12	10	.545	4.34	30	30	2	191	188	74	163	0	0	0	0	63	7	0	.111	12	28	5	1	1.5	.889
1994		2	2	.500	9.15	4	4	0	19.2	22	13	11	0	0	0	0	8	0	0	.000	1	0	0	0	0.5	1.000
8 yrs.		80	74	.519	4.05	193	186	26	1224.1	1193	482	889	4	3	0	0	71	7	0	.099	83	170	12	10	1.4	.955

Juan Guzman

GUZMAN, JUAN ANDRES
Born Juan Andres Guzman (Correa).
B. Oct. 28, 1966, Santo Domingo, Dominican Republic.

BR TR 5'11"   190 lbs.

Year	Team	W	L	PCT	ERA	G	GS	CG	IP	H	BB	SO	ShO	W	L	SV	AB	H	HR	BA	PO	A	E	DP	TC/G	FA
1991	TOR A	10	3	.769	2.99	23	23	1	138.2	98	66	123	0	0	0	0	0	0	0	–	5	9	3	1	0.7	.824
1992		16	5	.762	2.64	28	28	1	180.2	135	72	165	0	0	0	0	0	0	0	–	12	11	0	0	0.8	1.000
1993		14	3	.824	3.99	33	33	2	221	211	110	194	1	0	0	0	0	0	0	–	11	16	1	0	0.8	.964
1994		12	11	.522	5.68	25	25	2	147.1	165	76	124	0	0	0	0	0	0	0	–	5	12	2	1	0.8	.895
4 yrs.		52	22	.703	3.80	109	109	6	687.2	609	324	606	1	0	0	0	0	0	0	–	33	48	6	2	0.8	.931

LEAGUE CHAMPIONSHIP SERIES

Year	Team	W	L	PCT	ERA	G	GS	CG	IP	H	BB	SO	ShO	W	L	SV	AB	H	HR	BA	PO	A	E	DP	TC/G	FA
1991	TOR A	1	0	1.000	3.18	1	1	0	5.2	4	4	2	0	0	0	0	0	0	0	–	0	0	0	0	0.0	–
1992		2	0	1.000	2.08	2	2	0	13	12	5	11	0	0	0	0	0	0	0	–	0	0	0	0	0.0	–
1993		2	0	1.000	2.08	2	2	0	13	8	9	9	0	0	0	0	0	0	0	–	0	4	0	0	2.0	1.000
3 yrs.		5	0	1.000	2.27	5	5	0	31.2	24	18	22	0	0	0	0	0	0	0	–	0	4	0	0	0.8	1.000

WORLD SERIES

Year	Team	W	L	PCT	ERA	G	GS	CG	IP	H	BB	SO	ShO	W	L	SV	AB	H	HR	BA	PO	A	E	DP	TC/G	FA
1992	TOR A	0	0	–	1.13	1	1	0	8	8	1	7	0	0	0	0	0	0	0	–	2	0	0	0	2.0	1.000
1993		0	1	.000	3.75	2	2	0	12	10	8	12	0	0	0	0	2	0	0	.000	0	1	0	0	0.5	1.000
2 yrs.		0	1	.000	2.70	3	3	0	20	18	9	19	0	0	0	0	2	0	0	.000	2	1	0	0	1.000

John Habyan

HABYAN, JOHN GABRIEL
B. Jan. 29, 1964, Bay Shore, N. Y.

BR TR 6'1"   195 lbs.

Year	Team	W	L	PCT	ERA	G	GS	CG	IP	H	BB	SO	ShO	W	L	SV	AB	H	HR	BA	PO	A	E	DP	TC/G	FA
1985	BAL A	1	0	1.000	0.00	2	0	0	2	3	3	2	0	1	0	0	0	0	0	–	1	0	0	0	0.5	1.000
1986		1	3	.250	4.44	6	5	0	26.1	24	18	14	0	0	0	0	0	0	0	–	1	3	0	0	0.7	1.000
1987		6	7	.462	4.80	27	13	0	116.1	110	40	64	0	4	0	1	0	0	0	–	15	17	0	2	1.2	1.000
1988		1	0	1.000	4.30	7	0	0	14.2	22	4	4	0	1	0	0	0	0	0	–	5	1	0	0	0.9	1.000
1990	NY A	0	0	–	2.08	6	0	0	8.2	10	2	7	0	0	0	0	0	0	0	–	2	1	0	0	0.5	1.000
1991		4	2	.667	2.30	66	0	0	90	73	20	70	0	4	2	2	0	0	0	–	6	12	0	0	0.3	1.000
1992		5	6	.455	3.84	56	0	0	72.2	84	21	44	0	5	6	7	0	0	0	–	3	15	0	1	0.3	1.000
1993	2 teams	NY A	(36G 2–1)		KC A	(12G 0–0)																				
"	total	2	1	.667	4.15	48	0	0	56.1	59	20	39	0	2	1	1	0	0	0	–	5	7	0	0	0.3	1.000
1994	STL N	1	0	1.000	3.23	52	0	0	47.1	50	20	46	0	1	0	1	0	0	0	–	4	8	1	0	0.3	.923
9 yrs.		21	19	.525	3.74	270	18	0	435	435	145	287	0	18	9	12	0	0	0	–	42	63	1	3	0.4	.991

Year	Team	W	L	PCT	ERA	G	GS	CG	IP	H	BB	SO	ShO	Relief Pitching W	L	SV	Batting AB	H	HR	BA	PO	A	E	DP	TC/G	FA

Darren Hall
HALL, MICHAEL DARREN
B. July 14, 1964, Marysville, Ohio — BR TR 6'3" 205 lbs.

Year	Team	W	L	PCT	ERA	G	GS	CG	IP	H	BB	SO	ShO	W	L	SV	AB	H	HR	BA	PO	A	E	DP	TC/G	FA
1994	TOR A	2	3	.400	3.41	30	0	0	31.2	26	14	28	0	2	3	17	0	0	0	–	2	6	0	2	0.3	1.000

Joey Hamilton
HAMILTON, JOHNS JOSEPH
B. Sept. 9, 1970, Statesboro, Ga. — BR TR 6'4" 220 lbs.

Year	Team	W	L	PCT	ERA	G	GS	CG	IP	H	BB	SO	ShO	W	L	SV	AB	H	HR	BA	PO	A	E	DP	TC/G	FA
1994	SD N	9	6	.600	2.98	16	16	1	108.2	98	29	61	1	0	0	0	40	0	0	.000	7	16	1	3	1.5	.958

Atlee Hammaker
HAMMAKER, CHARLTON ATLEE
B. Jan. 24, 1958, Carmel, Calif. — BB TL 6'3" 200 lbs.

Year	Team	W	L	PCT	ERA	G	GS	CG	IP	H	BB	SO	ShO	W	L	SV	AB	H	HR	BA	PO	A	E	DP	TC/G	FA
1981	KC A	1	3	.250	5.54	10	6	0	39	44	12	11	0	0	0	0	0	0	0	–	1	4	0	1	0.5	1.000
1982	SF N	12	8	.600	4.11	29	27	4	175	189	28	102	1	0	0	0	59	4	0	.068	5	35	1	0	1.4	.976
1983		10	9	.526	**2.25**	23	23	8	172.1	147	32	127	3	0	0	0	59	6	0	.102	3	31	3	2	1.6	.919
1984		2	0	1.000	2.18	6	6	0	33	32	9	24	0	0	0	0	11	2	0	.182	0	6	0	0	1.0	1.000
1985		5	12	.294	3.74	29	29	1	170.2	161	47	100	1	0	0	0	47	4	0	.085	6	32	1	1	1.3	.974
1987		10	10	.500	3.58	31	27	2	168.1	159	57	107	0	1	0	0	57	7	0	.123	7	23	0	1	1.0	1.000
1988		9	9	.500	3.73	43	17	3	144.2	136	41	65	1	4	2	5	33	4	0	.121	7	33	0	3	0.9	1.000
1989		6	6	.500	3.76	28	9	0	76.2	78	23	30	0	3	3	0	19	7	0	.368	3	9	1	0	0.5	.923
1990	2 teams	SF N	(25G 4–5)			SD N	(9G 0–4)																			
"	total	4	9	.308	4.36	34	7	0	86.2	85	27	44	0	1	6	0	19	2	0	.105	6	7	0	2	0.4	1.000
1991	SD N	0	1	.000	5.79	1	1	0	4.2	8	3	1	0	0	0	0	1	0	0	.000	0	1	0	0	1.0	1.000
1994	CHI A	0	0	–	0.00	2	0	0	1.1	1	0	1	0	0	0	0	0	0	0	–	0	0	0	0	0.0	–
	11 yrs.	59	67	.468	3.61	236	152	18	1072.1	1040	279	612	6	9	11	5	305	36	0	.118	38	181	6	10	1.0	.973

LEAGUE CHAMPIONSHIP SERIES

Year	Team	W	L	PCT	ERA	G	GS	CG	IP	H	BB	SO	ShO	W	L	SV	AB	H	HR	BA	PO	A	E	DP	TC/G	FA
1987	SF N	0	1	.000	7.88	2	2	0	8	12	0	7	0	0	0	0	3	0	0	.000	0	1	0	0	0.5	1.000
1989		0	0	–	0.00	1	0	0	1	1	0	0	0	0	0	0	0	0	0	–	0	0	0	0	0.0	–
	2 yrs.	0	1	.000	7.00	3	2	0	9	13	0	7	0	0	0	0	3	0	0	.000	0	1	0	0	0.3	1.000

WORLD SERIES

Year	Team	W	L	PCT	ERA	G	GS	CG	IP	H	BB	SO	ShO	W	L	SV	AB	H	HR	BA	PO	A	E	DP	TC/G	FA
1989	SF N	0	0	–	15.43	2	0	0	2.1	8	0	2	0	0	0	0	0	0	0	–	0	1	0	0	0.5	1.000

Chris Hammond
HAMMOND, CHRISTOPHER ANDREW
B. Jan. 21, 1966, Atlanta, Ga. — BL TL 6'1" 190 lbs.

Year	Team	W	L	PCT	ERA	G	GS	CG	IP	H	BB	SO	ShO	W	L	SV	AB	H	HR	BA	PO	A	E	DP	TC/G	FA
1990	CIN N	0	2	.000	6.35	3	3	0	11.1	13	12	4	0	0	0	0	3	0	0	.000	0	3	2	0	1.7	.600
1991		7	7	.500	4.06	20	18	0	99.2	92	48	50	0	0	0	0	34	12	0	.353	6	18	2	1	1.3	.923
1992		7	10	.412	4.21	28	26	0	147.1	149	55	79	0	0	0	0	44	6	1	.136	9	22	2	1	1.2	.939
1993	FLA N	11	12	.478	4.66	32	32	1	191	207	66	108	0	0	0	0	63	12	2	.190	8	32	4	1	1.4	.909
1994		4	4	.500	3.07	13	13	1	73.1	79	23	40	1	0	0	0	22	3	0	.136	1	6	1	0	0.6	.875
	5 yrs.	29	35	.453	4.24	96	92	2	522.2	540	204	281	1	0	0	0	166	33	3	.199	24	81	11	3	1.2	.905

Mike Hampton
HAMPTON, MICHAEL WILLIAM
B. Sept. 9, 1972, Brooksville, Fla. — BR TL 5'10" 185 lbs.

Year	Team	W	L	PCT	ERA	G	GS	CG	IP	H	BB	SO	ShO	W	L	SV	AB	H	HR	BA	PO	A	E	DP	TC/G	FA
1993	SEA A	1	3	.250	9.53	13	3	0	17	28	17	8	0	1	0	1	0	0	0	–	0	2	1	0	0.2	.667
1994	HOU N	2	1	.667	3.70	44	0	0	41.1	46	16	24	0	2	1	0	1	0	0	.000	6	11	0	2	0.4	1.000
	2 yrs.	3	4	.429	5.40	57	3	0	58.1	74	33	32	0	3	1	1	1	0	0	.000	6	13	1	2	0.4	.950

Chris Haney
HANEY, CHRISTOPHER DEANE
Son of Larry Haney.
B. Nov. 16, 1968, Baltimore, Md. — BL TL 6'3" 185 lbs.

Year	Team	W	L	PCT	ERA	G	GS	CG	IP	H	BB	SO	ShO	W	L	SV	AB	H	HR	BA	PO	A	E	DP	TC/G	FA
1991	MON N	3	7	.300	4.04	16	16	0	84.2	94	43	51	0	0	0	0	27	2	0	.074	6	18	2	1	1.6	.923
1992	2 teams	MON N	(9G 2–3)			KC A	(7G 2–3)																			
"	total	4	6	.400	4.61	16	13	2	80	75	26	54	2	0	0	0	9	2	0	.222	2	6	0	0	0.5	1.000
1993	KC A	9	9	.500	6.02	23	23	1	124	141	53	65	1	0	0	0	0	0	0	–	7	19	0	0	1.1	1.000
1994		2	2	.500	7.31	6	6	0	28.1	36	11	18	0	0	0	0	0	0	0	–	3	5	0	2	1.3	1.000
	4 yrs.	18	24	.429	5.25	61	58	3	317	346	133	188	3	0	0	0	36	4	0	.111	18	48	2	3	1.1	.971

Erik Hanson
HANSON, ERIK BRIAN
B. May 18, 1965, Kinnelon, N. J. — BR TR 6'6" 210 lbs.

Year	Team	W	L	PCT	ERA	G	GS	CG	IP	H	BB	SO	ShO	W	L	SV	AB	H	HR	BA	PO	A	E	DP	TC/G	FA
1988	SEA A	2	3	.400	3.24	6	6	0	41.2	35	12	36	0	0	0	0	0	0	0	–	0	4	0	1	0.7	1.000
1989		9	5	.643	3.18	17	17	1	113.1	103	32	75	0	0	0	0	0	0	0	–	8	16	0	0	1.4	1.000
1990		18	9	.667	3.24	33	33	5	236	205	68	211	1	0	0	0	0	0	0	–	30	20	4	0	1.6	.926
1991		8	8	.500	3.81	27	27	2	174.2	182	56	143	1	0	0	0	0	0	0	–	14	16	1	0	1.1	.968
1992		8	**17**	.320	4.82	31	30	6	186.2	209	57	112	1	1	0	0	0	0	0	–	14	23	1	2	1.2	.974
1993		11	12	.478	3.47	31	30	7	215	215	60	163	0	0	1	0	0	0	0	–	25	25	3	3	1.7	.943
1994	CIN N	5	5	.500	4.11	22	21	0	122.2	137	23	101	0	0	0	0	39	6	0	.154	11	16	0	0	1.2	1.000
	7 yrs.	61	59	.508	3.74	167	164	21	1090	1086	308	841	3	1	1	0	39	6	0	.154	102	120	9	6	1.4	.961

Mike Harkey
HARKEY, MICHAEL ANTHONY
B. Oct. 25, 1966, San Diego, Calif. — BR TR 6'5" 220 lbs.

Year	Team	W	L	PCT	ERA	G	GS	CG	IP	H	BB	SO	ShO	W	L	SV	AB	H	HR	BA	PO	A	E	DP	TC/G	FA
1988	CHI N	0	3	.000	2.60	5	5	0	34.2	33	15	18	0	0	0	0	11	1	0	.091	2	3	2	0	1.4	.714
1990		12	6	.667	3.26	27	27	2	173.2	153	59	94	0	0	0	0	56	14	0	.250	19	16	1	0	1.3	.972
1991		0	2	.000	5.30	4	4	0	18.2	21	6	15	0	0	0	0	5	2	0	.400	1	3	0	0	1.0	1.000
1992		4	0	1.000	1.89	7	7	0	38	34	15	21	0	0	0	0	15	4	0	.267	1	6	0	1	1.0	1.000
1993		10	10	.500	5.26	28	28	1	157.1	187	43	67	0	0	0	0	54	5	0	.093	9	20	5	2	1.2	.853
1994	CLR N	1	6	.143	5.79	24	13	0	91.2	125	35	39	0	1	0	0	22	4	0	.182	10	15	0	3	1.0	1.000
	6 yrs.	27	27	.500	4.25	95	84	3	514	553	173	254	1	1	0	0	163	30	0	.184	42	63	8	6	1.2	.929

Pete Harnisch
HARNISCH, PETER THOMAS
B. Sept. 23, 1966, Commack, N. Y. — BB TR 6'1" 195 lbs.

Year	Team	W	L	PCT	ERA	G	GS	CG	IP	H	BB	SO	ShO	W	L	SV	AB	H	HR	BA	PO	A	E	DP	TC/G	FA
1988	BAL A	0	2	.000	5.54	2	2	0	13	13	9	10	0	0	0	0	0	0	0	–	2	2	0	0	2.0	1.000
1989		5	9	.357	4.62	18	17	2	103.1	97	64	70	0	0	0	0	0	0	0	–	7	9	0	2	0.9	1.000

Year	Team	W	L	PCT	ERA	G	GS	CG	IP	H	BB	SO	ShO	Relief Pitching W	L	SV	Batting AB	H	HR	BA	PO	A	E	DP	TC/G	FA

Pete Harnisch *continued*

Year	Team	W	L	PCT	ERA	G	GS	CG	IP	H	BB	SO	ShO	W	L	SV	AB	H	HR	BA	PO	A	E	DP	TC/G	FA
1990	HOU N	11	11	.500	4.34	31	31	3	188.2	189	86	122	0	0	0	0	0	0	0	–	12	14	1	0	0.9	.963
1991	HOU N	12	9	.571	2.70	33	33	4	216.2	169	83	172	2	0	0	0	62	6	0	.097	7	18	1	0	0.8	.962
1992		9	10	.474	3.70	34	34	0	206.2	182	64	164	0	0	0	0	67	11	0	.164	16	15	2	1	1.0	.939
1993		16	9	.640	2.98	33	33	5	217.2	171	79	185	4	0	0	0	67	7	0	.104	3	15	2	0	0.6	.900
1994		8	5	.615	5.40	17	17	1	95	100	39	62	0	0	0	0	35	6	0	.171	11	8	0	0	1.1	1.000
7 yrs.		61	55	.526	3.73	168	167	15	1041	921	424	785	6	0	0	0	231	30	0	.130	58	81	6	3	0.9	.959

Gene Harris

HARRIS, TYRONE EUGENE
B. Dec. 5, 1964, Sebring, Fla.

BR TR 5'11" 190 lbs.

Year	Team	W	L	PCT	ERA	G	GS	CG	IP	H	BB	SO	ShO	W	L	SV	AB	H	HR	BA	PO	A	E	DP	TC/G	FA
1989	2 teams						MON N (11G 1–1)			SEA A (10G 1–4)																	
"	total	2	5	.286	5.91	21	6	0	53.1	63	25	25	0	1	2	1	1	0	0	.000	2	13	0	0	0.7	1.000
1990	SEA A	1	2	.333	4.74	25	0	0	38	31	30	43	0	1	2	0	0	0	0	–	4	2	0	1	0.2	1.000
1991		0	0	–	4.05	8	0	0	13.1	15	10	6	0	0	0	1	0	0	0	–	0	2	0	0	0.3	1.000
1992	2 teams						SEA A (8G 0–2)			SD N (14G 0–2)																	
"	total	0	2	.000	4.15	22	0	0	30.1	23	15	25	0	0	2	0	3	1	0	.333	1	4	3	0	0.4	.625
1993	SD N	6	6	.500	3.03	59	0	0	59.1	57	37	39	0	6	6	23	1	0	0	.000	5	10	0	0	0.3	1.000
1994	2 teams						SD N (13G 1–1)			DET A (11G 0–0)																	
"	total	1	1	.500	7.61	24	0	0	23.2	34	12	19	0	1	1	1	1	0	0	.000	1	2	0	0	0.1	1.000
6 yrs.		10	16	.385	4.75	159	7	0	218	223	129	157	0	9	13	26	6	1	0	.167	13	33	3	1	0.3	.939

Greg Harris

HARRIS, GREG ALLEN
B. Nov. 2, 1955, Lynwood, Calif.

BB TR 6' 165 lbs.

Year	Team	W	L	PCT	ERA	G	GS	CG	IP	H	BB	SO	ShO	W	L	SV	AB	H	HR	BA	PO	A	E	DP	TC/G	FA
1981	NY N	3	5	.375	4.43	16	14	0	69	65	28	54	0	0	1	0	22	4	0	.182	3	7	1	2	0.7	.909
1982	CIN N	2	6	.250	4.83	34	10	1	91.1	96	37	67	0	0	1	1	18	3	0	.167	8	13	2	2	0.7	.913
1983		0	0	–	27.00	1	0	0	1	2	3	1	0	0	0	0	1	0	0	.000	0	1	0	0	1.0	1.000
1984	2 teams						MON N (15G 0–1)			SD N (19G 2–1)																	
"	total	2	2	.500	2.48	34	1	0	54.1	38	25	45	0	1	2	3	9	3	0	.333	3	7	1	0	0.3	.909
1985	TEX A	5	4	.556	2.47	58	0	0	113	74	43	111	0	5	4	11	0	0	0	–	8	16	1	4	0.4	.960
1986		10	8	.556	2.83	73	0	0	111.1	103	42	95	0	10	8	20	0	0	0	–	7	18	2	2	0.4	.926
1987		5	10	.333	4.86	42	19	0	140.2	157	56	106	0	1	4	0	0	0	0	–	14	20	5	1	0.9	.872
1988	PHI N	4	6	.400	2.36	66	1	0	107	80	52	71	0	4	5	1	9	3	0	.333	5	17	3	0	0.4	.880
1989	2 teams						PHI N (44G 2–2)			BOS A (15G 2–2)																	
"	total	4	4	.500	3.31	59	0	0	103.1	85	58	76	0	4	4	1	6	1	0	.167	4	20	3	0	0.5	.889
1990	BOS A	13	9	.591	4.00	34	30	1	184.1	186	77	117	0	1	0	0	0	0	0	–	23	36	4	1	1.9	.937
1991		11	12	.478	3.85	53	21	1	173	157	69	127	0	4	2	2	0	0	0	–	11	32	2	0	0.8	.956
1992		4	9	.308	2.51	70	2	1	107.2	82	60	73	0	4	8	4	0	0	0	–	3	16	2	0	0.3	.905
1993		6	7	.462	3.77	80	0	0	112.1	95	60	103	0	6	7	8	0	0	0	–	8	13	3	1	0.3	.875
1994	2 teams						BOS A (35G 3–4)			NY A (3G 0–1)																	
"	total	3	5	.375	7.99	38	2	0	50.2	64	26	48	0	3	5	2	0	0	0	–	1	7	1	1	0.2	.889
14 yrs.		72	87	.453	3.72	658	98	4	1419	1284	636	1094	0	43	50	54	65	14	0	.215	98	223	30	14	0.5	.915

LEAGUE CHAMPIONSHIP SERIES

Year	Team	W	L	PCT	ERA	G	GS	CG	IP	H	BB	SO	ShO	W	L	SV	AB	H	HR	BA	PO	A	E	DP	TC/G	FA
1984	SD N	0	0	–	31.50	1	0	0	2	9	3	2	0	0	0	0	0	0	0	–	0	0	0	0	0.0	–
1990	BOS A	0	1	.000	27.00	1	0	0	0.1	3	0	0	0	0	1	0	0	0	0	–	0	0	0	0	0.0	–
2 yrs.		0	1	.000	30.86	2	0	0	2.1	12	3	2	0	0	1	0	0	0	0	–	0	0	0	0	0.0	–

WORLD SERIES

Year	Team	W	L	PCT	ERA	G	GS	CG	IP	H	BB	SO	ShO	W	L	SV	AB	H	HR	BA	PO	A	E	DP	TC/G	FA
1984	SD N	0	0	–	0.00	1	0	0	5.1	3	3	5	0	0	0	0	0	0	0	–	0	0	0	0	0.0	–

Greg Harris

HARRIS, GREGORY WADE
B. Dec. 1, 1963, Greensboro, N. C.

BR TR 6'3" 190 lbs.

Year	Team	W	L	PCT	ERA	G	GS	CG	IP	H	BB	SO	ShO	W	L	SV	AB	H	HR	BA	PO	A	E	DP	TC/G	FA
1988	SD N	2	0	1.000	1.50	3	1	1	18	13	3	15	0	1	0	0	7	0	0	.000	0	2	0	1	0.7	1.000
1989		8	9	.471	2.60	56	8	0	135	106	52	106	0	5	5	6	19	1	0	.053	12	21	0	2	0.6	1.000
1990		8	8	.500	2.30	73	0	0	117.1	92	49	97	0	8	8	9	12	1	0	.083	4	17	0	1	0.3	1.000
1991		9	5	.643	2.23	20	20	3	133	116	27	95	2	0	0	0	36	3	0	.083	10	14	1	0	1.3	.960
1992		4	8	.333	4.12	20	20	1	118	113	35	66	0	0	0	0	31	4	0	.129	10	21	5	0	1.8	.861
1993	2 teams						SD N (22G 10–9)			CLR N (13G 1–8)																	
"	total	11	17	.393	4.59	35	35	4	225.1	239	69	123	0	0	0	0	73	10	0	.137	17	37	3	3	1.6	.947
1994	CLR N	3	12	.200	6.65	29	19	1	130	154	52	82	0	0	1	1	40	7	0	.175	8	22	2	1	1.1	.938
7 yrs.		45	59	.433	3.80	236	103	10	876.2	833	287	584	2	14	14	16	218	26	0	.119	61	134	11	8	0.9	.947

Bryan Harvey

HARVEY, BRYAN STANLEY
B. June 2, 1963, Chattanooga, Tenn.

BR TR 6'3" 235 lbs.

Year	Team	W	L	PCT	ERA	G	GS	CG	IP	H	BB	SO	ShO	W	L	SV	AB	H	HR	BA	PO	A	E	DP	TC/G	FA
1987	CAL A	0	0	–	0.00	3	0	0	5	6	2	3	0	0	0	0	0	0	0	–	0	0	0	0	0.0	–
1988		7	5	.583	2.13	50	0	0	76	59	20	67	0	7	5	17	0	0	0	–	4	2	1	0	0.1	.857
1989		3	3	.500	3.44	51	0	0	55	36	41	78	0	3	3	25	0	0	0	–	1	7	1	0	0.2	.889
1990		4	4	.500	3.22	54	0	0	64.1	45	35	82	0	4	4	25	0	0	0	–	3	4	0	1	0.1	1.000
1991		2	4	.333	1.60	67	0	0	78.2	51	17	101	0	2	4	46	0	0	0	–	2	8	2	0	0.2	.833
1992		0	4	.000	2.83	25	0	0	28.2	22	11	34	0	0	4	13	0	0	0	–	0	1	0	0	0.1	1.000
1993	FLA N	1	5	.167	1.70	59	0	0	69	45	13	73	0	1	5	45	0	0	0	–	3	5	0	0	0.1	1.000
1994		0	0	–	5.23	12	0	0	10.1	12	4	10	0	0	0	6	0	0	0	–	1	1	0	0	0.2	1.000
8 yrs.		17	25	.405	2.42	321	0	0	387	276	143	448	0	17	25	177	0	0	0	–	14	28	4	1	0.1	.913

Heath Haynes

HAYNES, HEATH BURNETT
B. Nov. 30, 1968, Wheeling, W. Va.

BR TR 6' 175 lbs.

Year	Team	W	L	PCT	ERA	G	GS	CG	IP	H	BB	SO	ShO	W	L	SV	AB	H	HR	BA	PO	A	E	DP	TC/G	FA
1994	MON N	0	0	–	0.00	4	0	0	3.2	3	3	1	0	0	0	0	0	0	0	–	0	0	0	0	0.0	–

Rick Helling

HELLING, RICKY ALLEN
B. Dec. 15, 1970, Devils Lake, N. D.

BR TR 6'3" 215 lbs.

Year	Team	W	L	PCT	ERA	G	GS	CG	IP	H	BB	SO	ShO	W	L	SV	AB	H	HR	BA	PO	A	E	DP	TC/G	FA
1994	TEX A	3	2	.600	5.88	9	9	1	52	62	18	25	0	0	0	0	0	0	0	–	2	3	0	0	0.6	1.000

Year	Team	W	L	PCT	ERA	G	GS	CG	IP	H	BB	SO	ShO	W	L	SV	AB	H	HR	BA	PO	A	E	DP	TC/G	FA
														Relief Pitching			Batting									

Rod Henderson

HENDERSON, RODNEY WOOD
B. Mar. 11, 1971, Greensburg, Ky.   BR TR 6'4"   195 lbs.

Year	Team	W	L	PCT	ERA	G	GS	CG	IP	H	BB	SO	ShO	W	L	SV	AB	H	HR	BA	PO	A	E	DP	TC/G	FA
1994	MON N	0	1	.000	9.45	3	2	0	6.2	9	7	3	0	0	0	0	1	0	0	.000	1	2	0	0	1.0	1.000

Tom Henke

HENKE, THOMAS ANTHONY (The Terminator)
B. Dec. 21, 1957, Kansas City, Mo.   BR TR 6'5"   215 lbs.

Year	Team	W	L	PCT	ERA	G	GS	CG	IP	H	BB	SO	ShO	W	L	SV	AB	H	HR	BA	PO	A	E	DP	TC/G	FA
1982	TEX A	1	0	1.000	1.15	8	0	0	15.2	14	8	9	0	1	0	0	0	0	0	–	2	2	0	0	0.5	1.000
1983		1	0	1.000	3.38	8	0	0	16	16	4	17	0	1	0	1	0	0	0	–	0	3	1	0	0.5	.750
1984		1	1	.500	6.35	25	0	0	28.1	36	20	25	0	1	1	2	0	0	0	–	1	2	0	0	0.1	1.000
1985	TOR A	3	3	.500	2.03	28	0	0	40	29	8	42	0	3	3	13	0	0	0	–	3	3	0	0	0.2	1.000
1986		9	5	.643	3.35	63	0	0	91.1	63	32	118	0	9	5	27	0	0	0	–	2	2	0	1	0.1	1.000
1987		0	6	.000	2.49	72	0	0	94	62	25	128	0	0	6	34	0	0	0	–	9	12	0	1	0.3	1.000
1988		4	4	.500	2.91	52	0	0	68	60	24	66	0	4	4	25	0	0	0	–	1	9	0	1	0.2	1.000
1989		8	3	.727	1.92	64	0	0	89	66	25	116	0	8	3	20	0	0	0	–	3	10	1	0	0.2	.929
1990		2	4	.333	2.17	61	0	0	74.2	58	19	75	0	2	4	32	0	0	0	–	6	5	0	0	0.2	1.000
1991		0	2	.000	2.32	49	0	0	50.1	33	11	53	0	0	2	32	0	0	0	–	2	1	0	0	0.1	1.000
1992		3	2	.600	2.26	57	0	0	55.2	40	22	46	0	3	2	34	0	0	0	–	2	2	0	0	0.1	1.000
1993	TEX A	5	5	.500	2.91	66	0	0	74.1	55	27	79	0	5	5	40	0	0	0	–	6	10	0	0	0.2	1.000
1994		3	6	.333	3.79	37	0	0	38	33	12	39	0	3	6	15	0	0	0	–	2	2	0	0	0.1	1.000
13 yrs.		40	41	.494	2.73	590	0	0	735.1	565	237	813	0	40	41	275 7th	0	0	0	–	39	63	2	3	0.2	.981

LEAGUE CHAMPIONSHIP SERIES

Year	Team	W	L	PCT	ERA	G	GS	CG	IP	H	BB	SO	ShO	W	L	SV	AB	H	HR	BA	PO	A	E	DP	TC/G	FA
1985	TOR A	2	0	1.000	4.26	3	0	0	6.1	5	4	4	0	2	0	0	0	0	0	–	1	0	0	0	0.3	1.000
1989		0	0	–	0.00	3	0	0	2.2	0	0	3	0	0	0	0	0	0	0	–	0	1	0	0	0.3	1.000
1991		0	0	–	0.00	2	0	0	2.2	0	1	5	0	0	0	0	0	0	0	–	0	2	0	0	1.0	1.000
1992		0	0	–	0.00	4	0	0	4.2	3	2	2	0	0	0	3	0	0	0	–	0	0	0	0	0.0	–
4 yrs.		2	0	1.000	1.65	12	0	0	16.1	8	7	14	0	2	0	3	0	0	0	–	1	3	0	0	0.3	1.000

WORLD SERIES

Year	Team	W	L	PCT	ERA	G	GS	CG	IP	H	BB	SO	ShO	W	L	SV	AB	H	HR	BA	PO	A	E	DP	TC/G	FA
1992	TOR A	0	0	–	2.70	3	0	0	3.1	2	2	1	0	0	0	2	0	0	0	–	0	2	0	0	0.7	1.000

Mike Henneman

HENNEMAN, MICHAEL ALAN
B. Dec. 11, 1961, St. Charles, Mo.   BR TR 6'4"   205 lbs.

Year	Team	W	L	PCT	ERA	G	GS	CG	IP	H	BB	SO	ShO	W	L	SV	AB	H	HR	BA	PO	A	E	DP	TC/G	FA
1987	DET A	11	3	.786	2.98	55	0	0	96.2	86	30	75	0	11	3	7	1	0	0	.000	8	11	0	2	0.3	1.000
1988		9	6	.600	1.87	65	0	0	91.1	72	24	58	0	9	6	22	0	0	0	–	4	8	1	0	0.2	.923
1989		11	4	.733	3.70	60	0	0	90	84	51	69	0	11	4	8	0	0	0	–	5	12	0	2	0.3	1.000
1990		8	6	.571	3.05	69	0	0	94.1	90	33	50	0	8	6	22	0	0	0	–	7	16	3	2	0.4	.885
1991		10	2	.833	2.88	60	0	0	84.1	81	34	61	0	10	2	21	0	0	0	–	6	10	2	1	0.3	.889
1992		2	6	.250	3.96	60	0	0	77.1	75	20	58	0	2	6	24	0	0	0	–	9	9	1	1	0.3	.947
1993		5	3	.625	2.64	63	0	0	71.2	69	32	58	0	5	3	24	0	0	0	–	6	5	1	0	0.2	.917
1994		1	3	.250	5.19	30	0	0	34.2	43	17	27	0	1	3	8	0	0	0	–	6	4	0	0	0.3	1.000
8 yrs.		57	33	.633	3.12	462	0	0	640.1	600	241	456	0	57	33	136	1	0	0	.000	51	75	8	8	0.3	.940

LEAGUE CHAMPIONSHIP SERIES

Year	Team	W	L	PCT	ERA	G	GS	CG	IP	H	BB	SO	ShO	W	L	SV	AB	H	HR	BA	PO	A	E	DP	TC/G	FA
1987	DET A	1	0	1.000	10.80	3	0	0	5	6	3	1	0	1	0	0	0	0	0	–	0	2	0	0	0.7	1.000

Butch Henry

HENRY, FLOYD BLUFORD
B. Oct. 7, 1968, El Paso, Tex.   BL TL 6'1"   195 lbs.

Year	Team	W	L	PCT	ERA	G	GS	CG	IP	H	BB	SO	ShO	W	L	SV	AB	H	HR	BA	PO	A	E	DP	TC/G	FA
1992	HOU N	6	9	.400	4.02	28	28	2	165.2	185	41	96	1	1	0	0	54	8	1	.148	13	30	3	2	1.6	.935
1993	2 teams	CLR N	(20G 2–8)		MON N	(10G 1–1)																				
"	total	3	9	.250	6.12	30	16	0	103	135	28	47	0	1	0	0	24	2	0	.083	5	12	1	1	0.6	.944
1994	MON N	8	3	.727	2.43	24	15	0	107.1	97	20	70	0	0	0	1	31	9	0	.290	8	13	0	3	0.9	1.000
3 yrs.		17	21	.447	4.14	82	59	3	376	417	89	213	1	0	1	1	109	19	1	.174	26	55	4	6	1.0	.953

Doug Henry

HENRY, RICHARD DOUGLAS
B. Dec. 10, 1963, Sacramento, Calif.   BR TR 6'4"   185 lbs.

Year	Team	W	L	PCT	ERA	G	GS	CG	IP	H	BB	SO	ShO	W	L	SV	AB	H	HR	BA	PO	A	E	DP	TC/G	FA
1991	MIL A	2	1	.667	0.25	32	0	0	36	16	14	28	0	2	1	15	0	0	0	–	4	1	0	0	0.2	1.000
1992		1	4	.200	4.02	68	0	0	65	64	24	52	0	1	4	29	0	0	0	–	10	4	0	2	0.2	1.000
1993		4	4	.500	5.56	54	0	0	55	67	25	38	0	4	4	17	0	0	0	–	5	7	0	0	0.2	1.000
1994		2	3	.400	4.60	25	0	0	31.1	32	23	20	0	2	3	0	1	0	0	.000	2	3	0	0	0.2	1.000
4 yrs.		9	12	.429	3.84	179	0	0	187.1	179	86	138	0	9	12	61	1	0	0	.000	21	15	0	2	0.2	1.000

Pat Hentgen

HENTGEN, PATRICK GEORGE
B. Nov. 13, 1968, Detroit, Mich.   BR TR 6'2"   210 lbs.

Year	Team	W	L	PCT	ERA	G	GS	CG	IP	H	BB	SO	ShO	W	L	SV	AB	H	HR	BA	PO	A	E	DP	TC/G	FA
1991	TOR A	0	0	–	2.45	3	1	0	7.1	5	3	3	0	0	0	0	0	0	0	–	0	2	0	1	0.7	1.000
1992		5	2	.714	5.36	28	2	0	50.1	49	32	39	0	5	1	0	0	0	0	–	0	4	0	1	0.1	1.000
1993		19	9	.679	3.87	34	32	3	216.1	215	74	122	0	0	1	0	0	0	0	–	12	22	1	1	1.0	.971
1994		13	8	.619	3.40	24	24	6	174.2	158	59	147	3	0	0	0	0	0	0	–	12	21	0	2	1.4	1.000
4 yrs.		37	19	.661	3.83	89	59	9	448.2	427	168	311	3	5	2	0	0	0	0	–	24	49	1	5	0.8	.986

LEAGUE CHAMPIONSHIP SERIES

Year	Team	W	L	PCT	ERA	G	GS	CG	IP	H	BB	SO	ShO	W	L	SV	AB	H	HR	BA	PO	A	E	DP	TC/G	FA
1993	TOR A	0	1	.000	18.00	1	1	0	3	9	2	3	0	0	0	0	0	0	0	–	1	0	0	0	1.0	1.000

WORLD SERIES

Year	Team	W	L	PCT	ERA	G	GS	CG	IP	H	BB	SO	ShO	W	L	SV	AB	H	HR	BA	PO	A	E	DP	TC/G	FA
1993	TOR A	1	0	1.000	1.50	1	1	0	6	5	3	6	0	0	0	0	3	0	0	.000	0	0	0	0	0.0	–

Gil Heredia

HEREDIA, GILBERT
B. Oct. 26, 1965, Nogales, Ariz.   BR TR 6'1"   190 lbs.

Year	Team	W	L	PCT	ERA	G	GS	CG	IP	H	BB	SO	ShO	W	L	SV	AB	H	HR	BA	PO	A	E	DP	TC/G	FA
1991	SF N	0	2	.000	3.82	7	4	0	33	27	7	13	0	0	0	0	7	3	0	.429	2	2	0	0	0.6	1.000
1992	2 teams	SF N	(13G 2–3)		MON N	(7G 0–0)																				
"	total	2	3	.400	4.23	20	5	0	44.2	44	20	22	0	2	0	0	9	1	0	.111	0	5	0	0	0.3	1.000
1993	MON N	4	2	.667	3.92	20	9	1	57.1	66	14	40	0	0	0	2	13	2	0	.154	4	11	0	1	0.8	1.000
1994		6	3	.667	3.46	39	3	0	75.1	85	13	62	0	4	3	0	16	5	0	.313	5	12	1	0	0.5	.944
4 yrs.		12	10	.545	3.81	86	21	1	210.1	222	54	137	0	6	3	2	45	11	0	.244	11	30	1	1	0.5	.976

Year	Team	W	L	PCT	ERA	G	GS	CG	IP	H	BB	SO	ShO	W	L	SV	AB	H	HR	BA	PO	A	E	DP	TC/G	FA

Jeremy Hernandez
HERNANDEZ, JEREMY STUART
B. July 6, 1966, Burbank, Calif.　　　　　　　　BR TR 6'5"　195 lbs.

Year	Team	W	L	PCT	ERA	G	GS	CG	IP	H	BB	SO	ShO	W	L	SV	AB	H	HR	BA	PO	A	E	DP	TC/G	FA
1991	SD N	0	0	–	0.00	9	0	0	14.1	8	5	9	0	0	0	2	2	0	0	.000	0	3	0	1	0.3	1.000
1992		1	4	.200	4.17	26	0	0	36.2	39	11	25	0	1	4	1	2	0	0	.000	2	6	0	2	0.3	1.000
1993	2 teams								SD N (21G 0–2)			CLE A (49G 6–5)															
"	total	6	7	.462	3.63	70	0	0	111.2	116	34	70	0	6	7	8	1	0	0	.000	3	17	1	1	0.3	.952
1994	FLA N	3	3	.500	2.70	21	0	0	23.1	16	14	13	0	3	3	9	1	0	0	.000	0	2	0	0	0.1	1.000
4 yrs.		10	14	.417	3.34	126	0	0	186	179	64	117	0	10	14	20	6	0	0	.000	5	28	1	4	0.3	.971

Roberto Hernandez
HERNANDEZ, ROBERTO MANUEL
Born Roberto Manuel Hernandez (Rodriguez).
B. Nov. 11, 1964, Santurce, Puerto Rico.　　　　　BR TR 6'4"　220 lbs.

Year	Team	W	L	PCT	ERA	G	GS	CG	IP	H	BB	SO	ShO	W	L	SV	AB	H	HR	BA	PO	A	E	DP	TC/G	FA
1991	CHI A	1	0	1.000	7.80	9	3	0	15	18	7	6	0	0	0	0	0	0	0	–	0	2	0	0	0.2	1.000
1992		7	3	.700	1.65	43	0	0	71	45	20	68	0	7	3	12	0	0	0	–	7	4	1	1	0.3	.917
1993		3	4	.429	2.29	70	0	0	78.2	66	20	71	0	3	4	38	0	0	0	–	2	11	1	1	0.2	.929
1994		4	4	.500	4.91	45	0	0	47.2	44	19	50	0	4	4	14	0	0	0	–	0	2	1	0	0.1	.667
4 yrs.		15	11	.577	3.05	167	3	0	212.1	173	66	195	0	14	11	64	0	0	0	–	9	19	3	2	0.2	.903

LEAGUE CHAMPIONSHIP SERIES

Year	Team	W	L	PCT	ERA	G	GS	CG	IP	H	BB	SO	ShO	W	L	SV	AB	H	HR	BA	PO	A	E	DP	TC/G	FA
1993	CHI A	0	0	–	0.00	4	0	0	4	4	0	1	0	0	0	1	0	0	0	–	0	0	0	0	0.0	–

Xavier Hernandez
HERNANDEZ, FRANCIS XAVIER
B. Aug. 16, 1965, Port Arthur, Tex.　　　　　　　BL TR 6'2"　185 lbs.

Year	Team	W	L	PCT	ERA	G	GS	CG	IP	H	BB	SO	ShO	W	L	SV	AB	H	HR	BA	PO	A	E	DP	TC/G	FA
1989	TOR A	1	0	1.000	4.76	7	0	0	22.2	25	8	7	0	1	0	0	0	0	0	–	1	2	1	0	0.6	.750
1990	HOU N	2	1	.667	4.62	34	1	0	62.1	60	24	24	0	2	0	0	3	1	0	.333	3	5	0	0	0.2	1.000
1991		2	7	.222	4.71	32	6	0	63	66	32	55	0	2	2	3	10	0	0	.000	6	9	0	0	0.5	1.000
1992		9	1	.900	2.11	77	0	0	111	81	42	96	0	9	1	7	9	0	0	.000	9	7	1	0	0.2	.941
1993		4	5	.444	2.61	72	0	0	96.2	75	28	101	0	4	5	9	5	0	0	.000	1	8	0	1	0.1	1.000
1994	NY A	4	4	.500	5.85	31	0	0	40	48	21	37	0	4	4	6	0	0	0	–	2	8	0	3	0.3	1.000
6 yrs.		22	18	.550	3.57	253	7	0	395.2	355	155	320	0	22	12	25	27	1	0	.037	22	39	2	3	0.2	.968

Orel Hershiser
HERSHISER, OREL LEONARD QUINTON IV (Bulldog)
B. Sept. 16, 1958, Buffalo, N. Y.　　　　　　　BR TR 6'3"　190 lbs.

Year	Team	W	L	PCT	ERA	G	GS	CG	IP	H	BB	SO	ShO	W	L	SV	AB	H	HR	BA	PO	A	E	DP	TC/G	FA
1983	LA N	0	0	–	3.38	8	0	0	8	7	6	5	0	0	0	1	0	0	0	–	0	2	0	1	0.3	1.000
1984		11	8	.579	2.66	45	20	8	189.2	160	50	150	4	2	2	2	50	10	0	.200	17	28	5	2	1.1	.900
1985		19	3	.864	2.03	36	34	9	239.2	179	68	157	5	1	0	0	76	15	0	.197	20	45	7	4	2.0	.903
1986		14	14	.500	3.85	35	35	8	231.1	213	86	153	1	0	0	0	71	17	0	.239	22	36	3	6	1.7	.951
1987		16	16	.500	3.06	37	35	10	264.2	247	74	190	1	0	1	1	90	19	0	.211	37	34	5	6	2.1	.934
1988		23	8	.742	2.26	35	34	15	267	208	73	178	8	0	0	0	85	11	0	.129	32	60	6	6	2.8	.939
1989		15	15	.500	2.31	35	33	8	256.2	226	77	178	4	0	0	0	77	14	0	.182	24	51	4	2	2.3	.949
1990		1	1	.500	4.26	4	4	0	25.1	26	4	16	0	0	0	0	7	0	0	.000	1	3	0	0	1.0	1.000
1991		7	2	.778	3.46	21	21	0	112	112	32	73	0	0	0	0	31	8	0	.258	12	18	1	1	1.5	.968
1992		10	15	.400	3.67	33	33	1	210.2	209	69	130	0	0	0	0	68	15	0	.221	28	41	3	2	2.2	.958
1993		12	14	.462	3.59	33	33	5	215.2	201	72	141	1	0	0	0	73	26	0	.356	20	43	3	1	2.0	.955
1994		6	6	.500	3.79	21	21	1	135.1	146	42	72	0	0	0	0	44	9	0	.205	22	24	2	3	2.3	.958
12 yrs.		134	102	.568	3.00	343	303	65	2156	1934	653	1443	24	3	3	5	672	144	0	.214	235	385	39	34	1.9	.941

LEAGUE CHAMPIONSHIP SERIES

Year	Team	W	L	PCT	ERA	G	GS	CG	IP	H	BB	SO	ShO	W	L	SV	AB	H	HR	BA	PO	A	E	DP	TC/G	FA
1985	LA N	1	0	1.000	3.52	2	2	1	15.1	17	6	5	0	0	0	0	7	2	0	.286	2	2	0	1	2.0	1.000
1988		1	0	1.000	1.09	4	3	1	24.2	18	7	15	1	0	0	1	9	0	0	.000	3	3	0	0	1.5	1.000
2 yrs.		2	0	1.000	2.03	6	5	2	40	35	13	20	1	0	0	1	16	2	0	.125	5	5	0	1	1.7	1.000

WORLD SERIES

Year	Team	W	L	PCT	ERA	G	GS	CG	IP	H	BB	SO	ShO	W	L	SV	AB	H	HR	BA	PO	A	E	DP	TC/G	FA
1988	LA N	2	0	1.000	1.00	2	2	2	18	7	6	17	1	0	0	0	3	3	0	1.000	1	1	0	0	1.0	1.000

Joe Hesketh
HESKETH, JOSEPH THOMAS
B. Feb. 15, 1959, Lackawanna, N. Y.　　　　　　BL TL 6'2"　165 lbs.

Year	Team	W	L	PCT	ERA	G	GS	CG	IP	H	BB	SO	ShO	W	L	SV	AB	H	HR	BA	PO	A	E	DP	TC/G	FA
1984	MON N	2	2	.500	1.80	11	5	1	45	38	15	32	1	0	1	1	10	1	0	.100	2	6	1	1	0.8	.889
1985		10	5	.667	2.49	25	25	2	155.1	125	45	113	1	0	0	0	44	4	0	.091	3	22	0	0	1.0	1.000
1986		6	5	.545	5.01	15	15	0	82.2	92	31	67	0	0	0	0	23	0	0	.000	2	8	1	0	0.7	.909
1987		0	0	–	3.14	18	0	0	28.2	23	15	31	0	0	0	1	4	0	0	.000	1	1	1	0	0.2	.667
1988		4	3	.571	2.85	60	0	0	72.2	63	35	64	0	4	3	9	2	0	0	.000	6	14	0	2	0.3	1.000
1989		6	4	.600	5.77	43	0	0	48.1	54	26	44	0	6	4	3	2	1	0	.500	3	9	1	3	0.3	.923
1990	3 teams								MON N (2G 1–0)			ATL N (31G 0–2)			BOS A (12G 0–4)													
"	total	1	6	.143	4.53	45	2	0	59.2	69	25	50	0	1	4	5	1	0	0	.000	4	6	2	0	0.3	.833
1991	BOS A	12	4	.750	3.29	39	17	0	153.1	142	53	104	0	1	0	0	0	0	0	–	13	19	1	1	0.8	.970
1992		8	9	.471	4.36	30	25	1	148.2	162	58	104	0	1	0	1	0	0	0	–	6	22	4	1	1.1	.875
1993		3	4	.429	5.06	28	5	0	53.1	62	29	34	0	2	1	1	0	0	0	–	2	7	1	1	0.4	.900
1994		8	5	.615	4.26	25	20	0	114	117	46	83	0	0	0	0	0	0	0	–	5	9	4	0	0.7	.778
11 yrs.		60	47	.561	3.78	339	114	4	961.2	947	378	726	2	16	13	21	86	6	0	.070	47	123	16	9	0.5	.914

Greg Hibbard
HIBBARD, JAMES GREGORY
B. Sept. 13, 1964, New Orleans, La.　　　　　　BL TL 6'　180 lbs.

Year	Team	W	L	PCT	ERA	G	GS	CG	IP	H	BB	SO	ShO	W	L	SV	AB	H	HR	BA	PO	A	E	DP	TC/G	FA
1989	CHI A	6	7	.462	3.21	23	23	2	137.1	142	41	55	0	0	0	0	0	0	0	–	5	27	0	4	1.4	1.000
1990		14	9	.609	3.16	33	33	3	211	202	55	92	1	0	0	0	0	0	0	–	7	29	0	2	1.1	1.000
1991		11	11	.500	4.31	32	29	5	194	196	57	71	0	0	0	0	0	0	0	–	9	28	2	2	1.2	.949
1992		10	7	.588	4.40	31	28	0	176	187	57	69	0	0	0	0	0	0	0	–	6	36	3	4	1.5	.933
1993	CHI N	15	11	.577	3.96	31	31	0	191	209	47	82	0	0	0	0	65	6	0	.092	6	26	0	1	1.0	1.000
1994	SEA A	1	5	.167	6.69	15	14	0	80.2	115	31	39	0	0	0	0	0	0	0	–	3	15	1	1	1.3	.947
6 yrs.		57	50	.533	4.05	165	158	11	990	1051	288	408	1	1	0	0	65	6	0	.092	36	161	6	15	1.2	.970

Year	Team	W	L	PCT	ERA	G	GS	CG	IP	H	BB	SO	ShO	Relief Pitching W	L	SV	Batting AB	H	HR	BA	PO	A	E	DP	TC/G	FA

Bryan Hickerson

HICKERSON, BRYAN DAVID
B. Oct. 13, 1963, Bemidji, Minn.   BL TL 6'2"   195 lbs.

Year	Team	W	L	PCT	ERA	G	GS	CG	IP	H	BB	SO	ShO	W	L	SV	AB	H	HR	BA	PO	A	E	DP	TC/G	FA
1991	SF N	2	2	.500	3.60	17	6	0	50	53	17	43	0	0	0	0	12	0	0	.000	0	1	0	0	0.1	1.000
1992		5	3	.625	3.09	61	1	0	87.1	74	21	68	0	5	3	0	4	0	0	.000	1	5	0	0	0.1	1.000
1993		7	5	.583	4.26	47	15	0	120.1	137	39	69	0	0	2	0	28	4	0	.143	4	12	1	0	0.4	.941
1994		4	8	.333	5.40	28	14	0	98.1	118	38	59	0	1	1	1	27	5	0	.185	1	9	0	1	0.4	1.000
4 yrs.		18	18	.500	4.20	153	36	0	356	382	115	239	0	6	6	1	71	9	0	.127	6	27	1	1	0.2	.971

Ted Higuera

HIGUERA, TEODORO
Born Teodoro Valenzuela Higuera (Valenzuela).
B. Nov. 9, 1958, Los Mochis, Mexico.   BB TL 5'10"   180 lbs.

Year	Team	W	L	PCT	ERA	G	GS	CG	IP	H	BB	SO	ShO	W	L	SV	AB	H	HR	BA	PO	A	E	DP	TC/G	FA
1985	MIL A	15	8	.652	3.90	32	30	7	212.1	186	63	127	2	0	0	0	0	0	0	–	8	18	1	2	0.8	.963
1986		20	11	.645	2.79	34	34	15	248.1	226	74	207	4	0	0	0	0	0	0	–	9	26	0	1	1.0	1.000
1987		18	10	.643	3.85	35	35	14	261.2	236	87	240	3	0	0	0	0	0	0	–	9	23	2	3	1.0	.941
1988		16	9	.640	2.45	31	31	8	227.1	168	59	192	1	0	0	0	0	0	0	–	12	33	0	1	1.5	1.000
1989		9	6	.600	3.46	22	22	2	135.1	125	48	91	1	0	0	0	0	0	0	–	5	10	1	0	0.7	.938
1990		11	10	.524	3.76	27	27	4	170	167	50	129	1	0	0	0	0	0	0	–	7	18	2	2	1.0	.926
1991		3	2	.600	4.46	7	6	0	36.1	37	10	33	0	0	0	0	0	0	0	–	1	5	1	0	1.0	.857
1993		1	3	.250	7.20	8	8	0	30	43	16	27	0	0	0	0	0	0	0	–	3	0	0	0	0.4	1.000
1994		1	5	.167	7.06	17	12	0	58.2	74	36	35	0	0	0	0	0	0	0	–	1	10	0	3	0.6	1.000
9 yrs.		94	64	.595	3.61	213	205	50	1380	1262	443	1081	12	0	0	0	0	0	0	–	55	143	7	12	1.0	.966

Ken Hill

HILL, KENNETH WADE (Thrill)
B. Dec. 14, 1965, Lynn, Mass.   BR TR 6'4"   200 lbs.

Year	Team	W	L	PCT	ERA	G	GS	CG	IP	H	BB	SO	ShO	W	L	SV	AB	H	HR	BA	PO	A	E	DP	TC/G	FA
1988	STL N	0	1	.000	5.14	4	1	0	14	16	6	6	0	0	0	0	3	0	0	.000	0	3	0	0	0.8	1.000
1989		7	15	.318	3.80	33	33	2	196.2	186	99	112	1	0	0	0	59	9	0	.153	12	31	1	1	1.3	.977
1990		5	6	.455	5.49	17	14	1	78.2	79	33	58	0	0	0	0	19	4	0	.211	7	10	1	1	1.1	.944
1991		11	10	.524	3.57	30	30	0	181.1	147	67	121	0	0	0	0	50	5	0	.100	15	26	2	1	1.4	.953
1992	MON N	16	9	.640	2.68	33	33	3	218	187	75	150	3	0	0	0	62	11	1	.177	21	36	4	3	1.8	.934
1993		9	7	.563	3.23	28	28	3	183.2	163	74	90	0	0	0	0	52	6	0	.115	24	38	1	2	2.3	.984
1994		16	5	.762	3.32	23	23	2	154.2	145	44	85	1	0	0	0	48	7	0	.146	15	33	2	2	2.2	.960
7 yrs.		64	53	.547	3.50	168	162	10	1027	923	398	622	5	0	0	0	293	42	1	.143	94	177	11	10	1.7	.961

Milt Hill

HILL, MILTON GILES
B. Aug. 22, 1965, Atlanta, Ga.   BR TR 6'   180 lbs.

Year	Team	W	L	PCT	ERA	G	GS	CG	IP	H	BB	SO	ShO	W	L	SV	AB	H	HR	BA	PO	A	E	DP	TC/G	FA
1991	CIN N	1	1	.500	3.78	22	0	0	33.1	36	8	20	0	1	1	0	1	0	0	.000	2	5	0	0	0.2	1.000
1992		0	0	–	3.15	14	0	0	20	15	5	10	0	0	0	1	0	0	0	–	3	2	0	0	0.4	1.000
1993		3	0	1.000	5.65	19	0	0	28.2	34	9	23	0	3	0	0	2	0	0	.000	4	0	1	0	0.3	.800
1994	2 teams	ATL N	(10G 0–0)		SEA A	(13G 1–0)																				
"	total	1	0	1.000	6.94	23	0	0	35	48	17	26	0	1	0	0	0	0	0	–	2	0	0	0	0.2	1.000
4 yrs.		5	1	.833	5.08	78	0	0	117	133	39	79	0	5	1	1	3	0	0	.000	11	7	1	0	0.2	.947

Eric Hillman

HILLMAN, JOHN ERIC
B. Apr. 27, 1966, Gary, Ind.   BL TL 6'10"   235 lbs.

Year	Team	W	L	PCT	ERA	G	GS	CG	IP	H	BB	SO	ShO	W	L	SV	AB	H	HR	BA	PO	A	E	DP	TC/G	FA
1992	NY N	2	2	.500	5.33	11	8	0	52.1	67	10	16	0	0	0	0	13	1	0	.077	1	7	0	0	0.7	1.000
1993		2	9	.182	3.97	27	22	3	145	173	24	60	1	0	1	0	44	7	0	.159	11	21	4	1	1.3	.889
1994		0	3	.000	7.79	11	6	0	34.2	45	11	20	0	0	0	0	8	0	0	.000	2	4	0	0	0.5	1.000
3 yrs.		4	14	.222	4.85	49	36	3	232	285	45	96	1	0	1	0	65	8	0	.123	14	32	4	1	1.0	.920

Sterling Hitchcock

HITCHCOCK, STERLING ALEX
B. Apr. 29, 1971, Fayetteville, N. C.   BL TL 6'1"   200 lbs.

Year	Team	W	L	PCT	ERA	G	GS	CG	IP	H	BB	SO	ShO	W	L	SV	AB	H	HR	BA	PO	A	E	DP	TC/G	FA
1992	NY A	0	2	.000	8.31	3	3	0	13	23	6	6	0	0	0	0	0	0	0	–	0	2	0	0	0.7	1.000
1993		1	2	.333	4.65	6	6	0	31	32	14	26	0	0	0	0	0	0	0	–	1	3	0	1	0.7	1.000
1994		4	1	.800	4.20	23	5	1	49.1	48	29	37	0	1	1	2	0	0	0	–	1	7	2	0	0.4	.800
3 yrs.		5	5	.500	4.92	32	14	1	93.1	103	49	69	0	1	1	2	0	0	0	–	2	12	2	1	0.5	.875

Trevor Hoffman

HOFFMAN, TREVOR WILLIAM
Brother of Glenn Hoffman.
B. Oct. 13, 1967, Bellflower, Calif.   BR TR 6'1"   200 lbs.

Year	Team	W	L	PCT	ERA	G	GS	CG	IP	H	BB	SO	ShO	W	L	SV	AB	H	HR	BA	PO	A	E	DP	TC/G	FA
1993	2 teams	FLA N	(28G 2–2)		SD N	(39G 2–4)																				
"	total	4	6	.400	3.90	67	0	0	90	80	39	79	0	4	6	5	7	1	0	.143	6	11	0	0	0.3	1.000
1994	SD N	4	4	.500	2.57	47	0	0	56	39	20	68	0	4	4	20	3	0	0	.000	4	5	0	1	0.2	1.000
2 yrs.		8	10	.444	3.39	114	0	0	146	119	59	147	0	8	10	25	10	1	0	.100	10	16	0	1	0.2	1.000

Darren Holmes

HOLMES, DARREN LEE
B. Apr. 25, 1966, Asheville, N. C.   BR TR 6'   199 lbs.

Year	Team	W	L	PCT	ERA	G	GS	CG	IP	H	BB	SO	ShO	W	L	SV	AB	H	HR	BA	PO	A	E	DP	TC/G	FA
1990	LA N	0	1	.000	5.19	14	0	0	17.1	15	11	19	0	0	1	0	0	0	0	–	1	1	0	0	0.1	1.000
1991	MIL A	1	4	.200	4.72	40	0	0	76.1	90	27	59	0	1	4	3	0	0	0	–	4	14	1	0	0.5	.947
1992		4	4	.500	2.55	41	0	0	42.1	35	11	31	0	4	4	6	0	0	0	–	5	4	1	1	0.2	.900
1993	CLR N	3	3	.500	4.05	62	0	0	66.2	56	20	60	0	3	3	25	0	0	0	–	7	6	1	1	0.2	.929
1994		0	3	.000	6.35	29	0	0	28.1	35	24	33	0	0	3	3	1	0	0	.000	2	3	1	0	0.2	.833
5 yrs.		8	15	.348	4.36	186	0	0	231	231	93	202	0	8	15	37	1	0	0	.000	19	28	4	2	0.3	.922

Rick Honeycutt

HONEYCUTT, FREDERICK WAYNE
B. June 29, 1952, Chattanooga, Tenn.   BL TL 6'1"   185 lbs.

Year	Team	W	L	PCT	ERA	G	GS	CG	IP	H	BB	SO	ShO	W	L	SV	AB	H	HR	BA	PO	A	E	DP	TC/G	FA
1977	SEA A	0	1	.000	4.34	10	3	0	29	26	11	17	0	0	0	0	0	0	0	–	0	2	0	0	0.2	1.000
1978		5	11	.313	4.89	26	24	4	134.1	150	49	50	1	0	0	0	0	0	0	–	9	28	2	1	1.5	.949
1979		11	12	.478	4.04	33	28	8	194	201	67	83	0	1	3	0	0	0	0	–	6	28	5	2	1.2	.872
1980		10	17	.370	3.95	30	30	9	203	221	60	79	0	0	0	0	0	0	0	–	9	32	2	1	1.4	.953
1981	TEX A	11	6	.647	3.30	20	20	8	128	120	17	40	2	0	0	0	0	0	0	–	3	30	3	1	1.8	.917

Year	Team	W	L	PCT	ERA	G	GS	CG	IP	H	BB	SO	ShO	Relief Pitching W	L	SV	Batting AB	H	HR	BA	PO	A	E	DP	TC/G	FA

Rick Honeycutt *continued*

Year	Team	W	L	PCT	ERA	G	GS	CG	IP	H	BB	SO	ShO	W	L	SV	AB	H	HR	BA	PO	A	E	DP	TC/G	FA
1982		5	17	.227	5.27	30	26	4	164	201	54	64	1	0	0	0	0	0	0	–	3	35	2	0	1.3	.950
1983	2 teams	TEX A	(25G 14–8)		LA N	(9G 2–3)																				
"	total	16	11	.593	3.03	34	32	6	213.2	214	50	74	2	0	0	0	12	1	0	.083	13	55	1	5	2.0	.986
1984	LA N	10	9	.526	2.84	29	28	6	183.2	180	51	75	2	0	0	0	56	8	0	.143	10	42	3	2	1.9	.945
1985		8	12	.400	3.42	31	25	1	142	141	49	67	0	0	1	1	38	5	0	.132	9	37	2	1	1.5	.958
1986		11	9	.550	3.32	32	28	0	171	164	45	100	0	1	0	0	43	3	0	.070	9	35	1	2	1.4	.978
1987	2 teams	LA N	(27G 2–12)		OAK A	(7G 1–4)																				
"	total	3	16	.158	4.72	34	24	1	139.1	158	54	102	1	0	1	0	30	7	0	.233	5	20	2	0	0.8	.926
1988	OAK A	3	2	.600	3.50	55	0	0	79.2	74	25	47	0	3	2	7	0	0	0	–	3	18	2	3	0.4	.913
1989		2	2	.500	2.35	64	0	0	76.2	56	26	52	0	2	2	12	0	0	0	–	4	16	1	1	0.3	.952
1990		2	2	.500	2.70	63	0	0	63.1	46	22	38	0	2	2	7	2	0	0	.000	0	15	1	0	0.3	.938
1991		2	4	.333	3.58	43	0	0	37.2	37	20	26	0	2	4	0	0	0	0	–	4	4	0	1	0.2	1.000
1992		1	4	.200	3.69	54	0	0	39	41	10	32	0	1	4	3	0	0	0	–	3	2	1	0	0.1	.833
1993		1	4	.200	2.81	52	0	0	41.2	30	20	21	0	1	4	1	0	0	0	–	2	5	1	1	0.2	.875
1994	TEX A	1	2	.333	7.20	42	0	0	25	37	9	18	0	1	2	1	0	0	0	–	2	7	1	0	0.2	.900
18 yrs.		102	141	.420	3.75	682	268	47	2065	2097	639	985	11	14	25	32	181	24	0	.133	94	411	30	21	0.8	.944

LEAGUE CHAMPIONSHIP SERIES

Year	Team	W	L	PCT	ERA	G	GS	CG	IP	H	BB	SO	ShO	W	L	SV	AB	H	HR	BA	PO	A	E	DP	TC/G	FA
1983	LA N	0	0	–	21.60	2	0	0	1.2	4	0	2	0	0	0	0	0	0	0	–	1	0	0	0	0.5	1.000
1985		0	0	–	13.50	2	0	0	1.1	4	2	1	0	0	0	0	0	0	0	–	0	1	0	0	0.5	1.000
1988	OAK A	1	0	1.000	0.00	3	0	0	2	0	2	0	0	1	0	0	0	0	0	–	0	0	0	0	0.0	–
1989		0	0	–	32.40	3	0	0	1.2	6	5	1	0	0	0	0	0	0	0	–	0	0	0	0	0.0	–
1990		0	0	–	0.00	3	0	0	1.2	0	0	0	0	0	0	1	0	0	0	–	1	0	0	0	0.3	1.000
1992		0	0	–	0.00	2	0	0	2	0	0	1	0	0	0	0	0	0	0	–	0	0	0	0	0.0	–
6 yrs.		1	0	1.000	10.45	15	0	0	10.1	14	9	5	0	1	0	1	0	0	0	–	2	1	0	0	0.2	1.000

WORLD SERIES

Year	Team	W	L	PCT	ERA	G	GS	CG	IP	H	BB	SO	ShO	W	L	SV	AB	H	HR	BA	PO	A	E	DP	TC/G	FA
1988	OAK A	1	0	1.000	0.00	3	0	0	3.1	0	0	5	0	1	0	0	0	0	0	–	0	0	0	0	0.0	–
1989		0	0	–	6.75	3	0	0	2.2	4	0	2	0	0	0	0	0	0	0	–	0	0	0	0	0.0	–
1990		0	0	–	0.00	1	0	0	1.2	2	1	0	0	0	0	0	0	0	0	–	0	0	0	0	0.0	–
3 yrs.		1	0	1.000	2.35	7	0	0	7.2	6	1	7	0	1	0	0	0	0	0	–	0	0	0	0	0.0	–

John Hope

HOPE, JOHN ALAN
B. Dec. 21, 1970, Ft. Lauderdale, Fla.

BR TR 6'3" 195 lbs.

Year	Team	W	L	PCT	ERA	G	GS	CG	IP	H	BB	SO	ShO	W	L	SV	AB	H	HR	BA	PO	A	E	DP	TC/G	FA
1993	PIT N	0	2	.000	4.03	7	7	0	38	47	8	8	0	0	0	0	13	1	0	.077	1	10	1	0	1.7	.917
1994		0	0	–	5.79	9	0	0	14	18	4	6	0	0	0	0	3	1	0	.333	1	3	0	0	0.4	1.000
2 yrs.		0	2	.000	4.50	16	7	0	52	65	12	14	0	0	0	0	16	2	0	.125	2	13	1	0	1.0	.938

Vince Horsman

HORSMAN, VINCENT STANLEY JOSEPH
B. Mar. 9, 1967, Halifax, N. S., Canada.

BR TL 6'2" 175 lbs.

Year	Team	W	L	PCT	ERA	G	GS	CG	IP	H	BB	SO	ShO	W	L	SV	AB	H	HR	BA	PO	A	E	DP	TC/G	FA
1991	TOR A	0	0	–	0.00	4	0	0	4	2	3	2	0	0	0	0	0	0	0	–	0	0	0	0	0.0	–
1992	OAK A	2	1	.667	2.49	58	0	0	43.1	39	21	18	0	2	1	1	0	0	0	–	1	5	0	0	0.1	1.000
1993		2	0	1.000	5.40	40	0	0	25	25	15	17	0	2	0	0	0	0	0	–	0	2	0	0	0.1	1.000
1994		0	1	.000	4.91	33	0	0	29.1	29	11	20	0	0	1	0	0	0	0	–	2	6	0	0	0.2	1.000
4 yrs.		4	2	.667	3.81	135	0	0	101.2	95	50	57	0	4	2	1	0	0	0	–	3	13	0	0	0.1	1.000

Charlie Hough

HOUGH, CHARLES OLIVER
B. Jan. 5, 1948, Honolulu, Hawaii.

BR TR 6'2" 190 lbs.

Year	Team	W	L	PCT	ERA	G	GS	CG	IP	H	BB	SO	ShO	W	L	SV	AB	H	HR	BA	PO	A	E	DP	TC/G	FA
1970	LA N	0	0	–	5.29	8	0	0	17	18	11	8	0	0	0	2	3	1	0	.333	1	3	0	0	0.5	1.000
1971		0	0	–	4.50	4	0	0	4	3	3	4	0	0	0	0	0	0	0	–	0	1	0	0	0.3	1.000
1972		0	0	–	3.38	2	0	0	2.2	2	2	4	0	0	0	0	0	0	0	–	0	1	0	0	0.5	1.000
1973		4	2	.667	2.76	37	0	0	71.2	52	45	70	0	4	2	5	14	3	0	.214	4	11	1	1	0.4	.938
1974		9	4	.692	3.75	49	0	0	96	65	40	63	0	9	4	1	12	0	0	.000	3	14	1	1	0.4	.944
1975		3	7	.300	2.95	38	0	0	61	43	34	34	0	3	7	4	6	2	0	.333	4	7	2	0	0.3	.846
1976		12	8	.600	2.21	77	0	0	142.2	102	77	81	0	12	8	18	21	6	0	.286	3	22	1	0	0.3	.962
1977		6	12	.333	3.33	70	1	0	127	98	70	105	0	5	12	22	22	4	1	.182	6	15	1	1	0.3	.955
1978		5	5	.500	3.29	55	0	0	93	69	48	66	0	5	5	7	12	4	0	.333	5	11	0	2	0.3	1.000
1979		7	5	.583	4.77	42	14	0	151	152	66	76	0	1	2	0	38	6	0	.158	5	26	1	0	0.8	.969
1980	2 teams	LA N	(19G 1–3)		TEX A	(16G 2–2)																				
"	total	3	5	.375	4.55	35	3	2	93	91	58	72	1	2	3	1	2	1	0	.500	2	10	1	0	0.4	.923
1981	TEX A	4	1	.800	2.96	21	5	2	82	61	31	69	0	0	0	1	0	0	0	–	2	8	0	1	0.5	1.000
1982		16	13	.552	3.95	34	34	12	228	217	72	128	2	0	0	0	0	0	0	–	14	35	1	4	1.5	.980
1983		15	13	.536	3.18	34	33	11	252	219	95	152	3	1	0	0	0	0	0	–	25	46	2	4	2.1	.973
1984		16	14	.533	3.76	36	**36**	**17**	266	**260**	94	165	1	0	0	0	0	0	0	–	12	51	1	2	1.8	.984
1985		14	16	.467	3.31	34	34	14	250.1	198	83	141	1	0	0	0	0	0	0	–	18	35	2	5	1.6	.964
1986		17	10	.630	3.79	33	33	7	230.1	188	89	146	2	0	0	0	0	0	0	–	20	32	1	2	1.6	.981
1987		18	13	.581	3.79	40	**40**	13	**285.1**	238	124	223	0	0	0	0	0	0	0	–	30	46	1	3	1.9	.987
1988		15	16	.484	3.32	34	34	10	252	202	**126**	174	0	0	0	0	0	0	0	–	27	43	1	4	2.1	.986
1989		10	13	.435	4.35	30	30	5	182	168	95	94	1	0	0	0	0	0	0	–	13	18	1	3	1.1	.969
1990		12	12	.500	4.07	32	32	5	218.2	190	119	114	0	0	0	0	0	0	0	–	11	31	2	1	1.4	.955
1991	CHI A	9	10	.474	4.02	31	29	4	199.1	167	94	107	1	0	0	0	0	0	0	–	12	31	1	1	1.4	.977
1992		7	12	.368	3.93	27	27	4	176.1	160	66	76	0	0	0	0	0	0	0	–	7	20	0	1	1.0	1.000
1993	FLA N	9	16	.360	4.27	34	34	0	204.1	202	71	126	0	0	0	0	63	2	0	.032	6	41	1	1	1.4	.979
1994		5	9	.357	5.15	21	21	1	113.2	118	52	65	0	0	0	0	33	4	0	.121	5	20	0	0	1.2	1.000
25 yrs.		216	216	.500	3.75	858	440	107	3799.1	3283	1665	2363	13	42	43	61	226	33	1	.146	235	578	22	38	1.0	.974
									8th																		

LEAGUE CHAMPIONSHIP SERIES

Year	Team	W	L	PCT	ERA	G	GS	CG	IP	H	BB	SO	ShO	W	L	SV	AB	H	HR	BA	PO	A	E	DP	TC/G	FA
1974	LA N	0	0	–	7.71	1	0	0	2.1	4	0	2	0	0	0	0	0	0	0	–	0	0	1	0	1.0	.000
1977		0	0	–	4.50	1	0	0	2	2	0	3	0	0	0	0	0	0	0	–	0	1	0	0	1.0	1.000
1978		0	0	–	4.50	1	0	0	2	1	0	1	0	0	0	0	0	0	0	–	1	1	0	0	2.0	1.000
3 yrs.		0	0	–	5.68	3	0	0	6.1	7	0	6	0	0	0	0	0	0	0	–	1	2	1	0	1.3	.750

Year	Team	W	L	PCT	ERA	G	GS	CG	IP	H	BB	SO	ShO	Relief Pitching W	L	SV	Batting AB	H	HR	BA	PO	A	E	DP	TC/G	FA

Charlie Hough *continued*

WORLD SERIES

Year	Team	W	L	PCT	ERA	G	GS	CG	IP	H	BB	SO	ShO	W	L	SV	AB	H	HR	BA	PO	A	E	DP	TC/G	FA
1974	LA N	0	0	–	0.00	1	0	0	2	0	1	4	0	0	0	0	0	0	0	–	0	0	0	0	0.0	–
1977		0	0	–	1.80	2	0	0	5	3	0	5	0	0	0	0	0	0	0	–	0	0	0	0	0.0	–
1978		0	0	–	8.44	2	0	0	5.1	10	2	5	0	0	0	0	0	0	0	–	1	0	0	0	0.5	1.000
3 yrs.		0	0	–	4.38	5	0	0	12.1	13	3	14	0	0	0	0	0	0	0	–	1	0	0	0	0.2	1.000

Chris Howard

HOWARD, CHRISTIAN
B. Nov. 18, 1965, Lynn, Mass.

BR TL 6' 185 lbs.

Year	Team	W	L	PCT	ERA	G	GS	CG	IP	H	BB	SO	ShO	W	L	SV	AB	H	HR	BA	PO	A	E	DP	TC/G	FA
1993	CHI A	1	0	1.000	0.00	3	0	0	2.1	2	3	1	0	1	0	0	0	0	0	–	0	0	0	0	0.0	–
1994	BOS A	1	0	1.000	3.63	37	0	0	39.2	35	12	22	0	1	0	1	0	0	0	–	2	4	0	0	0.2	1.000
2 yrs.		2	0	1.000	3.43	40	0	0	42	37	15	23	0	2	0	1	0	0	0	–	2	4	0	0	0.2	1.000

Dave Howard

HOWARD, DAVID WAYNE
Son of Bruce Howard.
B. Feb. 26, 1967, Sarasota, Fla.

BB TR 6' 165 lbs.

Year	Team	W	L	PCT	ERA	G	GS	CG	IP	H	BB	SO	ShO	W	L	SV	AB	H	HR	BA	PO	A	E	DP	TC/G	FA
1994	KC A	0	0	–	4.50	1	0	0	2	2	5	0	0	0	0	0	*				0	0	0	0	0.0	–

Steve Howe

HOWE, STEVEN ROY
B. Mar. 10, 1958, Pontiac, Mich.

BL TL 6'1" 180 lbs.

Year	Team	W	L	PCT	ERA	G	GS	CG	IP	H	BB	SO	ShO	W	L	SV	AB	H	HR	BA	PO	A	E	DP	TC/G	FA
1980	LA N	7	9	.438	2.65	59	0	0	85	83	22	39	0	7	9	17	11	1	0	.091	3	20	1	0	0.4	.958
1981		5	3	.625	2.50	41	0	0	54	51	18	32	0	5	3	8	1	0	0	.000	1	5	0	0	0.1	1.000
1982		7	5	.583	2.08	66	0	0	99.1	87	17	49	0	7	5	13	7	0	0	.000	2	17	1	0	0.3	.950
1983		4	7	.364	1.44	46	0	0	68.2	55	12	52	0	4	7	18	8	1	0	.125	4	15	0	0	0.4	1.000
1985	2 teams				LA N (19G 1–1)				MIN A (13G 2–3)																	
"	total	3	4	.429	5.49	32	0	0	41	58	12	21	0	3	4	3	0	0	0	–	3	7	1	0	0.3	.909
1987	TEX A	3	3	.500	4.31	24	0	0	31.1	33	8	19	0	3	3	1	0	0	0	–	4	4	0	0	0.3	1.000
1991	NY A	3	1	.750	1.68	37	0	0	48.1	39	7	34	0	3	1	3	0	0	0	–	5	6	3	1	0.4	.786
1992		3	0	1.000	2.45	20	0	0	22	9	3	12	0	3	0	6	0	0	0	–	2	7	1	0	0.5	.900
1993		3	5	.375	4.97	51	0	0	50.2	58	10	19	0	3	5	4	0	0	0	–	2	13	1	0	0.3	.938
1994		3	0	1.000	1.80	40	0	0	40	28	7	18	0	3	0	15	0	0	0	–	2	4	0	0	0.2	1.000
10 yrs.		41	37	.526	2.75	416	0	0	540.1	501	116	295	0	41	37	88	27	2	0	.074	28	98	8	1	0.3	.940

DIVISIONAL PLAYOFF SERIES

Year	Team	W	L	PCT	ERA	G	GS	CG	IP	H	BB	SO	ShO	W	L	SV	AB	H	HR	BA	PO	A	E	DP	TC/G	FA
1981	LA N	0	0	–	0.00	2	0	0	2	1	0	2	0	0	0	0	0	0	0	–	0	0	0	0	0.0	–

LEAGUE CHAMPIONSHIP SERIES

Year	Team	W	L	PCT	ERA	G	GS	CG	IP	H	BB	SO	ShO	W	L	SV	AB	H	HR	BA	PO	A	E	DP	TC/G	FA
1981	LA N	0	0	–	0.00	2	0	0	2	1	0	2	0	0	0	0	0	0	0	–	0	0	0	0	0.0	–

WORLD SERIES

Year	Team	W	L	PCT	ERA	G	GS	CG	IP	H	BB	SO	ShO	W	L	SV	AB	H	HR	BA	PO	A	E	DP	TC/G	FA
1981	LA N	1	0	1.000	3.86	3	0	0	7	7	1	4	0	1	0	1	2	0	0	.000	0	1	1	0	0.7	.500

Jay Howell

HOWELL, JAY CANFIELD
B. Nov. 26, 1955, Miami, Fla.

BR TR 6'3" 200 lbs.

Year	Team	W	L	PCT	ERA	G	GS	CG	IP	H	BB	SO	ShO	W	L	SV	AB	H	HR	BA	PO	A	E	DP	TC/G	FA
1980	CIN N	0	0	–	15.00	5	0	0	3	8	1	1	0	0	0	0	0	0	0	–	0	0	0	0	0.0	–
1981	CHI N	2	0	1.000	4.91	10	2	0	22	23	10	10	0	0	0	0	2	0	0	.000	2	9	0	1	1.1	1.000
1982	NY A	2	3	.400	7.71	6	6	0	28	42	13	21	0	0	0	0	0	0	0	–	2	2	0	0	0.7	1.000
1983		1	5	.167	5.38	19	12	2	82	89	35	61	0	0	0	0	0	0	0	–	7	10	1	0	0.9	.944
1984		9	4	.692	2.69	61	1	0	103.2	86	34	109	0	8	4	7	0	0	0	–	11	16	1	3	0.5	.964
1985	OAK A	9	8	.529	2.85	63	0	0	98	98	31	68	0	9	8	29	0	0	0	–	1	15	0	1	0.3	1.000
1986		3	6	.333	3.38	38	0	0	53.1	53	23	42	0	3	6	16	0	0	0	–	2	6	0	0	0.2	1.000
1987		3	4	.429	5.89	36	0	0	44.1	48	21	35	0	3	4	16	0	0	0	–	3	4	1	0	0.2	.875
1988	LA N	5	3	.625	2.08	50	0	0	65	44	21	70	0	5	3	21	2	0	0	.000	7	6	1	0	0.3	.929
1989		5	3	.625	1.58	56	0	0	79.2	60	22	55	0	5	3	28	3	0	0	.000	5	10	1	2	0.3	.938
1990		5	5	.500	2.18	45	0	0	66	59	20	59	0	5	5	16	0	0	0	.000	3	8	0	0	0.2	1.000
1991		6	5	.545	3.18	44	0	0	51	39	11	40	0	6	5	16	0	0	0	–	5	6	1	0	0.3	.917
1992		1	3	.250	1.54	41	0	0	46.2	41	18	36	0	1	3	4	0	0	0	–	6	7	0	0	0.3	1.000
1993	ATL N	3	3	.500	2.31	54	0	0	58.1	48	16	37	0	3	3	0	0	0	0	–	4	7	0	0	0.2	1.000
1994	TEX A	4	1	.800	5.44	40	0	0	43	44	16	22	0	4	1	2	0	0	0	–	5	6	2	1	0.3	.846
15 yrs.		58	53	.523	3.34	568	21	2	844	782	291	666	0	52	45	155	9	0	0	.000	63	112	8	9	0.3	.956

LEAGUE CHAMPIONSHIP SERIES

Year	Team	W	L	PCT	ERA	G	GS	CG	IP	H	BB	SO	ShO	W	L	SV	AB	H	HR	BA	PO	A	E	DP	TC/G	FA
1988	LA N	0	1	.000	27.00	2	0	0	0.2	1	2	1	0	0	1	0	0	0	0	–	0	0	0	0	0.0	–

WORLD SERIES

Year	Team	W	L	PCT	ERA	G	GS	CG	IP	H	BB	SO	ShO	W	L	SV	AB	H	HR	BA	PO	A	E	DP	TC/G	FA
1988	LA N	0	1	.000	3.38	2	0	0	2.2	3	1	2	0	0	1	1	0	0	0	–	0	0	0	0	0.0	–

John Hudek

HUDEK, JOHN RAYMOND
B. Aug. 8, 1966, Tampa, Fla.

BB TR 6'1" 200 lbs.

Year	Team	W	L	PCT	ERA	G	GS	CG	IP	H	BB	SO	ShO	W	L	SV	AB	H	HR	BA	PO	A	E	DP	TC/G	FA
1994	HOU N	0	2	.000	2.97	42	0	0	39.1	24	18	39	0	0	2	16	0	0	0	–	4	3	0	0	0.2	1.000

Bruce Hurst

HURST, BRUCE VEE
B. Mar. 24, 1958, St. George, Utah.

BL TL 6'4" 200 lbs.

Year	Team	W	L	PCT	ERA	G	GS	CG	IP	H	BB	SO	ShO	W	L	SV	AB	H	HR	BA	PO	A	E	DP	TC/G	FA
1980	BOS A	2	2	.500	9.00	12	7	0	31	39	16	16	0	0	0	0	0	0	0	–	1	4	0	0	0.4	1.000
1981		2	0	1.000	4.30	5	5	0	23	23	12	11	0	0	0	0	0	0	0	–	0	2	0	0	0.4	1.000
1982		3	7	.300	5.77	28	19	0	117	161	40	53	0	0	0	1	0	0	0	–	6	22	1	1	1.0	.966
1983		12	12	.500	4.09	33	32	6	211.1	241	62	115	2	0	0	0	0	0	0	–	12	34	2	2	1.5	.958
1984		12	12	.500	3.92	33	33	9	218	232	88	136	2	0	0	0	0	0	0	–	10	30	0	1	1.2	1.000
1985		11	13	.458	4.51	35	31	6	229.1	243	70	189	1	0	2	0	0	0	0	–	11	32	3	0	1.3	.935
1986		13	8	.619	2.99	25	25	11	174.1	169	50	167	4	0	0	0	0	0	0	–	7	18	2	2	1.1	.926
1987		15	13	.536	4.41	33	33	15	238.2	239	76	190	3	0	0	0	0	0	0	–	12	34	3	2	1.5	.939
1988		18	6	.750	3.66	33	32	7	216.2	222	65	166	1	0	0	0	0	0	0	–	7	31	0	0	1.2	1.000
1989	SD N	15	11	.577	2.69	33	33	10	244.2	214	66	179	2	0	0	0	70	5	0	.071	8	42	0	2	1.5	1.000
1990		11	9	.550	3.14	33	33	9	223.2	188	63	162	4	0	0	0	67	6	0	.090	7	34	1	3	1.3	.976
1991		15	8	.652	3.29	31	31	4	221.2	201	59	141	0	0	0	0	67	9	0	.134	7	33	2	2	1.4	.952

Year	Team		W	L	PCT	ERA	G	GS	CG	IP	H	BB	SO	ShO	Relief Pitching W	L	SV	Batting AB	H	HR	BA	PO	A	E	DP	TC/G	FA

Bruce Hurst *continued*

Year	Team	W	L	PCT	ERA	G	GS	CG	IP	H	BB	SO	ShO	W	L	SV	AB	H	HR	BA	PO	A	E	DP	TC/G	FA
1992		14	9	.609	3.85	32	32	6	217.1	223	51	131	4	0	0	0	69	11	0	.159	10	32	1	0	1.3	.977
1993	**2 teams** SD N (2G 0–1) CLR N (3G 0–1)																									
"	total	0	2	.000	7.62	5	5	0	13	15	6	9	0	0	0	0	1	0	0	.000	0	4	0	0	0.8	1.000
1994	TEX A	2	1	.667	7.11	8	8	0	38	53	16	24	0	0	0	0	0	0	0	–	0	3	0	0	0.4	1.000
15 yrs.		145	113	.562	3.92	379	359	83	2417.2	2463	740	1689	23	0	3	0	274	31	0	.113	98	355	15	15	1.2	.968

LEAGUE CHAMPIONSHIP SERIES

Year	Team	W	L	PCT	ERA	G	GS	CG	IP	H	BB	SO	ShO	W	L	SV	AB	H	HR	BA	PO	A	E	DP	TC/G	FA
1986	BOS A	1	0	1.000	2.40	2	2	1	15	18	1	8	0	0	0	0	0	0	0	–	1	2	0	0	1.5	1.000
1988		0	2	.000	2.77	2	2	1	13	10	5	12	0	0	0	0	0	0	0	–	0	4	0	0	2.0	1.000
2 yrs.		1	2	.333	2.57	4	4	2	28	28	6	20	0	0	0	0	0	0	0	–	1	6	0	0	1.8	1.000

WORLD SERIES

Year	Team	W	L	PCT	ERA	G	GS	CG	IP	H	BB	SO	ShO	W	L	SV	AB	H	HR	BA	PO	A	E	DP	TC/G	FA
1986	BOS A	2	0	1.000	1.96	3	3	1	23	18	6	17	0	0	0	0	3	0	0	.000	1	3	0	0	1.3	1.000

James Hurst

HURST, JAMES LAVON
B. June 1, 1967, Plantation, Fla.

BL TL 6' 160 lbs.

Year	Team	W	L	PCT	ERA	G	GS	CG	IP	H	BB	SO	ShO	W	L	SV	AB	H	HR	BA	PO	A	E	DP	TC/G	FA
1994	TEX A	0	0	–	10.13	8	0	0	10.2	17	8	5	0	0	0	0	0	0	0	–	0	2	0	0	0.3	1.000

Jonathan Hurst

HURST, JONATHAN
B. Oct. 20, 1966, New York, N. Y.

BR TR 6'3" 175 lbs.

Year	Team	W	L	PCT	ERA	G	GS	CG	IP	H	BB	SO	ShO	W	L	SV	AB	H	HR	BA	PO	A	E	DP	TC/G	FA
1992	MON N	1	1	.500	5.51	3	3	0	16.1	18	7	4	0	0	0	0	4	0	0	.000	2	2	0	0	1.3	1.000
1994	NY N	0	1	.000	12.60	7	0	0	10	15	5	6	0	0	1	0	0	0	0	–	1	1	0	0	0.3	1.000
2 yrs.		1	2	.333	8.20	10	3	0	26.1	33	12	10	0	0	1	0	4	0	0	.000	3	3	0	0	0.6	1.000

Mark Hutton

HUTTON, MARK STEVEN
B. Feb. 6, 1970, South Adelaide, Australia

BR TR 6'6" 240 lbs.

Year	Team	W	L	PCT	ERA	G	GS	CG	IP	H	BB	SO	ShO	W	L	SV	AB	H	HR	BA	PO	A	E	DP	TC/G	FA
1993	NY A	1	1	.500	5.73	7	4	0	22	24	17	12	0	0	0	0	0	0	0	–	1	2	1	0	0.6	.750
1994		0	0	–	4.91	2	0	0	3.2	4	0	1	0	0	0	0	0	0	0	–	0	0	0	0	0.0	–
2 yrs.		1	1	.500	5.61	9	4	0	25.2	28	17	13	0	0	0	0	0	0	0	–	1	2	1	0	0.4	.750

Mike Ignasiak

IGNASIAK, MICHAEL JAMES
Brother of Gary Ignasiak.
B. Mar. 12, 1967, Anchorville, Mich.

BR TR 5'11" 175 lbs.

Year	Team	W	L	PCT	ERA	G	GS	CG	IP	H	BB	SO	ShO	W	L	SV	AB	H	HR	BA	PO	A	E	DP	TC/G	FA
1991	MIL A	2	1	.667	5.68	4	1	0	12.2	7	8	10	0	2	1	0	0	0	0	–	1	0	0	0	0.3	1.000
1993		1	1	.500	3.65	27	0	0	37	32	21	28	0	1	1	0	0	0	0	–	0	3	0	0	0.1	1.000
1994		3	1	.750	4.53	23	5	0	47.2	51	13	24	0	2	0	0	0	0	0	–	2	4	0	1	0.3	1.000
3 yrs.		6	3	.667	4.35	54	6	0	97.1	90	42	62	0	5	2	0	0	0	0	–	3	7	0	1	0.2	1.000

Blaise Ilsley

ILSLEY, BLAISE FRANCIS
B. Apr. 9, 1964, Alpena, Mich.

BL TL 6'1" 195 lbs.

Year	Team	W	L	PCT	ERA	G	GS	CG	IP	H	BB	SO	ShO	W	L	SV	AB	H	HR	BA	PO	A	E	DP	TC/G	FA
1994	CHI N	0	0	–	7.80	10	0	0	15	25	9	9	0	0	0	0	1	0	0	.000	4	1	0	0	0.5	1.000

Danny Jackson

JACKSON, DANNY LYNN
B. Jan. 5, 1962, San Antonio, Tex.

BR TL 6' 205 lbs.

Year	Team	W	L	PCT	ERA	G	GS	CG	IP	H	BB	SO	ShO	W	L	SV	AB	H	HR	BA	PO	A	E	DP	TC/G	FA
1983	KC A	1	1	.500	5.21	4	3	0	19	26	6	9	0	1	0	0	0	0	0	–	2	3	0	0	1.3	1.000
1984		2	6	.250	4.26	15	11	1	76	84	35	40	0	1	0	0	0	0	0	–	6	7	1	2	0.9	.929
1985		14	12	.538	3.42	32	32	4	208	209	76	114	3	0	0	0	0	0	0	–	8	27	3	2	1.2	.921
1986		11	12	.478	3.20	32	27	4	185.2	177	79	115	1	0	0	1	0	0	0	–	14	21	2	1	1.2	.946
1987		9	18	.333	4.02	36	34	11	224	219	109	152	2	0	0	0	0	0	0	–	13	23	2	2	1.1	.947
1988	CIN N	**23**	8	.742	2.73	35	35	**15**	260.2	206	71	161	6	0	0	0	90	13	0	.144	10	52	3	2	1.9	.954
1989		6	11	.353	5.60	20	20	1	115.2	122	57	70	0	0	0	0	36	8	0	.222	5	15	0	0	1.0	1.000
1990		6	6	.500	3.61	22	21	0	117.1	119	40	76	0	0	0	0	37	2	0	.054	4	13	1	0	0.8	.944
1991	CHI N	1	5	.167	6.75	17	14	0	70.2	89	48	31	0	0	0	0	23	2	0	.087	4	7	1	0	0.7	.917
1992	**2 teams** CHI N (19G 4–9) PIT N (15G 4–4)																									
"	total	8	13	.381	3.84	34	34	0	201.1	211	77	97	0	0	0	0	60	5	0	.083	9	33	8	2	1.5	.840
1993	PHI N	12	11	.522	3.77	32	32	2	210.1	214	80	120	1	0	0	0	65	5	0	.077	7	26	4	3	1.2	.892
1994		14	6	.700	3.26	25	25	4	179.1	183	46	129	1	0	0	0	57	9	0	.158	12	30	0	3	1.7	1.000
12 yrs.		107	109	.495	3.77	304	288	42	1868	1859	724	1114	14	2	0	1	368	44	0	.120	94	257	25	17	1.2	.934

LEAGUE CHAMPIONSHIP SERIES

Year	Team	W	L	PCT	ERA	G	GS	CG	IP	H	BB	SO	ShO	W	L	SV	AB	H	HR	BA	PO	A	E	DP	TC/G	FA
1985	KC A	1	0	1.000	0.00	2	1	1	10	10	1	7	1	0	0	0	0	0	0	–	0	0	0	0	0.0	–
1990	CIN N	1	0	1.000	2.38	2	2	0	11.1	8	7	8	0	0	0	0	3	0	0	.000	0	2	0	0	1.0	1.000
1992	PIT N	0	1	.000	21.60	1	1	0	1.2	4	2	0	0	0	0	0	0	0	0	–	0	0	0	0	0.0	–
1993	PHI N	1	0	1.000	1.17	1	1	0	7.2	9	2	6	0	0	0	0	4	1	0	.250	0	0	0	0	0.0	–
4 yrs.		3	1	.750	2.35	6	5	1	30.2	31	12	21	1	0	0	0	7	1	0	.143	0	2	0	0	0.3	1.000

WORLD SERIES

Year	Team	W	L	PCT	ERA	G	GS	CG	IP	H	BB	SO	ShO	W	L	SV	AB	H	HR	BA	PO	A	E	DP	TC/G	FA
1985	KC A	1	1	.500	1.69	2	2	1	16	9	5	12	0	0	0	0	6	0	0	.000	0	4	1	0	2.5	.800
1990	CIN N	0	0	–	10.13	1	1	0	2.2	6	2	0	0	0	0	0	1	0	0	.000	0	1	1	0	2.0	.500
1993	PHI N	0	1	.000	7.20	1	1	0	5	6	1	1	0	0	0	0	1	0	0	.000	0	0	0	0	0.0	–
3 yrs.		1	2	.333	3.80	4	4	1	23.2	21	8	13	0	0	0	0	8	0	0	.000	0	5	2	0	1.8	.714

Darrin Jackson

JACKSON, DARRIN JAY
B. Aug. 22, 1963, Los Angeles, Calif.

BR TR 6' 185 lbs.

Year	Team	W	L	PCT	ERA	G	GS	CG	IP	H	BB	SO	ShO	W	L	SV	AB	H	HR	BA	PO	A	E	DP	TC/G	FA
1991	SD N	0	0	–	9.00	1	0	0	2	3	1	2	0	0	0	0	*				1	0	0	0	0.0	–

Mike Jackson

JACKSON, MICHAEL RAY
B. Dec. 22, 1964, Houston, Tex.

BR TR 6'1" 185 lbs.

Year	Team	W	L	PCT	ERA	G	GS	CG	IP	H	BB	SO	ShO	W	L	SV	AB	H	HR	BA	PO	A	E	DP	TC/G	FA
1986	PHI N	0	0	–	3.38	9	0	0	13.1	12	4	3	0	0	0	0	2	0	0	–	2	0	0	0	0.2	1.000
1987		3	10	.231	4.20	55	7	0	109.1	88	56	93	0	2	6	1	17	2	0	.118	5	12	1	0	0.3	.944
1988	SEA A	6	5	.545	2.63	62	0	0	99.1	74	43	76	0	6	5	4	0	0	0	–	4	11	0	0	0.2	1.000
1989		4	6	.400	3.17	65	0	0	99.1	81	54	94	0	4	6	7	0	0	0	–	3	11	2	0	0.2	.875
1990		5	7	.417	4.54	63	0	0	77.1	64	44	69	0	5	7	3	0	0	0	–	5	14	0	3	0.3	1.000

Year	Team	W	L	PCT	ERA	G	GS	CG	IP	H	BB	SO	ShO	W	L	SV	AB	H	HR	BA	PO	A	E	DP	TC/G	FA
														Relief Pitching			**Batting**									

Mike Jackson *continued*

Year	Team	W	L	PCT	ERA	G	GS	CG	IP	H	BB	SO	ShO	W	L	SV	AB	H	HR	BA	PO	A	E	DP	TC/G	FA
1991		7	7	.500	3.25	72	0	0	88.2	64	34	74	0	7	7	14	0	0	0	–	2	8	1	1	0.2	.909
1992	SF N	6	6	.500	3.73	67	0	0	82	76	33	80	0	6	6	2	2	0	0	.000	6	9	1	0	0.2	.938
1993		6	6	.500	3.03	81	0	0	77.1	58	24	70	0	6	6	1	3	2	0	.667	3	13	1	0	0.2	.941
1994		3	2	.600	1.49	36	0	0	42.1	23	11	51	0	3	2	4	1	0	0	.000	0	7	0	1	0.2	1.000
9 yrs.		40	49	.449	3.37	510	7	0	689	540	303	610	0	39	45	36	23	4	0	.174	30	83	6	5	0.2	.950

Jason Jacome

JACOME, JASON JAMES
B. Nov. 24, 1970, Tulsa, Okla.

BL TL 6'1" 155 lbs.

Year	Team	W	L	PCT	ERA	G	GS	CG	IP	H	BB	SO	ShO	W	L	SV	AB	H	HR	BA	PO	A	E	DP	TC/G	FA
1994	NY N	4	3	.571	2.67	8	8	1	54	54	17	30	1	0	0	0	16	1	0	.063	4	9	0	2	1.6	1.000

Kevin Jarvis

JARVIS, KEVIN THOMAS
B. Aug. 1, 1969, Lexington, Ky.

BL TR 6'2" 200 lbs.

Year	Team	W	L	PCT	ERA	G	GS	CG	IP	H	BB	SO	ShO	W	L	SV	AB	H	HR	BA	PO	A	E	DP	TC/G	FA
1994	CIN N	1	1	.500	7.13	6	3	0	17.2	22	5	10	0	1	0	0	4	1	0	.250	2	3	1	0	1.0	.833

Mike Jeffcoat

JEFFCOAT, JAMES MICHAEL
B. Aug. 3, 1959, Pine Bluff, Ark.

BL TL 6'2" 185 lbs.

Year	Team	W	L	PCT	ERA	G	GS	CG	IP	H	BB	SO	ShO	W	L	SV	AB	H	HR	BA	PO	A	E	DP	TC/G	FA
1983	CLE A	1	3	.250	3.31	11	2	0	32.2	32	13	9	0	1	0	0	0	0	0	–	2	4	0	0	0.5	1.000
1984		5	2	.714	2.99	63	1	0	75.1	82	24	41	0	4	2	1	0	0	0	–	2	13	0	3	0.2	1.000
1985	2 teams								CLE A (9G 0–0)		SF N	(19G 0–2)														
"	total	0	2	.000	4.55	28	1	0	31.2	35	12	14	0	0	2	0	1	0	0	.000	2	12	1	0	0.5	.933
1987	TEX A	0	1	.000	12.86	2	2	0	7	11	4	1	0	0	0	0	0	0	0	–	0	0	0	0	0.0	–
1988		0	2	.000	11.70	5	2	0	10	19	5	5	0	0	0	0	0	0	0	–	0	2	0	0	0.4	1.000
1989		9	6	.600	3.58	22	22	2	130.2	139	33	64	2	0	0	0	0	0	0	–	13	18	1	1	1.5	.969
1990		5	6	.455	4.47	44	12	1	110.2	122	28	58	0	2	1	5	0	0	0	–	4	10	1	3	0.3	.933
1991		5	3	.625	4.63	70	0	0	79.2	104	25	43	0	5	3	1	0	0	0	1.000	2	13	0	0	0.2	1.000
1992		0	1	.000	7.32	6	3	0	19.2	28	5	6	0	0	0	0	0	0	0	–	1	3	0	1	0.7	1.000
1994	FLA N	0	0	–	10.13	4	0	0	2.2	4	0	1	0	0	0	0	0	0	0	–	0	0	0	0	0.0	–
10 yrs.		25	26	.490	4.37	255	45	3	500	576	149	242	2	12	9	7	2	1	0	.500	26	75	3	8	0.4	.971

Miguel Jimenez

JIMENEZ, MIGUEL ANTHONY
B. Aug. 19, 1969, New York, N. Y.

BR TR 6'2" 205 lbs.

Year	Team	W	L	PCT	ERA	G	GS	CG	IP	H	BB	SO	ShO	W	L	SV	AB	H	HR	BA	PO	A	E	DP	TC/G	FA
1993	OAK A	1	0	1.000	4.00	5	4	0	27	27	16	13	0	0	0	0	0	0	0	–	0	0	0	0	0.0	–
1994		1	4	.200	7.41	8	7	0	34	38	32	22	0	0	0	0	0	0	0	–	2	6	1	1	1.1	.889
2 yrs.		2	4	.333	5.90	13	11	0	61	65	48	35	0	0	0	0	0	0	0	–	2	6	1	1	0.7	.889

Dane Johnson

JOHNSON, DANE EDWARD
B. Feb. 10, 1963, Coral Gables, Fla.

BR TR 6'5" 205 lbs.

Year	Team	W	L	PCT	ERA	G	GS	CG	IP	H	BB	SO	ShO	W	L	SV	AB	H	HR	BA	PO	A	E	DP	TC/G	FA
1994	CHI A	2	1	.667	6.57	15	0	0	12.1	16	11	7	0	2	1	0	0	0	0	–	0	1	0	0	0.1	1.000

Randy Johnson

JOHNSON, RANDALL DAVID
B. Sept. 10, 1963, Walnut Creek, Calif.

BL TR 6'10" 225 lbs.

Year	Team	W	L	PCT	ERA	G	GS	CG	IP	H	BB	SO	ShO	W	L	SV	AB	H	HR	BA	PO	A	E	DP	TC/G	FA
1988	MON N	3	0	1.000	2.42	4	4	1	26	23	7	25	0	0	0	0	9	1	0	.111	0	0	1	0	0.3	.000
1989	2 teams								MON N (7G 0–4)		SEA A	(22G 7–9)														
"	total	7	13	.350	4.82	29	28	2	160.2	147	96	130	0	0	0	0	7	1	0	.143	8	26	7	1	1.4	.829
1990	SEA A	14	11	.560	3.65	33	33	5	219.2	174	120	194	2	0	0	0	0	0	0	–	6	24	5	2	1.1	.857
1991		13	10	.565	3.98	33	33	2	201.1	151	152	228	1	0	0	0	0	0	0	–	0	23	5	3	0.8	.821
1992		12	14	.462	3.77	31	31	6	210.1	154	144	241	2	0	0	0	0	0	0	–	5	20	3	0	0.9	.893
1993		19	8	.704	3.24	35	34	10	255.1	185	99	308	3	0	0	1	0	0	0	–	10	29	0	2	1.1	1.000
1994		13	6	.684	3.19	23	23	9	172	132	72	204	4	0	0	0	0	0	0	–	12	27	0	0	1.7	1.000
7 yrs.		81	62	.566	3.70	188	186	35	1245.1	966	690	1330	12	0	0	1	16	2	0	.125	41	149	21	8	1.1	.900

Joel Johnston

JOHNSTON, JOEL RAYMOND
B. Mar. 8, 1967, West Chester, Pa.

BR TR 6'5" 218 lbs.

Year	Team	W	L	PCT	ERA	G	GS	CG	IP	H	BB	SO	ShO	W	L	SV	AB	H	HR	BA	PO	A	E	DP	TC/G	FA
1991	KC A	1	0	1.000	0.40	13	0	0	22.1	9	9	21	0	1	0	0	0	0	0	–	1	2	0	0	0.2	1.000
1992		0	0	–	13.50	5	0	0	2.2	3	2	0	0	0	0	0	0	0	0	–	0	0	0	0	0.0	–
1993	PIT N	2	4	.333	3.38	33	0	0	53.1	38	19	31	0	2	4	2	6	2	0	.333	4	5	0	0	0.3	1.000
1994		0	0	–	29.70	4	0	0	3.1	14	4	5	0	0	0	0	0	0	0	–	0	1	2	0	0.8	.333
4 yrs.		3	4	.429	3.97	55	0	0	81.2	64	34	57	0	3	4	2	6	2	0	.333	5	8	2	0	0.3	.867

John Johnstone

JOHNSTONE, JOHN WILLIAM
B. Nov. 25, 1968, Liverpool, N. Y.

BR TR 6'3" 195 lbs.

Year	Team	W	L	PCT	ERA	G	GS	CG	IP	H	BB	SO	ShO	W	L	SV	AB	H	HR	BA	PO	A	E	DP	TC/G	FA
1993	FLA N	0	2	.000	5.91	7	0	0	10.2	16	7	5	0	0	2	0	0	0	0	–	2	0	0	0	0.3	1.000
1994		1	2	.333	5.91	17	0	0	21.1	23	16	23	0	1	2	0	0	0	0	–	0	3	0	0	0.2	1.000
2 yrs.		1	4	.200	5.91	24	0	0	32	39	23	28	0	1	4	0	0	0	0	–	2	3	0	0	0.2	1.000

Bobby Jones

JONES, ROBERT JOSEPH
B. Feb. 10, 1970, Fresno, Calif.

BR TR 6'4" 210 lbs.

Year	Team	W	L	PCT	ERA	G	GS	CG	IP	H	BB	SO	ShO	W	L	SV	AB	H	HR	BA	PO	A	E	DP	TC/G	FA
1993	NY N	2	4	.333	3.65	9	9	0	61.2	61	22	35	0	0	0	0	20	1	0	.050	5	8	0	0	1.4	1.000
1994		12	7	.632	3.15	24	24	1	160	157	56	80	1	0	0	0	46	5	0	.109	11	33	0	3	1.8	1.000
2 yrs.		14	11	.560	3.29	33	33	1	221.2	218	78	115	1	0	0	0	66	6	0	.091	16	41	0	3	1.7	1.000

Doug Jones

JONES, DOUGLAS REID
B. June 24, 1957, Covina, Calif.

BR TR 6'3" 195 lbs.

Year	Team	W	L	PCT	ERA	G	GS	CG	IP	H	BB	SO	ShO	W	L	SV	AB	H	HR	BA	PO	A	E	DP	TC/G	FA
1982	MIL A	0	0	–	10.13	4	0	0	2.2	5	1	1	0	0	0	0	0	0	0	–	1	0	0	0	0.3	1.000
1986	CLE A	1	0	1.000	2.50	11	0	0	18	18	6	12	0	1	0	1	0	0	0	–	1	4	0	1	0.5	1.000
1987		6	5	.545	3.15	49	0	0	91.1	101	24	87	0	6	5	8	0	0	0	–	8	13	5	3	0.5	.808
1988		3	4	.429	2.27	51	0	0	83.1	69	16	72	0	3	4	37	0	0	0	–	7	11	2	0	0.4	.900
1989		7	10	.412	2.34	59	0	0	80.2	76	13	65	0	7	10	32	0	0	0	–	3	14	0	1	0.3	1.000

Year	Team	W	L	PCT	ERA	G	GS	CG	IP	H	BB	SO	ShO	Relief Pitching W	L	SV	Batting AB	H	HR	BA	PO	A	E	DP	TC/G	FA

Doug Jones *continued*

Year	Team	W	L	PCT	ERA	G	GS	CG	IP	H	BB	SO	ShO	W	L	SV	AB	H	HR	BA	PO	A	E	DP	TC/G	FA
1990		5	5	.500	2.56	66	0	0	84.1	66	22	55	0	5	5	43	0	0	0	–	0	9	2	0	0.2	.818
1991		4	8	.333	5.54	36	4	0	63.1	87	17	48	0	1	7	7	0	0	0	–	7	10	0	1	0.5	1.000
1992	HOU N	11	8	.579	1.85	80	0	0	111.2	96	17	93	0	11	8	36	4	0	0	.000	5	12	2	0	0.2	.895
1993		4	10	.286	4.54	71	0	0	85.1	102	21	66	0	4	10	26	0	0	0	–	2	12	1	0	0.2	.933
1994	PHI N	2	4	.333	2.17	47	0	0	54	55	6	38	0	2	4	27	1	1	0	1.000	2	10	2	0	0.3	.857
10 yrs.		43	54	.443	2.99	474	0	0	674.2	675	143	537	0	40	53	217	5	1	0	.200	36	95	14	6	0.3	.903

Todd Jones

JONES, TODD BARTON GIVIN
B. Apr. 24, 1968, Marietta, Ga.

BL TR 6'3" 200 lbs.

Year	Team	W	L	PCT	ERA	G	GS	CG	IP	H	BB	SO	ShO	W	L	SV	AB	H	HR	BA	PO	A	E	DP	TC/G	FA
1993	HOU N	1	2	.333	3.13	27	0	0	37.1	28	15	25	0	1	2	2	0	0	0	–	4	2	0	0	0.2	1.000
1994		5	2	.714	2.72	48	0	0	72.2	52	26	63	0	5	2	5	5	2	0	.400	4	3	0	0	0.1	1.000
2 yrs.		6	4	.600	2.86	75	0	0	110	80	41	88	0	6	4	7	5	2	0	.400	8	5	0	0	0.2	1.000

Jeff Juden

JUDEN, JEFFREY DANIEL
B. Jan. 19, 1971, Salem, Mass.

BR TR 6'7" 245 lbs.

Year	Team	W	L	PCT	ERA	G	GS	CG	IP	H	BB	SO	ShO	W	L	SV	AB	H	HR	BA	PO	A	E	DP	TC/G	FA
1991	HOU N	0	2	.000	6.00	4	3	0	18	19	7	11	0	0	0	0	5	0	0	.000	0	2	3	0	1.3	.400
1993		0	1	.000	5.40	2	0	0	5	4	4	7	0	0	1	0	0	0	0	–	0	0	0	0	0.0	–
1994	PHI N	1	4	.200	6.18	6	5	0	27.2	29	12	22	0	0	0	0	9	1	0	.111	1	3	1	0	0.8	.800
3 yrs.		1	7	.125	6.04	12	8	0	50.2	52	23	40	0	0	0	0	14	1	0	.071	1	5	4	0	0.8	.600

Scott Kamieniecki

KAMIENIECKI, SCOTT ANDREW
B. Apr. 19, 1964, Mt. Clemens, Mich.

BR TR 6' 195 lbs.

Year	Team	W	L	PCT	ERA	G	GS	CG	IP	H	BB	SO	ShO	W	L	SV	AB	H	HR	BA	PO	A	E	DP	TC/G	FA
1991	NY A	4	4	.500	3.90	9	9	0	55.1	54	22	34	0	0	0	0	0	0	0	–	5	9	0	0	1.6	1.000
1992		6	14	.300	4.36	28	28	4	188	193	74	88	0	0	0	0	0	0	0	–	15	20	0	3	1.3	1.000
1993		10	7	.588	4.08	30	20	2	154.1	163	59	72	0	0	1	1	0	0	0	–	17	23	0	1	1.3	1.000
1994		8	6	.571	3.76	22	16	1	117.1	115	59	71	0	1	0	0	0	0	0	–	8	17	1	1	1.2	.962
4 yrs.		28	31	.475	4.09	89	73	7	515	525	214	265	0	1	1	1	0	0	0	–	45	69	1	5	1.3	.991

Steve Karsay

KARSAY, STEFAN ANDREW
B. Mar. 24, 1972, Flushing, N. Y.

BR TR 6'3" 210 lbs.

Year	Team	W	L	PCT	ERA	G	GS	CG	IP	H	BB	SO	ShO	W	L	SV	AB	H	HR	BA	PO	A	E	DP	TC/G	FA
1993	OAK A	3	3	.500	4.04	8	8	0	49	49	16	33	0	0	0	0	0	0	0	–	2	3	0	0	0.6	1.000
1994		1	1	.500	2.57	4	4	1	28	26	8	15	0	0	0	0	0	0	0	–	3	4	0	0	1.8	1.000
2 yrs.		4	4	.500	3.51	12	12	1	77	75	24	48	0	0	0	0	0	0	0	–	5	7	0	0	1.0	1.000

Jimmy Key

KEY, JAMES EDWARD
B. Apr. 22, 1961, Huntsville, Ala.

BR TL 6'1" 180 lbs.

Year	Team	W	L	PCT	ERA	G	GS	CG	IP	H	BB	SO	ShO	W	L	SV	AB	H	HR	BA	PO	A	E	DP	TC/G	FA
1984	TOR A	4	5	.444	4.65	63	0	0	62	70	32	44	0	4	5	10	0	0	0	–	9	11	1	0	0.3	.952
1985		14	6	.700	3.00	35	32	3	212.2	188	50	85	0	1	0	0	0	0	0	–	15	52	3	3	2.0	.957
1986		14	11	.560	3.57	36	35	4	232	222	74	141	2	0	0	0	0	0	0	–	18	42	0	4	1.7	1.000
1987		17	8	.680	2.76	36	36	8	261	210	66	161	1	0	0	0	0	0	0	–	17	44	3	5	1.8	.953
1988		12	5	.706	3.29	21	21	2	131.1	127	30	65	2	0	0	0	0	0	0	–	5	19	0	1	1.1	1.000
1989		13	14	.481	3.88	33	33	5	216	226	27	118	1	0	0	0	0	0	0	–	11	44	2	2	1.7	.965
1990		13	7	.650	4.25	27	27	0	154.2	169	22	88	0	0	0	0	0	0	0	–	8	22	1	3	1.1	.968
1991		16	12	.571	3.05	33	33	2	209.1	207	44	125	2	0	0	0	0	0	0	–	22	37	2	3	1.8	.967
1992		13	13	.500	3.53	33	33	4	216.2	205	59	117	2	0	0	0	0	0	0	–	18	27	1	2	1.4	.978
1993	NY A	18	6	.750	3.00	34	34	4	236.2	219	43	173	2	0	0	0	0	0	0	–	14	33	4	1	1.5	.922
1994		17	4	.810	3.27	25	25	1	168	177	52	97	0	0	0	0	0	0	0	–	6	40	2	3	1.9	.958
11 yrs.		151	91	.624	3.36	376	309	33	2100.1	2020	499	1214	12	5	5	10	0	0	0	–	143	371	19	27	1.4	.964

LEAGUE CHAMPIONSHIP SERIES

Year	Team	W	L	PCT	ERA	G	GS	CG	IP	H	BB	SO	ShO	W	L	SV	AB	H	HR	BA	PO	A	E	DP	TC/G	FA
1985	TOR A	0	1	.000	5.19	2	2	0	8.2	15	2	5	0	0	0	0	0	0	0	–	0	3	0	0	1.5	1.000
1989		1	0	1.000	4.50	1	1	0	6	7	2	2	0	0	0	0	0	0	0	–	0	0	0	0	0.0	–
1991		0	0	–	3.00	1	1	0	6	5	1	1	0	0	0	0	0	0	0	–	0	3	0	1	3.0	1.000
1992		0	0	–	0.00	1	0	0	3	2	2	1	0	0	0	0	0	0	0	–	0	0	0	0	0.0	–
4 yrs.		1	1	.500	3.80	5	4	0	23.2	29	7	9	0	0	0	0	0	0	0	–	0	6	0	1	1.2	1.000

WORLD SERIES

Year	Team	W	L	PCT	ERA	G	GS	CG	IP	H	BB	SO	ShO	W	L	SV	AB	H	HR	BA	PO	A	E	DP	TC/G	FA
1992	TOR A	2	0	1.000	1.00	2	1	0	9	6	0	6	0	1	0	0	1	0	0	.000	2	4	0	0	3.0	1.000

Mark Kiefer

KIEFER, MARK ANDREW
Brother of Steve Kiefer.
B. Nov. 13, 1968, Orange, Calif.

BR TR 6'4" 175 lbs.

Year	Team	W	L	PCT	ERA	G	GS	CG	IP	H	BB	SO	ShO	W	L	SV	AB	H	HR	BA	PO	A	E	DP	TC/G	FA
1993	MIL A	0	0	–	0.00	6	0	0	9.1	3	5	7	0	0	0	1	0	0	0	–	1	1	0	0	0.3	1.000
1994		1	0	1.000	8.44	7	0	0	10.2	15	8	8	0	1	0	0	0	0	0	–	0	1	0	0	0.1	1.000
2 yrs.		1	0	1.000	4.50	13	0	0	20	18	13	15	0	1	0	1	0	0	0	–	1	2	0	0	0.2	1.000

Darryl Kile

KILE, DARRYL ANDREW
B. Dec. 2, 1968, Garden Grove, Calif.

BR TR 6'5" 185 lbs.

Year	Team	W	L	PCT	ERA	G	GS	CG	IP	H	BB	SO	ShO	W	L	SV	AB	H	HR	BA	PO	A	E	DP	TC/G	FA
1991	HOU N	7	11	.389	3.69	37	22	0	153.2	144	84	100	0	0	2	0	38	0	0	.000	7	17	3	1	0.7	.889
1992		5	10	.333	3.95	22	22	0	125.1	124	63	90	0	0	0	0	32	5	0	.156	2	12	5	0	0.9	.737
1993		15	8	.652	3.51	32	26	4	171.2	152	69	141	2	1	0	0	53	5	0	.094	9	15	3	0	0.8	.889
1994		9	6	.600	4.57	24	24	0	147.2	153	82	105	0	0	0	0	47	7	0	.149	9	19	1	0	1.2	.966
4 yrs.		36	35	.507	3.91	115	94	6	598.1	573	298	436	2	1	2	0	170	17	1	.100	27	63	12	1	0.9	.882

Kevin King

KING, KEVIN RAY
B. Feb. 11, 1969, Atwater, Calif.

BL TL 6'4" 170 lbs.

Year	Team	W	L	PCT	ERA	G	GS	CG	IP	H	BB	SO	ShO	W	L	SV	AB	H	HR	BA	PO	A	E	DP	TC/G	FA
1993	SEA A	0	1	.000	6.17	13	0	0	11.2	9	4	8	0	0	1	0	0	0	0	–	1	1	1	0	0.2	.500
1994		0	2	.000	7.04	19	0	0	15.1	21	17	6	0	0	2	0	0	0	0	–	1	3	0	0	0.2	1.000
2 yrs.		0	3	.000	6.67	32	0	0	27	30	21	14	0	0	3	0	0	0	0	–	1	4	1	0	0.2	.833

Year	Team	W	L	PCT	ERA	G	GS	CG	IP	H	BB	SO	ShO	Relief Pitching W	L	SV	Batting AB	H	HR	BA	PO	A	E	DP	TC/G	FA

Scott Klingenbeck

KLINGENBECK, SCOTT EDWARD
B. Feb. 3, 1971, Cincinnati, Ohio
BR TR 6'2" 205 lbs.

Year	Team	W	L	PCT	ERA	G	GS	CG	IP	H	BB	SO	ShO	RW	RL	SV	AB	H	HR	BA	PO	A	E	DP	TC/G	FA
1994	BAL A	1	0	1.000	3.86	1	1	0	7	6	4	5	0	0	0	0	0	0	0	–	1	0	0	0	1.0	1.000

Kurt Knudsen

KNUDSEN, KURT DAVID
B. Feb. 20, 1967, Arlington Heights, Ill.
BR TR 6'2" 185 lbs.

Year	Team	W	L	PCT	ERA	G	GS	CG	IP	H	BB	SO	ShO	RW	RL	SV	AB	H	HR	BA	PO	A	E	DP	TC/G	FA
1992	DET A	2	3	.400	4.58	48	1	0	70.2	70	41	51	0	2	2	5	0	0	0	–	6	7	0	0	0.3	1.000
1993		3	2	.600	4.78	30	0	0	37.2	41	16	29	0	3	2	2	0	0	0	–	4	3	0	0	0.2	1.000
1994		1	0	1.000	13.50	4	0	0	5.1	7	11	1	0	1	0	0	0	0	0	–	0	0	0	0	0.0	–
3 yrs.		6	5	.545	5.07	82	1	0	113.2	118	68	81	0	6	4	7	0	0	0	–	10	10	0	2	0.2	1.000

Bill Krueger

KRUEGER, WILLIAM CULP
B. Apr. 24, 1958, Waukegan, Ill.
BL TL 6'5" 205 lbs.

Year	Team	W	L	PCT	ERA	G	GS	CG	IP	H	BB	SO	ShO	RW	RL	SV	AB	H	HR	BA	PO	A	E	DP	TC/G	FA
1983	OAK A	7	6	.538	3.61	17	16	2	109.2	104	53	58	0	1	0	0	0	0	0	–	3	7	1	0	0.6	.909
1984		10	10	.500	4.75	26	24	1	142	156	85	61	0	0	0	0	0	0	0	–	6	12	0	1	0.7	1.000
1985		9	10	.474	4.52	32	23	0	151.1	165	69	56	0	1	0	0	0	0	0	–	3	23	2	0	0.9	.929
1986		1	2	.333	6.03	11	3	0	34.1	40	13	10	0	0	1	1	0	0	0	–	2	8	1	1	1.0	.909
1987	2 teams	OAK A (9G 0–3)				LA N (2G 0–0)																				
"	total	0	3	.000	6.75	11	0	0	8	12	9	4	0	0	3	0	0	0	0	–	0	0	0	0	–	
1988	LA N	0	0	–	11.57	1	1	0	2.1	4	2	1	0	0	0	0	0	0	0	–	0	2	0	0	2.0	1.000
1989	MIL A	3	2	.600	3.84	34	5	0	93.2	96	33	72	0	1	0	3	0	0	0	–	5	11	0	0	0.5	1.000
1990		6	8	.429	3.98	30	17	0	129	137	54	64	0	2	3	0	0	0	0	–	2	17	0	2	0.6	1.000
1991	SEA A	11	8	.579	3.60	35	25	1	175	194	60	91	0	1	0	0	0	0	0	–	5	30	0	2	1.0	1.000
1992	2 teams	MIN A (27G 10–6)				MON N (9G 0–2)																				
"	total	10	8	.556	4.53	36	29	2	178.2	189	53	99	0	0	0	0	3	0	0	.000	4	11	0	0	0.4	1.000
1993	DET A	6	4	.600	3.40	32	7	0	82	90	30	60	0	3	2	0	0	0	0	–	2	10	0	1	0.4	1.000
1994	2 teams	DET A (16G 0–2)				SD N (8G 3–2)																				
"	total	3	4	.429	6.38	24	9	1	60.2	68	24	47	0	0	0	0	12	6	0	.500	1	11	0	1	0.5	1.000
12 yrs.		66	65	.504	4.30	289	159	9	1166.2	1255	485	623	2	9	12	4	15	6	0	.400	33	142	4	8	0.6	.978

Mark Langston

LANGSTON, MARK EDWARD
B. Aug. 20, 1960, San Diego, Calif.
BR TL 6'2" 175 lbs.

Year	Team	W	L	PCT	ERA	G	GS	CG	IP	H	BB	SO	ShO	RW	RL	SV	AB	H	HR	BA	PO	A	E	DP	TC/G	FA
1984	SEA A	17	10	.630	3.40	35	33	5	225	188	118	204	2	1	0	0	0	0	0	–	15	30	2	2	1.3	.957
1985		7	14	.333	5.47	24	24	2	126.2	122	91	72	0	0	0	0	0	0	0	–	9	26	2	4	1.5	.946
1986		12	14	.462	4.85	37	36	9	239.1	234	123	245	0	0	0	0	0	0	0	–	7	27	6	3	1.1	.850
1987		19	13	.594	3.84	35	35	14	272	242	114	262	3	0	0	0	0	0	0	–	8	41	2	3	1.5	.961
1988		15	11	.577	3.34	35	35	9	261.1	222	110	235	3	0	0	0	0	0	0	–	11	45	4	6	1.7	.933
1989	2 teams	SEA A (10G 4–5)				MON N (24G 12–9)																				
"	total	16	14	.533	2.74	34	34	8	250	198	112	235	5	0	0	0	64	11	0	.172	15	28	2	2	1.3	.956
1990	CAL A	10	17	.370	4.40	33	33	5	223	215	104	195	1	0	0	0	0	0	0	–	7	42	3	0	1.6	.942
1991		19	8	.704	3.00	34	34	7	246.1	190	96	183	0	0	0	0	0	0	0	–	15	34	3	2	1.5	.942
1992		13	14	.481	3.66	32	32	9	229	206	74	174	2	0	0	0	2	0	0	.000	7	41	3	1	1.6	.941
1993		16	11	.593	3.20	35	35	7	256.1	220	85	196	0	0	0	0	0	0	0	–	10	47	2	4	1.7	.966
1994		7	8	.467	4.68	18	18	2	119.1	121	54	109	1	0	0	0	0	0	0	–	3	27	1	1	1.8	.938
11 yrs.		151	134	.530	3.74	352	349	77	2448.1	2158	1081	2110	17	1	0	0	66	11	0	.167	107	388	31	28	1.5	.941

Tim Leary

LEARY, TIMOTHY JAMES
B. Mar. 21, 1958, Santa Monica, Calif.
BR TR 6'3" 205 lbs.

Year	Team	W	L	PCT	ERA	G	GS	CG	IP	H	BB	SO	ShO	RW	RL	SV	AB	H	HR	BA	PO	A	E	DP	TC/G	FA
1981	NY N	0	0	–	0.00	1	1	0	2	0	1	3	0	0	0	0	1	0	0	.000	0	0	0	0	0.0	–
1983		1	1	.500	3.38	2	2	1	10.2	15	4	9	0	0	0	0	3	1	0	.333	1	3	0	0	2.0	1.000
1984		3	3	.500	4.02	20	7	0	53.2	61	18	29	0	3	0	0	10	3	1	.300	3	4	1	0	0.4	.875
1985	MIL A	1	4	.200	4.05	5	5	0	33.1	40	8	29	0	0	0	0	0	0	0	–	1	7	0	0	1.6	1.000
1986		12	12	.500	4.21	33	30	3	188.1	216	53	110	2	0	0	0	0	0	0	–	22	26	1	1	1.5	.980
1987	LA N	3	11	.214	4.76	39	12	0	107.2	121	36	61	0	1	4	1	23	7	0	.304	9	18	0	2	0.7	1.000
1988		17	11	.607	2.91	35	34	9	228.2	201	56	180	6	0	0	0	67	18	0	.269	24	34	1	4	1.7	.983
1989	2 teams	LA N (19G 6–7)				CIN N (14G 2–7)																				
"	total	8	14	.364	3.52	33	31	2	207	205	68	123	0	1	1	0	59	7	0	.119	20	31	2	1	1.6	.962
1990	NY A	9	19	.321	4.11	31	31	6	208	202	78	138	1	0	0	0	0	0	0	–	14	36	4	4	1.7	.926
1991		4	10	.286	6.49	28	18	1	120.2	150	57	83	0	0	0	0	0	0	0	–	9	12	1	3	0.8	.955
1992	2 teams	NY A (18G 5–6)				SEA A (8G 3–4)																				
"	total	8	10	.444	5.36	26	23	3	141	131	87	46	0	0	0	0	0	0	0	–	10	18	0	1	1.1	1.000
1993	SEA A	11	9	.550	5.05	33	27	0	169.1	202	58	68	0	0	1	0	0	0	0	–	14	28	0	3	1.3	1.000
1994	TEX A	1	1	.500	8.14	6	3	0	21	26	11	9	0	0	0	0	0	0	0	–	3	4	0	0	1.2	1.000
13 yrs.		78	105	.426	4.36	292	224	25	1491.1	1570	535	888	9	5	8	1	163	36	1	.221	130	221	10	22	1.2	.972

LEAGUE CHAMPIONSHIP SERIES

Year	Team	W	L	PCT	ERA	G	GS	CG	IP	H	BB	SO	ShO	RW	RL	SV	AB	H	HR	BA	PO	A	E	DP	TC/G	FA
1988	LA N	0	1	.000	6.23	2	1	0	4.1	8	3	3	0	0	1	0	1	0	0	.000	0	1	0	0	0.5	1.000

WORLD SERIES

Year	Team	W	L	PCT	ERA	G	GS	CG	IP	H	BB	SO	ShO	RW	RL	SV	AB	H	HR	BA	PO	A	E	DP	TC/G	FA
1988	LA N	0	0	–	1.35	2	0	0	6.2	6	2	4	0	0	0	0	0	0	0	–	1	3	0	1	2.0	1.000

Craig Lefferts

LEFFERTS, CRAIG LINDSAY
B. Sept. 29, 1957, Munich, West Germany.
BL TL 6'1" 180 lbs.

Year	Team	W	L	PCT	ERA	G	GS	CG	IP	H	BB	SO	ShO	RW	RL	SV	AB	H	HR	BA	PO	A	E	DP	TC/G	FA
1983	CHI N	3	4	.429	3.13	56	5	0	89	80	29	60	0	2	3	1	18	2	0	.111	8	13	1	0	0.4	.955
1984	SD N	3	4	.429	2.13	62	0	0	105.2	88	24	56	0	3	4	10	17	5	0	.294	5	10	1	2	0.3	.938
1985		7	6	.538	3.35	60	0	0	83.1	75	30	48	0	7	6	2	4	1	0	.250	4	11	0	1	0.3	1.000
1986		9	8	.529	3.09	83	0	0	107.2	98	44	72	0	9	8	4	8	1	1	.125	3	24	0	3	0.3	1.000
1987	2 teams	SD N (33G 2–2)				SF N (44G 3–3)																				
"	total	5	5	.500	3.83	77	0	0	98.2	92	33	57	0	5	5	6	7	2	0	.286	5	11	2	1	0.2	.889
1988	SF N	3	8	.273	2.92	64	0	0	92.1	74	23	58	0	3	8	11	9	0	0	.000	2	11	0	0	0.2	1.000
1989		2	4	.333	2.69	70	0	0	107	93	22	71	0	2	4	20	7	0	0	.000	5	9	0	2	0.2	1.000
1990	SD N	7	5	.583	2.52	56	0	0	78.2	68	22	60	0	7	5	23	4	1	0	.250	6	10	0	2	0.3	1.000
1991		1	6	.143	3.91	54	0	0	69	74	14	48	0	1	6	23	6	0	0	.000	3	12	0	1	0.3	1.000
1992	2 teams	SD N (27G 13–9)				BAL A (5G 1–3)																				
"	total	14	12	.538	3.76	32	32	1	196.1	214	41	104	0	0	0	0	52	4	0	.077	8	28	2	0	1.2	.947

Year	Team		W	L	PCT	ERA	G	GS	CG	IP	H	BB	SO	ShO	W	L	SV	AB	H	HR	BA	PO	A	E	DP	TC/G	FA

Craig Lefferts *continued*

1993	TEX	A	3	9	.250	6.05	52	8	0	83.1	102	28	58	0	2	4	0	0	0	0	–	6	12	1	0	0.4	.947
1994	CAL	A	1	1	.500	4.67	30	0	0	34.2	50	12	27	0	1	1	1	0	0	0	–	1	3	1	0	0.2	.800
12 yrs.			58	72	.446	3.43	696	45	1	1145.2	1108	322	719	0	42	54	101	132	16	1	.121	56	154	8	12	0.3	.963

LEAGUE CHAMPIONSHIP SERIES

1984	SD	N	2	0	1.000	0.00	3	0	0	4	1	1	1	0	2	0	0	0	0	0	–	0	0	0	0	0.0	–
1987	SF	N	0	0	–	0.00	3	0	0	2	3	1	0	0	0	0	0	0	0	0	–	0	2	0	1	0.7	1.000
1989			0	0	–	9.00	2	0	0	1	1	2	1	0	0	0	0	0	0	0	–	0	0	0	0	0.0	–
3 yrs.			2	0	1.000	1.29	8	0	0	7	5	4	2	0	2	0	0	0	0	0	–	0	2	0	1	0.3	1.000

WORLD SERIES

1984	SD	N	0	0	–	0.00	3	0	0	6	2	1	7	0	0	0	1	0	0	0	–	0	0	0	0	0.0	–
1989	SF	N	0	0	–	3.38	3	0	0	2.2	2	2	1	0	0	0	0	0	0	0	–	0	1	1	0	0.7	.500
2 yrs.			0	0	–	1.04	6	0	0	8.2	4	3	8	0	0	0	1	0	0	0	–	0	1	1	0	0.3	.500

Phil Leftwich

LEFTWICH, PHILLIP DALE
B. May 19, 1969, Lynchburg, Va. — BR TR 6'5" 205 lbs.

1993	CAL	A	4	6	.400	3.79	12	12	1	80.2	81	27	31	0	0	0	0	0	0	0	–	5	11	1	2	1.4	.941
1994			5	10	.333	5.68	20	20	1	114	127	42	67	0	0	0	0	0	0	0	–	9	15	3	0	1.4	.889
2 yrs.			9	16	.360	4.90	32	32	2	194.2	208	69	98	0	0	0	0	0	0	0	–	14	26	4	2	1.4	.909

Dave Leiper

LEIPER, DAVID PAUL
B. June 18, 1962, Whittier, Calif. — BL TL 6'1" 160 lbs.

1984	OAK	A	1	0	1.000	9.00	8	0	0	7	12	5	3	0	1	0	0	0	0	0	–	1	2	0	0	0.4	1.000
1986			2	2	.500	4.83	33	0	0	31.2	28	18	15	0	2	2	1	0	0	0	–	0	6	0	0	0.2	1.000
1987	2 teams		OAK A (45G 2–1)			SD N (12G 1–0)																					
"	total		3	1	.750	3.95	57	0	0	68.1	65	23	43	0	3	1	2	0	0	0	–	5	14	2	1	0.4	.905
1988	SD	N	3	0	1.000	2.17	35	0	0	54	45	14	33	0	3	0	1	2	1	0	.500	3	9	0	1	0.3	1.000
1989			0	1	.000	5.02	22	0	0	28.2	40	20	7	0	0	1	0	1	0	0	.000	4	7	1	0	0.5	.917
1994	OAK	A	0	0	–	1.93	26	0	0	18.2	13	6	14	0	0	0	1	0	0	0	–	0	1	0	1	0.0	1.000
6 yrs.			9	4	.692	3.76	181	0	0	208.1	203	86	115	0	9	4	5	3	1	0	.333	13	39	3	3	0.3	.945

Al Leiter

LEITER, ALOIS TERRY
Brother of Mark Leiter.
B. Oct. 23, 1965, Toms River, N. J. — BL TL 6'2" 200 lbs.

1987	NY	A	2	2	.500	6.35	4	4	0	22.2	24	15	28	0	0	0	0	0	0	0	–	0	2	0	0	0.5	1.000
1988			4	4	.500	3.92	14	14	0	57.1	49	33	60	0	0	0	0	0	0	0	–	0	11	1	0	0.9	.917
1989	2 teams		NY A (4G 1–2)			TOR A (1G 0–0)																					
"	total		1	2	.333	5.67	5	5	0	33.1	32	23	26	0	0	0	0	0	0	0	–	1	2	0	0	0.6	1.000
1990	TOR	A	0	0	–	0.00	4	0	0	6.1	1	2	5	0	0	0	0	0	0	0	–	1	1	0	0	0.5	1.000
1991			0	0	–	27.00	3	0	0	1.2	3	5	1	0	0	0	0	0	0	0	–	0	1	0	0	0.3	1.000
1992			0	0	–	9.00	1	0	0	1	1	2	0	0	0	0	0	0	0	0	–	0	0	0	0	0.0	–
1993			9	6	.600	4.11	34	12	1	105	93	56	66	1	3	1	2	0	0	0	–	4	12	1	0	0.5	.941
1994			6	7	.462	5.08	20	20	1	111.2	125	65	100	0	0	0	0	0	0	0	–	3	13	0	1	0.8	1.000
8 yrs.			22	21	.512	4.75	85	55	2	339	328	201	286	1	3	1	2	0	0	0	–	9	42	2	1	0.6	.962

LEAGUE CHAMPIONSHIP SERIES

| 1993 | TOR | A | 0 | 0 | – | 3.38 | 2 | 0 | 0 | 2.2 | 4 | 2 | 2 | 0 | 0 | 0 | 0 | 0 | 0 | 0 | – | 0 | 0 | 0 | 0 | 0.0 | – |

WORLD SERIES

| 1993 | TOR | A | 1 | 0 | 1.000 | 7.71 | 3 | 0 | 0 | 7 | 12 | 2 | 5 | 0 | 1 | 0 | 0 | 1 | 1 | 0 | 1.000 | 0 | 0 | 0 | 0 | 0.0 | – |

Mark Leiter

LEITER, MARK EDWARD
Brother of Al Leiter.
B. Apr. 13, 1963, Joliet, Ill. — BR TR 6'3" 200 lbs.

1990	NY	A	1	1	.500	6.84	8	3	0	26.1	33	9	21	0	0	1	0	0	0	0	–	0	8	0	1	1.0	1.000
1991	DET	A	9	7	.563	4.21	38	15	1	134.2	125	50	103	0	2	1	1	0	0	0	–	3	17	1	1	0.6	.952
1992			8	5	.615	4.18	35	14	1	112	116	43	75	0	3	2	0	0	0	0	–	8	15	1	0	0.7	.958
1993			6	6	.500	4.73	27	13	1	106.2	111	44	70	0	1	2	0	0	0	0	–	5	11	2	1	0.7	.889
1994	CAL	A	4	7	.364	4.72	40	7	0	95.1	99	35	71	0	2	4	2	0	0	0	–	5	16	1	0	0.6	.955
5 yrs.			28	26	.519	4.57	148	52	3	475	484	181	340	0	8	10	3	0	0	0	–	21	67	5	3	0.6	.946

Curtis Leskanic

LESKANIC, CURTIS JOHN
B. Apr. 2, 1968, Homestead, Pa. — BR TR 6' 180 lbs.

1993	CLR	N	1	5	.167	5.37	18	8	0	57	59	27	30	0	0	1	0	13	2	0	.154	5	5	1	2	0.6	.909
1994			1	1	.500	5.64	8	3	0	22.1	27	10	17	0	0	0	0	6	1	0	.167	1	2	0	0	0.4	1.000
2 yrs.			2	6	.250	5.45	26	11	0	79.1	86	37	47	0	0	1	0	19	3	0	.158	6	7	1	2	0.5	.929

Richie Lewis

LEWIS, RICHIE TODD
B. Jan. 25, 1966, Muncie, Ind. — BR TR 5'10" 175 lbs.

1992	BAL	A	1	1	.500	10.80	2	2	0	6.2	13	7	4	0	0	0	0	0	0	0	–	1	1	0	0	1.0	1.000
1993	FLA	N	6	3	.667	3.26	57	2	0	77.1	68	43	65	0	6	3	0	2	1	0	.500	3	13	1	1	0.3	.941
1994			1	4	.200	5.67	45	0	0	54	62	38	45	0	1	4	0	5	0	0	.000	6	5	2	1	0.3	.846
3 yrs.			8	8	.500	4.57	104	2	0	138	143	88	114	0	7	7	0	7	1	0	.143	10	19	3	2	0.3	.906

Scott Lewis

LEWIS, SCOTT ALLEN
B. Dec. 5, 1965, Grant's Pass, Ore. — BR TR 6'3" 190 lbs.

1990	CAL	A	1	1	.500	2.20	2	2	1	16.1	10	2	9	0	0	0	0	0	0	0	–	0	6	0	0	0.5	1.000
1991			3	5	.375	6.27	16	11	0	60.1	81	21	37	0	1	0	0	0	0	0	–	4	8	1	0	0.8	.923
1992			4	0	1.000	3.99	21	2	0	38.1	36	14	18	0	3	0	0	0	0	0	–	3	8	0	2	0.5	1.000
1993			1	2	.333	4.22	15	4	0	32	37	12	10	0	0	1	0	0	0	0	–	5	1	2	0	0.5	.750
1994			0	1	.000	6.10	20	0	0	31	46	10	10	0	0	1	0	0	0	0	–	0	5	0	0	0.3	1.000
5 yrs.			9	9	.500	5.01	74	19	1	178	210	59	84	0	4	2	0	0	0	0	–	12	23	3	2	0.5	.921

Year	Team		W	L	PCT	ERA	G	GS	CG	IP	H	BB	SO	ShO	W	L	SV	AB	H	HR	BA	PO	A	E	DP	TC/G	FA
															Relief Pitching			**Batting**									

Jon Lieber
LIEBER, JONATHAN RAY
B. Apr. 2, 1970, Council Bluffs, Iowa
BL TR 6'3" 220 lbs.

Year	Team		W	L	PCT	ERA	G	GS	CG	IP	H	BB	SO	ShO	W	L	SV	AB	H	HR	BA	PO	A	E	DP	TC/G	FA
1994	PIT	N	6	7	.462	3.73	17	17	1	108.2	116	25	71	0	0	0	0	39	4	0	.103	10	8	2	1	1.2	.900

Derek Lilliquist
LILLIQUIST, DEREK JANSEN
B. Feb. 20, 1966, Winter Park, Fla.
BL TL 6' 200 lbs.

Year	Team		W	L	PCT	ERA	G	GS	CG	IP	H	BB	SO	ShO	W	L	SV	AB	H	HR	BA	PO	A	E	DP	TC/G	FA
1989	ATL	N	8	10	.444	3.97	32	30	0	165.2	202	34	79	0	0	0	0	63	12	0	.190	9	20	2	1	1.0	.935
1990	2 teams			ATL N (12G 2–8)		SD N (16G 3–3)																					
"	total		5	11	.313	5.31	28	18	1	122	136	42	63	1	0	1	0	43	11	2	.256	4	7	0	0	0.4	1.000
1991	SD	N	0	2	.000	8.79	6	2	0	14.1	25	4	7	0	0	0	0	2	0	0	.000	1	4	0	0	0.8	1.000
1992	CLE	A	5	3	.625	1.75	71	0	0	61.2	39	18	47	0	5	3	6	0	0	0	–	3	9	0	0	0.2	1.000
1993			4	4	.500	2.25	56	2	0	64	64	19	40	0	4	4	10	0	0	0	–	1	9	1	0	0.2	.909
1994			1	3	.250	4.91	36	0	0	29.1	34	8	15	0	1	3	1	0	0	0	–	0	2	0	0	0.1	1.000
	6 yrs.		23	33	.411	4.00	229	52	1	457	500	125	251	1	10	11	17	108	23	2	.213	18	51	3	1	0.3	.958

Jose Lima
LIMA, JOSE DESIDERIO RODRIGUEZ
B. Sept. 20, 1972, Santiago, Dominican Republic
BR TR 6'2" 170 lbs.

Year	Team		W	L	PCT	ERA	G	GS	CG	IP	H	BB	SO	ShO	W	L	SV	AB	H	HR	BA	PO	A	E	DP	TC/G	FA
1994	DET	A	0	1	.000	13.50	3	1	0	6.2	11	3	7	0	0	0	0	0	0	0	–	1	0	0	0	0.3	1.000

Doug Linton
LINTON, DOUGLAS WARREN
B. Feb. 9, 1965, Santa Ana, Calif.
BR TR 6'1" 185 lbs.

Year	Team		W	L	PCT	ERA	G	GS	CG	IP	H	BB	SO	ShO	W	L	SV	AB	H	HR	BA	PO	A	E	DP	TC/G	FA
1992	TOR	A	1	3	.250	8.63	8	3	0	24	31	17	16	0	1	0	0	0	0	0	–	0	2	0	1	0.3	1.000
1993	2 teams			TOR A (4G 0–1)		CAL A (19G 2–0)																					
"	total		2	1	.667	7.36	23	1	0	36.2	46	23	23	0	2	0	0	0	0	0	–	2	3	0	0	0.2	1.000
1994	NY	N	6	2	.750	4.47	32	3	0	50.1	74	20	29	0	5	1	0	7	0	0	.000	1	6	1	0	0.3	.875
	3 yrs.		9	6	.600	6.32	63	7	0	111	151	60	68	0	7	2	0	7	0	0	.000	3	11	1	1	0.2	.933

Greg Litton
LITTON, JON GREGORY
B. July 13, 1964, New Orleans, La.
BR TR 6' 175 lbs.

Year	Team		W	L	PCT	ERA	G	GS	CG	IP	H	BB	SO	ShO	W	L	SV	AB	H	HR	BA	PO	A	E	DP	TC/G	FA
1991	SF	N	0	0	–	9.00	1	0	0	1	1	3	0	0	0	0	0	*				0	0	0	0	0.0	–

Graeme Lloyd
LLOYD, GRAEME JOHN
B. Apr. 9, 1967, Geelong, Australia
BL TL 6'8" 225 lbs.

Year	Team		W	L	PCT	ERA	G	GS	CG	IP	H	BB	SO	ShO	W	L	SV	AB	H	HR	BA	PO	A	E	DP	TC/G	FA
1993	MIL	A	3	4	.429	2.83	55	0	0	63.2	64	13	31	0	3	4	0	0	0	0	–	3	13	1	1	0.3	.941
1994			2	3	.400	5.17	43	0	0	47	49	15	31	0	2	3	3	0	0	0	–	6	2	0	1	0.2	1.000
	2 yrs.		5	7	.417	3.82	98	0	0	110.2	113	28	62	0	5	7	3	0	0	0	–	9	15	1	2	0.3	.960

Brian Looney
LOONEY, BRIAN JAMES
B. Sept. 26, 1969, New Haven, Conn.
BL TL 5'10" 180 lbs.

Year	Team		W	L	PCT	ERA	G	GS	CG	IP	H	BB	SO	ShO	W	L	SV	AB	H	HR	BA	PO	A	E	DP	TC/G	FA
1993	MON	N	0	0	–	3.00	3	1	0	6	8	2	7	0	0	0	0	1	0	0	.000	0	1	0	0	0.3	1.000
1994			0	0	–	22.50	1	0	0	2	4	0	2	0	0	0	0	0	0	0	–	0	0	0	0	0.0	–
	2 yrs.		0	0	–	7.88	4	1	0	8	12	2	9	0	0	0	0	1	0	0	.000	0	1	0	0	0.3	1.000

Albie Lopez
LOPEZ, ALBERT ANTHONY
B. Aug. 18, 1971, Mesa, Ariz.
BR TR 6'1" 205 lbs.

Year	Team		W	L	PCT	ERA	G	GS	CG	IP	H	BB	SO	ShO	W	L	SV	AB	H	HR	BA	PO	A	E	DP	TC/G	FA
1993	CLE	A	3	1	.750	5.98	9	9	0	49.2	49	32	25	0	0	0	0	0	0	0	–	5	6	3	0	1.4	.846
1994			1	2	.333	4.24	4	4	1	17	20	6	18	1	0	0	0	0	0	0	–	2	0	1	0	0.8	.667
	2 yrs.		4	3	.571	5.54	13	13	1	66.2	69	38	43	1	0	0	0	0	0	0	–	7	6	3	0	1.2	.813

Andrew Lorraine
LORRAINE, ANDREW JASON
B. Aug. 11, 1972, Los Angeles, Calif.
BL TL 6'3" 195 lbs.

Year	Team		W	L	PCT	ERA	G	GS	CG	IP	H	BB	SO	ShO	W	L	SV	AB	H	HR	BA	PO	A	E	DP	TC/G	FA
1994	CAL	A	0	2	.000	10.61	4	3	0	18.2	30	11	10	0	0	0	0	0	0	0	–	2	3	0	0	1.3	1.000

Greg Maddux
MADDUX, GREGORY ALAN
Brother of Mike Maddux.
B. Apr. 14, 1966, San Angelo, Tex.
BR TR 6' 170 lbs.

Year	Team		W	L	PCT	ERA	G	GS	CG	IP	H	BB	SO	ShO	W	L	SV	AB	H	HR	BA	PO	A	E	DP	TC/G	FA
1986	CHI	N	2	4	.333	5.52	6	5	1	31	44	11	20	0	0	1	0	12	4	0	.333	1	6	1	0	1.3	.875
1987			6	14	.300	5.61	30	27	1	155.2	181	74	101	1	0	0	0	42	5	0	.119	16	50	4	7	2.3	.943
1988			18	8	.692	3.18	34	34	9	249	230	81	140	3	0	0	0	96	19	0	.198	28	45	3	3	2.2	.961
1989			19	12	.613	2.95	35	35	7	238.1	222	82	135	1	0	0	0	81	17	0	.210	35	41	3	4	2.3	.962
1990			15	15	.500	3.46	35	**35**	8	237	**242**	71	144	2	0	0	0	83	12	0	.145	39	55	0	6	2.7	1.000
1991			15	11	.577	3.35	37	**37**	7	263	232	66	198	2	0	0	0	88	18	1	.205	39	50	2	5	2.5	.978
1992			**20**	11	.645	2.18	35	**35**	9	**268**	201	70	199	4	0	0	0	88	15	1	.170	30	64	3	1	2.8	.969
1993	ATL	N	20	10	.667	**2.36**	36	**36**	8	267	228	52	197	1	0	0	0	91	15	0	.165	39	59	7	5	2.9	.933
1994			16	6	.727	**1.56**	25	25	**10**	**202**	150	31	156	**3**	0	0	0	63	14	0	.222	20	37	4	4	2.4	.934
	9 yrs.		131	91	.590	3.02	273	269	60	1911	1730	538	1290	17	0	1	0	644	119	2	.185	247	407	27	35	2.5	.960

LEAGUE CHAMPIONSHIP SERIES

Year	Team		W	L	PCT	ERA	G	GS	CG	IP	H	BB	SO	ShO	W	L	SV	AB	H	HR	BA	PO	A	E	DP	TC/G	FA
1989	CHI	N	0	1	.000	13.50	2	2	0	7.1	13	4	5	0	0	0	0	3	0	0	.000	0	6	1	0	0.5	.000
1993	ATL	N	1	1	.500	4.97	2	2	0	12.2	11	7	11	0	0	0	0	4	1	0	.250	3	5	1	0	4.5	.889
	2 yrs.		1	2	.333	8.10	4	4	0	20	24	11	16	0	0	0	0	7	1	0	.143	3	5	2	0	2.5	.800

Mike Maddux
MADDUX, MICHAEL AUSLEY
Brother of Greg Maddux.
B. Aug. 27, 1961, Dayton, Ohio.
BL TR 6'2" 180 lbs.

Year	Team		W	L	PCT	ERA	G	GS	CG	IP	H	BB	SO	ShO	W	L	SV	AB	H	HR	BA	PO	A	E	DP	TC/G	FA
1986	PHI	N	3	7	.300	5.42	16	16	0	78	88	34	44	0	0	0	0	22	1	0	.045	5	10	2	0	1.1	.882
1987			2	0	1.000	2.65	7	2	0	17	17	5	15	0	1	0	0	3	0	0	.000	1	1	1	0	0.4	.667
1988			4	3	.571	3.76	25	11	0	88.2	91	34	59	0	2	0	0	23	3	0	.130	8	18	4	1	1.2	.867
1989			1	3	.250	5.15	16	4	0	43.2	52	14	26	1	0	0	0	10	0	0	.000	7	12	0	1	1.2	1.000
1990	LA	N	0	1	.000	6.53	11	2	0	20.2	24	4	11	0	0	0	0	2	0	0	.000	0	2	0	0	0.2	1.000
1991	SD	N	7	2	.778	2.46	64	1	0	98.2	78	27	57	0	6	2	5	13	1	0	.077	9	18	1	1	0.4	.964
1992			2	2	.500	2.37	50	1	0	79.2	71	24	60	0	2	1	5	9	1	0	.111	9	18	1	1	0.6	.964

Year	Team		W	L	PCT	ERA	G	GS	CG	IP	H	BB	SO	ShO	W	L	SV	AB	H	HR	BA	PO	A	E	DP	TC/G	FA

Mike Maddux *continued*

Year	Team	W	L	PCT	ERA	G	GS	CG	IP	H	BB	SO	ShO	W	L	SV	AB	H	HR	BA	PO	A	E	DP	TC/G	FA
1993	NY N	3	8	.273	3.60	58	0	0	75	67	27	57	0	3	8	5	3	0	0	.000	6	16	1	1	0.4	.957
1994		2	1	.667	5.11	27	0	0	44	45	13	32	0	2	1	2	3	0	0	.000	2	11	1	2	0.5	.929
9 yrs.		24	27	.471	3.83	274	37	2	545.1	533	182	361	1	16	13	18	88	6	0	.068	47	106	11	7	0.6	.933

Mike Magnante

MAGNANTE, MICHAEL ANTHONY
B. June 17, 1965, Glendale, Calif.

BL TL 6'1" 180 lbs.

Year	Team	W	L	PCT	ERA	G	GS	CG	IP	H	BB	SO	ShO	W	L	SV	AB	H	HR	BA	PO	A	E	DP	TC/G	FA
1991	KC A	0	1	.000	2.45	38	0	0	55	55	23	42	0	0	1	0	0	0	0	–	3	6	1	1	0.3	.900
1992		4	9	.308	4.94	44	12	0	89.1	115	35	31	0	1	4	0	0	0	0	–	9	20	0	3	0.7	1.000
1993		1	2	.333	4.08	7	6	0	35.1	37	11	16	0	0	0	0	0	0	0	–	4	6	0	0	1.4	1.000
1994		2	3	.400	4.60	36	1	0	47	55	16	21	0	2	2	0	0	0	0	–	4	7	1	1	0.3	.917
4 yrs.		7	15	.318	4.13	125	19	0	226.2	262	85	110	0	3	7	0	0	0	0	–	20	39	2	5	0.5	.967

Joe Magrane

MAGRANE, JOSEPH DAVID
B. July 2, 1964, Des Moines, Iowa.

BR TL 6'6" 225 lbs.

Year	Team		W	L	PCT	ERA	G	GS	CG	IP	H	BB	SO	ShO	W	L	SV	AB	H	HR	BA	PO	A	E	DP	TC/G	FA
1987	STL N		9	7	.563	3.54	27	26	4	170.1	157	60	101	2	0	0	0	52	7	1	.135	10	26	3	3	1.4	.923
1988			5	9	.357	**2.18**	24	24	4	165.1	133	51	100	3	0	0	0	48	8	1	.167	16	37	5	0	2.4	.914
1989			18	9	.667	2.91	34	33	9	234.2	219	72	127	3	0	0	0	80	11	1	.138	11	31	2	1	1.3	.955
1990			10	17	.370	3.59	31	31	3	203.1	204	59	100	2	0	0	0	55	7	0	.127	8	38	1	1	1.5	.979
1992			1	2	.333	4.02	5	5	0	31.1	34	15	20	0	0	0	0	10	2	1	.200	1	5	0	0	1.2	1.000
1993	2 teams	STL N (22G 8–10)				CAL A	(8G 3–2)																				
"	total		11	12	.478	4.66	30	28	0	164	175	58	62	0	0	0	0	35	4	0	.114	12	36	2	3	1.7	.960
1994	CAL A		2	6	.250	7.30	20	11	1	74	89	51	33	0	0	1	0	0	0	0	–	2	10	0	1	0.6	1.000
7 yrs.			56	62	.475	3.65	171	158	21	1043	1011	366	543	10	0	2	0	280	39	4	.139	60	183	13	9	1.5	.949

LEAGUE CHAMPIONSHIP SERIES

Year	Team	W	L	PCT	ERA	G	GS	CG	IP	H	BB	SO	ShO	W	L	SV	AB	H	HR	BA	PO	A	E	DP	TC/G	FA
1987	STL N	0	0	–	9.00	1	1	0	4	4	2	3	0	0	0	0	1	0	0	.000	0	1	0	0	1.0	1.000

WORLD SERIES

Year	Team	W	L	PCT	ERA	G	GS	CG	IP	H	BB	SO	ShO	W	L	SV	AB	H	HR	BA	PO	A	E	DP	TC/G	FA
1987	STL N	0	1	.000	8.59	2	2	0	7.1	9	5	5	0	0	0	0	0	0	0	–	1	1	0	0	1.0	1.000

Pat Mahomes

MAHOMES, PATRICK LAVON
B. Aug. 9, 1970, Bryan, Tex.

BR TR 6'1" 175 lbs.

Year	Team	W	L	PCT	ERA	G	GS	CG	IP	H	BB	SO	ShO	W	L	SV	AB	H	HR	BA	PO	A	E	DP	TC/G	FA
1992	MIN A	3	4	.429	5.04	14	13	0	69.2	73	37	44	0	0	0	0	0	0	0	–	5	4	0	0	0.6	1.000
1993		1	5	.167	7.71	12	5	0	37.1	47	16	23	0	1	0	0	0	0	0	–	4	4	0	1	0.7	1.000
1994		9	5	.643	4.73	21	21	0	120	121	62	53	0	0	0	0	0	0	0	–	11	12	1	2	1.1	.958
3 yrs.		13	14	.481	5.31	47	39	0	227	241	115	120	0	1	0	0	0	0	0	–	20	20	1	3	0.9	.976

Josias Manzanillo

MANZANILLO, JOSIAS
Born Josias Manzanillo (Adams).
Brother of Ravelo Manzanillo.
B. Oct. 16, 1967, San Pedro de Macoris, Dominican Republic.

BR TR 6' 190 lbs.

Year	Team		W	L	PCT	ERA	G	GS	CG	IP	H	BB	SO	ShO	W	L	SV	AB	H	HR	BA	PO	A	E	DP	TC/G	FA
1991	BOS A		0	0	–	18.00	1	0	0	1	2	3	1	0	0	0	0	0	0	0	–	0	0	0	0	0.0	–
1993	2 teams	MIL A (10G 1–1)				NY N	(6G 0–0)																				
"	total		1	1	.500	6.83	16	1	0	29	30	19	21	0	1	0	1	1	0	0	.000	2	5	0	1	0.4	1.000
1994	NY N		3	2	.600	2.66	37	0	0	47.1	34	13	48	0	3	2	2	4	0	0	.000	7	3	1	0	0.3	.909
3 yrs.			4	3	.571	4.42	54	1	0	77.1	66	35	70	0	4	2	3	5	0	0	.000	9	8	1	1	0.3	.944

Ravelo Manzanillo

MANZANILLO, RAVELO
Born Ravelo Manzanillo (Adams).
Brother of Josias Manzanillo.
B. Oct. 17, 1963, San Pedro de Macoris, Dominican Republic.

BL TL 6' 210 lbs.

Year	Team	W	L	PCT	ERA	G	GS	CG	IP	H	BB	SO	ShO	W	L	SV	AB	H	HR	BA	PO	A	E	DP	TC/G	FA
1988	CHI A	0	1	.000	5.79	2	2	0	9.1	7	12	10	0	0	0	0	0	0	0	–	0	1	0	0	0.5	1.000
1994	PIT N	4	2	.667	4.14	46	0	0	50	45	42	39	0	4	2	1	3	2	0	.667	2	8	1	0	0.2	.909
2 yrs.		4	3	.571	4.40	48	2	0	59.1	52	54	49	0	4	2	1	3	2	0	.667	2	9	1	0	0.3	.917

Dave Martinez

MARTINEZ, DAVID
B. Sept. 26, 1964, New York, N. Y.

BL TL 5'10" 150 lbs.

Year	Team	W	L	PCT	ERA	G	GS	CG	IP	H	BB	SO	ShO	W	L	SV	AB	H	HR	BA	PO	A	E	DP	TC/G	FA
1990	MON N	0	0	–	54.00	1	0	0	0.1	2	2	0	0	0	0	0	*				0	0	0	0	0.0	–

Dennis Martinez

MARTINEZ, JOSE DENNIS
Born Jose Dennis Martinez (Emilia).
B. May 14, 1955, Granada, Nicaragua.

BR TR 6'1" 175 lbs.

Year	Team		W	L	PCT	ERA	G	GS	CG	IP	H	BB	SO	ShO	W	L	SV	AB	H	HR	BA	PO	A	E	DP	TC/G	FA
1976	BAL A		1	2	.333	2.57	4	2	1	28	23	8	18	0	1	0	0	0	0	0	–	3	4	0	0	1.8	1.000
1977			14	7	.667	4.10	42	13	5	167	157	64	107	0	8	4	4	0	0	0	–	9	26	1	2	0.9	.972
1978			16	11	.593	3.52	40	38	15	276.1	257	93	142	2	0	0	0	0	0	0	–	27	51	1	6	2.0	.987
1979			15	16	.484	3.67	40	**39**	**18**	**292**	279	78	132	3	0	0	0	0	0	0	–	26	59	5	3	2.3	.944
1980			6	4	.600	3.96	25	12	2	100	103	44	42	0	0	1	1	0	0	0	–	5	16	0	1	0.8	1.000
1981			**14**	5	.737	3.32	25	24	9	179	173	62	88	0	0	0	0	0	0	0	–	20	44	2	4	2.6	.970
1982			16	12	.571	4.21	40	39	10	252	262	87	111	2	0	0	0	0	0	0	–	13	38	1	2	1.3	.981
1983			7	16	.304	5.53	32	25	4	153	209	45	71	0	1	0	0	0	0	0	–	16	42	1	0	1.8	.983
1984			6	9	.400	5.02	34	20	2	141.2	145	37	77	0	1	2	0	0	0	0	–	17	19	2	4	1.1	.947
1985			13	11	.542	5.15	33	31	3	180	203	63	68	1	1	0	0	0	0	0	–	17	26	1	0	1.3	.977
1986	2 teams	BAL A (4G 0–0)				MON N	(19G 3–6)																				
"	total		3	6	.333	4.73	23	15	1	104.2	114	30	65	1	0	0	0	30	3	0	.100	4	25	1	1	1.3	.967
1987	MON N		11	4	.733	3.30	22	22	2	144.2	133	40	84	1	0	0	0	46	3	0	.065	10	23	1	3	1.5	.971
1988			15	13	.536	2.72	34	34	9	235.1	215	55	120	2	0	0	0	78	15	0	.192	19	39	6	3	1.9	.906
1989			16	7	.696	3.18	34	33	5	232	227	49	142	2	0	0	0	72	9	0	.125	11	50	2	6	1.9	.968
1990			10	11	.476	2.95	32	32	7	226	191	49	156	2	0	0	0	68	7	0	.103	16	35	1	2	1.6	.981
1991			14	11	.560	**2.39**	31	31	**9**	222	187	62	123	5	0	0	0	72	11	0	.153	21	48	4	5	2.4	.945
1992			16	11	.593	2.47	32	32	6	226.1	172	60	147	0	0	0	0	74	14	0	.189	20	45	4	3	2.2	.942
1993			15	9	.625	3.85	35	34	2	224.2	211	64	138	0	0	0	1	69	11	0	.159	17	46	1	1	1.8	.984
1994	CLE A		11	6	.647	3.52	24	24	2	176.2	166	44	92	1	0	0	0	0	0	0	–	11	33	0	0	1.8	1.000
19 yrs.			219	171	.562	3.63	582	500	117	3561.1	3427	1034	1923	26	12	8	6	509	73	0	.143	282	669	34	47	1.7	.965

Year	Team		W	L	PCT	ERA	G	GS	CG	IP	H	BB	SO	ShO	Relief Pitching W	L	SV	Batting AB	H	HR	BA	PO	A	E	DP	TC/G	FA

Dennis Martinez *continued*

LEAGUE CHAMPIONSHIP SERIES
| 1979 | BAL A | | 0 | 0 | – | 3.24 | 1 | 1 | 0 | 8.1 | 8 | 0 | 4 | 0 | 0 | 0 | 0 | 0 | 0 | 0 | – | 2 | 0 | 0 | 0 | 2.0 | 1.000 |

WORLD SERIES
| 1979 | BAL A | | 0 | 0 | – | 18.00 | 2 | 1 | 0 | 2 | 6 | 0 | 0 | 0 | 0 | 0 | 0 | 0 | 0 | 0 | – | 0 | 1 | 0 | 1 | 0.5 | 1.000 |

Jose Martinez

MARTINEZ, JOSE MIGUEL
Born Jose Martinez (Martinez).
B. Apr. 1, 1971, Guayabin, Dominican Republic

BR TR 6'2" 180 lbs.

| 1994 | SD N | | 0 | 2 | .000 | 6.75 | 4 | 1 | 0 | 12 | 18 | 5 | 7 | 0 | 0 | 0 | 1 | 2 | 0 | 0 | .000 | 0 | 2 | 0 | 0 | 0.5 | 1.000 |

Pedro Martinez

MARTINEZ, PEDRO
Born Pedro Jaime (Martinez).
Brother of Ramon Martinez.
B. July 25, 1971, Manoguayabo, Dominican Republic.

BR TR 5'11" 150 lbs.

1992	LA N		0	1	.000	2.25	2	1	0	8	6	1	8	0	0	0	0	2	0	0	.000	0	0	0	0	0.0	–
1993			10	5	.667	2.61	65	2	0	107	76	57	119	0	10	3	2	4	0	0	.000	4	4	0	1	0.1	1.000
1994	MON N		11	5	.688	3.42	24	23	1	144.2	115	45	142	1	0	0	1	44	4	0	.091	9	15	4	0	1.2	.857
	3 yrs.		21	11	.656	3.05	91	26	1	259.2	197	103	269	1	10	3	3	50	4	0	.080	13	19	4	1	0.4	.889

Pedro Martinez

MARTINEZ, PEDRO
Born Pedro Martinez (Aquino).
B. Nov. 29, 1968, Villa Mella, Dominican Republic

BL TL 6'2" 155 lbs.

1993	SD N		3	1	.750	2.43	32	0	0	37	23	13	32	0	3	1	0	4	0	0	.000	2	4	1	0	0.2	.857
1994			3	2	.600	2.90	48	1	0	68.1	52	49	52	0	3	2	3	5	0	0	.000	5	17	4	1	0.5	.846
	2 yrs.		6	3	.667	2.73	80	1	0	105.1	75	62	84	0	6	3	3	9	0	0	.000	7	21	5	1	0.4	.848

Ramon Martinez

MARTINEZ, RAMON
Born Ramon Jaime (Martinez).
Brother of Pedro Martinez.
B. Mar. 22, 1968, Santo Domingo, Dominican Republic.

BR TR 6'4" 165 lbs.

1988	LA N		1	3	.250	3.79	9	6	0	35.2	27	22	23	0	0	0	0	7	0	0	.000	1	5	0	0	0.7	1.000
1989			6	4	.600	3.19	15	15	2	98.2	79	41	89	2	0	0	0	37	6	0	.162	11	14	0	1	1.7	1.000
1990			20	6	.769	2.92	33	33	12	234.1	191	67	223	3	0	0	0	80	10	0	.125	16	27	1	0	1.3	.977
1991			17	13	.567	3.27	33	33	6	220.1	190	69	150	4	0	0	0	77	9	1	.117	22	21	2	0	1.4	.956
1992			8	11	.421	4.00	25	25	1	150.2	141	69	101	1	0	0	0	50	6	0	.120	10	18	2	1	1.2	.933
1993			10	12	.455	3.44	32	32	4	211.2	202	104	127	3	0	0	0	70	9	0	.129	28	31	0	4	1.8	1.000
1994			12	7	.632	3.97	24	24	4	170	160	56	119	3	0	0	0	66	18	0	.273	21	17	3	0	1.7	.927
	7 yrs.		74	56	.569	3.44	171	168	29	1121.1	990	428	832	16	0	0	0	387	58	1	.150	109	133	8	6	1.5	.968

Roger Mason

MASON, ROGER LeROY
B. Sept. 18, 1958, Bellaire, Mich.

BR TR 6'6" 215 lbs.

1984	DET A		1	1	.500	4.50	5	2	0	22	23	10	15	0	0	0	1	0	0	0	–	5	1	0	0	1.2	1.000
1985	SF N		1	3	.250	2.12	5	5	1	29.2	28	11	26	1	0	0	0	11	1	0	.091	4	2	0	0	1.2	1.000
1986			3	4	.429	4.80	11	11	1	60	56	30	43	0	0	0	0	21	1	0	.048	6	4	1	0	1.0	.909
1987			1	1	.500	4.50	5	5	0	26	30	10	18	0	0	0	0	8	1	0	.125	3	3	2	2	1.2	1.000
1989	HOU N		0	0	–	20.25	2	0	0	1.1	2	2	3	0	0	0	0	0	0	0	–	1	0	0	0	0.5	1.000
1991	PIT N		3	2	.600	3.03	24	0	0	29.2	21	6	21	0	3	2	3	0	0	0	–	1	5	0	1	0.3	1.000
1992			5	7	.417	4.09	65	0	0	88	80	33	56	0	5	7	8	10	0	0	.000	6	7	1	0	0.2	.929
1993	2 teams		SD N	(34G 0-7)		PHI N	(34G	5-5)																			
"	total		5	12	.294	4.06	68	0	0	99.2	90	34	71	0	5	12	0	6	1	0	.167	2	8	0	0	0.1	1.000
1994	2 teams		PHI N	(6G 1-1)		NY N	(41G	2-4)																			
"	total		3	5	.375	3.75	47	0	0	60	55	25	33	0	3	5	1	0	0	0	–	3	3	0	0	0.1	1.000
	9 yrs.		22	35	.386	4.02	232	23	2	416.1	385	161	286	1	16	26	13	56	4	0	.071	31	33	2	3	0.3	.970

LEAGUE CHAMPIONSHIP SERIES
1991	PIT N		0	0	–	0.00	3	0	0	4.1	3	1	2	0	0	0	0	1	0	0	.000	0	0	0	0	0.0	–
1992			0	0	–	0.00	2	0	0	3.1	1	2	1	0	0	0	0	0	0	0	–	2	0	0	0	1.0	1.000
1993	PHI N		0	0	–	0.00	2	0	0	3	0	0	2	0	0	0	0	0	0	0	–	0	0	0	0	0.0	–
	3 yrs.		0	0	–	0.00	7	0	0	10.2	4	3	5	0	0	0	1	1	0	0	.000	2	0	0	0	0.3	1.000

WORLD SERIES
| 1993 | PHI N | | 0 | 0 | – | 1.17 | 4 | 0 | 0 | 7.2 | 4 | 1 | 7 | 0 | 0 | 0 | 0 | 0 | 0 | 0 | .000 | 0 | 0 | 0 | 0 | 0.0 | – |

Terry Mathews

MATHEWS, TERRY ALAN
B. Oct. 5, 1964, Alexandria, Va.

BL TR 6'2" 200 lbs.

1991	TEX A		4	0	1.000	3.61	34	2	0	57.1	54	18	51	0	4	0	1	0	0	0	–	8	5	0	0	0.4	1.000
1992			2	4	.333	5.95	40	0	0	42.1	48	31	26	0	2	4	0	0	0	0	–	5	4	0	1	0.2	1.000
1994	FLA N		2	1	.667	3.35	24	2	0	43	45	9	21	0	1	0	0	6	3	0	.500	5	6	0	1	0.5	1.000
	3 yrs.		8	5	.615	4.23	98	4	0	142.2	147	58	98	0	7	4	1	6	3	0	.500	18	15	0	2	0.3	1.000

Tim Mauser

MAUSER, TIMOTHY EDWARD
B. Oct. 4, 1966, Fort Worth, Tex.

BR TR 6' 185 lbs.

1991	PHI N		0	0	–	7.59	3	0	0	10.2	18	3	6	0	0	0	0	3	0	0	.000	0	1	0	0	0.3	1.000
1993	2 teams		PHI N	(8G 0-0)		SD N	(28G	0-1)																			
"	total		0	1	.000	4.00	36	0	0	54	51	24	46	0	0	1	0	6	0	0	.000	6	11	1	2	0.5	.944
1994	SD N		0	4	.333	3.49	35	0	0	49	50	19	32	0	2	4	2	4	1	0	.250	2	5	0	2	0.2	1.000
	3 yrs.		2	5	.286	4.12	74	0	0	113.2	119	46	84	0	2	5	2	13	1	0	.077	8	17	1	4	0.4	.962

Year	Team	W	L	PCT	ERA	G	GS	CG	IP	H	BB	SO	ShO	Relief Pitching W	L	SV	Batting AB	H	HR	BA	PO	A	E	DP	TC/G	FA

Kirk McCaskill

McCASKILL, KIRK EDWARD
B. Apr. 9, 1961, Kapuskasing, Ont., Canada.   BR TR 6'1"   185 lbs.

Year	Team	W	L	PCT	ERA	G	GS	CG	IP	H	BB	SO	ShO	W	L	SV	AB	H	HR	BA	PO	A	E	DP	TC/G	FA
1985	CAL A	12	12	.500	4.70	30	29	6	189.2	189	64	102	1	0	0	0	0	0	0	–	11	27	3	1	1.4	.927
1986		17	10	.630	3.36	34	33	10	246.1	207	92	202	2	0	0	0	0	0	0	–	24	26	1	0	1.5	.980
1987		4	6	.400	5.67	14	13	1	74.2	84	34	56	1	0	0	0	0	0	0	–	8	12	1	1	1.5	.952
1988		8	6	.571	4.31	23	23	4	146.1	155	61	98	2	0	0	0	0	0	0	–	12	18	3	2	1.4	.909
1989		15	10	.600	2.93	32	32	6	212	202	59	107	4	0	0	0	0	0	0	–	16	42	3	5	1.9	.951
1990		12	11	.522	3.25	29	29	2	174.1	161	72	78	1	0	0	0	0	0	0	–	19	29	3	2	1.8	.941
1991		10	19	.345	4.26	30	30	1	177.2	193	66	71	0	0	0	0	0	0	0	–	17	25	1	4	1.4	.977
1992	CHI A	12	13	.480	4.18	34	34	0	209	193	95	109	0	0	0	0	0	0	0	–	24	31	2	0	1.7	.965
1993		4	8	.333	5.23	30	14	0	113.2	144	36	65	0	0	1	2	0	0	0	–	7	23	2	4	1.1	.938
1994		1	4	.200	3.42	40	0	0	52.2	51	22	37	0	1	4	3	0	0	0	–	4	8	0	0	0.3	1.000
10 yrs.		95	99	.490	3.99	296	237	30	1596.1	1579	601	925	11	1	5	5	0	0	0	–	142	241	19	19	1.4	.953

LEAGUE CHAMPIONSHIP SERIES

Year	Team	W	L	PCT	ERA	G	GS	CG	IP	H	BB	SO	ShO	W	L	SV	AB	H	HR	BA	PO	A	E	DP	TC/G	FA
1986	CAL A	0	2	.000	7.71	2	2	0	9.1	16	5	7	0	0	0	0	0	0	0	–	0	0	0	0	0.0	–
1993	CHI A	0	0	–	0.00	3	0	0	3.2	3	1	3	0	0	0	0	0	0	0	–	0	2	0	0	0.7	1.000
2 yrs.		0	2	.000	5.54	5	2	0	13	19	6	10	0	0	0	0	0	0	0	–	0	2	0	0	0.4	1.000

Ben McDonald

McDONALD, LARRY BENARD
B. Nov. 14, 1967, Baton Rouge, La.   BR TR 6'7"   212 lbs.

Year	Team	W	L	PCT	ERA	G	GS	CG	IP	H	BB	SO	ShO	W	L	SV	AB	H	HR	BA	PO	A	E	DP	TC/G	FA
1989	BAL A	1	0	1.000	8.59	6	0	0	7.1	8	4	3	0	1	0	0	0	0	0	–	0	2	0	0	0.3	1.000
1990		8	5	.615	2.43	21	15	3	118.2	88	35	65	2	0	0	0	0	0	0	–	15	14	1	1	1.4	.967
1991		6	8	.429	4.84	21	21	1	126.1	126	43	85	0	0	0	0	0	0	0	–	12	8	0	1	1.0	1.000
1992		13	13	.500	4.24	35	35	4	227	213	74	158	2	0	0	0	0	0	0	–	22	29	0	2	1.5	1.000
1993		13	14	.481	3.39	34	34	7	220.1	185	86	171	1	0	0	0	0	0	0	–	15	42	2	2	1.7	.966
1994		14	7	.667	4.06	24	24	5	157.1	151	54	94	1	0	0	0	0	0	0	–	7	25	0	1	1.3	1.000
6 yrs.		55	47	.539	3.86	141	129	20	857	771	296	576	6	1	0	0	0	0	0	–	71	120	3	7	1.4	.985

Jack McDowell

McDOWELL, JACK BURNS
B. Jan. 16, 1966, Van Nuys, Calif.   BR TR 6'5"   180 lbs.

Year	Team	W	L	PCT	ERA	G	GS	CG	IP	H	BB	SO	ShO	W	L	SV	AB	H	HR	BA	PO	A	E	DP	TC/G	FA
1987	CHI A	3	0	1.000	1.93	4	4	0	28	16	6	15	0	0	0	0	0	0	0	–	1	6	0	0	1.8	1.000
1988		5	10	.333	3.97	26	26	1	158.2	147	68	84	0	0	0	0	0	0	0	–	12	16	5	1	1.3	.848
1990		14	9	.609	3.82	33	33	4	205	189	77	165	0	0	0	0	0	0	0	–	17	20	1	3	1.2	.974
1991		17	10	.630	3.41	35	35	15	253.2	212	82	191	3	0	0	0	0	0	0	–	19	32	0	1	1.5	1.000
1992		20	10	.667	3.18	34	34	13	260.2	247	75	178	1	0	0	0	0	0	0	–	16	27	2	3	1.3	.956
1993		22	10	.688	3.37	34	34	10	256.2	261	69	158	4	0	0	0	0	0	0	–	23	43	3	2	2.0	.957
1994		10	9	.526	3.73	25	25	6	181	186	42	127	2	0	0	0	0	0	0	–	8	24	0	0	1.3	1.000
7 yrs.		91	58	.611	3.50	191	191	49	1343.2	1258	419	918	10	0	0	0	0	0	0	–	96	168	11	10	1.4	.960

LEAGUE CHAMPIONSHIP SERIES

Year	Team	W	L	PCT	ERA	G	GS	CG	IP	H	BB	SO	ShO	W	L	SV	AB	H	HR	BA	PO	A	E	DP	TC/G	FA
1993	CHI A	0	2	.000	10.00	2	2	0	9	18	5	5	0	0	0	0	0	0	0	–	0	1	1	0	1.0	.500

Roger McDowell

McDOWELL, ROGER ALAN
B. Dec. 21, 1960, Cincinnati, Ohio.   BR TR 6'1"   175 lbs.

Year	Team	W	L	PCT	ERA	G	GS	CG	IP	H	BB	SO	ShO	W	L	SV	AB	H	HR	BA	PO	A	E	DP	TC/G	FA
1985	NY N	6	5	.545	2.83	62	2	0	127.1	108	37	70	0	6	4	17	19	2	0	.158	17	27	4	2	0.8	.917
1986		14	9	.609	3.02	75	0	0	128	107	42	65	0	14	9	22	18	5	0	.278	17	30	0	0	0.6	1.000
1987		7	5	.583	4.16	56	0	0	88.2	95	28	32	0	7	5	25	13	3	0	.231	10	17	0	1	0.5	1.000
1988		5	5	.500	2.63	62	0	0	89	80	31	46	0	5	5	16	11	3	0	.333	11	19	1	2	0.5	.968
1989	2 teams		NY N (25G 1–5)			PHI N (44G 3–3)																				
"	total	4	8	.333	1.96	69	0	0	92	79	38	47	0	4	8	23	3	1	0	.333	17	25	3	3	0.7	.933
1990	PHI N	6	8	.429	3.86	72	0	0	86.1	92	35	39	0	6	8	22	1	0	0	.000	1	23	5	2	0.4	.828
1991	2 teams		PHI N (38G 3–6)			LA N (33G 6–3)																				
"	total	9	9	.500	2.93	71	0	0	101.1	100	48	50	0	9	9	10	2	0	0	.000	8	25	3	3	0.5	.917
1992	LA N	6	10	.375	4.09	65	0	0	83.2	103	42	50	0	6	10	14	3	0	0	.000	8	21	3	2	0.5	.906
1993		5	3	.625	2.25	54	0	0	68	76	30	27	0	5	3	2	2	1	0	.500	11	24	3	3	0.7	.921
1994		0	3	.000	5.23	32	0	0	41.1	50	22	29	0	0	3	0	1	0	0	.000	2	7	0	0	0.3	1.000
10 yrs.		62	65	.488	3.17	618	2	0	905.2	890	353	455	0	62	64	151	72	16	0	.222	102	218	22	18	0.6	.936

LEAGUE CHAMPIONSHIP SERIES

Year	Team	W	L	PCT	ERA	G	GS	CG	IP	H	BB	SO	ShO	W	L	SV	AB	H	HR	BA	PO	A	E	DP	TC/G	FA
1986	NY N	0	0	–	0.00	2	0	0	7	1	0	4	0	0	0	0	1	0	0	.000	3	1	0	0	2.0	1.000
1988		0	1	.000	4.50	4	0	0	6	6	2	5	0	0	1	0	0	0	0	–	0	3	1	0	1.0	.750
2 yrs.		0	1	.000	2.08	6	0	0	13	7	2	8	0	0	1	0	1	0	0	.000	3	4	1	0	1.3	.875

WORLD SERIES

Year	Team	W	L	PCT	ERA	G	GS	CG	IP	H	BB	SO	ShO	W	L	SV	AB	H	HR	BA	PO	A	E	DP	TC/G	FA
1986	NY N	1	0	1.000	4.91	5	0	0	7.1	10	6	2	0	1	0	0	0	0	0	–	1	4	0	0	1.0	1.000

Chuck McElroy

McELROY, CHARLES DWAYNE
B. Oct. 1, 1967, Galveston, Tex.   BL TL 6'   160 lbs.

Year	Team	W	L	PCT	ERA	G	GS	CG	IP	H	BB	SO	ShO	W	L	SV	AB	H	HR	BA	PO	A	E	DP	TC/G	FA
1989	PHI N	0	0	–	1.74	11	0	0	10.1	12	4	8	0	0	0	0	0	0	0	–	1	0	0	0	0.1	1.000
1990		0	1	.000	7.71	16	0	0	14	24	10	16	0	0	1	0	0	0	0	–	1	0	0	0	0.1	.500
1991	CHI N	6	2	.750	1.95	71	0	0	101.1	73	57	92	0	6	2	3	10	3	0	.300	8	14	0	1	0.3	1.000
1992		4	7	.364	3.55	72	0	0	83.2	73	51	83	0	4	7	6	6	4	0	.667	3	8	1	2	0.2	.917
1993		2	2	.500	4.56	49	0	0	47.1	51	25	31	0	2	2	0	6	0	0	.000	3	5	0	1	0.2	1.000
1994	CIN N	1	2	.333	2.34	52	0	0	57.2	52	15	38	0	1	2	5	6	1	0	.167	1	5	0	0	0.1	1.000
6 yrs.		13	14	.481	3.09	271	0	0	314.1	285	162	268	0	13	14	14	28	8	0	.286	17	32	2	4	0.2	.961

Greg McMichael

McMICHAEL, GREGORY WINSTON
B. Dec. 1, 1966, Knoxville, Tenn.   BR TR 6'3"   215 lbs.

Year	Team	W	L	PCT	ERA	G	GS	CG	IP	H	BB	SO	ShO	W	L	SV	AB	H	HR	BA	PO	A	E	DP	TC/G	FA
1993	ATL N	2	3	.400	2.06	74	0	0	91.2	68	29	89	0	2	3	19	12	2	0	.000	7	18	1	2	0.4	.962
1994		4	6	.400	3.84	51	0	0	58.2	66	19	47	0	4	6	21	1	0	0	.000	2	6	2	0	0.2	.800
2 yrs.		6	9	.400	2.75	125	0	0	150.1	134	48	136	0	6	9	40	5	0	0	.000	9	24	3	2	0.3	.917

LEAGUE CHAMPIONSHIP SERIES

Year	Team	W	L	PCT	ERA	G	GS	CG	IP	H	BB	SO	ShO	W	L	SV	AB	H	HR	BA	PO	A	E	DP	TC/G	FA
1993	ATL N	0	1	.000	6.75	4	0	0	4	7	2	1	0	0	1	0	1	0	0	–	0	0	0	0	0.3	1.000

Year	Team		W	L	PCT	ERA	G	GS	CG	IP	H	BB	SO	ShO	W	L	SV	AB	H	HR	BA	PO	A	E	DP	TC/G	FA

Rusty Meacham

MEACHAM, RUSSELL LOREN
B. Jan. 27, 1968, Stuart, Fla. BR TR 6'3" 155 lbs.

1991	DET A		2	1	.667	5.20	10	4	0	27.2	35	11	14	0	0	0	0	0	0	0	–	4	4	0	0	0.8	1.000
1992	KC A		10	4	.714	2.74	64	0	0	101.2	88	21	64	0	10	4	2	0	0	0	–	13	18	1	1	0.5	.969
1993			2	2	.500	5.57	15	0	0	21	31	5	13	0	2	2	0	0	0	0	–	2	4	0	1	0.4	1.000
1994			3	3	.500	3.73	36	0	0	50.2	51	12	36	0	3	3	4	0	0	0	–	1	9	0	1	0.3	1.000
4 yrs.			17	10	.630	3.63	125	4	0	201	205	49	127	0	15	9	6	0	0	0	–	20	35	1	3	0.4	.982

Jose Melendez

MELENDEZ, JOSE LUIS
Born Jose Luis Melendez (Garcia).
B. Sept. 2, 1965, Naguabo, Puerto Rico. BR TR 6'2" 175 lbs.

1990	SEA A		0	0	–	11.81	3	0	0	5.1	8	3	7	0	0	0	0	0	0	0	–	0	0	0	0	0.0	–
1991	SD N		8	5	.615	3.27	31	9	0	93.2	77	24	60	0	3	2	3	20	2	0	.100	4	11	2	0	0.5	.882
1992			6	7	.462	2.92	56	3	0	89.1	82	20	82	0	6	4	0	5	0	0	.000	2	8	1	1	0.2	.909
1993	BOS A		2	1	.667	2.25	9	0	0	16	10	5	14	0	2	1	0	0	0	0	–	1	3	0	0	0.4	1.000
1994			0	1	.000	6.06	10	0	0	16.1	20	8	9	0	0	1	0	0	0	0	–	0	3	0	0	0.3	1.000
5 yrs.			16	14	.533	3.47	109	12	0	220.2	197	60	172	0	11	8	3	25	2	0	.080	7	25	3	1	0.3	.914

Tony Menendez

MENENDEZ, ANTONIO GUSTAVO
Born Antonio Gustavo Menendez (Remon).
B. Feb. 20, 1965, Havana, Cuba. BR TR 6'2" 190 lbs.

1992	CIN N		1	0	1.000	1.93	3	0	0	4.2	1	0	5	0	1	0	0	0	0	0	–	0	0	0	0	0.0	–
1993	PIT N		2	0	1.000	3.00	14	0	0	21	20	4	13	0	2	0	0	1	0	0	.000	1	2	1	0	0.3	.750
1994	SF N		0	1	.000	21.60	6	0	0	3.1	8	2	2	0	0	1	0	0	0	0	–	0	0	0	0	0.0	–
3 yrs.			3	1	.750	4.97	23	0	0	29	29	6	20	0	3	1	0	1	0	0	.000	1	2	1	0	0.2	.750

Jose Mercedes

MERCEDES, JOSE MIGUEL
B. Mar. 5, 1971, El Seibo, Dominican Republic BR TR 6'1" 180 lbs.

| 1994 | MIL A | | 2 | 0 | 1.000 | 2.32 | 19 | 0 | 0 | 31 | 22 | 16 | 11 | 0 | 2 | 0 | 0 | 0 | 0 | 0 | – | 1 | 3 | 1 | 0 | 0.3 | .800 |

Kent Mercker

MERCKER, KENT FRANKLIN
B. Feb. 1, 1968, Dublin, Ohio. BL TL 6'1" 175 lbs.

1989	ATL N		0	0	–	12.46	2	1	0	4.1	8	6	4	0	0	0	0	1	0	0	.000	0	0	0	0	0.0	–
1990			4	7	.364	3.17	36	0	0	48.1	43	24	39	0	4	7	7	3	0	0	.000	2	1	1	0	0.1	.750
1991			5	3	.625	2.58	50	4	0	73.1	56	35	62	0	4	3	6	10	1	0	.100	2	7	1	1	0.2	.900
1992			3	2	.600	3.42	53	0	0	68.1	51	35	49	0	3	2	6	5	0	0	.000	1	2	0	0	0.1	1.000
1993			3	1	.750	2.86	43	6	0	66	52	36	59	0	2	0	0	13	0	0	.000	1	4	1	0	0.1	.833
1994			9	4	.692	3.45	20	17	0	112.1	90	45	111	1	0	0	0	37	2	0	.054	4	15	0	1	1.0	1.000
6 yrs.			24	17	.585	3.24	204	28	2	372.2	300	181	324	1	13	12	19	69	3	0	.043	10	29	3	2	0.2	.929

LEAGUE CHAMPIONSHIP SERIES

1991	ATL N		0	1	.000	13.50	1	0	0	0.2	0	2	0	0	0	1	0	0	0	0	–	0	0	0	0	0.0	–
1992			0	0	–	0.00	2	0	0	3	1	1	1	0	0	0	0	0	0	0	–	0	0	0	0	0.0	–
1993			0	0	–	1.80	5	0	0	5	3	2	4	0	0	0	0	0	0	0	–	0	0	0	0	0.0	–
3 yrs.			0	1	.000	2.08	8	0	0	8.2	4	5	5	0	0	1	0	0	0	0	–	0	0	0	0	0.0	–

WORLD SERIES

| 1991 | ATL N | | 0 | 0 | – | 0.00 | 2 | 0 | 0 | 1 | 0 | 1 | 1 | 0 | 0 | 0 | 0 | 0 | 0 | 0 | – | 0 | 0 | 0 | 0 | 0.0 | – |

Brett Merriman

MERRIMAN, BRETT ALAN
B. July 15, 1966, Jacksonville, Ill. BR TR 6'2" 210 lbs.

1993	MIN A		1	1	.500	9.67	19	0	0	27	36	23	14	0	1	1	0	0	0	0	–	1	4	0	0	0.3	1.000
1994			0	1	.000	6.35	15	0	0	17	18	14	10	0	0	1	0	0	0	0	–	0	1	0	0	0.1	1.000
2 yrs.			1	2	.333	8.39	34	0	0	44	54	37	24	0	1	2	0	0	0	0	–	1	5	0	0	0.2	1.000

Jose Mesa

MESA, JOSE RAMON
Born Jose Ramon Nova (Mesa).
B. May 22, 1966, Pueblo Viejo, Dominican Republic. BR TR 6'3" 170 lbs.

1987	BAL A		1	3	.250	6.03	6	5	0	31.1	38	15	17	0	0	0	0	0	0	0	–	1	1	0	0	0.3	1.000
1990			3	2	.600	3.86	7	7	0	46.2	37	27	24	0	0	0	0	0	0	0	–	3	5	1	1	1.3	.889
1991			6	11	.353	5.97	23	23	2	123.2	151	62	64	1	0	0	0	0	0	0	–	17	17	0	0	1.5	1.000
1992	2 teams	BAL A (13G 3–8)								CLE A	(15G 4–4)																
"	total		7	12	.368	4.59	28	27	1	160.2	169	70	62	1	0	0	0	0	0	0	–	12	21	2	0	1.3	.943
1993	CLE A		10	12	.455	4.92	34	33	3	208.2	232	62	118	0	0	0	0	0	0	0	–	15	29	3	0	1.4	.936
1994			7	5	.583	3.82	51	0	0	73	71	26	63	0	7	5	2	0	0	0	–	3	11	2	0	0.3	.875
6 yrs.			34	45	.430	4.89	149	95	6	644	698	262	348	2	7	5	2	0	0	0	–	51	84	8	1	1.0	.944

Dan Miceli

MICELI, DANIEL
B. Sept. 9, 1970, Newark, N. J. BR TR 6'1" 185 lbs.

1993	PIT N		0	0	–	5.06	9	0	0	5.1	6	3	4	0	0	0	0	0	0	0	–	0	0	0	0	0.0	–
1994			2	1	.667	5.93	28	0	0	27.1	28	11	27	0	2	1	2	3	0	0	.000	1	5	0	0	0.2	1.000
2 yrs.			2	1	.667	5.79	37	0	0	32.2	34	14	31	0	2	1	2	3	0	0	.000	1	5	0	0	0.2	1.000

Bob Milacki

MILACKI, ROBERT
B. July 28, 1964, Trenton, N. J. BR TR 6'4" 220 lbs.

1988	BAL A		2	0	1.000	0.72	3	3	1	25	9	9	18	1	0	0	0	0	0	0	–	4	3	0	1	2.3	1.000
1989			14	12	.538	3.74	37	36	3	243	233	88	113	2	0	0	0	0	0	0	–	27	28	2	5	1.5	.965
1990			5	8	.385	4.46	27	24	1	135.1	143	61	60	1	0	0	0	0	0	0	–	21	16	1	2	1.4	.974
1991			10	9	.526	4.01	31	26	3	184	175	53	108	1	1	0	0	0	0	0	–	23	24	2	4	1.6	.959
1992			6	8	.429	5.84	23	20	0	115.2	140	44	51	0	0	1	0	0	0	0	–	14	10	0	0	1.0	1.000
1993	CLE A		1	1	.500	3.38	5	2	0	16	19	11	7	0	1	0	0	0	0	0	–	0	3	0	0	0.6	1.000
1994	KC A		0	5	.000	6.14	10	10	0	55.2	68	20	17	0	0	0	0	0	0	0	–	8	13	1	0	2.2	.955
7 yrs.			38	43	.469	4.31	136	121	8	774.2	787	286	374	5	2	0	1	0	0	0	–	97	97	6	12	1.5	.970

Year	Team		W	L	PCT	ERA	G	GS	CG	IP	H	BB	SO	ShO	Relief Pitching W	L	SV	Batting AB	H	HR	BA	PO	A	E	DP	TC/G	FA

Kurt Miller

MILLER, KURT EVERETT
B. Aug. 24, 1972, Tucson, Ariz.

BR TR 6'5" 205 lbs.

Year	Team		W	L	PCT	ERA	G	GS	CG	IP	H	BB	SO	ShO	W	L	SV	AB	H	HR	BA	PO	A	E	DP	TC/G	FA
1994	FLA	N	1	3	.250	8.10	4	4	0	20	26	7	11	0	0	0	0	6	1	0	.167	3	4	0	2	1.8	1.000

Alan Mills

MILLS, ALAN BERNARD
B. Oct. 18, 1966, Lakeland, Fla.

BR TR 6'1" 190 lbs.

Year	Team		W	L	PCT	ERA	G	GS	CG	IP	H	BB	SO	ShO	W	L	SV	AB	H	HR	BA	PO	A	E	DP	TC/G	FA
1990	NY	A	1	5	.167	4.10	36	0	0	41.2	48	33	24	0	1	5	0	0	0	0	–	3	10	2	0	0.4	.867
1991			1	1	.500	4.41	6	2	0	16.1	16	8	11	0	1	0	0	0	0	0	–	0	5	0	0	0.8	1.000
1992	BAL	A	10	4	.714	2.61	35	3	0	103.1	78	54	60	0	9	3	2	0	0	0	–	9	17	0	2	0.7	1.000
1993			5	4	.556	3.23	45	0	0	100.1	80	51	68	0	5	4	4	0	0	0	–	7	11	3	2	0.5	.857
1994			3	3	.500	5.16	47	0	0	45.1	43	24	44	0	3	3	2	0	0	0	–	3	2	0	0	0.1	1.000
5 yrs.			20	17	.541	3.49	169	5	0	307	265	170	207	0	19	15	8	0	0	0	–	22	45	5	4	0.4	.931

Nate Minchey

MINCHEY, NATHAN DEREK
B. Aug. 31, 1969, Austin, Tex.

BR TR 6'8" 225 lbs.

Year	Team		W	L	PCT	ERA	G	GS	CG	IP	H	BB	SO	ShO	W	L	SV	AB	H	HR	BA	PO	A	E	DP	TC/G	FA
1993	BOS	A	1	2	.333	3.55	5	5	1	33	35	8	18	0	0	0	0	0	0	0	–	1	3	1	0	1.0	.800
1994			2	3	.400	8.61	6	5	0	23	44	14	15	0	0	0	0	0	0	0	–	0	4	0	0	0.7	1.000
2 yrs.			3	5	.375	5.63	11	10	1	56	79	22	33	0	0	0	0	0	0	0	–	1	7	1	0	0.8	.889

Blas Minor

MINOR, BLAS
B. Mar. 20, 1966, Merced, Calif.

BR TR 6'3" 195 lbs.

Year	Team		W	L	PCT	ERA	G	GS	CG	IP	H	BB	SO	ShO	W	L	SV	AB	H	HR	BA	PO	A	E	DP	TC/G	FA
1992	PIT	N	0	0	–	4.50	1	0	0	2	3	0	0	0	0	0	0	0	0	0	–	0	1	1	1	2.0	.500
1993			8	6	.571	4.10	65	0	0	94.1	94	26	84	0	8	6	2	10	2	0	.200	8	15	0	0	0.4	1.000
1994			0	1	.000	8.05	17	0	0	19	27	9	17	0	0	1	1	0	0	0	–	1	2	0	0	0.2	1.000
3 yrs.			8	7	.533	4.76	83	0	0	115.1	124	35	101	0	8	7	3	10	2	0	.200	9	18	1	1	0.3	.964

Angel Miranda

MIRANDA, ANGEL
B. Nov. 9, 1969, Arecibo, Puerto Rico

BL TL 6'1" 160 lbs.

Year	Team		W	L	PCT	ERA	G	GS	CG	IP	H	BB	SO	ShO	W	L	SV	AB	H	HR	BA	PO	A	E	DP	TC/G	FA
1993	MIL	A	4	5	.444	3.30	22	17	2	120	100	52	88	0	0	0	0	0	0	0	–	4	13	2	1	0.9	.895
1994			2	5	.286	5.28	8	8	1	46	39	27	24	0	0	0	0	0	0	0	–	1	3	0	0	0.5	1.000
2 yrs.			6	10	.375	3.85	30	25	3	166	139	79	112	0	0	0	0	0	0	0	–	5	16	2	1	0.8	.913

Mike Mohler

MOHLER, MICHAEL ROSS
B. July 26, 1968, Dayton, Ohio

BR TL 6'2" 195 lbs.

Year	Team		W	L	PCT	ERA	G	GS	CG	IP	H	BB	SO	ShO	W	L	SV	AB	H	HR	BA	PO	A	E	DP	TC/G	FA
1993	OAK	A	1	6	.143	5.60	42	9	0	64.1	57	44	42	0	1	1	0	0	0	0	–	2	9	1	2	0.3	.917
1994			0	1	.000	7.71	1	1	0	2.1	2	2	4	0	0	0	0	0	0	0	–	0	0	0	0	0.0	–
2 yrs.			1	7	.125	5.67	43	10	0	66.2	59	46	46	0	1	1	0	0	0	0	–	2	9	1	2	0.3	.917

Rich Monteleone

MONTELEONE, RICHARD
B. Mar. 22, 1963, Tampa, Fla.

BR TR 6'2" 205 lbs.

Year	Team		W	L	PCT	ERA	G	GS	CG	IP	H	BB	SO	ShO	W	L	SV	AB	H	HR	BA	PO	A	E	DP	TC/G	FA
1987	SEA	A	0	0	–	6.43	3	0	0	7	10	4	2	0	0	0	0	0	0	0	–	0	3	0	0	1.0	1.000
1988	CAL	A	0	0	–	0.00	3	0	0	4.1	4	1	3	0	0	0	0	0	0	0	–	0	1	0	0	0.3	1.000
1989			2	2	.500	3.18	24	0	0	39.2	39	13	27	0	2	2	0	0	0	0	–	1	9	1	1	0.5	.909
1990	NY	A	0	1	.000	6.14	5	0	0	7.1	8	2	8	0	0	1	0	0	0	0	–	1	1	0	0	0.4	1.000
1991			3	1	.750	3.64	26	0	0	47	42	19	34	0	3	1	0	0	0	0	–	1	9	1	1	0.5	.917
1992			7	3	.700	3.30	47	0	0	92.2	82	27	62	0	7	3	0	0	0	0	–	6	7	0	1	0.3	1.000
1993			7	4	.636	4.94	42	0	0	85.2	85	35	50	0	7	4	0	0	0	0	–	9	11	1	0	0.5	.952
1994	SF	N	4	3	.571	3.18	39	0	0	45.1	43	13	16	0	4	3	0	3	0	0	.000	2	3	0	0	0.1	1.000
8 yrs.			23	14	.622	3.83	189	0	0	329	313	114	202	0	23	14	0	3	0	0	.000	20	45	3	3	0.4	.956

Jeff Montgomery

MONTGOMERY, JEFFREY THOMAS
B. Jan. 7, 1962, Wellston, Ohio.

BR TR 5'11" 170 lbs.

Year	Team		W	L	PCT	ERA	G	GS	CG	IP	H	BB	SO	ShO	W	L	SV	AB	H	HR	BA	PO	A	E	DP	TC/G	FA
1987	CIN	N	2	2	.500	6.52	14	1	0	19.1	25	9	13	0	2	1	0	2	0	0	.000	1	3	0	0	0.3	1.000
1988	KC	A	7	2	.778	3.45	45	0	0	62.2	54	30	47	0	7	2	1	0	0	0	–	3	10	1	0	0.3	.929
1989			7	3	.700	1.37	63	0	0	92	66	25	94	0	7	3	18	0	0	0	–	11	6	2	1	0.3	.895
1990			6	5	.545	2.39	73	0	0	94.1	81	34	94	0	6	5	24	0	0	0	–	3	13	0	0	0.2	1.000
1991			4	4	.500	2.90	67	0	0	90	83	28	77	0	4	4	33	0	0	0	–	10	8	0	0	0.3	1.000
1992			1	6	.143	2.18	65	0	0	82.2	61	27	69	0	1	6	39	0	0	0	–	12	13	1	2	0.4	.962
1993			7	5	.583	2.27	69	0	0	87.1	65	23	66	0	7	5	**45**	0	0	0	–	6	13	0	0	0.3	1.000
1994			2	3	.400	4.03	42	0	0	44.2	48	15	50	0	2	3	27	0	0	0	–	2	2	1	0	0.1	.800
8 yrs.			36	30	.545	2.64	438	1	0	573	483	191	510	0	36	29	187	2	0	0	.000	48	68	5	3	0.3	.959

Marcus Moore

MOORE, MARCUS BRAYMONT
B. Nov. 2, 1970, Oakland, Calif.

BB TR 6'5" 195 lbs.

Year	Team		W	L	PCT	ERA	G	GS	CG	IP	H	BB	SO	ShO	W	L	SV	AB	H	HR	BA	PO	A	E	DP	TC/G	FA
1993	CLR	N	3	1	.750	6.84	27	0	0	26.1	30	20	13	0	3	1	0	1	0	0	.000	0	1	2	0	0.1	.333
1994			1	1	.500	6.15	29	0	0	33.2	33	21	33	0	1	1	0	1	0	0	–	2	3	0	0	0.2	1.000
2 yrs.			4	2	.667	6.45	56	0	0	60	63	41	46	0	4	2	0	2	0	0	.000	2	4	2	0	0.1	.750

Mike Moore

MOORE, MICHAEL WAYNE
B. Nov. 26, 1959, Carnegie, Okla.

BR TR 6'4" 205 lbs.

Year	Team		W	L	PCT	ERA	G	GS	CG	IP	H	BB	SO	ShO	W	L	SV	AB	H	HR	BA	PO	A	E	DP	TC/G	FA
1982	SEA	A	7	14	.333	5.36	28	27	1	144.1	159	79	73	1	0	0	0	0	0	0	–	13	27	5	2	1.6	.889
1983			6	8	.429	4.71	22	21	3	128	130	60	108	2	0	0	0	0	0	0	–	7	24	1	0	1.5	.969
1984			7	17	.292	4.97	34	33	6	212	236	85	158	0	0	0	0	0	0	0	–	18	41	7	0	1.9	.894
1985			17	10	.630	3.46	35	34	14	247	230	70	155	2	0	0	0	0	0	0	–	21	43	2	1	1.9	.970
1986			11	13	.458	4.30	38	**37**	11	266	**279**	94	146	1	0	0	1	0	0	0	–	23	33	4	1	1.6	.933
1987			9	**19**	.321	4.71	33	33	12	231	**268**	84	115	0	0	0	0	1	0	0	.000	22	34	2	4	1.8	.966
1988			9	15	.375	3.78	37	32	9	228.2	196	63	182	3	1	0	0	0	0	0	–	19	29	1	3	1.3	.980
1989	OAK	A	19	11	.633	2.61	35	35	6	241.2	193	83	172	3	0	0	0	0	0	0	–	25	37	2	5	1.8	.969
1990			13	15	.464	4.65	33	33	3	199.1	204	84	73	0	0	0	0	0	0	0	–	22	31	1	1	1.6	.981
1991			17	8	.680	2.96	33	33	3	210	176	105	153	1	0	0	0	0	0	0	–	28	30	2	3	1.8	.967

Year	Team		W	L	PCT	ERA	G	GS	CG	IP	H	BB	SO	ShO	Relief Pitching W	L	SV	Batting AB	H	HR	BA	PO	A	E	DP	TC/G	FA

Mike Moore *continued*

Year	Team		W	L	PCT	ERA	G	GS	CG	IP	H	BB	SO	ShO	W	L	SV	AB	H	HR	BA	PO	A	E	DP	TC/G	FA
1992			17	12	.586	4.12	36	36	2	223	229	103	117	0	0	0	0	0	0	0	—	17	22	3	5	1.2	.929
1993	DET	A	13	9	.591	5.22	36	36	4	213.2	227	89	89	3	0	0	0	0	0	0	—	27	43	2	3	2.0	.972
1994			11	10	.524	5.42	25	25	1	154.1	152	89	62	0	0	0	0	0	0	0	—	21	30	0	2	2.0	1.000
13 yrs.			156	161	.492	4.23	425	415	78	2699	2679	1088	1603	16	1	0	2	1	0	0	.000	263	424	32	30	1.7	.955

LEAGUE CHAMPIONSHIP SERIES

Year	Team		W	L	PCT	ERA	G	GS	CG	IP	H	BB	SO	ShO	W	L	SV	AB	H	HR	BA	PO	A	E	DP	TC/G	FA
1989	OAK	A	1	0	1.000	0.00	1	1	0	7	3	2	3	0	0	0	0	0	0	0	—	0	1	0	0	1.0	1.000
1990			1	0	1.000	1.50	1	1	0	6	4	1	5	0	0	0	0	0	0	0	—	0	0	0	0	0.0	—
1992			0	2	.000	7.45	2	2	0	9.2	11	5	7	0	0	0	0	0	0	0	—	1	1	0	0	1.0	1.000
3 yrs.			2	2	.500	3.57	4	4	0	22.2	18	8	15	0	0	0	0	0	0	0	—	1	2	0	0	0.8	1.000

WORLD SERIES

Year	Team		W	L	PCT	ERA	G	GS	CG	IP	H	BB	SO	ShO	W	L	SV	AB	H	HR	BA	PO	A	E	DP	TC/G	FA
1989	OAK	A	2	0	1.000	2.08	2	2	0	13	9	3	10	0	0	0	0	3	1	0	.333	0	1	0	0	1.5	1.000
1990			0	1	.000	6.75	1	1	0	2.2	8	0	1	0	0	0	0	0	0	0	—	0	0	0	0	0.0	—
2 yrs.			2	1	.667	2.87	3	3	0	15.2	17	3	11	0	0	0	0	3	1	0	.333	0	3	0	0	1.0	1.000

Mike Morgan

MORGAN, MICHAEL THOMAS
B. Oct. 8, 1959, Tulare, Calif.

BR TR 6'3" 195 lbs.

Year	Team		W	L	PCT	ERA	G	GS	CG	IP	H	BB	SO	ShO	W	L	SV	AB	H	HR	BA	PO	A	E	DP	TC/G	FA
1978	OAK	A	0	3	.000	7.30	3	3	1	12.1	19	8	0	0	0	0	0	0	0	0	—	1	4	0	1	1.7	1.000
1979			2	10	.167	5.96	13	13	2	77	102	50	17	0	0	0	0	0	0	0	—	9	15	1	0	1.9	.960
1982	NY	A	7	11	.389	4.37	30	23	2	150.1	167	67	71	0	2	1	0	0	0	0	—	4	26	0	3	1.0	1.000
1983	TOR	A	0	3	.000	5.16	16	4	0	45.1	48	21	22	0	0	1	0	0	0	0	—	2	10	1	0	0.8	.923
1985	SEA	A	1	1	.500	12.00	2	2	0	6	11	5	2	0	0	0	0	0	0	0	—	0	1	0	0	0.5	1.000
1986			11	17	.393	4.53	37	33	9	216.1	243	86	116	1	0	0	1	0	0	0	—	14	27	2	5	1.2	.953
1987			12	17	.414	4.65	34	31	8	207	245	53	85	2	0	0	0	0	0	0	—	18	35	2	5	1.6	.964
1988	BAL	A	1	6	.143	5.43	22	10	2	71.1	70	23	29	0	1	0	1	0	0	0	—	9	9	0	1	0.8	1.000
1989	LA	N	8	11	.421	2.53	40	19	0	152.2	130	33	72	0	2	0	0	36	3	0	.083	20	41	2	2	1.6	.968
1990			11	15	.423	3.75	33	33	6	211	216	60	106	4	0	0	0	71	8	0	.113	25	39	1	3	2.0	.985
1991			14	10	.583	2.78	34	33	5	236.1	197	61	140	1	0	0	1	76	7	0	.092	25	41	2	3	2.0	.971
1992	CHI	N	16	8	.667	2.55	34	34	6	240	203	79	123	1	0	0	0	74	8	0	.108	19	45	3	3	2.0	.955
1993			10	15	.400	4.03	32	32	1	207.2	206	74	111	1	0	0	0	66	4	0	.061	11	33	1	3	1.4	.978
1994			2	10	.167	6.69	15	15	1	80.2	111	35	57	0	0	0	0	24	3	0	.125	3	8	3	0	0.9	.786
14 yrs.			95	137	.409	4.01	345	285	43	1914	1968	655	951	10	5	2	3	347	33	0	.095	160	334	18	29	1.5	.965

Jack Morris

MORRIS, JOHN SCOTT
B. May 16, 1955, St. Paul, Minn.

BR TR 6'3" 195 lbs.

Year	Team		W	L	PCT	ERA	G	GS	CG	IP	H	BB	SO	ShO	W	L	SV	AB	H	HR	BA	PO	A	E	DP	TC/G	FA
1977	DET	A	1	1	.500	3.72	7	6	1	46	38	23	28	0	0	0	0	0	0	0	—	2	8	0	0	1.4	1.000
1978			3	5	.375	4.33	28	7	0	106	107	49	48	0	3	4	0	0	0	0	—	5	15	2	3	0.8	.909
1979			17	7	.708	3.27	27	27	9	198	179	59	113	1	0	0	0	0	0	0	—	14	23	2	3	1.4	.949
1980			16	15	.516	4.18	36	36	11	250	252	87	112	2	0	0	0	0	0	0	—	31	43	2	2	2.1	.974
1981			14	7	.667	3.05	25	25	15	198	153	78	97	1	0	0	0	0	0	0	—	16	28	0	2	1.8	1.000
1982			17	16	.515	4.06	37	37	17	266.1	247	96	135	3	0	0	0	0	0	0	—	26	31	1	2	1.6	.983
1983			20	13	.606	3.34	37	37	20	293.2	257	83	232	1	0	0	0	0	0	0	—	29	26	2	2	1.5	.965
1984			19	11	.633	3.60	35	35	9	240.1	221	87	148	1	0	0	0	0	0	0	—	29	32	3	4	1.8	.953
1985			16	11	.593	3.33	35	35	13	257	212	110	191	4	0	0	0	0	0	0	—	25	25	4	2	1.5	.926
1986			21	8	.724	3.27	35	35	15	267	229	82	223	6	0	0	0	0	0	0	—	27	27	2	4	1.6	.964
1987			18	11	.621	3.38	34	34	13	266	227	93	208	0	0	0	0	1	0	0	.000	31	18	0	1	1.4	1.000
1988			15	13	.536	3.94	34	34	10	235	225	83	168	2	0	0	0	0	0	0	—	31	21	1	1	1.6	.981
1989			6	14	.300	4.86	24	24	10	170.1	189	59	115	0	0	0	0	0	0	0	—	17	22	1	3	1.7	.975
1990			15	18	.455	4.51	36	36	11	249.2	231	97	162	3	0	0	0	0	0	0	—	38	14	2	2	1.5	.963
1991	MIN	A	18	12	.600	3.43	35	35	10	246.2	226	92	163	2	0	0	0	0	0	0	—	23	25	0	2	1.4	1.000
1992	TOR	A	21	6	.778	4.04	34	34	6	240.2	222	80	132	1	0	0	0	0	0	0	—	20	26	1	1	1.4	.979
1993			7	12	.368	6.19	27	27	4	152.2	189	65	103	1	0	0	0	0	0	0	—	11	10	2	1	0.9	.913
1994	CLE	A	10	6	.625	5.60	23	23	1	141.1	163	67	100	0	0	0	0	0	0	0	—	12	19	4	1	1.5	.886
18 yrs.			254	186	.577	3.90	549	527	175	3824.2	3567	1390	2478	28	3	4	0	1	0	0	.000	387	413	29	36	1.5	.965

LEAGUE CHAMPIONSHIP SERIES

Year	Team		W	L	PCT	ERA	G	GS	CG	IP	H	BB	SO	ShO	W	L	SV	AB	H	HR	BA	PO	A	E	DP	TC/G	FA
1984	DET	A	1	0	1.000	1.29	1	1	0	7	5	1	4	0	0	0	0	0	0	0	—	1	1	0	0	2.0	1.000
1987			0	1	.000	6.75	1	1	1	8	6	3	7	0	0	0	0	0	0	0	—	0	0	0	0	0.0	—
1991	MIN	A	2	0	1.000	4.05	2	2	0	13.1	17	1	7	0	0	0	0	0	0	0	—	3	2	0	0	2.5	1.000
1992	TOR	A	0	1	.000	6.57	2	2	1	12.1	11	9	6	0	0	0	0	0	0	0	—	0	4	0	1	2.0	1.000
4 yrs.			3	2	.600	4.87	6	6	2	40.2	39	14	24	0	0	0	0	0	0	0	—	4	7	0	1	1.8	1.000

WORLD SERIES

Year	Team		W	L	PCT	ERA	G	GS	CG	IP	H	BB	SO	ShO	W	L	SV	AB	H	HR	BA	PO	A	E	DP	TC/G	FA
1984	DET	A	2	0	1.000	2.00	2	2	2	18	13	3	13	0	0	0	0	0	0	0	—	5	1	0	0	3.0	1.000
1991	MIN	A	2	0	1.000	1.17	3	3	1	23	18	9	15	1	0	0	0	2	0	0	.000	3	3	0	0	2.0	1.000
1992	TOR	A	0	2	.000	8.44	2	2	0	10.2	13	6	12	0	0	0	0	2	0	0	.000	0	1	0	0	0.5	1.000
3 yrs.			4	2	.667	2.96	7	7	3	51.2	44	18	40	1	0	0	0	4	0	0	.000	8	5	0	0	1.9	1.000

Jamie Moyer

MOYER, JAMIE
B. Nov. 11, 1962, Sellersville, Pa.

BL TL 6' 170 lbs.

Year	Team		W	L	PCT	ERA	G	GS	CG	IP	H	BB	SO	ShO	W	L	SV	AB	H	HR	BA	PO	A	E	DP	TC/G	FA
1986	CHI	N	7	4	.636	5.05	16	16	1	87.1	107	42	45	1	0	0	0	22	2	0	.091	2	22	0	0	1.5	1.000
1987			12	15	.444	5.10	35	33	1	201	210	97	147	0	1	0	0	61	14	0	.230	15	37	4	3	1.6	.929
1988			9	15	.375	3.48	34	30	3	202	212	55	121	1	1	0	0	60	5	0	.083	11	45	1	3	1.7	.982
1989	TEX	A	4	9	.308	4.86	15	15	1	76	84	33	44	0	0	0	0	0	0	0	—	5	14	0	2	1.3	1.000
1990			2	6	.250	4.66	33	10	1	102.1	115	39	58	0	1	1	0	0	0	0	—	6	14	0	2	0.6	1.000
1991	STL	N	0	5	.000	5.74	8	7	0	31.1	38	16	20	0	0	0	0	8	0	0	.000	0	5	0	0	0.6	1.000
1993	BAL	A	12	9	.571	3.43	25	25	3	152	154	38	90	1	0	0	0	0	0	0	—	14	25	1	1	1.6	.975
1994			5	7	.417	4.77	23	23	0	149	158	38	87	0	0	0	0	0	0	0	—	12	17	0	1	1.3	1.000
8 yrs.			51	70	.421	4.42	189	159	10	1001	1078	358	612	3	3	1	0	151	21	0	.139	65	179	6	12	1.3	.976

Year	Team		W	L	PCT	ERA	G	GS	CG	IP	H	BB	SO	ShO	Relief Pitching W	L	SV	Batting AB	H	HR	BA	PO	A	E	DP	TC/G	FA

Terry Mulholland

MULHOLLAND, TERENCE JOHN
B. Mar. 9, 1963, Uniontown, Pa.

BR TL 6'3" 200 lbs.

Year	Team		W	L	PCT	ERA	G	GS	CG	IP	H	BB	SO	ShO	W	L	SV	AB	H	HR	BA	PO	A	E	DP	TC/G	FA
1986	SF	N	1	7	.125	4.94	15	10	0	54.2	51	35	27	0	0	0	0	19	1	0	.053	1	9	3	0	0.9	.769
1988			2	1	.667	3.72	9	6	2	46	50	7	18	1	0	0	0	14	0	0	.000	7	7	0	0	1.6	1.000
1989	2 teams	SF N (5G 0–0)	PHI N (20G 4–7)																								
"	total		4	7	.364	4.92	25	18	2	115.1	137	36	66	0	0	0	0	36	2	0	.056	2	25	4	1	1.2	.871
1990	PHI	N	9	10	.474	3.34	33	26	6	180.2	172	42	75	1	0	0	0	62	6	0	.097	8	17	3	0	0.8	.893
1991			16	13	.552	3.61	34	34	8	232	231	49	142	3	0	0	0	80	7	0	.088	12	28	5	2	1.3	.889
1992			13	11	.542	3.81	32	32	**12**	229	227	46	125	2	0	0	0	83	8	0	.096	6	47	3	0	1.8	.946
1993			12	9	.571	3.25	29	28	7	191	177	40	116	2	0	0	0	62	4	0	.065	5	27	2	1	1.2	.941
1994	NY	A	6	7	.462	6.49	24	19	2	120.2	150	37	72	0	0	0	0	0	0	0	—	4	15	1	0	0.8	.950
8 yrs.			63	65	.492	4.04	201	173	39	1169.1	1195	292	641	10	0	0	0	356	28	0	.079	45	175	21	4	1.2	.913

LEAGUE CHAMPIONSHIP SERIES

| 1993 | PHI | N | 0 | 1 | .000 | 7.20 | 1 | 1 | 0 | 5 | 9 | 1 | 2 | 0 | 0 | 0 | 0 | 2 | 0 | 0 | .000 | 0 | 2 | 0 | 0 | 2.0 | 1.000 |

WORLD SERIES

| 1993 | PHI | N | 1 | 0 | 1.000 | 6.75 | 2 | 2 | 0 | 10.2 | 14 | 3 | 5 | 0 | 0 | 0 | 0 | 0 | 0 | 0 | — | 1 | 1 | 0 | 0 | 1.0 | 1.000 |

Bobby Munoz

MUNOZ, ROBERTO
Born Roberto Munoz (Sbert).
B. Mar. 3, 1968, Rio Piedras, Puerto Rico

BR TR 6'7" 237 lbs.

Year	Team		W	L	PCT	ERA	G	GS	CG	IP	H	BB	SO	ShO	W	L	SV	AB	H	HR	BA	PO	A	E	DP	TC/G	FA
1993	NY	A	3	3	.500	5.32	38	0	0	45.2	48	26	33	0	3	3	0	0	0	0	—	1	6	0	1	0.2	1.000
1994	PHI	N	7	5	.583	2.67	21	14	1	104.1	101	35	59	0	0	0	1	34	7	1	.206	8	18	1	1	1.3	.963
2 yrs.			10	8	.556	3.48	59	14	1	150	149	61	92	0	3	3	1	34	7	1	.206	9	24	1	2	0.6	.971

Mike Munoz

MUNOZ, MICHAEL ANTHONY
B. July 12, 1965, Baldwin Park, Calif.

BL TL 6'2" 190 lbs.

Year	Team		W	L	PCT	ERA	G	GS	CG	IP	H	BB	SO	ShO	W	L	SV	AB	H	HR	BA	PO	A	E	DP	TC/G	FA
1989	LA	N	0	0	—	16.88	3	0	0	2.2	5	2	3	0	0	0	0	0	0	0	—	1	1	0	0	0.7	1.000
1990			0	1	.000	3.18	8	0	0	5.2	6	3	2	0	0	1	0	1	0	0	.000	0	0	0	0	0.0	—
1991	DET	A	0	0	—	9.64	6	0	0	9.1	14	5	3	0	0	0	0	0	0	0	—	0	3	0	0	0.5	1.000
1992			1	2	.333	3.00	65	0	0	48	44	25	23	0	1	2	2	0	0	0	—	8	12	0	0	0.3	1.000
1993	2 teams	DET A (8G 0–1)	CLR N (21G 2–1)																								
"	total		2	2	.500	4.71	29	0	0	21	25	15	17	0	2	2	0	0	0	0	—	1	5	0	0	0.2	1.000
1994	CLR	N	4	2	.667	3.74	57	0	0	45.2	37	31	32	0	4	2	1	0	0	0	—	6	12	1	2	0.3	.947
6 yrs.			7	7	.500	4.28	168	0	0	132.1	131	81	80	0	7	7	3	1	0	0	.000	16	33	1	2	0.3	.980

Rob Murphy

MURPHY, ROBERT ALBERT, JR.
B. May 26, 1960, Miami, Fla.

BL TL 6'2" 200 lbs.

Year	Team		W	L	PCT	ERA	G	GS	CG	IP	H	BB	SO	ShO	W	L	SV	AB	H	HR	BA	PO	A	E	DP	TC/G	FA
1985	CIN	N	0	0	—	6.00	2	0	0	3	2	2	1	0	0	0	0	0	0	0	—	0	0	0	0	0.0	—
1986			6	0	1.000	0.72	34	0	0	50.1	26	21	36	0	6	0	1	3	0	0	.000	1	9	0	0	0.3	1.000
1987			8	5	.615	3.04	87	0	0	100.2	91	32	99	0	8	5	3	5	1	0	.200	7	14	0	0	0.2	1.000
1988			0	6	.000	3.08	**76**	0	0	84.2	69	38	74	0	0	6	3	0	0	0	—	4	14	0	2	0.2	1.000
1989	BOS	A	5	7	.417	2.74	74	0	0	105	97	41	107	0	5	7	9	0	0	0	—	7	15	0	1	0.3	1.000
1990			0	6	.000	6.32	68	0	0	57	85	32	54	0	0	6	7	0	0	0	—	4	7	1	2	0.2	.917
1991	SEA	A	0	1	.000	3.00	57	0	0	48	47	19	34	0	0	1	4	0	0	0	—	2	8	2	0	0.2	.833
1992	HOU	N	3	1	.750	4.04	59	0	0	55.2	56	21	42	0	3	1	0	1	0	0	.000	2	12	0	0	0.2	1.000
1993	STL	N	5	7	.417	4.87	73	0	0	64.2	73	20	41	0	5	7	1	2	1	0	.500	3	8	1	1	0.2	.917
1994	2 teams	STL N (50G 4–3)	NY A (3G 0–0)																								
"	total		4	3	.571	4.29	53	0	0	42	38	13	25	0	4	3	2	0	0	0	—	0	7	0	1	0.1	1.000
10 yrs.			31	36	.463	3.49	583	0	0	611	584	239	513	0	31	36	30	11	2	0	.182	30	94	4	7	0.2	.969

LEAGUE CHAMPIONSHIP SERIES

| 1990 | BOS | A | 0 | 0 | — | 13.50 | 1 | 0 | 0 | 0.2 | 2 | 1 | 0 | 0 | 0 | 0 | 0 | 0 | 0 | 0 | — | 0 | 0 | 0 | 0 | 0.0 | — |

Mike Mussina

MUSSINA, MICHAEL COLE
B. Dec. 8, 1968, Williamsport, Pa.

BR TR 6'2" 185 lbs.

Year	Team		W	L	PCT	ERA	G	GS	CG	IP	H	BB	SO	ShO	W	L	SV	AB	H	HR	BA	PO	A	E	DP	TC/G	FA
1991	BAL	A	4	5	.444	2.87	12	12	2	87.2	77	21	52	0	0	0	0	0	0	0	—	4	11	0	1	1.3	1.000
1992			18	5	**.783**	2.54	32	32	8	241	212	48	130	4	0	0	0	0	0	0	—	13	31	1	0	1.4	.978
1993			14	6	.700	4.46	25	25	3	167.2	163	44	117	2	0	0	0	0	0	0	—	12	19	0	1	1.2	1.000
1994			16	5	.762	3.06	24	24	3	176.1	163	42	99	0	0	0	0	0	0	0	—	14	28	1	1	1.8	.977
4 yrs.			52	21	.712	3.20	93	93	16	672.2	615	155	398	6	0	0	0	0	0	0	—	43	89	2	3	1.4	.985

Jeff Mutis

MUTIS, JEFFREY THOMAS
B. Dec. 20, 1966, Allentown, Pa.

BL TL 6'2" 185 lbs.

Year	Team		W	L	PCT	ERA	G	GS	CG	IP	H	BB	SO	ShO	W	L	SV	AB	H	HR	BA	PO	A	E	DP	TC/G	FA
1991	CLE	A	0	3	.000	11.68	3	3	0	12.1	23	7	6	0	0	0	0	0	0	0	—	1	1	0	0	0.7	1.000
1992			0	2	.000	9.53	3	2	0	11.1	24	6	8	0	0	0	0	0	0	0	—	0	2	0	0	0.7	1.000
1993			3	6	.333	5.78	17	13	1	81	93	33	29	1	0	0	0	0	0	0	—	3	17	0	1	1.2	1.000
1994	FLA	N	1	0	1.000	5.40	35	0	0	38.1	51	15	30	0	1	0	0	3	0	0	.000	2	6	1	1	0.3	.889
4 yrs.			4	11	.267	6.48	58	18	1	143	191	61	73	1	1	0	0	3	0	0	.000	6	26	1	2	0.6	.970

Randy Myers

MYERS, RANDALL KIRK
B. Sept. 19, 1962, Vancouver, Wash.

BL TL 6'1" 190 lbs.

Year	Team		W	L	PCT	ERA	G	GS	CG	IP	H	BB	SO	ShO	W	L	SV	AB	H	HR	BA	PO	A	E	DP	TC/G	FA
1985	NY	N	0	0	—	0.00	1	0	0	2	0	1	2	0	0	0	0	0	0	0	—	0	1	0	0	1.0	1.000
1986			0	0	—	4.22	10	0	0	10.2	11	9	13	0	0	0	0	0	0	0	—	0	2	0	0	0.2	1.000
1987			3	6	.333	3.96	54	0	0	75	61	30	92	0	3	6	6	7	2	0	.286	5	9	1	0	0.3	.933
1988			7	3	.700	1.72	55	0	0	68	45	17	69	0	7	3	26	4	1	0	.250	4	3	0	1	0.1	1.000
1989			7	4	.636	2.35	65	0	0	84.1	62	40	88	0	7	4	24	5	0	0	.000	3	11	0	0	0.2	1.000
1990	CIN	N	4	6	.400	2.08	66	0	0	86.2	59	38	98	0	4	6	31	4	1	0	.250	1	12	0	0	0.2	1.000
1991			6	13	.316	3.55	58	12	0	132	116	80	108	0	4	7	6	29	5	0	.172	6	12	2	0	0.3	.900
1992	SD	N	3	6	.333	4.29	66	0	0	79.2	84	38	66	0	3	6	38	7	1	0	.143	2	12	0	0	0.2	1.000
1993	CHI	N	2	4	.333	3.11	73	0	0	75.1	65	26	86	0	2	4	**53**	2	1	0	.500	1	7	0	0	0.1	1.000
1994			1	5	.167	3.79	38	0	0	40.1	40	16	32	0	1	5	21	1	0	0	.000	0	3	1	0	0.1	.750
10 yrs.			33	47	.413	3.11	486	12	1	654	543	291	654	0	31	41	205	59	11	0	.186	22	72	4	1	0.2	.959

Year	Team	W	L	PCT	ERA	G	GS	CG	IP	H	BB	SO	ShO	Relief Pitching W	L	SV	Batting AB	H	HR	BA	PO	A	E	DP	TC/G	FA

Randy Myers *continued*

LEAGUE CHAMPIONSHIP SERIES

1988	NY N	2	0	1.000	0.00	3	0	0	4.2	1	2	0	0	2	0	0	0	0	0	–	0	1	0	0	0.3	1.000
1990	CIN N	0	0	–	0.00	4	0	0	5.2	2	3	7	0	0	0	3	0	0	0	–	0	0	0	0	0.0	–
2 yrs.		2	0	1.000	0.00	7	0	0	10.1	3	5	7	0	2	0	3	0	0	0	–	0	1	0	0	0.1	1.000

WORLD SERIES

| 1990 | CIN N | 0 | 0 | – | 0.00 | 3 | 0 | 0 | 3 | 2 | 0 | 3 | 0 | 0 | 0 | 1 | 0 | 0 | 0 | – | 0 | 0 | 0 | 0 | 0.0 | – |

Chris Nabholz

NABHOLZ, CHRISTOPHER WILLIAM
B. Jan. 5, 1967, Harrisburg, Pa.

BL TL 6'5" 210 lbs.

1990	MON N	6	2	.750	2.83	11	11	1	70	43	32	53	1	0	0	0	21	0	0	.000	3	10	1	0	1.3	.929
1991		8	7	.533	3.63	24	24	1	153.2	134	57	99	0	0	0	0	52	6	0	.115	9	28	1	2	1.6	.974
1992		11	12	.478	3.32	32	32	1	195	176	74	130	1	0	0	0	65	8	0	.123	14	41	2	3	1.8	.965
1993		9	8	.529	4.09	26	21	1	116.2	100	63	74	0	0	0	0	39	5	0	.128	6	17	0	2	0.9	1.000
1994	2 teams	CLE A	(6G 0–1)		BOS A	(8G 3–4)																				
"	total	3	5	.375	7.64	14	12	0	53	67	38	28	0	0	0	0	0	0	0	–	1	9	0	2	0.7	1.000
5 yrs.		37	34	.521	3.89	107	100	4	588.1	520	264	384	2	0	0	0	177	19	0	.107	33	105	4	9	1.3	.972

Charles Nagy

NAGY, CHARLES HARRISON
B. May 5, 1967, Bridgeport, Conn.

BL TR 6'3" 200 lbs.

1990	CLE A	2	4	.333	5.91	9	8	0	45.2	58	21	26	0	0	0	0	0	0	0	–	3	8	1	2	1.3	.917
1991		10	15	.400	4.13	33	33	6	211.1	228	66	109	1	0	0	0	0	0	0	–	17	20	2	4	1.2	.949
1992		17	10	.630	2.96	33	33	10	252	245	57	169	3	0	0	0	0	0	0	–	22	43	1	3	2.0	.985
1993		2	6	.250	6.29	9	9	1	48.2	66	13	30	0	0	0	0	0	0	0	–	8	14	1	2	2.6	.957
1994		10	8	.556	3.45	23	23	3	169.1	175	48	108	0	0	0	0	0	0	0	–	9	26	2	1	1.6	.946
5 yrs.		41	43	.488	3.83	107	106	20	727	772	205	442	4	0	0	0	0	0	0	–	59	111	7	12	1.7	.960

Jaime Navarro

NAVARRO, JAIME
Born Jaime Navarro (Cintron).
Son of Julio Navarro.
B. Mar. 27, 1967, Bayamon, Puerto Rico.

BR TR 6'4" 210 lbs.

1989	MIL A	7	8	.467	3.12	19	17	1	109.2	119	32	56	0	1	0	0	0	0	0	–	6	16	2	0	1.3	.917
1990		8	7	.533	4.46	32	22	3	149.1	176	41	75	0	0	0	1	0	0	0	–	10	19	1	2	0.9	.967
1991		15	12	.556	3.92	34	34	10	234	237	73	114	2	0	0	0	0	0	0	–	16	28	3	3	1.4	.936
1992		17	11	.607	3.33	34	34	5	246	224	64	100	3	0	0	0	0	0	0	–	17	18	4	1	1.1	.897
1993		11	12	.478	5.33	35	34	5	214.1	254	73	114	1	0	0	0	0	0	0	–	14	21	2	2	1.1	.946
1994		4	9	.308	6.62	29	10	0	89.2	115	35	65	0	2	3	0	0	0	0	–	4	7	0	1	0.4	1.000
6 yrs.		62	59	.512	4.30	183	151	24	1043	1125	318	524	6	3	3	1	0	0	0	–	67	109	12	9	1.0	.936

Denny Neagle

NEAGLE, DENNIS EDWARD
B. Sept. 13, 1968, Gambrills, Md.

BL TL 6'4" 200 lbs.

1991	MIN A	0	1	.000	4.05	7	3	0	20	28	7	14	0	0	0	0	0	0	0	–	0	1	0	0	0.1	1.000
1992	PIT N	4	6	.400	4.48	55	6	0	86.1	81	43	77	0	3	3	2	11	0	0	.000	2	12	0	0	0.3	1.000
1993		3	5	.375	5.31	50	7	0	81.1	82	37	73	0	1	2	1	14	0	0	.000	1	5	0	0	0.1	1.000
1994		9	10	.474	5.12	24	24	2	137	135	49	122	0	0	0	0	42	8	1	.190	3	21	1	2	1.0	.960
4 yrs.		16	22	.421	4.93	136	40	2	324.2	326	136	286	0	4	5	3	67	8	1	.119	6	39	1	2	0.3	.978

LEAGUE CHAMPIONSHIP SERIES

| 1992 | PIT N | 0 | 0 | – | 27.00 | 2 | 0 | 0 | 1.2 | 4 | 3 | 0 | 0 | 0 | 0 | 0 | 0 | 0 | 0 | – | 0 | 0 | 0 | 0 | 0.0 | – |

Jeff Nelson

NELSON, JEFFREY ALLAN
B. Nov. 17, 1966, Baltimore, Md.

BR TR 6'8" 225 lbs.

1992	SEA A	1	7	.125	3.44	66	0	0	81	71	44	46	0	1	7	6	0	0	0	–	3	12	2	2	0.3	.882
1993		5	3	.625	4.35	71	0	0	60	57	34	61	0	5	3	1	0	0	0	–	3	12	0	2	0.2	1.000
1994		0	0	–	2.76	28	0	0	42.1	35	20	44	0	0	0	0	0	0	0	–	1	5	2	1	0.3	.750
3 yrs.		6	10	.375	3.58	165	0	0	183.1	163	98	151	0	6	10	7	0	0	0	–	7	29	4	5	0.2	.900

Robb Nen

NEN, ROBERT ALLEN
Son of Dick Nen.
B. Nov. 28, 1969, San Pedro, Calif.

BR TR 6'4" 200 lbs.

1993	2 teams	TEX A	(9G 1–1)		FLA N	(15G 1–0)																				
"	total	2	1	.667	6.75	24	4	0	56	63	46	39	0	0	0	0	4	0	0	.000	6	6	0	0	0.5	1.000
1994	FLA N	5	5	.500	2.95	44	0	0	58	46	17	60	0	5	5	15	3	0	0	.000	3	6	1	1	0.2	.900
2 yrs.		7	6	.538	4.82	68	4	0	114	109	63	99	0	5	5	15	7	0	0	.000	9	12	1	3	0.3	.955

Dave Nied

NIED, DAVID GLEN
B. Dec. 22, 1968, Dallas, Tex.

BR TR 6'2" 175 lbs.

1992	ATL N	3	0	1.000	1.17	6	2	0	23	10	5	19	0	2	0	0	7	2	0	.286	0	2	0	0	0.3	1.000
1993	CLR N	5	9	.357	5.17	16	16	1	87	99	42	46	0	0	0	0	23	4	0	.174	4	16	0	0	1.3	1.000
1994		9	7	.563	4.80	22	22	2	122	137	47	74	1	0	0	0	40	4	0	.100	4	12	0	2	0.7	1.000
3 yrs.		17	16	.515	4.58	44	40	3	232	246	94	139	1	2	0	0	70	10	0	.143	8	30	0	2	0.9	1.000

Junior Noboa

NOBOA, MILCIADES ARTURO
Born Milciades Arturo Noboa (Diaz).
B. Nov. 10, 1964, Azua, Dominican Republic.

BR TR 5'10" 155 lbs.

| 1990 | MON N | 0 | 0 | – | 0.00 | 1 | 0 | 0 | 0.2 | 0 | 1 | 0 | 0 | 0 | 0 | 0 | * | | | | 1 | 0 | 0 | 0 | 0.0 | – |

Year	Team	W	L	PCT	ERA	G	GS	CG	IP	H	BB	SO	ShO	Relief Pitching W	L	SV	Batting AB	H	HR	BA	PO	A	E	DP	TC/G	FA

Edwin Nunez

NUNEZ, EDWIN
Born Edwin Nunez (Martinez).
B. May 27, 1963, Humacao, Puerto Rico.
BR TR 6'5" 207 lbs.

Year	Team	W	L	PCT	ERA	G	GS	CG	IP	H	BB	SO	ShO	W	L	SV	AB	H	HR	BA	PO	A	E	DP	TC/G	FA
1982	SEA A	1	2	.333	4.58	8	5	0	35.1	36	16	27	0	0	0	0	0	0	0	–	2	5	1	0	1.0	.875
1983		0	4	.000	4.38	14	5	0	37	40	22	35	0	0	0	0	0	0	0	–	0	6	0	1	0.4	1.000
1984		2	2	.500	3.18	37	0	0	68	55	21	57	0	2	2	7	0	0	0	–	4	6	1	0	0.3	.909
1985		7	3	.700	3.09	70	0	0	90.1	79	34	58	0	7	3	16	0	0	0	–	5	12	1	0	0.2	1.000
1986		1	2	.333	5.82	14	1	0	21.2	25	5	17	0	0	2	0	0	0	0	–	1	1	0	0	0.1	1.000
1987		3	4	.429	3.80	48	0	0	47.1	45	18	34	0	3	4	12	0	0	0	–	2	5	0	0	0.1	1.000
1988	2 teams	SEA A (14G 1-4)							NY N (10G 1-0)																	
"	total	2	4	.333	6.85	24	3	0	43.1	66	17	27	0	2	1	0	0	0	0	–	6	8	2	1	0.7	.875
1989	DET A	3	4	.429	4.17	27	0	0	54	49	36	41	0	3	4	1	0	0	0	–	3	9	0	2	0.4	1.000
1990		3	1	.750	2.24	42	0	0	80.1	65	37	66	0	3	1	6	0	0	0	–	7	5	1	1	0.3	.923
1991	MIL A	2	1	.667	6.04	23	0	0	25.1	28	13	24	0	2	1	8	0	0	0	–	0	3	1	0	0.2	.750
1992	2 teams	MIL A (10G 1-1)							TEX A (39G 0-2)																	
"	total	1	3	.250	4.85	49	0	0	59.1	63	22	49	0	1	3	3	0	0	0	–	3	4	1	0	0.2	.875
1993	OAK A	3	6	.333	3.81	56	0	0	75.2	89	29	58	0	3	6	1	0	0	0	–	7	8	1	1	0.3	.938
1994		0	0	–	12.00	15	0	0	15	26	10	15	0	0	0	0	0	0	0	–	0	4	0	0	0.3	1.000
13 yrs.		28	36	.438	4.19	427	14	0	652.2	666	280	508	0	26	27	54	0	0	0	–	40	76	8	7	0.3	.935

Chad Ogea

OGEA, CHAD WAYNE
B. Nov. 9, 1970, Lake Charles, La.
BR TR 6'2" 200 lbs.

Year	Team	W	L	PCT	ERA	G	GS	CG	IP	H	BB	SO	ShO	W	L	SV	AB	H	HR	BA	PO	A	E	DP	TC/G	FA
1994	CLE A	0	1	.000	6.06	4	1	0	16.1	21	10	11	0	0	0	0	0	0	0	–	0	2	0	0	0.5	1.000

Bob Ojeda

OJEDA, ROBERT MICHAEL (Bobby O.)
B. Dec. 17, 1957, Los Angeles, Calif.
BL TL 6'1" 185 lbs.

Year	Team	W	L	PCT	ERA	G	GS	CG	IP	H	BB	SO	ShO	W	L	SV	AB	H	HR	BA	PO	A	E	DP	TC/G	FA
1980	BOS A	1	1	.500	6.92	7	7	0	26	39	14	12	0	0	0	0	0	0	0	–	1	3	0	0	0.6	1.000
1981		6	2	.750	3.14	10	10	2	66	50	25	28	0	0	0	0	0	0	0	–	3	10	1	1	1.4	.929
1982		4	6	.400	5.63	22	14	0	78.1	95	29	52	0	1	0	0	0	0	0	–	2	7	1	0	0.5	.900
1983		12	7	.632	4.04	29	28	5	173.2	173	73	94	0	0	0	0	0	0	0	–	11	23	1	2	1.2	.971
1984		12	12	.500	3.99	33	32	8	216.2	211	96	137	5	0	0	0	0	0	0	–	10	32	2	3	1.3	.955
1985		9	11	.450	4.00	39	22	5	157.2	166	48	102	0	2	1	1	0	0	0	–	13	23	3	0	1.0	.923
1986	NY N	18	5	.783	2.57	32	30	7	217.1	185	52	148	2	1	0	0	71	8	0	.113	9	37	1	3	1.5	.979
1987		3	5	.375	3.88	10	7	0	46.1	45	10	21	0	0	1	0	14	1	0	.071	5	6	0	2	1.1	1.000
1988		10	13	.435	2.88	29	29	5	190.1	158	33	133	5	0	0	0	61	10	0	.164	13	36	2	5	1.8	.961
1989		13	11	.542	3.47	31	31	5	192	179	78	95	2	0	0	0	66	7	0	.106	16	36	1	3	1.7	.981
1990		7	6	.538	3.66	38	12	0	118	123	40	62	0	3	1	0	30	4	0	.133	8	31	2	1	1.1	.951
1991	LA N	12	9	.571	3.18	31	31	2	189.1	181	70	120	1	0	0	0	56	9	1	.161	14	32	0	1	1.5	1.000
1992		6	9	.400	3.63	29	29	2	166.1	169	81	94	1	0	0	0	49	5	0	.102	5	37	2	0	1.5	.955
1993	CLE A	2	1	.667	4.40	9	7	0	43	48	21	27	0	0	0	0	3	0	0	–	3	9	0	1	1.3	1.000
1994	NY A	0	0	–	24.00	2	2	0	3	11	6	3	0	0	0	0	0	0	0	–	0	1	0	0	0.5	1.000
15 yrs.		115	98	.540	3.65	351	291	41	1884	1833	676	1128	16	7	3	1	347	44	1	.127	113	323	16	22	1.3	.965

LEAGUE CHAMPIONSHIP SERIES

Year	Team	W	L	PCT	ERA	G	GS	CG	IP	H	BB	SO	ShO	W	L	SV	AB	H	HR	BA	PO	A	E	DP	TC/G	FA
1986	NY N	1	0	1.000	2.57	2	2	1	14	15	4	6	0	0	0	0	5	0	0	.000	2	4	0	0	3.0	1.000

WORLD SERIES

Year	Team	W	L	PCT	ERA	G	GS	CG	IP	H	BB	SO	ShO	W	L	SV	AB	H	HR	BA	PO	A	E	DP	TC/G	FA
1986	NY N	1	0	1.000	2.08	2	2	0	13	13	5	9	0	0	0	0	2	0	0	.000	0	2	0	0	1.0	1.000

Omar Olivares

OLIVARES, OMAR
Born Omar Olivares (Palqu).
Son of Ed Olivares.
B. July 6, 1967, Mayaguez, Puerto Rico.
BR TR 6'1" 185 lbs.

Year	Team	W	L	PCT	ERA	G	GS	CG	IP	H	BB	SO	ShO	W	L	SV	AB	H	HR	BA	PO	A	E	DP	TC/G	FA
1990	STL N	1	1	.500	2.92	9	6	0	49.1	45	17	20	0	0	0	0	17	3	1	.176	7	8	0	0	1.7	1.000
1991		11	7	.611	3.71	28	24	0	167.1	148	61	91	0	0	0	1	53	12	0	.226	16	30	2	5	1.7	.958
1992		9	9	.500	3.84	32	30	1	197	189	63	124	0	0	0	0	68	16	1	.235	15	40	0	4	1.7	1.000
1993		5	3	.625	4.17	58	9	0	118.2	134	54	63	0	3	0	1	26	7	0	.269	9	36	4	3	0.8	.918
1994		3	4	.429	5.74	14	12	1	73.2	84	37	26	0	0	0	0	28	6	1	.214	7	14	1	1	1.6	.955
5 yrs.		29	24	.547	4.02	141	81	2	606	600	232	324	0	3	0	3	192	44	3	.229	54	128	7	13	1.3	.963

Darren Oliver

OLIVER, DARREN CHRISTOPHER
Son of Bob Oliver.
B. Oct. 6, 1970, Kansas City, Mo.
BR TL 6' 170 lbs.

Year	Team	W	L	PCT	ERA	G	GS	CG	IP	H	BB	SO	ShO	W	L	SV	AB	H	HR	BA	PO	A	E	DP	TC/G	FA
1993	TEX A	0	0	–	2.70	2	0	0	3.1	2	1	4	0	0	0	0	0	0	0	–	0	1	1	0	1.0	.500
1994		4	0	1.000	3.42	43	0	0	50	40	35	50	0	4	0	2	0	0	0	–	5	14	0	3	0.4	1.000
2 yrs.		4	0	1.000	3.38	45	0	0	53.1	42	36	54	0	4	0	2	0	0	0	–	5	15	1	3	0.5	.952

Gregg Olson

OLSON, GREGGORY WILLIAM
B. Oct. 11, 1966, Scribner, Neb.
BR TR 6'4" 210 lbs.

Year	Team	W	L	PCT	ERA	G	GS	CG	IP	H	BB	SO	ShO	W	L	SV	AB	H	HR	BA	PO	A	E	DP	TC/G	FA
1988	BAL A	1	1	.500	3.27	10	0	0	11	10	10	9	0	1	1	0	0	0	0	–	1	2	0	0	0.3	1.000
1989		5	2	.714	1.69	64	0	0	85	57	46	90	0	5	2	27	0	0	0	–	5	12	1	0	0.3	.944
1990		6	5	.545	2.42	64	0	0	74.1	57	31	74	0	6	5	37	0	0	0	–	4	4	0	1	0.1	1.000
1991		4	6	.400	3.18	72	0	0	73.2	74	29	72	0	4	6	31	0	0	0	–	6	11	3	0	0.3	.850
1992		1	5	.167	2.05	60	0	0	61.1	46	24	58	0	1	5	36	0	0	0	–	5	9	0	2	0.2	1.000
1993		0	2	.000	1.60	50	0	0	45	37	18	44	0	0	2	29	1	0	0	.000	2	7	0	0	0.2	1.000
1994	ATL N	0	2	.000	9.20	16	0	0	14.2	19	13	10	0	0	2	1	0	0	0	.000	0	0	0	0	0.0	–
7 yrs.		17	23	.425	2.54	336	0	0	365	300	171	357	0	17	23	161	2	0	0	.000	23	45	4	3	0.2	.944

Paul O'Neill

O'NEILL, PAUL ANDREW
B. Feb. 25, 1963, Columbus, Ohio.
BL TL 6'4" 200 lbs.

Year	Team	W	L	PCT	ERA	G	GS	CG	IP	H	BB	SO	ShO	W	L	SV	AB	H	HR	BA	PO	A	E	DP	TC/G	FA
1987	CIN N	0	0	–	13.50	1	0	0	2	2	4	2	0	0	0	0	0	0	0	*	0	0	0	0	0.0	–

Year	Team	W	L	PCT	ERA	G	GS	CG	IP	H	BB	SO	ShO	W	L	SV	AB	H	HR	BA	PO	A	E	DP	TC/G	FA

Steve Ontiveros — ONTIVEROS, STEVEN — B. Mar. 5, 1961, Tularosa, N. M. — BR TR 6' 180 lbs.

Year	Team	W	L	PCT	ERA	G	GS	CG	IP	H	BB	SO	ShO	W	L	SV	AB	H	HR	BA	PO	A	E	DP	TC/G	FA
1985	OAK A	1	3	.250	1.93	39	0	0	74.2	45	19	36	0	1	3	8	0	0	0	–	7	14	1	1	0.6	.955
1986		2	2	.500	4.71	46	0	0	72.2	72	25	54	0	2	2	10	0	0	0	–	2	10	0	1	0.3	1.000
1987		10	8	.556	4.00	35	22	2	150.2	141	50	97	1	1	2	1	0	0	0	–	14	29	1	0	1.3	.977
1988		3	4	.429	4.61	10	10	0	54.2	57	21	30	0	0	0	0	0	0	0	–	6	12	0	1	1.8	1.000
1989	PHI N	2	1	.667	3.82	6	5	0	30.2	34	15	12	0	0	0	0	12	1	0	.083	4	9	0	2	2.2	1.000
1990		0	0	–	2.70	5	0	0	10	9	3	6	0	0	0	0	0	0	0	–	2	3	0	0	1.0	1.000
1993	SEA A	0	2	.000	1.00	14	0	0	18	18	6	13	0	0	2	0	0	0	0	–	0	2	1	2	0.2	.667
1994	OAK A	6	4	.600	2.65	27	13	2	115.1	93	26	56	0	1	2	0	0	0	0	–	15	22	0	2	1.4	1.000
8 yrs.		24	24	.500	3.43	182	50	4	526.2	469	165	304	1	5	11	19	12	1	0	.083	50	101	3	8	0.8	.981

Jose Oquendo — OQUENDO, JOSE MANUEL — Born Jose Manuel Oquendo (Contreras). B. July 4, 1963, Rio Piedras, Puerto Rico. — BB TR 5'10" 160 lbs. BR 1984

Year	Team	W	L	PCT	ERA	G	GS	CG	IP	H	BB	SO	ShO	W	L	SV	AB	H	HR	BA	PO	A	E	DP	TC/G	FA
1987	STL N	0	0	–	27.00	1	0	0	1	4	1	0	0	0	0	0	248	71	1	.286	0	0	0	0	0.0	–
1988		0	1	.000	4.50	1	0	0	4	4	6	1	0	0	1	0	451	125	7	.277	0	0	0	0	0.0	–
1991		0	0	–	27.00	1	0	0	1	2	2	1	0	0	0	0	366	88	1	.240	0	0	0	0	0.0	–
3 yrs.		0	1	.000	12.00	3	0	0	6	10	9	2	0	0	1	0	*				0	0	0	0	0.0	–

Mike Oquist — OQUIST, MICHAEL LEE — B. May 30, 1968, La Junta, Colo. — BR TR 6'2" 170 lbs.

Year	Team	W	L	PCT	ERA	G	GS	CG	IP	H	BB	SO	ShO	W	L	SV	AB	H	HR	BA	PO	A	E	DP	TC/G	FA
1993	BAL A	0	0	–	3.86	5	0	0	11.2	4	4	8	0	0	0	0	0	0	0	–	1	0	0	0	0.2	1.000
1994		3	3	.500	6.17	15	9	0	58.1	75	30	39	0	2	0	0	0	0	0	–	6	7	0	0	0.9	1.000
2 yrs.		3	3	.500	5.79	20	9	0	70	87	34	47	0	2	0	0	0	0	0	–	7	7	0	0	0.7	1.000

Jesse Orosco — OROSCO, JESSE RUSSELL — B. Apr. 21, 1957, Santa Barbara, Calif. — BR TL 6'2" 174 lbs.

Year	Team	W	L	PCT	ERA	G	GS	CG	IP	H	BB	SO	ShO	W	L	SV	AB	H	HR	BA	PO	A	E	DP	TC/G	FA
1979	NY N	1	2	.333	4.89	18	2	0	35	33	22	22	0	1	2	0	6	0	0	.000	2	9	0	1	0.6	1.000
1981		0	1	.000	1.59	8	0	0	17	13	6	18	0	0	1	1	2	0	0	.000	1	2	0	0	0.4	1.000
1982		4	10	.286	2.72	54	2	0	109.1	92	40	89	0	4	8	4	14	2	0	.143	4	16	0	1	0.4	1.000
1983		13	7	.650	1.47	62	0	0	110	76	38	84	0	13	7	17	12	4	0	.333	5	19	0	1	0.4	1.000
1984		10	6	.625	2.59	60	0	0	87	58	34	85	0	10	6	31	4	1	0	.250	2	11	1	1	0.2	.929
1985		8	6	.571	2.73	54	0	0	79	66	34	68	0	8	6	17	7	3	0	.429	3	8	1	2	0.2	.917
1986		8	6	.571	2.33	58	0	0	81	64	35	62	0	8	6	21	3	0	0	.000	4	8	0	0	0.2	1.000
1987		3	9	.250	4.44	58	0	0	77	78	31	78	0	3	9	16	8	0	0	.000	4	9	0	1	0.2	1.000
1988	LA N	3	2	.600	2.72	55	0	0	53	41	30	43	0	3	2	9	2	0	0	.000	1	10	0	1	0.2	1.000
1989	CLE A	3	4	.429	2.08	69	0	0	78	54	26	79	0	3	4	3	0	0	0	–	6	13	0	1	0.3	1.000
1990		5	4	.556	3.90	55	0	0	64.2	58	38	55	0	5	4	2	0	0	0	–	1	14	1	1	0.3	.938
1991		2	0	1.000	3.74	47	0	0	45.2	52	15	36	0	2	0	0	0	0	0	–	3	3	0	0	0.1	1.000
1992	MIL A	3	1	.750	3.23	59	0	0	39	33	13	40	0	3	1	1	0	0	0	–	2	3	0	0	0.1	1.000
1993		3	5	.375	3.18	57	0	0	56.2	47	17	67	0	3	5	8	1	0	0	.000	1	19	0	0	0.4	1.000
1994		3	1	.750	5.08	40	0	0	39	32	26	36	0	3	1	0	0	0	0	–	3	3	0	1	0.2	1.000
15 yrs.		69	64	.519	2.95	754	4	0	971.1	797	405	862	0	69	62	130	59	10	0	.169	42	147	3	10	0.3	.984

LEAGUE CHAMPIONSHIP SERIES

Year	Team	W	L	PCT	ERA	G	GS	CG	IP	H	BB	SO	ShO	W	L	SV	AB	H	HR	BA	PO	A	E	DP	TC/G	FA
1986	NY N	3	0	1.000	3.38	4	0	0	8	5	2	10	0	3	0	0	0	0	0	–	1	1	0	0	0.5	1.000
1988	LA N	0	0	–	7.71	4	0	0	2.1	4	3	0	0	0	0	0	0	0	0	–	1	0	0	0	0.3	1.000
2 yrs.		3	0	1.000	4.35	8	0	0	10.1	9	5	10	0	3	0	0	0	0	0	–	2	1	0	0	0.4	1.000

WORLD SERIES

Year	Team	W	L	PCT	ERA	G	GS	CG	IP	H	BB	SO	ShO	W	L	SV	AB	H	HR	BA	PO	A	E	DP	TC/G	FA
1986	NY N	0	0	–	0.00	4	0	0	5.2	2	0	6	0	0	0	2	1	1	0	1.000	0	0	0	0	0.0	–

Al Osuna — OSUNA, ALFONSO — B. Aug. 10, 1965, Inglewood, Calif. — BR TL 6'3" 200 lbs.

Year	Team	W	L	PCT	ERA	G	GS	CG	IP	H	BB	SO	ShO	W	L	SV	AB	H	HR	BA	PO	A	E	DP	TC/G	FA
1990	HOU N	2	0	1.000	4.76	12	0	0	11.1	10	6	6	0	2	0	0	0	0	0	–	1	1	0	0	0.2	1.000
1991		7	6	.538	3.42	71	0	0	81.2	59	46	68	0	7	6	12	2	0	0	.000	4	10	1	2	0.2	.933
1992		6	3	.667	4.23	66	0	0	61.2	52	38	37	0	6	3	0	0	0	0	–	2	11	0	0	0.2	1.000
1993		1	1	.500	3.20	44	0	0	25.1	17	13	21	0	1	1	2	0	0	0	–	2	1	0	0	0.1	.667
1994	LA N	2	0	1.000	6.23	15	0	0	8.2	13	4	7	0	2	0	0	0	0	0	–	0	0	0	0	0.0	–
5 yrs.		18	10	.643	3.86	208	0	0	188.2	151	107	139	0	18	10	14	2	0	0	.000	7	24	2	2	0.2	.939

Dave Otto — OTTO, DAVID ALAN — B. Nov. 12, 1964, Chicago, Ill. — BL TL 6'7" 210 lbs.

Year	Team	W	L	PCT	ERA	G	GS	CG	IP	H	BB	SO	ShO	W	L	SV	AB	H	HR	BA	PO	A	E	DP	TC/G	FA
1987	OAK A	0	0	–	9.00	3	0	0	6	7	1	3	0	0	0	0	0	0	0	–	1	0	0	0	0.3	1.000
1988		0	0	–	1.80	3	2	0	10	9	6	7	0	0	0	0	0	0	0	–	1	1	0	0	0.7	1.000
1989		0	0	–	2.70	1	1	0	6.2	6	2	4	0	0	0	0	0	0	0	–	0	1	0	0	1.0	1.000
1990		0	0	–	7.71	2	1	0	2.1	3	3	2	0	0	0	0	0	0	0	–	0	2	0	1	1.0	1.000
1991	CLE A	2	8	.200	4.23	18	14	1	100	108	27	47	0	0	0	0	0	0	0	–	1	16	1	0	1.0	.944
1992		5	9	.357	7.06	18	16	0	80.1	110	33	32	0	0	0	0	0	0	0	–	3	14	1	1	1.0	.944
1993	PIT N	3	4	.429	5.03	28	8	0	68	85	28	30	0	1	1	0	18	4	0	.222	4	13	0	1	0.6	1.000
1994	CHI N	0	1	.000	3.80	36	0	0	45	49	22	19	0	0	1	0	2	0	0	.000	1	5	1	1	0.2	.857
8 yrs.		10	22	.313	5.06	109	41	1	318.1	377	122	144	0	1	2	0	20	4	0	.200	11	52	3	4	0.6	.955

Lance Painter — PAINTER, LANCE TELFORD — B. July 21, 1967, Bedford, England — BL TL 6'1" 195 lbs.

Year	Team	W	L	PCT	ERA	G	GS	CG	IP	H	BB	SO	ShO	W	L	SV	AB	H	HR	BA	PO	A	E	DP	TC/G	FA
1993	CLR N	2	2	.500	6.00	10	6	1	39	52	9	16	0	0	0	0	10	3	0	.300	1	9	0	0	1.0	1.000
1994		4	6	.400	6.11	15	14	0	73.2	91	26	41	0	0	0	0	21	3	0	.143	5	11	0	0	1.1	1.000
2 yrs.		6	8	.429	6.07	25	20	1	112.2	143	35	57	0	0	0	0	31	6	0	.194	6	20	0	0	1.0	1.000

Year	Team		W	L	PCT	ERA	G	GS	CG	IP	H	BB	SO	ShO	Relief Pitching W	L	SV	Batting AB	H	HR	BA	PO	A	E	DP	TC/G	FA

Vicente Palacios

PALACIOS, VICENTE
Born Vicente Palacios (Diaz).
B. July 19, 1963, Veracruz, Mexico.　　　　　BR TR 6'3"　　165 lbs.

Year	Team		W	L	PCT	ERA	G	GS	CG	IP	H	BB	SO	ShO	W	L	SV	AB	H	HR	BA	PO	A	E	DP	TC/G	FA
1987	PIT	N	2	1	.667	4.30	6	4	0	29.1	27	9	13	0	0	0	0	9	1	0	.111	2	1	0	0	0.5	1.000
1988			1	2	.333	6.66	7	3	0	24.1	28	15	15	0	0	1	0	8	0	0	.000	3	5	0	0	1.1	1.000
1990			0	0	–	0.00	7	0	0	15	4	2	8	0	0	0	3	4	0	0	.000	2	0	0	0	0.3	1.000
1991			6	3	.667	3.75	36	7	1	81.2	69	38	64	1	4	1	3	14	1	0	.071	4	9	0	0	0.4	1.000
1992			3	2	.600	4.25	20	8	0	53	56	27	33	0	2	0	0	14	1	0	.071	5	7	1	1	0.7	.923
1994	STL	N	3	8	.273	4.44	31	17	1	117.2	104	43	95	1	1	1	1	33	0	0	.000	6	16	2	0	0.8	.917
6 yrs.			15	16	.484	4.18	107	39	2	321	288	134	228	2	7	3	7	82	3	0	.037	22	38	3	1	0.6	.952

Donn Pall

PALL, DONN STEVEN
B. Jan. 11, 1962, Chicago, Ill.　　　　　BR TR 6'2"　　185 lbs.

Year	Team		W	L	PCT	ERA	G	GS	CG	IP	H	BB	SO	ShO	W	L	SV	AB	H	HR	BA	PO	A	E	DP	TC/G	FA
1988	CHI	A	0	2	.000	3.45	17	0	0	28.2	39	8	16	0	0	2	0	0	0	0	–	4	6	0	1	0.6	1.000
1989			4	5	.444	3.31	53	0	0	87	90	19	58	0	4	5	6	0	0	0	–	5	7	2	0	0.3	.857
1990			3	5	.375	3.32	56	0	0	76	63	24	39	0	3	5	2	0	0	0	–	1	11	0	2	0.2	1.000
1991			7	2	.778	2.41	51	0	0	71	59	20	40	0	7	2	0	0	0	0	–	4	8	1	0	0.3	.923
1992			5	2	.714	4.93	39	0	0	73	79	27	27	0	5	2	1	0	0	0	–	5	6	1	2	0.3	.917
1993	2 teams	CHI A (39G 2–3)								PHI N	(8G 1–0)																
"	total		3	3	.500	3.07	47	0	0	76.1	77	14	40	0	3	3	1	0	0	0	–	5	13	1	0	0.4	.947
1994	2 teams	NY A (26G 1–2)								CHI N	(2G 0–0)																
"	total		1	2	.333	3.69	28	0	0	39	51	10	23	0	1	2	0	0	0	0	–	4	4	0	0	0.3	1.000
7 yrs.			23	21	.523	3.43	291	0	0	451	458	122	243	0	23	21	10	0	0	0	–	28	55	5	5	0.3	.943

Chan Ho Park

PARK, CHAN HO
B. June 3, 1973, Kong Ju City, Korea　　　　　BR TR 6'2"　　185 lbs.

Year	Team		W	L	PCT	ERA	G	GS	CG	IP	H	BB	SO	ShO	W	L	SV	AB	H	HR	BA	PO	A	E	DP	TC/G	FA
1994	LA	N	0	0	–	11.25	2	0	0	4	5	5	6	0	0	0	0	0	0	0	–	0	0	0	0	0.0	–

Bob Patterson

PATTERSON, ROBERT CHANDLER
B. May 16, 1959, Jacksonville, Fla.　　　　　BR TR 6'2"　　185 lbs.

Year	Team		W	L	PCT	ERA	G	GS	CG	IP	H	BB	SO	ShO	W	L	SV	AB	H	HR	BA	PO	A	E	DP	TC/G	FA
1985	SD	N	0	0	–	24.75	3	0	0	4	13	3	1	0	0	0	0	0	0	0	–	0	0	0	0	0.0	–
1986	PIT	N	2	3	.400	4.95	11	5	0	36.1	49	5	20	0	1	2	0	8	1	0	.125	1	9	0	1	0.9	1.000
1987			1	4	.200	6.70	15	7	0	43	49	22	27	0	0	0	0	12	1	0	.083	0	7	0	0	0.5	1.000
1989			4	3	.571	4.05	12	3	0	26.2	23	8	20	0	3	1	1	3	0	0	.000	1	2	0	0	0.3	1.000
1990			8	5	.615	2.95	55	5	0	94.2	88	21	70	0	6	3	5	19	1	0	.053	9	10	0	0	0.3	1.000
1991			4	3	.571	4.11	54	1	0	65.2	67	15	57	0	4	3	2	4	1	0	.250	4	9	0	1	0.2	1.000
1992			6	3	.667	2.92	60	0	0	64.2	59	23	43	0	6	3	9	6	2	0	.333	3	7	0	1	0.2	1.000
1993	TEX	A	2	4	.333	4.78	52	0	0	52.2	59	11	46	0	2	4	1	0	0	0	–	3	7	0	0	0.2	1.000
1994	CAL	A	2	3	.400	4.07	47	0	0	42	35	15	30	0	2	3	1	0	0	0	–	2	1	0	0	0.1	1.000
9 yrs.			29	28	.509	4.27	309	21	0	429.2	442	123	314	0	24	19	19	52	6	0	.115	23	52	0	3	0.2	1.000

LEAGUE CHAMPIONSHIP SERIES

Year	Team		W	L	PCT	ERA	G	GS	CG	IP	H	BB	SO	ShO	W	L	SV	AB	H	HR	BA	PO	A	E	DP	TC/G	FA
1990	PIT	N	0	0	–	0.00	2	0	0	1	1	2	0	0	0	0	1	0	0	0	–	0	1	0	0	0.5	1.000
1991			0	0	–	0.00	1	0	0	2	1	0	3	0	0	0	0	0	0	0	–	0	0	0	0	0.0	–
1992			0	0	–	5.40	2	0	0	1.2	3	1	1	0	0	0	0	0	0	0	–	0	0	0	0	0.0	–
3 yrs.			0	0	–	1.93	5	0	0	4.2	5	3	4	0	0	0	1	0	0	0	–	0	1	0	0	0.2	1.000

Ken Patterson

PATTERSON, KENNETH BRIAN
B. July 8, 1964, Costa Mesa, Calif.　　　　　BL TL 6'4"　　210 lbs.

Year	Team		W	L	PCT	ERA	G	GS	CG	IP	H	BB	SO	ShO	W	L	SV	AB	H	HR	BA	PO	A	E	DP	TC/G	FA
1988	CHI	A	0	2	.000	4.79	9	2	0	20.2	25	7	8	0	0	1	1	0	0	0	–	1	2	0	0	0.3	1.000
1989			6	1	.857	4.52	50	1	0	65.2	64	28	43	0	6	1	0	0	0	0	–	3	4	0	1	0.1	1.000
1990			2	1	.667	3.39	43	0	0	66.1	58	34	40	0	2	1	2	0	0	0	–	2	12	1	0	0.3	.933
1991			3	0	1.000	2.83	43	0	0	63.2	48	35	32	0	3	0	1	0	0	0	–	1	6	3	1	0.2	.700
1992	CHI	N	2	3	.400	3.89	32	1	0	41.2	41	27	23	0	2	3	0	1	0	0	.000	4	6	1	0	0.3	.909
1993	CAL	A	1	1	.500	4.58	46	0	0	59	54	35	36	0	1	1	1	0	0	0	–	1	8	1	0	0.2	.900
1994			0	0	–	0.00	1	0	0	0.2	0	0	1	0	0	0	0	0	0	0	–	0	0	0	0	0.0	–
7 yrs.			14	8	.636	3.88	224	4	0	317.2	290	166	183	0	14	7	5	1	0	0	.000	12	38	6	2	0.3	.893

Roger Pavlik

PAVLIK, ROGER ALLEN
B. Oct. 4, 1967, Houston, Tex.　　　　　BR TR 6'3"　　220 lbs.

Year	Team		W	L	PCT	ERA	G	GS	CG	IP	H	BB	SO	ShO	W	L	SV	AB	H	HR	BA	PO	A	E	DP	TC/G	FA
1992	TEX	A	4	4	.500	4.21	13	12	1	62	66	34	45	0	0	0	0	0	0	0	–	6	3	1	0	0.8	.900
1993			12	6	.667	3.41	26	26	2	166.1	151	80	131	0	0	0	0	0	0	0	–	10	27	3	2	1.5	.925
1994			2	5	.286	7.69	11	11	0	50.1	61	30	31	0	0	0	0	0	0	0	–	2	8	0	1	0.9	1.000
3 yrs.			18	15	.545	4.36	50	49	3	278.2	278	144	207	0	0	0	0	0	0	0	–	18	38	4	3	1.2	.933

Bill Pecota

PECOTA, WILLIAM JOSEPH
B. Feb. 16, 1960, Redwood City, Calif.　　　　　BR TR 6'2"　　195 lbs.

Year	Team		W	L	PCT	ERA	G	GS	CG	IP	H	BB	SO	ShO	W	L	SV	AB	H	HR	BA	PO	A	E	DP	TC/G	FA
1991	KC	A	0	0	–	4.50	1	0	0	2	4	0	0	0	0	0	0	398	114	6	.286	0	0	0	0	0.0	–
1992	NY	N	0	0	–	9.00	1	0	0	1	1	0	0	0	0	0	0	269	61	2	.227	0	0	0	0	0.0	–
2 yrs.			0	0	–	6.00	2	0	0	3	5	0	0	0	0	0	0	*				0	0	0	0	0.0	–

Alejandro Pena

PENA, ALEJANDRO
Born Alejandro Pena (Vasquez).
B. June 25, 1959, Cambiaso Puerto Plata, Dominican Republic.　　　　　BR TR 6'1"　　200 lbs.

Year	Team		W	L	PCT	ERA	G	GS	CG	IP	H	BB	SO	ShO	W	L	SV	AB	H	HR	BA	PO	A	E	DP	TC/G	FA
1981	LA	N	1	1	.500	2.88	14	0	0	25	18	11	14	0	1	1	2	6	0	0	.000	1	5	1	0	0.5	.857
1982			0	2	.000	4.79	29	0	0	35.2	37	21	20	0	0	2	0	0	0	0	–	3	11	2	1	0.6	.875
1983			12	9	.571	2.75	34	26	4	177	152	51	120	3	2	1	1	60	6	1	.100	13	32	4	4	1.4	.918
1984			12	6	.667	2.48	28	28	8	199.1	186	46	135	4	0	0	0	66	8	0	.121	17	21	4	1	1.5	.905
1985			0	1	.000	8.31	2	1	0	4.1	7	3	2	0	0	1	0	1	0	0	.000	0	1	1	0	1.0	.500
1986			1	2	.333	4.89	24	10	0	70	74	30	46	0	0	1	1	17	3	0	.176	1	8	0	0	0.4	1.000
1987			2	7	.222	3.50	37	7	0	87.1	82	37	76	0	2	2	11	13	1	0	.077	4	1	0	0	0.2	.833

Year	Team	W	L	PCT	ERA	G	GS	CG	IP	H	BB	SO	ShO	Relief Pitching W	L	SV	Batting AB	H	HR	BA	PO	A	E	DP	TC/G	FA

Alejandro Pena *continued*

Year	Team	W	L	PCT	ERA	G	GS	CG	IP	H	BB	SO	ShO	W	L	SV	AB	H	HR	BA	PO	A	E	DP	TC/G	FA
1988		6	7	.462	1.91	60	0	0	94.1	75	27	83	0	6	7	12	6	0	0	.000	9	10	2	1	0.4	.905
1989		4	3	.571	2.13	53	0	0	76	62	18	75	0	4	3	5	1	1	0	1.000	1	5	1	0	0.1	.857
1990	NY N	3	3	.500	3.20	52	0	0	76	71	22	76	0	3	3	5	6	1	0	.167	2	4	0	0	0.1	1.000
1991	2 teams	NY N		(44G 6-1)	ATL N	(15G 2-0)														.						
"	total	8	1	.889	2.40	59	0	0	82.1	74	22	62	0	8	1	15	1	0	0	.000	6	9	1	1	0.3	.938
1992	ATL N	1	6	.143	4.07	41	0	0	42	40	13	34	0	1	6	15	2	0	0	.000	2	1	0	0	0.1	1.000
1994	PIT N	3	2	.600	5.02	22	0	0	28.2	22	10	27	0	3	2	7	1	0	0	.000	1	1	1	0	0.1	.667
13 yrs.		53	50	.515	3.01	455	72	12	998	900	311	770	7	30	30	74	180	20	1	.111	60	109	18	8	0.4	.904

LEAGUE CHAMPIONSHIP SERIES

Year	Team	W	L	PCT	ERA	G	GS	CG	IP	H	BB	SO	ShO	W	L	SV	AB	H	HR	BA	PO	A	E	DP	TC/G	FA
1981	LA N	0	0	–	0.00	2	0	0	2.1	1	0	0	0	0	0	0	0	0	0	–	0	0	0	0	0.0	–
1983		0	0	–	6.75	1	0	0	2.2	4	1	3	0	0	0	0	1	1	0	1.000	0	0	0	0	0.0	–
1988		1	1	.500	4.15	3	0	0	4.1	1	5	1	0	1	1	1	0	0	0	–	0	0	0	0	0.0	–
1991	ATL N	0	0	–	0.00	4	0	0	4.1	1	0	4	0	0	0	3	0	0	0	–	1	2	0	0	0.8	1.000
4 yrs.		1	1	.500	2.63	10	0	0	13.2	7	6	8	0	1	1	4	1	1	0	1.000	1	2	0	0	0.3	1.000

WORLD SERIES

Year	Team	W	L	PCT	ERA	G	GS	CG	IP	H	BB	SO	ShO	W	L	SV	AB	H	HR	BA	PO	A	E	DP	TC/G	FA
1988	LA N	1	0	1.000	0.00	2	0	0	5	2	1	7	0	1	0	0	0	0	0	–	0	0	0	0	0.0	–
1991	ATL N	0	1	.000	3.38	3	0	0	5.1	6	3	7	0	0	1	0	0	0	0	–	0	0	0	0	0.0	–
2 yrs.		1	1	.500	1.74	5	0	0	10.1	8	4	14	0	1	1	0	0	0	0	–	0	0	0	0	0.0	–

Brad Pennington

PENNINGTON, BRAD LEE
B. Apr. 14, 1969, Salem, Ind.

BL TL 6'5" 205 lbs.

Year	Team	W	L	PCT	ERA	G	GS	CG	IP	H	BB	SO	ShO	W	L	SV	AB	H	HR	BA	PO	A	E	DP	TC/G	FA
1993	BAL A	3	2	.600	6.55	34	0	0	33	34	25	39	0	3	2	4	0	0	0	–	1	2	0	0	0.1	1.000
1994		0	1	.000	12.00	8	0	0	6	9	8	7	0	0	1	0	0	0	0	–	0	0	1	0	0.1	.000
2 yrs.		3	3	.500	7.38	42	0	0	39	43	33	46	0	3	3	4	0	0	0	–	1	2	1	0	0.1	.750

Melido Perez

PEREZ, MELIDO TURPEN
Born Melido Turpen Gross (Perez).
Brother of Pascual Perez.
B. Feb. 15, 1966, San Cristobal, Dominican Republic.

BR TR 6'4" 180 lbs.

Year	Team	W	L	PCT	ERA	G	GS	CG	IP	H	BB	SO	ShO	W	L	SV	AB	H	HR	BA	PO	A	E	DP	TC/G	FA
1987	KC A	1	1	.500	7.84	3	3	0	10.1	18	5	5	0	0	0	0	0	0	0	–	0	0	1	0	0.3	.000
1988	CHI A	12	10	.545	3.79	32	32	3	197	186	72	138	1	0	0	0	0	0	0	–	8	18	1	1	0.8	.963
1989		11	14	.440	5.01	31	31	2	183.1	187	90	141	0	0	0	0	0	0	0	–	9	19	1	3	0.9	.966
1990		13	14	.481	4.61	35	35	3	197	177	86	161	3	0	0	0	0	0	0	–	4	20	1	0	0.7	.960
1991		8	7	.533	3.12	49	8	0	135.2	111	52	128	0	7	3	1	0	0	0	–	9	19	3	1	0.6	.903
1992	NY A	13	16	.448	2.87	33	33	10	247.2	212	93	218	1	0	0	0	0	0	0	–	15	28	10	0	1.6	.811
1993		6	14	.300	5.19	25	25	0	163	173	64	148	0	0	0	0	0	0	0	–	5	17	0	0	0.9	1.000
1994		9	4	.692	4.10	22	22	1	151.1	134	58	109	0	0	0	0	0	0	0	–	15	15	1	1	1.4	.968
8 yrs.		73	80	.477	4.09	230	189	19	1285.1	1198	520	1048	5	7	3	1	0	0	0	–	65	136	18	6	1.0	.918

Mike Perez

PEREZ, MICHAEL IRVIN
Born Michael Irvin Perez (Ortega).
B. Oct. 19, 1964, Yauco, Puerto Rico.

BR TR 6' 185 lbs.

Year	Team	W	L	PCT	ERA	G	GS	CG	IP	H	BB	SO	ShO	W	L	SV	AB	H	HR	BA	PO	A	E	DP	TC/G	FA
1990	STL N	1	0	1.000	3.95	13	0	0	13.2	12	3	5	0	1	0	1	1	0	0	.000	3	2	0	0	0.4	1.000
1991		0	2	.000	5.82	14	0	0	17	19	7	7	0	0	2	0	0	0	0	–	0	2	0	0	0.1	1.000
1992		9	3	.750	1.84	77	0	0	93	70	32	46	0	9	3	0	4	0	0	.000	9	15	0	2	0.3	1.000
1993		7	2	.778	2.48	65	0	0	72.2	65	20	58	0	7	2	7	1	0	0	.000	2	12	0	2	0.2	1.000
1994		2	3	.400	8.71	36	0	0	31	52	10	20	0	2	3	12	0	0	0	–	1	4	2	1	0.2	.714
5 yrs.		19	10	.655	3.40	205	0	0	227.1	218	72	136	0	19	10	20	6	0	0	.000	15	35	2	5	0.3	.962

Yorkis Perez

PEREZ, YORKIS MIGUEL
Born Yorkis Miguel Perez (Vargas).
B. Sept. 30, 1967, Bajos de Haina, Dominican Republic.

BL TL 6' 180 lbs.

Year	Team	W	L	PCT	ERA	G	GS	CG	IP	H	BB	SO	ShO	W	L	SV	AB	H	HR	BA	PO	A	E	DP	TC/G	FA
1991	CHI N	1	0	1.000	2.08	3	0	0	4.1	2	2	3	0	1	0	0	0	0	0	–	0	1	0	0	0.3	1.000
1994	FLA N	3	0	1.000	3.54	44	0	0	40.2	33	14	41	0	3	0	0	2	0	0	.000	5	1	0	0	0.1	1.000
2 yrs.		4	0	1.000	3.40	47	0	0	45	35	16	44	0	4	0	0	2	0	0	.000	5	2	0	0	0.1	1.000

Steve Phoenix

PHOENIX, STEVEN ROBERT
B. Jan. 31, 1968, Phoenix, Ariz.

BR TR 6'2" 175 lbs.

Year	Team	W	L	PCT	ERA	G	GS	CG	IP	H	BB	SO	ShO	W	L	SV	AB	H	HR	BA	PO	A	E	DP	TC/G	FA
1994	OAK A	0	0	–	6.23	2	0	0	4.1	4	2	3	0	0	0	0	0	0	0	–	0	0	0	0	0.0	–

Hipolito Pichardo

PICHARDO, HIPOLITO ANTONIO
Born Hipolito Antonio Pichardo (Balbina).
B. Aug. 22, 1969, Esperanza, Dominican Republic.

BR TR 6'1" . 160 lbs.

Year	Team	W	L	PCT	ERA	G	GS	CG	IP	H	BB	SO	ShO	W	L	SV	AB	H	HR	BA	PO	A	E	DP	TC/G	FA
1992	KC A	9	6	.600	3.95	31	24	1	143.2	148	49	59	1	0	1	0	0	0	0	–	19	16	2	2	1.2	.946
1993		7	8	.467	4.04	30	25	2	165	183	53	70	0	0	1	0	0	0	0	–	20	27	0	1	1.6	1.000
1994		5	3	.625	4.92	45	0	0	67.2	82	24	36	0	5	3	3	0	0	0	–	4	16	5	2	0.6	.800
3 yrs.		21	17	.553	4.16	106	49	3	376.1	413	126	165	1	5	5	3	0	0	0	–	43	59	7	5	1.0	.936

Erik Plantenberg

PLANTENBERG, ERIK JOHN
B. Oct. 30, 1968, Renton, Wash.

BR TL 6'1" 190 lbs.

Year	Team	W	L	PCT	ERA	G	GS	CG	IP	H	BB	SO	ShO	W	L	SV	AB	H	HR	BA	PO	A	E	DP	TC/G	FA
1993	SEA A	0	0	–	6.52	20	0	0	9.2	11	12	3	0	0	0	1	0	0	0	–	3	1	0	1	0.2	1.000
1994		0	0	–	0.00	6	0	0	7	4	7	1	0	0	0	0	0	0	0	–	0	3	1	0	0.7	.750
2 yrs.		0	0	–	3.78	26	0	0	16.2	15	19	4	0	0	0	1	0	0	0	–	3	4	1	1	0.3	.875

Dan Plesac

PLESAC, DANIEL THOMAS
B. Feb. 4, 1962, Gary, Ind.

BL TL 6'5" 205 lbs.

Year	Team	W	L	PCT	ERA	G	GS	CG	IP	H	BB	SO	ShO	W	L	SV	AB	H	HR	BA	PO	A	E	DP	TC/G	FA
1986	MIL A	10	7	.588	2.97	51	0	0	91	81	29	75	0	10	7	14	0	0	0	–	1	11	0	0	0.2	1.000
1987		5	6	.455	2.61	57	0	0	79.1	63	23	89	0	5	6	23	0	0	0	–	0	12	2	1	0.2	.857

Year	Team	W	L	PCT	ERA	G	GS	CG	IP	H	BB	SO	ShO	Relief Pitching W	L	SV	Batting AB	H	HR	BA	PO	A	E	DP	TC/G	FA

Dan Plesac *continued*

Year	Team	W	L	PCT	ERA	G	GS	CG	IP	H	BB	SO	ShO	W	L	SV	AB	H	HR	BA	PO	A	E	DP	TC/G	FA
1988		1	2	.333	2.41	50	0	0	52.1	46	12	52	0	1	2	30	0	0	0	–	0	6	0	0	0.1	1.000
1989		3	4	.429	2.35	52	0	0	61.1	47	17	52	0	3	4	33	0	0	0	–	2	8	0	0	0.2	1.000·
1990		3	7	.300	4.43	66	0	0	69	67	31	65	0	3	7	24	0	0	0	–	1	7	0	1	0.1	1.000
1991		2	7	.222	4.29	45	10	0	92.1	92	39	61	0	0	4	8	0	0	0	–	2	5	0	0	0.2	1.000
1992		5	4	.556	2.96	44	4	0	79	64	35	54	0	4	3	1	0	0	0	–	1	8	0	1	0.2	1.000
1993	CHI N	2	1	.667	4.74	57	0	0	62.2	74	21	47	0	2	1	0	1	0	0	.000	0	9	1	2	0.2	.900
1994		2	3	.400	4.61	54	0	0	54.2	61	13	53	0	2	3	1	4	0	0	.000	0	3	0	0	0.1	1.000
9 yrs.		33	41	.446	3.48	476	14	0	641.2	595	220	548	0	30	37	134	5	0	0	.000	7	69	3	5	0.2	.962

Eric Plunk

PLUNK, ERIC VAUGHN
B. Sept. 3, 1963, Wilmington, Calif.

BR TR 6'5" 210 lbs.

Year	Team	W	L	PCT	ERA	G	GS	CG	IP	H	BB	SO	ShO	W	L	SV	AB	H	HR	BA	PO	A	E	DP	TC/G	FA
1986	OAK A	4	7	.364	5.31	26	15	0	120.1	91	102	98	0	0	1	0	0	0	0	–	3	6	1	0	0.4	.900
1987		4	6	.400	4.74	32	11	0	95	91	62	90	0	3	2	2	0	0	0	–	1	9	0	0	0.3	1.000
1988		7	2	.778	3.00	49	0	0	78	62	39	79	0	7	2	5	0	0	0	–	2	5	1	0	0.2	.875
1989	2 teams									OAK A	(23G 1–1)					NY A	(27G 7–5)									
"	total	8	6	.571	3.28	50	7	0	104.1	82	64	85	0	4	3	1	0	0	0	–	2	7	1	0	0.2	.900
1990	NY A	6	3	.667	2.72	47	0	0	72.2	58	43	67	0	6	3	0	0	0	0	–	3	18	2	2	0.5	.913
1991		2	5	.286	4.76	43	8	0	111.2	128	62	103	0	2	2	0	0	0	0	–	4	7	2	0	0.3	.846
1992	CLE A	9	6	.600	3.64	58	0	0	71.2	61	38	50	0	9	6	4	0	0	0	–	7	7	1	0	0.3	.933
1993		4	5	.444	2.79	70	0	0	71	61	30	77	0	4	5	15	0	0	0	–	5	2	1	0	0.1	.875
1994		7	2	.778	2.54	41	0	0	71	61	37	73	0	7	2	3	0	0	0	–	8	3	0	0	0.3	1.000
9 yrs.		51	42	.548	3.81	416	41	0	795.2	695	477	722	0	42	26	30	0	0	0	–	35	64	9	2	0.3	.917

LEAGUE CHAMPIONSHIP SERIES

Year	Team	W	L	PCT	ERA	G	GS	CG	IP	H	BB	SO	ShO	W	L	SV	AB	H	HR	BA	PO	A	E	DP	TC/G	FA
1988	OAK A	0	0	–	0.00	1	0	0	0.1	0	1	1	0	0	0	0	0	0	0	–	0	0	0	0	0.0	–

WORLD SERIES

Year	Team	W	L	PCT	ERA	G	GS	CG	IP	H	BB	SO	ShO	W	L	SV	AB	H	HR	BA	PO	A	E	DP	TC/G	FA
1988	OAK A	0	0	–	0.00	2	0	0	1.2	0	1	0	3	0	0	0	0	0	0	–	0	0	0	0	0.0	–

Jim Poole

POOLE, JAMES RICHARD
B. Apr. 28, 1966, Rochester, N. Y.

BL TL 6'2" 190 lbs.

Year	Team	W	L	PCT	ERA	G	GS	CG	IP	H	BB	SO	ShO	W	L	SV	AB	H	HR	BA	PO	A	E	DP	TC/G	FA
1990	LA N	0	0	–	4.22	16	0	0	10.2	7	8	6	0	0	0	0	0	0	0	–	0	1	0	0	0.1	1.000
1991	2 teams									TEX A	(5G 0–0)					BAL A	(24G 3–2)									
"	total	3	2	.600	2.36	29	0	0	42	29	12	38	0	3	2	1	0	0	0	–	2	6	1	0	0.3	.889
1992	BAL A	0	0	–	0.00	6	0	0	3.1	3	1	3	0	0	0	0	0	0	0	–	0	2	0	0	0.3	1.000
1993		2	1	.667	2.15	55	0	0	50.1	30	21	29	0	2	1	2	0	0	0	–	4	7	1	0	0.2	.917
1994		1	0	1.000	6.64	38	0	0	20.1	32	11	18	0	1	0	0	0	0	0	–	3	4	0	0	0.2	1.000
5 yrs.		6	3	.667	3.06	144	0	0	126.2	101	53	94	0	6	3	3	0	0	0	–	9	20	2	0	0.2	.935

Mark Portugal

PORTUGAL, MARK STEVEN
B. Oct. 30, 1962, Los Angeles, Calif.

BR TR 6' 170 lbs.

Year	Team	W	L	PCT	ERA	G	GS	CG	IP	H	BB	SO	ShO	W	L	SV	AB	H	HR	BA	PO	A	E	DP	TC/G	FA
1985	MIN A	1	3	.250	5.55	6	4	0	24.1	24	14	12	0	0	0	0	0	0	0	–	4	7	1	1	2.0	.917
1986		6	10	.375	4.31	27	15	3	112.2	112	50	67	0	2	4	1	0	0	0	–	5	14	1	3	0.7	.950
1987		1	3	.250	7.77	13	7	0	44	58	24	28	0	0	1	0	0	0	0	–	1	6	0	2	0.5	1.000
1988		3	3	.500	4.53	26	0	0	57.2	60	17	31	0	3	3	3	0	0	0	–	2	1	1	0	0.2	.750
1989	HOU N	7	1	.875	2.75	20	15	2	108	91	37	86	1	0	0	0	34	7	1	.206	11	15	2	0	1.4	.929
1990		11	10	.524	3.62	32	32	1	196.2	187	67	136	0	0	0	0	66	9	0	.136	23	19	1	2	1.3	.977
1991		10	12	.455	4.49	32	27	1	168.1	163	59	120	0	0	2	1	46	9	0	.196	16	7	3	1	1.1	.917
1992		6	3	.667	2.66	18	16	1	101.1	76	41	62	1	1	0	0	28	3	0	.107	16	13	3	1	1.8	.906
1993		18	4	**.818**	2.77	33	33	1	208	194	77	131	1	0	0	0	65	15	1	.231	21	28	2	2	1.5	.961
1994	SF N	10	8	.556	3.93	21	21	1	137.1	135	45	87	0	0	0	0	48	17	0	.354	10	12	1	1	1.1	.957
10 yrs.		73	57	.562	3.78	228	170	10	1158.1	1100	431	760	3	6	10	5	287	60	2	.209	109	132	15	13	1.1	.941

Ross Powell

POWELL, ROSS JOHN
B. Jan. 24, 1968, Grand Rapids, Mich.

BL TL 6' 180 lbs.

Year	Team	W	L	PCT	ERA	G	GS	CG	IP	H	BB	SO	ShO	W	L	SV	AB	H	HR	BA	PO	A	E	DP	TC/G	FA
1993	CIN N	0	3	.000	4.41	9	1	0	16.1	13	6	17	0	0	2	0	1	0	0	.000	0	2	1	0	0.3	.667
1994	HOU N	0	0	–	1.23	12	0	0	7.1	6	5	5	0	0	0	0	0	0	0	–	0	2	0	0	0.2	1.000
2 yrs.		0	3	.000	3.42	21	1	0	23.2	19	11	22	0	0	2	0	1	0	0	.000	0	4	1	0	0.2	.800

Tim Pugh

PUGH, TIMOTHY DEAN
B. Jan. 26, 1967, Lake Tahoe, Calif.

BR TR 6'6" 225 lbs.

Year	Team	W	L	PCT	ERA	G	GS	CG	IP	H	BB	SO	ShO	W	L	SV	AB	H	HR	BA	PO	A	E	DP	TC/G	FA
1992	CIN N	4	2	.667	2.58	7	7	0	45.1	47	13	18	0	0	0	0	13	1	0	.077	2	6	0	0	1.1	1.000
1993		10	15	.400	5.26	31	27	3	164.1	200	59	94	1	0	1	0	54	12	0	.222	9	23	1	1	1.1	.970
1994		3	3	.500	6.04	10	9	1	47.2	60	26	24	0	0	0	0	14	5	0	.357	5	7	1	0	1.3	.923
3 yrs.		17	20	.459	4.93	48	43	4	257.1	307	98	136	1	0	1	0	81	18	0	.222	16	36	2	1	1.1	.963

Carlos Pulido

PULIDO, JUAN CARLOS
B. Aug. 5, 1971, Caracas, Venezuela

BL TL 6' 194 lbs.

Year	Team	W	L	PCT	ERA	G	GS	CG	IP	H	BB	SO	ShO	W	L	SV	AB	H	HR	BA	PO	A	E	DP	TC/G	FA
1994	MIN A	3	7	.300	5.98	19	14	0	84.1	87	40	32	0	0	0	0	0	0	0	–	2	11	1	2	0.7	.929

Paul Quantrill

QUANTRILL, PAUL JOHN
B. Nov. 3, 1968, London, Ont., Canada.

BL TR 6'1" 175 lbs.

Year	Team	W	L	PCT	ERA	G	GS	CG	IP	H	BB	SO	ShO	W	L	SV	AB	H	HR	BA	PO	A	E	DP	TC/G	FA
1992	BOS A	2	3	.400	2.19	27	0	0	49.1	55	15	24	0	2	3	1	0	0	0	–	4	6	2	0	0.4	.833
1993		6	12	.333	3.91	49	14	1	138	151	44	66	1	4	5	1	0	0	0	–	4	18	1	3	0.5	.957
1994	2 teams									BOS A	(17G 1–1)					PHI N	(18G 2–2)									
"	total	3	3	.500	4.92	35	1	0	53	64	15	28	0	3	2	1	3	0	0	.000	2	8	1	1	0.3	.909
3 yrs.		11	18	.379	3.78	111	15	1	240.1	270	74	118	1	9	10	3	3	0	0	.000	10	32	4	4	0.4	.913

Pat Rapp

RAPP, PATRICK LELAND
B. July 13, 1967, Jennings, La.

BR TR 6'3" 195 lbs.

Year	Team	W	L	PCT	ERA	G	GS	CG	IP	H	BB	SO	ShO	W	L	SV	AB	H	HR	BA	PO	A	E	DP	TC/G	FA
1992	SF N	0	2	.000	7.20	3	2	0	10	8	6	3	0	0	0	0	2	0	0	.000	2	2	0	0	1.3	1.000
1993	FLA N	4	6	.400	4.02	16	16	1	94	101	39	57	0	0	0	0	31	6	0	.194	5	15	1	0	1.3	.952

Year	Team	W	L	PCT	ERA	G	GS	CG	IP	H	BB	SO	ShO	Relief Pitching W	L	SV	Batting AB	H	HR	BA	PO	A	E	DP	TC/G	FA

Pat Rapp *continued*

Year	Team	W	L	PCT	ERA	G	GS	CG	IP	H	BB	SO	ShO	W	L	SV	AB	H	HR	BA	PO	A	E	DP	TC/G	FA
1994		7	8	.467	3.85	24	23	2	133.1	132	69	75	1	0	0	0	41	5	0	.122	8	15	0	1	1.0	1.000
3 yrs.		11	16	.407	4.06	43	41	3	237.1	241	114	135	1	0	0	0	74	11	0	.149	15	32	1	1	1.1	.979

Jeff Reardon

REARDON, JEFFREY JAMES
B. Oct. 1, 1955, Pittsfield, Mass.

BR TR 6' 190 lbs.

Year	Team	W	L	PCT	ERA	G	GS	CG	IP	H	BB	SO	ShO	W	L	SV	AB	H	HR	BA	PO	A	E	DP	TC/G	FA
1979	NY N	1	2	.333	1.71	18	0	0	21	12	9	10	0	1	2	2	0	0	0	–	1	1	0	1	0.1	1.000
1980		8	7	.533	2.62	61	0	0	110	96	47	101	0	8	7	6	0	0	0	.000	1	7	4	0	0.2	.667
1981	2 teams	NY N	(18G 1–0)		MON N	(25G 2–0)																				
"	total	3	0	1.000	2.18	43	0	0	70.1	48	21	49	0	3	0	8	5	0	0	.000	1	4	0	0	0.1	1.000
1982	MON N	7	4	.636	2.06	75	0	0	109	87	36	86	0	7	4	26	10	1	0	.100	6	9	1	0	0.2	.938
1983		7	9	.438	3.03	66	0	0	92	87	44	78	0	7	9	21	8	1	0	.125	3	4	2	0	0.1	.778
1984		7	7	.500	2.90	68	0	0	87	70	37	79	0	7	7	23	9	0	0	.000	2	5	1	0	0.1	.875
1985		2	8	.200	3.18	63	0	0	87.2	68	26	67	0	2	8	41	7	2	0	.286	9	8	0	0	0.3	1.000
1986		7	9	.438	3.94	62	0	0	89	83	26	67	0	7	9	35	8	1	0	.125	8	10	0	1	0.3	1.000
1987	MIN A	8	8	.500	4.48	63	0	0	80.1	70	28	83	0	8	8	31	0	0	0	–	2	6	0	1	0.1	1.000
1988		2	4	.333	2.47	63	0	0	73	68	15	56	0	2	4	42	0	0	0	–	1	2	0	0	0.1	1.000
1989		5	4	.556	4.07	65	0	0	73	68	12	46	0	5	4	31	0	0	0	–	1	3	0	0	0.1	1.000
1990	BOS A	5	3	.625	3.16	47	0	0	51.1	39	19	33	0	5	3	21	0	0	0	–	1	4	1	0	0.1	.833
1991		1	4	.200	3.03	57	0	0	59.1	54	16	44	0	1	4	40	0	0	0	–	2	1	0	0	0.1	1.000
1992	2 teams	BOS A	(46G 2–2)		ATL N	(14G 3–0)																				
"	total	5	2	.714	3.41	60	0	0	58	67	9	39	0	5	2	30	0	0	0	–	2	4	0	1	0.1	1.000
1993	CIN N	4	6	.400	4.09	58	0	0	61.2	66	10	35	0	4	6	8	2	0	0	.000	4	6	2	0	0.2	.833
1994	NY A	1	0	1.000	8.38	11	0	0	9.2	17	3	4	0	1	0	2	0	0	0	–	0	1	0	0	0.1	1.000
16 yrs.		73	77	.487	3.16	880	0	0	1132.1	1000	358	877	0	73	77	367 2nd	57	5	0	.088	44	75	11	4	0.1	.915

DIVISIONAL PLAYOFF SERIES

Year	Team	W	L	PCT	ERA	G	GS	CG	IP	H	BB	SO	ShO	W	L	SV	AB	H	HR	BA	PO	A	E	DP	TC/G	FA
1981	MON N	0	1	.000	2.08	3	0	0	4.1	1	1	2	0	0	1	2	1	0	0	.000	0	0	0	0	0.0	–

LEAGUE CHAMPIONSHIP SERIES

Year	Team	W	L	PCT	ERA	G	GS	CG	IP	H	BB	SO	ShO	W	L	SV	AB	H	HR	BA	PO	A	E	DP	TC/G	FA
1981	MON N	0	0	–	27.00	1	0	0	1	3	0	0	0	0	0	0	0	0	0	–	0	0	0	0	0.0	–
1987	MIN A	1	1	.500	5.06	4	0	0	5.1	7	3	5	0	1	1	2	0	0	0	–	0	1	0	0	0.3	1.000
1990	BOS A	0	0	–	9.00	1	0	0	2	3	1	0	0	0	0	0	0	0	0	–	0	0	0	0	0.0	–
1992	ATL N	1	0	1.000	0.00	3	0	0	3	0	2	3	0	1	0	1	0	0	0	–	0	0	0	0	0.0	–
4 yrs.		2	1	.667	6.35	9	0	0	11.1	13	6	8	0	2	1	3	0	0	0	–	0	0	0	0	0.1	1.000

WORLD SERIES

Year	Team	W	L	PCT	ERA	G	GS	CG	IP	H	BB	SO	ShO	W	L	SV	AB	H	HR	BA	PO	A	E	DP	TC/G	FA
1987	MIN A	0	0	–	0.00	4	0	0	4.2	5	0	3	0	0	0	1	0	0	0	–	0	0	0	0	0.0	–
1992	ATL N	0	1	.000	13.50	2	0	0	1.1	2	1	1	0	0	1	0	0	0	0	–	0	0	0	0	0.0	–
2 yrs.		0	1	.000	3.00	6	0	0	6	7	1	4	0	0	1	1	0	0	0	–	0	0	0	0	0.0	–

Rick Reed

REED, RICHARD ALLEN
B. Aug. 16, 1964, Huntington, W. Va.

BR TR 6' 195 lbs.

Year	Team	W	L	PCT	ERA	G	GS	CG	IP	H	BB	SO	ShO	W	L	SV	AB	H	HR	BA	PO	A	E	DP	TC/G	FA
1988	PIT N	1	0	1.000	3.00	2	2	0	12	10	2	6	0	0	0	0	4	0	0	.000	0	3	0	1	1.5	1.000
1989		1	4	.200	5.60	15	7	0	54.2	62	11	34	0	0	0	0	13	1	0	.077	6	5	0	0	0.7	1.000
1990		2	3	.400	4.36	13	8	1	53.2	62	12	27	1	0	0	1	16	4	0	.250	6	4	1	0	0.8	.909
1991		0	0	–	10.38	1	1	0	4.1	8	1	2	0	0	0	0	2	1	0	.500	0	0	0	0	0.0	–
1992	KC A	3	7	.300	3.68	19	18	1	100.1	105	20	49	1	1	0	0	0	0	0	–	6	18	1	0	1.3	.960
1993	2 teams	KC A	(1G 0–0)		TEX A	(2G 1–0)																				
"	total	1	0	1.000	5.87	3	0	0	7.2	12	2	5	0	1	0	0	0	0	0	–	3	1	0	1	1.3	1.000
1994	TEX A	1	1	.500	5.94	4	3	0	16.2	17	7	12	0	0	0	0	0	0	0	–	2	2	0	0	1.0	1.000
7 yrs.		9	15	.375	4.55	57	39	2	249.1	276	55	135	2	2	0	1	35	6	0	.171	23	33	2	1	1.0	.966

Steve Reed

REED, STEVEN VINCENT
B. Mar. 11, 1966, Los Angeles, Calif.

BR TR 6'2" 200 lbs.

Year	Team	W	L	PCT	ERA	G	GS	CG	IP	H	BB	SO	ShO	W	L	SV	AB	H	HR	BA	PO	A	E	DP	TC/G	FA
1992	SF N	1	0	1.000	2.30	18	0	0	15.2	13	3	11	0	1	0	0	0	0	0	–	3	4	0	0	0.4	1.000
1993	CLR N	9	5	.643	4.48	64	0	0	84.1	80	30	51	0	9	5	3	9	0	0	.000	3	14	1	1	0.3	.944
1994		3	2	.600	3.94	61	0	0	64	79	26	51	0	3	2	3	2	0	0	.000	0	5	0	0	0.1	1.000
3 yrs.		13	7	.650	4.06	143	0	0	164	172	59	113	0	13	7	6	11	0	0	.000	6	23	1	1	0.2	.967

Mike Remlinger

REMLINGER, MICHAEL JOHN
B. Mar. 23, 1966, Middletown, N. Y.

BL TL 6' 195 lbs.

Year	Team	W	L	PCT	ERA	G	GS	CG	IP	H	BB	SO	ShO	W	L	SV	AB	H	HR	BA	PO	A	E	DP	TC/G	FA
1991	SF N	2	1	.667	4.37	8	6	0	35	36	20	19	1	0	0	0	7	0	0	.000	1	6	0	0	1.0	.875
1994	NY N	1	5	.167	4.61	10	9	0	54.2	55	35	33	0	0	0	0	16	0	0	.000	1	4	0	0	0.5	1.000
2 yrs.		3	6	.333	4.52	18	15	1	89.2	91	55	52	1	0	0	0	23	0	0	.000	2	10	1	0	0.7	.923

Carlos Reyes

REYES, CARLOS ALBERTO, JR.
B. Apr. 4, 1969, Miami, Fla.

BR TR 6'1" 190 lbs.

Year	Team	W	L	PCT	ERA	G	GS	CG	IP	H	BB	SO	ShO	W	L	SV	AB	H	HR	BA	PO	A	E	DP	TC/G	FA
1994	OAK A	0	3	.000	4.15	27	9	0	78	71	44	57	0	0	1	1	0	0	0	–	3	7	0	1	0.4	1.000

Shane Reynolds

REYNOLDS, RICHARD SHANE
B. Mar. 26, 1968, Bastrop, La.

BR TR 6'3" 210 lbs.

Year	Team	W	L	PCT	ERA	G	GS	CG	IP	H	BB	SO	ShO	W	L	SV	AB	H	HR	BA	PO	A	E	DP	TC/G	FA
1992	HOU N	1	3	.250	7.11	8	5	0	25.1	42	6	10	0	0	0	0	4	2	0	.500	0	7	1	0	1.0	.875
1993		0	0	–	0.82	5	1	0	11	11	6	10	0	0	0	0	2	1	0	.500	0	1	0	0	0.2	1.000
1994		8	5	.615	3.05	33	14	1	124	128	21	110	0	3	1	0	33	3	0	.091	10	16	0	0	0.8	1.000
3 yrs.		9	8	.529	3.54	46	20	1	160.1	181	33	130	1	3	1	0	39	6	0	.154	10	24	1	0	0.8	.971

Armando Reynoso

REYNOSO, ARMANDO MARTIN
Born Armando Martin Reynoso (Gutierrez).
B. May 1, 1966, San Luis Potosi, Mexico.

BR TR 6' 186 lbs.

Year	Team	W	L	PCT	ERA	G	GS	CG	IP	H	BB	SO	ShO	W	L	SV	AB	H	HR	BA	PO	A	E	DP	TC/G	FA
1991	ATL N	2	1	.667	6.17	6	5	0	23.1	26	10	10	0	0	0	0	7	0	0	.000	3	12	0	0	2.5	1.000
1992		1	0	1.000	4.70	3	1	0	7.2	11	2	2	0	0	0	1	2	0	0	.000	0	2	0	1	0.7	1.000

Year	Team	W	L	PCT	ERA	G	GS	CG	IP	H	BB	SO	ShO	Relief Pitching W	L	SV	Batting AB	H	HR	BA	PO	A	E	DP	TC/G	FA

Armando Reynoso *continued*

Year	Team	W	L	PCT	ERA	G	GS	CG	IP	H	BB	SO	ShO	W	L	SV	AB	H	HR	BA	PO	A	E	DP	TC/G	FA
1993	CLR N	12	11	.522	4.00	30	30	4	189	206	63	117	0	0	0	0	63	8	2	.127	16	35	6	5	1.9	.895
1994		3	4	.429	4.82	9	9	1	52.1	54	22	25	0	0	0	0	17	3	0	.176	1	20	0	0	2.3	1.000
4 yrs.		18	16	.529	4.36	48	45	5	272.1	297	97	154	0	0	0	1	89	11	2	.124	20	69	6	6	2.0	.937

Arthur Rhodes

RHODES, ARTHUR LEE   BL TL 6'2" 190 lbs.
B. Oct. 24, 1969, Waco, Tex.

Year	Team	W	L	PCT	ERA	G	GS	CG	IP	H	BB	SO	ShO	W	L	SV	AB	H	HR	BA	PO	A	E	DP	TC/G	FA
1991	BAL A	0	3	.000	8.00	8	8	0	36	47	23	23	0	0	0	0	0	0	0	–	0	1	0	0	0.1	1.000
1992		7	5	.583	3.63	15	15	2	94.1	87	38	77	1	0	0	0	0	0	0	–	1	13	0	2	0.9	1.000
1993		5	6	.455	6.51	17	17	0	85.2	91	49	49	0	0	0	0	0	0	0	–	2	9	1	0	0.7	.917
1994		3	5	.375	5.81	10	10	3	52.2	51	30	47	2	0	0	0	0	0	0	–	0	2	1	0	0.3	.667
4 yrs.		15	19	.441	5.56	50	50	5	268.2	276	140	196	3	0	0	0	0	0	0	–	3	25	2	2	0.6	.933

Dave Righetti

RIGHETTI, DAVID ALLAN (Rags)   BL TL 6'4" 195 lbs.
B. Nov. 28, 1958, San Jose, Calif.

Year	Team	W	L	PCT	ERA	G	GS	CG	IP	H	BB	SO	ShO	W	L	SV	AB	H	HR	BA	PO	A	E	DP	TC/G	FA
1979	NY A	0	1	.000	3.71	3	3	0	17	10	10	13	0	0	0	0	0	0	0	–	1	3	0	1	1.3	1.000
1981		8	4	.667	2.06	15	15	2	105	75	38	89	0	0	0	0	0	0	0	–	6	9	1	0	1.1	.938
1982		11	10	.524	3.79	33	27	4	183	155	108	163	0	0	0	1	0	0	0	–	5	18	3	1	0.8	.885
1983		14	8	.636	3.44	31	31	7	217	194	67	169	2	0	0	0	0	0	0	–	3	24	1	2	0.9	.964
1984		5	6	.455	2.34	64	0	0	96.1	79	37	90	0	5	6	31	0	0	0	–	2	13	2	0	0.3	.882
1985		12	7	.632	2.78	74	0	0	107	96	45	92	0	12	7	29	0	0	0	–	1	12	1	2	0.2	.929
1986		8	8	.500	2.45	74	0	0	106.2	88	35	83	0	8	8	46	0	0	0	–	1	10	0	2	0.1	1.000
1987		8	6	.571	3.51	60	0	0	95	95	44	77	0	8	6	31	0	0	0	–	3	12	1	0	0.3	.938
1988		5	4	.556	3.52	60	0	0	87	86	37	70	0	5	4	25	0	0	0	–	2	8	0	0	0.2	1.000
1989		2	6	.250	3.00	55	0	0	69	73	26	51	0	2	6	25	0	0	0	–	0	9	0	0	0.2	1.000
1990		1	1	.500	3.57	53	0	0	53	48	26	43	0	1	1	36	0	0	0	–	3	1	1	0	0.1	.800
1991	SF N	2	7	.222	3.39	61	0	0	71.2	64	28	51	0	2	7	24	3	0	0	.000	3	13	0	1	0.3	1.000
1992		2	7	.222	5.06	54	4	0	78.1	79	36	47	0	2	5	3	7	1	0	.143	3	5	1	0	0.2	.889
1993		1	1	.500	5.70	51	0	0	47.1	58	17	31	0	1	1	1	1	1	0	1.000	2	5	0	0	0.1	1.000
1994	2 teams	OAK A	(7G 0-0)		TOR A	(13G 0-1)																				
"	total	0	1	.000	10.18	20	0	0	20.1	22	19	14	0	0	1	0	0	0	0	–	0	3	0	0	0.2	1.000
15 yrs.		79	77	.506	3.44	708	80	13	1353.2	1222	573	1083	2	46	52	252 9th	11	2	0	.182	35	145	11	9	0.3	.942

DIVISIONAL PLAYOFF SERIES

| 1981 | NY A | 2 | 0 | 1.000 | 1.00 | 2 | 1 | 0 | 9 | 8 | 3 | 13 | 0 | 0 | 0 | 0 | 0 | 0 | 0 | – | 0 | 0 | 0 | 0 | 0.0 | – |

LEAGUE CHAMPIONSHIP SERIES

| 1981 | NY A | 1 | 0 | 1.000 | 0.00 | 1 | 1 | 0 | 6 | 4 | 2 | 4 | 0 | 0 | 0 | 0 | 0 | 0 | 0 | – | 0 | 1 | 0 | 0 | 1.0 | 1.000 |

WORLD SERIES

| 1981 | NY A | 0 | 0 | – | 13.50 | 1 | 1 | 0 | 2 | 5 | 2 | 1 | 0 | 0 | 0 | 0 | 1 | 0 | 0 | .000 | 0 | 0 | 0 | 0 | 0.0 | – |

Jose Rijo

RIJO, JOSE ANTONIO   BR TR 6'1" 200 lbs.
Born Jose Antonio Rijo (Abreu).
B. May 13, 1965, San Cristobal, Dominican Republic.

Year	Team	W	L	PCT	ERA	G	GS	CG	IP	H	BB	SO	ShO	W	L	SV	AB	H	HR	BA	PO	A	E	DP	TC/G	FA
1984	NY A	2	8	.200	4.76	24	5	0	62.1	74	33	47	0	2	4	2	0	0	0	–	2	12	1	0	0.6	.933
1985	OAK A	6	4	.600	3.53	12	9	0	63.2	57	28	65	0	2	1	0	0	0	0	–	2	5	0	0	0.6	1.000
1986		9	11	.450	4.65	39	26	4	193.2	172	108	176	0	0	4	1	0	0	0	–	13	18	3	0	0.9	.912
1987		2	7	.222	5.90	21	14	1	82.1	106	41	67	0	0	0	0	0	0	0	–	10	10	1	0	1.0	.952
1988	CIN N	13	8	.619	2.39	49	19	0	162	120	63	160	0	6	1	0	37	2	1	.054	7	23	1	1	0.6	.968
1989		7	6	.538	2.84	19	19	1	111	101	48	86	1	0	0	0	38	8	0	.211	6	14	0	1	1.1	1.000
1990		14	8	.636	2.70	29	29	7	197	151	78	152	1	0	0	0	62	10	0	.161	19	27	2	0	1.7	.958
1991		15	6	.714	2.51	30	30	3	204.1	165	55	172	1	0	0	0	67	14	0	.209	17	22	3	2	1.4	.929
1992		15	10	.600	2.56	33	33	2	211	185	44	171	0	0	0	0	72	14	0	.194	19	31	2	1	1.6	.962
1993		14	9	.609	2.48	36	36	2	257.1	218	62	227	1	0	0	0	82	22	1	.268	27	35	0	8	1.7	1.000
1994		9	6	.600	3.08	26	26	2	172.1	177	52	171	0	0	0	0	49	10	0	.204	14	27	0	0	1.6	1.000
11 yrs.		106	83	.561	3.12	318	246	22	1717	1526	612	1494	4	10	10	3	407	80	2	.197	136	224	13	12	1.2	.965

LEAGUE CHAMPIONSHIP SERIES

| 1990 | CIN N | 1 | 0 | 1.000 | 4.38 | 2 | 2 | 0 | 12.1 | 10 | 7 | 15 | 0 | 0 | 0 | 0 | 5 | 0 | 0 | .000 | 0 | 0 | 0 | 0 | 0.0 | – |

WORLD SERIES

| 1990 | CIN N | 2 | 0 | 1.000 | 0.59 | 2 | 2 | 0 | 15.1 | 9 | 5 | 14 | 0 | 0 | 0 | 0 | 3 | 1 | 0 | .333 | 0 | 2 | 0 | 0 | 1.0 | 1.000 |

Bill Risley

RISLEY, WILLIAM CHARLES   BR TR 6'2" 215 lbs.
B. May 29, 1967, Chicago, Ill.

Year	Team	W	L	PCT	ERA	G	GS	CG	IP	H	BB	SO	ShO	W	L	SV	AB	H	HR	BA	PO	A	E	DP	TC/G	FA
1992	MON N	1	0	1.000	1.80	1	1	0	5	4	1	2	0	0	0	0	2	0	0	.000	0	1	0	0	1.0	1.000
1993		0	0	–	6.00	2	0	0	3	2	2	2	0	0	0	0	0	0	0	–	1	0	0	0	0.5	1.000
1994	SEA A	9	6	.600	3.44	37	0	0	52.1	31	19	61	0	9	6	0	0	0	0	–	5	2	1	1	0.2	.875
3 yrs.		10	6	.625	3.43	40	1	0	60.1	37	22	65	0	9	6	0	2	0	0	.000	6	3	1	1	0.3	.900

Kevin Ritz

RITZ, KEVIN D.   BR TR 6'4" 195 lbs.
B. June 8, 1965, Eatontown, N. J.

Year	Team	W	L	PCT	ERA	G	GS	CG	IP	H	BB	SO	ShO	W	L	SV	AB	H	HR	BA	PO	A	E	DP	TC/G	FA
1989	DET A	4	6	.400	4.38	12	12	1	74	75	44	56	0	0	0	0	0	0	0	–	4	10	0	0	1.2	1.000
1990		0	4	.000	11.05	4	4	0	7.1	14	14	3	0	0	0	0	0	0	0	–	2	4	1	0	1.8	.857
1991		0	3	.000	11.74	11	5	0	15.1	17	22	9	0	0	0	0	0	0	0	–	1	4	1	0	0.5	.833
1992		2	5	.286	5.60	23	11	0	80.1	88	44	57	0	0	0	0	0	0	0	–	6	10	0	1	0.6	1.000
1994	CLR N	5	6	.455	5.62	15	15	0	73.2	88	35	53	0	0	0	0	20	0	0	.000	6	13	0	3	1.3	1.000
5 yrs.		11	24	.314	5.78	65	47	1	250.2	282	159	178	0	0	0	0	20	0	0	.000	17	41	2	4	0.9	.967

Ben Rivera

RIVERA, BIENVENIDO   BR TR 6'6" 210 lbs.
Born Bienvenido Rivera (Santana).
B. Jan. 11, 1968, San Pedro de Macoris, Dominican Republic.

Year	Team	W	L	PCT	ERA	G	GS	CG	IP	H	BB	SO	ShO	W	L	SV	AB	H	HR	BA	PO	A	E	DP	TC/G	FA
1992	2 teams	ATL N	(8G 0-1)		PHI N	(20G 7-3)																				
"	total	7	4	.636	3.07	28	14	4	117.1	99	45	77	1	0	1	0	33	3	0	.091	3	19	0	1	0.8	1.000

Year	Team	W	L	PCT	ERA	G	GS	CG	IP	H	BB	SO	ShO	W	L	SV	AB	H	HR	BA	PO	A	E	DP	TC/G	FA
														Relief Pitching			**Batting**									

Ben Rivera *continued*

Year	Team		W	L	PCT	ERA	G	GS	CG	IP	H	BB	SO	ShO	W	L	SV	AB	H	HR	BA	PO	A	E	DP	TC/G	FA
1993	PHI	N	13	9	.591	5.02	30	28	1	163	175	85	123	1	0	0	0	51	5	0	.098	8	14	1	1	0.8	.957
1994			3	4	.429	6.87	9	7	0	38	40	22	19	0	1	1	0	9	0	0	.000	1	6	0	1	0.8	1.000
3 yrs.			23	17	.575	4.52	67	49	5	318.1	314	152	219	2	1	2	0	93	8	0	.086	12	39	1	3	0.8	.981

LEAGUE CHAMPIONSHIP SERIES

| 1993 | PHI | N | 0 | 0 | — | 4.50 | 1 | 0 | 0 | 2 | 1 | 1 | 2 | 0 | 0 | 0 | 0 | 0 | 0 | 0 | — | 0 | 0 | 0 | 0 | 0.0 | — |

WORLD SERIES

| 1993 | PHI | N | 0 | 0 | — | 27.00 | 1 | 0 | 0 | 1.1 | 4 | 2 | 3 | 0 | 0 | 0 | 0 | 0 | 0 | 0 | — | 0 | 0 | 0 | 0 | 0.0 | — |

Rich Robertson

ROBERTSON, RICHARD WAYNE
B. Sept. 15, 1968, Nacogdoches, Tex.

BL TL 6'4" 175 lbs.

Year	Team		W	L	PCT	ERA	G	GS	CG	IP	H	BB	SO	ShO	W	L	SV	AB	H	HR	BA	PO	A	E	DP	TC/G	FA
1993	PIT	N	0	1	.000	6.00	9	0	0	9	15	4	5	0	0	1	0	0	0	0	—	0	0	0	0	0.0	—
1994			0	0	—	6.89	8	0	0	15.2	20	10	8	0	0	0	0	4	1	0	.250	0	2	0	0	0.3	1.000
2 yrs.			0	1	.000	6.57	17	0	0	24.2	35	14	13	0	0	1	0	4	1	0	.250	0	2	0	0	0.1	1.000

Rich Rodriguez

RODRIGUEZ, RICHARD ANTHONY
B. Mar. 1, 1963, Downey, Calif.

BL TL 5'10" 185 lbs.

Year	Team		W	L	PCT	ERA	G	GS	CG	IP	H	BB	SO	ShO	W	L	SV	AB	H	HR	BA	PO	A	E	DP	TC/G	FA
1990	SD	N	1	1	.500	2.83	32	0	0	47.2	52	16	22	0	1	1	1	3	0	0	.000	1	10	0	1	0.3	1.000
1991			3	1	.750	3.26	64	1	0	80	66	44	40	0	3	1	0	5	0	0	.000	2	13	0	1	0.2	1.000
1992			6	3	.667	2.37	61	1	0	91	77	29	64	0	6	2	0	6	0	0	.000	4	17	1	2	0.4	.955
1993	2 teams	SD N (34G 2-3)													FLA N (36G 0-1)												
"	total		2	4	.333	3.79	70	0	0	76	73	33	43	0	2	4	3	2	0	0	.000	7	9	1	2	0.2	.941
1994	STL	N	3	5	.375	4.03	56	0	0	60.1	62	26	43	0	3	5	0	1	0	0	.000	1	3	1	0	0.1	.800
5 yrs.			15	14	.517	3.22	283	2	0	355	330	148	212	0	15	13	4	17	0	0	.000	15	52	3	6	0.2	.957

Kenny Rogers

ROGERS, KENNETH SCOTT
B. Nov. 10, 1964, Savannah, Ga.

BL TL 6'1" 200 lbs.

Year	Team		W	L	PCT	ERA	G	GS	CG	IP	H	BB	SO	ShO	W	L	SV	AB	H	HR	BA	PO	A	E	DP	TC/G	FA
1989	TEX	A	3	4	.429	2.93	73	0	0	73.2	60	42	63	0	3	4	2	0	0	0	—	1	22	0	0	0.3	1.000
1990			10	6	.625	3.13	69	3	0	97.2	93	42	74	0	9	4	15	0	0	0	—	5	22	2	1	0.4	.931
1991			10	10	.500	5.42	63	9	0	109.2	121	61	73	0	6	6	5	0	0	0	—	5	15	3	1	0.4	.870
1992			3	6	.333	3.09	81	0	0	78.2	80	26	70	0	3	6	6	0	0	0	—	4	17	2	0	0.3	.913
1993			16	10	.615	4.10	35	33	5	208.1	210	71	140	0	0	0	0	0	0	0	—	18	46	4	4	1.9	.941
1994			11	8	.579	4.46	24	24	6	167.1	169	52	120	2	0	0	0	0	0	0	—	9	33	4	4	1.9	.913
6 yrs.			53	44	.546	4.03	345	69	11	735.1	733	294	540	2	21	20	28	0	0	0	—	42	155	15	10	0.6	.929

Kevin Rogers

ROGERS, CHARLES KEVIN
B. Aug. 20, 1968, Cleveland, Miss.

BB TL 6'2" 190 lbs.

Year	Team		W	L	PCT	ERA	G	GS	CG	IP	H	BB	SO	ShO	W	L	SV	AB	H	HR	BA	PO	A	E	DP	TC/G	FA
1992	SF	N	0	2	.000	4.24	6	6	0	34	37	13	26	0	0	0	0	9	2	0	.222	1	3	0	0	0.7	1.000
1993			2	2	.500	2.68	64	0	0	80.2	71	28	62	0	2	2	0	3	0	0	.000	2	7	1	1	0.2	.900
1994			0	0	—	3.48	9	0	0	10.1	10	6	7	0	0	0	0	0	0	0	—	0	1	0	0	0.1	1.000
3 yrs.			2	4	.333	3.17	79	6	0	125	118	47	95	0	2	2	0	12	2	0	.167	3	11	1	1	0.2	.933

Mel Rojas

ROJAS, MELQUIADES
Born Melquiades Rojas (Medrano).
B. Dec. 10, 1966, Haina, Dominican Republic.

BR TR 5'11" 175 lbs.

Year	Team		W	L	PCT	ERA	G	GS	CG	IP	H	BB	SO	ShO	W	L	SV	AB	H	HR	BA	PO	A	E	DP	TC/G	FA
1990	MON	N	3	1	.750	3.60	23	0	0	40	34	24	26	0	3	1	1	3	0	0	.000	2	4	1	0	0.3	.857
1991			3	3	.500	3.75	37	0	0	48	42	13	37	0	3	3	6	4	0	0	.000	2	5	0	0	0.2	1.000
1992			7	1	.875	1.43	68	0	0	100.2	71	34	70	0	7	1	10	15	1	0	.067	9	12	2	1	0.3	.913
1993			5	8	.385	2.95	66	0	0	88.1	80	30	48	0	5	8	10	12	1	0	.083	7	9	0	1	0.2	1.000
1994			3	2	.600	3.32	58	0	0	84	71	21	84	0	3	2	16	10	2	0	.200	8	10	0	1	0.3	1.000
5 yrs.			21	15	.583	2.79	252	0	0	361	298	122	265	0	21	15	43	44	4	0	.091	28	40	3	3	0.3	.958

John Roper

ROPER, JOHN CHRISTOPHER
B. Nov. 21, 1971, Southern Pines, N. C.

BR TR 6' 175 lbs.

Year	Team		W	L	PCT	ERA	G	GS	CG	IP	H	BB	SO	ShO	W	L	SV	AB	H	HR	BA	PO	A	E	DP	TC/G	FA
1993	CIN	N	2	5	.286	5.63	16	15	0	80	92	36	54	0	0	0	0	28	5	0	.179	7	8	0	0	0.9	1.000
1994			6	2	.750	4.50	16	15	0	92	90	30	51	0	0	0	0	33	6	0	.182	5	13	2	2	1.3	.900
2 yrs.			8	7	.533	5.02	32	30	0	172	182	66	105	0	0	0	0	61	11	0	.180	12	21	2	2	1.1	.943

Kirk Rueter

RUETER, KIRK WESLEY
B. Dec. 1, 1970, Hoyleton, Ill.

BL TL 6'3" 190 lbs.

Year	Team		W	L	PCT	ERA	G	GS	CG	IP	H	BB	SO	ShO	W	L	SV	AB	H	HR	BA	PO	A	E	DP	TC/G	FA
1993	MON	N	8	0	1.000	2.73	14	14	1	85.2	85	18	31	0	0	0	0	26	2	0	.077	7	19	1	4	1.9	.963
1994			7	3	.700	5.17	20	20	0	92.1	106	23	50	0	0	0	0	34	4	0	.118	4	17	1	0	1.1	.955
2 yrs.			15	3	.833	3.99	34	34	1	178	191	41	81	0	0	0	0	60	6	0	.100	11	36	2	4	1.4	.959

Scott Ruffcorn

RUFFCORN, SCOTT PATRICK
B. Dec. 29, 1969, New Braunfels, Tex.

BR TR 6'4" 215 lbs.

Year	Team		W	L	PCT	ERA	G	GS	CG	IP	H	BB	SO	ShO	W	L	SV	AB	H	HR	BA	PO	A	E	DP	TC/G	FA
1993	CHI	A	0	2	.000	8.10	3	2	0	10	9	10	2	0	0	0	0	0	0	0	—	0	0	3	0	1.0	.000
1994			0	2	.000	12.79	2	2	0	6.1	15	5	3	0	0	0	0	0	0	0	—	0	0	0	0	0.0	—
2 yrs.			0	4	.000	9.92	5	4	0	16.1	24	15	5	0	0	0	0	0	0	0	—	0	0	3	0	0.6	.000

Bruce Ruffin

RUFFIN, BRUCE WAYNE
B. Oct. 4, 1963, Lubbock, Tex.

BB TL 6'2" 205 lbs.
BR 1986-87

Year	Team		W	L	PCT	ERA	G	GS	CG	IP	H	BB	SO	ShO	W	L	SV	AB	H	HR	BA	PO	A	E	DP	TC/G	FA
1986	PHI	N	9	4	.692	2.46	21	21	6	146.1	138	44	70	0	0	0	0	55	4	0	.073	8	20	1	0	1.4	.966
1987			11	14	.440	4.35	35	35	3	204.2	236	73	93	1	0	0	0	73	4	0	.055	7	32	2	3	1.2	.951
1988			6	10	.375	4.43	55	15	3	144.1	151	80	82	0	2	4	3	33	4	0	.121	11	25	2	2	0.7	.947
1989			6	10	.375	4.44	24	23	1	125.2	152	62	70	0	0	0	0	34	6	0	.176	3	34	4	0	1.7	.902
1990			6	13	.316	5.38	32	25	2	149	178	62	79	1	0	0	0	44	3	0	.068	5	23	0	2	0.9	1.000
1991			4	7	.364	3.78	31	15	1	119	125	38	85	1	1	0	0	24	0	0	.000	8	15	2	1	0.8	.920
1992	MIL	A	1	6	.143	6.67	25	6	1	58	66	41	45	0	1	2	0	0	0	0	—	4	5	0	0	0.4	1.000

Year	Team	W	L	PCT	ERA	G	GS	CG	IP	H	BB	SO	ShO	Relief Pitching W	L	SV	Batting AB	H	HR	BA	PO	A	E	DP	TC/G	FA

Bruce Ruffin *continued*

1993	CLR N	6	5	.545	3.87	59	12	0	139.2	145	69	126	0	3	1	2	25	2	0	.080	7	16	1	3	0.4	.958
1994		4	5	.444	4.04	56	0	0	55.2	55	30	65	0	4	5	16	4	1	0	.250	2	10	0	0	0.2	1.000
9 yrs.		53	74	.417	4.25	338	152	17	1142.1	1246	499	715	3	11	12	21	292	24	0	.082	55	180	12	11	0.7	.951

Johnny Ruffin

RUFFIN, JOHNNY RENANDO
B. July 29, 1971, Butler, Ala.

BR TR 6'3" 172 lbs.

1993	CIN N	2	1	.667	3.58	21	0	0	37.2	36	11	30	0	2	1	2	3	1	0	.333	4	5	0	0	0.4	1.000
1994		7	2	.778	3.09	51	0	0	70	57	27	44	0	7	2	1	8	0	0	.000	10	2	0	0	0.2	1.000
2 yrs.		9	3	.750	3.26	72	0	0	107.2	93	38	74	0	9	3	3	11	1	0	.091	14	7	0	0	0.3	1.000

Jeff Russell

RUSSELL, JEFFREY LEE
B. Sept. 2, 1961, Cincinnati, Ohio.

BR TR 6'4" 200 lbs.

1983	CIN N	4	5	.444	3.03	10	10	2	68.1	58	22	40	0	0	0	0	21	3	1	.143	2	10	1	0	1.3	.923
1984		6	18	.250	4.26	33	30	4	181.2	186	65	101	2	0	0	0	57	8	0	.140	7	34	2	4	1.3	.953
1985	TEX A	3	6	.333	7.55	13	13	0	62	85	27	44	0	0	0	0	0	0	0	–	6	10	0	1	1.2	1.000
1986		5	2	.714	3.40	37	0	0	82	74	31	54	0	5	2	2	0	0	0	–	6	17	0	3	0.6	1.000
1987		5	4	.556	4.44	52	2	0	97.1	109	52	56	0	5	3	3	0	0	0	–	11	17	0	2	0.5	1.000
1988		10	9	.526	3.82	34	24	5	188.2	183	66	88	0	1	0	0	1	0	0	.000	12	37	5	3	1.6	.907
1989		6	4	.600	1.98	71	0	0	72.2	45	24	77	0	6	4	38	0	0	0	–	6	14	0	3	0.3	1.000
1990		1	5	.167	4.26	27	0	0	25.1	23	16	16	0	1	5	10	0	0	0	–	1	5	1	0	0.3	.857
1991		6	4	.600	3.29	68	0	0	79.1	71	26	52	0	6	4	30	0	0	0	–	6	18	1	1	0.4	.960
1992	2 teams	TEX A	(51G 2–3)	OAK A	(8G 2–0)																					
"	total	4	3	.571	1.63	59	0	0	66.1	55	25	48	0	4	3	30	0	0	0	–	8	8	0	0	0.3	1.000
1993	BOS A	1	4	.200	2.70	51	0	0	46.2	39	14	45	0	1	4	33	0	0	0	–	2	5	0	0	0.2	1.000
1994	2 teams	BOS A	(29G 0–5)	CLE A	(13G 1–1)																					
"	total	1	6	.143	5.09	42	0	0	40.2	43	16	28	0	1	6	17	0	0	0	–	1	2	0	0	0.1	1.000
12 yrs.		52	70	.426	3.79	497	79	11	1011	971	384	649	2	30	31	163	79	11	1	.139	68	182	10	17	0.5	.962

LEAGUE CHAMPIONSHIP SERIES

| 1992 | OAK A | 1 | 0 | 1.000 | 9.00 | 3 | 0 | 0 | 2 | 2 | 4 | 0 | 0 | 1 | 0 | 0 | 0 | 0 | 0 | – | 0 | 0 | 0 | 0 | 0.0 | – |

Ken Ryan

RYAN, KENNETH FREDERICK
B. Oct. 24, 1968, Pawtucket, R. I.

BR TR 6'3" 200 lbs.

1992	BOS A	0	0	–	6.43	7	0	0	7	4	5	5	0	0	0	1	0	0	0	–	1	2	0	0	0.4	1.000
1993		7	2	.778	3.60	47	0	0	50	43	29	49	0	7	2	1	0	0	0	–	3	7	1	0	0.2	.909
1994		2	3	.400	2.44	42	0	0	48	46	17	32	0	2	3	13	0	0	0	–	2	4	0	0	0.1	1.000
3 yrs.		9	5	.643	3.26	96	0	0	105	93	51	86	0	9	5	15	0	0	0	–	6	13	1	0	0.2	.950

Bret Saberhagen

SABERHAGEN, BRET WILLIAM
B. Apr. 11, 1964, Chicago Heights, Ill.

BR TR 6'1" 160 lbs.

1984	KC A	10	11	.476	3.48	38	18	2	157.2	138	36	73	1	4	1	1	0	0	0	–	15	22	1	1	1.0	.974
1985		20	6	.769	2.87	32	32	10	235.1	211	38	158	1	0	0	0	0	0	0	–	22	38	2	4	1.9	.968
1986		7	12	.368	4.15	30	25	4	156	165	29	112	2	1	0	0	0	0	0	–	14	26	2	0	1.4	.952
1987		18	10	.643	3.36	33	33	15	257	246	53	163	4	0	0	0	0	0	0	–	21	34	2	5	1.7	.965
1988		14	16	.467	3.80	35	35	9	260.2	271	59	171	0	0	0	0	0	0	0	–	15	34	3	3	1.5	.942
1989		23	6	.793	2.16	36	35	12	262.1	209	43	193	4	0	1	0	0	0	0	–	21	36	4	1	1.7	.934
1990		5	9	.357	3.27	20	20	5	135	146	28	87	0	0	0	0	0	0	0	–	16	28	1	2	2.3	.978
1991		13	8	.619	3.07	28	28	7	196.1	165	45	136	2	0	0	0	0	0	0	–	17	30	2	2	1.8	.959
1992	NY N	3	5	.375	3.50	17	15	1	97.2	84	27	81	1	0	1	0	28	3	0	.107	7	26	0	2	1.9	1.000
1993		7	7	.500	3.29	19	19	4	139.1	131	17	93	1	0	0	0	45	5	0	.111	14	30	2	0	2.4	.957
1994		14	4	.778	2.74	24	24	4	177.1	169	13	143	0	0	0	0	58	10	0	.172	13	34	2	1	2.0	.959
11 yrs.		134	94	.588	3.19	312	284	73	2074.2	1935	388	1410	16	5	3	1	131	18	0	.137	175	338	21	21	1.7	.961

LEAGUE CHAMPIONSHIP SERIES

1984	KC A	0	0	–	2.25	1	1	0	8	6	1	5	0	0	0	0	0	0	0	–	1	1	0	0	3.0	.667
1985		0	0	–	6.14	2	2	0	7.1	12	2	6	0	0	0	0	0	0	0	–	2	1	0	0	1.5	1.000
2 yrs.		0	0	–	4.11	3	3	0	15.1	18	3	11	0	0	0	0	0	0	0	–	3	2	1	0	2.0	.833

WORLD SERIES

| 1985 | KC A | 2 | 0 | 1.000 | 0.50 | 2 | 2 | 2 | 18 | 11 | 1 | 10 | 1 | 0 | 0 | 0 | 7 | 0 | 0 | .000 | 0 | 0 | 0 | 0 | 0.0 | – |

A. J. Sager

SAGER, ANTHONY JOSEPH
B. Mar. 3, 1965, Columbus, Ohio

BR TR 6'4" 220 lbs.

| 1994 | SD N | 1 | 4 | .200 | 5.98 | 22 | 3 | 0 | 46.2 | 62 | 16 | 26 | 0 | 0 | 3 | 0 | 10 | 1 | 0 | .100 | 6 | 15 | 0 | 1 | 1.0 | 1.000 |

Roger Salkeld

SALKELD, ROGER WILLIAM
B. Mar. 6, 1971, Burbank, Calif.

BR TR 6'5" 215 lbs.

1993	SEA A	0	0	–	2.51	3	3	0	14.1	13	4	13	0	0	0	0	0	0	0	–	0	2	0	0	0.7	1.000
1994		2	5	.286	7.17	13	13	0	59	76	45	46	0	0	0	0	0	0	0	–	1	3	0	0	0.3	1.000
2 yrs.		2	5	.286	6.26	16	15	0	73.1	89	49	59	0	0	0	0	0	0	0	–	1	5	0	0	0.4	1.000

Bill Sampen

SAMPEN, WILLIAM ALBERT
B. Jan. 18, 1963, Lincoln, Ill.

BR TR 6'1" 185 lbs.

1990	MON N	12	7	.632	2.99	59	4	0	90.1	94	33	69	0	11	6	2	8	0	0	.000	5	9	0	0	0.2	1.000
1991		9	5	.643	4.00	43	8	0	92.1	96	46	52	0	6	3	0	13	3	0	.231	3	9	1	0	0.3	.923
1992	2 teams	MON N	(44G 1–4)	KC A	(8G 0–2)																					
"	total	1	6	.143	3.25	52	2	0	83	83	32	37	0	1	4	0	6	0	0	.000	10	15	0	0	0.5	1.000
1993	KC A	2	2	.500	5.89	18	0	0	18.1	25	9	9	0	2	2	0	0	0	0	–	2	2	0	0	0.2	1.000
1994	CAL A	1	1	.500	6.46	10	0	0	15.1	14	13	9	0	1	1	0	0	0	0	–	1	3	0	0	0.4	1.000
5 yrs.		25	21	.543	3.73	182	14	0	299.1	312	133	176	0	21	16	2	27	3	0	.111	21	38	1	1	0.3	.983

Year	Team	W	L	PCT	ERA	G	GS	CG	IP	H	BB	SO	ShO	Relief Pitching W	L	SV	Batting AB	H	HR	BA	PO	A	E	DP	TC/G	FA

Scott Sanders

SANDERS, SCOTT GERALD
B. Mar. 25, 1969, Hannibal, Mo. BR TR 6'4" 210 lbs.

Year	Team	W	L	PCT	ERA	G	GS	CG	IP	H	BB	SO	ShO	W	L	SV	AB	H	HR	BA	PO	A	E	DP	TC/G	FA
1993	SD N	3	3	.500	4.13	9	9	0	52.1	54	23	37	0	0	0	0	16	1	0	.063	3	2	0	0	0.6	1.000
1994		4	8	.333	4.78	23	20	0	111	103	48	109	0	0	0	1	32	4	0	.125	9	15	0	0	1.0	1.000
2 yrs.		7	11	.389	4.57	32	29	0	163.1	157	71	146	0	0	0	1	48	5	0	.104	12	17	0	0	0.9	1.000

Scott Sanderson

SANDERSON, SCOTT DOUGLAS
B. July 22, 1956, Dearborn, Mich. BR TR 6'5" 195 lbs.

Year	Team	W	L	PCT	ERA	G	GS	CG	IP	H	BB	SO	ShO	W	L	SV	AB	H	HR	BA	PO	A	E	DP	TC/G	FA
1978	MON N	4	2	.667	2.51	10	9	1	61	52	21	50	1	0	0	0	19	2	0	.105	2	6	1	0	0.9	.889
1979		9	8	.529	3.43	34	24	5	168	148	54	138	3	1	1	1	50	8	0	.160	9	13	1	1	0.7	.957
1980		16	11	.593	3.11	33	33	7	211	206	56	125	3	0	0	0	64	5	0	.078	14	21	1	0	1.1	.972
1981		9	7	.563	2.96	22	22	4	137	122	31	77	1	0	0	0	35	4	0	.114	6	14	0	0	0.9	1.000
1982		12	12	.500	3.46	32	32	7	224	212	58	158	0	0	0	0	57	8	1	.140	13	16	1	1	0.9	.967
1983		6	7	.462	4.65	18	16	0	81.1	98	20	55	0	0	0	1	28	4	0	.143	4	6	2	0	0.7	.833
1984	CHI N	8	5	.615	3.14	24	24	3	140.2	140	24	76	0	0	0	0	42	5	0	.119	11	24	1	0	1.5	.972
1985		5	6	.455	3.12	19	19	2	121	100	27	80	0	0	0	0	31	2	0	.065	11	21	0	2	1.7	1.000
1986		9	11	.450	4.19	37	28	1	169.2	165	37	124	1	2	0	1	51	3	0	.059	11	20	2	3	0.9	.939
1987		8	9	.471	4.29	32	22	0	144.2	156	50	106	0	1	2	2	40	3	1	.075	10	14	2	3	0.8	.923
1988		1	2	.333	5.28	11	0	0	15.1	13	3	6	0	1	2	0	0	0	0	–	0	1	0	0	0.1	1.000
1989		11	9	.550	3.94	37	23	2	146.1	155	31	86	0	1	2	0	43	2	0	.047	10	12	0	1	0.6	1.000
1990	OAK A	17	11	.607	3.88	34	34	2	206.1	205	66	128	1	0	0	0	0	0	0	–	11	18	2	2	0.9	.935
1991	NY A	16	10	.615	3.81	34	34	2	208	200	29	130	2	0	0	0	0	0	0	–	15	13	1	0	0.9	.966
1992		12	11	.522	4.93	33	33	2	193.1	220	64	104	1	0	0	0	0	0	0	–	4	18	2	1	0.7	.917
1993	2 teams	CAL A	(21G 7–11)		SF N	(11G 4–2)																				
"	total	11	13	.458	4.21	32	29	4	184	201	34	102	1	0	0	0	14	0	0	.000	13	23	2	1	1.2	.947
1994	CHI A	8	4	.667	5.09	18	14	1	92	110	12	36	0	0	0	0	0	0	0	–	4	18	0	1	1.2	1.000
17 yrs.		162	138	.540	3.81	460	396	43	2503.2	2503	617	1581	14	6	8	5	474	46	2	.097	148	258	18	16	0.9	.958

DIVISIONAL PLAYOFF SERIES

| 1981 | MON N | 0 | 0 | – | 6.75 | 1 | 1 | 0 | 2.2 | 4 | 2 | 2 | 0 | 0 | 0 | 0 | 1 | 0 | 0 | .000 | 0 | 0 | 0 | 0 | 0.0 | – |

LEAGUE CHAMPIONSHIP SERIES

1984	CHI N	0	0	–	5.79	1	1	0	4.2	1	1	2	0	0	0	0	2	0	0	.000	0	1	0	0	1.0	1.000
1989		0	0	–	0.00	1	0	0	2	2	0	1	0	0	0	0	0	0	0	–	0	0	0	0	0.0	–
2 yrs.		0	0	–	4.05	2	1	0	6.2	8	1	3	0	0	0	0	2	0	0	.000	0	1	0	0	0.5	1.000

WORLD SERIES

| 1990 | OAK A | 0 | 0 | – | 10.80 | 1 | 0 | 0 | 1.2 | 4 | 1 | 0 | 0 | 0 | 0 | 0 | 0 | 0 | 0 | – | 0 | 0 | 0 | 0 | 0.0 | – |

Bob Scanlan

SCANLAN, ROBERT GUY
B. Aug. 9, 1966, Los Angeles, Calif. BR TR 6'7" 215 lbs.

Year	Team	W	L	PCT	ERA	G	GS	CG	IP	H	BB	SO	ShO	W	L	SV	AB	H	HR	BA	PO	A	E	DP	TC/G	FA
1991	CHI N	7	8	.467	3.89	40	13	0	111	114	40	44	0	5	4	1	24	1	0	.042	9	16	2	0	0.7	.926
1992		3	6	.333	2.89	69	0	0	87.1	76	30	42	0	3	6	14	4	0	0	.000	5	22	2	0	0.4	.931
1993		4	5	.444	4.54	70	0	0	75.1	79	28	44	0	4	5	0	2	1	0	.500	3	6	0	0	0.1	1.000
1994	MIL A	2	6	.250	4.11	30	12	0	103	117	28	65	0	0	3	2	0	0	0	–	8	12	1	1	0.7	.952
4 yrs.		16	25	.390	3.85	209	25	0	376.2	386	126	195	0	12	18	17	30	2	0	.067	25	56	5	1	0.4	.942

Rich Scheid

SCHEID, RICHARD PAUL
B. Feb. 3, 1965, Staten Island, N. Y. BL TL 6'3" 185 lbs.

Year	Team	W	L	PCT	ERA	G	GS	CG	IP	H	BB	SO	ShO	W	L	SV	AB	H	HR	BA	PO	A	E	DP	TC/G	FA
1992	HOU N	0	1	.000	6.00	7	1	0	12	14	6	8	0	0	0	0	1	0	0	.000	1	1	0	0	0.3	1.000
1994	FLA N	1	3	.250	3.34	8	5	0	32.1	35	8	17	0	1	0	0	7	0	0	.000	0	4	1	0	0.6	.800
2 yrs.		1	4	.200	4.06	15	6	0	44.1	49	14	25	0	1	0	0	8	0	0	.000	1	5	1	0	0.5	.857

Curt Schilling

SCHILLING, CURTIS MONTAGUE
B. Nov. 14, 1966, Anchorage, Alaska. BR TR 6'5" 205 lbs.

Year	Team	W	L	PCT	ERA	G	GS	CG	IP	H	BB	SO	ShO	W	L	SV	AB	H	HR	BA	PO	A	E	DP	TC/G	FA
1988	BAL A	0	3	.000	9.82	4	4	0	14.2	22	10	4	0	0	0	0	0	0	0	–	0	0	1	0	0.3	.000
1989		0	1	.000	6.23	5	1	0	8.2	10	3	6	0	0	0	0	0	0	0	–	1	0	0	0	0.2	1.000
1990		1	2	.333	2.54	35	0	0	46	38	19	32	0	1	2	3	0	0	0	–	1	4	0	0	0.1	1.000
1991	HOU N	3	5	.375	3.81	56	0	0	75.2	79	39	71	0	3	5	8	3	1	0	.333	6	4	1	0	0.2	.909
1992	PHI N	14	11	.560	2.35	42	26	10	226.1	165	59	147	4	2	2	2	64	10	0	.156	14	21	3	1	0.9	.921
1993		16	7	.696	4.02	34	34	7	235.1	234	57	186	2	0	0	0	75	11	0	.147	6	36	0	1	1.2	1.000
1994		2	8	.200	4.48	13	13	1	82.1	87	28	58	0	0	0	0	28	3	0	.107	2	11	1	0	1.1	.929
7 yrs.		36	37	.493	3.55	189	78	18	689	635	215	504	6	6	9	13	170	25	0	.147	30	76	6	2	0.6	.946

LEAGUE CHAMPIONSHIP SERIES

| 1993 | PHI N | 0 | 0 | – | 1.69 | 2 | 2 | 0 | 16 | 11 | 5 | 19 | 0 | 0 | 0 | 0 | 5 | 0 | 0 | .000 | 0 | 0 | 0 | 0 | 0.0 | – |

WORLD SERIES

| 1993 | PHI N | 1 | 1 | .500 | 3.52 | 2 | 2 | 0 | 15.1 | 13 | 5 | 9 | 1 | 0 | 0 | 0 | 2 | 1 | 0 | .500 | 0 | 3 | 0 | 0 | 1.5 | 1.000 |

Pete Schourek

SCHOUREK, PETER ALAN
B. May 10, 1969, Austin, Tex. BL TL 6'5" 195 lbs.

Year	Team	W	L	PCT	ERA	G	GS	CG	IP	H	BB	SO	ShO	W	L	SV	AB	H	HR	BA	PO	A	E	DP	TC/G	FA
1991	NY N	5	4	.556	4.27	35	8	1	86.1	82	43	67	1	2	1	2	22	3	0	.136	6	14	0	1	0.6	1.000
1992		6	8	.429	3.64	22	21	0	136	137	44	60	0	1	0	0	42	2	0	.048	7	13	0	1	0.9	1.000
1993		5	12	.294	5.96	41	18	0	128.1	168	45	72	0	0	1	0	32	7	0	.219	5	17	0	2	0.5	1.000
1994	CIN N	7	2	.778	4.09	22	10	0	81.1	90	29	69	0	3	0	0	23	4	1	.174	1	13	0	2	0.6	1.000
4 yrs.		23	26	.469	4.54	120	57	1	432	477	161	268	1	6	2	2	119	16	1	.134	19	57	0	6	0.6	1.000

Erik Schullstrom

SCHULLSTROM, ERIK PAUL
B. Mar. 25, 1969, San Diego, Calif. BR TR 6'5" 220 lbs.

Year	Team	W	L	PCT	ERA	G	GS	CG	IP	H	BB	SO	ShO	W	L	SV	AB	H	HR	BA	PO	A	E	DP	TC/G	FA
1994	MIN A	0	0	–	2.77	9	0	0	13	13	5	13	0	0	0	1	0	0	0	–	1	0	1	0	0.2	.500

Year	Team	W	L	PCT	ERA	G	GS	CG	IP	H	BB	SO	ShO	Relief Pitching W	L	SV	Batting AB	H	HR	BA	PO	A	E	DP	TC/G	FA

Jeff Schwarz
SCHWARZ, JEFFREY WILLIAM
B. May 20, 1964, Fort Pierce, Fla. — BR TR 6'5" 190 lbs.

Year	Team	W	L	PCT	ERA	G	GS	CG	IP	H	BB	SO	ShO	W	L	SV	AB	H	HR	BA	PO	A	E	DP	TC/G	FA
1993	CHI A	2	2	.500	3.71	41	0	0	51	35	38	41	0	2	2	0	0	0	0	–	3	1	1	0	0.1	.800
1994	2 teams	CHI A	(9G 0–0)	CAL A	(4G 0–0)																					
"	total	0	0	–	5.50	13	0	0	18	14	22	18	0	0	0	0	0	0	0	–	0	1	0	0	0.1	1.000
	2 yrs.	2	2	.500	4.17	54	0	0	69	49	60	59	0	2	2	0	0	0	0	–	3	2	1	0	0.1	.833

Tim Scott
SCOTT, TIMOTHY DALE
B. Nov. 16, 1966, Hanford, Calif. — BR TR 6'2" 185 lbs.

Year	Team	W	L	PCT	ERA	G	GS	CG	IP	H	BB	SO	ShO	W	L	SV	AB	H	HR	BA	PO	A	E	DP	TC/G	FA
1991	SD N	0	0	–	9.00	2	0	0	1	2	0	1	0	0	0	0	0	0	0	–	0	0	0	0	0.0	–
1992		4	1	.800	5.26	34	0	0	37.2	39	21	30	0	4	1	0	0	0	0	–	0	4	0	0	0.1	1.000
1993	2 teams	SD N	(24G 2–0)	MON N	(32G 5–2)																					
"	total	7	2	.778	3.01	56	0	0	71.2	69	34	65	0	7	2	1	4	0	0	.000	3	8	1	1	0.2	.917
1994	MON N	5	2	.714	2.70	40	0	0	53.1	51	18	37	0	5	2	1	2	0	0	.000	2	0	0	0	0.1	1.000
	4 yrs.	16	5	.762	3.46	132	0	0	163.2	161	73	133	0	16	5	2	6	0	0	.000	5	12	1	1	0.1	.944

Rudy Seanez
SEANEZ, RUDY CABALLERO
B. Oct. 20, 1968, Brawley, Calif. — BR TR 5'10" 185 lbs.

Year	Team	W	L	PCT	ERA	G	GS	CG	IP	H	BB	SO	ShO	W	L	SV	AB	H	HR	BA	PO	A	E	DP	TC/G	FA
1989	CLE A	0	0	–	3.60	5	0	0	5	1	4	7	0	0	0	0	0	0	0	–	0	0	0	0	0.0	–
1990		2	1	.667	5.60	24	0	0	27.1	22	25	24	0	2	1	0	0	0	0	–	1	1	0	0	0.1	1.000
1991		0	0	–	16.20	5	0	0	5	10	7	7	0	0	0	0	0	0	0	–	0	0	0	0	0.0	–
1993	SD N	0	0	–	13.50	3	0	0	3.1	8	2	1	0	0	0	0	0	0	0	–	0	1	0	0	0.3	1.000
1994	LA N	1	1	.500	2.66	17	0	0	23.2	24	9	18	0	1	1	0	1	0	0	.000	0	4	0	0	0.2	1.000
	5 yrs.	3	2	.600	5.60	54	0	0	64.1	65	47	57	0	3	2	0	1	0	0	.000	1	6	0	0	0.1	1.000

Kevin Seitzer
SEITZER, KEVIN LEE
B. Mar. 26, 1962, Springfield, Ill. — BR TR 5'11" 180 lbs.

Year	Team	W	L	PCT	ERA	G	GS	CG	IP	H	BB	SO	ShO	W	L	SV	AB	H	HR	BA	PO	A	E	DP	TC/G	FA
1993	OAK A	0	0	–	0.00	1	0	0	0.1	0	0	1	0	0	0	0	*				0	0	0	0	0.0	–

Aaron Sele
SELE, AARON HELMER
B. June 25, 1970, Golden Valley, Minn. — BR TR 6'5" 205 lbs.

Year	Team	W	L	PCT	ERA	G	GS	CG	IP	H	BB	SO	ShO	W	L	SV	AB	H	HR	BA	PO	A	E	DP	TC/G	FA
1993	BOS A	7	2	.778	2.74	18	18	0	111.2	100	48	93	0	0	0	0	0	0	0	–	3	9	5	1	0.9	.706
1994		8	7	.533	3.83	22	22	2	143.1	140	60	105	0	0	0	0	0	0	0	–	6	14	0	0	0.9	1.000
	2 yrs.	15	9	.625	3.35	40	40	2	255	240	108	198	0	0	0	0	0	0	0	–	9	23	5	1	0.9	.865

Frank Seminara
SEMINARA, FRANK PETER
B. May 16, 1967, Brooklyn, N. Y. — BR TR 6'2" 205 lbs.

Year	Team	W	L	PCT	ERA	G	GS	CG	IP	H	BB	SO	ShO	W	L	SV	AB	H	HR	BA	PO	A	E	DP	TC/G	FA
1992	SD N	9	4	.692	3.68	19	18	0	100.1	98	46	61	0	0	0	0	34	4	0	.118	9	23	2	1	1.8	.941
1993		3	3	.500	4.47	18	7	0	46.1	53	21	22	0	2	1	0	10	2	0	.200	8	6	2	0	0.9	.875
1994	NY N	0	2	.000	5.82	10	1	0	17	20	8	7	0	0	2	0	3	0	0	.000	2	0	2	0	0.4	.500
	3 yrs.	12	9	.571	4.12	47	26	0	163.2	171	75	90	0	2	3	0	47	6	0	.128	19	29	6	1	1.1	.889

Scott Service
SERVICE, DAVID SCOTT
B. Feb. 26, 1967, Cincinnati, Ohio. — BR TR 6'6" 225 lbs.

Year	Team	W	L	PCT	ERA	G	GS	CG	IP	H	BB	SO	ShO	W	L	SV	AB	H	HR	BA	PO	A	E	DP	TC/G	FA
1988	PHI N	0	0	–	1.69	5	0	0	5.1	7	1	6	0	0	0	0	0	0	0	–	0	0	0	0	0.0	–
1992	MON N	0	0	–	14.14	5	0	0	7	15	5	11	0	0	0	0	2	0	0	.000	0	0	0	0	0.0	–
1993	2 teams	CLR N	(3G 0–0)	CIN N	(26G 2–2)																					
"	total	2	2	.500	4.30	29	0	0	46	44	16	43	0	2	2	2	7	1	0	.143	6	5	0	0	0.4	1.000
1994	CIN N	1	2	.333	7.36	6	0	0	7.1	8	3	5	0	1	2	0	0	0	0	–	0	3	0	0	0.5	1.000
	4 yrs.	3	4	.429	5.48	45	0	0	65.2	74	25	65	0	3	4	2	9	1	0	.111	6	8	0	0	0.3	1.000

Jeff Shaw
SHAW, JEFFREY LEE
B. July 7, 1966, Washington Court House, Ohio. — BR TR 6'2" 185 lbs.

Year	Team	W	L	PCT	ERA	G	GS	CG	IP	H	BB	SO	ShO	W	L	SV	AB	H	HR	BA	PO	A	E	DP	TC/G	FA
1990	CLE A	3	4	.429	6.66	12	9	0	48.2	73	20	25	0	0	0	0	0	0	0	–	4	7	0	0	0.9	1.000
1991		0	5	.000	3.36	29	1	0	72.1	72	27	31	0	0	4	1	0	0	0	–	4	11	2	2	0.6	.882
1992		0	1	.000	8.22	2	1	0	7.2	7	4	3	0	0	0	0	0	0	0	–	0	2	1	0	1.5	.667
1993	MON N	2	7	.222	4.14	55	8	0	95.2	91	32	50	0	1	3	0	15	1	0	.067	8	16	0	1	0.4	1.000
1994		5	2	.714	3.88	46	0	0	67.1	67	15	47	0	5	2	1	7	2	0	.286	8	12	0	0	0.4	1.000
	5 yrs.	10	19	.345	4.41	144	19	0	291.2	310	98	156	0	6	9	2	22	3	0	.136	24	48	3	3	0.5	.960

Paul Shuey
SHUEY, PAUL KENNETH
B. Sept. 16, 1970, Lima, Ohio — BR TR 6'3" 215 lbs.

Year	Team	W	L	PCT	ERA	G	GS	CG	IP	H	BB	SO	ShO	W	L	SV	AB	H	HR	BA	PO	A	E	DP	TC/G	FA
1994	CLE A	0	1	.000	8.49	14	0	0	11.2	14	12	16	0	0	1	5	0	0	0	–	0	0	0	0	0.0	–

Heathcliff Slocumb
SLOCUMB, HEATHCLIFF
B. June 7, 1966, Jamaica, N. Y. — BR TR 6'3" 180 lbs.

Year	Team	W	L	PCT	ERA	G	GS	CG	IP	H	BB	SO	ShO	W	L	SV	AB	H	HR	BA	PO	A	E	DP	TC/G	FA
1991	CHI N	2	1	.667	3.45	52	0	0	62.2	53	30	34	0	2	1	1	1	0	0	.000	5	10	1	0	0.3	.938
1992		0	3	.000	6.50	30	0	0	36	52	21	27	0	0	3	1	4	0	0	.000	3	4	2	0	0.3	.778
1993	2 teams	CHI N	(10G 1–0)	CLE A	(20G 3–1)																					
"	total	4	1	.800	4.03	30	0	0	38	35	20	22	0	4	1	0	1	0	0	.000	3	4	0	2	0.2	1.000
1994	PHI N	5	1	.833	2.86	52	0	0	72.1	75	28	58	0	5	1	0	4	1	0	.250	2	13	3	1	0.3	.833
	4 yrs.	11	6	.647	3.88	164	0	0	209	215	99	141	0	11	6	2	10	1	0	.100	13	31	6	3	0.3	.880

Aaron Small
SMALL, AARON JAMES
B. Nov. 23, 1971, Oxnard, Calif. — BR TR 6'5" 200 lbs.

Year	Team	W	L	PCT	ERA	G	GS	CG	IP	H	BB	SO	ShO	W	L	SV	AB	H	HR	BA	PO	A	E	DP	TC/G	FA
1994	TOR A	0	0	–	9.00	1	0	0	2	5	2	0	0	0	0	0	0	0	0	–	0	1	0	0	1.0	1.000

John Smiley
SMILEY, JOHN PATRICK
B. Mar. 17, 1965, Phoenixville, Pa. — BL TL 6'4" 180 lbs.

Year	Team	W	L	PCT	ERA	G	GS	CG	IP	H	BB	SO	ShO	W	L	SV	AB	H	HR	BA	PO	A	E	DP	TC/G	FA
1986	PIT N	1	0	1.000	3.86	12	0	0	11.2	4	4	9	0	1	0	0	0	0	0	–	1	2	0	0	0.3	1.000
1987		5	5	.500	5.76	63	0	0	75	69	50	58	0	5	5	4	7	1	0	.143	7	9	0	2	0.3	1.000

John Smiley *continued*

Year	Team	W	L	PCT	ERA	G	GS	CG	IP	H	BB	SO	ShO	W	L	SV	AB	H	HR	BA	PO	A	E	DP	TC/G	FA
1988		13	11	.542	3.25	34	32	5	205	185	46	129	1	0	0	0	63	5	0	.079	14	27	0	3	1.2	1.000
1989		12	8	.600	2.81	28	28	8	205.1	174	49	123	1	0	0	0	65	9	0	.138	7	23	4	2	1.2	.882
1990		9	10	.474	4.64	26	25	2	149.1	161	36	86	0	0	0	0	49	6	0	.122	8	24	2	1	1.3	.941
1991		**20**	8	**.714**	3.08	33	32	2	207.2	194	44	129	1	1	0	0	70	7	0	.100	5	34	1	0	1.2	.975
1992	MIN A	16	9	.640	3.21	34	34	5	241	205	65	163	2	0	0	0	0	0	0	–	4	35	0	2	1.1	1.000
1993	CIN N	3	9	.250	5.62	18	18	2	105.2	117	31	60	0	0	0	0	32	8	0	.250	7	16	0	0	1.3	1.000
1994		11	10	.524	3.86	24	24	1	158.2	169	37	112	1	0	0	0	55	11	0	.200	8	19	2	1	1.2	.931
9 yrs.		90	70	.563	3.70	272	193	25	1359.1	1278	362	869	6	7	5	4	341	47	0	.138	61	189	9	11	1.0	.965

LEAGUE CHAMPIONSHIP SERIES

Year	Team	W	L	PCT	ERA	G	GS	CG	IP	H	BB	SO	ShO	W	L	SV	AB	H	HR	BA	PO	A	E	DP	TC/G	FA
1990	PIT N	0	0	–	0.00	1	0	0	2	2	0	0	0	0	0	0	0	0	0	–	0	0	0	0	0.0	–
1991		0	2	.000	23.63	2	2	0	2.2	8	1	3	0	0	0	0	0	0	0	–	0	1	0	0	0.5	1.000
2 yrs.		0	2	.000	13.50	3	2	0	4.2	10	1	3	0	0	0	0	0	0	0	–	0	1	0	0	0.3	1.000

Dan Smith

SMITH, DANIEL SCOTT
B. Apr. 20, 1969, St. Paul, Minn.

BL TL 6'5" 190 lbs.

Year	Team	W	L	PCT	ERA	G	GS	CG	IP	H	BB	SO	ShO	W	L	SV	AB	H	HR	BA	PO	A	E	DP	TC/G	FA
1992	TEX A	0	3	.000	5.02	4	2	0	14.1	18	8	5	0	0	1	0	0	0	0	–	1	1	0	0	0.5	1.000
1994		1	2	.333	4.30	13	0	0	14.2	18	12	9	0	1	2	0	0	0	0	–	0	1	0	0	0.1	1.000
2 yrs.		1	5	.167	4.66	17	2	0	29	36	20	14	0	1	3	0	0	0	0	–	1	2	0	0	0.2	1.000

Lee Smith

SMITH, LEE ARTHUR, JR.
B. Dec. 4, 1957, Jamestown, La.

BR TR 6'5" 220 lbs.

Year	Team	W	L	PCT	ERA	G	GS	CG	IP	H	BB	SO	ShO	W	L	SV	AB	H	HR	BA	PO	A	E	DP	TC/G	FA
1980	CHI N	2	0	1.000	2.86	18	0	0	22	21	14	17	0	2	0	0	0	0	0	–	0	3	0	0	0.2	1.000
1981		3	6	.333	3.49	40	1	0	67	57	31	50	0	3	5	1	9	0	0	.000	3	9	0	0	0.3	1.000
1982		2	5	.286	2.69	72	5	0	117	105	37	99	0	2	1	17	16	1	1	.063	9	10	1	2	0.3	.950
1983		4	10	.286	1.65	66	0	0	103.1	70	41	91	0	4	10	**29**	9	1	0	.111	8	9	0	0	0.3	1.000
1984		9	7	.563	3.65	69	0	0	101	98	35	86	0	9	7	33	13	1	0	.077	6	13	0	0	0.3	1.000
1985		7	4	.636	3.04	65	0	0	97.2	87	32	112	0	7	4	33	6	0	0	.000	3	9	0	1	0.2	1.000
1986		9	9	.500	3.09	66	0	0	90.1	69	42	93	0	9	9	31	5	0	0	.000	1	12	0	2	0.2	1.000
1987		4	10	.286	3.12	62	0	0	83.2	84	32	96	0	4	**10**	36	2	0	0	.000	3	8	0	0	0.2	1.000
1988	BOS A	4	5	.444	2.80	64	0	0	83.2	72	37	96	0	4	5	29	0	0	0	–	5	4	1	0	0.2	.900
1989		6	1	.857	3.57	64	0	0	70.2	53	33	96	0	6	1	25	0	0	0	–	1	1	0	0	0.1	1.000
1990 2 teams	BOS A (11G 2–1) STL N (53G 3–4)																									
" total		5	5	.500	2.06	64	0	0	83	71	29	87	0	5	5	31	2	0	0	.000	2	3	0	0	0.1	1.000
1991	STL N	6	3	.667	2.34	67	0	0	73	70	13	67	0	6	3	**47**	0	0	0	–	3	6	0	0	0.1	1.000
1992		4	9	.308	3.12	70	0	0	75	62	26	60	0	4	9	**43**	0	0	0	–	1	7	1	1	0.1	.889
1993 2 teams	STL N (55G 2–4) NY A (8G 0–0)																									
" total		2	4	.333	3.88	63	0	0	58	53	14	60	0	2	4	46	2	0	0	.000	0	2	0	0	0.0	1.000
1994	BAL A	1	4	.200	3.29	41	0	0	38.1	34	11	42	0	1	4	**33**	0	0	0	–	2	2	1	0	0.1	.800
15 yrs.		68	82	.453	2.92	891	6	0	1163.2	1006	427	1152	0	68	77	434	64	3	1	.047	47	98	4	8	0.2	.973
					10th											1st										

LEAGUE CHAMPIONSHIP SERIES

Year	Team	W	L	PCT	ERA	G	GS	CG	IP	H	BB	SO	ShO	W	L	SV	AB	H	HR	BA	PO	A	E	DP	TC/G	FA
1984	CHI N	0	1	.000	9.00	2	0	0	2	3	0	3	0	0	1	1	0	0	0	–	0	0	0	0	0.0	–
1988	BOS A	0	1	.000	8.10	2	0	0	3.1	6	1	4	0	0	1	0	0	0	0	–	0	0	0	0	0.0	–
2 yrs.		0	2	.000	8.44	4	0	0	5.1	9	1	7	0	0	2	1	0	0	0	–	0	0	0	0	0.0	–

Pete Smith

SMITH, PETER JOHN
B. Feb. 27, 1966, Abington, Mass.

BR TR 6'2" 185 lbs.

Year	Team	W	L	PCT	ERA	G	GS	CG	IP	H	BB	SO	ShO	W	L	SV	AB	H	HR	BA	PO	A	E	DP	TC/G	FA
1987	ATL N	1	2	.333	4.83	6	6	0	31.2	39	14	11	0	0	0	0	11	1	0	.091	1	2	0	1	0.7	.750
1988		7	15	.318	3.69	32	32	5	195.1	183	88	124	3	0	0	0	53	6	0	.113	12	19	3	0	1.1	.912
1989		5	14	.263	4.75	28	27	1	142	144	57	115	0	0	0	0	41	4	0	.098	11	11	1	2	0.8	.957
1990		5	6	.455	4.79	13	13	3	77	77	24	56	0	0	0	0	23	2	0	.087	5	5	0	0	0.8	1.000
1991		1	3	.250	5.06	14	10	0	48	48	22	29	0	0	0	0	12	2	0	.167	3	6	0	0	0.6	1.000
1992		7	0	1.000	2.05	12	11	2	79	63	28	43	1	0	0	0	26	1	0	.038	3	13	1	2	1.4	.941
1993		4	8	.333	4.37	20	14	0	90.2	92	36	53	0	1	0	0	27	6	0	.222	7	14	0	1	1.1	1.000
1994	NY N	4	10	.286	5.55	21	21	1	131.1	145	42	62	0	0	0	0	37	5	0	.135	12	21	0	1	1.6	1.000
8 yrs.		34	58	.370	4.34	146	134	12	795	791	311	493	4	1	0	0	230	27	0	.117	54	91	6	5	1.0	.960

LEAGUE CHAMPIONSHIP SERIES

Year	Team	W	L	PCT	ERA	G	GS	CG	IP	H	BB	SO	ShO	W	L	SV	AB	H	HR	BA	PO	A	E	DP	TC/G	FA
1992	ATL N	0	0	–	2.45	2	0	0	3.2	2	3	3	0	0	0	0	1	0	0	.000	0	1	0	0	0.5	1.000

WORLD SERIES

Year	Team	W	L	PCT	ERA	G	GS	CG	IP	H	BB	SO	ShO	W	L	SV	AB	H	HR	BA	PO	A	E	DP	TC/G	FA
1992	ATL N	0	0	–	0.00	1	0	0	3	3	0	0	0	0	0	0	1	0	0	.000	0	0	0	0	0.0	–

Willie Smith

SMITH, WILLIE EVERETT
B. Aug. 27, 1967, Savannah, Ga.

BR TR 6'6" 250 lbs.

Year	Team	W	L	PCT	ERA	G	GS	CG	IP	H	BB	SO	ShO	W	L	SV	AB	H	HR	BA	PO	A	E	DP	TC/G	FA
1994	STL N	1	1	.500	9.00	8	0	0	7	9	3	7	0	1	1	0	0	0	0	–	0	0	0	0	0.0	–

Zane Smith

SMITH, ZANE WILLIAM
B. Dec. 28, 1960, Madison, Wis.

BL TL 6'2" 195 lbs.

Year	Team	W	L	PCT	ERA	G	GS	CG	IP	H	BB	SO	ShO	W	L	SV	AB	H	HR	BA	PO	A	E	DP	TC/G	FA
1984	ATL N	1	0	1.000	2.25	3	3	0	20	16	13	16	0	0	0	0	9	5	0	.556	2	3	1	1	2.0	.833
1985		9	10	.474	3.80	42	18	2	147	135	80	85	2	3	4	0	37	6	0	.162	7	35	3	2	1.1	.933
1986		8	16	.333	4.05	38	32	3	204.2	209	105	139	1	1	0	1	59	5	0	.085	7	45	1	4	1.4	.981
1987		15	10	.600	4.09	36	**36**	9	242	245	91	130	3	0	0	0	76	10	0	.132	15	43	0	4	1.6	1.000
1988		5	10	.333	4.30	23	22	3	140.1	159	44	59	0	0	0	0	42	7	0	.167	16	33	1	6	2.2	.980
1989 2 teams	ATL N (17G 1–12) MON N (31G 0–1)																									
" total		1	13	.071	3.49	48	17	0	147	141	52	93	0	0	0	2	32	6	0	.188	7	39	3	0	1.0	.939
1990 2 teams	MON N (22G 6–7) PIT N (11G 6–2)																									
" total		12	9	.571	2.55	33	31	4	215.1	196	50	130	3	0	0	0	68	11	0	.162	10	35	3	5	1.5	.938
1991	PIT N	16	10	.615	3.20	35	35	6	228	234	29	120	3	0	0	0	71	13	0	.183	12	39	3	5	1.5	.944
1992		8	8	.500	3.06	23	22	4	141	138	19	56	3	0	0	0	49	6	0	.122	6	29	0	2	1.5	1.000
1993		3	7	.300	4.55	14	14	1	83	97	22	32	0	0	0	0	25	2	0	.080	8	8	0	2	1.1	1.000
1994		10	8	.556	3.27	25	24	2	157	162	34	57	0	0	0	0	57	12	0	.211	8	40	0	1	1.9	1.000
11 yrs.		88	101	.466	3.56	320	254	34	1725.1	1732	539	917	15	4	5	3	525	83	0	.158	98	349	15	32	1.4	.968

Year	Team	W	L	PCT	ERA	G	GS	CG	IP	H	BB	SO	ShO	Relief Pitching W	L	SV	Batting AB	H	HR	BA	PO	A	E	DP	TC/G	FA

Zane Smith *continued*

LEAGUE CHAMPIONSHIP SERIES

Year	Team	W	L	PCT	ERA	G	GS	CG	IP	H	BB	SO	ShO	W	L	SV	AB	H	HR	BA	PO	A	E	DP	TC/G	FA
1990	PIT N	0	2	.000	6.00	2	1	0	9	14	1	8	0	0	1	0	3	0	0	.000	0	1	0	0	0.5	1.000
1991		1	1	.500	0.61	2	2	0	14.2	15	3	10	0	0	0	0	5	0	0	.000	0	3	0	0	1.5	1.000
2 yrs.		1	3	.250	2.66	4	3	0	23.2	29	4	18	0	0	1	0	8	0	0	.000	0	4	0	0	1.0	1.000

Roger Smithberg

SMITHBERG, ROGER CRAIG
B. Mar. 21, 1966, Elgin, Ill.   BR TR 6'3"   205 lbs.

Year	Team	W	L	PCT	ERA	G	GS	CG	IP	H	BB	SO	ShO	W	L	SV	AB	H	HR	BA	PO	A	E	DP	TC/G	FA
1993	OAK A	1	2	.333	2.75	13	0	0	19.2	13	7	4	0	1	2	3	0	0	0	–	2	6	0	0	0.6	1.000
1994		0	0	–	15.43	2	0	0	2.1	6	1	3	0	0	0	0	0	0	0	–	0	0	0	0	0.0	–
2 yrs.		1	2	.333	4.09	15	0	0	22	19	8	7	0	1	2	3	0	0	0	–	2	6	0	0	0.5	1.000

John Smoltz

SMOLTZ, JOHN ANDREW
B. May 15, 1967, Detroit, Mich.   BR TR 6'3"   210 lbs.

Year	Team	W	L	PCT	ERA	G	GS	CG	IP	H	BB	SO	ShO	W	L	SV	AB	H	HR	BA	PO	A	E	DP	TC/G	FA
1988	ATL N	2	7	.222	5.48	12	12	0	64	74	33	37	0	0	0	0	17	2	0	.118	4	6	0	1	0.8	1.000
1989		12	11	.522	2.94	29	29	5	208	160	72	168	0	0	0	0	62	7	1	.113	23	32	7	2	2.1	.887
1990		14	11	.560	3.85	34	34	6	231.1	206	90	170	2	0	0	0	74	12	0	.162	26	27	3	4	1.6	.946
1991		14	13	.519	3.80	36	36	5	229.2	206	77	148	0	0	0	0	65	7	0	.108	15	34	1	1	1.4	.980
1992		15	12	.556	2.85	35	35	9	246.2	206	80	215	3	0	0	0	75	12	1	.160	23	26	1	3	1.4	.980
1993		15	11	.577	3.62	35	35	3	243.2	208	100	208	1	0	0	0	71	13	0	.183	29	23	0	1	1.5	1.000
1994		6	10	.375	4.14	21	21	1	134.2	120	48	113	0	0	0	0	37	6	1	.162	10	18	1	1	1.4	.966
7 yrs.		78	75	.510	3.59	202	202	29	1358	1180	500	1059	6	0	0	0	401	59	3	.147	130	166	13	13	1.5	.958

LEAGUE CHAMPIONSHIP SERIES

Year	Team	W	L	PCT	ERA	G	GS	CG	IP	H	BB	SO	ShO	W	L	SV	AB	H	HR	BA	PO	A	E	DP	TC/G	FA
1991	ATL N	2	0	1.000	1.76	2	2	1	15.1	14	3	15	1	0	0	0	5	1	0	.200	3	0	0	0	1.5	1.000
1992		2	0	1.000	2.66	3	3	0	20.1	14	10	19	0	0	0	0	7	2	0	.286	0	1	0	0	0.3	1.000
1993		0	1	.000	0.00	1	1	0	6.1	8	5	10	0	0	0	0	1	0	0	.000	0	0	0	0	0.0	–
3 yrs.		4	1	.800	1.93	6	6	1	42	36	18	44	1	0	0	0	13	3	0	.231	3	1	0	0	0.7	1.000

WORLD SERIES

Year	Team	W	L	PCT	ERA	G	GS	CG	IP	H	BB	SO	ShO	W	L	SV	AB	H	HR	BA	PO	A	E	DP	TC/G	FA
1991	ATL N	0	0	–	1.26	2	2	0	14.1	13	1	11	0	0	0	0	2	0	0	.000	2	1	0	0	1.5	1.000
1992		1	0	1.000	2.70	2	2	0	13.1	13	7	12	0	0	0	0	3	0	0	.000	1	2	0	0	1.5	1.000
2 yrs.		1	0	1.000	1.95	4	4	0	27.2	26	8	23	0	0	0	0	5	0	0	.000	3	3	0	0	1.5	1.000
	1st																									

Paul Spoljaric

SPOLJARIC, PAUL NIKOLA
B. Sept. 24, 1970, Kelowna, B. C., Canada   BR TL 6'3"   205 lbs.

Year	Team	W	L	PCT	ERA	G	GS	CG	IP	H	BB	SO	ShO	W	L	SV	AB	H	HR	BA	PO	A	E	DP	TC/G	FA
1994	TOR A	0	1	.000	38.57	2	1	0	2.1	5	9	2	0	0	0	0	0	0	0	–	0	2	1	0	1.5	.667

Jerry Spradlin

SPRADLIN, JERRY CARL
B. June 14, 1967, Fullerton, Calif.   BB TR 6'7"   230 lbs.

Year	Team	W	L	PCT	ERA	G	GS	CG	IP	H	BB	SO	ShO	W	L	SV	AB	H	HR	BA	PO	A	E	DP	TC/G	FA
1993	CIN N	2	1	.667	3.49	37	0	0	49	44	9	24	0	2	1	2	2	0	0	.000	2	2	0	0	0.1	1.000
1994		0	0	–	10.13	6	0	0	8	12	2	4	0	0	0	0	0	0	0	–	1	1	0	0	0.3	1.000
2 yrs.		2	1	.667	4.42	43	0	0	57	56	11	28	0	2	1	2	2	0	0	.000	3	3	0	0	0.1	1.000

Russ Springer

SPRINGER, RUSSELL PAUL
B. Nov. 7, 1968, Alexandria, La.   BR TR 6'4"   195 lbs.

Year	Team	W	L	PCT	ERA	G	GS	CG	IP	H	BB	SO	ShO	W	L	SV	AB	H	HR	BA	PO	A	E	DP	TC/G	FA
1992	NY A	0	0	–	6.19	14	0	0	16	18	10	12	0	0	0	0	0	0	0	–	1	0	0	0	0.1	1.000
1993	CAL A	1	6	.143	7.20	14	9	1	60	73	32	31	0	0	0	0	0	0	0	–	3	2	0	0	0.4	1.000
1994		2	2	.500	5.52	18	5	0	45.2	53	14	28	0	1	0	2	0	0	0	–	2	3	0	1	0.3	1.000
3 yrs.		3	8	.273	6.44	46	14	1	121.2	144	56	71	0	1	0	2	0	0	0	–	5	6	0	1	0.2	1.000

Mike Stanton

STANTON, WILLIAM MICHAEL
B. June 2, 1967, Houston, Tex.   BL TL 6'1"   190 lbs.

Year	Team	W	L	PCT	ERA	G	GS	CG	IP	H	BB	SO	ShO	W	L	SV	AB	H	HR	BA	PO	A	E	DP	TC/G	FA
1989	ATL N	0	1	.000	1.50	20	0	0	24	17	8	27	0	0	1	7	0	0	0	–	1	2	1	0	0.2	.750
1990		0	3	.000	18.00	7	0	0	7	16	4	7	0	0	3	2	0	0	0	–	0	2	0	0	0.3	1.000
1991		5	5	.500	2.88	74	0	0	78	62	21	54	0	5	5	7	6	3	0	.500	6	16	0	0	0.3	1.000
1992		5	4	.556	4.10	65	0	0	63.2	59	20	44	0	5	4	8	2	1	0	.500	3	10	0	2	0.2	1.000
1993		4	6	.400	4.67	63	0	0	52	51	29	43	0	4	6	27	0	0	0	–	1	9	1	1	0.2	.909
1994		3	1	.750	3.55	49	0	0	45.2	41	26	35	0	3	1	3	3	2	0	.667	2	10	0	1	0.2	1.000
6 yrs.		17	20	.459	3.90	278	0	0	270.1	246	108	210	0	17	20	54	11	6	0	.545	13	49	2	4	0.2	.969

LEAGUE CHAMPIONSHIP SERIES

Year	Team	W	L	PCT	ERA	G	GS	CG	IP	H	BB	SO	ShO	W	L	SV	AB	H	HR	BA	PO	A	E	DP	TC/G	FA
1991	ATL N	0	0	–	∞	3	0	0		4	3	3	0	0	0	0	0	0	0	–	0	2	0	0	0.7	1.000
1992		0	0	–	0.00	5	0	0	4.1	2	2	5	0	0	0	0	1	1	0	1.000	0	1	0	0	0.2	1.000
1993		0	0	–	0.00	1	0	0	1	1	1	0	0	0	0	0	0	0	0	–	0	0	0	0	0.0	–
3 yrs.		0	0	–	1.69	9	0	0	5.1	7	6	8	0	0	0	0	1	1	0	1.000	0	3	0	0	0.3	1.000

WORLD SERIES

Year	Team	W	L	PCT	ERA	G	GS	CG	IP	H	BB	SO	ShO	W	L	SV	AB	H	HR	BA	PO	A	E	DP	TC/G	FA
1991	ATL N	1	0	1.000	0.00	5	0	0	7.1	5	2	7	0	1	0	0	0	0	0	–	0	0	0	0	0.0	–
1992		0	0	–	0.00	4	0	0	5	3	2	1	0	0	0	1	0	0	0	–	0	0	0	0	0.0	–
2 yrs.		1	0	1.000	0.00	9	0	0	12.1	8	4	8	0	1	0	1	0	0	0	–	0	0	0	0	0.0	–

Randy St. Claire

ST. CLAIRE, RANDY ANTHONY
Son of Ebba St. Claire.
B. Aug. 23, 1960, Glens Falls, N. Y.   BR TR 6'3"   180 lbs.

Year	Team	W	L	PCT	ERA	G	GS	CG	IP	H	BB	SO	ShO	W	L	SV	AB	H	HR	BA	PO	A	E	DP	TC/G	FA
1984	MON N	0	0	–	4.50	4	0	0	8	11	2	4	0	0	0	0	0	0	0	–	0	1	0	0	0.3	1.000
1985		5	3	.625	3.93	42	0	0	68.2	69	26	25	0	5	3	0	5	1	0	.200	4	13	0	2	0.4	1.000
1986		2	0	1.000	2.37	11	0	0	19	13	6	21	0	2	0	1	1	0	0	.000	1	5	0	0	0.5	1.000
1987		3	3	.500	4.03	44	0	0	67	64	20	43	0	3	3	7	6	2	0	.333	1	9	0	2	0.2	1.000
1988	2 teams	MON N	(6G 0–0)		CIN N	(10G 1–0)																				
"	total	1	0	1.000	3.86	16	0	0	21	24	10	14	0	1	0	0	1	0	0	.000	1	3	0	0	0.3	1.000
1989	MIN A	1	1	.500	5.24	14	0	0	22.1	19	10	14	0	1	1	1	0	0	0	–	4	2	0	1	0.4	1.000
1991	ATL N	0	0	–	4.08	19	0	0	28.2	31	9	30	0	0	0	0	2	1	0	.500	2	5	0	0	0.4	1.000
1992		0	0	–	5.87	10	0	0	15.1	17	8	7	0	0	0	0	0	0	0	–	0	4	0	0	0.4	1.000

Year	Team	W	L	PCT	ERA	G	GS	CG	IP	H	BB	SO	ShO	Relief Pitching W	L	SV	Batting AB	H	HR	BA	PO	A	E	DP	TC/G	FA

Randy St. Claire *continued*

Year	Team	W	L	PCT	ERA	G	GS	CG	IP	H	BB	SO	ShO	W	L	SV	AB	H	HR	BA	PO	A	E	DP	TC/G	FA
1994	TOR A	0	0	–	9.00	2	0	0	2	4	2	2	0	0	0	0	0	0	0	–	1	0	1	0	1.0	.500
9 yrs.		12	6	.667	4.14	162	0	0	252	252	93	160	0	12	6	9	15	4	0	.267	14	42	1	5	0.4	.982

WORLD SERIES

| 1991 | ATL N | 0 | 0 | – | 9.00 | 1 | 0 | 0 | 1 | 1 | 1 | 0 | 0 | 0 | 0 | 0 | 0 | 0 | 0 | – | 0 | 0 | 0 | 0 | 0.0 | – |

Dave Stevens

STEVENS, DAVID JAMES
B. Mar. 4, 1970, Fullerton, Calif.   BR TR 6'3" 210 lbs.

| 1994 | MIN A | 5 | 2 | .714 | 6.80 | 24 | 0 | 0 | 45 | 55 | 23 | 24 | 0 | 5 | 2 | 0 | 0 | 0 | 0 | – | 2 | 5 | 0 | 0 | 0.3 | 1.000 |

Dave Stewart

STEWART, DAVID KEITH
B. Feb. 19, 1957, Oakland, Calif.   BR TR 6'2" 200 lbs.

1978	LA N	0	0	–	0.00	1	0	0	2	1	0	1	0	0	0	0	0	0	0	–	0	0	0	0	0.0	–
1981		4	3	.571	2.51	32	0	0	43	40	14	29	0	4	3	6	5	2	0	.400	4	7	0	0	0.3	1.000
1982		9	8	.529	3.81	45	14	0	146.1	137	49	80	0	6	3	1	39	7	0	.179	15	16	3	2	0.8	.912
1983	2 teams					LA N (46G 5–2)			TEX A (8G 5–2)																	
"	total	10	4	.714	2.60	54	9	2	135	117	50	78	0	5	2	8	7	1	0	.143	9	17	1	2	0.5	.963
1984	TEX A	7	14	.333	4.73	32	27	3	192.1	193	87	119	0	0	1	0	0	0	0	–	11	19	3	2	1.0	.909
1985	2 teams					TEX A (42G 0–6)			PHI N (4G 0–0)																	
"	total	0	6	.000	5.46	46	5	0	85.2	91	41	66	0	0	4	4	0	0	0	–	6	10	3	2	0.4	.842
1986	2 teams					PHI N (8G 0–0)			OAK A (29G 9–5)																	
"	total	9	5	.643	3.95	37	17	4	161.2	152	69	111	1	0	0	0	0	0	0	–	10	18	1	2	0.8	.966
1987	OAK A	20	13	.606	3.68	37	37	8	261.1	224	105	205	1	0	0	0	0	0	0	–	18	20	1	0	1.1	.974
1988		21	12	.636	3.23	37	37	14	275.2	240	110	192	2	0	0	0	0	0	0	–	26	16	5	2	1.3	.894
1989		21	9	.700	3.32	36	36	8	257.2	260	69	155	0	0	0	0	0	0	0	–	22	28	4	4	1.5	.926
1990		22	11	.667	2.56	36	36	11	267	226	83	166	4	0	0	0	0	0	0	–	25	23	0	2	1.3	1.000
1991		11	11	.500	5.18	35	35	2	226	245	105	144	1	0	0	0	0	0	0	–	14	19	2	0	1.0	.943
1992		12	10	.545	3.66	31	31	2	199.1	175	79	130	0	0	0	0	0	0	0	–	8	13	3	2	0.8	.875
1993	TOR A	12	8	.600	4.44	26	26	0	162	146	72	96	0	0	0	0	0	0	0	–	13	9	0	1	0.8	1.000
1994		7	8	.467	5.87	22	22	1	133.1	151	62	111	0	0	0	0	0	0	0	–	11	6	0	0	0.8	1.000
15 yrs.		165	122	.575	3.86	507	332	55	2548.1	2398	995	1683	9	15	13	19	51	10	0	.196	192	221	26	21	0.9	.941

DIVISIONAL PLAYOFF SERIES

| 1981 | LA N | 0 | 2 | .000 | 40.50 | 2 | 0 | 0 | 0.2 | 4 | 0 | 1 | 0 | 0 | 2 | 0 | 0 | 0 | 0 | – | 0 | 0 | 0 | 0 | 0.0 | – |

LEAGUE CHAMPIONSHIP SERIES

1988	OAK A	1	0	1.000	1.35	2	2	0	13.1	9	6	11	0	0	0	0	0	0	0	–	0	2	0	0	1.0	1.000
1989		2	0	1.000	2.81	2	2	0	16	13	3	9	0	0	0	0	0	0	0	–	0	1	0	0	0.5	1.000
1990		2	0	1.000	1.13	2	2	0	16	8	2	4	0	0	0	0	0	0	0	–	0	3	0	0	1.5	1.000
1992		1	0	1.000	2.70	2	2	1	16.2	14	6	7	0	0	0	0	0	0	0	–	1	1	0	0	1.0	1.000
1993	TOR A	2	0	1.000	2.03	2	2	0	13.1	8	8	8	0	0	0	0	0	0	0	–	2	0	0	0	1.0	1.000
5 yrs.		8	0	1.000	2.03	10	10	1	75.1	52	25	39	0	0	0	0	0	0	0	–	3	7	0	0	1.0	1.000

WORLD SERIES

1981	LA N	0	0	–	0.00	2	0	0	1.2	1	2	1	0	0	0	0	0	0	0	–	0	0	1	0	0.5	.000
1988	OAK A	0	1	.000	3.14	2	2	0	14.1	12	5	5	0	0	0	0	3	0	0	.000	0	1	0	0	0.5	1.000
1989		2	0	1.000	1.69	2	2	1	16	10	2	14	1	0	0	0	3	0	0	.000	3	0	1	0	2.0	.750
1990		0	2	.000	3.46	2	2	1	13	10	6	5	0	0	0	0	0	0	0	.000	2	1	1	0	2.0	.750
1993	TOR A	0	1	.000	6.75	2	2	0	12	10	8	8	0	0	0	0	1	0	0	–	1	1	0	0	1.0	1.000
5 yrs.		2	4	.333	3.47	10	8	2	57	43	23	33	1	0	0	0	7	0	0	.000	6	3	3	0	1.2	.750
	10th																									

Phil Stidham

STIDHAM, PHILLIP WAYNE
B. Nov. 18, 1968, Tulsa, Okla.   BR TR 6' 180 lbs.

| 1994 | DET A | 0 | 0 | – | 24.92 | 5 | 0 | 0 | 4.1 | 12 | 4 | 4 | 0 | 0 | 0 | 0 | 0 | 0 | 0 | – | 0 | 0 | 0 | 0 | 0.0 | – |

Todd Stottlemyre

STOTTLEMYRE, TODD VERNON
Son of Mel Stottlemyre.   Brother of Mel Stottlemyre.
B. May 20, 1965, Sunnyside, Wash.   BL TR 6'3" 195 lbs.

1988	TOR A	4	8	.333	5.69	28	16	0	98	109	46	67	0	2	1	0	0	0	0	–	7	11	0	0	0.6	1.000
1989		7	7	.500	3.88	27	18	0	127.2	137	44	63	0	0	1	0	0	0	0	–	7	16	5	1	1.0	.821
1990		13	17	.433	4.34	33	33	4	203	214	69	115	0	0	0	0	0	0	0	–	17	30	1	5	1.5	.979
1991		15	8	.652	3.78	34	34	1	219	194	75	116	0	0	0	0	0	0	0	–	30	21	2	2	1.6	.962
1992		12	11	.522	4.50	28	27	6	174	175	63	98	2	1	0	0	0	0	0	–	15	17	1	2	1.2	.970
1993		11	12	.478	4.84	30	28	1	176.2	204	69	98	1	0	0	0	0	0	0	–	11	19	1	2	1.0	.968
1994		7	7	.500	4.22	26	19	3	140.2	149	48	105	0	2	0	1	0	0	0	–	10	12	0	0	0.8	1.000
7 yrs.		69	70	.496	4.39	206	175	15	1139	1182	414	662	4	5	2	1	0	0	0	–	97	126	10	12	1.1	.957

LEAGUE CHAMPIONSHIP SERIES

1989	TOR A	0	1	.000	7.20	1	1	0	5	7	2	3	0	0	0	0	0	0	0	–	0	0	0	0	0.0	–
1991		0	1	.000	9.82	1	1	0	3.2	7	1	3	0	0	0	0	0	0	0	–	1	0	0	0	1.0	1.000
1992		0	0	–	2.45	1	0	0	3.2	3	0	1	0	0	0	0	0	0	0	–	0	0	0	0	0.0	–
1993		0	1	.000	7.50	1	1	0	6	6	4	4	0	0	0	0	0	0	0	–	2	0	0	0	2.0	1.000
4 yrs.		0	3	.000	6.87	4	3	0	18.1	23	7	11	0	0	0	0	0	0	0	–	3	0	0	0	0.8	1.000

WORLD SERIES

1992	TOR A	0	0	–	0.00	4	0	0	3.2	4	0	4	0	0	0	0	0	0	0	–	0	0	0	0	0.0	–
1993		0	0	–	27.00	1	1	0	2	3	4	1	0	0	0	0	0	0	0	–	0	0	0	0	0.0	–
2 yrs.		0	0	–	9.53	5	1	0	5.2	7	4	5	0	0	0	0	0	0	0	–	0	0	0	0	0.0	–

Rick Sutcliffe

SUTCLIFFE, RICHARD LEE
B. June 21, 1956, Independence, Mo.   BL TR 6'7" 215 lbs.

| 1976 | LA N | 0 | 0 | – | 0.00 | 1 | 1 | 0 | 5 | 2 | 1 | 3 | 0 | 0 | 0 | 0 | 1 | 0 | 0 | .000 | 0 | 0 | 0 | 0 | 0.0 | – |
| 1978 | | 0 | 0 | – | 0.00 | 2 | 0 | 0 | 2 | 2 | 1 | 0 | 0 | 0 | 0 | 0 | 0 | 0 | 0 | – | 0 | 1 | 0 | 1 | 0.5 | 1.000 |

Year	Team	W	L	PCT	ERA	G	GS	CG	IP	H	BB	SO	ShO	Relief Pitching W	L	SV	Batting AB	H	HR	BA	PO	A	E	DP	TC/G	FA

Rick Sutcliffe *continued*

Year	Team	W	L	PCT	ERA	G	GS	CG	IP	H	BB	SO	ShO	W	L	SV	AB	H	HR	BA	PO	A	E	DP	TC/G	FA
1979		17	10	.630	3.46	39	30	5	242	217	97	117	1	1	2	0	85	21	1	.247	18	24	0	1	1.1	1.000
1980		3	9	.250	5.56	42	10	1	110	122	55	59	1	2	5	5	27	4	0	.148	6	13	0	0	0.5	1.000
1981		2	2	.500	4.02	14	6	0	47	41	20	16	0	0	0	0	11	2	0	.182	6	8	0	0	1.0	1.000
1982	CLE A	14	8	.636	2.96	34	27	6	216	174	98	142	1	2	1	1	0	0	0	—	14	32	1	1	1.4	.979
1983		17	11	.607	4.29	36	35	10	243.1	251	102	160	2	1	0	0	0	0	0	—	36	29	0	1	1.8	1.000
1984	2 teams	CLE A (15G 4–5)				CHI N (20G 16–1)																				
"	total	20	6	.769	3.64	35	35	9	244.2	234	85	213	3	0	0	0	56	14	0	.250	19	35	2	1	1.6	.964
1985	CHI N	8	8	.500	3.18	20	20	6	130	119	44	102	3	0	0	0	43	10	1	.233	12	23	1	0	1.8	.972
1986		5	14	.263	4.64	28	27	4	176.2	166	96	122	1	0	0	0	53	11	1	.208	8	30	1	4	1.4	.974
1987		18	10	.643	3.68	34	34	6	237.1	223	106	174	1	0	0	0	81	12	0	.148	12	54	4	4	2.1	.943
1988		13	14	.481	3.86	32	32	12	226	232	70	144	2	0	0	0	75	12	1	.160	21	37	3	2	1.9	.951
1989		16	11	.593	3.66	35	34	5	229	202	69	153	1	0	0	0	70	10	0	.143	22	31	1	3	1.5	.981
1990		0	2	.000	5.91	5	5	0	21.1	25	12	7	0	0	0	0	5	0	0	.000	2	5	0	0	1.4	1.000
1991		6	5	.545	4.10	19	18	0	96.2	96	45	52	0	0	0	0	32	3	0	.094	10	12	0	2	1.2	1.000
1992	BAL A	16	15	.516	4.47	36	36	5	237.1	251	74	109	2	0	0	0	0	0	0	—	11	24	3	2	1.1	.921
1993		10	10	.500	5.75	29	28	3	166	212	74	80	0	0	0	0	0	0	0	—	9	30	1	2	1.4	.975
1994	STL N	6	4	.600	6.52	16	14	0	67.2	93	32	26	0	0	0	0	23	3	0	.130	5	16	0	1	1.3	1.000
	18 yrs.	171	139	.552	4.08	457	392	72	2698	2662	1081	1679	18	6	8	6	562	102	4	.181	211	404	17	25	1.4	.973

LEAGUE CHAMPIONSHIP SERIES

Year	Team	W	L	PCT	ERA	G	GS	CG	IP	H	BB	SO	ShO	W	L	SV	AB	H	HR	BA	PO	A	E	DP	TC/G	FA
1984	CHI N	1	1	.500	3.38	2	2	0	13.1	9	8	10	0	0	0	0	6	3	1	.500	0	0	0	0	0.0	—
1989		0	0	—	4.50	1	1	0	6	5	4	2	0	0	0	0	2	1	0	.500	0	2	0	0	2.0	1.000
	2 yrs.	1	1	.500	3.72	3	3	0	19.1	14	12	12	0	0	0	0	8	4	1	.500	0	2	0	0	0.7	1.000

Russ Swan

SWAN, RUSSELL HOWARD
B. Jan. 3, 1964, Fremont, Calif.
BL TL 6'4" 210 lbs.

Year	Team	W	L	PCT	ERA	G	GS	CG	IP	H	BB	SO	ShO	W	L	SV	AB	H	HR	BA	PO	A	E	DP	TC/G	FA
1989	SF N	0	2	.000	10.80	2	2	0	6.2	11	4	2	0	0	0	0	2	0	0	.000	1	1	0	0	1.0	1.000
1990	2 teams	SF N (2G 0–1)			SEA A (11G 2–3)																					
"	total	2	4	.333	3.65	13	9	0	49.1	48	22	16	0	0	0	0	1	0	0	.000	3	8	0	0	0.8	1.000
1991	SEA A	6	2	.750	3.43	63	0	0	78.2	81	28	33	0	6	2	2	0	0	0	—	3	16	1	1	0.3	.950
1992		3	10	.231	4.74	55	9	1	104.1	104	45	45	0	1	5	9	0	0	0	—	7	23	1	0	0.6	.968
1993		3	3	.500	9.15	23	0	0	19.2	25	18	10	0	3	3	0	0	0	0	—	0	6	0	0	0.3	1.000
1994	CLE A	0	1	.000	11.25	12	0	0	8	13	7	2	0	0	1	0	0	0	0	—	0	2	0	0	0.2	1.000
	6 yrs.	14	22	.389	4.83	168	20	1	266.2	282	124	108	0	10	11	11	3	0	0	.000	14	56	2	1	0.4	.972

Bill Swift

SWIFT, WILLIAM CHARLES
B. Oct. 27, 1961, Portland, Me.
BR TR 6' 170 lbs.

Year	Team	W	L	PCT	ERA	G	GS	CG	IP	H	BB	SO	ShO	W	L	SV	AB	H	HR	BA	PO	A	E	DP	TC/G	FA
1985	SEA A	6	10	.375	4.77	23	21	0	120.2	131	48	55	0	1	0	0	0	0	0	—	10	18	1	1	1.3	.966
1986		2	9	.182	5.46	29	17	1	115.1	148	55	55	0	0	0	0	0	0	0	—	13	21	1	1	1.2	.971
1988		8	12	.400	4.59	38	24	6	174.2	199	65	47	1	3	1	0	0	0	0	—	19	33	4	3	1.5	.929
1989		7	3	.700	4.43	37	16	0	130	140	38	45	0	2	0	1	0	0	0	—	18	39	2	5	1.6	.966
1990		6	4	.600	2.39	55	8	0	128	135	21	42	0	3	2	6	0	0	0	—	10	21	2	1	0.6	.939
1991		1	2	.333	1.99	71	0	0	90.1	74	26	48	0	1	2	17	0	0	0	—	6	25	3	4	0.5	.912
1992	SF N	10	4	.714	2.08	30	22	3	164.2	144	43	77	2	1	1	1	51	8	0	.157	18	33	1	3	1.7	.981
1993		21	8	.724	2.82	34	34	1	232.2	195	55	157	1	0	0	0	80	21	0	.263	17	44	6	3	2.0	.910
1994		8	7	.533	3.38	17	17	0	109.1	109	31	62	0	0	0	0	32	6	0	.188	8	12	2	1	1.3	.909
	9 yrs.	69	59	.539	3.51	334	159	11	1265.2	1275	382	588	4	11	6	25	163	35	0	.215	119	246	22	22	1.2	.943

Greg Swindell

SWINDELL, FOREST GREGORY
B. Jan. 2, 1965, Fort Worth, Tex.
BR TL 6'2" 225 lbs.

Year	Team	W	L	PCT	ERA	G	GS	CG	IP	H	BB	SO	ShO	W	L	SV	AB	H	HR	BA	PO	A	E	DP	TC/G	FA
1986	CLE A	5	2	.714	4.23	9	9	1	61.2	57	15	46	0	0	0	0	0	0	0	—	2	12	0	1	1.6	1.000
1987		3	8	.273	5.10	16	15	4	102.1	112	37	97	1	0	0	0	0	0	0	—	0	13	1	1	0.9	.929
1988		18	14	.563	3.20	33	33	12	242	234	45	180	4	0	0	0	0	0	0	—	8	29	1	0	1.2	.974
1989		13	6	.684	3.37	28	28	5	184.1	170	51	129	2	0	0	0	0	0	0	—	7	25	0	1	1.1	1.000
1990		12	9	.571	4.40	34	34	3	214.2	245	47	135	0	0	0	0	0	0	0	—	8	20	1	1	0.9	.966
1991		9	16	.360	3.48	33	33	7	238	241	31	169	0	0	0	0	0	0	0	—	7	30	1	2	1.2	.974
1992	CIN N	12	8	.600	2.70	31	30	5	213.2	210	41	138	3	0	0	0	80	10	0	.125	6	33	1	2	1.3	.975
1993	HOU N	12	13	.480	4.16	31	30	1	190.1	215	40	124	1	0	0	0	60	11	0	.183	2	32	1	1	1.1	.971
1994		8	9	.471	4.37	24	24	1	148.1	175	26	74	0	0	0	0	44	11	0	.250	6	13	1	0	0.8	.950
	9 yrs.	92	85	.520	3.74	239	236	39	1595.1	1659	333	1092	11	0	0	0	184	32	0	.174	46	207	7	8	1.1	.973

Jeff Tabaka

TABAKA, JEFFREY JON
B. Jan. 17, 1964, Barberton, Ohio
BR TL 6'2" 195 lbs.

Year	Team	W	L	PCT	ERA	G	GS	CG	IP	H	BB	SO	ShO	W	L	SV	AB	H	HR	BA	PO	A	E	DP	TC/G	FA
1994	2 teams	PIT N (5G 0–0)			SD N (34G 3–1)																					
"	total	3	1	.750	5.27	39	0	0	41	32	27	32	0	3	1	1	1	1	0	1.000	3	4	1	0	0.2	.875

Jeff Tackett

TACKETT, JEFFREY WILSON
B. Dec. 1, 1965, Fresno, Calif.
BR TR 6'2" 200 lbs.

Year	Team	W	L	PCT	ERA	G	GS	CG	IP	H	BB	SO	ShO	W	L	SV	AB	H	HR	BA	PO	A	E	DP	TC/G	FA
1993	BAL A	0	0	—	0.00	1	0	0	1	1	1	1	0	0	0	0	0	0	0	*	0	0	0	0	0.0	—

Kevin Tapani

TAPANI, KEVIN RAY
B. Feb. 18, 1964, Des Moines, Iowa.
BR TR 6' 180 lbs.

Year	Team	W	L	PCT	ERA	G	GS	CG	IP	H	BB	SO	ShO	W	L	SV	AB	H	HR	BA	PO	A	E	DP	TC/G	FA
1989	2 teams	NY N (3G 0–0)			MIN A (5G 2–2)																					
"	total	2	2	.500	3.83	8	5	0	40	39	12	23	0	0	0	0	2	0	0	.000	4	4	0	1	1.0	1.000
1990	MIN A	12	8	.600	4.07	28	28	1	159.1	164	29	101	1	0	0	0	0	0	0	—	14	20	1	1	1.3	.971
1991		16	9	.640	2.99	34	34	4	244	225	40	135	1	0	0	0	0	0	0	—	26	26	1	2	1.6	.981
1992		16	11	.593	3.97	34	34	4	220	226	48	138	1	0	0	0	0	0	0	—	17	26	2	0	1.3	.956
1993		12	15	.444	4.43	36	35	3	225.2	243	57	150	1	0	0	0	0	0	0	—	17	32	0	2	1.4	1.000
1994		11	7	.611	4.62	24	24	4	156	181	39	91	1	0	0	0	0	0	0	—	11	27	1	2	1.6	.974
	6 yrs.	69	52	.570	3.94	164	160	16	1045	1078	225	638	5	0	0	0	2	0	0	.000	89	135	5	8	1.4	.978

Year	Team	W	L	PCT	ERA	G	GS	CG	IP	H	BB	SO	ShO	Relief Pitching W	L	SV	Batting AB	H	HR	BA	PO	A	E	DP	TC/G	FA

Kevin Tapani *continued*

LEAGUE CHAMPIONSHIP SERIES

| 1991 | MIN A | 0 | 1 | .000 | 7.84 | 2 | 2 | 0 | 10.1 | 16 | 3 | 9 | 0 | 0 | 0 | 0 | 0 | 0 | 0 | — | 3 | 0 | 0 | 0 | 1.5 | 1.000 |

WORLD SERIES

| 1991 | MIN A | 1 | 1 | .500 | 4.50 | 2 | 2 | 0 | 12 | 13 | 2 | 7 | 0 | 1 | 0 | 0 | 1 | 0 | 0 | .000 | 0 | 2 | 0 | 0 | 1.0 | 1.000 |

Julian Tavarez

TAVAREZ, JULIAN
Born Julian Tavarez (Carmen).
B. May 22, 1973, Santiago, Dominican Republic

BR TR 6'2" 165 lbs.

1993	CLE A	2	2	.500	6.57	8	7	0	37	53	13	19	0	0	0	0	0	0	0	—	2	3	0	2	0.6	1.000
1994		0	1	.000	21.60	1	1	0	1.2	6	1	0	0	0	0	0	0	0	0	—	0	0	0	0	0.0	—
2 yrs.		2	3	.400	7.22	9	8	0	38.2	59	14	19	0	0	0	0	0	0	0	—	2	3	0	2	0.6	1.000

Bill Taylor

TAYLOR, WILLIAM HOWELL
B. Oct. 16, 1961, Monticello, Fla.

BR TR 6'8" 200 lbs.

| 1994 | OAK A | 1 | 3 | .250 | 3.50 | 41 | 0 | 0 | 46.1 | 38 | 18 | 48 | 0 | 1 | 3 | 1 | 0 | 0 | 0 | — | 2 | 3 | 0 | 0 | 0.1 | 1.000 |

Kerry Taylor

TAYLOR, KERRY THOMAS
B. Jan. 25, 1971, Bemidji, Minn.

BR TR 6'3" 200 lbs.

1993	SD N	0	5	.000	6.45	36	7	0	68.1	72	49	45	0	0	0	0	12	0	0	.000	4	7	0	0	0.3	1.000
1994		0	0	—	8.31	1	1	0	4.1	9	1	3	0	0	0	0	2	0	0	.000	0	0	0	0	0.0	—
2 yrs.		0	5	.000	6.56	37	8	0	72.2	81	50	48	0	0	0	0	14	0	0	.000	4	7	0	0	0.3	1.000

Dave Telgheder

TELGHEDER, DAVID WILLIAM
B. Nov. 11, 1966, Middletown, N. Y.

BR TR 6'3" 212 lbs.

1993	NY N	6	2	.750	4.76	24	7	0	75.2	82	21	35	0	1	0	0	15	1	0	.067	4	9	0	0	0.5	1.000
1994		0	1	.000	7.20	6	0	0	10	11	8	4	0	0	1	0	0	0	0		0	0	1	0	0.2	.000
2 yrs.		6	3	.667	5.04	30	7	0	85.2	93	29	39	0	1	1	0	15	1	0	.067	4	9	1	0	0.5	.929

Bob Tewksbury

TEWKSBURY, ROBERT ALAN
B. Nov. 30, 1960, Concord, N. H.

BR TR 6'4" 200 lbs.

1986	NY A	9	5	.643	3.31	23	20	2	130.1	144	31	49	0	0	0	0	0	0	0	—	7	29	1	2	1.6	.973
1987	2 teams	NY A (8G 1–4)		CHI N (7G 0–4)																						
"	total	1	8	.111	6.66	15	9	0	51.1	79	20	22	0	0	1	0	5	0	0	.000	3	6	1	1	0.7	.900
1988	CHI N	0	0	—	8.10	1	1	0	3.1	6	2	1	0	0	0	0	2	0	0	.000	0	1	0	0	1.0	1.000
1989	STL N	1	0	1.000	3.30	7	4	1	30	25	10	17	1	0	0	0	9	1	0	.111	1	3	0	0	0.6	1.000
1990		10	9	.526	3.47	28	20	3	145.1	151	15	50	2	0	0	1	41	7	0	.171	6	20	1	2	1.0	.963
1991		11	12	.478	3.25	30	30	3	191	206	38	75	0	0	0	0	58	9	0	.155	9	34	2	2	1.5	.956
1992		16	5	.762	2.16	33	32	5	233	217	20	91	0	1	0	0	70	6	0	.086	14	42	1	2	1.7	.982
1993		17	10	.630	3.83	32	32	2	213.2	258	20	97	0	0	0	0	69	14	0	.203	19	46	0	2	2.0	1.000
1994		12	10	.545	5.32	24	24	4	155.2	190	22	79	1	0	0	0	54	10	0	.185	12	31	1	1	1.8	.977
9 yrs.		77	59	.566	3.62	193	172	20	1153.2	1276	178	481	4	1	1	1	308	47	0	.153	71	212	7	12	1.5	.976

Bobby Thigpen

THIGPEN, ROBERT THOMAS
B. July 17, 1963, Tallahassee, Fla.

BR TR 6'3" 195 lbs.

1986	CHI A	2	0	1.000	1.77	20	0	0	35.2	26	12	20	0	2	0	7	0	0	0	—	2	4	0	1	0.3	1.000
1987		7	5	.583	2.73	51	0	0	89	86	24	52	0	7	5	16	0	0	0	—	8	14	2	1	0.5	.917
1988		5	8	.385	3.30	68	0	0	90	96	33	62	0	5	8	34	0	0	0	—	5	11	0	2	0.2	1.000
1989		2	6	.250	3.76	61	0	0	79	62	40	47	0	2	6	34	0	0	0	—	7	7	0	0	0.2	1.000
1990		4	6	.400	1.83	77	0	0	88.2	60	32	70	0	4	6	57[1]	0	0	0	—	10	8	1	2	0.2	.947
1991		7	5	.583	3.49	67	0	0	69.2	63	38	47	0	7	5	30	0	0	0	—	3	15	1	0	0.3	.947
1992		1	3	.250	4.75	55	0	0	55	58	33	45	0	1	3	22	0	0	0	—	7	6	0	2	0.2	1.000
1993	2 teams	CHI A (25G 0–0)		PHI N (17G 3–1)																						
"	total	3	1	.750	5.83	42	0	0	54	74	21	29	0	3	1	1	1	0	0	.000	1	5	0	2	0.1	1.000
1994	SEA A	0	2	.000	9.39	7	0	0	7.2	12	5	4	0	0	2	0	0	0	0	—	0	1	0	0	0.1	1.000
9 yrs.		31	36	.463	3.43	448	0	0	568.2	537	238	376	0	31	36	201	1	0	0	.000	43	71	4	10	0.3	.966

LEAGUE CHAMPIONSHIP SERIES

| 1993 | PHI N | 0 | 0 | — | 5.40 | 1 | 0 | 0 | 1.2 | 1 | 1 | 3 | 0 | 0 | 0 | 0 | 0 | 0 | 0 | — | 0 | 0 | 0 | 0 | 0.0 | — |

WORLD SERIES

| 1993 | PHI N | 0 | 0 | — | 0.00 | 2 | 0 | 0 | 2.2 | 1 | 1 | 1 | 0 | 0 | 0 | 0 | 0 | 0 | 0 | — | 0 | 1 | 0 | 0 | 0.5 | 1.000 |

Mark Thompson

THOMPSON, MARK RADFORD
B. Apr. 7, 1971, Russellville, Ky.

BR TR 6'2" 205 lbs.

| 1994 | CLR N | 1 | 1 | .500 | 9.00 | 2 | 2 | 0 | 9 | 16 | 8 | 5 | 0 | 0 | 0 | 0 | 4 | 0 | 0 | .000 | 1 | 0 | 0 | 0 | 0.5 | 1.000 |

Mike Timlin

TIMLIN, MICHAEL AUGUST
B. Mar. 10, 1966, Midland, Tex.

BR TR 6'4" 205 lbs.

1991	TOR A	11	6	.647	3.16	63	3	0	108.1	94	50	85	0	10	5	3	0	0	0	—	9	17	2	0	0.4	.929
1992		0	2	.000	4.12	26	0	0	43.2	45	20	35	0	0	2	1	0	0	0	—	2	5	0	1	0.3	1.000
1993		4	2	.667	4.69	54	0	0	55.2	63	27	49	0	4	2	1	0	0	0	—	7	10	1	1	0.3	.944
1994		0	1	.000	5.18	34	0	0	40	41	20	38	0	0	1	2	0	0	0	—	5	5	0	0	0.3	1.000
4 yrs.		15	11	.577	4.00	177	3	0	247.2	243	117	207	0	14	10	7	0	0	0	—	23	37	3	2	0.4	.952

LEAGUE CHAMPIONSHIP SERIES

1991	TOR A	0	1	.000	3.18	4	0	0	5.2	5	2	5	0	0	1	0	0	0	0	—	0	2	1	0	0.8	.667
1992		0	0	—	6.75	2	0	0	1.1	4	0	1	0	0	0	0	0	0	0	—	0	0	0	0	0.0	—
1993		0	0	—	3.86	1	0	0	2.1	3	0	2	0	0	0	0	0	0	0	—	1	1	0	0	2.0	1.000
3 yrs.		0	1	.000	3.86	7	0	0	9.1	12	2	8	0	0	1	0	0	0	0	—	1	3	1	0	0.7	.800

Year	Team	W	L	PCT	ERA	G	GS	CG	IP	H	BB	SO	ShO	Relief Pitching W	L	SV	Batting AB	H	HR	BA	PO	A	E	DP	TC/G	FA

Mike Timlin *continued*

WORLD SERIES

1992	TOR A	0	0	–	0.00	2	0	0	1.1	0	0	0	0	0	0	1	0	0	0	–	0	1	0	0	0.5	1.000
1993		0	0	–	0.00	2	0	0	2.1	2	0	4	0	0	0	0	0	0	0	–	0	0	0	0	0.0	–
2 yrs.		0	0	–	0.00	4	0	0	3.2	2	0	4	0	0	0	1	0	0	0	–	0	1	0	0	0.3	1.000

Andy Tomberlin

TOMBERLIN, ANDY LEE
B. Nov. 7, 1966, Monroe, N. C.

BL TL 5'11" 160 lbs.

| 1994 | BOS A | 0 | 0 | – | 0.00 | 1 | 0 | 0 | 2 | 1 | 1 | 1 | 0 | 1 | 0 | 0 | 0 | 0 | 1 | * | 0 | 0 | 0 | 0 | 0.0 | – |

Randy Tomlin

TOMLIN, RANDY LEON
B. June 14, 1966, Bainbridge, Md.

BL TL 5'11" 179 lbs.

1990	PIT N	4	4	.500	2.55	12	12	2	77.2	62	12	42	0	0	0	0	25	1	0	.040	1	19	0	0	1.7	1.000
1991		8	7	.533	2.98	31	27	4	175	170	54	104	2	0	0	0	52	10	0	.192	9	36	2	0	1.5	.957
1992		14	9	.609	3.41	35	33	1	208.2	226	42	90	1	0	0	0	65	9	0	.138	12	52	1	3	1.9	.985
1993		4	8	.333	4.85	18	18	1	98.1	109	15	44	0	0	0	0	33	6	0	.182	9	18	1	2	1.6	.964
1994		0	3	.000	3.92	10	4	0	20.2	23	10	17	0	0	0	1	6	3	0	.500	1	3	0	0	0.4	1.000
5 yrs.		30	31	.492	3.43	106	94	8	580.1	590	133	297	3	0	1	0	181	29	0	.160	32	128	4	5	1.5	.976

LEAGUE CHAMPIONSHIP SERIES

1991	PIT N	0	0	–	3.00	1	1	0	6	6	2	1	0	0	0	0	2	0	0	.000	1	0	0	0	1.0	1.000
1992		0	0	–	6.75	2	0	0	2.2	5	1	0	0	0	0	0	0	0	0	–	0	1	0	0	0.5	1.000
2 yrs.		0	0	–	4.15	3	1	0	8.2	11	3	1	0	0	0	0	2	0	0	.000	1	1	0	0	0.7	1.000

Salomon Torres

TORRES, SALOMON
Born Salomon Torres (Ramirez).
B. Mar. 11, 1972, San Pedro de Macoris, Dominican Republic

BR TR 5'11" 150 lbs.

1993	SF N	3	5	.375	4.03	8	8	0	44.2	37	27	23	0	0	0	0	13	3	0	.231	4	9	0	0	1.6	1.000
1994		2	8	.200	5.44	16	14	1	84.1	95	34	42	0	0	0	0	26	4	0	.154	4	7	1	0	0.8	.917
2 yrs.		5	13	.278	4.95	24	22	1	129	132	61	65	0	0	0	0	39	7	0	.179	8	16	1	0	1.0	.960

Steve Trachsel

TRACHSEL, STEPHEN CHRISTOPHER
B. Oct. 31, 1970, Oxnard, Calif.

BR TR 6'3" 185 lbs.

1993	CHI N	0	2	.000	4.58	3	3	0	19.2	16	3	14	0	0	0	0	6	1	0	.167	1	5	0	0	2.0	1.000
1994		9	7	.563	3.21	22	22	1	146	133	54	108	0	0	0	0	43	8	0	.186	10	33	2	0	2.0	.956
2 yrs.		9	9	.500	3.37	25	25	1	165.2	149	57	122	0	0	0	0	49	9	0	.184	11	38	2	0	2.0	.961

Rick Trlicek

TRLICEK, RICHARD ALAN
B. Apr. 26, 1969, Houston, Tex.

BR TR 6'3" 200 lbs.

1992	TOR A	0	0	–	10.80	2	0	0	1.2	2	2	1	0	0	0	0	0	0	0	–	0	0	0	0	0.0	–
1993	LA N	1	2	.333	4.08	41	0	0	64	59	21	41	0	1	2	1	4	1	0	.250	7	12	0	2	0.5	1.000
1994	BOS A	1	1	.500	8.06	12	1	0	22.1	32	16	7	0	1	0	0	0	0	0	–	4	1	0	0	0.4	1.000
3 yrs.		2	3	.400	5.22	55	1	0	88	93	39	49	0	2	2	1	4	1	0	.250	11	13	0	2	0.4	1.000

Mike Trombley

TROMBLEY, MICHAEL SCOTT
B. Apr. 14, 1967, Springfield, Mass.

BR TR 6'2" 200 lbs.

1992	MIN A	3	2	.600	3.30	10	7	0	46.1	43	17	38	0	0	0	0	0	0	0	–	1	6	0	1	0.7	1.000
1993		6	6	.500	4.88	44	10	0	114.1	131	41	85	0	3	1	2	0	0	0	–	6	19	0	2	0.6	1.000
1994		2	0	1.000	6.33	24	0	0	48.1	56	18	32	0	2	0	0	0	0	0	–	5	3	1	0	0.4	.889
3 yrs.		11	8	.579	4.87	78	17	0	209	230	76	155	0	5	1	2	0	0	0	–	12	28	1	3	0.5	.976

Matt Turner

TURNER, WILLIAM MATTHEW
B. Feb. 18, 1967, Lexington, Ky.

BR TR 6'5" 215 lbs.

1993	FLA N	4	5	.444	2.91	55	0	0	68	55	26	59	0	4	5	0	2	0	0	.000	3	11	0	0	0.3	1.000
1994	CLE A	1	0	1.000	2.13	9	0	0	12.2	13	7	5	0	1	0	1	0	0	0	–	0	0	0	0	0.0	–
2 yrs.		5	5	.500	2.79	64	0	0	80.2	68	33	64	0	5	5	1	2	0	0	.000	3	11	0	0	0.2	1.000

Tom Urbani

URBANI, THOMAS JAMES
B. Jan. 21, 1968, Santa Cruz, Calif.

BL TL 6'1" 190 lbs.

1993	STL N	1	3	.250	4.65	18	9	0	62	73	26	33	0	0	1	0	16	3	0	.188	2	12	1	1	0.8	.933
1994		3	7	.300	5.15	20	10	0	80.1	98	21	43	0	0	2	0	24	6	0	.250	0	15	0	1	0.8	1.000
2 yrs.		4	10	.286	4.93	38	19	0	142.1	171	47	76	0	0	3	0	40	9	0	.225	2	27	1	2	0.8	.967

Ismael Valdes

VALDES, ISMAEL
B. Aug. 21, 1973, Victoria, Mexico

BR TR 6'3" 185 lbs.

| 1994 | LA N | 3 | 1 | .750 | 3.18 | 21 | 1 | 0 | 28.1 | 21 | 10 | 28 | 0 | 3 | 1 | 0 | 2 | 0 | 0 | .000 | 1 | 8 | 0 | 0 | 0.4 | 1.000 |

Sergio Valdez

VALDEZ, SERGIO
Born Sergio Sanchez (Valdez).
B. Sept. 7, 1964, Elias Pina, Dominican Republic.

BR TR 6' 165 lbs.

1986	MON N	0	4	.000	6.84	5	5	0	25	39	11	20	0	0	0	0	8	1	0	.125	3	1	1	1	1.0	.800
1989	ATL N	1	2	.333	6.06	19	1	0	32.2	31	17	26	0	1	1	0	1	1	0	1.000	2	2	0	0	0.2	1.000
1990	2 teams	ATL N	(6G 0–0)				CLE A	(24G 6–6)																		
"	total	6	6	.500	4.85	30	13	0	107.2	115	38	66	0	1	1	0	0	0	0	–	10	12	2	1	0.8	.917
1991	CLE A	1	0	1.000	5.51	6	0	0	16.1	15	5	11	0	1	0	0	0	0	0	–	0	0	0	0	0.0	–
1992	MON N	0	2	.000	2.41	27	0	0	37.1	25	12	32	0	0	2	0	3	0	0	.000	9	3	0	0	0.4	1.000
1993		0	0	–	9.00	4	0	0	3	4	1	2	0	0	0	0	0	0	0	–	0	0	0	0	0.0	–
1994	BOS A	0	1	.000	8.16	12	1	0	14.1	25	8	4	0	0	0	0	0	0	0	–	1	1	0	1	0.4	1.000
7 yrs.		8	15	.348	5.14	103	20	0	236.1	254	92	161	0	3	4	0	12	2	0	.167	25	22	3	2	0.5	.940

157

Year	Team		W	L	PCT	ERA	G	GS	CG	IP	H	BB	SO	ShO	Relief Pitching W	L	SV	Batting AB	H	HR	BA	PO	A	E	DP	TC/G	FA

Fernando Valenzuela

VALENZUELA, FERNANDO
Born Fernando Valenzuela (Anguamea).
B. Nov. 1, 1960, Navajoa, Mexico.   BL TL 5'11"   180 lbs.

Year	Team		W	L	PCT	ERA	G	GS	CG	IP	H	BB	SO	ShO	W	L	SV	AB	H	HR	BA	PO	A	E	DP	TC/G	FA
1980	LA	N	2	0	1.000	0.00	10	0	0	18	8	5	16	0	2	0	1	1	0	0	.000	0	3	0	1	0.3	1.000
1981			13	7	.650	2.48	25	**25**	11	192	140	61	**180**	8	0	0	0	64	16	0	.250	12	33	3	2	1.9	.938
1982			19	13	.594	2.87	37	37	18	285	247	83	199	4	0	0	0	95	16	1	.168	20	64	2	4	2.3	.977
1983			15	10	.600	3.75	35	35	9	257	245	99	189	4	0	0	0	91	17	1	.187	20	54	2	5	2.2	.974
1984			12	17	.414	3.03	34	34	12	261	218	106	240	2	0	0	0	79	15	3	.190	21	48	2	4	2.1	.972
1985			17	10	.630	2.45	35	35	14	272.1	211	101	208	5	0	0	0	97	21	1	.216	18	45	0	0	1.8	1.000
1986			**21**	11	.656	3.14	34	34	**20**	269.1	226	85	242	3	0	0	0	109	24	0	.220	29	47	1	2	2.3	.987
1987			14	14	.500	3.98	34	34	12	251	**254**	124	190	1	0	0	0	92	13	1	.141	15	53	4	2	2.1	.944
1988			5	8	.385	4.24	23	22	3	142.1	142	76	64	0	0	0	1	44	8	0	.182	6	38	1	2	2.0	.978
1989			10	13	.435	3.43	31	31	3	196.2	185	98	116	0	0	0	0	66	12	0	.182	18	35	5	4	1.9	.914
1990			13	13	.500	4.59	33	33	5	204	223	77	115	2	0	0	0	69	21	1	.304	5	31	3	2	1.2	.923
1991	CAL	A	0	2	.000	12.15	2	2	0	6.2	14	3	5	0	0	0	0	0	0	0	–	0	1	0	0	0.5	1.000
1993	BAL	A	8	10	.444	4.94	32	31	5	178.2	179	79	78	2	0	0	0	0	0	0	–	11	37	4	2	1.6	.923
1994	PHI	N	1	2	.333	3.00	8	7	0	45	42	7	19	0	0	0	0	12	3	0	.250	2	8	0	0	1.3	1.000
14 yrs.			150	130	.536	3.44	373	360	112	2579	2334	1004	1861	31	2	0	2	819	166	8	.203	177	497	27	30	1.9	.961

DIVISIONAL PLAYOFF SERIES

| 1981 | LA | N | 1 | 0 | 1.000 | 1.06 | 2 | 2 | 1 | 17 | 10 | 3 | 10 | 0 | 0 | 0 | 0 | 4 | 0 | 0 | .000 | 0 | 0 | 0 | 0 | 0.0 | – |

LEAGUE CHAMPIONSHIP SERIES

1981	LA	N	1	1	.500	2.45	2	2	0	14.2	10	5	10	0	0	0	0	5	0	0	.000	0	2	0	0	1.0	1.000
1983			1	0	1.000	1.13	1	1	0	8	7	4	5	0	0	0	0	3	0	0	.000	1	0	0	0	1.0	1.000
1985			1	0	1.000	1.88	2	2	0	14.1	11	10	13	0	0	0	0	5	1	0	.200	0	3	1	0	2.5	.800
3 yrs.			3	1	.750	1.95	5	5	0	37	28	19	28	0	0	0	0	13	1	0	.077	1	5	1	0	1.6	.875

WORLD SERIES

| 1981 | LA | N | 1 | 0 | 1.000 | 4.00 | 1 | 1 | 1 | 9 | 9 | 7 | 6 | 0 | 0 | 0 | 0 | 3 | 0 | 0 | .000 | 0 | 1 | 0 | 0 | 1.0 | 1.000 |

Tim Vanegmond

VANEGMOND, TIMOTHY LAYNE
B. May 31, 1969, Shreveport, La.   BR TR 6'2"   185 lbs.

| 1994 | BOS | A | 2 | 3 | .400 | 6.34 | 7 | 7 | 1 | 38.1 | 38 | 21 | 22 | 0 | 0 | 0 | 0 | 0 | 0 | 0 | – | 2 | 0 | 0 | 0 | 0.3 | 1.000 |

William VanLandingham

VANLANDINGHAM, WILLIAM JOSEPH
B. July 16, 1970, Columbia, Tenn.   BR TR 6'2"   210 lbs.

| 1994 | SF | N | 8 | 2 | .800 | 3.54 | 16 | 14 | 0 | 84 | 70 | 43 | 56 | 0 | 0 | 0 | 0 | 31 | 2 | 0 | .065 | 4 | 9 | 0 | 0 | 0.8 | 1.000 |

Todd Van Poppel

VAN POPPEL, TODD MATTHEW
B. Dec. 9, 1971, Hinsdale, Ill.   BR TR 6'5"   210 lbs.

1991	OAK	A	0	0	–	9.64	1	1	0	4.2	7	2	6	0	0	0	0	0	0	0	–	0	1	0	0	1.0	1.000
1993			6	6	.500	5.04	16	16	0	84	76	62	47	0	0	0	0	0	0	0	–	6	4	0	1	0.6	1.000
1994			7	10	.412	6.09	23	23	0	116.2	108	**89**	83	0	0	0	0	0	0	0	–	1	11	0	1	0.5	1.000
3 yrs.			13	16	.448	5.74	40	40	0	205.1	191	153	136	0	0	0	0	0	0	0	–	7	16	0	2	0.6	1.000

David Veres

VERES, DAVID SCOTT
B. Oct. 19, 1966, Montgomery, Ala.   BR TR 6'2"   195 lbs.

| 1994 | HOU | N | 3 | 3 | .500 | 2.41 | 32 | 0 | 0 | 41 | 39 | 7 | 28 | 0 | 3 | 3 | 1 | 2 | 1 | 0 | .500 | 5 | 2 | 0 | 0 | 0.2 | 1.000 |

Randy Veres

VERES, RANDOLF RUHLAND
B. Nov. 25, 1965, San Francisco, Calif.   BR TR 6'3"   190 lbs.

1989	MIL	A	0	1	.000	4.32	3	1	0	8.1	9	4	8	0	0	0	0	0	0	0	–	0	1	0	0	0.3	1.000
1990			0	3	.000	3.67	26	0	0	41.2	38	16	16	0	0	3	1	0	0	0	–	2	10	0	2	0.5	1.000
1994	CHI	N	1	1	.500	5.59	10	0	0	9.2	12	2	5	0	1	1	0	1	0	0	.000	0	2	0	0	0.2	1.000
3 yrs.			1	5	.167	4.07	39	1	0	59.2	59	22	29	0	1	4	1	1	0	0	.000	2	13	0	2	0.4	1.000

Frank Viola

VIOLA, FRANK JOHN, JR. (Sweet Music)
B. Apr. 19, 1960, Hempstead, N. Y.   BL TL 6'4"   195 lbs.

1982	MIN	A	4	10	.286	5.21	22	22	3	126	152	38	84	1	0	0	0	0	0	0	–	1	15	2	0	0.8	.889
1983			7	15	.318	5.49	35	34	4	210	242	92	127	0	0	0	0	0	0	0	–	7	23	1	2	0.9	.968
1984			18	12	.600	3.21	35	35	10	257.2	225	73	149	4	0	0	0	0	0	0	–	6	26	1	1	0.9	.970
1985			18	14	.563	4.09	36	36	9	250.2	262	68	135	0	0	0	0	0	0	0	–	6	33	5	0	1.2	.886
1986			16	13	.552	4.51	37	**37**	7	245.2	257	83	191	1	0	0	0	0	0	0	–	8	21	3	1	0.9	.906
1987			17	10	.630	2.90	36	36	7	251.2	230	66	197	1	0	0	0	0	0	0	–	6	34	3	1	1.2	.930
1988			**24**	7	**.774**	2.64	35	35	7	255.1	236	54	193	2	0	0	0	0	0	0	–	5	30	2	1	1.1	.946
1989	2 teams		MIN A	(24G 8–12)		NY N	(12G 5–5)																				
"	total		13	17	.433	3.66	36	36	9	261	246	74	211	2	0	0	0	23	3	0	.130	10	35	4	3	1.4	.918
1990	NY	N	20	12	.625	2.67	35	**35**	7	249.2	227	60	182	3	0	0	0	85	13	0	.153	11	34	1	1	1.3	.978
1991			13	15	.464	3.97	35	35	3	231.1	**259**	54	132	1	0	0	0	71	9	0	.127	6	34	4	1	1.3	.909
1992	BOS	A	13	12	.520	3.44	35	35	6	238	214	89	121	1	0	0	0	0	0	0	–	6	42	2	6	1.6	.964
1993			11	8	.579	3.14	29	29	2	183.2	180	72	91	1	0	0	0	0	0	0	–	10	31	4	1	1.6	.911
1994			1	1	.500	4.65	6	6	0	31	34	17	9	0	0	0	0	0	0	0	–	0	4	0	1	0.7	1.000
13 yrs.			175	146	.545	3.67	412	411	74	2791.2	2764	840	1822	16	0	0	0	179	25	0	.140	82	367	32	19	1.2	.933

LEAGUE CHAMPIONSHIP SERIES

| 1987 | MIN | A | 1 | 0 | 1.000 | 5.25 | 2 | 2 | 0 | 12 | 14 | 5 | 9 | 0 | 0 | 0 | 0 | 0 | 0 | 0 | – | 0 | 0 | 0 | 0 | 0.5 | 1.000 |

WORLD SERIES

| 1987 | MIN | A | 2 | 1 | .667 | 3.72 | 3 | 3 | 0 | 19.1 | 17 | 3 | 16 | 0 | 0 | 0 | 0 | 1 | 0 | 0 | .000 | 1 | 5 | 0 | 0 | 2.0 | 1.000 |

Ed Vosberg

VOSBERG, EDWARD JOHN
B. Sept. 28, 1961, Tucson, Ariz.   BL TL 6'1"   190 lbs.

| 1986 | SD | N | 0 | 1 | .000 | 6.59 | 5 | 3 | 0 | 13.2 | 17 | 9 | 8 | 0 | 0 | 0 | 0 | 2 | 0 | 0 | .000 | 0 | 1 | 1 | 0 | 0.4 | .500 |
| 1990 | SF | N | 1 | 1 | .500 | 5.55 | 18 | 0 | 0 | 24.1 | 21 | 12 | 12 | 0 | 1 | 1 | 0 | 0 | 0 | 0 | – | 1 | 5 | 0 | 0 | 0.3 | 1.000 |

Year	Team	W	L	PCT	ERA	G	GS	CG	IP	H	BB	SO	ShO	W	L	SV	AB	H	HR	BA	PO	A	E	DP	TC/G	FA
														Relief Pitching			**Batting**									

Ed Vosberg continued

Year	Team	W	L	PCT	ERA	G	GS	CG	IP	H	BB	SO	ShO	W	L	SV	AB	H	HR	BA	PO	A	E	DP	TC/G	FA
1994	OAK A	0	2	.000	3.95	16	0	0	13.2	16	5	12	0	0	2	0	0	0	0	–	2	5	0	1	0.4	1.000
3 yrs.		1	4	.200	5.40	39	3	0	51.2	54	26	32	0	1	3	0	2	0	0	.000	3	11	1	1	0.4	.933

Paul Wagner

WAGNER, PAUL ALAN
B. Nov. 14, 1967, Milwaukee, Wis.　　　　BR TR 6'3" 205 lbs.

Year	Team	W	L	PCT	ERA	G	GS	CG	IP	H	BB	SO	ShO	W	L	SV	AB	H	HR	BA	PO	A	E	DP	TC/G	FA
1992	PIT N	2	0	1.000	0.69	6	1	0	13	9	5	5	0	2	0	0	3	1	0	.333	2	2	0	0	0.7	1.000
1993		8	8	.500	4.27	44	17	1	141.1	143	42	114	1	2	3	2	42	8	0	.190	9	13	0	3	0.5	1.000
1994		7	8	.467	4.59	29	17	1	119.2	136	50	86	0	2	0	0	37	6	0	.162	14	22	0	3	1.2	1.000
3 yrs.		17	16	.515	4.24	79	35	2	274	288	97	205	1	6	3	2	82	15	0	.183	25	37	0	6	0.8	1.000

Tim Wallach

WALLACH, TIMOTHY CHARLES
B. Sept. 14, 1957, Huntington Park, Calif.　　　　BR TR 6'3" 220 lbs.

Year	Team	W	L	PCT	ERA	G	GS	CG	IP	H	BB	SO	ShO	W	L	SV	AB	H	HR	BA	PO	A	E	DP	TC/G	FA
1987	MON N	0	0	–	0.00	1	0	0	1	1	0	0	0	0	0	0	593	177	26	.298	0	0	0	0	0.0	–
1989		0	0	–	9.00	1	0	0	1	2	0	0	0	0	0	0	573	159	13	.277	0	0	0	0	0.0	–
2 yrs.		0	0	–	4.50	2	0	0	2	3	0	0	0	0	0	0	*				0	0	0	0	0.0	–

Bruce Walton

WALTON, BRUCE KENNETH
B. Dec. 25, 1962, Bakersfield, Calif.　　　　BR TR 6'2" 195 lbs.

Year	Team	W	L	PCT	ERA	G	GS	CG	IP	H	BB	SO	ShO	W	L	SV	AB	H	HR	BA	PO	A	E	DP	TC/G	FA
1991	OAK A	1	0	1.000	6.23	12	0	0	13	11	6	10	0	1	0	0	0	0	0	–	1	0	0	0	0.1	1.000
1992		0	0	–	9.90	7	0	0	10	17	3	7	0	0	0	0	0	0	0	–	0	1	0	0	0.1	1.000
1993	MON N	0	0	–	9.53	4	0	0	5.2	11	3	0	0	0	0	0	1	0	0	.000	1	1	0	0	0.5	1.000
1994	CLR N	1	0	1.000	8.44	4	0	0	5.1	6	3	1	0	1	0	0	0	0	0	–	0	1	1	0	0.5	.500
4 yrs.		2	0	1.000	8.21	27	0	0	34	45	15	18	0	2	0	0	1	0	0	.000	2	3	1	0	0.2	.833

Allen Watson

WATSON, ALLEN KENNETH
B. Nov. 18, 1970, Jamaica, N. Y.　　　　BL TL 6'3" 195 lbs.

Year	Team	W	L	PCT	ERA	G	GS	CG	IP	H	BB	SO	ShO	W	L	SV	AB	H	HR	BA	PO	A	E	DP	TC/G	FA
1993	STL N	6	7	.462	4.60	16	15	0	86	90	28	49	0	0	1	0	26	6	0	.231	3	10	1	1	0.9	.929
1994		6	5	.545	5.52	22	22	0	115.2	130	53	74	0	0	0	0	38	6	0	.158	4	14	1	0	0.9	.947
2 yrs.		12	12	.500	5.13	38	37	0	201.2	220	81	123	0	0	1	0	64	12	0	.188	7	24	2	1	0.9	.939

Gary Wayne

WAYNE, GARY ANTHONY
B. Nov. 30, 1962, Dearborn, Mich.　　　　BL TL 6'3" 185 lbs.

Year	Team	W	L	PCT	ERA	G	GS	CG	IP	H	BB	SO	ShO	W	L	SV	AB	H	HR	BA	PO	A	E	DP	TC/G	FA
1989	MIN A	3	4	.429	3.30	60	0	0	71	55	36	41	0	3	4	1	0	0	0	–	2	11	1	1	0.2	.929
1990		1	1	.500	4.19	38	0	0	38.2	38	13	28	0	1	1	1	0	0	0	–	1	4	0	1	0.1	1.000
1991		1	0	1.000	5.11	8	0	0	12.1	11	4	7	0	1	0	1	0	0	0	–	0	1	0	0	0.1	1.000
1992		3	3	.500	2.63	41	0	0	48	46	19	29	0	3	3	0	0	0	0	–	1	13	0	0	0.3	1.000
1993	CLR N	5	3	.625	5.05	65	0	0	62.1	68	26	49	0	5	3	1	1	1	0	1.000	0	9	0	1	0.1	1.000
1994	LA N	1	3	.250	4.67	19	0	0	17.1	19	6	10	0	1	3	0	1	0	0	.000	2	3	1	0	0.3	.833
6 yrs.		14	14	.500	3.93	231	0	0	249.2	237	104	164	0	14	14	4	2	1	0	.500	6	41	2	3	0.2	.959

Dave Weathers

WEATHERS, JOHN DAVID
B. Sept. 25, 1969, Lawrenceburg, Tenn.　　　　BR TR 6'3" 205 lbs.

Year	Team	W	L	PCT	ERA	G	GS	CG	IP	H	BB	SO	ShO	W	L	SV	AB	H	HR	BA	PO	A	E	DP	TC/G	FA
1991	TOR A	1	0	1.000	4.91	15	0	0	14.2	15	17	13	0	1	0	0	0	0	0	–	0	1	0	0	0.1	1.000
1992		0	0	–	8.10	2	0	0	3.1	5	2	3	0	0	0	0	0	0	0	–	0	0	0	0	0.0	–
1993	FLA N	2	3	.400	5.12	14	6	0	45.2	57	13	34	0	0	0	0	10	1	0	.100	5	3	0	0	0.6	1.000
1994		8	12	.400	5.27	24	24	0	135	166	59	72	0	0	0	0	44	3	0	.068	2	21	1	0	1.0	.958
4 yrs.		11	15	.423	5.26	55	30	0	198.2	243	91	122	0	1	0	0	54	4	0	.074	7	25	1	0	0.6	.970

Bill Wegman

WEGMAN, WILLIAM EDWARD
B. Dec. 19, 1962, Cincinnati, Ohio.　　　　BR TR 6'5" 200 lbs.

Year	Team	W	L	PCT	ERA	G	GS	CG	IP	H	BB	SO	ShO	W	L	SV	AB	H	HR	BA	PO	A	E	DP	TC/G	FA
1985	MIL A	2	0	1.000	3.57	3	3	0	17.2	17	3	6	0	0	0	0	0	0	0	–	3	0	0	0	1.0	1.000
1986		5	12	.294	5.13	35	32	3	198.1	217	43	82	0	0	0	0	0	0	0	–	20	19	1	4	1.1	.975
1987		12	11	.522	4.24	34	33	7	225	229	53	102	0	0	1	0	0	0	0	–	29	27	2	2	1.7	.966
1988		13	13	.500	4.12	32	31	4	199	207	50	84	1	0	0	0	0	0	0	–	14	24	3	3	1.3	.927
1989		2	6	.250	6.71	11	8	0	51	69	21	27	0	0	1	0	0	0	0	–	3	11	0	0	1.3	1.000
1990		2	2	.500	4.85	8	5	1	29.2	37	6	20	1	0	0	0	0	0	0	–	1	3	2	0	0.8	.667
1991		15	7	.682	2.84	28	28	7	193.1	176	40	89	2	0	0	0	0	0	0	–	28	34	4	1	2.4	.939
1992		13	14	.481	3.20	35	35	7	261.2	251	55	127	0	0	0	0	0	0	0	–	35	43	2	3	2.3	.975
1993		4	14	.222	4.48	20	18	5	120.2	135	34	50	0	0	0	0	0	0	0	–	12	21	2	4	1.8	.943
1994		8	4	.667	4.51	19	19	0	115.2	140	26	59	0	0	0	0	0	0	0	–	12	21	1	4	1.8	.971
10 yrs.		76	83	.478	4.10	225	212	33	1412	1478	331	646	4	0	0	0	0	0	0	–	157	203	17	21	1.7	.955

Bob Welch

WELCH, ROBERT LYNN
B. Nov. 3, 1956, Detroit, Mich.　　　　BR TR 6'3" 190 lbs.

Year	Team	W	L	PCT	ERA	G	GS	CG	IP	H	BB	SO	ShO	W	L	SV	AB	H	HR	BA	PO	A	E	DP	TC/G	FA
1978	LA N	7	4	.636	2.03	23	13	4	111	92	26	66	3	1	0	3	29	5	0	.172	6	12	1	0	0.8	.947
1979		5	6	.455	4.00	25	12	1	81	82	32	64	0	3	1	5	19	3	0	.158	2	8	3	3	0.5	.769
1980		14	9	.609	3.28	32	32	3	214	190	79	141	2	0	0	0	70	17	0	.243	15	26	1	3	1.3	.976
1981		9	5	.643	3.45	23	23	2	141	141	41	88	1	0	0	0	45	10	0	.222	4	18	0	1	1.0	1.000
1982		16	11	.593	3.36	36	36	9	235.2	199	81	176	3	0	0	0	85	12	0	.141	24	26	2	0	1.3	.957
1983		15	12	.556	2.65	31	31	4	204	164	72	156	3	0	0	0	73	7	1	.096	14	27	3	1	1.4	.932
1984		13	13	.500	3.78	31	29	3	178.2	191	58	126	1	0	0	0	51	4	0	.078	20	28	2	5	1.6	.960
1985		14	4	.778	2.31	23	23	8	167.1	141	35	96	3	0	0	0	50	9	0	.180	15	27	3	1	2.0	.933
1986		7	13	.350	3.28	33	33	7	235.2	227	55	183	0	0	0	0	76	8	1	.105	21	29	2	1	1.5	.959
1987		15	9	.625	3.22	35	35	6	251.2	204	86	196	4	0	0	0	83	13	0	.157	25	38	0	3	1.8	1.000
1988	OAK A	17	9	.654	3.64	36	36	4	244.2	237	81	158	2	0	0	0	0	0	0	–	16	32	1	2	1.4	.980
1989		17	8	.680	3.00	33	33	1	209.2	191	78	137	0	0	0	0	0	0	0	–	26	21	4	3	1.5	.922
1990		27	6	**.818**	2.95	35	35	2	238	214	77	127	2	0	0	0	0	0	0	–	20	31	0	2	1.5	1.000
1991		12	13	.480	4.58	35	**35**	7	220	220	91	101	1	0	0	0	0	0	0	–	15	29	2	1	1.3	.957
1992		11	7	.611	3.27	20	20	0	123.2	114	43	47	0	0	0	0	0	0	0	–	5	13	1	0	1.0	.947

Year	Team	W	L	PCT	ERA	G	GS	CG	IP	H	BB	SO	ShO	Relief Pitching W	L	SV	Batting AB	H	HR	BA	PO	A	E	DP	TC/G	FA

Bob Welch *continued*

Year	Team	W	L	PCT	ERA	G	GS	CG	IP	H	BB	SO	ShO	W	L	SV	AB	H	HR	BA	PO	A	E	DP	TC/G	FA
1993		9	11	.450	5.29	30	28	0	166.2	208	56	63	0	1	0	0	0	0	0	–	16	26	0	2	1.4	1.000
1994		3	6	.333	7.08	25	8	0	68.2	79	43	44	0	3	1	0	1	0	0	.000	4	6	1	0	0.4	.909
17 yrs.		211	146	.591	3.47	506	462	61	3091.1	2894	1034	1969	28	8	2	8	582	88	2	.151	243	394	26	30	1.3	.961

DIVISIONAL PLAYOFF SERIES

Year	Team	W	L	PCT	ERA	G	GS	CG	IP	H	BB	SO	ShO	W	L	SV	AB	H	HR	BA	PO	A	E	DP	TC/G	FA
1981	LA N	0	0	–	0.00	1	0	0	1	0	1	1	1	0	0	0	0	0	0	–	0	0	0	0	0.0	–

LEAGUE CHAMPIONSHIP SERIES

Year	Team	W	L	PCT	ERA	G	GS	CG	IP	H	BB	SO	ShO	W	L	SV	AB	H	HR	BA	PO	A	E	DP	TC/G	FA
1978	LA N	1	0	1.000	2.08	1	0	0	4.1	2	0	5	0	1	0	0	2	0	0	.000	0	1	0	0	1.0	1.000
1981		0	0	–	5.40	3	0	0	1.2	2	0	2	0	0	0	1	0	0	0	–	0	0	0	0	0.0	–
1983		0	1	.000	6.75	1	1	0	1.1	0	2	0	0	0	0	0	0	0	0	–	0	0	0	0	0.0	–
1985		0	1	.000	6.75	1	1	0	2.2	5	6	2	0	0	0	0	1	0	0	.000	0	0	1	0	1.0	.000
1988	OAK A	0	0	–	27.00	1	1	0	1.2	6	2	0	0	0	0	0	0	0	0	–	1	0	0	0	1.0	1.000
1989		1	0	1.000	3.18	1	1	0	5.2	8	1	4	0	0	0	0	0	0	0	–	1	0	0	0	1.0	1.000
1990		1	0	1.000	1.23	1	1	0	7.1	6	3	4	0	0	0	0	0	0	0	–	0	3	0	0	3.0	1.000
1992		0	0	–	2.57	1	1	0	7	7	1	7	0	0	0	0	0	0	0	–	0	1	0	0	1.0	1.000
8 yrs.		3	2	.600	4.26	10	6	0	31.2	36	15	24	0	1	0	1	3	0	0	.000	2	5	1	0	0.8	.875

WORLD SERIES

Year	Team	W	L	PCT	ERA	G	GS	CG	IP	H	BB	SO	ShO	W	L	SV	AB	H	HR	BA	PO	A	E	DP	TC/G	FA
1978	LA N	0	1	.000	6.23	3	0	0	4.1	4	2	6	0	0	1	1	0	0	0	–	0	0	0	0	0.0	–
1981		0	0	–	∞	1	1	0		3	1	0	0	0	0	0	0	0	0	–	0	0	0	0	0.0	–
1988	OAK A	0	0	–	1.80	1	1	0	5	6	3	8	0	0	0	0	0	0	0	–	1	1	0	0	2.0	1.000
1990		0	0	–	4.91	1	1	0	7.1	9	2	2	0	0	0	0	3	0	0	.000	0	2	0	0	2.0	1.000
4 yrs.		0	1	.000	5.40	6	3	0	16.2	22	8	16	0	0	1	1	3	0	0	.000	1	3	0	0	0.7	1.000

Bob Wells

WELLS, ROBERT LEE
B. Nov. 1, 1966, Yakima, Wash.

BR TR 6′   180 lbs.

Year	Team	W	L	PCT	ERA	G	GS	CG	IP	H	BB	SO	ShO	W	L	SV	AB	H	HR	BA	PO	A	E	DP	TC/G	FA
1994 2 teams	PHI N (6G 1–0)											SEA A (1G 1–0)														
" total		2	0	1.000	2.00	7	0	0	9	8	4	6	0	2	0	0	0	0	0	–	0	0	0	0	0.0	–

David Wells

WELLS, DAVID LEE
B. May 20, 1963, Torrance, Calif.

BL TL 6′3″   187 lbs.

Year	Team	W	L	PCT	ERA	G	GS	CG	IP	H	BB	SO	ShO	W	L	SV	AB	H	HR	BA	PO	A	E	DP	TC/G	FA
1987	TOR A	4	3	.571	3.99	18	2	0	29.1	37	12	32	0	4	1	1	0	0	0	–	2	4	0	1	0.3	1.000
1988		3	5	.375	4.62	41	0	0	64.1	65	31	56	0	3	5	4	0	0	0	–	5	5	0	1	0.2	1.000
1989		7	4	.636	2.40	54	0	0	86.1	66	28	78	0	7	4	2	0	0	0	–	9	11	1	0	0.4	.952
1990		11	6	.647	3.14	43	25	0	189	165	45	115	0	1	1	3	0	0	0	–	7	32	0	1	0.9	1.000
1991		15	10	.600	3.72	40	28	2	198.1	188	49	106	0	1	0	1	0	0	0	–	5	35	2	1	1.1	.952
1992		7	9	.438	5.40	41	14	0	120	138	36	62	0	1	2	2	0	0	0	–	9	14	1	1	0.6	.958
1993	DET A	11	9	.550	4.19	32	30	0	187	183	42	139	0	0	0	0	0	0	0	–	10	22	1	0	1.0	.970
1994		5	7	.417	3.96	16	16	5	111.1	113	24	71	1	0	0	0	0	0	0	–	6	11	0	0	1.1	1.000
8 yrs.		63	53	.543	3.88	285	115	7	985.2	955	267	659	1	17	13	13	0	0	0	–	53	134	5	5	0.7	.974

LEAGUE CHAMPIONSHIP SERIES

Year	Team	W	L	PCT	ERA	G	GS	CG	IP	H	BB	SO	ShO	W	L	SV	AB	H	HR	BA	PO	A	E	DP	TC/G	FA
1989	TOR A	0	0	–	0.00	1	0	0	1	0	2	1	0	0	0	0	0	0	0	–	0	0	0	0	0.0	–
1991		0	0	–	2.35	4	0	0	7.2	6	2	9	0	0	0	0	0	0	0	–	1	1	0	0	0.5	1.000
2 yrs.		0	0	–	2.08	5	0	0	8.2	6	4	10	0	0	0	0	0	0	0	–	1	1	0	0	0.4	1.000

WORLD SERIES

Year	Team	W	L	PCT	ERA	G	GS	CG	IP	H	BB	SO	ShO	W	L	SV	AB	H	HR	BA	PO	A	E	DP	TC/G	FA
1992	TOR A	0	0	–	0.00	4	0	0	4.1	1	2	3	0	0	0	0	0	0	0	–	0	0	0	0	0.0	–

Turk Wendell

WENDELL, STEVEN JOHN
B. May 19, 1967, Pittsfield, Mass.

BB TR 6′2″   185 lbs.

Year	Team	W	L	PCT	ERA	G	GS	CG	IP	H	BB	SO	ShO	W	L	SV	AB	H	HR	BA	PO	A	E	DP	TC/G	FA
1993	CHI N	1	2	.333	4.37	7	4	0	22.2	24	8	15	0	0	0	0	7	1	0	.143	7	1	0	0	1.1	1.000
1994		0	1	.000	11.93	6	2	0	14.1	22	10	9	0	0	0	0	2	0	0	.000	1	3	0	0	0.7	1.000
2 yrs.		1	3	.250	7.30	13	6	0	37	46	18	24	0	0	0	0	9	1	0	.111	8	4	0	0	0.9	1.000

Bill Wertz

WERTZ, WILLIAM CHARLES
B. Jan. 15, 1967, Cleveland, Ohio

BR TR 6′6″   220 lbs.

Year	Team	W	L	PCT	ERA	G	GS	CG	IP	H	BB	SO	ShO	W	L	SV	AB	H	HR	BA	PO	A	E	DP	TC/G	FA
1993	CLE A	2	3	.400	3.62	34	0	0	59.2	54	32	53	0	2	3	0	0	0	0	–	4	0	1	0	0.1	.800
1994		0	0	–	10.38	1	0	0	4.1	9	1	1	0	0	0	0	0	0	0	–	1	0	0	0	1.0	1.000
2 yrs.		2	3	.400	4.08	35	0	0	64	63	33	54	0	2	3	0	0	0	0	–	5	0	1	0	0.2	.833

David West

WEST, DAVID LEE
B. Sept. 1, 1964, Memphis, Tenn.

BL TL 6′6″   205 lbs.

Year	Team	W	L	PCT	ERA	G	GS	CG	IP	H	BB	SO	ShO	W	L	SV	AB	H	HR	BA	PO	A	E	DP	TC/G	FA
1988	NY N	1	0	1.000	3.00	2	1	0	6	6	3	3	0	0	0	0	2	2	0	1.000	1	0	0	0	0.5	1.000
1989 2 teams	NY N (11G 0–2)											MIN A (10G 3–2)														
" total		3	4	.429	6.79	21	7	0	63.2	73	33	50	0	0	0	0	5	1	0	.200	2	1	1	0	0.2	.800
1990	MIN A	7	9	.438	5.10	29	27	2	146.1	142	78	92	0	0	0	0	0	0	0	–	3	16	2	2	0.7	.905
1991		4	4	.500	4.54	15	12	0	71.1	66	28	52	0	0	0	0	0	0	0	–	1	11	1	1	0.9	.923
1992		1	3	.250	6.99	9	3	0	28.1	32	20	19	0	1	0	0	0	0	0	–	0	5	2	0	0.8	.714
1993	PHI N	6	4	.600	2.92	76	0	0	86.1	60	51	87	0	6	4	3	5	2	0	.400	2	4	2	1	0.1	.750
1994		4	10	.286	3.55	31	14	0	99	74	61	83	0	0	4	0	28	2	0	.071	3	6	0	1	0.3	1.000
7 yrs.		26	34	.433	4.63	183	64	2	501	453	274	386	0	7	8	3	40	7	0	.175	12	44	8	5	0.3	.875

LEAGUE CHAMPIONSHIP SERIES

Year	Team	W	L	PCT	ERA	G	GS	CG	IP	H	BB	SO	ShO	W	L	SV	AB	H	HR	BA	PO	A	E	DP	TC/G	FA
1991	MIN A	1	0	1.000	0.00	2	0	0	5.2	1	4	4	0	1	0	0	0	0	0	–	0	0	0	0	0.0	–
1993	PHI N	0	0	–	13.50	3	0	0	2.2	5	2	5	0	0	0	0	0	0	0	–	0	1	0	0	0.3	1.000
2 yrs.		1	0	1.000	4.32	5	0	0	8.1	6	6	9	0	1	0	0	0	0	0	–	0	1	0	0	0.2	1.000

WORLD SERIES

Year	Team	W	L	PCT	ERA	G	GS	CG	IP	H	BB	SO	ShO	W	L	SV	AB	H	HR	BA	PO	A	E	DP	TC/G	FA
1991	MIN A	0	0	–	∞	2	0	0		2	4	0	0	0	0	0	0	0	0	–	0	0	0	0	0.0	–
1993	PHI N	0	0	–	27.00	3	0	0	1	5	1	0	0	0	0	0	0	0	0	–	0	0	0	0	0.0	–
2 yrs.		0	0	–	63.00	5	0	0	1	7	5	0	0	0	0	0	0	0	0	–	0	0	0	0	0.0	–

Year	Team	W	L	PCT	ERA	G	GS	CG	IP	H	BB	SO	ShO	Relief Pitching W	L	SV	Batting AB	H	HR	BA	PO	A	E	DP	TC/G	FA

John Wetteland
WETTELAND, JOHN KARL
B. Aug. 22, 1966, San Mateo, Calif.   BR TR 6'2"   195 lbs.

Year	Team	W	L	PCT	ERA	G	GS	CG	IP	H	BB	SO	ShO	W	L	SV	AB	H	HR	BA	PO	A	E	DP	TC/G	FA
1989	LA N	5	8	.385	3.77	31	12	0	102.2	81	34	96	0	3	2	1	21	3	0	.143	5	8	2	0	0.5	.867
1990		2	4	.333	4.81	22	5	0	43	44	17	36	0	2	1	0	7	1	1	.143	1	3	1	0	0.2	.800
1991		1	0	1.000	0.00	6	0	0	9	5	3	9	0	1	0	0	0	0	0	.200	1	2	1	0	0.7	.750
1992	MON N	4	4	.500	2.92	67	0	0	83.1	64	36	99	0	4	4	37	5	1	0	.200	7	6	1	0	0.2	.929
1993		9	3	.750	1.37	70	0	0	85.1	58	28	113	0	9	3	43	4	0	0	.000	1	5	3	0	0.1	.667
1994		4	6	.400	2.83	52	0	0	63.2	46	21	68	0	4	6	25	4	1	0	.250	3	4	1	0	0.2	.875
6 yrs.		25	25	.500	2.93	248	17	0	387	298	139	421	0	23	16	106	41	6	1	.146	18	28	9	0	0.2	.836

Gabe White
WHITE, GABRIEL ALLEN
B. Nov. 20, 1971, Sebring, Fla.   BL TL 6'2"   200 lbs.

Year	Team	W	L	PCT	ERA	G	GS	CG	IP	H	BB	SO	ShO	W	L	SV	AB	H	HR	BA	PO	A	E	DP	TC/G	FA
1994	MON N	1	1	.500	6.08	7	5	0	23.2	24	11	17	0	0	0	1	4	0	0	.000	0	2	0	0	0.3	1.000

Rick White
WHITE, RICHARD ALLEN
B. Dec. 23, 1968, Springfield, Ohio   BR TR 6'4"   215 lbs.

Year	Team	W	L	PCT	ERA	G	GS	CG	IP	H	BB	SO	ShO	W	L	SV	AB	H	HR	BA	PO	A	E	DP	TC/G	FA
1994	PIT N	4	5	.444	3.82	43	5	0	75.1	79	17	38	0	2	4	6	13	1	0	.077	3	10	2	1	0.3	.867

Wally Whitehurst
WHITEHURST, WALTER RICHARD
B. Apr. 11, 1964, Shreveport, La.   BR TR 6'3"   180 lbs.

Year	Team	W	L	PCT	ERA	G	GS	CG	IP	H	BB	SO	ShO	W	L	SV	AB	H	HR	BA	PO	A	E	DP	TC/G	FA
1989	NY N	0	1	.000	4.50	9	0	0	14	17	5	9	0	0	0	0	1	0	0	.000	1	1	0	0	0.2	1.000
1990		1	0	1.000	3.29	38	0	0	65.2	63	9	46	0	1	0	2	8	2	0	.250	4	9	0	1	0.3	1.000
1991		7	12	.368	4.19	36	20	0	133.1	142	25	87	0	2	1	1	33	6	0	.182	11	24	2	2	1.0	.946
1992		3	9	.250	3.62	44	11	0	97	99	33	70	0	2	4	0	22	4	0	.182	6	17	1	1	0.5	.958
1993	SD N	4	7	.364	3.83	21	19	0	105.2	109	30	57	0	0	0	0	24	2	0	.083	3	18	2	2	1.1	.913
1994		4	7	.364	4.92	13	13	0	64	84	26	43	0	0	0	0	19	2	0	.105	4	10	1	0	1.2	.933
6 yrs.		19	36	.345	3.98	161	64	0	479.2	514	128	312	0	5	5	3	107	16	0	.150	29	79	6	6	0.7	.947

Matt Whiteside
WHITESIDE, MATTHEW CHRISTOPHER
B. Aug. 8, 1967, Charleston, Mo.   BR TR 6'   185 lbs.

Year	Team	W	L	PCT	ERA	G	GS	CG	IP	H	BB	SO	ShO	W	L	SV	AB	H	HR	BA	PO	A	E	DP	TC/G	FA
1992	TEX A	1	1	.500	1.93	20	0	0	28	26	11	13	0	1	1	4	0	0	0	–	3	2	1	0	0.3	.833
1993		2	1	.667	4.32	60	0	0	73	78	23	39	0	2	1	1	0	0	0	–	5	7	2	3	0.2	.857
1994		2	2	.500	5.02	47	0	0	61	68	28	37	0	2	2	1	0	0	0	–	4	6	1	0	0.2	.909
3 yrs.		5	4	.556	4.17	127	0	0	162	172	62	89	0	5	4	6	0	0	0	–	12	15	4	3	0.2	.871

Bob Wickman
WICKMAN, ROBERT JOE
B. Feb. 6, 1969, Green Bay, Wis.   BR TR 6'1"   207 lbs.

Year	Team	W	L	PCT	ERA	G	GS	CG	IP	H	BB	SO	ShO	W	L	SV	AB	H	HR	BA	PO	A	E	DP	TC/G	FA
1992	NY A	6	1	.857	4.11	8	8	0	50.1	51	20	21	0	0	0	0	0	0	0	–	4	6	0	3	1.3	1.000
1993		14	4	.778	4.63	41	19	1	140	156	69	70	1	6	4	4	0	0	0	–	7	19	2	1	0.7	.929
1994		5	4	.556	3.09	53	0	0	70	54	27	56	0	5	4	6	0	0	0	–	3	7	0	0	0.2	1.000
3 yrs.		25	9	.735	4.11	102	27	1	260.1	261	116	147	1	11	4	10	0	0	0	–	14	32	2	4	0.5	.958

Brian Williams
WILLIAMS, BRIAN O'NEAL
B. Feb. 15, 1969, Lancaster, S. C.   BR TR 6'3"   205 lbs.

Year	Team	W	L	PCT	ERA	G	GS	CG	IP	H	BB	SO	ShO	W	L	SV	AB	H	HR	BA	PO	A	E	DP	TC/G	FA
1991	HOU N	0	1	.000	3.75	2	2	0	12	11	4	4	0	0	0	0	3	0	0	.000	1	2	0	0	1.5	1.000
1992		7	6	.538	3.92	16	16	0	96.1	92	42	54	0	0	0	0	30	4	0	.133	8	15	2	0	1.6	.920
1993		4	4	.500	4.83	42	5	0	82	76	38	56	0	1	3	3	10	2	0	.200	7	20	1	0	0.7	.964
1994		6	5	.545	5.74	20	13	0	78.1	112	41	49	0	1	0	0	23	6	0	.261	8	9	4	0	1.1	.810
4 yrs.		17	16	.515	4.72	80	36	0	268.2	291	125	163	0	2	3	3	66	12	0	.182	24	46	7	0	1.0	.909

Mike Williams
WILLIAMS, MICHAEL DARREN
B. July 29, 1968, Radford, Va.   BR TR 6'2"   190 lbs.

Year	Team	W	L	PCT	ERA	G	GS	CG	IP	H	BB	SO	ShO	W	L	SV	AB	H	HR	BA	PO	A	E	DP	TC/G	FA
1992	PHI N	1	1	.500	5.34	5	5	1	28.2	29	7	5	0	0	0	0	10	4	0	.400	0	5	0	0	1.0	1.000
1993		1	3	.250	5.29	17	4	0	51	50	22	33	0	1	2	0	12	1	0	.083	2	6	0	1	0.5	1.000
1994		2	4	.333	5.01	12	8	0	50.1	61	20	29	0	0	0	0	12	2	0	.167	3	7	0	3	0.8	1.000
3 yrs.		4	8	.333	5.19	34	17	1	130	140	49	67	0	1	2	0	34	7	0	.206	5	18	0	4	0.7	1.000

Mitch Williams
WILLIAMS, MITCHELL STEVEN (Wild Thing)
B. Nov. 17, 1964, Santa Ana, Calif.   BL TL 6'3"   180 lbs.

Year	Team	W	L	PCT	ERA	G	GS	CG	IP	H	BB	SO	ShO	W	L	SV	AB	H	HR	BA	PO	A	E	DP	TC/G	FA
1986	TEX A	8	6	.571	3.58	80	0	0	98	69	79	90	0	8	6	8	0	0	0	–	1	10	2	1	0.2	.846
1987		8	6	.571	3.23	85	1	0	108.2	63	94	129	0	8	5	6	0	0	0	–	5	15	3	3	0.3	.870
1988		2	7	.222	4.63	67	0	0	68	48	47	61	0	2	7	18	0	0	0	–	3	10	1	0	0.2	.929
1989	CHI N	4	4	.500	2.64	76	0	0	81.2	71	52	67	0	4	4	36	5	1	1	.200	0	11	3	0	0.2	.786
1990		1	8	.111	3.93	59	2	0	66.1	60	50	55	0	1	7	16	5	0	0	.000	1	5	0	0	0.1	1.000
1991	PHI N	12	5	.706	2.34	69	0	0	88.1	56	62	84	0	12	5	30	1	0	0	.000	0	8	3	0	0.2	.727
1992		5	8	.385	3.78	66	0	0	81	69	64	74	0	5	8	29	4	1	0	.250	1	11	3	0	0.2	.800
1993		3	7	.300	3.34	65	0	0	62	56	44	60	0	3	7	43	1	1	0	1.000	2	3	2	0	0.1	.714
1994	HOU N	1	4	.200	7.65	25	0	0	20	21	24	21	0	1	4	6	0	0	0	–	0	1	0	0	0.0	1.000
9 yrs.		44	55	.444	3.51	592	0	0	674	513	516	641	0	44	53	192	16	3	1	.188	13	74	17	4	0.2	.837

LEAGUE CHAMPIONSHIP SERIES

Year	Team	W	L	PCT	ERA	G	GS	CG	IP	H	BB	SO	ShO	W	L	SV	AB	H	HR	BA	PO	A	E	DP	TC/G	FA
1989	CHI N	0	0	–	0.00	2	0	0	1	1	0	2	0	0	0	0	0	0	0	–	0	0	0	0	0.0	–
1993	PHI N	2	0	1.000	1.69	4	0	0	5.1	6	2	5	0	2	0	2	0	0	0	–	0	1	1	0	0.5	.500
2 yrs.		2	0	1.000	1.42	6	0	0	6.1	7	2	7	0	2	0	2	0	0	0	–	0	1	1	0	0.3	.500

WORLD SERIES

Year	Team	W	L	PCT	ERA	G	GS	CG	IP	H	BB	SO	ShO	W	L	SV	AB	H	HR	BA	PO	A	E	DP	TC/G	FA
1993	PHI N	0	2	.000	20.25	3	0	0	2.2	5	4	1	0	0	2	1	0	0	0	–	0	1	0	0	0.3	1.000

Woody Williams
WILLIAMS, GREGORY SCOTT
B. Aug. 19, 1966, Houston, Tex.   BR TR 6'   180 lbs.

Year	Team	W	L	PCT	ERA	G	GS	CG	IP	H	BB	SO	ShO	W	L	SV	AB	H	HR	BA	PO	A	E	DP	TC/G	FA
1993	TOR A	3	1	.750	4.38	30	0	0	37	40	22	24	0	3	1	0	0	0	0	–	5	6	0	1	0.4	1.000
1994		1	3	.250	3.64	38	0	0	59.1	44	33	56	0	1	3	0	0	0	0	–	2	6	1	2	0.2	.889
2 yrs.		4	4	.500	3.92	68	0	0	96.1	84	55	80	0	4	4	0	0	0	0	–	7	12	1	3	0.3	.950

Year	Team	W	L	PCT	ERA	G	GS	CG	IP	H	BB	SO	ShO	W	L	SV	AB	H	HR	BA	PO	A	E	DP	TC/G	FA
														Relief Pitching			**Batting**									

Mark Williamson

WILLIAMSON, MARK ALAN
B. July 21, 1959, Corpus Christi, Tex.

BR TR 6′ 155 lbs.

Year	Team	W	L	PCT	ERA	G	GS	CG	IP	H	BB	SO	ShO	W	L	SV	AB	H	HR	BA	PO	A	E	DP	TC/G	FA
1987	BAL A	8	9	.471	4.03	61	2	0	125	122	41	73	0	8	**8**	3	0	0	0	–	20	17	2	1	0.6	.949
1988		5	8	.385	4.90	37	10	2	117.2	125	40	69	0	4	2	2	0	0	0	–	9	14	1	0	0.6	.958
1989		10	5	.667	2.93	65	0	0	107.1	105	30	55	0	10	5	9	0	0	0	–	9	10	0	1	0.3	1.000
1990		8	2	.800	2.21	49	0	0	85.1	65	28	60	0	8	2	1	0	0	0	–	14	13	2	2	0.6	.931
1991		5	5	.500	4.48	65	0	0	80.1	87	35	53	0	5	5	4	0	0	0	–	7	9	2	0	0.3	.889
1992		0	0	–	0.96	12	0	0	18.2	16	10	14	0	0	0	1	0	0	0	–	1	0	0	0	0.1	1.000
1993		7	5	.583	4.91	48	1	0	88	106	25	45	0	7	5	0	0	0	0	–	8	10	0	0	0.4	1.000
1994		3	1	.750	4.01	28	2	0	67.1	75	17	28	0	3	0	1	0	0	0	–	8	3	0	0	0.4	1.000
8 yrs.		46	35	.568	3.86	365	15	2	689.2	701	226	397	0	45	27	21	0	0	0	–	76	76	7	4	0.4	.956

Carl Willis

WILLIS, CARL BLAKE
B. Dec. 28, 1960, Danville, Va.

BL TR 6′4″ 210 lbs.

Year	Team	W	L	PCT	ERA	G	GS	CG	IP	H	BB	SO	ShO	W	L	SV	AB	H	HR	BA	PO	A	E	DP	TC/G	FA
1984	**2 teams**	**DET A**	(10G	0–2)	**CIN N**	(7G	0–1)																			
"	total	0	3	.000	5.96	17	2	0	25.2	33	7	7	0	0	2	1	0	0	0	–	1	5	0	1	0.4	1.000
1985	CIN N	1	0	1.000	9.22	11	0	0	13.2	21	5	6	0	1	0	1	1	0	0	.000	0	1	1	0	0.2	.500
1986		1	3	.250	4.47	29	0	0	52.1	54	32	24	0	1	3	0	3	1	0	.333	4	10	0	3	0.5	1.000
1988	CHI A	0	0	–	8.25	6	0	0	12	17	7	6	0	0	0	0	0	0	0	–	3	0	0	0	0.5	1.000
1991	MIN A	8	3	.727	2.63	40	0	0	89	76	19	53	0	8	3	2	0	0	0	–	4	8	1	0	0.3	.923
1992		7	3	.700	2.72	59	0	0	79.1	73	11	45	0	7	3	1	0	0	0	–	6	6	1	1	0.2	.923
1993		3	0	1.000	3.10	53	0	0	58	56	17	44	0	3	0	5	0	0	0	–	2	6	0	0	0.2	1.000
1994		2	4	.333	5.92	49	0	0	59.1	89	12	37	0	2	4	3	0	0	0	–	2	5	0	0	0.1	1.000
8 yrs.		22	16	.579	4.09	264	2	0	389.1	419	110	222	0	22	15	13	4	1	0	.250	22	41	3	5	0.3	.955

LEAGUE CHAMPIONSHIP SERIES

| 1991 | MIN A | 0 | 0 | – | 0.00 | 3 | 0 | 0 | 5.1 | 2 | 1 | 3 | 0 | 0 | 0 | 0 | 0 | 0 | 0 | – | 0 | 0 | 0 | 0 | 0.0 | – |

WORLD SERIES

| 1991 | MIN A | 0 | 0 | – | 5.14 | 4 | 0 | 0 | 7 | 6 | 2 | 2 | 0 | 0 | 0 | 0 | 0 | 0 | 0 | – | 1 | 0 | 0 | 0 | 0.3 | 1.000 |

Bobby Witt

WITT, ROBERT ANDREW
B. May 11, 1964, Arlington, Va.

BR TR 6′2″ 190 lbs.

Year	Team	W	L	PCT	ERA	G	GS	CG	IP	H	BB	SO	ShO	W	L	SV	AB	H	HR	BA	PO	A	E	DP	TC/G	FA
1986	TEX A	11	9	.550	5.48	31	31	0	157.2	130	**143**	174	0	0	0	0	0	0	0	–	8	20	3	1	1.0	.903
1987		8	10	.444	4.91	26	25	1	143	114	**140**	160	0	0	0	0	1	0	0	.000	8	17	0	1	1.0	1.000
1988		8	10	.444	3.92	22	22	13	174.1	134	101	148	2	0	0	0	0	0	0	–	15	14	4	2	1.5	.882
1989		12	13	.480	5.14	31	31	5	194.1	182	**114**	166	1	0	0	0	0	0	0	–	13	22	1	1	1.2	.972
1990		17	10	.630	3.36	33	32	7	222	197	110	221	1	0	0	0	0	0	0	–	18	18	5	2	1.2	.878
1991		3	7	.300	6.09	17	16	1	88.2	84	74	82	1	0	0	0	0	0	0	–	7	6	2	1	0.9	.867
1992	**2 teams**	**TEX A**	(25G	9–13)	**OAK A**	(6G	1–1)																			
"	total	10	14	.417	4.29	31	31	0	193	183	114	125	0	0	0	0	0	0	0	–	14	20	1	2	1.1	.971
1993	OAK A	14	13	.519	4.21	35	33	5	220	226	91	131	1	0	0	0	0	0	0	–	12	39	3	5	1.5	.944
1994		8	10	.444	5.04	24	24	5	135.2	151	70	111	3	0	0	0	0	0	0	–	7	13	4	2	1.0	.833
9 yrs.		91	96	.487	4.56	250	245	37	1528.2	1401	957	1318	9	0	0	0	1	0	0	.000	102	170	23	17	1.2	.922

LEAGUE CHAMPIONSHIP SERIES

| 1992 | OAK A | 0 | 0 | – | 18.00 | 1 | 1 | 0 | 1 | 2 | 1 | 1 | 0 | 0 | 0 | 0 | 0 | 0 | 0 | – | 0 | 0 | 0 | 0 | 0.0 | – |

Mark Wohlers

WOHLERS, MARK EDWARD
B. Jan. 23, 1970, Holyoke, Mass.

BR TR 6′4″ 207 lbs.

Year	Team	W	L	PCT	ERA	G	GS	CG	IP	H	BB	SO	ShO	W	L	SV	AB	H	HR	BA	PO	A	E	DP	TC/G	FA
1991	ATL N	3	1	.750	3.20	17	0	0	19.2	17	13	13	0	3	1	2	1	0	0	.000	0	3	0	1	0.2	1.000
1992		1	2	.333	2.55	32	0	0	35.1	28	14	17	0	1	2	4	2	0	0	.000	2	7	0	0	0.3	1.000
1993		6	2	.750	4.50	46	0	0	48	37	22	45	0	6	2	0	0	0	0	–	6	6	0	1	0.3	1.000
1994		7	2	.778	4.59	51	0	0	51	51	33	58	0	7	2	1	1	1	0	1.000	3	7	1	0	0.2	.909
4 yrs.		17	7	.708	3.92	146	0	0	154	133	82	133	0	17	7	7	4	1	0	.250	11	23	1	2	0.2	.971

LEAGUE CHAMPIONSHIP SERIES

1991	ATL N	0	0	–	0.00	3	0	0	1.2	3	1	1	0	0	0	0	0	0	0	–	0	0	0	0	0.0	–
1992		0	0	–	0.00	3	0	0	3	2	1	2	0	0	0	0	0	0	0	–	1	0	0	0	0.3	1.000
1993		0	1	.000	3.38	4	0	0	5.1	2	3	10	0	0	1	0	0	0	0	–	0	0	0	0	0.0	–
3 yrs.		0	1	.000	1.80	10	0	0	10	7	5	13	0	0	1	0	0	0	0	–	1	0	0	0	0.1	1.000

WORLD SERIES

1991	ATL N	0	0	–	0.00	3	0	0	1.2	2	1	1	0	0	0	0	0	0	0	–	0	0	0	0	0.0	–
1992		0	0	–	0.00	2	0	0	0.2	0	1	0	0	0	0	0	0	0	0	–	0	0	0	0	0.0	–
2 yrs.		0	0	–	0.00	5	0	0	2.1	2	3	1	0	0	0	0	0	0	0	–	0	0	0	0	0.0	–

Brad Woodall

WOODALL, DAVID BRADLEY
B. June 25, 1969, Atlanta, Ga.

BB TL 6′ 175 lbs.

Year	Team	W	L	PCT	ERA	G	GS	CG	IP	H	BB	SO	ShO	W	L	SV	AB	H	HR	BA	PO	A	E	DP	TC/G	FA
1994	ATL N	0	1	.000	4.50	1	1	0	6	5	2	2	0	0	0	0	2	1	0	.500	0	3	0	1	3.0	1.000

Tim Worrell

WORRELL, TIMOTHY HOWARD
Brother of Todd Worrell.
B. July 5, 1967, Pasadena, Calif.

BR TR 6′4″ 210 lbs.

Year	Team	W	L	PCT	ERA	G	GS	CG	IP	H	BB	SO	ShO	W	L	SV	AB	H	HR	BA	PO	A	E	DP	TC/G	FA
1993	SD N	2	7	.222	4.92	21	16	0	100.2	104	43	52	0	0	0	0	31	1	0	.032	6	11	1	0	0.9	.944
1994		0	1	.000	3.68	3	3	0	14.2	9	5	14	0	0	0	0	2	1	0	.500	4	2	0	0	2.0	1.000
2 yrs.		2	8	.200	4.76	24	19	0	115.1	113	48	66	0	0	0	0	33	2	0	.061	10	13	1	0	1.0	.958

Todd Worrell

WORRELL, SCOTT ROLAND
Brother of Tim Worrell.
B. Sept. 28, 1959, Arcadia, Calif.

BR TR 6′5″ 215 lbs.

Year	Team	W	L	PCT	ERA	G	GS	CG	IP	H	BB	SO	ShO	W	L	SV	AB	H	HR	BA	PO	A	E	DP	TC/G	FA
1985	STL N	3	0	1.000	2.91	17	0	0	21.2	17	7	17	0	3	0	5	1	0	0	.000	3	0	0	0	0.2	1.000
1986		9	10	.474	2.08	74	0	0	103.2	86	41	73	0	9	10	**36**	7	1	0	.143	5	8	2	0	0.2	.867
1987		8	6	.571	2.66	75	0	0	94.2	86	34	92	0	8	6	33	10	1	0	.100	0	17	0	0	0.2	1.000
1988		5	9	.357	3.00	68	0	0	90	69	34	78	0	5	9	32	6	0	0	.000	3	10	0	4	0.2	1.000
1989		3	5	.375	2.96	47	0	0	51.2	42	26	41	0	3	5	20	1	0	0	.000	0	11	0	1	0.2	1.000

Year	Team	W	L	PCT	ERA	G	GS	CG	IP	H	BB	SO	ShO	Relief Pitching W	L	SV	Batting AB	H	HR	BA	PO	A	E	DP	TC/G	FA

Todd Worrell *continued*

Year	Team	W	L	PCT	ERA	G	GS	CG	IP	H	BB	SO	ShO	W	L	SV	AB	H	HR	BA	PO	A	E	DP	TC/G	FA
1992		5	3	.625	2.11	67	0	0	64	45	25	64	0	5	3	3	0	0	0	–	2	2	0	0	0.1	1.000
1993	LA N	1	1	.500	6.05	35	0	0	38.2	46	11	31	0	1	1	5	0	0	0	–	1	4	0	0	0.1	1.000
1994		6	5	.545	4.29	38	0	0	42	37	12	44	0	6	5	11	0	0	0	–	3	3	0	0	0.2	1.000
8 yrs.		40	39	.506	2.97	421	0	0	506.1	428	190	440	0	40	39	145	25	2	0	.080	17	55	2	5	0.2	.973

LEAGUE CHAMPIONSHIP SERIES

1985	STL N	1	0	1.000	1.42	4	0	0	6.1	4	2	3	0	1	0	0	0	0	0	–	0	1	0	0	0.3	1.000
1987		0	0	–	2.08	3	0	0	4.1	4	1	6	0	0	0	1	1	0	0	.000	0	0	0	0	0.0	–
2 yrs.		1	0	1.000	1.69	7	0	0	10.2	8	3	9	0	1	0	1	1	0	0	.000	0	1	0	0	0.1	1.000

WORLD SERIES

1985	STL N	0	1	.000	3.86	3	0	0	4.2	4	2	6	0	0	1	1	1	0	0	.000	0	0	0	0	0.3	1.000
1987		0	0	–	1.29	4	0	0	7	4	4	3	0	0	0	2	0	0	0	–	0	0	0	0	0.0	–
2 yrs.		0	1	.000	2.31	7	0	0	11.2	10	6	9	0	0	1	3 (4th)	1	0	0	.000	0	1	0	0	0.1	1.000

Anthony Young

YOUNG, ANTHONY WAYNE
B. Jan. 19, 1966, Houston, Tex.

BR TR 6'2"   200 lbs.

Year	Team	W	L	PCT	ERA	G	GS	CG	IP	H	BB	SO	ShO	W	L	SV	AB	H	HR	BA	PO	A	E	DP	TC/G	FA
1991	NY N	2	5	.286	3.10	10	8	0	49.1	48	12	20	0	0	0	0	14	2	0	.143	4	4	1	0	0.9	.889
1992		2	14	.125	4.17	52	13	1	121	134	31	64	0	1	7	15	27	3	0	.111	13	15	2	1	0.6	.933
1993		1	16	.059	3.77	39	10	1	100.1	103	42	62	0	1	8	3	14	2	0	.143	9	14	3	1	0.7	.885
1994	CHI N	4	6	.400	3.92	20	19	0	114.2	103	46	65	0	0	0	0	34	6	0	.176	13	18	1	1	1.6	.969
4 yrs.		9	41	.180	3.85	121	50	2	385.1	388	131	211	0	2	15	18	89	13	0	.146	39	51	7	3	0.8	.928

Manager Register

The Manager Register is an alphabetical listing of every man who managed in the major leagues in 1993. Most of the information is self-explanatory. Column headings include G for games managed, W for wins, L for losses, T for ties, N for no-decision games, PCT for winning percentage, and Standing.

The figures in the Standing column show where the team stood at the end of the season and when there was a managerial change. There are four possible cases:

Only Manager for the Team That Year. Indicated by a single boldfaced figure that appears in the extreme left-hand column and shows the final standing of the team.

Manager Started Season, but Did Not Finish. Indicated by two figures: the first is boldfaced and shows the standing of the team when this manager left; the second shows the final standing of the team. (See Tony LaRussa, Chicago, 1986.)

Manager Finished Season, but Did Not Start. Indicated by two figures: the first shows the standing of the team when this manager started; the second is boldfaced and shows the final standing of the team. (See Tony LaRussa, Oakland, 1986.)

Manager Did Not Start or Finish Season. Indicated by three figures: the first shows the standing of the team when this manager started; the second is boldfaced and shows the standing of the team when this manager left; the third shows the final standing of the team. (See Bobby Knoop, California, 1994.)

The managers' records for the 1981 split season are given separately for each half. "(1st)" or "(2nd)" will appear to the right of the standings to indicate which half.

| | G | W | L | T | N | PCT | Standing | | G | W | L | T | N | PCT | Standing | | G | W | L | T | N | PCT | Standing |

Felipe Alou

ALOU, FELIPE
Born Felipe Rojas (Alou).
Brother of Jesus Alou.
Brother of Matty Alou.
Father of Moises Alou.
B. May 12, 1935, Haina, Dominican Republic.

		G	W	L	T	N	PCT	Standing
1992	MON N	125	70	55	0	0	.560	4 2
1993		163	94	68	1	0	.580	2
1994		114	74	40	0	0	.649	1
3 yrs.		402	238	163	1	0	.594	

Sparky Anderson

ANDERSON, GEORGE LEE
B. Feb. 22, 1934, Bridgewater, S. D.

		G	W	L	T	N	PCT	Standing	
1970	CIN N	162	102	60	0	0	.630	1	
1971		162	79	83	0	0	.488	4	
1972		154	95	59	0	0	.617	1	
1973		162	99	63	0	0	.611	1	
1974		163	98	64	1	0	.605	2	
1975		162	108	54	0	0	.667	1	
1976		162	102	60	0	0	.630	1	
1977		162	88	74	0	0	.543	2	
1978		161	92	69	0	0	.571	2	
1979	DET A	106	56	50	0	0	.528	5 5	
1980		163	84	78	1	0	.519	4	
1981		57	31	26	0	0	.544	4	(1st)
1981		52	29	23	0	0	.558	2	(2nd)
1982		162	83	79	0	0	.512	4	
1983		162	92	70	0	0	.568	2	
1984		162	104	58	0	0	.642	1	
1985		161	84	77	0	0	.522	3	
1986		162	87	75	0	0	.537	3	
1987		162	98	64	0	0	.605	1	
1988		162	88	74	0	0	.543	2	
1989		162	59	103	0	0	.364	7	
1990		162	79	83	0	0	.488	3	
1991		162	84	78	0	0	.519	2	
1992		162	75	87	0	0	.463	6	
1993		162	85	77	0	0	.525	3	
1994		115	53	62	0	0	.461	5	
25 yrs.		3886	2134	1750	2	0	.549		
			5th	**4th**				**6th**	

LEAGUE CHAMPIONSHIP SERIES

		G	W	L	T	N	PCT	
1970	CIN N	3	3	0	0	0	1.000	
1972		5	3	2	0	0	.600	
1973		5	2	3	0	0	.400	
1975		3	3	0	0	0	1.000	
1976		3	3	0	0	0	1.000	
1984	DET A	3	3	0	0	0	1.000	
1987		5	1	4	0	0	.200	
7 yrs.		27	18	9	0	0	.667	
			2nd	**1st**			**5th**	**3rd**

WORLD SERIES

		G	W	L	T	N	PCT	
1970	CIN N	5	1	4	0	0	.200	
1972		7	3	4	0	0	.429	
1975		7	4	3	0	0	.571	
1976		4	4	0	0	0	1.000	
1984	DET A	5	4	1	0	0	.800	
5 yrs.		28	16	12	0	0	.571	
			6th	**7th**	**8th**			**3rd**

Dusty Baker

BAKER, JOHNNIE B., JR.
B. June 15, 1949, Riverside, Calif.

		G	W	L	T	N	PCT	Standing
1993	SF N	162	103	59	0	0	.636	2
1994		115	55	60	0	0	.478	2
2 yrs.		277	158	119	0	0	.570	

Don Baylor

BAYLOR, DON EDWARD
B. June 28, 1949, Austin, Tex.

		G	W	L	T	N	PCT	Standing
1993	CLR N	162	67	95	0	0	.414	6
1994		117	53	64	0	0	.453	3
2 yrs.		279	120	159	0	0	.430	

Terry Collins

COLLINS, TERRY LEE
B. May 27, 1949, Midland, Mich.

		G	W	L	T	N	PCT	Standing
1994	HOU N	115	66	49	0	0	.574	2

Bobby Cox

COX, ROBERT JOE
B. May 21, 1941, Tulsa, Okla.

		G	W	L	T	N	PCT	Standing	
1978	ATL N	162	69	93	0	0	.426	6	
1979		160	66	94	0	0	.413	6	
1980		161	81	80	0	0	.503	4	
1981		55	25	29	1	0	.463	4	(1st)
1981		52	25	27	0	0	.481	5	(2nd)
1982	TOR A	162	78	84	0	0	.481	6	
1983		162	89	73	0	0	.549	4	
1984		163	89	73	1	0	.549	2	
1985		161	99	62	0	0	.615	1	
1990	ATL N	97	40	57	0	0	.412	6 6	
1991		162	94	68	0	0	.580	1	
1992		162	98	64	0	0	.605	1	
1993		162	104	58	0	0	.642	1	
1994		114	68	46	0	0	.596	2	
13 yrs.		1935	1025	908	2	0	.530		

LEAGUE CHAMPIONSHIP SERIES

		G	W	L	T	N	PCT	
1985	TOR A	7	3	4	0	0	.429	
1991	ATL N	7	4	3	0	0	.571	
1992		7	4	3	0	0	.571	
1993		6	2	4	0	0	.333	
4 yrs.		27	13	14	0	0	.481	
			2nd	**4th**	**1st**			**9th**

WORLD SERIES

		G	W	L	T	N	PCT	
1991	ATL N	7	3	4	0	0	.429	
1992		6	2	4	0	0	.333	
2 yrs.		13	5	8	0	0	.385	

Jim Fregosi

FREGOSI, JAMES LOUIS
B. Apr. 4, 1942, San Francisco, Calif.

		G	W	L	T	N	PCT	Standing	
1978	CAL A	117	62	55	0	0	.530	3 2	
1979		162	88	74	0	0	.543	1	
1980		160	65	95	0	0	.406	6	
1981		48	22	25	0	1	.468	4 4	(1st)
1986	CHI A	96	45	51	0	0	.469	5 5	
1987		162	77	85	0	0	.475	5	
1988		161	71	90	0	0	.441	5	
1991	PHI N	149	74	75	0	0	.497	6 3	
1992		162	70	92	0	0	.432	6	
1993		162	97	65	0	0	.599	1	
1994		115	54	61	0	0	.470	4	
11 yrs.		1494	725	768	0	1	.486		

LEAGUE CHAMPIONSHIP SERIES

		G	W	L	T	N	PCT	
1979	CAL A	4	1	3	0	0	.250	
1993	PHI N	6	4	2	0	0	.667	
2 yrs.		10	5	5	0	0	.500	
			10th	**9th**				**8th**

WORLD SERIES

		G	W	L	T	N	PCT
1993	PHI N	6	2	4	0	0	.333

Phil Garner

GARNER, PHILIP MASON (Scrap Iron)
B. Apr. 30, 1949, Jefferson City, Tenn.

		G	W	L	T	N	PCT	Standing
1992	MIL A	162	92	70	0	0	.568	2
1993		162	69	93	0	0	.426	7
1994		115	53	62	0	0	.461	5
3 yrs.		439	214	225	0	0	.487	

Cito Gaston

GASTON, CLARENCE EDWIN
B. Mar. 17, 1944, San Antonio, Tex.

		G	W	L	T	N	PCT	Standing	
1989	TOR A	126	77	49	0	0	.611	6 1	
1990		162	86	76	0	0	.531	2	
1991		120	66	54	0	0	.550	1	
1991		9	6	3	0	0	.667	1 1	
1992		162	96	66	0	0	.593	1	

Cito Gaston continued

		G	W	L	T	N	PCT	Standing
1993		162	95	67	0	0	.586	1
1994		115	55	60	0	0	.478	3
6 yrs.		856	481	375	0	0	.562	

LEAGUE CHAMPIONSHIP SERIES

		G	W	L	T	N	PCT	
1989	TOR A	5	1	4	0	0	.200	
1991		5	1	4	0	0	.200	
1992		6	4	2	0	0	.667	
1993		6	4	2	0	0	.667	
4 yrs.		22	10	12	0	0	.455	
			4th	**5th**	**3rd**			**10th**

WORLD SERIES

		G	W	L	T	N	PCT
1992	TOR A	6	4	2	0	0	.667
1993		6	4	2	0	0	.667
2 yrs.		12	8	4	0	0	.667

Dallas Green

GREEN, GEORGE DALLAS
B. Aug. 4, 1934, Newport, Del.

		G	W	L	T	N	PCT	Standing	
1979	PHI N	30	19	11	0	0	.633	5 4	
1980		162	91	71	0	0	.562	1	
1981		56	34	21	1	0	.618	1	(1st)
1981		53	25	27	1	0	.481	3	(2nd)
1989	NY A	121	56	65	0	0	.463	6 5	
1993	NY N	124	46	78	0	0	.371	7 7	
1994		113	55	58	0	0	.487	3	
6 yrs.		659	326	331	2	0	.496		

DIVISIONAL PLAYOFF SERIES

		G	W	L	T	N	PCT
1981	PHI N	5	2	3	0	0	.400

LEAGUE CHAMPIONSHIP SERIES

		G	W	L	T	N	PCT
1980	PHI N	5	3	2	0	0	.600

WORLD SERIES

		G	W	L	T	N	PCT
1980	PHI N	6	4	2	0	0	.667

Mike Hargrove

HARGROVE, DUDLEY MICHAEL (The Human Rain Delay)
B. Oct. 26, 1949, Perryton, Tex.

		G	W	L	T	N	PCT	Standing
1991	CLE A	85	32	53	0	0	.376	7 7
1992		162	76	86	0	0	.469	4
1993		162	76	86	0	0	.469	6
1994		113	66	47	0	0	.584	2
4 yrs.		522	250	272	0	0	.479	

Butch Hobson

HOBSON, CLELL LAVERN, JR.
B. Aug. 17, 1951, Tuscaloosa, Ala.

		G	W	L	T	N	PCT	Standing
1992	BOS A	162	73	89	0	0	.451	7
1993		162	80	82	0	0	.494	5
1994		115	54	61	0	0	.470	4
3 yrs.		439	207	232	0	0	.472	

Davey Johnson

JOHNSON, DAVID ALLEN
B. Jan. 30, 1943, Orlando, Fla.

		G	W	L	T	N	PCT	Standing	
1984	NY N	162	90	72	0	0	.556	2	
1985		162	98	64	0	0	.605	2	
1986		162	108	54	0	0	.667	1	
1987		162	92	70	0	0	.568	2	
1988		160	100	60	0	0	.625	1	
1989		162	87	75	0	0	.537	2	
1990		42	20	22	0	0	.476	4 2	
1993	CIN N	118	53	65	0	0	.449	5 5	
1994		115	66	48	1	0	.579	1	
9 yrs.		1245	714	530	1	0	.574		

LEAGUE CHAMPIONSHIP SERIES

		G	W	L	T	N	PCT	
1986	NY N	6	4	2	0	0	.667	
1988		7	3	4	0	0	.429	
2 yrs.		13	7	6	0	0	.538	
			9th	**8th**	**8th**			**6th**

WORLD SERIES

		G	W	L	T	N	PCT
1986	NY N	7	4	3	0	0	.571

Tom Kelly

KELLY, JAY THOMAS
B. Aug. 15, 1950, Graceville, Minn.

Year	Tm	Lg	G	W	L	T	N	PCT	Standing	
1986	MIN	A	23	12	11	0	0	.522	7	6
1987			162	85	77	0	0	.525	1	
1988			162	91	71	0	0	.562	2	
1989			162	80	82	0	0	.494	5	
1990			162	74	88	0	0	.457	7	
1991			162	95	67	0	0	.586	1	
1992			162	90	72	0	0	.556	2	
1993			162	71	91	0	0	.438	5	
1994			113	53	60	0	0	.469	4	
9 yrs.			1270	651	619	0	0	.513		

LEAGUE CHAMPIONSHIP SERIES

Year	Tm	Lg	G	W	L	T	N	PCT
1987	MIN	A	5	4	1	0	0	.800
1991			5	4	1	0	0	.800
2 yrs.			10	8	2	0	0	.800
			7th					1st

WORLD SERIES

Year	Tm	Lg	G	W	L	T	N	PCT
1987	MIN	A	7	4	3	0	0	.571
1991			7	4	3	0	0	.571
2 yrs.			14	8	6	0	0	.571

Kevin Kennedy

KENNEDY, KEVIN CURTIS
B. May 26, 1954, Los Angeles, Calif.

Year	Tm	Lg	G	W	L	T	N	PCT	Standing
1993	TEX	A	162	86	76	0	0	.531	2
1994			114	52	62	0	0	.456	1
2 yrs.			276	138	138	0	0	.500	

Bobby Knoop

KNOOP, ROBERT FRANK
B. Oct. 18, 1938, Sioux City, Iowa.

Year	Tm	Lg	G	W	L	T	N	PCT	Standing		
1994	CAL	A	2	1	1	0	0	.500	3	2	4

Marcel Lachemann

LACHEMANN, MARCEL ERNEST
Brother of Rene Lachemann.
B. June 13, 1941, Los Angeles, Calif.

Year	Tm	Lg	G	W	L	T	N	PCT	Standing	
1994	CAL	A	74	30	44	0	0	.405	2	4

Rene Lachemann

LACHEMANN, RENE GEORGE
Brother of Marcel Lachemann.
B. May 4, 1945, Los Angeles, Calif.

Year	Tm	Lg	G	W	L	T	N	PCT	Standing		
1981	SEA	A	33	15	18	0	0	.455	7	6	(1st)
1981			52	23	29	0	0	.442	5		(2nd)
1982			162	76	86	0	0	.469	4		
1983			73	26	47	0	0	.356	7	7	
1984	MIL	A	161	67	94	0	0	.416	7		
1993	FLA	N	162	64	98	0	0	.395	6		
1994			115	51	64	0	0	.443	5		
6 yrs.			758	322	436	0	0	.425			

Gene Lamont

LAMONT, GENE WILLIAM
B. Dec. 25, 1946, Rockford, Ill.

Year	Tm	Lg	G	W	L	T	N	PCT	Standing
1992	CHI	A	162	86	76	0	0	.531	3
1993			162	94	68	0	0	.580	1
1994			113	67	46	0	0	.593	1
3 yrs.			437	247	190	0	0	.565	

LEAGUE CHAMPIONSHIP SERIES

Year	Tm	Lg	G	W	L	T	N	PCT
1993	CHI	A	6	2	4	0	0	.333

Tony LaRussa

LaRUSSA, ANTHONY
B. Oct. 4, 1944, Tampa, Fla.

Year	Tm	Lg	G	W	L	T	N	PCT	Standing		
1979	CHI	A	54	27	27	0	0	.500	5	5	
1980			162	70	90	2	0	.438	5		
1981			53	31	22	0	0	.585	3		(1st)
1981			53	23	30	0	0	.434	6		(2nd)
1982			162	87	75	0	0	.537	3		
1983			162	99	63	0	0	.611	1		
1984			162	74	88	0	0	.457	5		

Tony LaRussa *continued*

Year	Tm	Lg	G	W	L	T	N	PCT	Standing		
1985			163	85	77	1	0	.525	3		
1986			64	26	38	0	0	.406	6	5	
1986	OAK	A	79	45	34	0	0	.570	7	3	
1987			162	81	81	0	0	.500	3		
1988			162	104	58	0	0	.642	1		
1989			162	99	63	0	0	.611	1		
1990			162	103	59	0	0	.636	1		
1991			162	84	78	0	0	.519	4		
1992			162	96	66	0	0	.593	1		
1993			162	68	94	0	0	.420	7		
1994			114	51	63	0	0	.447	2		
16 yrs.			2362	1253	1106	3	0	.531			

LEAGUE CHAMPIONSHIP SERIES

Year	Tm	Lg	G	W	L	T	N	PCT
1983	CHI	A	4	1	3	0	0	.250
1988	OAK	A	4	4	0	0	0	1.000
1989			5	4	1	0	0	.800
1990			4	4	0	0	0	1.000
1992			6	2	4	0	0	.333
5 yrs.			23	15	8	0	0	.652
		3rd	3rd	6th				4th

WORLD SERIES

Year	Tm	Lg	G	W	L	T	N	PCT
1988	OAK	A	5	1	4	0	0	.200
1989			4	4	0	0	0	1.000
1990			4	0	4	0	0	.000
3 yrs.			13	5	8	0	0	.385

Tom Lasorda

LASORDA, THOMAS CHARLES
B. Sept. 22, 1927, Norristown, Pa.

Year	Tm	Lg	G	W	L	T	N	PCT	Standing		
1976	LA	N	4	2	2	0	0	.500	2	2	
1977			162	98	64	0	0	.605	1		
1978			162	95	67	0	0	.586	1		
1979			162	79	83	0	0	.488	3		
1980			163	92	71	0	0	.564	2		
1981			57	36	21	0	0	.632	1		(1st)
1981			53	27	26	0	0	.509	4		(2nd)
1982			162	88	74	0	0	.543	2		
1983			163	91	71	1	0	.562	1		
1984			162	79	83	0	0	.488	4		
1985			162	95	67	0	0	.586	1		
1986			162	73	89	0	0	.451	5		
1987			162	73	89	0	0	.451	4		
1988			162	94	67	1	0	.584	1		
1989			160	77	83	0	0	.481	4		
1990			162	86	76	0	0	.531	2		
1991			162	93	69	0	0	.574	2		
1992			162	63	99	0	0	.389	6		
1993			162	81	81	0	0	.500	4		
1994			114	58	56	0	0	.509	1		
19 yrs.			2820	1480	1338	2	0	.525			

DIVISIONAL PLAYOFF SERIES

Year	Tm	Lg	G	W	L	T	N	PCT
1981	LA	N	5	3	2	0	0	.600

LEAGUE CHAMPIONSHIP SERIES

Year	Tm	Lg	G	W	L	T	N	PCT
1977	LA	N	4	3	1	0	0	.750
1978			4	3	1	0	0	.750
1981			5	3	2	0	0	.600
1983			4	1	3	0	0	.250
1985			6	2	4	0	0	.333
1988			7	4	3	0	0	.571
6 yrs.			30	16	14	0	0	.533
		1st	2nd	1st				7th

WORLD SERIES

Year	Tm	Lg	G	W	L	T	N	PCT
1977	LA	N	6	2	4	0	0	.333
1978			6	2	4	0	0	.333
1981			6	4	2	0	0	.667
1988			5	4	1	0	0	.800
4 yrs.			23	12	11	0	0	.522
		9th	8th	9th				8th

Jim Leyland

LEYLAND, JAMES RICHARD
B. Dec. 15, 1944, Toledo, Ohio.

Year	Tm	Lg	G	W	L	T	N	PCT	Standing
1986	PIT	N	162	64	98	0	0	.395	6
1987			162	80	82	0	0	.494	4
1988			160	85	75	0	0	.531	2
1989			164	74	88	2	0	.457	5
1990			162	95	67	0	0	.586	1

Jim Leyland *continued*

Year	Tm	Lg	G	W	L	T	N	PCT	Standing
1991			162	98	64	0	0	.605	1
1992			162	96	66	0	0	.593	1
1993			162	75	87	0	0	.463	5
1994			114	53	61	0	0	.465	3
9 yrs.			1410	720	688	2	0	.511	

LEAGUE CHAMPIONSHIP SERIES

Year	Tm	Lg	G	W	L	T	N	PCT
1990	PIT	N	6	2	4	0	0	.333
1991			7	3	4	0	0	.429
1992			7	3	4	0	0	.429
3 yrs.			20	8	12	0	0	.400
		6th	7th	3rd				

Hal McRae

McRAE, HAROLD ABRAHAM
Father of Brian McRae.
B. July 10, 1945, Avon Park, Fla.

Year	Tm	Lg	G	W	L	T	N	PCT	Standing	
1991	KC	A	124	66	58	0	0	.532	7	6
1992			162	72	90	0	0	.444	5	
1993			162	84	78	0	0	.519	3	
1994			115	64	51	0	0	.557	3	
4 yrs.			563	286	277	0	0	.508		

Johnny Oates

OATES, JOHNNY LANE
B. Jan. 21, 1946, Sylva, N. C.

Year	Tm	Lg	G	W	L	T	N	PCT	Standing	
1991	BAL	A	125	54	71	0	0	.432	7	6
1992			162	89	73	0	0	.549	3	
1993			162	85	77	0	0	.525	3	
1994			112	63	49	0	0	.563	2	
4 yrs.			561	291	270	0	0	.519		

Lou Piniella

PINIELLA, LOUIS VICTOR (Sweet Lou)
B. Aug. 28, 1943, Tampa, Fla.

Year	Tm	Lg	G	W	L	T	N	PCT	Standing	
1986	NY	A	162	90	72	0	0	.556	2	
1987			162	89	73	0	0	.549	4	
1988			93	45	48	0	0	.484	2	5
1990	CIN	N	162	91	71	0	0	.562	1	
1991			162	74	88	0	0	.457	5	
1992			162	90	72	0	0	.556	2	
1993	SEA	A	162	82	80	0	0	.506	4	
1994			112	49	63	0	0	.438	3	
8 yrs.			1177	610	567	0	0	.518		

LEAGUE CHAMPIONSHIP SERIES

Year	Tm	Lg	G	W	L	T	N	PCT
1990	CIN	N	6	4	2	0	0	.667

WORLD SERIES

Year	Tm	Lg	G	W	L	T	N	PCT
1990	CIN	N	4	4	0	0	0	1.000

Jim Riggleman

RIGGLEMAN, JAMES DAVID
B. Nov. 9, 1952, Ft. Dix, N. J.

Year	Tm	Lg	G	W	L	T	N	PCT	Standing	
1992	SD	N	12	4	8	0	0	.333	3	3
1993			162	61	101	0	0	.377	7	
1994			117	47	70	0	0	.402	4	
3 yrs.			291	112	179	0	0	.385		

Buck Rodgers

RODGERS, ROBERT LEROY
B. Aug. 16, 1938, Delaware, Ohio.

Year	Tm	Lg	G	W	L	T	N	PCT	Standing		
1980	MIL	A	47	26	21	0	0	.553	2	3	
1980			23	13	10	0	0	.565	4	3	
1981			56	31	25	0	0	.554	3		(1st)
1981			53	31	22	0	0	.585	1		(2nd)
1982			47	23	24	0	0	.489	5	1	
1985	MON	N	161	84	77	0	0	.522	3		
1986			161	78	83	0	0	.484	4		
1987			162	91	71	0	0	.562	3		
1988			163	81	81	1	0	.500	3		
1989			162	81	81	0	0	.500	4		
1990			162	85	77	0	0	.525	3		
1991			49	20	29	0	0	.408	6	6	
1991	CAL	A	38	20	18	0	0	.526	7	7	
1992			39	19	20	0	0	.487	5	5	
1992			34	14	20	0	0	.412	5	5	

	G	W	L	T	N	PCT	Standing

Buck Rodgers *continued*

		G	W	L	T	N	PCT	Standing
1993		162	71	91	0	0	.438	5
1994		39	16	23	0	0	.410	3 4
13 yrs.		1558	784	773	1	0	.504	

DIVISIONAL PLAYOFF SERIES

1981	MIL	A	5	2	3	0	0	.400

Buck Showalter

SHOWALTER, WILLIAM NATHANIEL III
   B. May 23, 1956, DeFuniak, Fla.

1992	NY	A	162	76	86	0	0	.469	4
1993			162	88	74	0	0	.543	2
1994			113	70	43	0	0	.619	1
3 yrs.			437	234	203	0	0	.535	

Joe Torre

TORRE, JOSEPH PAUL
   Brother of Frank Torre.
   B. July 18, 1940, Brooklyn, N. Y.

			G	W	L	T	N	PCT	Standing	
1977	NY	N	117	49	68	0	0	.419	6 6	
1978			162	66	96	0	0	.407	6	
1979			163	63	99	1	0	.389	6	
1980			162	67	95	0	0	.414	5	
1981			52	17	34	1	0	.333	5	(1st)
1981			53	24	28	1	0	.462	4	(2nd)
1982	ATL	N	162	89	73	0	0	.549	1	
1983			162	88	74	0	0	.543	2	
1984			162	80	82	0	0	.494	2	
1990	STL	N	58	24	34	0	0	.414	6 6	
1991			162	84	78	0	0	.519	2	
1992			162	83	79	0	0	.512	3	

		G	W	L	T	N	PCT	Standing
1993		162	87	75	0	0	.537	3
1994		115	53	61	1	0	.465	3
13 yrs.		1854	874	976	4	0	.472	

LEAGUE CHAMPIONSHIP SERIES

1982	ATL	N	3	0	3	0	0	.000

Tom Trebelhorn

TREBELHORN, THOMAS LYNN
   B. Jan. 27, 1948, Portland, Ore.

1986	MIL	A	9	6	3	0	0	.667	6 6
1987			162	91	71	0	0	.562	3
1988			162	87	75	0	0	.537	3
1989			162	81	81	0	0	.500	4
1990			162	74	88	0	0	.457	6
1991			162	83	79	0	0	.512	4
1994	CHI	N	113	49	64	0	0	.434	5
7 yrs.			932	471	461	0	0	.505	